The Courthouse and the Depot

THE ARCHITECTURE OF HOPE IN AN AGE OF DESPAIR

THE ARCHITECTURE OF HOPE

The Courthouse

Wilber W. Caldwell

A Narrative Guide

to Railroad Expansion

and Its Impact

on Public Architecture

in Georgia, 1833-1910

IN AN AGE OF DISPAIR

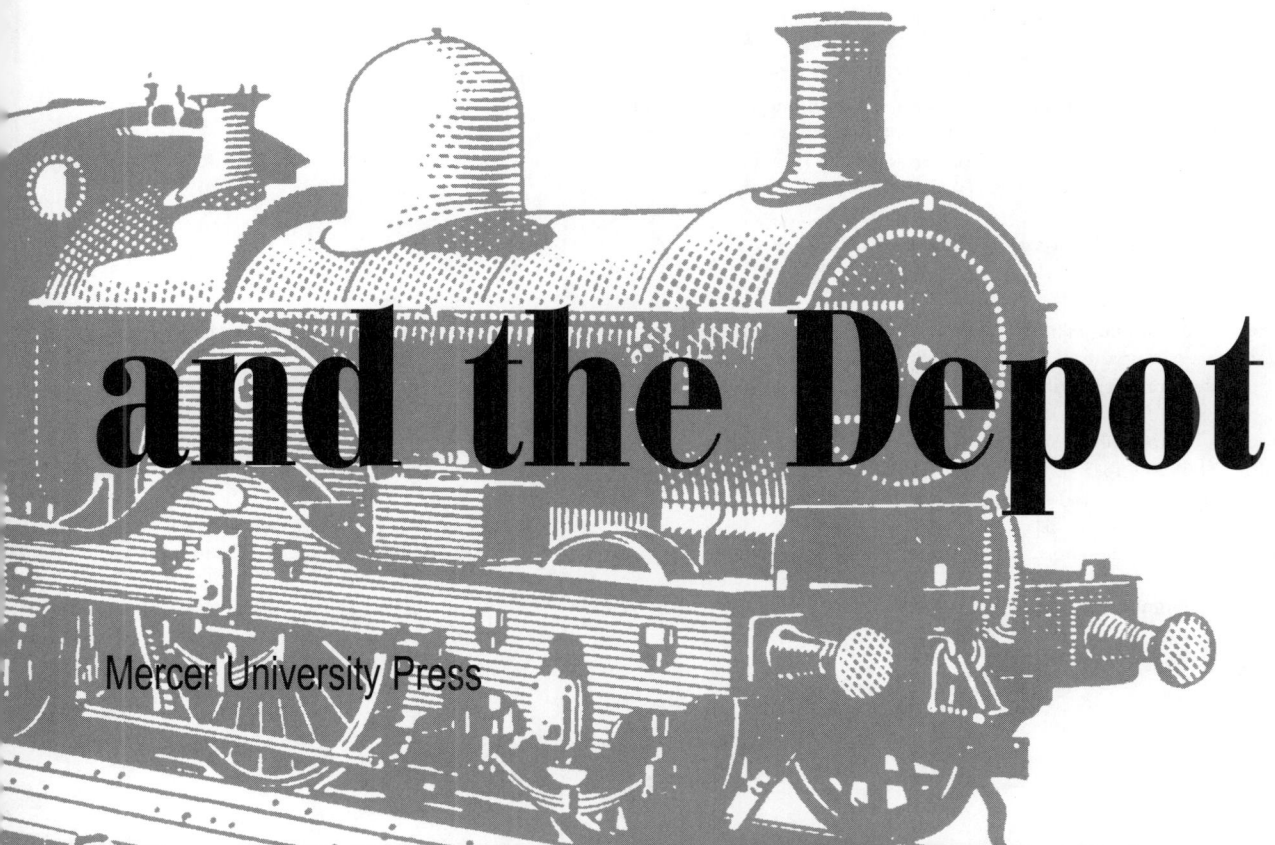

and the Depot

Mercer University Press

ISBN 0-86554-748-3
MUP/H564

© Mercer University Press
6316 Peake Road
Macon, Georgia 31210-3960
All rights reserved
2001

First Edition.

Book design by Mary-Frances Burt, Burt & Burt Studio

∞The paper used in this publication meets the minimum requirements
of American National Standard for Information Sciences—Permanence
of Paper for Printed Library Materials, ANSI Z39.48-1992.

Library of Congress Cataloging-in-Publication Data

Caldwell, Wilber W.
The courthouse and the depot : the architecture of hope in an age of
despair : a narrative guide to railroad expansion and its impact on pub-
lic architecture in Georgia, 1833-1910 / Wilber W. Caldwell.—1st ed.
p. cm.
Includes bibliographical references.
ISBN 0-86554-748-3
1. Architecture—Georgia—19th century. 2. Public architecture—
Georgia—19th century. 3.
Railroads—Georgia—History—19th century. I. Title.
NA730.G4 C35 2001
725'.15'0975809034—dc21

2001004526

Table of Contents

Notes Regarding Statistics

Unless otherwise noted, statistics for population, demographics and for agricultural and industrial production are taken from appropriate editions of The Census of the United States of America. Since this text cites numerous references to various editions of Adiel Sherwood's Gazetteer of Georgia, George White's Statistics of the State of Georgia, and A. E. Sholes's Georgia State Gazetteer and Business Directory, these sources are referenced by date in the text, but appear without footnote. All other statistical sources are documented in the traditional way.

Acknowledgments

The creation of *The Courthouse and the Depot* was a solitary endeavor, and yet, I did not write it alone. Over the many years I spent working on this book, scores of individuals and institutions lent me insight, support and encouragement. This brief acknowledgment seems small thanks for such extraordinary faith, scholarship and dedication.

First and foremost I would like to thank all of the institutions that amass and maintain the comprehensive special collections of local and regional historical documents and papers that made a book like this possible. Notable in this regard are the Robert W. Woodruff Library at Emory University and the collections of the Georgia Department of Archives and History. I am also deeply indebted to the Felix Hargrett Library and the Georgia Newspaper Project housed in the Main Library of University of Georgia at Athens. Thanks also to the Atlanta History Center and to the collections of hundreds of local libraries, private individuals and local historical societies all across the state.

Second, I would like to thank the Mercer University Press for publishing this volume. Additionally, I wish to acknowledge the contribution and unswerving support of Kenneth H. Thomas, Jr., historian for the Historical Preservation Division of the Georgia Department of Natural Resources, and the patronage of Mr. Tom Watson Brown. Without Ken's help and Mr. Brown's generous support, this book could not have been published.

Thanks also to Gail DeLoach at the Georgia Department of Archives and History, to Michael Rose at the Atlanta History Center and to Gary Doster, Les Winn and Ted Brooke for assistance with historic photos and post cards. A few very old photographs appear in this book without photo credits. These are images for which I was unable to locate an owner despite my considerable efforts to do so.

Finally, heartfelt thanks to some special friends and colleagues for their support, insight, ideas and encouragement, as well as for patience, tea and sympathy. Included in this long list are Mary Parra, Sue McAvoy, Margaret Knox, Dan Baum, Bill Chaloupka, Donna Scott, Krista Frangiamore, Merrilyn Crouch, Neill Herring, Seaborn Jones and Ross King.

Plate 1: The depot at Winder and the Barrow County Courthouse. (Photo: Wilber W. Caldwell)

Foreword

This is a book about small towns because the history of the South before 1910 is about small towns. It is a book about courthouses because the courthouse, more than any other building of the era, symbolized the aspirations and the collective self-image of the people of these towns. It is a book about depots because the depot is the architecture of the railroad, and, in this period, for these people, in these places, the railroad brought with it the singular, all consuming promise of the future. The focus of this inquiry is the period between 1870 and 1910. However, detailed treatment of the antebellum period beginning with Georgia's first railroads in 1833 establishes background and supplies contrast. Little consideration is given to structures built after 1910. It is my considered opinion that courthouse architecture in Georgia subsequent to 1910 ceased to be the architecture of the people and sadly became the architecture of the government.

Today, in almost every square in Georgia and along all of the state's half-forgotten railroad rights-of-way, we can hear the same compelling melody. It is a song that began around 1870 as Georgia's sturdy antebellum railroad network began to expand into the vast steel web that would eventually penetrate even the most remote corners of the state. As this proliferation of rail progressed, the appearance of so many tiny depots, architecturally unimaginative, often of wood and today usually found in ruin, if found at all, often created such hope that they inspired the construction of the architectural extravaganzas of brick and stone that were the courthouses of this era. Sadly, the hope so vibrantly expressed in these courthouses was in large part never realized. These grand buildings were monuments to the myths of an Old South imperfectly remembered and of the prosperous New South that stubbornly refused to arrive. Thus in a sense, the tiny depot was real and the grand courthouse was not.

The long awaited realization of the dreams of prosperity and industrialization were to be acted out primarily upon an urban, twentieth century stage, and when these long dreamt visions finally began to materialize, there commenced in these out-of-the-way places the inevitable exodus. The motor car ended what the railroad had begun. What were to be highways to prosperity for the South, became, at the same time, highways to oblivion for many small towns. Many of the courthouses of the era still stand in eerie testimony to the myths. Many of the depots are gone, taking with them all memory of the reality.

Architecture supplies us with a direct conduit to the spirit of the past. Through it we can hear ancient singing echoing all around us in profusion, not just in neatly preserved historical sites but in the simplest of shanties. Symphonies abound in various stages of use and decay on almost every city street, simple songs beside almost every cornfield. These structures sing to us in rhythms of hope and pride and sweat, dirges of ruin and failure and dashed dreams, anthems of triumph, broken waltzes of irony. In short, they sing for us the music of history.

It is my hope that these photographs and this text will combine to create a likeness of this most human of music.

Wilber W. Caldwell, 2001.

Introduction

I: ARCHITECTURE AS HISTORY

Strictly speaking, this is not a book of "architectural history." It is more a history book narrated by the record of architecture. In this context, unlike most "architectural histories," it does not necessarily concern itself with "great" buildings. Nor does it explore "important" or "exemplary" architecture. On the contrary, many of the buildings found in these pages are architecturally ordinary. It is not solely the story of architecture that the book seeks to relate, it is the story of a small piece of the American experience—the experience of the American South in the years between 1833 and 1910. There are perhaps no better narrators for this epic than Georgia's courthouses and depots. The grand courthouse narrates the aspiring mind of the postbellum South, while the humble depot speaks of a contradictory reality. Through the very real doorway of the unassuming little depot, we first glimpse the possibility of the mythical New South, while the courthouse remains a grand symbol for the myths of both the Old and the New South.

The central theme of this book is found in the extraordinary relationship that the structures shared. This relationship is defined by the illusive space in between, and in that short distance a compelling insight into the history of Georgia and the Deep South in the last third of the nineteenth century is revealed in peculiar detail. The mythical line that ended at the Southern courthouse led back to the myths of an agrarian past. The steel line that began at the Southern depot led to the reality of the Industrial Revolution and to the future. In most Southern towns of the late nineteenth and early twentieth century it was only about two blocks from the courthouse to the depot. Somewhere in that short distance between myth and reality lies the truth.

In 1910, Georgia was still a very rural place. It was primarily a state of small towns and of small farmers and merchants who were the collective product of the land, of hard times and of an agrarian, and in some ways dubious, common heritage. By the turn of the century, all of this had combined to create in the American South a strange inwardly turned amalgam of both the best and the worst elements of the emerging national character. It is a well-worn theme that the Southern experience was

Plate 2: The Lumpkin County Courthouse at Dahlonega, 1836. (Photo: Wilber W. Caldwell)

different from that of the rest of the nation. Without doubt the badge of defeat was unfamiliar to most Americans, but to Southerners it was to become more a badge of honor than of disgrace (a most un-American reaction. And if the South would hold itself up to be distinguished by defeat, then slavery's mark of guilt would hideously drag it down again as the region endlessly sought, not to prove its innocence, but to justify and compound its guilt in the most ignorant and base of white supremacy pageants. And yet while these two Southern distinctions are well known, poverty, a third and less celebrated difference, was perhaps more historically important in the era before the turn of the century. As C. Vann Woodward succinctly puts it, "Generations of scarcity and want constitute one of the historical experiences of the Southern people…"[1] Surely nothing could be farther from the popular American myth of plenty.

For all of its differences the South, like the North, had its roots in the America of the eighteenth century, an America born of the Enlightenment. In 1800, Americans, both Northern and Southern, were beginning as travelers on the same road. Just how far apart they would journey is part of this story. While the North embraced the new industrialism and espoused a maturing Federalism, it was the lofty ideals of eighteenth century French Humanism, the perfectibility of man, the purity of democratic justice and a preference for local forms of government that the South would cling to. The simple vernacular designs of her

early courthouses offer glimpses of this secular soul. These structures embodied an almost spiritual furor with a purely laic purpose that would gain strength and meaning until at the center of every town square in Georgia there stood a monument to the loftiest of dreams.

THE COURTHOUSE

Just how deeply the courthouse had become ingrained in the psyche of the average Southerner of the late nineteenth century is today impossible to guess. Just as the building stood at the center of the Southern town, it stood at the center of Southern life. Just as all roads in the county converged upon the courthouse square, all the twisting roads of Southern social being came together at that same place. The building was strangely wound around and through, not just Southern conscious life, but Southern heritage. In it were deeds to land, vouchers for inheritance, family trees, proofs of birth, marriage licenses, testaments to births of children, liens on property, receipts for taxes. Here Southerners voted, officially met to discuss matters of import, and judged their neighbors. Its bell rang out calamity, heralded victory, tolled death. In this one building, like no other, was the pattern of Southern life—hopes and fears and every detail in between. The courthouse evoked emotional images:

> But I have seen the old Courthouse. I have seen
> The flyspecked windows and the fading flag
> Over the judge's chair, touched the scuffed wall,
> Spat in the monumental brass spittoons
> and smelt the smell that never could be aired,
> Although one opened windows for a year,
> The unforgettable, intangible
> Mixture of cheap cigars, worm eaten books,
> Sweat, poverty, Negro hair-oil, grief and law.
> *John Browns Body*
> Stephen Vincent Benet

But above all the courthouse; the center, the focus, the hub; sitting looming in the center on the county's circumference like a single cloud in its ring of horizon, laying its vast shadow to the uttermost rim of the horizon; musing, brooding, symbolic, ponderable, tall as cloud, solid as rock, dominating all; protector of the weak, judiciate and curb of the passions and lusts, repository and guardian of the aspirations and hopes....

Requiem for a Nun
William Faulkner

In such an emotional context, it is perhaps best just to say that the manner in which the courthouse touched individual lives in both the North and the South was as powerful and as diverse as the new land itself. But as the South drifted out of the main current of the emerging American mind, she sought to entrench herself in her peculiarities, and thus her symbols developed in a pattern distinctly different from the rest of the nation. Foremost among these symbols was her architecture, and highly visible in the inventory of her architecture were her courthouses. Thus, emotionally holding the lives of its builders, while symbolically standing for their most cherished beliefs, the architecture of Georgia's courthouses speaks eloquently of the history of the South.

From early frontier beginnings Southerners seem to have been of a individualistic strain. In many places in Georgia, even after the turn of the century, the population lived not so far from that original frontier. It is upon the inherent themes in the idea of a persisting frontier that W. J. Cash bases a part of his well-known study:

...when the Southern backlandsman moved out into new cotton country..., he immediately set up the machinery of the State...everywhere he built his courthouse almost before he built anything else. And here in the South, as in all places in all times, the State, once established, inevitably asserted its inherent tendency to growth, to reach out and engross power.

[1] C. Vann Woodward, "The Search for A Southern Identity," *The Burden of Southern History* (Baton Rouge: Louisiana State University Press, 1960) 17.

[2] W. J. Cash, *The Mind of the South* (1941; reprint, New York: Vintage Books, 1991) 33.

[3] See Appendix A.

But against this was the fact that the tradition contained also, and as its ruling element, an intense distrust of, and, indeed, outright aversion to, any actual exercise of authority beyond the barest minimum essential to the social organism.[2]

Such individualism is the message of many of Georgia's early court buildings. Inheritors of the architectural tradition of the meeting houses of colonial New England and of a bold rectangular regional vernacular style which sometimes borrowed simple classical decorations from popular Georgian modes, the state's early courthouses sing songs of fierce frontier independence and local governmental prerogatives. Slavery was listed among these and this defames both the South and her anti-Federalism, although a ration of American regional diversity and independence may have been lost in the defeat of the latter cause. Scores of these often graceful but seldom sophisticated brick buildings were erected in Georgia in the first half of the nineteenth century[3]. Only thirteen unaltered early examples remain (see Table I). Perhaps the finest of these is the 1836 Lumpkin County Courthouse at Dahlonega (Plate 2). The style, like the frontier, followed Georgia into the postbellum era with buildings like the old 1869 Clayton County Courthouse at Jonesboro. Similarly, wooden courthouses once covered the state and four still remain to relate frontier individualism (see Table II). A stunning example is the old 1854 Chattahoochee County Courthouse, formerly at Cusseta (Plate 3), which has been restored and can now be seen at Westville in Stewart County.

Included in those authorities not beyond Wilbur Cash's "barest minimum essential to the social organism" is the Southern ideal of justice. Side by side, the messages that emanated from the bricks of Georgia's early court buildings were a distrust of big government and faith in the rule of law, concepts that varied little from the original French revolutionary ideals of Thomas Jefferson.

The courthouse as a "temple of justice" is the most obvious of images, and by the 1820s, with Jeffersonian Classicism well established in the region

Plate 3: The old Chattahoochee County Courthouse Formerly at Cusseta, now at Westville, 1854. (Photo: Wilber W. Caldwell)

TABLE I: BRICK

Columbia County at Appling, 1812 (rebuilt, 1856)

Fayette County at Fayetteville, 1825

Crawford County at Knoxville, 1832

Lumpkin County at Dahlonega, 1836

Marion County at Beuna Vista, 1856

Dawson County at Dawsonville, 1858

White County at Cleveland, 1860

Banks County at Homer, 1860-65

Clayton County at Jonesboro, 1869

Clay County at Fort Gaines, 1871

McDuffie County at Thomson, 1872

Bartow County at Cartersville, 1873

Clinch County at Homerville, 1896

TABLE II: FRAME

Marion County at Tazewell, 1848

Chattahoochee County, 1854, formerly at Cusseta
can now be seen at Westville in Stewart County

Glascock County at Gibson, 1858

The Pierce County Courthouse, 1876

and with the emerging popularity of the Greek Revival in America, Southern court buildings were sprouting columns in great numbers. In Georgia, considerable influence flowed from South Carolina and the work of Robert Mills, the first professionally trained American-born architect, who, in the 1820s, literally covered the state with Greek courthouses.

As the century wore on, the South hardened in defense of its economic and political peculiarities. Slavery was held close to the Southern heart and by 1850, the South had moved a long distance from any purely Jeffersonian ideal. The Greek democracy became the tool of John C. Calhoun and others and around it they wove a new myth of Southern society which, like their Greek model, flourished on the backs of slaves. The Greek Revival in the American South was thus denied its traditional messages and came to represent a grotesque distortion of classical ideals with the defense of slavery planted firmly at its very heart. These "Greek Temple" county court buildings filled Georgia's squares in the era before the Civil War. With a few notable exceptions, like Russell Warren's 1833 Chatham County Courthouse at Savannah, these were of a most vernacular sort. Although a great deal of fine Greek Revival architecture survives from antebellum times, only one courthouse survives from that early period. The 1849 Greene County Courthouse at Greensboro (Plate 4) is vernacular to its core, but exhibits a remarkable power and majesty despite its humble architectural credentials. After the war, the Greek tradition continued to gather symbolic force in the South, adding to its message the emotionalism of the Lost Cause and the brooding nostalgia that was draped about the growing myth of the Old South. Standing vernacular examples of postbellum Greek court buildings are the 1864 Banks County Courthouse at Homer and the 1871 Campbell County Courthouse in Fairburn.

The decades of poverty and ignorance that followed defeat encompass an epic that is little understood. It is in this era that Georgia's public architecture is most expressive, and it is of this era that her courthouses speak to us most clearly. As the cult of the Old South grew after the war, beside it there arose a second Southern creed, the New South, which envi-

Plate 4: The Greene County Courthouse at Greensboro, 1849. David Demarest and Atharates Atkinson, architects—builders. (Photo: Wilber W. Caldwell)

sioned a modern industrial South rising from the ashes of war to share in the progress of what Mark Twain coined "The Gilded Age." The primary focus of this book is the court buildings and the depots of the New South era, built between 1870 and 1910. They speak of what C. Vann Woodward calls "the divided mind of the south," a phrase which aptly describes the period. As Woodward so eloquently and correctly explains it, "One of the most significant inventions of the New South was 'the Old South', a legend of incalculable potentialities."[4] When John C. Calhoun began building his "citadel for the Southern mind" with its blatant manipulations of the principles of Greek democracy, he was laying the foundations for this legend. It was to become what Parrington later called "the most romantic ideal brought forth by our golden age of romance."[5] Even in defeat, while the rest of the country traded romanticism for an age of realism, the region clung to her romantic legacy, defending her agrarian institutions against the rapidly industrializing North and a much-despised Federalism, while simultaneously yearning for the bounty of the new age.

What Henry Grady and the New South spokesmen preached in the North was one thing, in the South another, and what Southerners heard and accepted in these messages was yet another. All of this confusion was coupled with an agricultural anarchy of labor and credit, a thoroughly backward looking regional mind-set and the immovable tenacity of blind

stubborn Southern pride. The result was decades of economic and cultural stagnation all wrapped in both the bright rhetoric of the New South and the comfortable mythology of the Old. Paul Gaston beautifully describes the scene under the apt title "The Emperor's New Clothes."[6] Southerners sang the songs of a by-gone age, danced to the seductive waltzes of the new industrial myth, and wore the superficial costumes of a transparent and short-lived progress in an effort to cover rags of abject poverty. In theory, the South would have the Industrial Revolution but only on its own terms. It would accept the machine and its associated "progress," but only to achieve the kind of success that would strengthen the region in her defense of ancient and cherished institutions. She would "out Yankee the Yankee" in order to secure her prerogatives. Put another way, the region would accept the economic rewards of industrialization, but would have none of the attendant political and social institutions. It was a one-sided bargain from the very beginning, and it resulted in the period of utter stagnation that this book seeks to examine.

At the center of such intransigence was a purely romantic obsession with the past that led to an impossible vision of the future. Romanticism in the North had followed the predictable path characterized by historical revivals, back-to-nature movements and exotic fascinations of all sorts. Northern romanticism sought an escape from the stern realities of unfettered capitalism, the monotony of industrial mechanization and its associated uncontrolled urban squalor, while Southerners practiced what Mark Twain described as "the jejune romanticism of an absurd past that is dead."[7] As Cash puts it: "The mind of the section… is continuous with the past. And its primary form is

[4] C. Vann Woodward, *Origins of the New South, 1877-1913* (1951; reprint, Baton Rouge: Louisiana State University Press, 1993) 154-5.

[5] Vernon L. Parrington, *Main Currents in American Thought, The Romantic Revolution in America, 1800 – 1860*, 3 Vols (New York: University of Oklahoma Press, 1927) 2:xii.

[6] Paul M. Gaston, *The New South Creed, A Study in Southern Mythmaking* (Baton Rouge: Louisiana State University Press, 1970) 187-214.

[7] Mark Twain, *Life on the Mississippi* (Boston: James R. Osgood and Company, 1883) 468.

Plate 5: The Jackson County Courthouse at Jefferson, 1879. W.W. Thomas, architect. (Photo: Wilber W. Caldwell)

Plate 6: The Newton County Courthouse at Covington, 1884. Bruce & Morgan architects. (Photo: Wilber W. Caldwell)

determined…by purely agricultural conditions… So …in many ways it has always marched away…from the present toward the past."[8]

The distinction between romanticism in the North and in the South is clearly voiced in the public buildings of the period. American architecture of the post-war age was characterized by a series of picturesque historical revivals that seemed perfect for the Southern mindset. But the symbolism that most of the country attached to the picturesque, and later to a Neoclassical Revival, was unacceptable in the extreme Southern view. In the North, a bold eclecticism employing first medieval and later classical forms was transformed into the architecture of American industrial power. Repugnant as this may have been in Dixie, the South would embrace some of these styles for her public buildings, but not before attaching her own peculiar symbolism. Then, through interaction with a healthy and poignant brick vernacular, she would reduce the wild beasts of Picturesque Eclecticism and Baroque Neoclassicism to more comfortable and familiar forms.

The Italianate was the first Romantic style to inspire Georgia's lagging tastes, and a number of courthouses were built in this mode just before and just after the war. Often more a voice of the American vernacular than the Italian Renaissance, the style was spread to unsophisticated rural builders by pattern books of the day. Although considered modern in the rural South, the style resulted in rather careful classical buildings like the 1879 Jackson County Courthouse at Jefferson (Plate 5).

Despite the early popularity of the Italianate Style, it was from an architectural catalogue of the wildly romantic Picturesque Eclectic Styles that Georgia would select her first truly eloquent spokesmen for the South's new split personality. In the decades before 1890, America's public building was generally dominated by three styles: the Gothic Revival, the Second Empire and the Romanesque Revival. In the South, Gothic remained almost exclusively the architecture of the church, and there were no pure Gothic Revival courthouses built in Georgia before 1910. Likewise, the national symbolism attached to the Second Empire Style was unacceptable to the South. It stood for the new industrialism, and, with it being French and nicknamed "the General Grant Style," there was much here for Southerners to hate. Still, a few of Georgia's more progressive cities built Second Empire courthouses, notably Atlanta, Athens and Macon. None of these structures survive. The only pure Second Empire courthouse still standing in Georgia is Alexander Bruce's fine 1884 Newton County Courthouse at Covington (Plate 6). As we shall see, it was built at a time when Covington mistakenly saw itself as an emerging hub, at the crossing of the rails from Atlanta to Augusta and from Macon to Athens. In addition to this urban monument at Covington, Alexander Bruce built three rural courthouses in Georgia with elements of the Second Empire Style. But these three almost identical buildings were subdued, rustic and utterly charming. They speak more of rural values than of revolutions, industrial or otherwise. They were the 1882 Hancock County Courthouse at Sparta (Plate 7), the 1883 Walton County Courthouse at Monroe and the no-longer-standing 1885 Hall County Courthouse at Gainesville, which was destroyed in 1936.

In the late 1880s and 1890s, the overwhelming choice of style to speak for the divided mind of the South was the Romanesque Revival, for at the heart of this style were two seemingly conflicting elements. At its most fundamental level the Romanesque Revival reflected the ancient architecture of medieval Europe, a surprisingly codified and primarily ecclesiastical architectural idiom, incorporating the arch, arcade and vault of Roman models, and combining these with primitive stone forms. At a contemporary level, the Romanesque Revival was a part of the modern Picturesque movement. Since mid-century, a highly eclectic picturesque architectural vocabulary had been flowing to America from Victorian England and creating in this county, as in England, an architectural riot of eclectic confusion.

Confusion may seem the appropriate motif for the Southern predicament in the 1880s, and many of the first Romanesque courthouses built in Georgia were of a highly Picturesque nature (see Table III). Most notable were those designed by William Parkins (Plate 8), the first professional architect to settle in

Plate 7: The Hancock County Courthouse at Sparta, 1882. Parkins & Bruce, architects. (Photo: Wilber W. Caldwell)

Plate 8: The Terrell County Courthouse at Dawson, 1892. William Parkins, architect. (Photo: Wilber W. Caldwell)

[8] Cash, *The Mind of the South*, lii.

Table III	HIGHLY PICTURESQUE ROMANESQUE REVIVAL COURTHOUSES STILL STANDING IN GEORGIA

Gwinnett County at Lawrenceville, 1885, E. G. Lind, architect.

Randolph County at Cuthbert, 1886, Kimball, Wheeler and Parkins, architects.

Oglethorpe County at Lexington, 1887, Kimball, Wheeler and Parkins, architects.

Dooly County at Vienna, 1890, William Parkins, architect.

Terrell County at Dawson, 1892, William Parkins, architects.

Table IV	ROMANESQUE REVIVAL COURTHOUSES STILL STANDING IN GEORGIA

Chatham County at Savannah, 1889, William G. Preston, architect.

Talbot County at Talbotton, 1892, Bruce and Morgan, architects.

Haralson County at Buchanan, 1892, Bruce and Morgan, architects.

Paulding County at Dallas, 1892, Bruce and Morgan, architects.

Floyd County at Rome, 1893, Bruce and Morgan, architects.

Elbert County at Elberton, 1894, Hunt and Lamar, V architects.

Macon County at Oglethorpe, 1894, W. Chamberlain, architect.

Bulloch County at Statesboro, 1894, Bruce and Morgan, architects.

Monroe County at Forsyth, 1896, Bruce and Morgan, architects.

Henry County at McDonough, 1897, J. W. Golucke, architects.

Clayton County at Jonesboro, 1898, J. W. Golucke, architect.

Berrien County at Nashville, 1898, Walter Chamberlain, architect.

Butts County at Jackson, 1898, Bruce and Morgan, architects.

Washington County at Sandersville, 1899, L. Goodrich, architect.

Union County at Blairsville, 1899, J. W. Golucke, architect.

Schley County at Ellaville, 1900, J. W. Golucke, architect.

Madison County at Danielsville, 1901, J. W. Golucke, architect.

Taliaferro County at Crawfordville, 1902, L F. Goodrich, architect.

Twiggs County at Jeffersonville, 1903, J. W. Golucke, architect.

Wayne County at Jesup, 1903, J. W. Golucke, architect.

Jones County at Gray, 1905, J. W. Golucke, architect.

Baker County at Newton, 1907, J. W. Golucke, architect.

Remodeled in the Romanesque Style

Burke County Waynesboro, 1898, Lewis Goodrich remodeling, architect.

Atlanta after the war and mentor to Atlanta's most successful Romanesque designers, Alexander Bruce and Thomas Morgan.

But such flamboyance proved the exception rather than the rule, and as with the Greek Revival, the South was quick to sort through the complex questions of style which baffled English and Eastern architects. Drawn to the style's inherent simplicity, the region would discard the frantic ornament of eclectic license and embrace a basic vocabulary of the Romanesque, which, when executed in Georgia's favored brick forms, yielded results not wholly dissimilar from the basic brick vernacular buildings to which the South had been drawn all along. Here is a chemistry in which the vernacular borrows from the styles of the day, while conversely the work of trained architects is shaped by simple local architectural traditions.

Thus, the region's consistent refusal to accept national symbols resulted in a Southern Romanesque Revival of a most fundamental nature. The brick vernacular had a sobering influence on the flowering eclectic of picturesque revivalism. This led the American South to a natural stylistic identification with the powerful fundamental forms inherent in the designs of Henry Hobson Richardson, the nation's pre-eminent architect of the era, and a pioneer in the quest for a national style. The Richardsonian Romanesque, as the style is called, was a highly individualistic codification of Romanesque elements. Richardson used this historical syntax to create a series of monumental public buildings which, although technically Romanesque in vocabulary, spoke a language yet unknown. Richardson's buildings seemed rooted, massive, primarily geometrical forms, and at the same time, fluid architectural statements of strange new mobility. Although none of the Romanesque Revival courthouses in Georgia begin to approach Richardson's inspirational standards, his influence is clear (Plate 9). Just as the force of the simple brick vernacular tamed the Picturesque Eclectic beast, so the monumentality of the Richardsonian Romanesque would be domesticated by the South's quest for a highly personal, comfortable, rural style.

Forty-seven Romanesque courthouses were built in Georgia between 1882 and 1907 (see Appendix A).

Plate 9: The Henry County Courthouse at McDonough, 1896. J. W. Golucke, architect. (Photo: Wilber W. Caldwell)

Thirteen of these were designed by Atlanta's Bruce and Morgan, who brought to the state's squares Romanesque buildings that hinted at Richardson's powerful vision but were tempered by an almost residential charm incorporating elements from many of the domestic styles the day, most notably the Queen Anne Style. Bruce's Queen Anne courthouses stand as apt symbols for the Southern dilemma. Here was a rudimentary Romanesque core transparently disguised by superficially up-to-date classical ornament. Additionally, eleven Romanesque court buildings were the products of the unlikely architectural career of James Wingfield Golucke. Perhaps more successfully than any in Georgia, Golucke drew pure forms from Richardson's well, but he too tempered his work. It may be that he understood that a drink from such modern waters would not quench Southern thirsts, or perhaps he simply tried and failed, like so many of Richardson's imitators.

Today thirty of these forty-seven Romanesque Revival courthouses still stand (see Tables III & IV). Richardson, himself a Southerner, chose a historical style as his vehicle to the future. Although many of

Georgia's courthouses owe a debt to H. H. Richardson, it was not his vision of the future that accounted for this connection, it was his chosen link to the past.

The death of the Romanesque Revival in America was sudden. In the North the buildings of the 1893 World's Fair and Columbian Exposition at Chicago sparked national enthusiasm for an excessively flowery Beaux-Arts Classicism. Before the turn of the century classical revivals spewed from the pens of architects like Richard Morris Hunt, Sanford White and Charles McKim. The old romantic champions of the picturesque were dispersed in full retreat. In 1893, Richardson was seven years dead, John Wellborn Root had died over a year before the fair opened and Louis Sullivan, perhaps the most capable traveler on Richardson's road from the picturesque to modernism, was soon to withdraw into bitter cynicism. In the meantime, the emerging world of American finance was quick to embrace the new classicism. Heralded as a return to order and a rejection of the chaotic reality of urban life reflected in the picturesque, Beaux-Arts Classicism and an attendant wave of classical revivals were suddenly proclaimed the new architecture of Wall Street, a symbol for the forces of a boastful American Imperialism.

This national rejection of the picturesque was achieved almost overnight, but the style died a lingering death in the South. Not surprisingly, the Southern post-mortem listed a very different cause of death. The towns of rural Georgia were neither "urban" nor "chaotic " and the architecture of Wall Street and American Imperialism found no relevance here. Oversized baroque statements of pure Beaux-Arts Classicism claimed few admirers in the American South before 1910. A few of J. W. Golucke's and Frank Milburn's Classical offerings wore Beaux-Arts trappings, but these stood as exceptions to prove the rule. It was not in the flamboyant ornament of Beaux-Arts Classicism but the familiar columns of the accompanying Neoclassical Revival that the South finally found what she had been waiting for, the perfect symbolic resolution to her precarious dilemma.

The tall white columns of the Neoclassical Revival in America were ready-made for Southerners.

Here was an architecture that could stand for the desired progress sought by the proponents of the New South. At the same time, and without seeming contradiction, it recalled the full-blown myth of the Old

Plate 10: The Meriwether County Courthouse at Greenville, 1903. J. W. Golucke, architect. (Photo: Wilber W. Caldwell)

South. Here was the individualistic agrarian idealism of Jefferson's classical legacy, the peculiar distortions of Calhoun's pseudo Greek democracy, and the tangled tapestry of Southern pride and bitterness that bound them all together into a grand symbol for the evolving mythologies of both Old and New South (Plate 10).

By 1900, the myth of the Old South bore little resemblance to any antebellum reality. It had become a pure romance, born of the Lost Cause and slowly transformed by years of poverty and pride into the backbone of a unique and often violent regional psyche. Between 1894 and 1910, Georgians built forty neoclassical courthouses (see Appendix A), thirty-five of which still stand today (See Table V). Most notable among their designers were J. W. Golucke, who created twelve classical court buildings between 1900 and 1907 (see Appendix C), and Frank Milburn whose masterpieces at Abbeville, Valdosta and Thomaston set the tone for the period. Surely more columns had sprung up in Georgia during this period then had ever been dreamt on the shady verandahs of the antebellum era.

Thus, beginning as monuments to rough-hewn American frontier individualism, to faith in the rule of law and to idealistic Jeffersonian democracy, by 1900 courthouses in the American South had made an architectural odyssey culminating in a dubious classical rebirth devoid of the usual high-minded symbolism. Turn-of-the-century Neoclassicism in Georgia had at its heart the sad encumbrances of

Table V

NEOCLASSICAL COURTHOUSES STILL STANDING IN GEORGIA

Johnson County, 1894, G. W. Golucke, architect.

Pike County, 1894, G. W. Golucke, architect.

Steward County, 1895, A. J. Bryan, architect.

DeKalb County, 1900, J. W. Golucke, architect.

Tattnall County, 1902, J. W. Golucke, architect.

Decatur County 1902, Alexander Blair, architect.

Bartow County, 1903, J. W. Golucke, architect.

Worth County, 1903, J. W. Golucke, architect.

Meriwether County, 1903, J. W. Golucke, architect.

Pierce County, 1903, J. W. Golucke, architect.

Wilcox County, 1903, Frank Milburn, architect.

Colquitt County, 1903, Andrew J. Bryan & Co, architects.

Coweta County, 1904, J. W. Golucke, architect.

Jefferson County, 1904, W.F. Denny, architect.

Putnam County, 1905, J. W. Golucke, architect.

Lowndes County, 1905, Frank Milburn, architect.

Morgan County, 1905, J. W. Golucke, architect.

Franklin County, 1906, W. Chamberlain, architect.

Early County, 1907, Morgan and Dillion, architects.

Dodge County, 1906, Ed C. Hosford, architect.

Montgomery County, 1907, Alexander Blair architect.

Turner County, 1907, Alexander Blair, architect.

Appling County, 1907, H. L. Lewman, architect.

Stephens County, 1907, H. L. Lewman, architect.

Glynn County, 1907, Charles Gifford, architect.

Ben Hill County, 1907, H. H. Huggins, architect.

Jasper County, 1908, Lockwood Brothers, architects.

Effingham County, 1908, N. W. Whitcover, architect.

Harris County, 1908, Ed C. Hosford, architect.

Upson County, 1908, Frank Milburn, architect.

Warren County, 1909, W. Chamberlain, architect.

Chattooga County, 1909, Bryan & Co. architects.

Irwin County, 1910, H. L Lewman, architect.

Jenkins County, 1910, Lewis F. Goodrich, architect.

regional myth, while it flaunted stubborn pride and a frustrated hope for progress.

The message of hope did not originate in most small Southern towns. It was a foreign doctrine. Imported by a tangle of railroad companies that had ensnared Georgia in a web of track, it was preached by the men who promoted, built and operated these roads. Thus, the frenzied dreams embodied in so many flamboyant Georgia courthouses had arrived through the doors of the most unassuming building of the era: the simple country depot.

THE DEPOT

Like the courthouse, the depot, too, stood on high ground in the Southern mind. Unlike the courthouse this was not a structure of myths and symbols, but one which occupied a very real place in most people's lives. The depot was often the one tangible manifestation of the industrial world in these out-of-the-way places. It was a narrow gateway to the progress that was otherwise passing the South by. If the courthouse stood for the social and political soul of the county and was a link to the past, then the depot stood for economic life and was a link to the future.

From their very beginnings in the 1840s, the shady platforms of Georgia's depots began to replace the courthouse steps as the center of informal gathering. Loitering at the depot was perhaps preferable to loitering at the courthouse, for several times a day the sublime mystery of the train would interrupt this pastoral world, and in an inferno of soot, steam, power and all of hell's imagery, the mail would arrive. People would come and go, freight would be loaded and unloaded, and the enigma of the telegraph would click out its magical messages. This was not the gossip and the worn-out news from the courthouse steps. This news was fresh, alive and filled with import and energy.

The depot was a new building type, and there was no ready national consensus as to an appropriate style. Indeed, to the extent that the depot represented the future, any historical style seemed inappropriate. Fittingly, Georgia's early railroads seem to have given all of this little thought. Early depots were designed by railroad civil engineers, not architects, and their forms were determined by the most utilitarian considerations. If these designs symbolized anything at all, it was a stern practical reality.

From the beginning, great emphasis was placed on the depots at the railheads of the early lines. Certainly much of this was due to the rather self-serving approach of Augusta and Savannah and later of Atlanta and Macon. These cities saw their railroads as private implements of "urban imperialism," designed to broaden the sponsoring city's trade and prosperity. The Georgia Railroad was the tool of Augusta and the Central of Georgia, of Savannah. The completion of

Plate 11: Atlanta's Stone Mountain Park features a miniature copy of architect E. A. Vincent's Atlantic & Western Depot, which was erected at Atlanta in 1853 and burned by Sherman in 1864. (Photo: Wilber W. Caldwell)

Table VI	**ANTEBELLUM DEPOTS STILL STANDING IN GEORGIA** Ringgold, 1849 Forsyth, 1852 Dalton, 1852 Calhoun, 1854 Cartersville, 1854, rebuilt 1902 Madison, c 1857 Crawford, c. 1857 Albany, 1857 Stone Mountain, 1852, rebuilt 1914 Thomson, 1860

stops on that line in the 1840s, by the 1850s many were replaced with brick depots.[10] Similarly on the Georgia Railroad, wooden sheds were replaced by stone or brick depots in the late 1850s.[11] On the Western and Atlantic, the late 1840s and 1850s saw the construction of fine brick or stone depots at almost every significant stop. The stunning detail of the 1852 depot at Dalton reflected national trends and was the model for postbellum design in the emerging American "Railroad Style" in the state. The Macon and Western, heir to the collapsed Monroe Railroad, built massive stone depots at Forsyth and

the Western and Atlantic from Atlanta to Chattanooga brought the upstart Atlanta into the contest, and Macon prospered on the success of the Southwestern Railroad. Undoubtedly the best-known antebellum railroad building in Georgia is the old Western and Atlantic "train shed" at Atlanta (Plate 11) designed by E. A. Vincent in 1853 and burned by Sherman in 1864. Similar structures stood at Macon (1855) and at West Point (1854) at the end of the Atlanta and LaGrange Railroad (later the Atlanta and West Point Railroad). In Savannah a great passenger shed, designed by Augustus Schwab, was begun before 1860. It was completed in 1876. Augusta's first Union Passenger Depot was of like design and was completed around 1870. The last of these grand train sheds rose at Columbus in 1882. Sadly, only the Central's great passenger depot at Savannah still stands today.

Most sources on the subject suggest that the typical small town depot of the antebellum era was a rough wooden shed. This does not wholly seem to have been the case in Georgia. The Central built a substantial brick depot at Millen in 1839,[9] and although rough wooden "store-houses" served most

Plate 12: The depot at Crawford, c. 1852. (Photo: Wilber W. Caldwell)

Barnesville in 1852. Remarkably today, ten antebellum depots survive (see Table VI).

After the war, despite devastating and widespread destruction or deterioration of roadbeds and rolling stock and the catastrophe of Sherman's march so ruinous to the Central, the re-emergence of Georgia's rail system was surprisingly rapid. By 1870, the Central had replaced most of the depots destroyed by Federal incendiaries, building substantial brick depots at Millen, Tennille, Bartow, Davisboro (no

[9] L. O. Reynolds, "The Third Chief Engineer's Report to the President of The Central Railroad and Banking Company" *The Annual Reports of the President of The Central Railroad and Banking Company*, 6 vols. (Savannah: J. M. Cooper and Co, 1839) 1:32.

[10] In his 1852 report to the president of the road, the Chief Engineer of the Central noted the "decay of our wood freight houses" and recommended the construction of 8 new structures "of brick." L. O. Reynolds, "The Eighteenth Chief Engineer's Report to the President of The Central Railroad and Banking Company" in *The Reports of the Presidents, Engineer-in-Chief and Superintendents of The Central Railroad and Banking Company*, 1/18 (Savannah 1854-1895). The 1858 report listed the cost of these depots at $4000 to $5000 each. Wooden depots of the era were estimated at about $600, so these must have been fine brick buildings. None escaped Sherman's attention.

[11] Charles C. Jones, Jr. and Salem Dutcher, *The Memorial History of Augusta* (Syracuse NY: D. Mason, 1890) 492.

Plate 13: The Central of Georgia Depot at Fort Valley, 1871. (Photo: Wilber W. Caldwell)

longer standing), and Toomsboro. In the same period, the Southwestern, leased by the Central in 1869, replaced its old wooden depots with similar brick structures at Fort Valley, Montezuma and Americus. All of these were built from essentially the same plan. All are stern, utilitarian warehouses with accommodations for passengers at one end (Plate 13).

By the late 1860s, out in the wilds of rural Georgia, traces of the American "Railroad Style" were beginning to materialize. Before the war, depot design in the rest of the country, although diverse, had gathered focus and the American "Railroad Style" had emerged out of a distinctly romantic and decidedly human need for symbolism. It began as a reflection of the gathering force of the Italian Villa Style that was the rage of the nation's domestic designers in the 1840s and 1850s. In its most fluent articulations, the

THE CENTRAL OF GEORGIA'S EARLY POSTBELLUM "RAILROAD STYLE" DEPOTS STILL STANDING IN GEORGIA
Millen , 1868
Tennille, 1869
Bartow, 1869
Toomsboro, 1869
Montezuma, 1870
Americus, 1870
Butler, 1870
Fort Valley, 1871
Hampton, 1874
Carrollton, c.1876

style featured low square towers, Italianate window treatments and broad eaves supported by large lacy brackets. In Georgia, towers and other Italianate finery were omitted. Occasionally we find a graceful classical doorway or cornice, but generally local iterations of the "Railroad Style" secure inclusion into the class solely through the vehicle of scrolling brackets supporting the eaves (Table VII).

With the completion of the Central of Georgia's depots at Butler on the Columbus Branch (1870) and

Plate 14: The depot at Ackert. (Photo: Wilber W. Caldwell)

at Hampton on the old Macon and Western (1880), we began to see the first move away from a purely functional approach to depot design. Although probably the work of a civil engineer and not a trained architect, these depots incorporate not only simple decorative motifs, but also exhibit a grace of form decidedly classical in origin.

But the influence of the "Railroad Style" was not to last long. Throughout the 1880s and 1890s and into the twentieth century the rank-and-file depot built in the average trackside hamlet in Georgia was most often wooden and of a rather fundamental design characterized by the oversized eaves supported by bold, masculine angular brackets. Details and ornamentation varied greatly from road to road and from region to region. In the pine barrens, in much of the old Cotton Belt and in very small towns, these structures were often quite plain (Plate 14). While in larger towns of the Piedmont and in the north and the western parts of the state many reflected the eclectic styles of the day, although in a rather crude but codified

Plate 15: The depot at Yatesville. (Photo: Wilber W. Caldwell)

Plate 16: The old Atlanta, Birmingham & Coast Depot at Tifton. (Photo: Wilber W. Caldwell)

"depot" sort of way. Some wore shingles and "carpenter style" jigsaw trim popular in vernacular domestic buildings of the era (Plate 15) while others incorporated practical considerations with a pleasingly simple and sometimes picturesque aesthetic (Plate 16). Standing examples are many.

While wood would serve for the "shake-rags" and "whistle-stops," larger upcountry county towns and virtually all of the regional market towns of the era built picturesque brick depots during the 1880s and 1890s. These were often the work of professional architects hired by the railroads. Many were cloned from standard plans, or were variations of reusable themes, and many achieved notable charm. Some of these buildings mirrored the ornament of architectural fads of the day (Plate 17). But most remained faithful to an emerging "depotesque" form characterized by broad eaves; heavy brackets; a long, low, sometimes flaring roofline; a string course at the level of the window sills and occasionally dormers or a low tower. Many survive today.

Meanwhile, the architectural saga of the great urban depots of the Railroad Era that was unfolding in the North and Midwest during the last decades of the nineteenth century had few parallels in Georgia. In the larger northern cities, the American urban depot had evolved as a distinct architectural form. In response to a long list of unique problems posed by rail travel and by the newly rediscovered art of city planning, late nineteenth century urban depot designers in the United States developed inventive architectural solutions to the most modern of puzzles. At the same time, the corporate egos of the growing railroad giants of the era demanded not only functional designs but flamboyant and self-serving architecture to flaunt the muscle of their monopolistic success and to broadcast their new-found pride in managerial capitalism. Turrets and towers, grand halls and gargantuan train sheds sprouted in the East and Midwest, but few of these monumental structures rose in Georgia.

There were a few exceptions. Thornton Marye's Atlanta Terminal Station, a baroque riot of Spanish Renaissance excess constructed of concrete, was completed in 1905 and demolished in 1971. Four years earlier, Savannah and Augusta had erected large depots in the same style designed with considerably more grace and art by Frank Milburn, who designed four courthouses in Georgia around the same time. A few rural depots in Georgia reflected current architectural appointments of the day rose. For example, Atlanta's Bruce and Morgan, whose Romanesque Revival court buildings had been popping up all over the state, designed stylish passenger stations at Forsyth (1895), Americus (1900) and Columbus (1901). Larger depots appeared in junction towns like Waycross, Fitzgerald, and Athens, but most of these were merely oversized cousins of the smaller brick stations that symbolized the railroads' extravagant promise. It was primarily these modest buildings, and in many cases the tiny rough-edged wooden warehouses that fostered the blind hope, which would fan the fires of courthouse building in Georgia between 1885 and 1910.

Plate 17: The depot at Forsyth, 1899. Bruce and Morgan, architects. (Photo: Wilber W. Caldwell)

Although decorated in the picturesque styles of their times, Georgia's courthouses and depots of the era seemed to have resisted the temptation to move beyond the limits of a rather strict Southern sensitivity concerning appropriate local architectural expression. Despite all the exuberance manifested in county courthouses between 1870 and 1910, none followed the lead of the lofty academic classicism of American public buildings erected by national and state governments. The Georgia State Capitol Building, designed by Edbrocke and Burnham and completed in 1889, was typical of the high governmental style. Like the national capitol, the building reflected an academic classical influence born of the Renaissance, which pressed on America out of eighteenth-century Europe. But out in Georgia's counties, considerable hostility was directed toward any centralizing force in government, and accordingly the architecture of county governments were reined in short of such formality. This prudence extended even to counties selecting styles that were inherently formal or ornately decorative. In classical modes like the Second Empire and the Neoclassical Revival, not only

was symbolism shamelessly localized, the styles themselves were held within the narrow boundaries of domestic tastes, sensitivities and proprieties. The courthouse, so close to the Southern heart and soul, was after all a court "house," and as such, a distinct modesty of scale and design was imposed. Like grand homes, monumentality was desired, but only of a specific sort and only within conservative limits. There is a comfortable quality to almost all of Georgia's late nineteenth-century court buildings, and it is no coincidence that the styles selected were generally the popular domestic styles of the day. Likewise, depot design in the period, although sometimes ornate and often picturesque, remained tame. Classicism was not the order of the day in railroad station design until after 1900, and even then, there was little of it erected beside Georgia's rails.

Even though the courthouse sang soaring songs of hope and the depot hummed the slow monotone of practical reality, the two structures had made a similar odyssey through the architectural minefield of the picturesque era. Both began the era as simple, functional, vernacular buildings. Both donned the clothing of popular styles, and both limited the application of this idiomatic wardrobe to local, acceptable, and comfortable executions. Lastly, both underwent a profound change after 1910. The architecture of Georgia's courthouses shifted drastically in the second decade of the new century. Although many were still designed in the Neoclassical Revival style, these twentieth-century buildings began to lose their comfortable, "hometown" quality. Depot design had begun to change at about the same time. The new generation of public buildings no longer represented monuments to the people of Georgia or to the South, Old or New. They appear cold and inorganic monuments to governmental and corporate efficiency and authority. The growing popularity of Beaux-Arts Classicism added greatly to this impression in both courthouse and depot design. The 1918 Walker County Courthouse at Lafayette and Macon's 1916 Union Depot are heartless standing examples.

The selection of the year 1910 as the end of this study is far from arbitrary. Perhaps it was at about this time that the New South was actually beginning to arrive in Georgia, that the old romance was starting to fade, and the forces of Eastern Industrialism were finally winning the peace that had followed the war fought almost a half century before. The overwhelming force of the homogony of the American middle-class with its cash-register morality was finally about to make itself known in Dixie. Or perhaps, as elsewhere in America, it was just the end of the frontier.

II: ARCHITECTURE AS ART

The best architecture reaches out, takes us by the hand and sings the most beautiful and personal of songs. But the appeal of these melodies is not purely aesthetic. Beauty cannot exist in a vacuum. Architectural beauty is an active force in an interactive world. As James Marston Fitch so aptly puts it, "In architecture there are no spectators, there are only protagonists, participants."[12] Thus all architecture must be considered in context. Its songs can be fully heard only in the context of its surroundings, its historical setting, and its own role in that history. Only then can it sing out and be properly judged, and judgment in this regard can not be purely aesthetic. It is by its ability to carry a symbol that architecture becomes art. A structure achieves greatness in its ability to

"stand for something," to relate, to evoke an image, to create emotions, to sing. Architecture does not "imitate life," it interacts with life and is thus held accountable to a sweeping artistic standard.

Most architectural histories work downward, following the forces of great buildings as they spill inspiration from on high to enrich the world. But there is a wealth of insight to be gleaned from looking at things from the ground up. In this case, we view the lofty heights of greatness from the obscurity of the wreckage of the Civil War and through the eyes of the South's second generation of trained architects. Viewed from this rural back-eddy in the American cultural mainstream, these mountains of inspiration must have seemed remote indeed.

In 1870, at the beginning of the period in question, the construction of the great court buildings of Europe was underway. G. E. Street won the competition among virtually all of England's great architects (Alfred Waterhouse, William Burges and Gilbert Scott among them), when he was selected to design London's wildly picturesque New Law Courts in 1868. The controversial new Criminal Wing of the French Courts designed by Louis Duc, was completed in Paris in that same year, and in Brussels, Joseph Poelaert's extraordinary Palace of Justice had been begun only two years before. In this country, the dome and the wings of the United States capitol were completed just as the Civil War ended.

Likewise, the era of the great urban train stations had arrived. In London, Philip Hardwick's 1849 Euston Station and his 1854 Paddington Station II were followed by Sir George Gilbert Scott's incredible St. Pancras Station begun in 1863 and Robert Hood's great train shed at Victoria Station completed in 1866. Similarly in France, Francois Duquesney's Gare de l'Est and Victor Lenoir's Gare Montparnasse were both completed in 1852, and the boldly Classical Gare du Nord, designed by J. I. Hittoff, was completed in 1865. In America, the age of the great urban train stations, which would reach a climax in the last

---

[12] James Marston Fitch, *American Building, The Environmental Forces that Shaped It*, 2nd ed. (Boston: Houghton Mifflin Company, 1972) 2.

quarter of the nineteenth century, had its beginnings in the 1850s in Baltimore, Harrisburg, and Chicago. New York's first Grand Central Station designed by Isaac Buckhout and J. B. Snook was begun in 1869.

What, if anything, did obscure Southern builders and designers find to be relevant in the great works of their era? How were their symbols applied? The Age of Enlightenment had passed, and the age of Romanticism was lingering. The great waves of Romantic Classicism and Picturesque Eclecticism had flowed from Europe to the cities of the American Northeast and then trickled southward where they mingled with a powerful vernacular. Thus, the primary artistic forces at work in the American South in years following the Civil War were not once but twice removed from cotton's weary fields where the vernacular was still a force. From the English influence in Colonial times and later from the dabbling of the francophile Thomas Jefferson in his search for a national architectural style, classicism had placed its mark on the American South. The region would return again and again to classical styles, each time re-manipulating the symbols to suit increasingly peculiar needs.

The manipulation of classical symbols was nothing new. The history of Europe was well documented by this changing imagery. Each period had adopted classical messages to suit its own ideals: the Renaissance in reaction to medieval dogma, later flowering neoclassicism to mirror governmental forms, Baroque classicism to reflect an aristocratic society, Napoleonic classicism to herald a thoroughly revolutionary era. In the wake of all this, it is not surprising that Jefferson sought to free his homeland from the heavy influence of English classicism manifested in the work of Christopher Wren, James Gibbs, Sir John Soane and others. Jefferson's designs endeavored to unearth a pure untarnished, national, democratic, architectural style, true to original Greek and Roman models. By the 1820s, a new wave of classicism had arrived. The Greek Revival seemed a natural democratic icon for the emerging nation. But the South would enthusiastically embrace the Greek Revival, draping it in her own unique imagery. This is part of the story to be told here. Likewise, the South's love affair with the

American Neoclassical Revival in the early years of the twentieth century is by no means consistent with the chosen national symbolism. At the turn of the century, the South sought to recall her past while the rest of the country found in flowery Beaux-Arts Classicism a flamboyant messenger to announce global financial power and the excesses of a budding imperialism, all of which had arrived on the steeds of industrialism.

Likewise, the full force of Romanticism was gathered into the picturesque movement, which had crossed the Atlantic from England. American picturesque architecture first flourished on the rising tide of the Gothic Revival and later on waves of historical European revivalism that often washed as much architectural confusion as romance. At the heart of the picturesque, most Southerners found architecture consisting of primal stone forms recalling a medieval agrarian countryside. This was the pure romantic essence of the picturesque, and it was this, and not the style's later "modern" imagery, which the South would embrace.

The Civil War marked the end of the Romantic era in most of America and silenced the voices of Whitman, Emerson and Thoreau. The forces of realism and the abuses of a grasping, exploitive industrialism and its attendant unsophisticated middle-class were loosed on the land. Whether one chooses, with Mark Twain, to sarcastically call the era "The Gilded Age" or to adopt Lewis Mumford's darker appellation, "The Brown Decades," the new American epic was generally devoid of artistic progress.

What brought such desolation? There is a school of thought that holds that the end of the aristocracy deprived artists of sophisticated patronage, and thus the period imposed a restrictive license on creativity, forcing it down to middle-class tastes. Europe's experience, however, seemed to refute this idea. The Industrial and Romantic Revolutions had produced Wordsworth, Byron, Shelly, and Keats; Hugo, Dumas and Balzac; Constable and Turner; Delacroix and Corot; and the late nineteenth century had replaced them with Dickens and Zola; Proust and Flaubert; Degas, Monet, Renoir, van Gogh, Seurat and Rodin. This was an art driven by arguably bourgeois tastes, but hardly restricted. But in America, none rose to replace the voices of Whitman, Emerson, Thoreau and Melville, or as Lewis Mumford would have us believe, the voices were there but were ignored. The forces that wrought an artistic wasteland in America in the late nineteenth century were complex and unlovely, but the clouds that covered the American South were darker still.

The region festered, due to her maudlin fixation on the past. The South clung to Romanticism long after it was dead and buried elsewhere, but in this habit, the region did not escape the artistic void which enveloped the rest of the country. To the contrary, the atmosphere in the South in the period beginning after the Civil War and continuing into the first decade of the twentieth century was as devoid of artistic promise as it was of economic progress. Wilbur Cash suggests that the South's predicament had deep roots. For Cash, before the war, the defense of slavery had rested at the heart of Southern intellectual, cultural and economic stagnation, and afterwards embittered racism fostered a similar intransigence. According to Cash, the defense of slavery "…not only eventuated…in a taboo of criticism; in the same process it set up a ban on all analysis and inquiry, a terrified truculence toward every new idea, a disposition to reject every invocation out of hand and hug the whole of the *status quo* with fanatical resolution."[13] And so it was that the nineteenth-century American South was barren soil for the arts. In fact, the region was doubly damned. It was bound to artistic sterility by its own narrow mindset, while at the same time, it was a stepchild to a national wasteland, so busy with its outward quest for real world plunder, that it allowed no place for inward reflection. But somewhere deep within the national vacuum, America's architects were beginning to sing.

It is one of history's many quirks that architecture was the exception to the drab artistic output of the American "Brown Decades." Ironically two of the country's architectural giants of the period were born in the South: H. H. Richardson was from Louisiana and John Wellborn Root was from Lumpkin, Georgia.

Like so many Southern artists, during and after the war, both men had left the South in search of more sympathetic atmospheres. Richardson landed in the East and Root in Chicago. American masters of the period, Richardson and Root, Sullivan and Wright, had begun to make something of the architectural confusion emanating from across the Atlantic while the rest of American art slept.

Architecture is the most functional of arts, and in the adolescence of industrialism, functionalism was becoming the watchword. The old rules were discarded, not by the new social and economic culture of the machine age, but in response to new needs and new building materials that the age created. If America began the period attempting to digest picturesque and Beaux-Arts designs handed down from the lofty heights of an European architectural Olympus, she ended the period exporting ideas for a sublimely engineered, functional new architecture of basic shapes and tall buildings. It was an architecture that responded to modern urban needs and egos. The Old World would gasp at the vision.

Sadly, most of this passed the South by. Richardson's appeal in Georgia was driven more by its historical vocabulary than by its modern message. Root designed the region's first modern tall building in 1892, The Equitable Building in Atlanta, and locally, Bruce and Morgan, a veteran firm of 18 Georgia courthouses (see Appendix C), designed the 10 story Grant Prudential Building in 1899. But Atlanta was only a symbol for a New South that was a long distance away in 1900. The art of Louis Sullivan and Frank Lloyd Wright would have little influence in cotton's struggling kingdom, although the grand Union Depot at Chattanooga, built in 1904, surely owes a debt to Sullivan, just as the fine 1913 Union Depot at Albany, owes something to Wright.

III: THE ARCHITECTURE OF THE NEW SOUTH

The premise of these pages involves the assumption that, in the period between the end of the Civil War and 1910, the New South was more a concept

---

[13] Cash, *The Mind of the South*, 98.

than a reality. And as this mythical concept grew, it impacted Southern history with a force every bit as potent as the concrete realities of the age. Likewise a part of the architecture of the New South was a product more of dreams that of substance. The wood and the stone were real enough, but the artistic force behind the design was often only false hope and empty bravado. As a result architectural style developed along untraveled paths, winding a perilous route, balanced on the cusp between two worlds, borrowing from both and fickle in allegiance. This book reveals an unsure architecture, often ambivalent in its symbols and chasing after a dream that its creators were half-afraid to catch. In order to understand the architecture of the New South, one must understand the New South itself. By examining real history found in the short distance between the courthouse and the depot, we find the key to these structures themselves—the myth of the New South.

By 1880, the columns of the Old South had seemingly inspired everyone, both Northern and Southern, to drink deeply of the potion of the antebellum period. In the years following the Civil War, America created an Old South to suit her changing needs. The individualistic young nation of once boundless frontiers was fast evolving into a grasping dominion of urban entrapment. The country's need for what she had lost was great, so she fabricated fantasies to soothe her once wild soul. Just as the legend of the Old West was born more of hunger for dime novels than of the lusty deeds of desperadoes and deputies, so the legend of the Old South conjured up aristocrats from simple farmers, soft breezes from malarial heat, gentle manners from slave owners, and the dying gasp of frontier individualism from brooding and often violent ignorance. Southerners had less vicarious reasons for clinging to the Lost Cause. The region did much to perpetuate that myth to soothe its own moody deprivations. But the full-blown myth of the Old South came, in large part, from the voracious appetites of an American middle class submerged in the drudgery of modern life and yearning for a romantic frontier that was disappearing before its eyes.

The purveyors of the myth of the New South were among the most adroit at weaving fabric for the myth of the Old South. Upon the smoldering stones of the Old South Henry Grady, Walter Hines Page, Henry Watterson, Richard Edmonds and others laid the foundation for their evangelical New South creed. Here was a complex dogma—every bit as enigmatic as the Southern mind to which it was designed to appeal, and every bit as corrupt as the Northern capitalistic impulse it was designed to attract. Upon the very foundations of the architecture of the Old South these men proposed to create the architecture of the New South. Out of ruin they proposed to design a new order. It was not to be an amalgam of the classical columns of agrarianism and the picturesque towers of industrialism. No such compromise was envisioned. The cold Romanesque stones of capitalism would be used only to build a bastion in which to protect the graceful verandahs of a bygone era. It was a paradoxical and inherently contradictory proposition, and although its blueprints were drawn with well-reasoned detail, few grand monuments would be built before 1910. Standing in puzzling exception to this rule are Georgia's courthouses. These buildings stood for all of the impossible hopes that turned on visions of prosperity. Thus, they were often the direct products of the real architecture of the New South, the countless unassuming little railroad depots that had begun to cover the state in the antebellum period and then multiplied like so many batten-board jack-rabbits in the post war period.

The concept of the New South was supported by three fundamental pillars: industrial and agricultural modernization, reconciliation with the North and racial peace. Attached to these great columns were all manner of supporting rafters and beams—lesser structural members each dedicated to its own form of progress: diversified and scientific agriculture, modern education, the region's abundant natural wealth, the creation of small farms, urbanization, industrial technology, Northern capital, a new patriotism, expanded markets, campaigns to lure immigrants, liberated racial attitudes and so much more. Inherent in all of this was the implication of a new social and economic order and a more liberal regional mindset.

The grand irony of the era is best revealed when one views both the promises and the failures of the

New South as two sides of the same coin. It was Newtonian—for every mythical promise, there was an equal and opposite realty. Against the myth of industrialization stood the dominating reality of a vast agricultural sea. Against the myth of entrepreneurial spirit and shopkeeper decorum stood the reality of a traditional simplicity of life tainted by a remarkable penchant for violence. Against the myth of boundless natural resources stood the reality of wholesale exploitation. Against the myth of education stood appalling illiteracy. Against the myth of immigration stood the reality that the South would accept few immigrants without white Anglo-Saxon pedigrees. Against the myth of diversified agriculture stood king cotton's impregnable kingdom. Against the myth of reconciliation stood the growing myth of the Lost Cause and the Old South itself. Against the myth of separate racial equality stood the dark realities of Jim Crow, disenfranchisement, lynching, terror and an insidious and pervasive mindset that vacillated between patronizing disdain on one hand and abject fear on the other. Against the myth of the small farmer stood the nightmare that was tenancy. Against the myth of Northern capital stood the fact that most of the cotton mills and railroads built in the South before 1895 were built with scraped-together local capital and the reality that mills built after 1895 were most often aimed at the exploitation of cheap labor.

The prosperity predicted by New South spokesmen required a radically changed Southern mindset. A new spirit had to be forged that welcomed change, threw off the yoke of the past, embraced capitalistic values, and sought a new liberal social order. This was not to be. The mind of the South was a metal that was deeply etched in tradition. The result of such intransigence was a period of stagnation, poverty, and cultural limbo. The South was trapped between two myths, and she vainly sought to have the best of both. She got the worst of the Old and little if any of the New.

As we have noted, architectural design is difficult to judge outside of its historical setting. Georgia's courthouse design in the era beginning in 1870 and ending in 1910 is a strange and mysterious alloy when viewed in the context of the region's ironic and compelling dilemma. It was a metal forged from equal parts of the Old South and the New South. It sought at once to move forward and back, and thus, it became fixed in a tortured present.

If the courthouses of the "New South Era" represented the architecture of Southern myth, then the depot represented the architecture of Southern reality. Standing firm among so many contradictions—so many promises unfulfilled and yet still stubbornly believed—the depot stood for the railroad, often the single shining reality in a foggy sea of myth. When reinforced by the enticing sermons flowing from the pulpits of the New South's overzealous spokesmen, so powerful was the illusion of progress imported by postbellum rails that the appearance of the depot and the few brick buildings which usually followed moved many counties to construct monuments to their dreams. The altogether new light shinning from the depot rendered many Southerners blind to a present rooted in poverty and ignorance, while it inspired visions of an impossible future.

———————

Although the mind of the South was slow to accept the gifts of a new era without qualification, it is impossible to deny that somewhere in all of this, one staggering change did take place. A comparison of the courthouses of the postbellum period with those built before the war clearly reveals that the rural population of Georgia changed. This history begins with those who would keep their treasures in a safe. It ends with those who would keep their treasures in a jewel box.

•

PART 1

Antebellum Railroads
1833–1860

The Georgia Railroad

THE MAIN LINE

Richmond County: Augusta • Columbia County: Appling • McDuffie County: Thomson • Taliaferro
County: Crawfordville • Greene County: Greensboro • Morgan County: Madison • Newton County: Covington
Rockdale County: Conyers • DeKalb County: Decatur • Fulton County: Atlanta (See chapters 4, 11, 26 & 32)

THE ATHENS BRANCH
Oglethorpe County: Lexington • Clarke County: Athens (See chapter 13)

THE WARRENTON BRANCH
Warren County: Warrenton (see Chapter 8)

THE WASHINGTON BRANCH
Wilkes County: Washington • Lincoln County: Lincolnton • Some Last Thoughts on the Georgia Railroad

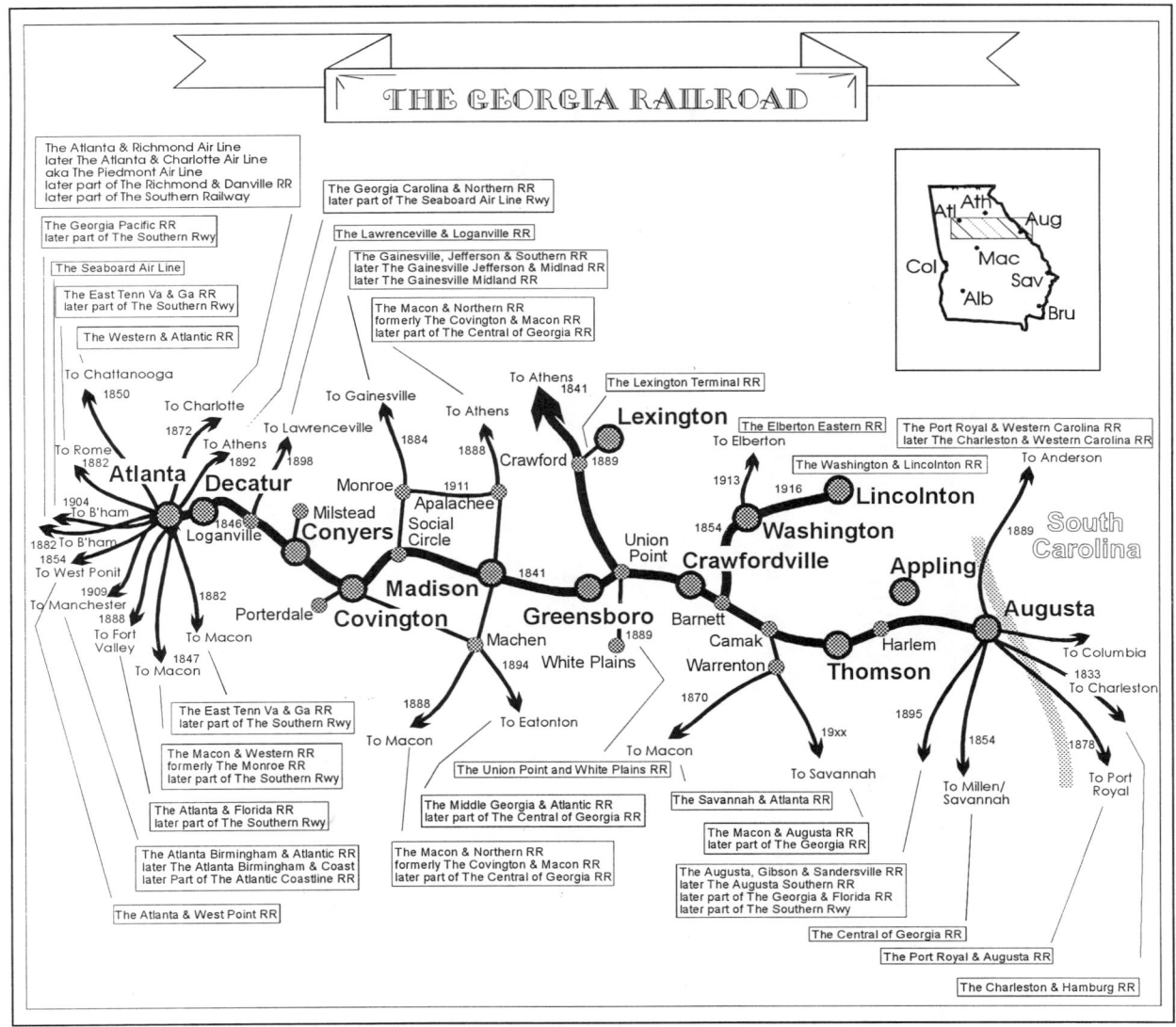

1 | The Georgia Railroad

THE MAIN LINE: AUGUSTA TO ATLANTA

RICHMOND COUNTY: AUGUSTA

Plate 1.1: Augusta: A View Across the Augusta Canal, built in 1847, to the Sibley Manufacturing Company, built in 1880.

There is neither depot nor courthouse here. Still we begin here not simply because Augusta is at the geographical and chronological beginning of our story, but also because Augusta has a voice. The canal speaks of what went before, and the mill speaks of what was later to come.

This is no ordinary canal—it is a power canal. Only 7 miles long and running parallel to the Savannah River, it was designed to take in water up stream and to control its flow in order to make the energy of falling water available for the mills along its route. It must have been considered a success for it was enlarged in 1875 to increase the horsepower from 600 to 14,000[1] —a remarkable fact considering the South was, at that time, still in the emotional throes of bitter defeat and paralyzed by the economic and political trauma of Reconstruction.

Canals had once been very much on the minds of Georgians. With the invention of the cotton gin in 1793 and subsequent advances in spinning technology, Sea Island cotton had proved wildly profitable along the coast in the first quarter of the nineteenth century. The central reality of Georgia was fast becoming cotton, and the central reality of cotton was expansion towards the west. The introduction of cotton into the Piedmont placed a premium on transportation. The challenge was to transverse the lonely expanses of Pine Barrens that separated the emerging "Cotton Belt" from the coast. Since the opening of the Erie Canal in 1819, Georgians had jealously eyed this success as they laboriously inched pole boats back up the Oconee and Ocmulgee, and watched steamboats filled with cotton founder on the shoals of the Savannah and the

---

[1] Charles C. Jones, Jr. and Salem Dutcher, *The Memorial History of Augusta* (Syracuse NY: D. Mason, 1890) 188.

Plate 1.1: The 1880 Sibley Manufacturing Company at Augusta flaunted the architecture of exuberance, hope, perhaps even excess, in a landscape still reeling from crushing defeat. (Photo: Wilber W. Caldwell)

Chattahoochee. Complex portage schemes were common, as were "disposable" barges, which were built for one trip down river and then sold for lumber on the coast. Floods and droughts added a desperate unpredictability, and all of this continued in the midst of an overland road system, which was, in a word, impossible. River and road maintenance was much discussed but nothing came of the discussions. Many canals were dreamt and very few built. In 1826, Georgia commissioned an English engineer, Hamilton Fulton, to investigate the possibility of linking either the Oconee or the Ocmulgee with the Tennessee River, thereby linking the Atlantic and the Mississippi River[2]. A similar study was begun to assess the feasibility of linking the Chattahoochee River with the

Savannah River via canals to the Oconee River.[3] A grand canal was discussed to connect Savannah with the Ogeechee River, running parallel to the Fall Line, and then crossing to the Oconee. A twelve-mile canal was actually dug using slave and later Irish labor linking Brunswick with the Altamaha River, but it was never used.[4]

Had the railroads not come along when they did, it is quite probable that some of these schemes would have come to fruition. In 1833 the city of Charleston, having no viable inland river to channel cotton from the Piedmont and feeling eclipsed by Savannah, built the Charleston and Hamburg Railroad from Charleston to Hamburg, South Carolina, just across the river from Augusta. The effect was electric. Both Savannah and Augusta scrambled to build railroads, and canals were soon forgotten. The names given to Georgia's earliest railroads suggest, however, a certain lack of faith in rail as the state's primary, transportation medium. The original 1833 charter of the Savannah line created the Central Railroad and Canal Company of Georgia (later the Central of Georgia Railroad), and the charter for the Augusta line created in that same year the Augusta and Eatonton Turnpike and Railroad Company (later the Georgia Railroad).

By 1847, when the Augusta Canal was built, railroads were becoming a reality in Georgia, and the best use for a canal seemed to be turning the wheels of the mills that everyone was sure would come. Falling water was the key, and thirty-three antebellum textile mills were built in Georgia including several in or near Augusta. Other textile centers emerged on moving water at Columbus and Macon, as well as on isolated streams and creeks along the Fall Line, and by 1860 Georgia's infantile industrialization was toddling along nicely. Then it all turned to ashes.

For most of Georgia, the path back from devastation proved a very long road indeed, and that is what

[2] Ulrich B. Phillips, *History of Transportation in the Eastern Cotton Belt to 1860* (1908, reprint, New York: McMillan, 1913) 110.

[3] James M. Russell, *Atlanta, 1847-1890: City Building in the Old South and New* (Baton Rouge: Louisiana State University of Press, 1988) 16.

[4] Kenneth Coleman, *The History of Georgia* (Athens GA: University of Georgia Press, 1977) 155-56.

makes structures like the Sibley Manufacturing Company so compelling. In truth, decade upon decade of stagnation marked the way, and except for Atlanta and a few Fall Line cities like Augusta, Georgia would lie wounded and nostalgically brooding for the remainder of the century and well into the next.

It is evident that the 1880 Sibley Manufacturing Company is no ordinary mill. The designers put aside the usual drab, utilitarian styles—the massive monotonies of brick interrupted only by a relentless array of unadorned windows. Here we find an architecture of hope. From whence did such hope spring? Nestled behind the Sibley Manufacturing Company is the spur of a railroad. In 1880, when this building was new, this railroad was called the Port Royal and Augusta. Its extension to Anderson, Walhalla and Greenville became the Charleston and Western Carolina, a latter day cousin of the Charleston and Hamburg Railway, which, in 1833, at a length of 133 miles, was the longest railroad in the world. These unassuming steel ribbons inspired the South to discard the unadorned, practical, vernacular styles of the past and adopt the joyous architectural expressions of the industrial period.

Plate 1.2: The Old Richmond County Courthouse at Augusta, built in 1821, demolished in 1959.

Augusta was the capital of Georgia from 1786 until 1795, and when George Washington visited the city in 1791, he found 250 dwellings, a courthouse, a stone jail, an academy, three warehouses for storing tobacco and 1100 inhabitants. In 1801, a small brick court building rose at Augusta, but this soon proved inadequate. In 1821, Augusta, with a population of about 2500, was emerging as a trading center at the head of navigation on the Savannah River. General Oglethorpe's little fort in "the back country" was awakening to the whistles of the first steamboats which had arrived in 1816.

Ignoring any emerging regional separatism, the old Richmond County Courthouse at Augusta reflected only an innocent early American self-awareness. This was a building in the "Federal Style," as much early American architecture is described. The more precise like to use it to refer to a reduction of the Adam Style of Neoclassicism brought from England and simplified into an American idiom. The less precise use "Federal" to describe most of the structures of quality built in the early days of our nation, which are not easily classified under any other Georgian style.

Although well executed detail and cohesive styling suggest the work of a professional architect, the design of this building is attributed to Mr. Middleton, a builder. Most early Georgia courthouses had no professional architect, and since there were very few trained architects in the entire country in 1821, speculation about the derivative nature of style in many of these early, builder-designed, public buildings is not complicated. At first glance one might suppose that Augusta's 1821 courthouse was a rough copy of Philadelphia's 1735 Independence Hall, and so it may have been. But influence also appears to have flowed from one of the best known of that small fraternity of professional architects then practicing in America, Charles Bulfinch, who had been appointed to work on the nation's capitol in 1817. Bulfinch was the architect of Bulfinch Hall, built in 1818, and the Harrison Gray Otis House, built in 1786, both in Massachusetts and both disarmingly similar to the Augusta courthouse in their rectangular massing and overall formal arrangement. It is unlikely that Mr. Middleton had been to Boston, but Bulfinch was well

Plate 1.2: Ignoring any emerging regional separatism, the old Courthouse at Augusta reflected only an innocent early American self-awareness. (Photo: From George White's Historical Collections of Georgia, 1855.)

Table 1.1
RAIL CONNECTIONS AT AUGUSTA, 1892 The Georgia Railroad, Augusta to Atlanta with branches to Athens, Warrenton and Washington. The Macon and Augusta, part of the Georgia Railroad, connections at Camak for Macon via Warrenton and Milledgeville. The Central of Georgia, connections with the Central main line to Savannah via Waynesboro and Millen. The Augusta Gibson and Sandersville (later Augusta Southern) (later part of the Georgia and Florida Railroad), Augusta to Sandersville. The Port Royal and Western Carolina, Port Royal to Augusta with branches to Anderson, Greenville and Spartanburg. The Richmond and Danville, to Columbia (later part of the Southern Railway. The South Carolina Railroad, the old Charleston and Hamburg to Charleston.

Plate 1.3: The first Union Depot at Augusta. Only Macon, Atlanta, Savannah, Columbus, and West Point could boast substantial brick train sheds of similar design. (Photo: Courtesy of Les R. Winn)

known for his Massachusetts State House built in 1789, and there were probably sketches or engravings of his buildings in circulation in 1821. Additionally, in wide circulation among builders of that era was *The American Builder's Companion* containing elevations by Asher Benjamin, a few of which bear a striking resemblance to Mr. Middleton's creation.

The American frontier is much closer to home than most Southerners today are inclined to think. To be sure in 1821, Augusta was on the edge of the frontier, and what these frontiersmen did not know about architecture they knew about robust durability. They knew how to build things to last. Eventually surrounded by numerous expansions and additions, this building stood at the core of the Richmond County Courthouse for almost 140 years.

Augusta seemed blessed. By 1880, her population was above 20,000. Textile factories were built and prospered, but although she enlarged the old court building in 1892, she built no great fantasy courthouse to substantiate the myth of the New South.

This courthouse had been good enough in 1821 when cotton began to trickle down the river to Savannah, and it was good enough in 1892 when seven railroads radiated from Augusta (see Table 1.1). As was often the case along the very early rails, Augusta came to view railroads as no great panacea. After the war, when so many towns dreamt of railroad salvation lifting them from ruin, Augusta could be seen not wearing her railroads and her courthouse like jewels, but wielding them like the tools that they were.

Plate 1.3: The first Union Depot at Augusta, built c.1870.

Today the great passenger depots of Augusta are gone. In the years following the Civil War, several depots served the city. In fact, an ordinance was passed allowing the Augusta and Summerville Railroad Company, a horse drawn, street railroad, not only to carry passengers between the depots of the Georgia Railroad, the Central of Georgia, and the South Carolina roads, but also to operate steam locomotives on the city streets.[5] In the 1870s, the first Union Depot was built in an effort to eliminate some of this confusion. In the entire state, only Macon, Atlanta, Savannah, Columbus and West Point could boast substantial brick train sheds of similar design.

Plate 1.4: The second Union Depot at Augusta, built in 1901. Demolished 1969. Frank Milburn, architect.

[5]Jones, Jr. Dutcher, *The Memorial History of Augusta*, 510-51.

[6]Lawrence Wodehouse,"Frank Pierce Milburn (1868-1926), A Major Soutern Architect," in *The North Carolina Historical Bulletin* 50/3 (1973):289-303.

[7]Jones, Jr. and Dutcher, *The Memorial History of Augusta*, 480.

[8]Florence F. Corley, *Augusta, Georgia: A Confederate City* (Columbia: University of South Carolina Press, 1955), Ray Rowland and Helen Callahan, *Yesterday's Augusta* (Miami: A. E. Seeman, 1976) 13.

Built in 1901, the second Union Depot, was designed in the Spanish Renaissance Style by Frank Milburn, who designed over twenty-five depots while in the employ of the Southern Railway. Milburn, operating out of Charlotte, Columbia, South Carolina, and later Washington, D. C., was one of the most successful Southern architects of the period.[6] His work in Georgia includes grand neoclassical courthouses at Abbeville, Thomaston, and Valdosta as well as the eclectic Dutch Renaissance Wilkes County Courthouse at Washington, Georgia.

The flamboyant parapets of Frank Milburn's Union Depot voiced the city's confidence in an era of New South prosperity and marked the end of an unsteady journey for Augusta. In the sixty-five years since 1836 when the first flimsy bridge connected the Georgia Railroad with the Charleston and Hamburg,[7] Augusta had struggled to come to grips with the power of her railroads. Long after the Georgia Railroad was completed to Atlanta, with a branch to Athens, city leaders in Augusta hesitated to maintain a permanent connection with the Charleston and Hamburg. There had been previous disputes with the city of Hamburg over bridges, but the real reason for inaction was deeper. Once Augusta sensed how powerful the railroad might become, she began to harbor mortal fears of becoming a forgotten stop along the way. It took South Carolinian threats of bypassing Augusta to make the connection a permanent reality in 1853.[8] Ironically, this was the beginning of the end for the city of Hamburg. Throughout the remainder of the nineteenth century, Augusta remained cautiously optimistic. With the construction of Frank Milburn's extravaganza in 1901, the city finally allowed herself a public architectural expression of her railroad-imported aspirations.

COLUMBIA COUNTY: APPLING

Plate 1.5: The Columbia County Courthouse, built 1808-1812, rebuilt in 1856.

If the arrival of the railroads were to inspire flights of architectural fantasy in so many Georgia towns after 1880, what happened in those places the railroads passed by? The answer, of course, is nothing.

Plate 1.4: The flamboyant scrolling parapets cf Frank Milburn's 1901 Union Depot at Augusta marked the end of an unsteady journey for Augusta. (Photo: Courtesy of Georgia Dept. of Archives and History.)

Appling, the county seat of Columbia County, is instructive in this regard, if in no other. It is, to say the least, small, and apparently it always has been. In 1849, just over ten years after the Georgia Railroad was built through Columbia County at Grovetown and Sawdust, 12 miles to the South of Appling, the great traveler George White could only say that Appling's population was about 100 and that it was "on the decline." Ten years later, Adiel Sherwood's last *Gazetteer of Georgia*, which seems hesitant to say anything negative about anyplace, offers the following understatement in reference to Appling: "the place has never reached eminence, nor attained large size."

By contrast, Grovetown and Sawdust, children of the Georgia Railroad in the southern part of the county, prospered. After the Civil War Sawdust disappeared

Plate 1.5: An occasional remodeling of the old 1812 courthouse was all Columbia County was moved to do. (Photo: Wilber W. Caldwell.)

giving way to nearby Harlem, which was founded in the 1870s about a mile down the line. A drive through Harlem today is far from an uplifting, urban experience, but the faint melodies of the New South myth can still be heard beside the row of fading, brick stores.

If one hears music at Harlem, at Appling there is only the old courthouse and the wind. Still, there is a lesson well worth learning here. It is a lesson taught by what is not here, what was never here. To assume that Columbia County was not prosperous because the county town never flourished is a mistake. The real prosperity of Columbia County in 1837, when the Georgia Railroad bypassed Appling, can be summed up in just one word: cotton. With regard to the prosperity of cotton, Columbia County was doing quite well. US Census figures document 3.7 million pounds in 1830, fifteenth among Georgia's 93 counties; 9525 bales in 1860, twenty-third among Georgia's 132 counties; and in the hard times of 1880, Columbia County, with 8313 bales, was still a respectable thirty-sixth among Georgia's 137 counties.

In the antebellum era, no towns were needed for the prosperity of cotton. The plantations and large farms were complete economic units, creating or importing all they needed to color the fields white each autumn. But they exacted a heavy price, exploiting men and land and insidiously erasing all sense of equilibrium on a treadmill of cotton. Success was based on slavery, a system as economically and socially out of balance, as it was morally indefensible. After the war, with slavery gone and the plantations a romantic memory, the tenant system galloped across the land unbridled, trampling down the men and women who toiled upon it and creating a new slavery of debt and stagnation. It too needed little of towns, only a few merchants to perpetuate the cashless, economic nightmare in which seed, fertilizer, victuals and the land itself were supplied against the only collateral available: future cotton, pledged before it was

planted. Some few of these merchants were to become the forbears of a new prosperity after 1900, but most were as hopelessly caught up in the ruthless stampede to oblivion as the poor tenants themselves. It is true that many of these barter bankers ended up taking land in payment, but what could they then do but cover it with more tenants and begin the cycle anew? They didn't need towns for that.

The railroads would later seem to promise so much, for there was to be much need. But in the beginning, before the war, before tenancy, before the proliferation of the myth, iron rails seemed to promise little more than access to new lands for the growing of more cotton, and an easier way to get more cotton to market. So when the railroad passed Appling by in 1837, few looked up from their plows to notice.

The contrast between the 1821 courthouse at Augusta and this courthouse only 20 miles away at Appling is enlightening. The Augusta courthouse spoke of sophistication and vision. At Appling, we see only a stern, practical reality. The appearance of a brick courthouse here as early as 1812 discourages the temptation to label Appling "the frontier," for not far from here on the true frontier, log courthouses were built long after 1812. Still, the original building readily reflected the rural character of its builders—a vernacular building, without ornament or pretense.

The question of style, and of derivative influence in these simple buildings is problematic. Most of these early courthouses had no professional architect. Questions of style arise in vernacular architecture when details and decorations like corbeling, window styling, porticos and the like appear. These are no doubt copied from more rigid disciplines with which these builders were seldom fully conversant. These details often conform only to some personal eclectic sense of propriety perceived solely by unsophisticated carpenters and masons. The results are sometimes charming, sometimes awkward, but almost always functional.

Further confusion is born of the fact that most of the recognized styles of the day were, at their root, inheritors of the classical orders, whether directly as with the Adam Style, the Federal Style and later the Greek Revival, or via Renaissance modes as with the

[9] *The McDuffie Progress*, July 21, 1971.

[10] *The Augusta Chronicle*, June 18, 1999.

[11] Jones, Jr. and Dutcher, *The Memorial History of Augusta*, 492.

[12] William C. MacCommons and Clara Stoval, *The History of McDuffie County, Georgia* (Tignall GA: Boyd Publishing, 1988) 86.

Plate 1.6: The stone section in the center of the depot at Thomson was built in 1860. (Photo: Wilber W. Caldwell.)

work of Christopher Wren, the disciples of Palladio and myriad other Georgian influences. The problem is made clear by the Columbia County courthouse. If one ignores the paired brackets supporting the eaves, this is simply a Georgian building. Its proportion and symmetry tell a rude but basically classical tale. Beyond that, it is difficult to assess. The thing about a vernacular architecture is that it knows no discipline, except that it tends to copy itself as much as anything else.

What of these paired brackets? Do they not tell a tale? Indeed they do. This building was rebuilt in 1856, and the brackets under the eaves are typical of those often associated with the Italian Villa Style popular in this county in the 1850s. Whether Italianate or vernacular, we find similar bracketing on the brick courthouses at Albany, 1855; Perry, 1856; Fairburn, 1871, and on the 1869 courthouse at Jonesboro.

The question remains as to how much, if any, of the old 1812 courthouse was incorporated into the 1856 rebuilding. We have the 1808 orders to the builder for the old courthouse itself, along with general specifications for dimensions and function.[9] These suggest that at least part of this structure dates from 1812, although this has been a matter of recent controversy.[10]

Whatever the case, no late nineteenth century fantasy courthouse rose at Appling. The Georgia Railroad had passed through only a tiny corner of the county in 1837, and the Port Royal and Western Carolina had skirted the northeastern border in 1892 on its way west. Cotton was planted year after year,

and the land grew weary. Since the railroads never came to Appling, the myth of the New South never arrived. As Reconstruction ended, all that Columbia County's farmers could see in any direction was hard times. The 1890s saw strong Populist sentiments here, but few dreamed of revolution, industrial or otherwise. The mythical courthouse was never built because no myth had been imported to inspire it.

McDuffie County: Thomson

Plate 1.6: The depot at Thomson.

In 1865, this depot witnessed one of the final pageants of the Confederacy. It was here on the Georgia Railroad that 100,000 newly freed, ragtag remnants of the Army of the Confederate States of America passed by on their way home.

Five years before those trains passed into history, this depot was built of stone. All along the line, beginning in 1857, the Georgia Railroad began to replace the first, crude, wooden depots with structures of brick or stone.[11] In this and many other connections, a recurring theme begins to speak from between the lines of many county histories: things having to do with the railroad are things of very high quality. The railroads brought to these out-of-the-way places the best men, the best equipment, the best mules, and in many early instances the best buildings these country folk had ever seen. In late 1837, the Georgia Railroad had arrived at the spot, which was to become Thomson, and by 1860 the place had become a town of several hundred inhabitants. It is a very good bet that this depot was the first building in Thomson constructed of any material other than wood. Here, as in so many Georgia towns before 1890, there were few brick structures, save the depot, the courthouse, a few churches and the Masonic Hall. Even as late as 1900 the majority of buildings were simple wooden cubes. Thomson's testimony to all of this is written in fire, which swept through the town regularly, most notably in 1886, 1888, and again in 1910.[12]

This was perhaps the first important town "born of the railroad," meaning that when the railroad arrived in Thomson there was nothing here at all. Fittingly they called the place Thomson, after J. Edgar

Thomson, then the Chief Engineer of the Georgia Railroad and later the president of the mighty Pennsylvania Railroad. Here we have the embryo of the New South myth, the first documentation of the power of the railroad to turn obscure pastures and woodlands into places of commerce. In 1849, George White's *Statistics of the State of Georgia* only mentions that there was a post office at Thomson. By 1879, Sholes's *Gazetteer of Georgia* relates that the town had a population of about 800 and was shipping 8000 bales of cotton annually on the Georgia Railroad. Not only was the town born of the railroad, a county was born as well. By 1870, in the heart of the nightmare that was Reconstruction, McDuffie County was created from Warren and Columbia Counties, and despite the corruption rampant in political creations of the day, we can still infer from this partition significant growth in and around Thomson.

This story was to be repeated again well into the twentieth century all across the face of Georgia. The pattern of the development of these railroad towns was almost always the same: population, local commerce, brick buildings, exciting comings and goings, a perception of sophistication, all the trappings of prosperity. County after county would embrace the growing myth and believe it to be true—believe these decorations to be indicative of prosperity itself. Oblivious to the ignorance and poverty that surrounded them, they would wear the railroad's sparkling gifts like the Emperor wore his new clothes.

Plate 1.7: The McDuffie County Courthouse, built in 1873.

The construction of this fine brick courthouse at Thomson in 1872-1873 is nothing short of a miracle. In the opening years of the decade of the 1870s, Georgia lay gasping, laid low by wounds of every sort: not only had the war destroyed her infrastructure, her resources, and her manpower, Reconstruction squeezed her penniless, leaving her without a system of credit much less credit itself. All of these woes left her powerless to deal with the horrors of the national depression following the Panic of 1873. Everything was disjointed, the slaves were free, former leaders could not lead or hold office, and corruption and

Plate 1.7: Erected in the midst of a sea of poverty and want, the construction of the McDuffie County Courthouse was a miraculous achievement in 1873. (Photo: Courtesy of Georgia Dept. of Archives and History.)

exploitation were loose upon the land. All things taken into account, this elegant courthouse represented quite an accomplishment for the newly formed McDuffie County in 1873.

It is difficult to picture the original building. The later addition of large, featureless wings leaves us only a view of the original facade with its classical shape and imposing pilasters, now coated over with stucco but originally bare brick. When this building was new, its floor plan described a Greek cross beneath a central hipped roof with pedimented dormers above the side entrances. The original cornice was decorated with brackets, which supported the eaves, and brick quoining, still visible where the old building connects to the newer wings, gave added detail. The classical treatment surrounding the main entrance is unchanged from the original. Architecturally, it seems just another builder-designed attempt at classical perfection, falling short of that mark by some distance, but in 1873 it was a miraculous achievement built in the midst of poverty and need.

As the postbellum era unfolded, the railroad-fueled success at Thomson would stand as a model for New South mythmakers. Why then did Thomson not place at its very heart a mythical courthouse? Part of the answer is timing. The powerful myth of a New South that would be the freight of so many postbellum railroads would not be fully developed for another decade. In addition, the great dream courthouses of the new era were most often created where the aggressively promoted railroads of the New South era crossed antebellum rails. It was beside such crossings that the myth was most persuasive. There was to be no such crossing at Thomson. Lastly, the myth that attended these crossings was part of the creed of the New South, a doctrine that sought to strip the South of her agrarian mindset, and open her mind to the industrial age. Such a fundamental intellectual and cultural upheaval was to prove exceptionally difficult in McDuffie County.

It was thought that only an almost spiritual conversion could pave the way for the new era. New South promoters sought reconciliation with the North, an influx of Northern capital and know-how, agricultural diversity, improved race relations, the immigration of farm and mill workers, and, of course, industrialization. But as many of the towns along the Georgia Railroad were to illustrate, the mind of the South was not so easily manipulated. Agrarian roots ran deep, and frontier individualism combined with rebel tenacity to create a stubborn intransigence. While newer towns across Georgia sought to drink from the waters of New South salvation, the citizens of Thomson, Crawfordville, Appling, Greensboro and Conyers wanted none of this potion. Many here viewed the New South's zealous spokesmen with angry resentment. While Henry Grady predicted a capitalist Eden in the American South, farmers watched agricultural conditions steadily worsen: cotton prices inexorably fell, while fertilizer prices rose. Perceived in all of this was the exploitation of Georgia's working farmers by a faceless machine, controlled by politicians, financiers and capitalists. Such perceptions were at the core of the Populist Movement in Georgia. In the early 1890s, the counties along the Georgia Railroad were to become Populism's political stronghold. At the center of this political fortress was Thomson, the home of Georgia's undisputed Populist leader, Thomas E. Watson, who was once a US Congressman, once a US Senator, twice a third party candidate for President of the United States, and all the time a very powerful man in Georgia politics between 1890 and 1922.

There can be little doubt of Populism's agrarian roots in Georgia. Although its followers espoused much of the physiocratic philosophies of Jefferson and sought seemingly Jacksonian grassroots political power for the common man, Populism was a far cry from the independent American ideals of the early part of the century. Populists sought Federal control of the railroads and a complex system of federally operated warehouses for farm produce. The Populist political agenda was as socialistic as it was reactionary. Since the railroads numbered among those institutions that the Populists perceived as exploitive, there is little likelihood that the followers of Thomas Watson attached much credence to the hopeful myths purveyed by postbellum railroad promoters. Accordingly, no fantastic courthouses rose on the squares of Populist strongholds like Columbia, McDuffie, Greene and Rockdale Counties. In the 1890s, the county that gave us Tom Watson would vainly pursue its own Populist dreams of prosperity. Thus there would be no architectural celebration of the new economic age erected on the square in Thomson.

TALIAFERRO COUNTY: CRAWFORDVILLE

Plate 1.8: The depot at Crawfordville, built c.1890.

One of the limitations of the early wood-burning locomotives was that they required fuel and water frequently. As a result, stops were created every 8 to 12 miles along early lines. Invariably these wood and water stops became towns. The line of the Georgia

Plate 1.8: The depot at Crawfordville. The combination of the broad eaves, the gentle curve of the roof and the distinctive broken based pediment is unique to depots built on the Georgia Railroad in the 1880s and early 1890s. Photo: Wilber W. Caldwell.)

Plate 1.9: The 1828 Taliaferro County Courthouse. Some of these buildings achieved near classical perfection, but more often they were charming at best, and at worst, merely functional.

Railroad around Crawfordville in Taliaferro County gives us a glimpse of these hamlets, which were the prolific creations of the railroads. Today, many of these places murmur only the faint, dissonant chords of decay.

Not far from Crawfordville in the depression year of 1837, the Georgia Railroad created Dearing, Camak and Cumming (now Barnett in Taliaferro County) all named for directors and organizers of the Georgia Railroad. In 1839, a spur was built from Camak four miles to Warrenton. This was intended to be the first link in a branch line to Eatonton via Sparta, but the branch was soon abandoned in favor of work on the main line via Madison to the planned terminus of the Western and Atlantic Railroad at the city soon to be called Atlanta. From the very beginning, the secondary status of a spur line location was demonstrated as Warrenton was often referred to a "Mule Town" because mules were used to pull passenger coaches into town from the depot on the main line at Camak.[13] Warrenton would lose its denigrating appellation soon enough, and in 1870, with the financial backing of the Georgia Railroad, the Macon and Augusta Railroad would extend this branch to Macon. The Warren County Courthouse is part of another story and is discussed in chapter 8.

[13] Virginia Hill Wilhoit, *History of Warren County Georgia, 1793-1974* (Washington GA: Wilkes Publishing Company, 1976) 59.

[14] *The Advocate Democrat* (Crawfordville GA), September 13, 1901.

Like Columbia, McDuffie, Warren, and Wilkes Counties, Taliaferro County was already white with cotton when the Georgia Railroad arrived in 1838. The county had been carved from its neighbors in 1825, and the county seat, Crawfordville, had been laid out in the same year at the intersection of the two main roads in the area: Washington to Sparta and Greensboro to Waynesboro. On the edge of town, this all but forgotten depot would bear silent witness to the insidious, self-destructive odyssey of cotton acted out, first by slaves and later by tenant farmers with predictable results.

Early records of depot construction are not to be found, but a telltale architectural detail helps us date this structure. The combination of the broad eaves, the gentle curve of the roof and the distinctive broken based pediment is unique to depots built on the Georgia Railroad in the 1880s and early 1890s. The large brick depot built at Covington in 1885 is good example, as is Bradford Gilbert's 1892 Conyers depot. Although this smaller depot at Crawfordville is built on an altogether different plan, the treatment of the roofline, eaves and pediment is identical.

By 1849, George White's *Statistics of the State of Georgia* put Crawfordville's population at 250, and Sherwood's 1860 Gazetteer states that the town "had not grown much." But with the end of the plantations, Crawfordville began to slowly grow as the merchant side of the tenancy equation began to expand. Sholes's *Gazetteer of Georgia* puts the 1879 population at 600 and the 1897 population at 800.

Plate 1.9: The Taliaferro County Courthouse, built in 1828. Demolished 1901.

James Carlton, who built many early buildings in Athens including the 1855 Georgia Railroad Depot, designed and built the original 1828 Taliaferro County Courthouse using brick he made himself. Only this one blurry photograph of Mr. Carlton's creation has been discovered, but it reveals a great deal despite the lack of focus. It is an excellent example of a typical builder-designed, vernacular courthouse of the era. Scores of such buildings graced Georgia's squares, but only thirteen remain (see Introduction, Table I). Most followed a similar pattern: a rectangular or square floor plan, with four entrances on the ground floor each flanked symmetrically by windows. All had two stories and gabled or hipped roofs. Decoration was Spartan on these predictable structures. Cupolas, cornices, corbels, modillions, dentals or brackets, are sometime used. Sometimes arched windows appear, and some employ a portico or decorative detail around the entrances. Rarely do we find a balustrade, rarely dormers, almost never quoining nor ornament beyond window and door treatments. The second floor almost always contained the courtroom, and occasionally the stairs were external with a court room entrance on the second floor. Some of these buildings achieved near classical perfection, but more often they were charming at best, and at worst merely functional.

Plate 1.10: The Taliaferro County Courthouse, built 1901-1902, Lewis F. Goodrich, architect.

If Tom Watson had stifled Thomson's enthusiasm for ornament and show, then Taliaferro's native son, Alexander H. Stephens, had a similar effect in Crawfordville. This former vice president of the Confederacy was one of the few Confederate leaders to pass morally unsinged through the fires of war and the corruption's which followed. No aristocrat, but a man of the people, he was much loved in Georgia throughout his political career. If there could have been a Southern hero in the midst of a war to preserve slavery, then it would have been Alexander Stephens, for it was his stalwart defense of both United States and Confederate States Constitutions that were at the core of all his actions. For Stephens, who opposed secession, only to then brilliantly take up its Constitutional defense, the war had not been so much about slavery as about freedom. He saw governments, North or South, all tending to grasp for power at the expense of individual rights, and it was that grasping tendency he sought to check at all costs. It is thus no surprise that Stephens's beloved Taliaferro County became a bastion of the fierce individualism of the American frontier. Here we find the roots of Populism, wrapped in individual rights, agrarianism and an unflagging loyalty to the Lost Cause.

In Crawfordville, few bonfires were laid before the myth of New South progress and no crossing rails arrived to ignite such blazes. Here New South prophets would encounter only hostility and skepticism. So when Taliaferro County finally built a new courthouse in 1901, it was only because she needed one. And even then, the building rose amidst considerable protest. According to the Crawfordville *Advocate Democrat*, supporters of the new courthouse movement had to demolish the old courthouse in the middle of the night in order to confirm the county's need for a new structure.[14]

The 1901 Taliaferro County Courthouse, designed by architect Lewis F. Goodrich of Augusta, was an almost exact copy of the courthouse Goodrich designed four years earlier at Sylvania in Screven County. This was not unique. The prestigious Atlanta architect, Alexander Bruce, designed nearly identical Second Empire court buildings at Sparta, Gainesville and Monroe in the early 1880s. The prolific J. W. Golucke would create twin Romanesque court buildings in Union and Henry Counties and triplets in Jones, Baker, and Schley Counties just after 1900.

Probably influenced by earlier Queen Anne designs by Atlanta architects, Bruce and Morgan, in Talbotton (1892), Buchanan (1892), Statesboro (1894) and Dublin (1895), Goodrich employed Queen Anne detail here in Crawfordville. The

Plate 1.10: The 1901 Taliaferro County Courthouse. The simplicity of this courthouse might be considered a stylistic lag, but perhaps it is more a statement made by the people of Taliaferro County. (Photo: Wilber W. Caldwell.)

Picturesque asymmetrical massing of the two corner towers with their bell domes, as well as the ornate chimneys and dormers that break the silhouette of the roof line and the sashed windows with grids of tiny panes above are all characteristic of the Queen Anne style. Like Bruce and Morgan, Goodrich undoubtedly employed Queen Anne ornament in order to achieve a more modern effect—dressing an older, fundamentally Romanesque form in up-to-date finery.

However in step with the times this structure might have been, there is a simplicity here which is unusual in buildings in this style. The Queen Anne is usually a jubilant expression—ornament for ornament's sake. Here we find a singularly un-ornate approach with simple lines and expanses of flat, unadorned brick. What little ornament there is, the corbeling beneath the eaves for example, is of a seemingly vernacular type found in infinite variation on almost every brick storefront built in Georgia after 1890.

The simplicity of this courthouse might be considered a stylistic lag, but perhaps it is also a statement. Although the people of Taliaferro County took a step toward monumentality, in truth they merely chose the natural extension of the vernacular, brick building that had served them for three-quarters of a century. Somewhere, not too far beneath the surface, is the

simple echo of James Carlton's old, brick courthouse torn down to make way for the new one.

Aye, there, indeed, was the rub, for the year was 1902.

GREENE COUNTY: GREENSBORO

Plate 1.11: The Greene County Courthouse, built 1848-1849. David Demarest and Atharates Atkinson, architects/builders.

In antebellum days, the railroad's ability to create civic euphoria was not so great as it was to become after the war. Nonetheless, the 1849 Greene County Courthouse fits the later pattern. The Georgia Railroad was completed to Greensboro by 1839, and the eighty-three long miles to Augusta were transformed into the astonishingly brief journey of only seven hours. Ten years later, this courthouse rose on the square in Greensboro. The Greensboro Cotton Factory was built in the same year. The first steam-powered cotton mill in Georgia, it complemented Greene County's two earlier water-powered textile mills. Greensboro was a healthy town of 600 by 1850, and no doubt its citizenry was attuned to the importance of iron rails. This courthouse is surely an echo of that intonation, but it also echoes more fundamental historical symbols.

We now come to the heart of the matter, the Greek Revival. The Greene County Courthouse, still in use today, speaks most articulately for the prewar period. This is not the architecture of the railroad: this is the architecture of the antebellum South, and its symbolism probes near the very nerve of what it meant to be Southern. To understand the Greene County Courthouse is to begin to understand the South in 1849.

The first Greek Revival building in America was the Second Bank of Pennsylvania built in Philadelphia in 1798. The architect, Henry Latrobe, had been trained in England and had arrived in America just two years before. The Elgin Marbles were about to make a stir in London (1801), and the fledgling study of archaeology was tempting architects to forsake Renaissance examples and seek a more direct connection with the classical orders. Nonetheless, most of

Plate 1.11: The Greene County Courthouse. Its symbolism probes near the very nerve of what it meant to be Southern in 1849. (Photo: Wilber W. Caldwell.)

Latrobe's work was of the older, European, neoclassical school. The Greek Revival did not begin in earnest in the United States until 1818 with the competition for the design of the Second Bank of the United States which was won by William Strickland, a former student of Latrobe. Stickland's creation was purely more Greek than Latrobe's was, and it launched a nationwide armada of Greek churches, schools, markets, especially banks, and of course, courthouses.

The popularity of the Greek Revival hinged on patriotic as well as romantic symbols. By the early 1820s, Americans were much in sympathy with the Greek War for Independence waged against the Turks, a sentiment made all the more heartfelt by the poetry of Lord Byron and later by his death in Greece in 1824. This struggle, it was felt, had much in common with our own revolution, and added a topical fervor to the image of American democracy and the "Temple of Justice." It may be that these images were even more alluring to Southerners owing to the region's emotionally romantic tradition, and perhaps to a sectional identification with Thomas Jefferson's early classical American architecture, despite the fact that Jefferson's influences were not Greek but Roman.

By the 1830s, the political philosophy of the cotton producing South had moved a long distance indeed from any recognizably Jeffersonian ideal. Although North and South may have begun as American states on the road to a common destiny, by the mid-nineteenth century they had drifted so far apart as to share little more than a common language. The North rushed to the Industrial Revolution and espoused a growing Federalism, while the South clung to its individualistic, agrarian ways and followed the lure of cotton, espousing local political prerogatives. Foremost among these prerogatives was, of course, cotton's handmaiden, slavery. As the century wore on the Greek Revival in the South was to be embraced with such fervor as to be an almost pervasive style. The South was to become so architecturally immersed in the Greek style, that it would lose some of its appeal in the North.[15]

The reasons for the Southern celebration of the Greek Revival are fundamentally symbolic. When John C. Calhoun and other Southern leaders looked at the historical ideal of the Greek democracy, they saw a loose confederation of city-states ruled by a wise gentry which prospered on the labor of slaves.[16] For the Southern politicians to so adroitly drape this classical metaphor about the shoulders of the Southern electorate is not surprising considering the relentlessly expanding need for slaves in cotton's kingdom. By 1840, the South had transformed the ideal of the Greek democracy into a theory of ethical and political balderdash which held that one portion of any community always lived upon the labor of another, and that the "wage slave" systems of industrial Europe and the North were not only less humane than bondage slavery, they were politically unstable.[17] So it was that the Greek Revival became a symbol for Greek democracy and thus for slavery in the antebellum South. So it is that beyond the columns of the Greene County Courthouse lies a myth—an impossible dream created and perpetuated by the same driving force that propelled almost everything else in the antebellum South: cotton.

The simplicity of the brick mass of this building is reminiscent of vernacular buildings of the era, but the Greek portico with its massive columns suggests disciplined influence. Two men are recorded as "architect/builders", Atharates Atkinson of Madison and David Demarest of Athens. David Demarest was an accomplished builder with an undeniably fine eye for design. Perhaps he alone served as architect, for the architectural credentials of Atharates Atkinson are more obscure. We know that both men came to Georgia in the 1830s, Demarest from New Jersey and Atkinson from New England. Both men prospered as builders and Atkinson quarried granite near Madison and marble in north Georgia. He also enjoyed the economic blessings of cotton as a planter.[18]

[15] James Marston Fitch, *American Building and the Historical Forces that Shaped It* 2nd ed (Cambridge: Houghton Mufflin Company, 1966) 88; and Robert J. Brink, ed., *Courthouses of the Commonwealth* (Amherst: University of Massachusetts Press,1984) 99.

[16] Vernon L. Parrington, *Main Currents in American Thought, The Romantic Revolution in American, 1800-1860* 3 vols. (New York: Harcourt, Brace & World, Inc., 1927) 2: xii-xii.

[17] Parrington, *Main Currents in American Thought*, 2:96.

Plate 1.12: Mercer Institute Chapel. The power and simplicity of the Greek Revival speak fluently from the middle of a lonely field only a few miles from Greensboro, in the tiny, forgotten hamlet of Penfield. (Photo: Wilber W. Caldwell.)

Greene County's first courthouse stood near this square, and was reportedly destroyed by Native Americans in 1787. A "more substantial" replacement was burned by a "Negro prisoner" jailed in the building in 1807, and the third Greene County Courthouse was erected in that same year.[19] The two-story, frame building was built at the same time as the stone jail, which still stands, on the rear of the square.

Except for a few brick churches, the first substantial public buildings in these rural places were usually the courthouse and the Masonic lodge. An odd alliance between the two structures was often forged. Many county histories tell of Masonic halls used for county functions after the all too frequent fires that were the ruin of so many early courthouses. Owing to mysterious fraternal bonds that transcended even Sherman's fiery resolve, Masonic halls again and again escaped destruction during the war. Many served as temporary courthouses during Reconstruction. A longstanding example of the courthouse—the Masonic lodge alliance occurs at Greensboro. Local tradition has it that the 1849 structure was originally to be a two-story structure, and that the local Masonic lodge proposed the addition of the third story for its own use.[20] We find similar scenarios in both the

1851 Lincoln County Courthouse at Lincolnton and the 1856 Catoosa County Courthouse at Ringgold.

Plate 1.12: The Mercer Institute Chapel at Penfield built in 1833. David Demarest, architect.

There were many fine examples of the Greek Revival near Greensboro. Columns had been sprouting in Athens long before 1849. Despite its nearly windowless facade, the 1836 Phi Kappa Hall with its simple two-story brick mass and four Doric columns is disarmingly similar to the later three-story Greene County Courthouse. Also notable is the University of Georgia Chapel (1832) built by James Carlton, builder of the 1828 Taliaferro County Courthouse. Modern speculation about the architect of the University of Georgia Chapel centers on Charles Cluskey. Savannah had a monumental Greek courthouse (1833), and Cluskey's Old Medical College in Augusta (1835) cannot be ignored in this context. Almost certainly influence also flowed from the work of Robert Mills in South Carolina. An early American master of the Greek orders and a student of Henry Latrobe, Mills designed fourteen courthouses in South Carolina in the 1820s.[21] He is perhaps best known for his design of the Washington Monument and the United States Treasury Building.

As with the earlier Federal Style, practical handbooks of the day aided unsophisticated local builders in their quest for Hellenic symmetry and proportion. The Greek orders were geometrically detailed for popular consumption in builder's guides published by Asher Benjamin, *The American Builder's Companion*, 1827, and *The Practical House Carpenter*, 1830; and by Minard Lefever, *The Beauties of Modern Architecture*, 1835.

Despite this abundance of Greek influence circulating in the antebellum south, it is likely that the real inspiration for 1849 Green county Courthouse grew close to home. Only a few miles from Greensboro one can still find what is left of the old Mercer Institute with its lovely chapel. Mercer Institute is the parent of Mercer University in Macon, and Jesse Mercer, one of its founders, commissioned "architect David Demarest of New England"[22] to build this chapel in 1833. Even today the power and simplicity of the

Greek Revival speaks fluently from the middle of a lonely field in the tiny, forgotten hamlet of Penfield. Although the history of Mercer University credits Demarest with being an architect, we find no mention of this title in Athens, Demarest's home. Rather he is referenced as a "carpenter" from New Jersey,[23] and as the "builder" of several fine homes. In fact his work on the Thomas Wray House in Athens was held up as the standard for workmanship for later Athenian construction.[24] Most probably David Demarest was one of those builders of the era who, although lacking formal architectural training, had a discerning eye and a gift for design. The heavy vernacular look and detail of the portico of the 1830 Phi Kappa Hall on the University of Georgia campus, whose architect is not known, are so similar to Demarest's Greene County Courthouse of 1849 that one is wont to speculate. Perhaps Demarest designed that famous University structure, or perhaps he copied it in Greene County.

Whatever the case, it is easy to see why Greene County chose Demarest to design their temple of justice. Surely his work in Athens and in Penfield is the inspiration for the columns of the Greene County Courthouse. It is the pure music of the Old South.

Plate 1.13: The depot at Greensboro built in 1917. S. R. Young, architect.

This is the first of the many depots designed by S. R. Young, an engineer, who later became president of the Georgia Railroad.[25] It typifies the better brick depots of the era. More graceful than their mid-nineteenth century predecessors, small brick depots built in Georgia after 1890 had more of a domestic feel. Excellent examples are at Forsyth, 1895; Marshallville, 1912; and Marietta, 1899. All are unmistakably depots but without the more massive warehouse look we find in older brick buildings like those at Thomson, Madison, Calhoun and Millen.

Typical also was Greensboro's history. Hard hit by Reconstruction, the town nonetheless experienced modest growth owing to an influx of merchants and factors who were the lending side of the sharecropping equation. By 1890, Greensboro's population was 1313, up from 910 in 1860. Any industrial fires, which may have burned before the war, were long

Plate 1.13: The 1917 Georgia Railroad Depot at Greensboro. (Photo: Wilber W. Caldwell.)

since extinguished, and as a Greene County history simply puts it, "those who controlled farm finances controlled the community."[26] And so it remained until the citizens of Greensboro decided to take matters into their own hands. For twenty years they had heard the New South spokesmen extol the dream of attracting Northern capital for the industrialization of Georgia, but none had come their way.

By the turn of the century, it was clear that if capital was going to be raised, it was going to have to come from a place nearer to home, and so, as was the case with so many Southern towns, the people of Greensboro did it themselves. A society for the development of industry and trade was organized in 1898, and by 1900, the Mary Leila Cotton Mill was incor-

[18] A conversation with Ms. Carroll Hart of Madison, Georgia, (Atkinson's grand daughter), March 2000.

[19] Thaddeus B. Rice, *The History of Greene County, Georgia* (Macon GA: J. W. Burke Company, 1961) 59.

[20] Dale Jaeger, Historic "Resources of Greensboro, Multiple Resource Nomination," unpublished nomination to the National Register of Historic Places, Greene County Library, Greensboro GA, 78.

[21] Mills Lane, *The Architecture of the South, South Carolina* (Savannah GA: Beehive Press, 1984) 171.

[22] Spright Dowell, *The History of Mercer University* (Macon GA: Mercer University Press, 1958) 64.

[23] Charlotte Marshall, *Historic Houses of Athens* (Athens GA: Athens Historical Society, 1987) 20.

[24] Marshall, *Historic Houses of Athens*, 33.

[25] Dale Jaeger, Historic "Resources of Greensboro, Multiple Resource Nomination," unpublished nomination to the National Register of Historic Places in the Greene County Library at Greensboro GA.

[26] A.F. Rapier, *Tenants of the Almighty* (New York:MacMillan, 1943) 86.

Plate 1.14: The depot at Madison built c.1857 is one of only five brick, antebellum depots still standing in Georgia. (Photo: Wilber W. Caldwell.)

porated. Located on five acres granted by the development committee, the plant was powered by steam generated in wood and coal-burning boilers. The first stockholders' meeting was held in the Greene County Courthouse, and by June of 1900, 100 workers were employed making C Class Cotton sheeting. The Mary Leila Cotton Mill illustrates part of the myth of the New South, the myth of Northern capital. Certainly Northern capital was to play a part in Georgia's eventual industrial growth, but this was usually in an exploitive, grasping, or consolidating role. The capital behind most of the railroads and most of the textile mills built before 1895 was scraped together by Georgians.[27]

The mill and the mill village erected around it are still very much a presence in Greensboro today, but the situation in 1900 was quite different. At its best the mill and its "mill village" exemplified a kind of paternalism of the sort manifested on plantations before the Civil War. At its worst, for the poor whites,

it was merely trading one form of tenancy for another. Men, women and children alike slaved long hours just as they had on the land. The mill owned their homes, gave credit against future hours worked, and paid the lowest of subsistence wages. These families were as trapped by the spinning of cotton as they had been by the growing of it. At the heart of the growth of the Southern textile industry lay the sad fact that almost all the region really had to offer was cheap, unskilled labor. Compared to national averages, wages were so low that all of these mills prospered.[28] Most could not have failed if they had tried.

So by 1910, Greensboro had a population of 2120 and needed a new depot. Cotton prices had doubled since 1900, and there was an air of progress in the wind. In 1907 the Bostick Railroad was begun from Appalachee to Bostick. It was renamed the Greene County Railroad in 1911 and extended all the way to Good Hope in 1912 and to Monroe in Walton County where it made the link with the Gainesville Midland Railroad in 1914. Still, beyond the perennial fields of white, which were only ten years away from the devastation of the boll weevil, it was a sad kind of progress which created the cheapest, coarsest of textile products with the meanest of unskilled labor working the longest of hours in the most unhealthy of conditions for the lowest of wages.

MORGAN COUNTY: MADISON

Plate 1.14: The depot at Madison built c.1857. John Byne Walker, Builder

Madison was an important place from a very early date. Adiel Sherwood's *Gazetteer of Georgia* published in the late 1820s recounts a population of over 1000, a male and a female academy with good libraries, a good brick courthouse and jail, a large Masonic Hall, numerous stores, and over sixty residences. By the time the Georgia Railroad arrived in 1841, Madison had a reputation for culture, learning, and a gay society life. To be sure, some of her early rivals like Milledgeville and Athens have passed her by. Still, the Georgia countryside is covered with the remains of towns which were once prosperous, and

[27] C. Vann Woodward, *Origins of the New South, 1877-1913* (1951; reprint, Baton Rogue: Louisiana State University Press, 1993) 134.

[28] Woodward, *Origins of the New South*, 133.

[29] William Chapman, *The Madison Historic Preservation Manual* (Madison: np, 1990) 8.

[30] Jones, Jr. and Dutcher, *The Memorial History of Augusta*, 492.

[31] The other four are at Dalton, 1852, Calhoun, 1854, Cartersville, 1854 (partial remains) and Albany, 1857.

[32] David Conyngham quoted in John M. Gibson, *Those 163 Days, A Southern Account of Sherman's March from Atlanta to Raleigh* (New York: Coward-McCann, 1961) 39-40.

[33] Chapman, *The Madison Historic Preservation Manual*, 9.

Madison with her two railroads has managed to hang on to a great deal of what was good in her past.

Why here and not elsewhere on the Georgia Railroad? There are three answers. First there is the growth and consolidation of very large plantations in Morgan County before the war. The fields of Morgan County sprouted such prosperity that many of the planters built elaborate town houses in Madison and created here a cultural wellspring to anoint their self-sanctioned entrance into the "gentry" of cotton. Producing over 8 million pounds of cotton in 1840, Morgan County was behind only Hancock County. Second, Madison was the temporary terminus of the Georgia Railroad for over four years (1841-1844) before completion to Terminus (Atlanta) in 1845. This was the key to shoring up an already solid economic underpinning. Madison shipped as many as 20,000 bales annually on the Georgia Railroad in the 1840s.[29] With this kind of commerce to build upon, cultural institutions could take deep root. Third, it was here in Madison that the rails of the postbellum line that was to become the Macon and Northern Railroad crossed the antebellum line of the Georgia Railroad. It was at such crossings that the myth of the New South seduced its most ardent followers.

The sign nailed above the door of this depot informs us that the Georgia Railroad reached Madison in 1841 and that the builder of this building was John B. Walker. It goes on to boast that this is the oldest brick depot in Georgia. The inference is that the building was built in the early 1840s when the railroad arrived. Neither Morgan County nor Georgia Railroad records can confirm this, but there is evidence to indicate that in 1857 and 1858 the Georgia Railroad replaced many early wooden depots with brick or stone structures.[30] It seems likely that this depot at Madison was one of these, and that the Western and Atlantic brick depots at Calhoun, 1854, and at Dalton, 1853, are probably older. Whatever the case, there are the only five brick, antebellum depots still standing in Georgia.[31] Almost all of the depots on the Central of Georgia and many on the Western and Atlantic and the Atlanta and West Point were destroyed during the war. This building was partially burned by Federal troops in 1864, but it was restored the next year. So just how much of the antebellum structure we see today is not known. Despite Sherman's standing orders limiting the infringement of private property rights, in Madison there were accounts of the ransacking of private homes by advance elements of Federal cavalry. Order was restored with the arrival of the main body of the Union force,[32] and as in most Georgia towns, incendiaries were primarily limited to manufacturing and rail facilities, raw cotton, and other supplies.

Ironically, what Sherman had failed to do came to pass of its own accord only six years later in 1869 when a large portion of Madison burned to the ground. Forty-two buildings including the Masonic Hall were destroyed. But resurgence was on the wind, and a new Madison emerged from the ashes. By 1880, the population was above 2000.[33] After the war, cotton production steadily grew in Morgan County: over 7,000 bales in 1870, and over 19,000 bales in 1890.

It was cotton that held Morgan County's farmers prisoner in a hopeless cycle of debt and frustration, and it was cotton that allowed Madison to prosper on the back of such servitude. In 1888, the arrival of the crossing rails of the Macon and Northern Railroad (originally called the Covington and Macon Railroad) helped to cement Madison's prosperity, but it was not yet time for a new courthouse.

Plate 1.15: The Morgan County Courthouse, built in 1844. Burned 1917. John Byne Walker, builder.

This is the second Morgan County Courthouse. It would be nice for the purpose of this text to say that this building was inspired by the Georgia Railroad, which arrived in Madison just two years before its construction. The truth of the matter is that the old brick courthouse, built in 1807, burned in 1844, and this one replaced it. A fine example of the simple, pervasive, vernacular antebellum courthouse form, this building reflected little exuberance.

The later addition of a clock tower was also typical. In the last decades of the nineteenth century, such towers were to become common features on Georgia's new crop of Picturesque courthouses, and many an

Plate 1.15: The 1844 Morgan County Courthouse was a fine example of the simple, pervasive, vernacular courthouse form which stood on so many of Georgia's squares before the Civil War. (Photo: Courtesy of The Cavin Collection, Morgan County Archives)

older court building would be fitted with a clock tower as a part of a post-war remodeling. This 1844 building remained in use until 1907. It burned ten years later.

Plate 1.16: The Morgan County Courthouse, built 1905-1907. J. W. Golucke, architect.

James Wingfield Golucke was the son of an Austrian immigrant cabinet-maker. With no connections, little money, and no formal training he fashioned a remarkable architectural career. The law creating a state board for the examination and registration of architects was not enacted by the Georgia legislature until 1919,[34] but by 1890, there was a small, tight cadre of trained architects in Atlanta who were members of the American Institute of Architects. No doubt men like Golucke, without academic credentials, were considered impostors by this group. Nonetheless, it was James Wingfield Golucke who proved the most prolific designer of the mythical mansions with their foundations of dreams and dust that were the courthouses of the fledgling New South era. Golucke designed twenty-six courthouses in Georgia, four in Alabama, and numerous churches, jails and

other public buildings between 1895 and 1907 (see Appendix C).

Mythical mansions well describes the neoclassical behemoths that began to dominate the squares of so many Georgia towns just after 1900. The idea that architecture is, at its very heart, not only a question of style, trend and fashion, but also a reflection of human aspirations and self-image is a large part of the fundamental premise of this book. In this regard, the courthouses built in Georgia during the last third of the nineteenth century and the first decade of the twentieth century are compelling. The architecture of these buildings is a remarkably direct reflection of the mind of these rural places.

Golucke's offering here in Madison is fitting. The usual symbolism attached to the Neoclassical Revival and Beaux-Arts Classicism, which dominated American public architecture at the turn of the century is that it celebrated the forces of Wall Street and the Industrial East. Its popularity was thought to represent the victory of Eastern industrialism over the values of American individualism in the West.[35] Perhaps such an interpretation was appropriate for the country at large, but for Madison, and for the South, this symbolism was unacceptable.

The South had already experienced the triumph of the forces of the East in 1865, and after the war, the Southern mind was balanced on a razor's edge. The bitterness of the Lost Cause and the romance of the Old South beckoned on one hand, and the promise of the new American dream sang seductively on the other. Sadly for the South, both concepts would prove mythical. Perhaps the new neoclassicism represented the myth of turn-of-the-century American prosperity to some Georgians, but its columned facades and airy porticos could not help but call to mind the myth of the Greek democracy and the Old South for most. Surely this dichotomy of aspiration was at the heart of Madison's persona in 1907, and J. W. Golucke's grand 1907 Morgan County Courthouse offered the perfect dual symbol.

There were forty neoclassical courthouses built in Georgia between 1894 and 1910. J. W. Golucke designed twelve of them (see Appendix C). The courthouse at Madison is not typical. The usual four-sided

[34] "Thomas Henry Morgan," in *The Atlanta Historical Bulletin* 7/23 (September 1943): 88.

[35] Fitch, *American Building and the Historical Forces that Shaped It*, 208-10.

symmetry of the "monument in the square" is not found here. Instead, we are confronted by a great Corinthian portico and dual wings heading off at forty-five degree angles. If the portico confronts us, the tower assaults us with its enormous masonry presence, a squared dome beneath a crowning belfry. The design and scale of the tower announce Beaux-Arts Classicism in the mold Richard Morris Hunt's Administration Building at the 1893 Columbian Exposition, which was itself modeled after the Renaissance dome of the Florence Cathedral. We might also be reminded of a squat version of the mausoleum-like tower that adorns Cuthbert Brodrick's famous 1853 Town Hall at Leeds, England. But in Georgia in 1905, there were other models closer at hand. Only two years before, Frank Milburn had designed a similar Beaux-Arts tower for his Lowndes County Courthouse at Valdosta.

Whatever Golucke's models for Madison's *palais de justice,* it is certain that the site plays a large part in his design. Most of Golucke's grand neoclassical courthouses are situated in the center of open squares: Eatonton, Cartersville and Newnan, for example. Their monumentality owes much to the great, voluminous, open spaces that surround their classical grandeur and complex ornament. They compete only with sky and clouds, and are the greater due to this backdrop. Here in Madison the courthouse occupies a corner lot facing a corner of the town square. The sidewalks hug the building. Street traffic runs all too close by, and despite Golucke's clever angling of the grand entrance to face the square, the scale of the building suddenly may seem wrong for the site.

This is not a surprising phenomenon. Certainly a grand site is best for a grand building. Still the Morgan County Courthouse shines more brightly than many neoclassical courthouses in Georgia built without the advantage of a great square: Monticello, Hamilton, Summerville and Baxley for example. Most importantly, its dual symbolism shines for the people of the county that built it. Like the legion of neoclassical courthouses built in Georgia after 1900, the portico of the Morgan County Courthouse is supported by both the columns of the Old South and the New. Both were beyond Madison's grasp in 1907.

Plate 1.16: The portico of the 1907 Morgan County Courthouse is supported by the columns of both the Old South and the New. (Photo: Wilber W. Caldwell.)

NEWTON COUNTY: COVINGTON

Plate 1.17: Brick Store, built in 1822.

Newton County was carved from Jasper, Henry and Walton Counties in 1821. The first court was held in this brick store which was built in 1822. Most counties formed in this early era took several years to select a county site, lay out a street plan and construct an official courthouse, so it was common for the first court to be held in a private home or even out in the open. Occasionally a small public building like this one was selected. There is considerable documentation throughout Georgia relating to the locations of these early court sessions, but few of the actual structures survive. Despite its simple lines and modest size, this building has a powerful presence. It quickly became an early landmark, for the existence of a brick building, however humble, in this remote wilderness in 1822 was noteworthy.

Plate 1.17: The existence of a brick building, however humble, in this remote wilderness in 1822, was noteworthy. (Photo: Wilber W. Caldwell.)

Like Greene and Morgan Counties, most of Newton County's early settlers came with the Georgia Land Lotteries following the Indian Cessions of 1805, 1818, and 1821. Immigrants from Carolina and Virginia poured into Georgia in successive waves to participate in these lotteries, and by 1825 the Middle Georgia wilderness was turning white with the progress of cotton.

The town of Covington, originally called Newtonsboro, was laid out in 1822, and a temporary

Plate 1.18: Compared to the other postbellum depots along the Georgia Railroad, the size of this 1885 depot at Covington reflects robust commercial ambitions. (Photo: Wilber W. Caldwell.)

log courthouse was built on the side of the square. A brick courthouse was completed a few years later. Early county records give the dimensions of this building as sixty feet by forty feet by twenty feet high.[36] Despite the absence of any description other than "elegant," it is easy to picture a building similar to the early, vernacular courthouses of the era like the ones we have already seen at Crawfordville and Madison. A second brick courthouse was built on the square in 1856 to replace the earlier brick structure which burned in that year. That courthouse, along with a sizable portion of the rest of the town, burned in 1883.[37]

Covington's early progress was so rapid that an early resident, J. E. Lawrence, was moved to relate in an 1824 letter that: "We could git anything there that we could git in North Carolina. It is two years since the town was laid off, and already it has 8 or 10 stores."[38] Immigrants from Carolina like Lawrence were chasing cotton, and so was the Georgia Railroad when it arrived near Covington nearly twenty-five years later.

Plate 1.18: The depot at Covington, built in 1885.

The Georgia Railroad arrived near Covington in 1844. Built around 1855, the original depot was not technically in Covington, but less than a mile away at Midway, a small hamlet between Covington and Oxford. It was burned by Federal troops in 1864, a new depot was built in 1867. It burned in 1884, and this brick depot, built in 1885, today occupies the same spot.[39]

From its very beginning, the town of Covington showed signs of a tenacious character when it came to business. Perhaps it is appropriate that the first court was held in a store, for it seems that a powerful mercantile instinct surged through the blood of Newton County's people. Compared to the other postbellum depots we have seen along the Georgia Railroad, the size of this building reflects robust commercial ambitions.

An early indication of a countywide mind for business came with the 1836 charter of the Middle Branch Railroad by a group from Newton County. These men had shrewdly guessed the importance of the plans for the state-owned Western and Atlantic Railroad to connect the area near present day Chattanooga with someplace south of the Chattahoochee River, a place which was later to be called Atlanta. The Middle Branch Railroad was chartered to run from Madison, through Covington to connect with that state-owned road. In 1837, the Georgia Railroad secured a similar charter and was beginning to survey a route from Madison to the Chattahoochee, which would pass north of Oxford and bypass Covington altogether. By 1838, the people of Covington, using the Middle Branch Railroad's charter as leverage, had negotiated with the Georgia Railroad and succeeded in getting the route changed to pass between Covington and Oxford. Emory College at Oxford sold a large tract of land to the Georgia Railroad, and as part of the compromise, the Middle Branch Railroad merged with the Georgia Railroad and disappeared. The first depot at Midway was connected to Covington via horse drawn street railway, and for all practical purposes Covington had her railroad.[40]

But one railroad was not enough for business-minded Covington. Ambitious business leaders in Covington hatched myriad schemes, but most came to nothing (See Table 1.2). Despite these repeated false starts, things began to look rosy for Covington in the early 1880s, and in 1885 the Covington and Macon Railroad was chartered. This was originally to be part of a connection between Florida and Knoxville, Tennessee.[41] The first leg of the road was to be Covington to Macon, but, alas, the route was changed, and the line was built from Macon to Athens in 1888, crossing the Georgia Railroad at Madison. Thus, the Covington and Macon Railroad never came near Covington at all, and in 1891 it was renamed the Macon and Northern Railroad.

Covington finally got her second railroad in 1894. The Eatonton and Machen Railroad was chartered in 1889 and immediately changed its name to the Middle Georgia and Atlantic Railroad. Following the proposed route of the ill-fated Eatonton and Covington Railroad chartered way back in 1854, it was completed from Eatonton to Machen where it crossed the Covington and Macon Railroad in 1891

COVINGTON RAILROADS CHARTERED BUT NEVER BUILT — Table 1.2

In 1847, the original plan for the Atlanta and West Point RR called for a line from Covington via Griffin to LaGrange or West Point.

The Eatonton and Covington Railroad, 1854.

The Middle Georgia Railroad, 1859, Covington and Thomaston via Barnesville.

The Covington and South River Railroad, 1880.

The Covington and South River Railroad, 1881, Covington to Brunswick via Macon.

The Covington and North Georgia Railroad, 1881, Covington to the Richmond and Danville main line at Lula.

The Covington and Macon Railroad, 1885. Macon to Knoxville, Tennessee, via Covington.

The Covington and Cedar Shoals Railroad, 1889, Covington to Cedar Shoals (now Porterdale).

The Alcovy and Northern Railroad, 1890, Alcovy station on the Georgia Railroad to Jersey in Walton County.

The Covington and Ocmulgee Railroad, rechartered 1891, Covington to the Ocmulgee River.

---

and later to Covington in 1894. An attractive wooden depot was built at Covington in 1897, and a spur was built from Covington to the mill at Porterdale in 1899.

The Newton County Courthouse, built in 1884. Bruce and Morgan, architects. (See Introduction, Plate 6)

In Covington, the power of the Georgia Railroad combined with a vigorous local entrepreneurial spirit to create a considerable success. When the railroad arrived in 1845 the town had about 300 residents,[42]

[36] *The History of Newton County, Georgia* (Covington GA: The Newton County Historical Society, 1988) 39.

[37] W.B. Williford, *The Glory of Covington* (Atlanta: Cherokee Publishing, 1973) 169.

[38] *The History of Newton County, Georgia* (Covington GA: The Newton County Historical Society, 1988) 39.

[39] *The History of Newton County, Georgia* (Covington GA: The Newton County Historical Society, 1988) 296.

[40] *The History of Newton County, Georgia* (Covington GA: The Newton County Historical Society, 1988) 286-88.

[41] *The History of Newton County, Georgia* (Covington GA: The Newton County Historical Society, 1988) 295.

[42] *The History of Newton County, Georgia* (Covington GA: The Newton County Historical Society, 1988) 288.

and by 1860 the population stood above 1300. It is clear from a list of proposed railroads (see Table 1.2) that there was an outbreak of "railroad fever" in Covington in the early 1880s. Surely, Bruce and Morgan's grand 1884 Newton County Courthouse, built not on the square but on a corner opposite the square, was to be a celebration of that railroad which everyone thought would run "right through the town square."

The selection of the Second Empire Style tells us much about the people of Covington and about the spirit that propelled the town in 1884. It strongly suggests the influence of the cities that lay at the other end of the rails, notably Atlanta, Macon, and Athens. Indeed, there were few courthouses built in Georgia that articulated the full flower of the Second Empire. Apart from the simple charm of Alexander Bruce's three nearly identical courthouses at Sparta, Monroe and Gainesville that reflected only a rather rural and reserved suggestion of the style's ornamental grandeur, there were only three true Second Empire courthouses built in the state. These were all in railroad centers: Atlanta (1883); Athens (1876); and Macon (1872). Covington must have viewed her fate as intertwined with these giants of commerce. Indeed, how could she not? After all, in the early 1880s, before the Covington and Macon Railroad was routed through Madison, Covington saw herself literally at the crossroads formed by the Augusta-Atlanta road and the proposed rails connecting Macon and Athens.

The choice of the Second Empire here at Covington reveals a great deal more about the town than a false sense of urbanity. In the late 1860s, and early 1870s, the style took the North by storm. Washington, DC, became so identified with Second Empire buildings that the style came to be called the General Grant Style. Its beginnings can be traced to France in 1853 when Baron Haussmann was placed in charge of what turned out to be a veritable rebuilding of the city of Paris. Louis Napoleon was determined to make Paris the premier city of Europe, and in his zeal, he swept aside old buildings by the block and replaced them with the new architecture of the Ecole des Beaux-Arts. For the French, the Second Empire was not so much a new style as a continuation of familiar Renaissance elements arranged to satisfy a modern functionality and the new French rationalism of the Ecole des Beaux Arts. But in America, it was unlike anything the county had seen. In the New World, the Second Empire models were scarce and its progress scribed a rather free and, some might say, creative course, while its symbolism became that of progress, high finance, industry, the railroads, and the Federal Government all rolled into one.

There was much in this for Southerners to hate in 1884. Indeed for the South, Second Empire architecture was triple damned: it was Parisian and thus implied a low moral character, it was Northern and thus represented the victory of industrialism over agrarianism and the individual, and it was called "General Grant" after the so-called "Butcher of The Wilderness." That the Second Empire graced the streets of Atlanta or Macon less than two decades after the Civil War was one thing. These cities were commercial centers and sought without reserve the riches of Northern capital. But for Covington to build a Second Empire courthouse is astounding—perhaps a bank or a railroad building—but a courthouse. Here local businessmen must have bought heavily the stock sold by the purveyors of the myth of the New South. They clothed themselves with the trappings of prosperity as their town grew, unaware that the foundations of their buildings, their railroads and indeed their dreams themselves were nothing but the flimsy fibers of cotton. Poverty cloaked the countryside. The price of cotton fell to just over 5¢ a pound

[43] Woodward, *The Origins of the New South*, 185.

[44] Paul R. Baker, *Richard Morris Hunt* (Cambridge MA: MIT Press, 1980) 105.

[45] T.D. O'Kelly and A.J. Guinn, eds., *Historical Souvenir of Conyers* (Conyers GA: n.p.,n.d.).

[46] Franklin M. Garrett, *Atlanta and Environs, A Chronicle of Its People and Places*, 3 vols. (New York: Lewis Publishing Company, 1954) 1:321-22.

[47] *The (Conyers) Solid South* (n.d.).

[48] E.L. Cowan and Francis A. King, *A History of Rockdale County* (Conyers GA: THP, 1978) 5.

[49] Jeff Wilkenson in an article published in *The Rockdale Citizen* is one of the local writers who have forwarded this idea. It is also said to have appeared in *The Rockdale Register*, although there is no date given for either of these sources and no authority or documentation.

Plate 1.19: Bradford Gilbert, who later became the principal architect in charge of the buildings for 1895 Cotton States Exposition at Atlanta, designed this depot for the Georgia Railroad in 1892. (Photo: Wilber W. Caldwell.)

by 1894,[43] while a miniature Parisian monument adorned the town square in Covington.

When it came to designing courthouses, the Atlanta architects, Alexander C. Bruce and Thomas Henry Morgan, were a team that was to prove almost as prolific as Atlanta's other premier courthouse architect of the era, J. W. Golucke (see Appendix C). The firm of Bruce and Morgan designed sixteen courthouses in Georgia between 1883 and 1898. Earlier, Bruce designed two courthouses in Georgia with William Parkins, and numerous others in his home state of Tennessee, before coming to Atlanta in 1879. Morgan designed two more Georgia courthouses after Bruce's retirement in 1904, thus bringing the total in Georgia to twenty. We don't have to look far to find Bruce's model for his creation at Covington. He had designed a similar Second Empire court building at the blossoming rail center of Chattanooga before establishing his practice in Atlanta in 1879.

Unlike Golucke, Bruce and Morgan were architects in every professional sense of the word. Both served long and arduous apprenticeships in architectural offices, Bruce in the shadow of William Strickland in the Nashville offices of H. M. Akeroyd, and the younger Morgan in that same office and later under Parkins and Bruce in Atlanta. Bruce attended school in Nashville, but did not study architecture. The first formal course in architecture in the United States was not begun until 1868 at M. I. T.[44]

Generally speaking, the work of Bruce and Morgan was more abreast of its times than that of

Golucke. Golucke's work before 1900 bears the reserved character of the Romanesque Revival, a hint of H. H. Richardson and perhaps even of a bit of the brick vernacular. On the other hand, the early courthouses of Bruce and Morgan not only flaunt the Romanesque Revival, but the Queen Anne and the Second Empire styles, incorporating all manner of high Victorian eclecticism. Nonetheless, formal architectural training and service to contemporary fads do not necessarily make the courthouses of Bruce and Morgan better than those of J. W. Golucke, merely different.

ROCKDALE COUNTY: CONYERS

Plate 1.19: The depot at Conyers, built in 1892. Bradford L. Gilbert, architect.[45]

Bradford Gilbert was a well-known railroad architect from New York whose work included plans for the remodeling of that city's old Grand Central Station as well as many other depots. He came to Atlanta in the early 1890s, and won the competition for chief architect of Atlanta's 1895 Cotton States Exposition. Gilbert would personally design five of the main buildings for this grand showcase for the New South,[46] and his bold uncomplicated symmetrical style would have a substantial impact on architecture in Georgia in the years just before the turn of the century.

When this depot was built in 1892, an article in *The Solid South* informed readers that this was "one of the best, if not the best, depot on the line."[47] It seems that *The Solid South* was unaware of the impressive new, brick depot at Covington, erected in 1885, not to mention the old Union Station at Augusta, built in the early 1870s. Still, this was certainly one of the finest wooden depots on the line.

The original depot built around 1845, shortly after the Georgia Railroad arrived, was called Conyers Station. It immediately became the focal point around which the town of Conyers blossomed. In 1855, Conyers Station burned in a disastrous fire, which destroyed a large portion of the business district of Conyers.[48] Several local authors suggest that "Federal raiders" set this fire.[49] This could hardly be other than myth. No historical confirmations exist outside of Conyers, and surely the appearance of armed "Federal raiders" burning an entire town 800 miles south of the Mason Dixon line in 1855 would have been seen as an event of sweeping historical import. Most likely "Federal raiders" were locally blamed long after the actual fire, and the legend grew without any basis in fact, or perhaps local historians somewhere along the way accidentally transposed the dates and causes of the various fires in Conyers's past.

Whatever the case, the depot was rebuilt only to be destroyed by real Federal troops in 1864. What Conyers did for a depot for the next 28 years is not known, but Bradford Giblet's 1892 depot served until 1975 when it was saved from destruction by a citizens' group which arranged for it to be leased to the City of Conyers. Renovated in 1977 and again in 1991, it is representative of depots all across Georgia which have been saved and used for all manner of assorted endeavors: city halls, historical society headquarters, antique shops, Lion's Clubs, craftsmen's workshops, and the like. For fifteen years beginning in 1977 this depot at Conyers was home to the Depot Players, a local theater group.

Rockdale County, like McDuffie County, is a child of the Georgia Railroad. It is hard to deny the preeminence of the railroad here, for Rockdale County, unlike its neighbors to the east, is a place endowed neither with promising farmland nor with great natural resources. Nonetheless, Conyers became quite a trading center after the arrival of the Georgia Railroad in 1845. Like her neighbor, Covington, Conyers built a spur, the Milstead Railroad, to a turn-of-the-century textile mill at Long Shoals, later called Milstead. As in so many Georgia towns, these first overtures to industrialism were accomplished with pri-

marily local capital.[50] The Milstead Railroad operated until 1977.

The story of Conyers Station is an extension of the Covington story, for it gives further example to the uncanny head for business, which characterized the early people of neighboring Newton County. The case in point is the prominent Covington citizen, Dr. W. D. Conyers. Dr. Conyers was a director of the Georgia Railroad,[51] and a delegate to the 1831 conference held in Eatonton to consider future railroads, turnpikes and canals for Georgia.[52] Around 1845, Dr. Conyers acquired the land that would soon become the town that today bears his name. Here was a man of insight when it came to railroads. He was one of the first Georgians to recognize the railroad's power to turn worthless plots of land into prime real estate. The land deal at Conyers Station was to be repeated again and again in every backwoods cow pasture that the railroads would touch. Land speculation would become a way of life for many, and fortunes would be made and lost betting on which way the tracks would run and which railroads would succeed.

All of this would soon become complex, ruthless and political, but in 1845 it was simple. A depot was built, and nine years later in 1854, when the town of Conyers was incorporated, the place had a population of about 400.[53] Rockdale County was created in

Plate 1.20: The architecture of the 1872 Rockdale County Courthouse reflected only the simple, unselfconscious, pioneer spirit of the frontier.

[50] E.L. Cowan and Francis A. King, *A History of Rockdale County*, 195.

[51] Charles C. Jones, Jr. and Salem Dutcher, *The Memorial History of Augusta*, 491; O'Kelly and Guinn, Historical Souvenir of Conyers, 4.

[52] Lucian Lamar Knight, *Georgia and Georgians*, 6 vols. (Chicago and New York: Lewis Publishing Company, 1917) 2:648.

[53] Cowan and King, *A History of Rockdale County*, 4.

[54] Cowan and King, *A History of Rockdale County*, 6.

[55] A good example of this is the town of Chatsworth, Georgia, in Murray County.

1870. By 1880, the population of Conyers was 1374; the town was shipping 12,000 bales of cotton annually and boasted: "forty stores, a fine hotel, one college, seven churches, ten or twelve lawyers, as many doctors, ...a large carriage manufacturer...."[54] Conyers was also an impressive regional livestock market, especially well known for the trading of mules.

Over the next fifty years, many towns would go to great ends to attract railroads. Gifts of land, reduction or even waiver of taxes and local bond issues were common. Some speculators would even go so far as to build brick yards and saw mills and the like out in the middle of nowhere in order to assure that a specific rural place would have every chance at becoming a town once the railroad was built.[55]

Plate 1.20: The Rockdale County Courthouse, built in 1872, demolished 1939.

The seeds of agrarianism and frontier individualism were planted deep here. Along the main line of the Georgia Railroad, only Covington and Madison with their postbellum crossing rails would be seduced by the allure of the myth of the New South. These were the only towns on the Georgia Railroad to build fantasy courthouses, and the only towns to voice those wild aspirations delivered on the crossing rails of the last third of the century. But here in Conyers, we encounter the same cool architectural reaction to the Georgia Railroad that we find all up and down the line. The railroad was almost single-handedly responsible for the existence of the town, and yet the architecture of the first Rockdale County Courthouse reflects only the simple, unselfconscious, pioneer spirit of the frontier.

The Rockdale County Courthouse was completed in early 1872 during the dark days of Reconstruction, and it reflected only a stern reality. Just to the northwest, in Milton County, the old courthouse at Alpharetta burned in 1876 and Milton County leaders erected a nearly exact copy of this building at Alpharetta, a town that had remained untouched by a railroad. Both buildings are simple, vernacular, brick structures whose only decoration derived from ordered pilasters, which divided the facades into vertical bays, small modillions beneath the eaves, and hooded arches decorating the arched doorway and one second story window. No record comes to us to identify the builder, who was probably the designer. Whoever he was, he created a kind of stylistic lag in his design of the Rockdale County Courthouse, for it is a pure replica of so many brick courthouses built in Georgia decades earlier. Like McDuffie, Greene, Columbia, Warren and Taliaferro Counties, Rockdale County, would become a formidable stronghold of Populism. Led by favorite son, Farmer's Alianceman and Populist leader, William L. Peek, many here came to view the railroad as an exploiter of hard working farmers and not the purveyor of riches of the New South myth.

The 1872 Rockdale County Courthouse served the county until 1939 when it was demolished to make way for the present courthouse.

DeKalb County: Decatur

Plate 1.21: The DeKalb County Courthouse, built in 1847, demolished 1898.

Decatur has not lived all of its life in the shadow of Atlanta. In 1829, Adiel Sherwood's *Gazetteer of Georgia* relates that Decatur had about forty houses and stores. About ten years later, in a subsequent edition, he states that the town was much improved. The Georgia Railroad arrived here in 1845 just four years before the publication of George White's *Statistics of Georgia*, in which Mr. White describes Decatur as a pleasant little village of about 600 with two schools, two churches, two hotels, and "several stores." Indeed, Decatur was a model town of the upper Piedmont, a modest and comfortable community on the edge of the frontier. Nowhere in any of this is Decatur linked to Atlanta, for in those days Atlanta was a nameless, virtually uninhabited tract of rolling woods and farmland. This all changed in a historical blink, and by 1860, Sherwood's description of Decatur would include the tell-tail phrase, "since the rapid growth of Atlanta, the town has ceased to improve." By 1880, Decatur's population was only 900. The railroad's power to turn obscure places into cities proved impotent here. This must have been especially

Plate 1.21: The 1842 DeKalb County Courthouse supplies an excellent example of how the fundamental forms of the Greek Revival were broadly manipulated and mixed with the vernacular as one moved closer to the frontier. (Photo: Courtesy of the Atlanta History Center.)

disappointing for Decatur, for neighboring Atlanta was the New South myth come to life.

The first DeKalb County Courthouse was a log structure built around 1824. It was replaced in 1829 by a brick building that burned in 1842. In 1847, this quaint brick courthouse was fashioned vaguely in the Greek mold. It is easy to see how even the fundamental forms of the Greek Revival were broadly manipulated and mixed with the vernacular as one moved closer to the frontier. Several basic departures from pure Hellenic classicism indicate a rather charming unfamiliarity with the Greek orders. Most striking among these is the absence of a row of supporting columns across the front of the building. Instead the portico's only support comes from two square columns at its corners. Additionally the rusticated quoining, although an elegant detail for such a rural structure, breaks the usual simplicity of the Greek and

recalls later classical models. Lastly there is the clock tower, which although it may have been original, was probably added later in the century. This building was demolished in 1898 to make way for a larger building.

Plate 1.22: The depot at Stone Mountain, built in 1852. Burned in 1864 and rebuilt in 1914.

It seems unlikely that 1845 and the coming of the Georgia Railroad brought celebration to Decatur. Focus was undoubtedly fixed on the linking of the Georgia Railroad and the Western and Atlantic a few miles beyond Decatur at the railhead then known as Terminus. Although the link was accomplished shortly after the Georgia Railroad reached Decatur, it would be almost four years before the first train ran between Atlanta and Chattanooga, signaling the commencement of the extraordinary growth of Atlanta and marking the beginning of a period of limbo for Decatur. Fulton County was set off from DeKalb in 1853. Decatur was too close to Atlanta to establish an identity of her own, and too far away to share in the prosperity. Stone Mountain on the other hand had experienced substantial growth as the size of this depot suggests. By 1897, Stone Mountain's progress would lead to a petition for the removal of the county seat from Decatur to Stone Mountain. A referendum was held to decide the question, and the popular vote favored Stone Mountain. However, this balloting failed to produce the statutory percentage of registered voters needed to mandate the change, and Decatur remained the county seat.[56] This 1914 rebuilding of

Plate 1.22: This 1914 rebuilding of the original 1852 stone depot speaks eloquently for Stone Mountain's progress. (Photo: Wilber W. Caldwell.)

the original 1852 stone depot speaks eloquently for Stone Mountain's progress, especially when compared to the small, ordinary wooden depot that still stands in Decatur. Despite its proximity to Atlanta, DeKalb remained primarily a rural place. As late as 1900, the county was eleventh among Georgia's 137 counties in cotton production. This state of affairs would, of course, slowly change as Atlanta grew and as links with Decatur were established.

As Atlanta grew as a rail center, the spokes of a great wheel began to radiate outward in all directions. Three of these passed through DeKalb County. The Georgia Railroad in 1845 was the first of these, hooking North to follow the ridgeline past the great stone mountain. In 1871, the Atlanta and Richmond Air Line (later the Atlanta and Charlotte and still later part of the Richmond and Danville Railroad) was built. The line passed out of Atlanta, begetting in DeKalb County the town of Chamblee which was originally called Roswell Junction, owing to the connection there with the "Buck" Line Railroad to Roswell. In 1888, the Georgia, Carolina and Northern Railroad (later the Seaboard) was built to Athens and Elberton, passing north of Decatur and through Tucker.

Plate 1.23: The DeKalb County Courthouse, built in 1898-1900. J. W. Golucke, architect.

James Wingfield Golucke's 1900 DeKalb County Courthouse was perhaps the most influential public building of its era in Georgia. Except for Atlanta architect, Andrew J. Bryan's less influential 1895 Stewart County Courthouse at Lumpkin and Bryan's 1896 remodeling of the old Muscogee County Courthouse at Columbus, Golucke's creation in Decatur was the first courthouse in the state to voice the passion of the American Neoclassical Revival. The new classicism had swept the county after the success of the "Florentine Renaissance" architecture of Chicago's "White City" at the 1893 Columbian Exposition.

A careful combination of modern neoclassical trends and the familiar classicism of the Old South, Golucke's granite centerpiece at in DeKalb was Georgia's most imitated public building of the first decade of the new century. Less than a year after it's

Plate 1.23: At the turn of the century, James W. Golucke's 1900 DeKalb County Courthouse was perhaps the most influential public architectural creation in Georgia. (Photo: Wilber W. Caldwell.)

completion, Golucke designed a brick court building in Hart County based on a nearly identical plan, and only a year later he followed that structure with his 1903 Meriwether County Courthouse at Greenville. By this time, county officials were flocking to Decatur to view Golucke's work, and newspaper reports in Eatonton and in Newnan confirm that Golucke's commissions for courthouses in those towns were awarded on the strength of the architect's work in DeKalb County. James Golucke would expand on his ideas in Putnam and Coweta Counties, adding more Beaux-Arts ornament and more expressive details. In all, he would design seven court buildings in Georgia modeled after the general form found here at in Decatur. In addition, Columbia's Frank Milburn, Eastman's Ed C. Hosford, Macon's Alexander Blair, Columbus's T. F. Lockwood, Augusta's Lewis Goodrich and Atlanta's Morgan and Dillon would all create court buildings in Georgia following Golucke's general "Decatur" plan.

Part of the success of the design turned on four more or less equal tetrastyle portico entrances, one at each of the four points of the compass. Elsewhere in America, the new classicism reflected a grasping com-

[56] Caroline McKinney Clarke, *The Story of Decatur* (Decatur GA: Caroline McKinney Clarke, 1973) 155.

mercialism and the aggressive nation's growing industrial might. To temper these uniquely un-Southern
images, Golucke was careful to retain, at the center of
each elevation, a bold Greek temple form, a grand
portico topped with a classical pediment supported by
imposing columns. Golucke thus balanced powerful
duel symbols that spoke to a deeply troubled region
teetering on the razor's edge between the Old South
and the New. Here, despite its granite monumentality, was a fundamentally Georgian classical form, not
much different from courthouse designs that appeared
in simple builder's guides of the early years of the nineteenth century.[57] Sadly the original building burned
1916 and was rebuilt along similar lines but without
the great lantern. The addition of wings in the 1930's
erased two of the grand entranceways, but the divided
mind of the American South at the turn of the century still radiates from the square in Decatur.

The absence of other granite or marble courthouses in Georgia before 1910 is puzzlement. Many
early courthouses had been wooden, but after 1884
there were only five wooden courthouses built in the
state (see Appendix A). Even counties, which boasted
huge quarries, like Elbert and Pickens, built brick
courthouses. Early in the twentieth century, a few concrete court buildings would rise, but with these few
exceptions, along with the limestone walls of the 1907
Appling County Courthouse at Baxley, all of Georgia's
courthouses constructed in between 1883 and 1910
were brick.

THE ATHENS BRANCH: UNION POINT TO ATHENS

OGLETHORPE COUNTY: LEXINGTON

The depot at Crawford, Georgia, built c.1857. (see Introduction, Plate 12)

Although Athens had been a driving force in the
organization of the Georgia Railroad, the line's 1833
charter was geographically broad. It prescribed a main
line to some undetermined point in the interior of
Georgia, and then proposed three branches: one to
Eatonton, one to Madison and one to Athens. In

1835, things looked rosy for Athens as a revised charter envisioned continuing the proposed Athens branch
to connect with "the railroad which the people of the
West have in contemplation between the city of
Cincinnati and the Southern Atlantic Coast."[58] But
in 1836, the State of Georgia began work on the
Western and Atlantic Railroad to connect the place we
now call Atlanta with the place we now call
Chattanooga. A western connection was about to
become a reality, but it would not pass through
Athens.

By 1838, the Georgia Railroad's branch point to
Athens was designated in Greene County and named
Union Point. The Eatonton branch, begun at Camak,
was extended only as far as Warrenton before it was
abandoned, and the Athens branch, although completed from Union Point to Athens in 1841, became a
stepchild. The branch through Madison became the
undisputed main line. It was completed to Atlanta in
1845, while the Athens and Warrenton branches were
used only as horse-drawn railroads. Completed to
Carr's Hill across the Oconee River from Athens, the
Athens branch did not know steam-power until
1847.[59]

Around 1840, the first wooden depot was built at
the place which later became Crawford, and the spot
was named Lexington Station. It was only three miles
from the Oglethorpe County seat at Lexington, and in
addition to handling passenger and freight connections to Lexington via hack and wagon, Lexington
Station was a relay point for horses on the Georgia
Railroad. Teams were changed ten times a day. By the
1850s when this stone depot was built,[60] steam was
the motive power, and Lexington Station was becoming an important place in its own right as cotton from
Elbert County and other nearby counties arrived here
for shipment on the Georgia Railroad. Just a buggy
ride away, once proud and prosperous Lexington was
beginning to slip.

By some accounts, the wound, which crippled
Lexington, was self-inflicted. One story holds that the
railroad was blocked from entering the town by
restrictions attached to the deed of Lexington's prestigious Meson Academy,[61] and it is widely accepted
that the citizens of Lexington wanted no part of the

Georgia Railroad when its surveyors arrived in Oglethorpe County around 1835. It was thought that the railroad would:"contaminate their choice society, import contagious diseases, and that the noise and the whistle of passing cars would disturb the quiet of their lovely village and cause much uneasiness and trouble by frightening carriage horses."[62] To be sure Lexington prided itself on its fine society, and just as surely there were many who viewed the railroad as noisy and intimidating. But all along the line, the established towns had contained factions that fought the Georgia Railroad. Why did the juggernaut suddenly capitulate in Lexington?

The answer is on the map. The Athens branch of the Georgia Railroad from Union Point to Crawford follows the straight back of a broad ridge, and Lexington was far enough down the slope and out of their way for them to quickly accept any hint of rejection. This theory is especially compelling in the light of the fact that in 1841 powerful men in Augusta were in control of the Georgia Railroad and the Athens branch had quickly become of secondary importance.

Plate 1.24: The Oglethorpe County Courthouse, built in 1887. Kimball, Wheeler and Parkins, architects.

This courthouse is a powerful example of the compelling nature of the myth created by the railroads. By 1880, Lexington had little to crow about. Her former prominence among the towns of the region had already begun to recede when the Athens branch of the Georgia Railroad passed her by in 1840. By the time Lexington got around to realizing the need for a rail line of her own, more than just the railroad had passed her by. Nonetheless in 1887, the Lexington Terminal Railroad was built from the Georgia Railroad at Crawford to Lexington. The entire railroad covered a distance of only three miles, yet it sparked wild visions of promise. Perhaps the citizens of Lexington believed that the Lexington Terminal could single-handedly return the place to prominence. Whatever the case, as the tiny railroad neared completion, they built a grand symbol to their New South aspirations.

Plate 1.24: The 1887 Oglethorpe County Courthouse, an eclectic hyperbole of the architecture of the age. (Photo: Wilber W. Caldwell.)

There is yet more testimony here concerning the power of the New South myth, more evidence to reveal how deeply Lexington swallowed the tempting bait of promise. Not twenty years after Appomattox, and only a handful of years after the end of Reconstruction, it is hard to believe that the citizens of Lexington would want much truck with Yankees. But so blinded were they by visions of a New South miracle in their town that they selected not one Yankee, but three to design their dream courthouse, and one of these was viewed by many as the most notorious carpetbagger in Georgia, Hannibal I. Kimball.

Kimball came South after the war, and along with his crony, Governor Rufus Bullock, he wove spells of promise, high finance and illusion all across Georgia. His schemes included the much-criticized lease of the

[57] Golucke's design is remarkably similar to the elevation of a design for a courthouse published in 1829 by Minard Lefever's in his *Young Builder's General Instructor*.

[58] Amendment to the Charter of the Georgia Railroad and Banking Company, 1835, quoted in T.P. Janes, *A Handbook of the State of Georgia* (Atlanta: Russell Brothers, 1876) 166.

[59] Jones, Jr. and Dutcher, *The Memorial History of Augusta*, 486.

[60] F.C. Smith, *The History of Oglethorpe County* (Washington GA: Wilkes Publishing Company, 1970) 206.

[61] Joan Niles Sears, *The First Hundred Years of Town Planning in Georgia* (Atlanta: Cherokee Press, 1979) 72.

[62] Smith, *History of Oglethorpe County*, 201.

Western and Atlantic Railroad from the State of Georgia, the organization and funding of numerous shaky railroading adventures and the sale of his unfinished Atlanta Opera House to the State of Georgia at an outrageous profit. Kimball was a promoter, a dreamer and a financier, not an architect. In 1869 and 1870, employing the considerable architectural skills of William Parkins, he financed and built the premier Southern hotel of the era, Atlanta's fabulous Kimball House.

Kimball left Georgia under the pressure brought by his financial dealings only to return in 1883 to organize the construction of the second Kimball House to replace the first building which had burned that same year. He formed a partnership with architect Lorenzo G. Wheeler of New York who arrived in Atlanta in 1884 with plans for the new building already begun. Wheeler remained seven years, completing the Atlanta Constitution Building in 1885 and the highly eclectic Kimball House II in 1886[63] William Parkins joined the firm in 1885. Parkins, also from New York, had been the first architect to practice in Atlanta after the war, and despite his northern roots and Union sympathies, he had earned much respect in Georgia. His many fine accomplishments included the Church of the Immaculate Conception, the original 1870 Kimball House, and the 1883 Fulton County Courthouse.[64]

But Oglethorpe County was a long way from Atlanta in a great many more respects than just miles, and seemingly there was much for Lexingtonians to distrust about carpetbagger Kimball and his Northern architectural cohorts. Still Kimball was, if nothing else, the consummate promoter, and thanks to the railroads and to men like these architects, the New South was becoming a reality in Atlanta. Perhaps these Northerners knew some secret. And if so, could they be all that bad? More importantly, would their magic work way out in the fields and woods of Oglethorpe County?

The first Oglethorpe County Courthouse was a log building constructed a few miles from what was to become Lexington soon after the county was created in 1793. Lexington became the county seat in 1806 and a more substantial brick courthouse was built on the square in 1819. The building was in "the shape of a cross" to afford an entrance at each of the four points of the compass,[65] and it remained on the square in Lexington for almost 70 years. In his *Gazetteer of Georgia*, Adiel Sherwood relates that Lexington had been preeminent among the villages of Georgia for its highly cultivated society." It had a courthouse, a jail, 28 dwellings, and 15 stores in 1829. By 1849, only a handful of years after the Georgia Railroad passed Lexington by, George White's *Statistics of the State of Georgia* would simply state that Lexington was "not the busy, thriving place that it once was."

Lexington was down, but the myth was powerful. That a town could stand still for so long, then suddenly lay down a few miles of track and aspire again to soar on the wind gives shape to the illusion of the New South. In 1886, when Lexington, with a population of only about 500, was hiring not just the best, but arguably two of the best architects in Atlanta to build her dream symbol, nearby Crawford with a population of 312 was unsuccessfully petitioning for the removal of the county seat from Lexington to Crawford.[66] With the completion of the Lexington Terminal Railroad and her new courthouse, Lexington would cement her hold of the county seat, but the town would only stagnate at the end of her tiny railroad. By 1900, when many of the small towns in Georgia were finally beginning to see a glimmer of progress among the shadows of poverty and backwardness, Lexington languished with a population of only 635. The last train on the Lexington Terminal Railroad passed into history in 1932.

Some architectural historians would call this building an example of "High Victorian" eclecticism, while others prefer the term "Picturesque Eclectic."[67] To call the 1887 Oglethorpe County Courthouse an example of the Picturesque Eclectic is

[63] Elizabeth Anne Mack Lyon, *Atlanta Architecture: The Victorian Heritage* (Atlanta: Atlanta Historical Society, 1976) 98.

[64] The 1883 Fulton County Courthouse at Atlanta was designed by the firm of Parkins and Bruce and is primarily the work of A.C. Bruce.

[65] Smith, *The History of Oglethorpe County*, 199.

[66] Smith, *The History of Oglethorpe County*, 200.

[67] Carroll L. V. Meeks, *The Railroad Station, An Architectural History* (New Haven: Castle Books, 1956) 1-25.

both to waffle and to accurately state the case. Is the Picturesque Eclectic actually a style? On one hand, it accurately describes what was happening in American architecture during the last quarter of the nineteenth century. However, difficulty arises from the freedom implied by the term "eclectic" which so defies discipline that an architectural style of the eclectic would seem inherently undefinable. This is to say that it could include just about anything, and in 1887, it often did.

At the end of the nineteenth century, architects in America were sorting through the wild extravagances emanating from the Victorian period in England, and a few were on the verge of extracting from this hodge-podge something uniquely American. In Great Britain, the early part of this period had been marked by a number of historical architectural revivals, including several articulations of Gothic Revival, a Tudor Revival, a Romanesque Revival, and the resurgence of the Italian Renaissance Style. By the late Victorian period several iterations of Renaissance Revival were added to the list, and a number of eclectic influences emerged including Dutch, Egyptian, Japanese, German *Rundbogenstil,* Byzantine, as well as a spattering of re-digested classical motifs. The result was an orgy of architectural decoration and excess.

Revivalism was more uniform on this side of the Atlantic and the resultant eclecticism was a bit less chaotic, but only a bit. Gothic architecture, although it did have its day, was generally limited to ecclesiastical applications in the American South. Not surprisingly, the Second Empire or "General Grant Style" never caught on in Dixie. Later, the Queen Anne Style, a rather codified and highly Picturesque form of eclecticism based on early English models adorned with a new "free classicism," became quite popular especially in domestic Southern architecture. The Romanesque Revival, which became the jumping off place for the first American architectural pathfinder, H. H. Richardson, flourished in the South. But as the Richardsonian Romanesque became more Richardsonian than Romanesque, few of the master's original ideas filtered southward.

Just two years before the courthouse cornerstone was laid at Lexington, Henry Hobson Richardson,

himself a Southerner, designed what is arguably the pre-eminent American Courthouse of this period. The Allegheny County Courthouse at Pittsburgh was designed in 1884 and completed in 1888, two years after Richardson's death. The influence of Richardson's design on the Oglethorpe County Courthouse is undeniable. A fundamental Richardsonian characteristic is a binary polychrome, usually expressed in contrasting colors of rough cut stone. Here, predictably, we find the prerequisite brick structure dressed in Richardsonian clothing by means of granite banding, granite arches, and the particularly Richardsonian granite columnettes flanking the main entrance and supporting the front of the tower. Also powerfully in the mold of H. H. Richardson is the central tower with its tall tourelles. This echoes not only the Allegheny County Courthouse, but also the earlier and less vertical Trinity Church tower in Boston (1878), one of Richardson's most lasting and monumental triumphs.

But to use the master's colors is not to create the masterpiece, and indeed the Oglethorpe County Courthouse is no masterpiece. Elements of the Richardsonian style are here, but the fundamental Richardsonian sense of mass is sadly absent. The result is more awkward than awe inspiring. The open air arches of the tower and the flanking second story arcades give a sense of emptiness where mass should prevail. Adding to the weightlessness are delicate, multi-pane windows at mid-tower and above the sashed windows all around. This building proves that the license of the eclectic, although enticing, is fraught with risk, and whether the result is more grotesque than picturesque might be a matter for debate.

Still, when we step away from the great shadows cast by Henry Hobson Richardson at Boston and Pittsburgh and into the humble but clear light of tiny, struggling Lexington, Georgia, in 1887, we can suddenly see the building for what it was and is: an inspiring announcement of courage, determination and hope; a deep and abiding prayer that maybe the industrial revolution itself might come and sweep little Lexington into the twentieth century.

It was not to be.

Plate 1.25: In 1817, the Wilkes County Courthouse was among the finest court buildings in the state. (Photo: Courtesy of Mary Willis Library, Washington, GA)

THE WASHINGTON BRANCH

WILKES COUNTY: WASHINGTON

Plate 1.25: The Wilkes County Courthouse built in 1817. Frederick Ball, architect.

With the single exception of the old colonial courthouse at Savannah, the only brick courthouses built in Georgia before 1820 were in the Piedmont. While counties in the Cotton Belt and the Coastal Plain settled for crude frame courthouses or even log structures, by 1817 brick court buildings graced the upcountry squares of Augusta, Madison, Sparta, Jefferson, Appling, Milledgeville, Washington, Greensboro and Clinton. Here was a convincing architectural testament to the growing allure of the Piedmont and to western population migration.

By 1790, over one third of Georgia's 82,548 inhabitants lived in Wilkes County. In that year, Washington was "a thriving village of thirty-four dwellings, a courthouse, a temporary jail and an academy."[68] Establishing a branch of the Georgia State Bank in 1820, the town flourished in the hospitable waters of cotton's rising tide. In that same year, Wilkes County counted 14,237 residents, 8960 of whom

were slaves laboring to turn Wilkes County white each fall.

In 1838, the Washington Railroad and Banking Company was chartered to connect Washington with the Georgia Railroad, but in the depression years of the late 1830s, the local company was unable to muster the financial resources to complete the 14 mile line. Washington's railroad aspirations remained frustrated until the business leaders of the town induced the Georgia Railroad to build the line in 1847. The Washington Branch of the Georgia Railroad was completed in 1854, connecting with the main line at the village of Cumming, which had formerly been called Double Wells and later became known as Barnett.

By the time the Georgia Railroad finally arrived at Washington, the 1817 Wilkes County Courthouse was almost 40 years old, and its cross-like floor plan had served as a pattern for many of the state's early brick court buildings. Only two years after this building's completion, the 1819 Oglethorpe County Courthouse rose at Lexington "in the shape of a cross."[69] Likewise Wilkes County's new centerpiece boasted Georgia's first court clock tower, a feature which was to become an almost obligatory part of courthouse architecture in the late nineteenth century. The tracery in the fan lights above the doorways and in the oval roundel in the pediment are hallmarks of the Federal Style. With its rather vernacular look, the 1817 building appears typical of the work of that generation of untrained "architect/builders" who practiced in rural America in the first decades of the nineteenth century. Of the "architect," Frederick Ball, we know little, except that he was a "carpenter" originally from New Jersey living in Savannah, and that he died in 1820 of a "fever."[70]

In the years that followed the Civil War, Ball's courthouse presided over a Wilkes County reeling from the collapse of the plantation system. As tenancy spread across the land, farms grew smaller and the crop lien system tightened its grip on the economy. Each year Wilkes county farmers planted more and more cotton, and each year cotton prices fell. From the reasonably high marks set just after the war, cotton prices fell to ten cents a pound in 1880 and slowly declined to barely half that by 1894. In 1860, the county had produced 8500 bales, by 1900, this number had reached a seemingly impossible 30,000 bales. There was little trace of fabled New South industrialization here. Still through it all, Washington slowly grew. Her population stood at 1500 just after the war. By 1900, it exceeded 3000. The town's progress was directly linked to success or failure out in the fields. The list of enterprises of the late century is predictable: an assortment of stores and mercantile houses, cotton warehouses and presses, grist and flour mills, carriage and wagon factory, two banks, two newspapers, two hotels and a small foundry. In addition, the town was noted throughout the region as a trading center for horses and mules.

Wilkes County's perennial favorite son was the flamboyant Robert Toombs. Standing between reactionary rural elements and the equally passionate apostles of the New South, Toombs led vigorous attacks on corruption and exploitation as he saw it, first against self-serving Reconstruction Republicans and later against Bourbon Democrats and their New South political "rings." He was perhaps most vocal in his attacks on the railroads whose unbridled exploitation of the citizens of rural Georgia he opposed at every turn. Robert Toombs set the tone for Washington and Wilkes County in the postbellum era, and while Toombs lived, there would be no euphoric New South fervor in Washington.

Plate 1.26: The Wilkes County Courthouse, built 1903-1904. Frank Milburn, architect.

Robert Toombs died in 1885, and by the late 1890s things had begun to change in Washington. Brick buildings began to sprout everywhere. Part of this was a result of a series of disastrous fires. Substantial portions of the town burned in 1895 and again in 1898, but in the 1890s, the mood was not simply rebuilding. Something else was on the wind, which sparked renewed vigor. A county history recounts "unprecedented commercial and civic activity."[71]

A close examination of period newspapers reveals the source of Washington's sudden hopeful boom. There can be little doubt that as early as 1890 the citizens of Washington, Georgia, were absolutely certain

Plate 1.26: Maimed by fire and an unfaithful restoration, Frank Milburn's 1903 Wilkes County Courthouse represents a dying gasp of the picturesque in Georgia. (Photo: Wilber W. Caldwell.)

that the arrival of a new railroad was eminent. In 1890, and again around the turn of the century, railroad rumors and speculations were so dense in the area that hopeful citizens could actually hear the whistle and smell the smoke.

Early railroad speculation surrounding a second connection to Washington was met with an odd combination of panic and elation. The panic seemed to stem from fears that, if the town did not respond to all budding railroad schemes, then rails would pass Washington by. In response to rumors of a line from Elberton to Washington the *Washington Chronicle* informed readers that it was "critical that the W & E...be built," and urged citizens to "lay all things aside and save (Washington's) position by recruiting the Washington and Elberton."[72] Likewise in discussing the need to capture the proposed line from Augusta to Chattanooga, the *Chronicle* urged civic action warning of competition from neighboring towns: "...a road is offered from Appling and another from Elberton via Lincolnton."[73] Upon a rumor

---

[68] *The Story of Washington-Wilkes* (Athens GA: The Writer's Program of the Works Projects Administration, 1941) 36.

[69] Smith, *The History of Oglethorpe County*, 199.

[70] *Registar of Deaths in Savannah, Georgia, 1984-1989* 6 vols. (Savannah GA: The Georgia Historical Society, 1989) 4:62.

[71] *The Story of Washington-Wilkes* (Athens GA: The Writer's Program of the Works Projects Administration, 1941) 70.

[72] *Washington Chronicle*, March 29, 1890.

[73] *Washington Chronicle*, March 29, 1890.

that the Georgia, Carolina and Northern would build a branch to Washington, the *Chronicle* went so far as to recommend that the town immediately subscribe $30,000 for the right of way.[74]

Most accounts of impending railroad connections in Washington were dripping with the honey of the New South myth. It was the stuff dreams (and courthouses) were made of. Responding to rumors of the Georgia, Carolina and Northern's branch to Washington, the Chronicle predicted that "another railroad would make Washington, one of the most prosperous trade centers in Georgia," and later in the same article the editors revealed the full bloom of the myth carried by postbellum rail: "...factories would spring into life, the enormous energy of steam would throw renewed life and vigor into our midst, and the time would be near when Washington would count her population at 5000."[75] Accompanying this flowery rhetoric was an accounting of what the new railroad would mean to the town. It reads like a textbook of New South dogma, promising increased land values, immigration of skilled labor from the North, development of the county's mineral resources, "manufacturing without end," and "new life, new spirit, and a world of happy changes."[76]

There was certainly no scarcity of railroad schemes to keep hopes burning brightly in Washington. In addition to the continual agitation for

Plate 1.27: Although he did not copy this earlier 1897 work at Anderson, South Carolina, Milburn captured exactly its soul in Wilkes County. (Photo: Wilber W. Caldwell.)

the extension of the Georgia Railroad to Lincolnton and a western connection to the Elberton Air Line at Elberton, other plans included the perennial attempts to build the Augusta and Chattanooga Railroad, a Macon to Elberton connection via Union Point; various branches from Athens, including the proposed spur of the Georgia, Carolina and Northern Railroad, and the grand, ongoing, dream-like saga of the Savannah, Augusta and Northern.

Here in Washington rumors of an impending rail connection fueled the dream of ending the town's isolation at the end of an insignificant antebellum spur line and created the same euphoria experienced by many towns where the crossing rails were real. It was a dream, which begot a dream, and it resulted in the one of the most bizarre courthouses in Georgia. By the mid-1890s, the new courthouse movement in Washington was well underway. In July of 1896, the *Manufacturer's Record* reported that there was "talk of a new courthouse" in Wilkes County.[77] As railroad speculation continued, the new courthouse movement gained strength, and the county commissioners finally purchased the courthouse lot in 1899.

The selection of Frank Milburn as architect for the new Wilkes County courthouse was no doubt accomplished by a survey of new courthouses in the area. The proximity of Milburn's 1897 Anderson County Courthouse in Anderson, South Carolina, (Plate 1.27) can be no coincidence for the similarities are striking. The county commissioners in Wilkes undoubtedly thought Milburn's work in nearby Anderson to be the very essence of the modern rail center they envisioned at Washington. Milburn was retained, and although he did not exactly copy his earlier work in South Carolina, he captured exactly its soul in Wilkes County. It is interesting to note that upon the completion of the Anderson County Courthouse in 1897, Milburn was accused of copying his own design for the 1893 Forsyth County Courthouse in Winston, North Carolina.[78]

In the years after the turn of the century, Frank Milburn became arguably the South's preeminent architect. His prestigious retainer by the Southern Railway added many depots to his lengthy credits including the main passenger depots at Augusta,

Rome and Savannah, Georgia; Columbia, Spartanburg, Greenville and Charleston, South Carolina, and Durham, North Carolina. He worked on the remodeling of four state capitol buildings and designed myriad courthouses across the south, including four in Georgia and three in South Carolina.[79] With his roots in nineteenth century eclecticism, Milburn designed in many Picturesque styles, and he later seemed equally comfortable and competent working in neoclassical and Beaux-Arts idioms.[80]

Here in Washington, we find a dying gasp of the picturesque in Milburn's highly eclectic court building. The structure burned in 1956 and was restored without its original clock tower. The squat misproportioned tower we see today is the product of a recent clumsy restoration. It lacks detail, appears compressed and bulky in scale and omits the central section of the original, stunningly tall and slender tower. Despite its wounds, the building is an enlightening example of the limits to which eclecticism was pushed.

The Wilkes County Courthouse and its older sibling at Anderson are bold and original mixtures incorporating elements of several picturesque modes of the day. The primary ingredients in these unlikely amalgams are the Richardsonian Romanesque and the Dutch Renaissance Revival. The bold low arch of the courthouse entrance at Washington is typically Richardsonian, as is the fenestration of both buildings with their ordered groupings and broad architraves. Richardsonian models are more clearly revealed at Anderson with the use of stone banding and massive stone voussoirs in the second story windows. These details are articulated in brick in the court building at Washington presumably owing to budgetary considerations. The patterned brick polychrome and scrolling parapets of the Northern European Renaissance cap these Romanesque elevations. The marriage of strikingly different styles is a great deal more graceful in Anderson, where decorative polychromatic brick courses are carried all the way around the building, and intricate brick designs flow into the high parapets with little interruption. In Washington, a broad cornice separates Dutch parapets from the Richardsonian mass of the building destroying continuity and compartmentalizing the historical elements. It is difficult

to say whether this cornice is original. It is probably an addition of recent restorations. As previously noted, the tower of the Washington restoration bears little resemblance to the original. Old photographs of the original building reveal a tower very much like the one at Anderson with Gothic elements in its upper stages.

Architectural historian, Carroll L. V. Meeks, has labored to paint Picturesque Eclecticism, not merely as a method for combining styles, but as the dominant architectural aesthetic of the era. The "synthetic type of eclecticism" he describes is the essence of Milburn's work here in Wilkes County. According to Meeks, a method of synthesis "underlay such nineteenth century styles as the Victorian Gothic, the Second Empire, the Queen Anne and the Richardsonian Romanesque. Meeks concludes: "Emancipation from archaeological accuracy and stylistic purity was the authorization for an increased degree of originality...which was distinguished...by the fact that...more and more emphasis was placed on the desire to be original than on the wish to be creative."[81] This is an apt distinction, and Milburn's courthouses at Washington and Anderson offer fine illustrations. Both were without doubt original, but the nobility of the creative aesthetic at work here is at best questionable.

When the Wilkes County Courthouse was completed in 1904, no new rails had arrived in Washington. Still, railroad hopes must have continued to soar. In 1907, the business association of the town petitioned the Georgia Railroad for a larger depot, and a new building was erected in response to these demands. Today the structure is nowhere to be found.

---

[74] *Washington Chronicle*, January 4, 1890.

[75] *Washington Chronicle*, January 4, 1890.

[76] *Washington Chronicle*, January 4, 1890.

[77] *The Manufacturer's Record*, July 3, 1896.

[78] John E. Wells and Robert E. Dalton, *South Carolina Architects, 1885-1935, A Biographical Dictionary* (Richmond VA: The New South Architectural Press, 1992) 122.

[79] Wells and Dalton, *South Carolina Architects, 1885-1935, A Biographical Dictionary*, 122- 27.

[80] Lawrence Wodehouse, "Frank Pierce Milburn (1868-1926), A Major Southern Architect," *The North Carolina Historical Review* 50/3 (1973): 295-96.

[81] Meeks, *The Railroad Station, An Architectural History*, 14.

It would be 1916 before the Washington and Lincolnton Railroad extended the Washington branch of the Georgia Railroad northward to Lincolnton, and 1919 before the Elberton Eastern finally gave Washington her long awaited connection to the west.

LINCOLN COUNTY: LINCOLNTON

Plate 1.28: The Lincoln County Courthouse, built in 1915-1916. G. Lloyd Preacher, architect.

After the Georgia Railroad built its branch line to Washington in 1854, there was immediate talk of an extension to Lincolnton, a hamlet of about 175 inhabitants about 25 miles to the east. Agitation for this line resurfaced in the post-war period reaching a peak in 1889 when the Washington and Lincolnton Railroad was chartered. In that same year, it seemed so certain that the Augusta and Chattanooga Railroad would pass through Lincolnton, that a depot site was actually selected.[82] Despite its poverty and obscurity, the tiny village was the subject of newspaper reports that dutifully spouted the prophecy of the railroads' powerful myth: "…when the line …the Augusta and Chattanooga… is built, Lincolnton will be one of the prettiest towns and best business points in Georgia."[83]

Notwithstanding myriad railroad schemes, the turn of the century came and went, and Lincoln remained without a railroad. Predictably no great architectural symbol for New South progress rose in Lincoln County during the period of our interest because no railroad had arrived to import the tempting myth of impending prosperity. In 1916, the Washington and Lincolnton Railroad finally materialized, and the very next year Lincoln County hired Augusta architect, G. Lloyd Preacher to design a courthouse that would reflect the progress everyone knew would arrive by rail. The Georgian elegance of Preacher's 1917 Lincoln County Courthouse was a fitting symbol for the county's hopes, and despite the fact that it was built well after the end of the period of this book's focus, it is illustrative of our theme.

Lincoln County had been cut from Wilkes County in 1796, and the town of Lincolnton was selected as the site of the new county's public build-

ings. A two-story courthouse was erected there in 1800. Exact descriptions of this building are lost to history, but local tradition holds that the building was constructed of rough stone masonry.[84] In 1851, a brick third story was added to house the local Masonic order, creating one of the few vernacular three-story court buildings of the antebellum era.[85] This old building was demolished in 1874, and a new courthouse was erected. Descriptions and photos recall typical brick vernacular buildings of the era. County historian, Clinton Perryman details: "an oblong, two-story hipped roof structure about 42 by 50 feet."[86]

By all accounts, Lincolnton was a very small, very poor place. Sholes's 1879 *Gazetteer of Georgia* estimates the town's population to have been around 150. By the turn of the century, Lincolnton could count only 220 residents. The arrival of the Washington and

Plate 1.28: Thanks to a fine restoration, the 1917 Lincoln County Courthouse still echoes that brief moment when the last murmurs of the myth of the New South were heard in Lincolnton. (Photo: Wilber W. Caldwell.)

Lincolnton Railroad in 1917 brought some progress, and by 1920, Lincolnton's population had reached 657. There was a flurry of lumbering activity, but as the virgin timber of Lincoln County began to disappear down her tiny new railroad, the boll weevil tightened his grip on the county's cotton crop. By the early 1930's, all of the large saw mills were gone, and depression griped the region. The last train on the Washington and Lincolnton Railroad passed into history in 1932. The depot at Lincolnton burned, and the road was sold for scrap in that same year.

SOME LAST THOUGHTS ON THE GEORGIA RAILROAD

It was the appearance of the Charleston and Hamburg Railroad that spurred the men of Augusta and of Athens to create the Georgia Railroad Company, but the story of how this railroad was born in a mud puddle has reached folklore status. The story details the events of the terrible winter of 1832 during which James Camak spent months agonizing over the hideous state of the roads in Georgia after a large piece of textile machinery became hopelessly mired in a mud hole between Augusta and Athens. We are told that the equipment had come from Philadelphia to Savannah by ship, tediously up the river by pole boat, and then by mule-drawn wagon to finally fulfill its destiny in that fateful quagmire in Greene County. Although this story may be true, it is of little significance, for the die was cast long before. It was cast by a thousand wagons in ten thousand mud holes in every road in Georgia.

It had taken almost ten years to build the 171 miles of track from Augusta to the Western and Atlantic railhead in DeKalb County. By 1845, when the Georgia Railroad was completed, the Western and Atlantic was already running as far north as Cartersville, and the finished connection linking Charleston, via Augusta, to the Tennessee River at Chattanooga was less than five years away. What had been started with the resolve of Athens had been finished with the money and power of Augusta. Indeed, Augusta first employed rails as the implements of her own personal prosperity. She wrought a bounteous

Plate 1.29: The Augusta Cotton Exchange, built in 1886. William Goodrich, architect. (Photo: Wilber W. Caldwell.)

steel river that flowed cotton from the Piedmont. But this proved to be only half of the equation. The promise of a connection to the West via the Western and Atlantic Railroad filled the merchants of Augusta and Charleston with even greater resolve. Since they first dreamed of canals, they had sought to tap the abundance of the American heartland. They envisioned not only boatloads of western staples bound for Europe and the North, but a cornucopia of western grain and pork to fill the bellies of Southerners so busy growing cotton that they sometimes scarcely took time to grow their own food.

[82] *The Elberton Star*, April 27,1889, quoted in Robert S. Davis and James E. Dorsey, Lincoln County Genealogy and History (Swainsboro GA: Magnolia Press, 1987) 349.

[83] *The Elberton Star*, April 27, 1889, quoted in Robert S. Davis and James E. Dorsey, Lincoln County Genealogy and History (Swainsboro GA: Magnolia Press, 1987) 349.

[84] Clinton J. Perryman, *History of Lincoln County* (1933; reprint, Tignall GA: Boyd Publishing Co., 1985) 47.

[85] The other three were the 1839 Jasper County Courthouse at Monticello, the 1849 Greene County Courthouse at Greensboro and the 1856 Catoosa County Courthouse at Ringgold.

[86] Perryman, *History of Lincoln County*, 67.

Despite all this vision and drive, the builders of Georgia's antebellum railroads were men of hard, calculating realism. Unlike the men who tangled the state with track after the war, their hope was pure and free from contrivance. They were not clawing their way back from defeat, nor were they bitter and filled with nostalgic despair. They were unencumbered by exploitation save their own. Their myths were not of a commercial sort, and they built little mythical architecture beyond the Greek Revival.

If one excepts the 1898-1900 DeKalb County Courthouse at Decatur and the unfounded hopes on the remote spur at Washington, a look back down the line of the Georgia Railroad reveals only three courthouses embodying architectural exuberance of a mythical sort: Bruce and Morgan's Second Empire centerpiece at Covington, 1884; Kimball, Wheeler and Parkins's wildly eclectic Oglethorpe County Courthouse at Lexington, 1887, and J. W. Golucke's grand neoclassical Morgan County Courthouse at Madison, 1907. To be sure, complex motives begot such exuberance, but certainly it is more than coincidence that these are the only three county seats on the line where postbellum rails crossed the Georgia Railroad. These buildings, built in response to the Covington and Macon, the Lexington Terminal and the Macon and Northern Railroads, stand in striking contrast to the simple brick courthouses which served the other counties along the right of way. The early railroads inspired few grand hopes and begot few grand illusions. Simple brick buildings were good enough for Appling, Thomson, Greensboro and Conyers. Likewise, Lewis Goodrich's 1902 monument at Crawfordville, although impressive, is far from a flowering statement of New South zeal and modernity. Indeed, even though blessed from the very beginning with the benefit of rail, most of the towns along the Georgia Railroad clung to their symbols of the past well into the twentieth century even as the allure of the New South was spinning a bright web of hope for places like Covington, Madison, and Lexington—places touched by the new rails of promise.

These were not the only early visions of steel rivers of cotton. Forever wildly jealous of Charleston, Savannah sought her own connection to the interior. At exactly the same time that the Georgia Railroad was chartered to connect Augusta with the interior, powerful interests in Savannah secured a charter for the Central Railroad and Banking Company of Georgia, the company which would become the Central of Georgia Railroad. They began to lay track for Macon in 1837.

•

2 | The Central of Georgia Railroad

THE MAIN LINE: SAVANNAH TO MACON

CHATHAM COUNTY: SAVANNAH

Plate 2.1: The Chatham County Courthouse, built in 1889. William Gibbons Preston, architect.

Mills Lane, who has written and edited a number of volumes on the architecture of the Old South, closes his 1977 edition of *Savannah Revisited, A Pictorial History* with a brief essay entitled, "Last Prosperity, 1865-1895." Here Mr. Lane assesses the economic problems of Savannah on the eve of the twentieth century in order to make the point that the city's flavor and charm were "preserved by the port's decline."[1] Such was the irony explicit in much of the city's architecture erected in the closing decades of the nineteenth century, just before the cotton kingdom began to unravel.

Unlike Augusta, which courted industry in 1880, Savannah was faithful in her marriage to trade. In that marriage she was bound to cotton, and in that bond lay a disappointing future. Despite dramatically increased yields in the decades following the Civil War, the bridegroom of cotton would be slowly broken by falling prices: $.25 per pound in 1868, $.12 in 1870, $.09 by 1880 and even lower just before the turn of the century. Although Savannah flourished again after 1870, it was only briefly.

The history of Savannah before 1910 is in many ways a paradigm for the history of Georgia and the cotton growing South, for Savannah, like most of Georgia, developed little or no industry and no significant middle class. Cotton was the central economic fact of the city, and when this building was new, no one foresaw the spiral of ruin to be wrought by the

---

[1] Mills Lane, *Savannah Revisited, A Pictorial History* (Savannah GA: Bee Hive Press, 1977) 82.

The Central of Georgia Railroad

THE MAIN LINE

Chatham County: Savannah • Jenkins County: Millen • Wilkinson County: Irwinton
Bibb County: Macon (see chapter 3 & 8)

THE AUGUSTA BRANCH

Burke County: Waynesboro

THE MILLEDGEVILLE-EATONTON BRANCH

Baldwin County: Milledgeville • Putnam County: Eatonton • Some Last Thoughts On the Central of Georgia Railroad

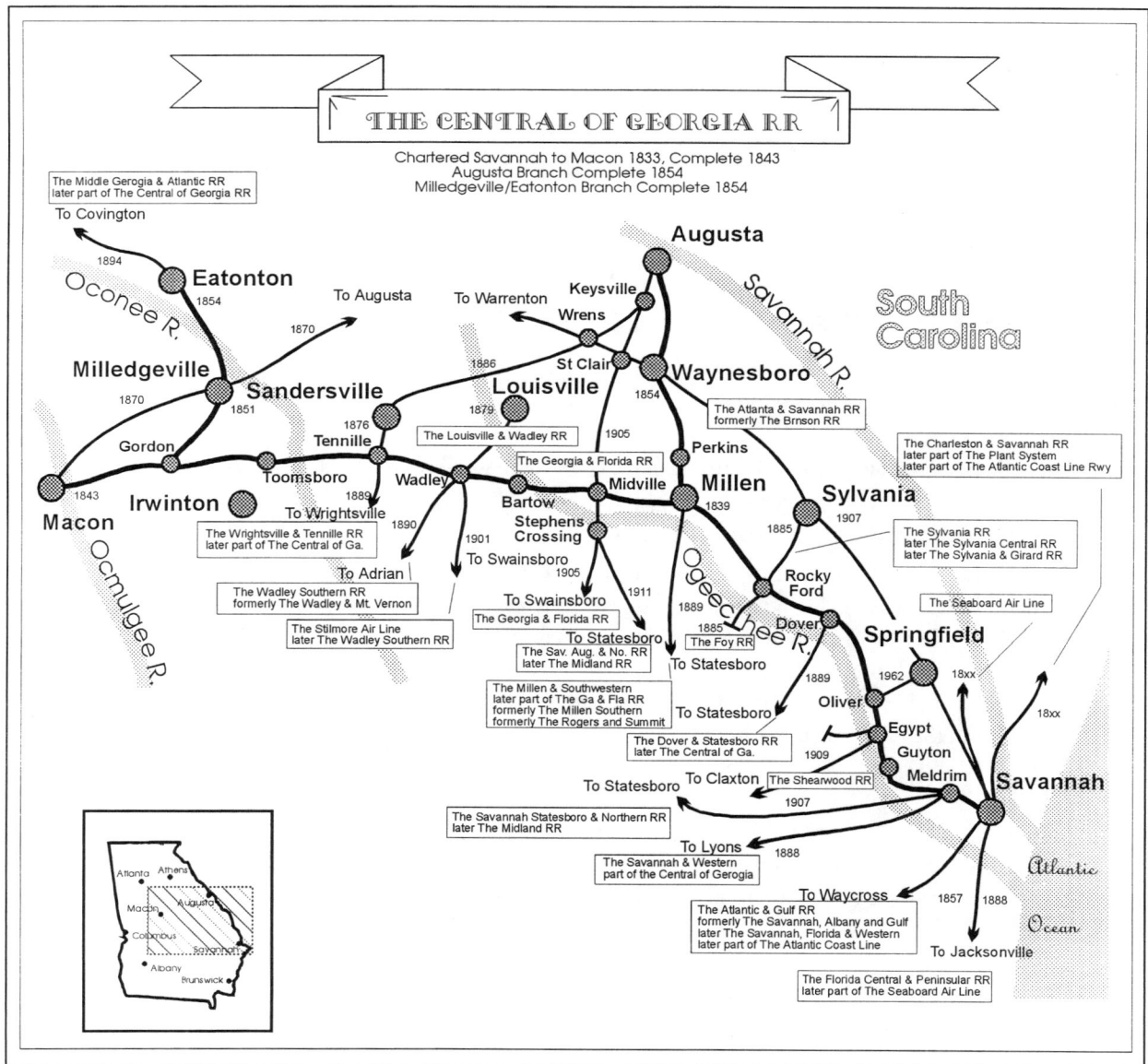

THE CENTRAL OF GEORGIA RR

Chartered Savannah to Macon 1833, Complete 1843
Augusta Branch Complete 1854
Milledgeville/Eatonton Branch Complete 1854

The Middle Georgia & Atlantic RR
later part of The Central of Georgia RR

To Covington

Eatonton 1854

To Augusta

To Warrenton

Keysville

Augusta

South Carolina

Milledgeville

Sandersville

Louisville

St Clair

Waynesboro

The Atlanta & Savannah RR
formerly The Brnson RR

The Charleston & Savannah RR
later part of The Plant System
later part of The Atlantic Coast Line Rwy

Gordon

Tennille

The Louisville & Wadley RR

The Georgia & Florida RR

Perkins

Midville

Millen

Sylvania

The Sylvania RR
later The Sylvania Central RR
later The Sylvania & Girard RR

Toomsboro

Wadley

Bartow

Stephens Crossing

Macon

Irwinton

To Wrightsville

The Wrightsville & Tennille RR
later part of The Central of Ga.

To Adrian

To Swainsboro

Rocky Ford

The Seaboard Air Line

The Wadley Southern RR
formerly The Wadley & Mt. Vernon

To Swainsboro

The Georgia & Florida RR

Dover

The Foy RR

Springfield

The Stilmore Air Line
later The Wadley Southern RR

To Statesboro

The Sav. Aug. & No. RR
later The Midland RR

To Statesboro

Oliver

The Millen & Southwestern
later part of The Ga & Fla RR
formerly The Millen Southern
formerly The Rogers and Summit

To Statesboro

Egypt

The Dover & Statesboro RR
later The Central of Ga.

Guyton

To Statesboro

To Claxton

The Shearwood RR

Meldrim

Savannah

The Savannah Statesboro & Northern RR
later The Midland RR

To Lyons

Atlantic

To Waycross

Ocean

The Savannah & Western
part of the Central of Georgia

The Atlantic & Gulf RR
formerly The Savannah, Albany and Gulf
later The Savannah, Florida & Western
later part of The Atlantic Coast Line

To Jacksonville

The Florida Central & Peninsular RR
later part of The Seaboard Air Line

Oconee R.

Ocmulgee R.

Ogeechee R.

Savannah R.

Atlanta Athens
Macon Augusta
Columbus Savannah
Albany
Brunswick

falling prices and glutted markets just before the turn of the century. Nor did anyone dare to dream the wildest nightmare of all, the boll weevil.

The year before this building was built, Thomas Gamble wrote, "everyone believed without reservation that Savannah was at the open door to an era of unprecedented progress."[2] Indeed, Savannah had always prospered on the cotton trade, and after the war, when cotton again began to flow down the river from Augusta and the railroads were rebuilt, it seemed logical to assume that the city would again rise to prominence. By the mid-1890s, five railroads converged on Savannah (Table 2.1) importing not only cotton from the interior but also vibrant hope for the future. Here again were the railroads and the myth of the New South, this time tempting old and stately Savannah to employ the Victorian fantasies of Boston architect, William Gibbons Preston.

Loosely the reign of Victoria saw revivalism flourish in England, and although the roots of American architecture of the period are similarly revivalist and decidedly English, a unique American character became increasingly distinct. The fact is, for the New World, the dates of Victoria's reign are of little historical significance, architecturally or otherwise. Although generally I refrain from calling American architecture "Victorian," in the case of Savannah I make an exception. Owing to her close mercantile ties with England in the cotton trade, Savannah developed architecturally as a remarkably English city. From the earliest Regency architecture of William Jay, the squares of the city have been uniformly lined with Georgian, brick buildings of a powerfully homogeneous nature. With this decidedly English base, Savannah became the natural host to a surprising amount of architecture of both the early and the late Victorian periods. In fact, Savannah's celebration of the myth of the New South made her home to the most diverse, and perhaps some of the best, Victorian buildings in Georgia. Of particular interest here are buildings of the early period especially in the Italianate and Early Gothic Revival styles. Equally at home in Savannah are buildings of the late Victorian period in representative array: Second Empire, Richardsonian Romanesque, Queen Anne, and the elaborate tracery

Plate 2.1: William Gibbons Preston's 1889 Chatham County Courthouse is another illustration of the inherent danger in the freedom of eclecticism. (Photo: Wilber W. Caldwell.)

RAILROAD CONNECTIONS AT SAVANNAH, 1892

The Central of Georgia, Savannah to Macon with a branch to Augusta.

The Central of Georgia (Savannah and Western Division), Savannah to Lyons to connect with the Savannah, Americus and Montgomery.

The Savannah, Florida and Western (Plant System) Savannah to Bainbridge (formerly the Atlantic and Gulf RR, later the Atlantic Coast Line Rwy.).

The Charleston and Savannah, (Plant System) (Later the Atlantic Coast Line Rwy.) Savannah to Charleston

The Florida Central and Peninsular RR (later the Seaboard Air Line Rwy.), Savannah to Jacksonville.

The Savannah and Tybee, Savannah to Tybee Island.

LATER:

The Seaboard Air Line Rwy., Savannah to Columbia, SC.

The Brinson Railway, Savannah to Sardis (later the Savannah and Atlanta RR, Savannah to Warrenton).

Table 2.1

[2] Thomas Gamble in Mills Lane, *Savannah Revisited, A Pictorial History* (Savannah GA: Bee Hive Press, 1977) 82.

Plate 2.2: The 1833 Chatham County Courthouse stood for a very different myth than the myth represented by the towers of William Gibbons Preston which replaced it.

of the various High Victorian domestic styles. It is this English uniformity and compactness of plan that gives Savannah her charm today, and in this context the work of William Gibbons Preston can be termed "Victorian," in spite of its debt to the American master, H. H. Richardson.

William G. Preston, a Bostonian and a graduate of the *Ecole des Beaux Arts* in Paris, designed twenty-three Victorian buildings in Savannah.[3] Among them were four significant public structures: The Cotton Exchange (1886), the DeSoto Hotel (1888), the Chatham County Courthouse (1889) and the Volunteer Armory (1892). Of the four, only the DeSoto Hotel, demolished in 1968, no longer stands. In contrast to his joyous Cotton Exchange and equally distinctive Armory, Mr. Preston seems to have missed the mark with his 1889 Chatham County Courthouse. The structure's dingy yellow brick set against the warmth and comfort of surrounding red brick buildings and the occasional gleaming white of nearby classical forms, seems shabby indeed. The east facade facing Wright Square seeks Richardsonian monumentality only to achieve a sort of institutional heaviness. Although the great arch below groupings of five arched windows above five lenteled windows is true to Richardson's ideas, the composition lacks the master's flare. The low tower detracts from the verticality of the high tower with its flamboyant Gothic decoration, which only serves to supply further dis-

traction from Preston's attempt at a Richardsonian facade. Indeed the squat, superfluous, low tower not only breaks the picturesque effect, but appears incongruous, more "prison-esque" than Romanesque. Its cornice and fenestration suggest a bastion, and its tourelles seem wholly out of scale and strangely out of place in Savannah. The southern elevation suffers a similar distracting lack of continuity, and when married to the two towers and the Richardsonian east facade, it is at best awkward. This is not one building but several, and it illustrates once again the inherent danger in the freedom of eclecticism. Just because the style gives license to draw from many wells is no guarantee that the resulting water will be sweet.

The recent history of this building parallels Savannah's fortunes. In the 1950s, the old courthouse was remodeled in order to save the expense of a new one. In the early 1970s, Savannah finally built a new court building, and this building was abandoned. It stood empty and neglected for almost twenty years until it was finally restored in 1990.

Plate 2.2: The Chatham County Courthouse, built in 1833, demolished in 1889. Russell Warren, architect (attributed).

In Savannah, the waters of architecture had been sweet indeed, and among the sweetest flowed from this building that Preston's 1889 courthouse replaced. It was among the finest examples of the Greek Revival in Georgia, standing equal to Charles Cluskey's notable achievements in the state and even rivaling Robert Mills's early work in South Carolina. Some sources attribute this building to Mills.[4] In fact there is a volume of opinion and speculation in this area. Talbot Hamlin in his exhaustive study of the Greek Revival in America mentions the possibilities of either Mills or William Jay in connection with this courthouse.[5] Chan Sieg attributes the building to Henry McAlpin[6], although it seems the ubiquitous McAlpin was more likely the builder.[7] Mills Lane is firm in his proclamation of Russell Warren who he describes as "a professional" from Rhode Island."[8] According to Professor Hamlin, Warren designed "extraordinarily vivid and original houses and was one of the architects responsible for the splendor of the

Greek Revival in Rhode Island."[9] Whoever the architect, this building graced Wright Square for almost sixty years, and its columns stood for a very different myth than the myth represented by the towers of William Gibbons Preston, that replaced them.

In 1833, in the American South, the columns of the Greek Revival were about to be twisted into a grotesque vision of the Greek democracy, in effect, idealizing that darker side of a classical society in which slavery had flourished. Elsewhere in adolescent America the Greek Revival mirrored more noble elements of classical culture as well as the new nation's strong anti-English sentiment. Jefferson himself had chosen classical architecture as the new national style, not only for its historical symbolism, but also because pure Classicism could look directly to original archeological sources for inspiration, thus bypassing English models. To be sure, the style flourished for a period in England; still it was ideal for this American architectural end-run. Although Savannah was not as drawn to the Greek Revival as many other important Southern cities, the style was perfect for the city's 1833 courthouse. With a Greek Temple of Justice the city could celebrate her American democratic spirit, her English mercantile ties, and her Southern attachments to cotton and to slavery.

The original Chatham County Courthouse, which this building replaced, was built before the Revolution. In fact an early guidebook to Savannah relates that the brick building was damaged during the Revolutionary War both by bombardment and later by British troops quartered in the building.[10] We know that it was quite small, having "no halls and no corridors,"[11] but we can only guess as to its appear-

ance. The building was repaired after that war and served the county for another fifty years.

The simple courthouse that served Savannah until 1833 speaks to the humble roots of Savannah herself. She began as "only the rude and crude military outpost of England's last and poorest colony in America." By 1760, the town had about 400 buildings, only three of which were brick.[12] In 1794, Savannah had a population of about 2500. By 1830, her population had grown to over 7000, but even years later the only "paved" street would be a plank road from the warehouses of the Central of Georgia Railroad on West Broad Street to the wharves.[13] Growth slowly brought refinement to Savannah. Still, just beyond her charming squares, lay a vast wilderness. In 1833, when this grand Greek courthouse was built the Central Railroad and Canal Company of Georgia was chartered to lay rails from Savannah to Macon and at that time, the country it sought to traverse was very wild indeed.

Plate 2.3: The Central of Georgia Depot at Savannah, designed in 1860, completed in 1876. Augustus Schwab, architect.

This 1860-1876 Central of Georgia depot, now a visitor's center, is one of several railway structures that still stand on West Broad Street. Along with an enormous 1856 freight depot, Alfred Eichberg's 1884 offices and warehouse and the extensive ruins of shops, engine houses and other service buildings in various stages of disrepair, this building supplies insight into the power of the Central of Georgia Railroad, which at its height was the region's dominant railroad.[14] Unlike Augusta, where little

[3] William Robert Mitchell, *Classic Savannah* (Savannah GA: Golden Coast Publishing, 1987) 118.

[4] *Historic Savannah* (Savannah GA: The Savannah Historical Foundation, 1968) 39; Talbot Hamlin, *Greek Revival Architecture in America* (1944; reprint, New York: Dover Publications, 1964) 202.

[5] Hamlin, *Greek Revival Architecture in America*, 202.

[6] Chan Sieg, *The Squares of Savannah* (Norfolk VA: Donning, 1984) 150.

[7] According to Chan Sieg, Henry McAlpin built the first railroad used in America on his plantation at the Hermitage. Chan Sieg, *The Squares of Savannah*, 149.

[8] Lane, *Savannah Revisited, A Pictorial History*, 114.

[9] Hamlin, *Greek Revival Architecture in America*, 180-1.

[10] Adelaide Wilson, *Historic and Picturesque Savannah* (Boston MA: 1899) 15.

[11] Sieg, *The Squares of Savannah*, 232.

[12] Lane, *Savannah Revisited, A Pictorial History*, 21.

[13] Lane, *Savannah Revisited, A Pictorial History*, 101.

[14] Jefferson Max Dixon, "The Central of Georgia 1833-1897, An Abstract" (Atlanta: George Peabody Teacher's College, RW Woodruff Library, Emory University, 1953) 9.

Plate 2.3: Augustus Schwab's 1876 Central of Georgia depot at Savannah represents the height of the Central of Georgia's power. (Photo: Wilber W. Caldwell.)

remains of the great warehouses and depots associated with the early days of the Georgia Railroad, Savannah is filled with the architecture of the railroad. It seems that only architect Frank Milburn's grand 1901 Union Depot, used by the Southern, the Seaboard and the Atlantic Coast Line Railroads after the turn of the century, has gone the way of the wrecker's ball. In fact, so impressive are the remains of the golden age of the Central, which boasted 2500 miles of track in 1882, that it is difficult to imagine Savannah nearly fifty years before when the very first rails were laid.

In 1833, just as Russell Warren's stunning Greek Revival Chatham County Courthouse rose on Wright Square in Savannah, the Central Railroad and Banking Company of Georgia was chartered. In that same year, the Charleston and Hamburg Railroad was completed. Augusta immediately moved to capitalize on her new connection to Charleston by chartering the Georgia Railroad to link Augusta with the then-prominent towns in the cotton-growing region of the Piedmont. Savannah, on the other hand, built directly from the coast, across the desolate expanse of the

Pine Barrens, to the interior cotton-growing regions below the Fall Line at Macon. It was an all-out effort to compete with Charleston for the position of pre-eminent Southern seaport.

Chartered only two days after the Georgia Railroad, The Central Railroad and Canal Company of Georgia, later the Central Railroad and Banking Company of Georgia, and finally just the Central of Georgia Railroad, was a prototype for early Southern railroads. U. B. Phillips describes the pattern of early rails in the South in his insightful *History of Transportation in the Eastern Cotton Belt to 1860*.

> The pine barrens were a stretch of infertile, pine-grown country intervening between the coast and the cotton belt...The population in the barrens was sparse and self-sufficing, producing no stable for export, and making little effective demand for articles for import. The transportation problem was...that of crossing the barrier and connecting the coast with the cotton growing areas. The obvious method in the railway era was to build a single trunk line from each seaport across the barrens, and then lay out a system of radiating lines in the cotton belt which would gather freight and serve as feeders to the main stem.[15]

Unlike the Georgia Railroad, which passed though most of the important towns of the Piedmont, the Central of Georgia would effectively traverse only open country before reaching Macon, her "radiating" hub. The branch system, which Professor Phillips describes, would later connect by-passed county seats along the way. Sylvania, Swainsboro, Statesboro, Waynesboro, Louisville, Sandersville and Milledgeville were all connected in due course along with smaller villages, which built rails to join the main line after 1870. In the process, some of the once obscure junction points for these branches, places like Millen, Midville, Wadley, Tennille, and Gordon, would become important towns in their own right. Sadly most of the junction towns would effectively fade from prominence after 1920.

By the 1830s, Savannah was slipping as Georgia's population center drifted westward. The predicament of Savannah is documented in the 1838 "First Report

[15] U. B. Phillips, *History of Transportation in the Eastern Cotton Belt to 1860* (1908; reprint, New York: McMillan, 1913) 4.

[16] L. O. Reynolds, "The First Chief Engineer's Report to the President of The Central Railroad and Banking Company" in *The Annual Reports of the President of The Central Railroad and Banking Company*, 6 vols. (Savannah GA: The Central Railroad and Banking Company, 1838) 1:13-14.

[17] James Michael Russell, *Atlanta, 1847-1890, City Building in the Old and the New* (Baton Rouge LA: Louisiana State University of Press, 1988) 26.

[18] Jefferson Max Dixon, "The Central of Georgia 1833-1897, An Abstract," 10.

of the Chief Engineer to the President of the Central Railroad and Banking Company of Georgia." The report stresses the advantages of the "Northern Route" surveyed through the powerful cotton-growing areas of Washington, Jefferson and Burke Counties:

> The introduction of Steam Boats on the Savannah River…placed Augusta near or on a level with this City (Savannah) as a mart for the purchase and sale of produce and merchandise. Then, the trade with these counties took that direction, merely on account of the shorter distance. The consequence has been the decline of Savannah and the advancement of Augusta. Can we doubt that the establishment of a permanent, certain, and cheap line of transportation through these counties would reclaim to our City her lost trade? The advantages of such a result would be not merely the transportation of the Cotton crop. The intercourse of the inhabitants would be with this City instead of Augusta and Charleston.[16]

From this it is clear that Savannah had slipped, and that the Central Railroad was chasing cotton in 1838, with her paramount economic goal the advancement of the city of Savannah. This kind of single-city myopia was common with Southern antebellum railroads, which were generally built with the investments of individual cities. Savannah was a prime example of what James Russell calls "urban imperialism," investing "$500,000 in city bonds in the Central of Georgia project even though the city's taxable wealth was only $2,357,250."[17]

As with the Georgia Railroad, plans for rails linking Georgia to the American West would soon complicate the picture. Despite opportunities to view a Western rail link as a path toward statewide progress, the Central of Georgia's aim remained the advancement of Savannah. Dreams of connections to the Mississippi Valley filled the heads of that city's merchants and traders with selfish fantasies of commerce to come.

Augustus Schwab's 1876 Central of Georgia depot at Savannah represents the height of the Central of Georgia's power. Just six years after the building was completed, the golden years of the Central came to an end with the death of her stalwart president William Wadley. For sixteen years Wadley had expanded the road while remaining true to Savannah's interests. Despite the grand alliance with the Louisville and Nashville, and the lease of the Georgia Railroad in 1881, the Central was brought to her knees in 1888 when the road came under the control of the giant railroad holding company, the Richmond and West Point Terminal and Warehouse Company. It is ironic that Wadley's loyalty to Savannah rendered part of the Central an anachronism. Savannah's interests had always been served by lines from the interior to the coast. After 1865, the trend was toward inland rails, parallel to the coast, a transportation trend that eventually forsook rail-sea routes to the Northeast in favor of all-rail alternatives. This, along with government regulation of railroads and the maturing of large railroad syndicates, marked the beginning of the end for the golden age of the Central of Georgia Railroad.[18] Along with the sinking fortunes of cotton, the Central of Georgia Railroad's decline foreshadowed the ebb of Savannah's prominence as a seaport.

JENKINS COUNTY: MILLEN

Plate 2.4: The depot at Millen, built in 1868.

Not only did the rails of the Central Railroad and Banking Company of Georgia by-pass the county seats of all seven counties they traversed on their northern loop from Savannah to Macon, but for all practical purposes they by-passed towns altogether. But even in the wildest country, where the trains

Plate 2.4: For the Central of Georgia, Millen was an important stop, and this was one of the first depots to be rebuilt after the war. (Photo: Wilber W. Caldwell.)

stopped there would be trade, and to prove this axiom, the first section of the Central, built in the late 1830s, would begin to concentrate pockets of population in some of the most malarial swamps in Georgia. The first half of this route, from Savannah to around Millen, traversed Pine Barrens. This was a very lonely place in the early nineteenth century.

The early locomotives needed a constant supply of wood and water so stations were established every ten miles. At first these were not towns but merely arbitrary spots in the wilderness chosen to fuel the ever-hungry steam engines. But when railroad buildings were built and people employed to feed the puffing iron beasts, towns naturally sprouted around these stations. Depots were established at Pooler, Bloomingdale, Eden, Brewer, Guyton, Egypt, Oliver, Dover, Halcyondale, Cameron, Outland, Ogeechee, Rocky Ford, and Scarboro. All of these places were born of the railroad, and many grew to become important local trading centers around the turn of the century. All are down on their luck today, and a few like Halcyondale and Cameron are hard to find. The only two depots still standing today between Savannah and Millen have been converted into private homes at Marlow and at Egypt.

An interesting note regarding the railroad's ability to create communities lies in the naming of these places. As a general rule the early railroads did not trouble to name these wood-and-water stops, and in the beginning they were referred to in two ways. The very early official documents of the Central refer to these depots by mileage, for example Guyton was called the "30 mile depot," Egypt the "40 mile depot," and so on. After a short time, a second tradition developed referring to these places not by miles but by numbering the depots starting with number one at Savannah. This system of numbering continued in popular reference long after proper names were applied to these towns, for example Halcyondale was #5, Dover-#6, Rocky Ford-#7, and so on. The Central's official reports were still using depot numbers to refer to these places well into the twentieth century. As new towns sprang up between the already numbered stations, the system accommodated them. Oliver became #4 1/2, Cameron-#6 1/2. Ogeechee-#7 1/2, etc.[19] I know of no subdivision on any railroad using fractions less than one half, but the depot numbering system was pervasive in Georgia on many of the early lines. Many people today can still remember their grandparents referring to a town by number.

Long before there was a Jenkins County, Millen, which straddled the line between old Screven and old Burke Counties, was born as the "The 80 Mile Depot" or "Old 9." The first proper name for the town was Brisonville, but in 1851 was changed to Millen Junction, probably for McPherson B. Millen, who became superintendent of the Central of Georgia in 1848.[20] This was shortened to Millen when the town was incorporated in 1881.[21] The first historical mention of this place came in the Third Report of the Chief Engineer, dated May of 1839, and it is clear that the Central Railroad had finally reached the edge of the Cotton Belt, for the buildings of commerce were to be constructed at the place which would later become Millen. "The site of the 80 mile depot has been designated, and preparations are now making to erect a large store-house for the receipt and forwarding of produce and merchandise. This will be completed in June."[22]

General Sherman's armies destroyed the depot and other railroad buildings along with a good portion of the town of Millen in 1864. The Union Army's

[19] Dixon Hollingsworth ed., *The History of Screven County, Georgia* (Dallas TX: Curtis Media, 1989) 29.

[20] Hollingsworth ed., *The History of Screven County, Georgia* , 68.

[21] Albert M. Hillhouse, *The History of Burke County, Georgia, 1777-1950* (Swainsboro GA: Magnolia Press 1985), 102.

[22] L. O. Reynolds in "The Third Chief Engineer's Report to the President of The Central Railroad and Banking Company" in *The Annual Reports of the President of The Central Railroad and Banking Company*, 1:32.

[23] G. W. Scatterwood in "The Thirty Second Roadmaster's Report to the President of The Central Railroad and Banking Company" in *The Annual Reports of the President of The Central Railroad and Banking Company*, 3: 26.

[24] G. W. Scatterwood in "The Thirty Third Roadmaster's Report to the President of The Central Railroad and Banking Company" in *The Annual Reports of the President of The Central Railroad and Banking Company*, 3: 23.

[25] Carroll L. V. Meeks, *The Railroad Station, An Architectural History* (New Haven: Yale University Press, 1956) 21, 43.

[26] The other seven counties created in 1905 were Crisp, Grady, Tift, Jeff Davis, Stephens, Toombs and Turner.

burning of Millen was one of the single most destructive acts on Sherman's march to the sea. Millen was an important stop on the road, and this was one of the first depots to be rebuilt after the war. The report of the Roadmaster of the Central of Georgia Railroad dated December, 1867, references the construction of a new depot at Millen with "four rooms for the accommodation of passengers and a Ticket Office." The Roadmaster further asserts that he thought it "best to defer…(a freight depot)…at Millen until one could be built of brick…"[23] In December of the next year, the Roadmaster reports that the new brick building was complete.[24] Although no longer used by the railroad, this building still stands in testimony to Millen's former prominence as a place of commerce.

This building, like most quality depots built before 1880, features decorative arched brackets supporting the deep overhang of the eaves. Often considered reflections of the Italian Villa Style, brackets decorated a diverse array of American buildings in the 1840s, 50s and 60s. Inspired by models published in pattern books like A. J. Downing's *Cottage Residences* (1842) and the *Architecture of Country Houses* (1850) and Samuel Sloan's *The Model Architect* (1852), brackets became so popular that they evolved as an independent force in American vernacular building. Thus a pronounced "bracketed" style emerged alongside Italianate modes and has been responsible for a great deal of confusion concerning mid-century stylistic development. The popularity of bracketed designs lingered in the South after the war. Elsewhere, so many depots of the very early railroad era, both in America and in Europe, had incorporated elements of the Italian Villa Style that stations of this type are often labeled "Railroad Style."[25] But depots in Georgia generally derive inclusion in this category solely by their bracketed eaves.

Millen was the first junction point on the Central of Georgia Railroad. A 51 mile branch line was first chartered in 1838 as the Augusta and Waynesboro Railroad and later as the Augusta and Savannah Railroad. It was completed from Millen to Waynesboro in 1851 and to Augusta in 1854. This branch road was leased to the Central of Georgia in 1862.

Plate 2.5: On January 10, 1910, Lewis Goodrich's brand new Jenkins County Courthouse at Millen burned to the ground. It was replaced in that same year by this structure built from nearly identical plans. (Photo: Wilber W. Caldwell.)

Plate 2.5: The Jenkins County Courthouse, built in 1910. Lewis F. Goodrich, architect.

Sholes's 1886 *Gazetteer of Georgia* places Millen's population at 350. Just ten years later this same publication declared Millen a "banking town" and listed the population as 900.

In the first decade of this century, controversy raged all across the state regarding the partition of older, established counties into smaller political units. To be sure, much of this was a result of pressure brought to bear by newer towns, born of the railroad. Many of these self-proclaimed "cities" of that time were drunk with the myth of impending prosperity imported by the railroads and by railroad promoters of the day, and some were just beginning to flex their newly-created muscles. Just after the turn of the century, many of these towns appeared to be running economic rings around older county seats that had been bypassed by the railroads. Things finally came to a head in 1904 when the legislature amended the state constitution lifting the limit on the number of counties in Georgia, which had stood at 137 since 1877. The next year, twenty-one perspective new counties applied to the state legislature for charters. Jenkins County was one of eight new counties created in 1905.[26]

Plate 2.6: The Central of Georgia's 1869 depot at Toomsboro. (Photo: Wilber W. Caldwell.)

Jenkins County's first courthouse, designed by Lewis Goodrich of Augusta, was completed shortly after the county's creation. It was Goodrich's fifth courthouse in Georgia (see Appendix C), and unlike his Romanesque offerings at Crawfordville, Sylvania and his extensive remodeling at Sandersville, this building wears the neoclassical clothes of the new era. On January 10, 1910, Goodrich's new creation at Millen burned to the ground. It was replaced in that same year by this structure, built from nearly identical plans.

Unlike the many flamboyant monuments to New South aspirations built in the first decade of the new century, Goodrich's Jenkins County Courthouse at Millen voices Georgian restraint. There is even a kind of simplicity in the flat, brick expanses of this building that sets it apart from many of the more baroque, neoclassical creations of J. W. Golucke, Frank Milburn and others in the same period. Take away the classical portico and the bell tower with its classical lantern and crowning statue of justice, and we find the unmistakable image of the simple, brick, Federal Style facade of the 1821 Richmond County Courthouse in

Goodrich's native Augusta. Perhaps Goodrich was just a simple kind of fellow, but most likely Millen in 1905, despite its success, was a simple kind of place with at least one foot planted firmly in the past.

WILKINSON COUNTY: IRWINTON

Plate 2.6: The depot at Toomsboro, built in 1869.

Despite engineering reports filled with technical verbiage concerning bridging the Ogeechee and swampy grounds to the south, it does not take any great insight to see through to the real reason for the selection of the long, looping northern route chosen by the Central Railroad and Banking Company of Georgia for the line from Savannah to Macon. The driving force behind this decision, like nearly all others in the antebellum South, was cotton. The southern route would have by-passed Burke and Jefferson Counties. With a cotton harvest of over 6 million pounds each in 1840, they stood fifth and sixth respectively in production of the intoxicating staple, and their close neighbor, Hancock County, was number one among the state's 93 counties. Together the three counties were responsible for nearly one-sixth of Georgia's total cotton crop in 1840. Hence, the northern route was the cotton route. Not coincidentally, this was the railroad that General William Tecumseh Sherman almost totally destroyed on his historic march to the sea.

The postwar rebuilding of the depots along the Central of Georgia gives insight into the relative importance of the region. The brick depot at Millen, built in 1868, announced the Central's entrance into the Cotton Belt, and a smaller clone built the next year at Bartow, announced the road's arrival at the heart of that region. In fact, the Roadmaster's Report to the President dated December, 1869, confirms the completion of four brick depots: Tennille,

[27]   Station #15 was originally at Emmit, about 1.5 miles from Toomsboro, but owning to friction with landowners the depot was moved to Toomsboro in 1856. Victor Davidson, *History of Wilkinson County* (Macon GA: J. W. Burke, 1930) 221-2.

[28]   G. W. Scatterwood in "The Thirty Fourth Roadmaster's Report to the President of The Central Railroad and Banking Company" in *The Annual Reports of the President of The Central Railroad and Banking Company*, 3:27.

[29]   Davidson, *History of Wilkinson County*, 221.

[30]   Edward L. Ayers, *Southern Crossing* (New York: Oxford University Press, 1995) 10.

[31]   J. Lanette O'Neal Faulk and Betty Walker Jones, eds., *History of Twiggs County, Georgia* (Jeffersonville GA: Major General John Twiggs Chapter, American Daughters of the American Revolution, 1960) 15.

Toomsboro,[27] Bartow and Davisboro (no longer standing)."[28] The speedy, postwar completion of these five, nearly identical, high quality, brick buildings, four of which are still standing, marked the railroad's commitment to these towns and the farmlands they supported even in the economic nightmare that was Reconstruction.

Like most of these towns, Toomsboro in Wilkinson County sprang up beside the railroad and served at cotton's bedside. The town seemed for a moment to soar, but achieved no real foundation for the accumulation of wealth or population. It aspired to the riches of the New South myth, shone briefly and then died. This depot, like its quintuplet sisters, was built with the brackets of the American "Railroad Style" in 1869 by the Central Railroad and Banking Company of Georgia. Its purpose was to serve Savannah. It served Wilkinson County as well. In 1890, the county had a population of almost 11,000, but this was considered a very rural place. According to Sholes's 1896 *Gazetteer of Georgia,* the largest towns were Gordon (400), Irwinton, the county seat, (300) and Toomsboro (200). Nearly one hundred years later, in 1990, the population of Wilkinson County remained at about 11,000, and the population of Irwinton was still only 641.

The Central of Georgia never came to Irwinton. It passed a few miles to the north creating Toomsboro, McIntyre and Gordon. Like most places bypassed by the early rails, Irwinton's history is filled with accounts of local opposition to the railroads. We are told that the citizens of the town were sure that "the train would run over all of the chickens and children."[29] Charming, self-effacing stories like this are very Southern and make entertaining reading. There is perhaps some truth to them, but it is doubtful that irrational, local fears of frightened chickens or even of dismembered children seriously stood in the way of the Central or any antebellum railroad in Georgia. The early railway companies were powerful institutions with the force of the law, and the weight of money and public opinion behind them. There is almost no mention of local opposition in any official railroad records, only notations of rising land prices. What local ire we do find recorded came from

bypassed towns and counties rather than those wanting to keep the railroads out. In short, public support of the railroads far outweighed any maverick opposition, no matter how colorful.

The fact is that the plantation economy had little need of towns. The large plantations tended to operate as independent economic entities. Successful planters often traded abroad through factors, and the small farmers had little cash to buy what they could not make for themselves.[30] This being the case, the early railroads too had little need of towns beyond fuel and water, depots and warehouses. Nonetheless, the railroad begot towns in profusion, and bypassed towns were quick to build connecting spurs to the main line after the war. Of the counties traversed by the Central of Georgia between Savannah and Macon, Irwinton was the only county seat that failed to make the connection. There would be no railroad at Irwinton, no myth, and no exuberant courthouse.

Plate 2.7: The Wilkinson County Courthouse, built in 1870, burned in 1924.

Although Wilkinson became a county in 1803, the county seat of Irwinton was not laid out until 1811. Twiggs County history tells us that when Twiggs was created from Wilkinson in 1809, a courthouse was under construction but had to be abandoned since its location was no longer in Wilkinson County.[31] There are conflicting accounts regarding the first courthouse. Victor Davidson's 1930 History of Wilkinson County relates that the county's first

Plate 2.7: The myth of the New South never arrived at Irwinton to inspire a grand courthouse to replace this simple court building which served until 1924.

Plate 2.8: The depot at Gordon, built in 1885. Tracks were never built to connect the county seat at Irwinton with the main line, and predictably Gordon became the economically prominent town of Wilkinson County. (Photo: Wilber W. Caldwell.)

courthouse was not completed until after 1818[32] and that it burned in 1828.[33] The Milledgeville *Southern Recorder* of March 17, 1828, reports that it was the home of the Wilkinson County Clerk which burned and that "despite great exertions, nearly all records in the Clerk's office (at Irwinton) were destroyed."[34] A 1973 county history cites this Milledgeville source and further suggests that the

[32] Davidson, *History of Wilkinson County*, 198.

[33] Davidson, *History of Wilkinson County*, 211.

[34] *Southern Recorder* (Milledgeville GA) March 17, 1828, quoted in Joseph T. Maddox, *Wilkinson County Historical Collections* (Irwinton GA: n.p., 1973) 14-15.

[35] Maddox, *Wilkinson County Historical Collections*, 15.

[36] Davidson, *History of Wilkinson County*, 212.

[37] Walter Hines Page, *The Rebuilding of the Old Commonwealth* (New York: Doubleday, Page, and Company, 1905) 26. Quoted in C.Vann Woodward, *Origins of the New South, 1877–1910* (Baton Rouge LA: Louisiana State University Press, 1951) 397.

[38] C. Vann Woodward, *Origins of the New South, 1877-1910* (1951; reprint, Baton Rouge: Louisiana State University, 1993), 397.

[39] Authority for this date comes from the Fiftieth Report of the Roadmaster, which states the completion of a structure 30 feet by 70 feet "at Gordon, a brick warehouse." William M. Stevens, "The Fiftieth Roadmaster's Report to the President of The Central Railroad and Banking Company" in *The Annual Reports of the of the President of The Central Railroad and Banking Company* 5/50 (Savannah GA: *The Annual Reports of the of the President of the Central Railroad and Banking Company*, 1885) 51.

[40] Victor Davidson, *History of Wilkinson County*, 218-19.

[41] Hillhouse, *History of Burke County, 1777 -1950*, 31.

[42] Hillhouse, *History of Burke County, 1777 -1950*, 102.

frame courthouse built sometime after 1828 was the county's first. Whether first or second, the c.1828 frame courthouse was destroyed by fire in 1854 and replaced with another two-story frame structure "built in Irwinton in the same place as the old and extended 50 feet long and 40 feet wide, with good materials and a nice workman-like manner."[35] General Sherman's forces burned the 1854 Wilkinson County Courthouse in 1864, and in 1870 Pat Ward, "...the Irishman erected this simple brick building in Irwinton."[36] It would serve well into the next century.

Wilkinson County's rather stagnant history illustrates the plight of what Walter Hines Page referred to as "The Forgotten Man." For Page his native South had failed to rise "after a century of unobstructed opportunity."[37] The problem as Page accurately saw it was one of stubborn, backward-looking, small-minded Southerners who were at once angry, nostalgic and sedentary. Page called them "mummies" in his sarcastic "Mummy Letters," and contended that Southern communities at the turn of the century were populated with "contemporary ancestors" who remained firmly set against anything that even hinted of progress. Indeed, "change" was likely an ugly word in places like Irwinton, and if the truth could be told, the atmosphere was not only immobile, it was reactionary. If they could have turned the hands of the clock back to 1840, they surely would have.

None of this was unique to Wilkinson County. Outside of Atlanta and a few other cities, this attitude existed, even prevailed, in most Georgia communities well into the twentieth century. If the railroads created the myth of the New South, the "mummies" fought it at every turn, and in places like Irwinton, where no rails ran, things stayed pretty much the same. As C. Vann Woodward so beautifully puts it, "Antiquated social institutions protruded like primeval rock from the smooth pavement to obstruct the traffic of progress."[38]

Plate 2.8: The depot at Gordon, built 1885.

This depot built in 1885[39] is similar to the five brick depots of the late 1860s built between Millen and Toomsboro, but here we see a fundamental change in detail that was to characterize depots of the next fifty years. The graceful, scrolling brackets of "The Railroad Style" have been replaced with the masculine, utilitarian, angular bracing of heavy beamed supports that are as straight as they are massive. Important depots would continue to be built, modifying and adapting the picturesque and eclectic styles of the day, but, from the 1880s until after the Second World War, work-horse, country depots like this one at Gordon would, more often than not, be recognized by these rudimentary angular wooden braces.

After the war the New South myth flourished in Gordon as the town's population grew to over 700 in 1910. In fact, there is evidence that the full myth was still abroad in Wilkinson County as late as 1930 when Victor Davidson, the county historian, wrote:

> The building of the Georgia White Brick Company at Gordon as a result of the railroad's extensive advertising, was followed by a visit here of the American Ceramic Society, and now the Harbison-Walker Refractories Company's development of deposits at Gordon is due to the railroad's activities… (developing) the promising growth of manufacturing establishments among the vast clay fields of this county…Therefore if the rapid growth of industries in this county seems imminent, it will be due to the policy of this road.[40]

Of course the "rapid growth of industries" in the county was not imminent. What was imminent was a vulgar and boldface exploitation of mineral resources by outside interests. Kaolin is mined on the surface from gaping pits here, as it is across a wide swath of Georgia along the Fall Line. This is exactly the kind of thing the "mummies" had feared. It is in part why they had rejected the myth of northern capital fifty years before. Indeed, what the railroads and the purveyors of the myth of the New South did not realize, or at least did not reveal, in the 1880s was the fact that when Northern capital came to Georgia, it seldom came to contribute; it came to exploit.

After 1880, Georgia could only watch as not only her cotton, but her forests, her clay, her stone, her turpentine and her coal were hauled away by the powerful young railroads which promised so much on one hand and took so much on the other.

THE AUGUSTA BRANCH: MILLEN TO AUGUSTA

BURKE COUNTY: WAYNESBORO

Plate 2.9: The Burke County Courthouse, built in 1857, remodeled in 1898. Lewis Goodrich, remodeling architect.

When it came to towns, Burke County was never really much of a place. But when it came to cotton, Burke was a giant, and she had little need for towns. With the exception of Waynesboro, and much later Midville, the history of towns in Burke County is a history of failure. 1836 records show five landings on the Savannah River in Burke County,[41] but like other small villages in the county, these would fade away. Waynesboro, the county seat, was the only incorporated town in Burke County during antebellum times.[42] The towns of Midville and Millen were placed on the map by the Central of Georgia in the 1840s. But Jenkins County took Millen in 1905,

Plate 2.9: The old 1857 Burke County Courthouse is encased inside 1898 and 1983 remodelings. (Photo: Wilber W. Caldwell.)

and with the coming of the Augusta and Florida Railroad in that same year, Midville soared only briefly, and then slowly slid back into oblivion like so many railroad towns in Georgia. A few tiny lumber settlements like Perkins were spawned by the Millen to Augusta line in the 1850s; still the 1860 manufacturing roster of the entire county was all but non-existent, listing only eleven grist mills, seven lumber companies, a boot factory, and a brick yard.[43] After the turn of the century the Augusta and Florida Railroad (later the Georgia and Florida Railroad) would spark hamlets and land speculation at places like Gough, Vidette, and Rosier, while the Brinson Railroad (later the Atlanta and Savannah), created Sardis. Predictably none of these places thrived. These frail, autumn blossoms of the railroad era were the last in a long line of heirs to the myth of the New South. But by 1905, theirs would be an impotent inheritance, stripped of its fervor by decades of disappointment, a tarnished legacy of dust and broken dreams. Waynesboro was, and is still, the only town in Burke County of any size at all.

The Augusta and Waynesboro Railroad was chartered in 1838 just as the first rails were beginning to penetrate the Georgia woodlands beyond Savannah and Augusta. Built from the Central of Georgia's main line at Millen to Augusta via Waynesboro, the road was finally completed in 1854 as the Augusta and Savannah Railroad. It was leased by the Central in 1862. Construction had been delayed for fifteen years by opposition from the businessmen of Augusta and by the Georgia Railroad who feared that the connection to Savannah would siphon Augusta's cotton trade from the counties southwest of their city.[44] Paramount among these counties was Burke, the largest cotton-producing county in the eastern part of the state, boasting over 19,000 bales in 1850.

Burke County was then, and is today, a very rural place. In 1860, the county had a population of over 17,000, while Waynesboro, the county seat and its only real town, had a population of only 307. Typical of towns that were to know antebellum rails, Waynesboro was never seduced by the New South myth. To be sure, the coming of the Augusta and Savannah Railroad brought a degree of urbanity to this rural place. The town's population increased to just over 1000 by 1880, but the last decades of the century proved difficult for Burke County. As the price of cotton fell, tenancy wrought its ruin on the already ruined land, and the exodus from the old Cotton Belt continued. Waynesboro was down to around 800 inhabitants in 1890, and was back to only 1200 in better times just after 1900.

The state of affairs in Waynesboro around the turn of the century bore little resemblance to the promises of the myth of industrial prosperity that postbellum rails had delivered to so many towns in the 1880s and 1890s. When new rails finally came to Burke County after 1905, it was too late to sell the shining wares of the New South to the farmers in these dried up fields. The people of Burke County were not buying. Waynesboro sang the rather sad song of the Eastern Cotton Belt. It was a song whose verses tolled the dirges of hard times, and whose choruses echoed the sweet music of better days gone by.

Along antebellum rails, the myth was hard pressed to take hold; still the 1898 remodeling of the Burke County Courthouse testifies to at least a hint of turn-of-the-century hope. Spirits were not high enough to set aside the old altogether, but the remodeling featured a monumental Romanesque facade and clock tower. This is recognizably the work of Lewis F. Goodrich of Augusta. Goodrich's remodeling and enlargement of the nearby Washington County Courthouse at Sandersville, 1899, and his twin courthouses at Crawfordville, 1902, and neighboring Sylvania, 1897, exhibit similar fenestration, and corbeling. All feature the architect's distinctive louvered openings in their towers. Like Goodrich's other courthouses, the Burke County addition plays architectural "lip service" to the styles of the day without the usual elaborate ornamentation. Just beneath the surface lies

[43] Hillhouse, *History of Burke County, 1777-1950*, 111.

[44] Phillips, *History of Transportation in the Eastern Cotton Belt to 1860*, 265.

[45] Hillhouse, *History of Burke County, 1777-1950*, 53.

[46] Joan Niles Sears, *The First Hundred Years of Town Planning in Georgia* (Atlanta: Cherokee Press, 1979) 157-81.

a simple, vernacular spirit that must have had great appeal in places like Waynesboro where the power of the myth was weak and the power of the past was compelling. The 1939 addition of a large annex to the rear of the old building completed the disguise, and the old 1857 courthouse was effectively hidden by successive efforts to enlarge, remodel and renovate its simple lines.

The original 1857 building was another of those simple vernacular brick buildings. But the power of cotton and of Burke County's prominence in antebellum cotton production was voiced by great double circular stairways which flanked an arched ground floor entrance and led to a second floor landing and the court room entrance above. Although not in the Greek mode, the forceful grace of this stairway flanking the deep arched portals recalled Robert Mills's early work in South Carolina, notably his courthouses in Union, Greenville, and Orangeburg Counties. These stairs were removed in the 1898 remodeling, but in 1983, an effort was made to recall the former elegance of the original building by recreating the exterior stairs. The result is unfortunate. The graceful curve of the stairs and their wrought iron rail are totally out of place against the backdrop of the massive, angular, Romanesque Revival, eastern elevation. The transformation of the typically Romanesque triple arched window grouping, into a second-story, triple entrance fails miserably, and the elongation of these three brick arches gives a surprisingly contemporary impression. The result is neither modern, Romanesque nor Federal, but an unhappy marriage of unlike elements and conflicting symbols.

The exact dates and locations of the early Burke County Courthouses are not known with any degree of certainty. In his *History of Burke County*, Albert Hillhouse hazards a "guess" that the first courthouse was built just outside of what is now Waynesboro sometime before 1783 when the town was laid out. He further speculates that the second Burke County Courthouse was built sometime between 1786 and 1791 on the present courthouse square.[45] This building burned in 1825 and was replaced by a third courthouse, probably a frame structure, which burned

in 1856 and was replaced by the brick building that lies at the heart of the present structure.

All across Georgia, the destruction wrought by courthouse fires has been fearful, but sadder still is the destruction wrought by the wrecker's ball during the 1960s and 70s (see Appendix D). It is not so much that architectural treasures were destroyed—few of these buildings were really that. It is that a piece of the soul of these counties was destroyed, a piece of history, and every Georgian is poorer for that. Slated for demolition in 1971, the Burke County Courthouse stands triumphant against a thoughtless and an all-too-common kind of "progress" that turns a deaf ear to the past. The successful effort by the people of Burke to save this building shines brightly in the otherwise dark story of late twentieth century courthouse demolition Georgia.

THE MILLEDGEVILLE / EATONTON BRANCH: GORDON TO EATONTON

BALDWIN COUNTY: MILLEDGEVILLE

Plate 2.10: The Old Georgia State House, built between 1807-37. 1807 architects, Smart and Lane. 1827 architect, Hamilton Fulton (attributed).

Laid out in 1803 to replace Louisville as the seat of government, Milledgeville is one of five Georgia towns created according to plans commissioned by the state. The others are Augusta, whose old colonial town plan was modified and expanded in 1783 on 1000 acres "confiscated from the royalists;" Louisville, laid out in 1796 as the new capital; Macon, surveyed in 1823, and Columbus, founded in 1828.[46] Not coincidentally each of these towns were located at the head of navigation on on one of Georgia's five main rivers, and not surprisingly the early relative success of each town was directly related to the navigability of the stream upon which it was built. Augusta and Columbus flourished by the robust waters of the Savannah and the Chattahoochee. Macon held her own on the less reliable Ocmulgee while Milledgeville's fortunes remained tenuous beside the

Plate 2.10: The old Georgia State House. For all the lure of its romantic symbolism and nostalgic embroidery, the Gothic Style seldom penetrated the American South beyond the architecture of the church. (Photo: Wilber W. Caldwell.)

shallow and capricious Oconee. Louisville stagnated in the swamps along the Ogeechee.

The choice of Louisville as the state capital was a mistake on almost every level. The river was impossible for navigation, the town site was a malarial swamp, and by 1800, it was clear that the population center of the state had shifted far to the west of Jefferson County and was moving farther westward at a healthy clip. The Creek Indian Cession of 1802-1805 provided the state with virtually all of the land between the Oconee and the Ocmulgee Rivers. Baldwin County and Milledgeville were born of this acquisition and the resulting land lottery, and in 1804 Milledgeville was declared the permanent capital of the state of Georgia. The English influence is undeniable here. Savannah was the cultural and economic capital of Georgia in 1800, and despite the anti-English sentiment of the period, Savannah's ties to England via the cotton trade were strong. The new town plan for Milledgeville mirrored Savannah, featuring four enormous squares.

In 1805, the state legislature passed the act authorizing the construction of a new capitol building in Milledgeville. James Bonner, Milledgeville historian, describes the structure, completed in 1811: "The state house was…in the form of a rectangle with neither porticos nor wings; yet its pointed arched windows and its battlements proclaimed the Gothic style. It is said by some to be the first use of this style in a public building in America."[47]

Bonner goes on to acknowledge subsequent remodeling and expansion, including the addition of the wings, begun in the 1820s and not completed until 1837. Mills Lane, in his "Georgia" volume of *The Architecture of the South,* tells a fundamentally different tale when he describes the original 1811 building as a "typical building of the Federal era…with plain brick walls, a hipped roof, and pedimented entrances."[48] According to Mr. Lane the Gothic elements, including the crenellation, the pointed arches, the re-designed roof, and the stucco exterior finish, were all part of the remodeling and expansion of the building which began in 1827. Some sources suggest that the design for the expanded building was the work of Hamilton Fulton, an English engineer who had been hired by the state to assess local waterways and to make recommendations regarding the construction of future canals and railroads in Georgia.[49]

If one examines the Gothic Revival in England, Mr. Lane's "later Gothic remodeling" scenario becomes all the more compelling, for although Gothic castles in a so-called "Castellated" mode were popular in England in the eighteenth century, in 1807 the historical Gothic Revival was still decades away. The full flower of the Gothic Revival appeared in English churches in the 1820s, and a broad awareness of the style became manifest after fire destroyed the Houses of Parliament in 1834, and Sir Charles Berry's New Palace of Westminster rose from these ashes to house parliament in Gothic array. The movement realized its fullness in the middle part of the century with the writings of John Ruskin and A. W. N. Pugin and the High Victorian Gothic designs of Alfred Waterhouse, George Gilbert Scott and others. But in 1807, when this capital building was begun and Milledgeville was being carved out of a remote wilderness, Ruskin, Pugin, Waterhouse and Scott were all yet to be born.

For all the lure of its romantic symbolism and nostalgic embroidery, the Gothic Style seldom penetrated the American South beyond the architecture of the church. As with the Greek, the South would attach its own symbols to the Gothic, and its message would remain primarily religious. Southerners, like the frontier people they were, preferred a simple, emotional religion devoid of ambiguities. One did not mistake a courthouse for a church any more than one mixed politics and religion.

The most influential proponents of the Gothic Style in England were Pugin and Ruskin. Both men sought to reach beyond the usual bounds of architectural symbolism and attach a moral character. For Pugin the only proper architecture of Christianity was the Sublime and glorious Gothic. Surely Southerners at least partially understood this line of thought, but Ruskin was to carry things farther, attaching a moral content to architecture itself. He was both a moral censor and an aesthete. According to Ruskin, "good architecture was the product of a state of Grace, and bad architecture betokened original sin."[50] To quote James Fitch, Ruskin saw the architecture around him as "a living falsehood, guilty of both structural and moral perversion."[51] This may have mixed well with the romanticism growing from Puritanical and Transcendental roots in the American North where the Gothic Style was the rage by the 1840s[52] and where Ruskin's works received both earlier and greater recognition than in England,[53] but the brand of romanticism that nourished Southern aesthetics included no such dogma.

Accordingly, the Old State House at Milledgeville is part of a very short list of antebellum, secular Gothic public architecture in Georgia. There were a few notable residences like the Albert Redd House in Columbus (1850-1860), the Charles Green House (1853) in Savannah and the James A. Sledge House (1860) in Athens. The Old Jail (1845) in Savannah is Gothic as is Richmond Academy (1856-1857) in Augusta and Brownward Female Institute (1830-1840) in LaGrange. After the war, as eclecticism flourished, Gothic elements begin to appear in combination with the elements of other styles and in "carpenter style homes," but there were few secular examples of anything approaching the pure Gothic Revival in Georgia. The exception in postbellum times appeared on campuses, for in most cases Georgia's small colleges had close religious ties, and the choice of the Gothic in this regard was merely an extension of ecclesiastical imagery that had already covered the state with Gothic churches. Perhaps the finest stand-

ing High Gothic Revival structure in Georgia is Mercer University's Administration Building designed by Chicago architect Gourdon P. Randall in 1872. Atlanta architects, Parkins and Bruce, designed the extraordinary, High Victorian Gothic Seney Hall (1881) at Emory at Oxford and earlier Bruce had been responsible for the original buildings of Shorter College (1877) in Rome. There is little else save A. C. Bruce's High Gothic gem, the 1877 Masonic Hall in Rome.

Beyond the Potomac the Gothic abounded, one of the fundamental architectural voices of romanticism. The whole county was reading Sir Walter Scott and Lord Byron, Keats and Goethe, but the Southern Faust bargained with Southern devils. From the antebellum era well into the twentieth century, Southerners pictured themselves locked in a struggle with a mechanized Mephistopheles who tempted them to exchange their agrarian Eden for the power of the Industrial Revolution. In this context the Gothic towers and tyrannies of medieval Europe seemed a stern escapism for Southern romantics who preferred the pure Elysian light of the Greek democracy with its enlightened aristocracy and, of course, its slaves. Although a few late century eclectic designs featured Gothic elements, no pure Gothic Revival courthouses were built in the state of Georgia before 1910.

Plate 2.11: The Central of Georgia Depot at Milledgeville, built in 1879-1880.

In contrast to the railroad's promise of progress in the antebellum era, early rails may have served to undermine what little commercial advantage Milledgeville had in the pre-war period. U. B. Phillips

[47] James Bonner, *Milledgeville, Georgia's Antebellum Capital* (Athens GA: University of Georgia Press, 1978) 21.

[48] Lane, *The Architecture of the South, Georgia* (Savannah GA: Beehive Press, 1986) 208.

[49] Lane, *The Architecture of the South, Georgia*.

[50] J. Mordaunt Crook, *The Dilemma of Style, Architectural Ideas from the Picturesque to the Post Modern* (London: Murray, 1987) 74.

[51] James Marston Fitch, *American Building and the Forces that Shaped It* (Boston: Houghton Mifflin Company, 1966) 129.

[52] Fitch, *American Building and the Forces that Shaped It*, 102.

[53] Fitch, *American Building and the Forces that Shaped It*, 127.

Plate 2.11: This 1880 depot gives us clues to the state of affairs in Milledgeville in the years following the war. (Photo: Wilber W. Caldwell.)

explains: "the building of the railroad, which put an end to river traffic,...destroyed the commercial advantage the city's (Milledgeville's) location on the river ...had secured in the early period. The town accordingly stagnated through Reconstruction and the following decades."[54]

Although Milledgeville was the capital of Georgia, its grasp of things commercial seemed lacking, and its grasp of things political was at best tenuous. Phillips describes antebellum Milledgeville as "a fairly typical, unprogressive village in Middle Georgia; a town in the midst of a region where town life was overshadowed by the prominence of the plantation system."[55] In spite of the town's importance as the seat of state government, the Central of Georgia was slow to connect Milledgeville with the main line. All through the 1840s, economic hard times persisted, and Milledgeville's hold on the political reins of Georgia seemed unsure. Phillips cites the reasons for the unenthusiastic attitudes with regard to Milledgeville:

> political importance and the possible advantages to accrue therefrom overshadowed the town's commercial and industrial interests and inclined people in a measure to look for favors instead of for opportunities to labor and invest earnings, and on the whole, stunted the growth and hampered the progress of the community. Then, too, the occurrence of movements for removal of the state capital to another place...added apprehension...and paralyzed the energies of the town.[56]

Not surprisingly, it was not until 1851 that the newly-chartered Milledgeville and Gordon Railroad completed the branch from Gordon to Milledgeville using old rails from the Central's original track, which was then being replaced by the new "T-rail." The Milledgeville and Gordon Railroad was leased to the Central Railroad and Banking Company of Georgia in 1855.

The original depot at Milledgeville was burned by Sherman's forces in 1864, but there was little else destroyed in Milledgeville save the Oconee bridge, a few warehouses and 1700 bales of cotton.[57] Even the Oconee Mill was spared, "probably because the owners were Northerners or men of foreign birth."[58] Sherman's standing orders for the entire campaign allowed the army to "forage liberally on the country," but instructed that "soldiers must not enter dwellings of the inhabitants." The written orders went on:

> To corps commanders alone is entrusted the power to destroy mills, houses, cotton gins, etc.; and for them this general principle is laid down:
>
> In districts...where the army is unmolested no destruction of such property should be permitted; but should guerrillas...molest our march...then army commanders should order and enforce devastation more or less relentless, according to the measure of such hostility.
>
> As to horses, mules, wagons, etc., belonging to the inhabitants the cavalry and artillery may appropriate freely without limit...[59]

With notable exceptions, like the looting and burning at Madison and Millen, these orders were generally followed wherever a main body of Union forces traveled. Unfortunately, incidents of abuse were commonplace, if not methodical, out in the countryside where units became scattered and military discipline was loose.

Milledgeville refutes the myth of Sherman's brutality. Thirty thousand Federal troops passed through the town, but only four private residences were burned, and most because they were being "too vigorously protected" by their owners.[60] This lack of destruction is remarkable in light of the fact that some resistance was offered, mostly by convicts released from the state penitentiary and by young students at the military academy. After what amounted to a non-battle, the town was surrendered with the usual request for the protection of private property. For the most part the taking of Milledgeville was an orderly affair.

We can not know whether Sherman would have burned the Baldwin County Courthouse or not, for the building had burned to the ground three years before the general's arrival, a suspected case of arson. Still, we can complete the record of Sherman's march in the context of courthouses and depots. How many depots did Sherman burn between Atlanta and Savannah on his march to the sea? He destroyed 139 miles of track and destroyed all the depots he could find. Only four survived. The 1865 report of the president of the Central relates that the depots at Stations 2 (Eden), 2 1/2 (Marlow), 10 (Bostick) and 14 (Oconee) survived or at least were not damaged beyond repair.[61] How many courthouses did Sherman burn between Atlanta and Savannah on his march to the sea? Only four, the Butts County Courthouse which was used to store "products for the maintenance of the Confederate States Army;"[62] the Wilkinson County Courthouse at Irwinton; the Washington County Courthouse at Sandersville after encountering local resistance to his advance outside these towns; and the Bulloch County Courthouse in Statesboro, which was at that time, a Pine Barrens settlement consisting of "one log courthouse, one saloon, and three or four dwelling houses."[63] On the other side of the account, after leaving Atlanta, Sherman

passed through and left the courthouses standing in DeKalb, Newton, Morgan, Jasper, Clayton, Henry, Spalding, Jones, Putnam, Jefferson, Burke, Emanuel, Screven, Effingham, Chatham and Liberty Counties. How many other structures were put to the torch between Atlanta and Savannah will never be known, but whatever the number, it is probably a great deal smaller than most Southerners have been led to believe.

This 1880 depot and its history, documented in the official records of the Central of Georgia, give us clues to the state of affairs in Milledgeville in the years following the war. We find that the original depot was only partially rebuilt in a makeshift way after the war. Clearly Milledgeville's importance was still in doubt as Reconstruction began. Although the State Capital at war's end, the city was stripped of this honor in 1868, and the end of Reconstruction found Milledgeville struggling. We can infer a city in decline from the Road Master's Report to the President of the Central of 1873: "The warehouse at Milledgeville, rebuilt since its destruction to less than half its original size, and one end left unfinished and roughly boarded up..."[64] It was not until 1879 that the building was expanded to its original pre-war dimensions.[65]

Despite this depot's neglected appearance today, here at Milledgeville we can get an excellent look at a simple, rural iteration of "The Railroad Style." In most simple county depots of the era, the only architectural details of the Italian Villa Style to be found are the flowing, graceful brackets supporting the eaves. Still this feature so dominates the look of these structures that not much more is needed to call such depots

---

[54] U. B. Phillips, "Historical Notes of Milledgeville, Georgia," in *The Gulf States Historical Magazine* (November 1903): 1.

[55] Phillips, "Historical Notes of Milledgeville, Georgia," in *The Gulf States Historical Magazine* (November 1903): 1.

[56] Phillips, *History of Transportation in the Eastern Cotton Belt to 1860*, 282.

[57] John Gibson, *Those 163 Days, A Southern Account of Sherman's March from Atlanta to Raleigh* (New York: Coward-McCann, 1961) 46.

[58] Bonner, *Milledgeville, Georgia's Antebellum Capital*, 187.

[59] William Sherman's Special Field Order No. 120, November 9, 1864, in *Richard Wheeler, Sherman's March* (New York: Crowell, 1978) 62-3.

[60] Bonner, *Milledgeville, Georgia's Antebellum Capital*, 187.

[61] George W. Adams, "The Thirteenth Superintendent's Report to the President of The Central Railroad and Banking Company" in *The Annual Reports of the President of The Central Railroad and Banking Company* 1/13, 278.

[62] Lois McMichael, *History of Butts County, Georgia, 1825-1976* (Atlanta: Cherokee Publishing Company, 1978) 41.

[63] Dorothy Brannen, *Life in Old Bulloch, The Story of a Wiregrass county in Georgia* (Gainesville GA: Magnolia Press, 1987) 51.

[64] W. G. Raoul, "The Thirty-eighth Road Master's Report to the President of The Central Railroad and Banking Company" in *The Annual Reports of the President of The Central Railroad and Banking Company* 3/38, 64-65.

[65] Raoul, "The Forty-fourth Superintendent's Report to the President of The Central Railroad and Banking Company" in *The Annual Reports of the President of The Central Railroad and Banking Company*, 44.

Plate 2.12: The Baldwin County Courthouse. Only from the sides, where the windows of the original courtroom are left unobstructed to gather the sunlight, can one retrieve a feel for the original 1886 structure. (Photo: Wilber W. Caldwell.)

Italian. Certainly there were many depots built in this period which incorporated more complete Italian Villa Style conventions, but most of these were in the larger cities of the North.

Plate 2.12: The Baldwin County Courthouse, built in 1886. Peter. E. Dennis, architect.

Baldwin County's first courthouse had been completed in 1814. In 1838, a more spacious building was begun, but the simple brick building was not fully completed until around 1847. Apparently the object of arson, it burned in 1861, just ten years after the first train steamed into Milledgeville on the Milledgeville and Gordon Railroad.

At war's end, Baldwin County was without a courthouse. Milledgeville's post-war fortunes would become so dire that it would be thirty years before one was built. In truth, the events immediately following

the war were perhaps more difficult for many Southerners to reckon than the military defeat. This was particularly true in the Cotton Belt owing to the ruin of the plantation economy, the enormous numbers of former slaves in population demographics, and a general, "Un-Reconstructed Rebel" attitude, which permeated almost every area of endeavor, erecting barricades to stand in the way of anything that smacked of progress. Like so many Georgia towns, Milledgeville, although effectively unscathed by Sherman, was laid low by Reconstruction.

After the fighting ended, Milledgeville had sought to pick up the pieces. The Masonic Hall was leased for a courthouse in 1866, the Central through Milledgeville began running again in 1865, and even in the teeth of the economic disaster, a new railroad was under construction. Completed to Milledgeville in 1867 and to Augusta in 1870, the Macon and Augusta Railroad created a direct connection linking Macon with Augusta via Milledgeville, Sparta, and Warrenton, joining the Georgia Railroad at Camak. Thus, Milledgeville became one of the first postbellum junction cities. But in that same year, the bottom dropped out. The end of Andrew Johnson's Presidential Reconstruction and the beginning of Radical Reconstruction, enforced by a Federal military presence, quickly put an end to Milledgeville's already tenuous hold on the state capital.

Any examination of the contrasting post-war economic and social climates in Milledgeville and Atlanta explains the reasons for the 1868 removal of the state capital to Atlanta. Milledgeville, like the rest of the rural South, languished in self-pity, bitterness and economic inertia, while Atlanta was unique among Southern cities. James Russell characterizes Atlanta's policies: "The city…accepted enthusiastically, Yankee capitalism and rejected the plantation system and other fundamentals of Old Southern culture. These policies signaled that the city did not adhere to restrictive Old South social norms and that Northern men and capital would be welcome."[66] Evidence of Atlanta's new "Northern" values is abundant. An elaborate Lincoln memorial was seriously considered by the city in 1867,[67] and by 1879 Sherman himself was cordially received by the Atlanta business community.[68] Atlanta businessmen saw all of this as progressive, forward thinking and modern, a paradigm of the New South itself. A brooding, bitter Milledgeville viewed the upstart capital with open hostility, connecting what the *Southern Recorder* termed the "Atlanta Ring" with the most despicable of tactics.[69] Some sources suggest that Milledgeville innkeepers were threatening to refuse lodging to black delegates. In light of Atlanta's hospitality and Milledgeville's hostility, it is little wonder that General John Pope, the Federal District Military Commander of Georgia, selected Atlanta as the site of the 1867 Constitutional Convention. By convention's end Georgia would, for all practical purposes, have both a new Constitution and a new capital.

In the 1867 election to select delegates to the Constitutional Convention, in all of Baldwin County, only 660 white men were registered and only seven voted.[70] Here were ignited the coals of anger and hatred, which were to power the engines of stagnation and narrow-mindedness for decades to come. To add insult to injury, Milledgeville's Oglethorpe University was moved to Atlanta in 1870, and the next decade saw not only a ruinous economic depression but also a devastating tornado and two fires that destroyed "fully half of the downtown business district including the new Milledgeville hotel..."[71]

All of these setbacks massed together to delay the construction of a new Baldwin County Courthouse. There seemed to be no hurry in 1868, for with the old capitol building now empty, there was plenty of room for courthouse functions. From 1880 to 1887 the county leased the Milledgeville Opera building for use as a temporary courthouse. By 1886 things had turned around enough for Baldwin County to consider a new courthouse, but the building completed in the next year reflected only a glimpse of "New South" exuberance. Like so many courthouses built in the postbellum period in towns beside antebellum rails, at heart, it reflected the earlier style.

Extensive additions to the building in 1937 and 1965 obscure much of the original structure. An imposing neoclassical portico and adjoining wings cover all but the old brick arch of the front entrance and a central Federal Style second-story window.

Large wings were added at each corner with cornices that relate to the portico. Sadly the old building is, in large part, encased in the expansion. Only from the sides, where the windows of the original courtroom are left unobstructed to gather the sunlight, can one retrieve a feel for the original 1886 structure. Apart from the remarkable clock tower, the 1886 Baldwin County Courthouse was a reflection of the old square two-story vernacular style. Suggesting the classical outline of the Federal mode, it echoes the simple design that typified antebellum courthouses built in an era when most of the state could lay claim to fellowship with an unsophisticated American frontier. But here, in 1886, we find richer detail: the regular brick pilasters and the stunningly tall arches of the court room windows beneath the traditional pyramidal roof supported by a studded cornice. With its flamboyant wooden decoration, its unique tower and its graceful arched courtroom windows, the 1886 Baldwin County Courthouse bridges the gap between the simple builder-designed architecture of that early period and the wild fantasies to come.

The tower is a bit of a puzzlement. Although its verticality is more emphatic, its general design is similar to Alexander Bruce's tower design atop the 1885 Hall County Courthouse in Gainesville, especially with regard to the three louvered panels in the center section, the square columns, the layered cornices and the inlaid square panel motif at the base. But unlike Bruce's Hall County tower, here the tower roof is straight-lined and severe. The effect is decidedly more High Gothic than Second Empire, perhaps a reflection of the stunning Gothic tower of G. P. Randall's 1872 Mercer University Administration Building in Macon. It is difficult to call this tower roof "mansard," rather it is a clever and complex eight sided affair, and the lines of the four main sides meet in points.

[66] Russell, *Atlanta, 1847-1890, City Building in the Old South and New*, 147.

[67] Russell, *Atlanta, 1847-1890, City Building in the Old South and New*, 149.

[68] Russell, *Atlanta, 1847-1890, City Building in the Old South and New*, 147.

[69] Bonner, *Milledgeville, Georgia's Antebellum Capital*, 218.

[70] Bonner, *Milledgeville, Georgia's Antebellum Capital*, 216-7.

[71] Bonner, *Milledgeville, Georgia's Antebellum Capital*, 231.

Plate 2.13: The Georgia Railroad Depot at Milledgeville may have been inspired by Frank Milburn's 1901 grand Spanish Renaissance Union Depot in Augusta. (Photo: Wilber W. Caldwell.)

The entire tower is made of wood, and its decoration is so elaborate that one suspects it to be the design of a master carpenter rather than a master architect. Perhaps this is the case. In the last part of the nineteenth Century a "Carpenter Style" was evolving everywhere in America, borrowing both Gothic and Italianate detail for wooden decorations of the most fantastic sort.

Most agree that the architect of the 1886 Baldwin County Courthouse was Peter E. Dennis of Macon, but unclear reference is also made to the McDonald Brothers of Louisville, Kentucky, who were somehow involved in the planning or the development of the specifications of the courthouse.[72] According to Russell Claxton writing in *Architecture/Georgia Magazine,* the Baldwin County Courthouse was P. E. Dennis's first professional commission in a career which would also include the design of the 1890 Turner County Courthouse at Ashburn created in cooperation with fellow Macon architect, Alexander Blair.[73]

This is not the grand, monumental architecture of state and national institutions. Here is an architecture of human scale, domestic, simple, proud, and rural, which looks to itself, more than anywhere else, for its forms. It is a very conservative, almost primitive art, which is so inwardly-turned. But after all, this was the art of a very inwardly turned people—a people who were confronted with visions of a new world while desperately clinging to distorted images of the old.

Plate 2.13: The Georgia Railroad Depot at Milledgeville, built c.1905, burned in 1995.

Inflated freight rates immediately following the war ignited powerful forces in Macon to resurrect pre-war plans for a railroad from Macon to Augusta, via Milledgeville, Sparta and Warrenton.[74] Originally chartered way back in 1837, the Milledgeville Railroad renamed the Macon and Augusta Railroad was begun before the war. Work on the road continued sporadically during the war years and, as Reconstruction began, the project gained financial momentum through a bond issue guaranteed by the State. This was one of the first in a long line of state-underwritten financial miscalculations and boondoggles that were to become infamous in Reconstruction Georgia. Not long after the State's promise to underwrite Macon and Augusta bonds, the Georgia Railroad offered financial support, thus rendering the State guarantee unnecessary, and so the Georgia Railroad controlled the Macon and Augusta from the beginning.

Thirty years after the war, Milledgeville still languished. Her population had been nearly 2500 at war's end, and by 1890, it was only about 3300. The last decade of the century finally saw progress as the town grew to 4200 residents by 1900. This depot built by the Georgia Railroad probably between 1900 and 1910 attests to this modest rebirth. The silhouette is that of the Spanish Renaissance, a more exuberant, more ornate style than this building implies. It was probably inspired by Frank Milburn's 1901 grand Spanish Renaissance Union Depot at Augusta.

PUTNAM COUNTY: EATONTON

Plate 2.14: The depot at Eatonton, built in 1884, burned c.1969.

The charred shell of this depot is all that remains to celebrate the arrival of the early railroads in Eatonton. Built in 1884,[75] this building replaced the one Sherman burned in 1864 which had been built shortly after the Eatonton Branch Railroad Company completed its extension from Milledgeville to Eatonton in 1854. In 1862, the line was leased by the Central, which had controlled it from its inception.

The completion of the first branch line to Eatonton in 1854 symbolically completed a circle, for it had been at Eatonton that the plans were laid for the first railroads in Georgia. By the end of 1831, a progressive Eatonton was host to the state's first railroad conference. Thirty-two of the state's seventy-eight counties sent representatives.[76] Acting on the conference's recommendation, the Georgia Legislature was quick to authorize the "formation of a company for the construction of a railroad or turnpike from the city of Augusta to Eatonton, and thence westward to the Chattahoochee River, with branches thereto." This was the first act to incorporate a railroad in the state of Georgia.[77] The company was called the Augusta and Eatonton Turnpike and Railroad Company, but no rails were laid, and after only two years the charter was rescinded to make way for the Georgia Railroad. Ironically it would be more than twenty years before Eatonton would be connected, and she would then find herself at the end of an insignificant spur line.

In 1831, the list of towns supporting the Augusta and Eatonton Railroad read like a "who's who" of the mid-eighteenth century Georgia Piedmont. Subscriptions were taken at Augusta, Milledgeville, Eatonton, Sparta, Greensboro, Warrenton and Monticello.[78] As the 1830s began, these towns were in blossom, and with cotton beginning to cover the up-country Piedmont, there was promise of a rich harvest for railroads and for the towns that spawned them. To be sure, Eatonton was anxious to reap a fair share for her part in birthing Georgia's early railroads. Adiel Sherwood's 1829 *Gazetteer of Georgia* describes Eatonton as a prosperous village of 726 persons containing "a courthouse, a jail, two academies, a Masonic

Plate 2.14: The charred shell of this 1884 depot is all that remains to celebrate the arrival of the early railroads in Eatonton. (Photo: Wilber W. Caldwell.)

hall, a branch of the State Bank, and sixty-nine houses...." In 1836, the Eatonton Manufacturing Company began spinning operations on the Little River. Like Madison's, Eatonton's antebellum culture was supported by newly rich cotton planters who had achieved enough success out in the fields to build elegant houses in town. Unlike Madison, Eatonton would not benefit from the commercial advantages of an early mainline railroad. Both towns struggled after the war, but Madison would retain her proud airs, while Eatonton grew rough around the edges.

Plate 2.15: The Putnam County Courthouse, built c.1832.

With a history so similar to Madison's, one might expect Eatonton's courthouse story to be similar. Indeed it is, right down to the finest detail. A sturdy, vernacular, mid-ninteenth century courthouse and a late century rail connection were followed by the construction of a monumental, turn-of-the-century, neoclassical courthouse dripping with the ornament of the new era, designed by the same architect and begun

[72] Janice Hardy, "Preservation of Georgia Courthouses through Historic Documentation and Photography" (c.1980). Unpublished manuscript in the Baldwin County Public Library in Milledgeville.

[73] Russell Claxton, "Dennis & Dennis," *Architecture/Georgia* (July 1991): 24.

[74] Peter S. McGuire, "The Railroads of Georgia, 1860-1880," *The Georgia Historical Quarterly* 16/3 (1932): 193.

[75] William M. Stevens, "The Forty-ninth Road Master's Report to the President of The Central Railroad and Banking Company" in *The Annual Reports of the President of The Central Railroad and Banking Company* 4/49, 54.

[76] John C. Butler, *Historical Record of Macon and Central Georgia* (Macon GA: National Association of the Colonial Dames of America, 1879) 78.

[77] Charles C. Jones, Jr. and Salem Dutcher, *The Memorial History of Augusta* (Syracuse NY: D. Mason, 1390) 481.

[78] Jones, Jr. and Dutcher, *The Memorial History of Augusta*, 481.

Plate 2.15: Sources vary as to the date of construction of the large vernacular brick building which was the second Putnam County Courthouse. (Photo Courtesy of the Georgia Dept. of Archives and History.)

in the same year as Madison's stunning Beaux-Arts Morgan County Courthouse.

The history of the first Putnam County Courthouse is obscure. The county had been carved from Baldwin County in 1807, and Eatonton, the county seat, was laid out in the following year. In 1810, the town had a population of only 107 whites and 73 slaves, while the rural population of the newly formed Putnam County was above 10,000. A hazy photo of the old courthouse was published in the county's 1895 *Guide to Immigration* and is captioned "Putnam County Courthouse built 1810."[79] It is very doubtful that a brick building of this size and quality was built here as early as 1810.

Of the first Putnam County Courthouse we know little except that there was a court building on the square in Eatonton before 1832. Sherwood lists a courthouse "of considerable taste" in his 1828 inventory of buildings in Eatonton. Sources vary as to the date of construction of the large vernacular brick building. In his summary work, *Courthouses in Georgia,* Robert Jordan dates this building from 1824, but he cites no authority.[80] Likewise, the Colonial Dames 1966 survey of Georgia courthouses cites an 1824-construction date.[81] There is authority for an 1832 dating, but it is far from perfect. According to *The Eatonton Messenger* of May 1905, the age of the old brick courthouse had long been a mystery in Eatonton. [82]

Despite the failure of the Augusta and Eatonton Railroad of 1831, railroads were on the minds of

Eatontonians throughout the century. A listing of Eatonton's unsuccessful efforts to get railroads built offers ample evidence (see Table 2.3). At least four Eatonton-sponsored railroads were chartered before the completion of the Eatonton Branch Railroad Company's spur from Milledgeville in 1854, and no less than eight more roads were chartered but never built before Eatonton finally closed the loop with the Middle Georgia and Atlantic Railroad to Machen in 1891. Originally chartered as the Eatonton and Machen Railroad Company, the line was extended to Covington in 1894. At last a frustrated Eatonton could breathe freely.

Plate 2.16: The Putnam County Courthouse, built in 1905. J. W. Golucke, architect.

The rush of fresh air that blew into Eatonton after the completion of the Middle Georgia and Atlantic must have been sweet indeed. In 1895, the county began efforts to promote itself and to attract new citizens and new commerce, and in a burst of New South frenzy two new cotton mills rose at Eatonton right after the turn of the century. Since the destruction of the Eatonton Manufacturing Company by Sherman's raiders in 1864, no effort had been put forth to replace this enterprise. But by 1900, the Middle Georgia Cotton Mill and the Eatonton Electric Cotton Mill were both under construction.

Plate 2.16: James W. Golucke's 1905 Putnam County Courthouse. With her embrace of the new American neoclassical Revival, the South would reaffirm her attachment to classical forms, but once again she would find the national symbolism inappropriate. (Photo: Wilber W. Caldwell.)

The fresh air of perceived progress is apparent in newspaper articles of the era, and most to the point, it is elegantly manifest in the monumental Putnam County Courthouse completed in 1905.

A survey of the *Eatonton Messenger* in the years between the completion of the Middle Georgia and Atlantic in 1894 and the construction of the new courthouse in 1905 reveals much about the myth of the New South. Like most myths, some of its aspects were grounded in elements of truth. The new railroad was real enough, and the fresh winds of economic change were themselves enough to raise capital and build two cotton mills in Eatonton. This was not myth; it was fact. Still, like most Georgia counties in 1900, at the heart of the psyche of Putnam County was not industry but agriculture, and in middle Georgia in 1900 "agriculture" was still spelled "cotton." Despite the new myth of industrial promise brought by the railroad, the lingering myth of the Old South continued to work its insidious mischief in the memories of these people. As a result, they were of a divided mind, caught between incompatible mythologies. The resulting reality left them in limbo, yearning for the new economic prosperity while they fought its political and social implications at every turn. A large part of what kept the myth of the New South mythical was a stubborn fixation on the myth of the Old South.

New South mythology offered numerous codified solutions to Southern problems. For the agricultural disaster that was tenancy, the myth of immigration was one such solution. In 1895, Putnam County prepared a booklet entitled *A Guide to Immigration, Putnam County, Georgia, and Its Resources*. From its pages we can clearly see a county alive with a hope, which rested squarely on the shoulders of vast hoards of immigrants who never came.[83] Immigrants to work smaller, diversified farms were thought to be a panacea.[84] But the problem in Putnam County was the same as elsewhere in the South. Despite flowery descriptions of an agrarian Paradise and warm invitations to attract immigrants, Southerners were far too selective about who these immigrants might be. They wanted white, Anglo-Saxon neighbors only. It is doubtful that the Southern and Eastern Europeans

EATONTON RAILROADS CHARTERED BUT NEVER BUILT
1838-The Eatonton Railroad Company
1853-Eatonton and Covington Railroad Company
1853-Eatonton and Monticello Railroad Company
1853-Madison, Eatonton, Watkinsville and Athens Railroad Company
1856-Eatonton and Hog Mountain Railroad Company
1859-Eatonton and Madison Railroad Company
1870-Eatonton and Union Point Railroad Company
1872-Athens and Eatonton Railroad Company
1885-Monticello and Eatonton Railroad Company
1887-Eatonton and Athens Railroad Company
1887-Eatonton and Madison Railway Company
1890-The Dalton, Spring Place and Eatonton Railroad Company
1891-Madison and Eatonton Dummy Line Company

Table 2.3

who were flowing into the United States by 1900 were welcome in Putnam County. As C. Vann Woodward sums up, "The flood tide of European immigration in 1899-1910 swept past the South leaving it almost untouched and further isolating it in its peculiarities from the rest of the country."[85]

The *Guide to Immigration* later turns from agriculture to articulate the full New South myth and reveal its most powerful messenger, postbellum railroads: "During the past four years another important road has been added, the Middle Georgia and Atlantic Railway...This is a most important connection for the town of Eatonton...The people now feel that they are

[79] D. T. Singleton, *Guide to Immigration, Putnam County, Georgia, and Its Resources* (Atlanta: Methodist Book & Publishing Co., 1895) 2.

[80] Robert H. Jordan and Gregg Puster, *Courthouses in Georgia, 1825-1983* (Norcross GA: The Harrison Company, 1984) 92.

[81] Eugenia Payne Wasden, *Historical Survey of 159 County Court Houses in the State of Georgia for the National Society of Colonial Dames of America* (Macon GA: n.p., 1976).

[82] *The Eatonton Messenger*, May 27, 1905.

[83] Singleton, ed., *A Guide to Immigration, Putnam County, Georgia, and Its Resources*, 4.

[84] Singleton, ed., *A Guide to Immigration, Putnam County, Georgia, and Its Resources*, 56.

[85] Woodward, *Origins of the New South, 1877-1910*, 299.

in close touch with the outside world…."[86] And the paragraph concludes: "…the day is not far distant when it will become the site of one of the most active industries in this section of the State."[87]

With this kind of elation in the air around Eatonton it is not hard to imagine the beginnings of the movement for a new courthouse. Again *The Eatonton Messenger* gives an account of the process. Editorials weighed the cost of a new courthouse ($30,000) against remodeling the old ($15,000).[88] A bond issue was proposed first in 1902 and again in 1904. Amid arguments of county pride, fire proofing of county records, and the attraction of immigrants,[89] the 1904 bond issue for a new courthouse was approved, 570 for to 61 against, in a remarkable turnout by the county's 758 registered voters.[90]

Next a search of *The Eatonton Messenger* details the county commissioners' quest for a design for the new courthouse. Just a week after the passage of the bond issue, they traveled to Forsyth to view Bruce and Morgan's 1896 Monroe County Courthouse,[91] and not two weeks later *The Eatonton Messenger* reported an excursion to Newnan by the commissioners to view J. W. Golucke's newly completed neoclassical creation there. A drawing of Golucke's 1900 DeKalb County Courthouse in Decatur appeared in the same issue identifying this building as the model for the new Putnam County Courthouse.[92] The hiring of Golucke was reported on December 12, 1904, and the budget for the new "brick, stone, terra-cotta and iron" building was set at $28,000.[93] Some sources indicate that this was technically a remodeling, and that Golucke designed his grand courthouse at Eatonton around the old building. If this was the case, it was a remodeling in name only, for the new structure completely encased the old.[94] The cornerstone was laid in May of 1905, and the building was completed around the end of the year. There can be little doubt that design criteria for the new Putnam County Courthouse had been derived from a survey of the immediate area, and it is clear that the columns of the new Classicism beckoned from places like Decatur and Newnan. The people of Putnam County got their grand neoclassical building, but by no stretch of the imagination was it a copy of the granite walls of the DeKalb County Courthouse. Like all of J. W. Golucke's courthouses except DeKalb, it was to be built of brick.

Today James Wingfield Golucke's neoclassical courthouses are windows on their times, revealing the collective mind of the people for whom they were designed. Golucke was undoubtedly aware of the monumental thrust of the neoclassical and Beaux-Arts buildings that were being constructed outside of the South around the turn of the century. Most of his ornamental vocabulary was derivative and flowed from the styles of day. Surely he was equally aware of the antebellum, classical tradition of the South beginning with the designs of Thomas Jefferson and culminating in the Southern celebration of the Greek Revival. At a fundamental level, his elevations are Georgian. Golucke must have known that any local appeal that the New Classicism might enjoy would be realized by recalling the architecture of the Old South. Accordingly his general plans always begin with a pedimented, classical portico attached to a horizontal rectangular mass in the popular style of older so-called Southern Colonial architecture. Possible antebellum sources are numerous. Among the obvious examples are: Robert Mills's Fireproof Building in Charleston (1828), William Strickland's College of Charleston (1828) and Tennessee Statehouse (1845), Charles Cluskey's Old Governor's Mansion at Milledgeville (1836) and the state capital buildings of both North and South Carolina. All adhere to this general form.

Additionally, it appears that Golucke was no stranger to the brick vernacular style, that rudimentary translation of the old Federal Style that was itself a simplification of Georgian models. It was in the vernacular that Georgia first saw the rectangular courthouse at the center of the square with four more or less equal entranceways. As the vernacular expanded its vocabulary, simple court buildings rose in the shape of a cross like the 1873 McDuffie County Courthouse at Thomson and the 1874 Cherokee County Courthouse at Canton. Five of Golucke's neoclassical courthouses, built before the Putnam County Courthouse had grand columned entrances to accommodate all four sides of a central town square without discrimination.[95]

In addition to the Old South and vernacular forces that molded Golucke's four-sided approach, the Palladian tradition is undeniable here. Golucke may have lacked formal architectural training, but it is unlikely that any serious American designer, of this or any other era, could have overlooked Palladio. Here at Eatonton, we find several basic Palladian themes. The basic form of classical portico attached to rectangular mass lies at the heart of many of Palladio's designs. In addition, several of the master's most famous villas, notably Villa Rotondo and Villa Meledo, embody the four-sided temple form. Palladio began with a circular center, squared it and then added a portico to each side of the square. It was a floor plan ready made for the American courthouse square. Golucke replaced Palladio's low, saucer-like domes with fanciful towers of more Baroque origin, packaged it all in Georgian symmetry, decorated it with Beaux-Arts finery, added a touch of Jefferson, a touch of the brick vernacular, and thus hammered out plans for the familiar local monuments we find on so many of Georgia's squares.

At Eatonton, Golucke decorated his creation with the ornament of the 1893 Chicago World's Fair: rusticated quoining, splayed window lintels with broad voussoirs, Corinthian capitals, roundels in the clerestory, and a Golucke trademark, the star patterned fenestration. This distinctive motif appears on 5 of Golucke's 10 neoclassical courthouses. It was a favorite of New York's most celebrated firm, McKim, Mead and White, appearing in many of their most important designs including the Agricultural Building at the Columbian Exposition (1893).[96] Additional-

ly, we find the star pattern in the designs of Bradford Gilbert at the 1895 Cotton States Exposition at Atlanta. Nonetheless, despite all of their up-to-date ornament, the courthouses of James Golucke spoke a uniquely Southern language that was largely foreign to the main stream critics of turn-of-the-century American architecture.

In 1904, the thrust of American architecture had shifted. A new torrent of Classicism had been loosed ten years earlier at the 1893 Columbian Exposition in Chicago, and in a matter of a few short years the picturesque had been reduced to a mere back eddy, at least as far as public building was concerned. The multiple currents of Neoclassical Revival, Beaux-Arts Classicism and Federal/Colonial Revival flowed from the financial centers in the East right into Main Street America. In his study of the pre-eminent American architectural firm of the day, McKim, Mead and White, Leland Roth explains that while older American Classicism had been "romantic" and "was nostalgic and meant to refer the observer's mind back to an equivalent period," this second American Neoclassical Revival was, "an attempt to introduce order and clarity into an urban environment which was growing exponentially and chaotically."[97] In Eatonton in 1904, there was no "urban environment" to clarify, and what little growth there was could hardly be termed "exponential" or "chaotic."

With her embrace of the turn-of-the-century main stream style, the South would reaffirm her attachment to classical forms, but once again she would find the national symbolism inappropriate.

[86] Singleton, ed., *A Guide to Immigration, Putnam County, Georgia, and Its Resources*, 74.

[87] Singleton, ed., *A Guide to Immigration, Putnam County, Georgia, and Its Resources*, 74.

[88] *The Eatonton Messenger*, May 14, 1904 and September 10, 1904.

[89] *The Eatonton Messenger*, September 24, 1904.

[90] *The Eatonton Messenger*, October 1, 1904.

[91] *The Eatonton Messenger*, October 8, 1904.

[92] *The Eatonton Messenger*, October 29, 1904

[93] *The Eatonton Messenger*, November 12, 1905.

[94] *The Eatonton Messenger*, October 29, 1904; Eugenia Payne Wasden, *Historical Survey of 159 County Court Houses in the State of Georgia for the National Society of Colonial Dames of America*.

[95] The 1900 DeKalb County Courthouse was of this design, although subsequent remodeling added wings in place of the east and west porticos. The Hart County Courthouse at Hartwell, 1902, the Bartow County Courthouse at Cartersville, 1902, the

Meriwether County Courthouse at Greenville, 1903 and the Coweta County Courthouse at Newnan, 1904, are the other four early examples.

[96] Other examples of this motif in the work of McKim, Mead and White include the Columbia University Library (1893), The Bowrey Savings Bank (1895), The Boston Public Library (1895) and the Cullen Memorial at West Point (1898).

[97] Leland M. Roth, *McKim, Mead and White, Architects* (New York: Harper and Row, 1983) 357.

Attaching her peculiar mythology, she draped the new Classicism in her own evolving romantic imagery. It no longer wore the robes of the democracy of Jefferson, nor of Calhoun's Greek Democracy. By 1900, the columns of Southern Neoclassicism were clothed in the myth of the Old South itself. It had become the Architecture of the Lost Cause, and if a little Beaux-Arts decoration crept into the blend, then all the better. The South had no problem with the ornaments of "progress" as long as she could manipulate their symbols on her own terms.

Even though 40 neoclassical courthouses would be built in Georgia between 1896 and the end of 1910, when the Putnam County Commissioners began their architectural quest in 1904, there were only fifteen such structures on Georgia's squares. Golucke had designed nine of these (see Appendix C). It seems the Putnam County Commissioners took one look at the glorious columns at Newnan and Decatur, and Golucke was hired. He had what they wanted, a mythical vision of both the past and the future all rolled into one.

SOME LAST THOUGHTS ON THE CENTRAL OF GEORGIA RAILROAD

The Central of Georgia Railroad from Savannah to Macon and the Georgia Railroad from Augusta to Atlanta both were chartered in 1833, both chased cotton and both later sought a westward connection via the Western and Atlantic Railroad at Atlanta. Beyond this the contrast between the two could hardly be more striking.

The Georgia Railroad served Augusta and ultimately Charleston via the Charleston and Hamburg. It traversed the rich Georgia Piedmont at a time when the region was in blossom, not only with cotton, but also with an agrarian and uniquely Southern brand of American, antebellum progress. It linked already prosperous towns in a mutually advantageous relationship, carrying cotton to the coast and importing goods and food from Charleston and later from the American heartland. The pre-war flowering of Madison and Covington and creation of Thomson and Conyers attest to the Georgia Railroad's power to invigorate an already healthy economic section of Georgia in the two decades that preceded the Civil War.

On the other hand, the Central of Georgia served Savannah, and for nearly the first half of its 195 miles to Macon it traversed some of the wildest terrain in Georgia, the swamps and scrub pine regions of the all-but-deserted coastal plain. When it reached the cotton belt it bypassed the county seats of Jefferson, Washington and Wilkinson Counties in a headlong rush to Macon, where it would spread a web of track north to Atlanta and south and southwest to Albany, Columbus and beyond. The growth of towns along the early route of the Central was not immediate. U. B. Phillips sums up this state of affairs: "In 1858 the directors (of the Central of Georgia) awoke to the fact that not a single town had grown up on the whole route from Savannah to Macon, and the stations were still known by their numbers in most cases, and devoid of all houses but a shanty at the roadside to accommodate a small volume of freight."[98] This awakening brought lower rates to stimulate growth along the road, rates that were especially favorable to the importation of guano and other commercial fertilizers to revitalize the already played-out land of the eastern Georgia Cotton Belt. Sadly, the war followed on the heels of this enlightenment, making it impossible to measure any result and creating looming barriers to future growth. To be sure, some of these places did grow after the war, but for the most part, their day in the sun was brief.

The history of the Central is a history of exploitation. Even Macon, the seeming beneficiary of a cotton trade vastly expanded by the arrival of the Central of Georgia, complained of the uneven rate policies of the road, and as early as the 1850s Macon sought a connection to Augusta in order to establish competitive tariffs. The antebellum rate policies of the Central are a confusing tangle, lowering "through rates" for freight originating on the Western and Atlantic in order to compete with the Georgia Railroad, while raising rates on short-haul, "way traffic," effectively gouging the small towns along the way. To compete with river traffic in Macon, a double standard was established, raising rates when the Ocmulgee was low and lowering rates when the water was high and easily navigable.[99] Not surprisingly, the Central flourished and eventually triumphed over the Georgia Railroad in 1882 by leasing the latter road. Ironically, four years later the Central itself was gobbled up by the giant holding company, the Richmond and West Point Terminal and Warehouse Company.

As we have noted the only flamboyant court-houses built beside the Georgia Railroad were sparked by the crossing of antebellum rails at Madison, Covington and Lexington. We see a similar pattern with the Central. If we discount Millen, which spawned a county of its own in 1905, the only three county seats on this portion of the Central were on its branches at Waynesboro, Milledgeville and Eatonton. All were touched by postbellum roads. In 1905, Eatonton created a fabulous courthouse that reflected the exuberance of the myths carried on the 1894 Middle Georgia and Atlantic Railroad. Milledgeville built its present courthouse in 1886 some fifteen years after the Macon and Augusta had arrived, and although the structure exhibited some of the fiery hope of the New South myth, it is fundamentally of the older type and probably better reflects a nostalgic spirit in the former capitol. In Waynesboro, the old 1856 Burke County Courthouse is still in use today. Postbellum rails did not come to Waynesboro until 1907, and by that time the lie of the New South myth had, for the most part, been exposed. The Brinson Railroad sparked only belated and half-hearted enthu-siasm in Burke County.

The real story of the Central of Georgia between Savannah and Macon is told by the bypassed towns. Most of these built their own rail connections to the Central after the war. Swainsboro and Statesboro built postbellum railroads to join the Central, followed by stunning courthouses. In 1899, Sandersville was final-ly moved to express its zeal in the architectural style of the day after the Augusta Gibson and Sandersville Railroad, which had closed the link with the earlier Sandersville and Tennille in 1885, was widened to standard gauge. Likewise, Louisville belatedly responded to the 1879 Louisville and Wadley and to the 1890 Wadley and Mount Vernon Railroad with neoclassical columns in 1904. These are stories for later. Only Irwinton, in Wilkinson County, remained

Plate 2.17: The Savannah Cotton Exchange, built in 1886. William Gibbons Preston, architect. (Photo: Wilber W. Caldwell.

unconnected, and her simple vernacular 1870 court-house that replaced the one burned by General Sherman in 1864 was used until it burned in 1924.

In the early 1840s, the directors of the Central Railroad and Banking Company of Georgia had seemed almost oblivious to all of these towns; their focus had been fixed on completing the line to Macon. By 1843, the road reached a spot across the Ocmulgee from that city. It would be eight years before a bridge was built, and by that time the Monroe Railroad, later the Macon and Western, was laying rails northward from Macon via Barnesville and Griffin to Atlanta.

•

[98] Phillips, *History of Transportation in the Eastern Cotton Belt to 1860*, 293.

[99] Phillips, *History of Transportation in the Eastern Cotton Belt to 1860*, 292

The Monroe Railroad

THE MAIN LINE

Bibb County: Macon, Part 1 • Monroe County: Forsyth • Lamar County: Barnesville
Spalding County: Griffin • Clayton County: Jonesboro • Fulton County: Atlanta
(see chapters 4, 11, 26 & 32)

THE THOMASTON BRANCH

Upson County: Thomaston Some Final Thoughts on the Monroe Railroad

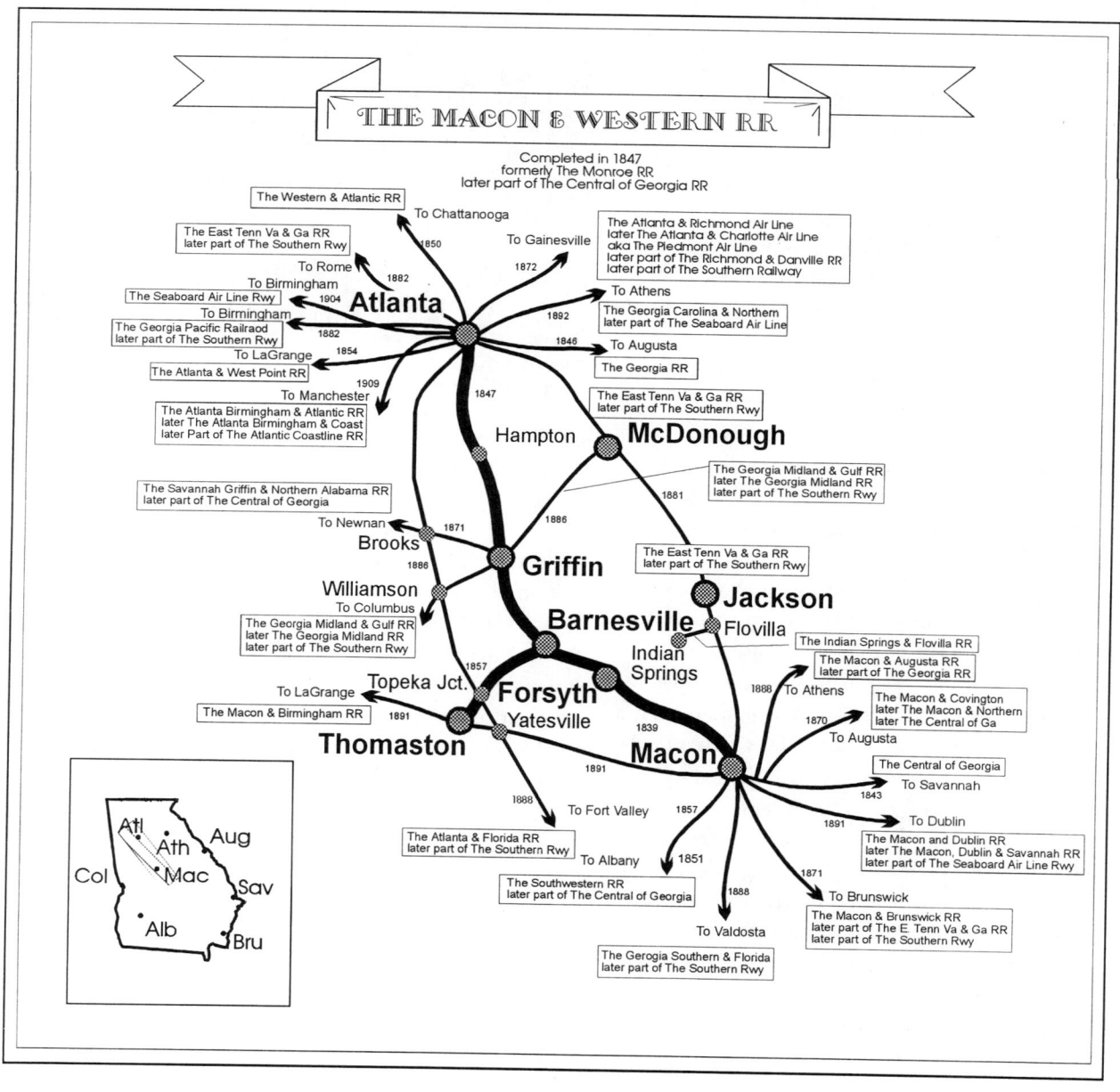

3 | The Monroe Railroad

THE MAIN LINE: MACON TO ATLANTA

BIBB COUNTY: MACON, PART 1

Plate 3.1: The Monroe Railroad and Banking Company, built in 1836.

This building is all that is left to sing the powerful music of early railroads in Macon, a song that began here in 1838 when the Monroe Railroad Company completed a line from Macon to Forsyth in nearby Monroe County. The Central of Georgia arrived in Macon from Savannah in 1843. By 1852 Macon was the railhead of the Southwestern Railroad upon which the riches of western Georgia flowed up out of the State's most productive cotton producing areas and into the city. When the first shells fell on Fort Sumter, grading on the Macon and Augusta had begun and the Macon and Brunswick was complete to somewhere in Twiggs County. By the turn of the century ten railroads would meet at Macon creating a complex opera of steam and steel (see Table 3.1).

The original 1836 structure was without pediment but featured six massive Doric columns. These columns celebrated more than Southern agrarian distortions of the Greek Democracy, more than the usual litany of cotton and slaves. These columns celebrated the railroad.

The history of Macon's original railroads is a history of many celebrations. The first of these came upon the occasion of the initial offering of stock in the Central Railroad and Banking Company of Georgia at Macon in 1835. "Bells were rung, guns were fired, the city was brilliantly lighted, and a ball was given…"[1] The year 1836 saw the celebration of the renewal of the original 1833 charter of the Monroe Railroad, planned from Macon to Forsyth. In that year, seven delegates from Macon attended a General Railroad Convention held in Knoxville, Tennessee. This convention recommended con-

---

[1] Ida Young, Julius Gholson and Clara Nell Hargrove, *The History of Macon, Georgia* (Macon GA: Lym, Marshall & Brooks, 1950) 78.

Plate 3.1: The Monroe Railroad and Banking Company building, built in 1836, is today Macon's City Hall. (Photo: Wilber W. Caldwell.)

Table 3.1

RAILROAD CONNECTIONS AT MACON 1900

The Central of Georgia Railroad, 1843. Savannah to Macon.

The Macon and Western Railroad, 1846. (formerly the Monroe Railroad. Macon to Atlanta; part of the Central of Georgia, 1872). Macon to Atlanta.

the Southwestern Railroad Company, 1852 (part of the Central of Georgia, 1869). Macon to Albany with branches to Opelika, Fort Gaines, Columbus and Perry.

The Macon and Brunswick Railroad, 1870 (later part of the East Tennessee, Virginia and Georgia Railroad; later part of the Southern Railway). Macon to Brunswick.

The Macon and Augusta Railroad, 1871 (part of the Georgia Railroad, 1877). Macon to Augusta via Camak.

The Covington and Macon Railroad, 1888 (later the Macon and Northern, 1891) (part of the Central of Georgia, 1895). Macon to Athens via Madison.

The Georgia, Southern and Florida Railroad, 1890 (later part of the Southern Railway). Macon to Palatka, Florida.

The Macon and Birmingham Railroad, 1891. Macon to La Grange.

The Macon, Dublin and Savannah Railroad, 1900. (later part of the Seaboard Air Line Railway). Macon to Vidalia via Dublin with connections to Savannah.

struction of a line from Cincinnati to Knoxville followed by a Southern extension to connect with the two Georgia roads already under construction. A Georgia railroad convention was held in Macon in November of the same year. This led to petitions for a state-supported railroad from the Chattahoochee to the Tennessee River. The result was the charter of the state-owned Western and Atlantic Railroad and the expansion of the charter of the Monroe Railroad and Banking Company granting rights to extend the line from Macon via Forsyth north to the future Western and Atlantic railhead planned in DeKalb County. More celebrations followed including the gala first trip from Macon to Forsyth in 1838 behind the steam engine "Ocmulgee" which had arrived in Macon, appropriately, by river boat.[2] A final celebration took place when the Central was completed to Macon in 1843. The first train to run the length of the line occasioned more festivities including a barbecue dinner with speeches that proclaimed the Central, "the longest railroad in the world" and predicted that the road would remain "until rivers and railroads are no longer needed."[3]

In 1844, amid all this bacchanal and merriment, the city of Macon went broke. The next year, the Monroe Railroad declared bankruptcy. Macon had danced and suddenly had to pay the piper. Having given municipal bonds in exchange for stock in the railroads (2500 shares of the Central and 500 shares of the Monroe Railroad) the city had interest to pay, and neither road had paid any dividends.[4] U. B. Phillips suggests that the cost of this elaborate headquarters building was part of the reckless management style that brought the Monroe Railroad to its financial knees in 1845.[5] The sale of the Monroe Railroad and Banking Company brought in Northern capital, and by 1846 the road was reborn as the Macon and Western Railroad and completed to the thriving rail camp that had just been christened Atlanta.

Even though Macon eventually had to sell her railroad stock at a loss, she would soon reap rich rewards from her investment. Macon's strength came from deep within the economic fabric of cotton. Before the railroads were even dreamt, Macon was a boomtown, and before track was laid, she had become a pillar of trade in central Georgia. In fact, the powerful city originally refused to let the Central cross the Ocmulgee, and the first depot was built on the east bank on the present site of the Bibb Manufacturing Company. The structure was described as "a copious warehouse together with a convenient passenger house, an engine shed, and a small shop for making repairs."[6]

Plate 3.2: The First Union Depot at Macon, built in 1855. Burned in 1891.

It was not until 1851 that the Central of Georgia was allowed to bridge the river and enter Macon proper to link up with the Monroe and the Southwestern Railroads. And it was not until 1855 that this General Passenger Depot was completed at the corner of 4th and Plum Streets for "the accommodation of all trains of all railroads."[7] Only six of these great train sheds were erected in Georgia.[8] Macon's reasons for denying the Central access to the city had been the same as Augusta's for denying the Georgia Railroad a connection across the Savannah River to the Charleston and Hamburg in the late 1840s. Both cities feared becoming forgotten stops along the line. Both were sure that the local drayage, hotel and warehouse trade would suffer in such a bargain. Like Augusta, Macon was finally forced to submit when the railroad threatened to by-pass the town all together and cross the Ocmulgee at some other point.

The relationship between Macon and the Central of Georgia would continue to be one of an odd mixture of conflict and mutual advantage. By the early 1850s when the Central of Georgia was waffling with regard to the construction of the Milledgeville branch, Macon's economic leadership was unquestioned, and it was Macon that rightly challenged Milledgeville for the title of capital city. At 5800, Macon's mid-century population was nearly three times that of Milledgeville. With or without her railroads, Macon was the bold and resourceful pretender whose claim to that crown was perhaps more legitimate than sleepy Milledgeville's had ever been.

Plate 3.3: The Bibb County Courthouse, built in 1829. Demolished in 1872. Elam Alexander, architect and builder.

This building is ample proof of Macon's early success. Macon had been laid out in 1823 as a state planned "trading town" in the heart of the vast lands ceded to the State of Georgia between the Oconee and the Flint Rivers by the Creek Indians in 1821. From the onset, every facet of the town reflected commerce, beginning with its location on the Fall Line at the head of navigation of the Ocmulgee River. Macon's early growth had been meteoric. When LaFayette passed through Macon in 1825 his secretary had noted: "Macon, which is a small handsome village,

Plate 3.2: Union Depot at Macon, completed 1855, burned in 1895. (Photo: Courtesy of The Georgia Department of Archives and History.)

[2] Young, Gholson and Hargrove, *The History of Macon, Georgia*, 79.

[3] John C. Butler, *A Historical Record of Macon and Central Georgia* (Macon GA: National Association of the Colonial Dames of America, 1879) 161.

[4] Butler, *A Historical Record of Macon and Central Georgia*, 167.

[5] U. B. Phillips, *History of Transportation in the Eastern Cotton Belt to 1860* (1908; reprint, New York: McMillan, 1913) 268.

[6] Young, Gholson and Hargrove, *The History of Macon, Georgia*, 82.

[7] Young, Gholson and Hargrove, *The History of Macon, Georgia*, 160.

[8] With its long arcaded bays, the structure was similar in plan to the Western and Atlantic's enormous passenger shed at Atlanta completed in 1853, the Atlanta and West Point's grand shed at West Point built in 1854, the Central of Georgia depot at Savannah designed in 1860 and completed in 1876, the old Union Depot (c.1870) at Augusta and the 1882 passenger shed at Columbus.

Plate 3.3: The 1829 Bibb County Courthouse. It is remarkable, but nonetheless apt, that a courthouse of this size was built at such an early date in the middle of what, not ten years before, had been wilderness. (Illustration: Courtesy of the Macon Museum of Arts and Sciences.)

tolerably populous, did not exist eighteen months since; it has risen from the midst of the forest as if by enchantment."[9] In his 1829 *Gazetteer of Georgia,* Adiel Sherwood describes a thriving community of 1140 inhabitants, with an Academy, two banks and two printing offices. He goes on to marvel at the town's growth and suggests that movements to usurp Milledgeville began at an early date: "Though it (Macon) was laid out in 1823, it already has one hundred houses, stores, warehouses, etc. and people are pressing to it with great zeal. Attempts have been made to remove the seat of government and make Macon the metropolis."

The history of Macon's trading fortunes is well documented. Sherwood describes vigorous pole boat

traffic on the Ocmulgee in 1829: "...boats carrying 400 to 500 bags of cotton descend (the Ocmulgee) from this place (Macon) and return with 70 tons of merchandise. Smaller boats ascend 50 miles above the confluence of the three branches of the river." In 1829, the first steam boat arrived, followed by a second in 1833, and by 1836, there were over sixty tow boats, fifty pole boats, and seven steamers trading on the Ocmulgee as far north as Macon.[10] John C. Butler's detailed chronicle of Macon reports that in 1834 the town's population was above 3000,[11] and in 1837 it passed 4000.[12]

This courthouse is fitting in many ways. The building reflects Macon's early growth and power. It is remarkable, but nonetheless apt, that a courthouse of this size was built at such an early date in the middle of what, not ten years before, had been wilderness. Although less graceful than Augusta's 1821 Richmond County Courthouse, the second Bibb County Courthouse rivaled Augusta's in size. With its three stories, this 90 x 43-foot building was a giant for its day. It replaced the first Bibb County Courthouse (1825) which was described as a "wooden, one room shack."[13]

Equally apt is the design. An awkward, although charming, brick vernacular structure with classical influences from both the Federal Style and the Greek Revival Style, the building celebrated a uniquely Southern version of the American frontier. The unusually tall and narrow Greek portico avoids the appearance of being "stuck" onto the front of the building through the device of the triglyph on the entablature, which is continued all the way around the building on a wide cornice. Probably not coincidentally, details of the Doric order and the triglyph motif appear in Asher Benjamin's 1827 *The American Builder's Companion* along with elevations for a similar three story courthouse. The Greek details of the triglyph and Doric columns are repeated on the cupola. The arched, hooded windows are incongruous with the Greek, but similar window and door treatments, borrowed from Federal Style and other Georgian modes, appear on many of the brick vernacular public buildings of the day.

[9] A. Lavasseur, *LaFayette in America in 1824 and 1825* in Joan Niles Sears, *The First Hundred Years of Town Planning in Georgia* (Atlanta: Cherokee Press, 1979) 172.

[10] E. H. Hinton, *A Historical Sketch of the Solution of Trade and Transportation at Macon, Georgia, Together with a Synopsis of the Rate Adjustment from the East* (Macon GA: n.p., 1912) 10.

[11] Butler, *A Historical Record of Macon and Central Georgia*, 113-5.

[12] Butler, *A Historical Record of Macon and Central Georgia*, 142-3.

[13] Young, Gholson and Hargrove, *The History of Macon, Georgia*, 58.

[14] Talbot Hamlin, *Greek Revival Architecture in America* (1944; reprint, New York: Dover Publications, 1944) 210.

The life of the designer of the 1829 Bibb County Courthouse reveals much about this building, about early nineteenth-century Georgia and about the progress of the Greek Revival in the American South. Most sources agree that Elam Alexander was of Scotch extraction. He came to Georgia from North Carolina as part of the state's first population explosion, an influx of settlers of Scottish, Irish and English ancestry who came primarily from the Carolinas and Virginia in response to the state's many land lotteries in the early decades of the century. Designing with no architectural training and little formal education, he stands for the best of the builder/architects of the era. It is the work of men like Elam Alexander, improvising on the examples of Robert Mills in South Carolina and William Strickland in Tennessee and on practical builders guides of the day, that moved Talbot Hamlin to write, "...behind such excellence of design as is apparent in the best of these houses one is forced to infer a designerça true architect in work if not in name."[14]

The 1829 Bibb County Courthouse was among Elam Alexander's first major commissions. It bears little of the grace and finished style manifest in his subsequent work in Macon like the Georgia Female College (Wesleyan), 1839; the Holt-Peeler House, 1840; and the Raines-Miller-Carmichael House, 1848, to name only a select few.

Our specialized investigation of Macon in the three decades preceding the Civil War would not be complete without reciting the rest of the achievements of Elam Alexander. In his life, the two essential elements of this book come together as one, for one side of Elam Alexander begot beautiful architecture; the other built railroads. He was a powerful stockholder in the Central of Georgia Railroad, the Monroe Railroad and also in the Southwestern Railroad, whose initial Board of Commissioners he chaired. He became the first president of this latter road in 1847. Five years earlier, he had been the general contractor in charge of the grading of the difficult last fifty miles of the Central of Georgia Railroad from the Oconee River to the east bank of the Ocmulgee at Macon.

Elam Alexander, perhaps more than any Southerner who lived before the Civil War, must have understood the possibilities for a joyous, hopeful relationship between the railroads and architecture. He died in 1863 before the erection of so many architectural ironies, created in hope, were destined only to bear witness to a seemingly endless pageant of disappointment.

Monroe County: Forsyth

Plate 3.4: The old depot at Forsyth, built c.1852.

At Forsyth we encounter another of the ten remaining antebellum depots in Georgia (see Table VI in the Introduction). This large, high-quality stone building attests to the early success of the town it served. There is nothing in Monroe County records to date this building, but we know that in 1852 a very similar structure was built at neighboring Barnesville, and it seems safe to assume that these depots were constructed at about the same time. With regular trains running on the newly built Monroe Railroad between Macon and Forsyth, in 1840 Monroe was the ninth largest cotton-producing county of Georgia's 93 counties. By 1850, she had risen to fourth, ginning over 15,000 bales. Forsyth was the first in a line of successful, cotton-fueled, Piedmont towns, which would realize rail connections to Savannah via the Central at Macon. By 1840, Eatonton and Milledgeville had shifted their railroad hopes from the Georgia Railroad to the Central of Georgia, and farther to the west, Thomaston and Talbotton were longingly eyeing the iron rails at Macon.

According to Monroe County lore, the passengers from Macon to Forsyth on the Monroe Railroad rode

Plate 3.4: The depot at Forsyth, one of only ten antebellum depots still standing in Georgia. (Photo: Wilber W. Caldwell.)

the first passenger train in Georgia. The year was 1838, and the 25-mile trip had taken a little over an hour. Anything in excess of 20 miles per hour was considered death defying for the era, and although the opening of the line must have created a gay occasion for Forsyth, reason to celebrate was primarily Macon's, for the bulk of the capital for the Monroe Railroad had come from that city.

Plate 3.5: The Monroe County Courthouse, built in 1825, demolished 1896.

Typical of many prosperous Piedmont counties that were the beneficiaries of early rails, Monroe County soon became comfortable with her railroad. As the nineteenth century wore on, she would resist the jubilant symbols of the myth of the New South, holding close to traditional architectural forms and keeping her 1825 courthouse for over seventy years. The old two-story brick structure, built in the vernacular style, featured a gabled roof, a broad cornice and four arched entrance doorways. Although the design was simplicity itself, the elegant proportion and considerable scale are particularly impressive, especially for such an early building in such a theretofore wild place.

There was wealth here as this building suggests, the wealth of cotton. Like Eatonton and Madison and other prosperous Piedmont towns, Forsyth would develop a society around well-to-do planters and their social urge to congregate in towns. But there would be

Plate 3.5: Although the design of the 1825 Monroe County Courthouse was simplicity itself, its elegant proportions and considerable scale are impressive for such an early building in such a theretofore wild place. (Photo: Courtesy of the Georgia Dept. of Archives and History.)

little railroad mania here, and Forsyth's population would remain static through the closing decades of the century (1105 in 1880, 1171 in 1900). Part of the reason for her unique rejection of the postbellum railroad myth is geographical. Proximity to both the sprawling railroad junctions at Macon and Atlanta made the dream of new rails in Forsyth seem an unlikely fantasy. Rails to the west were thought to be the common panacea in the post-war era, but the Monroe Railroad itself turned west at Forsyth on its way to Atlanta in order to reach the spine of the high ridge at Barnesville. The rails then branched farther westward to Thomaston or swung north again to Atlanta straddling the divide between the Flint and the Ocmulgee Rivers. With Macon and the Central's connection to Savannah nearby and the westward course of the Monroe Railroad from Forsyth to Barnesville, a second east-west line at Forsyth seemed fruitless. Similarly, an additional north-south connection seemed useless, especially after the East Tennessee, Virginia and Georgia connected Atlanta and Macon via nearby Jackson on the other side of the Ocmulgee in 1883 and the Atlanta and Florida Railroad connected Atlanta and Fort Valley via neighboring Zebulon on its way south in 1888. Seemingly surrounded by railroad mania, Forsyth apparently had no wild dreams of her own.

Finally on June 25, 1895, the Monroe *Advertiser* published the following notice:

> We the Commissioners of Monroe County... realizing that her Courthouse...has twice been condemned as unsafe by competent architects, and numerous grand juries, realizing that it was inadequate for the needs of the county, and that the progress of the court was often checked because jurors and witnesses could not be made comfortable in the building we now have recommended the building of a new Courthouse.[15]

And so in 1896, the county built a new courthouse, not out of any euphoric hopes for the future, but simply because one was needed.

Plate 3.6: The Monroe County Courthouse, built in 1896. Bruce and Morgan, architects.

Although the 1896 Monroe County Courthouse was not inspired by the promise of the New South as imported by so many postbellum railroads, the architecture of this building speaks for the period in several uniquely instructive voices. Despite the power of the American neoclassical Revival that had been ignited three years earlier by the buildings of the Columbian Exposition at the 1893 Chicago World's Fair, the silhouette here, despite its symmetry, still reflects the old picturesque Styles. There was a distinct lag in the South when it came to adopting the new classicism of the budding "American Renaissance." [16]

To be sure, this lag had been apparent all along. Italianate buildings were still popular in the South long after the style lost its appeal in the North. The streets of Washington and New York had been lined with Second Empire architecture long before the first courthouses of that style graced the streets of even the most progressive of Southern railroad cities. Despite the progressive verbiage of a generation of young Henry Grady's, architectural lags were something of a Southern tradition for fifty years after the Civil War. The depth of the South's wounds and the superficial nature of Southern "progress" cannot be underestimated in this context, as in so many others. As W. J. Cash so poignantly puts it: "it was the Yankee's fate to have strengthened it (the Southern mind) almost beyond reckoning, and to have made it one of the most solidly established, one of the least reconstructible ever developed."[17]

In 1896, Georgia courthouses may have been slow to don the new neoclassical garments, but the return to symmetry was apparently a welcome trend. For years the asymmetry of picturesque styles had dominated Georgia town squares, but by the time the Monroe County Commissioners began to consider a plan for the new courthouse at Forsyth, the return to symmetry was in full swing. In the space of only two years, six perfectly balanced Georgia courthouses had been completed.[18] All sang the songs of geometric balance. Several of these, including Reuben Hunt's stunning 1894 Elbert County Courthouse at Elberton, were quoined with low square pavilions

Plate 3.6: Although fundamentally Romanesque in silhouette, Bruce and Morgan's 1896 Monroe County Courthouse reflects Queen Anne styling, a new voice of eclecticism in which classical elements abound. (Photo: Wilber W. Caldwell.)

topped with pyramidal roofs. Here was the model for the formal arrangement found here at Forsyth. This studied symmetry undoubtedly flowed from the buildings of both the 1893 Chicago and the 1895 Atlanta Expositions, and form the Chateau-like pavilions following the French Renaissance Style exemplified by H. H. Richardson's New York State Capitol Building (1879) and Richard Morris Hunt's monumental work including the Biltmore House at Asheville, North Carolina, completed in 1895, the year this courthouse was begun. Just before his death in 1886, Henry Hobson Richardson had designed his Allegheny County Courthouse in Pittsburgh, a building that almost single-handedly defined the style of American Romanesque courthouses of the era. Here pavilions with pyramidal roofs defined the corners

[15] *The Monroe Advertiser* (Forsyth GA), June 25, 1895.

[16] The first neoclassical courthouses did not appear in Georgia until the completion of Andrew J. Bryan's Stewart County Courthouse at Lumpkin in 1895 and his Muscogee County Courthouse at Columbus in 1896. These court buildings and J. W. Golucke's 1900 DeKalb County Courthouse were the only courthouses built in the new style before 1902.

[17] W. J. Cash, *The Mind of the South* (1941; reprint, New York: Vintage Books, 1991) 107. Emphasis is original.

[18] These were the Whitfield County Courthouse, 1891, the Elbert County Courthouse, 1894, the Macon County Courthouse, 1894 (Plate 6.3), the Pike County Courthouse, 1895, the Johnson County Courthouse, 1895 and the Emanuel County Courthouse, 1895.

Plate 3.7: While hints of the new style would adorn the 1896 courthouse, the 1899 depot at Forsyth is firmly rooted in the older picturesque tradition. (Photo: Wilber W. Caldwell.)

and, like many of Richardson's later designs, the building followed symmetrical forms. By 1890, a decided national trend toward symmetry was under way even among Richardson's most ardent followers. The shift to symmetry was particularly radical for Bruce and Morgan. Although they had begun with symmetrical buildings influenced by the Second Empire Style, by 1895 much of the firm's reputation rested on highly picturesque designs in the Romanesque Style.[19]

But it appears that Bruce and Morgan borrowed more from the buildings of the 1893 Columbian Exposition than just a return to symmetry. County commissioners all across Georgia may not have been ready for the classical excesses of the World's Fair, but some of the architects were. Monroe County demanded and got a Romanesque building in the mold of Elbert and Emanuel Counties, but they got a little more in the bargain. This was still the age of eclecticism, and despite its fundamentally Romanesque silhouette, this building drips with neoclassical detail. Here we see the influence of the Queen Anne Style, not as a reflection of the earlier more historical Shavian Manorial mode, but as a new force of eclecticism in which classical elements abound in a sort of "free composition with classical detail."[20] classical pediments and elegant balustrades flank the central tower, which is decorated with Corinthian pilasters. The cornice is richly inscribed with a flowery Renaissance motif, and beneath the eaves we find bold

dentals in the classical tradition. Talbot Hamlin characterizes Southern architecture in his discussion of the earlier development of the Greek Revival in the region, "in general work was extremely conservative" and new forms "crept in only gradually."[21] In 1896 here in Monroe County the grandeur of the Renaissance was creeping into Central Georgia.

Plate 3.7: The depot at Forsyth, built in 1899. Bruce and Morgan, architects.

In 1898, as the citizens of Monroe County admired their new courthouse, the Atlanta architects, Bruce and Morgan, received another commission at Forsyth. Late in that year, the Central of Georgia retained that prestigious firm to design this passenger depot[22] next to the old 1852 depot which continued in use as a freight house. While hints of the new style had adorned the new courthouse, this depot is firmly rooted in the older picturesque tradition. It is an eclectic design, and one is hard to call it Queen Anne, Richardsonian, or Italianate, although it owes a debt to all of these styles. The roof line and ornate chimneys recall the Queen Anne, while bold window groupings and banded stone trim are Richardsonian as is a large arched window not seen in this photograph. At track side the building features a squat, square tower with a low pyramidal roof in the Italian Villa Style. In 1898, the coming trend for courthouses may have been the Neoclassicism of the Columbian Exposition, but Georgia's country depots would have little to do with the new style.

LAMAR COUNTY: BARNESVILLE

Plate 3.8: The depot at Barnesville, built in 1910.

Arriving in Barnesville in 1840, the Monroe Railroad came in the heart of the depression following the Panic of 1837. Times were so hard that the railroad could not get iron rails, and although the line from Macon to Forsyth had been iron, the original Forsyth to Barnesville road had used oak rails and relied not on steam power but horse-drawn railcars. As iron rail became available, it replaced the oak rail, which was pulled up and laid on the line from

Barnesville to Griffin. This "leap-frog" policy continued for several years..[23]

Before the creation of Lamar County in 1920, Barnesville was in Pike County. By 1850, it had become a prosperous rail junction virtually straddling the boundary between two counties. The fact that in 1852 the Macon and Western built a large stone depot here very much like the one in nearby Forsyth substantiates Barnesville's early success.[24] Local histories relate that in that year, the town had "2 hotels, 7 dry goods stores, 2 lawyers, 5 doctors, 4 teachers, and 2 preachers."[25] Before the Southwestern Railroad's branch from Fort Valley to Columbus was completed in 1853, Barnesville was the "overland" connecting point to Columbus for the Monroe Railroad. "Six-mule wagons" plied the bad roads to Columbus in the 1840s.[26] A western branch rail line, the Barnesville and Thomaston Railroad, was completed in 1857.

The old stone depot served until 1905 when it was demolished to make way for this depot which was erected by the Central of Georgia Railroad in 1910.[27] The 1910 design is typical of a number of brick depots in Georgia built in the early part of this century in the "Spanish" or Mission Style. The "Spanish Style" was one of the last flowerings of the architectural diversity that characterized American depot buildings before 1910.[28] "Spanish" depots had their beginnings on the Santa Fe Railroad in the last decade of the nineteenth century, and their popularity spread throughout the Southern States.[29] These designs generally fall into two types: the Spanish Renaissance Style, and the Mission Style, which had its roots in historical revivalism in California in the 1890s.

Small rural depots like this one seldom display elaborate detail in this or any other style. These were functional, austere structures, without excessive embellishment, and generally the only claim to a "Spanish" styling was found in the characteristic outline of a Mission Style parapet or dormer and an excellent tile roof. Just as the arching brackets of the Railroad Style often qualified a depot as Italianate, the distinct curves of these parapets qualified buildings like this as a Spanish or Mission Style depots.

Plate 3.8: The 1910 depot at Barnesville is typical of a number of brick depots in Georgia built in the early part of this century in the Spanish or Mission Style. (Photo: Wilber W. Caldwell.)

Interestingly, scrolling parapets like these are often associated with the Dutch Renaissance Style which itself drew inspiration from Spanish models.

In 1910, the railroad was attuned to Barnesville's importance. Perhaps the Central even foresaw the creation of a new county here. Back in 1894, when Pike County erected James Golucke's courthouse at Zebulon, leaders in Barnesville had proposed to build a second courthouse, relying on the notion that the county seat could be shared, alternating court sessions between Zebulon and Barnesville.[30] This was not to

[19] Bruce and Morgan's Romanesque court buildings designed before 1896 include the courthouses in Talbot, Sumter, Heard, Paulding, Haralson, Bulloch , Carroll , Laurens and Floyd Counties.

[20] Montgomery Schuyler, "Concerning Queen Anne,"in William H. Jordy and Ralph Coe, eds., *American Architecture and Other Writings*, 2 vols. (Cambridge: Belknap Press of Harvard University Press, 1961)..

[21] Hamlin, *Greek Revival Architecture in America*, 194.

[22] *The Manufacturer's Record*, November 4, 1898.

[23] Phillips, *History of Transportation in the Eastern Cotton Belt to 1860*, 268.

[24] Augusta Lambdin, ed., *The History of Lamar County* (Barnesville GA: The Barnesville News Gazette, 1932) 31 and 57.

[25] Leonora Ginn, ed., *Barnesville Days to Remember, 1826-1976* (Barnesville GA: Barnesville Lamar County Historical Society, 1976) 10.

[26] Lambdin, ed., *The History of Lamar County*, 31.

[27] *The Georgia Historical Society's Finders Guide of Plans and Maps of the Central of Georgia Railroad in the Georgia Department of Archives and History in Atlanta*.

[28] Jeffery Richards and John M. MacKenzie, *The Railway Station, A Social History* (New York: Oxford University Press, 1986) 47.

[29] Richards and MacKenzie, *The Railway Station, A Social History*, 48.

[30] *The Pike County Journal* (nd).

be, and although Zebulon retained the Pike County seat, she lay stagnant, while Barnesville's population exploded from 754 in 1870 to 3036 in 1900.

SPALDING COUNTY: GRIFFIN

Plate 3.9: Union Depot at Griffin built c.1889.

Griffin was laid out in 1840 as a planned stop on the Monroe Railroad. The town prospered as a jumping-off place to the West in the years before the Civil War. George White in his 1849 *Statistics of Georgia* describes Griffin as "the market town for Meriwether, Pike, a portion of Troup, Fayette, and parts of Upson, Monroe and Butts" Counties. According to White, by 1849, the town had a population of 2000 with "4 hotels, 5 warehouses, and 40 or 50 stores."

The city of Griffin was the dream of L. L. Griffin who exemplifies the most resourceful of Georgia's Western pioneers. Griffin came to Georgia from South Carolina as a young boy, and his family settled in Twiggs County in the early 1800s. The Indian Cession of 1802-1805 had brought this area officially into the state of Georgia. It is clear that the Griffins were hardy stock indeed, for L. L. Griffin made his early reputation as an "Indian" fighter, first in campaigns in Florida and later against the Creeks. By the 1830s, he was well known around Macon as "General" Griffin, and he achieved notable commercial success there as a merchant. But it is not for his exploits in war or in commerce that Lewis Lawrence

Plate 3.9: Ironically many of General Griffin's visions would eventually come true in the city of Griffin after the war, as this rather elaborate depot built in 1889 suggests. (Photo: Courtesy of Georgia Department of Archives and History.)

Griffin is remembered, for he was one of the first of a new breed. L. L. Griffin was "Railroad Man."

Griffin was one of the early promoters, a substantial stockholder, and the first president of the Monroe Railroad and Banking Company. Perhaps more than anyone else in Macon at the time, he recognized the potential of the railroad to turn obscure places into thriving communities. The story of the city of Griffin is the story of L. L. Griffin's efforts to exploit this unique power. Lewis Griffin was a true visionary. In 1836, he saw Georgia's future railroads, the Georgia Railroad, the Central of Georgia and the Western and Atlantic, as lines on the map, and it came to him that if all these lines could meet, the place of their joining would become the great city of the modern South. His vision was perfect, but as it turned out, his geography was slightly off.

L. L. Griffin drew an imaginary line straight from Madison to West Point, and at the place where this line crossed his proposed extension of the Monroe Railroad from Macon to the Western and Atlantic railhead he built his city: Griffin. According to local history, General Griffin laid out the town in a "primitive spot in the forest"[31] in 1840, a full two years before rails arrived at that spot.

In the depression years following the Panic of 1837, the Monroe Railroad struggled to complete its line to connect with the Western and Atlantic railhead in DeKalb County. The financial strain finally became too much, and with its goal almost in sight, the road folded in 1845 having graded the complete route and having laid rails as far north as Jonesboro.

L. L. Griffin had failed owing to a lack of capital, naive extravagance and perhaps to underestimating the resources, insight and skill of his early competitors. But by 1846, the Monroe Railroad, revitalized with Northern capital and reorganized as the Macon and Western Railroad, made the vital connection in DeKalb. By then, it was clear that General Griffin's dream would come true, but not in Griffin. The General's vision took life 30 miles to the north in the place soon to be called Atlanta. A ruined L. L. Griffin moved to Mississippi where he remade his fortune and died in 1867.

Ironically, many of General Griffin's visions would eventually come true in the city of Griffin after the war, as this rather elaborate depot suggests. Throughout her early history the town pressed for east-west rails (see Table 3.2), and by the mid-1880s Griffin had not one but two rail lines to the west (see Table 3.3). These lines became the key to growth, for they created, at least temporary, a critical intersection for both Atlanta-Columbus and Chattanooga-Columbus rails. This fine depot was completed sometime around 1889 to serve all of Griffin's railroads.

Generally speaking, the larger the depot, the more likely it was to don the trendy clothing of contemporary styles. Here in Griffin was a charming eclectic example. Despite its symmetry, the effect is picturesque indeed. The central octagonal tower and the bell-shaped roof recall the Queen Anne Style. Decorative woodwork abounds in carpenter Gothic array including a scalloped roofline and radiating motifs below the peaks of the six pediments.

Nationally towers had been almost a standard fixture of major American passenger stations since the rather squat square towers of the early Italian Villa Style depots. As the century progressed and the Gothic and the Romanesque became the predominant depot styles, the towers of the grand American railway stations became higher and thinner. By century's end depot towers were evolving back to "short, bulky" forms.[32]

In the large cities of the North and to a lesser degree after the turn of the century in the cities of the South, the urban picture was one of railroad competition and even railroad ego expressed in wildly elaborate railroad stations whose cost often taxed the individual roads to near financial ruin.[33] The effect of all of this on the simple, functional railway depots in rural Georgia was, of course, modest. In the 1880s and 1890s, in rural Georgia, we find only limited humble exuberance expressed in the occasional tower, a few decorative barge boards and other cheap, flowery trim. Generally in this period, the rural, work-a-day architecture of the railroads expressed a utilitarian aesthetic that allowed itself little flamboyant or symbolic expression. There was little need to voice

the promise of Southern rail in elaborate depot architecture, for in these poor, country places, the arrival of the railroad itself was enough to evoke the wild flights of elated fantasy and hope so often expressed in the courthouses of the era.

Plate 3.10: Spalding County Courthouse, built in 1859. Columbus Hughes, architect. David Demarest, builder.

In 1845, when L. L. Griffin lost his prized Monroe Railroad to the panicking creditors of the

GRIFFIN RAILROADS CHARTERED AND NEVER BUILT	Table 3.2
The original plan for what was become the Atlanta and West Point called for the road to run from Covington on the Georgia Railroad via Griffin to LaGrange. Monticello and Griffin Railroad Company, 1852. Griffin, and Madison Railroad Company, 1870. Griffin, Flat Shoals and Columbus Railroad Company, 1872. Griffin and Sandtown Railroad Company, 1872. Griffin Monticello and Madison, 1882 Griffin, LaGrange and Western, 1886 Middle Georgia Interurban RR Company. 1906 Griffin to Social Circle, c. 1906.	

RAILROAD CONNECTIONS AT GRIFFIN IN 1888	Table 3.3
The Monroe Railroad, 1840 (later the Macon and Western Railroad, 1846; part of the Central of Georgia Railroad 1872). Macon to Atlanta. The Savannah, Griffin and Northern Alabama RR, 1871 (part of the Savannah and Western, 1891; operated by the Central of Georgia Railroad). Griffin to Carrollton. Connections to Chattanooga at Newnan on the Chattanooga, Rome and Columbus Railroad, 1888. The Georgia, Midland and Gulf Railroad, 1886 (later the Georgia Midland Railroad). McDonough to Columbus via Griffin.	

[31] Quimby Melton, Jr., *History of Griffin* (Griffin GA: Quimby Melton, Jr., 1959) 7.

[32] Carrol L. V. Meeks, *The Railroad Station* (New Haven: Yale University Press, 1959) 105.

[33] Richards and MacKenzie, *The Railway Station, A Social History*, 37.

Plate 3.10: The 1859 Spalding County Courthouse. An enormous tower crowned the original building. (Photo: Wilber W. Caldwell.)

Monroe Railroad Banking Company, there was no Spalding County. In 1851, on the heels of the city of Griffin's growth, the county was carved from parts of Pike, Henry, Monroe, and Butts Counties with Griffin as its county seat. Despite its whirlwind success, the new county was not quick to build a courthouse. Adiel Sherwood estimated the 1859 population of Griffin at around 3000, and it was in 1859 that this building was completed. Although today it bears the scars and deformations of age and neglect, its details speak to us eloquently of the years immediately preceding the Civil War.

Just coming into vogue in the American South in the late 1850s were designs made popular a decade earlier in the North by Andrew Jackson Downing using the drawings of Alexander Jackson Davis in *Cottage Residences* (1842) and *The Architecture of Country Houses* (1850) and by Samuel Sloan in pattern books like *The Model Architect* (1852). So influential were these early "pattern books" in the unsophisticated adolescence of American building, that elements of the Gothic, the Italian and something vaguely called "bracketed" were hungrily and indiscriminately digested into an evolving vernacular style. Simultaneously, the domestic Italian Villa Style and a more formal commercial Italianate Style were emerging. The new styles incorporated a number of Renaissance elements including various classically inspired window decorations and elaborate supports beneath the eaves in the form of flowery modillions or more commonly heavy brackets. Perhaps not coincidentally one of the premiere Italianate homes in the

country, the William B. Johnston residence (later known as the Hay House), designed by Thomas Thomas of New York, had just been completed in Macon about the same time that the Spalding County Commissioners began to consider a design for a new courthouse. The Italian Renaissance influence here is clear in details like the courtroom windows with their elaborate, segmentally arched or pedimented hood-molds supported by decorative, carved braces. An additional classical feature, popularized by the Italian Villa Style, is the broken base of the pediment. Although of Roman and perhaps Hellenic origin,[34] this device was rare in earlier Southern classically derived styles.

Despite its classical details, the 1859 Spalding County Courthouse is, at least in part, a vernacular building. The original design included a massive central tower whose oversized first stage might be called Greek but for the arched louvered paired openings, and the graceless top stage with its clumsy roof line and dinky lantern. The symmetry of the building's intersecting dormered roof line is identical to many vernacular Georgia courthouses of the era including the 1825 Monroe County Courthouse in nearby Forsyth, the 1829 Troup County Courthouse at LaGrange and the 1835 Campbell County Courthouse at Campbellton. Evolving from courthouses on the square requiring four opposing entrances like the early example at Lexington (1819), the Greek cross-floor plan had become popular in many vernacular brick courthouses of the later era. John Wind's 1858 Thomas County Courthouse at Thomasville and his 1859 Brooks County Courthouse at Quitman were constructed from similar cross-like plans with Italianate details.

The architect, Columbus Hughes, was also the designer of the 1854, primarily Federal Style, Atlanta City Hall / Fulton County Courthouse. We know little of Mr. Hughes's work or his credentials as an architect. The builder was David Demarest of Athens, a man we know to have been familiar with Greek detail, a familiarity apparent in his compelling Mercer Academy Chapel at Penfield (1833), his domestic work in Athens, and his 1849 Greene County Courthouse. Here again we find the skilled craftsman and student of architectural details applying classical ornament to an otherwise vernacular building with pleasing but far from perfect results. Despite its architectural flaws, the 1859 Spalding County Courthouse is somehow a fitting symbol for the rustic character of L. L. Griffin and the first sturdy citizens of Griffin, who toiled not only to build a town in the wilderness, but to create the region's next great city. L. L. Griffin like David Demarest failed and at the same time succeeded. Neither accomplished what he set out to do, but in each case the results were impressive.

The history of Griffin's courthouses supplies excellent example for two themes. First, as we have repeatedly seen, towns along antebellum rails were slow to accept the wild promise implied by postbellum railroads. Surely some towns on old rails, like Madison, Eatonton and Covington, bought into the promise of the New South myth with the appearance of postbellum rails, but most, like Griffin, were slow to celebrate. Although the Spalding County grand jury recommended a new courthouse as early as 1895,[35] the old 1859 courthouse served until 1911.

The second theme exemplified by Griffin's courthouses is one we have yet to encounter. It involves the end of the period of focus for this book, the year 1910. After that year, we see a distinct shift in the look of courthouses in Georgia. They cease to speak in the wild, flamboyant voices of the promise of things to come. After 1910, we encounter not an architecture of the people, but rather an architecture of the government. Even though many of these later designs were fashioned in the same neoclassical mold as those built in the first decade of the century, these later buildings are by comparison, flat, lifeless and common. They appear somehow cheap. Of particular note in this regard is the work of J. J. Baldwin who, beginning in 1914, designed eight courthouses still in use in Georgia today.[36] Although generally in a somewhat Georgian Revival neoclassical mold, none of these buildings communicate much in the way of zeal or pride. Rather they seem quite ordinary and appear to stand only as obligatory clearinghouses for the functions of local government. It is as if the people of Georgia had suddenly accepted the conventional American symbolism attached to the neoclassical

Revival, seemingly knuckling under to the architecture of business—in this case the business of government.

In addition, massive Beaux-Arts courthouses began to appear after 1910. In 1911, Griffin built such a courthouse to replace this 1859 building, which was later converted into a jail. Despite its monumentality, a new rather calculated Beaux-Arts styling speaks not of popular exuberance, but of a stern, formal, governmental power. Far from a joyous manifestation of twentieth century American success, it conveyed mass without energy, ornament without symbolism, and classicism without grace. The building burned in 1981. Similar evidence of this rather clear dividing line is poignantly demonstrated by sub-

Plate 3.10a (Photo: Courtesy of Ted Brooke.)

[34] James S. Ackerman, *Palladio* (New York: Penguin Books, 1966), 43; Rudolph Wittower, *Architectural Principles in the Age of Humanism* (New York: WW Norton & Company, 1962) 53.

[35] *The Manufacturer's Record*, February 8, 1895.

[36] Today J. J. Baldwin-designed courthouses in Georgia can be found in Bleckley (1914), Barrow (1915), Bacon (1919), Atkinson (1920), Treutlen (1920), Candler (1921), Evans (1923) and Liberty (1926) Counties.

Plate 3.11: The 1869 Clayton County Courthouse is among the best standing reminders of seemingly countless brick vernacular court buildings built in so many Georgia counties before the war. (Photo: Wilber W. Caldwell.)

sequent courthouses built in the Beaux-Arts mode of the new century in Tift County (1913), Clarke County (1914), Fulton County (1914) and Walker County (1919), as well as by most of the flimsy Neo-Georgian work of J. J. Baldwin and others. This rule is not without exception. Most notably Alexander Blair's stunning 1916 Murray County Courthouse at Chatsworth voiced a late-arriving, railroad-imported promise of hope to a theretofore remote mountain people.

This text will not indulge in discussions of the architectural details of any of these post-1910 buildings. We pause here only to note the contrast. These buildings represent the beginning of a new era for the South. By 1910, Griffin was a city of almost 7500 people, and the New South, although far from a fully developed reality, had begun to evolve in earnest.

[37] The 1869 Georgia Railroad Depot at Atlanta was an impressive three-story affair (the first story still stands), with a somewhat Federal Style outline and Italian details including rusticated quoining, paired brackets and segmentally arched window headers. Elizabeth Lyon, *Atlanta Architecture, The Victorian Heritage* (Atlanta: Atlanta Historical Society, 1976) 24.

[38] Joseph Henry Hightower Moore, *A History of Clayton County, 1821-1983* (College Park GA: Ancestors Unlimited, Genealogical Society of Clayton County, Georgia, 1983) 40.

[39] Moore, *A History of Clayton County, 1821-1983*, 40.

[40] Moore, *A History of Clayton County, 1821-1983*, 39.

[41] Moore, *A History of Clayton County, 1821-1983*, 39.

With cities and factories and modern ways, came the first realizations of the modern loss of identity and personal style that is reflected in these grim structures. An appropriate, modern architecture would evolve elsewhere to capture the electric spirit of modern times, but not in Griffin—and not in the South for decades to come.

CLAYTON COUNTY: JONESBORO

Plate 3.11: The Clayton County Courthouse, built in 1869. Maxwell V. D. Corput, architect.

Despite its postbellum construction date, the simple brick cube of the 1869 Clayton County Courthouse at Jonesboro is today one of the best standing examples of the simple brick vernacular courthouse form that covered Georgia's public squares in the antebellum period. Here in Jonesboro, we find the fundamental essence of this rudimentary style. With its low, hipped roof, it stands next to the railroad, almost unadorned by ornament save the small paired brackets beneath the eaves and the simple arch of the entrance with its architrave in basic brick relief.

At the same time the vernacular style was thus evolving, trained architects were coming on the scene to erect buildings in codified styles that reflected schooled orders and carried deep-seeded, historical messages. The history of nineteenth century-public architecture in Georgia, as seen in its county courthouses, is a history of the cross breeding of these two architectural forces. Certainly the vernacular shamelessly, and often gracelessly, borrowed elements from disciplined designers, but in nineteenth century Georgia, trained architects also danced to vernacular tunes. Many of Atlanta's mighty masters of the picturesque would pay tribute to these humble brick vernacular buildings.

Although he began his career as a civil engineer, the designer of this building, Maxwell V. D. Corput, was well known in Atlanta for the architectural work of his firm, Corput and Bass. This included the 1869 Georgia Railroad Freight Terminal and the Union Passenger Depot II,[37] a colossal steel train shed completed in 1871. According to Clayton County historian Joseph Moore, Corput went into partnership with Atlanta architect Calvin Fay after the war[38] and designed this building on the very foundation of the first Clayton County Courthouse built in 1861. The earlier building had been burned by Kilpatrick's cavalry in 1864 along with a good part of the rest of Jonesboro. Corput was paid $25 for the design and specifications and 75 cents for his one inspection trip.[39]

That this courthouse still stands unaltered since its construction is a testament to hard times in Jonesboro. As late as 1893, The *Jonesboro News* complained of the unsightly burned-out walls of buildings destroyed during the war.[40] The county history relates that it was widely held in Clayton County before 1900 that, "Jonesboro never really recovered from the war."[41] Ironically we have this economic stagnation to thank for the preservation of the 1869 courthouse. For many years it, like almost everything else in Jonesboro before the turn of the century, remained frozen in time.

Plate 3.12: The Clayton County Courthouse, build in 1898. J. W. Golucke, architect.

By the end of the last decade of the nineteenth century, things had at last begun to show signs of change in Clayton County. Two southbound postbellum railroads passed through the countyçthe Atlanta and Florida and the East Tennessee, Virginia and Georgia—but neither would pass through Jonesboro. Jonesboro's proximity to Atlanta precluded any late nineteenth century growth, but Clayton County suddenly saw her fate hitched to Atlanta's prospects, and that future began to appear promising. Despite the fact that the population of Jonesboro had decreased by twenty percent between 1880 and 1900, by 1898 there was pressure for a new courthouse. After bond issues were defeated in 1896 and 1897, the county finally hired James Wingfield Golucke to design this symbol upon which to hang her dreams of the new prosperity.

The career and the designs of J. W. Golucke speak eloquently to the ten-year period surrounding the turn of the century in Georgia. The state was at last poised to move into the modern period. Although it would be a long slow process, the appearance of men like

Golucke signaled the beginning of the end for the long night of stagnation in the South. In 1890, James Golucke was listed in the Atlanta City Directory as an employee of the Woodward Lumber Company. The next year he was listed as a "architect." This overnight miracle had been made possible in part by the absence of official architectural certification, a condition that most certainly sustained vernacular forms in Georgia well into the twentieth century. But it had also been made possible by Golucke's personal ambition, ability and drive. That the son of an Austrian-born cabinetmaker could suddenly declare himself an architect was one thing. That he could rise to design 26 courthouses in Georgia and countless churches and other public

Plate **3.12:** For years, J. W. Golucke's 1898 eclectic creation in Clayton County was wrapped in a hideous 1962 remodeling leaving only the tower and the rear portions of the building exposed. (Photo: Wilber W. Caldwell.)

buildings in Georgia, Florida and Alabama was quite another.

Golucke's very first courthouses had been completed only three years before: the Johnson County Courthouse at Wrightsville, the Pike County Courthouse at Zebulon and the Emanuel County Courthouse at Swainsboro. Two years later in 1897 Golucke completed perhaps his most important Romanesque building, the Henry County Courthouse in nearby McDonough. Here we see the self-proclaimed architect prove his worth in a stunning building very much in the style of Henry Hobson Richardson. Here was the foundation for J. W. Golucke's Clayton County Courthouse, which was completed a year later at Jonesboro. If at McDonough Golucke had used Richardsonian restraint in his ornamentation, at Jonesboro he attempted to apply a stylish array of elaborately decorative tricks, adorning a fundamentally Romanesque building with rusticated quoining and rows of classical dentals. Repetitions of the scrolling motifs used in Henry County reappear, and twin pedimented bays are replaced with flanking pavilions. Perhaps Golucke too was gripped with the spirit of the Chicago's 1893 Columbian Exposition. Or perhaps he was influenced by Bruce and Morgan's newly completed 1896 Monroe County Courthouse at nearby Forsyth, a building dripping with ornament inspired by the rising tide of turn-of-the-century American Neoclassicism. Whatever the spirit, the results are very un-Richardsonian, and even a bit un-

Romanesque. The building fails to achieve the simple power of Golucke's design at McDonough, nor does it achieve the formal effect and the illusion of importance so well-stated in Bruce and Morgan's design at Forsyth. Nonetheless, this fundamental form with its central tower and flanking corner pavilions, which had first been tried by Golucke in Emanuel County in 1895, would become one of the architect's most popular plans. In subsequent years James Golucke would recreate this basic form in Habersham County at Clarkesville, Madison County at Danielsville, Fannin County at Blue Ridge, Twiggs County at Jeffersonville and in Wayne County at Jesup.

One might conclude from all of this that classical detail is best left to trained architects, and in most cases this axiom will prove serviceable, but in the case of James Wingfield Golucke, it greatly underestimates the man. The Clayton County Courthouse is not without architectural merit. Placed in the context of its time, it speaks well for the pride and the aspirations of the struggling county at the turn of the century. Most importantly, it is a stepping stone for James Wingfield Golucke, who would go on to design a host of neoclassical buildings whose quality was rarely matched in Georgia during this period.

For years, J. W. Golucke's eclectic creation in Clayton County is all but completely wrapped in a hideous 1962 remodeling leaving only the tower and the rear portions of the building exposed. Happily at this writing plans are today underway to demolish the newer building a restore Golucke's original design.

Plate 3.13: The Depot at Jonesboro, built in 1867.

Here we find a third stone depot on the Monroe Railroad to match the antebellum depots at Forsyth and Barnesville. Built in 1867 to replace the wooden depot at Jonesboro which had been burned by Union cavalry in 1864, this building was enlarged in 1910 using stone from the old 1852 depot at Barnesville which had been dismantled in the early years of the new century. Old photographs of this building at Jonesboro show a bold, square, white cupola atop the low hipped roof. The 1852 depot at Barnesville had an identical cupola, and it is not clear whether this decoration was original to the depot at Jonesboro, simply a

Plate 3.13: The 1867 stone depot at Jonesboro recalls the many stone depots of the antebellum era. (Photo: Wilber W. Caldwell.)

copy of the older building, or whether it was added as part of the 1910 enlargement which used materials from the recently demolished Barnesville depot. These old stone depots are rare, and they evoke the prewar era. Five stone depots still stand in Georgia (see Introduction: Table VI)

THE THOMASTON BRANCH:

UPSON COUNTY: THOMASTON

Adiel Sherwood notes in his 1827 *Gazetteer of Georgia* that all of the towns on the west side of the Ocmulgee seemed to spring up from wild and solitary wilderness as if by magic. Thomaston was typical of many robust West Georgia towns, but unlike its neighbors, Thomaston built three antebellum cotton mills. Meanwhile, a group of Upson County investors obtained a charter for the Thomaston and Barnesville Railroad in 1838, but not much was accomplished. For almost twenty years a lot of railroad talking begot a lot of railroad chartering but no railroad building (See Table 3.4). Finally, the Thomaston and Barnesville Railroad was completed in 1857. A "petty line" built by a "struggling company,"[42] the name was changed to the Upson County Railroad after the original company went bankrupt in 1860. The Central of Georgia acquired the sixteen-mile road in 1914.

Upson County was one of those "up by its own boot straps" kind of places. Ambitious and enterprising in her beginnings, after the war the county would languish at the end of this remote spur line until 1891 when the Macon and Birmingham Railroad was completed from Macon to La Grange. Thomaston's present depot, built in 1927,[43] is today a garden supply center, and it speaks not at all to the earlier period. It replaced an older depot all record of which seems to be lost to the ages. The charming little carpenter style depot at Yatesville (see Introduction, Plate 15), built probably around 1895, is about all that stands to recall late nineteenth century railroads in Upson County. It was at Yatesville in 1891 that the Macon and Birmingham on its way to Thomaston and La Grange crossed the Atlanta and Florida on its way to Fort Valley. These late century railroads, along

THOMASTON RAILROADS CHARTERED BUT NEVER BUILT	Table 3.4
1847 The Farmers Railroad: Talbotton to some point on the Macon and Western	
1854 The Thomaston Railroad: Thomaston to Geneva on the Muscogee Railroad (connections to Columbus).	
1854 The Thomaston Railroad: Thomaston to West Point and Milledgeville.	

with the 1899 organization of Thomaston Mills, created enough New South zeal to move Upson County leaders to hire one of the South's best-known architects, Frank Milburn, to design a new courthouse completed at Thomaston in 1908.

Upson County's first courthouse was completed in 1828, and the brick building was replaced by a larger, two-story, vernacular building in 1855. Sometime in the post war period an outrageous tower with a most bizarre, mansard-like roof was added. Only one photograph of this structure survives, and in it the courthouse is largely hidden by trees. Accordingly, it is hard to judge the building other than to say that enough is revealed in the photo to qualify the structure as truly unusual, if not comical. It is doubtless the creation of local builders blundering about in totally unfamiliar stylistic territory. It was replaced by Frank Milburn's neoclassical celebration in 1908.

Plate 3.14: The Upson County Courthouse, built in 1908. Frank Milburn, architect.

Perhaps the most successful architect in the South in the first decades of the twentieth century, Frank Pierce Milburn was born in Bowling Green, Kentucky, in 1868. We know little of his early life except that he attended the University of Arkansas and began the practice of architecture in Louisville, Kentucky, in 1894. Milburn built a large practice in Charlotte and

---

[42] Phillips, *History of Transportation in the Eastern Cotton Belt to 1860,* 272.

[43] *The Georgia Historical Society's Finders Guide to Plans and Maps of the Central of Georgia Railroad in the Georgia Department of Archives and History in Atlanta.*

[44] Lawrence Wodehouse, "Frank Pierce Milburn (1868-1926), A Major Southern Architect", in *The North Carolina Historical Review* 50/3 (July 1973): 289.

Plate 3.14: Frank Pierce Milburn seemed completely comfortable with the new, mixed classical vocabulary, and his 1908 Upson County Courthouse presses smoothly toward Parisian models especially in its ornate tower and strict Renaissance detail. (Photo: Wilber W. Caldwell.)

later in Columbia, South Carolina. Upon accepting the office of architect for the Southern Railway, he moved to Washington, D. C. in 1902, but maintained his Columbia offices, operating as Milburn, Hester and Company. Between 1895 and his death in 1926, he designed over 250 major structures in the South as well as numerous homes.[44] Any survey of the surviving body of his work reveals Frank Milburn to have been a man of his times. He was fluent in seemingly all of the styles of the late nineteenth century. In eclectic flights of imagination he was especially drawn to elements of the Italianate, the Richardsonian Romanesque, the Queen Anne and a rather personal, eclectic interpretation of the Northern European Renaissance Style exemplified in his 1903 Wilkes County Courthouse in Washington, Georgia. Of Milburn's four courthouses in Georgia, the 1903 Wilkes County Courthouse is his only picturesque offering.

Milburn's 1908 Upson County Courthouse was his last in Georgia, and it mirrors earlier neoclassical siblings: the 1903 Wilcox County Courthouse at Abbeville, and the 1905 Lowndes County Courthouse

at Valdosta. All three of these buildings follow the same general classical form that was becoming so familiar on Georgia's squares. The columns of the neo-classical Revival had great appeal in these out-of-the-way places, for they expressed a tempting new economic vision. At the same time, they recalled the misty moss-covered verandahs of the bygone era and the sweet sufferings of the Lost Cause. Milburn, like Golucke, was careful to fashion buildings with grand porticos attached to a rectangular mass in the Georgian mode, thus creating reflections of the cherished antebellum classical or so-called "Southern Colonial" style. Unlike Golucke, Frank Milburn seems to have been completely at home with Beaux-Arts ornament. While Golucke's results are effective, and perhaps even more appropriate, Milburn's work presses more smoothly toward Parisian models especially in his ornate towers and more strict Palladian and Renaissance details.

All three of Milburn's neoclassical court buildings in Georgia are loosely of the Ionic order, and all three employ a light golden brick bonded with dark mortar. It is not the gleaming alabaster magnificence of Chicago's 1893 "White City," but it is a far more classical choice than the ubiquitous Neo-Georgian red brick walls of Milburn's contemporaries. As to whether it is a more appropriate choice—more American or more Southern—it is difficult to say. Some Southerners might voice the opinion that a courthouse is supposed to be fashioned of red brick— one does not go changing such things just because of a bunch of Greek or Italian or (heaven forbid) French high-born ideas emanating from sources as distant as the Renaissance.

A complete list of Frank Milburn's courthouses in other areas of the South is not available. We do know that, in addition to four in Georgia, he designed at least six court buildings in North Carolina, at least two in South Carolina, as well as courthouses in Florida, Oklahoma and Kentucky.[45] Most of these were in the picturesque Eclectic Styles of the last century. It is quite likely that the construction of Milburn's first neoclassical building in Georgia, the elegant Wilcox County Courthouse at Abbeville, 1903, was one of the forces that set in motion the tidal

[45] Wodehouse, "Frank Pierce Milburn (1868-1926), A Major Southern Architect", in *The North Carolina Historical Review*, 289-303.

wave of neoclassical court buildings which was to again cover the state's squares with classical columns— this time symbolizing not John C. Calhoun's myth of the Greek democracy, but the modern clash of the dual mythologies of the Old and New South, a budding industrialism come face to face with a deep-rooted agrarianism.

SOME LAST THOUGHTS ON THE MONROE RAILROAD

The Monroe Railroad is representative of a very early shift in the thinking of railroad builders in Georgia. It began as a simple spur from Macon to the cotton-growing regions around Forsyth. It was designed as Macon's railroad in the same way that the Central was created to serve Savannah, and the Georgia Railroad to serve Augusta. All three roads began chasing cotton, and all three roads altered their focus as soon as the state of Georgia announced its plans to built the Western and Atlantic Railroad from the spot that was soon to become Atlanta to the spot that was soon to become Chattanooga. Without a doubt the prospect of a connection to the west was viewed by all three cities as an opportunity to funnel off the budding riches of the American interior. After the charter of the Western and Atlantic Railroad, it was not just cotton that these cities saw flowing down Georgia's railroads to the sea, it was all of the produce of the newly blooming American heartland.

It is quite clear that the Central quickly grasped the importance of the Monroe Railroad's link from Macon to the Western and Atlantic railhead, just as the Georgia Railroad had reacted to the upstart Middle Branch Railroad's plans to build from Covington to that same spot. It is certainly no coincidence that the Georgia Railroad was quick to strike a deal with the Middle Branch, just as the Central eventually gobbled up the Monroe Railroad's offspring the Macon and Western.

Along the line of the Monroe Railroad and its branch, the courthouses at Macon and Thomaston stand out as notable examples of the lure of postbellum rails and their power to inspire the architecture of hope. The Macon and Augusta and the Macon and

Brunswick Railroads sprouted out from Macon very soon after the end of the fighting, and despite the depth of the economic nightmare that began with the Reconstruction period, Macon had a new Second Empire courthouse by 1872. On the other end of the time line, Thomaston languished at the end of an insignificant antebellum spur line until the Macon and Birmingham Railroad arrived in the 1890s to inspire the county to employ the neoclassical fantasies of Frank Milburn a decade and a half later. Jonesboro finally began to feel the lure of the myth after the turn of the century, perhaps on her proximity to the Atlanta and Florida Railroad in the 1890s, but more likely on the proximity to the explosion that was the city of Atlanta.

Here on the Monroe Railroad, we also encounter two notable exceptions to the developing courthouse—depot pattern. Forsyth supplied an exception to the sobering influence of antebellum rails when the town built a celebration of progress in 1896 despite the fact that no postbellum rails had arrived to serve the wine of economic promise. On the other hand Griffin, the wild vision of a railroad dreamer, had resisted the lure of the myth of postbellum rails despite the town's success and the arrival of three different lines in the 1880s. When Griffin finally built her new courthouse in 1911, it would sing dirges of governmental formality not waltzes of economic fantasy.

L. L. Griffin's vision of a Southern city at the junction of the state's early railroads was indeed

Plate 3.15: Griffin. (Photo: Wilber W. Caldwel.)

prophetic, but in 1836, Lewis L. Griffin was not the only man in Georgia with such a vision. What Griffin failed to realize was that the location of that future great city was irrevocably set as soon as the Western and Atlantic's zero mile stake was driven into the ground near Standing Peachtree in DeKalb County. From then on, seemingly all roads would either converge on that point, or radiate outward from it. The Central of Georgia Railroad's connection between the future city of Atlanta and the city of Savannah was completed in 1846 by the Monroe Railroad's heir, the Macon and Western. The year before the Georgia Railroad had arrived at the same spot to complete its link to Augusta and to Charleston. It was a spot that was all about trade with the West. It had been a very long time in Georgia since a major event had not been all about cotton, and it would be a long time before another such event would occur.

•

4 | The Western and Atlantic Railroad

THE MAIN LINE: ATLANTA TO CHATTANOOGA

FULTON COUNTY: ATLANTA, PART 1

The Western and Atlantic Passenger Depot at Atlanta, built in 1853, burned in 1864. E. A. Vincent, architect. (See Introduction, Plate 11).

For most Georgians, images of Atlanta before the incendiaries in 1864 center on the Western and Atlantic Railroad's enormous train shed. Completed in the same year that Fulton County was created, the great depot at Atlanta spoke for a new kind of city. Atlanta had grown from a dusty, temporary railroad camp in 1840 to a bustling town of over 3500 by 1852 when this depot was ordered by Western and Atlantic Superintendent William Wadley. "Wadley appears to be grading off the whole of DeKalb County for his new depot," was the reaction of one Georgia Railroad engineer.[1] In demanding a structure of this size Wadley, a former superintendent and later president of the Central of Georgia Railroad, must have had a grand vision for both the city and the railroad. His 1852 "Report to the Governor of Georgia" contained the following regarding the new depot and other buildings then under construction on the line: "All of these improvements will be substantial in character—such, I flatter myself as will prove to be, not only useful ornaments to the Road, but monuments to the Enterprise and Liberality of the People of Georgia."[2]

---

[1] Fredrick C. Alms, quoted in James Michael Russell, *Atlanta, 1847-1890, City Building in the Old and New South* (Baton Rouge LA: Louisiana State University Press, 1988) 33.

[2] William Wadley, *Report of the Superintendent and Treasurer of The Western and Atlantic Railroad to his Excellency Howell Cobb* (Atlanta: Ware's Book and Job Office, 1852) 12.

The Western and Atlantic Railroad

THE MAIN LINE

Fulton County: Atlanta, Part One (also see chapters 11, 26 & 32) • Cobb County: Marietta • Bartow County: Cartersville • Gordon County: Calhoun Whitfield County: Dalton • Catoosa County: Ringgold

THE ROME RAILROAD

Floyd County: Rome • Some Final Thoughts on the Western and Atlantic Railroad

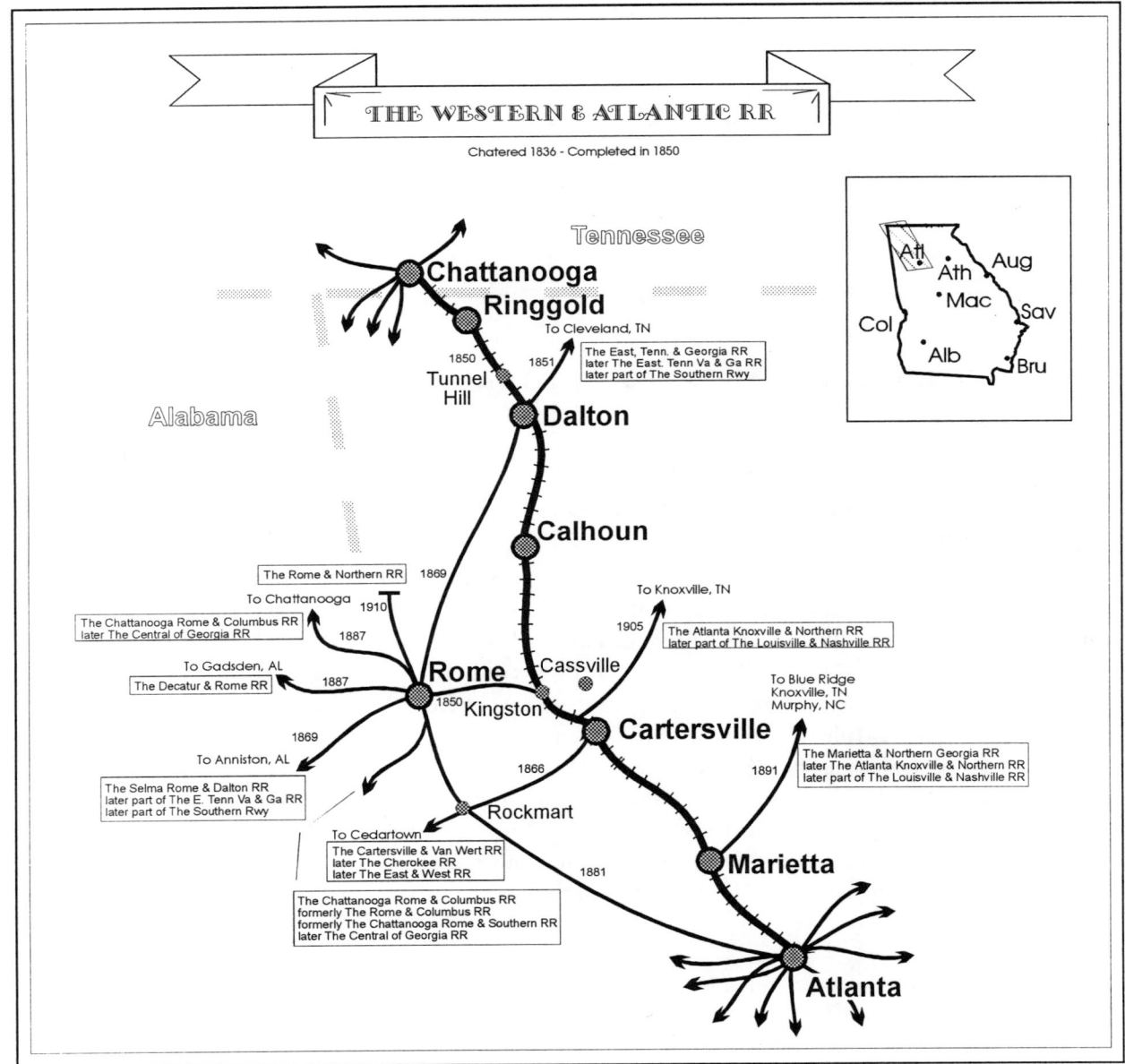

In a testament to the futility of monument building and a mockery of Wadley's fine words, William Tecumseh Sherman reduced this depot to ashes in 1864.

Of the architect, E. A. Vincent, we know little except that he came to Atlanta from England in the early 1850s and that he created a map of Savannah and one of the first maps of Atlanta.[3] Although Vincent was more likely an engineer than an architect, no structure could have spoken more eloquently for the new city than his purely utilitarian passenger depot. Here we find the liberal architecture of the Industrial Revolution blooming in cotton's conservative garden. To many Southerners, this building may have looked like a weed, but to the ambitious, citizens of Atlanta, it was surely an exotic flower.

Eighteen years earlier in 1836, the charter of the Western and Atlantic Railroad had been the culmination of a series of events going all the way back to the canal building schemes of the 1820s. For more than a decade the career of Wilson Lumpkin would represent the state's path from wilderness to transportation keystone. In 1826, Georgia's newly formed Board of Public Works selected Lumpkin to inspect the northwestern portion of the state. Lumpkin's tour was part of the investigation directed by the English-born engineer, Hamilton Fulton. Both men were investigating the feasibility of a canal system in Georgia to link principle waterways and to create a water route from the Oconee or the Ocmulgee to the Tennessee River. Both men eventually concluded that canals were not advisable in the state's northern mountains, and both cautiously suggested railroads as the solution.

In the fall of 1826, Wilson Lumpkin was elected to Congress, and at his own request he was appointed to the Committee for Indian Affairs. In 1827, he introduced the first legislation for the removal of the Cherokee. Lumpkin's bill did not pass, but in 1828 gold was discovered near Dahlonega, and in 1831 Lumpkin was elected governor of Georgia. By 1833, all of the Cherokee lands had been surveyed, divided and

assigned to white settlers in a lottery. The transparent legal proceedings that produced the 1835 Treaty of New Echota were followed by the charter of the Western and Atlantic Railroad and the infamous Trail of Tears. By 1838 the Cherokee were gone from Georgia.

Meanwhile, Governor Lumpkin had been assaulted by the promoters of western lines seeking a Southern connection. Foremost among these was E. P. Gaines's Atlantic and Mississippi Railroad planned from Memphis to Charleston via Athens. A second plan centered on the Charleston and Cincinnati Railroad, which also sought connection via Athens. Indeed spirits in Athens ran quite high for a brief time, but Governor Lumpkin withheld state support of either scheme and neither the Memphis nor the Cincinnati roads were built. Lumpkin's vision all along had been for a coordinated, statewide system of rails from the coast to the Piedmont with a centralized western connection feeding many branches. He rightly feared the uncooperative, competitive individualism of the state's infant railroads that were pawns of Augusta and Savannah.

The 1836 Railroad Convention at Macon brought together representatives of all of Georgia's railroads and resulted in a petition brought before the state legislature for a state-supported railroad to the west. Calling for a single line from the central Piedmont to the Tennessee River, the recommendation of the Macon Convention resembled the findings of Lumpkin's 1826 Board of Public Works. It was agreed in Macon in 1836 that, if the state would build such a road, privately funded extensions from its railhead would connect to the Georgia Railroad at Madison, the Central via the Monroe Railroad at Forsyth, as well as to Milledgeville and Columbus. When the act creating the Western and Atlantic was signed in December of 1836 only a few men could have guessed its

[3] Elizabeth Anne Mack Lyon, *Atlanta Architecture, The Victorian Heritage* (Atlanta: Atlanta Historical Society, 1976) 12.

Plate 4.1: The 1854 Fulton County Courthouse. The choice of the Federal Style seems to have purposely ignored the raging emotionalism of the controversy that gripped the county in the years preceding the Civil War. (Photo: Courtesy of The Atlanta History Center.)

importance. Surely Wilson Lumpkin was among them.

True to the recommendations of the 1836 Macon Railroad Convention, the Western and Atlantic's original charter called for the southern railhead to be at "the point on the Southeastern bank of the Chattahoochee River most eligible for the running of branch roads, thence to Athens, Madison, Milledgeville, Forsyth, Columbus." An amendment of the charter in 1837 authorized the extension of the terminating point 8 miles from the riverbank. Even though the original charter had authorized locating the railhead anywhere along a 70 mile stretch of the Chattahoochee from Hall County to Campbell County, the choice of the site had been obvious—the summit of a gentle ridge sloping up from the river with a grade of only

[4] Webb B. Garrison, *The Legacy of Atlanta* (Atlanta: Peachtree Publishing, 1987) 9-10.

[5] Russell, *Atlanta, 1847-1890, City Building in the Old South and New*, 11.

[6] Russell, *Atlanta, 1847-1890, City Building in the Old South and New*, 34.

[7] Russell, *Atlanta, 1847-1890, City Building in the Old South and New*, 32.

[8] Russell, *Atlanta, 1847-1890, City Building in the Old South and New*, 49.

285 feet in eight miles. The zero milepost was located amid rolling farmland. The remote and lonely place was called simply, "Terminus."

In 1843, there had been eight families living near "Terminus." To honor Lumpkin's daughter, the name was changed to Marthasville in that year.[4] By 1845, the place was incorporated and christened Atlanta, and by 1860 the city lay at the junction of four railroads and had a population of almost 10,000. Indeed Atlanta had grown, and this colossal depot had sprung up at its heart.

Plate 4.1: The Fulton County Courthouse and Atlanta City Hall, built in 1854, demolished in 1885. Columbus Hughes, architect.

Atlanta was not totally lost to the flames of 1864. Most probably Sherman had planned to torch only railroad buildings, warehouses, factories, and the like, but in a city of closely packed wooden buildings the uncontrolled spread of fire was inevitable, and surely little effort was made to prevent it. Still a sizable portion of the town survived, including the 1854 Fulton County Courthouse, which was located on the site of the present Georgia State Capitol Building.

This building's design is instructive for what it was not. It was not Greek Revival, and thus was not a symbol of mid-nineteenth century Southern agrarian imperialism. Like the 1821 Richmond County Courthouse at Augusta, the design of the first Fulton County Courthouse is reminiscent of American architecture in the first decades after independence, and the simplicity of its style recalls the work of Charles Bulfinch. The choice of the Federal Style seems to purposefully ignore the raging emotionalism of the controversy which gripped the country in the years preceding the Civil War, and this anachronism now appears disarmingly innocent, especially in light of the great and violent drama which was about to unfold in Atlanta.

As this courthouse suggests, in many ways Atlanta has always been a most un-Southern city. The image of the place as a progressive island in the midst of a stagnant Southern sea remains compelling. If the myth of the New South came true anywhere in the final decades of the last century, it was in Atlanta. From her very beginnings in the mid-1840s, Atlanta was a place apart from the rest of Georgia, and she developed with a spirit and a character all her own. Even before Sherman rendered the symbol of the Phoenix appropriate, Atlanta grew in an almost magical way. In truth, the city did not put the mythical bird on her official seal until 1887.[5] Atlanta's original city seal pictured a steam locomotive. All things considered, the steam engine was perhaps a more fitting metaphor. Only in myths can birds (or cities) magically rise from their own ashes. In the real world it takes work and money and steel. The New South may have been a myth in most of Georgia, but in Atlanta, where the spirit of the new age prevailed, it could hardly have been more real.

Atlanta's indomitable spirit is better proved by the tenacity and zeal of the city's postbellum promotional efforts than by the physical rebuilding after the fires of war. This spirit made Atlantans natural apostles of the New South Creed, and while the rest of Georgia sulked in self-pity and festered with bitterness, Atlanta shamelessly promoted herself.

In Atlanta, the seeds of this zeal had been planted at the junction of four antebellum railroads, and a modern crop had been blooming long before Sherman arrived. James Russell's *Atlanta, 1847-1890, City Building in the Old and New* paints a vivid picture of antebellum Atlanta and its unique breed of citizen. Russell points to the dominance of the middle class, the relatively small slave population, and the typical citizen who tended to be both vocationally and geographically mobile. Atlanta's spirit was driven by economic and business motives that tended to disassociate the city from the plantation South. A sizable "Yankee" presence before the war tended to set the stage for the post-war term "Georgia Yankees" which was used in rural Georgia to refer to Atlantans after the city became domi-

nant. Little wonder that Northerners before and after the war felt at home in Atlanta and were often uncomfortable in the rest of Georgia.

Atlanta's commercial and perhaps even "Yankee" character put the city at odds with the rest of the state on a number of issues. The most notable of these conflicts centered on the railroads. As we have seen, the Central was the tool of Savannah and the Georgia Railroad of Augusta and ultimately of Charleston. With the completion of the Western and Atlantic, Atlanta's interest lay across the path of both seaports and their railroads. The city's early history is a tale of continuing battles with the railroads over discriminatory rates and schedules,[6] as well as clashes regarding the physical encroachment of rails and roadbeds on Atlanta's ability to plan, grow and handle the overflow of traffic generated by success.[7] Differences grew and feelings ran deep. According to Russell, Atlantans of the 1850s saw their city as "a citadel of upcountry enterprise assailed by the 'unprogressive' lowland South."[8] Thus, it is no great surprise to find that, when Fulton County was carved from DeKalb in 1853, Atlanta's leaders spurned the columns of Old South solidarity. The architect, Columbus Hughes, also designed the 1859 Spalding County Courthouse in a rather rudimentary rendering of the so-called Italianate Style. Hughes's inspiration for Fulton County's first courthouse may have flowed from the work of John Boutell, one of the first professional architects to practice in Atlanta. Boutwell came to Atlanta from Massachusetts in 1852 and completed a remarkably similar building, the Atlanta Medical College, in the same year that Hughes's courthouse was accepted by the county. Both of these buildings rose from two-story, Federal Style designs featuring hipped roofs, octagonal cupolas and high balustrades above broad cornices. Hughes's courthouse features elegant brick detailing in the form of raised, rusticated quoining and staggered brick coursing creating a stone-like banding on the lower story.

Considering the South's passion for the Greek Revival, it might seem surprising, that Fulton County built a Federal Style courthouse only five years before Bull Run. And ironically not three years after Appomattox, when the state capitol was move from Milledgeville to Atlanta, this Federal Style building briefly served as the capitol building of the state of Georgia.[9] But as soon as the first state legislative session was held at Atlanta, it became clear that a much larger structure was needed. It was then that the notorious scheme to lease the new Kimball Opera House to the state was born.

The chain of events that left the enormous state House at Milledgeville empty in 1868, and crammed all of the machinery of Georgia's Reconstruction Military government into this tiny courthouse has many links. Certainly the referendum that called for Georgia's Reconstruction Constitutional Convention had been boycotted by enormous numbers of bitter, demoralized, white voters in every corner of the state. Certainly General Pope and his staff felt more welcome among the patronizing merchants of Atlanta, and preferred a state capitol close to their headquarters in that city. Certainly the new Carpetbagger Governor of Georgia, Rufus Bullock, wanted no part of the hostile intransigence and cold shoulders waiting for him in Milledgeville or Macon. But most certainly of all, the mobile, opportunistic citizens of Atlanta had jumped at the chance to steal the prize. In truth, the other cities of Georgia were pinned, not beneath the weight of defeat, but beneath the horrible weight of their own history. Atlanta, for all practical purposes, had no history. Where the rest of Georgia saw the ignominy of collaboration, Atlantans saw only opportunity.

COBB COUNTY: MARIETTA

Cobb County was carved from the enormity of Cherokee County in 1832 and Marietta was laid out as the county seat in the following year.

A crude log courthouse was built, and a frame court building replaced it in 1838.

In 1842, only four years after Marietta's frame court building was completed, the first train from Terminus to Marietta made the journey powered by the steam locomotive Florida, which had been transported sixty miles overland behind a sixteen mule team from the Georgia Railroad railhead at Madison. In 1850, the first train ran the complete route of the Western and Atlantic from Atlanta to Chattanooga. In the interim, Marietta prospered. The completion of the Western and Atlantic bolstered hopes and added fuel to the fires, which inspired Cobb to erect a grand Greek Revival courthouse in 1852. Other fires burned as well. The early 1850s had seen railroad schemes abound. The Marietta and Northern Georgia Railroad, although not consturcted until after the war, chartered in 1853, to consolidate the plans of the Marietta, Canton and Ellijay Railroad Company, formerly the Ellijay Railroad.

By all accounts, the 1852, Greek Revival Cobb County Courthouse at Marietta was a grand affair. Here we find what has called the "peripteral style" (columned porticos without pediment on all four sides.)[10] Beginning in the 1830s and gaining popularity throughout the 1840s and 1850s, this style, primarily employed in domestic architecture, took upcountry Georgia by storm. The "peripteral" Greek Revival manor house has become the stereotype for the "Southern Mansion." And indeed it should be, stunning houses of this style covered the Georgia countryside, and abundant examples can still be seen in Macon, Athens, Madison, Washington, Milledgeville and elsewhere. Many late 1850s remodelings of older Greek homes added porticos and columns[11] to surround Southern planters with their own personal adaptations of the Greek Revival. Where qualified architects or designers were not to be found, a "carpenter Greek" style produced a sometimes crude, sometimes charming, marriage of Greek and vernacular wooden forms. Well into the twentieth century, Georgians were fitting columned porticos onto old farmhouses and painting them white, a kind of instant architecture, often producing less than graceful results.

If a few columns were good, then an overdose was all the better. Perhaps the Southern planter's zeal for John C. Calhoun's clever distortions of the Greek Democracy inspired him to add columns until, in his regional patriotic fervor, he had "out-Greeked" even the Greeks. A number of local histories, including one in Marietta, conclude that this style is derivative of the Parthenon. It is more likely that the "peripteral" phenomenon was simply a natural growth of the practical side of architecture. Talbot Hamlin has suggested that the style developed as a combination of the porticos of the Greek Revival, and the high, airy porches of the planter's houses of the Caribbean,[12] where to create afternoon shade and to catch a little breeze was architecturally as important as all of the historical symbolism in the world.

Whatever the origin of its surrounding porticos, the 1852 Cobb County Courthouse spoke eloquently for the Old South. It is surely no coincidence that the "peripteral style" was developed primarily in domestic architecture. This leads to a compelling theme. In so many of these rural places, the quest for an appropriate style for the county's central and most visible symbol, its courthouse, had led Georgians to forsake the overblown monumentality of state and national governmental models, and aspire to a more personal statement of local pride and self-esteem. To these people it was indeed a court house. Time after time before 1910, we see Georgia courthouses built in the mold of fine local homes. Their styles were first Greek Revival, and later Queen Anne, which was the residential rage in the 1880s and 1890s. After 1900 the Neoclassical Revival inspired scores of Georgia's finest homes and most of the state's courthouses.

This domestic, personal side of the state's public architecture is certainly part of the reason there were so few Second Empire and Beaux-Arts

Style courthouses built in Georgia during this period. It is also undoubtedly part of the reason the full force of the Richardsonian Romanesque was not seen in Georgia's court buildings the way it was in other states. Although Richardson's powerful influence would be felt in Georgia, it was the simple shapes and symbols of the Romanesque that had appeal here, not the bold, new, industrial vision that the rest of the country was attaching to the designs of Henry Hobson Richardson. In much of the South, the pure Richardsonian Romanesque was not only seen as Northern and as overly monumental, but as bureaucratic and even (heaven forbid) modern. For Georgians a courthouse, like a grand home, needed a degree of monumentality and pomp, but only within the bounds of a soft, personal and most of all Southern temperance.

Marietta's 1853 temple of justice was built of brick on the north corner lot adjacent to the square, which was left an open park after the removal of the 1838 frame structure. The columns, and perhaps the outer walls of the building, were stuccoed white, and a graceful double arched stairway ascended to the second story court room entrance. The building reflected not only the Southern solidarity of cotton and slaves and the attendant agrarian ideal, but in Marietta it stood for substantial growth as well. George White in his 1849 *Statistics of Georgia* notes that "since 1848 more than sixty houses have been built."

By the time General Sherman arrived in 1864, Marietta was no stranger to fire. The town had experienced devastating fires in 1854, '55 and '57. But on November 13, 1864, only four days after Sherman's standing field orders

[9] Garrison, *The Legacy of Atlanta*, 37.

[10] Henry Russell Hitchcock, *Architecture–The Nineteenth and Twentieth Centuries* (1958; reprint, New Haven and London: Yale University Press, 1977) 23-142.

[11] G. E. Kidder Smith, *The Architecture of the United States, The South and Midwest*, 3 vols. (Camden City NJ: Anchor Books, 1981) 2:126-7.

[12] Talbot Hamlin, *The Greek Revival in America* (1944; reprint, New York: Dover Publications, 1964) 204.

restricting the destruction of private property were issued, Union troops burned not only the depot and warehouses, but over seventy-five other buildings in Marietta.[13] The courthouse was not spared. There is considerable documentation that Sherman himself, along with other Union officers, was appalled by the malicious burning at Marietta, but were unable to put a stop to it. Major Henry Hitchcock, a member of Sherman's staff, records in his diary that originally guards were posted to prevent unauthorized burning and vandalism, but when the guards "left with the column," much destruction followed despite active efforts by Union officers to extinguish the flames. Hitchcock's diary relates that Kilpatrick's aide, Major Rea, had personally attempted to save the courthouse. He "had three times put it out and tried hard to save it; but was kindled in the lathes under the plaster and 'twas no use."[14] The next morning Marietta was in ruin, and all that remained on the north corner

of the square were the blackened remnants of a few once stately columns.

Plate 4.2: The Cobb County Courthouse, built in 1872. William Hunt, architect.

The charred columns of the 1853 Cobb County Courthouse would stand for eight years as solemn reminders of a South that was no more. That the county would go so long without a courthouse is a testament to hard times. That a new one would be built as early as 1872 is testament to the economic resilience of the upcountry Piedmont. All of rural Georgia would lie in the grip of poverty and stagnation for decades following the war, but the towns along the Western and Atlantic and its branches were quicker to rebound than those farther to the south. Marietta, Cartersville, Rome and Dalton would all know a modicum of post-war prosperity not generally found in the rest of the state. This is evidence of the vitality of the western rail artery and the physical connection to Atlanta. These upcountry Georgians were less burdened by the myth of the Old South, and thus better able to believe in a new myth. By 1870, Marietta had resurrected the charter of the Marietta and Northern Georgia Railway, which had been conceived way back in 1854, and which was now planned all the way to Murphy, North Carolina. By the end of the decade, Marietta had a population of around 2500 with one of the largest flour mills in the state, a chair factory, paper mill, planing mill and tannery. To make way for a new courthouse, the blackened columns of the old courthouse were finally torn down in 1872. An article in the Marietta Journal seized on the image: "And thus, one by one, 'Sherman's sentinels' left in blackness on his March to the Sea, are disappearing, and out of this wreck of war, Phoenix-like, spring new and handsome buildings."[15]

This courthouse, built in the wake of the hopes generated by the Marietta and Northern Georgia Railway, was a charming mixture of two primary antebellum architectural forces: the

Plate 4.2: Despite post-war good fortune and ambitious aspirations in Marietta, the 1872 Cobb County Courthouse was far too early for any manifestation of the new hopeful styles to follow.

brick vernacular cube with its Federal Style underpinning, and the Greek Revival. Despite post-war good fortune and ambitious aspirations in Marietta, 1872 was far too early for any manifestation of the new styles to follow, for it was years too early for the new myth. No myth of a New South was afoot in 1872, and even the name "New South" did not come into widespread use until later in the decade.[16] Accordingly the architecture of the Old myth was still the popular choice. William Hunt, who is credited with the design, was probably a local builder. Apart from the clock tower, the building is strongly reminiscent of the work of Robert Mills in South Carolina fifty years earlier: a high second story set atop a low first, with a pedimented portico supported by four columns resting on a base of powerful masonry arches.[17] The main body of the building, however, recalls the simple lines of the two-story, brick vernacular with its hipped roof, and high arched second story windows.

Plate 4.3: The Cobb County Courthouse, remodeled in 1899, demolished in 1959. J. W. Golucke, architect.

Having almost doubled its 1880 population by the turn of the century, Marietta had grown into a town of almost 4500 persons. A knitting mill and a foundry had been added to the town's list of manufacturing concerns, and a handful of new railroads had been chartered. The Marietta and Alpharetta in 1884, the Marietta and Austell in 1885, the Carrollton, Marietta and Western in 1887 and the Marietta, Dahlonega and Northern in 1889, all created high spirits, speculation and hope although no rails were laid. In 1890, the Marietta and Northern Georgia Railroad joined the Knoxville and Southern at the Tennessee line north of Blue Ridge to connect Marietta with Knoxville in the fulfillment one of the earliest antebellum railroad dreams. Although the line declared bankruptcy in 1891, it was born again as the Atlanta, Knoxville and Northern Railroad in 1895. In 1898, the

Plate 4.3: James Golucke's 1899 rendering of the remodeled Cobb County Courthouse. (Illustration: *The Marietta Journal*, June 29, 1899.)

Western and Atlantic built a stylish brick depot just one block off the square in Marietta, and by 1899, riding a peak of railroad euphoria while bemoaning the inadequacies of the 1872 court building, three successive grand juries had recommended a new courthouse.

Despite her considerable success, Marietta's dreams of railroads, industry and growth were not so wild that they warranted a completely new courthouse, but they were sufficient to rad-

[13] From a list compiled by Enoch Faw quoted in Sarah Blackwell Gober Temple, *The First Hundred Years* (Atlanta: Walter W. Brown, 1935) 373.

[14] The personal diary of Major Henry Hitchcock, Nov. 13, 1864, quoted in Sarah Blackwell Gober Temple, *The First Hundred Years*, 354.

[15] *The Marietta Journal*, May 31, 1872, quoted in Sarah Blackwell Gober Temple, *The First Hundred Years*, 404.

[16] Paul M. Gaston, *The New South Creed, A Study of Southern Mythmaking* (Baton Rouge LA: Louisiana State University Press, 1970) 32. Gaston's study contends that the phrase "The New South" first appeared in 1872 in Edwin DeLeon's "The New South: What It is Doing, and What It Wants" which appeared in *Putnam's Magazine* in 1872, but that the term did come into general use until after 1874.

[17] Mills's South Carolina courthouses in this general style include his designs at Greenville, York, Orangeburg, Union, Horry, and Darlington.

Plate 4.4: The depot at Marietta. Despite the impending tidal wave of Neoclassicism, the Picturesque was still very much a central current in American railroad architecture in 1898. (Photo: Wilber W. Caldwell.)

ically enhance the town's self-image and to create enthusiasm enough to completely rebuild the old building. In truth, the renovation was so extensive, especially with regard to the exterior styling that it was a remodeling in name only. J. W. Golucke's design called for a completely new Romanesque façade, a grand clock tower and a large addition to the rear of the building. This, along with a Richardsonian "facelift" on the sides, resulted in an old structure effectively encased in a new one.

Here at Marietta, we find Golucke's most purely Richardsonian effort in Georgia. This was the Atlanta architect's fourth Romanesque effort (see Appendix C), and it owes much to H. H. Richardson's celebrated Allegheny County Courthouse in Pittsburgh, arguably the dominant Romanesque, American court building of the era. Richardson's influence on Golucke's design at Marietta is unmistakable. The thin verticality of the tower with its soft tourelles and its slot-like linteled windows; the window groupings offset by the large arched openings pointing to the major interior spaces; the polychrome accomplished here by white marble architraves and other marble details against a ubiquitous background of red brick are all distinctly Richardsonian elements. As are the pedimented dormers in the French Renaissance Style, even

the columnettes supporting the triple arched entrance.

Alas this was Marietta, not Pittsburgh, and J. W. Golucke, remarkable as he may have been, was no Henry Hobson Richardson. Part of the appeal of Richardson's buildings comes from a sense of mass and power born of function. The ornament, although rich, rarely calls attention to itself, and only exists in careful and correct support of the whole. In this regard, Golucke sadly missed the mark in Marietta. The flat walls press the decoration upon the beholder, and the contrast of white marble against ordinary brick lacks the rich subtlety of Richardson's favored textured, rough-hewn, rosy granite and rich, dark stone. Richardson's buildings appear to be single-minded expressions of a complete thought. Golucke's Cobb County Courthouse appears complicated. The master's vocabulary is here, but the building babbles in a language not fully understood.

Nonetheless, the 1899 remodeling of the Cobb County Courthouse spoke well for Marietta at the turn of the century, and all of Georgia is the poorer for its destruction in 1959. This building told a story of a county that was just beginning to ponder thoughts of a new prosperity.

Plate 4.4: The Western and Atlantic Depot at Marietta, built in 1898.

Here in Marietta, we find one of the finest late nineteenth century depots still standing in Georgia. Despite the impending tidal wave of Neoclassicism that swept across the county just before the turn of the century, the Picturesque was still very much a central current in American railroad architecture in 1898. The architect of this little depot brought the sweet waters of the Northern European Renaissance to humble Marietta. The stepped gables and the stepped parapet terminating one side of the roof recall the charm of the Netherlands and of Renaissance Flanders. The 1890s had seen a modest Northern Renaissance Revival in London characterized by the architecture of Earnest George and Harold Peto, and in the domestic designs of Grayson and Ould.[18] Some small ripples of this influence had crossed the Atlantic and even trickled South, as we can see here and in the examples of Frank Milburn's 1903 Wilkes County Courthouse in Washington, Georgia, and Lorenzo Wheeler's 1886 Randolph County Courthouse.

At Marietta we see a variation on the usual pattern of depot and courthouse. Generally the expectations created by the prospect of even the humblest of postbellum depots sparked the mythological fires that resulted in some of Georgia's most fantastic courthouses. In some places, however, the myth of the New South proved not altogether mythical. By the 1890s, a few of the towns on the Western and Atlantic—Marietta, Cartersville, Rome and Dalton for example—began to lay the footings upon which they would build the foundations of real economic success. Here we find not just the knee-jerk reaction of "humble depot inspires lofty courthouse," but a pattern in which quality depots and monumental court buildings evolved simultaneously. This fine depot was completed just as ground was broken for Golucke's monumental courthouse.

But in Marietta, as elsewhere on the Western and Atlantic, the prosperity that had been achieved existed in the midst of a sea of poverty and ignorance. Flourishing alongside the New South myth, the Lost Cause remained a very present ideal in Marietta. The year J. W. Golucke's grand courthouse was completed, census figures confirmed the fact that Cobb County was still operating on a fundamentally agrarian base and ranked a respectable 30th amongst Georgia's 137 counties in cotton production. The streets on the square in front of this courthouse were not paved until 1912, twelve years after Golucke's new courthouse was erected. In 1915, the dark shadows surrounding the lynching of Leo Frank in Cobb County would long remind the world that, even if the mind of Marietta was beginning

Plate 4.5: The 1873 Bartow County Courthouse is a rare standing example of a postbellum brick vernacular courthouse in Georgia. (Photo: Wilber W. Caldwell.)

to comprehend a New South, the heart of the place was still very much a part of the Old.

BARTOW COUNTY: CARTERSVILLE

Plate 4.5: The Bartow County Courthouse, built 1869. Fay and Corput, architects.

Cass County, as Bartow County was originally called, was created from Cherokee County in 1832, and the county town of Cassville was laid out the next year. In his *The History of Old Cassville, 1833-1866*, Joseph Mahan describes the first Cass County Courthouse built in 1836 as "a rectangular, two-story, brick structure with large double doors opening on each of the four sides."[19] In 1837, Adiel Sherwood describes this courthouse at Cassville as "one of the most elegant in the state." By 1850, according to George White, the town had three churches, a male and female academy, two hotels, seven stores, and a population of 800 to 900. Some historians speculate that Cassville was the largest town in Northwestern Georgia before the Western and Atlantic Railroad was built.

---

[18]   James Stephens Curl, *Victorian Architecture* (London: David and Charles, 1990) 124-27 and 175-77.

[19]   Joseph B. Mahan, Jr., *The History of Old Cassville, 1833-1866* (1950; reprint, Cartersville GA: n.p., 1994) 14.

Legend and lore surround the disappearance of Cassville, but it is no legend that Sherman burned the place to the ground in 1864. A local story blames this arson on the Federal reaction to the changing of the county's name to Bartow. This change had occurred in 1861 not so much in celebration of the heroics of martyred Confederate General, Francis S. Bartow, but in reaction to the fact that in that year Lewis Cass, for whom the county had originally been named, changed his mind about slavery, deciding it was wrong.

The truth of the matter is that Cassville and Canton were singled out for destruction by Sherman's orders. The continued presence of Confederate scouts in and around Cassville had finally led to the death of ten federal stragglers in Cassville on October 11th.[20] On October 30, 1864, Sherman ordered Cassville burned in reaction to this incident and to other Confederate guerrilla activity in the area.

This was not the first bit of bad luck to befall Bartow County's original county town. Over twenty years earlier, the survey of the Western and Atlantic bypassed Cassville. This resulted in related the usual myth: "…the citizens of Cassville did not want their town demoralized— nor their horses frightened—by having the railroad through town."[21] Additional local lore warrants that the chief engineer in charge of the survey demanded too much of a bribe to bring the road through Cassville. This is unlikely.[22] The truth is that the route of the state-owned railroad was surveyed by way of what is now Cartersville simply because Cassville was geographically inconvenient. This is borne out by the fact that Cassville later petitioned the state to build a branch to Cassville, but the resulting legislation called for the citizens of Cassville to pay for the line. The grading proved surprisingly expensive, and the idea died.[23] From the beginning, the route through the valley of the Etowah River passing about two miles from Cassville at Cass Station had been the obvious natural path.

After the war, a movement arose to locate the new county seat by the old stone depot at Cass Station. Before the idea was brought to a vote, Cartersville, which had prospered on this railroad from its beginning, offered to build a courthouse in exchange for the county seat. By all accounts, the 1867 election was a hot one, and the results of the record turnout were Cass Station 919, Cartersville 1085. Fay and Corput's 1869 courthouse at Cartersville is the fulfillment of Cartersville's pledge.

When the Western and Atlantic Railroad was begun, Cartersville was hardly a place at all. In 1850, when the first train ran the complete route from Atlanta to Chattanooga, George White placed the population of Cartersville at about 150 with four or five stores, a hotel and the impressive Cooper and Wyley Iron Works only 4 or 5 miles away employing 300 to 400 workers. The following decade saw growth. Although Cartersville, like Cassville, experienced Sherman's destructive fires, the town was quick to recover, garnering the seat of county government in 1867. By the time this courthouse was finished, Cartersville teemed with almost 2500 residents, many of whom had moved from Cassville which remains today an empty place populated primarily by legends and historical ghosts.

The years have not been kind to this building, but one can still be thankful for the structure's survival. It remains a fine example of a postbellum Italianate courthouse.

Plate 4.6: The Bartow County Courthouse, built in 1902-1903. J. W. Golucke, architect.

The year 1903 was one of unprecedented achievement for James Wingfield Golucke. Having begun designing courthouses in the Romanesque style, his experiment with neoclassical ornament in the 1898 Clayton County Courthouse at Jonesboro had led to three designs in the new Beaux Arts mode: Chambers County, Alabama, 1899, Calhoun County, Alabama, 1900, and Tattnall County Georgia,

1902. His early work employing the idioms of a distinctly Southern interpretation of the Neoclassical Revival began about the same time with the DeKalb County Courthouse at Decatur, 1900, and the Hart County Courthouse at Hartwell, 1902. The 1903 Bartow County Courthouse in Cartersville represents the emergence of Golucke's mature neoclassical courthouse style. In all, James Golucke designed six courthouses in Georgia based on this familiar plan (see Appendix C).

Here we find Golucke's favored four-sided Greek cross floor plan with porticos and entrances at all four points of the compass. Corinthian columns support simple entablatures with brick friezes. True to Corinthian order, the pediments are trimmed with both modillions and dentals beneath the eaves. The enormous clock tower displays Renaissance ornament like the broken based pediments that frame the openings and decorate the tower base. The fenestration is straight, linteled and simple, almost severe, like Golucke's Eatonton courthouse, but without the star patterned panes and the elaborate keystoning. Despite its Roman and Renaissance trim, the building relies on the Greek post and lentil form to articulate its fundamental organizing system. The façade is segmented by basic, brick pilasters with austere capitals, and there is little decoration beyond the portico, the tower and the masonry keystones above the second floor windows. This is truly a building for both the Old South and the New. Neoclassical elements and the enormous tower are true to the style of the day and seem to point to a modern future, but not far beneath the surface, strict Georgian simplicity, horizontal massing and red brick recall the work of Thomas Jefferson. This imagery was clear in the speeches of the prominent men of Bartow on January 12, 1903, when the courthouse was dedicated. Judge A. M. Foute's remarks were to this point: "...massive columns of the Corinthian order°lending a grace and beauty to the superstructure as enduring as the solid stone in which

Plate 4.6: The 1903 Bartow County Courthouse in Cartersville represents the emergence of James Golucke's mature Neoclassical Courthouse Style. (Photo: Wilber W. Caldwell.)

they are chiseled. These happily remind us of the old south, the dear old south, with her splendid homes and luxurious appointments of antebellum times."[24] Thus for Southerners in 1903, what may have appeared au currant to the rest of the country, spoke emotionally of the precious Lost Cause and other sad and cumbersome regional myths.

[20] Mahan, Jr., *The History of Old Cassville, 1833-1866.*

[21] Lucy Josephine Cunyus, *The History of Bartow County, Formerly Cass* (Cartersville GA: Tribune Publishing, 1933) 20.

[22] Mahan, Jr., *The History of Old Cassville, 1833-1866*, 34.

[23] Cunyus, *The History of Bartow County, Formerly Cass*, 20.

[24] *The Cartersville News and Courant* (Cartersville GA), January 15, 1903.

Local histories inform readers that the reason for the new courthouse was that the old one was too close to the railroad, and that the noise of the trains became so disruptive that trials were interrupted.[25] Here is another colorful, local story, and perhaps one with a grain of truth, but there was surely more motivation for James W. Golucke's Bartow County architectural commission than just a noisy courtroom. By 1900, Cartersville was a railroad junction town of over three thousand residents. There can be little doubt that the myth of the New South had taken root here.

As Cartersville's new courthouse rose in 1903, the Atlanta, Knoxville and Northern was at work on a new line leaving the Western and Atlantic near Cartersville at Junta, and passing through Gordon and Murray Counties and into Tennessee. The new line from Cartersville to Knoxville, Tennessee would be straighter and the grade less steep than Marietta's old Marietta and North Georgia Railroad. For Cartersville it must have seemed the fulfillment of a railroad dream that went back to antebellum times.

Cartersville had a rich, if not illustrious railroading history. After the completion of the Western and Atlantic in 1850, Cartersville had seen a number of railroad schemes come and go, beginning with an 1857 proposal for a road westward to Jacksonville, Alabama, and culminating in the odyssey of the Cartersville and Van Wert Railroad chartered in 1866. This road, which proposed to connect with Van Wert, the old Paulding County seat near Rockmart, was a microcosm of all the railroad swindles and boondoggles that flowed from the corruption of Radical Reconstruction. Controversy centered on the state's guarantee of railroad bonds issued by the Cartersville and Van Wert, which in 1870

became the Cherokee Railroad with that notable scoundrel/promoter, Hannibal I. Kimball, at the helm. At one time or another, Kimball was president of four railroads that received state assistance. A close confidant of Rufus Bullock, the unscrupulous governor of Georgia until 1871, Kimball fabricated several notoriously boldfaced and shameless railroad schemes. His Cherokee Railroad had built only a few miles out from Cartersville when it defaulted in 1871. It was sold in 1878 for $29,500 although it had received illegal state-endorsed bonds in the amount of $575,000,[26] while no private funds had even been paid in.[27] The Cartersville and Van Wert later became the property of the Cherokee Iron Company and was completed through Cedartown to the Alabama line. In 1882, it was leased to the East and West Railroad of Alabama. It became part of the Seaboard in 1902.

In 1886, Cartersville saw the charter of the Cartersville and Gainesville Air Line which became the Cartersville, Gainesville and Port Royal Railroad in 1891, and the Cartersville, Gainesville, Augusta and Charleston in that same year. All of this renaming failed to grease the proper financial gears, and no track was ever laid. Nonetheless, in the first years of the new century, Cartersville prospered at the junction of the Western and Atlantic and the Seaboard Air Line's branch to Alabama, while a new line directly to Knoxville was just over the horizon. It must have seemed high time for a new courthouse, and the man of the hour was James Wingfield Golucke, the self-taught, self-proclaimed master of public architecture.

Plate 4.7: The depot at Cartersville, built 1854, remodeled 1902.

The 1854 Western and Atlantic depot at Cartersville was one of several depots that William Wadley built in his brief but productive tenure as superintendent of the state-owned road. A number of depots on this line survived the harsh events of 1864 owing in part to the fact

[25] Cunyus, *The History of Bartow County, Formerly Cass*, 119.

[26] Peter S. McGuire, "The Railroads of Georgia, 1860-1880," *The Georgia Historical Quarterly* 16/3 (1932): 211.

[27] McGuire, "The Railroads of Georgia, 1860-1880," 200.

[28] *The Cartersville News and Courant* (Cartersville GA), April 24, 1902.

Plate 4.7: This depot at Cartersville, although remodeled and modified several times, still incorporates some of the 1854 brick walls. (Photo: Wilber W, Caldwell.)

that, once captured, the Western and Atlantic became Sherman's main supply line. This depot, although remodeled and modified several times, still incorporates some of the original brick walls. These ancient walls of locally fired brick are easily distinguishable from the hard, modern brick walls of twentieth century renovations and additions. The most notable alteration took place in 1902 and drastically changed the look of the building, adding the present high roofline and contemporary fenestration. In Cartersville, as in Marietta, we see the stones of a modern economic foundation being laid around the turn of the century, and as in Marietta, we find here a simultaneous emergence of depot and courthouse. As if to dramatically drive the point home, *The Cartersville News and Courant* for Thursday, April 24, 1902, features two headlines: "The Ceremonies for Today, Laying of Corner Stone for New Courthouse" and "Dirt Broken for New Depot."[28]

GORDON COUNTY: CALHOUN

Plate 4.8: The depot at Calhoun, built 1854.

At Tunnel Hill north of Dalton, the Western and Atlantic's only tunnel was finally completed in 1849, and the dream of western connection was at last approaching reality. The first train

from Atlanta to Chattanooga made the journey in 1850. In the years following the road's completion, three new counties were created along the line. Gordon County was cut from Cass, Murray and Floyd Counties in 1850, Whitfield County from Murray in 1851, and Catoosa County from Murray and Walker in 1853.

Despite the impact of the Western and Atlantic, northwest Georgia was still a very wild place in 1850. Compelling evidence of this is found in the fact that in that year the newly created Gordon County contained virtually no towns. Two crude hamlets came to vie for the title of county seat. One of these, a place called Center or Big Spring, was a full eight miles from the railroad. The other, Oothcaloga Station was selected, surveyed and laid out as the town of Calhoun. A brick courthouse was built the next year.

The choice of county and town names here is telling. In Georgia, in 1850, there could not have been two more impactful lives to revere. William Washington Gordon had supplied the driving force behind the Central of Georgia Railroad, and was perhaps the single most influential petitioner to the state legislature for the charter of the Western and Atlantic. South Carolina's John Caldwell Calhoun, the clearest and most eloquent voice of Southern agrarianism had forged a solid political philosophy that upheld the cause of minority rights in the face of

Plate 4.8: The depot at Calhoun, built 1854. One of five surviving antebellum brick depots in Georgia. (Photo: Wilber W. Caldwell.)

the unchecked juggernaut of the numerical majority. Both men were born in the eighteenth century into the Southern plantation aristocracy; both were educated in the North (Calhoun at Yale and Gordon at West Point), and both had recently died (Gordon in 1842 and Calhoun in March of 1850). Most of all, both men were in their own ways slaves to cotton. Gordon sought restore the fortunes of Savannah by bringing cotton from the interior of Georgia to that city's wharves. Calhoun sought to redefine the underlying principles of American democracy by bringing the nation's political philosophy in line with social and economic realities of slavery.

Calhoun and Gordon County chose well their namesakes, and by the end of 1850, the new county town had over 150 residents.[29] In 1854, the Western and Atlantic completed this fine brick depot, which stands today as one of five surviving antebellum brick depots in Georgia.

Plate 4.9: The Gordon County Courthouse, built in 1889, demolished in 1960. William Parkins, architect.

On March 15, 1888, the Gordon County grand jury found the original 1851 courthouse to be in good condition, recommending repairs to the roof and improvements to the privies.[30] Five days later a tornado touched down in Calhoun destroying a significant portion of the town. By most accounts the courthouse was destroyed. A closer examination of the situation reveals that indeed the courthouse was damaged, but not beyond repair. An initial survey of the damage published in *The Calhoun Times* suggested a new courthouse, but went on to say that repairs to the old building would probably cost only "one or two thousand dollars."[31] On April 12th, *The Times* reported that an architect from Atlanta had been engaged to assess the damage and make recommendations. That architect was William Parkins. Parkins was not only arguably Atlanta's most noted architect, but in 1888 he was fresh from his association with

perhaps the ablest New South promoter of all, the notorious Hannibal I. Kimball. There can be little doubt that Parkins, himself a Northerner, was an able and convincing spokesman for a New South brand of progress, and in Calhoun he must have found a receptive audience.

In 1888, with a population of only about 600, Calhoun lagged behind her sisters on the Western and Atlantic. Marietta, Cartersville and Dalton all were at least six times her size, and all had postbellum crossing rail lines. Surely the citizens of Calhoun were quick to seize on the hopes created by rumored plans for the extension of the Fort Payne and Eastern Railroad via Calhoun to connect with the Atlanta and Charlotte Air Line at Gainesville.[32] At the same time, additional hope was being generated by speculation surrounding the planned route of the Augusta and Chattanooga, as we read of the town's disappointment a year later in *The Times*: "...the Augusta and Chattanooga Railroad will be built by Ducktown, Tenn., and thence to Chattanooga. Calhoun's chances for this road grow...less with each rumor of its construction."[33]

Thus, railroad schemes surrounded Calhoun in 1888. Parkins's visit in April of that year surely stoked burning hopes for progress, and by May the fat was unquestionably in the fire as *The Times* held up the challenge of neighboring Pickens County with its plans for a new courthouse at Jasper on the Marietta and Northern Georgia: "Pickens County let the contract to build a $13,000 courthouse. If our mountain sister can build at that figure, Gordon can easily build one at $20,000."[34] Here again we see evidence of the effect of buildings in neighboring counties. In this period, again and again a competitive interaction proved potent with regard to both the initial motivations to build new courthouses and the selection of architectural styles.

The name William Parkins is connected to a number of courthouses in Georgia, and often the connection came by way of association with other architects. A close look at the work of

Plate 4.9: In 1889, William Parkins's Gordon County Courthouse brought the Picturesque to rural Georgia, as if the modern, eclectic styling of a new courthouse could lift a town up out of the economic doldrums and anoint it with the healing balms of the New South. (Photo: Courtesy of Georgia Dept. of Archives and History.)

Alexander Bruce in Tennessee, where he practiced before joining Parkins in Atlanta, leads to the conclusion that the Parkins and Bruce's court buildings at Sparta, (1882) and Atlanta, (1883) are primarily the work of Bruce, although Parkins probably had a hand in the Fulton County building. Similarly, with the firm Kimball, Wheeler and Parkins it appears that Parkins was part of the design team for the 1887 Oglethorpe County Courthouse at Lexington, but the firm's other Georgia court building, the 1886 Randolph County Courthouse at Cuthbert, appears to be primarily the work of Lorenzo Wheeler.

There is, however, a body of work that reflects the talent of William Parkins alone, including some of Atlanta's finest buildings of the period: the Church of the Immaculate Conception (1873); the Kimball Opera House (1869, later remodeled as the Capitol Building of the state of Georgia, burned 1893); the first Kimball House Hotel (1870, burned 1883); and the John James House (1869, later Atlanta's first Governor's Mansion, demolished 1924). Sadly, only the Church of the Immaculate Conception still stands today, and thus the 1960 demolition of Parkins's Gordon County Courthouse

deprived the people of Georgia of one more of the precious few William Parkins buildings left. Fortunately two excellent Parkins courthouses are still in use: the Dooly County Courthouse at Vienna, 1890, and the wildly eclectic Terrell County Courthouse in Dawson, 1892. Both of these buildings share numerous stylistic motifs with the Gordon County court building including stepped parapets and similar fenestration.

Parkins may not have been a great American Master, but his buildings symbolized the New South as he dreamed it, and he was one of a handful of architects in Georgia to design commercial buildings that unabashedly voiced the High Victorian styles of the day, incorporating imaginatively eclectic combinations and even elements of Gothic ornament into secular buildings. His picturesque designs for courthouses were far more eclectic than those of his former junior partners Bruce and Morgan.

In Gordon County, Parkins's approach is primarily Romanesque. The obligatory tower rises above large arched entrances, and the central portion of the façade, with its arcade, echoes the arches of the tower above. Henry Hobson Richardson's sublime 1888 Allegheny County Courthouse at Pittsburgh might have tempted most other followers of Richardson to frame corners in Romanesque pavilions with pyramidal roofs, but Parkins waxed free. Still, the circular bay of a staircase and stair-stepped fenestration continue in the Romanesque Revival tradition as do the small paned windows beneath the arcade and in the second story of the tower. The side elevations of the building suggest the Queen Anne Style in silhouette with hints of Northern European Renaissance in the stepped parapets

[29] Lucie Pitts, *History of Gordon County* (Calhoun GA: Press of the Calhoun Times, 1933) 17.

[30] *The Calhoun Times*, March 15, 1888.

[31] *The Calhoun Times*, March 29, 1888.

[32] *The Calhoun Times*, Feb. 6, 1890.

[33] *The Calhoun Times*, Feb. 28, 1889.

[34] *The Calhoun Times*, May 31, 1888.

framed by high chimneys. This is a complicated building which rambles a bit, but with considerable appeal.

The devastating cyclone of 1888 was no ill wind. It blew William Parkins to Gordon County and along with him, a few of the bricks of the dream of prosperity. Parkins's design for Gordon County is the prescription of a prophet of the New South. Here, as at Lexington, Cuthbert, Vienna, Cedartown and Dawson, Parkins brought the Picturesque to rural Georgia. Perhaps some believed that the modern, eclectic styling could lift a town up out of the economic doldrums of the postbellum South, and anoint these yokels with the healing balms of the industrial revolution.

This building is all the more remarkable in the face of Gordon County's strong Populist politics of the 1890s. Georgia's Populists bristled at the idea of a New South and at the flimsy promotions of its railroads. This is one a very few court buildings erected in Populist Counties. By 1900, the streets of Calhoun were lined with new brick buildings. By 1910, the town had a cotton mill and had more than doubled its 1888 population. Still, crossing rails never came to Gordon County, and the progress of a handful of brick buildings and a cotton mill to exploit cheap labor was a far cry from the flamboyantly aggressive New South that William Parkins had ventured to sell.

WHITFIELD COUNTY: DALTON

Plate 4.10: The depot at Dalton, built in 1852.

Dalton was already booming in 1851 when William Wadley became superintendent of the newly completed Western and Atlantic Railroad. In that same year, Whitfield County was created from parts of Murray, Cass and Floyd Counties, and with some financial support from the Georgia Railroad, the East Tennessee and Georgia Railroad completed track connecting Dalton with Loudon, Tennessee, on the way to Knoxville. The effect of the two railroads on the

new county seat of Dalton was electric. One local account contends that Dalton's population grew from 300 to over 1500 the year the railroad was completed.[35] While this is probably something of an exaggeration, it points to the fact of remarkable growth, as does the 1852 report of Superintendent Wadley to Governor Cobb:

> At Dalton it was found necessary to have increased accommodations for our passenger business: accordingly I have purchased a site, which is now being graded, preparatory to the laying of tracks and the erection of a suitable house. It is proposed to build upon such a scale as will accommodate the East-Tennessee and Georgia Road as well as our own.[36]

This depot reflected the town's success and signified the importance of the railroad, for as in so many towns born of the railroad, the depot was used to mark the exact center of the town, and "town limits" were measured in a circle with a depot benchmark as its focus. Of all of the antebellum depots still standing in Georgia, this is perhaps the finest. It is still a simple, rectangular box, yet details like the elegant paired brackets contrast with the coarse look of late 1860s and early 1870s Railroad Style depots on the Central of Georgia and the Southwestern Railroad. The Classical lines of the doorways suggest a sophistication unknown in early depots in the rest of the state.

Two years before Wadley's letter to Governor Cobb, George White had written of Dalton's prosperity in his *Statistics of the State of Georgia* declaring it: "the market town for large portions of Eastern Tennessee, Western North Carolina, and Northern Georgia…immense quantities of produce are hauled here by wagon." White goes on to describe Dalton in 1849 as a town with 3 or 4 hotels, 18 stores, 10 or 12 carpenters, 3 brick layers, a candle factory, a candy manufacturer, 3 lawyers, 14 doctors and its own newspaper.

Despite considerable war damage, the town's post-war resurgence was swift. In 1869, the Selma, Rome and Dalton Railroad was completed, and Dalton had her third line. This road, originally chartered in 1854 as the Dalton and Gadsden Railroad (later the Dalton and Jacksonville Railroad) became part of the East Tennessee, Virginia and Georgia system in 1881. By 1882, Dalton's population was above 3000, and *The Official Whitfield County History* lists an assortment of manufacturing endeavors: a flour mill, an ax handle factory, a planing mill, a furniture factory, a cotton press, two gins, several saw mills, and a meat packer.[37] A list like this is typical of this period in the South. On the surface, we might assume a prosperity born of entrepreneurial spirit, and to an extent this is a correct assessment, but there is a pattern here which belies real industrial progress. All of these "industries" arise either from an agricultural base or are exploitive of an abundant natural resource, in this case timber. We find only the processing of that which was locally at hand, and little of the complex process by which diverse raw materials are collected, refined and fashioned by labor and capital into products for far-flung distribution and mass consumption. Most of Georgia would follow this pattern for decades.

In the 1880s, a few of the more progressive places began to manufacture cotton textiles and thus cracked open the door to the industrial era, but only a slender shaft of the true light of the modern age would shine in. Dalton was such a place. In 1885, the town celebrated the opening of the Crown Cotton Mill. Much ado is made about the emergence of mills like Crown at Dalton. Indeed, most were locally financed and profitable, and most grew. Many gave birth to the idea that the bounties of the modern era were at hand, but this was not to be. The beginning of the drama of cotton textile manufacturing in Georgia, especially the creation of the very coarse varieties of cloth first produced in the state, was a far cry from a grand entrance onto the stage of American industry. It required workers of the

Plate 4.10: The 1854 depot at Dalton marked the center of town. (Photo: Wilber W. Caldwell.)

lowest skill levels, and placed them and their families on hopeless treadmills of low wages, long hours and sometimes ruthless exploitation. It might have been a start toward a New South, but in most ways it was a poor one, for at its heart this industrial revolution was, to use the words of W. J. Cash, "only a revolution in tactics." For Cash, the motivation behind the glossy rhetoric of the New South promoters was not a new South at all, but the Old South with new and more powerful weapons: "...what the New South meant and boasted of was mainly a South which would be new in this: that it would be so rich and powerful that it might rest serene in its

[35] Walter S. Bogle in the *Daily Citizen News* (Dalton GA), n.d.

[36] Wadley, *Report of the Superintendent of The Western and Atlantic Railroad to his Excellency Howell Cobb*, 12.

[37] Whitfield County History Commission, *Official History of Whitfield County* (Dalton GA: Whitfield County History Commission, 1936) 79-80.

ancient positions, forever impregnable."[38] It was an odd sort of progress that emerged with such a backward focus.

Plate 4.11: The Whitfield County Courthouse, built in 1892, demolished in 1960. W. Chamberlain, architects.

Dalton is typical of the handful of towns that experienced some semblance of economic growth immediately after the war. Certainly other towns on the Western and Atlantic and its branch are in this group including Marietta, Cartersville, and Rome, as well as Augusta, Columbus, Americus and a few others on other early roads. Here we find an early embrace of the New South Creed and a formidable, although transparent, form of boosterism fashioned after that shown by Atlanta, but somehow less convincing.

Plate 4.11: The 1892 Whitfield County Courthouse bridges the gap between vernacular and professionally designed architecture. (Photo: Courtesy of Ted Brooke.)

[38] W. J. Cash, *The Mind of the South* (1941; reprint, New York: Vintage Books,

1991) 184.

[39] *The Dalton Argus*, March 29, 1890.

[40] *The Dalton Argus*, March 1, 1890.

[41] *The Dalton Argus*, May 17, 1890.

[42] *The Dalton Argus*, November 29, 1890.

[43] *The Dalton Argus*, April 25, 1891.

Not surprisingly, much of this civic propaganda centered around the railroads, and often the target audience for these promotions was not potential investors and businessmen so much as the railroads themselves. An 1890 clip from *The Dalton Argus* speaks to the point as it urged the construction of additional mills. "There is a special need for cooperative activity of Dalton people right now. During the year the W & A will pass into new hands. First appearances have an impressive effect upon strangers. Dalton wants to meet the new managers, on first introduction, in full harness, head up and tail over dashboard. We must impress the new company..."[39]

Similarly, using the railroads as a focal point, *The Argus* had argued for a new courthouse in an editorial appearing a few weeks earlier. In it we again find evidence of a basic connection between depot and courthouse. "The county is without public debt, in good financial condition, and a decent courthouse should be built without further delay. The railroad manipulations of the past few years have entirely changed the [pliaze] of future prospects. The E.T.V. & G. is now, with a few movements to be accomplished, the mogul of the Southern transportation system as it relates to Georgia."[40]

Here we have come to the heart of the matter: that the depot, and all that it stood for, sparked expectations so bold as to demand an architecture of hope, not only here in Dalton, but in places where the economic realities of the postbellum South were far less promising.

Certainly there was more that just the East Tennessee, Virginia and Georgia's power and the Nashville, Chattanooga and St. Louis's lease of the Western and Atlantic to lure Daltonians into the sort of railroad-mania that led to courthouse building. Other railroad schemes abounded, but little came of it all (see Table 4.1).

Nonetheless, the momentum created by the speculation surrounding these ill-fated railroads induced dreams of a powerful Dalton at the center of a tangle of steel rails. This was enough to move the county commissioners to call for plans for a new court building in May of 1890.[41] There is no clue to how the design selection process proceeded. There is only a brief mention in *The Argus* on November 29 that "a most imposing plan of structure had been selected,"[42] and the announcement of the letting of the contract to build in April of the next year.[43] But if we look at the later work of the architectural firm W. Chamberlain and Company of Knoxville, Tennessee, we find compelling similarities to Dalton's 1890 monument to her dreams. Chamberlin's Berrien County Courthouse in Nashville, Georgia, (1898) and his Macon County Courthouse in Oglethorpe (1894) share rather fundamental details with the Dalton court building. Most notable are the square corner pavilions with their pyramidal caps and the distinctive, if not attractive, brick banding in the second story of these pavilions. A closer examination reveals similar brick detail accenting the window headers and other common details. The resemblances here are not mere similarities of style but of architectural plan, and there can be little doubt that the 1891 Whitfield County Courthouse is the work of the same designer who created the plans for Nashville and Oglethorpe.

One of the many restrictions placed upon architects creating buildings to be erected in rural areas was the necessity to design something within the capabilities of local masons and carpenters. The ability of these artisans to handle precise classical proportion and elaborate Renaissance decoration was very much in question. Thus the choice of brick and the Romanesque Revival Style was a natural. Similarly, a distinguishing characteristic of Walter Chamberlin's style is that he borrowed directly from the brick vernacular of the day. Buildings like this one and its sisters at Oglethorpe and Nashville, as well as Lewis Goodrich's courthouses at Sylvania and Crawfordville, are examples of architects taking a cue from the vernacular brick masonry forms of

DALTON RAILROADS CHARTERED BUT NEVER BUILT	Table 4.1
The Dalton & Morganton RR,. 1876	
The Georgia Northern RR (Dalton to Pickens Co.), 1889	
The Augusta & Chattanooga RR, 1888	
The Dalton & Spring Place RR, 1890	
The Stevenson, Sandhill & Dalton RR, 1890	
The Savannah, Augusta & Northern RR, 1901	
The Dalton & Alaculsey R, 1902	

the day and incorporating that type of decoration into simple buildings for simple folk. The results are aesthetically questionable, but remarkably appropriate. Whether this is designing down to the skill of the work force or to the tastes of the customer, is a question whose answer we can only guess. Perhaps it was simply the style that Chamberlain and Goodrich knew and preferred.

CATOOSA COUNTY: RINGGOLD

Plate 4.12: The depot at Ringgold, built c. 1849.

Of the ten antebellum depots still standing in Georgia, this is the oldest (see Introduction Table VI). In the late 1840s, while the tunnel at Tunnel Hill was under construction, The Western and Atlantic contracted for grading, track work, depots and bridges between Dalton

Plate 4.12: The depot at Ringgold. Of the ten antebellum depots still standing in Georgia, this is the oldest. (Photo: Wilber W. Caldwell.)

Plate 4.13: The 1856 Catoosa County Courthouse. Local legend contends that Sherman spared this courthouse in 1864 because it housed the Masonic Lodge.

Plate 4.13: The Catoosa County Courthouse, built in 1856. Demolished in 1939.

Not every town along the line of the Western and Atlantic Railroad came to embrace the myth of the New South. Ringgold, situated in a narrow gap between ridgelines, knew no postbellum crossing rails and experienced little growth. The town's population was listed as 319 in the 1870 census and 398 in 1910. With no hope of a postbellum railroad, Ringgold stood in marked contrast to Dalton, Cartersville and Marietta. As for the Catoosa County Courthouse, the predictable pattern held. In use, almost from the county's inception in 1854, until 1939, this courthouse attests to the town's economic stagnancy, and its basic vernacular lines softly speak of hard times.

Ringgold began its life as a town in 1847, the railroad arrived in 1848, Catoosa County was split off from Murray and Walker in 1854, and this courthouse was built in 1856. After that not much changed in Ringgold for the better part of a century. This simple structure is typical of a generation of spacious but plain court buildings built in so many out-of-the-way places in Georgia in the middle part of the nineteenth century. Its style was subservient to its function, and only the wide cornice and bold splayed window lintels suggest decoration.

The Catoosa County Courthouse was originally designed by the builder as a two-story affair, but with the addition of the third story, we find a familiar tale. As with the 1849 Greene County Courthouse at Greensboro, the Masons here made a pact with the county to add the extra floor for use as a lodge. The local legend contends that Sherman spared this courthouse because it housed the Masonic Lodge. This story is not unique. In the recorded histories of many Georgia counties we read of Masonic connections that reportedly saved buildings from Sherman's torch. These stories generally hold that Sherman and many of his officers were Masons and thus bound to an ideal of universal, humanistic brotherhood, a bond that often tran-

and Chattanooga. By inference, this depot is assumed to have been part of that construction order, and since the contract specified that the work be complete before December of 1849, that date is given to this depot. The building bears the visible signs of extensive Civil War damage, and repairs and stone patches are still obvious today.

These scarred stone walls stand at the very turning point of the war. In September of 1863, the South won a great victory only a few miles away at Chickamauga. But Southern leaders failed to press their advantage, and only two months after Chickamauga the Union army broke out of Chattanooga in heroic actions at Missionary Ridge and Lookout Mountain. Ringgold was the scene of a fierce delaying action in which Confederate rear guard forces engaged the pursuing Federal Army. The following May, Sherman began the long march down the line of the Western and Atlantic Railroad to Atlanta. Beginning with the Atlanta campaign and Sherman's subsequent march to the sea, the war suddenly took on an un-glorious complexion. This was the beginning of a new kind of war, a long, slow struggle to strip the South of its will to fight, characterized not by heroics on the battlefield, but by insidious campaigns designed to destroy the South's ability to make war. Thus, this depot and the tiny Battle of Ringgold are balanced on the cusp of modern military history.

scended Federal and Rebel causes alike. Again and again we are told of a Masonic sign or handshake or pleas made on Masonic oaths softening the hearts of Federal officers. Some stories relate that this tactic succeeded where entreaties by the clergy or even women and children failed. Whatever the case, here in Ringgold we are confronted with the same tale: that Sherman ordered the courthouse spared when he heard that it housed the Masonic Lodge. The story continues that he ordered the return of all Masonic property stolen by Union soldiers from the third floor of this building.

There is perhaps truth in many of these tales, but it must also be noted that along the Western and Atlantic on the march to Atlanta, just as along the Central on the march to the sea, the usual Federal pattern was to protect the courthouses, not to burn them. The record shows that on the way to Atlanta, only the courthouses at Cassville, Canton, and Marietta were destroyed. The first two were burned in reprisal for overt rebel guerrilla activity in these towns. The courthouse at Marietta was burned by stragglers despite valiant efforts by Union officers to save it. As we have seen, Sherman's record on the march to the sea was even less brutal: four courthouses were burned owing to rebel activities, and 16 courthouses were spared.[44] It is of note here that, only the Clayton County Courthouse was burned during a cavalry raid in the fighting surrounding the Battle of Atlanta, while the Fulton County Courthouse was left standing amid Atlanta's ashes.

THE ROME BRANCH

FLOYD COUNTY: ROME

Plate 4.14: Floyd County Courthouse, built in 1835. Demolished in 1892.

All of northwest Georgia was included in the enormous Cherokee County, which was chartered in 1832, three years before the Treaty of New Echota officially stripped the Indians of their heritage. Floyd County was split off from

Plate 4.14: The 1835 Floyd County Courthouse was demolished in 1892.

Cherokee almost immediately. A log courthouse was built at Livingston, the original county seat, but when Rome was founded in 1834, where the Coosa River begins at the confluence of the Etowah and the Oostanaula Rivers, it became clear that this place would be the region's hub. This brick courthouse was built in 1835 and remained in use until 1892. Unlike most early court buildings in Georgia, which were financed by the selling of lots in newly designated county towns, this building was paid for by donations solicited from the early citizens of Rome.[45] Apparently Rome was founded by speculators. The four men, who created the town, drawing the name from a hat, were men of business. Rome was laid out for trade and grew in that mold. From the earliest histories we read of little but ferries and bridges and river traffic. Like Macon, Rome flourished in her first decade.

In 1848, as the Western and Atlantic was nearing completion, insightful businessmen in Rome, who had been sorely disappointed that the road had not been surveyed through Rome in the first place, built the sixteen mile long Memphis Branch Railroad connecting Rome with the Western and Atlantic at Kingston. This

[44] A summary of courthouses burned and spared on the march to the sea appears in the Milledgeville section of Chapter 2.

[45] George M. Battey, *A History of Rome and Floyd County* (Atlanta: Webb, 1922) 38.

Table 4.2

RAILROAD CONNECTIONS AT ROME, 1890

The Rome Railroad (formerly the Memphis Branch RR, 1848), Rome to Kingston to connect with the Western and Atlantic

The East Tennessee, Virginia and Georgia Railroad (The Blue Mountain Line), (formerly the Georgia Southern Railroad) (formerly the Selma Rome and Dalton Railroad) (later part of the Southern Railway), Rome to Selma, Alabama, Rome to Dalton—Rome to Atlanta.

The Chattanooga, Rome and Columbus Railroad, (formerly the Rome and Carrollton Railroad 1887,) (later the Chattanooga, Rome and Southern Railroad; the Savannah & Western Railroad and the Central of Georgia). Chattanooga to Columbus via Carrollton

The Rome and Decatur Railroad, 1887, (later part of the East Tennessee, Virginia and Georgia Railroad)

The Rome Northern Railroad, 1910. Abandoned 1927.

line was built with some financial backing from the Georgia Railroad, which at the time was investing in "feeder" lines from the west. Notable among these were the East Tennessee and Georgia, the Nashville and Chattanooga and the Atlanta and LaGrange.[46] The original charter of 1838 had created the Memphis Branch Railroad and Steamship Company, and although the name was changed to the Rome Railroad in 1850, the original name is telling. As we have seen, a western rail connection to the Mississippi River through northern Alabama had been the dream of Georgians almost from the beginning, and the citizens of Rome, like those of Calhoun, Dalton, Marietta, Athens, Gainesville and, of course, Atlanta sought such a connection with a passion. But there was a great deal more to building a Memphis rail connection than the naming of a short spur, and rails to the west were not to be for Rome until after the war.

In the meantime, the railhead of the Rome Railroad at the confluence of the three navigable rivers in northwest Georgia and northeast Alabama made Rome the center of area trade. Like the other notable early river towns in Georgia—Macon, Augusta and Columbus— Rome achieved substantial pre-railroad success. By 1850 her population was above 3000. George White describes Rome in his 1849 *Statistics of the State of Georgia:* "...since 1834 it has increased rapidly....Property has increased in value and confidence is felt that capitalists will be induced to settle in this place." By 1860, Rome had a population of over 4000 with several large steam-powered flourmills and the Noble Foundry, which had just produced the first steam locomotive built in the state of Georgia.[47] Steamboats plied the Coosa River 200 miles below Rome and as far up the Oostanaula system as 100 miles.[48] Rome knew how to grab the golden ring, and by 1890, four railroads would meet at Rome (see Table 4.2).

In 1890, the golden ring would still be cotton, but for Rome it was cotton with a difference. Certainly the city was the site of factors and warehouses for the bounteous cotton-growing bottomlands along the Coosa River in Alabama. And certainly a "cash crop" in the creditless, Reconstruction economy lured even mountain farms into the insidious cycle of cotton growing, borrowing and tenancy. But just as certainly, Rome and the other cities along the Western and Atlantic had developed differently from the rest of Georgia before the war, thus they would respond differently to circumstances after the war. Rome was not so deeply immersed in the growing of cotton as in the buying and selling of it. Surely Rome was as crushed by defeat as any city in Georgia, but when it came to returning to what the city had been doing before the war, Romans found that their "business as usual" was a great deal more in line with the gospel preached by the apostles of the New South than with the sad, bitter, lament heard

[46] U. B. Phillips, *Transportation in the Eastern Cotton Belt to 1860* (1908; reprint, New York: McMillan, 1913) 247.

[47] Roger Aycock, *All Roads Lead to Rome* (Rome GA: The Rome Heritage Foundation, 1981) 66.

[48] Aycock, *All Roads Lead to Rome*, 164.

everywhere in cotton's defunct Kingdom. Accordingly, like many towns along the rails of the Western and Atlantic, Rome embraced the myth of the New South from its earliest glimmerings.

There were to be many apostles to preach the New South gospel—Richard Edmonds and his much-quoted *Manufacturer's Record,* Henry Waterson of the *Louisville Courier Journal,* Walter Hines Page of the *Raleigh State Chronicle* and the industrialist Daniel Thompkins of Charlotte to name just a few. But without doubt the best known and perhaps most persuasive of all was Georgia's Henry Woodfin Grady of the *Atlanta Constitution.* It is not coincidental that Grady's early career was linked to Rome. Rome's faith must have been great to achieve such success, and in the South such a faith often came from the pulpit of a great preacher. Such a one was Henry Grady.

When Grady came to Rome in 1869, he had just graduated from the University of Georgia and was only a minor contributor to the *Atlanta Constitution.* He came to cover a grand press "excursion" sponsored by the Western and Atlantic Railroad. By the time the excursion ended Grady had been employed as a reporter by the *Rome Tri-Weekly Courier.* The excursion by train and riverboat visited what was left of the industrial heart of the Confederacy.

We can only imagine how Henry Grady made his way from the ruin of the Confederate industrial base to the optimism of the New South. Like all zealots, his course was straight, and he was seldom deterred by the sobering facts of the Southern economic condition. Along the way, he and the other New South spokesmen would learn to manipulate the facts to suit their ends and to play on the nostalgic emotions and stubborn convictions of their audiences. In Grady's defense, he almost surely understood that, like all economic systems based on credit and capital, believing would make it so. Henry Grady and the other New South spokesmen promoted a plan that was at once the truth and a lie.

They knew that if they could convert a bitter and nostalgic South to a belief in industrial progress, in modern agriculture, in progressive race relations, education, and urbanization, the lie of Southern economic potential which they preached in the North would become truth. They also knew that if they could convert Northern capitalists to a belief in New South economic potential, the lie of New South progress, which they pressed so hard on backward Southerners, would also become truth. It was a snake eating its own tail. But if believing made it so, then perhaps Grady and the others were not lying at all, for none believed it more than they. For most of the South it was not to be, but in Rome and a few other cities in Georgia, believing made it so.

Plate 4.15: The Cherokee Lodge, built in 1877. Alexander Bruce, architect.

Alexander Bruce's 1877 High Gothic Revival Masonic Lodge at Rome is one of the first chapters in a history written in brick and mortar, and Bruce's 1892 Floyd County Courthouse is among the last. Like Savannah, Rome's success was not for the twentieth century. The city would be hard hit by the boll weevil depression of the twenties and the Great Depression of the thirties. As in Savannah the

Plate 4.15: Alexander Bruce's 1877 Cherokee Lodge at Rome is one of the first chapters in a history written in brick and mortar. (Photo: Wilber W. Caldwell.)

long period of economic downturn had a small, architectural "silver lining." Most of the postbellum, nineteenth century buildings served throughout the first half of the twentieth century, and thus were effectively preserved by the city's decline.

Today a drive down Rome's Broad Street articulately recounts the city's postbellum history in an architectural language that is rich in detail and unmistakable in overview. Here lies the evidence of a rare and early manifestation of an emerging prosperity. In 1877, the Atlanta architect, Alexander Bruce, who was then still practicing in Knoxville, Tennessee, designed Rome's fabulous Masonic Hall, the Cherokee Lodge, one of the premier High Gothic Revival secular buildings in Georgia. Also designed by Bruce in Gothic array, the buildings of Rome's Shorter College in Rome were begun in 1877. Sadly the old Shorter College buildings are gone, as is Bruce's grand, Second Empire Nevin Opera House at Rome which was the envy of Georgia in 1880. [49]

Rome's building boom continued on into the 1880s, and it was supported by real economic progress. Cotton factors prospered, trading an average of over 80,000 bales annually during this period. The 1880 census lists an astonishing 90 manufacturing concerns in Floyd County. Most are of the predictable sort for this era in the South: a tannery, gins, saw mills, fertilizer, flour and gristmills. But also on the list are a foundry, machine shop, and a manufacturer of farm implements. By 1890, a furniture factory, a brick manufacturer, a cotton mill, and a plow manufacturer had been added, and in 1896 the enormous Massachusetts Mills open the first of two cotton mills at Lindale only 4 miles south of Rome. This was not the hollow promise of New South platitude. It was a corner of the real Industrial Revolution, and in its wake, boosterism every bit as bold and brash as that generated by Atlanta flowed from Rome.

Plate 4.16: The East Tennessee, Virginia and Georgia Depot at Rome, built c.1884, burned 1899.

Leading Rome to this New South Promised Land were her railroads. The railroad from Alabama, the Selma, Rome and Dalton, arrived in 1869, and in 1881 this road became part of the powerful East Tennessee, Virginia and Georgia Railroad system, one of the South's earliest conglomerate railroads. In 1882, this company built a line from Rome via Atlanta to Macon to connect with its new acquisition, the Macon and Brunswick Railroad. In 1887, the Chattanooga, Rome and Columbus Railroad completed a north-south line from Rome to Carrollton and fanned already high spirits generated by Rome's own trade exposition, the Rome and Northern Alabama Exposition of 1888. In 1891, the Decatur (Alabama) and Rome Railroad arrived in Rome and built a handsome depot on the city's north side. In the shadow of what can only be termed civic euphoria, Rome commissioned a new courthouse, and it is perhaps fitting that it is arguably the finest Romanesque Revival Courthouse in Georgia.

Plate 4.17: The Floyd County Courthouse, built in 1892. Bruce and Morgan, architects

When Alexander Bruce returned to Rome in 1891-1892, a great deal had transpired in the fif-

Plate 4.16: The old East Tennessee, Virginia & Georgia depot at Rome burned just before the turn of the century.

teen years since he had designed the grand, Gothic façade of Rome's Masonic Lodge. Bruce, who had apprenticed in Nashville with H. M. Akeroyd in the office of William Strickland, an American master of the Greek Revival, had begun his own practice in Knoxville in 1869. In 1879, he joined William Parkins in Atlanta, forming the partnership of Parkins and Bruce. In that same year, Thomas Henry Morgan, a former associate of Bruce's in Knoxville, joined Parkins and Bruce as the firm's draftsman and apprentice. In 1882, Bruce and Morgan left Parkins to form what was to become the Deep South's most distinguished architectural partnership of the era. The firm of Bruce and Morgan designed sixteen courthouses in Georgia; (see Appendix C) monumental buildings at Auburn University, Clemson University, Georgia Tech, and Agnus Scott College; the Union Depot at Columbus, Georgia, several of the South's first tall buildings including Atlanta's Prudential and Empire Buildings; and numerous churches and grand residences. Of Bruce and Morgan's sixteen Georgia courthouses, thirteen were in the Romanesque Revival Style and many flaunted exquisite Queen Anne details.

To discuss the Romanesque Revival in America without discussing the work of Henry Hobson Richardson is almost pointless. There are several reasons for Richardson's all-pervasive influence. First and foremost is his talent and vision. He seized the picturesque possibilities inherent in the Romanesque Style and seemingly single-handedly molded them into an architectural force that took was to the first step in the unthinkably long journey from revivalism to American modernism.

However, to view Richardson's work as merely transitional is to slight the master. This brings us to the second reason for Richardson's domination in American architecture. Before the 1870s many schooled architects in America had come from abroad. The rest had come up through a totally unregulated apprentice system or had simply begun designing buildings with-

Plate 4.17: The 1892 Floyd County Courthouse. Photo: Wilber W. Caldwell.

out bothering with the formalities of an architectural educational background. The result of all of this was either strict, European thinking, or the rather static output of a journeyman system that was in itself medieval, and not at all conducive to original ideas. Henry Hobson Richardson was the among the first American architects to attend the Ecole Des Beaux Arts in Paris, and it was the combination of Richardson's remarkable genius and his French educational

[49] Alexander Bruce was a well-established architect in Knoxville before joining William Parkins in Atlanta in 1879. The commission for the buildings at Shorter College in Rome may have been the occasion for Bruce's first designs in Georgia. George M. Battey, *A History of Rome and Floyd County*, 38. *The Rome Courier* names Bruce as the Shorter College architect and mentions the ground breaking for the Masonic Hall in the same article. *The Rome Courier*, May 28, 1877. Alexander Bruce's profile in *The Dictionary of Georgia Biography* credits Bruce with the 1880 design of the Nevin Opera House and with Rome's "New" City Hall. Arne Harman and Janice Hardy, *Dictionary of Georgia Biography*, 2 vols. in Kenneth Coleman and Charles Stephen Gurr, eds. (Athens GA: University of Georgia Press, 1983) 127.

experience that placed him at the focus of the American architectural scene. At first, almost alone among American architects, Richardson saw the need, understood the challenge, and possessed both the knowledge and the talent to begin the task of creating an American architectural style.

The third reason for the power of Richardson's presence in the 1880s is purely technical. Before 1876, there was no regular architectural journal in the United States. Some of the more affluent American professionals like Richardson himself, subscribed to English publications like *The Builder* or *The Building News.* Beyond this and a few standard texts and the ubiquitous builder's guides and pattern books, there was little to keep budding architects abreast of the times, and only architects in urban areas were able to avoid working in a vacuum. The publication of the first issue of *The American Architect* in 1876 had an electric effect. With the subsequent widespread inclusion of photographic plates in the 1880s, architecture, not to mention eclecticism, in America was given an enormous boost, and the work of Richardson and his followers, was suddenly available for all to see. In 1885, the ten best buildings in America as selected by the American Institute of Architects included five buildings by H. H. Richardson.[50] Never before had the designs of one American been so visible, and thus never before had one man had such influence.

Still a young man, Richardson died in 1886, and his defining courthouse, the Allegheny County Courthouse at Pittsburgh, was not completed until 1888. Down in lowly Atlanta, Alexander Bruce and Thomas Morgan had no doubt been carefully studying the pages of *The American Architect.* They built a fine Romanesque courthouse in Sumter County at Americus in 1887 and by the time the Floyd County Courthouse was begun, Bruce and Morgan designs for Romanesque court buildings were under construction in Carroll County at Carrollton, Talbot County at Talbotton,

Paulding County at Dallas, and Haralson County at Buchanan.

At the time, only a few men would be given to understand what it was that Richardson was trying to do. These few, among them John Wellborn Root, Lewis Sullivan, and of course Frank Lloyd Wright, would continue along, creating a winding and often treacherous path toward a modern American architectural style. The rest, architects like Bruce and Morgan, would look at the work of Richardson, adopt his vocabulary, and design buildings that were a great deal more Romanesque than Richardsonian. Still it was, in large part, Richardson who gave them this language and demonstrated its use. Here in Rome, Bruce and Morgan's Floyd County Courthouse employs some of the master's vocabulary using ordinary brick syntax. The hipped roof and the broad cornice with its modillion course are Romanesque Revival to the core. At the base the three round arched openings on the façade with their broad architraves composed of massive voussoirs are typical of Richardson's designs. The stone banding and the pyramidal roof of the tower are also distinctly Richardsonian, and the duel arches of the belfry recall Richardson's Allegheny County Courthouse. Both the curved bay and the hexagonal bay, as well as the fenestration on the west side, are typical of buildings of the Romanesque Revival, and the entire courthouse is expertly decorated with various terra-cotta plaques and bands, devices common to both the Romanesque Revival and the Queen Anne Styles.

Here at Rome, Bruce and Morgan achieved a degree of monumentality not found in their previous court buildings. This is due, in part, to the height of the tower. Certainly a sense of verticality expressed in grand towers had been an integral part of the Romanesque Revival from the beginning, and towers were important elements in Richardson's own design for his powerful courthouse at Pittsburgh. By 1890, all across America, towers had been carried to almost impossible extremes.

Tower and all, the Floyd County Courthouse is undeniably a Picturesque building, but its monochromatic red brick mass, next to the deep green waters of the Oostanaula River presents us with something of the Sublime. In Georgia in 1892, this was a monumental structure indeed, a reflection of accomplishment and hope in Rome. The preservation of this courthouse is a credit to the citizens of Rome, for today as the city stirs again after more than a half century of sleep, she awakens to find her glorious courthouse looking not much different than it did the day it was built. If she looks around for her depots, she will find them all gone.

SOME LAST THOUGHTS ON THE WESTERN AND ATLANTIC RAILROAD.

Although it was not chartered until 1836, the Western and Atlantic Railroad owes much to Wilson Lumpkin's 1834 decision to deny state support to E. P. Gaines's proposed line from Memphis to Charleston, via Athens. There was great support for Gaines's plan in Floyd, Gordon, Cass and Paulding Counties as well as in Athens, but Georgia's early railroads and the cities that supported them wanted their own version of a western connection. The state-owned Western and Atlantic Railroad was chartered in response to pressure by the Central, the Georgia and the Monroe Railroads. Begun in the teeth of the financial Panic of 1837, the road would take fourteen years to complete. So dire and long lasting was this recession that in 1845 rails stretched only about fifty miles north of Atlanta.

The Western and Atlantic was the focus of unique political and economic storms. State ownership of a profit producing concern brought with it controversial issues concerning financing, rates, profitability, and the regulation of charters to competitive lines. In 1843, support for the road was so low that the entire line was

Plate 4.18: Rome. (Photo: Wilber W. Caldwell.)

offered for sale to the first buyer to tender one million dollars. No buyers appeared. By 1847, the Macon and Western and the Georgia Railroad had connected with the railhead at Atlanta, and with the prospects for profitable economic operation suddenly looking brighter, the state finally ordered the completion of the road providing a new bond issue of $375,000.[51] Throughout the 1850s, there was powerful political pressure on the state to lease the Western and Atlantic to a private operator,

[50] These were Trinity Church at Boston, Albany City Hall, Sever Hall at Cambridge, the New York State Capitol, and the Town Hall at North Easton, Massachusetts. Carrol L. V. Meeks, *The Railroad Station, An Architectural History* (New Haven : Yale University Press, 1956) 104.

[51] Phillips, *History of Transportation in the Eastern Cotton Belt to 1860*, 318.

but the road's political problems before the war were nothing when compared to the outright thievery of the Reconstruction period. At the very heart of the sideshow that was Georgia's state government in 1870 was the financial rape of the Western and Atlantic by the carpetbagger governor Rufus Bullock's appointed superintendent Foster Blodgett. U. B. Phillips describes Blodgett's administration as one of "wholesale mismanagement, extravagance, and plundering, shared by numerous politicians."[52] Bullock's hold on the Western and Atlantic came to an end with the scandalous lease of the road to a consortium of his cronies. This lease expired in 1890, and the line was leased to the Nashville, Chattanooga and St. Louis Railroad, the predecessor of the Louisville and Nashville.

For all of the questions arising out of state ownership of such an important road, there remains the fact that, in the face of extreme financial adversity, the Western and Atlantic was actually built. It seems highly unlikely that it could have been constructed in this period by any privately funded group. Proof of this supposition lies in the fact that it took the Georgia Railroad over ten years to build the sixty relatively flat miles from Madison to Atlanta, and the Monroe Railroad went broke trying to build on the gentle ridge line between Barnesville and Atlanta—a route that required no bridges. It is impossible to avoid speculation as to what the history of Georgia might have been had the state not undertaken the construction of the line. We might safely assume that the road could not have been completed before the late 1850s—perhaps not even before the beginning of the Civil War. Georgia's role as the keystone of Southern rail systems would have been adversely affected. It was the Western and Atlantic that transformed Georgia's antebellum rail system into an integrated network, and without its centralizing influence Georgia's railroads may have continued

at cross-purposes for decades, serving only the limited goals of their patron cities. The brief postbellum success of the Central and the city of Savannah would have undoubtedly been altered, and the emergence of the city of Atlanta may never have taken place. It may be too bold a speculation, but one might ponder the possibility that had the state not funded and built the Western and Atlantic when it did, Macon would now be the capital of Georgia.

———

Here along the Western and Atlantic, there is a very clear link between the hope generated by postbellum crossing rails and the construction of new and stylish courthouses. In Marietta, a connection to Knoxville was completed in 1890, and before the turn of the century J. W. Golucke had clothed the Cobb County Courthouse in Romanesque finery. In Cartersville, the new line to Knoxville was begun 1895, and Bartow County had a Neoclassical courthouse by 1903. In Dalton, the lease of the Western and Atlantic to the Nashville, Chattanooga and St. Louis and the crossing line of the equally powerful East Tennessee, Virginia and Georgia begot a Romanesque court building in 1891, and in Rome the completion of the Chattanooga, Rome and Columbus across the East Tennessee, Virginia and Georgia inspired Bruce and Morgan's monumental Floyd County Courthouse in 1892. Calhoun saw no crossing rails, but hopes for such a crossing were high in 1888 when a tornado wrecked the old courthouse. William Parkins's Picturesque fantasy spoke to the county's dream. It is left to hapless Ringgold, hemmed in her mountain pass, with no hope of crossing rails, to prove the point. The 1854 courthouse served Catoosa County until 1939.

It seems clear that there was something that set the towns served by the Western and Atlantic apart from other railroad towns in Georgia. Like

[52] Phillips, *History of Transportation in the Eastern Cotton Belt to 1860*, 332.

other towns spawned by the state's early rails, they all experienced rapid growth and considerable prosperity. But before the war, cotton production here was comparatively small, and Rome and Dalton, like the other prosperous towns on the Western and Atlantic, developed in a more diverse economic pattern than Macon and the rest of Georgia. In 1850, the combined cotton production of Cobb, Cass, Gordon, Whitfield, Catoosa and Floyd Counties was only a fraction of 1% of the state's total, and by 1860 this was still below 3%. Corn, wheat and other grain crops flourished in this area, and thus a different agricultural base evolved along with a slightly different cultural base. There were fewer blacks in this area, less dependence on slavery, and although Southern patriotic fervor was every bit as high along the Western and Atlantic, it was of a slightly different sort.

Certainly, the Western and Atlantic Railroad itself had its affect on culture as well. The only towns along its right-of-way were links in a chain between the economically progressive "outlaw," Atlanta, and the individualism of the American west. Different ideological breezes blew along these rails than along those connecting Macon with Savannah, or Augusta with the upcountry, Georgia Piedmont. In antebellum times, the towns along the Western and Atlantic prospered in a broader sense than did the rest of the state. It was a prosperity based on trade—a prosperity once removed from its agricultural base. Thus along with mercantile pursuits, we find early industry in the form of foundries and small factories. Accordingly, it should come as no great surprise that after the war, like Atlanta, these towns were quick to embrace the concept of the New South. In this embrace, as in few other places in the state, the New South became real. Still these were very Southern places with very Southern problems, and their prosperity was fleeting. After the turn-of-the-century many of these towns lost much of their momentum.

•

The Atlanta and West Point Railroad

Fulton County: Atlanta (see chapters 4, 11, 26 & 32) Campbell County: Fairburn
Coweta County: Newnan • Troup County: LaGrange • Heard County: Franklin
Some Last Thoughts on the Atlanta and West Point Railroad

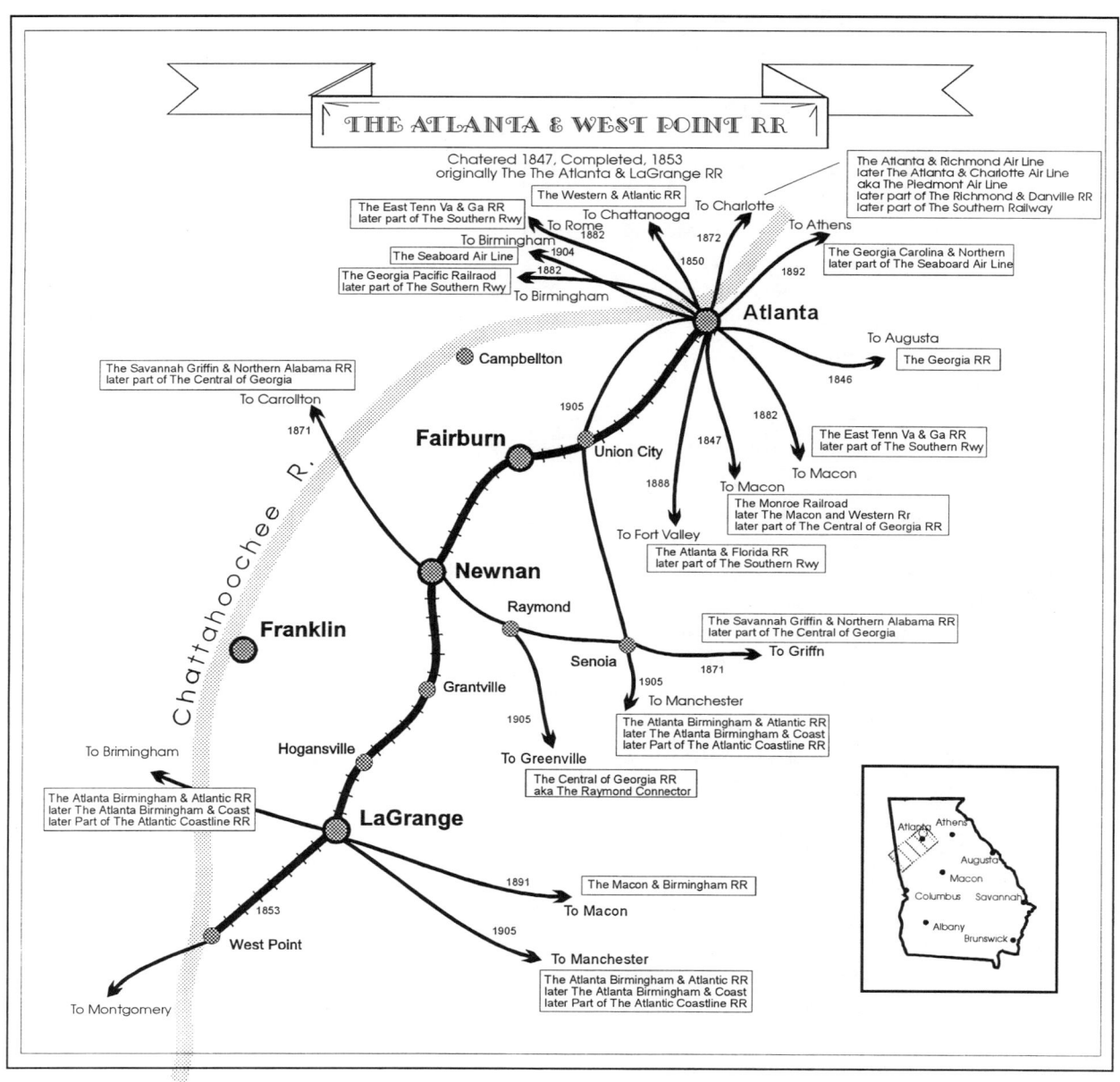

5 | The Atlanta and West Point Railroad

ATLANTA TO WEST POINT

CAMPBELL COUNTY: FAIRBURN

Plate 5.1: The Old Campbell County Courthouse at Campbellton, built 1835. Demolished c.1914.[1]

Campbellton, Campbell County's original county seat, was laid out in 1828 when Campbell County was cut from DeKalb, Coweta, Carroll and Fayette Counties. A wooden courthouse was completed in 1829 and was replaced by this fine brick structure in 1835. Similar to the early brick vernacular courthouses at Forsyth, 1825; LaGrange, 1830; Dahlonega, 1836; [2] and Rome, 1835, it was a sturdy example of the skill of local builders to employ simple classical details. With its crossing gabled roofs, the old building featured fine arched entranceways, and a high cornice supporting low pediments.

A Coweta County account relates that in 1830 Samuel Keller moved from Newnan to Campbellton "lured by expectations" of steamboats on the Chattahoochee River.[3] Troup County history recounts that in 1831 Colonel Reuben Thompson brought a load of goods upriver from West Point to Campbellton, but as far as we know he made the trip only once.[4] The dream of a Chattahoochee navigable all the way up to Atlanta persisted well into the second half of the twen-

---

[1] *The Campbell News*, July 19, 1916, reports that the old courthouse at Campbellton was partially demolished "two or three years ago."

[2] According to the 1974 News Letter of the Old Campbell County Historical Society 4, in the branch of the Fulton County Library at Fairburn, the courthouse at Dahlonega was built from the same plans as the original Campbell County Courthouse. This seems unlikely for, although the Dahlonega court building is of a very similar form, it embodies several significant differences in detail most particularly in the size and orientation of the pediment.

[3] The Newnan and Coweta County Historical Society, *The History of Coweta County, Georgia* (Roswell GA: Newnan and Coweta County Historical Society, 1988) 8.

[4] Clifford L. Smith, *History of Troup County* (Atlanta: Foote and Davies, 1933) 108.

Plate 5.1: The Old Campbell County Courthouse at Campbellton. (Photo Courtesy of the Ga. Department of Archives and History.)

tieth century, but it was never to be. Still, whatever the cause, Campbellton's initial growth must have been substantial, and according to Atlanta chronicler Franklin Garrett, the place was once a town of 1200 inhabitants.[5] Bypassed by the Atlanta and West Point Railroad in 1851, Campbellton counted only 239 white residents in 1860.

Here again we see the usual myth of the by-passed town: "The citizens of Campbellton chose not to allow the Atlanta and West Point Railroad to pass through their beautiful and carefully planned city on the banks of the Chattahoochee."[6] A quick look at the terrain "on the banks of the Chattahoochee" reveals some pretty rough county for railroad building while the natural ridge at Fairburn is flat and inviting. Thus, it seems unlikely that the opinions of the citizens of Campbellton had much influence on the survey of the Atlanta and West Point Railroad. By mid-1851 the road was completed as far as the town

of Palmetto, the highest spot on that long, comfortable ridge which runs from Atlanta to Newnan.

Along the line, the town of Fairburn sprang up near a small post office that had first been called Cartersville and later Berryville. By 1860, the place was home to 300 persons. Ten years later, the power of the steel rails of the Atlanta and West Point Railroad had energized Fairburn to such an extent that the citizens of Campbellton were moving to Fairburn in droves. One local account relates that in 1870 Campbellton residents were dismantling their homes and moving them as well.[7] In that same year, Fairburn became the Campbell County seat. By then, Campbellton was in decay. Today all that remains is a church, the old Masonic lodge and a stone monument on the top of a pleasant hill to mark the site of the 1835 courthouse.

Plate 5.2: The Campbell County Courthouse at Fairburn, built in 1871.

If a railroad ever built a courthouse, it was here at Fairburn in Old Campbell County. In many ways, the 1871 structure was a re-creation of the old 1835 courthouse Campbellton. If one ignores the Greek Revival portico and the lacy, paired brackets, the courthouse at Fairburn is a near replica of its predecessor which fell into disrepair after Campbellton was abandoned. The crumbling structure was pulled down early in this century. It is not remarkable that the builder-designers of the 1871 Campbell County Courthouse were anxious to re-create the old Campbellton court building beside the shiny new rails of the Atlanta and West Point at Fairburn. What is remarkable is the eclectic approach that they took in bringing the old building up to date. It is as if the citizens of Fairburn were of a divided mind. They sought first the older American tradition by copying the county's original vernacular courthouse; then the reactionary myth of the Old South by adding the Greek Revival portico; and lastly, a touch of the New South by decorating the cornice with paired brackets to gracefully bring the building out of the past and into the world of the 1870s.

This was not the stylish Victorian picturesque Eclectic so popular in the American North. This was a voice from within the American vernacular. From the

[5] Franklin M. Garrett, *Atlanta and Environs, The Chronicle of Its People and Event*, 3 vols.(New York: Lewis Publishing Company, 1954) 1:855. Mr. Garret's figure of 1200 seems high in light of George White's 1849 estimate of 175, published in his Statistics of the State of Georgia, and US Census figures for 1860 which puts Campbellton's population at 239 white residents.

[6] Nancy Jones Cornell, "Old Campbell County." Unpublished and undated article found in the Fairburn branch of the Fulton County Public Library, 1.

[7] Cornrell, "Old Campbell County," 1.

[8] *Atlanta Journal and Constitution*, January 13, 1991.

very beginning, American architects and builders had exercised a free hand redefining European ideas and fashioning an architecture that spoke both practically and symbolically to simple American resources and values. Certainly the Federal Style was a simplified departure from Georgian forms. Likewise, the Greek Revival in America had paid little heed to strict classical orders. Talbot Hamlin speaks of this American freedom of design in The Greek Revival in America:

> It is unlikely that the changes that American architects made in Greek forms were made from ignorance…the practice of changing the details and proportion of the Greek orders was thoroughly ingrained in the American tradition long before the Greek influence became common… except for the larger more monumental buildings…departure from any exact copying of Greek details was the rule rather than the exception.

It is true that this kind of freedom in the hands of untrained designers often led to questionable results. Aesthetically the urge to wander can create confusion, and symbolically the risk is utter ambiguity. Occasionally however, freedom's language is startlingly clear, as is the case here in Fairburn. This building is deeply rooted in multiple traditions of the past. What little the new Campbell County Courthouse had to say about the present in 1871 or about the future is carefully subordinated to dominant nostalgic motifs.

Despite the fact that Fairburn could call the antebellum railroad both father and mother, like so many places along early rails, little of the modern industrial myth imported by postbellum roads would penetrate the region's brooding armor. This courthouse echoes both the Greek Revival and the vernacular style of the earlier period, but it carries the imagery of the new age as well. Here is a symbol of two eras: a past lost forever in a tangle of nostalgia and a seemingly unattainable future. It would serve the county until it was merged and became part of Fulton County in 1932.

All of this notwithstanding, Fairburn did enjoy a brief boom after the turn of the century. In 1900, Fairburn's population was only 761. By 1910, it had

Plate 5.2: What little the new Campbell County Courthouse had to say about the present in 1871 or about the future is carefully subordinated to a dominant nostalgic motif. (Photo: Wilber W. Caldwell.)

nearly doubled. Today two depots stand at Fairburn. These were erected in 1916, to replace the town's old wooden depot.[8] We know that the town had some sort of depot as early as 1854 when Fairburn was chartered because the act which created the town defined the town limits as a 600 yard circle with the depot as its center. Federal forces destroyed this original depot 1864.

COWETA COUNTY: NEWNAN

Plate 5.3: The Coweta County Courthouse, built in 1904-1905. J. W. Golucke, architect.

Here in Newnan, we find one of the finest of James Wingfield Golucke's Neoclassical undertakings. This was his tenth commission in Georgia for a classical courthouse in six years (see Appendix C). Most of Golucke's designs in the neoclassical Revival Style had been based on similar plans: the Palladian, four-sided "Villa Rotonda" model with four more or less equal porticos forming temple-like entrances, one at each of the four points of the compass. Allowing equal treatment on all four sides, the Greek cross was the perfect solution to the challenge presented by the central town square. The result, when viewed from any of the four sides was familiar indeed to Southern eyes. Each side recalled the theme so often voiced by Mills, Cluskey and others—the simple, clean, classical mes-

Plate 5.3: The Coweta County Courthouse. Here at Newnan in 1904, James Wingfield Golucke made a bold and dramatic departure. (Photo: Wilber W. Caldwell.)

sage of the Greek Revival and all the magnolia-scented Old South mythology that had later been attached to it.

Despite Golucke's consistency in the use of this familiar Southern plan, his courthouse at Newnan draws boldly on the ornamental motifs of the Beaux-Arts Style. This flowery brand of Classicism was sweeping the country in the years following the Columbian Exposition in Chicago in 1893. It can be no coincidence that, in the same year that this courthouse was built, Americans were gaping at the fantasy buildings of the 1904 Louisiana Purchase Exposition in Saint Louis, whose architecture picked up where the designs of Columbian Exposition had left off, carrying the baroque ornamentation of the new Classicism to even more fantastic extremes. Unlike his earlier neoclassical buildings, like the simple but elegant 1903 Bartow County Courthouse at Cartersville, the Coweta County Courthouse incorporated, what

was for Georgia, a riot of stylish turn-of-the-century decoration. However, by the measure of the buildings at the Saint Louis Fair, Golucke's flourishes here at Newnan were quite tame indeed.

Here at Newnan, J. W. Golucke embroidered his loose interpretation of the Ionic order with a broad architrave and a bold frieze decorated with three roundels, each crisscrossed with Golucke's favored star pattern. The star pattern also appears above the sash and beneath the splayed lintels of the ground floor windows and in the small windows of the clerestory above the courtroom. Borrowing from the Corinthian order, the pediment features both modillions and dentals. The second story windows are of the arched type with bold, masonry and keystoned archivolts similar to the fenestration of Golucke's Meriwether County Courthouse in Greenville, 1903. The porticos on the north and south sides of the building feature only two columns, a design very much in keeping with the Beaux-Arts Style. The tower is high and thin. Broken based pediments are supported by paired Ionic columnettes, and the small roundels in the tower echo those of the porticos below.

Despite the trendy Beaux-Arts decoration, this building is a long distance indeed from the alabaster glow of Chicago's "White City" which so changed the course of American architecture after 1893. It is also a long distance from the simplicity of the Colonial Revival or the American Greek Revival. These classical revivals had contained a common element: the radiant uncompromising glow of pure white. In the early part of the nineteenth century when archeology was just beginning as a science, researchers had discovered the fact that Greek and Roman buildings had originally been brightly painted, but the latter-day architectural symbolism of pristine purity was already cast in stone, so to speak. Revivalist architects wanted nothing of polychromatic classical monuments, and color was left for more romantic builders. In short, classical buildings were white, and that was that. Even though the all-powerful, emerging American vernacular, with help from Georgian models, often substituted brick for white stone or stuccoed walls, the trim remained white.

Here at Newnan in 1904, James Wingfield Golucke made a bold and dramatic departure. In place of the almost obligatory white stone trim, he substituted the deep, mossy, almost black-green of oxidized copper. A copper dome was one thing, but here the entire tower and all of the building's cornice and sofit are of dark weathered metal. Only the stone columns and the arched archivolts and splayed lintels above the windows are of white stone. Against the deep red brick walls, the effect of the weathered trim is darkly powerful and strongly "un-classical."

Here again is that troublesome contradiction: "romantic-Classicism" which Henry Russell Hitchcock uses to describe an International classical Style which included the Greek Revival, among other early nineteenth century styles. Architectural historian, Vincent Scully, borrows the same term to describe the work of H. H. Richardson. Professor Scully's words seem fitting "...a latent and very American Classicism was embodied in warm and earthy forms, not in the bright humanistic vocabulary of earlier classical design."[9]

For most of America, the Neoclassical Revival constituted a return to order after the asymmetrical ramblings of the Picturesque Eclectic. It also represented an affirmation of Eastern financial and industrial power. At the turn of the century, these symbols were unacceptable to much of the American South. In most towns in Georgia, a rudimentary brick "store-front" vernacular was about the only evidence of "the ramblings of the picturesque," and Eastern financial and industrial power was undoubtedly the last cause these brooding rebels wanted to architecturally affirm. Nonetheless, the Neoclassical Revival knew great popularity in the South, for as with almost everything else, the region would attach her own unique and contrary symbols to the style. In Coweta County, as elsewhere in Dixie, these columns recalled the stubborn myth of the Old South and the Greek democracy of John C. Calhoun. Here in Newnan, as in Madison and Cartersville and a few other towns in the Georgia Piedmont, which by 1900 had realized small amounts of postbellum economic success, people remained of a divided mind. It was not that they could not decide upon a course of action, but that

they wanted it both ways. They dreamed of a uniquely Southern kind of economic progress, one that came without the price tag of a modern society. What they got was the worst the old, and little, if any, of the new.

J. W. Golucke knew his clients well. They teetered on the cusp between an emerging modern world and a romantic world that was lost forever. Both worlds beckoned with half-truths and lies. Both worlds seemed unreachable. They were thus in need of a dual symbol—Excalibur—the sword that cut two ways. This courthouse was such a symbol.

Plate 5.4: The old Atlanta and West Point Depot at Newnan, built in 1892, demolished in 1911.

To be sure, Reconstruction and the economic trials that followed had lulled Newnan into the impotency of poverty beside her antebellum railroad. But the town began to move forward in the late 1880s and 1890s. In 1904, J. W. Golucke's Coweta County Courthouse scribed the high water mark of the county's success.

The railroads had begun the work. The Savannah, Griffin and Northern Alabama Railroad had laid track through Newnan in 1871. This road had been chartered way back in 1854, and grading had begun before the Civil War. By 1874, it connect-

Plate 5.4: Newnan's new Union Depot replaced this charming 1892 building in 1911.

[9] Vincent Scully, *American Architecture and Urbanism* (1969; rev.ed., New York: Henry Hold and Company, 1988) 103.

ed Griffin with Carrollton via Newnan, and by 1888, with the connection to the Chattanooga, Rome and Columbus at Carrollton, the line ran all the way from Griffin to Chattanooga. Later part of the Central of Georgia's Savannah and Western Division, these rails were merged with the Columbus and Rome Railroad, which was acquired by the Central in 1895.

Meanwhile the 1880s had seen the charter of two Newnan-sponsored railroad companies which died aborning: The Newnan and Greenville Railroad whose dream was finally fulfilled by the Central in 1905, and the Newnan and Western, which contemplated a line to Franklin, Georgia, in Heard County. Golucke's courthouse reflected the fullest flowering of Newnan's economic zeal, which came around 1905 when the Central, operating briefly as the Greenville Railroad Company, completed the missing link in the Chattanooga to Columbus route, the 23 miles between Greenville and Newnan (with the junction at Raymond). Surely the new courthouse was, at least in part, a celebration of this railroad's promise. In fact, in 1905, Newnan must have seemed at the very center of the South, with her old east-west line from Montgomery to Atlanta, her north-south connection from Macon, via Griffin and Rome, to Chattanooga, and her long awaited direct line to Columbus.

This 1892 depot replaced an earlier Atlanta and West Point depot that had burned shortly after its completion in 1889.[10] A new Union Depot replaced this charming building in 1911.[11] It, like the 1904 Coweta County Courthouse, was the product of a new kind of progress that had begun to spread across the face of Georgia in the first decade of the new century. Like those which crossed at Newnan,

railroads all across the South were completing their web of raw steel and flimsy promises in this period, and a new wave of consolidation and exploitation was underway. By 1905, some of Georgia's regional banking towns like Newnan were realizing more than the veneer of New South economic promises and were beginning to evolve the frail skeleton of a modern economic infrastructure. Still, this framework was fragile, for its foundation still rested largely on the fickle economics of cotton.

Plate 5.5: The Coweta County Courthouse, built in 1829. William Hitchcock, builder/designer

Newnan stands as an example of the pattern experienced by so many fair-sized Georgia Piedmont towns in the period between 1865 and the middle of the twentieth century. The town suffered economic devastation, followed by a slow and shallow recovery that, in the final accounting, was not robust enough to secure prominence in the economic gales of the new century. The story of Newnan's progress in this period will prove useful, for it provides insight into why so many Georgia towns that had seemed so ripe for New South progress somehow failed to fully grasp the ring of opportunity.

The story begins with this courthouse built in 1829 by William Hitchcock who, according to Coweta County history, built over twenty such courthouses in Georgia.[12] The building is a stunning example of the marriage of the brick vernacular and the American Greek Revival, which in the 1820s was gaining momentum in Georgia partly as a result of acclaim for the many Greek public buildings designed by Robert Mills in South Carolina. Coweta County could have chosen no more appropriate symbol around which to build her county town. In 1829, the South shared the national sentiment for the Greek Revival, attaching the lofty imagery of democracy and justice to these columns. Only later would John C. Calhoun and others mold the Greek myth into a distorted and uniquely Southern metaphor for the imperialism of cotton and slavery.

Even as early as the Treaty of Indian Springs in 1825 and the opening up of all the lands between the Flint and the Chattahoochee Rivers in the subsequent

[10] Mary Jones Gibson and Lily Elizabeth Reynolds, *The Coweta Chronicles* (Atlanta: Stein Printing Company, 1928) 298, 306.

[11] The 1911 Union Depot at Newnan was demolished in 1970.

[12] The Newnan and Coweta County Historical Society, *The History of Coweta County, Georgia*, 8. My own research can document William Hitchcock as the builder of courthouses at Greenville, McDonough, Jackson, and Fayetteville.

[13] The Newnan and Coweta County Historical Society, *The History of Coweta County, Georgia*, 19.

[14] Edward L. Ayers, Southern Crossing, *A History of the American South, 1877 - 1906* (Oxford and New York: Oxford University Press, 1995) 16.

Land Lottery of 1827, Georgia's westward expansion was driven by cotton. Twenty five years later, when the Atlanta and LaGrange Railroad arrived at Newnan, the irreducible and unquestioned reason for the railroad and for the town was still cotton, and by 1860 Coweta County was ranked tenth among Georgia cotton-producing counties. This courthouse stood on the square at Newnan for seventy-five years. When it was replaced, the columns of J. W. Golucke's 1904 Coweta County Courthouse still stood for bastions of cotton. But in 1904, we can detect a least a slight crack in the seemingly impregnable wall that cotton had built around these places. It would still be decades before these walls would begin to crumble, and ironically the resulting freedom would come with the invasion of an unlikely liberator: the boll weevil.

It is only against this backdrop of cotton, tenancy and hard times that we can fully understand the development of Newnan and of Georgia's new crop of emerging towns in this era. In the last quarter of the nineteenth century, Newnan began to wear the unmistakable badge of progress: brick buildings. In the 1870s wooden buildings on the east and west side of the square were replaced by brick structures, and the last wooden building on the square came down in 1897.[13] In 1888, Newnan erected her cotton mill. Built in an early frenzy of New South zeal, like most early Southern mills, this enterprise followed a civic agenda, aimed at the progress of the town rather than purely capitalistic urges. At the same time, the R. D. Cole Manufacturing Company was growing into a strange hodgepodge of endeavors, erecting saw mills, cotton gins, water towers, water wheels and all types of buildings.

Thus by 1905, Newnan's new courthouse symbolized not only the age-old reality of cotton, but also a modern perception of progress. But in the mythical New South, things were not always what they seemed. In truth, Newnan's cotton mill was quite small and R. D. Cole's business only supplied a large agricultural area's demand for saw mills, boilers, gins and the like. If we place all the rest of Newnan's "progress" against the backdrop of cotton, we see not an emerging industrial revolution, but just another regional banking and trading town serving as cotton's handmaiden.

Plate 5.5: The 1829 Coweta County Courthouse was a stunning example of the marriage of the brick vernacular and the American Greek Revival.

Newnan's other "industries" of this period fit that mold: saw mills, a tannery, a mill, a small furniture factory, a cottonseed oil refinery—the usual extractive dabblings of the early postbellum South. The nature of the town's growth is documented in the Newnan Directory of 1905. Here we find grocers, hardware merchants, harness makers, blacksmiths, druggists, doctors, lawyers, bankers, dentists, dry goods merchants, all that is required of a regional center in support of an agricultural hinterland. This was never really a budding industrial center at all; it was just another trading center for the struggling planters and harvesters of cotton.

TROUP COUNTY: LAGRANGE

In his book *Southern Crossing,* Edward L. Ayers rightly declares that even as late as 1910, "to many Southerners, industry seemed more a charade than an actuality."[14] To illustrate this point he quotes a 1908 article in the *Southern Lumberman* poking fun at the zeal of one of the New South's most optimistic organs, *The Manufacturer's Record:*

If all of the saw mills, cotton mills, tobacco factories, new towns, and other enterprises and undertakings which it has heralded to its advertisers and subscribers as having been started up… had really been built and put into operation, there wouldn't be surface room for them to stand on, water enough under the earth to supply their boilers, nor room enough in the sky for the smoke from their chimneys.[15]

This cynicism may have been appropriate for places like Newnan where the end of the century brought what many had hoped would become the beginnings of industrialization, only to have such modern seeds fail to take hold among the monotonous and infertile rows of a deep rooted agrarian tradition. But, like so many aspects of the region's late century history, the story of the growth of the cotton textile industry in the American South is paradoxical. A comparison between Newnan's story with that of her neighbor, LaGrange, can only leave us with a renewed sense of wonder at the seemingly capricious and contradictory forces of history. LaGrange too had been at the center of an agrarian economy, and she too built a late century cotton mill. The results could hardly have been more different.

Plate 5.6: The Atlanta and West Point Depot at LaGrange, built c. 1890, demolished in 1910.

Newnan and LaGrange entered the last decade of the nineteenth century as almost identical twins. The citizens of Newnan organized the Newnan Cotton

Plate 5.6: The Atlanta and West Point Depot at LaGrange was similar to the lines 1892 depot at Newnan, and was probably built at about the same time.

Factory in 1888. In that same year, LaGrange Mills was built as an expansion of the 1883 LaGrange Oil and Manufacturing Company. At this time, LaGrange, with a population of about 3000, was about the same size as Newnan. The dominance of cotton was clear in both counties. In 1880, Troup County had produced over 18,000 bales compared to Coweta's 16,000. Yet by 1920 while Newnan bumped along with her single mill and a population of only about 7000, LaGrange had become home to eight large mills, and Troup County's population exceeded 36,000 with nearly half of that number living in the mill villages in and around LaGrange.

For once, the difference was not the railroads. The Atlanta and LaGrange Railroad, the forerunner of the Atlanta and West Point, reached Newnan in 1851 and LaGrange by 1853. Both towns saw postbellum crossing rails. The Savannah, Griffin and Northern Alabama arrived in Newnan in 1871 on its way to Carrollton to eventually make connections via Rome to Chattanooga. The Central later connected Newnan directly with Columbus. Likewise LaGrange became the end of the line for the Macon and Birmingham in 1891, and the Atlanta, Birmingham and Coast arrived around 1907. Additionally, both towns had seen the usual parade of railroads that had lived only in men's dreams—railroads that would never be built (See Table 5.1).

One could argue that Newnan's location on the divide between the Flint and the Chattahoochee deprived the town of sufficient waterpower. But by the late 1880s, steam was beginning to be considered more efficient than falling water, and electricity was coming into its own.[16] In fact, LaGrange Mills had electric lights and furnished the town of LaGrange with power for the city's first streetlights in 1890. Surely the explanation for the city's dynamic growth lies elsewhere, somewhere in the psyche of the place, for most of LaGrange's growth in textiles came well after the era of water-powered mills.

The history of early textile mills in the American South has been the subject of a disproportionate amount of scholarship. Early studies like Broadus Mitchell's 1921 *The Rise of Cotton Mills in the South* rightly describe the cotton mill movement as a form of civic piety, fraught with moral considerations and its own brand of philanthropic fervor.[17] While C. Vann Woodward points to financial profit as a possible force, he concludes: "As important as these inducements undoubtedly were, they cannot account for the public zeal that, in the Carolinas, Georgia and Alabama, converted economic development into a civic process inspired with a vision of social salvation."[18]

To be sure, the mills built before the mid-1890s were the product of local Southern civic concern, and they were built largely with local capital. Many studies list investors as local farmers, bankers, lawyers and merchants.[19] According to The History of Troup County, LaGrange Mills's investors in 1888 included "most of the business and professional men of the little town of LaGrange."[20] The promoters of these ventures combined the rhetoric of the New South spokesmen with the language of the pulpit: the salvation of the town, the elevation and purification of the poor whites and a prophecy of grace to herald a new age. Later studies look at the self-contained structure of the mill and its mill village and see a reflection of the antebellum plantation. W. J. Cash is among those who revel in this correlation.[21] Cash, of course, takes all of this much farther. He concludes that generally Southern efforts toward industrialism were designed to create enough economic power to successfully defend the region's old ways against any modern, outside meddling. More specifically he places the social significance of the Southern cotton mill at the center of a racial arena. Despite its strange rhetoric, Cash's work has the smell of truth about it, for in it we can sniff out the Old South social structure disguising itself in New South economics. Wilbur Cash knew that, as always, Southerners wanted progress, but only on their own terms.

Many mills were built along these lines, driven by both the purest and the meanest of motives. Mills like the Newnan Cotton Factory and the 1888 LaGrange Mills were the products of civic crusades. They made a profit to be sure. But all the Southern mills made a profit, for at the heart of the matter, what they had to sell was not cotton yarn but cheap labor, and in the abuse of that commodity lies the paradox of the "civic

LaGrange Railroads Chartered but Never Built

LaGrange and Oxford Railroad 1856

LaGrange and Troup Factory Railroad, 1857

North and South Railroad, 1870

LaGrange and Barnesville Railroad, 1871

LaGrange, North and South Railroad, 1885

Griffin, LaGrange and Western Railroad, 1886

Brunswick, LaGrange and Northwestern Railroad, 1893

Table 5.1

piety" of Southern "mill fever." Descriptions of these early mill villages are grim indeed. Living conditions were primitive and working conditions were often ghastly, hours were long, child labor was the rule not the exception, and the workers were every bit as destitute and as trapped as they had been as tenants on the farm.

Later mills in Georgia, those built after 1895 like the ones at Porterdale near Covington, Milstead near Conyers, New Holland near Gainesville and Lindale near Rome, were not wholly of this civic-spirited type. Many were driven by a more straightforward motive: profit. Ironically conditions in the mill villages of these later mills were, in many cases, improved over the horrors of the earlier period. Still, life was hard and hours were long. These later mills were built primarily for profit and, at least in part, with Northern capital. So it was with the later mills at LaGrange (See Table 5.2). It is unlikely that Yankee investors had any interest in the convoluted moral callings of early

[15] The Southern Lumberman, 1908 quoted in Edward L. Ayers, *Southern Crossing, A History of the American South, 1877 - 1906*, 16.

[16] David L. Carlton, *Mill and Town in South Carolina, 1880-1920* (Baton Rouge LA: Louisiana State University Press, 1982) 46.

[17] Broadus Mitchell, *The Rise of Cotton Mills in the South* (Baltimore: John Hopkins University Press, 1921) 127-36.

[18] C. Vann Woodward, *Origins of the New South, 1877-1913* (1951; reprint, Baton Rouge LA: Louisiana State University Press, 1993) 133.

[19] Broadus Mitchell, *The Rise of Cotton Mills in the South*, 160.

[20] Clifford L. Smith, *History of Troup County* (Atlanta: Foote and Davies, 1933) 115.

[21] W. J Cash, *The Mind of the South* (1941; reprint, New York: Vintage Books, 1941) 201.

COTTON MILLS AT LAGRANGE
LaGrange Mills, 1888
Dixie Cotton Mills, 1895
Unity Cotton Mills, 1900
Park Cotton Mills 1902
Elm City Cotton Mills, 1905
Unity Spinning Mills, 1909
Dunson Mills, 1910
Hillside Cotton Mills, 1915
Stark Mills, 1922
Valley Waste Mills, 1927
Valway Rug Mills, 1927
Rockweave Mills, 1927
Oakleaf Mills, 1928

not. It is probably safe to say that mills built for profit multiplied if successful, while mills built for the more complex civic reasons we have discussed did not. They had no place in a modern industrial equation, for they attempted to create something that no mill could manufacture.

Plate 5.7: The 1904 Troup County Courthouse at LaGrange. In many ways the classical songs heard here seem echoes of the simplicity of the old Federal Style. (Photo Courtesy of Georgia Dept. of Archives and History.)

Southern mill builders. As Professor Woodward writes with elegant understatement: "The profit motive did not necessarily preclude the philanthropic motive, but it does seem to have outweighed it in some instances."[22]

LaGrange's pattern of mill growth exemplifies the pattern of the growth of the textile industry all across the American South. In 1889, New England's mills counted over 10 million spindles while the South could boast only about 1.3 million, with Georgia's portion about 455, 000. By 1929, there were over 17 million spindles in the South, while New England's total was only a little over 11 million, down from 17.6 million in 1919. Georgia's 1929 total was about 3 million spindles, and 200,000 of them were in Troup County.[23]

Despite all the statistics, we may never know why LaGrange flourished as a mill town while Newnan did

Plate 5.7: The Troup County Courthouse, built 1904, burned 1936. A. J. Bryan and Company, architects.

Troup County's original courthouse was a temporary log structure built in 1829. Later that year, Benjamin Cameron built a fine brick court building very much like the ones at Forsyth, 1825; Campbellton, 1835, Rome, 1835, and Dahlonega, 1836. That simple building stood on the square at LaGrange until 1904 when a new courthouse was built. Atlanta architect, Andrew J. Bryan designed this building and seven other courthouses in Georgia (see Appendix C). In 1907, Bryan virtually duplicated this design with his Washington Parish Courthouse at Franklinton, Louisiana.

With the exception of the almost Roman arcades of the central rotunda, there was little flamboyance in A. J. Bryan's offering at LaGrange. Three stern pedimented sides adjoined the great rotunda of the

[22] Woodward, *Origins of the New South, 1877-1913*, 134.

[23] A. C. Galensen, *The Migration of the Cotton Textile Industry from New England to the South, 1880-1930* (New York: Garland, 1985) 2. Mr. Galensen tabulates statistics for six New England states (Connecticut, Maine, Massachusetts, New Hampshire, Rhode Island, and Vermont) and six Southern states (Alabama, Georgia, North Carolina, South Carolina, Tennessee and Virginia). Troup County's totals are found in Clifford L. Smith, History of Troup County, 121.

[24] In 1971 a short spur was built in the north east corner of Heard County to supply Georgia Power Company's Plant Wansley.

courtroom. The dome was placed at the transept of a familiar cross-like plan, like so many of Georgia's neo-classical court buildings of the day. But apart from the rotunda itself and the curious round turrets with their tiny columned porticos and domed caps, the classical songs heard here seem echoes of Georgian simplicity and of the old American Federal Style. There had, in fact, been a renewed national interest in this style in conjunction with the Colonial Revival that began in the early 1880s, shortly after America's centennial celebrations.

Federal and Georgian Revival buildings were still in vogue after the turn of the century. Like most revivalist architecture of the new century, these buildings incorporated more elaborate decoration than the originals. Here at LaGrange in 1904, we find the Federal Style according to A. J. Bryan and Company. Although the quality of Bryan's design is subject to debate, the Federal elements are true to the historical style: rectangular massing, bays defined by stern brick pilasters, the simple broad cornice, bold pediments with their semicircular brick relief suggesting Federal Style fan windows, rooftop stone balustrades and a clock tower that in this context becomes a more large domed cupola than tower.

The symbolism here is unmistakable: this is the architecture of New England, which still ruled the American textile industry in 1904. Like New England's early brick public buildings, this courthouse at LaGrange delivered a message that was practical and puritan. It stood in stark contrast to the fantasy architecture of grand but hollow illusions that decorated so many of Georgia's squares in 1904. There were few illusions needed here in LaGrange. The railroads were real just as they were in the rest of Georgia, but here the progress they implied was also real. No dream symbol was needed to remind LaGrange of a promise that had already been fulfilled.

In truth, the severe, unadorned lines of the 1904 Troup County Courthouse were perhaps even more appropriate than all of this might suggest. By 1904, not only had Troup County achieved some degree of industrial progress, she had seen both sides of the true face of the new industrial era, and what she saw was every bit as frightening as it was alluring. One side of

the face of progress was that familiar, promising smile which beckoned to every town in Georgia. The other side was a visage of exploitation and human agony that was ugly beyond imagination. As the century wore on, LaGrange would first grow, and then her prominence would fade. This courthouse burned in 1936.

HEARD COUNTY: FRANKLIN

Plate 5.8: The depot at Hogansville.

This impressive depot, on the Atlanta and West Point Railroad at Hogansville in Troup County, is as close to rail service as Heard County would ever come. No track was ever laid in Heard County.[24] Franklin, the county seat, is another of those bypassed places, like Irwinton in Wilkinson County and Appling in Columbia County. In the absence of a rail connection, it remained virtually unchanged well into this century. At the turn of the century, Heard County had over 11,000 residents, but only 218 lived in Franklin, the county's largest town. By 1960, Franklin residents numbered only 620 while the county's population had fallen dramatically to 5333.

Postbellum times were hard all over Georgia, and to single out Heard County to illustrate the South's woes may seem unfair. Still the isolation imposed by the absence of rails in this marginally fertile area seems to have magnified the common problems of the age. As late as 1917, Heard County schools took students only as far as the seventh grade and the annual school

Plate 5.8: The depot at Hogansville was as close to rail service as Heard County would ever come. (Photo: Wilber W. Caldwell.)

term was only five months.[25] In 1910, illiteracy in Heard among males of voting age remained above 25%.[26] Browsing through old issues of the Franklin *News and Banner* plays like a stuck record of typhoid fever, tuberculosis, hook worm and the like. The frightfully high infant death rate in the county continued well into this century. In 1900, in all of Heard County there were only seven doctors.[27] Likewise no industry at all was in evidence, and even as late as 1900 the county could list only the following enterprises: 30 gins, 27 stores, and 20 gristmills.[28]

By contrast, Hogansville, which sprang up less than 20 miles away on the Atlanta and West Point Railroad shortly after rails reached Troup County, had a population of over 1200 in 1910, with a new cotton mill, electric lights, a large flour mill and important

Plate 5.9: The 1894 Heard County Courthouse, a compact and charming building that echoed the emotional and uniquely rural message of home and hearth. (Photo Courtesy of Ted Brooke.)

brick kilns at nearby Trimble.[29] This depot replaced a stone depot built in the 1850s, and its size and style speak of the prosperity of Hogansville in the years after the turn of the century. As the closest depot to Franklin, Hogansville was the trading center for most of Heard County. Post office records show all of Heard County's mail service originated here. Likewise, before the arrival of the Columbus and Rome Railroad at nearby Greenville, the county seat of Meriwether County, the depot at Hogansville served that area as well.

Plate 5.9: The Heard County Courthouse, built in 1894, demolished in 1965. Bruce and Morgan, architects.

What compelled a county so destitute to employ the state's most prestigious architects to build such a courthouse? Before answering the question, we must recall that most counties in Georgia were doubly destitute in the depression year of 1894. Few had experienced any real progress, but many were beginning to nurture railroad-imported dreams conjured up by the sermons preached by New South prophets. If the design of 1894 Heard County Courthouse was driven by such dreams, which it certainly appears to have been, then hope built this courthouse. The real question is: where did this hope come from since there had been no rails to import it?

Perhaps this kind of hope spontaneously sprang up without the usual euphoria created by the arrival of a railroad. This seems very unlikely, although there is some evidence that such far-fetched optimism did occur here. A movement for the construction of a cotton mill was under way in Franklin at about the same time that this courthouse was erected. The absence of rail connections was glossed over as a detail by The Franklin *News and Banner*, which declared, "everything would be right here and hauling it to the railroad would be a small matter."[30] Descriptions of the county's roads of the period make this laughable. Newsprint was plentiful, but without a railroad, real capital for such a mill was nonexistent, and surely everyone knew it. It seems a wildly remote assumption that the investors of Heard County, if there were any, no matter how unsophisticated, could have taken any of this seriously, and even less likely that such a scheme could have attracted outside capital. Thus, it is doubtful that much hope for progress could have arrived in Franklin without rails.

There is, however, another explanation for whatever hopes may have been brewing in Franklin in 1894. Perhaps it was not so much hope brought by a railroad, but hope for a railroad. Indeed, history reveals a number of plans for rails through Franklin. Since antebellum times there had been various schemes for the construction of a rail line north from Columbus to Rome. As early as 1851, the Columbus and West Point Railroad was chartered to supersede the earlier Columbus and West Point Railroad and Plank Road Company. Later in 1870, this plan was adopted by the North and South Railroad Company, which completed a line as far north as Hamilton in 1874. In 1879, the company was reorganized as the Columbus and Rome Railroad, and its rails were extended to Greenville in 1884. Meanwhile in LaGrange, a Columbus to Rome route was on the minds of investors there. According to Troup County history, grading of a link in this line was begun northward from LaGrange toward Franklin first under the charter of the North and South Railroad and later under a new company, the North and South Railroad of LaGrange.[31] Confirmation of this comes in Sholes's 1879 *Gazetteer of Georgia,* which describes Franklin as "on the proposed line of the North and South Railroad." Similarly the North and South's successor, the Columbus and Rome, must have planned its route through Franklin for Sholes's Gazetteer of 1887 describes Franklin as "on the survey of the Columbus and Rome Railroad."

In the meantime, the Columbus-Rome connection was being pursued from the other end by the Chattanooga, Rome and Columbus Railroad, and track was complete from Rome to Carrollton by 1888. Hopes soared on the prospect that the line would extend through Franklin to LaGrange and on to Columbus.[32] Sadly for Franklin, the existence of the Savannah, Griffin and North Alabama's line from Newnan to Carrollton brought Columbus-Rome traffic eastward through Newnan and Griffin. All the while Franklin must have been on a roller coaster of

expectation and disappointment. It is probably safe to say that Franklin's hopes were still alive in 1894 when this courthouse was built, for only three years before the *Newnan Herald* had reported that a survey had been completed for "The Newnan and Franklin Railroad."[33] Although there is no record of a line by this name chartered in the State of Georgia, this may have been the final thrashing on the old Newnan and Western. Chartered back in 1885, the survey of this line alone could have been enough to send spirits soaring in Franklin. Add to this the fact that the Chattahoochee River divides Heard County, and in 1894 the first steel bridge in the county was built at Franklin, thus uniting a county divided and generating much excitement among the merchants of Franklin.[34] All of this could easily have combined to propel the citizens of Franklin to indulge in a few New South fantasies of their own despite their notable lack of progress theretofore.

Perhaps optimism of this sort contributed to the grand style of the 1894 Heard County Courthouse, but we do not have to look so far for the real reason it was built. In the final accounting, it is not really so remarkable that a new courthouse came to be built in such a remote place without the driving hope supplied by new rails. The disappointing truth of the matter is that the original old brick courthouse, which had severed the county from the very beginning, burned to the ground in 1894. A petition for relocation of the county seat to the west bank of the Chattahoochee followed the fire, but by the summer of 1894 with the new steel bridge in place, The Franklin *News and*

---

[25] James C. Bonner, *A Short History of Heard County* (Milledgeville GA: Georgia College, 1967) 11.

[26] U.S. Bureau of the Census. 1910. Population, 385.

[27] Bonner, *A Short History of Heard County,* 9.

[28] Bonner, *A Short History of Heard County,* 2.

[29] Jane M. Strain, ed., *History of the Town of Hogansville, 1870 - 1970* (Hogansville GA: n.p., 1970).

[30] *The News and Banner* (Franklin GA), March 1, 1895.

[31] Smith, *History of Troup County,* 110.

[32] *The Carroll Free Press* (Carrollton GA), June 29, 1888.

[33] Jones and Reynolds, *The Coweta Chronicles,* 305.

[34] *The News and Banner* (Franklin GA), April 20, 1894.

Banner was again waxing eloquent: "...the matter is now settled and patriotic citizens can all go to work together now to fly phoenix-like from the ashes."[35]

Sad to say, very little, save the walls of Bruce and Morgan's dramatic new Romanesque Revival courthouse, would rise above the ground in Heard County, for the ashes here symbolically included a great deal more than the charred remains of the old courthouse. Although the Civil War had not physically touched Heard County, the kind of ashes it left here represented a deeper destruction than did the blacken remains at Atlanta. The fires of Heard County burned not in war, but in the wake of war. They left the cinders of a ruined economic system. As tenancy spread across the land, the consequences for counties like Heard were grim indeed. Here we find the source of all those wretched families who later populated the sprawling mill villages at LaGrange. But as we have seen, there was still hope here 1894, and the full force of exodus did not begin until after the boll weevil in the 1920s.

Even before the death of H. H. Richardson in 1886 and the completion of his landmark Allegheny County Courthouse at Pittsburgh in 1888, the Romanesque Revival had become the style for courthouses in America. It would remain so until the 1893 Columbian Exposition at Chicago unleashed an often tastelessly reactionary and gushingly flamboyant American Neoclassical Revival. Even in Georgia, where America's styles of the day were either rejected out of hand or lagged well behind the rest of the nation, Romanesque buildings had an appeal, as long as they were made of brick. After the success of their grand, Romanesque Revival Sumter County Courthouse at Americus, 1887, the Atlanta firm of Bruce and Morgan designed thirteen Romanesque court buildings between 1892 and 1898 (see Appendix C).

Certainly part of the appeal of this style in places like Heard County came from the fact that, at its very heart, the Romanesque Revival was a reflection of a crude, medieval, rural architecture. When executed in the ubiquitous local red brick, it is little wonder that these buildings recalled older Southern vernacular models. In the hands of less accomplished architects, the style seemed only a more complicated extension of the familiar old brick Federal courthouse style. Buildings like Lewis Goodrich's 1902 Taliaferro County Courthouse at Crawfordville and W. Chamberlain's 1892 Whitfield County Courthouse at Dalton plainly reveal their vernacular roots. Bruce and Morgan, on the other hand, walked a much finer line. Just as they had done a decade earlier with their surprisingly appropriate manipulations of Second Empire designs in rural places like Sparta, 1882; Monroe, 1883, and Gainesville, 1885, the firm built compact, charming Romanesque Revival courthouses which echoed an emotional and uniquely rural message of home and hearth. In all of their Romanesque massing and Queen Anne detail, these buildings were singularly appropriate for small-town Georgia's squares. Their measured monumentality seems at once important and familiar, while picturesque Romanesque arches, towers and stone banding exemplified the contemporary stylistic idiom. One is reminded that the goal of the picturesque is to recall pastoral scenes.

It is bold indeed to compare Alexander Bruce and Thomas Morgan to the great H. H. Richardson. There can be little doubt that Richardson's blinding lamp is historic and far-reaching, while Bruce and Morgan are at best flickering candles in the gales of architectural history. But, in one regard, comparison is instructive. Henry Hobson Richardson took the Romanesque as his vehicle and molded it to reflect his vision of the shape and the motion of a new era. The sweeping movement implied in Richardson's buildings set against their fundamental yet fluid mass attempts the journey from the picturesque to the Sublime, and thus begins the journey to the modern age. Bruce and Morgan on the other hand took the Romanesque for exactly what it was: an ancient rural tradition which was developed in the darkest epoch of Europe's history and carried with it the most rudimentary of classical forms. What could have been more appropriate for Heard County in 1894?

---

[35] *The News and Banner* (Franklin GA), April 6, 1894.

[36] Jonathan Norcross quoted in an interview by Henry Grady quoted in Franklin M. Garrett, *Atlanta and Environs, The Chronicle of Its People and Events*, 3 vols. (New York: Lewis Publishing Company, 1954) 1:258.

SOME LAST THOUGHTS ON THE ATLANTA AND WEST POINT RAILROAD

From the very beginnings of railroads in Georgia, the concept had been the trunk line fed by the branches of many "feeder" lines. The Georgia Railroad had originally been conceived as a trunk from Augusta through the central Piedmont with branches to Eatonton, Madison and Athens. The Central built its trunk from Savannah, to Macon with lines branching along the way, and from its hub at Macon, branches penetrated the newly developing cotton growing regions of southwest Georgia. Likewise employing existing roads as "feeders" to distribute the bounty of the emerging American West, the Western and Atlantic had been chartered with branches in mind, thus uniting Georgia's antebellum rail system at Atlanta.

In 1847, when the forerunner of the Atlanta and West Point, the Atlanta and LaGrange, was chartered, the Georgia Railroad was having limited success with her original "feeder" lines to Washington, Warrenton and Athens. Seeking an expanded and more rewarding "feeder" system, the road invested in branches to the Western and Atlantic and elsewhere. the Rome Railroad, the East Tennessee and Georgia, the Nashville and Chattanooga and the Atlanta and LaGrange all received substantial financial support from the Georgia Railroad in the form of stock subscriptions or bond purchases

Just a few years after its tracks reached Atlanta, the Georgia Railroad formulated the plan for what was to become the Atlanta and West Point Railroad. The stock subscription books were opened at Charleston, Campbellton, Newnan, LaGrange and at Corinth and Franklin in Heard County. As it turned out Campbellton, Franklin and Corinth were not to be on the line, and according to one of Atlanta's most influential early citizens, Jonathan Norcross, Atlanta itself was nearly bypassed.[36] The original plan called for a line from Covington via Griffin to LaGrange. Without doubt this was celebrated in Griffin, adding credence to newly-bankrupt L. L. Griffin's vision of a Southern rail center in that town. But it was not to be for Griffin nor for Covington, and in the end this plan

was seen as a transparent scheme to force freight coming down the Western and Atlantic, bound for western Georgia and LaGrange, over the rails of the Georgia Railroad to Covington. Atlanta was recognized as the natural center, and the geography of the ridgeline from Atlanta to Newnan was deemed perfect. Atlanta's future was thus further cemented, although the Atlanta and West Point chose as its railhead an obscure spot just south of Atlanta on the Macon and Western,

Plate 5.10: Newnan. (Photo: Wilber W. Caldwell.)

a spot which would later become known as East Point. Rails were completed via Fairburn to Newnan in 1851 and all the way to West Point in 1853 where they connected with the newly completed Montgomery and West Point Railroad in Alabama.

In the antebellum period, the rails of the Atlanta and West Point Railroad were chasing cotton all the way from East Point to West Point.[37] The Georgia Piedmont, south and west of Atlanta, was turning white with prosperity in 1853 when this road joined with the Montgomery and West Point Railroad. This Alabama road was built using a different gauge track so all "through passengers" and "through freight" had to be transferred at West Point. Thus the town became a notable railroad center although no crossing or junction occurred there. Attesting to her prominence was an enormous central train shed built in 1854. The only other antebellum buildings of this sort in Georgia were at Atlanta, 1853 and Macon, 1855. Later, similar passenger sheds were completed at Savannah, 1876, Augusta c.1875 and Columbus, 1882 .

The Civil War took its toll on the Atlanta and West Point. Miles of track were destroyed, and Federal forces burned the depots at Fairburn, Palmetto, LaGrange and West Point. By 1868, the road was again in operation, but the awkward mismatch of track gauges at West Point remained a problem long after Reconstruction ended. Track gauges all across the South were standardized in 1886, and soon after, West Point's importance faded. Her great train shed was demolished in 1910. Similarly the stylish passenger depots at LaGrange and Newnan were demolished shortly after the turn of the century to make way for more commodious replacements. Ironically the forces of prosperity that built these charming buildings were the same forces which would later destroy them.

Similarly, courthouse building along the line of the Atlanta and West Point would reflect New South aspirations. Fairburn, born of the railroad in the 1850s, became a county seat in 1870, but no postbellum rails would cross the Atlanta and West Point there, and Campbell County's 1871 court building

would remain the only one the county ever built at Fairburn. Creating less than the usual optimism in Newnan, postbellum rails arrived from Griffin in 1871 on their way to Carrollton in 1874, and the connection of this line through to Rome and Chattanooga was accomplished in 1888. But J. W. Golucke's 1904 Coweta County Courthouse was not a celebration of such ancient history. This grand building may nonetheless owe its inspiration to a railroad, for the Central of Georgia built the line from Newnan to Greenville via Raymond in the same year this courthouse was completed. Thus in 1904, there was much in these new rails for Newnan to celebrate. That short stretch of new track meant that the direct route from Columbus via Rome to Chattanooga no longer passed through Griffin, while Newnan remained an important junction point. In that same year, LaGrange built a classical courthouse, which in part may have reflected the completion of the Macon and Birmingham over a decade earlier. But from the look of the New England-style simplicity of Andrew J. Bryan's Federal Revival Style creation, the building reflected more of the city's textile mills than of any railroad. And so it should have. Only Franklin remained without rails. With her population still below 250 in 1894, when fire destroyed her original courthouse, she built a fine Romanesque Revival courthouse more on wild railroad rumor and vain hope than on anything else.

History is a fickle lover. On LaGrange she bestowed an industrial boon that few cities in Georgia matched, while Newnan remained in the Old South mold, a charming, slow-moving center of area agriculture. In the wings, tiny Fairburn waited, too close to the emerging giant Atlanta to evolve her own identity. And all the while tiny Franklin could only hope, waiting for rails that never came, while the county's population slowly trickled away.

Still, despite history's apparent caprice, there is something in all of this that seems steady and true, something constant in each story. If we go back before the arrival of the railroad and consult that most well traveled of Georgians, George White, we find that the character of each of these places was set almost from their very beginning. White journeyed across the state in the late 1840s, and he published *Statistics of the*

---

[37] West Point had originally been called Franklin until the nearby county town of Heard County was incorporated with the same name in 1831

State of Georgia in 1849. Of course, White has nothing at all to say about Fairburn, for there was no Fairburn in 1849. In Newnan, White found perhaps only what he expected, 8 stores, 3 taverns, 12 lawyers, 3 doctors and "a good sidewalk." It is difficult to read much into this until we compare it with his stunning impressions of LaGrange, which at that time was about the same size as Newnan. Of LaGrange George White waxes exuberant: "No place in Georgia can boast a population from its foundations to the present time, possessing greater merits in point of refinement of manners, benevolence of feeling, intelligence, and moral worth." As for Franklin, we find a suggestion that this was a pretty rough place from the very beginning. White, who is the master of understatement and has absolutely nothing negative to say about even the meanest of mud holes, relates that Franklin had: "much republican simplicity in the manners of the people. They are improving in everything calculated to make good citizens and honest men." Republican simplicity for manners may have been George White's way of saying that these were some very unsophisticated folk, and to say that they were improving in the area of citizenship and honesty certainly implies that they possessed no acceptable level of either. This is all far from scholarly or scientific, but still, the clear inference from this trusted chronicler is this: that Newnan was a comfortable, ordinary kind of place; LaGrange was exceptional and Franklin was rough around the edges. So it was to be.

In 1849, when George White wrote his *Statistics of the State of Georgia,* Atlanta to West Point was not the only route being planned to penetrate the vast and blooming new cotton lands of Western Georgia. Just as the Georgia Railroad had watched over the progress of the Atlanta and LaGrange, down in Macon the Central of Georgia was closely eyeing plans to build a line south and west from Macon with branches to Albany and Columbus. Before the Atlanta and LaGrange reached West Point in 1853, the Southwestern Railroad had laid track from Macon southward through Fort Valley crossing the Flint River at Oglethorpe and was pressing on to Americus. Additionally, the Southwestern had joined with the struggling Muscogee Railroad to connect Macon with

Columbus via Butler, making the junction at Fort Valley.

Even as late as 1853, southwestern Georgia was still a very wild place, but each fall its fertile landscape turned so white that even the most "civilized" parts of the state were quick to forgive these newly landed planters their rough edged ways. The bloodlines of cotton were the most respected pedigree in the state.

•

The Southwestern Railroad

THE MAIN LINE

Bibb County: Macon (see chapters 3 & 8) Peach County: Fort Valley • Macon County: Oglethorpe
Sumter County: Americus • Lee County: Leesburg • Dougherty County: Albany

THE FORT GAINES—GEORGETOWN BRANCH

Terrell County: Dawson • Randolph County: Cuthbert • Quitman County: Georgetown • Clay County: Fort Gaines

THE COLUMBUS BRANCH

Taylor County: Butler • Muscogee County: Columbus • Some Last Thoughts on the Southwestern Railroad

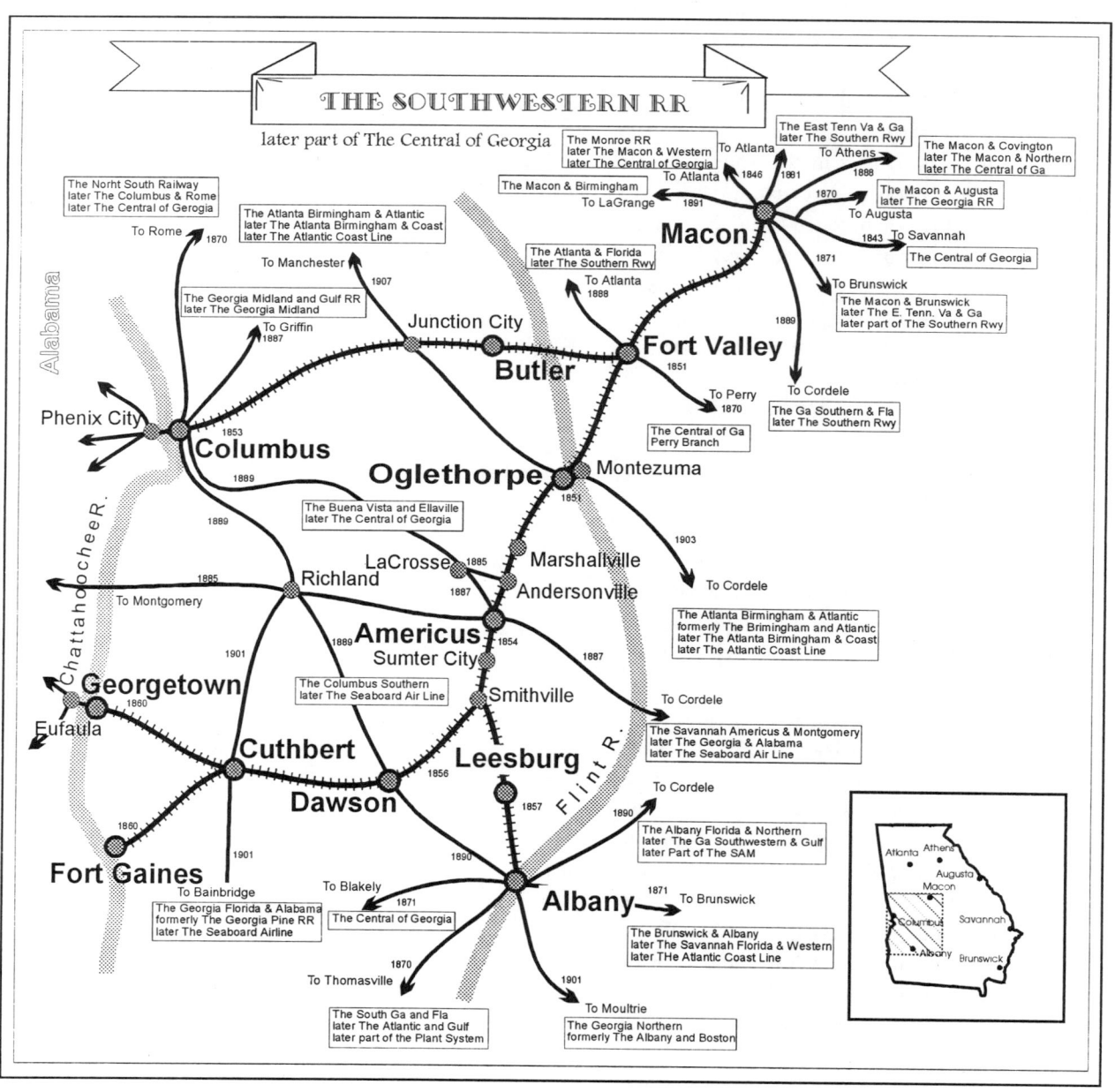

6 | The Southwestern Railroad

THE MAIN LINE: MACON TO ALBANY

PEACH COUNTY: FORT VALLEY

Plate 6.1: The depot at Fort Valley, built 1871.

In 1868, the year after a disastrous fire destroyed almost all of the business section of Fort Valley, Virgil Powers, the superintendent of the Southwestern Railroad, reported to the road's president, Richard Cuyler, that he had built a, "substantial brick Warehouse…at Fort Valley, 40 x 145, with roof projecting over a ten foot platform on three sides…"[1] Two years later, that depot mysteriously burned to the ground. It was replaced in 1871[2] by this early post-war depot. With its graceful brackets, it is similar to the depots built along the Central of Georgia in the late 1860s at places like Tennille, 1869; Millen, 1868; and Toomsboro, 1868. In its quest for cotton, the Central of Georgia had backed the Southwestern Railroad from the very beginning, and the Central would lease the road in 1869, only two years before the completion of this depot at Fort Valley, then in Houston County.

The enormous structure does not sing just songs, but entire operas of cotton. When the Southwestern Railroad arrived at Fort Valley in 1851, Houston County rivaled even Burke County, that perennial giant of the eastern Cotton Belt, in the production of the pivotal staple. The story this depot has to tell, along with those of two additional depots, both built after the turn of the century and both still standing in Fort Valley, can be told in the lives of two men: James Everett and Samuel Rumph.

---

[1] Virgil Powers, "Superintendent's Report" in *Report of the Chief Engineers, Presidents and Superintendents of The Southwestern Railroad* (Macon GA: JW Burke & Co., 1869) 582.

[2] Virgil Powers, "The Superintendent's Report" in *The Annual Reports of the President of The Central Railroad and Banking Company* 3/35 (Savannah GA: The Central Railroad and Banking Company, 1870) 30.

Plate 6.1: The depot at Fort Valley. This enormous structure sings not just songs, but entire operas of cotton. (Photo: Wilber W. Caldwell.)

Houston County records relate that the county's first court session was held in "the blacksmith shop of James Everett," one of southwest Georgia's earliest pioneers.[3] Everett operated an early trading post at the present site of the town of Fort Valley, and in 1834 he arranged for a post office of that name to be moved there from Crawford County. When the Southwestern Railroad was chartered in 1845, James Everett was among the line's first supporters. Seeking a connection between Macon and the Chattahoochee River, the Southwestern struggled to gain support in its early years. Zeal for this project in Macon was only lukewarm. Like Augusta, Macon harbored deep fears that the extension of the railroad would render the town just another stop along the line. Just as these fears delayed the construction of the Central's bridge across the Ocmulgee at Macon, they also spoiled Macon's appetite for stock in the new rail line. Meanwhile, the white promise of rich returns was beginning to cover the fields of southwest Georgia, and while Macon delayed, the fluffy bounty of the west was drifting down the Chattahoochee and the Flint Rivers to Apalachicola. The Central and the city of Savannah greedily came to the rescue of the new line, together pledging $500,000 toward the completion of the road if a like amount could be raised from the counties along the proposed route.

Thus, despite the Southewestern's slow start and the Central's powerful support, it was investors like James Everett who finally made the line a reality. The list of subscribers from Houston County is headed by James Everett, who subscribed a substantial 200 shares. As a cotton grower, Everett prized the railroad.

As a land speculator, he saw to it that the line came to Fort Valley, for he sensed the power of rail. It was James Everett who donated the land for the depot and the right of way through Fort Valley to the new railroad company. It is said that the Southwestern was his greatest dream, but he did not live to see its arrival in Houston County. He died in 1848, before the tracks of the Southwestern were complete to Fort Valley, and at his own request he was buried along the right of way somewhere near the future site of this depot.

Plate 6.2: The depot at Marshallville, built 1912.

In 1851, the year the Southwestern arrived at Fort Valley, Samuel Rumph was born on his father's plantation near Marshallville in Macon County only 8 miles south of James Everett's still fresh grave. In the early 1870s, when Rumph developed the Elberta Peach, the Houston County town of Perry, bypassed by the main line of the Southwestern, had just over 800 residents while Fort Valley counted over 1300 and was the junction point for the Southwestern Railroad's branches to Columbus and to Perry. Realizing handsome profits from his robust Elberta as early as 1875, Rumph had successfully shipped large quantities of the new variety to New York. By 1886, when a substantial new wooden depot rose at Marshallville,[4] his orchards contained over 65,000 peach trees covering over 400 acres.[5] So prosperous were Rumph's efforts, that the Central built a spur from the main line to the Rumph packing house, and before 1900 the area around Fort Valley no longer turned white each Fall, but pink each Spring, as the county tended 829,000 peach trees. Rumph died in 1922, ten years after the 1886 wooden depot burned and was replaced by this fine brick structure. Two years after Rumph's death, Peach County was carved from cotton's defunct kingdom in Houston, Crawford and Macon Counties.

This was a success story that New South promoters could sink their teeth into. Here was the very image of the agricultural diversity they had so long preached and so deceitfully described to Northern capitalists in their fanciful accounts of the region's thriving good health and boundless possibilities. Here was a cash crop that was not cotton. Still, peaches were no staple crop, and their impact on the state's agricultural woes was negligible before cotton's decline. Despite Rumph's considerable success in Houston County and some modest successes in a few other counties, it would be years before peaches came close to toppling King Cotton from his throne. Cotton's eventual fall would come only after the boll weevil, after the stern Federal regulations of the 1930s and after the reorganization of the nation's agricultural credit system in the New Deal.

Nonetheless, Samuel Rumph proved that it was not solely a lack of alternative crops that bound Georgia's farmers to their continued groveling at the feet of the cotton king. Samuel Rumph, himself a successful cotton planter, demonstrated profitable diversity with peaches in the 1880s, and other counties would demonstrate pockets of local diversity with livestock, vegetables, apples, corn, tobacco, grain, and a variety of other agricultural products well before 1900. But a look at the aggregate value of the cotton and the peach crops for the year 1900 reveals what New South promoters refused to acknowledge: the truth veiled by the myth of diversified agriculture. In 1900, Georgia's fruits, nuts and all other orchard products were valued at $672,000. Her cotton harvest for that year totaled $57,171,000.[6]

While Samuel Rumph and his uncle, Lewis, were covering Houston and Macon Counties with peach orchards in the 1880s, aspirations in Fort Valley were soaring on the prospect of crossing rails. Most notable were several schemes to build lines from Dublin to Fort Valley in 1886 and 1887. All of this speculation came to nothing, but one new railroad did come steaming south out of Atlanta and into Fort Valley carrying with it the full-blown myth of a New South. The Atlanta and Florida Railroad Company acted on the charter of the old Atlanta and Hawkinsville Railroad and built southward from Atlanta through Fayetteville and Zebulon, passing near Knoxville at Roberta, and arrived in Fort Valley in 1888. Initially the line had visions of continuing to Cordele, Waycross, and on to Florida.[7] The effect of this new road was electric. Had Fort Valley been the Houston County seat, she surely would have been compelled to build a new courthouse just as Fayetteville,[8] and Zebulon had

Plate 6.2: In 1886, when the wooden predecessor of this fine depot at Marshallville was built, Samuel Rumph's nearby orchards contained over 65,000 peach trees. (Photo: Wilber W. Caldwell.)

been moved to do. The festivities at Fort Valley were reportedly gala. A great barbecue was held to celebrate the new road's arrival, and *The Fort Valley Enterprise* described the grand events that followed in an extravagant "Barbecue Edition."[9] In 1888, the air around Fort Valley was charged with expectation, but hard times still lay ahead.

[3] Bobbe S. Hickson, *A Land So Dedicated, A History of Houston County* (Perry GA: Houston County Library Board, 1976) 56.

[4] Theodore D. Kline, "The Superintendents Report to the President of The Central Railroad and Banking Company" in *The Annual Reports of the President of The Central Railroad and Banking Company*, 6 vols. (Savannah GA: JW Burke & Co., 1886) 42.

[5] *Atlanta Journal*, July 1, 1889.

[6] Willard Range, *A Century of Georgia Agriculture, 1850-1950* (1954; reprint, Athens GA: University of Georgia Press, 1969) 117. The choice of the year 1900 may be misleading for the statewide peach crop of only 259,000 bushels was extraordinarily low. Even, in the good year of 1910, when Georgia produced over 2.5 million bushels of peaches at a value exceeding 2.5 million dollars, revenues from cotton (including cottonseed sales) were nearly 150 million dollars.

[7] *The Pike County Journal*, February 26, 1889, and May 5, 1889.

[8] Courthouse building in Fayetteville was limited to a complete remodeling and the addition of a grand tower designed by Atlanta's Alexander Bruce and Thomas Henry Morgan.

[9] *The Fort Valley Enterprise*, June 15, 1888.

MACON COUNTY: OGLETHORPE

Plate 6.3: The depot at Montezuma, built c. 1905. Moved to Tifton for restoration and display at the Georgia Agrirama.

The story of the courthouse and the depot in Macon County is a tale of four cities all built along the same short stretch of the Flint River. Two of these towns, Oglethorpe and Montezuma, remain today, and two, Traveler's Rest and Lanier, are among the dead towns of Georgia, barely even memories of a long past era.

For Oglethorpe, the moment of hope arrived with the railroad in 1851. But in the blink of a few years, the crest of any perceived progress had passed, trampled before the horsemen of a uniquely Southern Apocalypse: disease and war, followed by cotton's tyranny of tenancy and widespread economic stagnation. Still, the struggling town managed to retain distinction as the seat of county government, despite the growth of her sister railroad city, Montezuma, which lay just across the river.

Oglethorpe's decline, although sudden, was not nearly so complete nor dramatic as that of the two original towns that occupied the opposite side of the Flint. Before the arrival of the railroad in the early 1850s, Lanier and Traveler's Rest graced the east bank of the Flint near the present site of Montezuma. Lanier, the original county seat, had been laid out in

1837 shortly after Macon County was created. About two miles to the South, Traveler's Rest was much older. Just how old no one can say. We know that around 1790 Timothy Barnard, one of the earliest settlers in this area, had established a trading post on the Flint's west bank on the very spot where the town of Oglethorpe stands today and that he operated a ferry at "Barnard's Crossing." Traveler's Rest grew up at this crossing.

Before the end of 1851, the Southwestern Railroad had bridged the Flint and built a large wooden depot on the west bank at Oglethorpe.[10] By 1854, Oglethorpe had grown so that the county's 700 voters elected to move the county seat there from its original site at Lanier. About this time, Montezuma appeared on the east bank across from Oglethorpe. The old 1838 frame courthouse at Lanier was moved to Schley County in 1854 and used as a private residence for over 100 years. It was recently demolished. Lanier and Traveler's Rest soon faded from memory. Today nothing remains of either save a few crumbling headstones. Oglethorpe appropriated its old market building as a temporary courthouse. When this building burned in 1857, the county moved into a fine brick building which, although not originally designed to be a courthouse, still stands today on the main corner in Oglethorpe and bears a striking resemblance to the old courthouse at nearby Knoxville.

The old Union Depot at Oglethorpe, which once stood at the very crossing of the tracks of the Central of Georgia and the Atlanta, Birmingham and Atlantic was demolished long ago. Only the relics of the ticket office and the waiting rooms remain, rotting in a dense thicket not two hundred yards from their former foundations. The rescue of the old Atlanta, Birmingham and Atlantic depot at Montezuma by the Georgia Agrirama at Tifton resulted in what is today arguably the finest restoration of a wooden depot in the state. This building with its picturesque corner tower is typical of the early A. B. A. depots. Nearly identical buildings can be seen at the village of Ideal in Macon County, in downtown Tifton and at Andersonville, where the old 1904 A. B. A. depot from Mauk in Taylor County has been relocated and restored.

Plate 6.3: The rescue of this old Atlanta, Birmingham and Atlantic depot by the Georgia Agrirama at Tifton resulted in arguably the finest restoration of wooden depot in the state. (Photo: Wilber W. Caldwell)

Plate 6.4: The Macon County Courthouse, built in 1894. Walter Chamberlain, architect.

If this courthouse has a story to tell, it is the story of Oglethorpe's fight to keep the county seat against the larger and perhaps more progressive Montezuma. By 1890, with a population of 486, Oglethorpe had realized little growth since before 1860 while Montezuma's residents numbered above 700. A memorable fight for the honor of the county seat ensued with Montezuma promising to build a $20,000 courthouse should the seat of local government be relocated. Oglethorpe countered with its own plans for a courthouse, apparently purchasing the design from W. Chamberlain of Knoxville, Tennessee.

The courthouse battle in Macon County finally came to a vote in 1894, and according to county histories more than 2000 votes were cast in a county with less than 1000 registered voters. Ever since the enfranchisement of multitudes of Freedmen at the end of the war and the political corruption that followed during Reconstruction, the power of the votes of Georgia's black population had been shamelessly manipulated and abused in election after election. By the 1890s, with Populism a serious challenge to Georgia's Democratic machine, blatant and fraudulent manipulation of black votes was pervasive, and things had reached depths so alarmingly low, that even those who manipulated the elections were beginning to worry.[11] According to Macon County sources, "whiskey flowed like water" and "special trains" were chartered to bring "Negroes from Albany" to vote in the election.[12] The conservative "rural" vote sided with tradition,[13] and Oglethorpe prevailed.

Although designed generally in the Romanesque Revival style, Walter Chamberlain's court buildings here and at Nashville, 1898, and Dalton, 1894, reflect little of the eclectic fantasies of the age. These buildings convey a stern and fundamental message, and appear quite crude. The brick corbeling, banding and other decoration is of an almost vernacular sort. It is possible that the most compelling attribute of these designs was the promise that they could be built by ordinary masons who did not possess any of the special skills needed to produce the fantasy courthouses that were going up elsewhere in the state. Romanesque

Plate 6.4: Walter Chamberlain's 1894 Macon County Courthouse was erected to fend off Montezuma's attempts to wrestle the county seat away from Oglethorpe. (Photo: Wilber W. Caldwell.)

court buildings in the adjacent counties of Sumter at Americus, 1887; Talbot at Talbotton, 1892; Dooly at Vienna, 1892, and Schley at Ellaville, 1900, all exuberantly and eloquently celebrated the arrival of the pervasive New South myth of better times. But Macon County's strange new courthouse at Oglethorpe contemplated what is perhaps a more appropriate Southern reality: a desperate attempt to simply hang on to what little progress hapless Oglethorpe had achieved.

This is a building of desperation, just as the fraudulent votes, which indirectly created it, were products of desperation and fear. It was a very Southern kind of fear, at the heart of which lay the nebulous horror of loss of identity. With large parts of the South still in economic ruin, the Southern identity in 1894 had become fragile indeed. Propped up

[10] According to the Chief Engineer's Report to the President of the Southwestern, in 1850 a warehouse (depot) 33' x 103' was "in an advanced state towards completion." E. P. Holcomb, "Superintendent's Report" in the *Report of the Chief Engineers, Presidents and Superintendents of The Southwestern Railroad* (Macon GA: JW Burke & Co., 1869) 140.

[11] C. Vann Woodward, *Origins of the New South, 1877-1913* (1951; reprint, Baton Rouge LA: Louisiana State University Press, 1993) 326-27.

[12] Louise Frederick Hays, *History of Macon County, Georgia* (Atlanta: Stein Printing, 1933) 367.

[13] Hays, *History of Macon County, Georgia*, 222.

only by the fallacious myths of both the Old South and the New, Southern pride was bolstered by rose-colored remembrances and unrealistic hopes, all held motionless in the horrific politics of white supremacy.

All the rusty metals of fear and crumbling identity would combine with that particularly bold braggadocio seemingly inherent in the Southern character. The resulting alloy was a pervasive civic spirit that penetrated the very fabric of Southern society. As hopes for New South progress mushroomed in the heady atmosphere created by postbellum railroads, local competition increased and the accompanying boasts grew bolder and strayed farther from reality, creating their own absurd mythology. Claiming enormous growth after the arrival of the Southwestern Railroad, Oglethorpe propagated particularly bald-faced exaggerations with regard to her population, progress and importance. In his 1849 *Statistics of Georgia* the reliable George White makes no mention of Oglethorpe in his descriptions of Macon County, but in his 1855 *Historical Collections of Georgia* he describes Oglethorpe as "situated as to command trade of a large portion of Southwest Georgia. The place is rapidly improved." Here was fuel for myth. Writing in the first half of the twentieth century, local historians reading White's words would translate this "commanding situation" into wild flights of fancy regarding the town's growth after the arrival of the Southwestern. Several books, pamphlets and articles, including an official 1933 *History of Macon County*, go into elaborate detail to describe a "hey-day" in Oglethorpe in the mid-1850s. These sources claim that the town grew to over 20,000 with 80 "business houses" becoming "the largest city in southwest Georgia"[14] before a mass exodus occurred after the extension of the Southwestern Railroad to Americus in 1854 followed by a devastating small pox epidemic in 1858.[15] Additionally, these histories claim that the town was under consideration to replace Milledgeville as capital of the state. According to historian, Spencer Bidwell King, many Georgia boomtowns of the era were proposed as possible sites for the state capital. Among these were Griffin, Atlanta, Savannah, Madison, Stone Mountain, and Indian Springs, but according to Prof. King, "there is

no evidence that the legislature ever seriously considered making Oglethorpe the state's capital."[16] According to United States Census figures, Oglethorpe had a population of 113 whites and an unrecorded number of blacks in 1850, and in 1860 the town reported a total of only 454 residents. It appears that the ten-year period in between these census reports is the subject of a rather enlightening episode of exaggeration and myth-making.

To be sure, Oglethorpe experienced a brief prominence as the terminus of the Southwestern Railroad, but the road arrived in 1851, and by 1852, stock was being sold to finance the road's extension. By 1854, the Southwestern had reached Americus, and by 1857, Albany. Thus the period during which Oglethorpe was perceived as "terminus" was quite brief. As to the smallpox reported to have begun in 1858, there is evidence that there was incidence of the disease in 1853[17] and again as late as 1862,[18] but the claim of hundreds of deaths before 1860 seems as bogus as the 20,000 population.[19]

Although smallpox was undoubtedly a factor in ending Oglethorpe's boom, it seems more likely that the fear of the disease put a premature end to the town's sudden growth rather than wiping out a vast entrenched population. This probably hastened the inevitable exodus that was a consequence of the railroad's extension to Americus. We might hazard a guess as to Oglethorpe's size at the height of its "heyday" by considering a few comparisons. In 1860, the population of Macon was only 8247 and Columbus, with all of its mills, only 9621; Atlanta, the quintessential boomtown, had reached 9554. Atlanta is perhaps a good measuring stick. Construction on the Western and Atlantic was begun in the early 1840s, and by 1846 both the Central and the Georgia Railroads had also reached the "terminus." Three years later, in 1849, Atlanta's population stood at about 2000.[20] If we give Oglethorpe the benefit of the doubt, and compare it to the South's most successful city, Atlanta, a few years after the arrival of the railroad, we might stretch and say that the town reached a population of between 1500 and 2000, but this is probably generous. The loss of trade and the exodus of railroad crews along with the riffraff that generally attach themselves to transient work camps could easily account for a substantial out-migration in Oglethorpe before 1860, thus returning the town to its former population of about 500.

After all of the fireworks created by local pride and amateur historians, consulting a professional like U. B. Phillips can place things in perspective. Of Oglethorpe's boom Phillips simply says: "the town had a boom of trade so long as it was the head of the railroad, and then sank to village status."[21]

Sumter County: Americus

Plate 6.5: The Sumter County Courthouse, built in 1847. Clock tower added 1866. Demolished 1887.

The life Samuel Hugh Hawkins is a paradigm for the story of Americus. With all its twists and turns, history seldom provides such startling parallels. In 1835, the year after Sumter County erected its first simple frame courthouse on the square at Americus, Samuel Hawkins was born in Jones County. In 1847, the year this fine brick structure replaced that first crude court building, Hawkins moved with his family to Sumter County, establishing a cotton plantation

Plate 6.5: The 1847 Sumter County Courthouse.

near Magnolia Springs. At that time, Americus had a population of 117.[22] Southwestern Georgia between the Flint and the Chattahoochee Rivers had

[14] The population claim seems to stem from a 1914 publication by Lucian Lamar Knight. Knight was a prolific amateur historian, and writing after the turn of the century, he produced biography, historical sketchbooks, collections of oratory, and collections of Georgia lore. His work, while extremely useful, bears the unmistakable bias of his era. In the case of Oglethorpe's population claim of 20,000, the statistic first appeared in Knight's work entitled *Georgia's Landmarks, Memorials and Legends*. Lucian Lamar Knight, *Georgia's Landmarks, Memorials and Legends* 2 vols. (Atlanta: Lucian Lamar Knight, 1914) 2:857.

[15] Hays, *History of Macon County, Georgia*, 177; and Lois Payne, Historical Sketches of Oglethorpe (1933; reprint, Spartanburg SC: Reprint Company, 1979). Both of these references claim population to have reached 20,000. Ryland D. Fowler, *Macon County Life* (Montezuma GA: Macon County Historical Society, 1983) claims a population exceeding 12,000.

[16] Spencer Bidwell King, ed., "Rebel Lawyer: The Letters of Lt. Theodorick W.

Montfort, 1861-1862" *The Georgia Historical Quarterly* 68/3 (June 1964): 319.

[17] In his report to the president of the Southwestern Railroad in 1853, Superintendent, George Adams, mentions small pox in Oglethorpe and Marshallville "for several months." George Adams, "Superintendent's Report" in *Report of the Chief Engineers, Presidents and Superintendents of The Southwestern Railroad* (Macon, 1869), 174. A letter to the editor of Macon's *Georgia Journal and Messenger* signed mysteriously by "M." recounts Oglethorpe's boom following the railroad's arrival and the town's sudden stagnation, being "cut off from the world" owning to "not more than 20 cases of "Chicken Pox." According to M. there were six fatalities, so undoubtedly this was small pox. The letter goes on to detail quarantine enforcement and vaccination efforts. *The Journal and Messenger*, March 16, 1853. Only five months later, Robert Toombs addressed a crowd of 700 in Oglethorpe, so it seems the scare was quickly over. *The Georgia Journal and Messenger*, Aug. 31, 1853.

[18] County Historian Louise Hays cites records of the State of Georgia, which list reimbursements to medical personnel for expenses incurred in the course of their efforts to treat 25 cases of small pox in Macon County in 1862. Hays, *History of Macon County, Georgia*, 181.

[19] A review of Macon's *Georgia Journal and Messenger* between 1858 and 1862 reveals several references to smallpox: six possible cases in Dalton in 1858, one outbreak along the Chattahoochee River in 1859 with about 20 cases and "several deaths," and fifteen non-fatal cases just south of Macon itself in 1860. If a few suspected cases in Dalton made headlines in Macon, certainly "hundreds of deaths" in Oglethorpe would have incited panic.

[20] James Mitchell Russell, Atlanta, 1847-1890, *City Building in the Old South and the New* (Baton Rouge LA: Louisiana State University Press, 1988) 27.

[22] Daisy Malard and Virginia Culpepper, "Americus", in *The Georgia Review* 4/1 (Athens 1950): 116, and Jack F. Cox, *History of Sumter County, Georgia* (Roswell GA: W.H. Wolfe, 1983) 4.

been opened to settlers in the land lottery of 1827, and in the 1840s planters like Ezekiel Hawkins, Samuel's father, were still arriving eager to extract the rewards of cotton from the rich soil of western Georgia.

In 1854, the Southwestern Railroad arrived at Americus ready for business, and progress was on the wind as *The Sumter Republican* faithfully reports: "New Buildings are being erected in every direction, north, south, east and west. The mechanic is to be seen busily applying the implements of his profession, and every breeze wafts to the ear the hum of industry and enterprise."[23] *The Sumter Republican* goes on to describe the construction of entire blocks of wooden stores and warehouses. Three years later in 1857, Samuel Hugh Hawkins, returning to Americus from Columbus where he had passed the Georgia bar, was also ready for business.

Plate 6.6: The depot at Americus, built c.1870.

In 1931, *The Americus Daily Times Reporter* published an interview with long time Americus resident, C. A. Fricher, who remembered the old antebellum wooden depot that this building replaced: "We had a little old wooden box of a depot before and sometime after the war...we didn't aspire to much then."[24] In 1869, Virgil Powers, the Superintendent of the Southwestern Railroad, had reported to the president of the road regarding that very structure: "The Warehouse at Americus...will have to be thoroughly

repaired at heavy comparative cost. I believe it will be an economy in the end to take it down and build a good, substantial brick warehouse; I recommend that this be done."[25]

Power's depot at Americus was cloned from the Central of Georgia's standard brick warehouse-depot plan. It is nearly identical to depots at Montezuma, c.1870, and Fort Valley, 1871, as well as several structures on the Central's main line between Savannah and Macon, notably those at Millen, 1868; Tennille, 1869; Bartow, 1869, and Toomsboro, 1869. Despite this architectural similarity, Americus was different. The seeds of her early success seem to lie in a shrewd ambition. That she believed in the power of the railroad is clear from her aggressive courtship of the southward extension of the Southwestern beyond the temporary railhead at Oglethorpe. The original 1847 survey had called for a more westerly route from

Plate 6.6: The 1870 depot at Americus was cloned from the Central of Georgia's standard warehouse plan. (Photo: Wilber W. Caldwell.)

[23] *The Weekly Sumter Republican,* September 21, 1854, quoted in William Williford, *Americus Through the Years* rev.ed. (Atlanta: Cherokee Publishing, 1960) 8.

[24] C. A. Fricher quoted in *The Americus Times Reporter*, December 8, 1931.

[25] Virgil Powers, "Superintendent's Report" in *Report of the Chief Engineers, Presidents and Superintendents of The Southwestern Railroad*, 582.

[26] L. O. Reynolds, "Superintendent's Report: in the *Report of the Chief Engineers, Presidents and Superintendents of The Southwestern Railroad*, 161.

[27] Phillips, *History of Transportation in the Eastern Cotton Belt to 1860*, 279.

[28] Phillips, *History of Transportation in the Eastern Cotton Belt to 1860*, 295 This date is more likely 1858, Albany Patriot, February 18, 1858, quoted in Historical Background of Dougherty County, 1836 - 1940 (Atlanta: 1981), 15-16.

Oglethorpe to Richland in Stewart County with the main trunk south to the Chattahoochee River and branches to Columbus, Albany and Cuthbert. But the directors of the Southwestern made it clear that their plans could be coerced. The President's report of 1852 states the case: "RESOLVED: This Board has always shown its willingness to extend the Road wherever a sufficient sum of money should be subscribed to authorize an extension."[26] And this account from the reliable U. B. Phillips: "In 1852-53 the citizens of Americus and vicinity subscribed and had paid $75,000 to secure the extension to their town costing $125,000 in addition to that amount…. The policy of allowing local subscriptions was thus successful after the company had built its initial stem mostly with resources contributed by Savannah and the Central of Georgia Railroad."[27] As further enticement, business interests in Albany had, at about this same time, incorporated the Georgia and Florida Railroad Company and begun construction of a line southward from Americus toward Albany. Only 25 miles of this road were completed when it was absorbed by the Southwestern in 1857.[28]

An architectural stroll around Americus's former courthouse square today reveals the town's early progress. Few antebellum structures remain, but unlike most Georgia towns, whose progress is marked by brick buildings built in the years just before and after the turn of the century, Americus's streets are lined with graceful structures of an earlier period. The effect is unusual for southwest Georgia. In fact, the stylish facades of brick buildings from the 1870s, 1880s, and early 1890s, built at a time when most of Georgia was balanced on the brink of economic ruin, recall Northern and Midwestern towns which flourished in mid-century. Today the elegant details of the Italianate Style still frame the windows and decorate the cornices of the many fine commercial buildings. Like Virgil Powers's sturdy depot at Americus, this too is the architecture of cotton, and it testifies to Americus's railroad dreams (see Table 6.1) and to the city's importance as a center for factors and merchants.

About the same time that this depot was completed, Samuel Hawkins and a few associates obtained a charter for the Bank of Americus, and in an atmos-

phere of growth, he began his remarkable rise and fall as a financier and railroad baron—a most un-Southern career.

Plate 6.7: The completion of G. L. Norrman's stunning Windsor Hotel in 1891 scribed the high water mark of an economic surge in Americus that came just before financial disaster. (Photo: Wilber W. Caldwell.)

Plate 6.7: The Windsor Hotel, built in 1891. G. L. Norrman, architect.

This building, built in 1891 by Samuel Hawkins's Americus Investment Company, sounds the music of Americus at its peak, thus it sings of Col. Samuel Hawkins at the peak of an extraordinary career.

The conventional mythologies of America as a whole, and of the American South in particular, maintain that part of the Southern dilemma after the war was rooted in a refusal of the region to shed the old agrarian clothing and don the garments of the industrial age. Surely there was much for Southerners to despise in the national corruptions of the early post-war era. In many minds, the Old South had

RAILROADS PROPOSED FOR AMERICUS BUT NEVER BUILT
The Americus and Jacksonville Railroad
The Americus and Florence, Alabama, Railroad
The Americus and Isabella Railroad
The Atlanta, Americus and Florida Railroad
The Newnan and Americus Railroad

Table 6.1

represented the last barrier to this advancing juggernaut and its accompanying Federalism. Everywhere the claw of American industry greedily raked in the abundance a once virgin land. Samuel Hawkins was a member of that rare breed of Southerners who would attempt such exploitation.

At the center of Samuel Hawkins' aspirations for himself and for Americus was the railroad. Even before the war, cotton's all-powerful interests had become so intermingled with Georgia's steel highways that the railroads had come to be a part of almost every aspect of Southern economic life. Hawkins was among those who not only comprehended the power of rail, but recognized the exploitive policies by which the railroads in general and the Central of Georgia in particular manipulated the towns along their routes. By the mid-1870s, the Central's uneven and boldly monopolistic rate policies had created in Samuel Hawkins an early and most unlikely advocate of state control of the railroads. The son of a planter, Col. Hawkins appeared the prototypical Southern gentleman, complete with a little white goatee. During the war he had been a lieutenant following Forrest and Cheatham to both glory and defeat.[29]

Despite his legal training, he was a strange candidate to champion a cause of such liberal content. Nonetheless, Hawkins and others like him, helped Georgia to become the first Southern State to create a Railroad Commission.

The Georgia Constitutional Convention of 1877 had mandated the creation of a body to oversee Georgia's railroads, and the Georgia Railroad Commission was chartered in 1879. With broad powers to regulate rates, Georgia's Commission became a model for many of the turn-of-the-century reorganizations in other Southern states whose early railroad regulatory organizations had functioned only in advisory capacities.[30] But the Central was powerful, and like so many railroads of the era, it justified a wide variety of rate structures on the grounds of low population density, low-grade cargo, and a predominance of one-way and local traffic.[31] According to Maxwell Furgeson's study, *State Regulation of Railroads in the South:* "The railroads, on the whole, simply refused to conform to the regulation of the

board….Whatever complaint was made to the commission the offending railroad promptly refunded the overcharge—amounting, in some cases, to but a few dollars; and having thus disposed of that particular complaint, continued its extra-legal policy as before."[32] The law that created the Georgia Commission and the performance of the commission in its early years are perhaps best judged by the charges of corruption and the cries for reform that echoed through the state in the 1890s. Suffice it to say, in the early 1880s, the Georgia Railroad Commission had proved impotent to fully control the Central, which continued to exploit with an ever-widening web of track.

In 1889, the Central acquired the Buena Vista and Ellaville Railroad. Originally chartered in 1883 as the Buena Vista Railroad, the line was proposed from Buena Vista to Oglethorpe, but in 1885 it was built from Buena Vista to Andersonville. This line, which was controlled by the Central from it beginning, threatened Americus. Things were nearing a crisis when Hawkins and his associates took a bold step. If the state could not control what they perceived to be the abuses of the Central, then they would take matters into their own hands and build a competitive line. Just as Macon's early rebellion against the abusive rate structures of the Central of Georgia had created the Macon and Augusta, so a similar situation in Americus created the Savannah, Americus and Montgomery Railroad. Later, simply called "The S.A.M.," the original line was chartered in 1884 as the narrow gauge Americus, Preston and Lumpkin Railroad. Its initial purpose was to connect Americus with the Chattahoochee River in Stewart County. The Americus, Preston and Lumpkin was complete by 1886. This forced the Central's pawn, the Buena Vista and Ellaville, to forsake Andersonville and build from Ellaville to Americus in 1887. Connections from Buena Vista to Columbus followed in 1889. Meanwhile, the Americus, Preston and Lumpkin continued to expand. Crossing the Ocmulgee at Abbeville in 1887, the line was rechartered in 1889 as the Savannah, Americus and Montgomery. It ran as far east as Lyons where it connected with the Central of Georgia's subsidiary, the Savannah and Western, in

1890. In 1891, a reciprocal agreement had been reached whereby the SAM was allowed to use the Savannah and Western's tracks from Lyons to Savannah, in exchange for track rights from Lyons into Americus.[33] In that same year, at the other end if the line, the SAM reached its western terminus at Montgomery.

Plate 6.8: The Sumter County Courthouse, built in 1887. Demolished 1959. Bruce and Morgan, architects.

By 1887, the success of the SAM must have created a kind of missionary zeal in Samuel Hawkins and his associates. If ever the euphoria brought by antebellum rails created a monument to mercantile dreams, it was here, where the rails of hope were a local product not an exploitive import. Hawkins himself was on the building committee that sought to create at Americus, a grand symbol for that city's newfound expectations—a courthouse unlike anything then found in Georgia. As if to confirm her aggressive commercialism, the city sold her square to Hawkins's Americus Investment Company for $5000 and a guaranteed expenditure of $75,000 for the Windsor Hotel and $25,000 for promotional efforts to attract industry. Selecting a less central site, the committee hired what was arguably the premiere architectural firm in Georgia, Bruce and Morgan, who were fresh from Second Empire courthouse successes most recently in 1884 in Newton County at Covington. With the construction of the SAM, Americus had been quick to take up the banner of the New South, and given the American architectural horizon in 1887, the choice of the Romanesque Revival Style for the new Sumter County Courthouse must have seemed obvious.

With Henry Hobson Richardson's death in 1886, the Richardsonian Romanesque became the new architectural symbol for emerging American industrialism. Richardson had died a young man the year before Bruce and Morgan's Sumter County Courthouse was completed. While Richardson was alive there had been little of the Richardsonian Romanesque that did not come from the master's own office, but immediately following his death, there was a rush to embrace his style, which many proclaimed

Plate 6.8: The 1887 Sumter County Courthouse at Americus was the first of Atlanta architects, Bruce and Morgan's thirteen Romanesque Revival court buildings. (Photo: Courtesy of Georgia Dept. of Archives and History.)

not revivalist, but "reformist."[34] A monograph of his work published soon after his death had a major influence throughout the country. In 1891, Montgomery Schuyler describes the rush to worship at the altar of Richardson: "While he was living and practicing architecture, architects who regarded themselves as in any degree his rivals were naturally loath to introduce in a design dispositions or features or details, of which the suggestion plainly came from him. Since his death has extinguished envy and ended rivalry the admiration his work excited has been free to express either in direst imitation or in the adoption or elaboration of the suggestions his work furnished."[35] Alexander Bruce and Thomas Henry Morgan shared the sudden national enthusiasm for H.

[29] Knight, *Georgia and Georgians*, 4:3245.

[30] Arthur S. Link, "The Progressive Movement in the South, 1870-1914" in Patrick Gerster and Nicholas Cords, eds., *Myth and Southern History* 2nd ed. 2 vols. (Urbana and Chicago: University of Illinois Press, 1989) 1: 71.

[31] Woodward, *Origins of the New South*, 1877-1913, 312.

[32] Maxwell Ferguson, *State Regulation of Railroads in the South* (New York: Columbia University Press, 1916) 102.

[33] Les R. Winn, *Ghost Trains and Depots in Georgia* (Chamblee GA: Big Shanty Press, 1995) 168.

[34] Henry Van Brunt, "Henry Hobson Richardson, Architect"(1886) in William A. Coles, ed., *Architecture and Society, The Essays of Henry Van Brunt* (Cambridge: Belknap Press of Harvard University, 1969) 178.

[35] Montgomery Schuyler (1891) quoted in Marcus Wiffen, *American Architecture Since 1870, A Guide to Styles* (Cambridge MA and London: MIT Press, 1960) 137.

H. Richardson's work. After 1886, they designed nine Romanesque courthouses in Georgia, most with substantial Richardsonian influence.[36] This was the first.

While there was much of the Romanesque Revival already in Georgia, Richardson's ideas represented something more than just another voice in the picturesque choir of nineteenth century revivalism. Rooted in the simplicity and strength of the ancient architecture of the Avergne, Anjou and Provence, Richardson's historical vocabulary was remarkably small. Nonetheless, he brought to his buildings a personal force that transcended any mere stylistic historical revival and supplied what many believe to be the foundations for a unique and long-awaited American architectural style. In 1887, Bruce and Morgan, as admirers of Richardson, were probably unaware that, they were offered the opportunity to pioneer a new architecture. Sadly, like many of Richardson's followers of the next decade, they would produce only diluted imitations. The Sumter County Courthouse is such a building. It lacks the powerful sense of continuous mass and motion characteristic of Richardson's public buildings. The stone voussoirs of the dual arched entrance and the stone banding defining the second story and segmenting the tower are in the Richardsonian mold. But the smooth surface of the structure's brick skin lacks the power of Richardson's favored rough hewn stone, and the picturesque plan with all of its towers and bays fails to project the master's sense of motion and flow. The building drips with superfluous and confusing Renaissance ornament like the pediments above the clocks, the star motif in the triple arched windows and

the terra-cotta decorations in the tower. Although a notable achievement in the history of public building in Georgia, the Sumter County Courthouse hardly defines any new national architectural horizons. On the contrary, its songs mouth the familiar lyric of the eclectic age, and that, after all, is what the citizens of Americus had commissioned.

In the end, only a few would comprehend the direction implied by Henry Hobson Richardson's remarkable genius and far-sighted vision. Only Lewis Sullivan and Frank Lloyd Wright and, to a lesser degree, a small handful of others, like John Wellborn Root and Bruce Price would grasp the implications of Richardson's ideas and set the course toward a new and uniquely American modern style. Way down South in Georgia, the Sumter County Courthouse and the Windsor Hotel turned out to be not much more than monumental ironies. Designed to herald the coming of a new age in Americus, they only served to scribe the high-water mark of the economic surge that came just before financial disaster.

Plate 6.9: The depot at Americus, built in 1900.

In 1888, the Richmond and West Point Terminal and Warehouse Company, the holding Company for the Richmond and Danville, which later became the Southern Railway, acquired the Central and its pawn, the Savannah and Western. As a result of financial manipulations that grew out of this acquisition, the Central failed in 1892. It was another step in the long march that created in the American South a sort of colony to be exploited by the Industrial North. By the end of this era, a series of railway consolidations left most of Georgia's railroads snugly locked in the grasp of three corporate giants: the Southern, the Seaboard, and the Atlantic Coast Line.

The demise of the SAM began in 1891 when the Richmond and Danville refused the SAM her link to Savannah at Lyons.[37] Unable to stand before the enormous power of the Richmond and Danville, Samuel Hawkins's tenacious Savannah, Americus and Montgomery Railroad failed in November of 1892. High costs of expansion were cited as the cause, but doubtless an 1892 Georgia bill to protect railroad investors by limiting the issuance of railroad securities

---

[36] Bruce and Morgan's built nine Romanesque Georgia courthouses. The other eight were Haralson County at Buchanan, 1892; Talbot County at Talbutton, 1892; Paulding County at Dallas, 1892; Floyd County at Rome, 1893; Bulloch County at Statesboro, 1884; Heard County at Franklin, 1894; the Monroe County Courthouse at Forsyth, 1896; and Butts County Courthouse at Jackson, 1898. Additionally the firm designed numerous other public buildings in the Romanesque style including monumental structures at Auburn University, Georgia Institute of Technology and Clemson University.

[37] *The Macon Telegraph*, November 13, 1891 in Williford, *Americus Through the Years*, 92.

[38] Williford, *Americus Through the Years*, 103.

dealt a critical blow, along with increased pressures by the Richmond and Danville. It is a tribute to the power of Americus and to the skill and nerve of Samuel Hawkins that the SAM was built and operated successfully, but times were changing. Men like Col. Hawkins were rare in the South and most were falling prey to powerful exploitive consolidating elements in the North before which no man, no matter how bold, could stand.

The downfall of Americus is a sadly representative chapter in the Southern experience in the late nineteenth century. In this period, Georgia and the South became a kind of third world, exploited and picked over by the unfettered greed of an expanding Eastern industrial behemoth. In the depression that followed the collapse of the SAM and the Panic of 1893, both Col. Hawkins and the city of Americus stood near financial ruin. Hawkins is said to have lost nearly one million dollars of his own money in his vain attempts to save the SAM, the Bank of Americus failed in January of 1893 and the Americus Land Development Company was placed in the hands of a receiver only a month later.[38]

The SAM was reorganized as the Georgia and Alabama Railroad in 1895, and by 1901, the line was part of the rising giant of the Seaboard Air Line Railway, By this time, the Central had re-emerged as an independent line, and Sumter County appeared economically back on track. Cotton prices were up, but things were never really quite the same for Americus. The town continued to grow—from 3200 in 1870, the year the Central built its old brick depot, to 6000 in 1887, the year Bruce and Morgan designed their grand Romanesque vision of the Gilded Age. When Bruce and Morgan designed this fine depot at Americus in 1900, Americus's population had leveled off at about 7500. Just to the south, the extraordinary growth of Cordele had created a brash new competitor, and farther south, Albany, which had lived these early years in the shadow of Americus, was beginning to grow. Even though the 1890s had been punctuated by the charter of the Atlanta, Americus and Florida Railroad and by other ambitious railroading schemes, the fires of New South zeal that had burned in

Plate 6.9: The Southwestern's Depot at Americus, built in 1900. Bruce and Morgan, architects. (Photo: Courtesy of Les R. Winn.)

Americus had been all but extinguished by the collapse of the SAM

Before his death in Americus in 1905, Samuel Hawkins made another fortune in timber on the edge of the great swamp in Clinch County. Still, the image of Col. Hawkins as a rough and ready timberman is a long way indeed from the vision of him smoking cigars in his private Pullman car (which he called the Nannie Lou after his second daughter) as he chugged along the SAM with his family, newly returned from the grand tour of Europe. The story is told that it was Hawkins's daughters, all aglow with the glamour of Europe, who named many of the towns along the route of the Savannah, Americus and Montgomery: Seville, Rhine, Rochelle—also Cordele after Samuel Hawkins's wife, Cordelia.

LEE COUNTY: LEESBURG

The enormous Lee County was one of the original counties created in the land lotteries that followed the Creek Indian cessation of 1825-1826. By the time the Southwestern Railroad arrived in 1857, the great empty expanses of Lee had come alive with the music of cotton. Randolph, Stewart and Sumter Counties were created from Lee's once vast wilderness, and as the railroad began to push south and west from Americus in the mid-1850s, Clay, Quitman, Webster and Terrell Counties were also cut from lands that were once a part of the dwindling Lee.

The original county seat of Lee County was at Starkville, established in 1832. Starkville today is not so much a ghost town, as it is a vanished remembrance. No trace remains. Searching for Starkville, one unearths bits and pieces of Old South and American frontier myths layered one on top of the other.

We first encounter the usual myth of a golden era of social grace and refinement. Local histories recall a town of 1800 to 2000[39] residents, "once famous for wealth, refinement, hospitality and outstanding citizens."[40] According to one local historian, the cultural and economic achievements of the place were substantial in the years before 1850: "All roads went there (Starkville). It did an enormous business and thousands of visitors attended the centers of amusement. It was the social, intellectual and sporting center of this section of Georgia."[41]

One need only consult the reliable traveler George White to obtain a more accurate picture of old Starkville. In his 1849 *Statistics of the State of Georgia* White has little to say about Starkville other than its population was about 100, its courthouse and jail were "inferior buildings, built of wood," and the water was "not good." This does little to establish the place as an intellectual center of "wealth, refinement and hospitality." Likewise it disputes local population claims by twice a full order of magnitude. Still, if we dig deeper, we find another myth developing alongside the first. Some local accounts of Starkville relate "a wide open town" inhabited by "pistol packing men"—a place known for its "12 saloons" and many "gambling halls."[42] According to the same myth, it was the "scene of many tragedies," and peopled by men whose favorite pastimes were "pistol shooting," horse racing and cock fighting. We are told: "down

near Muckalee Creek there was a 'Primrose Path' where raucous music and revelries reigned."[43]

In the first account, we find the typical myth of the Old South radiating social grace and refinement, applied to a rustic and rough-edged place, which in other accounts has been the subject of some frontier mythmaking not unlike legends of the American West. If we are to believe the frontier stories which, although undoubtedly exaggerated and embellished with age, are probably closer to the truth, then Starkville's legends clearly illustrate the misleading "spin" of Old South mythmaking. Saloons are turned into "social centers" and gambling halls and horse races are transformed into "centers of amusement" and "the sporting center of this section of Georgia." The true nature of the place is sadly lost in a muddle of nostalgia and tales too often told.

According to local tradition, the first court in Lee County was held under an oak tree. The county's original courthouse, built before 1837 was probably the simple frame building described as "inferior" by George White in 1849. County records indicate that in 1854 William Love built a new courthouse at Starkville, yet in that same year, the county seat was inexplicably moved to Webster, another present day ghost town, where yet another frame court building was erected by Charles P. Kelley. It appears that the seat of county government returned to Starkville in 1856. This account is unclear, but we do know with reasonable certainty that the courthouse at Starkville burned in 1858. At this point, with the county seat having bounced to Webster and back, there was still considerable controversy in Lee. According to *The Albany Patriot* of April 1858: Lee County's "citizens are very much divided in opinion as to the course to be pursued since their new and elegant courthouse burned. Some are in favor of building a new one at Adams—about that same number at Wooten's (now Leesburg)—and others think Starkville the suitable place."[44] Starkville carried the day, and a new courthouse was completed in 1861. One local account offers photographic evidence that the 1861 courthouse was a monumental, three-story brick structure. This is most unlikely. The photo depicts a large public building in the style of the turn of the century,

[39] *The History of Lee County, Georgia* (Leesburg GA: Lee County Historical Society, 1983) 100.

[40] Tom Love in "50th Anniversary Edition," *The Lee County Journal*, September 29, 1944.

[41] Tom Love in "50th Anniversary Edition," *The Lee County Journal*, September 29, 1944.

[42] Lee County Historical Society, *The History of Lee County, Georgia* (Leesburg: 1983) 100.

[43] Tom Love in "50th Anniversary Edition," *The Lee County Journal*, September 29, 1944.

[44] Albany Patriot, April 29, 1858.

[45] Lee County Historical Society, *The History of Lee County, Georgia* (Leesburg: 1983) 100.

[46] Helen Terrill, *The History of Stewart County, Georgia* (Columbus GA: Columbus Office Supply, 1958) 371.

probably a school. Sadly, we may never know for the history of this building. Like the history of Starkville, it remains shrouded. Just how large Starkville was and just which myth properly reflects the town's character is not known. Just as the two myths continue side by side today, perhaps they existed side by side in old Starkville, with a fine courthouse on the high ground and a shabby row of saloons down by the creek.

Plate 6.10: The Lee County Courthouse, built in 1880. Demolished c.1921.

One part of the history of Starkville is no myth or mystery: after the railroad arrived "the courthouse was moved and the people moved with it."[45] The establishment of trade at Wooten's Station beginning with the arrival of the railroad in 1857 marked the beginning of a period of decline for Starkville. The county seat was removed to Wooten's Station in 1872, and the new county town was christened Leesburg. A temporary wooden courthouse was built and burned almost immediately. In 1874, bonds were approved for a brick courthouse, but the work on the uncompleted structure was halted in the following years apparently owing to the county's "financial embarrassments." Finally, this substantial building was completed in 1880. By the most accounts, it was the county's sixth court building

With its broad cornice and brackets supporting the eaves, this structure is typical of vernacular brick court buildings built in the first two decades after the war. It bears a strong resemblance to Fay and Corput's 1873 Bartow County Courthouse at Cartersville, although the fenestration here is of the segmentally arched type.

In 1880, when this building was new, Leesburg had a population of 358. Nearby, Albany, Americus and Dawson were all vying to become the region's trading center, while tiny Leesburg had humble roots and a late start. Here was a place, which seemed unlikely to achieve much in the way of New South progress. This simple court building served well into the twentieth century in unimposing testament to the rural South's stagnancy. There were to be no crossing rails here. With the junction of the old Southwestern Railroad's branch to Cuthbert only 13 miles to the

Plate 6.10: By 1880, when the Lee County Courthouse was built at Leesburg, the county's great plantations were deteriorating into so many dirt farms.

north at Smithville, and Albany's tangle of track only 8 miles to the south, there was little hope for such progress. In 1884, the Central of Georgia considered a line from Smithville northwestward via Preston toward Columbus, but this scheme came to nothing.[46]

Reflected in these solid but uninspired brick walls is cotton's post-war legacy of tenancy and poverty. The great plantations, which had been the rising hope of the thriving cotton culture of Southwest Georgia in the antebellum era, were deteriorating into so many dirt farms by 1880. The year this courthouse was built, there were 715 farms Lee County, and the average size was down to 270 acres. By 1900, the county had over 1300 farms with an average size of only 127 acres; 717 of these were under 50 acres and almost a thousand were worked either by renters or by "croppers" through some sort of crop sharing arrangement. No New South mythology was to find root here, and the myths of the Old South and perhaps the Old West would have to do.

DOUGHERTY COUNTY: ALBANY

The early history of the city of Albany is told in the career of Nelson Tift. Seldom in American history do we encounter a city whose development was so dominated by one man. The son of a merchant, Tift was born in 1810 in Groton, Connecticut. In 1830, after an apprenticeship with his father's mercantile firm in Key West, he moved first to Charleston, then to Augusta and later to Hawkinsville. There, in 1836, he became the operating partner in Rawls, Tift and Company, a firm organized to establish a trading center on the Flint River in the fledgling Baker County, which had been cut from the empty expanses of Early County in 1825. From the beginning Tift's progress and the growth of the city of Albany were linked in the firmest of unions. In 1837, Tift launched the steamboat Mary Emeline on the Flint and built a sawmill at Albany. After Dougherty County was created in 1853, it was Nelson Tift who sold the new county the land for its first courthouse at Albany. By 1855, Tift was president of the newly chartered Georgia and Florida Railroad. This pioneer line was quickly acquired by the Southwestern Railroad and completed from Americus to Albany in 1857. The very next year, Tift built and operated the first bridge across the Flint at Albany. After a wartime career building ships and acting as paymaster for the Confederate Navy, Tift was back in Albany establishing a cotton factory in 1866. In 1869, he tried in vain to revive the charter of the old Georgia and Florida Railroad to built a line to Alabama.

Tift's political successes were every bit as impressive as his commercial ambitions. In addition to local and state offices, he was twice elected to the United States House of Representatives. All the while, Nelson Tift continued to be a railroad man. Only two years before his death in 1891, he was instrumental in the organization of The Albany, Florida and Northern Railroad Company which ambitiously contemplated three lines from Albany to Florida, and which, after much ado, came to nothing.

Plate 6.11: The Dougherty County Courthouse, built in 1856. Demolished in 1903.

Dougherty County records afford us a unique and remarkably detailed look at courthouse construction in the antebellum period. Here no general contractor was used, and as a result, the county's books contain a record of every brick and nail used in the construction of this building. We find that the structure was erected in large part using slave labor at a cost of $20 to $35 per month for each hand.[47] Architecturally, the courthouse is typical of the best of the vernacular brick court buildings of the era. With

its traditional two stories, the 52 x 64-foot structure achieved notable charm via a simple but well-proportioned lantern, a broad cornice and deep eaves supported by scrolling paired brackets. Also notable here are pairs of Gothic arched windows in the cupola, a rare example of Gothic decoration in the architectural inventory of Georgia's courthouses. The 1856 Dougherty County Courthouse was similar to many Georgia court buildings built in the 1840s and 1850s. It is sad and a little surprising that so few of these charming structures remain, for they were so many.

This building's story is a tale of competition between Albany and Americus. In 1856, builders at Albany undoubtedly took for their model the 1847 Sumter County Courthouse at Americus. The arched fenestration and an ornate lantern were later added in an effort to out-do the neighboring county. Not to be outdone, Americus later added a similar crown to her old court building.

The year after this courthouse was completed, the first train arrived in Albany on the rails of Nelson Tift's Georgia and Florida Railroad, which by 1857 had been acquired by the Southwestern and extended

Plate 6.11: The 1856 Dougherty County Courthouse achieved notable charm via a simple but well-proportioned lantern, a broad cornice and deep eaves supported by scrolling paired brackets.

from Americus to Albany. From her beginnings as a trading port on the Flint River in 1836, Albany appeared destined to become the dominant trading center of the rich and rapidly developing cotton growing area of southwest Georgia. But the completion of the Southwestern Railroad to Americus in 1854 and the dead-end of the line at Albany in 1857 marked the beginning of a period of struggle for the town. It was to be a struggle which would not be fully resolved until this charming building was demolished and replaced by T. F Lockwood's neoclassical Dougherty County Courthouse completed in 1903. By that time, seven railroad lines met in Albany, and Americus's day in the sun was over (see Table 6.2). In the beginning, the river had appeared to be the key to Albany's destiny, but from a very early date Nelson Tift understood that the real key to Albany's future was the railroad. Tift knew well that steamboat operations on the Flint River had been one long epic of raging floods, low water, snags, sinkings and groundings. In 1837, Tift's first steamboat, the Mary Emeline, attempted to ascend the Flint beyond Bainbridge, an undertaking that left the craft grounded on the shoals south of Albany. Freight had to be unloaded and hauled up river by barge. Extensive damage occurred on the return to Apalachicola, and on the second voyage up river the Mary Emeline reached Albany, but not without multiple groundings, much delay and a generally perilous passage. Tift was not deterred, although his partners were quick to sell him their shares in Rawls, Tift and Company.

Almost from the beginning, Nelson Tift seem to know that in the end the railroads would put an end to river freight. But in 1837, vast amount of freight flowed down the Flint and Chattahoochee rivers to the Gulf to the harbor at Apalachicola. In that year, 327 vessels had sailed from that port.[48] By 1914, only ten vessels cleared the port, and by 1917, only two steamboats were left on the Flint. Almost from the day it was built, this courthouse would witness a pageant seemingly determined to prove that Albany's power in the trading of the white fiber would not come from her location on the river but from her railroads.

Table 6.2

RAILROAD CONNECTIONS AT ALBANY 1901

1857, the Southwestern Railroad, Macon to Albany (later the Central of Georgia).

1870, South Georgia and Florida Railroad, Albany to Thomasville (later the Atlantic and Gulf, later part of the Plant System).

1871, the Brunswick and Albany, Brunswick to Albany (later part of the Plant System)

1871, the Central of Georgia, Albany to Blakeley.

1890, the Albany, Florida and Northern, Albany to Cordele, (later leased by the Savannah, Americus and Montgomery, later Georgia Southwestern & Gulf).

1890, the Columbus Southern, Columbus to Albany (later part of the Georgia and Alabama, later part of the Seaboard Air Line).

1901, the Georgia Northern, Albany to Boston, Georgia, (built under the charter of the Boston and Albany RR).

Plate 6.12: The Southwestern Railroad Depot at Albany, built in 1857.

Although similar in design to many of the Central of Georgia Railroad's early depots, this building, completed in 1857, was the work of Nelson Tift's Georgia and Florida Railroad. Perhaps Tift copied the Central's early depot style, or perhaps the similarity is the product of later additions and remodelings completed by the Central after it acquired the Southwestern. In either case, this enormous depot speaks well for Albany's early railroad resolve.

By the time this depot was completed, Albany had already been a party to several failed railroad schemes. Ten years before the first train steamed into Albany on the Southwestern Railroad from Americus, a charter had been granted for the Savannah and Albany Railroad. Nelson Tift became this road's first president in 1849. Wildly ambitious plans were laid for rails connecting Savannah, via Albany to Mobile and even to San Diego, California, but the hoped-for European funding was not forthcoming, and controversy over the route ensued. The completed line was

[47] Minutes of the Inferior Court of Dougherty County between December, 1854, and January, 1855 in *The Historical Background of Dougherty County, 1836-1941* (1941; reprint, Atlanta: Cherokee Publishing Company, 1981) 7.

[48] Edward A. Meuller, *Perilous Journey, A History of Steamboating on the Chattahoochee, Apalachicola and Flint Rivers*, 1828-1928 (Eufaula GA: Historic Chattahoochee Commission, 1990) 48.

financed primarily by subscriptions from the city of Savannah, and it was built, not to Albany, but to Thomasville. Along the way, the name had been changed first to the Savannah, Albany and Gulf and later to the Atlantic and Gulf. At about this same time in Brunswick, plans were being laid to construct the Brunswick and Florida Railroad to connect Albany with Brunswick. $200,000 was subscribed at Albany toward the construction of this road, but boondoggles and flimflams blocked progress.[49] When the war put an end to construction in 1861, the road was complete only from Brunswick to Waresboro in Ware County. At about this time, the name was changed to the Brunswick and Albany Railroad.

But all of this is modern history when compared to the wooden rails and horse-drawn cars proposed on the Flint and Ocmulgee Railroad, a thoroughly strange story from its very beginning. In 1827, a full six years before the charter of the Central of Georgia and the Georgia Railroad and thirty years before this depot was constructed, Thomas Spalding, a wealthy planter on Sapelo Island obtained a charter to build a "railroad or a canal" to connect the Flint with the Ocmulgee River. The new company, the Flint and Ocmulgee Railroad and Canal Company was chartered just a year after Hamilton Fulton completed his aforementioned survey to determine the feasibility of a canal connecting the Tennessee River with either the

Plate 6.12: Nelson Tift's 1857 depot at Albany was similar to the Central of Georgia Railroad's early depot designs. (Photo: Wilber W. Caldwell)

Oconee or the Ocmulgee. By 1835, Spalding had purchased land overlooking the great bend of the Ocmulgee at Mobley's Bluff in old Irwin County, and some time after that he began grading his railroad. In 1840, Spalding hired Abbott Brisbane to supervise the grading. A West Point graduate, a veteran of the Seminole Indian Wars in Florida and a newly converted Irish Catholic, Brisbane proved to be a zealot in many regards. At a time when most Southern railroads were graded with slave labor, Brisbane procured a small army of newly-arrived Irish Catholic immigrants by promising them subsistence, small wages, stock in the railroad, and a place in his planned Roman Catholic colony in Georgia. It was a vision of Utopia, and Abbott Brisbane along with the Catholic Priest, Father James Graham, proposed a "Catholic domain" in South Georgia. Grading proceeded quickly, wooden ties and wooden rails were laid, and the work brought the line near the present-day city of Fitzgerald and through to the old Irwin County seat, at Irwinville.

Like all Utopian dreams, the Flint and Ocmulgee Railroad ended in failure. With the end of the grading almost in sight, Father Graham died, and Abbot Brisbane, strapped for cash and low on magical promises, was unable to pay his increasingly uneasy workers. According the Russell Chalker's account, rails had been laid as the grading progressed, and in September of 1843 Brisbane was surrounded by an angry mob of disgruntled Irish workers and then rescued a few days later by a military force sent from Albany under the command of Nelson Tift.[50] According to U. B. Phillips, no rails had been laid when the starving Irish: "beat the plausible Brisbane with stones and cudgels. Brisbane fled for his life and that was the end of the Flint and Ocmulgee Railroad story."[51]

The Flint and Ocmulgee Railroad was the first viable plan to connect the Atlantic and the Gulf of Mexico. Conceived in 1827, it relied primarily on river passage. Even as early as 1843, when this proposed horse-drawn line was simultaneously nearing completion and approaching its ultimate end, it must have been clear to some Georgians that rail routes were not destined to supplement river routes, but to replace them altogether. To be sure, this was clear to everyone by 1850, and by 1880 it was becoming equally clear that railroads could replace sea routes up the North American coast for all save the bulkiest of cargoes.

Albany's antebellum railroad schemes seemed snake-bit from the beginning. The end of the Civil War would find Albany a town of about 1500 at the end of a remote spur of the Southwestern Railroad, while Americus had blossomed to above 3000. The Brunswick and Albany Railroad arrived in 1870 and, for most of the early postbellum era, Albany's best links to Savannah were the circuitous Southwestern via Macon or the Brunswick and Albany via Jesup. The completion of the Albany, Florida and Northern Railroad to Cordele in 1890 finally provided a slightly more direct link to the Atlantic coast via the Savannah, Americus and Montgomery Railroad. But it was only after the failure of the SAM in 1894 and the completion of the Columbus Southern in 1890 and the Georgia Northern to Boston, Georgia in 1901 that Albany would take her place as the growing center of area trade that had appeared to be her destiny from the beginning.

As we have seen, the winds that blew along postbellum rails brought hope and with it a burning need for fresh symbols. With the arrival of her seventh railroad, it was time for a new courthouse at Albany.

Plate 6.13: The Dougherty County Courthouse, built in 1903. Burned in 1966. T. F. Lockwood, architect.

With the completion of the Georgia Northern in 1901 seven railroads met at Albany (see Table 6.2), and at last prospects appeared promising. With her population only just above 4500, Albany still lay in the shadow of Americus, which boasted over 7500 residents in 1900. But things had turned sour for Americus, and Albany felt the surge of change riding on the power of rail. By 1910, a blossoming Albany with 8193 residents would pass a stalled Americus. This kind of urban growth was the stuff of the New South myth, and a long-suffering Albany was about to step out of darkness to glimpse a sliver of the light of the modern age. Still Albanians, like most Georgians,

Plate 6.13: T. F. Lockwood's 1903 Dougherty Courthouse. Albany, rich in the pride and tradition of the Old South, was among the first Georgia cities to embrace the dual symbolism of the columns of the Neoclassical Revival. (Photo: Courtesy of Georgia Dept. of Archives and History.)

had to walk the razor's precarious edge between two myths. Without doubt, a taste of the New South had arrived, but not at the expense of the Old. In 1903, Albany, rich in the pride and tradition of the Old South, was among the first Georgia cities to embrace the dual symbolism of the columns of the American Neoclassical Revival. Again and again all across Georgia these tall pillars would beckon with the promises of a new American dream while at the same time recalling the fabled elysian agrarianism of the Old South. In this clash of symbols, the citizens of Albany found no contradiction.

With progress seemingly at hand, Albany turned to the Lockwood Brothers of Columbus for the design of her new courthouse. This is one of four Georgia courthouses designed by the Columbus firm (see Appendix C). T. F. Lockwood's similar Jasper County Courthouse at Monticello was built in 1907, and his best work in Georgia, the Crisp County Courthouse at Cordele was completed in 1908.

The Lockwood brothers were from Trenton, New Jersey. The better known of the two, Frank Lockwood, received his architectural training in New York and began to practice with his brother, Thomas Frith

[49] *The Historical Background of Dougherty County, 1836-1941*, 16.

[50] Russell Chalker, "Irish Catholics in the Building of the Ocmulgee and Flint Railroad," *The Georgia Historical Quarterly* 54/4 (Atlanta 1970): 513.

[51] Phillips, *History of Transportation in the Eastern Cotton Belt to 1860*, 274-75.

Lockwood,[52] in Columbus, Georgia, in the early 1890s. In 1895, while maintaining an office in Columbus, Frank Lockwood moved to Montgomery. Most of his important commissions were in Alabama.

The Lockwood brothers' portico at Albany draws inspiration from Thomas Jefferson's Virginia State House built in 1786. Based on a Roman model, the Mason Carree at Nimes, France, Jefferson's Virginia Capitol became an early ideal for Southern builders. Like Jefferson, the Lockwood Brothers substituted Ionic columns into what is fundamentally a Corinthian form. Here in Albany, all similarities to Jeffersonian Classicism or to his Roman models ended with the portico's attachment to the undistinguished rectangular mass of the main building, which was topped with a crude and slightly oversized octagonal tower with a squat dome, and crowned by an odd lantern. In an effort to effect the look of finished stone work so popular in the Renaissance Revival and Beaux-Arts styles of the day, the first story of the building was decorated with brick banding patterned to resemble the rusticated stone work of more monumental masonry. Lockwood's choice of light gray brick was meant to further the stone illusion. Unfortunately, dust from Georgia's red soil has always had a nasty tendency to slowly adorn light colored masonry with a brownish and distinctly unlovely hue. Even though the new Dougherty County Courthouse was built on a spacious square, little effort was made to decorate the sides or the rear of the building. The structure stood in sharp contrast to many of Frank Milburn's and J. W. Golucke's buildings also based on the Greek cross plan, which were so well suited to the central square. Despite its shortcomings, Lockwood's

design must have looked good on paper, for *The Albany Daily Herald* waxed poetic when the plans were revealed in 1902, calling it: "a magnificent structure of colonial lines, capped by a huge dome, and with symmetry in every line."[53]

A county courthouse was an emotional symbol, and such deeply personal icons did not always come and go without a fight. In this regard, Albany was typical. From the beginning, a vocal and active faction in Dougherty County opposed the new courthouse in favor of remodeling the old building. The battle that ensued would be far more monumental than the new building itself. In a heated election held in the spring of 1902, a bond issue to fund the new courthouse carried the day. But opponents were not so easily set aside. Dissidents challenged the legality of the bond election, and the election was declared fraudulent in November of 1902. Although the county commissioners had threatened to simply levy a tax to finance the building, a new election was held December. The bond issue passed again and the contract for the construction of the new building was finally let in May of 1903, a full year after Lockwood had presented the original plans.

The building suffered considerable damage in a tornado in 1940 loosing the clock tower and a large portion of the roof. The ghastly results of a half-hearted restoration remained on Albany's square until 1966 when the building burned while awaiting demolition. The present courthouse replaced it in 1968. T. F. Lockwood's 1903 Dougherty County Courthouse was far from the most distinguished of its era. Ironically, the old 1856 vernacular building it replaced was one of the finest of its genre built in Georgia.

Plate 6.14: The Union Depot at Albany, built in 1911-1913.

This fine depot begun only twenty years after the completion of the Central's 1891 depot at Albany, vividly illustrates Albany's victory over Americus. Before 1890, Albany, with a population of just over 4000, had been at the crossing of the rails connecting Savannah with Blakely, and the rails connecting Macon with Thomasville. Her stern vernacular Romanesque depot of 1891 voiced little beyond a

Plate 6.14: The architect of Albany's stunning 1913 passenger station was attuned to the winds of architectural change which were blowing in the American West. (Photo: Wilber W. Caldwell.)

vague sense of outdated architectural trends and a need for expanded passenger accommodations. By 1911, when this second Union Depot was begun, seven railroads met at an Albany of over 8000 residents, and the city had become the unquestionable center of regional trade and society.

Albany's second Union Depot, completed in 1913, was a remarkably up-to-date architectural statement for southwest Georgia. Often lagging far behind national trends, architectural fashion in the South had been in a kind of time warp since before the Civil War. But here, only a decade after the turn of the century, is a structure which recalls the low horizontal profile and the hovering roof lines of Frank Lloyd Wright's Prairie Style and the exposed joists of the so-called California Stick Style or Craftsman Style of San Francisco's Benard Maybeck and Pasadena's Henry Mather Greene. The style was a natural for horizontal massing, a low roofline, deep eaves, and exposed supports had all been intrinsic features of small depot design almost from the beginning. Whatever the sources of its design, the architect of Albany's new passenger station was attuned to the winds of change which were blowing in the American West. For Albany, it was an oddly modern statement: perhaps an indication of a small hesitant step toward the New South.

THE EUFAULA / FT. GAINES BRANCH

TERRELL COUNTY: DAWSON

Plate 6.15: The Terrell County Courthouse, built in 1892. William Parkins, architect.

Terrell County had its beginnings in 1856, only three years before the Southwestern Railroad arrived on its way to Eufaula. A large frame courthouse was erected at the new county town of Dawson. Only thirty-four years later in 1890, when the Columbus Southern Railroad crossed the Southwestern at Dawson, the town boasted over 3000 residents, and saw herself as a rival to both Americus and Albany.[54]

Yet in 1890, manufacturing in Terrell County was all but non-existent: fifteen "manufacturing establishments" employed only 173 of Terrell's population of

Plate 6.15: William Parkins's 1892 Terrell County Courthouse is Georgia's most elaborate Picturesque Eclectic architectural proclamation. (Photo: Wilber W. Caldwell.)

over 14,000. Almost half of Terrell County's 88,000 acres of improved farmland were planted in cotton. In that year, county growers produced 16,000 bales worth about $650,000. This accounted for over two-thirds of the county's total agricultural gross of $939,000. Here, before the turn of the century, was a rural South still economically crushed beneath the dual boot heels of tenancy and cotton's unrelenting tyranny. Ironically it was here, in the midst of such poverty that Georgia's most elaborate picturesque Eclectic architectural proclamation came to be built.

This remarkable courthouse clearly delivers the message of The Courthouse and the Depot: that the fantasies of brick and stone that were the courthouses

---

[52] T. F. Lockwood's son, T. F. Lockwood Jr., designed and built several courthouses in Georgia in the 1920s and 30s.

[53] *The Albany Daily Herald*, May 3, 1902.

[54] United States Census figures place Dawson's 1890 population at 2284, but a population of above 3000 was routinely quoted by *The Dawson News* in that same year, for example *The Dawson News*, March 26, 1890.

of the postbellum era were monuments to the hope delivered by Georgia's ever growing web of rail. Crossing the old line of the Southwestern Railroad at Dawson to connect Columbus with Albany, the Columbus Southern Railroad was completed in 1890. Adding to expectations were abundant rumors that the town would soon get a third railroad, the Florida, Dawson and Northern planned from Tallahassee, Florida, to Dawson.[55] To define the wave of euphoria that postbellum crossing-rails, or even rumors of such crossings, brought to towns like Dawson, we need look no farther than William Parkins's flamboyant towers. Without question this is the most wildly eclectic courthouse ever built in Georgia. It presses hard against the outer boundaries of period architectural tastes if not against the frontiers of the bizarre, just as the hope it symbolized pressed hard against the borders of reality.

Three factors influenced Dawson's selection of Parkins. First was the town's enthusiasm for prospects kindled by the new railroad. Second, only a few years before and only 32 miles away, neighboring Cuthbert had employed Parkins's old firm, Kimball, Wheeler and Parkins, to design a truly elegant court building, the 1886 Randolph County Courthouse. With the arrival of The Columbus Southern, it seems sure that Dawson was moved to attempt to out-do her neighbor. Third, Parkins, in association with Alexander Bruce, was the designer of what was at the time arguably the state's grandest court building, Atlanta's 1883 Fulton County Courthouse. Additionally, Parkins had just completed three courthouses which expressed wildly eclectic flights of fancy: the 1887 Oglethorpe County Courthouse at Lexington designed in association with Lorenzo Wheeler, the 1888 Gordon County Courthouse at Calhoun and the 1890 Dooly County Courthouse at Vienna. If there was an architect in Georgia in 1890 who could top the fantastically picturesque edifice of the Randolph County Courthouse at Cuthbert, it was William Parkins himself, a man about to be commissioned to out-do his own firm's best effort.

Some architectural historians consider the Picturesque Eclectic a codified style. This line of thinking is not without its problems, but however one chooses to classify the styles of the era, eclecticism marked the beginning of the end for the romance of the picturesque. The movement began in England with the strict historicism of the Gothic Revival. Along with the Queen Anne and a kind of Free Classicism, the Picturesque Eclectic (or Free Eclecticism or Progressive Eclecticism as some scholars choose to call it) was the last voice of the picturesque Movement. In America, as in England, it punctuated the end of the architectural era not with a whimper, but with a decided bang.

It is interesting that such a grand public building came to be built in a region almost devoid of High Gothic architecture. In the American South, even the tamer elements of the Gothic Revival had been almost exclusively reserved for churches. Many scholars view the Picturesque Eclectic Movement as heir to the Gothic Revival, but broader perspective would characterize the picturesque era as an epic filled with waves of historical revivals, all of which eventually came together in eclecticism. This latter view is perhaps more appropriate, and is certainly more descriptive of the progress of the picturesque in the New World. Nonetheless, here in Dawson there is an almost uncomfortable echo of the High Gothic in Parkins's Terrell County Courthouse, despite the absence of any strict Gothic details.

Composed of almost everything but Gothic ornament, Parkins's details here comprise a smorgasbord of styles. The central entrance bay lends ample example. The great double arches of rough stone masonry are Romanesque to the core. Above, the two segmentally arched window openings, with the delicate beveled sashes and tiny panes are characteristic of the Queen Anne Style. The window grouping in the parapet is of a sort often referred to as "Palladian." It is typical of the broad span of the Renaissance Revival, or could flow just as easily from the Colonial Revival whose Georgian roots also lead back to the Renaissance. On

---

[55] *The Dawson News*, April 2, 1890.

[56] *The Dawson News*, March 26, 1890.

[57] Richard Cuyler, "Superintendent's Report" in *Report of the Chief Engineers, Presidents and Superintendents of The Southwestern Railroad*, 262.

top, the stepped parapet recalls the Northern European Renaissance, a favored motif of Lorenzo Wheeler, Parkins's former partner.

It would be a simple but exhausting matter to inventory each section of Parkins's fantasy at Dawson, but it is perhaps best to simply point out his eclecticism in a broader sweep. With the exception of the great square columnar corner piers with their classical capitals and the Queen Anne oval window at the base, the central tower is fundamentally Romanesque with its stone banding and spired tourelles in the top quarter. The lower tower is similar to the small tower of Parkins's 1888 Gordon County Courthouse at Calhoun but for the addition of a wildly Romantic oriel or turret which becomes a narrow minaret with its pointed dome and miniature balcony. Also notably eclectic are the small tower's stylized urns, which serve as classical finials.

One of the fundamental weaknesses of the picturesque was its tendency to bind design to a purely scenic agenda. The license of the eclectic offered even more enticing temptations for architects to "paint pictures" with their buildings. With his design for the Terrell County Courthouse, Parkins fell into this uniquely picturesque trap. The results are at best questionable. Although striking, William Parkins's heavy-handed design here in Terrell County does not come close to the graceful delicacy of his offering in neighboring Randolph County. Yet it would be difficult to find another building better suited to illustrate the freedom incorporate in eclecticism and the dangers it presents. Here in Dawson, William Parkins was apparently given both the mandate and the liberty to outdo his own firm's creation in neighboring Cuthbert. Only a great artists could avoid disaster in such a situation, and William Parkins, although thoroughly competent, was not a member of that group. The results were predictable. Like Icarus, Parkins flew too near the sun. A little eclectic license had yielded success in Cuthbert, and the citizens of Dawson demanded more. The orgy of ornament they received passed well beyond the edges of good taste. But in 1890, in the middle of cotton's sadly depressed kingdom, the citizens of Terrell County may have received exactly what they ordered: a grand symbol, like no

other, for their desperate illusions of economic salvation created by the arrival of yet another steel highway.

Despite the surrounding sea of rural poverty, in 1890 and again around the turn of the century, Dawson, like so many market towns in Georgia, had experienced a brief blossoming. The fullest flower of Dawson's false spring came around 1910 when the town achieved a population near 4000. Still in 1906, the citizens of Dawson had been waiting for 16 years "for an architect to be sent by the Central" to construct a new depot.[56] All the while, The Dawson News had been spewing forth boosterism and self-congratulatory articles tirelessly cataloguing Dawson's prospects for the future. But the Central remaned slow to respond. In its first year, the Columbus Southern was denied the use of the Central's old depot. Passengers on the new road had to detrain "in the middle of a field." A proper depot was finally built in 1906. Here again we find illustration of the strong tendency of small town public buildings to mirror popular domestic styles. At Dawson, the Central's 1906 depot reflected another picturesque historical style, the Tudor Revival, a fashionable domestic style of the late nineteen and early twentieth century.

RANDOLPH COUNTY: CUTHBERT

Plate 6.16: The Randolph County Courthouse, built in 1886. Kimball, Wheeler and Parkins, architects.

In 1856, Randolph and Terrell Counties together subscribed $175,000 for stock in the Southwestern Railroad,[57] which arrived in Cuthbert in 1859. The Southwestern's first sturdy depot, built of limestone block quarried only three miles from Cuthbert, was unique in South Georgia. Over two feet thick, its walls were completed just two years before war was declared. Although untouched by the actual fighting, the Civil War left its ruinous mark on the economy of southwest Georgia, thus further entrenching the region in proud and defiant agrarian traditions.

Plate 6.16: William Parkins's 1886 Randolph County Courthouse is undoubtedly one of the finest picturesque court buildings in the state. (Photo: Wilber W. Caldwell.)

At first blush, it may seem odd that such a place as Cuthbert would eventually turn to a notorious Carpetbagger for help. But Cuthbert did: not once but twice. Under the leadership of a Northern railroad promoter, the Bainbridge, Cuthbert and Columbus Railroad, chartered in 1869, was brought to financial ruin by 1872. The town then languished for ten years yearning for north-south rails. Just as railroad progress seemed again on the wind, she once more turned to the very same promoter, this time for a new courthouse. That man was Hannibal I. Kimball. To consider such a story odd is to underestimate Kimball, to stereotype Carpetbaggers, and to miscalculate the plight of those who sought their counsel and influence. Cuthbert's story may be a tale of desperation, still, such desperation, described by C. Vann Woodward, accounts for only part of the phenomenon:

Involved in the downfall of the old planter class were the leading financial, commercial and industrial families of the region. The hard struggle of these people to get back on their feet and recoup their losses took on a measure of desperation...the more desperate of them were said by one of their number to be 'willing for almost anything to turn up which gives promise or possibility of change.' Numerous leaders of old families attached themselves to Yankee capitalists, economic Carpetbaggers, who came South for profits. These adventurers often prospered with the aid of extravagant subsidies from Carpetbagger state governments.[58]

Without doubt this describes Hannibal Kimball perfectly, and yet there was a great deal more to the infamous Mr. Kimball, and to many of the Carpetbaggers, than popular myth recalls. The record regarding Kimball describes a New England Yankee, with New York banking connections and a very close relationship to Georgia's Reconstruction Governor, Rufus Bullock, a New Yorker who had settled in Augusta before the war. Bullock, having served in the Confederate Army, was not technically a Carpetbagger, yet his alleged scoundrelly cronyism and unscrupulous financial dealings as governor beginning in 1868 ultimately forced him to flee the state in 1871 just ahead of a criminal indictment. Although he was never criminally charged, Kimball left Georgia at about the same time under similar pressures. The scandal surrounding Hannibal Kimball was fired by numerous financial flimflams. Included in these were the state's purchase of allegedly fictitious railroad cars from Kimball Car Works, the questionable lease of the state-owned Western and Atlantic Railroad, the remodeling and subsequent sale to the state of the Kimball Opera House and the issuance of state endorsed bonds to fund several of Kimball's railroad schemes including the Cartersville and Van Wert, the Atlanta and Blue Ridge, the Brunswick and Albany and the ill-fated Bainbridge, Cuthbert and Columbus Railroad, which Kimball took over at the behest of that road's stock holders in 1871.

Cuthbert had become the county seat of Randolph County back in the 1830 when Stewart County had been split off from Randolph. A crude frame courthouse had been erected in 1837. It was replaced by a slightly more respectable wooden structure in 1840. The Southwestern Railroad had arrived in Cuthbert in 1859, and at war's end. After the war the town suddenly saw itself at the proposed crossing of north-south rails connecting Bainbridge and Columbus and the Southwestern's east-west branch from Smithville to Eufaula, Alabama. The town's hopes began to turn first on the Camilla and Cuthbert Railroad and then on the Bainbridge, Cuthbert and Columbus Railroad. Out of the ruin of Reconstruction, the town somehow scraped together $100,000 for stock in the proposed road. Columbus and Bainbridge showed similar financial zeal for the project. Thus, it is not surprising to find that, as early as 1872, there was a faction in Cuthbert demanding a new courthouse. None was forthcoming. The Camilla and Cuthbert Railroad never got off the ground and the Bainbridge, Cuthbert and Columbus, like so many Reconstruction railroads, was hopelessly underfinanced. There can be little doubt that the impossible financial condition of the Bainbridge, Cuthbert and Columbus was apparent to subscribers almost from the very beginning. And yet they pressed on, for like so many early railroad and cotton mill building endeavors, this was more than a matter of finance and profit; this was a matter of civic duty, pride and an odd sort of localized Southern patriotism. It was also a reflection of chaotic times.

With the election of Rufus Bullock, the state of Georgia began a period of financial manipulations that would take years to untangle. Part of Bullock's freewheeling policy involved the state's wholesale endorsement of private railroad bonds. This began a period of "railroad mania" of which the Bainbridge, Cuthbert and Columbus, chartered in 1869, was but a small part. At the center of this whirlwind was Hannibal I. Kimball. In the active years of state aid, 1869-1870, thirty-nine railroads were chartered. All but four that received state aid came to grief before any track was laid.[59] In 1869, the state had authorized bond endorsements for the Bainbridge,

Cuthbert and Columbus in the amount of $12,000 per mile, conditional on the usual stipulations regarding ample stock subscription and physical progress in construction. By 1871, the road had made little progress, and only a fraction of the stock subscriptions had been paid in. In a transaction typical of the era, Kimball convinced Governor Bullock to endorse $240,000 of the company's bonds despite the fact that only 35 miles of the road had been graded and none completed. This, along with other questionable financial arrangements made by Kimball in New York, was not enough to save the Bainbridge, Cuthbert and Columbus, which defaulted in 1872. When Bullock and the Radicals fell from power, a committee was appointed to investigate the ex-governor's dealings. As the dust settled, the state's endorsement of Bainbridge, Cuthbert and Columbus bonds was found to be improperly granted and the state refused to honor its obligation.

Kimball's appeal in places like Cuthbert is understandable. Despite the fact that he was a Yankee, he was charming, enthusiastic, and he had the governor's ear. Men like Kimball are often viewed as ruthless swindlers driven by exploitive motives for personal gain, but there was a great deal more to Hannibal Kimball than that. In her biography, *Hannibal I. Kimball, Entrepreneur,* Alice Reagan paints a picture of a man of his age. She depicts Kimball as a promoter in an age of promoters, a flimflam man in an age when business ethics as we know them today were undreamed, a financial exploiter in an age of exploitation, and a slick denizen of the Gilded Age. But there was still something more to the man, and this final element may explain Kimball's appeal to Southerners. It may even explain why so many Georgians continually forgave Kimball his faults and frauds. Kimball was a true believer. He was convinced of the South's potential. This zeal and confidence, when combined with his notable promotional skills and personal charm made him a force to be reckoned. Hannibal Kimball may have been among the first of

[58] Woodward, *Origins of the New South, 1877-1913*, 29-30.

[59] Peter S. McGuire, "The Railroads of Georgia, 1860-1880," *The Georgia Historical Quarterly* 16/3 (September 1932): 200-201.

the New South spokesmen. Here was the familiar message of hope and prosperity delivered years before the New South even had a name. Perhaps the citizens of Cuthbert never considered Kimball a swindler. Or, if he had swindled, they had to admit that it was for their cause, in which Kimball had no doubt been the staunchest believer.

Hannibal Kimball dreamed big dreams. To accomplish these dreams he schemed big schemes. In his zeal to succeed he regularly crossed over ethical or even legal boundaries. Thus, like the Bainbridge, Cuthbert and Columbus, many of his teetering towers of finance came tumbling down. Like all good New South spokesmen, Kimball believed his own propaganda. Regardless of all the signs to the contrary, Kimball saw Georgia as a vast untapped resource about to rise from the ashes of war. He must have been powerfully convincing, for not two years after he fled the state, he was back. In the following years, progressive Atlantans sought his considerable promotional skills to head their new Atlanta Cotton Mill and to organize and promote their ambitious 1881 Cotton States Exposition. Along the way he built Atlanta's Oglethorpe Park, a second grand Kimball House Hotel, and managed several elaborate land development projects including Kimball City near Chattanooga. Among his associates of that era was Henry Grady, perhaps the only man in Georgia able to surpass Kimball in New South zeal and ardor.

One of Kimball's many enterprises of this era was the architectural firm of Kimball, Wheeler and Parkins. Hannibal Kimball was not an architect, and the inclusion of his name on the shingle of Kimball, Wheeler and Parkins tells us something about Kimball the man: he was not one to let facts get in the way of dreams. Armed with this mindset and seemingly endless supplies of optimism, zeal and pure gall, Hannibal Ingalls Kimball might have gone down in history as only another Carpetbagger had he not become caught up in a personal vision of a New South. Instead of exploiting the South, he was seduced by her, and it was often his undoing.

Like many Georgians, the people of Cuthbert were quick to forgive Kimball. When the assets of the old Bainbridge, Cuthbert and Columbus were pur-

chased by an Alabama company in 1881 and re-chartered as the Chattanooga, Columbus and Southern, hopes in Cuthbert again began to soar. Later that same year, the proposed road became the Chattanooga, Columbus and Florida and renewed hope for crossing rails rekindled talk of a new courthouse. At that time, the finest courthouse in the state was going up in Atlanta with William Parkins and Alexander Bruce as architects. When Hannibal Kimball began his second Kimball House Hotel in Atlanta in 1883, he teamed with Parkins, who had designed the first Kimball House in 1870 and Lorenzo Wheeler of New York whose eclectic Dutch Renaissance designs were a novelty in Georgia. We will never know what moved Cuthbert to select the new firm of Kimball, Wheeler and Parkins to design their new courthouse. Perhaps it was the town's former association with Kimball and his incredible enthusiasm for Georgia's economic prospects. Perhaps it was William Parkins's reputation as an architect, or Lorenzo Wheeler's new "modern" style. Whatever the reason, Kimball's firm was hired, and in 1885, the plans were unveiled. Always the promoter, Kimball managed a little editorial comment in the Atlanta papers, which had called the design: "unique and attractive...and departs from the ordinary, old-fashioned style, so prevailing throughout the South....It marks a new era in the development of architectural taste, that we are glad to notice."[60] *The Cuthbert Enterprise and Appeal* also remarked on the new style labeling it correctly as Dutch Renaissance and adding: "This is rapidly becoming the leading style in the nation."[61] While far from "the leading style in the nation," Northern European Renaissance motifs were in vogue during the eclecticism of the late 1880s and early 1890s. Some of its details, notably the scrolling gables were popularized by the work of Norman Shaw who was at the center of the English architectural scene beginning in the late 1870s.

The Randolph County Courthouse was completed in 1886. Although local sources in Cuthbert establish Parkins as the supervising architect on the project,[62] the style here leads us to speculate that possibly Wheeler was the primary designer. After all, it was he who brought the Northern European Renaissance or Dutch Renaissance Style to Georgia.

Georgians first glimpsed graceful Netherlandish scrolling gables in Wheeler's 1884 design for Atlanta's Kimball House II. The scrolling effects are achieved here in Cuthbert through the use of quarter-round terra cotta castings. Also notable is Wheeler's use of wrought iron decoration around the entrance to compliment the terra cotta and the elaborate patterned reliefs above courtroom windows framed by a great bearing arch. Further ornamental detail is achieved through the use of brick polychromy around window openings also in Dutch 16th century style. There is little here of William Parkins's early work, but many of Parkins's later court buildings reflect Wheeler's influence in their Northern European Renaissance detail and in their tall thin quoining tourelles like those adorning Wheeler's Kimball House II.

If Hannibal Kimball brought failure to Cuthbert in 1871 with the collapse of the Bainbridge, Cuthbert and Columbus Railroad, he brought success a decade and a half later when his firm designed the 1886 Randolph County Courthouse. It is undoubtedly one of the finest picturesque courthouses in Georgia. Ironically Cuthbert's mid-eighties railroad dreams were as disappointing as her dreams of fifteen years earlier. The Chattanooga, Columbus and Florida Railroad never came to be, and it was not until 1901 and the completion of the Georgia, Florida and Alabama Railroad from Richland to Arlington that Cuthbert got her longed for north-south crossing line.

QUITMAN COUNTY: GEORGETOWN

Plate 6.17: The Vicksburg and Brunswick Depot at Eufaula, Alabama, built in 1872.

This fine depot, originally built by the Vicksburg and Brunswick Railroad, is one of the many glorious architectural treasures of Eufaula, the main cotton-trading hub for the lower Chattahoochee Valley. With its extraordinarily high arched windows, delicate wooden shutters, regular brick corbeling and bold angular brackets, this building surpasses in architectural grace and ornament any depot of the era built along South Georgia's rails. Here, in these high arches and broad bracketed eaves, is a clearer voice of the "Railroad Style," than those previously heard in

Plate 6.17: In 1872, across the river from Georgetown this fine depot rose at Eufaula. In architectural grace and ornament, it surpassed any depot of the era built along South Georgia's rails. (Photo: Wilber W. Caldwell.)

Georgia where, across the river from Eufaula, tiny Georgetown languished in the deep shadow of her neighbor's success.

Back in 1847, when the Southwestern Railroad first published its plans to connect Macon with Columbus, Eufaula and Albany, the directors of the new road were shrewd and politically sensitive. They were playing a coy financial game, dangling the bait of iron rails in order to garner the largest stock subscription possible from secondary towns along the way, and hoping to ward off the threats of planned rival roads from Columbus to Barnesville, from Macon to Columbus and from Savannah to Albany or Thomasville. Thus as she progressed, the Southwestern subtly implied that further westward progress was for sale. In 1856, Richard Cuyler, president of the Southwestern wrote:

> "...this Company,...feels that the people of these places ...Cuthbert, Eufaula and Fort Gaines) and of the country tributary to them, respectively, should unite themselves to the Southwestern Railroad, and through the Road connect and

[60] *Atlanta Constitution*, April 30, 1885.

[61] *The Enterprise and Appeal* (Cuthbert GA), May 6, 1886 in Ira Goolsby, Florence Moye, and Cornelia Mattox, *Randolph County, A Compilation of Facts, Recollections and Family Sketches* (Cuthbert GA: Randolph County Historical Society, 1977) 17.

[62] *The Enterprise and Appeal* (Cuthbert GA), May 6, 1886 in Ira Goolsby, Florence Moye, and Cornelia Mattox, *Randolph County, A Compilation of Facts, Recollections and Family Sketches*, 17.

identify themselves with Macon and Savannah—with the Seat of Government, the mountain country of Georgia and the General Railroad system of the Union."[63]

Cuyler continued in veiled terms: "Further extension to Cuthbert, and points beyond, depends on the efforts the people may make to carry out the views of the Company. The Board hopes that those efforts may lead at once to continuation of the survey from Cuthbert to Eufaula, and to the speedy building of the Road to that place."[64] By "efforts…to carry out the views of the Company" Cuyler meant cash investments, and he spelled this out in 1857 when he promised the extension of the road if the citizens of Cuthbert and Eufaula would subscribe $150,000 and $300,000 respectively. Ultimately $633,000 was subscribed including $200,000 from Fort Gaines, and the line was finished to Georgetown, opposite Eufaula, by 1860. A branch to Fort Gaines was completed in that same year.

Quitman County was split off from Randolph in 1858, and the next year a two-story frame courthouse was constructed at Georgetown. In that same year, the Southwestern began constructing a small wooden depot there. From the very beginning the focus in Georgetown was fixed on Eufaula across the river. Upon completing the line to Georgetown, the Southwestern immediately set out to bridge the Chattahoochee, a project that struggled forward throughout the war. Finally in 1865, the span was complete, and Georgetown, with a population below 250, was thrust into obscurity. The simple frame courthouse served the county until it burned in 1921. At that time, Georgetown's population was still about 250, and court was held in a commercial warehouse until 1939 when a new court building was designed by T. F. Lockwood Jr., the son of the Columbus architect who had developed the plans for Albany's 1903 court building. No photograph survives of either the first Quitman County Courthouse or of Georgetown's tiny wooden depot, but fittingly photographs of the Southwestern's remarkable 1865 bridge at Georgetown are abundant. Resting on four massive

piers, the completely covered, 900-foot wooden span soared 80 feet above the river.

This impressive bit of engineering spelled stagnancy for Georgetown and more growth for Eufaula, which was already a thriving trading center of the river-bound cotton trade. When the Southwestern arrived, Eufaula boasted over 3000 citizens. By 1886, with her population above 5000, the largest of Eufaula's many factors traded a staggering 30,000 bales.[65] Although the arrival of the railroad would eventually all but end river traffic on the Flint and the Chattahoochee, the immediate effect was to complement steamboating interests. In the late 1860s the Atlantic and Gulf Railroad, operating between Bainbridge and Savannah, offered shippers a river-rail link connecting the lower portions of the Flint and the Chattahoochee with Savannah. To counter this competitive thrust the Southwestern announced the purchase of two iron-hulled steamboats in 1868. These arrived at Apalachicola in that same year.

Eufaula was not the end of the line for the Southwestern. In 1860 the Montgomery and Eufaula Railroad began operations eventually connecting Eufaula and most of southwest Georgia with Alabama's growing rail system. The Vicksburg and Brunswick was only completed as far as Clayton, Alabama, when the line was leased by the Central of Georgia in 1879. Through it all, Georgetown was never more than an insignificant stop along the way. Then one day the trains ceased to stop there at all.

CLAY COUNTY: FORT GAINES

Plate 6.18: The Clay County Courthouse, built in 1871-1873.

Fort Gaines had passed the moment of its fullness by the time the Southwestern arrived in 1860. Located on a high bluff overlooking the Chattahoochee River, the town prospered from its early beginnings as the river port of the once enormous Early County. In 1854, Clay County was split off from Early and Randolph Counties with Fort Gaines as the county seat. A one-room frame courthouse was erected, and it served the county until this building was completed in Reconstruction times. Part of the original one room structure still stands today, remodeled as the kitchen to the old McAllister home on Jefferson Street.

As a very early trading center, Fort Gaines's importance cannot be understated, and today some of the finest structures from the frontier period in southwest Georgia can be found here in various stages of renovation and decay. In 1849, George White described Fort Gaines as "a place of considerable trade" with a population of about 400." But Eufaula was fast becoming the unquestioned trading center for traffic on the lower Chattahoochee, and ironically the arrival of the Southwestern ended what little hope Fort Gaines may have had left. Although the town had gathered resources enough to subscribe $200,000 to construct the spur from Cuthbert Junction, the line was doomed to be a dead-end from the beginning, and no serious effort at bridging the Chattahoochee at Fort Gaines was ever made by the Southwestern or by the Central. The rail connection to Macon and thus to Savannah was to greatly diminish Fort Gaines's importance, and as the nineteenth century drew to a close, river transport slowly declined.

It may be that enough railroad zeal survived the war to prompt the citizens of Clay County to build a new courthouse in 1871, but this structure, built in the face of the stern realities of the Reconstruction years, reflects little exuberance. Like most of Georgia's court buildings of the era, this is a sober vernacular statement of practical needs and modest expectations. Of thirty-nine courthouses built in Georgia between 1865 and 1877 (see Appendix A), three were log buildings, nineteen were vernacular frame structures and twenty were brick. Most of these brick buildings reflected various local builders' architectural interpretations of hard times. Only the Second Empire monuments to the new age at the rail centers of Athens and Macon, sang up-to-date architectural tunes. These were the only court buildings of style built in the period. Two of the remaining brick buildings were of a crude Greek vernacular sort, and the remaining fifteen, like the 1871 Clay County Courthouse, were of predictable brick vernacular design similar to many built before the war. With their hipped or pyramidal roofs, their flat unadorned walls were divided into neat bays by simple brick pilasters.

Plate 6.18: The 1871 Clay County Courthouse exemplifies many vernacular designs, which typified public building in Georgia during the Reconstruction period. (Photo: Wilber W. Caldwell.)

Even before this simple courthouse was constructed, Fort Gaines was becoming something of a stepchild. During the war when Federal raiders destroyed a portion of the Atlanta and West Point Railroad near LaGrange, replacement rails had been supplied by pulling up the Fort Gaines branch of the Southwestern. After the war, few trains ran to Fort Gaines, and in 1966 the Central abandoned the line only five years before this courthouse celebrated is 100th birthday. A very old wind blows in the lonely streets of Fort Gaines today. It is a place rich in history, but its history is of a time long before there were railroads to inspire courthouse towers.

THE COLUMBUS BRANCH

TAYLOR COUNTY: BUTLER

Plate 6.19: The depot at Butler, built in 1868.

In 1868, Virgil Powers reported to the president of the Southwestern Railroad: "The new Brick Warehouse at Bulter, which had but recently been completed, was destroyed by fire on the morning of the 14th of June. The walls are not seriously damaged,

[63] Richard Cuyler, "Superintendent's Report" in *Report of the Chief Engineers, Presidents and Superintendents of The Southwestern Railroad*, 236.

[64] Cuyler, "Superintendent's Report," 238.

[65] Anne Kendrick Walker, *Backtracking in Barbour County, A Narrative of the Last Alabama Frontier* (Richmond: Dietz Press, 1941) 303.

Plate 6.19: This 1868 depot at Butler supplies a rare and early example of ornamentation in rural railroad architecture in Georgia. (Photo: Wilber W. Caldwell.)

and it will cost about $3000 to rebuild it."[66] Most of Georgia's antebellum and Reconstruction depots were quite plain, but these walls with their elegant brick corbeling supply a rare and early example of architectural ornamentation in rural railroad architecture in Georgia.

In 1853, the Southwestern met the stalled Muscogee Railroad at Butler thus completing a rail link between Macon and Columbus. From its beginning, the Southwestern had been drawn toward Columbus, which, from its inception in 1827, seemed destined to become one of the great trading centers of Georgia. In 1847, when the civil engineer, F. P Holcolm, delivered the results of his preliminary survey to the Southwestern Railroad's board of directors, the Columbus connection seemed essential, and his report was quick to cite the predictable motivation: "Eighty-thousand bales of cotton, which are now annually received at Columbus, would be a rich harvest.... Until the completion of the Muscogee Road...the whole travel (of) light goods now hauled in wagons from Barnesville to Columbus would take that route."[67] Holcomb maintained that if the Southwestern simply passed within 30 or 40 miles of Columbus, that city would be moved to build a connecting link. This prophecy proved insightful, and by 1852, aiming for a junction at Fort Valley, the newly chartered Muscogee Railroad had laid track as far as Bulter. In the interim, the Columbus connection was growing even more attractive to the Southwestern owing to the progress and promise of new Alabama

roads, notably the Columbus and Opelika and the Mobile and Girard. After reaching Butler, the Muscogee Railroad ran short of funding, and completion of the line was left to the Southwestern, which absorbed the Muscogee Railroad in 1852. The entire branch was completed in 1853, and Columbus was finally connected to Savannah via the Central, and to the American heartland via the Macon and Western and the Western and Atlantic.

The railroad's power to shape history is again illustrated in Butler. In the same year that the Muscogee Railroad arrived, Taylor County was cut from Talbot County with Butler as her county town. The next year, a fine brick courthouse was constructed on the square. In 1860, Adiel Sherwood's *Gazetteer of Georgia* described Butler as "yet a small place." After the war, Butler was not to know crossing rails, and the county's resources remained small. In 1880, Taylor County cotton production stood at only 18,000 bales compared to 36,000 and 31,000 respectively in neighboring Talbot and Macon Counties. The early 1890s saw a strong Populist faction rise in Taylor County. As in other places where Populism was strong, the New South myth remained weak. Predictably the euphoria imported by postbellum rails would not find voice in Taylor County, and she would retain her original courthouse until 1935.

MUSCOGEE COUNTY: COLUMBUS

Plate 6.20: The Muscogee County Courthouse, built in 1838. John Goodwin, builder.

Almost from the moment the first bolls exploded into white fibrous profusion along of the state's central and western Fall Line, Georgia's state government began to envision trading towns in the interior. But as we have seen, the plantations of the antebellum era had little need of towns, and the state's early leaders knew that, "if urban centers were to exist in Georgia, the state would have to bring them into existence."[68] Macon and Columbus were thus created via state level legislation as "trading centers." Both blossomed in wild and unexpected bursts of frontier exuberance and frenzy: Macon was founded in 1823 at the Fall Line on the Ocmulgee and Columbus five years later in 1828 at the Fall Line on the Chattahoochee.

Only two years after her wide streets were laid out, Columbus boasted seventy-five frame buildings, twelve stores, two hotels,[69] and a crude wooden courthouse. That first court building burned in 1838, and the second Muscogee County Courthouse, built by John Goodwin who we assume was also the designer, was remarkably similar in form to the 1829 Bibb County Courthouse in Macon. Like Macon's early court building, the grand scale of this courthouse sings a convincing song of a frontier city's early growth. Although more horizontal in massing than its sister at Macon, its hipped roof and two stories set on a massive half-basement pierced by arched openings beneath a Doric Greek portico, reflect Robert Mills's early designs in South Carolina. It is also consistent with early American visions of the Greek Revival published in builders guides of the day, most notably Asher Benjamin's *The American Builder's Companion* (1827) and *The Practical House Carpenter* (1830) and Minard Lefever's *The Beauties of Modern Architecture* (1835). The horizontal form and the central high portico are typical of antebellum models, which influenced legions of neoclassical Revival court buildings built in Georgia just after the turn of the century.

Although later in beginning and deeper into the wild country newly acquired from the hapless and reluctant Creeks, Columbus quickly seized upon advantages that Macon lacked. The Chattahoochee was a far more reliably navigable stream than the Ocmulgee, and the power of the falls at Columbus, dropping 125 feet in less than 2.5 miles, produced a staggering 66,000 horsepower even in low water seasons. Together with a certain frontier entrepreneurial spirit, all of this resulted in the first semblance of a truly industrial city in Georgia, eventually eclipsing even the venerable Augusta in that regard. Water wheels were turning in Columbus by 1834, and by 1860, four large cotton textile mills were in operation. The Civil War brought additional prosperity to Columbus before it brought ruin. The town's population of about 9000 in 1860 had grown to over 15,000 by 1863,[70] as Columbus produced a long list of goods for the industry-starved Confederacy including

Plate 6.20: Like Macon's early court building, the grand scale of the 1838 Muscogee County Courthouse sings a convincing song of a frontier city's early growth.

cartridges, shoes, tents, rope, swords, steam engines, boilers, harnesses, knapsacks, and uniforms. Frederick Law Olmsted maintained that Columbus, with its mills and foundries, was the largest industrial city in the Confederacy south of Richmond.[71] Tragically, seven days after Appomattox all this was turned to ashes by Federal forces opposed by only sparse and ineffective Rebel resistance none of whom had received word of Lee's surrender. Destruction was limited in large part to industrial and military targets, and the next day Union forces had set out for Macon when they received word that the war was over. Macon was thus spared, but the news had come a day late for Columbus.

[66] Holcomb, "Supplement to the Report of the Civil Engineer" in *Reports of the Chief Engineers, Presidents and Superintendents of The Southwestern Railroad*, 54-55.

[67] Holcomb, "Civil Engineer's Report" in *Reports of the Chief Engineers, Presidents and Superintendents of The Southwestern Railroad* , 28-29.

[68] Joan Niles Sears, *The First Hundred Years of Town Planning in Georgia* (Atlanta: Cherokee Press, 1979) 157.

[69] *The Columbus Enquirer*, February 27, 1830 in Historical Preservation in Columbus Georgia.

[70] John S. Lupold, *Columbus, Georgia, 1828-1978* (Columbus GA: Columbus Sesquicentennial, Inc., 1978) 31.

[71] Fredkick Law Olmsted in Leopold, *Columbus, Georgia, 1828-1978*, 23.

Plate 6.21: As Columbus cemented her position as a rail center in the 1880s, Bruce and Morgan's Central of Georgia office building and the last of Georgia's great train sheds rose in 1882. (Illustration: Columbus Daily Enquirer, October 1, 1895.)

Plate 6.21 The Central of Georgia's offices, depot and train shed at Columbus, built in 1882. Bruce and Morgan, architects.

When the Western and Atlantic was chartered back in 1836, Columbus chartered the Chattahoochee Railroad aiming for a connection with that railhead at the place soon to be called Atlanta. But the financial decline of the late 1830s put an end to the scheme, and the company finally collapsed in 1841. The river remained Columbus's trading link as the town struggled for rail connection. With the Monroe Railroad complete to Barnesville in 1840, a steady awkward flow of wagon trade crept along the muddy roads connecting Columbus to that early railhead. In the meanwhile, as the Southwestern Railroad approached Fort Valley, Columbus's fledgling railroad entrepreneurs saw a connection there as the course of least resistance. By the time, the Muscogee Railroad made the link with the Southwestern at Butler in 1853, several more rail schemes were afoot to the west in Alabama. The city of Columbus had invested $300,000 in the Mobile and Girard Railroad chartered in 1846, and by 1860 that road was complete from Columbus to Union Springs, Alabama. Likewise in the 1850s, Columbus sought connection to the main line of rail traffic flowing along the Atlanta and West Point Railroad to Montgomery, and in 1855 a spur was completed from Columbus to Opelika. Originally called the Savannah and Memphis Railroad, the line was later renamed the Columbus

and Western. Thus, the beginning of the war found Columbus connected to the cotton country of Black Belt Alabama by the Mobile and Girard, to the Atlanta-Montgomery line at Opelika by the Savannah and Memphis and to Macon and Savannah via the Muscogee and the Southwestern Railroads.

After the war, with the shadow of hard times dark upon the land, Columbus, like Augusta, was remarkably quick to recover. Her mills and foundries attracted Northern capitalists. In the 1870s New England entrepreneurs created Muscogee Mills, and New Jersey investors revived the enormous Eagle and Phenix Mill. The rebuilding of these and other resources painted a picture of what the New South spokesmen would envision for the rest of Georgia. Like Rome and the cities along the Western and Atlantic Railroad, Columbus had known industrial growth before the war, and although she was steeped in the culture of cotton, she was not so myopically afflicted as to overlook the opportunities afforded by manufacturing.

Railroad progress in the 1870s was less impressive. Of the five roads proposed for Columbus in the 1870s only two laid any track. The Savannah and Memphis was extended to Birmingham and the North and South Railroad (later the Columbus and Atlanta Air Line) began a link to the north, but only completed a short stretch of track before it stalled at Hamilton in 1877. It was not until 1885 that the line was extended to Greenville, Georgia by the Columbus and Rome Railroad, which in turn became part of the Savannah and Western. In the difficult times of the 1870s, river traffic on the Chattahoochee flourished, and it was not until the late 1880s that new rail construction cemented Columbus's position as a rail center. As things picked up, Bruce and Morgan's sober office building and the last and most elegant of Georgia's great brick train sheds were built by the Central at Columbus. By 1980, seven railroads converged on the city (see Table 6.3). Intended for the joint use of the Central, the Mobile and Girard and the Columbus and Western, the Central's great shed was similar to those at Macon, Augusta, Savannah and West Point.

---

[72] Lupold, *Columbus, Georgia, 1828-1978*, 14.

[73] *Columbus Daily Enquirer*, May 24, 1895.

Plate 6.22: The Muscogee County Courthouse, Built, 1838. Remodeled 1895-1896. Andrew J. Bryan, remodeling architect. Demolished, 1972.

With such power expressed by the ordinarily utilitarian architecture of the railroad, it would seem that Columbus might have been quick to express her success in a new courthouse. But it must be remembered that the irony of the relationship between the courthouse and the depot is that fantasy courthouse building was sparked by the railroads most often in places where the promises of the New South were dreams rather than reality. In Columbus, like Augusta and Atlanta, the New South was fast becoming a reality, in spite of the vast stagnant rural sea of poverty and ignorance that festered just beyond the town limit.

By 1890, Columbus had fourteen textile mills, four foundries, four hosiery mills, seven brick yards, two clothing manufacturers, a wagon factory and a population of almost 20,000.[72] Like Augusta, which had simply enlarged her 1821 court building in 1892 to growing needs, Columbus too operated on a keen sense of practicality and probably felt little need to create the mythical architecture of dreamers. Although she built a new courthouse in 1895, it was in reality just an elaborate remodeling and expansion of the old 1838 building.[73] In adding to the old building, Columbus, unlike Augusta, grasped the opportunity to completely change the appearance of the structure, effectively encasing the old courthouse in a radically modern neoclassical monument. This was neither the architecture of New South aspirations nor of Old South reverie. It was the self-celebrating architecture of modern American industry and finance. This was the only court building of this type built in Georgia before 1910.

As we have noted, the impact of the flowery Florentine Classicism of the buildings of the 1893 Columbian Exposition at Chicago had enormous effect on American public building. The success of "The White City," as it was called, swept aside the slow steady progress made by H. H. Richardson and his followers toward a modern national style. It all but extinguished the Romantic flames lit by John Wellborn Root, Lewis Sullivan and others. From the

RAILROAD CONNECTIONS AT COLUMBUS IN 1890 — Table 6.3

The Central of Georgia Railroad, 1853 (formerly the Muscogee and the Southwestern Railroads), Columbus to Macon.

The Mobile & Girard Railroad, 1845, (later part of the Central of Georgia) Columbus to Mobile, Al.

The Savannah & Memphis Railroad, 1855 (later the Columbus & Western Railroad), Columbus to Birmingham via Opelika.

The Georgia, Midland & Gulf Railroad, 1886, (later the Georgia Midland), Columbus to McDonough via Griffin.

The Buena Vista & Ellaville Railroad, 1889 (formerly the Buena Vista Railroad, later the Buena Vista & Anderson Railroad, later the Central of Georgia Railroad), Columbus to Americus.

The Savannah & Western Railroad, a division of the Central of Georgia, 1888, (formerly the Columbus & Rome Railroad, formerly the North and South Railroad), Columbus to Chattanooga via Griffin and Rome.

The Columbus Southern Railroad, 1890, (later the Georgia & Alabama Railroad) Columbus via Richland to Albany.

glowing coals of Renaissance Revival, begun in the late 1870s, the architecture of the fair ignited an academic classical bonfire that almost overnight became the chosen national architectural beacon and the new symbol for American business, imperialism and finance. Waves of classical revivals followed in the United States including American Neoclassical Revival, invigorated Georgian (or Colonial) and Italian Renaissance Revivals, begun way back in the early 1880s, and the most flamboyant and bombastic of all, the American Beaux-Arts Style.

Plate 6.22: In an extensive 1896 remodeling, the old 1838 Muscogee County Courthouse was effectively encased in a radically modern Beaux Arts monument. (Photo: Courtesy of Georgia Dept. of Archives and History)

It is difficult to overstate the national importance of the buildings of the Chicago Exposition. Led by a veritable "who's who" of American architects of the day, including George B Post; Henry Van Brunt, Richard Morris Hunt, New York's Mead, McKim and White and Boston's Peabody and Sterns, the awe-inspiring alabaster classical vision created by these buildings took the country by storm. In an architectural heartbeat, the wellspring of American architectural inspiration had shifted from London to Paris.

Not surprisingly, this new architecture with its whigish symbolism found few patrons in the South before 1900. Still, it is predictable that it had appeal in Columbus. The direct architectural connection between Chicago in 1893 and Columbus, Georgia in 1895 is easy to trace, and the trail leads through Atlanta. In 1895, just as Columbus was considering a design for her courthouse remodeling, the Cotton States Exposition opened in Atlanta. Like the Columbian Exposition, the effect of this fair was electric. Most of the central architecture was the work of New York architect, Bradford Gilbert. Executed in conservative compositions of gray shingle and green roofs, Gilbert's work at Atlanta, with its studied symmetry, was a tame and only slightly picturesque voice of dying Southern romanticism.

Only a few major buildings were not of this type. Distinctive among the exceptions was Walter Downing's 65,000 square foot Fine Arts Building, which most certainly had as its model Charles B. Atwood's Fine Arts Building at the 1893 Columbian Exposition in Chicago. There can be little doubt that this enormous structure in Atlanta's Piedmont Park was in turn the model for Atlanta architect, Andrew J. Bryan's 1895 Muscogee County Courthouse. Bryan was the architect of eight courthouses in Georgia. He would prove himself a versatile innovator on varied projects including Romanesque offerings at Douglasville (1895) and at Douglas (1900), several neoclassical court buildings like the Colquitt County Courthouse at Moultrie (1903) and a generally Federal Style or Neo-Georgian Troup County Courthouse at LaGrange (1904). Here in Columbus, the central mass of his Muscogee County Courthouse

was laid in almost identical form to Downing's Cotton States Exposition design with a deep central portico supported by an Ionic colonnade. The high cornice and the balustrade are typical of the style introduced in Chicago, and the low dome with its ring of roundels is a miniature of the crown of Atwood's grand Fine Arts Building at Chicago.

The up-to-date styling of Bryan's design at Columbus points directly to a remarkably progressive spirit in that city. The architectural style of court buildings of this period was driven more by local hopes and attitudes than it was by the artistic tastes and convictions of the architects who designed them. The record of architectural review in connection with the 1896 Muscogee County Courthouse points to this conclusion. *The Columbus Daily Enquirer* of July 14 and 16, 1895, details the selection process. Seven different architects presented plans on July 16 and 17. Each had met with the county commissioners to discuss the county's needs and desires regarding the building. With such input and seven plans to choose from, it is likely that the citizens of Columbus got exactly what they wanted.

Plate 6.23: Union Depot at Columbus, built in 1901. Bruce and Morgan, architects.

In the early period in Georgia, most depot architecture was the work of the railroad's own engineers. By the 1890s, many large roads had retained notable architects to handle the job of creating the larger urban depots that were so important in maintaining the prestige and symbolizing the power of the new corporate giants. We encounter several examples in this connection as we survey Georgia's public architecture around the turn of the century. Bradford Gilbert had an extensive railroad career in New York before coming south. Frank Milburn as the chief architect for the giant Southern Railway designed grand depots at both Augusta (1901) and Savannah (1901) and P. Thornton Mayer created the plan for Atlanta's 1905 Terminal Station. Meanwhile, Atlanta architects, Bruce and Morgan, designed stunning smaller depots at Forsyth (1895), Americus (1900), and here at Columbus in 1901.

Bruce and Morgan's extensive courthouse work in Georgia had been limited to picturesque variations on Second Empire, Romanesque Revival and Queen Anne themes. Here the firm departs from this tradition to create what is fundamentally a classical form with its low hipped roof and broad classical cornice. Beyond this, the structure presents an odd, although pleasing, mixture which betrays the return to order of the budding American academic classical tradition and reminds us that in 1901 eclecticism was not yet dead in the American South. The stone entrance arch is clearly Richardsonian. This is echoed by the over-sized, broad arched windows of the central mass of the building. Although the central feature of the rounded parapet breaking the line of the cornice recalls many Mission Style depots in smaller towns, the impression here is more of the Northern European Renaissance. In overall effect, we are again reminded that depot architecture of this era often looked to domestic models. Fittingly this successful but unusual building, today masterfully restored, stands to remind us that Columbus at the turn of the century was indeed a successful and in many ways an unusual Southern city.

SOME LAST THOUGHTS ON THE SOUTHWESTERN RAILROAD

In 1845, when the newly chartered Southwestern Railroad completed its initial survey, the rich cotton lands southwest of Macon were bursting into inviting bloom. Cotton's promise was moving west, and the virgin lands of Southwest Georgia, Alabama and Mississippi beckoned to ambitious planters and yeomen in the tired fields of the eastern Cotton Belt. The railroad's survey was quick to point out opportunities for potential investors, noting that the port of Apalachicola was shipping 150,000 bales annually, and that the prosperous city of Columbus on the Chattahoochee was ripe for rail connection. In a prophetic bit of rhetoric the survey waxed poetic: "(the Chattahoochee), like most other rivers of the country, ultimately destined to yield the palm to superior speed, certainly, and safety of that great revolutionist, the railroad. The great Mississippi itself will be deserted...."[74]

Plate 6.23: The Union Depot at Columbus. By the 1890s, most large roads had retained notable architects to handle the job of creating larger urban depots so important in maintaining the prestige and symbolizing the power of the new corporate giants. (Photo: Wilber W. Caldwell.)

But the "great revolutionist" of the Southwestern was slow to attract investors. Initial stock subscriptions at Macon and elsewhere along the proposed line were disappointing, and had it not been for substantial support from the Central, which would effectively control the road from the beginning, the Southwestern would have long remained only a paper survey.

As it turned out, zeal for the road seemed in increase as track was laid. This was due in part to the natural momentum of the project, and to the Southwestern's practice of "dangling the carrot" of rail connection before the hungry planters and merchants of one town after another: first Americus, and later Dawson, Cuthbert, Fort Gaines and Eufaula. Likewise Albany and Columbus were lured into the enterprise, building connecting rails to the main line, which were subsequently gobbled up by the Southwestern. By 1860, over thirty percent of the cotton produced in Georgia was coming from the counties served by the Southwestern, and the lion's share of this harvest was hauled up the line to Macon and on to Savannah via the Central of Georgia. Just as the Civil War ended the great bridge at Eufaula was completed, and a sizable

---

[74] E. P. Holcomb, *Report on the Preliminary Survey and Estimates for The Southwestern Railroad.*

195

Plate 6.24: Columbus. (Photo: Wilber W. Caldwell.)

Americus and Dawson had fought the good fight. Both had achieved postbellum crossing rails around 1890, and both had built elaborate fantasy court buildings in response to the promise of the new roads. The Savannah, Americus and Montgomery Railroad had been an extension of the Americus, Preston and Lumpkin Railroad built in 1886, and Americus had employed the notable skills of Alexander Bruce and Thomas Henry Morgan in 1887 to create what was one of the finest Romanesque Revival courthouses built in Georgia. Sadly the building was demolished in 1959, but today in Americus one can still enjoy a stunning sampling of the architecture of the last two decades of the nineteenth century. Notable are G. L. Norman's grand Windsor Hotel and his fine Americus City Hall building. In Dawson, the Columbus Southern crossed the old line of the Southwestern Railroad in 1890, and the expectations surrounding this event compelled the town to engage Atlanta's William Parkins to design Georgia's most extreme example of Picturesque Eclecticism. Built in 1892, Parkins' fantasy stands today to ironically scribe the high water mark in Dawson, which was not destined to be much more than a prosperous area center of trade in support of the agricultural base.

Cuthbert contemplated an early crossing line which failed to materialize, but not before the town had built a elegant courthouse from plans by Atlanta's Kimball, Wheeler, and Parkins. The design, probably the work of Lorenzo Wheeler, reflects Dutch Renaissance influence, and is perhaps the most aesthetically successful of Georgia's standing Picturesque Eclectic court buildings.

Elsewhere along the Southwestern, in towns where no crossing rails appeared, the story was predicable. Lee and Clay Counties kept their simple 1870s courthouses at Leesburg and Fort Gaines until well into this century. Likewise, the antebellum court buildings at Georgetown in Quitman County and Butler in Taylor County served until 1921 and 1935 respectively.

The story in Columbus is remarkably similar to Augusta's courthouse saga. Early antebellum prosperity was evidenced by enormous courthouses built in each county's infancy and remodeled or enlarged as

portion of the Alabama crop was added to the Southwestern's manifests. Thus, the iron hand of the Central of Georgia would control the cotton trade in southwest Georgia for decades to come.

The drama of courthouse building in the region was played out in the postbellum era as Americus, Albany and, to a lesser degree, Dawson vied for influence. Albany would eventually emerge the victor, but not before the town was established as the dominant rail center of the area. The question hung in the balance until well into the depression years of the 1890s. By the turn of the century, seven railroads met at Albany and the town's growth surged. In 1903, Albany replaced her exquisite 1847 vernacular courthouse with a neoclassical symbol of her victory, designed by Columbus architect T. F. Lockwood.

the county grew. Like Augusta. Columbus realized a rare helping of New South prosperity after the Civil War. Thus, the city did not know that odd combination of desperation and fear that drove so many of Georgia's county towns to erect hopeful monuments in the dark decades of the last third of the nineteenth century. Unlike Augusta, Columbus was moved to accomplish a complete facelift on her old court building in 1896. Andrew Bryan's remodeling yielded the first neoclassical Revival court building in Georgia.

The lure of cotton in Southwestern Georgia beckoned in the 1850s, and the Southwestern Railroad was not the only rail line to answer the cotton Siren's seductive call. While the Southwestern completed her web in the west of the state, the last of Georgia's antebellum railroads was underway farther to the south. Often called the Main Trunk Line, the road scribed a southerly loop from Savannah to Thomasville. Near present-day Waycross, it crossed a rival road building northward out of Brunswick bound for Albany. It seems Savannah had another seaport competitor beyond Charleston. Brunswick, like Charleston had a good harbor but was without viable water routes to the interior. She too sought to tap South Georgia's white bounty via rail, and so began a clash that resulted in the Atlantic and Gulf Railroad.

The Atlantic and Gulf Railroad

Savannah (see Chapter 2) Liberty County: Hinesville • Long County: Ludowici
Wayne County: Jesup • Pierce County: Blackshear • Ware County: Waycross
Clinch County: Homerville • Lanier County: Lakeland • Echols County: Statenville
Lowndes County: Valdosta • Brooks County: Quitman • Thomas County: Thomasville
Some Last Thoughts on the Atlantic and Gulf Railroad

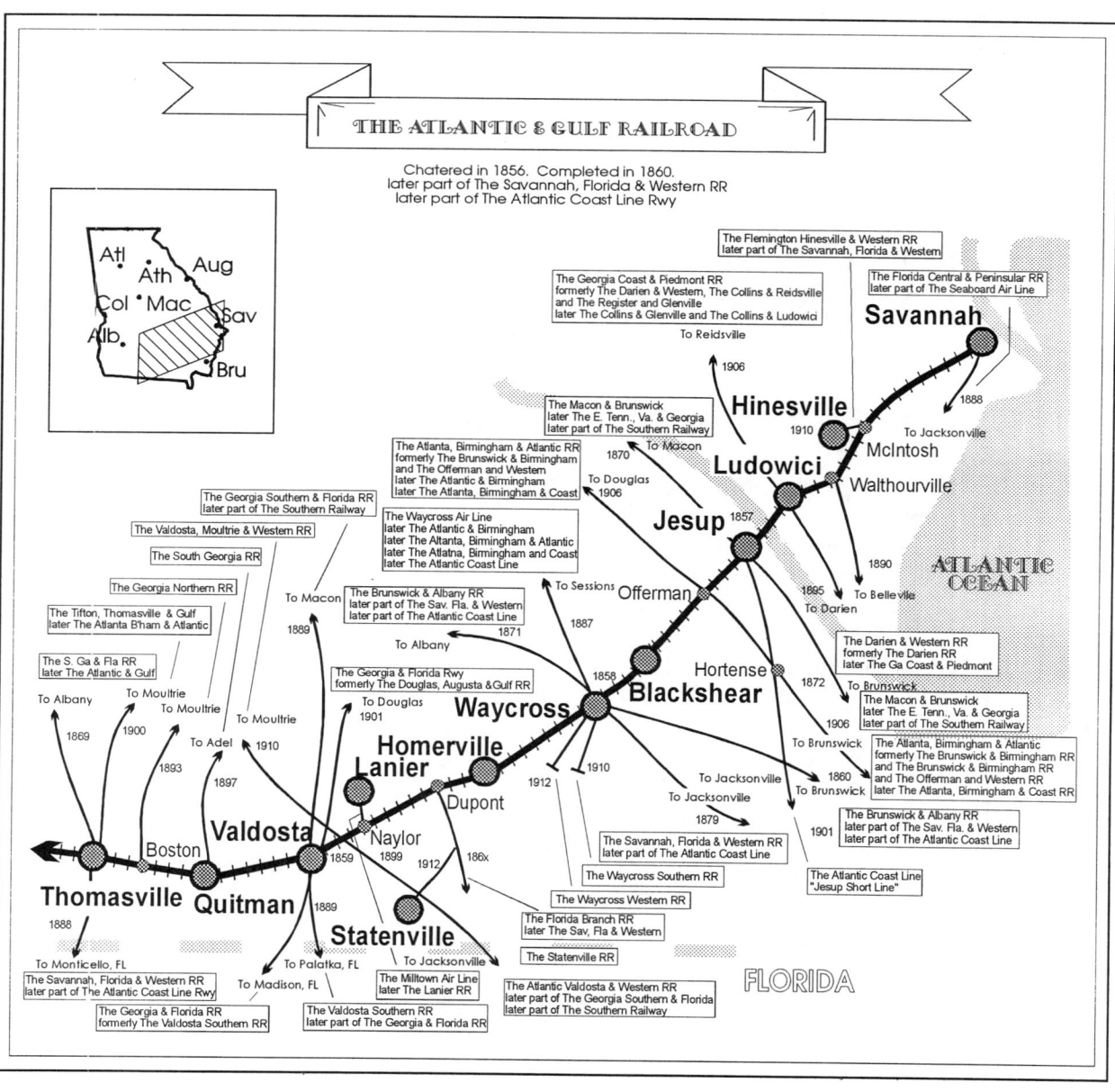

7 | The Atlantic and Gulf Railroad

SAVANNAH TO THOMASVILLE

LIBERTY COUNTY: HINESVILLE

Plate 7.1: R. Q. Cassel and Sons Store at McIntosh, built in 1887.

All across the state, the crumbling ruins of countless rural stores like this one at McIntosh in Liberty County recall an era of small farms and hard times. They also stand in dramatic contrast to the plantation economy that they helped to replace. This imposing structure was erected in 1887 across the tracks from the wooden shed of a depot in the tiny hamlet first called Hutchenson Plantation and later renamed McIntosh to honor some obscure depot agent who resided at the place the Savannah, Albany and Gulf Railroad originally called Station #3.[1] Before the Civil War, the plantations of Liberty County had little need for such stores. Theirs was an inwardly turned economy of rice, Sea Island cotton and indigo. In 1857-1858 when the Savannah, Albany and Gulf Railroad scribed its sweeping arc through some of the poorest country in Georgia on its way not to Albany but to Thomasville, Liberty County had over 100 plantations of over 1000 acres, many with over 100 slaves.[2] But, as we so often find in the Old South, things were not as they seemed.

Liberty County boasts two signers of the American Declaration of Independence, and was home to enough Revolutionary War heroes to supply names for five Georgia Counties.[3] But although rich in Colonial and Revolutionary history and despite her huge slave population and her fabled large plantations, the county had a surprisingly low agricultural output. County histories point to rice and Sea Island cotton as the staple crops, to support the usual myth of Old

---

[1] The popular assumption is that the village of McIntosh was named for Lachlan McIntosh, a Georgia Revolutionary War hero, but local historians hold to the contrary, Robert Long Groover, *Sweet Land of Liberty, A History of Liberty County* (Roswell GA: W. H. Wolfe, 1987) 41.

[2] Groover, *Sweet Land of Liberty, A History of Liberty County*, 39.

[3] Liberty County's Button Gwinnett and Lyman Hall signed the Declaration of Independence. Additionally Georgia Revolutionary War heroes from Liberty County lent their names to Gwinnett, Hall, Screven, Stewart, and Baker Counties.

Plate 7.1: The powerful remains of the R. Q. Cassel store at McIntosh near the village of McIntosh. (Photo: Wilber W. Caldwell.)

South prosperity. A quick check of Census agricultural statistics for the pre-war period reveals otherwise. In 1850, Liberty County reported only 1.8 million pounds of rice, making the county a distant "also ran" in a statewide twelve county harvest of 38 million pounds. This number pales when compared to neighboring Chatham County's bounteous 19 million pounds. Cotton was even less significant, for in the Pine Barrens cotton was not king. In 1850 the entire county counted only 1854 whites and 5517 slaves.

Predictably after the war, things were in ruin in Liberty. The county's only wealth had been in slaves. In 1864, General Sherman had visited his usual fiery wrath upon Liberty County's railroad, destroying track along the right of way and burning the depots at McIntosh, Walthourville and Johnson's Station (later Ludowici in Long County). In the wake of war, county-wide cotton production fell from 2400 bales in 1860 to only 600 bales in 1880, and while cotton production soared out of control in the rest of the state in the last decades of the century, Liberty would report only 330 bales in 1900. Likewise rice growing faded in the chaos following slavery's demise.

Despite its abuses in the cotton growing regions, tenancy had in many ways filled the void left by the collapse of the plantation system. On most Georgia farms the complex system of renters and croppers supplied labor and credit in a society that had been striped of its economic infrastructure by the collapse of the Confederacy and by the freeing of the slaves. With little or no cotton to harvest and rice devastated by hurricanes and nearly impossible to grow on small autonomous farms, tenancy did not take firm root in the coastal regions the way it did in the Cotton Belt. In 1880, of Liberty County's 100 antebellum plantations of over 1000 acres or more, over half were more or less intact and still farmed by owners. Improved acreage remained near its 1850 level, and almost two-thirds of the county's farms were worked by owners. Many turned to timber and the production of turpentine.

Against this back drop of poverty, railroad building in Liberty County can easily be seen for what it was: either the creation of mainline roads that were going somewhere else, or the temporary fabrications

Table 7.1

THE RAILROADS OF LIBERTY COUNTY

1857, The Savannah, Albany and Gulf Railroad (later part of the Atlantic and Gulf, later the Savannah, Florida and Western [Plant System]; later the Atlantic Coast Line Railroad; Savannah to Thomasville.

1890, A spur was constructed from Walthourville to Belleview on the Sapelo River to connect with the Darien Short Line Railroad which was completed to Darien in 1895 (later part of the Georgia Coast and Piedmont).

1892, The Florida Central and Peninsular Railroad (formerly the Florida Railway and Navigation Company, later part of the Seaboard Air Line); Savannah to Jacksonville, Florida.

1906, The Georgia Coast and Piedmont Railroad (formerly the Darien and Western, the Reidsville Southeastern, the Collins and Reidsville and the Register and Glenville) (later the Collins and Glenville and the Collins and Ludowici), Collins to Brunswick via Ludowici. a.k.a. the Gopher, Coon and Possum Railroad.

1910, the Flemington, Hinesville and Western (later the Savannah, Hinesville and Western), McIntosh to Hinesville. a.k.a. the Farmer's Horse and Wagon Railroad. a.k.a. Fold Hands and Weep Railroad.

1911, the Savannah Southern, Glenville to Lanier. According to Robert Groover's Liberty County history this road, built by G. W. Tuten, was operated as early as 1884. a.k.a. the Tuten Railroad.

The Southern Lumber Company and the Dunlevie Lumber Company at Allenhurst operated over 40 miles of rail around the turn of the century.

A spur was completed from Allenhurst via Hinesville to Fort Stewart in 1941.

of shaky lumber barons built to exploit timber, which was then viewed as an exhaustible resource. In towns along the main lines of the 1857 Savannah, Albany and Gulf and the 1892 Florida Central and Peninsular, it was the daily fate of Liberty County residents to longingly ponder the romance of rail as streams of cars flowed by bound for lands of perceived opportunity then blossoming in Florida or for the cotton growing regions of the west. These trains almost never stopped and seldom slowed down in Liberty County. Of logging roads and short lines, there were several (see Table 7.1). Additionally after the turn of the century, two roads emerged only to fade from memory after attempting to serve an area too poor to support serious railroading. In 1906, the Georgia Coast and Piedmont consolidated the rails of the Darien and Western, the Collins and Reidsville and the Reidsville and Southeastern Railroads which built the connecting link from Ludowici (then Liberty City) to Reidsville around 1906. After extending all the way to Brunswick in 1914, the line declared bankruptcy in 1916. In 1911, the Savannah Southern Railroad was constructed from Glenville to Lanier, but this ne'er-do-well line was abandoned in 1923. Another ill-fated scheme was the Flemington, Hinesville and Western, built around 1910 from McIntosh on the main line to Hinesville, a distance of 5.4 miles. A private home was converted to serve as a depot, and after the road failed in 1917 the building reverted to its original use on North Main Street in Hinesville.

Plate 7.2: The Liberty County Courthouse at Hinesville, built in 1837. Demolished in 1927.

The county's first town had been the port of Sunbury founded by Puritans in the 1750s. By the time of the Revolution, it was the second largest town in Georgia,[4] and it became the first Liberty County seat of justice in 1783. Riceboro replaced Sunbury as the county town in 1796, and a log courthouse was built there soon after the town was surveyed. In 1836, Liberty's citizens voted to move the county seat again, and the town of Hinesville was laid out. In 1837, this two-story frame courthouse was erected in a crude car-

penter Greek mode. Twenty years later the rails of the Savannah, Albany and Gulf would bypass Hinesville opting to serve the larger Walthourville, creating McIntosh and Allenhurst along the way. Through the years, Hinesville experienced little in the way of growth, and even as late as 1910 it counted only 174 residents. Little hope had arrived in Hinesville despite the brief folly of the Flemington, Hinesville and Western, and this simple court building would serve Liberty County until 1927.

Times remained hard as the late nineteenth-century rush of New South zeal failed to arrive on Georgia's coastal plain, and as the new century dawned, what few aspirations the railroads had delivered in Hinesville faded into the gray reality of poverty, ignorance and want. Highway 84 to Hinesville remained a dirt road until 1934, but the county would pulse with vigor after the creation of Fort Stewart in 1940. A spur passing near Hinesville was built from the main line at Allenhurst to Fort Stewart in 1941.

Plate 7.2: With its simple carpenter Greek portico, the 1837 Liberty County Courthouse at Hinesville would stand until 1927. (Photo: Courtesy of Georgia Dept. of Archives and History.)

[4] Joan Niles Sears, *The First One Hundred Years of Town Planning in Georgia* (Atlanta: Cherokee Press, 1979) 55.

Plate 7.3: Ludowici's depot recalls the short history of the Georgia Coast and Piedmont Railroad. (Photo: Wilber W. Caldwell.)

LONG COUNTY: LUDOWICI

Plate 7.3: The depot at Ludowici.

Ludowici's history as a small commercial and rail center is instructive. When the Savannah, Albany and Gulf Railroad arrived in 1858, there was nothing in the way of a town. The piney woods of what is now Long County were sparsely populated by poor hearty folk, most of whom scraped a living form subsistence agriculture, herding and from the products of the forest. A small wooden depot was erected and designated Station #5. The place was later named Johnston's Station, and in 1872 it was renamed Liberty City. It was later renamed yet again, this time Ludowici after

a German tile manufacturer who had established a small factory in the town. Although the tile factory is long ago moved, tile roofs still dot the landscape in this remote area.

The original depot was burned by General Sherman's forces in 1864, rebuilt after the war, burned again and was replaced by the present structure presumably some time before the turn of the century. In the last decades of the nineteenth century, Ludowici boasted the "largest store between Savannah and Waycross," a somewhat dubious claim, given the low density of the population in Wiregrass counties at the end of the last century. Various editions of Sholes's *Gazetteer of Georgia* place the town's population at 30 in 1879, 200 in 1886 and 350 a decade later. Along the way, the antebellum rails of the Savannah, Albany and Gulf had become the Atlantic and Gulf in 1863, the Savannah, Florida and Western in 1979 and the Atlantic Coast Line in 1902. In 1906, the new rails of the Georgia Coast and Piedmont Railroad crossed these antebellum rails near this depot, and by 1910, Ludowici had a population of 541.

Just as Ludowici can thank an antebellum railroad for her conception, the effect of the crossing of postbellum rails should not be underestimated in fueling of Ludowici's successful split from Liberty County in 1920. The creation of Long County is particularly notable in light of the fact that the timber industry was in sharp decline by 1920. In that year, the United States Forest Service reported that almost all of Georgia's virgin timber was harvested, and predicted that Georgia's large saw mills would be gone by 1930.[5] Likewise turpentine production had dropped, and the center of the naval stores industry had moved to Florida. But as we have seen, crossing rails often created optimism even in the face of economic despair. Certainly this was the case with the Georgia Coast and Piedmont. Spirits in Ludowici soared even though the line struggled from its inception and survived only ten years, from 1906 to 1916. The road's profits may have been mythical, but the rails were real enough. The Georgia Coast and Piedmont was purchased out of bankruptcy in 1919 and continued to run trains northward from Ludowici operating as the Collins and Ludowici until 1921. The first Long County Courthouse did not rise at Ludowici until 1926. The building is not a part of this study.

Wayne County: Jesup

Plate 7.4: The depot at Jesup, built c. 1885. Burned c. 1900.

Plate 7.4: Built in the mid-1880s, this depot at Jesup reflects elements of the American "Stick Style."

As we have noted, depot architecture in this era often looked to domestic sources for decoration. This depot, probably built in the mid-1880s, features curving beveled struts and open trusses forming the branched arches typical of what Vincent Scully has labeled the American Stick Style. The style rose from both a European taste for decorative rustic cottages and from an American fascination with carpenter styles and other wooden forms, which had emerged from vernacular interpretations of Gothic and Italian Villa Style cottages. The Stick Style, itself an emerging vernacular force, had swept domestic building in America in the 1870s. Conforming to the usual Southern stylistic lag and to the retarding economic conditions in the rural South after the war, Stick Style decoration was popular among homebuilders in Georgia in the last decades of the century. With its fondness for open verandahs and exposed supports, it was a natural for depots.

What became of this fine depot is something of a mystery. One old time Jesup resident recalled a depot fire just before 1900.[6] The history of the present depot is similarly clouded. It probably replaced this old Stick Style depot around 1900, and appears to have once been a structure of considerable charm with a graceful tile roof and decorative "eyebrow" dormers. Sadly additions, alterations and remodelings have today rendered the building architecturally uninteresting.

The story of depot building in Jesup is not the only missing page here. The early-recorded history of Wayne County is sketchy at best. One reason for the county's rather imprecise early records was its sparse population. In point of fact, there was little history to record, for there were few inhabitants to create any. Joan Sears cites this lack of population when she omits consideration of the early development of Wayne

County in her *The First Hundred Years of Town Planning in Georgia,* stating that the area was "less fertile" and "almost uninhabited".[7] Even the usually euphemistic rhetoric of official county history uses rather blunt language to describe Wayne's landscape, terming it simply "poor pine land with cypress ponds, palmetto and wiregrass." As late a 1850, the empty expanses of Wayne County, which at that time comprised most of present day Brantley and Charlton Counties as well as a portion of Pierce, contained only 1088 white settlers and 406 slaves

Wayne County was created in 1802 from land ceded to the state by the Creek Indians. The first courts were held in private homes. In 1829, Waynesville, today in Brantley County, became the county town. In that same year in his *Gazetteer of Georgia,* the reliable Adiel Sherwood reported that a "a tavern, a boarding house and 10 houses" made up this village, which had been laid out in 1825 twenty-five miles southeast of present-day Jesup. The history of early courthouses in Wayne County is a puzzle. Sherwood also mentions a courthouse on "Buffalo Creek," and twenty years later, in his *Statistics of the State of Georgia,* George White informs us that in Waynesville court was held "in the academy." There is also evidence suggesting that a village called Hortense, today in Pierce County, was the site of a courthouse

[5] Willard Range, *A Century of Georgia Agriculture, 1850-1950* (1954; reprint, Athens GA: University of Georgia Press, 1969) 208.

[6] Anna K. Clark's "Memories of Jesup" in Bobby M. Martin, *Wayne County, Georgia, Its History and Its People* (Dallas: Curtis Media, 1990) 41, This source mentions a two-story depot that burned before 1900. Despite the apparent discrepancy, it seems likely that the fire she remembers destroyed this building.

[7] Sears, *The First One Hundred Years of Town Planning in Georgia,* 95.

beginning in 1856, and there is mention of a two-story frame court building with a "dogtrot" opening in the first floor.[8]

Before the 1857 arrival of the Savannah, Albany and Gulf Railroad, none of these places could properly be called towns. But by the time this early line became the Atlantic and Gulf Railroad in 1863, simple wood and water stops had been transformed into centers of population. Station #5, became Doctortown where the railroad bridged the Altamaha, Station #6 became Jesup and Station #7 became Screven after James Screven, president of the Savannah, Albany and Gulf.

Even with the railroad's power to create towns, progress was slow and hard times prevailed in the Wiregrass after the war. Early records paint a stark picture of the scene at Jesup in 1869 relating that the entire town consisted of one wood rack to supply the ever hungry locomotives, one saw mill, one store, five bar rooms, and a few rows of "miscellaneous hutments."[9] In addition, a glance at early town ordinances suggests that there was a substantial "undesirable class." In short, when the city government was organized in 1870, Station #6 (or Jesup) was a pretty rough place. In that year, the Macon and Brunswick Railroad arrived, crossing the old line of the Atlantic and Gulf at Jesup and cementing the town's future.

Exactly when Station #6 began to be called Jesup is another matter for speculation as is the origin of the name.[10] The year in which Jesup became the county seat is also a matter of some conjecture. In 1855, Charlton County was created from the entire southern portion of Wayne County, thus leaving Waynesville on the extreme southern boundary of the County. The 1870 census lists four districts in Wayne County: Waynesville, Over River, Phinhalaway and Courthouse. Thus, it seems that we can safely conclude that Waynesville was no longer the County seat in that year. "Courthouse" may have referred to Hortense or to a yet-to-be-named Jesup, but this is unclear. Whatever the case, the courthouse lot in Jesup was sold to the county 1873[11] and a courthouse was completed in that same year. The building stood until shortly after the completion of the present courthouse in 1903. It was probably a two-story frame building

much like so many of its contemporary Wiregrass neighbors.

Plate 7.5: The Wayne County Courthouse, built in 1903. James W. Golucke, architect (attributed.)

There can be little doubt that Jesup had always been a "railroad town." One 1891 newspaper account relates that: "the majority of Jesup's population is connected in some way with the railroad."[12] At the turn of the century, Jesup, with a population of about 900, lay at the junction of two important rail links. H. B. Plant's Savannah, Florida and Western Railroad had consolidated the antebellum rails of the Atlantic and Gulf into a growing rail empire in 1879, and this all became part of the Atlantic Coast Line in 1902. The Macon and Brunswick had been completed in 1872, purchased by the East Tennessee, Virginia and Georgia Railroad in 1881 and acquired by the Southern Railway in 1894. Despite this important junction at Jesup, in 1900 Waycross, with its line to Florida, was at the true heart of the Plant System, and until 1901 Jesup seemed destined to live in the shadow of her western neighbor.

Accordingly, it is difficult to imagine the electricity that must have swept through Jesup when the following appeared in *The Jesup Sentinel* in 1901:

> It is now an assured fact that Jesup will have two new railroads. The charter was granted this week to the Jacksonville, St. Marys and Jesup Railroad, which will be a direct route to Jacksonville from Jesup via St. Marys. The Plant System's short line to Jacksonville via Folkston will also be built at an early date. With these valuable acquisitions, Jesup cannot help from building up and we predict that ere long we will have a city second to none in South Georgia.[13]

A building boom followed the completion of the 1902 "Jesup Short Line" to Jacksonville igniting the predictable urge to build a new courthouse. In April of 1902, after the obligatory lament over the condition of the county's roads, the grand jury recommended a new court building, and the county commissioners were quick to take up the torch.[14] By October, *The*

Jesup Sentinel was waxing proud: "There can be no denying that with the completion of our fine courthouse and the other handsome brick buildings already erected this year that Jesup will soon be up with the best towns in the state...."[15] In December of 1902, *The Jesup Sentinel* reports that there were ten firms bidding on the construction of Jesup's new courthouse, "some from as far as Atlanta."[16] In a blatant show of regional favoritism, T. J. Darling of Waycross was selected.[17] The courthouse cornerstone was laid in March of 1903 and the building was complete by the end of that year. Here was a late bloom of the myth of the New South flowering in the poorest expanse of the piney woods. Although Jesup may not have been magically transformed into "one of the best towns in the state," by 1910 her population was above 1400, and the power of the Atlantic Coast Line Railway's new "Jesup Short Line" was clear.

The corner stone of the 1903 Wayne County Courthouse lists S. A. Baker in the architect's usual spot, yet the title "Supt" appears beside his name, indicating that S. A. Baker supervised construction either for the county or for T. J. Darling. No S. A. Baker appears in any list of turn-of-the-century Georgia or Florida architects, but the name does appear on county tax records of 1909 indicating that Baker was a Wayne County resident,[18] and rendering his architectural credentials extremely questionable.

The completed building was an almost exact replica of James Golucke's Habersham County Courthouse erected three years earlier at Clarkesville. In addition, the massing reminds us of several other Golucke-designed court buildings including the 1898 Clayton County Courthouse at Jonesboro, its near twin, the 1901 Fannin County Courthouse at Blue Ridge, the 1903 Twiggs County Courthouse at Jeffersonville and its double, the 1901 Madison County Courthouse at Danielsville.

Beyond the building's similarity to other Golucke's designs, there is another connection adding credence to the theory that Golucke was the architect here in 1903. Only two years before, Golucke had opened an office in Jacksonville, a city newly connected to Jesup via the Atlantic Coast Line's 1902 "Jesup Short Line." Jacksonville had experienced a terrible

Plate 7.5: The 1903 Wayne County Courthouse is a most rudimentary statement of Romanesque Revival themes. (Photo: Wilber W. Caldwell.)

fire in 1901, and, teaming up with H. J. Klutho, Golucke hoped to make the most of the opportunities that abounded in that city's misfortune.[19]

Thus, it seems highly likely that James W. Golucke was the architect of the 1903 Wayne County Courthouse. Along with its twin in Clarkesville, it is

[8] Margaret Coleman Jordan, *Wayne County Miscellany* (Jesup GA: Jordan, 1976) 8.

[9] *The History of The First Baptist Church of Jesup, Georgia* quoted in Bobbie M. Martin, *Wayne County, Georgia, Its History and Its People*, 34.

[10] It could be that the town was named for James R. Jesup, a stock holder in the Macon and Brunswick Railroad and a land speculator who had purchased considerable interest in real estate in the county before the arrival of this crossing line. Most local histories hold that the town was named for Morris K. Jessup, a nationally known New York financier and a major stock holder in the Savannah, Albany and Gulf Railroad. This is probably correct, for Morris K. Jessup spelled his name with a double consonant, and the "Acts to Incorporate the Town of Jessup" of October, 1870, also spell the name with a double "s" throughout the document. The local D. A. R. published a history alleging that Jesup was named for Thomas S. Jesup, a hero of the Creek Indian Wars. This is not likely.

[11] Martin, *Wayne County, Its History and Its People*, 35.

[12] *The Jesup Sentinel*, 1891, in Bobby M. Martin, *Wayne County, Georgia, It History and Its People*, 34.

[13] *The Jesup Sentinel*, April 5, 1901.

[14] *The Jesup Sentinel*, May 22, 1902 and September 25, 1902.

[15] *The Jesup Sentinel*, October 15, 1902.

[16] *The Jesup Sentinel*, December 4, 1902.

[17] *The Jesup Sentinel*, December 4, 1902.

[18] Jordan, *Wayne County Miscellany*, 157.

[19] In Young's 1904 Business and Professional Directory of Georgia, J. W. Golucke and Company's ad boasts offices in Atlanta, Anniston and Jacksonville. Golucke's partnership with Henry John Klutho was short-lived. The team's only significant accomplishment was the six-story 1902 Dyal-Upchurch Building, Jacksonville's first "high-rise."

Golucke's most rudimentary romanesque design. If we strip away the great tower and the corner pavilions, we are left with that familiar, four-square, hipped-roofed, brick vernacular building form, which graced so many Georgia squares before the war. For all her zeal for the railroad-imported New South myth, Jesup was never really far from the inescapable reality of her simple Old South soul. In 1904, the grand jury praised this building and complimented the County Commissioners before impotently noting that the county's roads were still bad. The Jacksonville, St. Mary's and Jesup Railroad was never built.

PIERCE COUNTY: BLACKSHEAR

Plate 7.6: The Pierce County Courthouse, built c.1876

In 1857, just as the Savannah, Albany and Gulf Railroad began to lay track across the lonely expanses of pine forest southwest of the Altamaha River, Pierce County was created from Wayne and Appling Counties. Officially the first train hissed into Station #8 at Blackshear, the new county seat, on May 1, 1859. A small log structure served as the first courthouse and was replaced by a frame building probably sometime just after the war. In 1875, the building burned and was replaced by this fine frame structure.

Plate 7.6: Before it was converted to a private home in 1902, the 1876 Wayne County Courthouse featured an elegant cupola and Stick Style double verandahs in place of the present Greek portico. (Photo: Wilber W. Caldwell.)

Before it was converted to a private home in 1902, the original building, built in the usual two-story square vernacular courthouse form, featured an elegant cupola and Stick Style double verandahs in place of the present Greek portico. This was a uniquely graceful public building for such a remote area, and, it suggests that the situation in Pierce County after the war may not have been quite so dire as elsewhere. Cotton production had never been high in this land of poor soil, and the slave population was small. All of Pierce County reported only 233 slaves out of a total population of 1973 in 1860. Thus, the economic consequences of defeat and Reconstruction were less traumatic despite, and perhaps because of, the county's meager resources.

In 1875, when this courthouse was built, Blackshear was doing well at the center of the county's small truck farms and growing timber industry. The village had a population of above 800 with four churches, three bar rooms, one steam gristmill and cotton gin, one turpentine still, one saw mill and two schools.[20] But in 1875, this modest success and the prosperity to come would be based largely on the county's timber resources, which would yield to the most ruthless kind of exploitation. In the years before the turn of the century, Pierce County was to witness a small part of what one forestry official termed, "the most rapid and reckless destruction of forests known to history."[21]

Plate 7.7: The depot at Blackshear, built c.1910.

Postbellum rails finally came to Pierce County, but not to the county town of Blackshear. Around 1901, about ten years before this fine depot at Blackshear was built by the Atlantic Coast Line Railway, the Brunswick and Birmingham Railroad was completed from Brunswick to Offerman, a booming lumber town nine miles to the northeast of the county seat. There the new road crossed the main line of the old Atlantic and Gulf and connected with the Offerman and Western to Nichols. By 1903, these new lines had become part of the Atlantic and Birmingham Railroad, the forerunner of the mighty Atlanta, Birmingham and Atlantic. There can be little doubt that with the arrival of these postbellum crossing rails, new vigor steamed into Pierce County. At the junction town of Offerman, timber interests centered on the Southern Pine Lumber Company's enormous mill. According to local sources, the mill employed hundreds and featured an 80-foot smokestack and "the largest circular saw in the South."[22]

The rape of the county's virgin forests was accomplished by the construction of temporary log-railed "tram" railroads build out from the main line railroads at two-mile intervals. These probing fingers formed a dense web of mule-drawn feeder lines whose constant extension eventually denuded most of Pierce County. With the vast proliferation of rail around the turn of the century and new technology for extracting and transporting logs, private logging railroads multiplied, growing together to nearly cover the map of south Georgia. Like so many mills of the era, the Southern Pine mill at Offerman was a snake eating its own tail. Most of the mill's output was railroad ties and heavy timber for trestles used to build more railroads to extract more timber. In Pierce County the New South dream had become the typical Southern nightmare: a shallow industrialization which benefited few, exploited many, and begot a short-lived prosperity of false hope.

Plate 7.8: The Pierce County Courthouse, built in 1902-1903. J. W. Golucke, architect.

The "success" at Offerman may not have been enough to spark urges for a new courthouse at nearby Blackshear, but according to *The Waycross Herald*, at the time this building was conceived, everyone thought the main line of the new railroad planned from Brunswick to Birmingham would build through Blackshear.[23] In addition, according to *The Blackshear Times*, the old courthouse was "becoming rotten" and "really dangerous."[24] In 1903, J. W. Golucke was busy with several court buildings including classical designs in Meriwether and Bartow Counties. Both of these buildings flaunted up-to-date neoclassical ornament adorning a traditional Southern classical form. Here in Blackshear we find a surprising and most un-Southern departure, the unmistakable elements of the Beaux-Arts Style.

Plate 7.7: It is perhaps symbolic of the passing of Pierce County's virgin pine forests that this depot rose at Blackshear in 1910, the same year that the depot at Offerman burned. (Photo: Wilber W. Caldwell.)

For many, Beaux-Arts Classicism in American building is a broad term used to describe the academic return to order that transformed the nation's architectural scene in the late nineteenth and early twentieth centuries, especially after the success of the buildings at Chicago's Columbian Exposition in 1893. But, in addition to Neoclassical Revival and Renaissance Revival Styles, the turn of the century saw a more specifically Baroque form of Classicism emerging, which itself may be termed the "Beaux-Arts Style." This mode drew inspiration from the modern work of the students of the Ecole des Beaux-Arts in Paris, and as Vincent Scully reminds us, American architects were, as always, quick to have their way with the new idiom: "Once again, Americans eclecticized the European forms, loosened their rationale, and mixed up their programs. So the American Beaux-Arts became much less systematic than the French, less

[20] Dean Boone, *History of Pierce County, Georgia* (Blackshear GA: Broome Printing, 1973) 291.

[21] J. F. Duggar, "Areas of Cultivation in the South" in *The South in the Building of a Nation*, quoted in C. Vann Woodward, Origins of the New South (1951; reprint, Baton Rouge LA: Louisiana State University Press, 1993) 118.

[22] Boone, *History of Pierce County, Georgia*, 343.

[23] *The Waycross Herald*, August 16, 1902.

[24] *The Blackshear Times*, 1899, in Dean Boone, *History of Pierce County, Georgia*, 566.

Plate 7.8: The 1903 Pierce County Courthouse, the unmistakable elements of the up-to-date American Beaux-Arts Style deep in the heart of the Southern Pine Barrens. (Photo: Wilber W. Caldwell.)

intellectually rigorous, and more superficially tasteful."[25]

Blackshear, Georgia is as far from Chicago as James Golucke's Pierce County Courthouse is from the manifestly Rococo arcades of Richard Morris Hunt's 1893 Columbian Exposition Administration Building. Nonetheless and despite the seemingly obligatory use of ubiquitous red brick and a fundamentally neoclassical design, there are undeniable elements of the Beaux-Arts Style here. Most notable is the increased plasticity of the facade accomplished by bold pilasters which function more like enormous piers dividing the front elevation into its modular elements and projecting the portico and the corner bays forward in strong relief. The paired columns are also typical of the Beaux-Arts Style as are the high broad cornice and the decorative central parapet. In addition, the original design called for an ornate low dome

[25] Vincent Scully, *American Architecture and Urbanism*, rev.ed. (New York: Henry Hold and Company, 1969) 136-7.

[26] *The Waycross Herald*, October 25, 1902.

[27] James Marston Fitch, *American Building and the Historical Forces that Shaped It*, rev. ed. (Boston MA: Houghton Mifflin Company, 1947) 208-10.

[28] Scully, *American Architecture and Urbanism*, 136.

[29] The Centennial Issue of *The Blackshear Times*, November 26, 1959.

[30] Laura Singleton Walker, *History of Ware County* (Macon GA: JW Burke, 1934) 107.

[31] Jeffrey Richards and John M. MacMenzie, *The Railway Station, A Social History* (New York: Oxford University Press, 1986) 47.

very much in the Beaux-Arts mode and similar to several designs at the 1893 Columbian Exposition: notably Charles McKim's Agricultural Building and Charles Atwood's Fine Arts Building. An architectural rendering of the building with its crowning dome appeared in *The Waycross Herald* in October of 1902.[26] It is unclear whether the building was constructed as designed and the dome later removed, or whether the dome was simply omitted to hold the building within budget. Most likely the dome was never built, for the rendering reveals a number of ornamental elements, which were later omitted including ornate capitols crowing the pilasters, more fully articulated stone masonry around the windows in the facade and an elegant dental course along the cornice and the pediment. The completed building does only partial justice to Golucke's original design.

Elsewhere in the American North, the return to academic designs including the Beaux-Arts Style came to symbolize financial and industrial power, and even American Imperialism.[27] As Vincent Scully points out, the Ecole des Beaux-Arts had offered order to America's leading architects "just as the country entered its international, even imperial phase."[28] No record remains to document local reaction to the new style in the rough-edged village of Blackshear in 1903, but we can safely assume that way out on the logging lines of Pierce County these columns did not stand for Northeastern financial and industrial might. Whatever its symbolism, architecturally this is not a great building, but in this setting and at this time, it was certainly a monumental one. Perhaps that is all these loggers wanted.

Ironically in 1905, only two years after Golucke's grand courthouse at Blackshear was completed, the Southern Pine Lumber Company closed its mill at Offerman leaving lumbermen to ponder the barren expanses of Pierce County. Local citizens bought the flimsy wooden buildings at Offerman from the departed lumber company and tried to revitalize the community, but the great stands of virgin timber were gone, and little was accomplished. The depot at Offerman burned in 1910.[29] Today the rails of the old Atlanta, Birmingham and Atlantic have been pulled up for scrap, but the line of the old roadbed is still clear, and the spot where the rails crossed those of the old Atlantic and Gulf is easy to find. Sadly evidence of the original town of Offerman is more difficult to locate.

The continuing durges of hard times played on in Pierce County in monotonous rhythms. The county turned to Sea Island cotton to bolster its sagging prospects only to host the boll weevil in 1918. In a remarkable campaign, spear-headed by the railroads, Pierce County farmers switched to tobacco in 1919, and the stunning 40,000 square foot warehouse that still stands in Blackshear today was completed just in time for the first harvest. By that time, it was beginning to occur to some that perhaps there was value in second growth pine, and that Georgia's timber might be a renewable resource.

WARE COUNTY: WAYCROSS

Plate 7.9: Freight house adjacent to Union Depot at Waycross, built in 1910-1911.

The saga of Waycross's rise from a dusty junction town to a powerful railroad center is articulately told by her depots. The first of these, "a crude affair built of rough lumber,"[30] must have stood right at the junction of the rails, for in 1883 it was destroyed when the Savannah, Florida and Western's "Western Fast Mail" was hit at the crossing by a Brunswick and Albany passenger train. The building was replaced by the first Union Depot, a sprawling ragtag pile locally known as "Noah's Ark." Built of coarse batten boards, it seemed to expand of its own accord as the town blossomed and expanded until the building stretched for hundreds of feet along the track-side, a jumble of crude vernacular mansards and pediments, shacks and lean-to sheds. This in turn was replaced in 1911 by the orderly lines of the present Union Depot.

If ever there was a "Railroad Town," it was Waycross. The second Union Depot with its appropriate address on Plant Avenue adjoins this charming little freight house built at about the same time. These buildings occupy the center of town and reflect the city's soul. Here we find the graceful scrolling parapets often associated with Spanish influence that graced so many Southern depots after 1900[31] and today dec-

orate a surprisingly large number of public, commercial and residential buildings in Waycross. Depots of this type are often described as Mission Style or Spanish Style depots, and they usually derive inclusion into this architectural category only via their scrolling parapets and broad tile roofs. But, without additional stylistic detail, it is difficult to specifically call these buildings Spanish Renaissance Revival, Spanish Colonial Revival or Mission Style. In fact, we might make a case for calling the style here at Waycross Dutch or Northern European Renaissance based on the polychromatic banding, coping and corbeling and the elaborate brick work which in this case restates the characteristic polychromy in a pattern known as Flemish bond. Whatever name we choose, just after the turn of the century, this was the signature style of the Atlantic Coast Line Railroad which, with Waycross at its very heart, delivered the well-worn myth of the New South from Montgomery to Savannah and from Virginia to Florida. Similarly styled depots can be found today at Thomasville, Blackshear and Albany.

In order for the brash and often shameless promises of New South spokesmen to carry any illusion of real promise, the myth had to contain at least a few grains of truth. It was real enough in Atlanta, and few could deny that the Fall Line cities of Augusta, Macon and Columbus had realized enough industrial and financial success to be called New South

Plate 7.9: Here in Waycross we find the graceful scrolling parapets often described as Mission Style or Spanish Style. (Photo: Wilber W. Caldwell.)

cities. But perhaps nowhere in Georgia would the wild promises of New South promoters find better example than in Waycross, and nowhere would the railroads play a bigger part in keeping their often Faustian bargain. While other junction towns on the old Atlantic and Gulf struggled for crumbs, Waycross soared. Here in the most unlikely of spots, the pine barrens just to the north of the abundant desolation of the great Okefenokee Swamp, Waycross rose amid scrub pine and palmetto at the junction of the Atlantic and Gulf and the Brunswick and Albany Railroad. In 1880, Waycross had a population of only 628 and according to local county histories: "although it had captured the county seat, [it] was a most insignificant place....All the buildings in the place were rough...The half a dozen stores were dingy wooden structures and not very inviting...."[32] But by 1890, the town had over 3000 residents, and by 1910, with her population above 14,000, Waycross was known by many names. *The Savannah Morning News* called the it "The Magic City," "The Queen City" and "The Gate City."[33] By 1924, according to the *Atlanta Journal,* Waycross was the sixth largest city in Georgia, boasting a population of over 20,000 with nine railroad outlets and a staggering 62 passenger trains a day.

Behind Waycross's success was Henry B. Plant, a railroad visionary, who in 1879, began to create his "Plant System" out of the remains of the old Atlantic and Gulf. If New South promoters could hold Waycross up as a shining example of the accuracy of their vision, then the man responsible for Waycross's

skyrocket flight could likewise be pointed out as exemplary of New South drive and foresight. Nearly 2000 miles of railroad, myriad steamship lines and fabulous Florida resort hotels were all lead by Henry B. Plant. Here was a human symbol of New South success seemingly so compelling that even the most imaginative of the movement's promoters would have been hard-pressed to conjure up such a wildly successful idol.

A Connecticut Yankee, Plant had come South before the war as an officer of the Southern Express Company, and although he had not been sympathetic to the Southern cause and had returned to the North during the war, he had traveled on a Confederate passport. Thus upon his return in 1865, he could hardly have been termed a "Carpetbagger."

Throughout the 1870s Plant waited for his chance. By 1873, the Atlantic and Gulf was in the hands of a receiver. Unable to recover from the ravages of war, crippled by a poor cotton harvest in 1871 and ruined by national depression of 1873, the road was forced by the court to sell its assets in 1879. By that time, Henry B. Plant was in a financial position to buy it, thanks in large part to his marriage to a wealthy New York Senator's daughter and to a long list of willing investors that included Henry Flagler himself.

Plant was one of the first to realize that railroads would replace steamships up and down the eastern seaboard. In conjunction with Henry M. Flagler's emerging empire in Florida, Henry Plant's Savannah, Florida and Western; South Florida Railroad; and his Charleston and Savannah Railroad would control service in and out of Florida. Plant reasoned that from the east-west line of the Atlantic and Gulf, which he renamed the Savannah, Florida and Western, it would be a simple matter to run short lines to the south to connect with emerging rail systems in Florida, and thus capture enormous trade. When he bought the Atlantic and Gulf he obtained the old DuPont to Live Oak line, the first Georgia connection to Florida which had been built by the Confederacy during the war. The second link to Florida was Plant's new line from Climax near Bainbridge to River Junction, Florida, planned to connect to Pensacola, and the third, and by far the most important, was what

---

[32] Walker, History of Ware County, 107-108.

[33] *The Savannah Morning News,* 1911, in Robert L. Hurst, *This Magic Wilderness, Historical Features of the Wiregrass* (Waycross GA: Brantley Printing, 1982) 106.

[34] Walker, *History of Ware County,* 97.

[35] Walker, *History of Ware County,* 97.

[36] Walker, *History of Ware County,* 108.

[37] Hurst, *This Magic Wilderness, Historical Features of the Wiregrass,* 105.

[38] *The Waycross Evening Herald,* January 4, 1890.

[39] Both Robert L. Hurst in his *This Magic Wilderness* and Laura Singleton Walker in her *History of Ware County, Georgia* mentions a dedication of the building in 1887, but newspaper accounts of grand jury proceedings relate that in 1890 the grand jury found the courthouse in need of only "slight repairs" and make no mention of a new building in progress, *The Waycross Evening Herald,* January 4, 1890.

became known as the "Waycross Short Line." Originally built as the Waycross and Florida Railroad, the line from Waycross to Jacksonville was completed in April of 1881. Almost from that very moment Waycross began to stir.

Plate 7.10: The Ware County Courthouse, built 1891. G. L. Norrman, architect. Demolished in 1957.

Ware County had been split off from enormous expanses of Appling County in 1824, and the first county site was designated at Waresboro. The new town was laid out in 1825, and shortly thereafter a simple courthouse had been erected. Early county records relate that juries would often "retire to the woods" to deliberate.[34] This "large, one-story log building with two small interior rooms for offices"[35] was soon replaced by a frame building. In 1859, the Savannah, Albany and Gulf established its Station #9 at Tebeauville nine miles east of Waresboro. By 1860, the Brunswick and Florida Railroad was complete to Waresboro on its way from Brunswick to Albany, but this road's Northern ownership ceased construction in 1861 after fighting began. Two years later, the Confederate Government nationalized the line, and its rails were taken up for use elsewhere. After the war, the charter was renewed, and under the direction of the notorious railroad speculator, Hannibal Kimball, the Brunswick and Albany Railroad was completed in 1871 crossing the old Atlantic and Gulf near Tebeauville at the place soon to be called Waycross.

Enormous influence seems to have flowed from land speculation, and the power of crossing rails quickly won the day. Only a year after the completion of the Brunswick and Albany, the Ware County seat was moved from Waresboro to Waycross. A new court building was erected by Daniel Lott,[36] a developer who would later publish the town's first newspaper, *The Headlight,* and secure the charter for Plant's Waycross Short Line to Jacksonville.[37] When Lott's 1872 courthouse mysteriously burned in 1874, it was replaced in 1876. Some say that the old frame court building from Waresboro was moved to Waycross, thus further infuriating the residents of the original county town.

With the completion of H. B. Plant's "The Short Line" the promises of the New South in Waycross began to appear more real than mythical. Throughout the 1880s, the air in Waycross was charged with railroad building electricity. Notable schemes included the Cordele, Waynesville and South Brunswick Railroad chartered in 1888 and an extension of the Atlanta and Florida Railroad from Fort Valley to Waycross contemplated in 1890.[38] Neither road was built, but the "Short Line's" success and the atmosphere of railroad building frenzy, precipitated a cry for a new symbol for the county's rising hopes: a new courthouse.

By several accounts, plans were underway as early as 1887 for the construction of the building that subsequent generations in Waycross would come to call "The Castle." [39] Completed in August of 1891, the

Plate 7.10: In 1891, Atlanta architect, G. L. Norrman, designed the Ware County Courthouse that became locally known as "the Castle." (Photo Courtesy of Georgia Deptartment of Archives and History.)

Plate 7.11: By 1895, when the Clinch County Courthouse was completed, the old vernacular architecture of frontier individualism had become the architecture of despair. (Photo: Wilber W. Caldwell.)

new Ware County Courthouse was designed by Atlanta architect, G. L. Norrman, who at the time of this commission was overseeing the completion of his fabulous Windsor Hotel in Americus. Indeed, Norrman's design here in Waycross was in many ways similar to the Windsor: both have a low round towers balancing tall square spires, both feature deep-set upper story porches with decorative wooden trim, monumental arched entrances and elaborate brick corbeling. In short, both are typical picturesque eclectic buildings rooted in the tradition of the Romanesque Revival in America. But here in Waycross, something is missing. Norrman's grand Peters home in Atlanta and the fanciful delight that is the Windsor Hotel in Americus reflect picturesque compositions worthy of an accomplished architect. In Waycross, the results seem pedestrian by comparison. It is as if Norrman's picturesque elements were clumsily glued to the central rectangular mass of a vernacular brick count building. The details are missing, and the graceful blending of unlike elements that ordinarily make the picturesque sing, were here replaced by a rather crude "stuck together" effort. How could a proven artist like G. L. Norrman so miss the mark?

We find the answer in an 1891 newspaper account relating that Norrman had little hand in supervising construction. In fact, so unfamiliar a name was G. L. Norrman in Waycross, that *The Waycross Herald* misspells his name, citing "G. S. Norman" as the architect. The article goes on to reveal the culprit: "Mr. George Felthon...[was] superintendent in charge of construction, and afterward assumed the duties of architect and made important modifications in the plans."[40]

Still despite its awkwardness, "the Castle" constituted an appropriate symbol for Waycross's progress, and there can be little question that it was the product of a singularly volatile explosion in railroad building. By the time the cornerstone was laid, the Savannah, Florida and Western had built an extensive complex of at Waycross. In 1887, the Waycross Air Line began to build to the northwest of the city. That road would be completed to Fitzgerald by the turn of the century, and it would later become part of the Atlanta, Birmingham and Atlantic. In 1903, three years after Henry Plant's death, the Plant System became part of the Atlantic Coast Line and the "Short Line" from Jesup to Jacksonville was completed, thus in part preempting "The Waycross Short Line." But by then, Waycross's place as a railroad city was fixed, and in 1910 the Atlantic Coast Line cemented her relationship with Waycross by expanding her shops and other facilities into one of the largest rail complexes in the South.

CLINCH COUNTY: HOMERVILLE

Plate 7.11: The Clinch County Courthouse, built in 1896.

By 1896, when this simple brick structure was completed, Clinch County could see nothing but disappointment in one direction and hard times in the other. Here is a very late, but predictable, example of the old vernacular brick courthouse form which, fifty years before, had graced so many squares in Georgia. Before the war, this had been the practical architecture of frontier individualism, and although there was still plenty of frontier in Clinch County in 1895, by then this had become the architecture of despair.

[40] *The Waycross Herald*, April 23, 1891.

[41] Folks Huxford, History of Clinch County, Georgia (Macon GA: JW Burke, 1916) 47.

Clinch County had been cut from Ware and Lowndes Counties in 1850. The county seat was laid out in that same year at a place originally called Polk and later renamed Magnolia. The first wooden court building burned in 1856, and was replaced in that same year by a frame building. Meanwhile, the Atlantic and Gulf Railroad was preparing to pierce the piney wall of South Georgia, and in 1859, it arrived in Clinch County establishing its Station #11 on the farm of Homer Maddox, who would later, perhaps jokingly, call the place "Homerville." In addition to a keen sense of humor, Maddox had a practical nature, and his vision was clear regarding the power of rail. He gladly gave the railroad its right-of-way through his land, donated a large lot for the depot, laid out town lots and began a movement to have the county seat moved. The next year the voters of Clinch approved this move, and by the end of 1860, Homerville had a courthouse, "2 or 3 small stores" and "8 or 10 families" in residence.[41] The 1856 courthouse, which had been moved from Magnolia and reassembled in Homerville burned in 1867 and was replaced by a typical two-story frame building with the court room of the second floor and steps leading up the outside of the building. Despite several attempts to have the county seat moved to the junction town of DuPont, Homerville managed to retain the seat of county government, and this brick courthouse was built in 1896, perhaps to cement Homerville's lock on the prize. At DuPont, the Florida Branch Railroad to Live Oak, Florida, joined the main line of the Atlantic and Gulf. This road had been constructed in the closing stages of the war to aid Confederate communications and to transport beef from Florida to hungry rebel armies. It was the first rail connection between Georgia and Florida.

The east-west rails of the Atlantic and Gulf had penetrated some very wild and nearly uninhabited country before the Civil War. By the turn of the century, north-south crossing lines to Florida were generating the exuberant architecture of hope elsewhere along these antebellum rails, but not at here. Homerville, like so many other towns in Georgia, had reaped a disappointing harvest. The town languished in between Frank Milburn's 1905 classical wonder at Valdosta and G. L. Norrman's bizarre 1891 romanesque "Castle" at Waycross.

Plate 7.12: The depot at DuPont.

Built in 1900, the old depot still stands in Homerville today. Nine miles away, in the now all but deserted hamlet of DuPont, this depot is perhaps a better architectural narrator for the period. Both speak only of what might have been. Homerville, like Waycross, has its Plant Avenue, but similarity ends there. While the crossings of the Brunswick and Albany and the "Waycross Short Line" to Jacksonville turned Waycross's aspirations into a teeming metropolis of 14,000 by 1910 and crossing of the Georgia

Plate 7.12: The old depot at DuPont is perhaps a better architectural narrator for Clinch County's disappointing saga. (Photo: Wilber W. Caldwell.)

Southern and Florida Railroad and the Georgia and Florida Railway transformed Valdosta into a city of 7500, tiny Homerville knew no crossing rails, and her population held steady for decades at around 430. There had once been glimmers of hope. One of the original surveys for the Georgia Southern and Florida proposed a line through Homerville, only to build through Valdosta in 1888.

In 1887, two roads had been proposed through DuPont, only 8 miles west of Homerville. Hoping to revitalize the old DuPont to Live Oak, Florida, line built during the Civil War, the DuPont, Macon and Florida Railway and the DuPont, Decatur Alabama and Florida Air Line both failed to get beyond the planning stages. With her intersecting early road to Florida and her population above 500 in 1880, it is surprising that DuPont did not succeed in her efforts to capture the county seat. Had either of these later roads been built, it is very likely that DuPont would have prevailed in her late-century quest for the courthouse.

Finally in 1899, a line was built through the southern part of Clinch County. This road, the Atlantic, Valdosta and Western, consolidated the right of way of various timber interests to the west and south of the Okefenokee Swamp and created a link from Valdosta to Jacksonville passing through the remote piney wildness that was, and still is today, Clinch and Echols Counties.

LANIER COUNTY: LAKELAND

In 1901, G. V. Gress built a short line railroad to serve his sawmill at Milltown, then in Berrien County. The line terminated in a junction with the old Atlantic and Gulf Railroad (by then the Atlantic Coast Line Railway) at the village of Naylor in Lowndes County, twelve miles west of DuPont. This seven-mile line was called the Milltown Air Line, and it marked the beginning of an episode, which culminated in the creation of Lanier County almost twenty years later. In

Milltown, the events that followed the completion of the Milltown Air Line give testimony to the power of rail to transform out-of-the-way places into boom-towns, and to create new counties and build courthouses even in the face of extraordinary adversity and just plan bad luck.

Milltown had begun around 1825 when early settlers established a gristmill beside the great lake in what was then one of the most remote regions of the piney woods. By 1848, a saw mill was operating at Milltown, and forty years later as timber interests in the region multiplied, the place had a population of 175 according to Sholes's 1886 *Gazetteer of Georgia.* The real boom arrived with Gress's railroad and the large saw mill he built at Milltown just after the turn of the century. By 1910, Milltown had a population of over 1200, its own newspaper and two banks. In 1918, the first bill proposing the creation of Lanier County was put before the State Legislature. Lanier County was created in 1920.

In an odd chain of events, just as citizens began to lobby for a new county, everything began to fall apart beside South Georgia's great natural lake. In 1919, the enormous saw mill burned, never to be rebuilt. The mill had operated the railroad and furnished both water and electricity to the town. Local business men took up the challenge of restore city service and were quick to acquire the Milltown Air Line, but when fire destroyed a second mill in 1924, Milltown's population began to wane. By 1927, the Milltown Air Line was up for sale as scrap. The line was purchased by the city of Milltown, which by this time, with no mills to speak of, had changed its name to Lakeland. The tiny railroad was renamed the Lakeland Railroad, and it continued to limp along until 1957 when it was finally abandoned.

Meanwhile, Lanier County struggled to build a courthouse. A plan was put forward in 1922, but in the wake of the great fires, no building rose. Court was held on the second floor of a Lakeland mercantile building until 1942, when the first Lanier County Courthouse was finally completed. This building was demolished in 1972 to make way for the present court building.

[42] The last frame courthouse to be erected in Georgia rose in 1901 at Clyde in Bryan County.

Plate 7.13: The 1899 Echols County Courthouse at Statenville was one of the last frame court buildings to be erected in Georgia. (Photo: Courtesy of Ted Brooke.)

ECHOLS COUNTY: STATENVILLE

Plate 7.13: The Echols County Courthouse, built in 1899. Demolished in 1956.

Completed in 1899, this fine frame courthouse sounded a late vernacular voice of the Greek Revival in Echols County. In the same year, only eight miles north of this building the tiny county town of Statenville, the new rails of the Atlantic, Valdosta and Western Railroad cut through Echols on their way from Valdosta to Jacksonville, Florida. Several planned towns popped up along the new rails, including Haylow where the new line crossed the old "Live Oak Connector," and the ill-fated town of Fruitland which was laid out in 1906 and abandoned in 1909. All of this ushered in the new century in tiny Statenville, revealing a brief glimmer of New South promise that faded as quickly as it appeared.

If the 1864 "Live Oak Connector" from DuPont to Live Oak, Florida, was one of the first lines to branch off the "Main Trunk" of the old Atlantic and Gulf, the Statenville Railway was one of the last. This ne'er-do-well spur is illustrative of an on going epidemic of railroad building, which tangled steel rails into even the most isolated regions of the piney woods. Chartered in 1906 to serve A. G. Garbutt's expansive new lumber mill that was then rising near Statenville, the fourteen-mile line from Haylow was six years in the building. Less than a decade after the completion of the line, the vast tracts of virgin timber

were gone from Echols County. The great Garbutt mill was closed in 1920, and the Statenville Railway was abandoned four years later leaving tiny Statenville alone in an unlovely sea of stumps, and Haylow agitating to become the county seat.

Echols County was created in 1858, and the county's first courthouse rose in the tiny village of Troublesome. This dubious appellation was changed to Statenville straight away, and the original four room court building served until it burned in 1876. It was replaced by a two-story frame courthouse that burned in 1898. Erected in 1899, this "Carpenter Greek" structure was one of the last frame court buildings to be erected in Georgia.[42] Only four of these early frame courthouses survive today (see Introduction, Table II). The 1899 Echols County Courthouse stood at the center of tiny Statenville until its was demolished in 1956 to make way for the present building.

LOWNDES COUNTY: VALDOSTA

Plate 7.14: The Georgia Southern and Florida Depot at Valdosta, built in 1907. Demolished 1977, Curran Ellis, architect.

When the rails of the Georgia Southern and Florida Railroad, Macon's direct route to Central Florida, crossed the rails of the old Atlantic and Gulf at Valdosta in 1889, they set in motion a series of events that culminated in the construction of Frank

Plate 7.14: Curran Ellis's fine Georgia Southern and Florida Depot at Valdosta rose simultaneously with The Atlantic Coast Line's new depot. (Photo: Courtesy of Les R. Winn.)

Table 7.2

RAILROADS AT VALDOSTA

The Atlantic and Gulf Railroad, 1860 (later the Savannah. Florida and Western [Plant System], 1879) (later the Atlantic Coast Line, 1902) Savannah to Thomasville.

The Georgia Southern and Florida Railroad, 1889, (later part of the Southern Railway) Macon to Palatka, Florida.

The Atlantic, Valdosta and Western, 1899, (later part of the Georgia Southern and Florida, later part of the Southern Railway) Valdosta to Jacksonville, Florida.

The Georgia and Florida Railroad, 1908 (incorporating the Valdosta Southern, 1896 and the Augusta, Douglas and Gulf), Augusta to Madison, Florida.

The Valdosta, Moultrie and Western Railroad, 1910, Valdosta to Moultrie.

Milburn's 1905 Beaux-Arts Lowndes County Courthouse. Two years later, this impressive depot was completed. Designed by Macon's Curran Ellis, who later designed the present Bibb County Courthouse, the fine two-story building rose simultaneously with the Atlantic Coast Line's 1907 depot at Valdosta, a low rambling tile roofed affair, typical of so many depots built on that line after the turn of the century. But Valdosta's story is not a tale of one courthouse and two depots. Six courthouses had preceded Milburn's, and by 1910 the city would have five railroads, each with a depot of its own (see Table 7.2).

Architecture in Valdosta had moved a long distance indeed since 1860 and the first rough shack that was Station #12 on the newly completed Atlantic and Gulf Railroad from Savannah to Thomasville. The first train had arrived on July 4th, 1860. At that time, Valdosta with a population of about 200[43] had just been declared the county seat. A "rough frame building" had been hastily erected on the newly laid out square.[44] It was the county's fourth courthouse.

Lowndes County had been cut from Irwin and Early Counties in 1825, and the county seat had been established first at Franklinville in 1828 and later at Lowndesville in 1833. A rough courthouse was erected at Franklinville and probably a second at Lowndesville. By 1837, Troupville was the new county town, and a frame courthouse was completed there in 1847. This was wild and empty country before the railroad arrived, but Troupville prospered apparently

on trade with Florida. As early as 1836, there had been hope of rail connection at Troupville. Both the ill-fated Brunswick and Chattahoochee and the Brunswick and Florida had contemplated lines through Lowndes, but the early efforts of both roads came to nothing. Still Troupville grew, and the town had achieved a population of over 500 before 1850.[45] In the early 1850s, it appeared that the rails from Savannah, bound for Thomasville, would at last pass through Troupville. But alas, when the courthouse burned in 1858 and the Atlantic and Gulf began grading four miles south of the town, there was little left for the hapless and frustrated citizens of Lowndes to do but move the county seat again. That "rough frame building" was built at Valdosta only to be replaced by a larger frame structure in 1871, followed in 1875 by a substantial two-story brick courthouse with stylish broken based pediments and bracketed eaves. When the Georgia Southern and Florida Railroad arrived in 1889, Valdosta was a city of more than 2500 residents.

Plate 7.15: The Lowndes County Courthouse, built in 1904-1905. Frank Milburn, architect.

This courthouse completed in 1905 was the culmination of a grand celebration in Lowndes County that lasted for over a decade. In 1889, the Georgia Southern and Florida Railroad had reached Valdosta, crossing the antebellum rails of the Atlantic and Gulf, on its way from Macon to Palatka, Florida. By 1900, Valdosta had doubled its 1890 population boasting over 5500 residents, and a movement for a new courthouse was underway. Valdosta's growth fostered a self-congratulatory success story and created an aggressive boosterism, which in a down-home kind of way resembled the promotional efforts of many larger and more influential New South cities like Atlanta, Birmingham and Charlotte. With the arrival of the Georgia Southern and Florida, the city began a festive period of self-promotion and local mythmaking that exemplified the kind of zeal the New South's tempting promises could generate in out-of-the-way places. If Frank Milburn's 1905 Lowndes County Courthouse was the finale to these years of theatrical self-promotion, then the Georgia State Fair at Valdosta in 1900 was the centerpiece.

This was the age of great fairs. Between 1876 and 1915 more than 100 million people attended over a dozen major international expositions held in the United States. [46] Valdosta hosted the first State Fair to be held in South Georgia, and it was not only the State's hopeful celebration of the turn of the century, but an event of special significance for Valdosta. The town had struggled up and out of the post-war period, experiencing a terrible tornado, devastating fires and occasional skirmishes with yellow fever and cholera, in addition to poverty and the usual ongoing battle with those uniquely Southern demons, ignorance, intransigence and brooding nostalgia. But by the turn of the century, Valdosta had known a decade of growth despite the clouds of national depression that darkened the years after 1893. By 1900, the town was drunk on the new wine of prosperity that had been imported on the rails of the Georgia Southern and Florida Railroad. Along with population explosion had come the trappings of New South success including brick buildings, electric lights, improved sanitation, a proper fire department, beautification programs and finally a cotton mill in 1899. The Georgia Southern and Florida built a spur to the Fair Grounds, and the Valdosta Street Railway began operation. In 1900, Valdosta had visions of following in the footsteps of the 1895 Atlanta Cotton States Exposition, and the town looked ahead to the Pan American Exposition to be held in Buffalo, New York, in 1901 and even to the lofty heights of the 1900 World's Fair in Paris.

But it was a long way from the Wiregrass to Paris, and that distance was measured in more than miles. According to *The Valdosta Times* the Fair was: "sthe pronouncement that Lowndes County finally had become the prospering area in which 'new' and 'modern' were acceptable words."[47] Like the larger fairs, buildings were erected for administration, agriculture, machinery, live stock and education, but the entire proceeding had the expected agricultural focus and an element of carnival overshadowed attempts to emphasize industrial and cultural progress. One Valdosta observer recalled: "I remember thinking how the

Plate 7.15: Frank P. Milburn's 1905 Lowndes County Courthouse. Trickles of inspiration flowing into the American South from Paris and the Ecole des Beaux-Arts arrived via a circuitous route. (Photo: Wilber W. Caldwell.)

whole town looked like a poorly wrapped birthday present."[48] Still the emphasis was on celebration. The fair began with the "Wiregrass Parade" down "Joy Avenue," the central thoroughfare of the grounds. Attractions included a diving horse, and, as if that were not enough, a diving elk.[49]

Whatever unclear messages the 1900 Georgia State Fair may have implied about progress in Valdosta, there can be little doubt about the message broadcast by Frank Milburn's stunning 1905 Lowndes County Courthouse. Here is a work of architectural sophistication. Perhaps nothing could have better voiced Valdosta's self-proclaimed coming-of-age than the selection of Frank Milburn, who in 1905 was arguably the South's most successful architect. Permanently retained by the prestigious Southern

[43] Jane Twitty Shelton, *Pines and Pioneers, A History of Lowndes County, 1826-1900* (Atlanta: Cherokee Publishing, 1976) 136.

[44] Shelton, *Pines and Pioneers, A History of Lowndes County, 1826-1900*, 135.

[45] Shelton, *Pines and Pioneers, A History of Lowndes County, 1826-1900*, 93.

[46] Thomas J. Schlereth, *Victorian America, Transformations in Everyday Life* (1991; reprint, New York: Harpers Perennial, 1992) xv.

[47] *The Valdosta Times* in Louis E. Schmier, *Valdosta and Lowndes County* (Northridge CA: Windsor Publications, 1988) 42.

[48] *The Valdosta Times* in Schmier, *Valdosta and Lowndes County*, 41.

[49] *The Valdosta Times* in Schmier, *Valdosta and Lowndes County*, 41.

Plate 7.16: Proposed courthouse at Anniston, Alabama. J. W. Golucke rendering, c.1900. (Illustration: *The Anniston Evening Star,* August 27, 1900.)

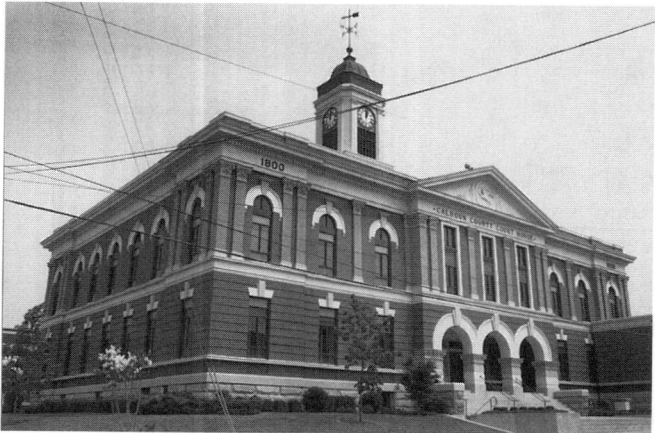

Plate 7.17: Calhoun County Courthouse in Anniston, Alabama, built in 1900. J. W. Golucke, architect. Burned 1931. Rebuild, 1932. (Photo: Wilber W. Caldwell.)

Plate 7.18: Chambers County Courthouse in Lafayette, Alabama, built in 1901. J. W. Golucke, architect. (Photo: Wilber W. Caldwell.)

Railway and designer of over 250 major structures[50] from Florida to Oklahoma, Milburn was at home with most of the picturesque modes. Additionally, unlike the previous generation of Southern architects, he also seemed comfortable with Beaux-Arts Classicism both architecturally and as the emerging voice of American economic success. Although there can be little doubt that the poetically pure neoclassical lines of Milburn's exceptional 1903 Wilcox County Courthouse at Abbeville inspired the Lowndes County Commissioners to engage this accomplished architect, here in Valdosta, Milburn would create an inspiring Beaux-Arts monument unlike any other Georgia court building of the era. The paired columns and the corner pavilions with their low domes sing Parisian songs as do the Ionic pilasters and the high balustrade. Although more modest in scale, the central tower recalls Cuthbert Brodrick's monumental Town Hall at Leeds, a rare English tribute to Napoleon III's building revolution in Paris.

This courthouse was the result of a long process that began with the arrival of the Georgia Southern and Florida Railroad and saw two more railroads intersect the old Atlantic and Gulf at Valdosta before it was over. The Atlantic, Valdosta and Western cut through from Jacksonville in 1899 and the Ocilla and Valdosta arrived in 1903. Movement for a new courthouse had originated before 1900. In fact just after the Georgia State Fair closed at Valdosta, the Lowndes County Commissioners approved a design by Atlanta's J. W. Golucke. An elegant rendering of the building appeared in *The Valdosta Times* on November 24, 1900.[51] The exuberant new courthouse was to be similar to Golucke's Calhoun County, Alabama, Courthouse just completed in Anniston, Alabama.[52] The exact same rendering had appeared in *The Anniston Evening Star* on August 27, 1900, (Plate 7.16).[53] Comparison today is difficult, because the Alabama building burned in 1931 destroying the tower and most of the central portion of the structure. It was rebuilt with notable simplifications (Plate 7. 17), but photos taken before the fire reveal that the original Anniston court building was erected with substantial variations from Golucke's original plan illustrated in the rendering. In February of 1901, the Lowndes County Commissioners decided to delay construction for what appears to have been political reasons.[54]

Two years later, as another Georgia State Fair opened at Macon's fairgrounds, a bond issue was pending for the construction of the Lowndes County Courthouse. This time a new courthouse would be built not from the original Golucke design but from plans by Frank Milburn. Golucke was apparently incensed at his dismissal, for he began legal proceedings against the county for the unpaid portion of his fee. The Lowndes County Commissioners balked at this demand on the grounds that the design was "too much like other buildings which have been made from his plans."[55] Indeed it was, for in the interim Golucke's plans had been used to build the Chambers County Courthouse at Lafayette, Alabama (Plate 7.18). Completed in 1901, the courthouse at Lafayette is far less graceful on that square than it was on Golucke's rendering. Despite the fact that the builders had taken considerable liberty during construction, omitting much of the Beaux-Arts ornamentation, the results nonetheless confirm that, at least in this case, Golucke's facility with Beaux-Arts design lay more in fanciful drawing than in architecture. Still, it is interesting to note that, despite J. W. Golucke's questionable results at Lafayette, Frank Milburn's later design for Valdosta, although far superior in detail, borrows a great deal from Golucke's original rendering. Not the least of the similarities are the domed corner pavilions. Additionally Milburn had designed a similar court building, also completed in 1905, at Lake City, Florida, which lay just across the state line from Lowndes County along the newly completed rails of the Georgia Southern and Florida Railroad. Perhaps these apparently derivative designs are what really galled James Golucke in Lowndes County, or perhaps he simply sought to sell his Parisian oddity to as many as would buy.

No matter which Parisian monument it selected, Lowndes County was still every bit as far from Paris in 1905 as it had been in 1900. Trickles of inspiration flowing into the American South from the Ecole des Beaux-Arts arrived via a circuitous route, being first filtered through an often insensitively commercial and shamelessly trendy American North. By the time modern architectural ideas arrived south of the Mason Dixon line and were diluted by the obligatory doses of Jeffersonian Classicism and Millsian Greek Revivalism, they often had acquired a regional character unlike anything on the Rue de Rivoli. For many, the elegant columns of the central portico breaking away from the familiar horizontal mass only sang the songs of an Old South not forgotten. All of this notwithstanding, Milburn's courthouse here at Valdosta is a fitting, and unusually pure, Beaux-Arts monument and a proper symbol for Valdosta's success.

As Valdosta entered the second decade of the new century with her up-to-date courthouse and her five railroads, she must have seemed the model of New South success. Perhaps she was. But between the lines of this story, a stubborn undercurrent was at work. A vocal, intransigent, backwardly focused element still offered resistance to progress at every turn. In an example that would be funny were it not so sadly true to life, local historian Louis Schimer points out that in 1884 Valdosta lined some of the downtown streets with pear trees, and one 'die-hard' applauded the new greenery noting that: "…they gave Valdosta the missing southern flavor it needed to overcome the…'Yankee stench' of ever-increasing construction in the town."[56]

Valdosta, like every other town in Georgia, had its fair share of "die-hards" who resisted change regardless of circumstance. In addition, almost two-thirds of

[50] Lawrence Wodehouse, "Frank Pierce Milburn (1868-1826), A Major Southern Architect," in *The North Carolina Historical Review* 50/3 (July 1973): 289.

[51] *The Valdosta Times*, December 3, 1900.

[52] *The Valdosta Times*, November 24, 1900.

[53] *The Anniston Evening Star*, August 27, 1900.

[54] *The Valdosta Times*, February 5, 1901.

[55] *The Valdosta Times*, November 7, 1903.

[56] Schimer, *Valdosta and Lowndes County*, 44.

Lowndes County's 1900 population lived out in the country. For these farmers, turpentiners and timbermen, the grand celebrations and Parisian architecture at Valdosta had little meaning beyond a pleasant and perhaps mystifying distraction from the poverty which would continue to engulf many of these lives for decades.

BROOKS COUNTY: QUITMAN

Plate 7.19: The Brooks County Courthouse, built 1859-1864. John Wind, architect. Remodeled 1892. Bruce and Morgan remodeling architects.

In the years just before the Civil War, the Atlantic and Gulf Railroad carved its narrow arching path from Savannah south and then westward through that seemingly endless monotony of pine known as the Wiregrass region of South Georgia. Almost magically it created counties and towns in the wilderness. Just as the new road was being surveyed west of Valdosta, Brooks County was split off from Lowndes, and the new county seat of Quitman was laid out on the line of the proposed railroad. Where the rails entered Brooks County the landscape subtly changed. Graceful stands of long leaf pine began to appear, and the marginal sandy soil of the Pine Barrens darkened. Here was cotton, that fickle lover that would at once become both the salvation and the undoing of the postbellum South.

That there was wealth here in 1860 is clear, for in that year the citizens of the newly established Brooks county began a fine brick court building unlike any built along the Atlantic and Gulf between Savannah

and Quitman before 1875. As county historian Folks Huxford so accurately puts it: "The undertaking to build such a pretentious and costly edifice in that day and time excited much surprise with some of the citizens…especially in the adjoining counties. Most Courthouses were small frame affairs of rough lumber and unpainted."[57]

To design their centerpiece, the Brooks County Commissioners turned to John Wind of Thomasville, one of the first architects to practice in South Georgia. A native of England, Wind had been brought to Thomasville by a wealthy planter, and in addition to the courthouse there, he had designed several large plantation houses. Although it is doubtful that John Wind had any formal architectural training, he, like Elam Alexander in Macon, may deserve the title "architect" based on the quality of the structures he designed, a few of which stand today in Thomas County in testament to Wind's artistry.

Sadly, we will never know the true extent of John Wind's vision here in Quitman for his design for the building was drastically altered during construction. This is one of only two courthouses in Georgia built during the Civil War,[58] and owing to extreme shortages of materials and skilled labor, substantial omissions to Wind's original design were necessary. Again according to county historian Folks Huxford: "the parapet, cupola, balustrade on the roof and certain ornate columns in the court room and porticos on the ends of the building were dispensed with on account of the war."[59] A temporary frame court building was erected, and the work stretched on through the war years. Although not fully completed, the County accepted the building with its familiar cross-like footprint in 1864. One sketch of the building survives from 1869,[60] and the presence of the balustrade, parapet and elaborate cupola lead one to suspect that this is not a copy of the "as built" structure, but rather a copy of one of Wind's drawings. Either way, the original structure bore a notable resemblance to both Wind's 1858 Thomas County Courthouse at Thomasville and Elam Alexander's 1829 Bibb County Courthouse at Macon. All were examples of the force of the brick vernacular style inspired, at least in part, by builder's guides of the era,

[57] Folks Huxford, *History of Brooks County, Georgia, 1858-1948* (1948; reprint, Spartanburg SC: Reprint Company, 1978) 66.

[58] The other is the Banks County Courthouse at Homer, which was under construction between 1860 and 1865.

[59] Huxford, *History of Brooks County, Georgia*, 67.

[60] Freehand drawing by W. Howend dated 1869, a copy of which can be found in the Main Branch of the Brooks County Library at Quitman.

[61] Huxford, *History of Brooks County, Georgia*, 181-82

[62] June Jackson Parrish, *The History of Cook County, Georgia* (Adel GA: n.p., 1967) 56.

[63] Henry Russell Hitchcock and William Seale, "Notes on the Architecture" in Richard Pare, ed., *Courthouse, A Photographic Document* (New York: Horizon Press, 1978) 225.

in this case almost surely by Asher Benjamin's *American Builder's Companion* (see Plate 7.22).

Quitman's progress in the years immediately following the war was unusual. By 1872, the town, although smaller than the older and well-established Thomasville to the west, was keeping pace with the upstart Valdosta to the east. With a population of about 1500, 35 stores, and a new three-story cotton mill,[61] Quitman seemed blessed. Kerosene streetlights were added in 1873 and concrete sidewalks added a most modern touch in 1875. Still crossing rails were slow to come. In the late 1880s, one of the original surveys of the Georgia and Florida Railroad proposed a line through Quitman. But after local landowners tried to charge the new railroad for the right-of-way, the route was changed to pass through Valdosta where residents granted free right-of-way and donated land for the depot site.[62]

By 1890, Quitman's population stood at about 1800. With no crossing rails to import hopeful creeds and her 1871 cotton mill failed for a second time, Quitman had little faith in the kind of the New South mythology which inspired courthouse building. The old court building, with its simplifications and omissions of wartime construction, did little to lift already sagging spirits in Brooks County. In 1892, leaders in Quitman were able to muster enough civic spirit to remodel the old pile, and the Atlanta partnership of Alexander Bruce and Thomas Henry Morgan was engaged. The result was stunning.

Bruce and Morgan designed sixteen courthouses in Georgia between 1882 and 1898. Twelve of these buildings were romanesque in form, and many incorporated elaborate Queen Anne detail. Here in Quitman, the massive twin arches of the main entrance are clearly Richardsonian, while much of the fenestration suggests Queen Anne influence. Interestingly, here we also find the clear mark of the Italian Renaissance Revival.

There are few references to Georgia's courthouses of this era in the literature of American architecture, but in the fine study, Courthouse edited by Richard Pare, Henry Russell Hitchcock and William Seale give due reverence to Bruce and Morgan's remodeling here in Brooks County. Citing the building as an early

Plate 7.19: Bruce and Morgan's 1892 remodeling of the 1864 Brooks County Courthouse at Quitman supplies a rare example of the Italian Renaissance Revival in Georgia. (Photo: Wilber W. Caldwell.)

example of the "return to order" in American architecture, they labor under the mistaken assumption that the stone monument in the building's facade which declares that the building was "remodeled 1882" correctly dates the remodeling.[63] Despite the fact that the actual remodeling took place ten years later, the design still represents an early example of Renaissance Revival elements in the architecture of the American South. Notable in this regard is the delicate garland that spans the entire facade, and the elaborate pediments above the central windows of the second stage. With respect to public architecture in Georgia in the last two decades of the nineteenth century, this is one of the only significant examples of the Italian Renaissance Revival apart from post offices and other buildings commissioned by the Federal government.

Although "Renaissance" may have been what the region needed, "Renaissance" spirit was hard to find in the devastated back eddies of rural Georgia and Alabama. Even after the turn of the century, when the voices of academic design were finally heard in Georgia, it was a stricter more pure Neoclassicism that was most often embraced. To be sure Renaissance elements had eventually crept in, but at the bottom of it all, it was the simplicity of the Greek Revival, not ornate Italian finery, that was so close to the Southern soul.

The old 1900 depot no longer stands to sing the song of the crossing rails that finally did come to Brooks County. At the town of Boston, 13 miles to the west of Quitman along Brooks County's border with Thomas County, the Georgia Northern Railroad completed rails to Moultrie in 1893. Four years later, in 1897, Quitman finally got her north-south line. The South Georgia Railroad was completed from Quitman to the village of Heartpine, on the Georgia Southern and Florida Railway. Subsequently, the northern terminus of the line was moved from Heartpine to Adel and the road was later extended from Quitman southward into Florida. Nestled between the Old South success story at Thomasville and the New South wonder at Valdosta, Quitman was not destined for greatness. But by 1910 her mill was up and running again and her population was nearing 4000. The town had experienced a decade of growth after the arrival of the crossing rails of the Georgia Southern Railroad.

THOMAS COUNTY: THOMASVILLE

Plate 7.20: The Thomas County Courthouse, built 1858. John Wind architect. Remodeled 1885.

Thomasville's early history is unique, and in many ways it sets the town apart from the rest of Southwest Georgia. Only fifty miles south of Albany, the village had its beginnings over a decade earlier, but unlike Albany, Thomasville had no navigable river. Here in the antebellum period, commercial connections were accomplished by an unreliable network of poorly maintained roads. The best and most direct of these led southward to Tallahassee. Thus, before the arrival of the Atlantic and Gulf Railroad in 1860, Thomasville must have seemed more a part of Florida than of Georgia. The town had endured the decades of her early growth without a bank. Planters, merchants and factors alike had perennially decried the flimsy paper received from Tallahassee bankers. It can be no coincidence that less than a year after the arrival of the Atlantic and Gulf, the Cotton Planters Bank was

established at Thomasville, and almost overnight this remote corner of Southwest Georgia became economically linked to Savannah.

Although the first depot was probably not much more than a shack, the establishment of the Atlantic and Gulf's Station #19 at Thomasville was a singularly monumental event. It meant that the 200-mile journey to Savannah could suddenly be accomplished in the unthinkably short span of thirteen hours, and it changed not only the town's orientation and allegiance, but altered its point of view.

The erection of the courthouse at Thomasville on the very eve of the arrival of the Atlantic and Gulf suggests the birth of a new and progressive railroad-inspired self-image in Thomasville, which may have foreshadowed the postbellum pattern of simple depot inspiring grand courthouse. But like many successful Georgia trading towns of the antebellum era, Thomasville probably also built in response to need. In 1858, this was still the frontier, and accordingly the Thomas County Courthouse undoubtedly reflected practical pioneer necessity more than railroad-inspired zeal for an industrial future.

From its early beginnings in 1825, Thomasville had quickly become the gateway to western Florida and the dominant trading center for the southernmost tip of the Cotton Belt in Georgia. The county's first courthouse was built in 1827 of "split pine logs covered with pine boards." In 1830, the entire county, which at that time included large portions of present-day Brooks, Colquitt and Grady Counties, had only about 3000 residents. In 1846-1847, a brick courthouse replaced this first crude structure but was badly damaged by a storm in 1853 and declared unsafe in 1855. By the early 1850s, the county's population had exceeded 10,000. As new settlers, eager to exploit the compelling promise of cotton, began to clear Thomas County's great expanses of pine, Thomasville sought to develop its own brand of culture and refinement in what still must have been a rather remote outpost of the vanishing American frontier.

As we have seen, most of the other court buildings built in the antebellum period along the line of the Atlantic and Gulf were of the crudest sort, log or wood-frame vernacular buildings with no attempt at ornament. Here in Thomasville we find an attempt at an architectural statement of refinement, culture, even monumentality designed by a transplanted Englishman, John Wind. To discover this building's soul, we must mentally peal away an extensive 1885 remodeling. To help us with this, a fine charcoal drawing (Plate 7.21) survives from 1860. It documents the building's original form,[64] and revealing that this courthouse was once a stunning example of the early brick vernacular style. This elementary style, which developed along the edges of the American frontier, was often inspired by details and elevations presented in various builders guides. In this case, as in the case of the early court building at Macon, the source seems sure. Asher Benjamin, who published a series of practical builder's guides between 1806 and 1857, includes "Plate 38: Elevation for a Courthouse" in his 1827 *The American Builder's Companion* (Plate 7.22). As William Mitchell, Jr. points out in his survey of Thomas County architecture, the general form of John Wind's 1858 Thomas, County Courthouse is astonishingly close to Benjamin's courthouse form, featuring a three-story, rectangular mass with a projecting tetrastyle portico, a hipped roof and a delicate cupola. In Thomasville, some of Wind's details depart from Benjamin's example, but probably only to avoid sophistication too ambitious for local builders. Benjamin's octagonal cupola, for example, was modified, here replaced by a cubical base supporting an airy round columned belfry, and instead of the expected classical pediment above the portico, Wind applied a rather crude stepped parapet. The use of builder's guides was so widespread in this era that serious questions of architectural credits often arise. As Alan Gowan puts it: "So successful and so widely used were it [*The American Builder's Companion*] and later guides by Benjamin (and others primarily Minard LeFever) that historians are still questioning the extent to which buildings should be attributed to him…"[65] Details of John Wind's fine plantation houses in Thomas County also bear the undeniable marks of Asher Benjamin's influence. That John Wind was a unique and talented man is beyond question. That John Wind was a trained architect is doubtful. Nonetheless,

Plate 7.20: The 1885 remodeling of John Wind's 1858 Thomas County Courthouse undoubtedly did much to affirm Thomasville's belief in Old South mythology. (Photo: Wilber W. Caldwell.

the quality of his work earned him inclusion into this category.

Wind came to Thomasville from England some time before 1840 at the expense of Jackson Jones Marsh, a wealthy planter. His background included a degree form Queens College. This is hardly an architectural credential. After taking up residence in Thomasville, Wind began to advertise himself as an architect. It is certain that, in the case of the Thomas County Courthouse, Wind was retained solely as a designer, the construction of the building having been awarded to the lowest bidder in 1855. In that same year, Wind had been paid $55 for the design. Despite Thomasville's growth, architectural commissions in

[64] William Mitchell, Jr., Landmarks, *The Architecture of Thomasville and Thomas County, Georgia* (Thomasville GA: Thomasville Landmarks, 1980).

[65] Alan Gowans, *Styles and Types of North American Architecture* (1992; reprint, New York: Icon Editions, 1993) 89-90.

Plate 7.21: Thomas County Courthouse as built 1858. (Author's line drawing from Wind's original sketch.)

Thomasville in 1850 were understandably scarce, and Wind, who was apparently something of a "Renaissance man," busied himself as a watch repairman, and an inventor, patenting a cotton thrashing machine.

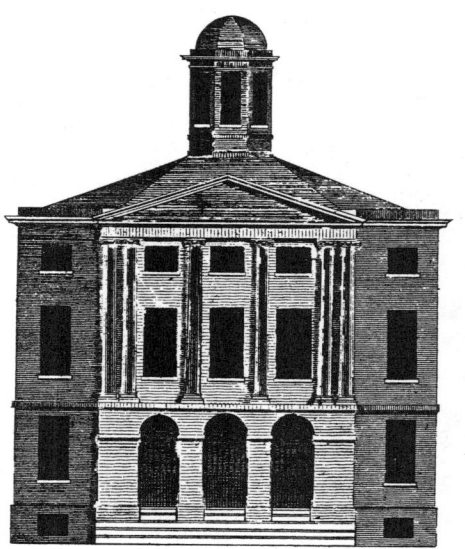

Plate 7.22: Asher Benjamin's "Elevation for a Courthouse" from *The American Builder's Companion,* 1827. (Illustration: Asher Benjamin (1827).)

In his *Statistics of the State of Georgia,* George White reports Thomasville's population at around 500 in 1849. By some accounts, the town experienced considerable growth in the 1850s, reaching 2500 residents by 1860.[66] Whatever the case, this 1858 courthouse was an enormous building for its place and time, and with the seeds of sophistication germinating in Thomas County's crude garden of pioneer pragmatism, symbolic architectural messages elevated this structure above mere practical considerations. Simple classical forms were used throughout America to convey images of purity, Justice, Democracy, Reason and so on, but by 1850 in the American South these symbols were becoming distorted to reflect a convoluted historical vision of a Greek Democracy which prospered on the labor of slaves.

Despite such imagery, the result of Wind's manipulations of Asher Benjamin's much copied form was probably more reflective of Thomasville's economic success and commercial growth than anything else. This building distinguished Thomasville more by its size and quality of construction than by its artistic qualities of design. This distinction is made even more radiant when the building is compared to many of its neighbors. Thomasville had undoubtedly managed some degree of cultural refinement by 1860 as wealthy planters achieved enough success in the fields to move their residences to town. Nonetheless Thomas County surely had its rough-edges on the eve of the Civil War, and this building, in its original form, spoke perhaps better for that practical frontier culture than it did for a planter "aristocracy." And so it should have, for in truth, most of Georgia's "aristocracy" before the Civil War was fabricated in myths of the Old South fashioned in the dark nostalgic decades of the last third of the nineteenth century. These myths endure today, and their force has erased, or at least blunted, any frontier mythology, which might have just as legitimately developed along side.

The 1885 remodeling of the Thomas County Courthouse undoubtedly did much to affirm Thomasville's belief in such Old South mythology. The Italian Renaissance details, presumably the design of local contractors Eaves and Chase, added considerable charm to what theretofore had been a rather stark

Plate 7.23: The Atlantic Coast Line's 1916 depot at Thomasville. More than any other railroad in Georgia, The Atlantic Coast Line maintained a consistent stylistic approach to depot building. (Photo: Wilber W. Caldwell.)

old red brick pile. After a few years, it became natural for Thomasvillians to simply assume that the building had always radiated this refined neoclassical aura. In an almost unavoidable inference, this late-century architectural sophistication has come to document a rose-colored vision of society in the earlier period, implying an antebellum cultural enlightenment similar to the one detailed in the myth.

The 1885 remodeling of the old vernacular building lifted the structure out of the frontier and into a more sophisticated, if not up-to-date, American architectural era. Here we find Renaissance themes, but details generally recall the older Italianate Style popular in the pre-war period rather than the modern clothing of the blossoming American Renaissance Revival which, in the 1880s, was just beginning to gain momentum in the North. Distinctly Italianate is the fenestration featuring both rounded and segmental arches with bold hoodmolds supported by ornamental braces. The enclosure of the portico and the addition of the pediment and its three massive supporting arches create an entrance true to the vision of the original Asher Benjamin design. Likewise the remodeled octagonal tower, although more grand than Benjamin's plan, is similar in effect. Unlike Bruce and Morgan's 1892 Brooks County remodeling of John Wind's 1860 courthouse at nearby Quitman, this is not a step forward into the architectural future, but rather a decided step backward into the past. In fact, if we disregard the delicate arched fenestration, the

effect of the 1885 remodeling created a greater likeness to Asher Benjamin's original 1827 "Elevation for a Courthouse." Perhaps this historical focus was more in tune with the mood in Thomasville in 1888 than any modern messages.

Plate 7.23: The Depot at Thomasville, built 1916.

Begun only five years after its near twin at Waycross, this grand depot is perhaps Georgia's best standing example of the architectural style employed by the Atlantic Coast Line Railway in the early decades of the twentieth century. More than any other road in Georgia in this era, the Atlantic Coast Line maintained a consistent stylistic approach to depot building. This line's depots were usually characterized by broad tile roofs, polychromatic brick banding and corbeling and patterned brick wall construction, while scrolling shaped parapets and gables often were crowned with masonry coping. This building replaced an 1885 two-story frame depot built vaguely in the Stick Style, which had presumably replaced the original 1860 depot.

Although Thomasville was eventually able to realize postbellum crossing rails, the saga of her struggle is without sequel in Georgia. The town had grown during the war, and the post war period began hopefully

[66] William Warren Rogers, "The Way They Were" *The Georgia Historical Quarterly* 60/2 (September 1976): 139.

THOMASVILLE RAILROADS
PROPOSED BUT NEVER BUILT

The Monticello and Thomasville RR, 1863, Thomasville to Monticello, Florida.

The Monticello and Georgia RR, 1870, Thomasville to Monticello, Florida.

The Thomasville RR, 1877, Thomasville to Monticello, Florida.

The Carrabelle and Thomasville RR, c.1882, Carrabell, Florida, to Thomasville via Tallahassee, Florida.

The Thomasville, Tallahassee and Gulf RR, 1883, Carrabell, Florida, to Thomasville via Tallahassee, Florida.

The Tallahassee and Thomasville RR, 1886, Thomasville to St. Marks, Florida, via Tallahassee, Florida.

The Tallahassee Branch of The Savannah, Florida and Western, 1887, Thomasville to Tallahassee, Florida

The Thomasville and Augusta RR, 1885, Augusta to Florida state line via Sandersville and Thomasville.

The Columbus and Florida RR, 1885, Columbus to Florida state line via Thomasville.

The Thomasville Branch of the Georgia Southern and Florida RR, 1888, Cordele to Thomasville.

The Thomasville and Ty Ty RR, 1887, Ty Ty to Thomasville.

The Thomasville Branch of the Atlanta and Florida RR, 1887, branch to Thomasville.

The Thomasville, Florida and Western RR, 1887, Columbus to the Florida state line via Thomasville.

The Augusta, Thomasville and Gulf RR, 1887, Augusta to Florida's west coast via Thomasville.

The Thomasville and Northern RR, 1887. Worth County to the Florida state line via Thomasville.

The Thomasville and Cordele Railroad, 1889, Cordele to Thomasville.

The Augusta and West Florida RR, 1889, Augusta to Florida state line via Sandersville and Thomasville.

The Augusta, Tallahassee and Gulf RR, 1889, Carrabell, Florida, to Thomasville via Tallahassee, Florida.

The Florida, Dawson and Northern RR, 1889, Dawson to Florida State line via Thomasville, Cairo or Bainbridge.

The Carrabelle, Tallahassee and Georgia RR, 1891, Carrabell, Florida, to Thomasville via Tallahassee, Florida.

The Richland, Gulf and Northern RR, c.1893, Richland to Florida state line, via Thomasville or Cairo.

The Atlanta, Americus and Florida RR, c.1895, Atlanta to Tampa, Florida, via Thomasville.

The McRae, Ocilla and Southwestern RR, c.1895, McRae to Thomasville.

enough. The Atlantic and Gulf was repaired and running to Thomasville by the end of 1866, and a line from Thomasville to Albany was begun by the South Georgia and Florida Railroad Company and completed by the Atlantic and Gulf in 1869. In the meantime, the Atlantic and Gulf's main line was extended through Cairo to Bainbridge.

But at the center of the Thomasville's railroad aspirations were connections to Florida. Two natural routes were pursued, one to renew the link with Tallahassee, and the other to connect with central Florida at Monticello, 25 miles southeast of Thomasville. Between 1863 and 1895 no fewer than 25 railroads were proposed in these connections (see Table 7.3). The line to Tallahassee was never built, and the Monticello road was not completed until the Savannah, Florida and Western Railroad finally built the link in 1888.

After a seemingly endless succession of unrealized hopes, Thomasville had become quite cynical when it came to the promise of postbellum rails. Examples of this frustration are many. In 1881, *The Thomasville Times* editor John Triplett remarked on the progress of the ill-fated Thomasville Railroad's progress toward Monticello, stating that, "It looks like we would have to get a shovel apiece, and go throwing dirt ourselves."[67] In 1883, upon reading that executives of the fledgling Thomasville, Tallahassee and Gulf Railroad had celebrated their ground breaking, digging a ceremonial first shovel of earth, *The Times* could only remark, "We should like to see the last one thrown."[68] And perhaps best of all, Thomasville historian William Rogers describes the "mock horror" feigned by *The Times* reporting the Thomasville and Augusta Railroad's application for a charter in 1887. The headline read: "Thomasville Threatened with Another Railroad."

Accordingly, it is small wonder that no lobby for a new fantasy courthouse materialized to celebrate the town's aspirations for a future filled with New South prosperity. Like so many older towns along the antebellum railroads of Georgia, Thomasville was not so quick to swallow the tempting bait offered by the New South's spokesmen. The city was rooted in tradition, and the myths of the Old South were in many ways

Plate 7.24: Architect J. A. Wood's Piney Woods Hotel in Thomasville was a forerunner to Plant and Flagler's fabulous Florida Resorts hotels.

preferable to the broken promises of the New South. An elegant remodeling of her old courthouse must have seemed just the thing in 1885, for at the time Thomasville was beginning to blossom, but in a graceful and distinctly Southern sort of way.

Plate 7.24: The Piney Woods Hotel at Thomasville, built in 1885. Burned in 1906. J. A. Wood, architect.

In 1885, two magnificent resort hotels were completed at Thomasville marking the period of the town's fullest flower. Mild winters and soft Southern airs had made Thomasville a popular winter resort with wealthy Northern vacationers, and these enormous facilities, the Mithchell House and the Piney Woods, added substantial elegance to the attractive natural scene. Both were designed by New York architect J. A. Wood who would later go on to design the Oglethorpe Hotel in Brunswick and Henry B. Plant's fabulous 511 room Tampa Bay Hotel completed in 1891.

By 1888, the long-awaited connection to Florida was realized when Henry Plant's Savannah, Florida and Western Railroad finally built the much-discussed line from Thomasville to Monticello, Florida. Thomasville's last major railroad connection came in July of 1900 when the Union Lumber Company announced the opening of the Tifton, Thomasville and Gulf Railroad. There was guarded hope for an extension of this line to Tallahassee, but as usual, these plans came to nothing. The line was acquired by the

Atlantic and Birmingham in 1903 and became part of the Atlanta, Birmingham and Atlantic in 1906. In 1907-1908, the ne'er-do-well Florida Central Railroad built a line from Thomasville southward 46 miles into Florida. This railroad proved a financial disaster, failed in 1912, and it was abandoned shortly thereafter. All the while, Thomasville's population remained rather static reporting about 5500 residents in 1890 and just above 6500 twenty years later. The town had settled into to a sort of refined complacency. It is unclear whether this came from so many disappointments striving to reach the future, or from an unswerving commitment to the past. In all likelihood it came from both. Thus, Thomasville, like so many Georgia towns of the era, was trapped between two conflicting and equally fallacious myths, and it was a town in danger of becoming at odds with itself.

SOME LAST THOUGHTS ON THE ATLANTIC AND GULF RAILROAD

The Atlantic and Gulf, the last of the great antebellum railroads in Georgia, was built to serve Savannah. By 1860, it had traversed almost 200 miles of desolate and virtually uninhabited swamps and pine barrens to siphon the riches of Southwest Georgia's

[67] *The Thomasville Times*, August 11, 1883, in William Warren Rogers, *Thomas County, 1865-1900* (Tallahassee: Florida State University Press, 1973) 111.

[68] *The Thomasville Times*, August 11, 1883, in Rogers, *Thomas County, 1865-1900*, 111

inland cotton belt to the sea. In the post-war period, this road, renamed the Savannah, Florida and Western, with southward branches sprouting into Florida and a coastwise connection to Charleston, would be among the first roads to demonstrate that railroads would soon replace coastal sea-going transportation systems. Ironically, Savannah had created the Atlantic and Gulf only to later be forsaken by it.

As Savannah's second handmaiden, the Atlantic and Gulf was in many way similar to the first, the Central of Georgia. Each made a looping path to its destination paying little heed to the few existing towns along the way. Each begot new towns, which eclipsed older settlements. And each would act as a main trunk for a host of postbellum branches and short line railroads in the last decades of the ninetieth century. It is certainly appropriate that the earliest popular name for the road was "The Main Trunk Railroad." In the 1880s and early 1890s, an inconceivably complex web

Plate 7.25: Thomasville. (Photo: Wilber W. Caldwell.)

of tiny tram lines snaked their way into the south Georgia forests and by the turn of the century, many of these had been expanded to become full-fledged commercial railroads connecting with the main line to Savannah. It was a classic case of railroad over-building in an area too poor to support such extensive infrastructure.

When the Atlantic and Gulf's ancestor, the Savannah and Albany Railroad, was chartered way back in 1849, investors had visions of a line from Savannah via Albany all the way to Mobile. But by the time construction began, Albany had been connected to the Southwestern Railroad and thus to Macon, and Thomasville somehow won the day. Opposition by the Central and its pawn, the Southwestern, may have played a part in this curious change of direction. Whatever the case, it was a grave loss from which Albany would be slow to recover, and although the choice of the southern route demonstrates the importance and financial power of Thomasville in the early era, it is telling that Thomasville was never able to fully capitalized on the connection.

As we have seen, in the desperate decades after Reconstruction, older towns that had known success in the antebellum period were less likely to fall prey to the enticements of the myth of the New South. Thomasville was such a place, and predictably the town retains her 1858 courthouse to this day. The only other old town along the route of the Atlantic and Gulf might have been Hinesville the county seat of Liberty County, but the line bypassed Hinesville, and until the middle of the twentieth century the town remained perhaps Georgia's best example of what happens where rails fail to arrive. In 1927, the old frame courthouse at Hinesville was ninety years old, but Hinesville still had a population of below 250 and was located on an unpaved highway

All of the other county towns along the route of the Atlantic and Gulf were created by that railroad, and those that knew postbellum crossing rails where quick to build the expected monuments to hope and progress which this book seeks to explain. Three of these towns were destined to become significant junction points for connections to Florida. All three celebrated their newfound prospects with monumental court buildings: G. L. Norrman's 1891 picturesque "Castle" at Waycross, James W. Golucke's rather stern 1903 romanesque courthouse at Jesup, and Frank Milburn's Beaux-Arts wonder at Valdosta completed in 1905. Fired by speculation that a Brunswick to Birmingham rail line would pass through Blackshear, Pierce County erected J. W. Golucke's Beaux-Arts monument in 1903. Despite its rocky financial history, the later crossing line of the 1906 Georgia Coast and Piedmont was enough to assure the creation of Long County in 1920 and help secure a courthouse for Ludowici. Likewise, the construction of the Milltown Air Line in 1901 begot growth at Milltown (later Lakeland) and sparked the subsequent creation of Lanier County in 1920.

In places where no rails crossed, the story was equally predictable. In 1895, tiny Homerville built a vernacular brick court building in the style of the antebellum period. Statenville in Echols County remained unconnected until 1910 and the county built one of the last vernacular frame court buildings in the state in 1899. Although crossing rails did finally come to Quitman, Brooks County was content to keep its fine 1864 courthouse with its brilliant 1892 remodeling.

The common link here is difficult to overlook. Except for comfortable old Thomasville, the Atlantic and Gulf's original destination, most of the county towns that lie along the line today did not exist before the construction of their antebellum railroad.

When the first shots of the Civil War echoed in Georgia, the basic skeleton of the state's future railroad network was almost complete. Four roads radiated from Atlanta and three from Macon. Farther south, the isolated curve of the Atlantic and Gulf stretched from Savannah to Thomasville. The great system of branches and connecting lines that was to come was barely begun. At war's onset, only ten branch lines were in operation: the Athens, Washington and Warrenton branches on the Georgia Railroad; the Milledgeville/Eatonton and Augusta branches on the

Central of Georgia; the Thomaston branch on the Macon and Western; the Rome branch on the Western and Atlantic and the Eufaula and Fort Gaines branches on the Southwestern.

In addition, the beginning of the war interrupted several railroad construction projects in progress. In 1861, the Brunswick and Albany was complete from Brunswick to Waresboro just northwest of Waycross. Although this line might properly be considered part of the antebellum rail system, it was dismantled during the war, and its history more logically belongs with the Reconstruction era, which saw it completion in 1870. In addition, two lines were under construction from Macon in 1861. The Macon and Brunswick was graded southward from that city to somewhere in Twiggs County, and the Macon and Augusta was well underway via Milledgeville.

The Reconstruction period would see the completion of all of these lines. Remarkably, despite the economic chaos that engulfed Georgia and a severe national depression in 1873, a handful of new railroads, branches and connectors would be completed before the end of Reconstruction. All of these would be main line roads.

•

PART 2

Reconstruction Railroads
1865–1873

The Macon and Augusta Railroad

Bibb County: Macon, Part 2 • Baldwin County: Milledgeville (see chapter 2)
Hancock County: Sparta • Warren County: Warrenton
Some Last Thoughts on the Macon and Augusta Railroad

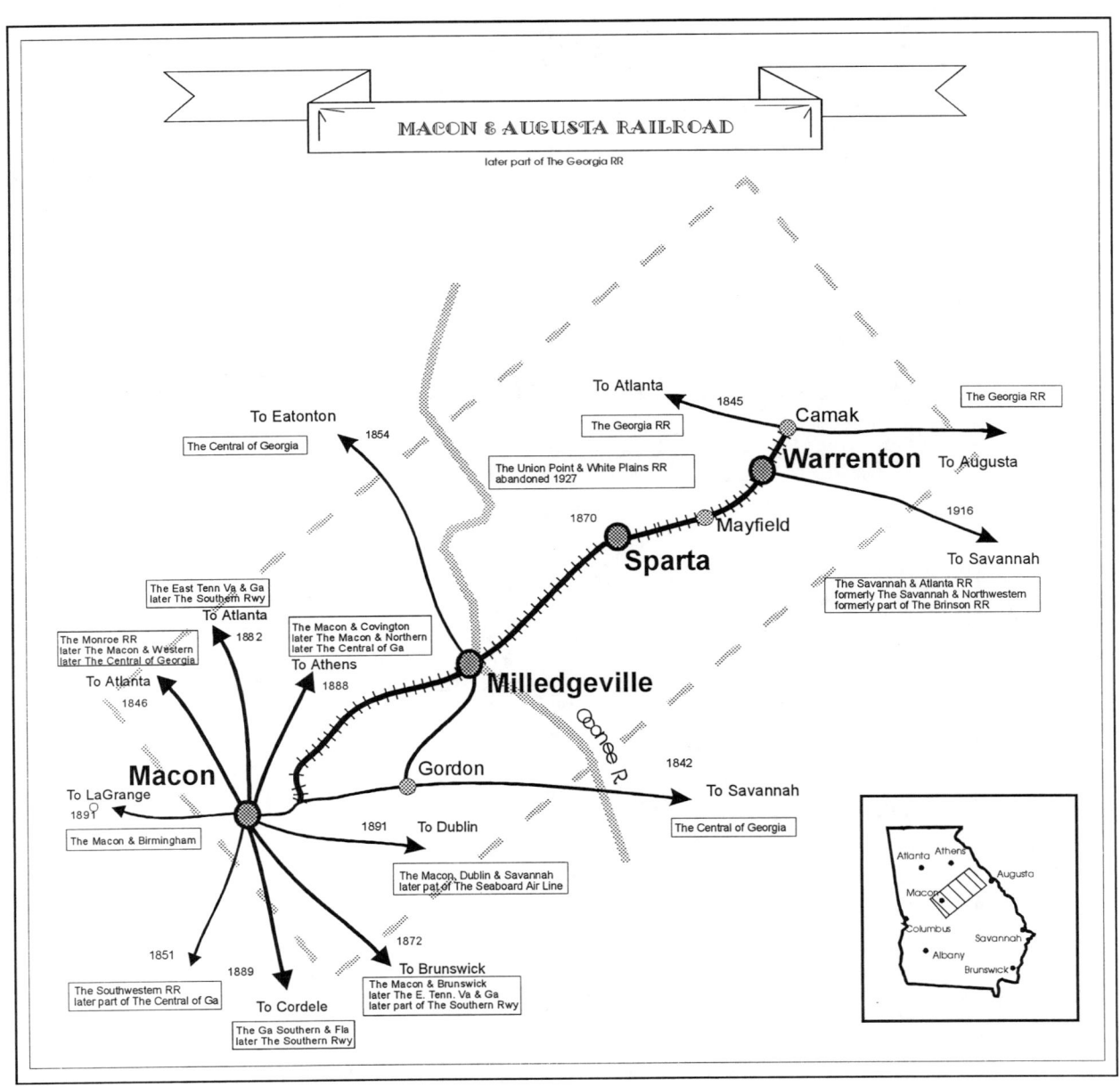

MACON & AUGUSTA RAILROAD

later part of The Georgia RR

To Atlanta

The Georgia RR

To Eatonton

1854

The Central of Georgia

1845   Camak

The Georgia RR

The Georgia RR

Warrenton

The Union Point & White Plains RR
abandoned 1927

To Augusta

1870   Mayfield

Sparta

1916

To Savannah

The East Tenn Va & Ga
later The Southern Rwy
To Atlanta

1882

The Macon & Covington
later The Macon & Northern
later The Central of Ga
To Athens

1888

The Savannah & Atlanta RR
formerly The Savannah & Northwestern
formerly part of The Brinson RR

The Monroe RR
later The Macon & Western
later The Central of Georgia
To Atlanta

1846

Milledgeville

Oconee R.

Macon

Gordon

1842

To Savannah

To LaGrange
1891

1891   To Dublin

The Central of Georgia

The Macon & Birmingham

The Macon, Dublin & Savannah
later part of The Seaboard Air Line

1851

1889

1872

To Brunswick

The Southwestern RR
later part of The Central of Ga

To Cordele

The Macon & Brunswick
later The E. Tenn. Va & Ga
later part of The Southern Rwy

The Ga Southern & Fla
later The Southern Rwy

Atlanta   Athens

Augusta

Macon

Columbus

Savannah

Albany

Brunswick

8 | The Macon and Augusta Railroad

MACON TO CAMAK

BIBB COUNTY: MACON, PART 2

Plate 8.1: The Bibb County Courthouse built in 1872. Demolished 1922. Gourdon P. Randall, architect.

As the Reconstruction era began, many white Georgians looked to Macon for leadership. By 1868, two years before the cornerstone for this courthouse was laid, Milledgeville, the old state capitol, had been forced to yield the palm to that brash upstart, Atlanta. Despite its destruction at the hand of General Sherman four years before, there was much for ex-Confederate Georgians to hate about the resurgent Atlanta in 1868. Perhaps a little too cozily, it was headquarters for the Federal occupation forces in Georgia. It was the site of the loathed "nigger-New England" Constitutional Convention made up of a newly assembled predominantly Republican coalition of freedmen, carpetbaggers, and Union sympathizing scalawags. And it was blatantly self-promotional in its approach to almost everything, especially its shameless quest for Northern capital.

In 1868, with a population of just over 10,000, Macon was about the same size as Atlanta. It was every bit the railroad center that Atlanta was, and perhaps most importantly, it had been the center of Georgia's vast agricultural economy before the war. Thus, many looked to Macon to redeem their downtrodden culture, to lead their desperate political struggle for control of the state's destiny and to bolster their hopes for economic relief from the nightmare that was Radical Reconstruction. Accordingly, while Atlanta's 1867 Constitutional Convention set the wheels in motion to ratify the Fourteenth Amendment and repudiate all Confederate debts, Georgia Democrats met in Macon to declare Reconstruction itself a "crime" and to lay the organizational framework for what was to become the Bourbon Democracy in Georgia.

By 1877, Democrats would redraft the state's Constitution into one of the narrowest and most reactionary documents in American history. It was an act that "prohibited virtually everything that might encourage the emergence of the New

No. 30.   Court House.

Plate 8.1: With the completion of the 1872 Bibb County Courthouse, G. P. Randall could legitimately claim the finest Second Empire building in Georgia. (Photo: Courtesy of Georgia Dept. of Archives and History.)

South in Georgia."[1] As the 1877 Democratic Constitution was being written in Atlanta, Federal troops returned home from the South, Bourbon Democrats cemented their power in Georgia, and black Georgians were either denied the franchise or sadly manipulated by increasingly corrupt white political machines. For decades, the Bourbons would accomplish little, except their re-election. Their platform rested firmly on a stable social order, the center post of which was white supremacy. Ironically, all of the top leadership in the Bourbon Democracy, despite its grassroots beginnings in Macon, ended up in what became known as the Atlanta Ring. One chapter in

the history of the Democratic Party in Georgia is the story of Macon and her downstate allies' effort to break the monopoly of power held by the Atlanta-oriented leadership.

In the post-war era, Macon, like much of the American South, and like the Bourbon Democracy itself, was trapped and held immobile between the past and future. The city could never re-cross the treacherous barricades of war to re-live her past, and she was equally incapable of significant forward progress owing to her bitter intransigence and reactionary social focus. Atlanta, with virtually no past at all, was unaffected by this kind of paralysis. While Atlanta welcomed William T. Sherman with open arms in 1879, Macon erected an enormous monument to her Confederate dead, and dedicated it in a memorable orgy of Old South fervor.

Still, Macon only flaunted the outward symbols of progress, not the least of which were her railroads and this courthouse, built in the up-to-date Second Empire Style. Macon built the very first railroads after the war, and she set the pattern for the period by celebrating the promise of these new rails with a grand and stylish courthouse. In 1870, the Macon and Augusta Railroad was complete and the Macon and Brunswick had reached Jesup. The next year, the construction of this monumental building spoke for only one side of the split personality of Bibb County. Its message bears no hint of the wounded, nostalgic brooding that dominated so much of the Southern mind after the war. Here is the architecture of the railroad, a symbol of the age, fresh from Paris by way of England and the American Northeast. Here is the Republican message of American big business and big government.

There were only three other authentic Second Empire courthouses built in Georgia: Athens, 1876, Atlanta, 1883, and Covington 1884. The three would-be railroad centers of Atlanta, Macon and Athens attempted to cast off the past and leap into the future. As it turned out, only Atlanta, with no real past to hold her down, was able to successfully make the jump. In Macon, the 1872 Bibb County Courthouse represented only the illusion of modern possibilities for a city pinned beneath the burden of its own history.

[1] Numan V. Bartly, *The Creation of Modern Georgia* (1983; reprint, Athens GA: University of Georgia Press, 1990) 79.

[2] Henry Russell Hitchcock, *Architecture: Eighteenth and Nineteenth Centuries* (1958; reprint, New Haven and London: Yale University Press, 1977) 243.

To design her symbol of "progress to come," Macon employed the services of Chicago architect, Gourdon P. Randall, who was well known for his spectacular Second Empire court buildings in Illinois, Indiana and Michigan. While working on Macon's new palace of justice, Randall simultaneously designed Macon's Mercer University Administration Building, arguably the finest standing example of the High Gothic Revival in Georgia. With the completion of the 1872 Bibb County Courthouse, Randall likewise could legitimately claim the finest Second Empire building in Georgia. It was preceded in the style by William Parkins's rather bulky 1869 Kimball Opera House which later became the State Capitol Building and Parkins's lavish but less than graceful 1870 Kimball House Hotel, both in Atlanta.

Despite its Renaissance vocabulary, the Second Empire Style in America derived its models not from distant historical periods but from Napoleon III's contemporary rebuilding of the city of Paris. Thus Randall's courthouse brought to Macon a truly modern architectural idiom. Typical of most American architectural trends before 1880, a great deal of the Second Empire had arrived via England. Especially influential were drawings for both the British War Office and Foreign Office that were widely reproduced in architectural publications in the late 1850s, despite the fact that neither building was built. These drawings provided the models for many American Second Empire designs in the 1860s.[2] By 1870, Washington was so filled with Second Empire buildings, that the style became known as the "General Grant Style," an appellation that must have stuck in the throats of Maconites. In truth, beyond the drawings for Britain's War Office and Foreign Office there were very few visual guides to instruct American architects in Second Empire disciplines, and the result was a freedom and originality that yielded uniquely American results. Typical Americanization is present here in Macon: the use of brick transports the building away from academic purity and into a rich world of picturesque texture and color, likewise the asymmetrical arrangement of the high tower illustrates a typically English and American taste for the picturesque.

Despite her modern architectural symbols, Macon quickly lost her battle with Atlanta, whose population soared to above 60,000 by 1890 while Macon counted barely 20,000 residents. Atlanta's growth had been meteoric, while Macon's had remained steady and predictable, primarily reflecting the town's regional prominence as an agricultural, commercial and railroad center. Cotton warehouses and wholesalers typified Macon's progress in this era punctuated by periodic expansions of her cotton mill or an occasional shirt factory. Her only other substantial industry centered on the foundries, which supported her extensive array of railroad shops and maintenance facilities. In the late 1880s, Macon experienced a ground swell of light manufacturing growth only to be laid low again by the depression following the Panic of 1893.

Plate 8.2: The East Tennessee, Virginia and Georgia Railroad Depot at Macon, built in 1886.

By the time this fine depot was erected, Macon seemed to be on the edge of real progress, and the contemporary lines and Queen Anne details of this structure spoke for a city that saw itself on the threshold of a new age. Here again is a depot that wore the clothing of domestic architecture. In this case elements of an American version of the Queen Anne

Plate 8.2: The contemporary lines and Queen Anne details of the East Tennessee, Virginia and Georgia Railroad Depot at Macon spoke for a city that saw itself on the threshold of a new age. (Photo: Courtesy of Les R. Winn.)

Table 8.1

RAILROAD CONNECTIONS AT MACON 1900

The Central of Georgia Railroad, 1843 Savannah to Macon.

The Macon and Western Railroad, 1846. (formerly the Monroe Railroad; part of the Central of Georgia, 1872). Macon to Atlanta

The Southwest Railroad Company, 1852 (part of the Central of Georgia, 1869). Macon to Albany with branches to Eufaula, Fort Gaines, Columbus and Perry.

The Macon and Brunswick Railroad, 1870 (part of the East Tennessee, Virginia and Georgia Railroad, 1881; later part of the Southern Railway). Macon to Brunswick.

The Macon and Augusta Railroad, 1870 (later part of the Georgia Railroad, 1877). Macon to Augusta via Camak.

The East Tennessee, Virginia and Georgia Railroad, 1881 a.k.a. the Macon and Brunswick Extension) (later part of the Southern Railway), Macon to Atlanta.

The Covington and Macon Railroad, 1888 (later the Macon and Northern, 1891; later part of the Central of Georgia, 1895). Macon to Athens via Madison.

The Georgia, Southern and Florida, 1890 (later part of the Southern Railway). Macon to the Florida line via Valdosta.

The Macon and Birmingham Railroad, 1891. Macon to LaGrange.

The Macon, Dublin and Savannah Railroad, 1900. Macon to Vidalia via Dublin with connections to Savannah.

United States. A vague and unlikely marriage, the Queen Anne represented a reaction to High Victorian exuberances while it retained a pronounced picturesque quality. Accordingly, there was considerable controversy over the true character of the style.

This building was much loved in Macon, for at the very heart of the city's existence lay her railroads (see Table 8.1). The vast complex of shops maintained by the Central was in time mirrored by shops serving the Macon and Brunswick, which later became part of the East Tennessee, Virginia and Georgia; the Georgia Southern and Florida; the Macon and Northern and later the Macon and Dublin Railroad. The old Union depot, built way back in 1855, served most lines until it burned in 1891, but several roads maintained separate passenger facilities. The Monroe Railroad depot stood at Forsyth and College Streets until 1884, and this grand depot built by the East Tennessee, Virginia and Georgia Railroad in 1886 served that road, and later its successor, the Southern Railway. It appears that the Covington and Macon built its own depot sometime around 1891 and that the Macon and Dublin later used the facility, but the record here is unclear. The first depot built in the post-war era was erected by the Macon and Augusta at the foot of Poplar Street in 1870.

———————

The Macon and Augusta Railroad, was begun well before the war and work on the road continued even while the fighting raged. During the war, it represented a strategic link, and after the fighting ended it represented Macon's first futile effort to free herself from the monopolistic tyranny of the Central of Georgia. Spurred by the Central's soaring passenger and freight rates, work resumed almost immediately after the fighting stopped.

It is little wonder that rates were high in 1865. Georgia and her railroads lay in ruin. Rails and rolling stock had been either destroyed by Federal Troops or commandeered by Southern forces for use elsewhere in the Confederacy. What little roadbed and other equipment that remained had become almost unus-

Style are evident in the irregular silhouette of the roof line, elaborate flaring chimneys, dog's tooth terra cotta decoration above the windows and lacy bargeboards in the pediment. The Queen Anne had first appeared in America following the praise of the English half-timbered houses that were part of the English exhibit at the 1876 Philadelphia Centennial Exposition. The new style was driven by the success of Norman Shaw in England, and its first phase, often termed the Shavian Manorial, gained popularity in America in the late 1870s. By the mid-1880s, the Queen Anne Style had evolved into its second or "Free Classic" phase, which sprang from the later efforts of Shaw and others to combine free composition with classical detail. This developed into an uneven idiom in the

[3] Peter S. McGuire, "The Railroads of Georgia, 1860 -1880," *The Georgia Historical Quarterly 16/3 (Savannah 1932)*: 187.

[4] McGuire, "The Railroads of Georgia, 1860 -1880," *The Georgia Historical Quarterly*, 193.

able for want of maintenance. Even the unfinished Macon and Augusta had suffered during the war when Confederate authorities had seized iron for fifty miles of new track for use in the construction of ironclads.[3] Most roads were in financial distress, having invested in Confederate bonds and extended enormous lines of credit to the Confederate government and other non-cash customers whose fortunes had rested on the worth of Confederate currency. Immediately following the war, progress on new roads was nearly non-existent. Ten new railroads were chartered in 1867-1868, but in the great financial void that was the South's legacy of defeat, all ten of these efforts came to nothing.[4] Work on the Macon and Augusta lagged.

It was in this atmosphere that state aid for Georgia's railroads came to the front. The plan called for state endorsement of railroad bond issues upon the acquisition of set amounts of private capital and the actual construction of a prescribed number of miles of rail. It was a proposition which appealed to seemingly everyone. Railroad promoters saw it as a way to build extensive lines using the state's credit to attract investors, and legislators saw it as a way to boost Georgia's sagging fortunes with little or no financial risk. This last proved a disastrous miscalculation.

State endorsement of the bonds of the Macon and Augusta came with three justifications: it was in the best interest of the industrial progress of the state, it sought to reverse the financial embarrassments of the war and it compensated the company for the iron rails seized during the war. As it turned out, the Georgia Railroad offered to endorse $700,000 in bonds for the Macon and Augusta, and state aid proved unnecessary.

Ironically, just as the line was nearing completion, the Central and the Georgia Railroad agreed to jointly fix per-mile freight rates, thus depriving Macon of any hope for rate competition. The Macon and Augusta was completed in 1870, and like most Reconstruction Railroads, it almost immediately fell on hard times and failed. In 1880, it was purchased by the Georgia Railroad, which had guaranteed the road's initial bond issue.

HANCOCK COUNTY: SPARTA

Plate 8.3 and 8.5: The Hancock County Courthouse, built in 1881-1883. Parkins and Bruce, architects.

Alexander Bruce's 1883 Hancock County Courthouse marks a turning point in the history of public architecture in Georgia. When the first brick vernacular cubes rose to decorate the state's new courthouse squares, Georgians embraced an honest uncomplicated architecture that celebrated simple frontier values and fierce individualism. The unambiguous lines of the vernacular and later the unadorned chastity of the Greek Revival supplied ideal monuments for the early period. But the defense of slavery imposed a corruption upon Greek symbols in the years leading up to the Civil War and an increasing sophistication characterized national architectural models in the decade following Appomattox.

By 1880, the American South was in need of a new stylistic symbol to give form to both the old and the new visions that were beginning to rise from the ashes of surrender. Here in Hancock County, as in so many Georgia counties, new aspirations arrived by rail. After a long series of railroad disappointments (see Table 8.2), the first train arrived in Sparta on the Macon and Augusta Railroad in 1870. At last, Sparta had her long-awaited railroad. Movement for a new courthouse was quick to get underway. By 1874, *The Sparta Times and Planter* reported that a bond issue to

Plate 8.3: Alexander Bruce's Hancock County Courthouse, completed in 1883, marks a turning point in the history of public architecture in Georgia. (Photo: Wilber W. Caldwell.)

fund a new courthouse had been approved and that the Atlanta architectural firm of Parkins and Allen had been hired to design a new Hancock County Courthouse. There followed several years of controversy regarding the county's authority to issue such bonds, and in 1877 the Georgia Supreme Court apparently ruled in the county's favor.[5] By 1879, Alexander Bruce had replaced J. Warner Allen as William Parkins's partner, and one of Bruce's designs was selected for the new court building at Sparta. Further delays ensued, and the contract for the construction of Bruce's courthouse was not let until July of 1881.[6]

Alexander Campbell Bruce began his architectural career in Nashville as an apprentice to the English-born architect H. M. Akeroid, and in 1869 he moved to Knoxville to open his own office. Although the details of Bruce's work in Knoxville are incomplete, we know that he designed at least five court

Plate 8.4: Alexander Bruce's 1875 McMinn County, Courthouse at Athens, Tennessee. Illustration from c.1883 Bruce and Morgan Brochure. (Courtesy of the Atlanta History Center)

buildings in Tennessee including the 1879 Hamilton County Courthouse at Chattanooga.[7] In 1879, he arrived in Atlanta to begin his practice with William Parkins with a large portfolio of completed designs. The design for the Hancock County Courthouse was among these, for Bruce had originated the plan four years earlier. Completed in 1875 and destroyed by fire in 1964, Bruce's McMinn County Courthouse at Athens, Tennessee, (Plate 8.4) was identical in almost every detail to Sparta's 1883 courthouse. In this era, there was substantial precedent for the re-selling of designs as evidenced by the fact that Bruce himself re-created this fine building twice more in Georgia: first in 1883 in Walton County and later in 1885 in Hall County.

Alexander Bruce would go on to design 19 court buildings in Georgia (see Appendix C), but this may well be his masterpiece. Remarkably, Bruce's Hancock County Courthouse achieves success by copying both old and new models. Bruce's magical synthesis here in Sparta imparts grace and sophistication upon the coarse geometry of the old brick vernacular, while it

Table 8.2	HANCOCK COUNTY RAILROADS CHARTERED BUT NEVER BUILT
	1840s The Central of Georgia; a connector between the Central and the Georgia Railroad via Sparta.
	1840s The Georgia Railroad; Washington to some point on the Central of Georgia, via Sparta.
	1850 Sparta Plank Road and Turnpike Company; Sparta to Warrenton and Sandersville.
	1860s The Central of Georgia: Davisboro to Union Point via Sparta.
	1888 The Atlanta, Atlantic and Great Western Railway; Atlanta to Savannah via Sparta.
	1890 East and West Railroad; extension of the Union Point and White Plains Railroad to Sparta and beyond.

[5] *The Sparta Times and Planter,* October 24, 1874 in Janice Hardy, *Preservation of Georgia's Courthouses Through Documentation and Photography,* an unpublished manuscript in the Baldwin County Library at Milledgeville.

[6] *The Ishmaelite,* May 4, 1881, in Janice Hardy, *Preservation of Georgia's Courthouses Through Documentation and Photography,* an unpublished manuscript in the Baldwin County Library at Milledgeville.

[7] Bruce's Tennessee courthouses include the Loudon County Courthouse at Loudon (1871), the McMinn County Courthouse at Athens (1875), the Hamblen County Courthouse at Morristown (1874), the Smith County Courthouse at Carthage (1879), and the Hamilton County Courthouse at Chattanooga (1879).

Plate 8.5: The 1883 Hancock County Courthouse, side elevation. (Photo: Wilber W. Caldwell.)

reshapes the crassly Baroque and inappropriately formal Second Empire Style into a soft, personal, rural idiom, altogether fitting for the slow airy ways of Sparta's 800 inhabitants in 1883. On its hilltop site, the building achieves a proper degree of monumentality while retaining a disarmingly comfortable charm.

Bruce's great gift here was his ability to preserve a fundamental vernacular form while gracefully adorning it with Second Empire plasticity and up-to-date ornament. He began with the familiar four-sided cross-like footprint, with its hipped roof and oversized second story widows. Thus the central form is similar to many of the state's antebellum brick vernacular court buildings. For his Second Empire model, Alexander Bruce chose a courthouse designed by Cyrus Porter, whose long career had taken him to New York, Chicago, Buffalo and Bay County, Michigan. Porter's Bay County Courthouse (Plate 8.6) had appeared in Bicknell's Village Builder and Supplement in 1872. This popular pattern book had contained Bruce's own design for "A Cottage Villa." With its central pedimented bay, and almost identical silhouette and floor plan, Porter's design is clearly the source of Bruce's inspiration. There can be no doubt of Porter's influence on Bruce's ideas, for in 1877, Bruce copied Porter's design almost verbatim in Carthage, Tennessee, where his 1879 Smith County Courthouse still stands today. Here in Sparta, the pedimented central bay balanced by mansard corner pavilions,

masonry quoining and segmental arched fenestration in the squat ground floor mirror Porter's model.

Neither vernacular models nor Porter's Bay County Courthouse rise to the heights achieved here in Hancock County where Bruce added his own gentle touch to their blending. The central section of the building is composed of several bays, and a decidedly French three-deminsionalism propels the central bay forward. This effect is heightened by the use of rustication in the second story quoining. The forward thrust of the central bay de-emphasizes the modern elements of the straight-roofed mansarded wings that flank more classical Second Empire convex mansards in the side elevations (see Plate 8.5). To continue the rustic effect, Bruce added a rambling Stick Style porch across the front of the building, thus emphasizing the diminutive scale of the lower story, which seems to be almost crushed beneath the weight of the enormous courtroom. Lastly, as with most of Bruce's subsequent work, the tower was his own. Certainly not French Second Empire, nor vernacular by any stretch of the imagination, the complex lantern adds the required verticality without detracting from the unity of all that lies below. The overall effect is a charming combination of classic brick vernacular and modern forms. Here is an eclecticism born more of stylistic lag than any vision of the future. Nothing could have been more apt for Sparta.

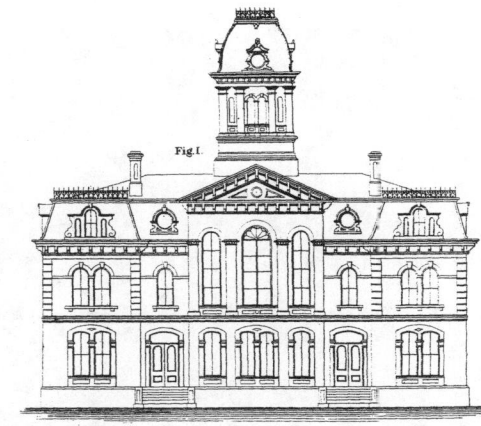

Plate 8.6: Cyrus Porter's Bay County Courthouse, 1872. (Illustration from *Bicknell's Village Builder and Supplement.*)

Sparta was laid out by Major Charles Abercrombie, a Revolutionary War soldier, who received state bounty land in the area that would become Hancock County. A simple wooden courthouse, "originally built elsewhere,"[8] was placed on the square sometime after 1793 when the county was formed. This burned in 1806 and was replaced by a 30 x 40-foot two-story brick vernacular building. Wings were added in 1824. By the end of the war, the building must have been in frightful condition. In 1879, the year Alexander Bruce was commissioned to design Sparta's new centerpiece, *The Sparta Times and Planter* reprinted an article that had appeared in *The Dalton Headlight* stating that Hancock County had the "worst looking courthouse in the state."[9]

The carefully crafted reflection of the earlier period that is one side of the 1883 Hancock County Courthouse's split personality was sadly appropriate for Sparta in the post-war era. Hancock County had good reason to look backward in 1879 for she was making the long journey from one of Georgia's richest counties to one of her poorest. Like most Cotton Belt counties, the root of her agricultural woes lay in the socio-economic chaos wrought by the freeing of the slaves. Before the war, the county's wealth had consisted of land and slaves. In 1865, the slaves were free men and land values had plummeted.

The year 1840 had been the high water mark for cotton in Hancock County. In that year, the county's plantations had produced over 13 million pounds,

first among the state's 93 counties. As war approached, cotton took its toll on the land, and although cotton production in the once fertile fields round Sparta remained flat, a healthy diversification replaced the staple. In 1860, with over 8000 slaves at work in her fields, Hancock County produced over 13,000 bales of cotton (15th among Georgia's 132 counties) and over 350,000 bushels of corn, almost 25,000 bushels of wheat, in addition to maintaining a population of over 24,000 swine and 10,000 cattle. Hard statistics in Hancock County document the lasting effect of the war on farm production and livestock populations in the Georgia Cotton Belt. By 1890, corn production in Hancock County had made its way back to only 70% of the 1860 harvest, and wheat production equaled only a third of the prewar level. The agricultural sector perhaps most devastated by the war was live stock. The county's cattle count in 1890 was still only 60% of the 1860 figure and swine production had been even slower to recover.

Plate 8.7: The depot at Sparta, built c. 1881.

When this depot was new, cotton production in Hancock County was again soaring despite the depressed condition of other agricultural sectors. With the arrival of the railroad, Hancock cotton growers enjoyed competitive shipping and began to import much needed commercial fertilizer. Hancock County was back among Georgia leaders in cotton production by 1880, but things had changed. As the insidious pattern of tenancy spread across the land, cotton prices plummeted and a once prosperous Hancock County watched as her farms shrank in size and grew leaner. In 1890, of the county's almost 2000 farms, over 1000 were smaller than 50 acres. In the prewar era, only 13 of the county's farms had been smaller than 50 acres.

Just as Hancock County's agricultural woes stand to exemplify post-war conditions in Georgia, the circus that was county politics in the Reconstruction era is equally typical. The short story of how black Georgians gained the franchise, were elected to office, ousted, and disenfranchised was played out in and around Sparta in a petty pageant of beatings, mob confrontations, and miscarriages of justice. At the center of all of this was a white jury system, white control

Plate 8.7: The depot at Sparta. In 1881, when this depot was new, cotton production in Hancock County was again soaring. (Photo: Wilber W. Caldwell.)

of the polls and white manipulation of a state law requiring the payment of back taxes in order to receive a ballot. All of this unfolded against a backdrop of violence and intimidation punctuated by unpunished murders. Three separate times Federal troops were called to Hancock County.

By the end of 1870, Sparta had her railroad, and firm control of political affairs again rested with white men. Plans for a new courthouse would soon be on everyone's lips. But the future held nothing but hard times for Hancock County. The county's only economic progress would come in support of agriculture: a slaughter house, a tannery, grist mills, a creamery, cannery and this graceful depot, which is nearly identical to one built in 1881 at nearby Warrenton. Here we find the distinctive signature roofline of the Georgia Railroad: the gentle curving flare of the roof's transition to eaves, and the broken base of the pediment. These architectural details are unique to the depots of the Georgia Railroad. Other fine examples are standing today at Thomson, Crawfordville, Covington and Conyers.

WARREN COUNTY: WARRENTON

Plate 8.8: The Warren County Courthouse, built in 1909-1910. Walter Chamberlain, architect.

Warren County built her first frame courthouse in 1798. The building burned in 1853 and was replaced by a fine two-story brick structure typical of so many of Georgia's antebellum vernacular court buildings. The 1853 courthouse burned in 1909 and was replaced by the present building designed by Walter Chamberlain. It is tempting to assert that this courthouse reflected the high hopes propelled by the rails of the Savannah and Northwestern Railroad, which had consolidated the rails of the older Brinson Railroad and was pressing westward out of Savannah through Burke and Jenkins Counties to eventually join the Georgia Railroad at Warrenton. This, however, was not the case. Although the connection between Savannah and Atlanta was finally made by the Savannah and Atlanta Railroad in 1916, and a simple wooden depot built at East Warrenton in 1917, any New South fires that may have once burned in Warren

Plate 8.8: The Warren County Courthouse straddles the line between the fantasy courthouses of the nineteenth century and those of the twentieth century that would reflect the architecture of an increasingly distant government. Photo: Wilber W. Caldwell.)

County were long since quenched before 1910. The truth of the matter is that Warrenton reluctantly built a new courthouse only because she needed one.

Like so many towns along the antebellum rails of the Georgia Railroad, Warrenton clung to cautious and practical philosophies. Originally conceived as the first leg of a line to Eatonton, a branch to Warrenton was completed in 1839, but efforts to continue the Eatonton line were abandoned as plans to connect with the state's proposed Western and Atlantic Railroad at Atlanta became the Georgia Railroad's central focus. Although this three and a half mile

[8]   Forrest Shivers, *The Land Between, A History of Hancock County, Georgia to 1940* (1940; reprint, Spartanburg GA: Reprint Company, 1990) 121.

[9]   *The Sparta Times and Planter*, May 31, 1879 in Shivers, *The Land Between, A History of Hancock County, Georgia to 1940*, 240.

mule-powered spur undoubtedly improved the town's prospects, it also brought with it the appellation of "Mule Town," an ignominy that did nothing to inspire the wild dreams of prosperity, which so commonly accompanied rail construction. The harsh realities of Reconstruction and the difficult times that followed entrenched the town in skepticism for New South dogma and reinforced a nostalgic agrarianism, which enriched the political soil in this garden of late century Populism.

The two decades before the war were punctuated by numerous proposals to connect the Georgia Railroad with the Central. As these roads jealously maneuvered for position, Warrenton's spur line was often viewed as the beginning of such a link, but these schemes begot more disappointment than zeal in Warrenton. In 1854, the Central completed its Savannah and Augusta line well to the east of Warrenton. In 1861, the Georgia Railroad, backed an effort by the citizens of Warrenton, Sparta and Milledgeville, began construction on the newly chartered Milledgeville Railroad from Warrenton to Milledgeville. This road contemplated a connection with a line then being graded from Macon to Milledgeville. With track completed as only far as Mayfield, construction was halted in 1864.[10] After the war, propelled by enthusiasm flowing from Macon, the line was finally completed from Warrenton via Milledgeville to Macon in 1870. Like so many Reconstruction lines, the Macon and Augusta Railroad immediately fell on hard times, and failed. The Georgia Railroad, which had guaranteed the new road bonds from the beginning, acquired the bankrupt line in 1880, and in 1881 built a fine brick depot at Warrenton which was almost identical to the one at Sparta. It was demolished sometime in the mid-twentieth century.

All of this sporadic and uncertain railroad progress did little to make Warrenton a hotbed of New

South zeal. As we have seen, towns located along antebellum rails were slow to grasp at the golden ring of postbellum promise. In 1909, immediately following the destruction of the old 1853 courthouse, the grand jury recommended that the county retain Augusta architect, Lewis F. Goodrich[11] well known in the area for his 1902 Taliaferro County Courthouse at nearby Crawfordville, his 1905 Athens City Hall and for his 1905 Jenkins County Courthouse at Millen. But the county commissioners met serious resistance to any reasonable budget for the new courthouse. It appears that the choice of Walter Chamberlain and Company was driven by conservative financial considerations and not by any artistic or architecturally competitive agenda. The architectural selection process was hampered by strong opposition to every design. Every financing scheme the county commissioners put forward precipitated protests. The Chamberlain plan was finally selected from the "many plans examined,"[12] but a lawsuit followed seeking the rejection of the design. Matters were not settled until the Georgia Supreme Court the ruled on issue.

Walter Chamberlain, with offices in Knoxville and later in Birmingham, designed courthouses all over the South in the two decades surrounding the turn of the century. Six of these were in Georgia (see Appendix C). Most of his early work represents crude brick interpretations of the Romanesque Revival, designed for limited budgets and mindful of the limited skills of local masons. Examples are the 1894 Macon County Courthouse at Oglethorpe, and the 1898 Berrien County Courthouse at Nashville, Georgia. In addition to these rudimentary and somewhat bizarre brick forms, Chamberlain was a pioneer in the use of concrete block construction as evidenced in his 1906 Franklin County Courthouse at Carnesville and his Jeff Davis County Courthouse at Hazlehurst built in that same year. Here at Warrenton, there was considerable use of concrete construction to form thick walls for the fireproofing of the ground floor. Additionally, the decorative quoining is of concrete block.

Beaux-Arts influence is clear here in the low dome, the irregularly spaced columns and the three-dimensional forward trust of the corner bays.

[10] U. B. Phillips contends that the Macon and Augusta was actually completed "after a fashion for most of it length" during the war. U. B. Phillips, *History of Transportation in the Eastern Cotton Belt to 1860* (1908; reprint, New York: McMillan, 1913) 291.

[11] *The Warrenton Clipper*, April 9, 1909.

[12] *The Warrenton Clipper*, July 9, 1909

Doubtless many in Warren County would look at Walter Chamberlain's stout columns and dream of the columns of a bygone era. But the overall effect is sadly as far from the purity of the Greek Revival as it is from the Baroque facades of the great fairs at Chicago, St. Louis and San Francisco that propelled Beaux-Arts Classicism in the North. Perhaps the best thing that can be said about this building is that it is transitional. One of several rather ordinary court buildings erected in Georgia by the Falls City Construction Company of Louisville, Kentucky, the Warren County Courthouse straddles the line between Georgia's fantasy courthouses of the nineteenth century, which were so often reflections of the railroad's tempting but hollow promises, and the courthouses of the twentieth century, which would soon to reflect the cold institutional architecture of an increasingly distant government.

SOME LAST THOUGHTS ON THE MACON AND AUGUSTA RAILROAD

Like many of Georgia's Reconstruction railroads, the Macon and Augusta was the culmination of a series of events that transpired well before the Civil War. In the early 1840s when the Central of Georgia was building through the Pine Barrens, across the Eastern Cotton Belt and into Macon and the Georgia railroad was following the Fall Line from Augusta to Atlanta, there was talk of connecting the two pioneer roads. Both lines were cautious, not wanting to bestow on its competitor any advantage that might flow from the connection. Nonetheless, the wealth of Burke, Washington, Jefferson and Hancock Counties, which lay between the two roads, could hardly be overlooked. In 1850, these four counties represented 10% of Georgia's cotton harvest. This number was still 8% in 1860 despite cotton's continued progress in western Georgia. Not only cotton but culture flowed from places like the old state capitol at Louisville, and from cotton rich centers like Sandersville and Sparta. But when the Central finally took the plunge, she chose to connect directly to Augusta via Waynesboro so as not to pass any freight over the Georgia Railroad. Conversely the Georgia Railroad had sought connec-

tion from a more central point on the line in numerous proposals like the ill-fated Sparta Plank Road and Turnpike Company of the 1850s.

The war put an end to all these schemes, but after the fighting ceased, Macon was quick to pick up the pieces of the Georgia Railroad's Warrenton to Milledgeville plan, which at war's end ran to Mayfield in Warren County. Continuing grading begun toward Milledgeville before the war, Macon completed the Macon and Augusta Railroad in 1870. It was the Georgia Railroad's answer to the Central's Savannah to Augusta line, and it was Macon's answer to the Central's outrageous rates immediately following the Civil War. The road represented myriad interests, convoluted jealousies and gripes, but had little firm basis in economic reality. The success of antebellum railroads in Georgia had been so complete, that it must have appeared to Reconstruction promoters that any route would prosper. This cavalier attitude, combined with the state's indiscriminate endorsement of railroad bond issues resulted in the construction of a handful of Reconstruction railroads, most of which could not be reliably supported by the areas they served.

The Macon and Augusta was thus typical of the era. It failed to serve Macon, for in 1870 the Georgia Railroad pledged to match the Central's per mile freight rates thus negating any competitive position the Macon and Augusta might have offered. It failed to serve Augusta or Charleston, for the connection to Macon and to the cotton growing regions of Southwestern Georgia was not as direct as the Central's Macon to Savannah line. That it served Milledgeville, Sparta and Warrenton is sure, but in 1870 these towns like the rest of the Eastern Cotton Belt were just beginning an era of social upheaval and economic decline that would last for decades.

Thus, it is not surprising that Milledgeville and Warrenton were slow to reflect New South frenzy by building fantasy court buildings. On the other hand, Sparta would fall victim to the railroad's allure. Having vainly sought a rail connection throughout the antebellum period, Sparta would rejoice at the arrival of the Macon and Augusta, commissioning A. C. Bruce to create one of Georgia's most compelling court buildings.

Still, it was Macon who set the tone for the post-war period by building a fabulous Second Empire monument of a courthouse in 1872. Certainly the completion of the Macon and Augusta in 1870 fueled Macon's aspirations, which were already beginning to blossom nourished by the rich bounty flowing up the Southwestern Railroad and by her connection via Atlanta to the American heartland. In addition, the year 1870 would see the beginning of another new railroad in Macon, for in the same year the Macon and Augusta was completed, the first trains ran from Macon to Jesup on the Macon and Brunswick, another railroad whose construction had been interrupted by the war.

•

9 | The Macon and Brunswick Railroad

MACON TO BRUNSWICK

BLECKLEY COUNTY: COCHRAN

By the time Bleckley County was formed in 1912, the age of flamboyant courthouse building was over in Georgia. As if to mark the beginning of the new era, Bleckley County employed J. J. Baldwin of the architectural firm Gayre and Baldwin to design her new courthouse. This is perhaps the best of J. J. Baldwin's eight Georgia courthouses. Although a pleasant and serviceable brick building with the obligatory white columns and stone trim, it lacks exuberance and flair. Baldwin's designs typify a new breed of Southern court buildings expressing settled emotions: more resignation than hope, more complacency than lust for movement toward either the past or the future. Similar architectural restraint all across the state suggests that by 1910 most rural areas were beginning to recognize the myth of the New South for the lie that it was.

At the beginning of Reconstruction, a pine forest occupied the site of the present town of Cochran. Originally called Dykesboro, the town could date its first breath from the arrival of the Macon and Brunswick Railroad. Later named for the road's president, A. E. Cochran of Brunswick, Station No. 15 was the site of the junction of a branch line to Hawkinsville, which was completed to the Ocmulgee River in 1866. A bridge was built in 1868. By 1870, the Macon and Brunswick was complete from Macon to Jesup. Two years later, just as the new railroad reached Brunswick, the company went bankrupt. Despite its lack of financial success, the Macon and Brunswick had created towns in a theretofore nearly unoccupied part of Georgia. In 1880, less than ten years after the first train from Macon entered Brunswick, the East Tennessee, Virginia and Georgia Railroad bought the failed road. In that same year Sholes's *Gazetteer of Georgia* described Cochran as a town of over 1000 residents.

The Macon and Brunswick established the pattern for railroads in the Reconstruction era. Like so many of the roads completed in this period, it had its beginnings in the 1850s. Chartered in 1856, the proposed line began on the strength of a $200,000 subscription from the city of Macon and the promise of a free right-of-way through that city. Unlike many

The Macon and Brunswick Railroad

Bibb County: Macon (see chapters 3 & 8) • Bleckley County: Cochran
Pulaski County: Hawkinsville • Dodge County: Eastman • Telfair County: McRae
Jeff Davis County: Hazlehurst Appling County: Baxley • Wayne County: Jesup (see chapter 7)
Glynn County: Brunswick • Some Last Thoughts on the Macon and Brunswick Railroad

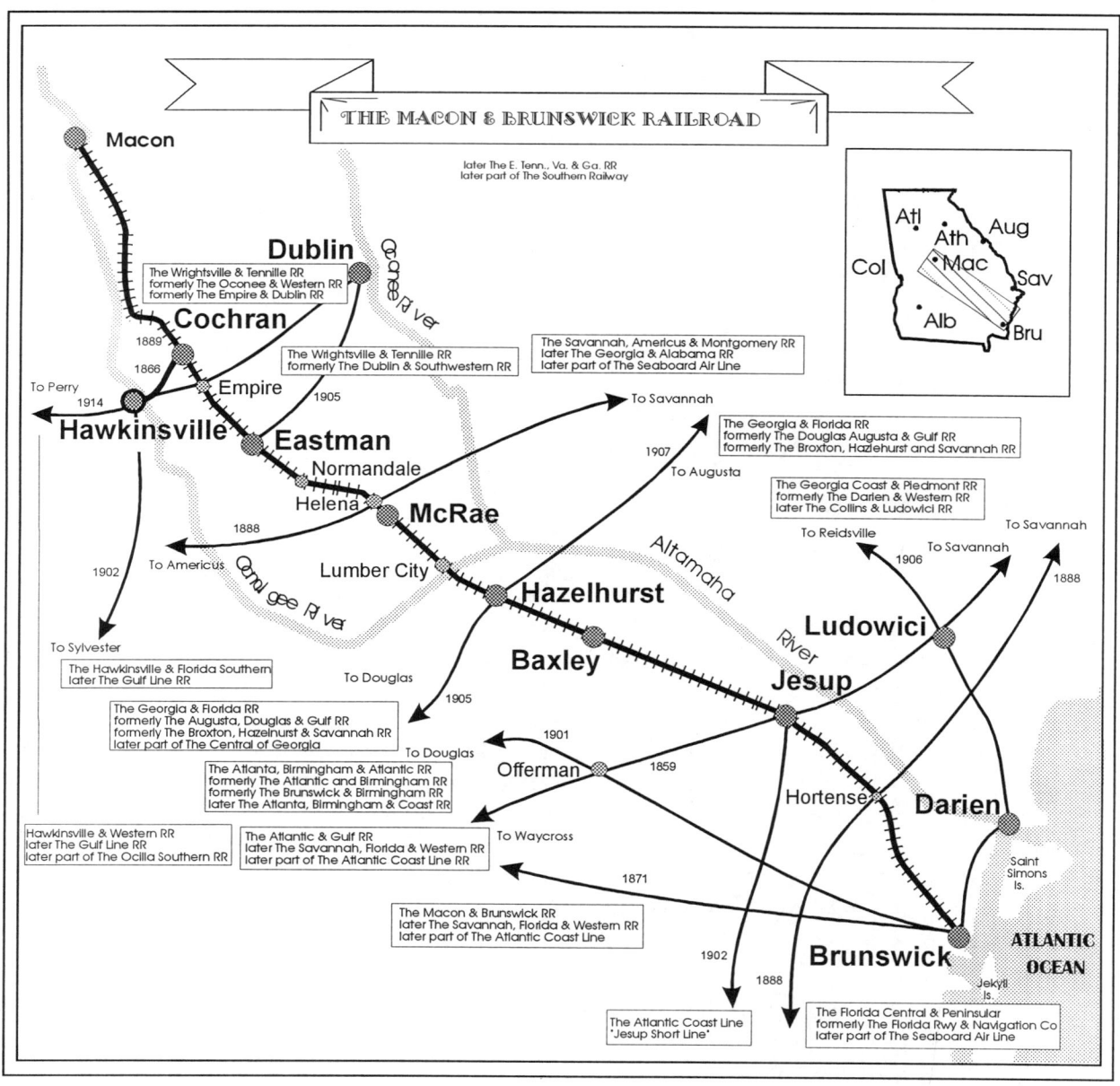

antebellum roads, the Macon and Brunswick would realize little financial support from the towns along her proposed route, owing to the fact that, for all practical purposes, there were no towns along her proposed route. Nonetheless, by the time the first shells fell on Fort Sumter, grading was underway south of Macon and trains ran the first twenty-five miles of the line.[1] About fifteen more miles of track were completed during the war. Immediately following the war, there was agitation in both Macon and Brunswick to resume construction of the line, and a bill was put before the State legislature proposing state credit to back the new road. State aid was granted based on an odd combination of appeals including the dubious argument that the area to be served by the proposed road was too poor to fund the undertaking. At the time there was apparently no concern that this might also mean that the area served by the road would be too poor to support it's operation.

Just as the Macon and Brunswick was among the first railroads in Georgia to receive the state's endorsement of its bonded debt, it was among the first in the state to employ leased convict labor. In 1866, with the state penitentiary at Milledgeville still smoldering from Union incendiaries, state prisoners had been "farmed out" to the highest bidder. In 1868, the state had entered into a contract with Grant, Alexander and Company to "obtain from 100 to 500 convicts at $10 each per annum for work on the Macon and Brunswick Railroad. With its roots in the Reconstruction era, the convict lease system remained a bastion of petty fraud, unpardonable cruelty and unspeakable human suffering for over four decades."[2] This horror would continue in Georgia until 1908. Leased convicts were also used in mining, agriculture, brick making and other labor-intensive endeavors, but it was the railroads that proved the most ravenous consumer of this hideously abused source of cheap labor.

Despite state endorsed bonds to finance the new line and an ample supply of state convict labor to build it, the Macon and Brunswick quickly failed, leaving the state to buy the bankrupt railroad for $1,000,000 in order to protect its $2,500,000 in guarantees.[3] This was the first of many such failures.

Nonetheless, the great piney wilderness south of Macon was opened up, and towns like Cochran blossomed amidst the ruthless exploitation of Georgia's virgin pine forests. It was the beginning of a thoughtless harvest, which the Macon and Brunswick and scores of similar railroads made possible.

PULASKI COUNTY: HAWKINSVILLE

Plate 9.1: The Pulaski County Courthouse, built in 1874. Remodeled in 1897. Andrew J. Bryan remodeling architect.[4]

Beneath the classical raiment of A. J. Bryan's 1897 remodeling, the Pulaski County Courthouse is a rare treasure. To find it, we need only to mentally remove Bryan's stylish turn-of-the-century decoration; peel away the great lantern, the neoclassical portico with its fluted white columns and do away with clumsy attachments like the Palladian pediment over the entrance, and the false balustrades beneath the upper story windows. This mental exercise is perhaps easier

Plate 9.1: In his 1897 remodeling of the Pulaski County Courthouse, Andrew J. Bryan was able to create a modern symbol without doing unconscionable damage to a revered icon of the past. (Photo: Wilber W. Caldwell.)

[1] Mrs. Wallace Leigh Harris, ed., *History of Pulaski and Bleckley Counties* (Macon GA: Daughters of the American Revolution, Georgia State Society, Hawkinsville Chapter, 1957) 276.

[2] Judson Clements Ward, Jr., *Georgia Under the Bourbon Democrats, 1872-1890* (Chapel Hill: University of North Carolina, 1947) 279-80.

[3] Peter S. McGuire, "The Railroads of Georgia, 1860-1880," *The Georgia Historical Quarterly* 16/3 (Savannah 1932): 200-1.

	HAWKINSVILLE RAILROADS CHARTERED BUT NEVER BUILT
Table 9.1	The Americus and Hawkinsville, 1870
	The Fort Valley and Hawkinsville, 1870
	The Hawkinsville and Eufaula, 1871
	The Atlantic, Fort Valley and Memphis Railroad, 1871.
	The Augusta and Hawkinsville, 1874
	The Atlanta and Hawkinsville Railroad, 1886 (built from Atlanta to Fort Valley as the Atlanta and Florida Railroad)
	The Hawkinsville and Dublin Railroad, 1887
	The Hawkinsville, Americus and Eastman Railroad, 1988

to perform on the side elevations where the adornments of 1897 are fewer and more easily distinguishable for what they are: the overlaid trappings of a later age. If we then mentally replace Bryan's elegant modillion course with the paired brackets of the earlier era and add a cupola similar to the one on, say, the 1856 Dougherty County Courthouse at Albany, then we have before us one of the state's only standing examples of the old brick vernacular hipped roofed courthouse that graced scores of Southern squares before the railroads sparked the fires of hope that led to the fantastic monuments of the closing decades of the last century. It is a sad parenthesis to our story that so few of the grand ladies of mid-century were spared in the frenzy of the late nineteenth century building zeal.

Of his nine courthouses in Georgia, this is one of Andrew Bryan's finest efforts. Here, despite the superficiality of his classical ornament, he was able to create a modern symbol to voice Hawkinsville's turn-of-the-century aspirations for the future, without doing unconscionable damage to the old symbol of her revered past. In 1874, the newly completed Pulaski County Courthouse had numbered among Georgia's finest public buildings. That the people of Pulaski County erected such a monument in the teeth of a national depression that had only served to worsen the

economic, political and social upheavals of Reconstruction in Georgia is a convincing testament to the railroad's power to evoke hope and pride even in the worst of times.

Hawkinsville's past was a potent mixture of frontier moxie and commercial enterprise. Pulaski County was created in 1808 after the Creek Indians ceded the land between the Oconee and the Ocmulgee Rivers to the state of Georgia. By 1809, ten counties had been carved out of this vast tract, and Hartford, the new county town of Pulaski County, was one of two county seats laid out right on Ocmulgee River.[5] Truly a frontier town, Hartford's early history is that of the interaction of a new land, a great river and a vast wilderness. With the 1821 Treaty of Indian Springs, the huge tract between the Ocmulgee and the Flint was ceded to the state, and Hartford was suddenly transformed from frontier outpost to center of transportation. By 1830, Hartford was on the decline, eclipsed by progress in the newer settlement of Hawkinsville on the west bank of the river. In 1831, the Bank of Darien opened a branch at Hawkinsville, and in 1837 the new town captured the county seat from a disappearing Hartford. The old wooden courthouse, originally erected at Hartford, was moved to Hawkinsville in that year. The decades preceding the American Civil War brought prosperity. Cotton from the fertile new lands west of the Ocmulgee flowed down that river from Hawkinsville. In 1849, George White described the town as having six stores, two churches, two hotels and a population of 175.

The Macon and Brunswick Railroad completed its spur to Hartford in 1866, bridged the Ocmulgee and built a depot at Hawkinsville in 1868. With this connection, Reconstruction railroad speculation flourished in Hawkinsville (see Table 9.1). But none of these schemes bore fruit, and even though the 1874 courthouse at Hawkinsville rose too early to reflect the architecture of the New South myth, it was nonetheless a product, at least in part, of the railroads' seductive promises of progress.

By 1890 Hawkinsville had seen her great lumber mills come and go, and the town was becoming an important cotton market. These changes brought a new wave of railroad speculation. In 1889, the Empire

---

[4] *The Hawkinsville Dispatch and News*, July 1, 1897.

[5] The other was Jacksonville, which was the county seat of Telfair County from 1810 to 1871.

[6] *The Hawkinsville Dispatch and News*, July 22, 1897.

and Dublin Railroad built from Dublin southward toward Hawkinsville, crossing the Macon and Brunswick, at the village of Empire. Three years later the road was extended to Hawkinsville as the Oconee and Western, which later became part of the Wrightsville and Tennille. In 1895, the Hawkinsville and Florida Southern began to lay track northward toward Hawkinsville from Worth, Georgia, on the main line of the Georgia Southern and Florida south of Cordele. Slow progress on this line did not dampen spirits in Hawkinsville, and county leaders commissioned Andrew J. Bryan to remodel the Pulaski County Courthouse in 1897. The building would wear the up-to-date attire of the railroad age well before the Hawkinsville and Florida Southern arrived in Hawkinsville in 1902.

Plate 9.2: The Southern Railway Depot at Hawkinsville, c.1900.

Shortly after the acceptance of A. J. Bryan's plans for the remodeling of the Pulaski County Courthouse, the Southern Railway announced plans to build a new depot at Hawkinsville.[6] With its low broad roof line, curving brackets and lattice-like fenestration this building is typical of the Southern's simple turn-of-the-century depot style, and in 1900 Hawkinsville was well on its way to becoming a railroad town.

In 1914, the last of Hawkinsville's railroads was completed. The Hawkinsville and Western built across Houston County to Perry where it connected with the Central's spur from Fort Valley. Thus, by 1914, four railroads radiated from Hawkinsville.

Today none remain. The Hawkinsville and Florida Southern became part of the Gulf Line

Railway and ceased operations in 1921. The Hawkinsville and Western was leased by the Ocilla Southern in 1917 and was abandoned some time after 1925. The Wrightsville and Tennille from Dublin to Hawkinsville was abandoned in 1941. The first to arrive would be the last to go, and the original spur of the old Macon and Brunswick was abandoned in 1995, leaving Hawkinsville without a railroad.

DODGE COUNTY: EASTMAN

Plate 9.3: The depot at Eastman, built in 1906.

Built only a year before E. C. Hosford's grand 1907 courthouse rose at Eastman, this depot marks the end of an era for Dodge County. The saga of the

Plate 9.3: This 1906 depot at Eastman marked the end of an era for Dodge County. (Photo: Wilber W. Caldwell.)

Plate 9.2: With its low broad roofline, curving brackets and lattice-like fenestration this passenger station at Hawkinsville is typical of the Southern's simple turn-of-the-century depot style. (Photo: Wilber W. Caldwell.)

three and a half decades before this building was erected is a compelling tale of a Reconstruction railroad and how it turned a vast and virtually uninhabited wilderness of virgin pine into the lumber empire of two notable Northern entrepreneurs, William E. Dodge and William Pitt Eastman. It is also a story that sheds considerable light upon so-called Carpetbaggers in the American South, a myth grown wildly beyond any semblance of reality.

William Pitt Eastman was born in Gilmanton, New Hampshire, in 1813, and by the time the Civil War began, he had amassed a sizable fortune in the woolen underwear business in New Jersey. In 1868, partly on the urgings of his friend George Hazlehurst, then president of the Macon and Brunswick Railroad, Eastman bought more than 300,000 acres of timberland in the northern reaches of the great pine forests that stretched south and east across central Georgia from the Fall Line to the sea. In 1869, Eastman and another New Englander, the great American merchant, industrialist, railroad baron and lumberman, William E. Dodge, established the Georgia Land and Lumber Company with a capitalization of over $500,000 and over 400,000 acres of virgin forest including large portions of Laurens, Telfair, Pulaski and Montgomery Counties. The company's holdings comprised much of the land between the Oconee and the Ocmulgee Rivers and extended southward to the confluence of these two streams where the Altamaha River begins.

So pleased was George Hazlehurst with Eastman's investments in Georgia that he named the place at the Macon and Brunswick's new Station #13, Eastman, in the New Englander's honor. William Eastman in turn quickly used the considerable influence of his financial

situation to induce the State Legislature to create a new County and name it after his well-known new business associate, William Dodge. In 1870, the Georgia Legislature created Dodge County and wrote to Dodge declaring that they were: "mindful...of the great interest taken by yourself and your friends in the commercial prosperity of the State of Georgia."[7]

In the early 1870s, the new village of Eastman gained a notable reputation as a winter resort for Northern tourists. But by 1880, the Georgia Land and Lumber Company had "transformed a bucolic former resort into a noisy timber colony."[8] As the fingers of tiny tram railroads spread throughout the region between the two great rivers, Dodge built two enormous lumber mills: one at Normandale, south of Eastman, and one on the Ocmulgee River at Wilcox Lake. Finished lumber was shipped down the Macon and Brunswick and logs were floated down the Ocmulgee and the Altamaha to Darien where they were nursed by steam tugs to the Dodge Lumber Company's great new mills on Saint Simon's Island.

Eastman and Dodge brought to Georgia enormous sums of that scarce commodity, which New South promoters would later term "Northern capital." But as their story unfolded, it became clear that, despite their capital investments in the area's future, Eastman and Dodge were far from unilaterally welcome in the county that bore Dodge's name. William Eastman's great land purchase and William Dodge's magnificent entrepreneurial empire of timber and rail were the target of one of the largest and most persistent legal actions in Georgia's history. In a series of cases that lasted from 1877 to 1923, Dodge and his heirs were continually in court defending title to their domain against hundreds of claimants. This period was punctuated by evictions, injunctions, intimidation and even a brutal murder. All attempts to discredit Dodge's title failed. As the battle raged, the people of Dodge County elected officials who opposed the man for whom the county was named, developed a thoroughly unhealthy opinion of the Federal justice system, and became further entrenched in their prejudices against Northern men of business.

The events surrounding these land trials give substance to the Carpetbagger myth. Although he was

[7] From a letter to William E. Dodge from the Georgia State Legislature, October 26, 1870 in Richard Lowitt, *Merchant Prince of the Nineteenth Century*, William E. Dodge (New York: Columbia University Press, 1954) 265.

[8] Mark V. Wetherington, *The New South Comes to Wiregrass Georgia* (Knoxville TN: University of Tennessee Press, 1993) 246.

[9] W. J. Cash, *The Mind of the South* (1941; reprint, New York: Vintage Books, 1991) 109.

[10] Wetherington, *The New South Comes to Wiregrass Georgia*, 247.

[11] *The Times Journal* (Eastman GA), February 28, 1907.

committed to the exploitation of the resources of the area, Dodge had done nothing legally wrong. He was a citizen of an age of exploitation. Indeed he had been almost solely responsible for the county's growth, even its very existence. Yet he was opposed by legions of squatters, maverick turpentiners, "peckerwood" loggers and dirt farmers who had been on the land so long that they claimed it for their own. Perhaps a portion of this ragtag army had arguable legal claims to their land, while others blindly grasped at any scheme, no matter how fraudulent or ill-founded that would offer them prospects of retaining what they considered to be their own. All of this was stirred in a pot seasoned with greed, malice, regional hatred, Confederate zeal, violence and outright fraud. The resulting attitudes typify a widely held Southern opinion regarding economic Carpetbaggers. Like so many of the New South promoters' visions, the dream of Northern capital ran contrary to the convictions of many poor white Southerners. As the last decades of the nineteenth century flowed by, much of the old Southern ruling class sold out to the Yankees, leaving the poor whites alone to fight the economic and social changes that came with the new age.[9]

William Dodge died in 1883 leaving his vast empire in Georgia in hands of his son, Norman. The year before, the East Tennessee, Virginia and Georgia Railroad had acquired the failed Macon and Brunswick Railroad and built northward from Macon to Rome, thus linking South Georgia's vast timber lands to the timber hungry cities of the American interior. A new wave of lumbering began, and large mills popped up all across Dodge County. By the time 1906 rolled around, and this depot was built, all of the vast stands of virgin timber were gone from Dodge county, and the heirs of William Dodge had begun to sell his empire piecemeal. The great mill at Normandale had burned in 1892 never to be rebuilt. Other large mills at Empire and Eastman were dismantled and moved to Southwest Georgia. The age of exploitation was passing as farmers converted the denuded timberland into fields of cotton. As if to symbolize the end of "King Timber" and the rise of "King Cotton," Eastman erected a turn-of-the-century cotton mill on

the site of the enormous Eastman Lumber Company's mill, which had been abandoned in 1900.[10]

With timber's demise, Eastman became a cotton market. Meanwhile a new era of railroading arrived in Dodge County. The old Macon and Brunswick, which had become the East Tennessee, Virginia and Georgia in 1882, became the main line to Florida of the emerging railroad giant, the Southern Railway. Just to the south of Eastman, the Savannah, Americus and Montgomery traversed Dodge County in 1889. In 1891, consolidating the old Empire and Dublin Railroad, the Oconee and Western built north of Eastman across Dodge County on its way from Dublin to Hawkinsville. The Dublin and Southwestern ran its first train into Eastman in 1905, and the town finally had its second railroad.

Plate 9.4: The Dodge County Courthouse, built in 1907-1908. Ed C. Hosford, architect.

Norman Dodge died in 1907, the year this courthouse was begun. *The Times Journal* claimed that Dodge had once been the "the largest single land owner in Georgia."[11] But times were changing, the lumber barons were gone, cotton covered the county, Eastman's population was nearing 3000 and rail schemes abounded. The Georgia Eastern Railroad and the Waycross, Chattanooga and Jacksonville Railroad were proposed to run through Eastman, along with a new road to Fitzgerald. In this atmosphere of impend-

Plate 9.4: The Dodge County Courthouse is difficult to assess after the devastation of a 1939 fire that gutted the central section of the building. Gone are the grand lantern and the columns of the main entrance. Only the side entrances remain. (Photo: Wilber W. Caldwell.)

ing high times, Dodge County looked to Atlanta architect, Ed Hosford, to design a new courthouse to replace the county's original frame court building, which had been a gift back in 1874 from none other than William E. Dodge. The bond issue to fund the new courthouse was passed by the seemingly impossible margin of 2029 for, 65 against.[12] The grand jury congratulated all parties involved and concluded that: "(the prospects are bright for a still more glorious progress and improvement than we have ever before enjoyed."[13]

By early March of 1906, the Dodge County Commissioners had delegated a committee to inspect various new court buildings across the state. Not surprisingly the unanimous choice for a model was James Wingfield Golucke's stunning Coweta County Courthouse at Newnan, which had been completed only two years before.[14] On March 8, 1908, *The Eastman Times Journal* lists C. C. Hosford of Empire, Georgia, as a member of the building committee. Predictably on April 19, after "many of the leading architects of the state" submitted proposals, the committee announced the selection of C. C. Hosford's son, Ed C. Hosford of Atlanta as architect. Rumors circulated in Eastman that J. W. Golucke would supervise the project, but E. C. Hosford denied this, stating that the work would be his alone, and that he would move to Eastman to supervise the project.[15]

Ed C. Hosford did eventually move back to Eastman. He went on the design at least eight more court buildings (see Appendix C): two in Georgia—the 1909 Harris County Courthouse at Hamilton and the 1917 Wheeler County Courthouse at Alamo—two in Texas, and at least four in Florida including the 1909 Jefferson County Courthouse at Monticello, Florida, which was quite similar to his effort here at Eastman. Hosford was also the architect of an extensive remodeling of the Bulloch County Courthouse in 1914.

Although competent, Hosford's work never had Golucke's unique flair. Hosford borrowed from Golucke in fashioning a great horizontal mass with a central portico and flanking wings, but the results here in Eastman are ordinary at best. Today Hosford's courthouse at Eastman is difficult to assess, for in 1939 the building was completely gutted by a devastating fire which swept through the central section causing the grand lantern to collapse and destroying the porticos at the center of the structure. The building was rebuilt to function like the original, but gone are the great clock tower and the monumental columns of the main entranceways. Only the columned side porticos remain, serving today as the main entrance.

In 1906, like so many Georgia towns, Eastman saw itself on the edge of a new era of prosperity, but disappointment lay ahead. As Hosford's courthouse rose, cotton was proving a capricious provider, and the age of railroad building in Dodge County was over. After the arrival of the Dublin and Southwestern in 1905, none of the proposed new rail lines that had fueled the county's enthusiasm for a new courthouse would be built. The Southern Railway's prestigious mainline traffic to Florida would begin to forsake the old Macon and Brunswick and follow the rails of the former Georgia Southern and Florida down from Macon through Valdosta. By 1920, the scream of the crack "Kansas City Express" would no longer pierce the damp night air in Dodge County, and passengers departing Eastman would be at the mercy of the local train, the Southern's tediously unpredictable and dubiously named "Georgia Cracker."

TELFAIR COUNTY: MCRAE

Plate 9.5: The depot at Helena, built in 1899.

Only one mile from the courthouse at McRae, where the rails of the Savannah, Americus and Montgomery Railroad crossed the old Macon and Brunswick, this picturesque depot at Helena eloquently voiced a story of two towns and two railroads.

In 1869, under supervision of its chief engineer, William McRae, the Macon and Brunswick arrived at the farm of Daniel McRae (no relation) and established Station No. 11, which to no one's great surprise, became known as McRae. Telfair had been carved from Wilkinson County in 1810, and for over sixty years not much had transpired in that vast wilderness of pine. The county's first courthouse at Jacksonville, a log structure completed in 1812, was replaced by a frame court building in 1860. George White in his reliable 1849 *Statistic of Georgia* informs us that villages like Lumber City and Temperance were populated with "persons engaged in the lumber business" while he cites Jacksonville, the old trading town in the "Big Bend" of the Ocmulgee as the county's largest town, boasting four stores and a population of about 60. Only two years after the arrival of the Macon and Brunswick, the county seat of Telfair County was moved to McRae, and by 1879 the town's population had exploded to over 400 according to Sholes's' *Gazetteer of Georgia*. A frame courthouse was erected at McRae in 1872, and this was replaced by a simple brick building in 1888.

In that year, the Savannah, Americus and Montgomery Railroad was complete from Americus to Cordele and was headed straight for a crossing with the old Macon and Brunswick near McRae. It was clear to almost everyone that the crossing of these two railroads would create a place of considerable economic opportunity in Telfair County. Most assumed that McRae was the natural choice for such an intersection. But Americus railroad promoter, Samuel Hawkins, had closely allied his Savannah, Americus and Montgomery Railroad with his Americus Investment Company, an organization whose sole purpose was to exploit the rising value of land occasioned by the arrival of new rails in theretofore remote and undeveloped places. The wisdom of such an arrangement would soon be made abundantly clear in places like Cordele, Rochelle and Richland.

The exact sequence of events surrounding the bypassing of McRae and the creation of Helena is clouded by local legends, and sadly most of the Telfair County newspapers from the era are lost. Nonetheless, we can piece together a reasonable scenario. The county history recounts the usual myth, relating that the people of McRae "didn't want to bother with the noise and smoke of a second railroad."[16] This is highly unlikely. It is another example of the bad wine frequently encountered when the "sour grapes" of a bypassed town are aged. *The Hawkinsville News* of March 13, 1889, relates a substantially different story. Readers were informed that the residents of McRae, confident that their town was the new railroad's only

Plate 9.5: The 1899 depot at Helena told a story of two towns and two railroads. (Photo: Courtesy of Les R. Winn.)

logical crossing point, refused to invest the $10,000 requested by the S. A. M:

> The Americus Investment Company, which owns a majority of the stock of the S. A. M. road, did not propose to pay a premium on selfishness by building a road to a town which proposed to reap all of the benefits without paying anything in return." (It) "purchased two thousand acres about two miles south (this should be one mile northwest) of McRae paying an average of three dollars an acre for it....The S. A. M. will form its junction in the center on that tract.(The Investment Company will soon lay a portion of its tract out into town lots and place them on the market.[17]

All of this notwithstanding, it is quite possible that the S. A. M. and its real-estate arm never intended to pass through McRae in the first place. The new road sought a direct connection between Savannah and the cotton growing lands in southwest Georgia and Alabama. It cared little for established towns in the Pine Barrens, and probably considered the power of the railroad to create new towns an appealing side

[12] *The Times Journal* (Eastman GA), August 6, 1906.

[13] *The Times Journal* (Eastman GA), March 19, 1908.

[14] *The Times Journal* (Eastman GA), March 22, 1906.

[15] *The Times Journal* (Eastman GA), April 19, 1906.

[16] Kevin J. Cheek, in *The History of Telfair County, Georgia* (Dallas TX: Curtis Media, 1987) 10.

[17] *The Hawkinsville News*, March 13, 1889 in The History of Telfair County, Georgia, 52.

effect of their endeavor. Thus in 1889, one mile north of McRae in the middle of an empty forest, the Savannah, Americus and Montgomery crossed the old Macon and Brunswick, which by then had been acquired by the East Tennessee, Virginia and Georgia. The place was called Helena after the wife of Henry Clay Bagley, the president of the Americus Investment Company. Ten years later, this fine depot replaced the original shed, and before another decade went by, the upstart Helena made a bid to steal the county seat away from McRae.

Plate 9.6: The Telfair County Courthouse, built in 1906. Burned 1934. Alexander Blair III, architect.

Like so many court buildings of the period, the 1906 Telfair County Courthouse rose as a direct consequence of the arrival of a crossing rail line. But here the circumstances were a little different. Only a few years after laying out the town of Helena, the Americus Investment Company, the S. A. M. and Samuel Hawkins's entire empire came crashing down in the economic uncertainty which lead to the Panic of 1893. Out of the depression that followed, the S. A. M. was reorganized as the Georgia and Alabama Railroad, which became part of the Seaboard Air Line Railway just after the turn of the century. By this time,

Plate 9.6: With his 1906 Telfair County Courthouse, Macon's Alexander Blair achieved a strange monumentality of mismatched elements and bizarre proportions.

the Americus Investment Company, which owned much of Helena, was in the hands of "a Northern syndicate" according to sources in neighboring McRae, where the citizens had quickly developed an unhealthy dislike for the upstart community that had stolen away the prized railroad junction.

By 1900, grand juries in Telfair were recommending the construction of a new courthouse to celebrate the county's progress. By 1905, an outright battle was in progress over whether the new courthouse should be in McRae or a mile away in Helena. Sensing the rising competition from Helena, political forces in McRae sought to "railroad" the matter, demolishing the old court building and quietly hiring Macon's Alexander Blair to design and supervise the construction of a new building on the old site. The citizens of Helena were quick to secure an injunction, balking at the $40,000 price tag and seeking to bring the matter of location to a countywide vote. Leaders in McRae accused Helena of "pandering to petty jealousies against the town of McRae"[18] The conservative rural vote sided with McRae, and Alexander Blair's monument was erected in McRae in 1906.

Alexander Blair III was the son of an English-born Macon architect of the same name. Before his death in 1894, Alexander Blair II had been the preeminent architect in Macon, designing numerous homes, and commercial blocks as well as Macon's notable Academy of Music. His son had taken over the practice, continuing his father's work in Macon and rising to design eight courthouses in Georgia between 1902 and 1912 (see Appendix C). His first, the 1902 Decatur County Courthouse at Bainbridge, was among his finest. Certainly it must have been a significant credential in gaining the commission here in Telfair County. Although the two buildings are quite different, there is an element of similarity. Both designs incorporate rather formal Renaissance ornament. Particularly notable is the use of heavy balustrades and so-called "Palladian" fenestration. Here in McRae, the effect is particularly jarring against the backdrop of what fundamentally appears to be the familiar vernacular brick courthouse form with its hipped roof and simple two-story rectangular mass. A vastly over-sized lantern created a strange monumentality of mismatched elements and bizarre proportion. It is likely that Andrew J. Bryan's 1897 remodeling of the old Pulaski County Courthouse at neighboring Hawkinsville had influence here. In Hawkinsville, Bryan had done in remodeling what Blair attempted from scratch in McRae: adorn a fundamentally vernacular form with uncomfortably formal and slightly oversized Renaissance trappings.

Whatever the citizens of McRae thought of Alexander's Blair's artistry, they were doubtless pleased with their situation in 1906. Blair's courthouse was proof that the threat from Helena had been repulsed. Despite her rail crossing, Helena would never be the place McRae was. The truth of the matter was that she was too close to McRae to develop an identity of her own. Still the people of McRae were so wary of the power of Helena's railroads that they built a rail line of their own. Sometime around the turn of the century, the town of McRae built the McRae Terminal Railroad. Less than one mile long, the road connected the north side of McRae with the Seaboard Air Line near Helena.

JEFF DAVIS COUNTY: HAZLEHURST

Plate 9.7: The Jeff Davis County Courthouse, built in 1906-1907. W. Chamberlain, architect.

Almost forty years before Jeff Davis County was created and this solid courthouse built, two crews began work on the Macon and Brunswick Railroad. Employing convict labor leased form the state, one group worked southward from Macon and one built northward from Jesup. The line was completed in 1870 when the rails met at Station #8-1/2, which was fittingly named Hazlehurst, for George Hazlehurst, who had replaced A. E. Cochran as the road's president in 1865. Originally a small settlement of turpentiners and lumbermen, the place today called Hazlehurst had been first called Handtown.

Like most places in the Pine Barrens where timber was king, there appeared in Hazlehurst along side the lumber business, considerable trading in naval stores. Naval stores comprise all of the products derived from pine gum, notably turpentine, rosin, and

pine tar used in the construction and maintenance of wooden ships. To be sure timbermen were a rough and ready lot, but turpentiners were even rougher. The collection and processing of naval stores centered on hundreds of "camps," which were the subject of legendary tales of hard work and harder men. Early oral histories of Hazlehurst describe the place as "wild and rowdy" with "plenty of whisky fighting among the citizens."[19] By 1880, when the town's population was still under 250, there were said to have been over twenty turpentine stills in what is today Jeff Davis County. By 1900, the production of naval stores was a $20 million industry in the United States, and of the nation's 1503 stills, 524 of them were in Georgia. Certainly many of these were in the area around Hazlehurst. Nonetheless by 1900, the town was loosing its rough edge, had tripled its 1880 population and was looking for its second railroad.

At the turn of the century, a glance at the railroad map of Georgia would have revealed a broken line created by several small independent railroads beginning in Augusta, passing through Hazlehurst and pointing

Plate 9.7: The 1906 Jeff Davis County Courthouse, remodeled in 1995. (Photo: Wilber W. Caldwell)

[18] *The Telfair Enterprise* (nd).

[19] A. D. Findley in *Jeff Davis County Ledger*, January 25, 1973.

toward Valdosta and beyond to Florida. The combination of these short lines with strategically placed new track would become the Georgia and Florida Railway, which would connect Augusta with Madison, Florida, via Hazlehurst. It was a jigsaw puzzle created by the ousted ex-president of the Seaboard Air Line Railway, John Skelton Williams. Williams sought to piece together parts of the Augusta Southern, the Augusta and Florida, the old Midville, Swainsboro and Red Bluff, the Millen Southwestern, and the Valdosta Southern Railroads. The perfecting link in what was to become the Georgia and Florida Railway was the Douglas, Augusta and Gulf, and part of that link was the Broxton, Hazlehurst and Savannah Railroad, which had completed track to Hazlehurst in 1900. Here was the spark that helped give life to Jeff Davis County, one of eight new counties created in Georgia in 1905.[20] Thus, at Hazlehurst, the crossing of steel rails would inspire yet another Georgia courthouse.

Originally promoted as Cromartie County, Jeff Davis County, like the seven other new counties created in 1905, was largely the result of the maturation of the seeds of railroad power that had been planted in earlier decades. The rising rail centers of Tifton, Cordele, and Toccoa were among the new crop of county seats created in that year. Although Hazlehurst, with her population above 1000 in 1905 had outgrown nearby Baxley, the county seat of old Appling County, she was no match for these robust railroad towns. She occupied an extremely remote part of the Wiregrass, and it is hard to compare the modest progress here with the meteoric success of places like of Cordele or Tifton. Nonetheless, a new railroad cultivated a late bloom of New South zeal and built a new courthouse at Hazlehurst. Still the building was not designed without that sense of cautious moderation appropriate to the relatively depressed conditions in Pine Barrens.

Walter Chamberlain's 1905 Jeff Davis County Courthouse is a testament to both the new county's modest zeal and this rather thrifty sense of restraint. As we have noted, Chamberlain's 1909 courthouse at Warrenton was no monument to New South fantasies. It was a simple building designed to address an immediate need and a limited budget. A brief comparison of building costs illustrates the point. Chamberlain's 1906 courthouse here at Hazlehurst cost $24,000. His court buildings at Warrenton (1910) and Nashville (1898) cost $25,000 and $17,000 respectively. Elsewhere in Georgia, where the myth was stronger and economic prospects more enticing, budgets were higher. J. W. Golucke's 1904 Coweta County Courthouse at Newnan cost $57,000, his 1905 Worth County Courthouse at Sylvester, $46,000, and Frank Milburn's 1905 Lowndes County Courthouse at Valdosta $60,000.[21] To place all of this in a national perspective, by the turn of the century, court buildings in small towns in the American Midwest had been commanding budgets in excess of $200,000 for over 25 years, and budgets of twice that size were common in the mid-sized cities of Ohio, Indiana and Illinois around 1900.[22]

The 1906 Jeff Davis County Courthouse was the first court building in Georgia to be constructed of concrete. Stucco covered concrete block was doubtless selected for its economy and exceptional fireproofing qualities, but there is an element of style involved here as well. In 1906, reinforced concrete was emerging as the preferred material of American industrial architecture. As the monolithic concrete creations that were the American factories and grain elevators of the day grew larger and more elaborate, they began to capture the imagination of a new generation of European architects who would lead the Western world into the modern architectural era. Walter Gropius would compare American industrial buildings to the "work of ancient Egyptians," and Le Corbusier himself would

[20] They were Jenkins, Crisp, Grady, Jeff Davis, Stephens, Tift, Toombs and Turner.

[21] Robert H. Jordan and J. Gregg Puster, *Courthouses in Georgia* (Norcross GA: The Harrison Company, 1984).

[22] Richard Pare, ed., *Courthouse, A Photographic Document* (New York: Horizon Press, 1978).

[23] *American Architect and Building News*, (June 14, 1911): 109: 214; *Engineering News*, (July 7, 1898): 60: 15; in Reyner Banham, *A Concrete Atlantis, United States Industrial Building and European Modern Architecture* (Cambridge: MIT Press 1986) 6.

[24] Banham, *A Concrete Atlantis, United States Industrial Building and European Modern Architecture*, 82.

announce that "American engineers overwhelm with their calculations our expiring architecture."[23] Concrete led the way to the appearance of industrial elements in non-industrial architecture. With the work of Auguste Perrett and others in France, and the American genius, Earnest L. Ransom, new techniques for the use of reinforced concrete would revolutionize building. According to Banham in his insightful study, *A Concrete Atlantis,* the construction of concrete framed factories by both Packard Motor Company in Detroit and Pierce Arrow in Buffalo made 1906 the critical year in the emergence of the new material.[24]

To be sure there was nothing revolutionary about Walter Chamberlain's work in Jeff Davis County in that year. Concrete had been widely used since before Roman times, and Portland cement had been around since the middle of the nineteenth century. By the turn of the century concrete block was widely used owing partly to Ransom's experiments with the material in California in the 1870s and 1880s. Still the use of concrete block, cast right at the building site, typified a distinctly American frugality and honesty in design, which was, in a crude way, ahead of its time.

Stylistically, Chamberlain's frugal efforts in Hazlehurst reflected the passing of the Romanesque Revival, which had been favored in his earlier court buildings at Dalton (1891), Oglethorpe (1894) and Nashville, Georgia, (1899). Although the choice of concrete block may have been primarily a budgetary consideration, it also provided a coarse approximation of the smooth stone ashlar of the buildings of the Renaissance Revival, which had been growing as a fundamental force in American public architecture since the early 1880s. Oddly, here in Hazlehurst, Chamberlain retained the same general plan he had used in his Romanesque buildings, a central rectangular mass with four corner pavilions, which in this case are octagonal, adding further to a picturesque effect. Predictably, the result falls short of monumental elegance. The simple louvered lantern would be a graceful addition but for its crude base and, although the broken based pediment above the central bay is elegant, the cornices and other decorative features appear undersized and lack detail. Nonetheless, with its recent remodeling completed in 1995, the old Jeff

Davis County Courthouse today sings a strangely charming song.

APPLING COUNTY: BAXLEY

Plate 9.8: The Appling County Courthouse, built 1907-1908. H. L. Lewman, architect.

Surprisingly, this was the only limestone courthouse built in Georgia during the period of our interest. In remote areas of the state, wooden court buildings were erected right up until 1900, and as we have seen, there were a few courthouses constructed of concrete block in the first decade of the new century. But, except for the granite hulk of J. W. Golucke's 1900 DeKalb County Courthouse at Decatur, all of the state's great court buildings of the New South era were built of brick. In the Wiregrass, the myth of a New South would appear late. It arrived with considerable thrust after the turn of the century, and it arrived on the promise of so many crossing rails. As timberlands played out, many logging railroads were converted to common carrier lines, and a wave of courthouse building followed.

Here in Baxley, a town that had sustained only modest growth in the closing decades of the nineteenth century, this promise must have seemed enticing indeed. In 1906, just as a fine wooden depot was going up in Baxley, the county's citizens approved the expenditure of over $50,000 for the construction of H. L. Lewman's neoclassical monument to their aspirations for the new century. Built at over twice the

Plate 9.8: Simple dignity. The 1907 Appling County Courthouse. (Photo: Wilber W. Caldwell.)

cost of the nearby 1906 Jeff Davis County Courthouse at Hazlehurst, this building reflects not only the hope for crossing rails but a considerable competition with Appling County's neighbors. Ironically, both of Baxley's neighbors, Jesup and Hazlehurst, would get their crossing rails, but despite the many promising schemes for new rails in the first decade of the twentieth century, no new railroads would cross the old Macon and Brunswick in Appling County.

According to Joan Niles Sears in *The First Hundred Years of Town Planing in Georgia,* the land which comprised the original Appling County, created in 1818, was at first "considered useless."[25] Until lumbermen began to clear the vast reaches of virgin pine, the area was only sparsely populated by struggling farmers and stockmen. In the late 1820s, the population of the sprawling new county was only about 1200, and it was not until 1828 that a location for the county seat was established. In that year, the now extinct town of Holmesville was laid out as the seat of government, and a log courthouse was erected. Twenty years later, the noted traveler George White noted in his 1849 *Statistics of Georgia* that the town had two stores and a population of 20. In 1870, the trains of the Macon and Brunswick began to traverse the county, and in 1872, the voters of Appling County voted 249 "for" and 121 "against" to move the county town to Station #7. Later called Baxley for Wilson Baxley, a local cattlemen and merchant, the new town centered on the depot, which county histories describe as an "old box car".[26] Most of the residents of Holmesville moved to Baxley in the first year of the town's existence. As timber and cattle interests began to develop, Baxley slowly grew reaching a population of 175 by 1879, 250 by 1886 and 350 by 1896 according to various Sholes's *Gazetteers of Georgia.* A simple frame courthouse was erected in 1874, and replaced by a larger frame building in 1876. A rudimentary brick courthouse was completed in 1886. As the years passed, the huge expanses of the county were slowly whittled away. Eleven counties would claim lands contained in the original Appling County.[27]

In the closing decades of the nineteenth centruy, there seemed little here in the deep piney woods to

inspire much in the way of New South zeal. Trees were cut, turpentine was distilled, and, as was the case in much of the Wiregrass, cattle were raised, free ranging among the pines. Although the thin cattle roaming the Pine Barrens were a far cry from their more robust cousins in the pastures of the Piedmont, they represented a sizable agricultural endeavor in the area. The "open range" of Georgia's piney woods remained free long after the great ranges of the American West were fenced in. According to Ruth T. Barrow's account, Appling County's fence laws were not enacted until 1953.[28] The maintenance of "open range" in the deep woods was common in many Wiregrass areas. Undergrowth was burned off each winter, identification branding was employed and roundups were held annually.

In the sandy soil of the Pine Barrens, as elsewhere in Georgia during the decades surrounding the turn of the century, dreams were not the products of agricultural prospects. They sprang from the modern promises of a new age of steel, and steam and electricity. To the residents of Baxley in 1905, the only symbol available to suggest the possibility of such an age was the impossibly straight line of the two shiny steel rails that disappeared out of sight into the pines at either end of the tiny town. Although her old Reconstruction railroad, the Macon and Brunswick, had brought progress, it was of a modest sort. The New South myth insisted that a modern crossing railroad would bring the gifts of the industrial era as it had in Waycross and Cordele. Thus, it is little wonder that Judge A. M. Crosby "decided" to erect a new courthouse at Baxley in 1905.[29] In that year the Waycross, Baxley and Vidalia Railroad had been chartered, and rumors were on the wind whispering that the great enterprise that was to become the Atlanta, Birmingham and Atlantic Railroad would pass right through Baxley, extending a line to Savannah.[30]

The debate regarding the wisdom of Judge Crosby's plan was short, and arguments for the new building were convincing. An editorial in the Baxley News Banner argued that the old courthouse was "injurious to those who frequented its halls from a sanitary point of view," and that the records were not safe in the old structure. In the end, most convincing of all was the argument that a new courthouse was needed because the old building had been pulled down in an orgy of premature support for Judge Crosby's proposal to erect a new building.[31] It mattered little, for when the matter of a bond issue for the new building came to a vote in September of 1907, the count was 1158 "for" and only 164 "against."

Despite its expensive limestone walls, the building, like all of those built in Georgia by Louisville's Falls City Construction Company, lacked the exuberance and force of the neoclassical court buildings of the first half of the decade. As we have noted, Walter Chamberlain's Warren County Courthouse at Warrenton was such a building, a transitional link between the flamboyant symbols of nineteenth century aspirations and the governmental architectural doldrums which were to come. Originally called M. T. Lewman and Company, the Fall City Construction Company was organized in 1907 by the three sons of M. T. Lewman who had drowned in Savannah while building the DeSoto Hotel.[32] The company built eight courthouses in Georgia. Three of these are quite similar in design to H. L. Lewman's 1907 court building here in Appling County. Although executed in brick, the 1905 Stephens County Courthouse at Toccoa, the 1909 Chatooga County Courthouse at Summerville and the 1910 Irwin County Courthouse at Ocilla all have front elevations, rooflines and lanterns that match Lewnam's design here in Baxley.

The first decade of the twentieth century witnessed the construction of 55 courthouses in Georgia. Some architects, like J. W. Golucke had developed their own personal versions of neoclassicism that were mindful of both flamboyant national trends and the simpler Old South classicism of Jefferson and of the Greek Revival. Others like Frank Milburn, who were more at home with Beaux-Arts Classicism, were able to fashion modern symbols that were still acceptable to conservative, even reactionary, Southern tastes. The third group of neoclassicists working in Georgia in this period were designers like H. L. Lewman and Walter Chamberlain, men who were denizens of the age they were seeking to introduce. Theirs was an ordinary, fundamentally commercial brand of architecture. They employed classical symbols, yet failed to

achieve emotional effects. Before 1910, classical architectural success in Georgia would only come from men who understood Southern predicaments as well as Southern prospects, only from men who sought to express this confused essence in their buildings.

All of this notwithstanding, there is a simple dignity in Lewman's Appling County Courthouse, and with its 1966 remodeling, the old building proudly occupies a prominent corner in the center of town. Of all of the wild hopes that brought this building to life in 1907, none were realized. The Waycross, Baxley and Vidalia Railroad was never built. Likewise, the Atlanta, Birmingham and Atlantic's branch line to Savannah died aborning. In 1910, with its population above 800, Baxley must have seemed to be riding a surge, but the first half of the new century held little for Appling County except hard times.

GLYNN COUNTY: BRUNSWICK

Plate 9.9: J. A. Wood's Oglethorpe Hotel, built in 1889.

Plate 9.10: The clubhouse of the Jekyll Island Club, built in 1889. Charles Alexander, architect.

Individual works of architecture are voices in the chorus of history. Each adds its own unique texture to richly orchestrated themes, and each, no matter how humble, sounds a note in an evolving symphony of complex polyphonic content. The voices are often geographically and temporally far flung, obstructing overview and making melodic analysis difficult. Occasionally, however, we encounter a location in which architectural and historical forces come togeth-

[25] Joan Niles Sears, *The First Hundred Years of Town Planning in Georgia* (Atlanta: Cherokee Press, 1979) 135.

[26] Ruth T. Barron, *Footprints in Appling County* (Baxley GA: The Appling County Board of Commissioners, 1981) 104.

[27] Present day Atkinson, Bacon, Brantley, Charlton, Clinch, Coffee, Echols, Jeff Davis, Pierce, Ware, and Wayne Counties all contain lands which were part of the original Appling County.

[28] Barron, *Footprints in Appling County*, 43

[29] *The Baxley News Banner*, June 6, 1907.

[30] *The Baxley News Banner*, April 19, 1907.

[31] *The Baxley News Banner*, August 23, 1907.

[32] *The Jackson Herald*, April 25, 1907.

Plate 9.9: The Oglethorpe Hotel and the Plant System's depot at Brunswick, built in 1889. Demolished in 1959. J. A. Wood, architect. (Photo: Courtesy of Les R. Winn.)

er to reveal the bizarre and ironic fantasia of human endeavor. In the decades surrounding the turn of the century, Brunswick, Georgia, was such a place.

In and around Brunswick, the architecture of the 1890s sings an odd and compelling song. Still standing today are the 1889 Jekyll Island Club House designed by Chicago architect, Charles Alexander and Brunswick's fine 1892 City Hall designed by Savannah architect, Alfred Eichberg. No longer standing, but looming large in Brunswick's history, are a fine depot built for the Plant System and the fabulous 300 room Oglethorpe Hotel, both completed in 1889 and demolished in 1959. Both were designed by J. A. Wood of New York, who would go on to create Plant's grand Tampa Bay Hotel in 1891.

When all of these buildings were new, the heirs of William E. Dodge were operating the third largest lumber mill in the world only a few miles away. Long ago destroyed and today almost forgotten, the colossal Dodge-Meigs Mill #2 stood at Gascoigne Bluff on St. Simon's Island on the banks of the McKay River across

the marsh from Brunswick. This most un-architectual structure loomed on the opposite side of the entrance to Brunswick Harbor from the architectural fairyland that was the Jekyll Island "Millionaire's Club," a playground for the first crop of American industrialists. The sprawling Dodge-Miegs mill was the perfect architectural symbol to represent the ruthless exploitation that built the Millionaire's Club. In a unique way, all of this was a product of the Macon and Brunswick Railroad.

In 1872, when the Macon and Brunswick and the Brunswick and Albany Railroads were newly completed and William Dodge was beginning to exploit the vast pine forests between the Oconee and the Ocmulgee Rivers, Brunswick had a population of about 2300. The port lay in the shadow of Savannah. Failure to follow through on the completion of a canal to connect the port with the Altamaha River estuary way back in the 1830s had proved nearly fatal for the city. Likewise, the Confederate government's confiscation of the rails of the city's only antebellum railroad, the Brunswick and Florida, which, in 1860, had been completed to Waresboro, connecting with the Atlantic and Gulf near present day Waycross, proved equally crippling. But the arrival of the Macon and Brunswick Railroad in 1872 meant new life. As the rest of the South struggled to pull itself from the quagmire of Reconstruction, Brunswick began to soar. The town's self-promotional efforts were notable. In 1869, Brunswick's mayor spoke to a railroad conference in Memphis advocating Brunswick as: "the only suitable point for the Atlantic terminus of the Southern Pacific Railroad and the great emigrant depot of the states of the South and the West."[33] *The Brunswick Advertiser and Appeal* published startling statistics in 1882, claiming that the town's population had increased from 2900 in 1880 to over 3800 by the end of 1881.[34] In 1878, 193 ships cleared the port. This number doubled by 1881.[35] Brunswick would never approach Savannah's maritime success, but her timber and naval stores export tonnage would be similar in the decades before the turn of the century. Both ports shipped about 160 million board feet in 1900, and Brunswick's naval stores trade was unsurpassed. But most vessels trading at Brunswick were small, and

[33]   James Houston, in a address to the members of the Southern Commercial Convention held in Memphis, Tennessee, on May 18, 1869, quoted in a leaflet entitled James Houston, *The Port of Brunswick, Georgia* (Brunswick GA: The Office of the Mayor of the City Brunswick, 1869).

[34]   *The Brunswick Advertiser and Appeal*, March 25, 1882.

[35]   *The Brunswick Advertiser and Appeal*, September 30, 1882.

[36]   Georgia Department of Agriculture, *Georgia Historical and Industrial* (Atlanta: 1901), 583 and 685.

[37]   *The Brunswick Advertiser and Appeal*, April 19, 1885.

in other areas Savannah dwarfed her southern neighbor. For example, Savannah shipped over 600,000 bales of cotton in 1900 compared to Brunswick's 25,000.[36] Nonetheless, there was good reason for optimism in Brunswick, railroad schemes abounded (see Table 9.2), and in 1885 *The Brunswick Advertiser and Appeal* published an article dripping with the sort of exuberant boosterism common in the era. The article concluded with the following historical insight: "Until a year or two ago there was not a single brick building in the city...and now fully 100 new buildings are in the course of construction...many of brick."[37]

Henry Plant's purchase of the old Brunswick and Albany Railroad and the East Tennessee, Virginia and Georgia Railroad's acquisition of the Macon and Brunswick represented increased power for the port of Brunswick, and the population continued to grow reaching almost 8500 by 1890. All of this was fueled by the Herculean efforts of the successors of William Dodge and others who led the ruthless campaign to strip Georgia's pine forests of virgin timber. Before the turn of the century, theirs would be a cruel and decisive victory, and the spoils of battle, dripping with the blood of pine gum, would flow down the rails to Brunswick and down the Altamaha to Darien or to Dodge's enormous Mill #2 on St. Simon's Island.

In 1890, there was more than just lumber passing over the rails of the old Macon and Brunswick Railroad heading for the sea at Brunswick. Oblivious to the piney spoils of exploitation that accompanied them on their journey, America's wealthiest families boarded their private rail cars each Spring to alight at Brunswick's fine new depot. From there it was only a short boat ride to Jekyll Island, where in 1886 a pleasure palace had been decreed by such latter-day khans as J. P. Morgan, Vincent Astor, Joseph Pulitzer and William Rockefeller. From 1886 to 1947, Jekyll Island was the site of the Jekyll Island Club, the most exclusive private club in America, whose few hundred members numbered among the country's social and economic elite. Across the sound from the log ripping saws of Dodge's fiery Mill #2, summer cottages designed by the nation's best architects were built on a low bluff overlooking the peaceful marsh.

Table 9.2

BRUNSWICK POSTBELLUM RAILROADS CHARTERED BUT NEVER BUILT
The Brunswick and Augusta Railroad, 1870
The Brunswick and Great Northern Railroad, 1874
The Brunswick and Flint River Railroad, 1881
The Brunswick and Atlanta Railroad, 1887
The Cordele, Waynesville and South Brunswick Railroad, 1888
The Brunswick, Athens and Northwestern Railroad, 1889
The Brunswick and Northern Railroad, 1890
The Brunswick and St. Simon's Railway 1890
The Altamaha and Northern Railroad, 1891
The Brunswick St. Mary's and Florida Railroad, 1891

This clubhouse was designed by Charles Alexander, a well-known Chicago architect. Later renovations and additions, along with the elegant "Sans Souci" apartment building, are the work of Charles Gifford of New York, who had made quite a name for himself designing resort hotels. His best known

Plate 9.10: The clubhouse of the Jekyll Island Club is a fairy tale silhouette framing a fragile maze of fantastic wooden detail and ornament. (Photo: Wilber W. Caldwell.)

accomplishments were the Bretton Woods Hotel in New Hampshire and Clifton Hall at Niagara Falls, New York. Working in a highly picturesque fantasy style which borrowed from contemporary Queen Anne, Stick Style, Shingle Style and Eastlake elements, Alexander and Gifford gave the Club House and its additions a kind of fairy tale brick silhouette. A fragile maze of fantastic wooden detail and imaginative ornament, the club house was surrounded by the cottages

Plate 9.11: Brunswick City Hall, built in 1892. Its details are a bit heavy for Queen Anne decorative tastes of the day, but they are consistent with the monumental Richardsonian entrance and befitting the importance of a public building. (Photo Wilber W. Caldwell.)

of members, designed by such turn-of-the-century architectural luminaries as Philadelphia's Furness, Evans and Company, New York's Carrere and Hastings (designers of Henry Flagler's exotic Ponce de Leon Hotel in St. Augustine) and the eminent American Classicist, John Russell Pope.

Across the Marshes of Glynn in Brunswick, New York architect, J. A. Wood, designer of the elegant 1885 Piney Woods Hotel at Thomasville, supervised the construction of his elegant Oglethorpe Hotel. Completed almost simultaneously with Alexander's Jekyll Island Club, the building would be the prototype for Wood's $2.5 million Tampa Bay Hotel commissioned the next year by Henry Plant, who must have been viewing the progress in Brunswick with considerable satisfaction.

Plate 9.11: Brunswick City Hall, built in 1892. Alfred Eichberg, architect.

As Brunswick entered the last decade of the nineteenth century, the stage was set for a new courthouse. Here, at least for the moment, the promise imported by postbellum rail had proved anything but mythical, and the New South appeared to be blossoming in Brunswick. In 1884, when the port's boom had just begun, a wooden court building had been erected. It appears that citizens of Glynn were well pleased with the building. The grand jury called the structure a "credit to this thriving city".[38] There is record of an early courthouse built sometime before 1829 when the town consisted of only about 30 structures, but we can only guess at this building's fate. Most likely it burned. Previous to the erection of the 1884 structure, court had been held in rented space.[39] There is considerable evidence that in 1897 county leaders in Brunswick waged a significant campaign to erect a new Glynn County Courthouse. A $60,000 bond issue for construction was proposed early in that year. Plans by Frank Milburn were accepted in April, but in August, construction plans were delayed. Apparently the bond issue failed to pass, and plans for a new courthouse were scrapped.[40]

Five years earlier, in 1892, Brunswick had built a city court building to symbolize her railroad-born prosperity and hope. The city's new City Hall

Building was designed by Atlanta architect Alfred Eichberg, who had moved to Savannah in 1886 and designed the Central of Georgia's fine headquarters building in 1888. Eichberg's City Hall at Brunswick housed the city courts, and the courtroom was also used by the county. With its massive Richardsonian granite entrance, it rivaled any county court building in Georgia in 1892. The style here is predominantly Queen Anne. It was a remarkably up-to-date building for Georgia in 1890. Most of the state's public architecture suffered from a decided stylistic lag in the post-war era, and most had its symbolism regionalized to reflect a rather inwardly turned Southern worldview. It is not surprising that Brunswick with her coast-wise connections to Northern ports and a constant stream of wealthy Yankees passing through on their way to Jekyll Island would select such a modern style.

The building once had an impossibly slender tower, which collapsed early in this century. Despite this loss, the structure still sings elegant songs today with its masonry lower story, flaring chimneys, scrolling brackets, octagonal turrets and arched transoms. Although the stone banding and rusticated fenestration are perhaps a bit heavy for Queen Anne decorative tastes of the day, which usually favored smaller, more detailed ornamentation, the massive effect is consistent with the monumental Richardsonian entrance and befits an important public building.

The City Hall was completed in 1892, but while Brunswick was rejoicing in her new symbol of success, 120 miles up the rails of the old Macon and Brunswick Railroad, the Dodge Lumber Company's great mill at Normandale burned. It was not rebuilt. The handwriting was on the wall. The great pine forests of central Georgia were being depleted.

Plate 9.12: The Glynn County Courthouse, built in 1907. Charles A. Gifford and E. S. Betts, architects.

By the middle of the first decade of the new century, the big loggers were gone from the lands adjacent to the old Macon and Brunswick, which by that time had become part of the mighty Southern Railway. The

Plate 9.12: The 1907 Glynn County Courthouse, moody and nostalgic, recalling a shadowy classical ruin, more emotionally poignant and appropriately Southern than any new structure. (Photo: Wilber W. Caldwell.)

period of Brunswick's decline was eminent, but few understood the dilemma. In 1906, when this courthouse was begun, most of the citizens of Glynn County placed their hopes in the Atlantic and Birmingham Railroad, later the Atlanta, Birmingham and Atlantic, which was in the process of connecting Brunswick with the iron-rich new city of Birmingham, Alabama. The new road built an enormous new depot in Brunswick in 1902-1903 and later purchased the Oglethorpe Hotel. It must have looked like a made-to-order formula for more New South success, and as the Atlanta, Birmingham and Atlantic extended its rails across Georgia, this courthouse was erected in a shady square off Brunswick's Glouchester Street. In 1907, it was unquestionably one of Georgia's finest court buildings of the new century.

Once again Brunswick had forsaken regional architectural symbols and selected a style popular in the American North. Appropriately the architect was New Yorker Charles A. Gifford who had designed so many of the buildings at the Jekyll Island Club. Although the building follows the familiar four sided cross-like plan employed by so many Southern

[38] *The Brunswick Advertiser and Appeal*, April 31, 1884.

[39] *The Brunswick Advertiser and Appeal*, May 27, 1882.

[40] *The Manufacturers Record*, January 29, 1897, April 16, 1897 and August 13, 1897.

Neoclassical Revival courthouse designers in the first decade of the new century, the style here is decidedly influenced by the American Renaissance Revival. A heavy hand of academic classicism is at work here recalling not the usual Greek or Roman or Georgian designs in up-to-date neoclassical garb, but the Italian Renaissance as recreated in so many governmental buildings in the American North. Unlike Frank Milburn's earlier Beaux-Arts effort at Valdosta, which employed similar light colored brick with limestone trim, the theme here is formally historical. Particularly notable is the pedimented fenestration in the so-called "Palladian" mold and the substantial balustrade. Almost hidden in the moss covered oaks of a large square, the effect of this building today is moody and nostalgic, recalling not the pure light of the Renaissance but a shadowy classical ruin, more emotionally poignant and appropriately Southern than any new structure.

A classical ruin was fitting for Brunswick, for like Savannah, her days as a thriving seaport were numbered. In 1907, this fine new building stood ironically at the brink of the port's decline. The recent arrival of the much celebrated Atlanta, Birmingham and Atlantic Railroad and the extension of the Georgia Coast and Piedmont into Brunswick around 1912 would do little except open up new forests to be quickly depleted by the ever-ravenous saw mills. By 1920, Georgia's timber industry was in decline, and the vast hinterland that drained into the sea near Brunswick had been transformed into so many dirt farms. Throughout the last part of this century, these marginal farms would slowly revert to timber, which is today again the dominant industry in the area. Meanwhile Brunswick would have to look elsewhere for the rebirth promised by the Atlanta, Birmingham and Atlantic. In the harsh light of the new century, it was nowhere to be found.

SOME LAST THOUGHTS ON THE MACON AND BRUNSWICK RAILROAD

According to the 1876 *Handbook of Georgia,* the Macon and Brunswick Railroad traversed "sparsely populated country" on its way to Brunswick, which

was described as "not a place of large trade."[41] Half of the new railroad's $7 million construction cost had come from bonds guaranteed by the State of Georgia, which assumed operating ownership of the road after it failed in 1873. To be sure, the Macon and Brunswick could never have been built had it not been for the state's financial backing, and a generous supply of leased convict labor. The fact that it failed almost before it began is not surprising.

But, as this book seeks to make clear, the wisdom of the era held that any railroad, in and of itself, contained the seeds of its own success, even in the face of adverse economic circumstance. Although this notion proved mythical in most cases, in a strange way, by the end of the century, it would briefly prove true for the Macon and Brunswick. In the last decade of the nineteenth century, all of the empty spaces between Macon and Brunswick would come alive with the woodsman's ax, and an enormous region that had previously contained almost no towns would be dotted with tiny villages all privately spinning their own silver webs of rail. With the completion of the Jesup "Short Line" to Florida in 1902, the old Macon and Brunswick, would become the mighty Southern Railway's main line to Florida. Although the Industrial Revolution beckoned from beyond the rails, prosperity proved only a brief illusion. Like so many places in the South, the region had no way to turn the lure of its resources to its own advantage, and Georgia could only watch as her forests were felled and hauled away down the very rails that and promised so much. By the time Valdosta captured the Southern's main line to Florida, the great pine forests of the Wiregrass were gone. Only an endless sea of stumps remained.

Before the arrival of the Macon and Brunswick, the distance between Brunswick and Macon had been measured in days if not weeks. In 1872, when this same journey was reduced to but a few hours, Brunswick almost literally came to Macon, and the space in between the two cities was transformed. Towns were created almost overnight. Except for Hawkinsville, which got its own branch to attest to its previous history, every depot built on the line would become a new town, new counties were later created and in all cases county seats were moved to the closest depot. The list is impressive. Bleckley, Dodge and Jeff Davis Counties were created and the railroad-born towns of Cochran, Eastman, McRae, Hazlehurst, Baxley, and Jesup almost magically materialized to become county seats.

As for courthouse building and its relation to the humble wooden depots along the line, the record remains consistent. It was the crossing of postbellum rail lines, or the prospect for such roads, that triggered the urge to build monuments to each county's dreams for the future. Hawkinsville was moved to build a lovely brick court building in 1874, only six years after the arrival of the spur from Cochran. The extension of the Oconee and Western Railroad and the prospects for the Hawkinsville and Florida Southern Railroad sparked Andrew J. Bryan's elaborate remodeling in 1897. Both Eastman and Dodge County had been created almost simultaneously by the railroad's arrival, and amid speculation concerning new rails in the first decade of the new century, Eastman erected an enormous new court building. The arrival of the Savannah, Americus and Montgomery Railroad, near McRae, created her sister city, Helena, and begot a fight for the courthouse, the result of which was Alexander Blair's 1906 Telfair County Courthouse. Jeff Davis County was created in 1905 amid the excitement surrounding the arrival of what was to become the Georgia and Florida Railway, and the very next year Walter Chamberlain was retained to create a new courthouse there. Only Baxley failed to attract crossing rails, but in 1907 when a new court building was erected, prospects for a new line appeared quite good. One of the perfecting links in the rise to prominence of the old Macon and Brunswick was Jesup's 1902 "Short Line" to Florida, and as we have seen, the town erected James Golucke's Romanesque Revival court building in 1903.

At either end of the line the two terminals bracketed courthouse building in the period of our interest. Macon, the great rail hub of central Georgia, set the tone for the era with the construction of G. P. Randall's bold Second Empire 1872 Bibb County Courthouse. Brunswick, afire with the new hope sparked by the construction of the mighty Atlanta, Birmingham and Atlantic Railroad, erected Charles

Gifford's Renaissance Revival fantasy courthouse in 1907.

While the Macon and Brunswick Railroad was erecting the simple depots that would create towns in the wilderness, another railroad was seeking to transform another part of the piney woods just to the north of the great Okeefanokee Swamp. In 1870, the Brunswick and Albany Railroad penetrated the wilds of what was then, and still remains, some of the most desolate country in Georgia.

•

Plate 9.13: Brunswick City Hall, 1892. (Photo: Wilber W. Caldwell.)

[41] Thomas P. Janes, ed., *Handbook of The State of Georgia* (New York: Russell Brothers, 1876) 174

The Brunswick and Albany Railroad

Glynn County: Brunswick (see chapter 9) • Brantley County: Nahunta • Ware County: Waycross (see chapter 7) Atkinson County: Pearson • Tift County: Tifton • Worth County: Sylvester • Dougherty County: Albany (see chapter 6) • Some Last Thoughts on the Brunswick and Albany Railroad

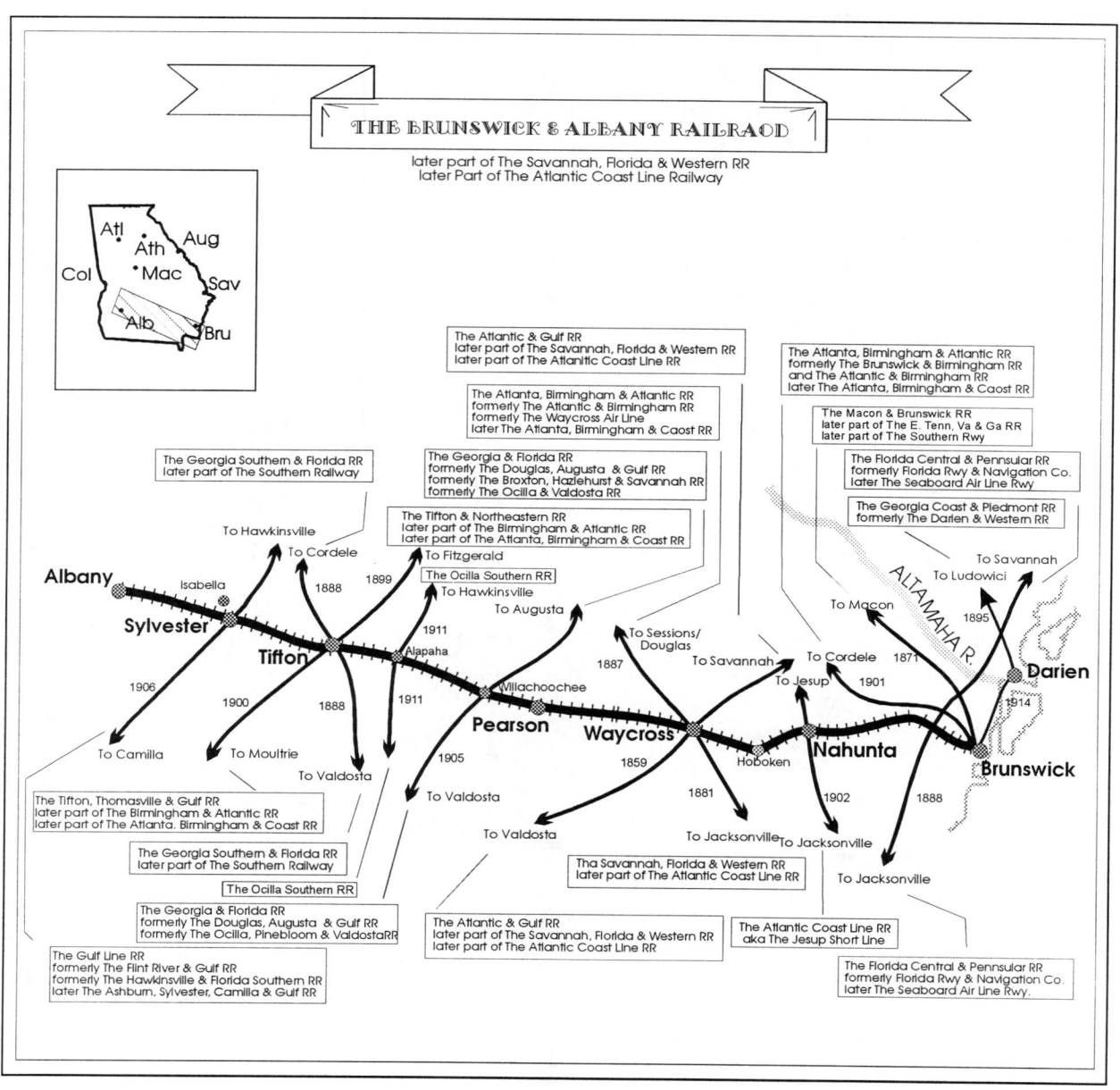

10 | The Brunswick and Albany Railroad

BRUNSWICK TO ALBANY

BRANTLEY COUNTY: NAHUNTA

Plate 10.1: The depot at Hoboken, now restored at the Okefenokee Heritage Center in Waycross.

This old depot which once stood beside the rails of the Brunswick and Albany at Hoboken is all that is left to remind us of the early railroads in the vast reaches of the great pine forest which became Brantley County in 1920. In the years following Appomattox, the Brunswick and Albany Railroad was built through a flat piney wilderness in the southern portion of what was then Wayne County. So sparse was the population here that the tiny depots at places like Nahunta and Hoboken were slow to beget towns. As late as 1879, Sholes's *Gazetteer of Georgia* places the population of Hoboken, Brantley County's original county seat, at only 50.

When the Civil War began the Brunswick and Florida Railroad had completed grading to Albany and beyond toward Eufaula, Alabama.[1] Passing through what is today Brantley County in 1860, about 65 miles of track was laid from Brunswick to Waresboro, which lies just to the west of present day Waycross and was, at that time, the county seat of Ware County. In 1863, a critical shortage of steel moved the Confederate government to nationalized the line, which was largely owned by Northern investors. The rails were removed for use elsewhere in the Confederacy. Renamed the Brunswick and Albany, by 1870 the line was again in operation to Waresboro and work was underway to extend the rails to Albany.

At the helm of this grand enterprise was Hannibal I. Kimball of New England, New South promoter, railroad entrepreneur and crony of Georgia's Republican Reconstruction Governor Rufus Bullock. Promoting the road as the "Union Pacific of Georgia," Kimball envisioned the last and perfecting link in a "great trunk line from the Pacific."[2] After orga-

---

[1] Peter S. McGuire, "The Railroads of Georgia, 1860-1880," *The Georgia Historical Quarterly* 16/3 (Savannah 1932): 200.

[2] Peter S. McGuire, "The Railroads of Georgia, 1860-1880," *The Georgia Historical Quarterly* 16/3 (Savannah 1932): 196-97.

Plate 10.1: The old depot from Hoboken is all that is left to remind us of the early railroads in the vast reaches of the great pine forest which became Brantley County in 1920. (Photo: Wilber W. Caldwell.)

through the heart of what was to become Brantley County, crossing the Atlanta, Birmingham and Coast at the tiny village of Hortense and the Brunswick and Albany at Nahunta. Reliable population statistics for these remote villages in the early part of this century are difficult to find. For the year 1896, Sholes's *Gazetteer of Georgia* places the population of Hoboken at 20 and Nahunta at 100, but the 1906 *Cyclopedia of Georgia* lists Nahunta as a town of 173.[3] The county seat was first established at Hoboken, but in 1923 that town yielded the palm to Nahunta based on its central location and its rail junction. Brantley County erected its first and only courthouse in 1930, well after the period of our interest, but it is notable that, even as late as 1930, crossing rails were still acting as a catalyst for courthouse construction.

The new county town of Nahunta was most certainly born of the railroad, for the name, although mistakenly thought by many to be of native American origin, was derived from a shortening of the original place name that appeared on early maps as the rail siding owner by "N. A. Hunter."

ATKINSON COUNTY: PEARSON

Plate 10.2: The Georgia and Florida Railway Depot at Willacoochee, built c. 1907.

Today in Atkinson County, the only depot still standing by the old road bed of the Brunswick and Albany Railroad is this aging Georgia and Florida Railway Depot at Willacoochee/Pinebloom. Here, in the years just before 1910, the Georgia and Florida Railway crossed the rails of the old Brunswick and Albany. This crossing line, originally built in 1901 by the Gray Lumber Company from the Satilla River south of Douglas via Pinebloom to Nashville, soon became the Ocilla, Pinebloom and Valdosta Railroad. It was acquired by the Douglas, Augusta and Gulf in 1905 and later became a key link in John Skelton Williams's Georgia and Florida Railway. With the creation of this junction, Willacoochee became the largest town in what was later to become Atkinson County. Her population shot up from 471 in 1900 to almost 1000 by 1910.

nizing the original investors of the defunct Brunswick and Florida Railroad and claiming damages of over $3,000,000, including claims against the state for the 1863 Confederate rape of the old line to Waresboro, Kimball succeeded in obtaining authorization to issue paid up stock to former bond holders. In 1869 the state granted endorsement of new bonds in the amount of $15,000 per mile. The Brunswick and Albany was completed to Albany and graded all the way to Eufaula by the end of 1871. Typical of the pattern of Reconstruction railroads in Georgia, the line immediately fell upon hard times, defaulted after only six month of operation and was sold in foreclosure in 1873.

Formed from parts of Wayne, Charlton and Pierce Counties, Brantley County was a place of few towns when it was created in 1920. On the line of the old Brunswick and Albany, which by then had become the Brunswick and Western Division of the Atlantic Coast Line Railway, two hamlets, Nahunta and Hoboken, wrestled to become the county seat. Almost three decades earlier, in 1902, the Atlantic Coast Line had completed its "Jesup Short Line" to Florida

---

[3] Allen D. Candler and Clement A. Evans, *The Cyclopedia of Georgia* (Atlanta: State Historical Association, 1906) 647.

[4] The new Counties created in 1905 were Crisp, Grady, Jeff Davis, Jenkins, Stephens, Tift, Toombs and Turner. Ben Hill County was created in 1906.

[5] *The Tifton Gazette*, September 30, 1904.

In 1917, Atkinson County was created from Coffee and Clinch Counties with the centrally located town of Pearson as its seat of justice. Also located on the rails of the old Brunswick and Albany Railroad, Pearson was a town of just over five hundred persons in 1910. To celebrate its creation, the new county engaged the services of J. J. Baldwin to design a courthouse at Pearson. Although the 1920 Neoclassical Revival Atkinson County Courthouse is arguably Baldwin's most monumental accomplishment, it, like virtually all of J. J. Baldwin's courthouses, delivers a somewhat unemotional message typical of the court buildings erected in Georgia after 1910. These buildings are not part of this study.

Today both of Willachoochee's railroads have been pulled up for scrap, and the depot at tiny Pearson is gone. All that remains is the faint trace of the old roadbed cutting razor straight through the pines all the way to Albany. Here in the remote reaches of the piney woods is a telling snapshot of the myth of the New South, a last glimpse at the forgotten dream that was the "Union Pacific of Georgia." The rails which were to connect Brunswick with the Pacific coast never got any farther west than Albany.

Tift County: Tifton

Plate 10.3: The Atlantic Coast Line Depot at Tifton.

In 1905, Tifton and her many depots were at the center of Georgia's "New County Movement." The 1877 State Constitution had limited the number of counties in Georgia to 137. In 1904, this Constitution was amended, and out of 21 applications for charter in 1905, Tift County was created, one of the eight granted new county status in that year.[4] It was the culmination of a decade of political agitation, primarily in South Georgia, by a new breed of late converts to the doctrines of the New South. Webs of rail lines had created formidable population centers almost over-night, and suddenly the New South's promise was proving more than mythical in a few south Georgia cities like Tifton, Cordele and Fitzgerald.

The argument behind the "New County Movement" was direct. In Tifton, *The Tifton Gazette*

Plate 10.2: The Georgia and Florida Railway Depot at Willacoochee. All that remains is the faint trace of the old roadbed cutting razor straight through the pines. (Photo: Wilber W. Caldwell.)

of September 30, 1904, phrased the cause appropriately: "In recent years a network of railroads have been built over South Georgia, and now some of the largest towns—the centers of population, the centers of wealth, the trade centers, are situated thirty or forty miles from their county seats, on the edge of very large counties.... The county of Berrien contains as many square miles as the five counties of Fulton, Bibb, Clarke, Clayton and Rockdale."[5]

Tifton, originally in Berrien County, was indeed a prime example of the situation. Located on the old rails of the Brunswick and Albany, which by 1905 was part of the growing railroad empire of the Atlantic Coast Line Railway, the town had grown up around her lumber industry. The crossing rails of the Georgia Southern and Florida Railroad had arrived in 1888,

Plate 10.3: The Atlantic Coast Line depot at Tifton. (Photo: Wilber W. Caldwell.)

and by 1900, Tifton was booming. Agitation for a new county with Tifton as the county seat began just as Tifton erected her first Union Depot in 1899, a building *The Gazette* called "the finest passenger depot south of Macon."[6] Also built in the years just before the turn of the century, the Tifton, Thomasville and Gulf and the Tifton and Northeastern Railroads were later acquired by the Atlantic and Birmingham. By 1904, talk of a courthouse at Tifton was being kindled by the merger of the Atlantic and Birmingham with the Brunswick and Birmingham in one of the first moves toward the creation of the giant Atlanta, Birmingham and Atlantic Railroad.

The Atlantic and Birmingham built a its own depot at Tifton in 1904. This building burned only two years later and was replaced by the picturesque old depot that still stands in Tifton today. Oozing New South boosterism, *The Gazette* flaunted Tifton's railroads as it lobbied for the new county: "Tifton has, most appropriately, been spoken of as a Hub, because this place radiates, as the spokes of a wheel, railroads in six directions, touching every part of the proposed new county. North and south to Macon and Jacksonville, the Georgia Southern and Florida; east and west to Albany, Brunswick and Savannah, the Atlantic Coast Line; northeast and southwest to Fitzgerald and Thomasville, the Atlantic and Birmingham, giving us the three greatest railway systems in the state."[7]

Previous to a statewide election, there appears to have been scattered resistance to the creation of new counties in South Georgia. A few Northern counties feared increased political power in the southern part of the state. But in September of 1904, reports from Atlanta listed "scarcely a tangible objection"[8] to the Cromartie Bill, and in October of 1904 the voters of Georgia ratified the amendment to the state's Constitution, allowing for eight new counties. In Tifton the vote had been unanimous: 367 for, 0 against. In testament to Tifton's power, we find little opposition to the creation of Tift County from surrounding counties, even Worth and Berrien Counties, which were to loose considerable territory to the upstart, favored the new county. *The Worth County Local* speculated that "the good would be in excess of

the harm done,"[9] and the Berrien County Grand Jury actually recommended the creation of the new county.[10]

Indeed, Tifton's success had been so notable, that in 1905, few would oppose the creation of Tift County. Remarkably, just over thirty years before, the countryside around the old Brunswick and Albany Depot had been a vast wildness of pine. Sholes's 1879 *Gazetteer of Georgia* gives no population figure and describes Tifton as "a small post office 25 miles northwest of Nashville, the Berrien County seat." According to Sholes, the only enterprises in Tifton in 1879 were a general store and steam saw mill run by H. H. Tift.

Henry Harding Tift had come to Georgia from Connecticut at the behest of his uncle, Nelson Tift, who had almost single-handedly founded and developed the city of Albany. In 1871, the Brunswick and Albany built its first depot at the spot that was to become Tifton, and less than a year later, H. H. Tift arrived to set up his sawmill. He had acquired the land from his uncle, Nelson Tift, who had bought the parcel from none other than Abbott Brisbane, after the collapse of the old Flint River and Ocmulgee Railroad way back in 1842. In 1886, Sholes again lists Tifton in his gazetteer, and this time he describes it as "an important station."

Like his uncle, Nelson, Henry Tift had the gift. By 1900, there were seven lumber mills operating in Tifton and H. H. Tift's mill was producing over 7 million board feet annually.[11] In addition, Henry Tift was successfully operating a foundry, a large nursery, an extensive wholesale business, was a director of the Georgia Southern and Florida Railroad and president of both the Tifton Cotton Mill and the Tifton and Northeastern Railroad. Under Tift's direction, Tifton was on the way to becoming to a city of almost 3000 by 1910. As the new county became a reality, Tifton installed electric streetlights, built a new water works, and boasted four banks and a five-story "skyscraper." It was a microcosm of the elusive New South come to life almost magically out in the wasteland of the Wiregrass. Here was an example of the railroad's seemingly capricious nature. Some towns blossomed and prospered, while others shriveled up and disappeared.

But Tifton's success was more than New South caprice. Despite their railroads, a great many prosperous saw mill towns in the Wiregrass had faded from sight after the virgin forests had disappeared. Unlike so many Wiregrass communities that were left gasping after the rape of Georgia's pine forests, Tifton had been quick to diversify. By the time Tift County was created in 1905, there was not much left of the great pine forests along the old Brunswick and Albany. The Tift Lumber Mill would limp along until 1916, but all the while diversity was on the wind. H. H. Tift and his brother W. O. Tift were cultivating significant fruit crops as early as 1890, and the brothers developed an enormous commercial nursery business in the fields around Tifton, shipping tomato plants and onion sets to Florida. Sweet potatoes became a money crop, and as in many South Georgia counties, tobacco would replace cotton as a cash crop after the ravages of the boll weevil. The Atlanta, Birmingham and Atlantic promoted tobacco growing all up and down its line in 1916.[12]

New South promoters had long promised that if agriculture could be diversified, industrial progress would follow. Although few places in Georgia would test the theory, Tifton proved it true. Tifton Knitting Mills, more foundries and warehouses, an enormous guano plant and the agricultural education center at Abraham Baldwin College all followed agricultural success in rapid succession. Like Waycross, Tifton's story was an unlikely tale, and she owed much of her New South success to her railroads. In 1901, *The Gazette* reported that there were over 16 miles of railroad track inside the city limits of Tifton.[13]

Despite Tifton's jubilation over the creation of Tift County, the city was slow to build a courthouse. Three times the electorate of Tift County would fail to muster the two-thirds majority required to pass a bond issue to fund a court building. At one point opponents even obtained an injunction to stop direct taxation. Finally in 1912, *The Gazette* would wail: "The situation is a reproach to every citizen of our county. Tift is the wealthiest of the nine counties created six years ago, yet every one except it has a substantial home. Indeed it is said that this is the only county in the state whose only public building is a

jail."[14] Finally in May of that year, $60,000 in county bonds was approved, and the Tift County Courthouse was completed in 1913, eight years after the new county had been created.

The success at Tifton and a few other places like it marked the beginning of the new era. Here, rays of the light of a long awaited New South were clearly visible. Accordingly, an altogether different architectural symbol was needed. The symbols of reality are seldom as uplifting as the symbols of hope. Tifton would have none of the confused mythical symbols of fantasy and nostalgia that decorated so many of Georgia's squares. Instead, we find one of the first court buildings in Georgia designed to fully express the architecture of the new age, of financial might and governmental power. Like the 1911 Spalding County Courthouse at Griffin, the 1913 Fulton County Courthouse at Atlanta, and the 1914 Clarke County Courthouse at Athens, the Beaux-Arts flamboyance of Atlanta architect W. A. Edwards's 1912 Tift County Courthouse voiced the conviction that the New South might, after all, be at hand. It also whispered the foreboding warning that the rewards of the industrial age would be attainable only at a considerable price.

WORTH COUNTY: SYLVESTER

Plate 10.4: The depot at Sylvester.

This little depot's story is one of the most compelling in Georgia. In 1871, as the Brunswick and Albany Railroad approached the edge of the Pine Barrens, its rails brought new possibilities to the southwest Georgia Cotton Belt. With the addition of commercial fertilizer and tons of railroad-imported

[6] *The Tifton Gazette*, November 17, 1899.

[7] *The Tifton Gazette*, June 2, 1905.

[8] Atlanta "Evening News" in *The Tifton Gazette*, September 29, 1904.

[9] Worth County Local quoted in *The Tifton Gazette*, April 8, 1904.

[10] *The Tifton Gazette*, April 14, 1905.

[11] *The Tifton Gazette*, November 17, 1899.

[12] Ida Belle Williams, *The History of Tift County* (Macon GA: J. W. Burke, 1948) 297.

[13] *The Tifton Gazette*, June 21, 1901, quoted in Ida Belle Williams, The History of Tift County, 37.

Plate 10.4: The depot at Sylvester. The community that sprouted next to the ancestor of this depot would voice some of the most fantastically optimistic New South proclamations ever heard in Georgia. (Photo: Wilber W. Caldwell.)

guano, even the sandy soil of Worth County began to bear fruit. Just after the turn of the century, the heady, mature wine of New South aspirations arrived with the news that the Flint River and Gulf Railroad would be built from Ashburn to Sylvester. Under the influence of this potent concoction, Sylvester would voice some of the most fantastically optimistic New South proclamations ever heard in Georgia. *The Worth County Local* of September 22, 1904 offers ample example.

> The industrial development of this magnificent country is something wonderful. Fifteen years ago, the spot where now stands the ambitious prosperous town of Sylvester was a waste country. Behold its development. See what the natives have done for their state and marvel. (Proclaim it from the housetops, North, South, East and West, that the Wiregrass country is the place to locate, and place your investments. The best climate and the best water and the best people under the sun.[15]

It was the intoxicated gibberish of a drunkard's dream. Although Sylvester knew a brief prosperity after the turn of the century, captured the county seat in 1904 and immediately built a fantasy courthouse, hard times still lay ahead for Worth County. The realities of the new century would bare little resemblance to Sylvester's turn-of-the-century ravings.

Only 3.5 miles from the old county seat at Isabella, Sylvester could mark its beginning from the arrival of the railroad in 1871. The community that sprouted next to the ancestor of this depot grew slowly at first. Sholes's 1879 *Gazetteer of Georgia* makes no mention of Sylvester and places the population of Isabella, the county seat, at only 50. In the 1886 edition, Isabella had grown to a town of 150 and its location is given as "3 miles from Isabella Station (Sylvania P.O.) its depot." No population figure is given for "Isabella Station" in 1886, but just ten years later "Sylvania P.O." had become Sylvester with a population of 500 while Isabella counted only 350 residents. With the arrival of the Brunswick and Albany in 1871, a chain of new towns blossomed along the new rails. In addition to the growth at "Isabella Station," substantial villages appeared at Sumner and Poulan. Each of these hamlets would eventually make its bid for the county seat.

Isabella had been laid out as Worth County's seat of justice just after the county's creation from Dooly and Irwin Counties in 1853. The original county seat had been designated at San Bernard, once the proposed site of General Abbott Brisbane's Catholic mission, a wild utopian dream of the 1840s that centered around hopes for the ill-fated Flint River and Ocmulgee Railroad and an associated Irish Catholic colony in Georgia. This site was rejected very early in the county's history, and a frame courthouse was erected at Isabella less than a mile away. This building burned in 1879, sparking the first wave of assaults on the county seat by Poulon, Sumner and Sylvester. Isabella managed to hang on the prize and erected another frame court building that burned in 1893. Again Isabella's hold on the county seat was challenged, and again Isabella prevailed, building a large two-story brick vernacular courthouse in 1895. Apparently the building was poorly constructed, for in 1903 the grand jury was charging inadequacy and bemoaning the sad condition of the structure."[16]

Business leaders in Sylvester hungrily seized on the grand jury's condemnation of the courthouse at Isabella as a brass ring of opportunity. By 1903, Sylvester's power in Worth County was unquestioned, and spirits were soaring on news of the Flint River and Gulf Railroad. The line would arrive in Sylvester in 1906. It later became part of the Gulf Line Railroad from Hawkinsville via Sylvester to Bridgeboro where it connected with the Georgia Northern, which had been built from Moultrie to Albany in 1902. Contemplating the arrival of crossing rails, Sylvester boomed. The year 1904 saw over 10,000 bales of cotton shipped from this tiny depot. All of the old wooden buildings in the business district of the town were coming down to make way for brick structures,[17] and the Sylvester Banking Company was inviting everyone to inspect its new safe.[18] Residents exuded boundless enthusiasm. To counter the objections of a skeptical and frugal rural population, fifty-five business men in Sylvester raised $10,000, which was deposited with the Ordinary of Worth County in order to "relieve the county of any expense incurred by the change of site should the election result in removal."[19] The election of 1904 brought the county seat to Sylvester and closed the book on: "a hard fight of more than twenty years trying to move the county seat from Isabella in the woods, to some place on the railroad. Almost every town on the railroad has tried at some time to get the county seat."[20]

There is still a small village at Isabella today, and despite the grand jury's condemnation, the old brick courthouse at Isabella stood at the center of the disappearing town for over fifty years.

Plate 10.5: The Worth County Courthouse, built in 1905-1906, burned in 1965, rebuilt in 1966. James W. Golucke, architect.

In 1905, one of the premiere courthouses in Georgia was James Wingfield Golucke's Coweta County Courthouse just completed at Newnan. It is perhaps the most mature statement of Golucke's neoclassical courthouse form with four more of less equal porticoed entrances, one to face each side of the traditional courthouse square. Upon inspecting the building at Newnan, the Worth County Courthouse Committee was quick to retain Golucke. It mattered little that this designer was without formal architectural training. His imposing neoclassical monuments at Newnan and Decatur supplied all the required credentials. Golucke's original rendering of the Coweta County court building appeared in *The Worth County*

Plate 10.5: The Worth County Courthouse, built in 1906 typifies James W. Golucke's delicate balancing act. (Photo: Wilber W. Caldwell.)

Local on September 9, 1904, along with a caption identifying it as the new Worth County Courthouse and promising that the building would be "commodious, substantial and of great architectural beauty."[21] There was no mention in the Local that the building pictured already existed in Georgia.

The 1906 Worth County Courthouse was built from substantially the same plans as the building that inspired it. Still some details differed. Most notable among the variations was the absence of that copper clad trim used in Newnan to create a dramatically dark persona. In contrast, traditional white classical wood and stone trim was used to achieve a rather traditional Georgian effect in Sylvester. Both buildings are crowned with distinctively slender and markedly vertical lanterns. Sadly the 1966 reconstruction of the building at Sylvester lacks much of the delicate detail of Golucke's original. It is nonetheless a credible, even impressive, likeness, especially in light to its birth in

[14] *The Tifton Gazette*, April 12, 1912.
[15] *Worth County Local*, September 22, 1905.
[16] *Worth County Local*, December 4, 1903.
[17] *Worth County Local*, March 20, 1903.
[18] *Worth County Local*, March 27, 1903.
[19] *Worth County Local*, March 11, 1904.
[20] *Worth County Local*, July 8, 1904.
[21] *Worth County Local*, September 9, 1904.

an era now infamous for the destruction of the state's architectural treasures.

Here in Sylvester, we find another example of J. W. Golucke's delicate balancing act: on one hand modern Neoclassical and Beaux-Arts forms reflected national architectural trends and symbolized American industrial and financial power. On the other hand, soft nostalgic "Southern Colonial" columns and verandahs recalled the Lost Cause, that all-powerful myth, which still dominated the Southern mind. Two ideals existing simultaneously in one building is a contradiction that reveals Sylvester's story in 1904. Here was a young city breathing its first gasps of the promised air of the New South, but for all its zeal for the new age, the new courthouse, and the new railroad which inspired them, there was a deeper Southern soul to be reckoned with. Half of the mind of Worth County was drunk on the wine of a mythical new prosperity, and half remained soberly loyal to the myths of the past. As if to amplify this conflict, in June of that year, a heated debate arose in Sylvester to underscore the divided mind of the place and boldly outlined the obstacle that still lay across the path of real modern economic progress. The burning question of that day was, "had the time finally arrived for the South to again celebrate the Fourth of July?"[22]

SOME LAST THOUGHTS ON THE BRUNSWICK AND ALBANY RAILROAD

The corruptions of the Reconstruction era and of the Bullock administration along with the exploits of Governor Bullock's crony and "financial advisor," Hannibal I. Kimball, are well worn themes in Georgia's history. To be sure political power, public funds and governmental influence were imprudently, if not illegally, used to further the ends of a select group of entrepreneurs many of whom have since generally been termed "Carpetbaggers." But in order to render a fair assessment of the operations of Bullock and his cronies or of "Carpetbaggers" in general, it is useful to place events in historical perspective. The history of the Brunswick and Albany Railroad provides a useful backdrop for this task.

Arriving in Georgia after the war, the New Englander, Hannibal Kimball was a man who dreamed big dreams. In championing the cause of the Brunswick and Albany Railroad he envisioned a great deal more than a link to the sea for cotton factored at Albany. Kimball envisioned a "Union Pacific of Georgia," a road which would eventually become the final link in the Southern Pacific Railroad and make the port of Brunswick the premiere Atlantic seaport for the Deep South and the West. To fund such a grand scheme, Kimball, with the help of his friend Bullock, obtained the State's endorsement for the road's bonds in March of 1869. Typical of the few state endorsed railroads of the era that were actually built, the Brunswick and Albany Railroad was completed in 1871, and defaulted after less than six months of operation.

As damning as this may sound, our judgment of Bullock and Kimball may be tempered when we view their activities against the backdrop of the corruption of the Gilded Age in America. Only two months before Kimball obtained the state's endorsement of the Brunswick and Albany's bonds, a golden spike had marked the completion of the Union Pacific Railroad, a project fraught with scandals and private manipulations of the public trust. The culmination of this enormous flimflam was the infamous Credit Mobilier disgrace that shook the Grant administration to the core. This outrage was typical in this age of manipulation and exploitation whose only ethic seemed material.

This is not to imply that abuses at the national level forgive local chicanery, but they go a long way toward softening our opinions of men like Rufus Bullock and Hannibal Kimball. These men were buccaneers in an age of piracy; this is undeniable. Still, one continually gets the feeling that their visions were a great deal larger than the accumulation of personal wealth.

[22] *Worth County Local*, June 5, 1904.

[23] Ellis Melton Coulter, *The South During Reconstruction* (Baton Rouge LA: University of Louisiana Press, 1949) 150-51.

[24] Numan Bartley, *The Creation of Modern Georgia* (1983; reprint, Athens GA and London: University of Georgia Press, 1990) 71

Whatever the case, all over the South, similar scenarios where acted out during Reconstruction. Hannibal Kimball had his counterparts in almost every Southern State. In North Carolina, Martin S. Littlefield concocted identical railroad funding schemes, while John and Daniel Stanton did the same in Alabama, a state which became so entangled in fraud that no one has ever been able to accurately access the extent of these swindles.[23] Indeed the magnitude of the crimes resulting from Reconstruction railroad funding in America are difficult to reckon. In most cases the bond endorsements themselves were legal, and wrongdoing could only be charged when bonds were issued before certain statutory conditions of were met. There were many such cases, but often railroad promoters and executives were guilty only of imprudence, excessive zeal and bad judgment. As Numan Bartley observes, when the Republicans lost power in Georgia in 1871, the Democrats convened committees which promptly found the Bullock Administration "guilty of most known crimes."[24] Nonetheless, Bullock and Kimball were never convicted of any wrongdoing in a court of law, and it is likely that a great deal of their alleged villainy stemmed more from politically motivated allegations than from real crimes.

Perhaps these so-called "Carpetbaggers" defrauded the people of Georgia, but they succeeded in building railroads. Despite its initial failure, the Brunswick and Albany quickly turned an empty wilderness into an economically viable part of the state. Two great rail centers of South Georgia were a direct result of crossings on the Brunswick and Albany. Waycross appeared where her rails crossed the antebellum rails of the Atlantic and Gulf in 1871, and Tifton blossomed at the line's crossing of the Georgia, Southern and Florida in 1888.

With the arrival of the Brunswick and Albany, the town of Waycross was created and that village almost immediately captured the county seat of Ware County away from tiny Tebeauville. Only twenty years later, amid wild railroad speculation, G. L. Norrman's Ware County Courthouse rose to become one of South Georgia's first fantasy court buildings.

But, as we have seen, the pattern of the courthouse and the depot was slow to develop elsewhere in the Wiregrass. In Worth County, it took Sylvester on the Brunswick and Albany over thirty years to wrestle the county seat away from Isabella "in the woods." But with the arrival of the crossing rails of the Flint River and Gulf, Sylvester captured the prize and built a courthouse to manifest her dreams in 1906. When Tift County was finally created in 1905 Tifton was beyond dreaming of New South prosperity. Like few places in Georgia, the young city was reaping a modern harvest. Her courthouse would symbolize not dreams but reality, and accordingly she built a Beaux-Arts symbol of the modern age in 1912. By the time Brantley and Atkinson Counties were created in 1917 and 1921 respectively, the Eldorado of the New South myth had been exposed for the half-truth that it was,

Plate 10.6: Tifton (Photo: Wilber W. Caldwell.)

and the stern face of the modern age had been revealed.

Just as the Brunswick and Albany Railroad created South Georgia's shining examples of New South cities at Tifton and Waycross, another Reconstruction railroad was accomplishing similar work in northeast Georgia. The Atlanta and Richmond Air Line was completed from Atlanta to Charlotte, North Carolina, in 1873, and the towns of Gainesville and Toccoa were set on their way to becoming two more rare indications that the myth of a New South was not completely without foundation. Such cities fueled the fires of the myth and gave it force. Modest successes in places like Waycross and Tifton, Gainesville and Toccoa, Rome and LaGrange were held up by New South promoters to inspire hope for that vast forgotten host of places that seemed destined for nothing but hard times.

•

11 | The Atlanta and Richmond Air Line

ATLANTA TO RICHMOND, VA.

FULTON COUNTY: ATLANTA PART 2

Plate 11.1: Atlanta's Union Depot, built in 1871. Maxwell V. D. Corput, architect. Demolished in 1930.

Immediately following the war, the charred remains of the Western and Atlantic's great train shed at Atlanta were replaced by a temporary wooden depot, which by 1870 was completely inadequate for the needs of the growing city. In that year, officials of all four lines serving Atlanta reached an agreement concerning a new depot.[1] Completed in 1871, this building perhaps best symbolizes Atlanta during the Reconstruction period. The great iron train shed was designed by Maxwell V. D. Corput, a civil engineer and a partner in the architectural firm, Corput and Bass, which designed a number of structures in and around Atlanta in the years following the Civil War, including the 1869 Clayton County Courthouse at Jonesboro and the 1869 Georgia Railroad Freight Terminal. Contemporary reports described Atlanta's new Union Depot as one of the country's "handsomest, largest, and most commodious iron depots."[2]

But in 1871, this was not the nation's "handsomest" depot by any architectural standard, nor was it the most commodious. The great cities of the North had been erecting far more artistically pleasing and functionally hospitable structures since the mid-1850s. Most of these included train sheds supported by trussing systems employing combinations of cast iron and wood. The 1852 S&W Railroad depot at Philadelphia boasted the nation's largest span, 200 feet supported by arched Howe trusses. By 1870, a number of larger European train sheds spanned well over 200 feet using iron arched lattice supports. New York's first Grand Central Station, which was built simultaneously with Atlanta's 1871 Union Depot,

---

[1] *Atlanta Constitution*, June 22, 1870 in Franklin Garrett, *Atlanta and Environs, A Chronicle of Its People and Events*, 3 vols. (New York: Lewis Publishing Company, 1954) 1:839-40.

[2] Elinor Hillyer in Franklin Garrett, *Atlanta and Environs, A Chronicle of Its People and Events*, 1:840.

The Atlanta and Richmond Air Line

Fulton County: Atlanta Part 2 (also see chapters 4, 26 & 32) • Milton County: Alpharetta
Hall County: Gainesville • Banks County: Homer • Stephens County: Toccoa
Some Last Thoughts on the Atlanta and Richmond Air Line

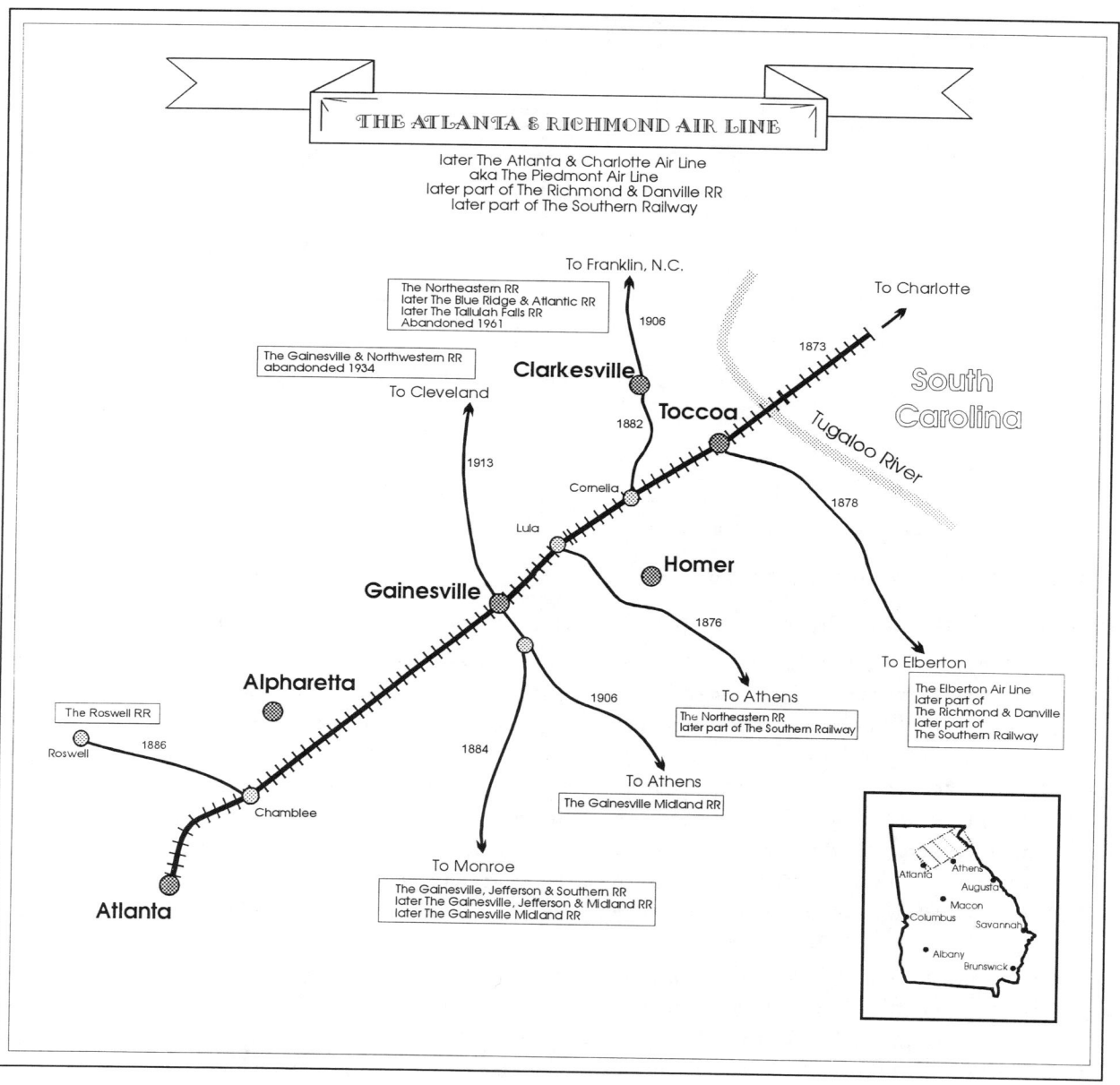

was an attempt to emulate London's grand St. Pancras Station. Like Atlanta's new Union Depot, Commodore Vanderbilt's first Grand Central Station wore Second Empire clothing of the so-called "General Grant Style."

In Atlanta, the Second Empire appeared to be something of an architectural enigma, and Max Corput's vision of Napoleon III's Paris was a long distance from Commodore Vanderbilt's refinements on 42nd Street and even farther from anything on the Rue de Rivoli. The rather crude brick corner pavilions with their mansard caps and odd spires demonstrated just how unfamiliar early Southern engineers-turned-architects were with the new international Second Empire Style. As Henry Russell Hitchcock reminds us, the American Second Empire Style developed without "accurate visual documents, or even a codified body of precedent, to be followed."[3] Although inferior to many earlier New World depots in its architectural elements, Atlanta's Union Depot was indeed an important symbol for its time. More than any other structure in the city, it spoke for Atlanta's progress in an era that found most of the American South destitute.

There were over 400 buildings erected in Atlanta in 1871.[4] Notable among these were the famous Kimball House Hotel and the remodeling and completion of the Kimball Opera House, which soon became the state capitol building. Both buildings were boxy examples of the Second Empire mode designed by Atlanta's pre-eminent architect of the era, William Parkins, and, like Corput's new Union Depot, both were associated with the notorious promoter and financier, Hannibal I. Kimball. In fact, there were few Atlanta-born schemes of the era not somehow connected with the ubiquitous Kimball. History suggests that Kimball was a far better promoter than financier. Almost all of his dealings appear fraught with complex financial, contractual and ethical problems. His close ties to with Georgia's Republican administration was well known, as was his cronyism with Rufus Bullock, Georgia's Reconstruction governor, who would flee Georgia in 1871. Hannibal Kimball left Atlanta on Bullock's heels. By that time, he had been a party to the leasing of the state owned Western and Atlantic

Plate 11.1: Atlanta's 1871 Union Depot. Max Corput's vision of Napoleon III's Paris was a long distance from anything on the Rue de Rivoli. (Photo: Courtesy of Georgia Dept. of Archives and History.)

Railroad, erected the enormous Kimball Opera House and sold it to the state for an obscene profit. He had also built the finest hotel in the South, headed at least nine railroads, and established the Atlanta Fair Grounds.

Much to the indignation, if not outright disgust, of the rest of Georgia, Atlanta's Reconstruction success was accomplished on the backs of men like Kimball. The city's notable progress was the result of a number of factors, many of which had been at work since before the war. Certainly a boldly self-promotional spirit prevailed and, Atlanta's boosterism was all but shameless. Hand in hand with this exaggerated civic salesmanship was openness to Northern ideas and a beckoning hospitality, even deference, to Northern men unlike anything found elsewhere in the state. While other cities in Georgia were mourning the Lost Cause, as early as 1867 Atlanta was planning a Lincoln memorial.[5] Economically, Atlanta's success in the period was tied to her substantial cotton warehouses and to a robust and aggressive wholesale trading establishment. With the help of far-reaching rail

---

[3] Henry Russell Hitchcock, *Architecture, Nineteenth and Twentieth Centuries* (1958; reprint, New Haven: Yale University Press, 1977) 243.

[4] Webb B. Garrison, *The Legacy of Atlanta* (Atlanta: Peachtree Publishing, 1987) 43.

[5] James Michael Russell, *Atlanta, 1847-1890, City Building in the Old South and the New* (Baton Rouge LA: Louisiana State University Press, 1988) 149.

connections and rate-conscious fast freight associations, like the famous Green Line uniting the city with St. Louis and Louisville, Atlanta wove a web of commerce from "Richmond to Key West and Charleston to the Mississippi River."[6] In the midst of it all, the name of Hannibal Kimball seems to pop up at every turn.

As we have seen, Kimball was probably not so much a scoundrel as an over zealous salesman, and even though he came from New England, he was no ordinary Carpetbagger. He was a consummate promoter in an age of promoters, and like all good promoters he believed in his schemes—perhaps too fervently to carefully consider the risks or to tend to details of business like contract terms and other legalities. He was a denizen of the Gilded Age, and if an architectural Style could fit a man, the Second Empire Style was made for Hannibal Ingalls Kimball, and he for it.

Shaken by the Panic of 1873 and the corruptions of the Grant administration, the popularity of the Second Empire Style did not last long in the United States.[7] What had begun in triumph as a proud flamboyant statement of American industrial and economic power, ended as a garish statement of the exploitation and the financial flimflams of the Gilded Age. Even in the lagging fashions of the American South, by the early 1880s the style was loosing what little appeal it had achieved. That the buildings of Hannibal Kimball and the architecture of Reconstruction Atlanta reflected the "General Grant Style" seems fitting. Equally fitting is the notable lack of popularity of the style in the rest of the rural Deep South.

Despite his former questionable financial dealings, by 1874, Hannibal Kimball was back in Atlanta at the invitation of local business leaders. This time he

led promotional efforts to finance the construction of what was to be Georgia's largest textile factory, the Atlanta Cotton Mill, and to launch the city's International Cotton Exposition. He would eventually become the mill's first president and the director of Atlanta's International Cotton Exposition. According to James Russell, it was these two projects, along with the construction of the city's fifth railroad, the Atlanta and Richmond Air Line, in 1873, "which established the city as a regional center for New South urban-industrial boosterism."[8]

Like Macon, Atlanta had often found herself at the mercy of hostile railroads. Since well before the Civil War, she had fought discriminatory freight rates, and had long sought to establish railroads of her own. As early as 1856, the city had moved to build competing lines that she alone could control. This was aimed at leveling the playing field, which was then steeply tilted in favor of Savannah, Augusta and Charleston, cities that controlled the rails radiating from Atlanta. With freight rates soaring in the years following the war, Atlanta revived her plans for the Georgia Western Railroad to the coal rich areas of Alabama and for the Georgia Air Line, a road designed to connect the city with Charlotte, North Carolina. The Georgia Western was not begun until 1882 when the Georgia Pacific Railroad was constructed from Atlanta to Birmingham, but the Georgia Air Line proved more alluring. Even though the primary force behind Atlanta's enthusiasm for the line was a short-sighted desire for lower shipping costs, the early promoters of this railroad were among the first to raise the insightful argument that such an inland line, parallel to the coast, might compete favorably with coastwise sea transportation.[9]

In 1868, the Richmond and Danville Railroad was expressing interest in a coastwise railroad, and in that year the promoters of the Georgia Air Line invited Richmond and Danville president, A. S. Buford to Atlanta. In a memorable speech, Buford stirred Atlantans to action, and before the dust had settled, the city had subscribed $300,000, the state $240,000 and private citizens $210,000 to build the first twenty miles of the Atlanta and Richmond Air Line. By 1871, the road was complete to Gainesville, and the

[6] Russell, *Atlanta, 1847-1890, City Building in the Old South and the New*, 126.

[7] Hitchcock, *Architecture, Nineteenth and Twentieth Centuries*, 241-43.

[8] Russell, *Atlanta, 1847-1890, City Building in the Old South and the New*, 132.

[9] Russell, *Atlanta, 1847-1890, City Building in the Old South and the New*, 133.

entire line to Charlotte was in operation by late 1873. Although state aid had been offered, it was eventually refused, and the Air Line became one of the few railroads built in Georgia during the Reconstruction period without the aid of state endorsed bonds. The lion's share of the staggering $8 million construction cost came from the Richmond and Danville Railroad, which would control the line from the beginning. The Atlanta and Richmond Air Line (also known as the Piedmont Air Line) failed in 1876 and was reorganized as the Atlanta and Charlotte Air Line. In the end, the loss of control of the Air Line made little difference to Atlanta, for the age of city-controlled railroads was nearing an end. The early 1880s saw the completion of the Georgia Pacific and the East Tennessee, Virginia and Georgia, and competition among Atlanta's various railroads began to create competitive rail rates. By that time, Reconstruction and the ruinous effect of the Panic of 1873 were over, and Atlanta was beginning to feel the full power of her seven railroads.

It was time for a new courthouse.

Plate 11.2: The Fulton County Courthouse, built in 1883. Parkins and Bruce, architects. Demolished in 1911.

Although this courthouse was completed well after the end of Reconstruction in Georgia, it is included here because its spiritual message is deeply rooted in the soil of the Atlanta's unique Reconstruction growth. Here is the city's last gasp of Second Empire architecture.

To discover the driving force behind Atlanta's choice of the Second Empire Style, we need look no farther than Macon. As we have seen, in 1872, that city, seeking to compete with the upstart Atlanta, had employed the considerable skills of Chicago architect, Gourdon P. Randall, to design the state's most up-to-date courthouse, a fine Second Empire brick edifice with an asymmetrically placed clock tower. Both cities had entered the Reconstruction era with populations of about 10,000, but by 1881, when Atlanta answered Macon's challenge by breaking ground for this fine court building, her population had exceeded 40,000, well over twice that of Macon. Although Atlanta's

Plate 11.2: The 1883 Fulton County Courthouse. The city's last gasp of Second Empire architecture. (Photo: Courtesy of Georgia Dept. of Archives and History.)

Second Empire courthouse outshines her earlier rival in Macon in size, detail and quality of construction, there are fundamental similarities. Most notable is the overall plan featuring three balanced corner pavilions offset by the asymmetry of a high tower.

To be sure, Parkins and Bruce employed more refined Renaissance ornament in Atlanta, and this detailed ornamentation lifts the building well above Randall's Bibb County Courthouse of a decade earlier. But, on the whole, this appears to be more the result of a generous budget than of a superior architectural vision. Despite the building's fine stone quoining, classical pilasters and lacy balustrades, the 1883 Fulton County Courthouse lacked the bold plasticity and flowery classical ornament of the landmark Second Empire public buildings of the era in the North and Midwest. Still, if the 1871 Union Depot reflected the railroad's promise at the close of the Civil War, then the 1883 Fulton County Courthouse reflected the fact that, at least in one place in the American South, that enticing promise was to be real.

MILTON COUNTY: ALPHARETTA

Plate 11.3: The Milton County Courthouse, built in 1876. Demolished in 1955.

This simple brick court building was erected at Alpharetta in 1876 almost immediately after Milton County's original 1858 courthouse burned. Its predictable vernacular lines have two short stories to tell.

First, the appearance of new counties around Atlanta in the years following the creation of Fulton County in 1854 attests to the area's remarkable growth and growing political power. Milton County, created in 1857, was one of three new counties that would surround Fulton. Clayton County had been created in 1858 and Rockdale County followed in 1870. All three of these new counties built almost identical two-story, square, brick vernacular courthouses in the years immediately following the Civil War. The old 1869 Clayton County Courthouse at Jonesboro was the simplest of the three and is the only one still standing today. The 1872 Rockdale County Courthouse was almost identical to this court building at Alpharetta and was perhaps the later building's model. Both buildings were distinguished by tall brick pilasters that created vertical bays. Both have a hipped roof, a simple cornice and shallow eaves supported by

Plate 11.3: The 1876 Milton County Courthouse. The appearance of new counties around Atlanta in the years following the creation of Fulton County in 1854 attests to the area's remarkable growth and growing political power. (Photo: Courtesy of the Atlanta History Center.)

modillions. Here in Alpharetta, as in Jonesboro, there are also paired brackets beneath the eaves.

The second narrative emanating from the memory of the old 1876 Milton County Courthouse is a familiar one. Commanding the main crossroads in Alpharetta long after the county merged with Fulton in 1931, this building, gave stirring example to what happens in places where the railroads never arrived to spread their shaky gospel of New South hope and prosperity. In 1857, when Alpharetta became the county seat of Milton County, the nearest railhead was at Marietta, over 20 miles away. By the time this courthouse was completed, the Atlanta and Richmond Air Line was up and running, and Sholes's *Gazetteer of Georgia* relates that Alpharetta was 11 miles from the depot at Norcross and had a population of 200. By 1886, the spur known as the "Buck Line Railroad" had been completed from Chamblee to Roswell, and in that year Sholes relates that Alpharetta was only 7 miles from the depot at Roswell and had a population of 250. Ten years later Sholes counts Alpharetta's population at 300, and in a telling phrase, describes the place as "an interior town." Although here these words obviously refer to the town's lack of rail connection, historically they had been used to describe places not on a major waterway.

However one chooses to describe Alpharetta, its saga ran true to form. By 1910, the year, which perhaps most often scribed the high water mark for small towns in Georgia, Alpharetta's population was still under 350, and without a humble depot, there would be no notions regarding a grand courthouse in Milton County.

HALL COUNTY: GAINESVILLE

Plate 11.4: The Hall County Courthouse, built in 1884. Bruce and Morgan architects. Destroyed by tornado in 1936.

Gainesville was the location of the last of Alexander Bruce's four nearly identical courthouses. Sadly this building was completely destroyed in 1936 by a devastating tornado that wrecked a substantial portion of Gainesville and killed more than 200 people there. Before its untimely end, this building invited comparison with its three triplet sisters, Bruce's 1875 McMinn County Courthouse at Athens, Tennessee, his 1882 Hancock County Courthouse at Sparta and his 1884 Walton County Courthouse at Monroe. These four Second Empire court buildings all attested to the architect's considerable skill in combining the modernity of the fashionable Second Empire Style with soft comfortably Southern forms.

The Second Empire in the American North had begun as a fashionable voice of growing financial and industrial might, and by 1865 it was much employed in public building and especially popular with governmental builders. With the abuses of the Gilded Age and the corruption of the Grant Administration, the style quickly became tainted by the vices of the era. Needless to say, it knew little popularity in the rural South. All of this makes Alexander Bruce's achievement in Gainesville the more remarkable. Here, as in Sparta and Monroe, he fashioned an essentially Second Empire courthouse that succeeded despite the mansard-roofed perils inherent in its Yankee symbolism. Through a careful synthesis with more familiar forms, Bruce softened the building's modern effect by infusing a comfortable local vocabulary, like the high arched windows of the courtroom and the simple classicism of the lantern. In 1885, Alexander Bruce's Hall County Courthouse was an apt symbol for the postwar South, for stylistically it looked backward and forward at the same time.

The likeness of this structure to its sisters on two other squares in the Georgia Piedmont seems to have drawn little remark in either Gainesville, Sparta, or in Monroe. Although there were some differences, they were minor. The roofline of the lantern here in Gainesville is of a cleaner, more classical type, the low porch is smaller, and there are some variations in the fenestration, banding and the decorative quoining. Nonetheless, it appears that exclusivity of design was not expected, or at least was of little importance at this early date in these then rather remote places. The connectivity that was provided by Georgia's blossoming rail system would soon put an end to such tolerance. But in 1885, when professional architects were just beginning to make their mark in the far-flung corners

Plate 11.4: The 1884 Hall County Courthouse. A Second Empire design that succeeded despite the mansard-roofed perils inherent in its Yankee symbolism. (Photo: Courtesy of Georgia Dept. of Archives and History.)

of the state, this sort of self-plagiarism was apparently acceptable.

Alexander Bruce was not the only architect in Georgia who was copying himself by reselling plans. As we have seen Augusta's Lewis Goodrich would build nearly identical court buildings at Crawfordville and Sylvania and Walter Chamberlain at Nashville and Oglethorpe. James W. Golucke would resell plans of several types, most notably those of the 1900 Schley County Courthouse at Ellaville, which was recreated in Jones County at Gray in 1905 and in Baker County at Newton in 1907.

For the purposes of this book, it would be nice to say that the 1885 Hall County Courthouse was built in a flurry of New South zeal generated by the completion of the city's first postbellum railroad, as had clearly been the case with its two triplet sisters at Sparta and Monroe. In 1884, the Gainesville, Jefferson and Southern Railroad, chartered back in 1872, was completed to connect Gainesville with the

Georgia Railroad at Social Circle. This new road included a branch line to Jefferson and later extended it to Athens. As economically uplifting as this may have been, the simple truth is that the old Hall County Courthouse burned in 1882, and this building rose to replace it. Still the choice of the then modern Second Empire Style suggests high expectations in Gainesville.

The charred remains upon which this building rose marked the site of a fine brick court building that had been erected in 1852. By all accounts, this was a typical vernacular courthouse, and one local history includes a drawing of a building very similar to the 1836 Lumpkin County Courthouse at Dahlonega.[10] The two-story structure was the county's fourth courthouse. The first, a log structure built in 1818, had been replaced by a frame structure shortly thereafter, and in 1832, a simple brick building was erected. It burned in 1852 and was replaced by the fine brick building that stood until it too was consumed by fire thirty years later.

Plate 11.5: The Southern Railway Depot at Gainesville, built c.1910.

The 1873 arrival of the Atlanta and Richmond Air Line triggered a period of steady growth for Gainesville. In stark contrast to most places in the Deep South, a few Georgia towns had been able to establish and maintain a healthy pattern of growth after the arrival of postbellum rails. Although the modest progress here in Gainesville was a long distance from the economic Elysiums promised by New

South promoters, the pattern here is similar to many of the towns along the rails of the Western and Atlantic Railroad, where the vision of a New South had, at least in part, been made real. Before the arrival of the Atlanta and Richmond Air Line, Gainesville had been a town of only about 500 residents. By 1880, the city's population had reached almost 2000, and by 1910, almost 6000. With its rail connections, the city found itself the trading town for a vast mountainous area to the north, which with few exceptions would remain unconnected by rail. While trade flourished, industry made modest strides, and by the 1890s Gainesville could boast a 30,000 square foot carriage factory, a large shoe factory producing over 600 pairs a day, a foundry, and a tannery.[11] As early as 1880, the poultry industry upon which the area would come to rely was beginning to develop. Additionally, thanks to the railroads, the area was gaining a reputation as a resort with several large spas advertising cures for "rheumatism, blood poisoning, dyspepsia and all kidney troubles." In 1888, the area around Gainesville boasted 12 hotels and 6 spas.

In 1901, the first of Gainesville's several textile mills, the enormous Pacolet Mill #4, was erected at New Holland. The mill with its modern mill village was flaunted by Southern textile promoters as a model of industrial efficiency and an example of the region's idyllic labor relations. The propaganda of the era often centered on such modern mills. One pamphlet claimed that 89% of the mills in Georgia owned their own mill villages and lifted up the mill at New Holland as evidence that: "The dirty, muddy streets of base frame shacks of the old time mill village are passing...(replaced by) the modern mill village today with its low rent, paved streets and all of the modern sanitary convinces and inviting parks."[12] The pamphlet continues, emphasizing a theme familiar to New South promoters and a prejudice typical of the era: "Southern mills are operated by native Americans exclusively. No foreign mill labor ever has been invited to the South, and it cannot be foreseen that any ever will be wanted in this section."[13] The authors of this damning passage might well have truthfully mentioned the black man's exclusion from the Southern textile mill, but part of the New South

Plate 11.5: The Southern Railway Depot at Gainesville. Similar to the Southern's fine passenger depot at Athens built in 1913. (Photo: Wilber W. Caldwell.)

Creed was the myth that racial relations in the American South were a picture of sweetness and light, and any mention of blacks in these publications was usually limited to glowing reports of racial harmony.

All of this took place in an atmosphere charged with railroad schemes and dreams. Between 1847 and 1910, no fewer than 12 railroads were chartered with the intent of passing through Gainesville (See Table 11.1). Although some progress was made on the Gainesville and Dahlonega Railroad, it was never completed, and only the Atlanta and Richmond Air Line and the Gainesville, Jefferson and Southern were built in the period of our interest. The Gainesville Northwestern Railroad was completed to Cleveland and on to Helen in 1913. This shaky timber road failed in 1934.

Plate 11.6: The Gainesville, Midland Depot at Gainesville, built in 1914.

The terrible tornado of 1936 had not been the first to ravage Gainesville. The predecessor to this fine depot, built by the Gainesville Jefferson and Southern in 1913-1914, had been destroyed in a tornado that killed 90 and damaged a considerable portion of the town in 1903.

Thirty years earlier, the completion of the Atlanta and Richmond Air Line had sparked considerable railroad building in northeast Georgia. Several successful lines stretched eastward from the main trunk of the Air Line into the central Piedmont. Joining the Air Line at Lula a few miles north of Gainesville, the Northeastern Railroad, chartered way back in 1854 by the people of Athens, was completed in 1876. Likewise, about the same time, the Elberton Air Line was completed from Elberton connecting with the Atlanta-Charlotte road at Toccoa. Railroad building to the west was not so successful. With the exception of the Northeastern Railroad's 1882 branch from Cornelia on the Atlanta and Richmond Air Line to Tallulah Falls and later reorganization and extension to Franklin, North Carolina, there was no chartered railroad penetration of the mountains of northeast Georgia in the period before 1910.

The largest of the railroads connecting the Atlanta and Richmond Air Line with the central

GAINESVILLE RAILROADS CHARTERED BUT NEVER BUILT
1847, The Gainesville Railroad
1856, The Gainesville and Chattahoochee Railroad, later the Gainesville Ridge Railroad
1866, The Gainesville and Dahlonega Railroad (begun but never completed.)
1870, The Gainesville and Ellijay Railroad
1873, The Gainesville, Blairsville and Northwestern Railroad
1874, The Northwestern Railroad
1880, The State Line Railroad
1885, The Gainesville and Western Railroad
1885, The Augusta and Chattanooga Railroad
1886, The Cartersville and Gainesville Railroad
1887, The Gainesville and Columbia Railroad
1891, The Cartersville, Gainesville and Port Royal Railroad
1891, The Cartersville, Gainesville and Augusta Railroad

Table 11.1

Plate 11.6: The Gainesville, Midland Depot at Gainesville. (Photo: Wilber W. Caldwell.)

[10] Sibyl McRae, ed., *A Pictorial History of Hall County* (Gainesville GA: Hall County Library Committee, 1985) 26.

[11] Eleanor Ripley in a 1973 unpublished manuscript found in the Hall County Public Library in Gainesville.

[12] Georgia Power Company, *Industrial Georgia, Cotton Manufacturers* (Atlanta: The Georgia Power Company, 1925) 34.

[13] Georgia Power Company, *Industrial Georgia, Cotton Manufacturers*, 15.

Piedmont was the Gainesville, Jefferson and Southern, which was completed from Gainesville to join the Georgia Railroad at Social Circle in 1884. This had been accomplished with the help of the Georgia Railroad, which leased the unfinished line in that same year and arranged a consolidation with the Walton Railroad, which operated between Monroe and Social Circle. The Gainesville, Jefferson and Southern began as a narrow gauge railroad. It struggled through the last decades of the nineteenth century, bankrupted in 1904, was reorganized and extended a branch to Athens in 1906 and bankrupted again in 1921. In that year, it was reorganized again, this time as the Gainesville Midland Railroad.

Despite this road's recurring financial difficulties, its impact on Gainesville and on the city's architecture was considerable. Sadly two tornadoes have stripped the town of most of the notable buildings of the era, but fittingly one remains to speak for the period. The stunning Auditorium Building at Gainesville's Brenau College stands today to voice the city's New South progress. Completed in 1897, this building may have been an early Southern attempt to copy the mature French neoclassical styles popular in the North at the turn of the century, but it appears to be more of an extremely late articulation of the Second Empire style, which had been dead in the United States for almost two decades. The appearance of such a grand building in such an outdated mode is fitting here. It speaks well for one of the few places in Georgia to achieve even a

modicum of prosperity during the nineteenth century. And it reminds us that, at the turn of the century, although progress was made in Gainesville, like the rest of the American South, the place was still far behind the times.

BANKS COUNTY: HOMER

Plate 11.7: The Banks County Courthouse, built 1860-1865.

In 1858, Banks County was created from Franklin and Habersham Counties. At that time, the initial survey for the Georgia Air Line, Atlanta's grand scheme for a railroad across the Piedmont via Charlotte to Richmond, sketched a line parallel to the Chattahoochee River to Gainesville and then to Anderson, South Carolina, via Carnesville and Hartwell, passing through or near the present site of the Banks County seat at Homer.[14] Surely this was a factor in locating the new county's seat of justice. The town of Homer was laid out in 1859. In that same year, county officials published the specifications for this courthouse, which is today one of the best standing examples of the brick vernacular courthouse form in Georgia. A thoroughly detailed description of the proposed building, the document includes remarkably complete specifications regarding dimensions, materials and design. These specifications provide insight into the development of vernacular public architecture in America.

Most scholars correctly ascribe the progress of vernacular forms to an evolution in the designs of local builders who fashioned their buildings using time-honored techniques and traditional designs, often influenced by early pattern books and builder's guides. These designs are most often viewed as the products of a surprisingly consistent architectural stew, which was stirred by hometown carpenters and masons in a stock pot filled with local materials, undisciplined ideas and other random stylistic ingredients. Accurate as this image may be, the 1859 specifications for this courthouse at Homer represented another force in the American vernacular. The document is typical of written specifications found in many other places in Georgia in the age before professional architects began

Plate 11.7: The Banks County Courthouse. An antebellum vision of what a courthouse was supposed to look like. (Photo: Wilber W. Caldwell.)

to spin their web of fantasy and symbolism in the South. Although local builders, using their familiar "design as you go" methods were influential, the true essence of public buildings was often on paper in the form of this type of specification well before the builders began. In short, these specifications constitute a plan as detailed as a professional architectural drawing of the era might have provided. For example, the 1859 Bank County Courthouse specifications don't simply call for columns supporting a portico, they specify four columns supported by "pedestals two and one half feet square," and they go on to define the spacing as well as detail the precise taper of the columns. In this case, the vernacular was not only a product of the experience, taste and whim of an individual builder, it represented the collective will of the people, or at least of the early officials, of the new county. They had a vision of what a courthouse should look like, and they committed that vision to paper in much the same way an architect would have done.

This courthouse, built in part with slave labor, would serve for well over 100 years. It stands today in the still tiny hamlet to remind us of what happened in places bypassed by rail. Sadly for Homer, Atlanta's original plans for the Georgia Air Line stalled in the late 1850s, only to re-emerge after the war as the Atlanta and Richmond Air Line. In 1870, the route was re-surveyed and, like the Northeastern Railroad a few years later, the new line would only skirt the edge of Banks County, and no rails would come near Homer. North of Gainesville, the Atlanta and Richmond Air Line ran the high ground just to the east of the Chattahoochee River passing through the sparsely populated foot hills on its was to the South Carolina border, and creating towns at the future junctions of Lula, Cornelia and Toccoa. The entire population of Banks County was less than 5000 when the Air Line was completed to Charlotte. Although we have no record of the exact population of Homer at that time, six years later Sholes's 1879 *Gazetteer of Georgia* approximated the town's size at about 175 persons and related that mail arrived "tri-weekly by horseback." By 1900, the county had doubled in size and was producing a little cotton and a lot of corn, but Homer was still a town of only 221.

Today the Banks County Courthouse has another tale to tell. It is a story of the era that followed the period of our interest. Like so many rural counties in Georgia, Banks County would know a brief and modest prosperity around 1910 only to plunge once again into decades of need. In 1910, when 80% of Georgia's population lived in rural areas, Banks County had expanded its population to over 11,000. By 1960, this figure had shrunk to 6400, and the county was much the same size as when this courthouse was new. In the meanwhile, not much had happened in Homer.

STEPHENS COUNTY: TOCCOA

Plate 11.8: The 1897 Habersham County Courthouse proposed for Toccoa but never built. Andrew J. Bryan, architect.

In 1881, the Atlanta and Charlotte Air Line was acquired by the great Richmond and Danville Railroad. This line would later become the centerpiece in J. P. Morgan's giant Southern Railway. The present depot at Toccoa was built by the Southern well after the end of the period of our interest. Like so many railroad buildings of the mid-twentieth century, this utilitarian little structure is of little architectural interest and is a sadly inadequate symbol for the power of the Atlanta and Richmond Air Line, which created the town in 1873.

The story of Toccoa and the Air Line and ultimately of the Southern Railway itself is a tale rooted in the lust of the Gilded Age, an era that released from deep within the American spirit a ruthless quest for material wealth. In 1871, when the Air Line began to build, a new American political state was being fashioned to serve a new age of big business. The way was being cleared for the cash-register morality that was arriving on the rising tide of industrialism and laissez faire capitalism.

The creation of the city of Toccoa in 1873 and the subsequent war waged between this child of the Gilded Age and the neighboring foot hills of Habersham County in the decades surrounding the

[14] John William Baker, *History of Hart County* (Atlanta: Foote and Davies, 1933) 80.

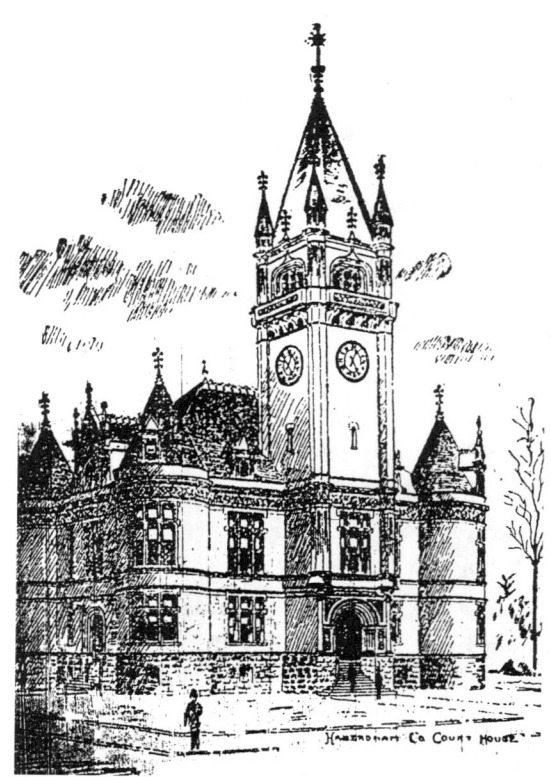

Plate 11.8: Andrew J. Bryan's design for a new courthouse at Toccoa contemplated an architectural style to flaunt the excessive wealth of the emerging elite of American capitalism. (Illustration: *The Southern Record*, August 16, 1897.)

turn of the century presents in microcosm the confrontation between the decaying pastoral order and the rising age of American capitalism, or more simply put, between town and country.

At the very heart of the new age, was the creation of towns like Toccoa, and at the center of these towns was the new ethic of wealth. Everywhere was the desire to grow rich. If we could strip away all of the superfluous wrappings of the myth of the New South, at the very core of the movement we would find this same emerging American materialism. In fashioning the myth, Henry Grady and many others sought a second Southern surrender, this time to the ideological forces of a new Northern middle-class morality, which recognized the machine as its high priest. Perhaps that is why the New South offered such strong resistance in some quarters. It was not so much a movement asso-

ciated with "Yankee" ideas, as it was a mode of thinking that ran contrary to the fundamental frontier ideals, which would remain strong in the American South and West for decades to come.

Despite frontier hardened idealism and poverty in the region, a new breed of Georgia towns began to appear. Born of a railroad inseminated seed, Toccoa was heir to the new lustful grasping American spirit. As offspring of the railroad's combination of rape and seduction, the children of such a father would prove divisive. In 1873, when the Atlanta and Richmond Railroad passed through the sparsely populated foothills of Habersham County, there was little in the region to suggest that the industrial age was at hand. There were virtually no significant towns. The county seat of Clarkesville, located well to the west of the Air Line's route, was a village of only a few hundred residents, and Toccoa, once established on the rails between Atlanta and Charlotte, would soon eclipse her stagnant rival. Appropriately, Toccoa was the product of land speculation. Developers laid out their city next to the Air Line's depot at the place previously known as Dry Pond. With the completion of the Elberton Air Line, which made its junction with the Atlanta-Charlotte road at Toccoa in 1878, extensive switching and yard facilities began to sprout. Twenty years later, the aggressive child had grown up and would confirm her material appetites by making a bid to wrestle the county seat of Habersham County away from Clarkesville.

By 1897, Toccoa had a cotton mill, a large furniture factory and numerous other timber related enterprises, as well as growing mercantile interests. In that year, with her population approaching 2000 and Clarkesville's below 500, Toccoa moved to become Habersham County's seat of justice. The battle lines were drawn between the forces of New South materialism and the Old South agrarian order. The citizens of Toccoa espoused the new American materialism, and the city's values are clear in a Toccoa resident's 1898 letter in *Southern Field Magazine,* which praises that publication for "representing the material interests of those whose fortunes are cast in this fair country." If Toccoa strutted the stuff of progress, then Clarkesville and the county's rural population countered with indignation at the upstart's brazen urban ways and the accompanying affront to tradition.

In exchange for the prize of the county seat, Toccoa offered to build an elaborate courthouse at no cost to the taxpayers of the county. The "Courthouse Club" of Toccoa, the organization that directed the movement to capture the county seat, commissioned Atlanta architect, Andrew J. Bryan to designed the proposed courthouse at Toccoa.[15] Not to be outdone, county officials in Clarkesville also commissioned Andrew J. Bryan to design a new courthouse to strengthen Clarkesville's hold on the county seat. But county leaders in Clarkesville had acted without legal authority. After considerable debate, Bryan was unable to collect his fee for the design, and sued the county, precipitating yet another round of accusations from Toccoa.[16]

Meanwhile, the response from the rural faction to Toccoa's proposed new court building was typified in a letter "To the Taxpayers of Habersham County" published in Toccoa's *Southern Record* in August of 1897: "Do you propose to sell your vote to Toccoa? They can ride around the county in their fine buggies and think that they can buy your God-given right of a free ballot. Do you intend to let them to do so? The intelligent voters of Habersham County say no. We are not slaves to be bought and sold at Toccoa's bidding."[17]

In August of 1897, The Toccoa *Southern Record* published this rendering of Toccoa's proposed courthouse.[18] The selection of the so-called Chateauesque styling is indeed telling. Often called Francois I, the popularity of the style in the United States owes much to the work of Richard Morris Hunt, the first American architect to attend the Ecole des Beaux Arts in Paris and the designer of a number of Chateauesque mansions in the North. Here was an architectural style to flaunt the excessive wealth of the emerging elite of American capitalism. It cannot be coincidental that not very far away in Asheville, North Carolina, Hunt had just completed George Washington Vanderbilt's fabulous Biltmore House, arguably the most lavish American private residence ever built. Except for its symmetry, this courthouse typifies the Chateauesque Style with its high pinna-

cled gables, heavy linteled windows, "basket handle" arch and rounded turrets with their conical caps.

The style of Toccoa's proposed courthouse may have appeared an apt choice to the fledgling New South capitalists in that city, but to the residents to Clarkesville and the rural areas of Habersham County, the flamboyant French castle undoubtedly symbolized everything that they abhorred. Only a few weeks after the sketch appeared, Toccoa was defeated in her effort to capture the county seat. Clarkesville built James Golucke's austere new Romanesque Revival brick courthouse the following year.

The loss of the 1897 election left the matter far from settled. When in 1904, the State Legislature amended the State Constitution relating to the creation of new counties, the Toccoa courthouse faction was quick to join the ranks of 21 other growing adolescent New South railroad towns seeking a county of their own. Again the battle lines were drawn in Habersham County, but this time the forces of the new urban materialism were far too powerful for the dwindling resistance offered by a decaying rural order. Sponsored by business interests in Toccoa, the future Stephens County was originally promoted as Piedmont County and later as Bleckley County.

Whatever the appellation, Toccoa boasted all of the trappings of the arriving new age: a railroad junction with over $275,000 in freight receipts in 1904, the transfer of over 40,000 bales of cotton, two cotton mills, several other small industries, electric power, a plan for a new water works, and almost 3000 inhabitants.[19] Claiming that the wagon road from

[15] Although Bryan's design for a Chateauesque courthouse at Toccoa was never used, in 1899 Bryan presented virtually the same design to leaders in Douglas, Georgia, and with a few modifications, the Coffee County Courthouse rose to reflect Toccoa's earlier plan in 1900.

[16] The record here is a bit unclear. In May of 1897 *The Manufacturer's Record* names Bryan as the architect commissioned at Clarkesville, but less than two months later that publication retracted the report stating that Golucke received the commission. *The Manufacturer's Record*, May 21, 1897 and June 18, 1897. In August of that same year *The (Toccoa) Southern Record* related that Bryan had brought suit against the county for payment of his fee. *The Toccoa Southern Record*, August 6, 1897

[17] *The Toccoa Southern Record*, August 6, 1897.

[18] *The Toccoa Southern Record*, August 16, 1897.

[19] *The Toccoa Southern Record*, June 16, 1905.

Clarkesville to Toccoa actually "destroyed time," the promoters of the new county raged that it usually took a day and half to travel the 17 miles from the Toccoa area to Clarkesville. As for rail travel to Clarkesville, *The Southern Record* held that the trip required over seven hours owing to connections at Cornelia, and that one could easily go to Atlanta and back in that time.[20] It seems odd that in this age of increasing railroad connectivity, the primary argument in favor of new counties in Georgia was bad roads and a long journey to the courthouse. While this argument most often appeared on the surface of the struggle in 1905, the real force behind what was referred to as "the new county movement" was the growing economic and political power of emerging railroad towns like Toccoa, Tifton, Millen, Hazlehurst, Cordele, Ashburn, Cairo, Lyons and Fitzgerald, which all became county seats of new Georgia counties in 1905-1906.

Plate 11.9: The Stephens County Courthouse, built in 1907-1908. H. L. Lewman, architect.

With the creation of Stephens County spirits ran high in Toccoa. Free at last from the retarding yoke of ruralism that had bound the new city to a backward mountain county and to the past, the new county set about the work of creating the machinery of government. High on the list was a new courthouse. An election was held in January of 1907 to approve bonds to fund the new building, and we need look no farther

Plate 11.9: The 1907 Stephens County Courthouse. A stern symbol of new-found political power. (Photo: Wilber W. Caldwell.)

than the results of that polling to assess the measure of the optimism that abounded in and around Toccoa. The vote was unanimous: 1107 for, 0 against.[21]

With such solidarity behind the courthouse movement, one might expect the architectural results to reflect the new county's zeal. This was curiously not the case. H. L. Lewman's Stephens County Courthouse was built from substantially the same plan Lewman had used for the Appling County Courthouse at Baxley in 1906 which, although uninspiring in design, was constructed entirely of elegant limestone. Here we find only limestone trim to accent the ubiquitous red brick walls. The effect is disappointing, and like most of the courthouses built in Georgia in the first decade of the new century by Lewman's Fall City Construction Company of Louisville, Kentucky, this building echoes little zest for either the Old South or the New. Costing just under $40,000 to construct, Lewman's design in Toccoa lacks the exuberance of similarly styled neoclassical court structures built earlier in the decade at similar cost. One can only conclude that like all of Lewman's courthouses in Georgia, this building is not so much a reflection of hope for a new age of prosperity, but a stern symbol for the new found political power which accompanied its arrival. If the people of Toccoa could have shed their enthusiasm long enough to carefully contemplate their new courthouse, they might have perceived in it a warning that the fruits of the new material prosperity they sought would not come without a substantial price.

SOME LAST THOUGHTS ON THE ATLANTA AND RICHMOND AIR LINE

The rails of the Atlanta and Charlotte Air Line straddle a distinct turning point in the history of railroad building in Georgia. At one end of the road's history is the old Georgia and Western Railroad chartered way back in 1856 and promoted as Atlanta's champion. At the other end of the line's history is a series of bankruptcies and acquisitions, which culminated in the acquisition of the Air Line by John Pierpont Morgan's mighty Southern Railway, the juggernaut of Morgan's Southern railroad monopoly. In between are the excesses of America's Gilded Age and the unlovely consequences of that era's unfettered capitalistic cravings. The Atlanta and Richmond Air Line failed only three years after its completion and was reorganized as the Atlanta and Charlotte Air Line. Also widely known as the Piedmont Air Line it was part of the grand railroading scheme of New York shipping tycoons, William and Thomas Clyde. After the line failed again, it was acquired by the emerging giant, the Richmond and Danville. The Atlanta and Charlotte Air Line ultimately came under the control of the Richmond and West Point Terminal and Warehouse Company, the railroad giant whose downfall in a great swindle of 1889 preceded both national depression and the creation of J. P. Morgan's Southern Railway.

As the history of the Air Line illustrates, the price of the Gilded Age's orgy of expansion and exploitation was great. It drowned out the soft voices of romanticism and idealism that the South had heard so clearly, and attempted to replace them with a noisy cynical realism and a growing Federalism that catered to the interests of big business. All of this echoed in a seemingly uncontrollable monopolistic cacophony of failures and reorganizations.

As the era progressed, America began to answer to a new material ethic, which was little understood in a still predominantly rural nation. The result was a national feast that Vernon L. Parrington has called "The Great Barbecue." It was a party to which the American South had not been invited. While the South endured the abuses of Radical Reconstruction, the rest of the nation gorged itself at the feast of the Gilded Age. When the table was cleared, the South would not even be offered the leftovers. It had, in fact, been served up as part of the banquet. Typical of this emerging pattern, the Atlanta and Richmond Air Line was ultimately controlled by Northern men.[22] The region, as a whole, would languish for decades, while the North would be forever reforged in the mold of a new grasping American capitalism.

Along the way, the face of Southern rail would change, and the Atlanta and Richmond Air Line would again be at the center of transition. The early railroads of Georgia had been the servants of trading

Plate 11.10: Gainesville, 1897. (Photo: Wilber W. Caldwell.)

towns like Savannah and Augusta and generally ran from the sea to the inland cotton producing areas of the Cotton Belt and the Piedmont. After the war, the trend began toward rails parallel to the coast, and it became increasingly clear that railroads would in many cases replace coastwise ocean transportation. In addition, the decade following the war saw the emergence of fast freight associations, and cooperative efforts involving numerous Southern railroads to establish favorable rates and reliable schedules for long distance interstate rail shipments.[23] Connecting

[20] *The Toccoa Southern Record*, June 16, 1905.

[21] Kathryn C. Trogdon, ed., *The History of Stephens County, 1715-1972* (Toccoa GA: Toccoa Women's Club, 1973) 52.

[22] C. Vann Woodward, *Origins of the New South, 1877-1913* (1951; reprint, Baton Rouge LA: University of Louisiana Press, 1977) 121.

Atlanta with the industrial centers of the Northeast via Charlotte and Richmond, the Air Line was a pioneer.

Lastly, the Atlanta and Richmond Air Line was transitional with respect to its construction. Georgia's antebellum railroads, like most early American lines, had tended to follow the geographical course of least resistance with little regard for distance. Unlike early railroads in Europe where land was expensive and labor cheap, American's pioneer railroad builders found quite the opposite condition, and they generally skirted natural obstacles seeking to hold down labor costs by moving as little earth as possible.[24] The result was often an inefficient serpentine road with steep grades and sharp curves. In its name as well as its philosophy, the Air Line rejected this concept. This was among the first railroads in Georgia to employ extensive cut and fill techniques to create a straight level passage in order to achieve long term economy of operation.

Builders who followed this new direct approach to the geography of railroad building paid little heed to towns. The driving force behind the creation of the Atlanta and Richmond Air Line had been to connect Atlanta with Charlotte and Richmond by the most direct route. Accordingly, as the new road passed through five Georgia counties, it bypassed all of the region's significant towns except Gainesville.

Remarkable as this may sound, in the foothills of the Appalachians in 1873 few towns existed before the Air Line arrived to create them. The tiny short line of the old Buck Line Railroad from Chamblee on the Air Line to Roswell was as close as Alpharetta, the county seat of old Milton County, would come to steel rails. The county retained its simple vernacular courthouse until it merged with Fulton County in 1931. Likewise the Air Line skirted the western edge of Banks County. Predictably the old 1865 courthouse at Homer stands today as one of the best examples of the fundamental brick design that typified Georgia court-

houses in the era before the railroads spread the myth of promise that would father so many flamboyant architectural expressions of hope in the decades before 1910. The Air Line also passed through Habersham County, bypassing the county seat of Clarkesville. In 1878, the Elberton Air Line made its junction with the new Atlanta-Richmond line at Toccoa, and set off a chain of events, which would see Toccoa mushroom into a town of 2000 by the time the city unsuccessfully bid for the county seat of Habersham in 1897. At the end of this railroad-forged chain of history was the creation of Stephens County in 1905. The Stephens County Courthouse was erected at Toccoa in 1907.

Gainesville, the only old county seat on the Air Line's route, was a modest village before the arrival of the new railroad. It quickly grew to a relatively prosperous New South hub along side the steel rails. With the completion of the Gainesville, Jefferson and Southern Railroad in 1884, Gainesville became a junction town and a new courthouse was erected in 1885. One of Alexander Bruce's quadruplet sister court buildings, the exceptional Second Empire building flaunted the architectural style of the Gilded Age but in a soft hometown sort of way. There can be little doubt that the choice of Alexander Bruce in Gainesville was a direct result of the success of that architect's stunning Second Empire Fulton County Courthouse completed only three years before. We might also argue that Atlanta herself commissioned Parkins and Bruce's Fulton County Courthouse as a monument to her own New South dreams induced by the completion of the Atlanta and Richmond Air Line. While there may be some truth in the suggestion, the completion of the Air Line gave Atlanta her fifth railroad. Thus, by 1882, when her new courthouse was completed, her celebrations were not those of mythical hope but of concrete reality.

•

---

[23] Russell, *Atlanta, 1847-1890, City Building in the Old South and the New*, 120.

[24] Wolfgang Schivelbusch, *The Railroad Journey, The Industrialization of Time and Space in the Nineteenth Century* (1941; reprint, Leamington Spa UK, Hamburg and New York: Berg Publishers, Inc., 1986) 96

12 | Reconstruction Branches, Extensions and Short Lines

GRADY COUNTY: CAIRO

Plate 12.1: The Grady County Courthouse, built in 1908-1909. Alexander Blair III, architect. Burned, February 18, 1980.

Grady County was one of eight new counties created in 1905.[1] But unlike Tifton, Cordele, Toccoa and the other progressive rail crossings that sought new county status in that year, Cairo was not a hotbed of New South zeal. Most to the beneficiaries of the "new county movement" centered on railroad "boom towns" that had achieved their independence as the apparent heirs to the New South's capricious legacy. But here in Cairo, the county soon to be ironically named Grady, after the New South's most influential spokesman, based her appeal on no such progress. The extension of the Atlantic and Gulf had arrived on its way to Thomasville almost forty years earlier. Cairo had clung to her rural ways and in 1905 simply argued for the partition of Decatur and Thomas Counties on the grounds that they were the two largest counties in Georgia.[2]

Cairo's agrarian ideological focus was dramatically revealed in the fight with Thomas and Decatur Counties over the creation of the new county. The region that was soon to become Grady County was considered a "hot bed of Populism" by many in Thomas County. In response *The Cairo Messenger* lashed out at her prosperous neighbor in a torrent of emotion that exposed reactionary passions and bitter resentment in Cairo.

> Why should the people of Grady County, after 80 years of faithful service, any longer help to pay taxes to…work the Thomasville roads so their 'distinguished winter visitors' can air themselves luxuriously around in rubber tire carriages and four horse tallyhos?…Thomasville people…have permitted the foreign and privileged millionaire class to gobble up all her lands (and have) allowed…agricultural hopes to go blighted. Who should stagger and pay taxes…for the curse of this stag-

---

[1] The others were Crisp, Jeff Davis, Jenkins, Stephens, Tift, Toombs and Turner.

[2] *The Cairo Messenger*, December 30, 1904.

Reconstruction Branches, Extensions and Short Lines

THE ATLANTIC AND GULF RAILROAD
Bainbridge Extension Grady County: Cairo • Decatur County: Bainbridge
Seminole County: Donalsonville

THE ATLANTIC AND GULF RAILROAD
Thomasville to Albany—Mitchell County: Camilla

THE SOUTHWESTERN RAILROAD
Blakely Extension - Early County: Blakely • Perry Branch - Houston County: Perry

THE ALABAMA AND CHATTANOOGA RAILROAD
Dade County: Trenton • Some Last Thoughts on Reconstruction Railroads

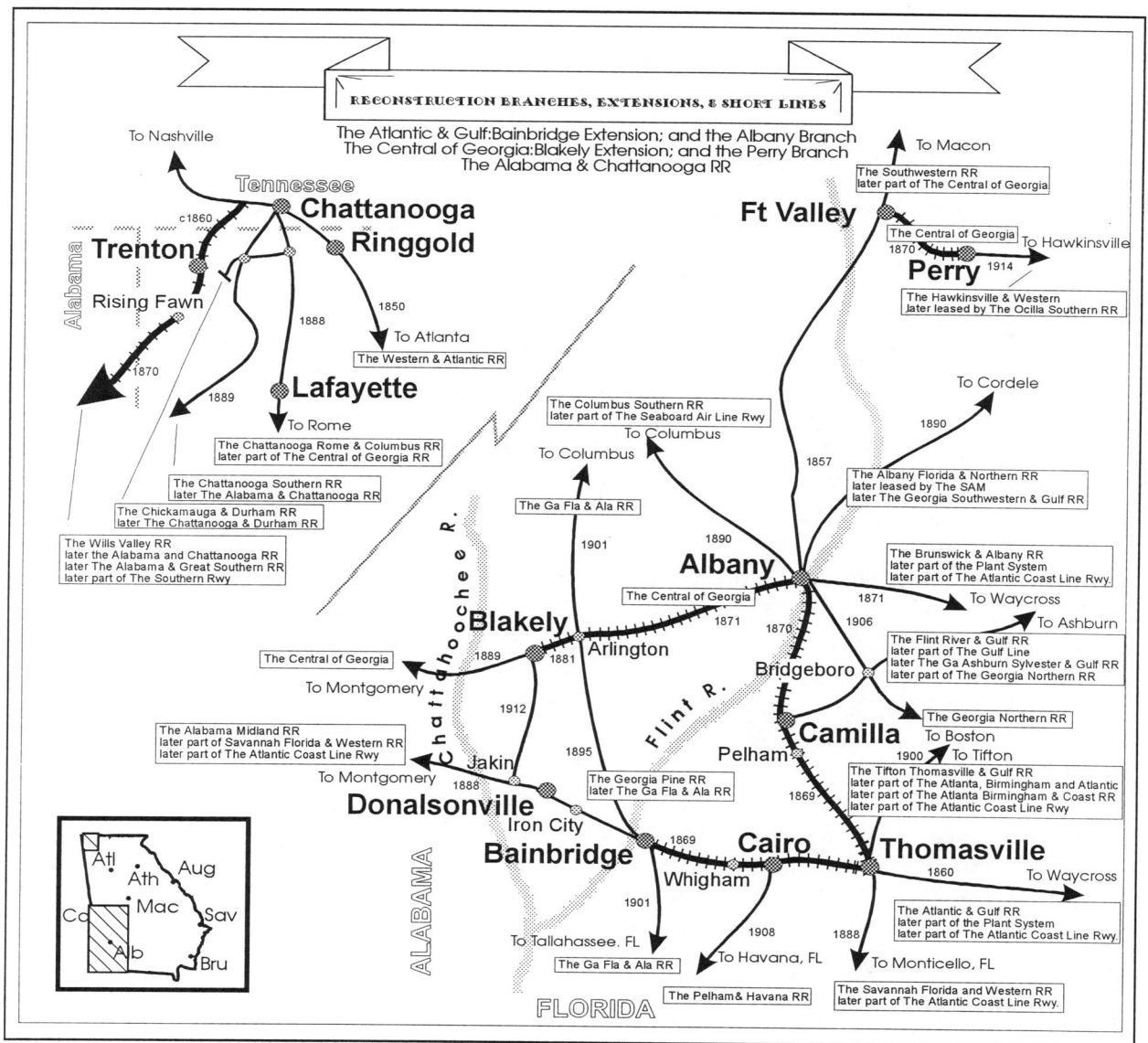

nant poison…? The Crackers over here will run the new county and look out for their taxes if you will run the Yankees and look out for your taxes.[3]

After an attempt to move the county seat from Cairo to nearby Whigham and three failed attempts to pass a bond issue to fund a new courthouse, the newly-created Grady County opted to finance courthouse construction out of general revenues and broke ground on this building in 1908. Despite the county's decided lack of New South fervor, Alexander Blair's 1908 Grady County Courthouse at Cairo appeared to be a thoroughly up-to-date affair. But here the bold neoclassicism, which elsewhere in America stood for the nation's growing financial and industrial power, also recalled the soft columns of a bygone era in the Deep South. What passed for the architecture of Wall Street in the Northeast was the architecture of the Lost Cause in Cairo. Here is one of the last of the dual architectural symbols like those perfected by J. W. Golucke and Frank Milburn just after the turn of the century. By 1908, there were many models close at hand for Blair to follow. A. J. Bryan's compelling 1902 Colquitt County Courthouse, T. F. Lockwood's 1903 Dougherty County Courthouse and J. W. Golucke's stunning 1906 Worth County Courthouse stood on the squares of nearby Moultrie, Albany and Sylvester respectively. But here in Cairo, second generation Macon architect, Alexander Blair III, who had designed the remarkable Decatur County Courthouse in nearby Bainbridge in 1901, ignored all of these models and copied his own Montgomery County Courthouse, which had been completed at Mt. Vernon in 1907.

Blair's building is transitional. Gone are the four more or less equal entrances with their bold pediments so reminiscent of the Greek temple and of the Old South. In their place, Renaissance ornament abounded in bold rusticated quoining, splayed window lentils and elaborate fenestration featuring scrolling hood supports in the second story. Like Blair's court buildings at Colquitt and Mount Vernon, the Grady County Courthouse takes a step on the road toward modern renaissance-inspired forms at the extreme of

Plate 12.1: Built in 1908, Alexander Blair's Grady County Courthouse symbolized Cairo's precarious progress, which balanced on the razor's edge between the Old South and the New. (Photo: Courtesy of Georgia Dept. of Archives and History.)

which would be Beaux-Arts classicism, an excessively baroque governmental style that emotionally recalled little of times gone by. Its appearance in the South would mark the end of an architecture of the people and the beginning of an architecture of the government. The emergence of Beaux-Arts architecture in Georgia celebrated a New South that, to some, appeared real. But its pompous impersonal styling warned others that the modern era would not arrive without a numbing cost.

In Grady County in 1908, American industrialism and its flamboyant symbols were still a very long distance away. Cairo remained balanced on the razor's edge between the old and the new, while the more modern neoclassicism of Alexander Blair III's 1908 Grady County Courthouse supplied a rare glimpse into a distant future.

Plate 12.2: The Depot at Cairo, built in 1905.

Like almost all of Georgia's railroads built in the Reconstruction period, the extension of the Atlantic and Gulf to Bainbridge via Cairo was a realization of pre-war plans. The right-of-way for this portion of the road had been secured in 1859, and the usual land speculations had ensued. Large tracts around Cairo

[3] *The Cairo Messenger*, February 10, 1905.

Plate 12.2: In 1905, many citizens of the newly formed Grady County took the Atlantic Coast Line's sturdy new brick depot at Cairo to stand for the road's "confidence" in Cairo's future. (Photo: Wilber W. Caldwell.)

were sold in 1861 and divided into town lots and resold in 1866. The resulting town was called Cairo after an old Post office in the area. In October of the next year, *The Thomasville Enterprise* published the following notice: "This railroad will be open to Station #20 (Cairo) 14 miles west of Thomasville, on October 10."[4]

After the arrival of the railroad, growth in Cairo was steady. By 1880, there were 55 households at the place that before the arrival of the Atlantic and Gulf, had contained little save the old Cairo Post Office located "five days from Tallahassee by ox cart."[5] By 1900, despite the intransigence of many of Grady County's independent farmers, there were hints of New South zeal churning just beneath the surface in Cairo. This fine brick depot was completed by the Atlantic Coast Line Railroad in 1905, and citizens of the new county took it to stand for the road's "confidence" in Cairo's future.[6] Such confidence begot the familiar exaggeration that so often accompanied a sip of New South's intoxicating wine. Stating that the new depot would "be a dandy," *The Cairo Messenger* pre-

dicted that, upon the new building's completion, Cairo "would not be far behind Atlanta."[7]

Although one is hard pressed to attribute the creation of Grady County and the construction of Alexander Blair's grand neoclassical architectural symbol to the arrival of crossing rails in Cairo, crossing rails did arrive just as the new courthouse was nearing completion. The early years of the century had been filled with railroad schemes in southwest Georgia, and Cairo had listened to her share of these dreams. The Thomasville and Gulf Railroad was proposed to pass through Grady County on its way to St. Joseph's Bay, Florida. A road was planned from Meigs on the Mitchell County border, to Quincy, Florida, via Cairo, and spirits soared on the prospects for the Albany, Camilla and Newton Railroad and the Albany, Cairo and Gulf. Nothing came of these railroad plans. But one tiny railroad was begun. In 1908, just as throngs paraded in the streets of Cairo to celebrate the new courthouse, [8] the Pelham and Havana Railroad completed rails into Cairo from Havana, Florida.

The road was never extended to Pelham, but the fact that Cairo sought connection with that extraordinary place is testament to a budding New South spirit in Grady County. Pelham was the creation of the remarkable J. L. Hand. By 1900 it was a microcosm of New South growth and prosperity in a most unlikely setting, a boomtown in the piney wilderness 17 miles north of Cairo. Although the town's hay-day was brief, Pelham with her large cotton mill and fabulous 100,000 square foot Hand Trading Company was a beacon for New South aspirations in Southwest Georgia in the first two decades of the new century. Cairo reluctantly sought the light. In November of 1908, *The Cairo Messenger* observed: "The citizens of Cairo are admirers of thrifty Pelham and are anxious for railroad connection between the towns. Railroad connections would put in closer relation two of the best towns in this section, and give Pelham a splendid opening to the sea."[9]

By 1908, the end of an era was approaching for Cairo. Although she was still a long way from standing in the modern light of the new age, she was at least beginning to reveal her divided mind, and like so

[4] *The Enterprise* (Thomasville GA), October 8, 1867.

[5] Yvonne Miller Brunton, Grady County Georgia, *Some of Its History, Folk Architecture and Families* (Jackson MS: Quality Printers, 1979) 37.

[6] *The Cairo Messenger*, December 30, 1904.

[7] *The Cairo Messenger*, May, 1904.

[8] *The Cairo Messenger*, April 30, 1909 and May 7, 1909.

[9] *The Cairo Messenger*, November 20, 1908.

[10] William S. Holt, "Report to the Superintendents, Chief Engineers, Presidents and Superintendents of The Southwestern Railroad," (Macon GA: The JW Burke and Company, 1869) 575.

many blossoming villages all across Dixie, Cairo was forced to begin to address the fundamental dilemma which stood at the center of the real New South.

DECATUR COUNTY: BAINBRIDGE

Plate 12.3: The Atlantic Coast Line Depot at Bainbridge, built c. 1908.

In 1868, when the Atlantic and Gulf Railroad reached Bainbridge, the air on the banks of the Flint became highly charged with railroad energy. Almost simultaneously with the extension of the rails from Savannah, the promise of crossing rails loomed large in Decatur County. The Bainbridge, Cuthbert and Columbus Railroad was chartered in March of 1869, and in 1871 the ubiquitous Hannibal Kimball, Atlanta's consummate railroad promoter and self-styled entrepreneur, obtained state endorsement for the new road's bonds. In the heart of the economic nightmare that followed the war, the city of Bainbridge subscribed $50,000 in Atlantic and Gulf stock and then again dug deep into her dwindling coffers in order to muster financial support for Kimball's new north-south crossing line. Hopes for crossing rails were quickly dashed as the Bainbridge, Cuthbert and Columbus, defaulted in 1872, having laid no rails. Citing various irregularities, a new Democratic legislature refused to honor the state's endorsement of the road's bonds. Despite increased traffic on the Flint River flowing to the Atlantic and Gulf's railhead at Bainbridge, the town lay stagnant for almost twenty years. Finally in 1888, the Alabama Midland Railroad extended the line to Montgomery, Alabama, and the extension became part of the Plant System in 1890.

In 1823, long before America's first railroads were constructed, Decatur County had been cut from the giant Early County. A year later, on the site of an older Indian trading post, Bainbridge, was designated the county seat. A crude courthouse was erected in 1826, and the first steamboat arrived a year later. In his 1829 *Gazetteer of Georgia*, the reliable Adiel Sherwood described Bainbridge as a village containing a court-house, a jail and about twenty stores and houses. The original court building was replaced with a 20 x 40-foot brick courthouse begun in 1831 but not

Plate 12.3: The Atlantic Coast Line Depot at Bainbridge was probably built in response to Bainbridge's population boom in the years just before 1910. (Photo: Wilber W. Caldwell.)

completed until 1838. George White estimatated Bainbridge's population at only 200 in 1849, but the 1850s saw significant growth as cotton began to flow down the Flint. A fine two-story brick courthouse rose on the square in 1855. Although the town was not technically at the head of navigation of the Flint River, and steamboats regularly plied the waters northward to Albany, navigation above Bainbridge was unpredictable. Before the arrival of the railroad, the town's economic focus had been her river connection to the shallow harbor at Apalachicola.

Surprisingly, the arrival of the Atlantic and Gulf Railroad in 1868 had the initial effect of increasing the importance of river transportation for Bainbridge. In southwest Georgia in the years immediately following the Civil War, the Atlantic and Gulf operated her own steam boats on the Chattahoochee and the Flint Rivers, promoting a water-rail route to Savannah with the rail link originating at Bainbridge. This forced the Central of Georgia to lower her rates for cotton shipped from Ft. Gaines and Eufaula, and in 1868 the Central began operating her own steamboats on the Chattahoochee.[10]

Although Bainbridge saw little progress in the years following the 1872 failure of the Bainbridge, Cuthbert and Columbus, by 1889 several more railroad schemes had emerged including those of the Bainbridge, Cuthbert and Western and the Bainbridge and Northeastern Railroad, but these were to quickly disappear into obscurity. Only the Bainbridge Northern Railroad managed to lay any track, but this tiny lumber road, begun in 1896, stretched only 32 miles out into the piney woods reaching the village of

Paulina in 1904. The line was abandoned around 1925.

Despite these frustrations, Hannibal Kimball's old dream of a connection from Tallahassee to Columbus was never far from the hearts of citizens of Bainbridge. In 1895, the old fires were kindled with the completion of the Georgia Pine Railroad from Bainbridge to Arlington. The embers of expectancy sparked by the Georgia Pine, which by 1901 had become part of the Georgia, Florida and Alabama Railroad, were fanned into a notable conflagration of New South passion as Bainbridge's Tallahassee to Columbus railroad dream finally began to come true. Here again was the inferno of seemingly boundless hope in which the girders of so many fantasy courthouses were forged.

It is clear that the old dream of the Bainbridge, Cuthbert and Columbus was never forgotten in Decatur County. In 1902, *The Bainbridge Search Light* wrote: "The completion of the Ga., Fla. and Ala. (Georgia Pine) road to Tallahassee is a consummation we have been devotedly wishing ever since the first dirt was broken on the B. C. & C. in 1870."[11] Such remembrances were accompanied by the predictable outpourings of unfettered enthusiasm. These issued forth in contemplation of the mythical gifts that everyone was sure would soon be bestowed upon Bainbridge in reward for her long-suffering vigil. The rhetoric spewed in all directions. Waves of mindless optimism proclaimed that Bainbridge was "destined to be one of the greatest commercial towns in the South"[12] and that there was no reason why Bainbridge "should remain long behind Columbus in point of population."[13] This last dramatic quote relates the fantastic power of the myth to overpower logic and reason, for in the 1902, when this was published, Bainbridge's population stood just above 2500 and Columbus was a town of almost 20,000.

Amid all of this fervor, the citizens of Bainbridge continually heckled the Atlantic Coast Line for a new depot. The sad condition of the old building was inconsistent with the town's new self-image, and when in 1903, the Georgia, Florida and Alabama announced plans for new depot in Bainbridge, *The Search Light* seized upon the opportunity to regale the Atlantic Coast Line for not replacing its "antediluvian structure."[14] It is highly unlikely that the railroad paid much attention to such ravings, and although we do not know exactly when this depot was erected, it was most likely built in response to Bainbridge's population boom in the years just before 1910.

In the meantime, undeterred by reality, the full-blown myth of the New South appeared at Bainbridge, and the apparition beckoned:

> Now let manufacturing interests be promoted and built up in keeping with our great opportunities. No other town in Georgia has fortune knocking harder for entrance, in no other town is there so many natural advantages for every prosperous enterprise and thrifty industry. Let the onward march of progress be welcomed far and wide.[15]

In 1903, two more railroads would appear headed for Bainbridge, but like so many of the promises of the New South, the St. Andrews, Quincy and Northern and the Apalachicola and Northern never arrived. Nonetheless, spirits briefly soared, the town grew, and part of Bainbridge's perceived "onward march of progress" was the construction of Alexander Blair III's 1902 Decatur County Courthouse.

Plate 12.4: The Decatur County Courthouse, built in 1902. Alexander Blair III, architect.

Many in Bainbridge found it unthinkable that a courthouse might be built in any location other than the center of the town square, but after a year of controversy over budget, funding and location, Alexander Blair III's Decatur County Courthouse rose on a corner lot adjacent to the square. The old courthouse was pulled down and the square remains a public park today.

Alexander Blair was the son of the English born architect of the same name who had made a successful career in Macon in the last decades of the nineteenth century. Following in his father's foot steps, the son went on to design eight courthouses in Georgia (see Appendix C). This was his first, and it was perhaps his best. The year 1901 found courthouse design in Georgia at a crossroads. Picturesque designs had covered the state in the years before the depression of 1893. Right up until the turn of the century Romanesque designs continued to find favor in Georgia despite the growing national fascination with the neoclassical theatrics spawned by the 1893 Columbian Exposition at Chicago and the ensuing City Beautiful Movement. In 1901, only two neoclassical court buildings had appeared in Georgia, and it would be two more years before J. W. Golucke's courthouses at Greenville and Newnan and Frank Milburn's Wilcox County Courthouse at Abbeville would firmly establish the popularity of the classical courthouse form that was to capture the imagination of rural Georgians.

In this void, Alexander Blair labored to create in Bainbridge a design that would bridge the turbulent waters of changing times. He sought to capture the essence of New South economic passions imported on the rails of the Georgia, Florida and Alabama Railroad while retaining the distinctly Southern (which is to say reactionary) social character of the place. The result is a remarkable tapestry of architectural symbols. With its high corner tower, the building presents a picturesque silhouette. The east elevation includes a monumentally tall and slender classical portico of the Composite Order. But the fundamental thrust of the design is what Henry Russell Hitchcock and William Seale properly term "Neocolonial," and "of a loosely Georgian order."[16] The whole is overlaid with rather bold Renaissance ornament. Here is a symbol that, despite its complexity, clearly spoke the language of the divided mind of the South.

At first blush it might seem surprising that the Georgian Revival did not find an early audience in Georgia, but the power of the Greek Revival in the Southern mind can not be understated. J. W. Golucke's much imitated four-sided symmetrical designs at Decatur, Greenville, Cartersville, Newnan, Eatonton, Hartwell, and Sylvester would brush aside everything in their wake until 1910. Alexander Blair's later court buildings at Colquitt (1903), Mount Vernon (1907) and Cairo (1908) would reflect this popular neoclassical form. With their studied balance and airy porticos these buildings would combine the power of the Greek Revival and the brick and stone

Plate 12.4: The Decatur County Courthouse, built in 1902. Alexander Blair III's design sought to bridge the turbulent waters of changing times. (Photo: Wilber W. Caldwell.)

classicism of Jefferson with the modern classical forms emanating from the American Northeast. It was to become the ambiguous architecture of both the Old and the New South, and its self-contradictory symbolism spoke the troubled mythical language of hope, pride and despair.

[11] *The Bainbridge Search Light*, May 23, 1902.

[12] *The Bainbridge Search Light*, August 3, 1901.

[13] *The Bainbridge Search Light*, September 19, 1902.

[14] *The Bainbridge Search Light*, October 20 1903

[15] *The Bainbridge Search Light*, May 23, 1902.

[16] Henry Russell Hitchcock and William Seale, "Notes on the Architecture," in Richard Pare, ed., *Courthouse, A Photographic Document* (New York: Horizon Press, 1978) 235.

SEMINOLE COUNTY: DONALSONVILLE

Plate 12.5: The depot at Iron City.

Like so many South Georgia villages, Donalsonville's early history is rooted in the lumber and turpentine industry. Before the arrival of the railroad, there were minor timber related activities and scattered farms in what is today Seminole County, but there were no proper towns until 1888, when the Alabama Midland Railroad laid its rails from Bainbridge to Montgomery, Alabama. This line was acquired by the Plant System in 1890.

Donalsonville's early history is a record of struggle. The town grew out of the successful operations of the Donalson Lumber Company until her great saw

Plate 12.5: Today the depot at Donalsonville is gone, but its sister still stands only 4 miles away at Iron City. (Photo: Wilber W. Caldwell.)

mill burned just before the turn of the century. In the wake of this disaster, Donalsonville faltered, becoming a near "ghost town."[17] She rebounded slowly, but in 1902 a devastating fire again laid her low. Three years later, the region was part of the "new county movement," vying for new county status, but this dream was not realized until 1920 when Seminole County was cut from Decatur and Early Counties. In the meantime, the Wainhurst Railroad had come and gone. This tiny timber road was built from Brinson, on the old Atlantic Coast Line Railway nine miles east of Donalsonville to the Chattahoochee River in 1903. It was abandoned in 1916.

Seminole County's 1921 Beaux-Arts courthouse, designed by Atlanta's William J. J. Chase, is still in use today. Typical of the court buildings of the era, the Seminole County Courthouse seems inappropriately formal, even pompous, in its rural and unassuming setting. Like so many court buildings of the era, this structure's message seems to be one of governmental authority rather than communal celebration. Buildings of this era are not included in this study.

Today, the depot at Donalsonville is gone, but its sister stands only 4 miles away at Iron City. With her great virgin forest leveled, a surprisingly diverse agricultural base blossomed in Seminole County in the first decades of this century. But Donalsonville remained a remote and very rural spectator, watching from the wings as the New South struggled to become reality on the uneven stage of the new century.

MITCHELL COUNTY: CAMILLA

Plate 12.6: The Mitchell County Courthouse, built in 1890. Demolished in 1936. Bruce and Morgan, architects.

Even before the Atlantic and Gulf reached Thomasville in 1860, forward-thinkers there had begun plans for a rail connection via Camilla to Albany. To that end the South Georgia and Florida Railway was chartered in 1857. As Thomasville awaited the long promised rails of the Atlantic and Gulf, her enterprising factors envisioned the rich cotton harvests of Southwest Georgia transported to Savannah not northward over the Southwestern Railroad from

Albany via Macon, but southward over the South Georgia and Florida via Thomasville and then eastward over the Atlantic and Gulf. Albany was cool to this scheme, for she harbored a similar vision. In Albany's dreams, the cotton route to Savannah followed the proposed Brunswick and Florida Railroad from Albany down to its junction with the Atlantic and Gulf at the place soon to be called Waycross. As the first shells fell on Fort Sumter and the Atlantic and Gulf had reached Thomasville, the Brunswick and Florida (later called the Brunswick and Albany) was laying track west of Waycross, and the South Georgia and Florida was newly surveyed. But it would be ten years before either line was completed.

Despite the economic chaos that gripped Georgia after the war and the deplorable condition of her war-torn rails and rolling stock, the state's railroads were surprisingly quick to resume service after the fighting ended. The Western and Atlantic, the Georgia Railroad, the Atlanta and West Point and the Macon and Western were all running again by the end of 1865, and the thoroughly ravaged Central of Georgia was back in service by the end of 1866. The Atlantic and Gulf, which had been mutilated by Sherman between Savannah and the Altamaha River crossing near Jesup, was up and running again in April of 1866.[18] With passenger and freight rates on the incline and cotton again beginning to cover southwest Georgia, railroad expansion was on the wind. The restoration of the "Live Oak Connector" from DuPont to Florida and the extension of the main line to Bainbridge were the Atlantic and Gulf's first priorities.

This meant that Thomasville's dreams of a connection to Albany via Camilla had to wait. Such a delay did not sit well in Thomas County, where fears arose that, without crossing rails, the town would become nothing more than a stop along the way. Thus, with the help of state-endorsed bonds, the old charter of the South Georgia and Florida was revived by local interests in Thomasville. By 1869 rails were complete to Pelham in Mitchell County, but the South Georgia and Florida was financially unable to continue, and the struggling company was sold to the

Plate 12.6: The Mitchell County Courthouse built in 1890, was a bridge for from Bruce and Morgan's Second Empire work of the 1880s to their grand Richardsonian and Queen Anne creations of the 1890s. (Photo: Courtesy of Ted Brooke.)

Atlantic and Gulf, which completed the line through Camilla and on to Albany before 1870.

Like the South Georgia and Florida Railroad, the new county town of Camilla was a work in progress when the Civil War ended. Created from Baker County in 1858 and reflecting the allure of the state's rich western cotton growing lands, Mitchell County was part of a huge crop of new counties created in southwest Georgia in the decade before 1860.[19] The county's first courthouse, a two-story frame building, had been erected in 1858. The building burned in 1869, the same year that the rails of the Atlantic and Gulf arrived at Camilla, and the county's second courthouse, an exact replica of the first, rose on the same spot.

At the beginning of the war, only three years after the first Mitchell County Courthouse was completed,

[17] Mary Kirkland, ed., *Cornerstone of Georgia, Seminole County, 1920-1991* (Roswell GA: Seminole County Historical Society, 1991) 21.

[18] Peter S. McGuire, "The Railroads of Georgia, 1860-1880," in *The Georgia Historical Quarterly* 16/3 (Savannah 1932): 189-90.

[19] Southwestern Georgia saw the creation of ten new counties in the 1850s. They were Brooks, Calhoun, Clay, Colquitt, Dougherty, Miller, Mitchell, Quitman, Terrell and Worth.

Camilla contained only three frame dwellings.[20] By 1890, her population was just above 800, but the town's early hopes for crossing rails had died with the Camilla and Cuthbert Railroad which, despite its privileged state-endorsed bonds, had failed way back in the early 1870s after grading only a few miles of roadbed. With no aggressive railroad promoters to spread New South dogma, there would be few mythical promises abroad in the streets of Camilla. While the late 1880s and early 1890s saw fanciful court buildings rise all across the state where crossing rails beckoned, the 1890 Mitchell County Courthouse was a predictably simple affair. Here there would be none of the picturesque fantasies of William Parkins and Lorenzo Wheeler's 1886 Randolph County Courthouse at nearby Cuthbert nor the wild eclectic excesses voiced in Parkins's 1892 Terrell County Courthouse at neighboring Dawson. Alexander Bruce's 1890 Mitchell County Courthouse at Camilla echoed the softer voices of an earlier age. It bore a marked similarity to Bruce's very first courthouse design, the 1871 Loudon County Courthouse at Loudon, Tennessee, (Plate 12.7) and it was an almost exact copy of his 1888 Pickens County Courthouse at Jasper. Although the Pickens County Courthouse at Jasper displayed a bit more elegance with its stone banding, both buildings flaunt only modest decoration. Their overall plans are so similar that they lead one to conclude that the original Pickens County court building was originally topped with a similar clock tower.

All of these buildings evolved from the simple hipped roofed rectangular central mass flanked by hipped roofed wings, and are reminiscent of the American brick vernacular. Nonetheless, they achieve notable plasticity with their multiple wall surfaces projecting outward from the central mass and from the wings in a series of three-dimensional elevations typical of the French Second Empire mode. Here at Camilla, the lantern's low silhouette and multifaceted roof recalled Bruce's 1882 Hancock County court building at Sparta, and there can be little doubt that Alexander Bruce was treading on familiar soil when he designed his 1890 courthouse at Camilla. It is as if, with the Second Empire long out of vogue, Bruce simply stripped away the mansards and the Parisian ornamentation, leaving behind a simple unadorned form. Although this building could never be termed Romanesque, it may have been a stepping stone for Bruce and Morgan, a bridge from their Second Empire work of the 1880s to their grand and highly picturesque creations of the 1890s. Whatever the case, it contains many of the elements of Bruce's earlier work. Here is a late reminder of the foundation upon which his Second Empire designs were based, a stylistic lag that reveals vernacular roots. What could have been more apt for Mitchell County almost twenty years before crossing rails would reach Camilla?

Plate 12.8: The Atlantic Coast Line Railway Depot at Camilla, built c. 1915.

Camilla was finally blessed with crossing rails in 1908 when the Gulf Line Railroad arrived from Sylvester. This was a late link in a railroad scheme begun by the old Hawkinsville and Florida Southern Railroad, which had become part of the Gulf Line in 1906. This fine depot was built to service the junction of the Gulf Line with the Thomasville to Albany line, which by that time had become part of the Atlantic Coast Line Railway. When this depot was built, Mitchell County's new courthouse was only about twenty-five years old, but despite the prosperity on the wind in much of South Georgia in the years around 1910, Camilla was not sufficiently moved by an outpouring of New South zeal to erect another.

Just to the south of Camilla, along the rails of the old Atlantic and Gulf's branch from Thomasville to Albany, other crossing rails were aborning. As if to contrast with Camilla's sobriety, the intoxicating elixir of the myth of the New South would be heartily consumed in the neighboring hamlet of Pelham. It was a strange and ultimately doomed enterprise, but before it was over, the unbridled raptures wrought by the promises of the myth of prosperity in that village would equal the outpourings of New South zeal anywhere in Georgia. Like so many of the stories attached to the myth of the New South, Pelham's tale centers on the drive and convictions of one man.

Judson Larrabee Hand was born near Perry, Georgia, in 1851, and came to Pelham in 1871 just after the town had been founded beside the tiny depot of the Atlantic and Gulf's fledgling Thomasville and Albany branch. Like so many other successful regional entrepreneurs of the era when the railroads first penetrated the piney woods, Hand began as a lumberman.

If J. L. Hand's story could be narrated by the record of architecture in Pelham, it would be a story told by two buildings. His residence recounts his early success in the lumber business. Designed by Atlanta's noted architect, Gustav Leo, Hand's home at Pelham was built just over a decade after his arrival in Mitchell County. After Pelham's demise, the elaborate wooden house slowly fell into a state of decay and was demolished late in the twentieth century, but when it was completed in 1885, it was surely one of the finest houses in Southwest Georgia. The other architectural narrator of J. L. Hand's story is the Hand Trading Company building in Pelham. Designed by Atlanta's Walker and Chase and completed in 1916 just before the streets of Pelham were paved, the 100,000 square foot, four-story building still looms above the tiny town. Standing empty on a prominent corner in Pelham today, it dwarfs the now dwindling village whose population had risen from about 250 when Hand built his fine home in 1885 to well over 2000 when the enormous Hand Trading Company Building was begun in 1914. In between, were saw mills and turpentine stills; a cotton gin built in 1893 reputed to have been "the largest in the South;" a fertilizer plant; a cotton seed oil factory; a bank; melons and tobacco and tomatoes; two railroads, the Flint River and Northeastern and the Pelham and Havana (which never got all the way to Pelham); and a cotton mill which was said to be south Georgia's largest in 1900.[21]

Hand's success in Pelham so eclipsed anything else in the area that an effort was made to create a new county from parts of Mitchell, Grady, Thomas and Colquitt with Pelham as the county seat. Hansel County, as the new county was to be called, failed to secure legislative approval in 1913 as concerns grew that too many counties in South Georgia had begun to tip political scales in the state. Three years later, J. L. Hand died, just as his grand Trading Company

Plate 12.7: Alexander Bruce's 1871 Loudon County Courthouse at Loudon, Tennessee. (Photo: Wilber W. Caldwell.)

Plate 12.8: The Atlantic Coast Line Depot at Camilla was built to service the junction of the Gulf Line and the Atlantic Coast Line. (Photo: Wilber W. Caldwell.)

Building was completed. Today only the wind passes through the Hand Trading Company and the great smoke stack is all that is left of south Georgia's largest cotton mill. Here in Pelham, we come face to face with the myth of the New South.

The reason no fantasy courthouse rose at Camilla is the same reason Pelham slowly faded. When the New South finally arrived in Georgia, it would act on an urban stage. When J. L. Hand's empire was nearing its peak, Mitchell County, like most of Georgia was a very rural place. In 1901, 62% of Georgia's work force

[20] Margaret Spence and Anna M. Fleming, *History of Mitchell County, Georgia, 1857-1976* (Camilla GA: Camilla Rotary Club, 1976) 101.

[21] Marion Rogers, *The Building of a Town, A Partial History of Pelham, Georgia,and Surrounding Areas, 1880-1974* (Tallahassee FL: Rose Printing, 1976) 60.

labored in agriculture. This was a state of farmers, pure and simple, and all of the railroads and railroad promoters in the world would not quickly change this central agricultural fact of Southern life, any more than they could change the fact that, in 1910, cotton was still the central fact of Southern agriculture. All of the state's corps combined were valued at $226 million in 1909, and almost two thirds of this total, $146 million, was derived from cotton. Nonetheless, a few glimmers of the new age appeared in the heart of cotton's kingdom. Places like Pelham reveal the New South in microcosm. They were built as shimmering multifoliate dreams of prosperity erected on foundations of sand, and in a blink they were gone.

EARLY COUNTY: BLAKELY

Plate 12.9: The Early County Courthouse, built in 1857, Demolished 1904.

Unlike the many "boom towns" that blossomed all across South Georgia at the beginning of the twentieth century, Blakely's roots ran deep into the nineteenth century. The town had been established as Early County's permanent seat of justice in 1825. Chartered in 1818, Early County along with Appling and Irwin was one of the three enormous counties that originally spanned the vast empty reaches of south central and southwestern Georgia. Eleven new counties would later be fashioned, in whole or in part, from

Plate 12.9: The 1857 Early County Courthouse with its ample portico supported by four, square columns remained in use until 1904.

Early's original territory. Located only 9 miles from Howard's Landing on the Chattahoochee River, Blakely began as cotton's servant. In 1849, George White described the town as having twenty-five or thirty families with two stores and two hotels. The first Early County Courthouse had been a "heavy hewn log building"[22] built some time after 1825. This was replaced by a frame structure in 1836, which in turn gave way to a "Colonial Style" court building in 1857. This vernacular building with its ample portico supported by foursquare columns remained in use until 1904.

In 1873, Virgil Powers, Superintendent of the Southwestern Division of the Central of Georgia Railroad, reported to the road's president that the new "Blakely Extension" of the Southwestern Railroad was running between Albany and Arlington and that grading was completed all the way to Blakely.[23] But in the wake of the depression following the Panic of 1873, it would be eight years before rails reached Blakely. Meanwhile, the financial disaster of the seventies had forced the closing of Early County's antebellum cotton mill, which had been established in 1855 on Harrod Creek nine miles from the courthouse.

In 1881, the Central finally completed the "Blakely Extension," and unloaded the usual cargo of high spirits. Reporting on the arrival of the first train in Blakely in 1881, *The Early County News* observed that: "everybody moved with a more lively step, a smile was on every countenance, and expressions of satisfaction came from every mouth."[24] This effect was short-lived. Although the Central extended the "Blakely Extension" to the Chattahoochee River at Columbia, Alabama, in 1889, Blakely remained true to her agrarian ways, and the town showed only brief signs of conversion to the creed of New South progress.

Plate 12.10: The Early County Courthouse, built in 1904-1905. Morgan and Dillion, architects.

By 1890, with her population under 500, Blakely was sputtering. By the turn of the century, when the Central completed the "Blakely Extension" to Dothan, Alabama, the town still counted only 800 residents. But nearby, progress was on the wind. In 1901, the Georgia, Florida and Alabama Railroad crossed the Central at Arlington only 14 miles east of Blakely, and by 1904 political forces in Arlington were lobbying in vain for the creation of Griggs County, with Arlington as the County seat. Meanwhile only a few miles west of Blakely in Alabama, the news was that the Birmingham, Columbus, and St. Andrews Bay Railroad would cross the Central at Dothan.[25] Although crossing rails seemed to surround her, none arrived at Blakely. As a result, the town began to feel exploited by the Central's uneven rate structure. It was at about this time that the first proponents of the Blakely Southern Railroad surfaced. In January of 1903, *The Early County News* supported plans for a 25-mile line from Blakely southward to Jakin west of Donalsonville on the Atlantic Coast Line Railway. Without this connection, *The News* warned, "we are at the mercy of the Central."[26]

At this point spirits seem to have soared in Blakely, and the grand jury began to recommend a new courthouse. Not all of this was the usual railroad-imported New South propaganda. The old courthouse was in bad shape. The News related that the building was "all rotten," and "becoming unsafe."[27] The grand jury called the old courthouse "thoroughly worn out."[28] Nonetheless, the rhetoric surrounding the construction of a new court building in Blakely was tinted with a light wash of New South fervor and an outpouring of self-promotion. In January of 1905, *The News* published an architectural rendering of Morgan and Dillon's proposed design calling it "the handsomest structure of its kind in Southern Georgia," and promising that it would "be in keeping with the wealth and prosperity of Early County—the Garden spot of Georgia."[29]

By 1905, the Romanesque Revival, which had died earlier in the North, was almost dead in Georgia. The last picturesque courthouse erected in the state would be J. W. Golucke's 1907 Baker County Courthouse at Newton, which was a copy of earlier designs by that architect. To replace the picturesque, waves of classical revival were washing southward from urban centers in the North. At the source of much of this deluge lay the gleaming white "Florentine

Plate 12.10: The Early County Courthouse, built in 1904-1905. The rush was on to build courthouses that would affirm both New South aspirations and Old South traditions. (Photo: Wilber W. Caldwell.)

Renaissance" buildings of the 1893 Columbian Exposition in Chicago. But by 1904, another orgy of classical excess was afoot, this time in Saint Louis at the Louisiana Purchase Exposition and World's Fair where the already Baroque excesses of the Chicago Fair were being pressed to even more Rococo extremes. Georgia had been slow to accept even the simplest forms of the new classicism, but when the slender columns of classical revival finally began to rise on Southern squares, Southerners were quick to attach their own symbolism. Such buildings may have stood for American financial and industrial progress in Saint Louis, but in Blakely, Georgia, the columns of

[22] The Early County Historical Society, *Collections of the Early County Historical Society* 2 vols. (Blakely GA: The Early County Historical Society, 1971) 1:6.

[23] Virgil Powers in "The Thirty Eighth Report to the President of The Central Railroad and Banking Company" in *The Annual Reports of the President, Superintendents, and Engineers in Chief of The Central Railroad and Banking Company* 20/38 (Savannah 1895): 43.

[24] *The Early County News*, November 3, 1881 quoted in *The Early County Historical Society, Collections of the Early County Historical Society*, 1:102.

[25] *The Early County News*, December 1, 1904.

[26] *The Early County News*, January 8, 1903.

[27] *The Early County News*, April 7, 1904.

[28] *The Early County News*, April 14, 1904.

[29] *The Early County News*, January 1, 1904.

Plate 12.11: The simple brick Houston County Courthouse built in 1855 remained in use until 1948. (Photo: Courtesy of Georgia Dept. of Archives and History.)

Morgan and Dillion's 1904 Early County Courthouse recalled the comfortable columns of the Old South.

John Robert Dillon, an apprentice at the Atlanta architectural firm of Bruce and Morgan, was made a partner in 1903, and upon Bruce's retirement the next year, the firm became known as Morgan and Dillion. The 1904 Early County Courthouse represented the prestigious firm's first neoclassical courthouse. The firm's founder, Alexander Bruce had led Atlanta's small architectural community through the picturesque era. After a brief association with William Parkins that began in 1879, Bruce had joined forces with Thomas Henry Morgan in 1882 to form the firm of Bruce and Morgan. Designing first in the Second Empire mode and later in softly personal voices of the Romanesque and Queen Anne Styles, the partnership remained Georgia's preeminent architectural firm for over two decades. Bruce and Morgan designed sixteen courthouses in Georgia between 1882 and 1898. The last two of these, the 1896 Monroe County Courthouse at Forsyth and the 1898 Butts County Courthouse at Jackson, although Romanesque in character, displayed an eclectic mix of classical ornament, which was as much a signal of the rising tide of neoclassicism in the South as it was a reflection of the Queen Anne Style which sought to combine free composition with classical detail.

Despite this obvious concession to the classical revivals that were sweeping the country in the last years of their partnership, Bruce and Morgan did not design any neoclassical court buildings. As the early

years of the new century unfolded, a bumper crop of classical courthouses had begun to rise on town squares all across the state, and Bruce and Morgan's once thriving career as courthouse designers took a sudden dip. In the six years previous to 1898 the firm had designed seven Romanesque court buildings in Georgia, but Bruce and Morgan received no commissions for courthouses between 1898 and 1904. While the firm enhanced its reputation designing many of the South's first tall buildings in Atlanta during this period, out in the countryside, the old Romanesque forms were falling from favor, and the rage was becoming the columns of the neoclassical and Georgian Revivals. James W. Golucke, Frank Milburn, T. F. Lockwood, W. F. Denny and others were carefully manipulating these classical forms to recall the architecture of a bygone era while simultaneously symbolizing the aggressive American financial and industrial progress that so invigorated the rest of the country and so tantalized the American South where it had failed to materialize outside of a few urban centers.

Like most of the state's early neoclassical courthouses, Morgan and Dillon's plan at Blakely featured a cross-like plan with classical porticoed entrances facing all four sides of the square. The new Early County Courthouse presented a fundamentally Georgian silhouette with its horizontal rectangular massing and brick construction accented with white stone trim. But the new firm's approach to ornament was a great deal more modern than either Golucke's careful reserve or Frank Milburn's more properly Palladian decoration. Here in Blakely, in place of the grand lanterns typical of Golucke and Milburn's designs, we find a low dome of the most up-to-date Beaux-Arts styling. Also unique to Georgia are columns of a "rusticated order." These had appeared in the American North early in the new century, but were little known in the South. Following Roman models, particularly those commissioned by Caligula in the 1st century AD, Renaissance examples of this textural detail abound.

Despite its unquestionable architectural quality, the 1905 Early County Courthouse may have tipped the delicate balance away from the Old South and toward Beaux-Arts bombast. In 1912, Blakely finally completed the Blakely Southern Railroad to Jakin. Only two years later, just as the boll weevil crept into Georgia, the new line failed and was abandoned. In the decades to come, Morgan and Dillon's grand Renaissance symbol would represent little more than a grand irony. Its hopeful symbols were perhaps a bit too modern for rural Georgia in 1904, where despite dreams of a new prosperity, the past still lingered, forming an unyielding barrier to progress.

HOUSTON COUNTY: PERRY

Plate 12.11: The Houston County Courthouse, built in 1855. Demolished in 1948.

Stretching all the way from the Ocmulgee to the Flint, the original Houston County was one of five counties created from the vast tract that was ceded to the State of Georgia by the Creek Indians in the 1821 Treaty of Indian Springs. The ensuing land lottery extended cotton's powerful grip westward along with an attendant regional culture of land and slaves. As the first and most easterly county of the new western Cotton Belt, Houston County was balanced on the cusp between the older established cotton culture in the east and a new breed of ambitious individualistic yeoman farmers who sought fortune on the frontier of western Georgia. Perry, first called Wattsville, was established as the county seat in 1823, and a fine frame courthouse rose on her square the next year. By 1859, eight years after the Southwestern Railroad arrived at neighboring Fort Valley, then in Houston County, and only four years after this fine brick courthouse replaced the original court building at Perry, Houston County was the number one cotton producing county in Georgia, producing an incredible 28,852 bales.

Although Perry was physically untouched by the Civil War, like the county towns of the old Eastern Cotton Belt, she was laid low by the Reconstruction. In 1869, Houston County produced only 3819 bales of cotton, barely 13 percent of her pre-war total. Few places in Georgia were harder hit by the social and economic changes of the postwar era, and few faced change with a more stubborn intransigence. Although

a spur of the Southwestern Railroad was completed from Fort Valley to Perry in 1873, no crossing rails were to follow. While Fort Valley slowly began to reap the rewards of the modern era, Perry remained fixed, doggedly agrarian and inflexibly opposed to social and economic change while she draped herself in the growing myth of the Old South.

In the context of the courthouse and the depot, it is not surprising that in such a place the simple brick courthouse erected in 1855 would serve until 1948. Here stood one of the last of the old brick vernacular court buildings built to reflect the individualism of the frontier. Only the scrolling paired brackets beneath the eaves betray mid-century styling. As cotton covered Houston County and the war and Reconstruction came and went, much of the individualism that these simple court buildings symbolized would be slowly corrupted and fashioned into a brooding backwardly focused intransigence, blind to any progress that might undermine the archaic social institutions that had prevailed at the time of this building's construction.

Plate 12.12: The Depot at Perry.

This modest wooden depot, rescued from demolition in 1985 by a clothing store and later renovated by a travel agency, remains is an appropriate symbol for Perry's humble railroad history. When the first survey for the Southwestern Railroad was completed back in 1847, the civil engineer, F. P. Holcomb, reported to the president of the new road that the natural route of the road should lead through Perry because it would "afford the greatest revenue to the road when completed." But he recommend a route via neighboring Fort Valley on the grounds that efforts by that city to secure the passage of the railroad "had so far excelled" those in Perry. [30] In short, Fort Valley had been forthcoming with stock subscriptions while Perry, true to her conservative nature, had not. Perry's agrarian fixations were no doubt further hardened by the events of the Reconstruction period, but despite her

[30] F. P. Holcomb, "Supplement to the Report of the Civil Engineer", in *Reports of the Chief Engineers, Presidents and Superintendents of The Southwestern Railroad*, 10.

seemingly inflexible mind-set, she had later lamented her failure to secure a railroad and sought to correct the situation. In 1870, a group in Perry acquired a charter for the Fort Valley and Hawkinsville Railroad, but this project stalled. It was not until the Southwestern agreed to build the line, that Perry got her railroad. The Southwestern required a contribution from the city of Perry of six thousand dollars along with the usual stock subscriptions, and in May of 1871 *The Houston Home Journal* was literally pleading with citizens: "Make up this amount citizens, make it up, oh make it up. It is easy to get a railroad.

Plate 12.12: The simple batten board depot at Perry is an appropriate symbol for Perry's humble railroad history. (Photo: Wilber W. Caldwell.)

[31] *The Houston Home Journal*, May 25,1871.

[32] The other two were at Skull Shoals in Greene County and near Albany in Dougherty County. Jusdon Clements Ward, Jr., *Georgia Under the Bourbon Democrats, 1872-1890* (Chapel Hill NC: University of North Carolina Press, 1947) 390.

Let's have it."[31] The spur was completed to Perry in February of 1873.

Here we begin to see the first strange inconsistencies that characterize what C. Vann Woodward calls "the divided mind of the South." Like many small Georgia towns, Perry wanted at least a part of the bounty of the industrial age, but she was unwilling to sacrifice the traditions of her past. It was a modern dilemma. While she labored to build her 12-mile spur from Fort Valley, she received with contempt the early New South rhetoric emanating from progressive cities like Atlanta.

Fifteen years later, another railroad would bypass Perry. Pressing southward from Macon heading for Palatka, Florida, the Georgia, Southern and Florida Railroad cut through the eastern part of Houston County in 1888, creating a string of tiny towns: Centerville, Bonaire, Kathleen, Coreen and Elko. The entire line was complete by the end of 1890, and in the 1930s it would become the giant Southern Railway's main line to Florida. But the old "Shoo Fly" local from Macon to Valdosta only skirted the edge of Houston County, and the romantic whistles of crack passenger trains like "The Ponce de Leon" and "The Royal Palm" could not be heard in Perry. In 1914, the spur from Fort Valley to Perry was finally extended to Hawkinsville by the ill-fated Hawkinsville and Western Railroad, which became part of the Ocilla Southern in 1917. Sometime around 1925, the railroad from Hawkinsville to Perry was abandoned, and Perry was again left to wait beside her antebellum courthouse at the end of her half-forgotten spur.

DADE COUNTY: TRENTON

Plate 12.13: The depot at Trenton.

This charming little depot at Trenton was built sometime around the turn of the century by the Alabama Great Southern Railroad. Isolated in its narrow valley, the ancestor of the Alabama Great Southern, the Alabama and Chattanooga Railroad, cut through Dade County headed for Meridian, Mississippi, in 1870. It was part of an enormous railroad flimflam devised by financier, John C. Stanton of Boston, Alabama's most infamous Carpetbagger, whose ambitious state-backed railroad schemes surpassed even those of Georgia's Hannibal I. Kimball. Stanton's Alabama and Chattanooga gobbled up the tiny Will's Valley Railroad, which had been chartered in 1853 and built southward toward Trenton from its junction on the Nashville and Chattanooga Railroad just before the Civil War erupted.

This railroad belonged more to the states of Alabama and Tennessee than to Georgia and this is no surprise, for Dade County itself, although politically part of Georgia, could claim little attachment to that state. Isolated for the rest of Georgia by the massive barrier of Lookout Mountain, Dade has often been referred to as Georgia's "Lost County." Although Dade County was created from Walker County in 1837, it is not mentioned in Adiel Sherwood's 1839 *Gazetteer of Georgia,* nor does the usually thorough George White list it in his 1849 *Statistic of Georgia.*

Like almost all of the state-financed Reconstruction railroads in the South, the Alabama and Chattanooga failed shortly after its completion. It was reorganized as the Alabama Great Southern Railroad in 1877, and served to exploit the coal and iron resources in the northwest corner of Georgia. The enormous iron furnaces at Rising Fawn, only a few miles south of Trenton, had been fired up just as the Alabama and Chattanooga was completed, and reached peak production in the 1890s. Smelting operations continued until the second decade of the twentieth century. The Dade County Coal Mines, which employed leased convict labor until 1908, were active until 1947. These mines were the site of Penitentiary Camp #1, one of three camps established after the restructuring of Georgia's convict lease system in 1876.[32]

This is a fiercely independent region. Its isolating geography made crossing rails impossible, and Trenton remained unexposed to the infections of the New South myth with its tempting promise of material progress and modern social and economic advancement. The exuberant hopes so often imported by Georgia's postbellum railroads were not to take root in the shadow of the great Lookout Mountain, and no monument to such dreams would be erected on Trenton's tiny courthouse square.

Plate 12.13: The depot at Trenton in Georgia's "Lost County." (Photo: Wilber W. Caldwell.)

Plate 12.14: The Dade County Courthouse built c. 1853. Demolished, 1926.

The record of courthouse building in Dade County is sketchy at best. The County was created in 1837, and Trenton became the county seat in 1841. A simple courthouse was probably built in the early 1840s, but there is no record of a courthouse before 1854 when county records reference of an 1853 courthouse fire. The building pictured above building was probably erected to replace the courthouse, which burned in 1853. With its Federal Style doorways and simple brackets beneath the eaves, the building strongly resembled many brick vernacular courthouses of the mid-1850s. There is speculation that this building was demolished and rebuilt in 1867. Some say it was destroyed by Federal forces just before the battle on Chickamauga in 1863. But there is no documented

Plate 12.14: The Dade County Courthouse built c. 1853. A purely vernacular affair, typical of the mid-1850s.

support for these tales, and they thus seem unlikely. Nor is there much evidence for the account that the building was replaced owing to its deteriorated condition in 1867, only a dozen or so years after it was first erected. Thus, the structure in the old photograph is probably the old 1854 courthouse, which was demolished in 1926 to make way for the present court building. Whatever its history, the old courthouse at Trenton was a purely vernacular affair, and its architecture reflected none of the exuberant styles that attended the growing myth of the New South.

SOME LAST THOUGHTS ON RECONSTRUCTION RAILROADS

The year 1873 marks a historical watershed. It saw the beginning of a period of national economic depression that would bring sweeping changes to a nation obsessed with a new material ethic. For most of the American South, 1873 marked the beginning of the end of the Reconstruction period because the North was then developing financial problems of her own. In the face of hard times, the materialistic forces of Northern big government and big business were quick to abandon the great fiasco that was Southern Reconstruction, leaving the region to wallow in the quagmire they had helped to create. Political arrangements would take another four years, but the economic dye was cast in 1873, and the waters of Southern history were forever colored. The south would remain a forgotten stepchild of the American Dream well into the next century.

Despite the great shroud of economic devastation draped across rural Georgia just after the Civil War, there were twenty-six new courthouses erected between 1867 and 1873 (see Appendix A).

Surprisingly only eight of these were replacements for buildings destroyed during the war. Courthouse building in the Reconstruction period was inspired primarily by railroad expansion. New counties or new county seats were created, and most erected simple vernacular wooden or brick court buildings of the type common before the war. In 1873, many of the railroads that would later carry the promises of the New South had been built, but few had delivered their mythical cargo of hope. Only Gourdon P. Randall's grand Second Empire Bibb County Courthouse erected in 1873 at the blossoming rail center that was Macon had risen to set the example for the period of railroad-borne hope which was to follow.

Interestingly, it was the much despised Radical Republicans who attempted to create the first foundations for an industrial New South, and it was the Bourbon Democrats, the champions of New South rhetoric, who were slow to build on this platform. The Democratic Redeemers were reactionary Old South traditionalists on one hand, and they preached the New South gospel on the other with little or no result. But the Radical Republicans were capitalist of the Gilded Age. Unencumbered by idealism, romanticism or the social and political baggage of the earlier period, they applied the machinery of government to the task of getting railroads for a starving Georgia, and in doing so they paid little attention to any legalities encountered along the way. Recent histories have sought to soften some of the charges of corruption and abuse of power that have been heaped upon the Radicals. In addressing the issue of Republican excesses with regard to state aid to railroads, Mark Summers concludes: "…no party was to blame. The true instigator…was a public mood, that is, the feverish zeal for railroad building at any price."[33]

Thus, ironically, the period of Georgia's deepest economic devastation was a period of remarkably productive railroad building. In 1860, there had been 682 miles of rail in Georgia. By 1880 there were 1420.[34] In 1869 and 1870, the state had agreed to endorse the bonds of over thirty-seven different railroad companies. Most of these existed only on paper, and in the end only seven actually received state endorsed bonds. The Macon and Brunswick, the Brunswick and

[33] Mark W. Summers, *Railroads, Reconstruction and the Gospel of Prosperity* (Princeton: Princeton University Press, 1984) 77.

[34] Peter S. McGuire, "The Railroads of Georgia, 1860-1880" *The Georgia Historical Quarterly* 16/3 (Savannah 1932): 179.

[35] John F. Stover, *The Railroads of the South, 1865-1900 A Study in Finance and Control* (Chapel Hill NC: University of North Carolina Press, 1955) 82.

[36] Stover, *The Railroads of the South, A Study in Finance and Control*, 122.

[37] C. Vann Woodward, *Origins of the New South* (1951; reprint, Baton Rouge LA: Louisiana State University Press, 1993) 295

Albany, the South Georgia and Florida, and the Alabama and Chattanooga, all discussed in the preceding chapters, as well as the Bainbridge, Cuthbert and Columbus, the Cartersville and Van Wert and its offspring the Cherokee Railroad all were granted state aid. Additionally the Macon and Augusta and the Atlanta and Richmond Air Line returned state-endorsed bonds when they later arranged private funding. By the fall of 1870, over $30,000,000 in state endorsed railroad bonds had been issued in Georgia, although the Democrats would later refuse to honor over $10,000,000 of these.[35]

All across the nation, the early 1870s saw remarkable increases in railroad construction. The nation's railroad mileage doubled between 1865 and 1873,[36] and with Carpetbagger governments at the helm, all ten Southern states funded new rails with state-endorsed bonds. Many of these lines were constructed using convict laborers leased from the states.

The early progress of Georgia's antebellum railroads had fostered the illusion that all railroads contained the seeds of success, regardless of their route, cost, financing or operating organization. Here was an ancestor of the New South myth that would be proved fallacious by virtually every railroad built in the state between 1865 and 1873. This cavalier line of thinking, along with the funding provided by state guaranteed bonds, created railroads whose economic prospects were questionable at best. Thus, many Southern railroads built in the economic nightmare of Reconstruction were doomed from the beginning. Most suffered gross mismanagement, were burdened with extremely heavy debt structures, and incurred enormous construction costs. Many traversed virtually uninhabited country.

Nonetheless, the single most significant factor in the failure of almost all of these roads was the regional, national and global financial conditions that arose out of the Panic of 1873. Even the well-established antebellum roads, which had opposed the state's unfair efforts to give a leg up to new competition, suffered in the financial collapse. Only the Central, the Georgia Railroad and the Western and Atlantic, along with their subsidiaries and leased holdings, remained solvent.

Out of the ashes of receivership came the first of many consolidations, re-organizations, financial manipulations and mergers that would characterize the development of Georgia's rail system for the next forty years. The failures of the early 1870s cleared the way for Northern control of Southern rail. The first of the great consolidations had begun by 1880, as the Connecticut Yankee, Henry Plant, built his giant Plant System out of the ruins of the Atlantic and Gulf, and as the East Tennessee, Virginia and Georgia gobbled up the pieces of the Macon and Brunswick and the Selma, Rome and Dalton. At the end of this path, would be three all-encompassing railroad giants, the Southern, the Atlantic Coast Line and the Seaboard which, by the turn of the century, were all dominated by John Pierpont Morgan.[37]

Despite chilling tales of financial irresponsibility and ruin, there is another side to the story of Reconstruction railroads. This is the story told by the courthouses of the period. New rails brought population to a formerly empty wilderness. Five new counties were created between 1865 and 1873, and in older counties, county seats were relocated to blossom beside the new rails. Where Reconstruction rails crossed antebellum rails, the future rail centers of Georgia materialized at places like Waycross and Albany. Most of the court buildings that rose during Reconstruction were of the simple brick vernacular sort, for the wild-eyed dreams of a New South were still incubating. As the Reconstruction period ended, intoxicating architectural visions sprang full-blown from the womb of the Gilded Age. In the following decades, riding on a growing web of connecting railroads, the myth of the New South would cover the land, and most of these simple brick Reconstruction era courthouses would be replaced by the extraordinary monuments built to symbolize the blind hope that emanated from so many tiny new depots.

•

PART 3

The Railroads and the Myth of the New South
1875–1910

The Northeastern Railroad

Clarke County: Athens Habersham County: Clarkesville Rabun County: Clayton
Some Last Thoughts on the Northeastern Railroad

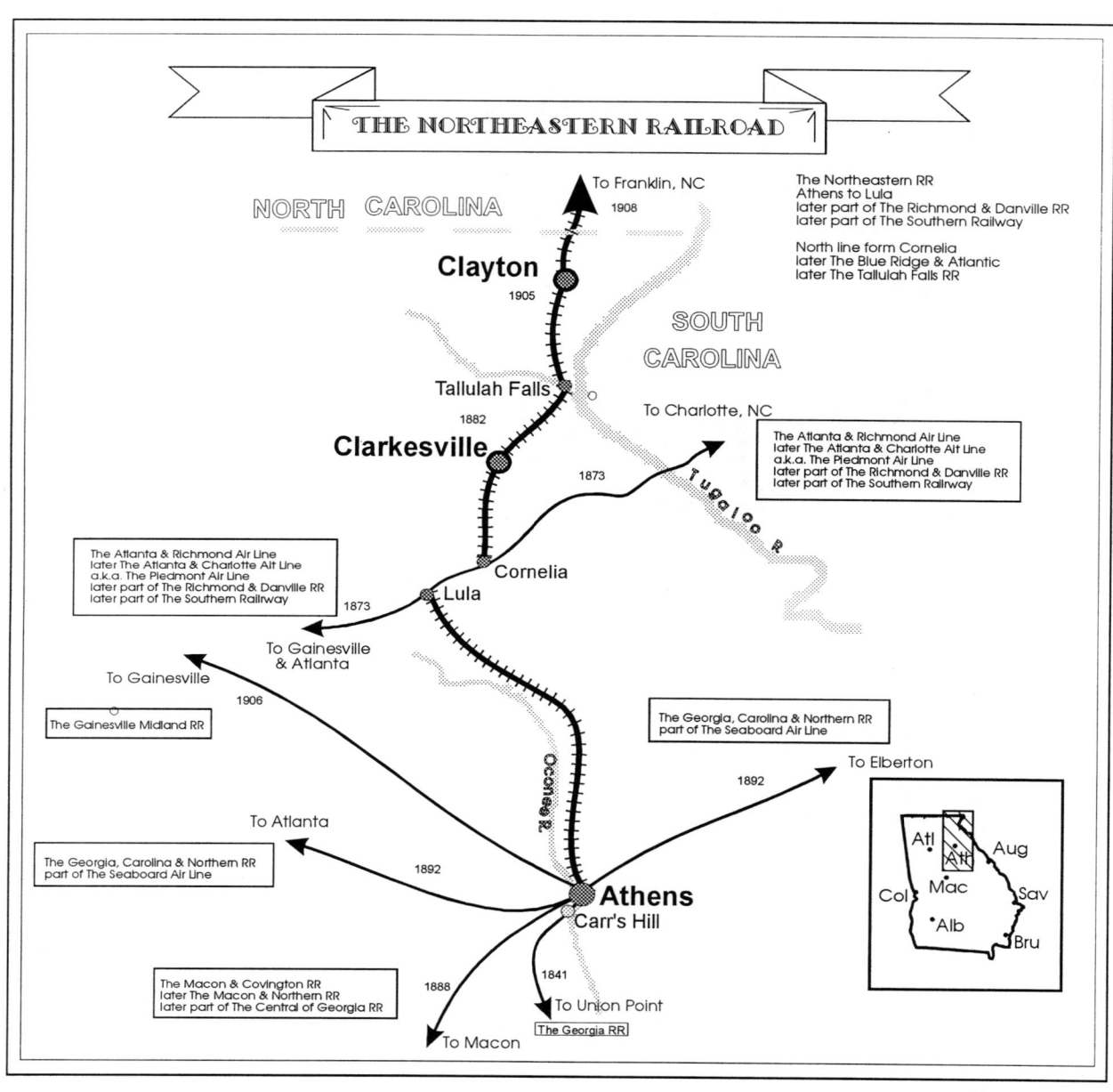

THE NORTHEASTERN RAILROAD

To Franklin, NC
1908

NORTH CAROLINA

Clayton
1905

The Northeastern RR
Athens to Lula
later part of The Richmond & Danville RR
later part of The Southern Railway

North line form Cornelia
later The Blue Ridge & Atlantic
later The Tallulah Falls RR

SOUTH CAROLINA

Tallulah Falls
1882

Clarkesville

To Charlotte, NC

Tugaloo R.

The Atlanta & Richmond Air Line
later The Atlanta & Charlotte Air Line
a.k.a. The Piedmont Air Line
later part of The Richmond & Danville RR
later part of The Southern Railway

1873

The Atlanta & Richmond Air Line
later The Atlanta & Charlotte Air Line
a.k.a. The Piedmont Air Line
later part of The Richmond & Danville RR
later part of The Southern Railway

Cornelia
Lula
1873

To Gainesville
& Atlanta

To Gainesville
1906

The Gainesville Midland RR

Oconee R.

The Georgia, Carolina & Northern RR
part of The Seaboard Air Line

To Elberton
1892

To Atlanta

The Georgia, Carolina & Northern RR
part of The Seaboard Air Line

1892

Athens
Carr's Hill

The Macon & Covington RR
later The Macon & Northern RR
later part of The Central of Georgia RR

1888

1841
To Union Point
The Georgia RR

To Macon

Atl Ath Aug
Col Mac Sav
Alb Bru

13   The Northeastern Railroad

CLARKE COUNTY: ATHENS

Plate 13.1: The Southern Railway Passenger Depot at Athens built in 1913.

This fine depot, built in 1913, on the site of the old Northeastern Railroad Depot at Athens, looked back on an ironic saga that spanned eighty years. In one sense, Georgia's vast nineteenth century rail network had begun at Athens in 1834 when James Camak, William Dearing and others met to gain control of the languishing Georgia Railroad, whose 1833 charter called for a railroad to link Augusta with Athens, Eatonton and Madison. It was the first of many disappointing episodes for Athens. From the perspective of investors in Clarke County, the most important branch of the line was to run from Athens to Augusta where it would accomplish connections to Charleston via the recently completed Charleston and Hamburg Railroad, one of the first railroads constructed in the United States.

From the very beginning, a connection from Athens westward across the mountains to Tennessee beckoned (see Table 13.1). But Athens's early dreams for a western connection were soon to be interrupted. By 1841, powerful factions in Augusta had gained control of the Georgia Railroad, and the idea of a western connection via Athens was loosing its allure. In 1836, when the state-owned Western and Atlantic Railroad began to build northwestward from the future Atlanta to the future Chattanooga, the Athens Branch of the Georgia Railroad was reduced to secondary status, and the main line from Augusta reached out to connect with the proposed railhead at Atlanta. Even though the Athens branch was completed to Carr's Hill just across the Oconee River from Athens in 1841, there can be little doubt of the secondary status of this line. For the first six years, the Athens Branch would remain a horse-drawn railroad, a proper depot was not built at Carr's Hill until 1855 and a bridge across the Oconee from Carr's Hill to Athens would not materialize for forty years.

Plate 13.1: The Southern Railway's fine 1913 passenger depot at Athens looked back on an ironic railroading saga that spanned eighty years. (Photo: Wilber W. Caldwell)

**ATHENS RAILROADS TO THE WEST
CHARTERED BUT NEVER BUILT**

Table 13.1

1833-The Georgia Railroad planned to be part of the grand "Charleston and Cincinnati Railroad," An early charter authorized the Athens branch to extend to the Tennessee River, crossing the Chattahoochee River near present day Duluth and then crossing the high ground between the Etowah and the Tallapoosa Rivers to join the Tennessee River at Decatur, Alabama.

1834-E. P. Gaines's Atlantic and Mississippi Railroad planned to link Memphis with Charleston via The Georgia Railroad at Athens.

1835-The Georgia Railroad (a later plan involved a connection with the Hiawassee Railroad, to link Athens with Knoxville. The Georgia portion of this route was actually surveyed by the Georgia Railroad in 1836).

1846-The Athens and Cartersville Railroad.

1854-The Northeastern Railroad Company (the original charter contemplated a connection with the ill-fated Blue Ridge Railroad near Clayton).

1889-The Brunswick, Athens and Northwestern Railroad.

1890-The Chattanooga Southern Railway.

1904-The Savannah, Statesboro and Northern Railroad

1906-The Georgia Traction Company

1907-The Savannah, Augusta and Northern Railroad

Thus, the Western and Atlantic stole away the dreams of Athens, as the railhead at Atlanta lured Georgia's railroads like a Siren. But even after the completion of the Western and Atlantic in 1850, a persistent Athens continued to look westward (see

Table 13.1). None of these wild visions would fully materialize, but like so many depots across Georgia, the predecessors of this fine passenger station at Athens flew the flag of eternal hope.

While grand railroading schemes surrounded early Athens, the city's later emergence as a rail center would eventually come to rest on more modest undertakings. As early as the 1840s, more realistic schemes for western connections had surfaced. Plans were laid for rail connections to Clarkesville in 1847 and to Gainesville at about that same time.[1] In addition, plans for overland plank roads abounded. All of this came to little. But in 1870, riding on a new wave of hope occasioned by the revival of plans for the illusive Blue Ridge Railroad, the Northeastern Railroad was re-chartered to build to "some point on the Blue Ridge Railroad near Clayton."[2] Ground was broken at Athens in 1872.[3]

Born in the railroad building frenzy that characterized the Reconstruction era, the first phase of the Northeastern Railroad sought to connect Athens with the new main trunk line of the Atlanta and Richmond Air Line. After considerable delay, the line was completed in 1876, joining the Air Line at Lula just north of Gainesville. With track rights granted by the Air Line from Lula to Cornelia and the state's endorsement of bonds granted in 1879, the Northeastern extended northwestward from Cornelia to Clarkesville in 1882 with an eye to the age-old Knoxville connection. After the Northeastern was leased to the Richmond and Danville Railroad in 1886, the Clarkesville Branch was sold off and became known as the Blue Ridge and Atlantic Railroad. This spur was promoted as a future connection between Savannah and the American heartland. The ill-fated scheme was fired in part by post-war speculations centering on the resurrection of the old Blue Ridge Railroad and renewed efforts to build a line from Knoxville to Charleston. Beginning at Cornelia, the Blue Ridge and Atlantic Railroad finally reached Franklin, North Carolina, in 1906 as the Tallulah Falls Railroad. Along the way she passed by the sad remains of the half-completed tunnels and abandoned roadbed of the frustrated dream that were all that remained of the Blue Ridge Railroad.

Just over ten years after the Northeastern Railroad made its connection with the Atlanta and Richmond Air Line at Lula, Athens got her third railroad, the Macon and Northern. Like Athens, Macon too had harbored grand visions of a connection to the west. In 1864, she had chartered the Macon and Cincinnati Railroad. This scheme, which envisioned a railroad passing through Covington and Dahlonega came to nothing. But in the early 1880s, a more modest version of this plan emerged as the Covington and Macon Railroad. The road's charter, revised in 1885, contemplated a line from Macon via Covington to connect with the Air Line near Lula with branches to Griffin and to Athens. Renamed the Macon and Northern Railroad, the line was finally built to Athens in 1887 via Madison, not Covington, and all plans for branches were abandoned. There can be little doubt that the earlier completion of the Northeastern Railroad from Athens to the Air Line at Lula acted as a lure, and deprived Covington of this crossing line.

Ironically, after all her struggles attempting to secure connections to the west, Athens finally got her trunk line. The coastwise main line of the Georgia, Carolina and Northern, the predecessor of the giant Seaboard Air Line Railway, was built through Athens in 1891 on its way to Atlanta from the Carolina coastal plain. Thus, by the turn of the century there were four depots in Athens, and the city had grown from a town of 2500 when the Georgia Railroad arrived in 1841 to a city of 10,000. In 1906, the last of Athens's railroads would arrive as the newly reorganized Gainesville Midland Railroad completed its branch from Gainesville to Athens.

Plate 13.2: The Clarke County Courthouse, built in 1876. Leon Henri Charbonnier, architect. Demolished c.1951.

Watkinsville, the original Clarke County seat of justice, had been laid out following the creation of Clarke County from Jackson County back in 1801. From an early date the growth of Athens as a trading center had exerted pressure on this tiny village to yield the palm of the county seat. Athens had been chartered in 1806, five years after the state legislature had created the University of Georgia, originally called

Plate 13.2: The Clarke County Courthouse. Despite its mansard-roofed tower and elaborate fenestration, the building retained the somewhat vernacular look of the earlier period.

Franklin College, on 633 acres. Adiel Sherwood's 1828 *Gazetteer of Georgia* describes Athens as having eighty-five houses and "a good appearance" and places the town's population above 1000. Early chronicles report heavy wagon trade with the upcountry. The town's factors quickly created a large cotton market, and a branch of the state bank was established at Athens in 1834. By the time the Georgia Railroad arrived in 1841, the area around Athens had three cotton factories, three tanneries, five flourmills, thirteen gristmills and fifteen saw mills. Meanwhile, Watkinsville languished. In 1849, George White's *Statistics of the State of Georgia* listed Watkinsville as a town of only 240 persons. By 1860, Athens's population was nearing 4000, while Watkinsville remained virtually unchanged.

Serious agitation for the moving of the courthouse to Athens flared in the 1853, and in 1855 there was an attempt to divide the county, followed by similar political rumblings in 1861.[4] In 1871, just as

[1] Ernest C. Hynds, *Antebellum Athens and Clarke County, Georgia* (Athens GA: University of Georgia Press, 1974) 57.

[2] "An Act to Create The Northeastern Railroad," Henry W. Thomas, *Digest of the Railroad Laws of Georgia* (Atlanta: Franklin Printing and Publishing Co., 1895) 275.

[3] Peter S. McGuire, "Athens and the Railroads," *The Georgia Historical Quarterly* 18/1 (Athens 1934): 18.

[4] Hynds, *Antebellum Athens and Clarke County, Georgia*, 58-59.

Plate 13.3: The Athens City Hall, built in 1904. A rare song of New South progress. (Photo: Wilber W. Caldwell.)

plans were maturing for the construction of the Northeasteren Railroad, Athens finally wrestled the county seat of Clarke County away from tiny Watkinsville. Four years later in 1875, Oconee County was split off from Clarke. Watkinsville became the Oconee County seat, and the old brick vernacular Clarke County Courthouse, built in 1829, would serve the new county until 1888.

As we have seen, there was to be little flowering of New South myths in Georgia before the early 1880s, and with only a few exceptions, court buildings erected in the 1870s reflected little of the fantasy designs which were to come. L. H. Charbonnier's 1876 Clarke County Courthouse at Athens is transitional. Although technically in the Second Empire Style, the building carried little of the exuberant force of that idiom. Despite its mansard-roofed tower and

elaborate fenestration, it retained the somewhat vernacular look of the earlier period. Like many of the "architects" practicing in rural areas in this era, the designer of this building was a civil engineer. Leon Henri Charbonnier was a professor of engineering, mathematics and astronomy at the University of Georgia. A native of France and a graduate of St. Cyr, the French "West Point," Charbonnier came to the United States in 1860, fought for the Confederacy in the Civil War, taught briefly at the Citadel and came to the University of Georgia around 1867. In 1874, he designed Moore College, the only Second Empire building on the University campus, and one of the most up-to-date public structures of its time in Athens. On the strength of this success, Charbonnier was given the commission for Clarke County's first courthouse at Athens. The building served the county until the completion of A. Ten Eyck Brown's imposing Beaux-Arts courthouse in 1918. In 1914, Charbonnier's old Clarke County Courthouse was enlarged, remodeled and served as a high school until it was demolished in the early 1950s.

Plate 13.3: The Athens City Hall, built in 1904. Lewis F. Goodrich, architect.

By the turn of the century, the promises of New South promoters were coming true in Clarke County. Still, no fantasy courthouse rose in Athens in the period of our interest. But one flamboyant architectural expression of New South zeal did appear in Athens in the first decade of the new century. Augusta architect, Lewis Goodrich, designed several courthouses in Georgia (see Appendix C) but his 1904 Athens City Hall building is unquestionably his finest public building. Its limestone base and bold Renaissance ornament sets it apart from most of Georgia's courthouses of the era, which sought to reflect both Old South and New South imagery. With its especially fine lantern, the building is particularly notable for its Renaissance Revival elements which, in this period of Georgia's history, sang rare songs of progress and were generally reserved for Federal buildings.

---

[5] *Tri-County Advertiser*, Centennial Edition, July 5, 1979.

[6] *The Manufacturer's Record*, June 18, 1897.

HABERSHAM COUNTY: CLARKESVILLE

Plate 13.4: The Habersham County Courthouse, built in 1832. Demolished 1898.

Habersham County was created form the Cherokee Cession of 1818. Early records indicate that the county's first court sessions were held in the open a few miles from present day Clarkesville, which was laid out and designated the county seat in 1823. The first Habersham County Courthouse was a small wooden building built in 1821. This structure was still standing in 1979,[5] but sadly it has since been demolished. It is unclear whether the old frame building was erected expressly as a courthouse, or whether it was a private residence used by the early court. Whatever the case, in 1829, Adiel Sherwood describes Clarkesville as having a "courthouse, a jail and 33 houses and stores." In 1832, only three years after Sherwood's publication, this monumental, if not graceful, brick courthouse was erected on Clarkesville's square.

In 1828, the discovery of gold in a narrow band stretching from Rabun County southwestward through Habersham, White and Lumpkin Counties attracted population to the virtually unsettled mountain regions of Georgia and precipitated the abrupt removal of nearly 14,000 Cherokee Indians in 1835. On the eastern edge of this vast wilderness, Habersham County was only ten years old when prospectors began to flood her theretofore-virgin forests in search of instant fortune. For the next twenty years mining activity was brisk in North Georgia. As late as 1849, George White, in his *Statistics of the State of Georgia*, lists six major mining sites in Habersham County. In the same 1849 text, White describes this massive courthouse as a building "of brick, but not very well arranged."

Thirty years later according to Sholes's 1879 *Gazetteer of Georgia,* Clarkesville had a population of about 400, and enjoyed a modest success as a mountain resort. Since the charter of the ill-fated Athens and Clarkesville Railroad in 1846, a line to Clarkesville had been part of Athens's vision of western connection. In 1882, the rails of the Northeastern

Plate 13.4: The Habersham County Courthouse, built in 1832, was an illustration of that crassly utilitarian side of the brick vernacular. (Photo: Courtesy of the Georgia Department of Archives and History)

Railroad finally passed by this great brick vernacular court building on their way northward to Tallulah Falls from their junction with the Atlanta and Richmond Air Line at Cornelia. By the time the old Habersham County Courthouse was demolished in 1898, the Northeastern had become the Blue Ridge and Atlantic, and that, in turn, had become the Tallulah Falls Railroad. But the line still came to a dead end at Tallulah Falls, and not much else had changed in Clarkesville.

Plate 13.5: The Habersham County Courthouse, built in 1898. James W. Golucke, architect.[6]

As the turn of the century approached, Clarkesville was still a very remote place. In a sense, it

Plate 13.5: The Habersham County Courthouse, built in 1898. A trend toward symmetry was creeping in as the new century approached. (Photo: Courtesy of the Georgia Department of Archives and History.)

was the rural and detached quality of her mountain setting that set in motion the odd progression of events that ended in the creation this courthouse. Fifty years after Clarkesville was laid out, the town of Toccoa appeared along the newly laid rails of the Atlanta and Richmond Air Line in the eastern part of Habersham County. Twenty-five years later, Toccoa had mushroomed into a city of over 2000, while Clarkesville languished, counting less than a quarter of that number. By 1897, enormous pressures to move the courthouse from Clarkesville to Toccoa had developed, and in that year, the matter came to a vote. It was the classic confrontation of town against country. It pitted modernity against tradition, materialism against agrarian ideals, New South zeal against Old South intransigence and commercial America against the frontier. With the help of the rural vote, Clarkesville fended off the upstart challenge in an emotional political battle fought in the poverty-stricken backwater of rural Georgia.

As much loved as the old 1832 courthouse at Clarkesville was, in the minds of many, the building represented the town's unprogressive character. Accordingly, as pressure from Toccoa mounted in 1897, county officers commissioned Atlanta architect, Andrew J. Bryan, to design a new court building in order to strengthen Clarkesville's grip on the county seat. To counter this tactic, the "Courthouse Club" of Toccoa offered to build a new court building in that city at no cost to the taxpayers. At the same time, Toccoans attacked county officials in Clarkesville, charging that they had acted without legal authority in the hiring of Bryan. The architect later had to sue Habersham County for his $880 charge for services.[7] A few weeks later Clarkesville defeated Toccoa in a countywide election and the county seat remained unchanged.

After Clarkesville's victory, County officials continued to press for the construction of a new courthouse to cement Clarkesville's hold on the county seat, and to replace the relic on the town square. Needless to say, Toccoa residents were not anxious to be taxed to pay for a new building in Clarkesville. Owing to the high emotions that accompanied this situation, two different accounts of subsequent events

survive. Both accounts agree that the old 1832 Habersham County Courthouse was demolished in January of 1898. Most agree that it was blown up, some say with a firebomb, some say with dynamite. Histories loyal to Clarkesville simply relate that "County Ordinary, W. D. Hill, labored to get a new courthouse."[8] With regard to the destruction of the old building, they state that it was "torn down during a dispute with Toccoa"[9] or "was destroyed in an explosion, the origin of which was suspected but never determined."[10] Sources in Toccoa offer a more specific account, charging that contractors hired by county officials blew up the old building in the middle of the night. *The Southern Banner* called for a Grand Jury investigation calling the incident "an outrage."[11] This tactic of gaining support for courthouse construction is not unique to Clarkesville. Similar accounts and rumors surrounded the destruction of the c.1852 Whitfield County Courthouse at Dalton in 1892. Likewise the old courthouses at Baxley and at McRae were reportedly illegally razed in advance of elections to ratify and approve financing for the construction of new buildings.

However the old Habersham County Courthouse came to be demolished, a new courthouse became a necessity, rather than a point of contention. And while residents of Toccoa and a conservative rural population might have condemned their leaders' tactics, they were suddenly hard pressed to oppose the construction of a new court building for Habersham County. Bryan's controversial design was abandoned, and Atlanta architect, James Golucke was retained.[12] The building was completed before the end of 1898.

Most of the early Romanesque Revival court buildings erected in Georgia reflected the style's powerfully picturesque asymmetrical tradition. Many incorporated stone banding and decoration in the Richardsonian mode. But as this building illustrates, a trend toward symmetry was emerging as the new century approached. R. H. Hunt's 1894 Elbert County Courthouse was among the first examples, and Georgia's preeminent Picturesque courthouse designers, Bruce and Morgan, had designed a symmetrical Romanesque court building at Forsyth (1896) before James Golucke began his plans for Clarkesville.

Perhaps here at Clarkesville, we find an echo of an older and more fundamental pre-Richardsonian American Romanesque Revival mixed with the American brick vernacular. This style, sometimes referred to as the American Round Windowed Style, may have sprung from the German *Rundboganstil*.[13] Still in the end, it seems more likely that Golucke's simplicity here in Clarkesville was rooted more in a turn-of-the-century return to symmetry coupled with a limited budget than in historical revivalism.

James W. Golucke's 1898 Habersham County Courthouse was badly damaged by fire in 1923, and was faithfully restored in that year. Much to the dismay of most present day residents of Clarkesville, the old building was demolished in the mid 1960s to make way for the present courthouse.

RABUN COUNTY: CLAYTON

Plate 13.6: Rabun County: Clayton depot at Tallulah Falls.

The original depot at Clayton was built in 1907, two years after the arrival of the Tallulah Falls Railroad. It burned in 1913 and was replaced by a stone structure. Sadly that sturdy station was later demolished to make way for commercial development in Clayton.

This fine depot at Tallulah Falls on the border between Habersham and Rabun Counties speaks eloquently for the resort that flourished on the lip of the great gorge. It is all that is left to narrate Raburn County's contribution to the saga of the courthouse and the depot. For over thirty years, this was the end on the line for the tiny spur of the Tallulah Falls Railroad, an extension of the frustrated dreams of the citizens of Athens who vainly sought connection with the ill-fated Blue Ridge Railroad through Rabun Gap. Originally part of the Northeastern Railroad, the line was built from Cornelia on the Atlanta and Charlotte Air Line and completed to Tallulah Falls in 1884. The dream of a western connection continued as the line became the Blue Ridge and Atlantic Railroad in 1887 and the Tallulah Falls Railroad in 1898. In 1905, it was extended to Clayton and on to Franklin, North

Plate 13.6: The depot at Tallulah Falls speaks eloquently of the resort that flourished on the lip of the great gorge. (Photo: Wilber W. Caldwell.)

Carolina, in 1908. Clayton built her new courthouse only two years after the arrival of steel rails.

Rabun County was created in 1819 from the great Cherokee Cession of the year before. In 1820, the population of the entire new county was only 524. By 1850, all of Rabun County counted under 2000 settlers, and this vast mountainous region remained only sparsely settled throughout the nineteenth century. The county seat, originally called Claytonville, was created in 1824, and a two-story log courthouse was erected on the square. This building was poorly constructed, and it was replaced in 1838 with a similar structure. In the 1839 edition of his *Gazetteer of Georgia*, Adiel Sherwood describes Clayton as having a courthouse, a jail and only 20 houses and stores. Ten years later, George White's Statistics of the State of Georgia offers a similar description and adds, "at the time of this notice, no trade of any kind was carried on at Clayton." To attest to her remote location and poor circumstances, Rabun County used her log courthouse for over fifty years. In 1878 the second log courthouse collapsed (while court was in session, the

---

[7] *The Southern Banner* (Toccoa GA), August 6, 1897.

[8] Mary L. Church, *The Hills of Habersham* (Clarkesville GA: n.p., 1962) 103.

[9] Undated and unidentified newspaper clipping in the Habersham County Library at Clarkesville.

[10] *Tri-County Advertiser*, Centennial Edition, July 5, 1979.

[11] *The Southern Banner* (Toccoa GA), January 21, 1898.

[12] *The Manufacturer's Record*, June 18, 1897.

[13] Kathleen Curran, "The German Rundbogenstil and Reflections of the American Round Windowed Style," *The Journal of the Society of American Architectural Historians* 67/4(December 1988) 366, and Carrol L. V. Meeks, "Romanesque before Richardson in the United States," Art Bulletin 35 (1953): 17-33.

story goes) and was replaced by a simple frame building. By the turn of the century, Clayton's population was still under 200.

Despite her remote location, Clayton had experienced a boom of sorts in the mid-1850s as crews labored in the nearby mountains in a futile effort to complete Charleston's fantasy, the Blue Ridge Railroad. This ambitious project followed in footsteps of the Hiawassee Railroad, which spent nearly a million dollars in grading and bridging the Hiawassee River in the 1830s in a failed effort to connect with Charleston via the Georgia Railroad at Athens.[14] In the 1850s, the Blue Ridge Railroad sought to connect with Charleston via Clayton and Anderson, South Carolina. The scheme involved four tunnels, the longest of which, the tunnel at Stump House Mountain, was to be over a mile in length. Charters for portions of the Blue Ridge had been granted in Tennessee, North and South Carolina and in Georgia. Work ceased in 1858,[15] dashing Charleston's hopes and ending Clayton's boom before the first shots of the Civil War were fired.

Plate 13.7: The Rabun County Courthouse, built in 1908. H. L. Lewman, architect, attributed. Demolished 1960.

With the arrival of the rails of the Tallulah Falls Railroad in 1905, Clayton at last surged. Lumbermen

Plate 13.7: The Rabun County Courthouse, built in 1908 projected a sobering, second-rate image of the new century, and little if any of the emotional traditions of the old. (Photo: Courtesy of the Georgia Dept. of Archives and History.)

began to work the mountains and tourists arrived at Clayton's new depot. By 1910, the town's population had reached 541, almost tripling the 1900 count.

The arrival of the railroad brought with it the usual high spirits, and of course, agitation for a new courthouse. It might be a bit of a stretch to characterize the new courthouse movement in Clayton as "New South zeal," for the inhabitants of the north Georgia mountains were a frugal, practical lot who were ever skeptical of change. By the first decade of the new century, even in the face of the economic "boom," the myth of the New South was beginning to be exposed as a hollow outpouring of overzealous boosterism. In Clayton, all of this was borne out by the fact that, despite the economic surge provided by the arrival of the Tallulah Falls Railroad and the deteriorating condition of the 1879 frame courthouse, the voters of Rabun County refused to approve a 1906 bond issue to fund a new court building. In 1907, the County Ordinary, M. H. James, ordered a direct tax to fund the new building. Mr. James was not re-elected.

The 1908 Rabun County Courthouse is a product of the Falls City Construction Company, which erected a number of courthouses in Georgia between 1905 and 1910. As with many of that company's court buildings, it appears that here in Clayton, the Louisville, Kentucky, contractor supplied the county with plans and specifications for its new courthouse and then turned around and bid on the erection of the structure. Exactly how this worked is not known. Perhaps the plan was free to the county if Falls City was awarded the job. Perhaps Falls City simply knew that it could compete with anyone when bidding on a structure of its own design. Perhaps all of these deals were in some way "fixed."

Many of the court buildings erected in Georgia by Falls City were designed by H. L. Lewman, a principal of the company, or by Walter Chamberlain, who apparently worked closely with this contractor on many projects. With its octagonal corner pavilions and central lantern, this concrete block building bears as strong resemblance to Chamberlain's 1906 Jeff Davis County Courthouse at Hazlehurst. The court building at Hazlehurst and the 1906 Franklin County Courthouse at Carnesville were the first court buildings in Georgia to be constructed of concrete block. Both were erected by Falls City, and both were designed by Chamberlain. Rabun County records indicate that H. L. Lewman was involved in the project as "representative of the construction company." From all of this, we might conclude that Lewman designed the building using Chamberlain's Hazlehurst plan as a point of beginning. Whatever the case, like most of the work of the Falls City Construction Company, the 1908 Rabun County Courthouse reflected little of the wild dreams of prosperity imported by the railroad. This was a building built on a "shoe-string" budget, and like Lewman's creation at Toccoa, it projected a sobering, second-rate image of the new century, and little if any of the romantic tradition of the old.

SOME LAST THOUGHTS ON THE NORTHEASTERN RAILROAD

The first section of the Northeastern Railroad belongs to the Reconstruction period. Like most Reconstruction railroads, it had its beginnings in the pre-war period. Originally chartered in 1854 "to strike the Blue Ridge Railroad at such a point as the directors may determine," the line's charter was revived in 1870 to build from Athens to "some point on the Blue Ridge Railroad near Clayton." [16] Also like most Reconstruction roads, the line received state aid in the form of bond endorsements. Unlike most Reconstruction Railroads, the Northeastern was slow to get started, and while most state-supported roads of the era were defaulting on their interest payments, the Northeastern remained unbuilt. The state's endorsement of the road's bonds did not come until 1878. Thus, it was not until after the Reconstruction period was over and the economic depression that followed the Panic of 1873 was abating that the first leg of the line was completed from Athens to Lula on the Richmond and Atlanta Air Line. The Northeastern Railroad, like earlier Reconstruction roads did finally default on its bonded debt, but this did not occur until another national financial catastrophe occurred in 1893.

Plate 13.8: Commerce, Georgia. (Photo: Wilber W. Caldwell.)

The second section of the road, from Cornelia to Tallulah Falls, was completed in 1884. This section of the road was sold off when the Richmond and Danville leased the Northeastern in 1886. It became the Blue Ridge and Atlantic Railroad and later the Tallulah Falls Railroad, which completed the extension to Clayton and finally to Franklin, North Carolina, in the first decade of the new century.

[14] U. B. Phillips, *History of Transportation in the Eastern Cotton Belt to 1860* (1908; reprint, New York: McMillan, 1913) 374.

[15] Phillips, *History of Transportation in the Eastern Cotton Belt to 1860*, 376.

[16] "An Act for the Building of the Northeastern Railroad," Thomas, *Digest of the Railroad Laws of Georgia*, 275

Although not a direct result of railroad imported frenzy, the partition of Clarke County and the designation of Athens as the new Clarke County seat in 1875 surely owned a debt to Athens's location on the Georgia Railroad and to the city's hopes for the Northeastern. Likewise the subsequent construction of H. L. Charbonnier's Second Empire Clarke County Courthouse in 1876 just as surely reflected hope for the prosperity that would arrive on the newly completed newly rail connection to the Atlanta and Charlotte Air Line.

In Clarkesville, a simple mountain town of fewer than 400 residents, the 1884 arrival of the Northeastern sparked no immediate agitation for a new courthouse. Nonetheless, it was a railroad that finally moved the county to engage architect James W. Golucke to design the 1898 Habersham County Courthouse. The Air Line had created the town of Toccoa in 1873, and only twenty-five years later Toccoa was aggressively trying to steal the county seat away from Clarkesville. Clarkesville's erection of a new courthouse was thus defensive, an effort to cement her position as the seat of county government against the onslaught of the railroad driven prosperity and zeal of her rival, Toccoa.

In 1908, with the completion of H. L. Lewman's Rabun County Courthouse at Clayton, we find a late example of the classic courthouse and depot phenomenon. The Tallulah Falls Railroad completed its line to Clayton in 1905, and almost immediately Clayton found her old building wanting, and sought to replace it with a symbol of her new-found status as a railroad town. Sadly, the county's choice of the Falls City Construction Company begot of a concrete oddity rather than a symbol of hope.

•

14 | The Elberton Air Line

ELBERT COUNTY: ELBERTON

Plate 14.1: The Elbert County Courthouse, built in 1893-1894. Hunt and Lamm, architects.

Elberton's story is the saga of the nearly thirty years between Chattanooga architect, Reuben Harrison Hunt's, humble departure from Elbert County as a child, and his triumphant return to design the 1894 Elbert County Courthouse. Hunt was born in Elbert County, Georgia, in 1862. In 1866, he left with his family,[1] and ten years later, he began his career as a builder, studying architecture informally on the side. Arriving in Chattanooga in 1883, Hunt "went to work for day wages as a carpenter."[2] He began his architectural practice in 1885. In a career that spanned six decades, R. H. Hunt designed churches, courthouses, and schools all across the South and in many other states.[3] His work is that of an accomplished designer reflecting many styles including Gothic Revival, Romanesque Revival, the Beaux-Arts Style, Georgian Revival and later Art Deco modes. Like this fine court building at Elberton, many of his early courthouses were influenced by the work of the American master, Henry Hobson Richardson.

When Hunt left Elbert County, Elberton was a very remote place. Its history was similar to many of the older counties in the upcountry Piedmont. Cut from Wilkes County in 1790, Elbert County established its county seat at the tiny hamlet first called Elbertville and later simply called "Elbert Courthouse." When the town was incorporated with the name, Elberton, in 1803, a log courthouse stood on the square. At this time, Elberton lay in the shadow of the now nearly forgotten city of Petersburg, which was situated in Elbert County between the Broad and Savannah Rivers. At the end of the

[1] *The Elberton Star*, June 9, 1893.

[2] Charles D. McGuffey, ed., *The Standard History of Chattanooga, Tennessee* (Knoxville TN: Crew and Dorey, 1911) 105.

[3] John E. Wells and Robert E. Dalton, *South Carolina Architects, 1885-1935* A Biographical Dictionary (Richmond: The New South Architectural Press, 1992) 122-27.

The Elberton Air Line

Elbert County: Elberton • Hart County: Hartwell • Franklin County: Carnesville
Some Last Thoughts on the Elberton Air Line

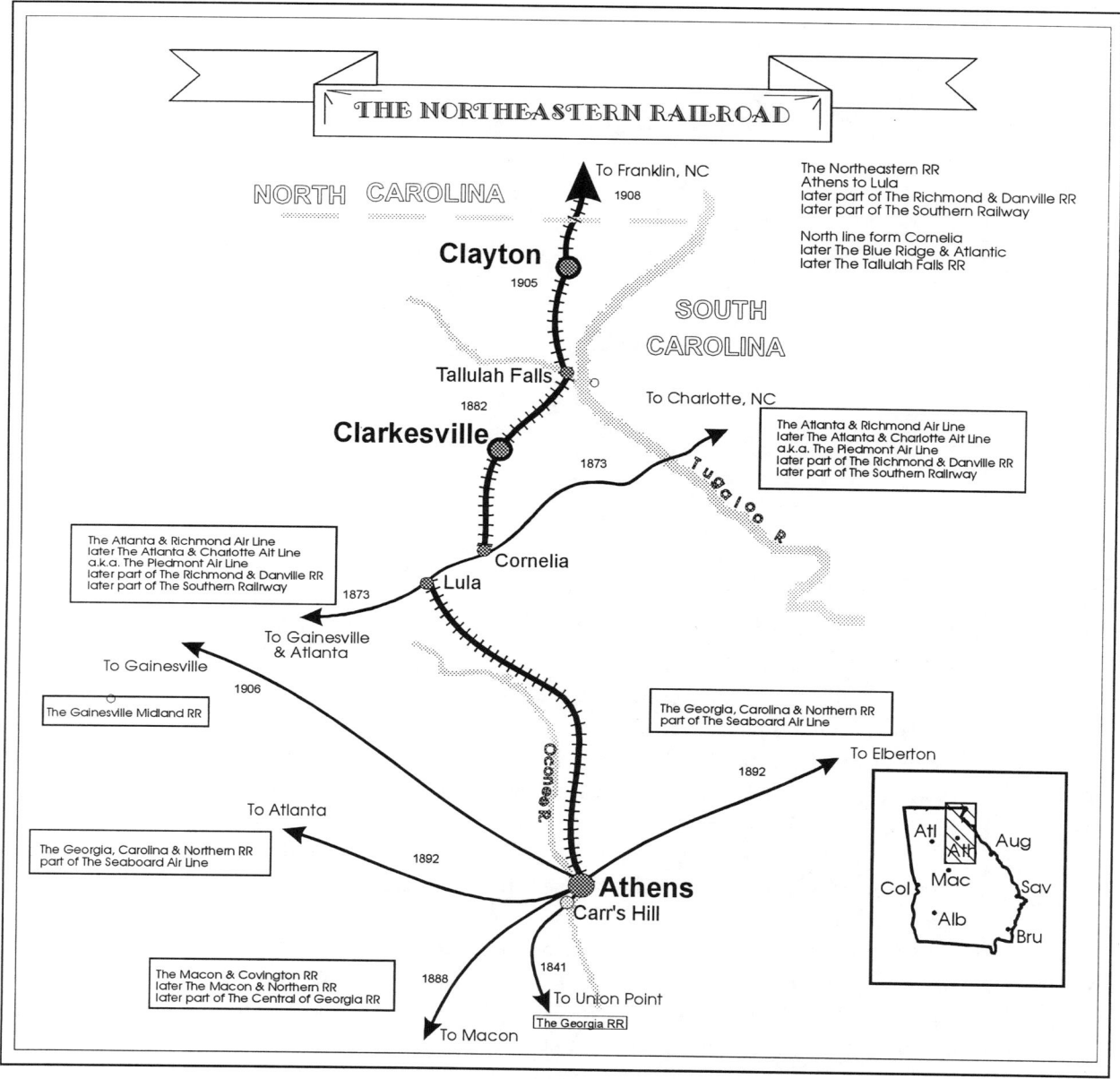

THE NORTHEASTERN RAILROAD

NORTH CAROLINA

To Franklin, NC
1908

The Northeastern RR
Athens to Lula
later part of The Richmond & Danville RR
later part of The Southern Railway

North line form Cornelia
later The Blue Ridge & Atlantic
later The Tallulah Falls RR

Clayton
1905

SOUTH CAROLINA

Tallulah Falls
1882

To Charlotte, NC

Clarkesville

1873

The Atlanta & Richmond Air Line
later The Atlanta & Charlotte Air Line
a.k.a. The Piedmont Air Line
later part of The Richmond & Danville RR
later part of The Southern Railway

The Atlanta & Richmond Air Line
later The Atlanta & Charlotte Air Line
a.k.a. The Piedmont Air Line
later part of The Richmond & Danville RR
later part of The Southern Railway

Cornelia

1873   Lula

To Gainesville
& Atlanta

To Gainesville

1906

The Gainesville Midland RR

The Georgia, Carolina & Northern RR
part of The Seaboard Air Line

To Elberton

1892

To Atlanta

The Georgia, Carolina & Northern RR
part of The Seaboard Air Line

1892

Oconee R.

Athens
Carr's Hill

The Macon & Covington RR
later The Macon & Northern RR
later part of The Central of Georgia RR

1888   1841

To Union Point
The Georgia RR

To Macon

Atl   Aug

Col   Mac   Sav

Alb   Bru

eighteenth century, Petersburg, with a population of over 2000, was among the largest settlements in Georgia and the center of a prosperous tobacco trade. According to Adiel Sherwood's *Gazetteer of Georgia,* by 1829, Elberton had "a courthouse, a jail, 2 academies, 1 church and 21 houses and stores." The early record of courthouse building in Elbert County is sketchy, but we know that a substantial brick court building was finally built around 1853.[4] Four years before that sturdy building was erected, the reliable George White had passed through Elbert County and described Elberton as a village of about 300 persons. As for Petersburg at mid-century, White waxed poetic, recounting feelings of "melancholy and loneliness" as he viewed the old town "in a state of dilapidation."

When the Washington Branch of the Georgia Railroad was completed in 1854, citizens in Elberton sought an extension to connect their town with the railhead at Washington. When none was forthcoming, railroad schemes in Elberton slept for over two decades. The Civil War came and went, and Elbert County continued in her isolation. Cotton remained king, but modern notions began to surface in Elberton in the late 1870s.

In the frenzied railroad building atmosphere of Reconstruction, even conservative Elberton awoke to the unfamiliar cacophony of opportunity. An early scheme to build a railroad from Augusta through Elberton to Hartwell failed in 1870, but shortly thereafter, leaders in Elberton chartered the Elberton Air Line, receiving $50,000 from the city of Elberton and additional capital from stock subscription along the proposed route of the road. After an uncertain beginning, the road was graded in 1874-1875 using leased convict labor, and completed along the 50-mile ridge running from Elberton to a junction with the Atlanta and Charlotte Air Line at Toccoa. According to Sholes's *Gazetteer of Georgia* Elberton shipped 10,000 bales of cotton on the Elberton Air Line in 1879, only a year after the line's completion.

The next thirty years brought sweeping change to Elberton as the place evolved from a sleepy village to a boomtown brimming with New South passion. By 1890, the town's population had reached 1500. At the apex of this period was the 1892 arrival of the crossing

Plate 14.1: The Elbert County Courthouse built in 1893-1894. Elberton's story is the saga of the nearly thirty years between Reuben Harrison Hunt's humble departure from the county as a child and his triumphant return to design the 1894 Elbert County Courthouse. (Photo: Wilber W. Caldwell.)

rails of the main line of the Georgia, Carolina and Northern Railroad and the erection of R. H. Hunt's grand Elbert County Courthouse in 1893-1894. The hopeful mood that accompanied the arrival of crossing rails was typical. In July of 1893, *The Elberton Star* spewed forth the usual high-spirited boosterism, informing readers that: "...the entire moral and spiritual condition of the people changed for the better and nowhere will you find a more marked improvement in every particular in so short a time than along the 50 miles between Elberton and Toccoa, the result of the Elberton Air Line."[5] As wildly fantastic as this may seem, it was based on a generous potion of real

---

[4] *The Elberton Star*, June 9, 1893. On the eve of the demolition of the Elbert County Courthouse, *The Star* eulogized the old building stating that it was forty years old.

[5] *The Elberton Star*, July 7, 1893.

progress. Only seven months before, *The Star* had joyfully detailed a boom in Elberton. The Swift Cotton Mill had been completed along with a new Opera House and a hotel. Additionally, we are informed that:"(over 100 dwellings have been built within the corporate limits of the town within the last year. There is scarcely a vacant house in Elberton."[6] Serious commercial granite quarrying operations were begun at about this time, and Elberton was in a battle with Abbeville, South Carolina, for the shops of the Georgia, Carolina and Northern, a contest that Elberton would soon win. A foundry followed within a year. In the midst of all of this progress, citizens suddenly began to demand modern improvements, and in the same civic breath that begot the new courthouse, agitation arose for bonds to finance street lights, sidewalks, a water works, and macadamized streets.[7]

Plate 14.2: The Elbert County Courthouse, built c1853. Demolished in 1893.

Elberton's new courthouse movement began right on cue after the arrival of the crossing rails of the Georgia, Carolina and Northern. As was so often the case, it had its beginnings not so much in dreams of a new court building, but in public outcry over the inadequacy of the old building. Poorly maintained, vernacular courthouses had stood crumbling on Georgia's squares for decades. In most cases these buildings would have to burn or fall down in order to arouse public support for their replacement, but over and over again we see the arrival of new rails rendering these old court buildings inconsistent with a community's new found aspirations and elevated self-image.

Plate 14.2: The Elbert County Courthouse built c. 1853. Elberton's 1893 new courthouse movement had its beginnings not so much in dreams of a new court building, but in public outcry over the inadequacy of the old building. (Illustration: The Elberton Star: June 9, 1893.)

Overnight, railroads transformed once proud symbols of tradition into shameful eyesores.

Such was the case in Elberton. This simple vernacular brick courthouse had first graced Elberton's square around 1853. With its crude wooden courtroom stairs tacked to the exterior the building, it displayed little architectural refinement save the brick corbeling of the cornice and the attractive parapet above. By all accounts the building had served the county well, but in March of 1893, *The Star* described the old court building as "unsightly," "inconveniently arranged," "located in the wrong place," "unsafe for records" and "badly in need of repair."[8] In a passage that cut directly to the heart of the matter, the editor declared: "When we reflect on…the arrival and departure of trains on two roads…we are at a loss to account for the condition of the public buildings."[9]

But the demolition of the old building was not to come without the obligatory nostalgic look backward that revealed the divided mind of the place. Recounting all the drama of its past *The Star* eulogized the old building that had been entered by "men with hearts trembling" and recalled the voices of Alexander Stephens and "the lion of the South," Robert Toombs, echoing in an old courtroom "imbued with reverence." In the end, however, *The Star* put aside myths of the Old South for the myths of the New declaring: "(progress and enterprise are iconoclast, and everything must yield to the march of the invaders and all

---

[6] *The Elberton Star*, January 2, 1893.

[7] *The Elberton Star*, March, 31, 1893.

[8] *The Elberton Star*, March 3, 1893.

[9] *The Elberton Star*, June 9, 1893.

[10] *The Elberton Star*, June 9, 1893.

[11] Richard Howland Hunt, the son of the great American architect, Richard Morris Hunt, became a nationally known architect in his own right with a particular fondness for Chattanooga. He designed buildings for the University of the South at Suwanee, Tennessee, and for Vanderbilt University at Nashville. Thus, two architects named R. H. Hunt worked in and around Chattanooga in the same time frame, and not surprisingly there has been considerable confusion in this regard.

alters and antiquities are swept away by their withering touch." [10] Here was the true metal of New South progress after it had been tempered with the emotions of a tragic past. The flamboyant zeal for prosperity when smelted by the fire of the mythical Lost Cause called forth an image of progress as invincible "invader" who, in many minds, no doubt, still wore Union blue.

Plate 14.3: The Elbert County Courthouse built in 1893-1894. Reuben H. Hunt, architect. The year 1893 was a watershed for American architecture. After the death of the great H. H. Richardson, only seven years before, the Richardsonian Romanesque had briefly dominated American's architectural imagination. But other forces were at work. A second Renaissance Revival was gaining momentum. With the overwhelming success of the "Florentine Renaissance" excesses of the buildings of the Columbian Exposition at the 1893 Chicago Worlds Fair, the picturesque would soon be in disarray, and a return to order would become the architectural voice of American economic progress in the coming century. As the great Chicago Fair opened, Reuben Hunt was selected from a field of six architects who presented plans for Elbert County's new courthouse.

When Hunt returned to the county of his birth, he had already designed many buildings in the Richardsonian mode. The influence of the American master's Romanesque designs is clear here at Elberton. The brick and stone polychromy, the grand arch of an entrance, the characteristic fenestration and the bold corner pavilions with their steep rooflines all recall Richardson's Allegheny County Courthouse at Pittsburgh, completed only five years before. Equally clear, however, are evolving classical elements. Most notable is Hunt's careful symmetry. By 1890, a national trend toward symmetry was emerging even among Richardson's most ardent disciples. Additionally, Hunt employed an eclectic array of Renaissance ornaments including the splayed voussoirs of the grand arch and the central tower with its purely classical lantern. Likewise, the brick banding in the lower story is carefully arranged to suggest rusticated stone masonry that was a hallmark of neoclassicism all across Europe.

It is also notable that in the early 1890s, two domestic works of another great American architect, Richard Morris Hunt,[11] were rising to further incorporate elements of the French Renaissance into the bubbling American architectural mix. R. M. Hunt's Ochre Court at Newport, Rhode Island, was completed in 1891, and the construction of his grand Biltmore House at Asheville, North Carolina, was begun in that same year. It is quite possible that in designing the roofline of the Elbert County Courthouse, Reuben Hunt drew inspiration from these grand homes. The steep hipped roofs of the front pavilions and the almost conical caps of the octagonal rear pavilions are typical of the French Renaissance, and are characteristic of Richard Morris Hunt's work in this style. Also, it may be that the second story arcade was inspired by Hunt's Ochre Court.

This was to be Reuben Hunt's only courthouse in Georgia, but its influence cannot be understated. In the last years of the old century and the first years of the new, this symmetrical design with its corner pavilions and central tower would become popular with many of Georgia's best architects, and soon similar buildings would decorate many of the state's courthouse squares. Bruce and Morgan would unveil their Monroe County Courthouse at Forsyth in 1895, the

Plate 14.3: Reuben Hunt's rendering of the 1894 Elbert County Courthouse. (Illustration: The Elberton Star , June 9, 1893.)

year after Walter Chamberlain completed his strange Macon County Courthouse at Oglethorpe. Likewise, James Golucke would build many court buildings in this mode.

Plate 14.4: The depot at Elberton, built in 1910.

In 1892, when the Georgia, Carolina and Northern Railroad was completed to Elberton, the trip to Atlanta was suddenly reduced to an impossibly brief four hours. The journey, with its seventeen stops, could be made for $4.03. By 1910, when this depot was built, Elberton was a city of 6500. The building is almost identical to the depot built in the same year by the Seaboard Air Line Railway at Winder. This fine restoration is a fitting symbol for Elberton's railroad borne success. According to one account, a representative for the business community of Elberton traveled all the way to Norfolk in 1910 to lobby the Seaboard for a new brick depot rather than the wooden structure first proposed by the railroad. Although this story may be true, it is unlikely that the man had to argue very hard, for by 1910 Elberton was booming, and her railroad-building dreams were not at an end. Incorporated as the Elberton Eastern Railroad, a new line was extended eastward to the village of Tignal in

Plate 14.4: When this depot was completed in 1910, Elberton's railroad dreams were not at an end. (Photo: Wilber W. Caldwell.)

[12] Baker, *History of Hart County*, 258.

[13] *The Hartwell Sun*, May 15, 1878.

[14] *The Hartwell Sun*, July 10, 1878.

[15] *The Hartwell Sun*, October 2, 1878.

[16] *The Hartwell Sun* in John William Baker, History of Hart County (Atlanta: Foote and Davies, 1933) 83.

[17] Baker, *History of Hart County*, 82.

1913. This extension reached Washington in 1917 to connect with the branch of the old Georgia Railroad. It was the fulfillment of a dream that went all the way back to 1854. But hard times still lay ahead for Elbert County, and the line was abandoned in 1933.

HART COUNTY: HARTWELL

Plate 14.5: The depot at Hartwell, built c. 1885.

In May of 1878, William F. Bowers, who "had much to do with the building of the Elberton Air Line,"[12] was the owner of a substantial piece of land along that railroad ten miles west of Hartwell at a place later called Bowersville. Like many in Hart County, Bowers was an individualist with firm opinions about that county's place in the universe. A staunch Unionist before the war, he led attempts to establish a Unionist party in Hart County in the late 1860s and was Hart County's representative to the 1868 Constitutional Convention in Atlanta. William Bowers was also a Baptist preacher of some renown. His political speeches and his rhetoric in support of a railroad from Hartwell to Bowersville retained the tone of the pulpit. At a railroad meeting in Hartwell, Bowers argued that God's way was the way of community, not individual ends, and that personal interests should be put aside in order to bring rails to Hartwell. "Vain is the man who opposes the progress of these things," Bowers declared, and in answer to the question of his own self-interest, he replied: "I have heard people say…Old Billy Bowers has a few acres of land and he wants to enhance its value. I tell you this is a mistake. I would be for a railroad if I had not an acre of land in the world. I see that there is great good to be effected by it."[13]

Despite William Bowers's "unselfish" appeals, there was little of the usual overstated New South boosterism attached to the birth of the Hartwell Railroad. The thrust of most arguments for the construction of the tiny short line was centered in practical agricultural considerations. In July of 1878, at another railroad meeting at Hartwell, promoters stressed the railroad's usefulness in cases "when the many products of your soil have outgrown home markets."[14] And in October, *The Hartwell Sun* reminded farmers that a rail line would subtract $10 per ton off the price of guano at Hartwell.[15]

This was a far cry from the extravagant visions of New South industry and wealth that filled the dreams of so many local railroad builders of the era. It seemed that the most Hartwell dared to hope for was that cotton growers in South Carolina would ship from the new railhead at Hartwell rather than continuing the traditional rocky float down the river to Augusta. When the narrow gauge Hartwell Railroad was completed in 1879 and a tiny four-wheeled locomotive, nicknamed the Nancy Hart, chugged into Hartwell, *The Sun*'s only excesses were an article entitled "Hartwell as a Cotton Market," and a long, awkward poem, entitled "The Nancy Hart" by "Uncle Billy" Bowers. Bowers was unquestionably a better railroad promoter that poet. His verse declared in part: "Yea, many a bale she'll make quiver. / Brought from far, far over the river. / Cotton shipped on the Elberton Railroad in part. / Will be furnished it by our Nancy Hart."[16]

This tiny depot replaced the original depot at Hartwell some time around 1885.[17] The diminutive locomotive, "Nancy Hart," served the town until 1904 when the line was converted to standard gauge. Meanwhile, Bowersville had been laid out in 1879, but a large portion of the town burned in 1888. Its population remained stagnate at around 300 well into the new century. Little remains today, save scattered dwellings and a few empty brick stores.

Plate 14.6: The Hart County Courthouse, built in 1856. Burned 1900.

In the antebellum period, cotton production was relatively low in Hart County and slaves were few. Farmers retained the fiercely individualistic ethic of the frontier. In 1854, only a year after Hart County was cut from Franklin and Elbert Counties, the new county town of Hartwell was laid out only 3 miles from the meeting place the Cherokees had called "The Center of the World." In that same year, a simple frame courthouse was erected. In 1856, that temporary structure was replaced by a brick building. Typical of the Greek inspired vernacular buildings of the period, the courthouse featured a fine portico supported

Plate 14.5: The depot at Hartwell, built c. 1885 was a far cry from the extravagant visions of New South industry and wealth that filled the dreams of so many local railroad builders of the era. (Photo Wilber W. Caldwell.)

by four Doric columns resting on brick piers. A delicate dental course decorated the entablature. Doubtless rendered with the aid of one of the many builders guides that detailed classical orders for unsophisticated carpenters of the era, the 1856 Hart County Courthouse is a crude reflection of the graceful lines of Robert Mills's many Greek Revival court

Plate 14.6: The Hart County Courthouse, built in 1856 is a crude reflection of the graceful lines of Robert Mills's many Greek Revival court buildings across the river in South Carolina.

buildings across the river in South Carolina. But unlike the pure Romantic symbolism of Mills's Greek Revival of the 1830s, the Greek Revival of the 1850s had become saturated with that uniquely Southern perversion that sought to align Southern society with ancient Greek institutions, which, of course, included slavery.

The same year this courthouse was completed, the original survey of the Georgia Air Line had scribed a right-of-way from Atlanta, through Homer, Carnesville and Hartwell, to Charlotte. After the war, this plan had been discarded when the Atlanta and Richmond Air Line was built through Toccoa. Since that time, a disappointed Hart County had been cool to railroad schemes. The empty railroad promises of the early 1870s, including the Augusta and Hartwell Railway and a line through Hartwell from Wallhalla, South Carolina, to Petersburg, Georgia, had fostered further skepticism. In 1877, *The Hartwell Sun* summed up the town's attitude in response to plans for the Augusta and Knoxville Railroad, declaring that, "the river suits us better(and water transportation is equally cheap."[18] Thus, the arrival of the Hartwell Railroad in 1879 stirred little in the way of New South fervor, and the usual outcry for a new courthouse that so often followed railroad connections was nowhere to be heard.

Hart County was not a place welcoming change with open arms. Populists had been strong here, barely loosing to the Democrats in 1892 and capturing all county level offices except Sheriff in 1896. Populism promoted an odd agenda. On one hand it advocated nearly socialistic notions aimed at weakening the power of big business, and on the other it seemed almost reactionary with regard to many social issues. This seemingly contradictory political blend resulted in a general opposition to most of the New South's capitalistic platform. Inherent in this was a powerful opposition to the railroad's freewheeling brand of monopolistic exploitation. In Populist strongholds, where opposition to the railroads was fierce few new courthouses rose.

The nature of the Hartwell Railroad itself reflected the county's lack of commitment to modern industrial notions. By any standard, the line was a

half-hearted effort. Like the narrow gauge Elberton Air Line, the flimsy spur with its single toy-like locomotive was "the subject of butts and amusement" in the other parts of the state.[19] Nonetheless, it brought change. Hartwell had a small cotton mill before 1900, and her population had blossomed from around 200 in 1860 to 1500 by the turn of the century.

As in so many hapless Deep South communities, the new railroad would beget only a few hollow trappings of the modern era. As elsewhere along Georgia's early postbellum rails, the most powerful agent of change to arrive on the Hartwell Railroad was commercial fertilizer. In 1869, Hart County produced only 1320 bales of cotton, a figure similar to the county's modest annual totals before the war. With the completion of the Elberton Air Line and the Hartwell Railroad, the sudden availability of commercial fertilizer raised the curtain on the sad pageant of cotton and tenancy in Hart County. In 1879, the county produced over 5000 bales. This number would reach an astounding 24,000 bales by 1911. All the while, farms became smaller and more desperate. In 1860, Hart County had counted 523 farms. In 1900, she counted over 2000. In that year, the old Hart County Courthouse burned to the ground.

Plate 14.7: The Hart County Courthouse, built in 1901. Burned 1967. James W. Golucke, architect.

Having little faith in New South prophets with their dizzy railroad induced dreams of impending prosperity, the practical citizens of Hart County harbored only modest hope for any progress that might arrive on the rails of the Hartwell Railroad. They clung to a traditional agrarian vision, and no doubt, the simple Greek portico of the old courthouse had been an appropriate symbol for the collective pragmatic mind of Hart County. Thus, when the old building burned, it is not surprising that county officials sought to replace it with a structure that projected similar imagery. In 1900, they did not have to look far to find such a building. James W. Golucke had just designed the first of his many neoclassical courthouses. The imposing granite walls of the 1900 DeKalb County Courthouse in Decatur represented

Golucke's answer to the dilemma of the South. Here was a duel symbol, balancing faithful memories of the old South with the modern Northern imagery of the Neoclassical Revival and Beaux-Arts Classicism. With its grand central lantern and four great Ionic porticos, the 1901 Hart County Courthouse, although constructed of brick, was remarkably similar to Golucke's 1900 DeKalb County Courthouse. Memories of the architecture of Thomas Jefferson and Robert Mills are voiced by the temple-like Greek porticos, while more modern neoclassical imagery is expressed in Renaissance ornament like the rusticated stone quoining and the pedimented openings adorning the lantern. Like so many of Golucke's neoclassical designs, the building follows the form of Palladio's Villa Rotondo with a squared dome and four more of less equal porticoed entrances, one facing each side of Hartwell's spacious square. The tragic loss of this building to fire in 1967 deprived the state of one of James Wingfield Golucke's early models, a simple, inexpensive building that would lead directly to Golucke's elaborate masterpieces at Newnan and Greenville, Georgia.

Only four years after this courthouse was completed, "Uncle Billy" Bowers died. For over twenty years, Bowers had led efforts to extend his Hartwell Railroad. In 1879, he championed a grand scheme to incorporate the tiny Hartwell Railroad into an Anderson, South Carolina, to Rome, Georgia, line.[20] After this effort failed, Bowers had worked for over a decade to complete a short line from Bowersville to the railroad hungry hamlet of Carnesville, the county seat of neighboring Franklin County. These efforts came to nothing, but in 1904 as Bowers lay on his death bed, his grand scheme surfaced again in the form the Atlanta and Carolina Railway, later called the Atlanta and Anderson Railway.[21] Rumors of this railroad continued to tantalize the remote and unconnected county seats of Homer and Carnesville for over a decade. In 1917, an Atlanta to Anderson line was actually surveyed before the project was abandoned.[22]

Meanwhile, the cautious skepticism of the farmers of Hart County had proved insightful. Unlike most of James Golucke's grand neoclassical court build-

Plate 14.7: With its grand central lantern and four great Ionic porticos, the 1901 Hart County Courthouse, although constructed of brick, was remarkably similar to Golucke's 1900 DeKalb County Courthouse at Decatur. (Photo: Courtesy of the Georgia Dept. of Archives and History.)

ings, the courthouse at Hartwell was not built as a result of railroad inspired zeal, nor would it come to stand for any modern, New South vision of progress. It is more likely that Golucke's graceful porticos were simply up-to-date reminders of the columns of the old Hart County Courthouse built way back in 1856.

FRANKLIN COUNTY: CARNESVILLE

Plate 14.8: The Franklin County Courthouse, built in 1826. Demolished 1906.

The second and third decades of the nineteenth century saw brick courthouses sprouting all across the Georgia Piedmont. With its external staircase beneath a classical portico supported by four Doric columns, the 1826 Franklin County Courthouse was typical of these sturdy brick vernacular buildings. Here was a building inspired by the Greek Revival creations of Robert Mills in South Carolina. This simple style defied change until after the Civil War. Created in

[18] *The Hartwell Sun*, April 4, 1877.

[19] *The Hartwell Sun*, May 15, 1878.

[20] *The Hartwell Sun*, September 17, 1879.

[21] *The Franklin County Register*, April 14, 1904, and June 24, 1904.

[22] Baker, *History of Hart County*, 83.

Plate 14.8: A crude reflection of the Greek Revival architecture of Robert Mills in South Carolina, the 1826 Franklin County Courthouse was typical of the sturdy brick vernacular court buildings that covered the Piedmont in the antebellum period.

1784, the enormous expanses of the original Franklin County were whittled away over the years. Nine new counties in Georgia were carved from Franklin.[23] Many of these "offspring" counties would build similar court buildings. As late as 1864, Banks County completed an extremely similar building which still stands today at Homer, one of the few remaining standing examples of this once pervasive style.

The history of Franklin County's first court buildings is sketchy. In appears that a log courthouse was built near the present site of Carnesville in 1793. The exact date of the settlement of Carnesville is not known, but county officials authorized the erection of a new courthouse there in 1805. The building was completed the next year, and Carnesville was incorporated in 1807. No description of the 1806 courthouse survives. It was replaced by this 1826 brick structure which would faithfully stand on the square in Carnesville for eighty years.

Plate 14.9: The depot at Lavonia, built in 1910.

This fine depot at Lavonia with its squat tower is typical of depots built by the Southern Railway in the first decade of the new century. It has two stories to tell: one of Lavonia's success and the other of Carnesville's failure. On the western border of Franklin County beside the shinny new rails of the Elberton Air Line, the first lots in Lavonia were offered for sale in 1878. Originally called Burgess

City, the town was renamed Lavonia to honor the wife of T. H. Jones of Elberton, the president of the new railroad. Lavonia's growth was meteoric. A modest village of 283 in 1890, the place became a hot bed of New South passion by 1910, boasting over 1700 residents. Only thirty years after her birth, Lavonia had a flour mill grinding 90 barrels a day, a cotton mill with almost 5000 spindles, a brick yard capable of firing 50,000 bricks a day, a prosperous cotton seed oil mill, two hotels and a bank.[24] Here was a shining example of the railroad's power to bestow the blessing of the new age in rural areas. Although these gifts would prove temporary, in 1910, Lavonia was everything Carnesville was not.

Carnesville's story is one of endless frustration. In 1856, Carnesville lay on the original survey of the Georgia Air Line, the antebellum predecessor to the Atlanta and Charlotte Air Line. Then in the early 1870s, the town had organized a concerted effort to

Plate 14.9: This fine depot built by the Southern Railway at Lavonia has two stories to tell: one of Lavonia's success and the other of Carnesville's failure. (Photo: Wilber W. Caldwell)

attract the Elberton Air Line. Both railroads eventually passed Carnesville by. The 1880s began a long period of railroad scheming in Carnesville, which would see the town's railroad dreams appear to materialize again and again only to vaporize in a series of agonizing failures. In stark contrast to the dizzying growth in the railroad city of Lavonia, only 10 miles away, Carnesville's population remained static. The town listed 275 residents in 1890, and in 1910 the village could count only 322. In this context, it is not surprising that in 1903 Lavonia, despite her location on the very western edge of Franklin County, made an all-out effort to capture the county seat.

Plate 14.10: The Franklin County Courthouse, built in 1906. Walter Chamberlain, architect.

Despite her conspicuous lack of rail connection, Carnesville was not without her own brand of New South zeal. Almost from the beginning, the town had ardently courted the railroads. With each new railroad scheme, the construction of the line would first be declared "assured," then, when rails failed to materialize, leaders would urge continued effort. In 1905, an editorial in *The Carnesville Advance* entitled "Carnesville's Future" was typical: "Because we have been disappointed…is not reason for giving up. True greatness consists not in never failing, but in rising every time we fail….Let us not abandon true hope for a railroad…. (Carnesville) lacks only a railroad to rapidly advance in material wealth…We MUST have a railroad."[25] Earlier in that same year *The Advance* had published a shopping list of New South dreams for Carnesville that included: "a standard gauge railroad (to any point, just so we get it), a new courthouse, a public library…, up to date sidewalks and streets, brick business houses…, a free public school system, manufactories of all kinds (and) an electric light system."[26]

But it was not only material trappings that the citizens of Carnesville sought. From an early date they were aware that the town was vulnerable without a railroad. In 1878, when the city of Lavonia consisted of nothing more than a few surveyors stakes beside the rails of the Elberton Air Line, an anonymous letter appeared in *The Franklin County Register:* "For lo

Plate 14.10: Although a long distance from the wild exuberance of the 1904 St. Louis World's Fair, Walter Chamberlain's 1906 Franklin County Courthouse reflects the influence of American Beaux Art Classicism. (Photo: Wilber W. Caldwell)

these many years the citizens of Carnesville…have done all in their power to build a railroad to their town. But alas it was all in vain. What must they do? I would suggest that, as they cannot get a railroad, they consider the question of moving their county site to some eligible point on the Elberton Air Line.[27] Undoubtedly this kind of talk added fuel to the fires of railroad building in Carnesville. The next thirty years saw numerous futile efforts to connect with the Elberton Air Line at Lavonia, Canon, Bowersville, and

[23] Franklin County originally contained territory that today comprises all or part of Stephens, Banks, Oconee, Clarke, Jackson, Barrow, Hall, Hart and Madison Counties.

[24] Marie Haley Williams, Lavonia, *Gem of the Piedmont* (Lavonia GA: Library Committee, Lavonia Carnegie Library, 1977) 43-56.

[25] *Carnesville Advance*, December 15, 1905.

[26] *Carnesville Advance*, July 21, 1905.

[27] *Franklin County Register*, October, 12, 1878.

Toccoa, as well as plan to link with the Northeastern Railroad at Commerce. In 1888, Carnesville's hopes rose with the charter of the Smithsonia, Danielsville and Carnesville Railroad, but this line sputtered in 1895 having laid only five miles of track from Smithsonia to Colbert. In 1903, as Lavonia mounted her assault on the courthouse, the Georgia Traction Company applied for a charter, and plans for a thirty-three mile electric railroad from Carnesville to Athens were well under way in December of 1903.[28] Like so many previous schemes, the line's construction seem assured. A contract for grading had been signed earlier in the year,[29] and two weeks after the announcement of the application for charter, *The Advance* advertised for hands to work on the road and published a locally composed poem that voiced the dreams of so many towns on the era:

"Over the hills, the streams,
A roadbed now is building;
the fondest hope of all our dreams
It's surface fair is gliding.
When fifteen months have passed away,
Fortunes hand will beckon;
Trade to turn in Carnesville's way,
At least that's what we reckon.
On the roadbed soon we'll look,
To see the tie and railing;
And down the grade, around the crook,
An electric engine sailing.
The cars behind all loaded up,
With produce from the farms:
The farmer brings along his pup,
Both free from all alarms.
Outbound cars will take them back,
The farmer, pup and wares;
To every big or little shack,
The railroad's killed our cares.[30]

---

[28] *Carnesville Advance*, December 4, 1903.

[29] *Carnesville Advance*, April 17, 1903.

[30] *Carnesville Advance*, December 18, 1903.

[31] *Carnesville Advance,* July 3, 1903.[32] *Carnesville Advance*, May 22, 1903.

[33] *Carnesville Advance*, April 28, 1904, and June 6, 1904

In an effort to steal away the county seat, Lavonia voiced skepticism concerning the viability of an electric road, and offered to build a new courthouse at no cost to the taxpayers. Additionally, Lavonia charged that Carnesville simply advocated continued use of the old 1826 building in order to save the expense of a new building, and that, after the election, county officials in Carnesville would dynamite the aging building in order to get a new courthouse in Carnesville built at taxpayer's expense.[31] It was a foul charge, but by all appearances county leaders in Clarkesville had done exactly that in 1898, after a notable battle with Toccoa over the Habersham County seat of justice. Leaders in Carnesville were incensed by the charge calling it "false, slanderous and contemptuous." They doubled their arguments against Lavonia on geographical grounds, citing its peripheral location, and on financial grounds, claiming that the tax revenues from the operation of Carnesville's new railroad would be more than enough to fund a new courthouse in Carnesville.[32]

Lavonia lost her bid for the Franklin County seat, and Carnesville began plans to construct a new courthouse to cement her victory. In the midst of all of this, plans were announced for the construction of the Atlanta and Carolina Railroad. Also known as the Atlanta and Anderson Railroad, the line was surveyed through Carnesville in 1904.[33]

With two railroads apparently on the way, Carnesville surely envisioned herself on the threshold of the modern age and sought a monument to voice her dreams. On the page opposite the announcement of the Atlanta and Carolina Railroad's plans to put Carnesville of the map, *The Franklin County Advance* ran an article about the great Louisiana Purchase Exposition then underway in St. Louis. The paper included a picture of New York architect Cass Gilbert's Palace of Fine Arts, a building literally dripping with the Baroque excesses of Beaux-Arts Classicism. Although a long distance, indeed, from the wild exuberance of the 1904 St. Louis World's Fair, Walter Chamberlain's 1906 Franklin County Courthouse at Carnesville reveals the influence of American Beaux-Arts Classicism which was then dominating the nation's public architecture in the North. Here, as in

Hazlehurst the year before, Chamberlain employed the modern material of solid concrete block. At Carnesville, he fashioned four equal porticos, one facing each side of the town's ample square, each supported by paired columns flanked by massive block piers in the Beaux-Arts mode.

This building is another product of the Falls City Construction Company of Louisville, Kentucky. With its imposing lantern, the concrete block and yellow brick walls of Chamberlain's 1906 Franklin County Courthouse represents what is arguably this architect's best work in Georgia. Still, like most of Fall City's work in the state, the building evokes little flamboyance and even less purely Southern imagery. It is thus a far cry from the many uniquely appropriate duel neoclassical symbols designed by J. W. Golucke and Frank Milburn.

The last page of Carnesville's story is filled with irony. It appears that, based upon her newfound prospects of becoming a stop on the Atlanta and Anderson Railroad, Carnesville abandoned plans for her electric short line to Athens. No sooner had the Georgia Traction Company been dissolved, then plans for the Atlanta and Anderson line vaporized leaving Carnesville again unconnected and despondent beside her sparkling new courthouse.

SOME LAST THOUGHTS ON THE ELBERTON AIR LINE

The Elberton Air Line supplies an excellent illustration of the pattern of railroad expansion that began in Georgia around 1880. The period was characterized first by a proliferation of locally financed short line railroads, all seeking to connect remote villages to the state's network of antebellum and Reconstruction mainline railroads, and second by the acquisition of these connecting roads by the consolidating forces of the giant Northern railroad conglomerates that would come to control virtually all of the state's main line railroads. Built with local capital scraped together by farmers and local merchants struggling in the midst of the economic stagnation that gripped the rural South after the Panic of 1873, the fifty mile, narrow gauge Elberton Air Line was begun in that very year. After

considerable difficulty, the line was completed in 1878 using leased convict labor. By 1888, the Elberton Air Line was part of the advancing transportation juggernaut known as the Richmond and Danville Railroad, which was soon to emerge as the centerpiece of J. P. Morgan's powerful Southern Railway.

As to courthouse building along the Elberton Air Line, only Elberton, greedily swallowed the bait offered by the tempting myths of New South prosperity. In 1892, promises of progress seduced Elberton with the arrival of the crossing rails of the main trunk of the Georgia, Carolina and Northern Railroad. Accordingly, the next year, Elbert County employed native son, Reuben Hunt of Chattanooga to design one of the state's finest Romanesque court buildings. Despite her tiny short line railroad, Hartwell, a Populist stronghold, was not so quick to embrace the New South creed. Nonetheless, when the old 1856 courthouse burned in 1900, she employed James W. Golucke to copy his new DeKalb County Courthouse on the square in Hartwell.

In 1906, in tiny Carnesville, Walter Chamberlain's Franklin County Courthouse had been inspired by hopes generated first by the locally financed Georgia Traction Company, an electric railroad proposed to run the 33 miles from Carnesville to Athens, and later by plans for the Atlanta and Anderson Railroad, which contemplated a main line through Carnesville. Ironically, just as the Beaux-Arts columns of Chamberlain's courthouse were finally set in place, plans for both railroads vaporized, leaving Carnesville unconnected. The village remains today a sadly charming example of what happened in towns that were bypassed by rail.

•

The East Tennessee, Virginia and Georgia Railroad

Whitfield County: Dalton (see chapter 4) • Floyd County: Rome (see chapter 4)

Paulding County: Dallas Douglas • County: Douglasville

Fulton County: Atlanta (see chapters 4, 11, 26 & 32)

Henry County: McDonough • Butts County: Jackson • Macon to Brunswick (see chapter 9)

Some Last Thoughts on the East Tennessee, Virginia and Georgia Railroad

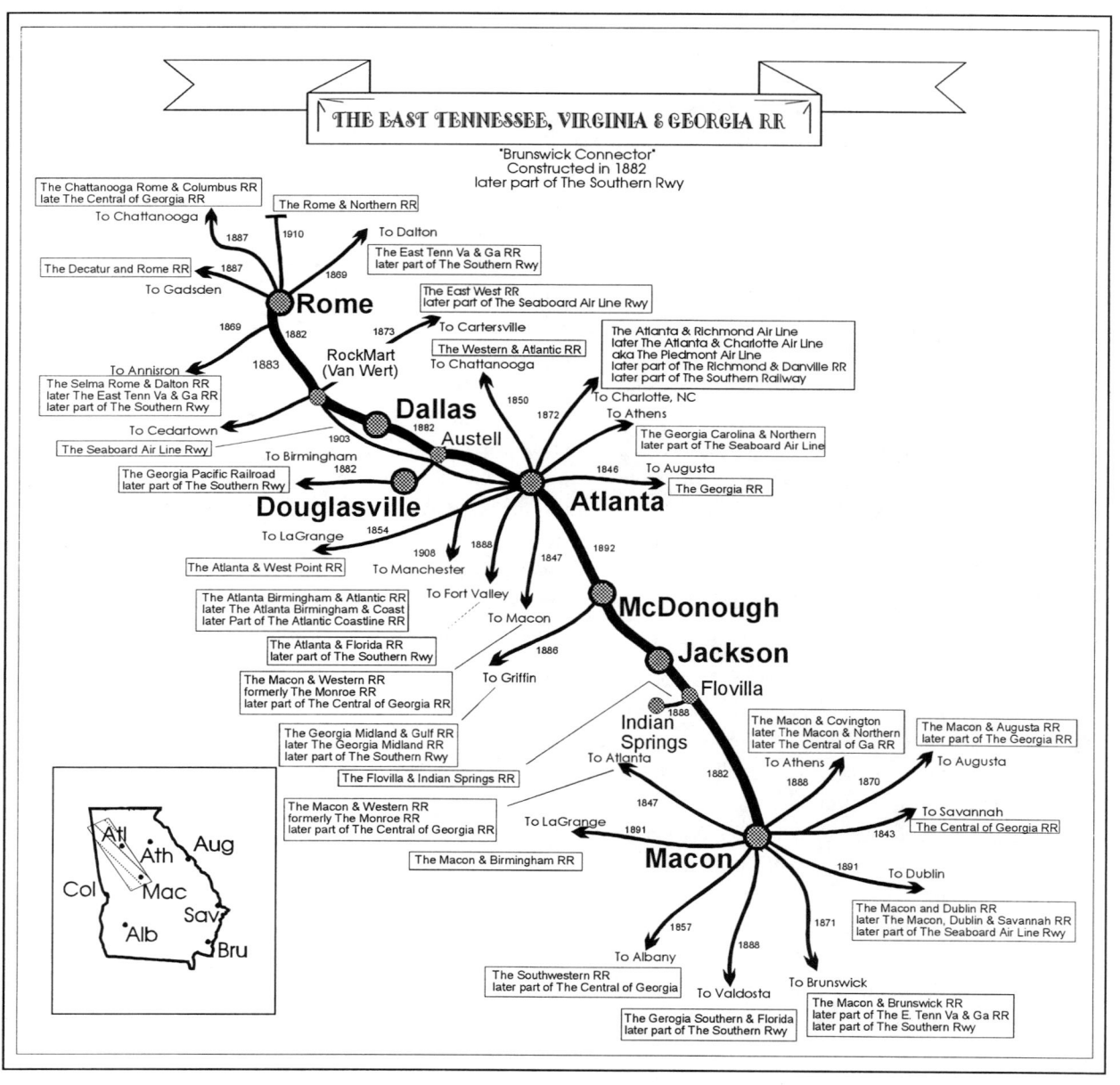

15 | The East Tennessee, Virginia and Georgia Railroad

PAULDING COUNTY: DALLAS

Plate 15.1: The Paulding County Courthouse built in 1892, Bruce and Morgan, architects.

Paudling County was one of many battlegrounds in an epic political confrontation of the late nineteenth century. In the 1880s, the county's farmers organized under the broad wings of the Farmers Alliance and later became politically active as the Peoples Party. These Populists viewed themselves as victims of ruthless economic exploitation, both real and perceived, which was thought to flow from the manipulations of American big business and big government. Very few grand courthouses rose in counties where Populism was strong. Paulding is a rare exception. This elegant courthouse was erected by the political faction led by progressive merchants and professionals in Dallas who embraced the myth of a New South in the face of an outraged rural population of economically beleaguered Populist farmers.

In 1892, when Paulding County's simple vernacular court building was replaced by this stunning new palace of justice designed by Atlanta architects, Bruce and Morgan, the event punctuated the ongoing struggle between town and county. As elsewhere, the battle lines had been drawn between rural conservative agrarian factions and the overzealous proponents of New South progress. As if to perpetuate the conflict, the old brick vernacular court building that had served the county since antebellum times, was left standing. For over thirty years it occupied a site directly across the street from Paulding County's gleaming new monument to the new age. The old building, which finally burned in 1924, had been erected in 1852, after Polk County had been cut from Paulding. Paulding's original 1836 court building at Van Wert, was described by George White in 1849 as "an unimposing wooden structure" in an "unhealthy" village of about 100 inhabi-

Plate 15.1: The grand new Paulding County Courthouse was not universally embraced as an appropriate symbol for the county's aspirations. (Photo: Wilber W. Caldwell.)

tants. After becoming the county seat in 1852, Dallas struggled through her early years. A poor county producing only 2300 bales of cotton in 1860, Paulding could boast little progress. In 1864, Dallas was described as "a village of squalid tenements, ragged appearance and very few citizens."[1]

The arrival of the East Tennessee, Virginia and Georgia Railroad in 1882 found Paulding County locked in the grip of the same economic stagnation that paralyzed much of rural Georgia in the decades following the Civil War. But by 1883, Dallas had erupted with the usual high-spirited aspirations that invariably accompanied the arrival of railroads in out-of-the-way places. It is telling that the local newspaper declared the most important contribution of the new road to be the income it supplied to destitute farmers who were widely employed in the road's construction: "...nothing could have conduced more to the maintenance and support of a vast number of our population, who, driven to the very verge of suffering

and want for the necessities of life,...were enabled to...support their families with the proceeds of their labor."[2]

The East Tennessee, Virginia and Georgia Railroad was the first of the Northern corporate transportation giants to begin the consolidation of Georgia's antebellum and Reconstruction railroads. In 1852, the same year the old brick vernacular courthouse at Dallas was built, the East Tennessee and Georgia Railroad entered Georgia laying track from Loudon, Tennessee, to Dalton, Georgia. After a merger with the East Tennessee and Virginia Railroad in 1869, the emerging giant became the East Tennessee, Virginia and Georgia operating a 212-mile interstate railroad from Bristol, Virginia, through Knoxville, Tennessee, to Dalton. In 1881, this company acquired two of Georgia's bankrupt Reconstruction lines, the Selma, Rome and Dalton and the Macon and Brunswick. Seeking a continuous connection between Cincinnati and Brunswick, the aggressive company set out to span the 141 mile gap between Rome and Macon with new rails. This connection, often called "The Macon and Brunswick Extension," was completed in October of 1882. Tiny Dallas, Georgia, the county seat of Paulding County lay along this route.

With the arrival of the railroad, a rising tide of the propaganda of progress washed over the county. Just as a flashy new depot rose in Dallas, the town celebrated the publication of her first newspaper, the Paulding *New Era*. As the name suggests, early issues of *The New Era* abounded with New South rhetoric:

> The completion of the E. T. V. & G. to this point has brought activity with it in each branch of industry, and now the quietude that formerly reigned supreme has been succeeded by the bustle of a live railroad town—the puffing and blowing of the locomotives as they pass with their heavy loaded and rumbling trains, the sound of the carpenter's saw and the ringing of the blacksmith's anvil and the bricklayers trowel.[3]

The next week *The New Era* waxed poetic declaring: "Your towns, which have long been as dormant as The Dead Sea, are now awakening to the new order of things, and putting on the shining garments of enterprise and pride."[4] *The New Era* maintained that the volume of trade during the first year of Paulding County's new railroad had seen a "ten-fold" increase and applauded the construction of 23 new buildings, nine of which were of brick.[5]

Bolstered by the force of such a boom, county officers backed by New South believers in Dallas hired Georgia's premier architectural firm of the era to design a new courthouse. Bruce and Morgan designed twelve courthouses in Georgia in the Romanesque Revival Style (see Appendix C). Many of these manifested reflections of H. H. Richardson's up-to-date Romanesque visions, and many were overlaid with abundant Queen Anne detail.

The Queen Anne Style had its beginnings in the United States following the appearance of the half-timber houses in the British exhibit at the 1876 Centennial Exposition at Philadelphia. Following the fashion set by Norman Shaw in England, the style reached its apex in America in the late 1880s passing through a historical Jacobethan Revival, often referred to as the Shavian Manorial Style, and into a new form of eclectic excess in which picturesque forms were combined with classical ornament. As the license of eclecticism became broader, the style tended toward confusion and ambiguity.

Bruce and Morgan's Paulding County Courthouse is an excellent example of such ambiguities. Queen Anne elements dominate the decoration. Especially notable in this context are the segmentally arched windows in the side elevation with their incised decoration above the headers and the bracketed cornice supporting the small balcony above the side entrance. The liberal use of terra cotta decoration is also typical of brick Queen Anne buildings of the era, especially the dogstooth pattern in the octagonal tower and in the massive pediment crowning the large side bay. Likewise, the classical pediments of various dormers and the flared capitals of the pilasters in the main tower are reflections of the Queen Anne style. All of this not withstanding, like many brick Queen Anne designs, these buildings are not without fundamental Romanesque elements. The massive tower and arched entrance appear Romanesque, while the ornate terra cotta banding, the recurring use of small window

panes and the smaller octagonal tower with its massive stone masonry base are all elements that are equally common to both Romanesque and Queen Anne forms.

Not surprisingly, the grand new courthouse was not universally embraced as an appropriate symbol for the county's aspirations. Dripping with ornate finery so popular in the North, the Queen Anne courthouse undoubtedly represented an apt symbol to those who had swallowed the tempting bait of New South mythology. On the other hand, there was perhaps no style that could have seemed more abhorrent to the simple farmers who opposed the onrushing tide of capitalism and despised such frilly Yankee bombast. The roots of conflict ran deep. As C. Vann Woodward reminds us, there remained in most rural areas "an elaborately reasoned critique of The Brave New South" that attached itself to the Lost Cause, viewed large cities as "sores on the body politic" and placed little trust in capitalism or technology. In 1892, the year this fine courthouse was erected in Dallas, the forces of the New South were solidly confronted by this "elaborately reasoned critique," in the form of Paulding County's Populist Party.

Just after Alexander Bruce's grand Queen Anne courthouse was completed, the first issue of *The Herald* appeared in Dallas. One of many locally published Populist journals, *The Herald* put forward a rather polarized view of society and politics, contending that human history was a record of the conflict between: "...the masses of people who bring from the earth its treasured wealth by their toil, and that class of people who live in arrogant idleness upon the wealth thus produced."[6]

As for the new courthouse, *The Herald*'s editors took a firm stand in opposition to bonds to finance

---

[1] *The Augusta Constitutionalist*, May 30, 1864, in Lucien Roberts, *A History of Paulding County* (Dallas GA: Lucien Roberts, 1933) 45.

[2] *The Paulding New Era*, February 15, 1883.

[3] *The Paulding New Era*, February 4, 1883.

[4] *The Paulding New Era*, February 15, 1883.

[5] W. A. Foster, Jr., *Paulding County, Its People and Places* (Roswell GA: WH Wolfe, 1983) 231.

[6] *The Dallas Herald*, May 4, 1893.

the new building, observing that the bond system was "the bottom rung of the Shylock's ladder" and applauding those who refused "to dance to the music of the bosses."[7] Today, in Dallas, Bruce and Morgan's 1892 Paulding County Courthouse supplies a dramatic reminder of the ongoing confrontation that, in Professor Woodward's words, "set the New South back on its heels." [8]

Douglas County: Douglasville

Douglasville's story is a tale of two railroads. In 1882, the East Tennessee, Virginia and Georgia reached a junction with the newly laid rails of the Georgia Pacific Railroad, on the boarder between Cobb and Douglas County. The junction point, later called Austell Junction, was first called Cincinnati Junction. Construction on the Georgia Pacific had begun less than a year before. This line sought to connect Atlanta and Birmingham, and as the name implies, it's ambitious creators harbored grand visions for a transcontinental railroad.

Among these visionaries was steamship magnate, William Clyde of New York, who embodied the financial force behind another growing Southern railroad cartel known as the Piedmont Air Line. Chartered in 1877 in a reorganization of the antebellum Georgia Western Railroad, the Georgia Pacific made little progress under the leadership of its first president, Georgia's beloved Civil War Hero turned Bourbon Democrat, General John B. Gordon. Then in January of 1882, with the support of Clyde's Piedmont Air Line, rails were laid through "Cincinnati Junction" and reached Birmingham less than two years later. In May of 1882, the first train on the Georgia Pacific arrived at Douglasville. A crowd estimated at 2000 persons witnessed the event. The majority of whom, according to county historian Fannie Mae Davis, "had never seen a train."[9]

Be this as it may, the residents of Douglasville were no strangers to railroads. From its very inception, Douglasville had been a town with its sights set on a railroad. The Georgia Western Railroad, the forerunner of the Georgia Pacific had been chartered in 1854, and by the beginning of the Civil War, grading had

been completed from Atlanta to a point two miles west of present day Douglasville. Work on the Georgia Western was halted by the war. In the 1870s, numerous efforts to revive the road came to nothing. Meanwhile, Douglas County was created from Cobb and Carroll Counties and a monumental struggle regarding the location of the county seat ensued. The dispute raged between those who advocated a central location, and those who sought a location on the proposed line of the railroad. After four years of conflict, the winner of the contest was a village colorfully known as Skint Chestnut, where a temporary 30' by 30' courthouse had already been built of "roughly dressed lumber."[10] In 1875, Skint Chestnut was incorporated as Douglasville, and within a few years, a two-story brick vernacular courthouse had been erected there to replace the first temporary wooden structure.

The arrival of the Georgia Pacific in 1882 brought the usual clamor regarding a new courthouse. In 1884, the grand jury suggested that the old courthouse, which was only a few years old, "was in bad shape and perhaps dangerous" and recommended that the building be "bolted and banded without delay."[11] Local legend holds that the bricks for the building had been improperly fired, some say owing to alcohol induced negligence on the part of the local brickmaker. Whatever the case, like neighboring Paulding County, Populism had a strong following here, and despite the usual efforts by New South prophets in Douglasville, change was slow to come. It would be twelve years before Andrew Bryan's new courthouse finally rose.

With the arrival of the Georgia Pacific Railroad, county officials, merchants and professionals in Douglasville set to work to transform Douglasville from a rough frontier village where "much drinking took place…(and) fighting and knife cutting was prevalent,"[12] to a place of business and commerce. Prohibition laws were passed in 1885 and in 1886 city leaders organized committees to promote a bank, a warehouse, a cotton mill, and a hotel.

But it was not only the railroad that delivered the New South's tempting promises to Douglas County. Just as Douglasville began to court the mythical prosperity of the industrial age, the tantalizing aroma of the New South's bounty began to blow in from tiny Salt Springs, only 6 miles to the east, near the junction of the Georgia Pacific and the East Tennessee, Virginia and Georgia Railroads. In 1886, at Salt Springs (first called Deer Lick and later called Lithia Springs), the New South's most powerful prophets, led by none other than Henry Woodfin Grady himself, were erecting monuments to their creed. In that year, construction of the grand Sweetwater Park Hotel was begun near John C. Bowden's mineral spring, which had acquired a national reputation for its healing waters. Built with financial backing from Atlanta's business elite and promoted by the powerful pen of Grady, the 250 room Sweetwater Park Hotel, opened its doors on July 4, 1888. In the following decade, it would play host to a parade of the nation's wealthiest families including the Vanderbilts, Astors and four US presidents.[13] As the sumptuous hotel with its elegant landscaping, modern electric lights and indoor plumbing took shape at the place soon referred to by Grady as "The Saratoga of the South," the Salt Springs and Bowden Lithia Railroad began operations carrying guests to the springs and bottled water to the depot at Austell.

In that same year, Henry Grady, again with the financial help of Atlanta's top businessmen, organized and built the Piedmont Chautauqua at Lithia Springs, a grand Southern version of the 1874 Chautauqua Institution at Lake Chautauqua, New York. The Piedmont Chautauqua featured instruction in foreign languages, natural sciences, the fine arts, and physical education taught by the nations top educators including visiting faculty from Harvard, Princeton, Yale and Johns Hopkins. Adjacent to the Sweetwater Park Hotel, Grady's Chautauqua was housed in a fantastic Moorish style complex which included a 1000 seat restaurant, a 7000 seat auditorium and various other classroom buildings all designed by New York architect, Lorenzo Wheeler, who had designed Grady's Atlanta Constitution Building in Atlanta in 1884. Using his national reputation as an orator and journalist as his platform, Grady spewed forth a stream of rhetoric promoting both the hotel and the Chautauqua.

The complex at Lithia Springs was at once a health spa, a grand resort, a place of learning and perhaps a bit of a circus. It was also a financial failure. The original project included a sizable land speculation scheme that met with little success. At heart, the undertaking rested on a series of flashy promotional events designed to draw crowds to a host of illusions that included a miracle cure and the equally miraculous promise of personal enlightenment emanating from the odd marriage of shameless boosterism and ostentatious spectacle masquerading as an educational institution. Like the New South itself, Grady's Piedmont Chautauqua amounted to little more that a grand promotion. Its doors were closed in 1891, only two years after Grady's death. The buildings soon fell into disuse and were demolished in 1910. The Sweetwater Park Hotel remained stylish throughout the 1890s, but lost its allure after the turn of the century as the capricious fads of the wealthy turned elsewhere for cures. The building burned in 1912.

Back in Douglasville prospects seemed suddenly hitched to the progress at Salt Springs. As construction of the Sweetwater Park Hotel began in 1886, *The Weekly Star* reported that the town would have a bank, a hotel and "several manufacturing enterprises within 12 months." In 1887, the editor declared that "as soon as the (Sweetwater Park) hotel is complete, a cotton factory that will employ four hundred hands will be built."[14] But no cotton mill rose and manufacturing enterprises were slow to arrive to fulfill *The Weekly Star's* prophesy. Douglasville did finally get a bank, but it did not open until 1891, and by that time the

[7] *The Dallas Herald*, July 27, 1893.

[8] C. Vann Woodward, *Origins of the New South, 1877-1913* (1951; reprint, Baton Rouge LA: Louisiana State University Press, 1993) 173-7_4.

[9] Fannie Mae Davis, *Douglas County, Georgia, From Indian Trails to Interstate 20* (Roswell GA: W fH Wolfe, 1987) 156.

[10] Davis, *Douglas County, Georgia, From Indian Trails to Interstate 20*, 78.

[11] *The Weekly Star* (Douglasville GA), January 18, 1884, in Fannie Mae Davis, *Douglas County, Georgia, From Indian Trails to Interstate 20*, 79.

[12] *The Douglasville Weekly Star*, in Fannie Mae Davis, *Douglas County, Georgia, From Indian Trails to Interstate 20*, 87.

[13] Inez Watson Croft, "Lithia Springs, Recollections of the Golden Age of a Southern Resort," *The Atlanta Historical Bulletin* 12/1 (March 1868): 10.

[14] *The Weekly Star*, January 18, 1884, in Fannie Mae Davis, *Douglas County, Georgia, From Indian Trails to Interstate 20*, 118.

old courthouse was crumbling. In 1895, county offi-cials hired Atlanta architect, Andrew J. Bryan, to design a new courthouse for Douglas County.

Plate 15.2: The Douglas County Courthouse, built in 1896. Andrew J. Bryan, architect. Burned in 1956.

A. J. Bryan's 1896 Douglas County Courthouse was the architect's first Romanesque court building in Georgia. The choice of the Romanesque Revival Style was driven by courthouse construction in neighboring counties. To be sure, Parkins and Bruce's 1883 Fulton County Courthouse was a stylistic beacon, and by 1895 highly picturesque Romanesque court buildings designed by Atlanta's Bruce and Morgan stood on the nearby squares of Paulding, Haralson, and Heard Counties while Bruce's more formally Richardsonian courthouse graced the square at nearby Carrollton in Carroll County. Although clearly influenced by Alexander Bruce's earlier work, Andrew Bryan's more formal version of the Romanesque Revival contains few lacy Queen Anne frills nor does it echo the fanci-ful personal elements of Bruce and Morgan's elaborate decorative style. What little ornament Bryan allowed himself, like the balustrades above the court room windows and the finials which punctuate various dormers, sounded a distinctly Renaissance note, although massive corner pavilions, some window groupings and the stone banding recall Richardsonian themes.

Plate 15.2: The fire which destroyed the 1896 Douglas County courthouse was as tragic as it was spectacular for it robbed the county of a fitting symbol for its entrance into a new century.

In 1899, the original 1883 Georgia Pacific depot at Douglasville burned. By the time it was replaced in 1900, the town's population had reached 1140. The second depot was replaced in 1916, and its successor stood in Douglasville until the early 1970s, when it was moved to a private farm. Although progress was often slowed by adverse economic conditions in the region, by stubborn elements clinging to Old South myth and by a more modern form of intransigence born of misconceptions regarding progress and social reform, Douglasville had come a long way in the six-teen years that the old 1883 Georgia Pacific depot had lasted. The town that built this courthouse was a long distance indeed from the dusty rough-edged village of Skint Chestnut. The 1956 fire that destroyed this building, was as tragic as it was spectacular, for it robbed Douglas County of the landmark that symbol-ized her entrance into a new century.

HENRY COUNTY: MCDONOUGH

Henry County was created from land ceded to the State of Georgia by the Creek Indians in the 1821 Treaty of Indian Springs. One of five counties cut from this massive tract between the Ocmulgee and Flint Rivers,[15] Henry established its county seat at McDonough in 1823 and completed a fine brick ver-nacular courthouse there in 1831. In the 1840s, when the Macon and Western Railroad was constructed through the eastern corner of the county, on its way from Macon to the place soon to be called Atlanta, the event marked the beginning of a period of decline for the bypassed county town of McDonough. Meanwhile, Griffin and Hampton had appeared on the Macon and Western in the early 1840s. By 1849, these new railroad towns were booming while, accord-ing to George White in his *Statistics of the State of Georgia,* McDonough counted only about 500 resi-dents. White went on to recount that McDonough "had declined in business when Griffin was first set-tled." McDonough's woes continued after the war. By 1880, her population had dwindled to only 325, while a wildly prosperous upstart, Griffin, boasted over 4000 residents, and the once minuscule village of Hampton counted more than 600.

Plate 15.3: The depot at Hampton, built in 1880.[16]

At Hampton this enormous brick depot still marks the center of town, and it reveals much about the town's history. Here we find an early hint of postbellum architectural enthusiasm in the stylish brick corbeling beneath the eaves. This form of decoration flowed from the Italian Villa Style, which inspired the so-called American "Railroad Style." In the closing decades of the nineteenth century, vernacular brick buildings across the South would display seemingly endless variations on the theme of brick edging, corbeling, and other ornamental brick detailing that became the personal signature of local mason-builder-designers in countless nearly-forgotten Southern towns.

But beyond its ornament, the Macon and Western Depot at Hampton voices a flowing continuity of form, and thus separates itself from the usually unimaginative architecture of most of Georgia's brick depots of the era. Here brick pilasters divide the building into ten bays each with an elegant, segmental arch to form a classical arcade. The simple grace of the brick hoods adorning these arched doorways is reminiscent of the arcaded openings of Augustus Schwab's Central of Georgia Depot at Savannah, designed in 1860 and not completed until 1876. Like the Central's depot at Savannah, the depot at Hampton appears to be the work of a professional architect.

A brief inquiry into Hampton's past reveals this building's story. The Monroe Railroad had traversed the Western edge of Henry County in the early 1840s, and by 1858 two new counties, Spalding and Clayton had been carved, in part, from Henry's western flank. In the meantime, virtually all of Henry County's sizable cotton crop began to flow through Hampton, originally known as Bear Creek, on the Macon and Western. According to an 1879 *Gazetteer of Georgia*, the town shipped over 8000 bales each year. There was regular hack service between Hampton and the county seat at McDonough, a trip of over two hours.[17] So attractive was the railroad location that McDonough's lawyers chose to live in Hampton, 15 miles to the west of the courthouse.[18] By 1870, a serious exodus had begun, and a substantial number of houses were actually picked up and moved out of McDonough to Griffin or Hampton on the Macon and Western.[19] But after the East Tennessee, Virginia and Georgia Railroad, and later the Georgia Midland and Gulf, arrived at McDonough, Hampton returned to obscurity. Her population was down to near 400 by 1890.

In the early 1880s, news of the East Tennessee, Virginia and Georgia's purchase of the Macon and Brunswick and subsequent plans to connect this newly acquired south Georgia railroad to the company's main line to Knoxville had blown through Henry County on welcome winds of optimism. Although a preliminary survey bypassed McDonough, town leaders were quick to convince the new railroad to perfect a route through the rail-hungry town. A telegraph line began operation in McDonough in September of 1881, and the first train arrived in June of 1882. A

Plate 15.3: The Macon and Western Depot at Hampton voices a flowing continuity of form, and thus separates itself from the usually unimaginative architecture of most of Georgia's brick depots of the era. (Photo: Wilber W. Caldwell.)

[15] The others were Dooly, Houston, Monroe, and Fayette. Over the years Henry County's vast lands dwindled, becoming parts of Walton, Fulton, DeKalb, Clayton, Rockdale, Newton, Butts, and Spalding Counties.

[16] William Rogers, "The Superintendents Report to the President of The Central Railroad and Banking Company" *The Annual Reports of the President, Superintendent s, and Engineer in Chief of The Central Railroad and Banking Company*, 6 vols. (Savannah 1880): 6:16n.45.

[17] Vessie Thrasher Rainer, *Henry County, Georgia, The Mother of Counties* (McDonough GA: Boyd Publishing Company, 1971) 142.

[18] Rainer, *Henry County, Georgia, The Mother of Counties*, 142.

[19] Rainer, *Henry County, Georgia, The Mother of Counties*, 141.

wave of euphoric rhetoric was unleashed by these events. Referring to the East Tennessee, Virginia and Georgia in a letter to *The Griffin Sun,* Henry County leaders recited almost verbatim from the catechism of the New South declaring: "A day of prosperity is beginning to dawn upon Georgia and the influx of Northern capital into our midst is destined to develop the resources of our state to a degree that will make it not only in name but in fact 'The Empire State of the South.'"[20]

As soon as the railroad appeared headed for McDonough, the town began to grow. By 1880, the village had regained most of its lost population, reporting 515 residents in the US Census of that year. By then, both of the county's newspapers had moved from Hampton back to McDonough, where, led by factors who migrated from Hampton and from Jonesboro, a substantial cotton market developed. In 1886, McDonough got her second railroad. In that year, the Georgia Midland and Gulf, which soon became the Georgia Midland, was completed from McDonough through Griffin to Columbus. Nonetheless, this railroad-inspired "boom" did little more than return McDonough to her former status of a small farm-market town. Real industry-based economic progress abided only in the realm of vague speculation and vain hope. These modern dreams, along with agitation for a new courthouse, were temporarily snuffed out by the depression that followed the Panic of 1893 and by falling cotton prices. But as the turn of the century neared, things improved. A bank was finally established, the Southern Railway (which was by then controlled the old East Tennessee, Virginia and Georgia and the Georgia Midland Railroad) built a fine new depot at McDonough, and

talk of a cotton mill once again floated hopefully on the breeze.

Plate 15.4: The Henry County Courthouse, built in 1897. Golucke and Stewart, architects.

There is perhaps no courthouse in Georgia that better sings the songs of resurgence and hope than James Wingfield Golucke's 1897 Henry County Courthouse at McDonough. Appropriately, there is perhaps no place in Georgia that better illustrates the railroad's power to first withhold the New South's illusive promise, and then, later, to abundantly bestow its tantalizing hope for prosperity.

Although the rails of the East Tennessee, Virginia and Georgia and the Georgia Midland and Gulf brought the possibilities of the New South to McDonough, the town initially realized little more than an abundant helping of hope. Fifteen years after the arrival of the railroad, and despite the shallowness of any real progress, hope continued to be the railroad's most important import. In 1900, the editor of *The Griffin News* reported on McDonough's progress:

> [Over at McDonough in Henry County, there are unmistakable evidence of activity and prosperity. A few years ago McDonough was one of the most dilapidated and unsightly old towns in Georgia, but a building boom struck the old place and the old courthouse gave way to a magnificent temple of justice and almost all of the stores are now brick and plate glass front and present a splendid appearance, a marked contrast to the old wooden shacks that formerly stood on the square.... McDonough only needs some diversified manufacturing industry to make it a greater center of business...[21]

Thus, we see James Golucke's fine courthouse at McDonough for what it was, an illusion of prosperity. Like the new brick stores which surrounded it, the building was merely part of the window dressing of a hollow progress, built upon a capricious agricultural economic base and supported by social institutions that were as archaic as they were blind to the changing world around them.

---

[20] A letter to the editors of *The Griffin Sun* dated August 5, 1881, in Vessie Thrasher Ranier, *Henry County, Georgia, The Mother of Counties*, 152.

[21] *The Henry County Weekly*, May 17, 1901 in Vessie Thrasher Rainer, *Henry County, Georgia, The Mother of Counties* (McDonough GA: Boyd Publishing Company, 1971) 155-6.

[22] *The Henry County Weekly*, November 13, 1896 in Vessie Thrasher Rainer, *Henry County, Georgia, The Mother of Counties*, 183.

[23] *The Henry County Weekly*, February , 1896 in Vessie Thrasher Rainer, *Henry County, Georgia, The Mother of Counties*, 183.

In November of 1896, county records reveal that Atlanta architect Andrew J. Bryan had been selected to design Henry's monument to the county's expectations.[22] But by the time the notice to contractors appeared in *The Henry County Weekly* in February of 1897, James Golucke's plans were cited as the accepted design.[23] We are given no reason for the last minute switch, and we can only presume that when Golucke presented his new Richardsonian design, the quality and charm of his creation easily eclipsed Bryan's more Spartan visions of the Romanesque Revival. Indeed, Bryan's Romanesque forms pale before the boldly modern Richardsonian detail of Golucke's design. Although modest in scale and restricted by a surprisingly small budget (the building's original contracted cost was only $13,789), the Henry County Courthouse is a comfortable combination of Henry Hobson Richardson's monumental style and Henry County's comfortable rural tastes. Golucke applies Richardson's vocabulary freely, featuring a massive arched entrance, distinctly Richardsonian window groupings and employing granite banding and bold voussoirs to achieve polychromy This was Golucke's first Richardsonian Courthouse, and it is certainly his finest.

Just as the Atlanta architect would later tame the wildly Baroque excesses of American Beaux-Arts classicism, he would first wrestle with the massive masculinity of the Richardsonian beast. Here was architecture to capture the divided mind of the South. It spoke to the South's modern aspirations, and at the same time, it seemingly reveled in the brooding nostalgic distorted sense of history that soothed the angry tormented spirit of a defeated agrarian Old South come face to face with the modern age. Golucke approached the Romanesque Revival with divided aims. Despite the rising tide of classicism in the North, in the 1890s the Richardsonian Romanesque remained a potent symbol for both emerging American industrial might and a brash new national self-image. Henry Hobson Richardson's buildings transcended their Romanesque vocabulary to create a unique language, a strangely modern and yet unmistakably picturesque tongue that combined mass and movement and projected a singularly American and

Plate 15.4: Employing the Romanesque vocabulary of H. H. Richardson, J. W. Golucke fashioned his own intimately personal Romanesque Revival, which although modern, was also softly rural, disarmingly rustic and strangely pastoral. (Photo: Wilber W. Caldwell.)

powerfully urban aura. On the face of it, nothing could have been more inappropriate for tiny McDonough, Georgia, in 1897. It is at this point that Golucke's genius surfaces. Employing the Romanesque vocabulary of Richardson, Golucke fashioned his own intimately personal Romanesque Revival, which although modern, was also softly rural, disarmingly rustic, and strangely pastoral. Like the pure Romanesque architecture of Richardson's medieval models in France and Spain, it was an architecture of a simple, struggling people who lived very close to the land.

Butts County: Jackson

Plate 15.5: The Butts County Courthouse, built in 1898. Bruce and Morgan, architects.

In 1849, in his *Statistics of the State of Georgia*, George White described Jackson as a village of about 300 inhabitants with a courthouse, a jail, two churches and three stores. The courthouse, a two-story brick vernacular structure, had been built in 1828 to replace the log court building erected in 1825 when Butts County had been cut from Monroe and Henry Counties. Jackson was roughly treated by Federal forces in 1864 owing to scattered resistance in the area, and to large quantities of Confederate supplies warehoused there. The old courthouse had been used to store grain for the Rebel Army and was burned to the ground. A second brick vernacular court building was erected in 1870. When the East Tennessee, Virginia and Georgia Railroad arrived in 1882, Jackson still counted only about 300 residents and not much had changed since White's visit. *The Middle Georgia Argus* described the town on the eve of the railroad's arrival: "...an old dilapidated town with only about half a dozen business houses, and they doing a very small business, and but a few decent dwelling houses...."[24] As was usually the case, the arrival of steel rails created a frenzy of expectation and excess. *The Argus* heralded the arrival of the railroad as "the greatest day to remembrance for the people of Butts County,"[25] and spewed forth myths lifted verbatim from the New South's catechism of progress:

Plate 15.5: Alexander Bruce's courthouse here at Jackson reflected the beginning of the end for the Romanesque Revival in Georgia. (Photo: Wilber W. Caldwell. (Photo: Wilber W. Caldwell.)

"Now that Northern capital has been induced...who can imagine the future that awaits our section?"[26] *The Jackson News* was beside itself: "...businessmen are alive, energetic, moral, intelligent, progressive...the young men are gallant, the young ladies beautiful. Upon the whole Jackson is destined to be the business town between Macon and Atlanta."[27]

A year after the coming of the railroad, *The Argus* listed numerous improvements including new stores and warehouses and observed: "The extreme quiet that reigned here one year ago is counter balanced today by a general rush and a continuous rattle of the many drays, wagons, hacks, buggies, and other rolling stock, that continually throng our streets."[28] With such a beginning, prospects for the future appeared boundless. *The News* went so far as to publish predictions that Jackson's population would "triple in 12 months" and reach 1500 in two years.[29]

For a brief moment, the New South's promises for the enduring prosperity of the industrial age appeared real, but all of this amounted to little. In fact, Jackson's boom had included no real industry at all. By 1890, although the town's population had more than doubled since the arrival of the railroad, Jackson's economy still rested on the upward spiral of cotton production and the downward spiral of cotton prices. In 1891, Jackson shipped 18,000 bales (compared to 8000 reported by Sholes' *Gazetteer of Georgia* in 1886). A list of Jackson's "industries" in 1890 reveal only the shaky infrastructure of cotton: gins and a cotton seed oil plant, factors and fertilized dealers; a livery stable, two small planing mills, a carriage manufacturer plus a handful of merchants, professionals and bankers to serve the vast rural economy of cotton. Nonetheless, the people of Jackson saw in the town's fine new brick buildings the glorious beginnings of the long promised New South. Sadly, these facades concealed little more than the utter hopelessness of the same old economic treadmill of cotton.

Throughout the period of Jackson's "boom," there persisted a present hope for a second major crossing railroad. This was later accompanied by the usual agitation for a new courthouse. Beginning in 1870, the Griffin and Madison Railroad had chartered a line through Jackson and Monticello. In the mid-1880s, operating under a renewed charter as the Griffin, Monticello and Madison Railroad, the company actually completed grading from Griffin to Jackson before financial troubles engulfed the undertaking. A second railroad did arrive in Butts County when in 1888 the Flovilla and Indian Springs Railroad was completed. Originally a horse drawn line, the tiny railroad operated until 1918 connecting the main line of the East Tennessee, Virginia and Georgia (later the Southern Railway) to the popular resort at Indian Springs only a mile or so away.

Again believing that the riches of a New South were at hand, leaders in Jackson proposed a new courthouse for Butts County, but met a solid wall of resistance from rural factions who perceived none of the mythical progress that Jackson flaunted like the Emperor his new clothes. Rural opposition to a new court building was clearly visible well into the 1890s. In 1895, the editor of *The Flovilla National Headlight,* a Populist journal, emphatically wrote, "Build no new courthouse. The old one is as good as we can afford at present....to talk of building a new courthouse when hundreds of people in the country are without a cent of money, is something that should not for a moment be considered.... Seldom we see any appearance of progress in the county, and a gloom seems to hang over the entire land."[30] This was a long distance indeed for the rhetoric of sweetness and light that flowed from leaders in Jackson with their dreams of a new age of prosperity, and who by this time were fixed on the idea of building a cotton factory.

The shallow nature of Jackson's "boom" is revealed in the rhetoric of the cotton factory movement. In the wake of the depression following the Panic of 1893, promoters of the new cotton factory advocated their scheme on the grounds that it would "help relieve hard times."[31] As we have seen in nearby Newnan, Griffin and LaGrange, these early cotton mills were part of a sweeping regional movement that had at its heart, a great deal more than the usual capitalist profit motive. Most mills of this era grew out of a strange combination of civil pride, economic desperation and abiding faith that the presence of a locally funded "Industrial Revolution" would lift

these places out of backwardness and poverty and thrust them into the modern age. Although most of these mills were successful, it would take a great deal more than a few rows of secondhand spindles exploiting cheap labor to establish the institutions of an industrial society.

No sooner was the Pepperton Mill completed than a new wave of optimism broke, and Jackson began anew her assault of the old courthouse. In 1896, *The Argus* spouted the usual myths: "Once the wheels are in motion, there will be erected a home market to every product of the farm, and thousands of dollars will be kept in circulation where only a hundred circulate now." In a notable non sequitur *The Argus* continued: "What else does Jackson and Butts County need? The answer is(a new and modern courthouse...." The article concluded with a familiar prediction that was no more correct in 1896 than it had been back in 1882: "With the improvements and enterprises mentioned once established and in operation it would be reasonable to expect Jackson's population to be doubled within a few years."[32] As if to belie such urban visions, the next month *The Argus* reminded readers that the courthouse square was a "not a good place to tie stock."[33]

Although the spirit of progress that was first created by the railroad and later by the Pepperton Mill added fuel to the fires of the new courthouse move-

[24] *The Middle Georgia Argus*, May 12, 1883 in Lois McMichael, ed., *History of Butts County, 1825-1976* (Atlanta, 1978), 81.

[25] The Middle Georgia Argus, May 12, 1883 in Lois McMichael, ed., *History of Butts County, 1825-1976* (Atlanta: Cherokee Publishing Company, 1978) 81.

[26] *The Middle Georgia Argus*, June 2, 1881.

[27] *From The Greenback Cause* (Atlanta: n.p., 1882) reprinted in the *Jackson News*, September 20, 1882, in Lois McMichael, ed., *History of Butts County, 1825-1976*, 142.

[28] *The Middle Georgia Argus*, May 12, 1883, in Lois McMichael, ed., *History of Butts County, 1825-1976*, 81.

[29] *The Jackson News*, April 9, 1882.

[30] *The National Headlight* (Flovilla, GA), March 8, 1895.

[31] *The Jackson Argus*, August 16, 1895.

[32] *The Jackson Argus*, January 24, 1896.

[33] *The Jackson Argus*, February 26, 1896

ment in Jackson, in the final analysis, it was a highly competitive local pride that won the day for those in favor of a new court building in Butts County. Local newspapers had been quick to point out the gleaming towers of new courthouses in nearby Zebulon in 1895 and in neighboring Forsyth in 1896. In March of 1897, only a few weeks after neighboring Henry County accepted James W. Golucke's plan for a new courthouse at McDonough, the Butts County grand jury recommended a new courthouse. A building committee was appointed, and in April, after a survey of new court buildings in Laurens, Douglas and Monroe Counties, the committee selected the Atlanta firm of Bruce and Morgan as architects. The selection was probably made on the strength of the firm's recent work at Forsyth which, although still romanesque in form, was adorned with Renaissance detail that foreshadowed the emerging Neoclassical Revival. By May, the old courthouse had been demolished and the project opened for bids.

Not only did courthouse building in neighboring counties hasten the construction of a new court building in Jackson, it also influenced the county's choice of architects and the style of the building. Indeed, the 1898 Butts County Courthouse owes a considerable stylistic debt to Bruce and Morgan's earlier work at Forsyth. Although Alexander Bruce, the principle designer, returned to a more picturesque, asymmetrical silhouette in Jackson, his design here, like his earlier work in Forsyth, flaunts a profusion of classical decoration. Bruce's earlier Queen Anne courthouses can not be overlooked in this context. The broad classical entablature above the arched entrance at the west side of the building is a dominant feature. Likewise, the balustrades decorating the large open arches of the tower, and the rusticated quoining of the northeast corner pavilions are of classical origin as are the Ionic capitols of the many brick pilasters and the rather formal decoration surrounding the clocks which crown the high tower. Further, the central mass of the building, with its dormered roofline terminated in bold pediments, appears classical in proportion, despite the picturesque addition of the tower and pavilions that break the silhouette.

This was Alexander Bruce's last courthouse in Georgia before his retirement in 1904. Although a number of Romanesque courthouses would rise in Georgia after the turn of the century, Bruce's "swan song" here at Jackson reflects the beginning of the end for the Romanesque Revival.

SOME LAST THOUGHTS ON THE EAST TENNESSEE, VIRGINIA AND GEORGIA RAILROAD.

By 1875, all of Georgia's Reconstruction railroads and many of her antebellum lines were in financial ruin. After the war, state financing of Southern rail had resulted in a banquet of railroad building all across the South. Beginning in the Panic of 1873, a series of bankruptcies had cleared this feast from the table set by state governments, leaving a tempting array of leftovers to be gobbled up by hungry Northern capitalists who saw sweeping opportunities for what was to amount to a second conquest of the American South. As Henry Plant's Plant System lunched on the spoils of the Atlantic and Gulf and the Brunswick and Albany, William Clyde's growing conglomerate digested the Selma Rome and Dalton and the Macon and Brunswick. Even the mighty Central of Georgia, the Georgia Railroad and the Western and Atlantic, the only roads in Georgia to survive the crisis of 1873, would eventually fall prey to Northern consolidations.

To be sure, the 1880s also saw the continued construction of locally funded railroads designed to bolster the economy of selected trading cities. But by 1880, the handwriting was on the wall, and before the end of the decade, most of these lines would be consumed by railroad giants. Atlanta would strive to build the Atlanta and Charlotte Air Line and the Georgia Pacific to further her own mercantile interests. But the force behind the completion of these interstate lines would ultimately come from William Clyde's emerging Piedmont Air Line, which would soon form the keystone of J. P Morgan's mighty the Southern Railway. Along the way, the Southern's predecessor, the Richmond and Danville, would hungrily consume myriad smaller local roads like the Elberton Airline, and the Northeastern Railroad.

In 1882, the East Tennessee, Virginia and Georgia Railroad, which was also destined to become part of Morgan's Southern Railway, sought to connect the newly acquired Macon and Brunswick with her main line out of Rome via Dalton to Knoxville, Tennessee, and beyond. Built in part using leased convict labor, 141 miles of new track linked Macon and Rome. This new line gave Atlanta another connection to the American heartland and created a considerable stir in the poor counties of the upcountry Piedmont west of Atlanta and on the east bank of the Ocmulgee between Atlanta and Macon. A handful of theretofore sleepy bypassed villages suddenly awoke to the mythical promises of the New South, which arrived on the rails of the East Tennessee, Virginia and Georgia Railroad.

The messages of progress and prosperity that flowed along these new rails begot remarkably consistent architectural symbols. "The Macon and Brunswick Connector," as the line from Rome to Macon was first called, is marked by a string of Romanesque Revival courthouses all built in the 1890s. The line began at Rome where Bruce and Morgan's extraordinary Floyd County Courthouse rose in 1893. Pushing south, the railroad inspired another Bruce and Morgan romanesque court building at tiny Dallas, Georgia, in 1894. In Douglasville on the crossing line of the Georgia Pacific Railroad, which was built simultaneously with the East Tennessee, Virginia and Georgia, Andrew J. Bryan fashioned the Romanesque arches of his second courthouse in Georgia in 1896. The rails passed through Atlanta and on into Henry Country where James W. Golucke designed what is arguably the finest Richardsonian Romanesque Courthouse in Georgia in 1897. Lastly, before reaching Macon and its connection to the Macon and Brunswick, the road passed through Jackson where Bruce and Morgan built their last Romanesque courthouse in 1898.

A trip down the old East Tennessee Virginia and Georgia Railroad today will confirm the powerful influence of the American master, Henry Hobson Richardson. There can be little doubt that the

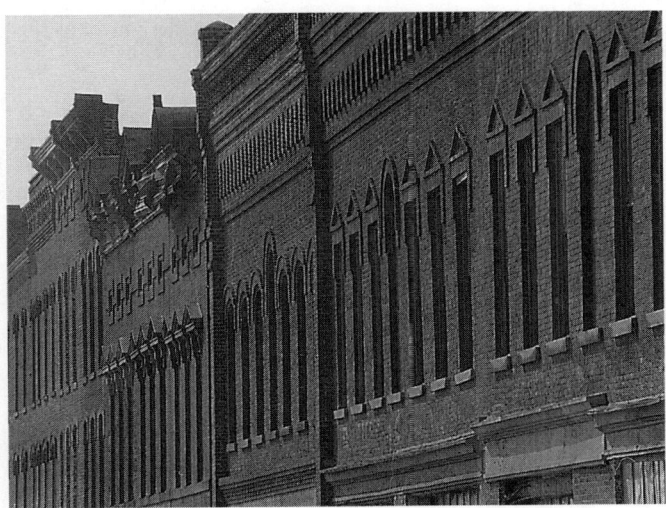

Plate 15.6: Macon. (Photo: Wilber W. Caldwell.)

Richardsonian Romanesque was architecture inspired by American industrial might. But in Georgia in the 1890s, the railroads were about the only evidence of the Industrial Revolution to be found. Nonetheless, as the courthouses along "The Macon and Brunswick Connector" illustrate that Richardsonian buildings rose even in the back eddies of an economically devastated Deep South. Still, the region would embrace this Northern style only to the extent that she could attach her own symbols. In the hands of Georgia's first generation of local architects, the style was subtly manipulated to appeal to rural Southern sensitivities. Alexander Bruce and James Golucke understood Southern suspicions and fears regarding the industrial age, and although they employed the vocabulary of H. H. Richardson and his imitators, they rejected the American master's imposing monumentality, seeking an intimate rural architecture, which, although unquestionably Romanesque, was also softly comfortable and even unassuming. Alexander Bruce often achieved an almost domestic effect by adorning his Romanesque Revival buildings with Queen Anne Style ornament and later with bolder classical detail. J. W. Golucke's work was more directly in the Richardsonian tradition. There can be little doubt that James Golucke understood Richardsonian restraint when it came to the disciplined use of ornament, but unlike Richardson's awe-inspiring monuments, Golucke's buildings are notable for their very personal sense of scale, and for an almost humble symmetry. To be sure, neither Alexander Bruce nor J. W. Golucke stood on any architectural high ground, especially when compared to Henry Hobson Richardson. Nonetheless, their work is particularly instructive when we consider architecture as a reflection of history. It is also an enlightening insight into the far-reaching scope of Richardson's influence.

•

16 | The Gainesville, Jefferson and Southern Railroad

JACKSON COUNTY: JEFFERSON

The Jackson County Courthouse, built in 1879. William W. Thomas, architect. Remodeled in 1906, H. L. Lewman, architect (see Plate 5 in the Introduction).

The full-blown myth of the New South did not penetrate the tangled forest of the Southern mind until after 1880. In the fifteen years following Appomattox, a few voices urged education, Northern capitalization, agricultural diversity, and industrial growth in Georgia, but as Paul Gaston observes in his study, *The New South Creed,* "none of these long range issues was in focus in the mid-seventies."[1] It was not until the North grew tired of the great Reconstruction experiment that the laborious process of Southern self-reconstruction began, and the New South myth emerged to meet the occasion. Thus, the handful of Georgia courthouses erected in the 1870s reflected the simple styles of the pre-war period and did not voice the architectural exuberance that the tempting myth of New South prosperity would inspire in the following three decades.

Like many antebellum courthouses in Georgia, William Thomas's 1879 Jackson County Courthouse was built on the familiar Greek cross plan. The classical lantern and the stucco finish are the products of a later remodeling. The original brick structure, with its bold window hoods and elegant brackets supporting the eaves, featured prominent raised brick quoining and was typical of what many have termed the Italianate Style. Italian Renaissance ideas were spread to less sophisticated builders and architects by elevations and details published in popular pattern books of the day. Notable among these were A. J. Davis's drawings of buildings "in the Italian Style" in Andrew Jackson Downing's *Cottage Residences* (1850) and Samuel Sloan's "Italian Villas" in *The Model Architect* (1851). Whatever the source, in rural America, decorative ideas of

[1] Paul M. Gaston, *The New South Creed, A Study in Southern Mythmaking* (1970; reprint, Baton Rouge LA: Louisiana State University, 1976) 41.

The Gainesville, Jefferson and Southern Railroad

Hall County: Gainesville (see chapter 11) • Jackson County: Jefferson • Barrow County: Winder
Walton County: Monroe • Clarke County: Athens (see chapter 13)
Some Last Thoughts on the Gainesville, Jefferson and Southern Railroad

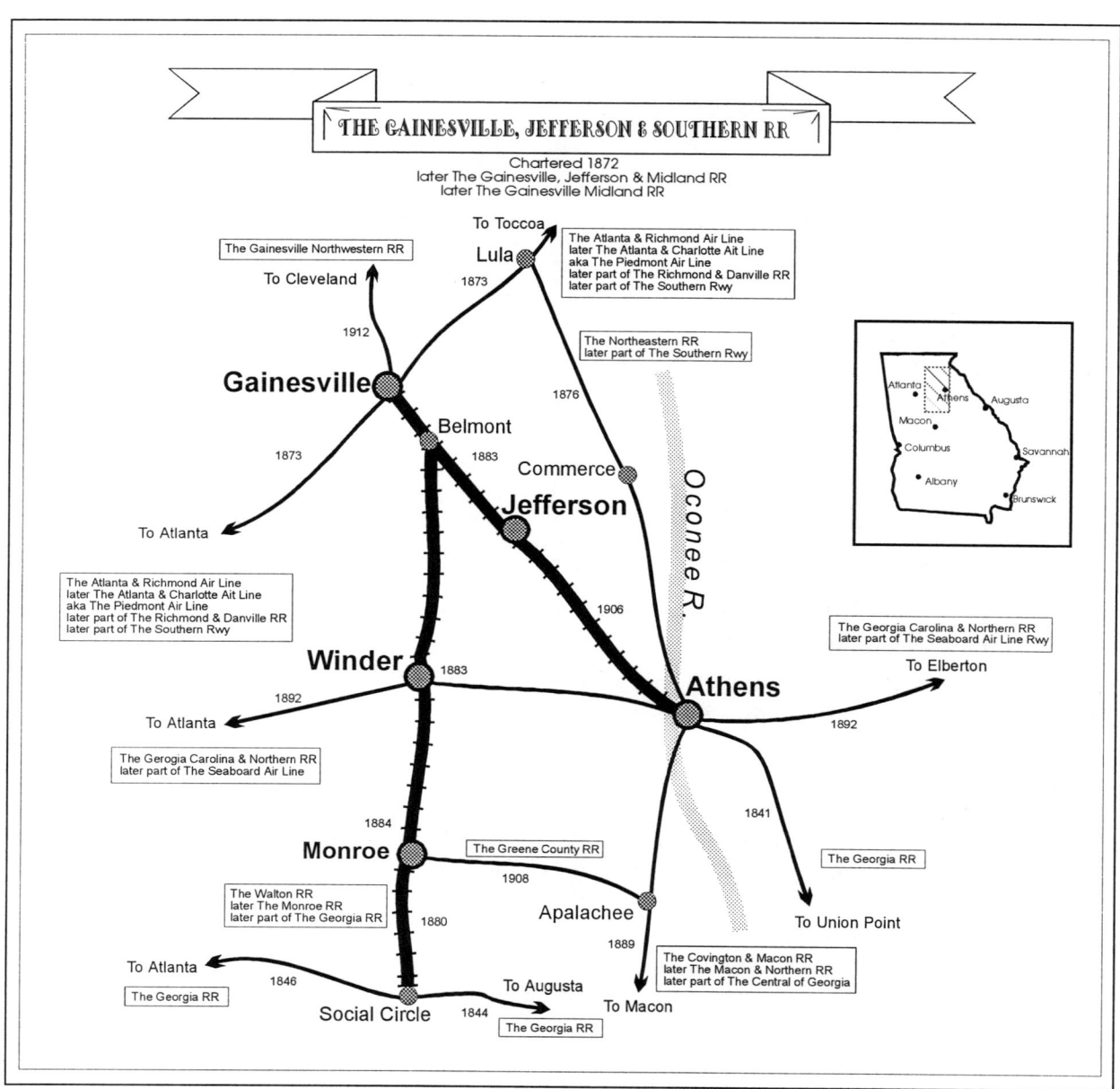

neoclassical Italian origin met head on with the brick vernacular, and the results, although often charming, were usually a great deal less sophisticated then any of this terminology implies. The 1879 Jackson County Courthouse is typical if this meeting.

In Jefferson, the atmosphere that surrounded the construction of William Thomas's 1879 courthouse was far from typical of the wildly hopeful flights of railroad inspired fancy that fathered so many later Georgia court buildings. Although many of the circumstances here fit the later pattern, including the impending arrival of the rails of the Gainesville, Jefferson and Southern Railroad, the elevated spirit of enterprise so often associated with the construction of later railroads was absent in Jefferson in 1879. In fact, the prevailing attitude relating to the town's future remained stoically dark, and the question of a new courthouse was so vigorously debated that some leaders in Jefferson were afraid that the town would lose interest in the railroad after so heated a fight over the courthouse.[2] Two grand juries had recommend a new court building to replace the old brick vernacular courthouse which had been built in 1817 in place of the county's original c.1806 log courthouse. According to Jackson County historian, Frary Elrod, the problem with the old building was its low-lying location and the "sea of mud" that surrounded the old court building and mired wagons and buggies "to their axles and horses to their bellies."[3] Twice bond issues were rejected by county voters. The second of these elections was held after the demolition of the old brick courthouse and the signing of a cash contract for the construction of a new building. Bitter resentments festered among Jackson County's farmers who felt manipulated by a "Jefferson clique of concentrated selfishness and unmitigated meanness."[4] When the County Ordinary pressed ahead with the construction of a new building in spite of the election results, *The Forest News* could observe that: "...the people of the county, or the vast majority of them, do not want the new courthouse under any circumstance(the people do not like the way that they were forced into the matter altogether against their wishes."[5] Here we find a well worn theme, an ongoing conflict between the local merchants and professionals living in Jefferson

who made up Jackson County's "courthouse gang" and the great faceless mass of the county's rural population who were suspicious of change in almost any form. In 1879, the next generation of courthouse architecture in Georgia would reflect the growing political power of "courthouse gangs" with their extravagant railroad-inspired boosterism and soaring aspirations.

Alongside the courthouse controversy there arose a heated battle over the location of the county seat. When Jackson County was cut from Franklin County in 1796, it covered all or part of present-day Walton, Banks, Oconee, Clarke, Madison, Gwinnett and Hall Counties. The original county seat had been at Clarkesboro, but after Clarke County was created in 1801, Jefferson was designated the new county seat of Jackson County. By 1879, as the courthouse controversy raged, a large rural faction favored a more central location, and in the debate that followed, Jefferson was much maligned. The town was described as a place of "dilapidated appearance" where "natural beauties were few and dwellings and business houses were unsightly." In addition, Jefferson residents were said to be morally suspect and generally of a "non-progressive" character.[6] After a committee appointed to study the matter failed to reach consensus and delivered conflicting majority and minority opinions, the County Ordinary decided the matter in favor of the minority. This left the county site at Jefferson where the first court session to be held in William Thomas's fine Jackson County Courthouse convened in February of 1880.

The son of a director of the Georgia Railroad, architect William Winstead Thomas was born in Athens in 1849. We know little of his architectural education, but his work in and around Athens stands as testament to his skill. In the last decades of the 19th century, William Thomas designed the Seney Stovall

---

[2] *The Forest News*, June 12, 1879, and November 1879.

[3] Frary Elrod, *Historical Notes on Jackson County, Georgia* (Jefferson GA: n.p., 1967) 42.

[4] *The Forest News*, September 12, 1879.

[5] *The Forest News*, September 26, 1879.

[6] *The Forest News*, May 23, 1879.

Chapel, the Lucy Cobb Institute and many fine residences in Athens. His finest domestic work is elaborately picturesque, much of it in the popular Queen Anne Style. In addition to the Jackson County Courthouse, Thomas designed one other courthouse in Georgia, the 1888 Oconee County Courthouse at Watkinsville, a building which reflected the influence of H. H. Richardson.

Plate 16.1: The depot at Jefferson, built in 1906.

As Jackson County's new courthouse rose at Jefferson, railroad organizers in Gainesville garnered the financial support of the Atlanta and Charlotte Air Line and pressed ahead with the Gainesville Jefferson and Southern Railroad's plans to link Gainesville with the Georgia Railroad at Social Circle via Monroe. A thirteen-mile branch from Belmont to Jefferson was proposed, but the fate of this spur hung in the balance, awaiting the tender of stock subscriptions from the citizens of Jefferson. These same citizens had experienced previous railroad disappointments. The original 1856 survey of the Georgia Air Line had run through their village, and in the 1870s the Northeastern Railroad out of Athens had offered to build through Jefferson to Gainesville. But the progressive town of Harmony Grove (later Commerce) had been quick to tender $50,000 subscription leaving Jefferson again bypassed. The late 1870s had spawned another Jefferson to Athens railroad plan as well as a scheme to build a line from Jefferson to Flowery Branch on the Atlanta and Charlotte Air

Plate 16.1: Promises of prosperity glimmered briefly in Jefferson in 1906 when this depot was built and the Jefferson branch of the Gainesville Midland was extended to Athens. (Photo: Wilber W. Caldwell.)

Line, but all of this had come to nothing.[7] By 1880, leaders in Jefferson feared that the courthouse fiasco had so damaged their credibility that local support for the branch of the Gainesville, Jefferson and Southern might erode. In February of 1881, *The Jackson Herald* declared that the line would be built if everyone honored their financial commitments calling the moment a: "…golden opportunity…to better your own fortunes while you add to the material wealth of this magnificent County."[8] This time Jefferson's railroad investors were true to their commitments, and the branch line to Jefferson was completed in 1883.

The conventional wisdom in Jefferson is that this depot was built shortly after the arrival of rails in Jefferson, but we have nothing to document the exact date of its construction. We know that in 1898, the depot was moved "nearer to the business part of the city,"[9] and that it remained in use as a freight depot after a new passenger depot was built in 1906.[10] It is not completely clear from the evidence available, but it appears that this depot, which still stands in Jefferson today, is the 1906 structure and not the earlier building.

The Gainesville, Jefferson and Southern Railroad struggled throughout the 1880s and 1890s and finally declared bankruptcy in 1897. In 1904, the Gainesville to Monroe and the Belmont to Jefferson portions of the road were purchased by a Savannah group and reorganized as the Gainesville Midland Railroad. In 1906, as the people of Jefferson celebrated their village's centennial, the Jefferson branch was extended to Athens, and the entire line began a painfully slow upgrade from narrow gauge to standard gauge track. This ended a long period of isolation at the end of an insignificant branch line for Jefferson. Overnight the spirit of the myth of the New South swept through the village. The once downtrodden town came alive with spunk as it contemplated "the springing up of industries of every class."[11] Wild railroad speculation swirled. Reports assured citizens that a crossing north-south railroad to Carnesville "was a certainty."[12] Quoting reports in Savannah, *The Jackson Herald* noted George Brinson's efforts to build from Savannah to Athens, and linked them to a rumored extension of the Jefferson Branch of the

Gainesville Midland that would "push through the mountains of Georgia and up to Tennessee."[13] Not surprisingly, the town celebrated by remodeling W. W. Thomas's courthouse. Here at last, in the classical lines of architect, H. L. Lewman's great white lantern, we see Jefferson's version of the grand courthouse as a manifestation of the railroad-borne myth of the New South. In the same issue that detailed plans for the courthouse additions, *The Herald* reported the application for a charter of the Savannah, Augusta and Northern Railway Company, which proposed to build a railroad through Jefferson from Savannah to Chattanooga.[14]

George Brinson's line from Savannah was finally built, but only as far as Warrenton. Dreams of the Savannah, Augusta and Northern came to nothing, and as we have seen, no line was built to Carnesville. Even if all of these wild railroad dreams had come true, Jefferson's celebration was a little late. By 1906, when Jefferson was finally connected to the rail hub at Athens, two competing railroad boomtowns already flourished in Jackson County.

In 1876, when the Northeastern Railroad had arrived at Harmony Grove on Jackson County's northeastern broader, that tiny hamlet had begun an extraordinary period of growth. By 1884, when the town was incorporated, Harmony Grove boasted a population of over 500. The first brick building rose in 1886, and by 1910, seven years after changing her name to Commerce, the former whistle-stop had blossomed into a thriving cotton market of over 2000 inhabitants with a flourishing cotton mill, electric lights and a new water works. On Jackson County's southwestern border at the village of Jug Tavern, the Georgia, Carolina and Northern Railroad, which would later become the giant Seaboard Air Line, crossed the rails of the Gainesville, Jefferson and Southern in 1892, and the town (later called Winder) blossomed. By 1910, Winder with its foot in three counties counted almost 2500 residents. In 1914, after a long struggle that began in the New County Movement of 1905, Barrow County was created from Jackson, Walton and Gwinnett with Winder as the seat of government.

Meanwhile, despite the success of her 1899 cotton mill, Jefferson's progress remained slow, and fifteen years later, as, Winder laid plans for a courthouse in the newly formed Barrow County, Jefferson still counted fewer than 750 residents. Promises of prosperity had glimmered briefly in Jefferson in 1906 when the Jefferson branch of the Gainesville Midland was extended to Athens, but these promises were rooted in nothing more than the familiar but elusive myth of a New South, which appeared and disappeared with tantalizing and capricious cruelty.

BARROW COUNTY: WINDER

Plate 16.2: The depot at Winder, built in 1910.

Although the creation of Barrow County in 1914 and the subsequent completion of J. J. Baldwin's neo-colonial Barrow County Courthouse in 1920 took place well after the end of the period of our interest, the railroad-inspired growth that transformed the village of Jug Tavern into the city of Winder is illustrative of our theme. Here on the boarder of three counties, the 1883 arrival of the Gainesville, Jefferson and

Plate 16.2: The depot at Winder is remarkably similar to the Seaboard's depot at Elberton, which was built in the same year. (Photo: Wilber W. Caldwell.)

[7] *The Forest News*, July 4, 1879.

[8] *Jackson Herald*, February 25, 1881.

[9] *Jackson Herald*, November 16, 1905.

[10] *Jackson Herald*, December 14, 1905, and September 13, 1906.

[11] *Jackson Herald*, April 26, 1906.

[12] *Jackson Herald*, October 25, 1906.

[13] *Jackson Herald*, May 24, 1906.

[14] *Jackson Herald*, November 29, 1906.

Southern Railroad had stirred the residents of Jug Tavern. A village of 200 in 1880 became a town of 500 by 1890. In 1892, the Georgia, Carolina and Northern Railroad, which soon became part of the powerful Seaboard Air Line Railway, crossed the Gainesville, Jefferson and Southern here, and in 1894, Jug Tavern was renamed to honor Seaboard president, John H. Winder. Despite the name change, the old Gainesville, Jefferson and Southern from Gainesville via Monroe to Social Circle continued for many years to be lovingly called by many "The Jug Tavern Route."

By 1900, Winder counted almost 1200 residents. Ten years later, the Gainesville Jefferson and Southern had become the Gainesville Midland, Winder's population had reached 2500, and the town had sprouted a cotton mill, a large foundry, and considerable banking interests. As the first decade of the new century ended, this stylish depot was constructed to serve the growing city. The building is remarkably similar to the Seaboard's depot at Elberton, which was built in the same year.

The growth at Winder and the subsequent creation of Barrow County illustrate the economic force of crossing rails and exemplify their power to create the great waves of zeal that characterized the myth of the New South. First applying to the state legislature in 1905, residents in Winder proposed the creation of a new county to be called "Stephens." Like most of the twenty-one new county advocates in the New County Movement of 1905, Winder residents were disappointed. Undeterred by the setback Winder, which lay in three different counties, continued her pressure for a county of her own, and in 1914 Barrow Country was created from Jackson, Gwinnett and Walton. But the progress at Winder symbolized by J. J. Baldwin's grand courthouse and Atlanta architect, A. F. N. Everett's four story Beaux Arts "sky scraper," the Winder Banking Company Building, was more symbolic than real. The city had donned the uniform of a sailor of the industrial age, but she remained adrift on a sea of poverty. In 1920, there were 2774 families in the newly created Barrow County; of them 1851 worked farms with an average size of 43 acres, and over two thirds of them were tenants. This was no place for "sky scrapers."

WALTON COUNTY: MONROE

Plate 16.3: The depot at Monroe, built c. 1885.

In 1880, the first train arrived at the village of Monroe on the newly completed Walton Railroad, a ten mile short line, which had been chartered back in 1872 to connect Monroe with the main line of the Georgia Railroad at Social Circle. The line was funded by local subscription with financial backing from the Georgia Railroad. This wooden depot, which was encased in brick at a much later date, was built soon after the completion of the short line. Architecturally, the influence of the Georgia Railroad is clear. The hallmark of this road's late nineteenth century depots between Atlanta and Augusta is the gentle curve of the roof line as it flares out into the broad overhang of the eaves and the broken based pediment below. Georgia Railroad depots at Thomson, Crawfordville, Covington and Conyers all display these details, as do

Plate 16.3: The last narrow gauge track in Georgia was replaced beside this depot at Monroe in 1913. (Photo: Wilber W. Caldwell.)

the depots at Warrenton (no longer standing) and Sparta on the Macon and Augusta Railroad, which was controlled by the Georgia Railroad almost from its beginning.

In 1884, the Gainesville, Jefferson and Southern arrived in Monroe, and the next year this narrow gauge line purchased the Walton Railroad thus completing the link from Gainesville on the Atlanta and Charlotte Air Line to Social Circle on the Georgia Railroad. The Walton Railroad was a standard gauge line, and all freight on the Gainesville, Jefferson and Southern had to be off-loaded and re-loaded at Monroe owing to the difference in track width between the two lines. In the late 1880s, while the South struggled to convert all of her mainline railroads to standard gauge, the Gainesville, Jefferson and Southern took a step backwards, converting the ten miles of the old Walton Railroad to narrow gauge. The entire line would remain narrow gauge until its reorganization as the Gainesville Midland Railroad in 1904 when the section from Monroe to Social Circle was sold and became the Monroe Railroad, which operated until 1917 when it was leased by the Georgia Railroad. At the time of the sale, the Monroe Railroad was converted back to standard gauge thus recreating a cumbersome mismatch of rails at Monroe. Shortly after its organization, the Gainesville Midland began the process of converting to standard gauge, but owing to financial difficulties, it would take the struggling line almost ten years to complete the change. The last narrow gauge track in Georgia was replaced at Monroe in 1913.

The differential between the Northern "standard" gauge and the Southern narrow gauge had created bottlenecks similar to the one at Monroe all across the South. In May of 1886, after "prolonged preparations" some 1300 miles of Southern mainline railroads were changed to standard gauge,[15] but mismatches of track gauges would remain a problem in the South well into the twentieth century. Passenger service

between Monroe[16] and Social Circle was discontinued in 1930. The Gainesville Midland's tracks from Belmont to Monroe were abandoned in 1947.

Plate 16.4: The Walton County Courthouse, built in 1883-1884. Bruce and Morgan, architects.

In the early 1880s, railroads were creating a stir in Monroe. A comfortable trading center in the heart of the cotton growing Piedmont, Monroe, originally called "Walton Courthouse," had its beginnings in 1821, three years after Walton County was created from lands ceded to the state of Georgia by the Creek Indians. In that year, the county seat was moved from its original location at Cowpens, and the new county's first courthouse was erected. Two years later the crude log building that had cost the county $50 was replaced by a $2500 brick building. This, in turn, was replaced in 1841 by a $5000, 40' x 50' brick courthouse typi-

Plate 16.4: In his 1883 Walton County Courthouse, Alexander Bruce was careful to subdue modern Parisian Second Empire elements in the design and impose the simple rural blend of Italianate and Gothic decorative ideas that had characterized the American brick vernacular in the years before the Civil War. (Photo: Wilber W. Caldwell.)

[15] C. Vann Woodward, *Origins of the New South, 1877-1913* (1951; reprint, Baton Rouge LA: Louisiana State University 1993) 124.

[16] Anita Sams, *Wayfarers in Walton* (Monroe GA: General Charitable Foundation of Monroe, 1967) 103.

cal of so many early brick vernacular court buildings of that era. According to George White's description of the town in his 1849 *Statistics of the State of Georgia*, Monroe had a population of about 500 and contained forty-one houses, eleven stores and two hotels. Over thirty years later, when the first train ran on the Walton Railroad from Social Circle to Monroe, not much had changed since White's visit, but the arrival of steel rails set in motion the usual frenzy. This outpouring of zeal led directly to the erection of Alexander Bruce's grand Walton County Courthouse. The building was completed in 1883, just in time to see the first train arrive in Monroe on the Gainesville, Jefferson and Southern.

Here at Monroe, we find the third of Alexander Bruce's quadruplet courthouses. The building claims two identical older sisters: Bruce's 1875 McMinn County Courthouse at Athens, Tennessee, and his 1882 Hancock County Courthouse at Sparta. The last sister was born when Bruce's Hall County Courthouse at Gainesville was completed in 1885. In the early 1880s, along with Gourdon P. Randall's 1872 Bibb County Courthouse at Macon and Parkins and Bruce's 1883 Fulton County Courthouse at Atlanta, this courthouse and its sister at Sparta were arguably the finest, most up to date court buildings in Georgia.

There can be little doubt that in this period, designs were considered the property of the architect, and that little attention was attracted by the designer who resold his own work. Self-plagiarism of this sort was doubtless encouraged by unsophisticated clients, who were often so awed by these fine modern buildings that they demanded similar if not identical designs for their own squares. All of this was driven by a distorted sense of competition among neighboring counties. Fueled by the wild myths of New South prosperity imported by the railroads of the era, the resulting boosterism and aggressive civic scheming clearly exaggerated the inherently Southern tendency toward boasting into ongoing duels of "oneupsmanship."

The earlier Hancock County Courthouse at Sparta bares such a striking resemblance to this building that it is easier to point out the differences than to enumerate the similarities. There is considerable vari-

ation in the decoration especially in the fenestration. Notably only the three central courtroom windows have hooded arches in Monroe, while the remaining windows are adorned with masonry keystones and splays, which are absent at Sparta. The dormers in the mansard roof of the wings appear more Gothic here in Monroe and the elegant rusticated stone quoining found at Sparta is omitted here.

The most notable difference is the clock tower. The original tower was apparently destroyed in a windstorm shortly after the building was completed. Although few local newspapers from this era survive, and there is no official record of this event, in March of 1890 *The Banner Messenger* reported that "the tower of the courthouse at Monroe has been declared dangerous and will be removed."[17] One of Monroe's few surviving nineteenth century newspapers is an 1897 edition of *The Walton News* which contains a photograph of this courthouse with a tower identical to the one we see today minus the clock. We know that the clock was installed in 1910, but records regarding the 1910 remodeling are sketchy. It is possible that in 1890 the county removed only the dome that crowned the tower. If this is the case, then the abbreviated tower we see today is original, and the 1910 "remodeling" involved only the installation of new clock. It is more likely that the original tower was removed in 1890 and replaced shortly thereafter.

Although these buildings clearly mirror the vocabulary of the Second Empire architecture so popular a decade earlier in the American North, Bruce apparently understood the dangers of employing "Yankee finery" to appeal to a Southern aesthetic. Thus, he was careful to subdue modern Parisian elements in the design and impose a simple rural blend of those Italianate and Gothic decorative ideas that had crept into the American brick vernacular in the years before the Civil War. The result was a stunning combination of the modern architecture of the Gilded Age and the comfortable but archaic vernacular architecture of the American frontier. Nothing could have been more appropriate for Monroe in 1883 for, like most Southern towns, the place dreamed of the prosperity of a new age while it desperately struggled to retain frontier traditions and the social order of earlier times. Here was what C. Vann Woodward has called the "Divided Mind of the South." Here were the elements that make up W. J. Cash's "Of Quandary - the Birth of a Dream." Indeed, as Cash so forcefully points out, the American Civil War had left part of the mind of the South defiant and unshaken in her old frontier ethic. At the heart of this defiance was "an intense distrust of, and, indeed, a downright aversion to any actual exercise of authority."[18]

It seems clear that Alexander Bruce, too, understood the inherent Southern aversion to big government. Like his Second Empire work here in Monroe, all of his court buildings avoid the pompous formality of the stiff Renaissance forms so often associated with American governmental architecture of the era. All of Bruce's courthouses are comfortably draped in a cloak of simple rural charm. Although they reflect the contemporary styles, unlike the monumental behemoths which were filling the town squares of the Ohio, Indiana and Michigan in the same period, Alexander Bruce's court buildings retain a personal unassuming charm - an architecture of an independent people, not of a grasping government. Here is the architecture of Wilbur J. Cash's "quandary."

SOME LAST THOUGHTS ON THE GAINESVILLE, JEFFERSON AND SOUTHERN RAILROAD

The myth of the New South was blind to the economic viability of the individual railroads upon which it rode. Seemingly any railroad would do, regardless of its financial prospects. It then followed that virtually any new railroad town could expect to soar on the wings of progress, regardless of its ability to attract capital, supply labor, or embrace the social institutions of the new age.

The Gainesville, Jefferson and Southern had few profitable years, yet the mere rumor of its conception contributed to a new courthouse movement in Jefferson where William Thomas's Jackson County Courthouse rose in the face of seemingly overwhelming opposition in 1879. Likewise, despite the cumbersome bottleneck at Monroe arising from the mismatch of rail gauges between the Walton Railroad

and the Gainesville, Jefferson and Southern, town leaders there were quick to commission Alexander Bruce's magnificent 1883 Walton County Courthouse, certainly one of the finest Georgia court buildings of its day. After reorganization and the extension of the line's Jefferson Branch to Athens in 1906, the road's successor, the Gainesville Midland met with only limited success. Yet by this time, opposition in Jefferson had eroded, and a brief epidemic of New South zeal seized the town, despite the fact that compared to her neighbors, Winder and Commerce, Jefferson had profited little from the arrival of the railroad. The song of her newfound fervor was voiced in H. L. Lewman's grand domed clock tower added to the old Jackson County Courthouse in 1906. Similar songs echoed in Winder at the junction of the Gainesville Midland and the Seaboard Air Line. The old town of Jug Tavern had blossomed and in 1905 sought the creation of her own county. This dream was realized in 1914 with the creation of Barrow County, and J. J. Baldwin's 1920 Barrow County Courthouse followed.

The Gainesville, Jefferson and Southern was not the only narrow gauge line born of the railroad-building frenzies of the 1870s. Construction of the state's first narrow gauge railroad had begun in Columbus in 1870 when the North and South Railroad was chartered with the aid of state endorsed bonds. Like all of the state-aided undertakings of the era, the road quickly failed. But not before it built the first short link in what would become the Columbus and Rome Railroad, a line that would eventually come under the control of the mighty Central of Georgia and reach all the way to Chattanooga, inspiring a string of grand courthouses on western edge of the state.

•

[17] *The Harris County Banner-Messenger*, March 7, 1890.

[18] W. J. Cash, *The Mind of the South* (1941; reprint, New York: Vintage Books, 1991) 33.

Chattanooga to Columbus

THE COLUMBUS AND ROME RAILROAD
Muscogee County: Columbus (See chapter 6) • Harris County: Hamilton • Meriwether County: Greenville

THE SAVANNAH, GRIFFIN AND NORTH ALABAMA
Coweta County: Newnan (see chapter 5)

THE CHATTANOOGA, ROME AND COLUMBUS RAILROAD
Carroll County: Carrollton • Haralson County: Buchanan • Polk County: Cedartown
Floyd County: Rome (See chapter 4) • Chattooga County: Summerville • Walker County: LaFayette
Some Last Thoughts on the Columbus and Rome and the Chattanooga, Rome and Columbus Railroads

17 | Chattanooga to Columbus

HARRIS COUNTY: HAMILTON

Plate 17.1: The depot at Cataula.

Today about 23 miles north of Columbus, along the rails of the old North and South Railroad at the village of Hamilton, the old depot no longer stands to remind us of Harris County's brief encounter with the promise of a New South. Only this nearly forgotten little depot at Cataula, 8 miles to the south of Hamilton, remains to tell the tale. Hamilton, the county town of Harris County was incorporated in 1828, less than a year after the county was created. A temporary log courthouse was erected in 1829, and two years later a two-story brick vernacular courthouse rose on the square. This simple building would stand for over three-quarters of a century, a testament to the static nature of things in Hamilton.

Part of the vast tract west of the Flint River ceded to the state by the Creek Indians in the 1825 Treaty of Indian Springs, Harris County counted over 5000 residents by 1830. For the next two decades, settlers rushed to west Georgia seeking new cotton-growing lands, and by 1860, with slaves accounting for almost two-thirds of the county's 13,000 inhabitants, Harris ranked ninth among Georgia's cotton growing counties. Through it all, Hamilton remained a tiny village.

In 1870, Hamilton's hopes rose as investors in Columbus chartered the North and South Railroad with bonds endorsed by the state. Like all of the state-aided railroads of this era, the North and South Railroad failed almost immediately. In 1877, with 23 miles of narrow gauge track stretching only as far north as Hamilton, the line was reorganized as the Columbus and Atlanta Air Line. In 1882, it was reorganized again and renamed the Columbus and Rome Railroad. The struggling company's accomplishments did not live up to either of her ambitious new names, and progress northward was halting. By 1885, the tracks had reached Greenville, only 26 miles north of Hamilton. In 1888, the Columbus and Rome was purchased by the Savannah and Western Railroad, a venture organized to spearhead the Central of Georgia's westward expansion. But the track from Columbus north to Greenville proved of little value to the mighty Central, and for years it was operated as an unimportant branch line.[1]

Harris County's population would reach her peak of just over 18,000 in 1900, while Hamilton remained a hamlet of 418. But by 1905, the fragrant aroma of hope was again on the wind. In that year, the Central of Georgia announced plans to extend the dead-end of the old Columbus and Rome Railroad at Greenville through to Raymond just south of Newnan, thus finally completing the long dreamt direct link from Chattanooga to Columbus. Before the construction of the Central's 1905 Raymond to Greenville link, all traffic between Rome and Columbus had followed a circuitous route along the broken pieces of a series of half-completed older railroads. Bypassing Hamilton, travelers followed the rails of the old Georgia Midland

Plate 17.1: Today the old depot at Hamilton is gone, but its near twin still stands today only eight miles away at Cataula. (Photo: Wilber W. Caldwell.)

and Gulf Railroad up to Waverly Hall, through the old Pine Mountain tunnel at Shiloh to Griffin. Then they traveled along the former Savannah, Griffin and North Alabama Railroad through Newnan to Carrollton and a connection to Rome with the rails of the old Chattanooga, Rome and Columbus which had never made it any farther south than Carroll County. As part of the 1905 improvement, the Central also announced that it would widen the full length of the old Columbus and Rome to standard gauge. These plans sent waves of euphoria cascading through Hamilton, and a late tide of New South fervor rose on the surety that the town's long sleep was at last over. In April of 1905, *The Hamilton Journal* predicted: "When we get a regular through train on a standard gauge railroad there will be no section of the country more desirable then the territory between Columbus and Greenville."[2] Rumors began to circulate that the Central would extend a line southward to Pensacola. Additional speculation centered on the possibility that the Atlantic and Birmingham, which was soon to become the powerful Atlanta, Birmingham and Atlantic, would abandon its plans for a northern route through Talbotton to LaGrange in favor of a southern path through Hamilton and West Point. Leaders in Hamilton urged support of this scheme, and suggested that the town donate the right of way and offer to build a depot free of charge.[3]

Plate 17.2: The Harris County Courthouse, built in 1908. Ed C. Hosford, architect.

As elsewhere, railroad-inspired boosterism sparked lofty aspirations in Hamilton. In 1905, the town opened its first bank, the Bank of Hamilton, and the inevitable talk of a new courthouse began to circulate. Simultaneously with speculation concerning the route of the Atlantic and Birmingham, came a proposal for the construction of the Columbus and Northern Railway through Hamilton, and in the heat of this frenzy, the old courthouse was declared "inadequate."[4] It is surprising how quickly the building's "inadequacy" deteriorated into abject ruin. The next two years saw the building declared first "rotten" and then "unsafe," and by August of 1907 it was condemned. Supporters of many new courthouse movements of this era veiled their cause in the cloak of necessity in order not to arouse the opposition of rural elements who often viewed the promises of the New South with skepticism or even with overt hostility. Hamilton is an excellent example of this political strategy. In March of 1905, when the Central announced plans for the Raymond to Greenville connector and the courthouse movement began, supporters argued that a building was needed not as "an ornament to Harris County" but to serve a "pressing need."[5] But as hopes rose, the language slowly changed, and it become clear that the building represented a great deal more than utility to its supporters. By 1906, as a bond election approached, supporters pressed for a building that would be "the envy of other counties" and declared, "There is no reason why we should live in the backwoods and be called the heathen of the state."[6] It was only a short jump from this point of view to a direct refutation of the original claim of "pressing need," and as the cornerstone was laid, *The Journal* pronounced the building, "an ornament and a crown," and declared it a "monument to the...progress of our age."[7]

Here again was the courthouse as an unabashed symbol for the myth of the New South. But as was so often the case, the architectural music of aspiring progress would be drowned out by the old songs of ignorance and poverty. Despite all of the hollow music of prosperity flowing up and down the rails from Chattanooga to Columbus, by the time Ed C. Hosford's grand courthouse at Hamilton was completed in 1908, the Atlantic and Birmingham had bypassed Hamilton, plans for the Columbus and Northern had been abandoned and Hamilton's population had fallen below her 1900 level.

Meanwhile, the powerful myth of railroad-borne New South prosperity was working its mischief elsewhere along the rails of the old Columbus and Rome Railroad. In 1905, in the northern part of Harris County at Chipley, town leaders proposed that a new county called Treutlen be cut from Harris, Meriwether, and Troup with Chipley (later called Pine Mountain) as the county seat. Although Chipley's bid for a new county failed, it seems certain that all of this added fuel to the fires of the new courthouse move-

Plate 17.2: The Harris County Courthouse at Hamilton was an unabashed symbol for the myth of the New South. (Photo: Wilber W. Caldwell.)

ment in Hamilton in 1905. In July of 1906, *The Journal* reported that a number of architects, including the ubiquitous J. W. Golucke, had presented designs to county leaders.[8] With the first bond election set for December of 1906, architect Ed C. Hosford's design was selected and a notice to contractors appeared in *The Journal* on November 9, 1906. Despite lofty aspirations, there was considerable opposition to the Harris County Courthouse at Hamilton, and it would take more than a year and two more bond elections before work was begun on the new building.

Ed C. Hosford had designed his first courthouse in Georgia in his native Eastman in 1906 where his father had been on the building committee. Despite such nepotism, Hosford's work in Dodge County was credible, and his second effort here at Hamilton, although smaller, surpassed his first design. Since the new building was not situated on the square, Hosford centered his attention on a grand facade. His fine six

[1] Les R. Winn, *Ghost Trains and Depots in Georgia* (Chamblee GA: Big Shanty Press, 1995) 168.

[2] *The Hamilton Journal*, April 21, 1905.

[3] *The Hamilton Journal*, March 24, 1905.

[4] *The Hamilton Journal*, March 24, 1905.

[5] *The Hamilton Journal*, March 24, 1905.

[6] *The Hamilton Journal*, November 23, 1906.

[7] *The Hamilton Journal*, February 7, 1908.

[8] *The Hamilton Journal*, July 6, 1906 and August 10, 1906.

column Doric portico supported a broad entablature, adding a low comfortable mass to the simple building, which was originally crowned by a massive octagonal clock tower encompassed by a fine balustrade. Sometime in the middle part of this century, the grand lantern was deemed unsafe and demolished. This brutally maimed Hosford's design, destroying the building's former monumentality, and leaving a rather low ordinary looking governmental clearinghouse. At this writing, planners discussing the remodeling of and additions to the Harris County Courthouse are considering recreating Hosford's original clock tower.

MERIWETHER COUNTY: GREENVILLE

Plate 17.3: The Meriwether County Courthouse, built in 1832. William Hitchcock, builder.

Created in 1827, Meriwether County was part of the enormous tract west of the Flint River that was ceded to the state of Georgia by the Creek Indians in the 1825 Treaty of Indian Springs. This controversial cession and the land lotteries that followed opened the floodgates for a wild rush to claim new cotton-growing lands in the western part of the state. In 1830, Meriwether County counted over 4000 residents. By 1840, this number had grown to over 14,000. As the county grew, William Hitchcock's 1832 courthouse rose on the square in Greenville.[9] This sturdy brick

Plate 17.3: The 1832 Meriwether County Courthouse. In the antebellum period, this sturdy brick building stood for simple frontier individualism and bore witness to a modest prosperity centered on the growing of cotton.

building would serve for over seventy years. In the antebellum period, it stood for simple frontier individualism and bore witness to a modest prosperity centered on the growing of cotton. In 1860, the county produced over 18,000 bales of the staple, fifth among Georgia's 132 counties. This rich harvest flowed up the old Atlanta and West Point Railroad from the depot at Hogansville to Atlanta. In 1885, the narrow gauge rails of the Columbus and Rome finally made their way from Columbus into Greenville, a town that had remained a comfortable village of about 500 residents.

Hastily chartered in the Reconstruction railroad-building frenzy of 1870, the predecessor of the Columbus and Rome was the North and South Railroad, which declared bankruptcy in 1877 having built only 23 miles of track from Columbus to Hamilton in Harris County. In subsequent reorganizations, the Columbus and Atlanta Air Line and later the Columbus and Rome Railroad struggled to extend the line northward. Sadly, after eight years, only 26 miles of new track had been completed, and the line stretched only as far north as Greenville whose citizens had subscribed $16,000 toward the construction of the extension. For twenty years the village would remain a simple agricultural trading town at the end of a ne'er-do-well narrow gauge rail spur.

Meanwhile, a flurry of railroad building was astir elsewhere in Meriwether County. In 1886, the Georgia Midland and Gulf built from Griffin to Columbus, and in 1891, the ill-fated Macon and Birmingham Railroad was completed from Macon to LaGrange. These lines crossed at the village of Woodbury, which boomed in the last decade of the nineteenth century. Passing only 4 miles south of Greenville, the Macon and Birmingham crossed the rails of the Columbus and Rome at the place that would become Harris City. For years Greenville's connection to the outside world lay through this tiny hamlet. As if to demonstrate Greenville's isolation, passengers bound for Greenville would take the Macon and Birmingham out of Macon and change at Harris City to the "Back Back," the regular passenger train on the Columbus and Rome, which, having arrived at Greenville earlier in the day, would simply "back back" down the line to Harris City every evening to pick up Greenville bound passengers.

This was a long distance from crack rail service, but it did spur a brief boom in Greenville. In the early 1890s, this progress was followed by a notable fire and a brutal tornado that damaged the old courthouse and swept the town clear of many old wooden buildings. Local historians report that in this period sixteen brick buildings rose to replace those destroyed. By 1900, the town's population was above 800. In 1901, news of the Central of Georgia's efforts to purchase the Chattanooga, Rome and Southern reached Greenville. Spirits soared on the speculation that the Central would extend the Columbus and Rome from Greenville through to Newnan,[10] thus realizing the town's age-old dream of a railroad from Columbus via Greenville all the way to Chattanooga.

The Meriwether County Courthouse, built in 1902-1903. J. W. Golucke, architect. Burned 1976. Restored 1980. (See Plate 10 in the Introduction.)

By 1901, the old 1832 courthouse at Greenville was aging. Its renovation after the tornado damage of 1893 remained less than perfect, and, as railroad speculation grew, the need for a new court building appeared more and more pressing. In addition to the rumors surrounding the Central's plan for a north-south line through Greenville, wild speculations began to surface regarding the future route of the Brunswick and Birmingham, the father of the powerful Atlanta, Birmingham and Atlantic Railroad, which in 1901, had just purchased its first locomotive. In that year, this line was beginning to fashion plans for the western end of its proposed connection between Brunswick and the coal fields and steel mills at Birmingham, Alabama.[11] Just as these railroad dreams appeared, county leaders in Greenville predictably declared the old courthouse unsafe, and were jealously eyeing J. W. Golucke's grand new classical creation in DeKalb County at Decatur.[12] By October of 1901, a plan created by Golucke and modeled after his work at Decatur was accepted. A contract for construction was let, the old courthouse was demolished and $30,000 in bonds were authorized and sold.[13] By June of 1902, as this grand

courthouse began to fill Greenville's tiny square, Meriwether County was buzzing which anticipation as *The Vindicator* declared, "The Brunswick and Birmingham is coming this way."[14]

James W. Golucke's 1900 DeKalb County Courthouse was perhaps Georgia's most influential public building of the era. With the exception of Andrew J. Bryan's 1895 Stewart County Courthouse at Lumpkin and an 1896 remodeling of the Muscogee County Courthouse at Columbus, Golucke's design at Decatur was the first courthouse in Georgia to reflect the pomp of the American Neoclassical Revival. After the wild success of the "Florentine Renaissance" architecture of the so-called "White City" at Chicago's 1893 Columbian Exposition, waves of the new classicism swept across the country. Great thrusts of modern American Neoclassical styling and an avant Beaux-Arts classicism eclipsed the picturesque and overshadowed the already popular Colonial and Renaissance Revivals to create a uniquely American Neoclassical Revival that found no counterpart abroad. Outside of the South, all of this architectural pomp and circumstance was part of the national celebration of a new sense of American industrial, financial, military and imperialist might that celebrated the questionable culmination of three decades of greed and unfettered commercial expansion. To be sure, no such celebration seemed appropriate in the American South. In 1900, the region still festered with bitterness, ignorance and intransigence, and, despite the myths of impending progress, the rural South was still desperately trapped in a spiral of exploitation and poverty.

Still, as James Golucke was soon to prove, the South would nonetheless have her Neoclassical Revival. And she would have it on her own terms. If

---

[9] Hitchcock designed and built several courthouses in this early period, notable among these were those at Newnan, 1829, Jackson, 1828 and McDonough, 1831 .

[10] *The Meriwether Vindicator*, June 6, 1901

[11] *The Meriwether Vindicator*, April 12, 1901.

[12] *The Meriwether Vindicator*, April 26, 1901.

[13] *The Meriwether Vindicator*, September 27, 1901 and October 11, 1901.

[14] *The Meriwether Vindicator*, June 27, 1902.

the national symbolism attached to the American Neoclassical Revival was abhorrent to Southern aesthetes, then the region would substitute her own symbols, and no one had to look far for an appropriate replacement. In the Southern mind of 1900, the columns of the Old South had come to stand for an idealized era dripping with sweetness and light. It was certainly not a great distance from the simple antebellum forms of Thomas Jefferson and Robert Mills to the ornate columns of J. W. Golucke's American Neoclassical Revival courthouses. And it can be no coincidence that James Golucke always employed grand porticos in the Greek temple form as the centerpiece of his court buildings. Although he employed Beaux-Arts ornament with increasing freedom, he always returned to the great temple-like portico. It was a choice that allowed his buildings to simultaneously speak two mythical languages. The modern myth of the New South teetered on the shaky foundations of the myth of the Old South.

In 1976, James Golucke's 1903 Meriwether County Courthouse was badly damaged by a fire. Rather than take such calamity as opportunity to construct a modern government building, the citizens of Meriwether rallied to restore the old courthouse. Restoration architect, Ed Neal, of Columbus called the project a "adaptive restoration," meaning that the exterior of the building would be faithfully restored while the interior would be remodeled and modern-

Plate 17.4: The 1906 depot at Greenville. Gone are the familiar hipped roof and the distinctive overhanging eaves. In their place we find unmistakably classical forms. (Photo: Wilber W. Caldwell.)

ized. The results are stunning. The solid stone columns today support hand carved pediments just as they did in 1903. In true Southern fashion, when the New South finally did arrive in Meriwether County, these columns still served to recall the decades of struggle and quandary that were her past.

Plate 17.4: The depot at Greenville, built in 1906.

James W. Golucke's stunning Meriwether County Courthouse was not the only voice of turn-of-the-century American Neoclassicism to be heard in Greenville. In 1904-1905, the Central of Georgia, having gained control of the old dead-end spur of the Columbus and Rome Railroad, widened the narrow gauge rails to standard gauge and extended them through to Newnan. In the shadow of Golucke's gleaming limestone columns, spirits in Greenville again briefly soared. With a direct line now completed from Chattanooga to Columbus, the Central celebrated with this fine brick depot, erected at Greenville in 1906.[15] Gone are the familiar hipped roof and the distinctive overhanging eaves. In their place we find unmistakably classical forms: a rather formal pediment defined by a bold cornice that projects outward offering only a suggestion of broad eaves, a mock brick dental course supporting the cornice, a series of cleanly articulated segmental arched doorways and emphatic brick quoining.

In 1906, the neoclassical grandeur of both Grand Central Station and Pennsylvania Station were rising in midtown Manhattan. While these simple classical details at Greenville may seem a long distance from New York City's blossoming "American Renaissance," this depot is a humble part of the same sweeping trend. The pragmatic civil engineers of the Central were being replaced by trained architects, and the utilitarian depot style that had characterized the line's nineteenth century depots was being discarded for expressions of style and order. As this fine depot illustrates, after the turn of the century, the new classicism began to appear even in the most rural of places.

In 1906, when this depot was built, Greenville's population was less than 1000. It would remain stagnant for the next 70 years. Despite the extension of her old rail line, the railroad-borne prosperity of the

New South would bypass the county town in favor of a remote spot in the southern part of the county. In 1907, the long-awaited rails of the Atlanta, Birmingham and Atlantic finally arrived in Meriwether County, and after considerable speculation, the route through Greenville was rejected. The new railroad selected a rural site to traverse the low mountains near Warm Springs and called it Manchester after the English industrial city that had been the terminus of the world's first commercial railroad. Here the Atlanta, Birmingham and Atlantic began its Atlanta branch, and here the company established extensive shops and yards. While Greenville stagnated, Manchester soared. Only two years after the new town was laid out, its population equaled that of Greenville. By 1909, Callaway Mills was employing 350 workers at Manchester, and this number would quickly reach 1000 with a mill village of 250 houses.[16]

As if to highlight the contrast between Greenville's static fortunes and Manchester's boom, the Macon and Birmingham through Harris City, 4 miles south of Greenville was abandoned in 1937. Likewise, the Central's Columbus to Newnan route through Greenville never prospered, and the rails from Greenville to Raymond were abandoned in 1981. While over in Manchester, the fortunes of the old Atlanta, Birmingham and Atlantic were invigorated by the Atlantic Coast Line Railroad, which acquired the line in 1946. It was just another example of the capricious nature of the myth of the New South.

Carroll County: Carrollton

Plate 17.5: The Carroll County Courthouse, built in 1851.

Carroll County was created in 1826, and her first court building was a 20' by 20' log structure erected at Carrollton around 1829 shortly after the county seat had been moved from its original site at "Old Carrollton." In 1837, Adiel Sherwood in his *Gazetteer of Georgia* reports that Carrollton consisted of eight or ten houses and two stores. In that year, a frame courthouse replaced the first crude building. By 1851, as the west Georgia fields turned white with cotton, this

Plate 17.5: The 1851 Carroll County Courthouse. An elegant air was achieved through the use of bold brick pilasters that divided the facade into narrow vertical bays.

typical brick vernacular court building rose to meet the growing administrative and judicial needs of the Carroll County's 9357 residents, only 250 of whom lived in Carrollton, the county's largest town.[17] It is interesting to note that Carrollton built this sturdy brick courthouse in the same year that the town's leaders spearheaded an attempt to build a short line railroad from Carrollton to connect with the Atlanta and West Point Railroad.[18] The broad cornice and paired brackets supporting the eaves are typical of vernacular rural public buildings of the era. A particularly elegant air was achieved through the use of bold brick pilasters that divided the facade into narrow vertical bays. The use of tied pairs of these great pier-like members to close the end bays and stress the sides of the composition is a rather sophisticated device for such a crude building. It is a technique that was often used in Italian Renaissance palaces, and was most likely inspired by one of the many builders' guides or pattern books available to builders of the day.

[15] *A Finders Guide to Plans and Maps of The Central of Georgia Railroad* in the Georgia Department of Archives and History in Atlanta.

[16] Regina Pinkston, ed., *Historical Account of Meriwether County, Georgia, 1827-1974* (Greenville GA: Gresham Printing Company, 1974) 118.

[17] Ben Griffin, *At Home in Carrollton, A History Illustrated* (Roswell GA: W H Wolfe, 1995) 20.

[18] Griffin, *At Home in Carrollton, A History Illustrated*, 20.

Plate 17.6: The depot at Carrollton, built in c.1875.

In 1872, the Central of Georgia Railroad acquired controlling interest in the struggling Savannah, Griffin and North Alabama Railroad, which had completed track from Griffin to Newnan but had stalled in rocky ground at Whitesburg while attempting to extend the line to Carrollton. Construction remained at a standstill for almost a year, while Whitesburg experienced a considerable boom, and Carrollton languished in frustrated concern for the $50,000 her citizens had subscribed for the purchase of the foundering road's stock, all of which was pledged "unconditionally."[19] In 1874, with the financial backing of the Central, the line finally entered Carrollton. This fine depot was completed shortly thereafter. Here in Carroll County, we find an early example of the Central's emerging brick depot style. Like the line's great passenger depot at Savannah completed in 1876, and the charming 1880 depot at Hampton in Henry County, we find an arcade of graceful segmental arches separated by bold brick pilasters.

With the arrival of the Central, Carrollton would experience her own brief boom as an area cotton market. One historian contends that the number of businesses in town doubled between 1871 and 1873.[20] Whatever the case, Carrollton's boom was brief. The Central abandoned work on the westward extension after its arrival in Carrollton, and the town was destined to occupy the end of this lonely spur for almost 15 years.

The size of this building offers convincing testament to the success of cotton growers in Carroll County. With the railroad's arrival, Carrollton prospered, shipping over 15,000 bales annually from this depot in the late 1880s.[21] As the decade ended, Carrollton had her own bank and a population of nearly 1500. But, as always, dreams of a New South would eventually crumble when supported only by the flimsy foundations of cotton.

Plate 17.6: The c.1875 depot at Carrollton. This characteristic arcade of graceful segmental arches separated by bold brick pilasters is an early reflection of the Central's emerging brick depot style. (Photo: Wilber W. Caldwell.)

Plate 17.7: The Carroll County Courthouse, built in 1892-1893. Burned 1928. Bruce and Morgan, architects.

More than ten years after the Central's great depot rose at Carrollton, the town's isolation at the western end of the Savannah, Griffin and North Alabama Railroad came to an end. In Rome in 1887, organizers with Northern financial backing had chartered the Rome and Carrollton Railroad and completed a narrow gauge line from Rome as far south as Cedartown before encountering financial problems. In 1888, the line was quickly reorganized as the Chattanooga, Rome and Columbus, widened to standard gauge and, using leased convict labor, completed to Carrollton to connect with the old Savannah, Griffin and North Alabama. As early as September of

1886, *The Carroll Free Press* reported that the construction of the Rome and Carrollton Railroad "was assured" and that Carrollton was "on a boom."[22] By January of 1888, hopes soared on the news that the new line planned to build through to LaGrange and on to Columbus.[23]

Despite the fact that the Columbus extension failed to materialize, there can be little doubt that the rising prospects created by the long awaited arrival of the Chattanooga, Rome and Columbus sparked a new courthouse movement in Carrollton. Only a little more than a year after the new rails arrived, county leaders put a bond issue to fund a new courthouse before the voters of Carroll County. Although the bonds failed to pass, beginning in 1891, two successive grand juries recommended a new courthouse, and in July of 1892, *The Free Press* reported that the county commissioners were "resolved to build a new courthouse," and had set up a meeting with an unnamed architectural firm.[24] Despite the fact that the issue of how to pay for the building was still unresolved, a plan was selected, and a contract for the construction of Bruce and Morgan's grand 1893 Carroll County Courthouse was let on December 9th of 1892. There followed the predictable political squabble, including a second bond election, which also failed to achieve the necessary voter support. In the end, the building was funded by a direct tax.

Just as the impetus behind the movement to build the 1893 Carroll County Courthouse had arrived on the rails of the Chattanooga, Rome and Columbus, the Romanesque Revival style flowed down to Carrollton on the same railroad. Beginning with William Parkins's 1888 Gordon County Courthouse at Calhoun, we can trace a line of Romanesque court buildings along the railroads of northwest Georgia. Parkins's 1889 Polk County Courthouse rose at Cedartown followed by Walter Chamberlain's 1891 Whitfield County Courthouse at Dalton. Only a year later, Bruce and Morgan Romanesque courthouses were going up at Rome and at Buchanan, only 20 miles up the line from Carrollton. Similarly, the same stylistic impetus must have flowed down the rails of the East Tennessee, Virginia and Georgia from Rome to Dallas where

Plate 17.7: The 1893 Carroll County Courthouse. The grand arches and towers of the Romanesque Revival flowed down to Carrollton on the Chattanooga, Rome and Columbus Railroad. (Photo: Courtesy of the Georgia Dept. of Archives and History.)

Bruce and Morgan designed the highly picturesque Paulding County Courthouse in 1892. Finally it wandered over to Douglasville where the bold Romanesque walls of Andrew Bryan's Douglas County Courthouse rose in 1896.

The 1893 Carroll County Courthouse owed a debt to a number these buildings. Although devoid of much of Alexander Bruce's earlier Queen Anne finery, this structure was in many ways similar to Bruce and Morgan's Haralson County Courthouse at nearby Buchanan, completed only a year earlier. The side elevation, with its shaped parapet flanked by small tourelles and the three bold arches of the courtroom windows, clearly mirrors the firm's earlier work at Buchanan. The stone banding and the great entrance arches reflect the work of H. H. Richardson in general, and the paired arches of the front entrance specifically recall Parkins's 1891 Polk County Courthouse at neighboring Cedartown. The round tower with its conical cap is unique among Bruce and Morgan's many Romanesque court buildings. But

[19] Tyrola, "The Railroad Subscription," *The Carroll County Times*, 1874, reprinted in *The Carroll County Historical Quarterly* 1/1 (1968): 17.

[20] James C. Bonner, *Georgia's Last Frontier, The Development of Carroll County* (Athens GA: University of Georgia Press, 1971) 99.

[21] Griffin, *At Home in Carrollton, A History Illustrated*, 37-38.

[22] *The Free Press* (Carrollton GA), September 3, 1886.

[23] *The Free Press* (Carrollton GA), January 20, 1888.

[24] *The Free Press* (Carrollton GA), July 29, 1892.

towers of all sorts characterized the Romanesque Revival in America, and the massive square tower with its arcaded arched window groupings and pyramidal roof is typical of all of this Atlanta firm's work in the style.

In Carrollton we find another conspicuous example of the intense competitive spirit that Georgia's counties exhibited as the railroads were beginning to tie these places together for the first time. The 1893 Carroll County Courthouse, and indeed the long string of 1890s Romanesque court buildings that stretched from Dalton to Franklin, Georgia, south of Carrollton in Heard County, stood in monumental testament to these place's compelling need to first emulate and then outdo their neighbors with architectural flights of fancy, which often far exceeded any practical consideration. These buildings not only stood for a uniquely Southern version of the promise of prosperity imported by the railroads, they also broadcast a boastful pride.

Despite the fact that most of these buildings represented a hollow promise and a false pride, for a brief moment Carrollton appeared to be the fulfillment of promises imported back in 1888 by the Chattanooga, Rome and Columbus. As the new courthouse neared completion, a devastating fire swept through Carrollton destroying fifteen wooden buildings. All of these were replaced by brick structures. By 1905, Carrollton's population, which had stood at around 1500 in 1890, had more than doubled. And the town boasted "53 business houses, 3 hotels 2 newspapers and 10 passenger trains a day."[25] Along the way, a cotton mill had been added in 1898, and ten years later the plant's capacity had almost doubled. Still, this was hardly the stuff of the modern age. All the while, Carroll remained a county of farmers, and cotton production continued to mushroom. In 1905, the county was the second largest producer in the state,[26] and by 1914 Carroll produced an incredible 43,000 bales. Three years later the boll weevil arrived, and by 1921 countywide cotton production was down to 26,000 bales. It was a disaster, for despite all of her fine new clothes, Carrollton's very soul was still inexorably bound to the production of cotton. Almost symbolically, Bruce and Morgan's grand symbol for the

mythical bounty of the New South burned to the ground in 1928.

There is a footnote to Carroll County's story, and it concerns the struggle of the town of Bowdon and her efforts to achieve a rail connection. The town suffered a dramatic disappointment after the Savannah, Griffin and North Alabama ceased westward construction and called Carrollton the end of the line in 1874. In that year, an article appeared in *The Carroll County Times* declaring that Bowdon had tendered thirty thousand dollars to secure the extension of the line from Carrollton to Bowdon. The article went on to relate that the road's failure to keep its bargain had dealt Bowdon a "staggering blow," "paralyzing trade" and bringing material improvement to a "standstill." It seems that the citizens of Bowdon had discovered what so many towns of the era were slow to grasp: that the railroads could destroy as well as create. The 1874 article sums it up nicely: "Railroads are the great civilizers of the Nineteenth century…but they sometimes inspire false hopes, excite the spirit of speculation and unreasonably inflate property values—and thus, in time comes disaster."[27]

Despite this setback Bowdon was quick to take another bite from the New South's tempting apple. In 1890, she chartered the Waco and Bowdon Railroad contemplating a 12-mile line to connect the town with the old Georgia Pacific at Waco. This scheme came to nothing, but in 1910 the town built the Bowdon Railroad, connecting Bowdon with the Central of Georgia at Bowdon Junction between Carrollton and Bremen. This line operated until 1963 when it was abandoned.

HARALSON COUNTY: BUCHANAN

Plate 17.8: The Haralson County Courthouse, built in 1891-1892. Bruce and Morgan, architects.

Most of Bruce and Morgan's Romanesque Revival designs were highly picturesque in silhouette and lavishly embellished with all manner of eclectic decoration. Elements of the Queen Anne Style were widely employed including towers with bell roofs, ornate terra cotta decorations, delicate classically inspired fenestration and other details. The 1892

Haralson County Courthouse at Buchanan is typical of Bruce's elegant and strangely personal Queen Anne courthouse style. Its story is typical of the struggle of so many tiny Georgia hamlets to retain the county seat in the face of the capricious forces of New South prosperity.

When Haralson County was created from Carroll and Polk Counties in 1856, the vast rocky expanses of this hilly section of western Georgia contained no towns large enough to claim the title of county seat. In 1857, a central location was selected and the county town was laid out. First called Pierceville, after President Franklin Pierce, the village soon discovered that the name was already in use in Georgia. One US President must have appeared as good as another to the county's founders, for the name was quickly changed to Buchanan for President James Buchanan, who had just been elected to replace the hapless Pierce. Both presidents were Democrats with an ear to the South's peculiar cause, but, in truth, both proved ineffective leaders in the hour of the nation's greatest need. As the west Georgia town that bore his name constructed its first courthouse James Buchanan stood helplessly by while Kansas burned, the Dred Scott decision affirmed slavery, and the union plummeted toward war.

The frame courthouse completed at Buchanan in 1857 presided over a place so remote that the initial business of Haralson County's first inferior court was to mandate the construction of roads from Buchanan to Villa Rica, Carrollton and Cedartown. The old frame building, erected back in 1857, would stand for more than thirty years. In 1889, only two years after the Chattanooga, Rome and Columbus Railroad finally arrived in Buchanan, the old building was badly damaged by fire. By 1890, agitation for a new courthouse was intense among Buchanan's 324 residents. But by that time, the town stood in the shadow of a bizarre boom at nearby Tallapoosa, a village that, almost overnight, had become a city of nearly 3000.[28] Only 8 miles away, the capricious whim of the New South myth had fabricated this brief but convincing success along the rails of the old Georgia Pacific Railroad on Haralson County's western side.

Plate 17.8: The 1892 Haralson County Courthouse. Elements of the Queen Anne Style were widely employed including towers with bell roofs, ornate terra cotta decorations and delicate classically inspired fenestration. (Photo: Wilber W. Caldwell.)

The story of Tallapoosa's boom illuminates the irony inherent in the myth of the New South and its endless quest for Northern capital. Just as the town of Buchanan had bound itself to the dubious memory of an ineffective American president, the city of Tallapoosa is linked to one of the most thoroughly disreputable American political figures of the postwar era. Tallapoosa was the product of the Georgia-Alabama Land Development Company, which was

[25] Private Joe Cobb, *Carroll County and Her People* (Carrollton GA: Private Joe Cobb, 1906) 53.

[26] Cobb, *Carroll County and Her People*, 51.

[27] Tyrola, "The Railroad Subscription," *The Carroll County Times*, 1874, reprinted in *The Carroll County Historical Quarterly* 1/1 (1968) 17-18.

organized by General Benjamin Franklin Bulter of Massachusetts, one the most disreputable characters of a shameful age. A powerful figure in American politics from the 1850s through the 1880s, Butler kept a perennially lustful eye on the presidency, and although he never garnered that prize, he left a mark on national policy in the era after the Civil War that was both indelible and unlovely. It is an odd chapter in the history of the American South that recounts the story of how the region, with its growing fascination with the myth of the Old South and its swelling allegiance to the Lost Cause, would welcome the exploitive investment of one of its most hated former protractors, Benjamin Franklin Butler.

Despite Butler's despicable career, the Georgia-Alabama Land Development Company was something of a success. The Company reputedly attracted 3000 new residents to Tallapoosa and boasted a prestigious list of investors including two former United States treasurers.[29] According to a prospectus published in 1891, Tallapoosa had grown from a village of 56 inhabitants in 1884 to a city that, accord-

ing to promoters, "enjoyed the reputation of being the pre-eminent Yankee city under the southern sky."[30] Like so many schemes of that era, success rested upon blatant promotionalism. An elaborate national campaign broadcast the idea that Tallapoosa, Georgia, was perhaps the finest place in the entire county. Brochures extolled Tallapoosa's merits, adding that the town was only 32 hours from New York by rail.[31]

The slick promotional literature that documented the hay-day of Tallapoosa's boom offers clear insight into the shameless manipulation employed by the purveyors of the myth of the New South. Promoters could not stop without including the full menu of New South propaganda which, despite the fervor of its apostles, amounted to nothing less than ridiculous verbiage and outright lies. A few examples will more than suffice:

"The new South will soon rival if not surpass the North and the West in the quality and value of its products and in the enterprise and resources of its people."[32] "...another decade will see the South the greatest manufacturing center of the United States."[33] The resources of the South "afford a solid foundation for a growth in trade surpassing anything ever known."[34] "...city building in the South marks an industrial revolution never before accomplished in times of peace in the world's history."[35]

At the center of it all was a mineral spring and the enormous 175 room Lithia Springs Hotel built in 1892. Designed by Chattanooga architect, Samuel Patton, the hotel was heralded by locals as the largest wooden building in the South.[36] This claim seemed to ignore the 250 room 1886 Sweetwater Park Hotel at Salt Springs (later called Lithia Springs) just up the rails of the Georgia Pacific near Douglasville. Whatever the case, unlike the resort at Salt Springs, the development in Tallapoosa described a much broader pattern. By the mid-1890s, the town had a mule drawn trolley line and a cotton mill under construction. In addition the place boasted three hotels, a large sash and door factory, a foundry, a cabinet factory, a chemical company, a wagon manufacturer, a knitting mill, a glass factory to support local vineyards'

[28] The Georgia-Alabama Land Development Company, *A Prospectus of the City of Tallapoosa, Haralson County, Georgia* (Boston GA: The Georgia-Alabama Land, 1891) 4.

[29] The Georgia-Alabama Land Development Company, *A Prospectus of the City of Tallapoosa, Haralson County, Georgia*, 3.

[30] The Georgia-Alabama Land Development Company, *A Prospectus of the City of Tallapoosa, Haralson County*, Georgia, 4.

[31] Lois Owen Newnan, *Haralson County, Georgia* (Roswell GA: W H Wolfe Associates, 1994) 101.

[32] The Georgia-Alabama Land Development Company, *A Prospectus of the City of Tallapoosa, Haralson County, Georgia*, 40.

[33] The Georgia-Alabama Land Development Company, *A Prospectus of the City of Tallapoosa, Haralson County, Georgia*, 40.

[34] The Manufacturer's Record quoted in The Georgia-Alabama Land Development Company, *A Prospectus of the City of Tallapoosa, Haralson County, Georgia*, 62.

[35] Henry W. Grady in The Georgia-Alabama Land Development Company, *A Prospectus of the City of Tallapoosa, Haralson County, Georgia*, 66.

[36] Newnan, *Haralson County, Georgia*, 100.

[37] The Georgia-Alabama Land Development Company, *A Prospectus of the City of Tallapoosa, Haralson County, Georgia*, 28-30.

[38] The Georgia-Alabama Land Development Company, *A Prospectus of the City of Tallapoosa, Haralson County, Georgia*, 26.

[39] *The Banner-Messenger* (Buchanan GA), February 28, 1890.

[40] *The Banner-Messenger* (Buchanan GA), June 4, 1891.

increasing wine production and a blast furnace producing fifty tons of pig iron daily.[37] Promoters also declared the town "a railroad center" primarily on the strength of plans to construct the Georgia, Tennessee and Illinois Railroad, which had been chartered in 1889 to connect Tallapoosa with "eleven railroads."[38]

The citizens of Buchanan could only admire the grand hotels and thriving commerce from afar. Thus, the thrust of the argument for a new courthouse in Buchanan in 1890 was of a distinctly defensive sort. Bruce and Morgan's Queen Anne elegance was not inspired by the wild dreams of railroad-borne prosperity that we find elsewhere along the rails of the Chattanooga, Rome and Columbus. It rose more from the fear of losing the status of county seat to nearby Tallapoosa. A letter published in *The Banner-Messenger* in 1890 clearly states the case: "...steps should be taken at once to build a commodious courthouse instead of the dilapidated structure that now occupies the public square. It is whispered now(that Buchanan is dead and that we (Tallapoosa and Bremen) will draw straws for the county seat."[39]

The construction of Bruce and Morgan's 1892 Haralson County Courthouse at Buchanan did little to stimulate growth in the tiny hamlet which in 1900 still counted only 359 residents, but it did cement the town's hold on the county seat. As the foundation for the new temple of justice was laid in Buchanan, *The Haralson Banner Messenger* called the construction the new courthouse "an event...that means more to Buchanan and Haralson County than anything that has ever occurred during the history of the county."[40]

Meanwhile, like most flashes of New South prosperity, the boom at Tallapoosa was short-lived. The Georgia, Tennessee and Illinois Railroad was never built, and the great Tallapoosa building boom collapsed in the Panic of 1893. By 1900, the town's population stood at just above 2000. In 1910, this figure remained unchanged. The economic prosperity of the earlier decade had depended upon growth, and as the language of the handsome brochures promoting a New South of industrial prosperity and racial harmony began to acquire a hollow ring, places like

Tallapoosa began to stagnate. In 1907, when Georgia passed a prohibition law effectively killing the region's prosperous wine industry, the iron deposits of west Georgia were beginning to show signs of depletion. By that time, the halls of the once grand Lithia Springs Hotel were filled with nothing more than the ghosts of a bygone era. The building was demolished in 1946.

POLK COUNTY: CEDARTOWN

Plate 17.9: The Polk County Courthouse, built in 1890. Demolished in 1951, William Parkins, architect.

Polk County was created in 1851 from Floyd and Paulding Counties, and Cedartown was laid out shortly thereafter. The county's first courthouse rose in 1852, and according to local historians, it was burned along with sixty-five other buildings in Cedartown by elements of Kilpatrick's Union cavalry in 1864. It

Plate 17.9: With its great tower destroyed the grandeur of William Parkins's 1890 Polk County Courthouse was gone, and just as the great thrust of Cedartown's boom disappeared, the town was left to contemplate a wounded symbol of its lost prosperity. (Photo: Courtesy of Ted Brooke.)

seems quite unlikely that there were 65 buildings in Cedartown in 1864. About all the reliable Adiel Sherwood could say about Cedartown in his 1860 *Gazetteer of Georgia* was that it was "not a large place." As to Federal incendiaries, Union Orders document a considerable Federal force at Cedartown in late 1864, but no Confederate or Union military records mention the destruction of the town. The record reveals only that Kilpatrick was needed at Cedartown on October 31st.[41] It unclear whether or not he ever arrived in Cedartown. We are told only that Federal soldiers foraged at Cedartown where they, "took much," but left "plenty of corn and pigs."[42] Whatever the case, local historians hold that a new courthouse was completed in 1867.

Although Cedartown had been nothing but a dusty hamlet before the war, the town experienced a post-Civil War boom, which was not typical in Georgia. At the heart of this progress were the region's iron deposits and efforts to establish pig iron production in western Georgia and eastern Alabama. These efforts met with considerable initial success. In Cedartown, under the direction of New Yorkers, Amos G. West and W. C. Browning, the Cherokee Iron Company built a blast furnace in 1873. At about the same time the company purchased the Cartersville and Van Wert Railroad, the bankrupt remains of one of Hannibal Kimball's flimflam Reconstruction railroading schemes, which at the time, extended only 14 miles from Cartersville to the village of Taylorsville. Reorganized as the Cherokee Railroad, the narrow gauge line was extended via Rockmart to Cedartown.

By 1882, the Cherokee Iron and Railroad Company was experiencing financial difficulties, and Browning organized the East and West Railroad Company of Alabama to lease the Cherokee Railroad.[43] By 1887, when the Chattanooga, Rome and Columbus crossed The East and West Railroad at Cedartown, Browning had widened the entire line to standard gauge and extended it to Pell City, Alabama.

New South promoters were quick to emphasize the implications of iron production in the South. Indeed, the initial outlook had been rosy, and by the mid-1880s, furnaces dotted the west Georgia countryside. Rising Fawn in Dade County, Rome, and Cedartown all boasted pig iron producing hearths. Over in Alabama, by 1887 there were 32 furnaces on the line of the L & N.[44] Despite the successes at Birmingham and Anniston, the Southern iron and steel industry would wither, either wiped out after the Panic of 1893 or gobbled up by Northern conglomerate interests,[45] which from the beginning had bludgeoned Southern competition with a series of brutal weapons drawn from the quiver of Eastern control of the nation's financial and transportation resources. At its height, Georgia's share of the nation's iron and steel production had amounted to no more than a small fraction of 1%, and most of the state's output was pig iron, which by 1900 had been eclipsed by steel.

Despite financial woes, the furnace at Cedartown was still chugging along in 1887, when the old courthouse at Cedartown burned to the ground. In that same year, the crossing rails of the Chattanooga, Rome and Columbus arrived to breathe new life into the town. By 1890, Cedartown had a population of 1625. As the walls of William Parkins's grand Polk County Courthouse began to rise in 1889, a new helping of Northern capital flowed into Cedartown when a Philadelphia native, Charles Adamson, chartered the Cedartown Land Company to promote the city and to exploit its already apparent potential. Adamson was typical of a class of Northern entrepreneurs who were tempted by the mythical potential of the New South dream in the last decade of the nineteenth century. This courthouse is an apt symbol for Adamson's vision and for Cedartown's boom. By 1905, the city had

[41] Major General O. O. Howard in *The War of the Rebellion, Official Records of Union and Confederate Armies*, Series 1, Vol. 39, Part 3, Orders, 532.

[42] L. M. Dalton, in a letter to General William Sherman, November 2, 1864, in *The War of the Rebellion, Official Records of Union and Confederate Armies*, Series 1, Vol. 39.

[43] Winn, *Ghost Trains and Depots in Georgia*, 294.

[44] C. Vann Woodward, *Origins of the New South* (1951; reprint, Baton Rouge LA: Louisiana State University Press, 1993) 127.

[45] Woodward, *Origins of the New South*, 299.

[46] Charles K. Henderson, "Polk County Persons and Things," unpublished manuscript in Polk County Library, Cedartown GA, 1937.

[47] Gordon D. Sargent, "The Legacy of Charles Adamson," in Olin Jackson, ed., *The Journal of North Georgia History*, 3 vols., 3:338.

three cotton mills, two knitting mills, four hotels, extensive car shops to serve both of her railroads, and eight passenger trains a day. Her population would top 3500 in 1910.

As we have seen, the rails of the Chattanooga, Rome and Columbus Railroad brought more than hope to the west Georgia villages south of Rome. They also delivered the most up-to-date fashions including the architectural ideas of Henry Hobson Richardson and the American Romanesque Revival. William Parkins's 1890 Polk County Courthouse enlarged on the themes voiced in his recently completed Gordon County Courthouse at nearby Calhoun. The grand tower was supported by a massive base featuring a pair of highly Richardsonian entrance arches beneath window groupings typical of Richardson's designs. Here was Parkins's most literal interpretation of the American master's work. But like his courthouse at Calhoun, the rest of the building was something of a controlled riot of eclectic ornament and form. Queen Anne elements abounded in classical pediments, foliate brackets, elaborate chimneys, lacy fenestration and an impossibly complex and romantically picturesque roofline. The entire building was of brick, and as was usually the case with buildings of this sort, the white stone trim served more to accent Queen Anne detail than to emulate Richardsonian polychromy.

Writing in 1937, county historian Charles K. Henderson, summed up the outlook in Cedartown after the 1887 arrival of the Chattanooga, Rome and Columbus: "Possessed of two railways…there seemed nothing in the way of indefinite prosperity."[46] Sadly, Mr. Henderson goes on to vividly describe the town's "ruin" as the new century progressed. In this regard, we learn that Charles Adamson died a pauper in 1931,[47] and that perhaps fittingly, the great tower of Parkins's courthouse was destroyed, leaving only its squat base attached to the complex mass of the rest of the building. Without the tower the grandeur was gone, and just as the great thrust of Cedartown's boom disappeared, the town was left to contemplate this wounded symbol of her lost prosperity. This fine courthouse was demolished in 1951 to make way for the present structure.

CHATTOOGA COUNTY: SUMMERVILLE

Plate 17.10: The depot at Summerville, built in 1895.

As soon as the Chattanooga, Rome and Columbus Railroad completed the line southward from Rome to Carrollton, the directors of the road turned their attention to the north and began construction from Rome up the valley of the Chattooga River toward Chattanooga. Unlike the wild white water fury of Georgia's better-known Rabun County Chattooga River in the northeastern part of the state, this softer, western Chattooga flows through the broad comfortable valley that forms a natural "backdoor" into Chattanooga. Building first westward from Rome, the Chattanooga, Rome and Columbus reached the mouth of the valley of the Chattooga, turned northward and completed the line through Summerville and Trion in 1888. Owing to the sheer walls of Taylor Ridge on the east and Pigeon Mountain of the west, the prospects for crossing rails anywhere in Chattooga County were very poor. Although the Chattanooga Southern built down the western edge of the valley on its way from Chattanooga to Gadsden, Alabama, in 1889, the single line of the Chattanooga Railroad, Rome and Columbus was the only railroad Summerville would know. The Reconstruction period was particularly difficult for this impoverished and often violent region. But for the growing of peaches and strawberries, agri-

Plate 17.10: The depot at Summerville. Isolated but for the thin steel line of the Chattanooga, Rome and Columbus Railroad, Summerville would be slow to accept any of the shining mythical wares sold by New South boosters. (Photo: Wilber W. Caldwell.)

culture remained at subsistence levels in the mountains, and for decades about the only profitable industry in Chattooga County beyond the old mill at Trion was the production of moonshine. Thus entrenched in her highly individual mountain culture and isolated but for the thin steel line of the Chattanooga, Rome and Columbus, Summerville would be slow to accept any of the shining mythical wares sold by New South boosters. By the time a helping of New South progress arrived, the shine of the myth had begun to tarnish.

Plate 17.11: The Chattooga County Courthouse, built in 1909. The Bryan Architectural Firm, St. Louis, Missouri. architects.

Plate 17.11: The 1909 Chattooga County Courthouse marks the beginning of an architecture of an increasingly detached government. (Photo: Wilber W. Caldwell.)

Chattooga County was cut from Walker and Floyd in 1838. Some sources maintain that James Hitchcock's brick courthouse, built around 1841, was the county's first. Others recall a log courthouse erected before 1841 at Summerville, which in that year consisted of "a few log houses and only 5 frame houses."[48] Whatever the case, when George White published his *Statistics of the State of Georgia* in 1849, he noted Hitchcock's "handsome brick courthouse" and observed that the town had two hotels, five stores and a population of about 275. After the war, Federal troops, called in to retain order in Chattooga County, were billeted in the old courthouse. Post-war growth was slow, and when the railroad finally arrived in Summerville, almost fifty years after Hitchcock's courthouse was constructed, the town's population was still under 500.

There is little here to echo the usual high hopes and soaring aspirations that inspired so many of Georgia's turn-of-the-century courthouses. The old 1841 courthouse simply grew old and had to be replaced. In 1906, *The Summerville News* noted that the old building "looked like the last rose of summer."[49] Bonds for a new structure were approved in a countywide referendum in December of 1908, and on July 22, 1909, a photograph of H. L. Lewman's Appling County Courthouse at Baxley appeared in *The News,* beneath the caption, "Chattooga County's New Courthouse."

It is easy to see why Lewman's court building at Baxley captured the imagination of Chattooga County leaders. Despite its rather uninspiring form, the building was the only Georgia courthouse of the era to be constructed of limestone. But if the use of limestone

[48] Robert S. Baker, Chattooga County, *A Story of a County and Its People* (Roswell GA: W H Wolfe Associates, 1988) 101

[49] The Summerville News, 1906, in Baker, *Chattooga County, A Story of a County and Its People*, 106.

[50] While the vast majority of the state's court buildings would continue to be constructed of brick, the Falls City Construction Company built several concrete block court buildings in the state including the Jeff Davis County Courthouse at Hazlehurst and the Franklin County Courthouse at Carnesville , both completed in 1906.

[51] Sir John Summerson in Marcus Wiffen, *American Architecture Since 1780* (Cambridge MA: MIT Press, 1969) 99.

distinguished the otherwise ordinary lines of Lewman's courthouse at Baxley, the use of concrete block here at Summerville yielded a rather cold institutional structure, whose lifeless material matched its unimaginative design.[50] Although the grand portico with its richly decorated pediment is an obvious attempt to convey lofty symbols, the building emerged a rather graceless and blocky pile that failed to describe any known classical proportions.

Here in Summerville, we find one of the first of the buildings of a new era of courthouse design in Georgia. This is no longer the architecture of individualism and hope. Like the similar court buildings built by the Falls City Construction Company at Toccoa (1907), Ocilla (1909), and Warrenton (1910), the Chattooga County Courthouse marks the beginning of an architecture of homogeny and resignation. Here is an unemotional symbol for an increasingly detached government.

Like so many Georgia towns at the foot of the mountains, Summerville and neighboring Trion stand as examples of the South's odyssey in the first years of the new century. By 1909, when the new Chattooga County Courthouse was completed, the picture in Summerville might have suggested that the promises of the New South were becoming real. In 1906, the Central of Georgia, which had acquired the Chattanooga, Rome and Columbus in 1901, built a spur from Lyerly, in the western part of Chattooga County, 9 miles to Dewey, Alabama, and in 1911, speculators in Rome completed the Rome and Northern Railroad from Rome to Gore. The county's first cotton mill, erected at Trion back in 1847, survived the Civil War only to burn in 1875. It was rebuilt in 1876, and by 1900 the Trion mill consisted of 3 mills operating 51,000 spindles. In Summerville, local entrepreneur, John D. Taylor built the Summerville Cotton Mill in 1906. But, like so many of the railroads and mills that sprung up in Georgia in the decades surrounding the turn of the century, these were part of a progress, which at its root adhered to a backwardly focused agenda. The prosperity of the New South was to be employed to secure the traditions of the Old. It was recipe for disaster. The great mill at Trion declared bankruptcy in 1911, both the

Rome and Northern and the Central's Lyerly spur were completely abandoned before 1923, and all of John D. Taylor's enterprises in Summerville, including the cotton mill, failed in the early years of the great depression of the 1930s.

WALKER COUNTY: LAFAYETTE

Plate 17.12: The Walker County Courthouse, built in 1883. Demolished 1922. J. B. Patton, builder / architect (attributed).

Originally containing all of present day Dade and Catoosa County, as well as parts of Whitfield and Chattooga, Walker County was created in 1833, and a brick courthouse was erected on the square at LaFayette in 1838. Although this fiercely independent mountainous region had opposed succession in 1861, the old Walker County Courthouse was ironically one of only a few court buildings in Georgia to see action in the Civil War. In June of 1864, Confederate troops repeatedly stormed the old courthouse in an unsuccessful attempt to dislodge its Yankee defenders. The old building survived this violence only to burn to the ground 18 years later. It was replaced by this building in 1883.

As Sir John Summerson so accurately observed, "The use of the term 'vernacular' by historians is a confession of ignorance."[51] Indeed, we know little of

Plate **17.12:** We know little of the 1883 Walker County Courthouse, and our ignorance temps us to call the structure vernacular.

the 1883 Walker County Courthouse, and our ignorance temps us to call the structure vernacular. But despite its simple unadorned lines, records survive that may place the building in the realm of formal architecture. To be sure, the structure had a formal plan, for in March of 1883, a notice in *The Walker County Messenger* invited prospective contractors to view drawings in the office of the County Ordinary. The winning contractor was J. B. Patton of Rome. *The Messenger* goes on to inform readers that a building committee appointed by the County Commissioners had visited Center, Alabama, where a new courthouse was nearing completion, in order to "investigate and suggest plans for a new courthouse" at LaFayette.[52] Inquires in Center, Alabama, reveal that indeed, the Cherokee County Alabama Courthouse burned in 1882 and was replaced in that year. Although no architect is referenced in connection with the construction at Center, we find that the builder was the same J. B. Patton of Rome. Although Mr. Patton's courthouse at Center burned in 1896 and no photographs survive, the obvious inference is that the 1883 Walker County Courthouse was a copy of, or a variation on, the earlier builder-designed court building erected in Alabama. As to whether Mr. Patton's skills as a designer lift the building up and out of the vernacular and into a more self-conscious realm is perhaps more a matter of taste than of history.

Only five years after the completion of Walker County's new courthouse, the Chattanooga, Rome and Columbus Railroad arrived in LaFayette. As we have seen, the power of steel rails to inspire New South zeal in the poor mountainous regions of the state was not so great as it was in the Piedmont. Although the growing of cotton had begun to impact Walker County's economy by the turn of the century, cotton was never king here. In these broad valleys, it was "King Corn," and large portions of area agriculture remained at subsistence levels well in the new century. Likewise, the boom of what little New South progress LaFayette was to enjoy came late. With her population below 350 when the railroad arrived in 1888, and despite the appearance of a locally funded cotton mill only two yeas later, the town continued to languish, counting only 491 residents in 1900. After

the turn of the century, some progress was finally realized, but it was of a modest sort. It was not until 1917 that Walker County began to feel the need for a new courthouse, and by this time the era of New South mythmaking was over.

The new age was at last arriving, and most were beginning to realize that it was to be nothing like the great age of Southern progress and prosperity that Henry Grady and so many others had envisioned. In 1918, the Beaux-Arts facade of Chattanooga architect, C. E. Bearden's, Walker County courthouse rose just a block off the square to announce the stern realities of the modern era. Here is further suggestion that Georgia's courthouses built after 1910 were no longer lavish symbols of individualism and hope. They had become monumental celebrations of growing bureaucracies. The South had always been slow to embrace national architectural trends, but by 1920 she was beginning to accept the new northern styles, and their aggressively materialistic national symbolism.

Although LaFayette had been largely untempted by the myth of the New South, elsewhere in Walker County we find its distinct remains. In the western part of the county on the line of the Chattanooga Southern Railroad, which had been built southward from Chattanooga into Alabama in 1889, the Kensington Land Company began the development of a proposed "industrial metropolis" at tiny Kensington just 22 miles south of Chattanooga. Financed by Northern speculators, many of whom already owned interests in iron and coal resources in the area, Kensington was named for a suburb of Philadelphia. By the end of 1890, investors had erected a water works, an electric light company, a cotton mill and the fabulous Kensington Hotel. In 1892, a fire destroyed the electric light plant and one of the mills, and the development company tumbled into bankruptcy. By 1915, Kensington was a "ghost town."[53]

Meanwhile up the line of the Chattanooga, Rome and Columbus Railroad at Chickamauga, the Crawfish Land Company began a similar development, completing the enormous Park Hotel in 1891. Sadly typhoid was discovered in the water, and the dreams of the Crawfish Land Company were dashed.

The year after the Park Hotel was completed, the Durham Railroad was constructed from the coalmines at Pigeon Mountain to connect with the Chattanooga, Rome and Columbus at Chickamauga.

In the decades following the Civil War, Walker County had remained poor. Her only resource, beyond cheap labor for the mills that rose at LaFayette and Kensington, lay in her rich iron and coal deposits. By 1890, this wealth was being hauled away down the exploiting rails of two shiny new railroads. It is no surprise that, except for the wild and ill-fated dreams at Kensington and at Chickamauga, the luster of the myth of the New South had generally failed to tempt the practical farmers of Walker County. And it is likewise not surprising that the old 1883 Walker County Courthouse remained on the square at LaFayette until 1922, when it was demolished due to its rundown condition. Eventually, even the old square itself would be removed to make way for a highway.

SOME LAST THOUGHTS ON THE COLUMBUS AND ROME AND THE CHATTANOOGA, ROME AND COLUMBUS RAILROADS

Charles Adamson, who built Cedartown's 1896 cotton mill and pioneered the town's development in the last decade of the nineteenth century, described his first impressions of Cedartown as, "a small county village on a railroad running from no place to nowhere…."[54] Indeed in 1890, the Chattanooga, Rome and Columbus Railroad stretched from Chattanooga only as far south as Carrollton, and the ne'er-do-well Columbus and Rome Railroad only reached from Columbus northward to the village of Greenville. Both roads struggled through the 1890s, and a direct connection from Columbus via Rome to Chattanooga would not be realized until 1906 when the Central of Georgia completed the "Raymond Connector" from Newnan to Greenville.

Apt as Mr. Adamson's description may have been, these struggling rail lines were more than enough to import a modest helping of New South zeal to the some of the villages along their right-of-way. The record of courthouse building along the Chattanooga,

Plate 17.13: Carrollton. (Photo: Wilber W. Caldwell.)

Rome and Columbus is particularly noteworthy in this regard. The line supplied a broad highway for the migration of the Romanesque Revival Style. Dalton and Calhoun, both on the Western and Atlantic and connected to Rome by the old Selma, Rome and Dalton Railroad, had erected stunning new Romanesque Revival courthouses around 1890 (the Whitfield County Courthouse, [1891] and the Gordon County Courthouse, [1888]). At about this same time, the rails of the Chattanooga, Rome and Columbus were stretching southward from Rome

[52] *The Walker County Messenger*, March 8, 1883.

[53] Walker County History Committee, *Walker County Heritage* (Dallas GA: Walker County History Committee, 1984) 23.

[54] Charles Adamson in Gordon D. Sargent, "The Legacy of Charles Adamson," in Olin Jackson ed., *The Journal of North Georgia History 3*, 337.

through Cedartown and Buchanan to Carrollton. All four of these towns would erect Romanesque Revival courthouses in the early 1890s: William Parkins's 1890 Polk County Courthouse at Cedartown and Bruce and Morgan's stunning courthouses at Rome (1892), Buchanan (1892) and Carrollton (1893).

Further south along the dead-end line of the Rome and Columbus Railroad, the arrival of visions of a New South would be delayed until the Central of Georgia purchased the old Columbus and Rome Railroad and sparked rumors of an extension of that lonely spur through to Newnan. This and other railroad speculation fired hope in Greenville, and James W. Golucke's Meriwether County Courthouse rose on that square in 1903. The Central built the "Raymond Connector" in 1905-1906, thus completing the long awaited Columbus to Chattanooga link, and Ed Hosford's Harris County Courthouse at Hamilton was completed in 1908.

Only the fiercely independent mountain counties resisted the lure of the myth of railroad-borne prosperity. Walker County's antebellum courthouse had burned in 1883 and was replaced in that same year. Thus, LaFayette already had a new court building when the railroad arrived. Of all of the stops on line, only tiny Summerville ignored the siren of the New South's mythical bounty. Chattooga County may have felt the stirrings of the modern age when the Chattooga County Courthouse was erected in 1909, but this structure voices little of the exuberance of the many earlier court buildings along the rails between Chattanooga and Columbus.

By 1910, the spindles were humming all up and down the line of the Chattanooga, Rome and Columbus, and the picture might have suggested that the dream of a New South was coming true. But as Wilbur Cash notes, "On all sides there was change, but everywhere it was taking place within the lines laid down in the past."[55] It was a recipe for tension. As the forces of social change, inherent in the arrival of industrial progress, met head on with the unbending social fabric of the Old South, there emerged unique-

ly Southern fears. The handmaiden of fear was hate, and in the South, the companion of hate was violence. Thus, the stage was set, not for real progress, but for the demagoguery of Hoke Smith, the fundamentalism of the Scopes trail, and the violence of the Ku Klux Klan.

It would be decades before any of these deep-seated tensions would be relaxed, and by that time, the grand courthouses would be growing old and the New South and its railroads would be all but forgotten. The Central of Georgia discontinued passenger service on the old Chattanooga, Rome and Columbus in 1950, and the line north of Cedartown was dismantled in 1981. Today, although the tracks remain, the rest of the old Chattanooga, Rome and Columbus lies virtually unused. The "Lyerly extension" was abandoned in 1920, and the old Chickamauga and Durham line was scraped in 1951. Likewise farther south, the Central's "Raymond Connector" was pulled up in 1981. All along these rails, few depots remain to recall the dream of a rail connection from Columbus to Rome and of the Central's turn-of-the-century "back door" to Chattanooga.

•

---

[55] W. J. Cash, *The Mind of the South* (1941; reprint, New York: Vintage Books, 1991) 233

18 | The Marietta and North Georgia Railway

CHEROKEE COUNTY: CANTON

Plate 18.1: The Cherokee County Courthouse, built in 1874. Burned 1927. Architect, unknown.

Almost thirty years before the first shells fell on Fort Sumter, Cherokee County had been created to establish the state's jurisdiction over the enormous Cherokee Nation. The discovery of gold in north Georgia in 1829 had added urgency to an already ugly controversy between the Cherokee Indians and the state of Georgia. There followed a period of increased friction, escalated by an epidemic of land grabbing. Even though the formal treaty for removal of the Cherokee Indians would not be signed until 1835, by 1832, Cherokee County had been split into ten new counties and land lotteries had begun. The first court sessions in Cherokee County were held at the tiny hamlet of Etowah, which soon became known as the Cherokee Courthouse. In 1832, the town's name was officially changed to Canton. This name was probably Chinese in origin, a remembrance of the misguided hopes of early entrepreneurs who sought to establish silk production in the area. Dreams of an empire of silk failed to materialize, and Canton's early growth was modest. In 1840, Cherokee County's first courthouse rose on the square in Canton. The two-story brick building was burned by Federal troops in 1864.

Interestingly, and contrary to popular misconceptions, only ten Georgia courthouses were destroyed by Union forces during the Civil War.[1] Here in Canton, we encounter one of those relatively rare instances. In response to guerrilla activity in the area, Union troops burned a large portion of Canton in May of 1864. The extent of the damage is a matter of some disagreement, and although some sources insist that "only two or three houses were left standing," other accounts maintain that only about half of the town was destroyed.[2] Whatever the case, it would be ten years before Canton recov-

---

[1] Federal forces destroyed the courthouses at Darien, Cassville, Canton, Marietta, Jonesboro, Jackson, Irwinton, Sandersville, Statesboro, and possibly Cedartown.

[2] Lloyd G. Marlin, *The History of Cherokee County* (Atlanta: Walter W. Brown Publishing Co., 1932) 77-8.

The Marietta and North Georgia Railway

Cobb County, Marietta (see chapter 4) • Cherokee County: Canton • Pickens County: Jasper
Gilmer County: Ellijay • Fannin County: Blue Ridge

THE ATLANTA, KNOXVILLE AND NORTHERN RAILROAD
Murray County: Chatsworth • Some Last Thoughts on the Marietta and North Georgia Railway

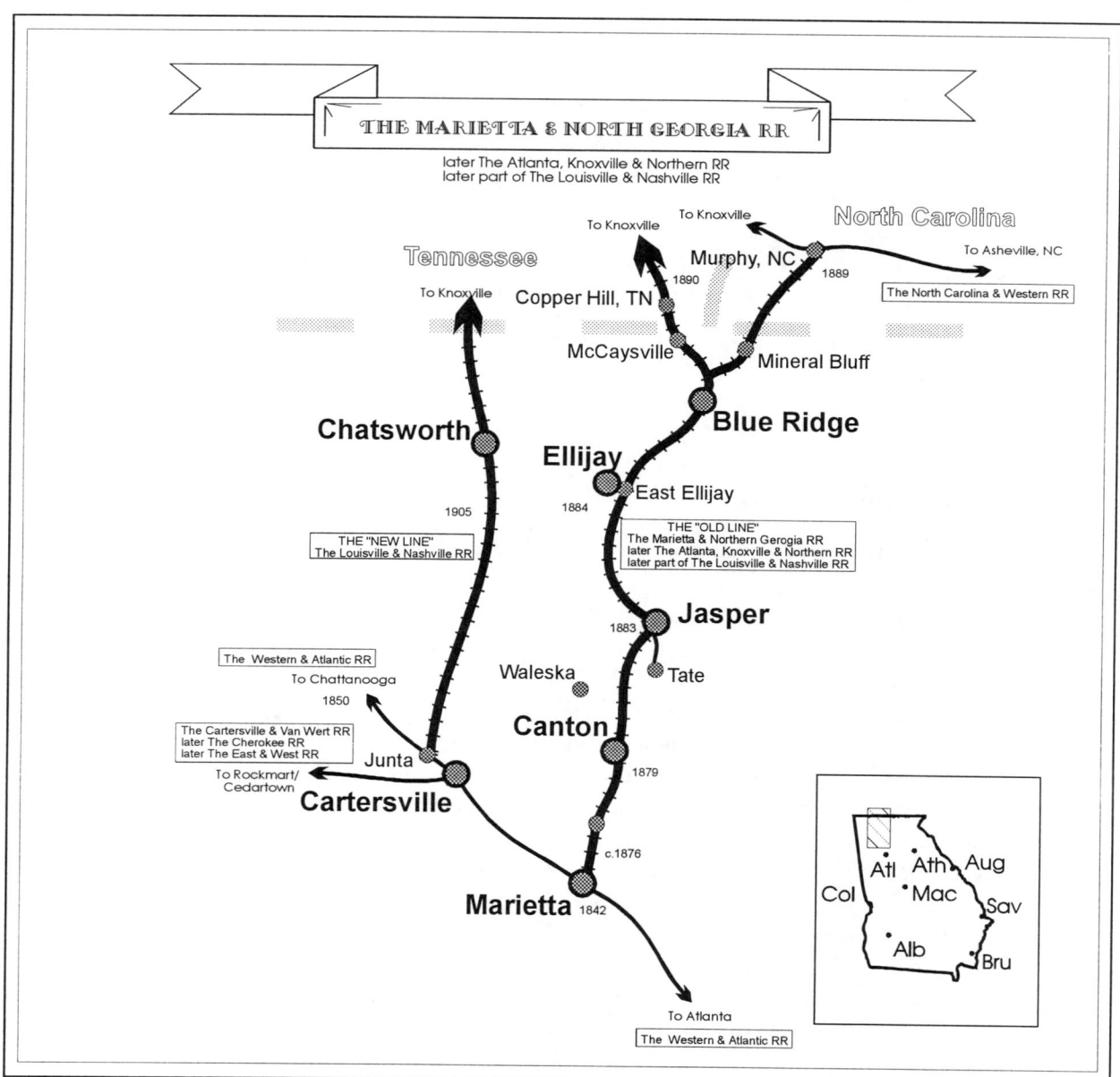

THE MARIETTA & NORTH GEORGIA RR

later The Atlanta, Knoxville & Northern RR
later part of The Louisville & Nashville RR

North Carolina

Tennessee

To Knoxville
To Knoxville

To Asheville, NC

Murphy, NC
1890
1889

The North Carolina & Western RR

To Knoxville

Copper Hill, TN

McCaysville

Mineral Bluff

Blue Ridge

Chatsworth

Ellijay
1884

East Ellijay

1905

THE "NEW LINE"
The Louisville & Nashville RR

THE "OLD LINE"
The Marietta & Northern Gerogia RR
later The Atlanta, Knoxville & Northern RR
later part of The Louisville & Nashville RR

Jasper
1883

The Western & Atlantic RR

To Chattanooga
1850

Waleska

Tate

The Cartersville & Van Wert RR
later The Cherokee RR
later The East & West RR

Junta

Canton

1879

To Rockmart/
Cedartown

Cartersville

c.1876

Marietta 1842

Atl Ath Aug
Col Mac Sav
Alb Bru

To Atlanta

The Western & Atlantic RR

Plate 18.1: The 1874 Cherokee County Courthouse may well have been the work of a trained architect whose name has been lost in the dusty labyrinths of history. (Photo: Courtesy Mr. Herman Cantrell)

ered sufficiently to rebuild her courthouse. The 1874 Cherokee County Courthouse was one of 44 courthouses erected in Georgia between 1866 and 1880. Of these, twenty were of brick. Ten still stand today (see Appendix A).

Most of these brick buildings reflected simple designs, with the notable exception of two Second Empire court buildings: G. P. Randall's fine 1872 Bibb County Courthouse at Macon and Henri Chamberlain's less imposing 1876 Clarke County Courthouse at Athens. With regard to the remaining twenty-two brick courthouses of the early post-war period, there is record of an architect or a skilled designer only at Jonesboro (1869), Marietta (1873) and Jefferson (1879). The remaining courthouses must be considered builder-designed vernacular buildings. Nonetheless a few, like this building at Canton, suggest professional architectural planning.

The 1874 Cherokee County Courthouse may well have been the work of a trained architect whose name has been lost in the dusty labyrinths of history. The mansard roofed clock tower, although a crude affair, points to more sophisticated stylistic influence as do the broken based pediments which crown the four distinct entrance bays. Still in 1874, before the construction of the Marietta and North Georgia Railway, Canton was a remote place, and the presence

of formal architecture in isolated areas was rare in Georgia before 1880.

This isolation lies at the center of Canton's history before the arrival of the railroad, and around the end of this isolation the story of the New South, both real and imagined, revolves. Canton was a little over fifteen years old when the town first dreamed of rail connections. In 1846, the Etowah and Blue Ridge Railroad was chartered, followed by the Etowah Railroad in 1847. Nothing came of these efforts. In 1854, the Ellijay Railroad was chartered to run northward through Canton from Marietta. This scheme also sputtered before any real progress was made. Four years later, expectations centered on the rekindling of earlier ambitions and on the charter of the Marietta, Canton and Ellijay Railroad, whose plans were eclipsed by the Civil War.

By 1874, when Cherokee County's courthouse was finally rebuilt, Canton had a population of between two and three hundred, and the town's railroad dreams had been resurrected. At the same time, the possibility of navigation on the Etowah River between Canton and Rome was also given serious consideration.[3] Well before the rails arrived in Canton, the rhetoric of the New South began to spew forth from *The Cherokee Georgian*. Aspirations must have been soaring in 1875, when the editor declared,

Build this railroad and then will come schools, mills, factories, furnaces, etc.: the people will become vitalized anew, and the country will become what God intended it to be. Build this railroad and the population will double...all of our misfortunes will pass away; we will be united by ligaments of steel, floods of light and life will break upon us, and old Georgia will once more be proud, grand and free.[4]

In 1870, the Marietta, Canton and Ellijay Railroad had received the state's endorsement of its bonds, and shortly thereafter the name was changed to the Marietta and North Georgia Railway. Despite

[3] *The Cherokee Georgian* (Canton GA), September 29, 1875.

[4] *The Cherokee Georgian* (Canton GA), September, 23, 1875.

high hopes, the state's endorsement and the extensive use of leased convict labor supplied by the state, progress was excruciatingly slow. With subscriptions from Cobb, Cherokee, Pickens, Gilmer and Fannin Counties, the flimsy narrow-gauge line began construction in the mid-1870s and reached Canton in 1879. It would be 1884 before the tracks reached Ellijay and five more years before the rails were complete to Murphy, North Carolina.

In 1890, the Knoxville Southern, a Tennessee Company operated by the Marietta and North Georgia Railway, completed its line from Etowah, Tennessee, through Copperhill, to a connection with the Marietta and North Georgia just north of Blue Ridge. Although this completed an important rail link between Atlanta and Knoxville, the route was a torturous nightmare of sharp curves and steep grades, incorporating a series of switchbacks in the mountains north of Copperhill. Even though tracks were converted to standard gauge in 1889, the line remained of limited economic value and was forced into bankruptcy in 1891. It was reorganized as the Atlanta, Knoxville and Northern Railroad in 1895, and sold to the Louisville and Nashville Railroad in 1902. Three years later, traffic to Knoxville was stolen away by a new line constructed by the L&N from near Cartersville northward through Chatsworth. Through it all, and despite desperate struggles and countless misfortunes, the rickety mountain rails of the Marietta and North Georgia would be heralded as nothing less than an economic miracle in Canton.

Plate 18.2: Although the old depot at Canton is gone, this fine depot built in by the L&N 1912 still stands today at nearby Woodstock. (Photo: Wilber W. Caldwell.)

Plate 18.2: The depot at Woodstock, built in 1912.

The old depot at Canton is gone. But along the old rails of the Marietta and North Georgia Railway, several fine L&N depots remain to remind us of the power of this first frail and treacherous connection to Knoxville and of the promises it delivered to the remote mountains of northwest Georgia. Only a few miles south of Canton, we find this 1912 depot at Woodstock in Cherokee County. Its almost identical sister at Ellijay in Gilmer County was built in the same year.

Most mountain counties were slow to accept the flashy wares of the New South myth, but in Canton, where high expectations had prevailed, the arrival of steel rails brought considerable change. Despite derailments and delays on the flimsy narrow gauge line's serpentine roadbed, the mail began to arrive daily in Canton, instead of on Tuesdays and Saturdays as in the pre-railroad era.[5] According to *The Cherokee Advance,* in 1884, five years after achieving her rail connection, Canton had added or improved "69 dwellings, 13 stores, 4 warehouses, 2 steam gins, 3 steam flour grist mills,…depot, jail, church, schoolhouse, feed stable, steam saw mill," and various other commercial structures.[6] All the while, spirits remained high on the prospects for an east-west line through Cherokee County. The Kingston, Waleska and Gainesville Railroad was chartered in 1881, and although this line was never built, it continued to spark hope in the Georgia foothills throughout the 1880s. By 1890, Canton's population had reached 654, nearly doubling in the ten years since the arrival of the Marietta and North Georgia. The Bank of Canton was established in 1892, and in that same year, local entrepreneurs opened the Georgia Marble Finishing Works. By this time, considerable New South passion had been kindled in Canton, and in 1899 local investors established the Canton Textile Mills. Twenty five years later, a second mill was added, and over 1100 textile workers toiled at Canton, whose population had soared past 2000 by 1910.

Sadly Canton would witness the rise and fall of all of these industries. Nonetheless, their existence surely suggests the presence of a progressive spirit and represents a small step toward modern progress. We can only speculate that, had Cherokee County not constructed a new courthouse on the very eve of the railroad's arrival, a grand monument to the myth of the new South might have risen at Canton. As it turned out, the simple 1874 Cherokee County Courthouse would serve the county until it burned in 1929. At that time, Atlanta architect, A. Ten Eyck Brown's, new white marble Renaissance Revival Courthouse was already under construction. It is a unique building of considerable distinction, but the story is that of a later time, and is not within the scope of this study.

PICKENS COUNTY: JASPER

Plate 18.3: The Pickens County Courthouse, built in 1888. Burned 1947. Bruce and Morgan, architects.

After Pickens County was created from Cherokee and Gilmer Counties in 1853 and the location of the county seat had been fixed at Jasper, construction of a brick courthouse began almost immediately. It took over six years to complete the building. The reasons for delays in construction do not come down to us, but surely they reflect hard times, and a slow-paced subsistence agrarian life in this remote region. In 1860, the county's population was below 6000. There were few slaves here, and cotton production was nil. The 1860 Census reports that only ten bales of cotton were produced in the entire county. By 1880, this figure was only a little over 700 bales while neighboring Cherokee County produced a respectable 5500 bales. In short, prosperity was a stranger in Pickens County, and with this backdrop, it is not difficult to imagine the atmosphere in Jasper when the rails of the Marietta and North Georgia arrived in 1883.

It had taken the Marietta and North Georgia Railway four years to build the 20 miles from Canton to Jasper, still the road's arrival in Jasper was met with enthusiasm. Small quantities of marble had been quarried in the area since the early 1840s, and with the arrival of the railroad, large scale exploitation of the county's great marble deposits began. Just as the arrival of steel rails would generate the great granite quarries of Elbert County and spawn Reuben Hunt's stunning

Plate 18.3: Alexander Bruce's 1888 Pickens County Courthouse at Jasper. Even in the heart of stone's inter-most keep the courthouse would be built of brick. (Photo: Courtesy of Ted Brooke.)

1894 Elbert County Courthouse at Elberton, farther to the west, new rails would give birth to the marble quarries of Pickens County and to Alexander Bruce's 1888 Pickens County Courthouse at Jasper. It is interesting to note that, even in the heart of the stone industry, both of these counties built courthouses out of brick, not stone. There were few exceptions to the unwritten code, which seemed to mandate that courthouses built in Georgia before 1910 were to be constructed of brick.

Only four years after the arrival of the Marietta and North Georgia Railway, speculation centered on the fable that the Augusta and Chattanooga Railroad would build through Pickens County. In Jasper, waves of New South zeal crested, and in 1887 plans for a new courthouse materialized just as *The Cherokee Advance* reported that: "The surveyors of the Augusta and Chattanooga Railroad are now in Pickens County. This road will cross the Marietta and Northern Georgia at Talking Rock, its building will prove a great developer of Pickens County. About six miles of railroad is also being surveyed to Tate."[7]

Despite the considerable zeal for the construction of a new courthouse that blossomed in the hothouse of railroad dreams at Jasper, there is no record of the architect here. Only a few old newspapers of the peri-

[5] *The Cherokee Georgian* (Canton GA), August 15, 1875.

[6] *The Cherokee Advance* (Canton GA), January 3, 1884.

[7] *The Cherokee Advance* in The Ellijay Courier, Augusta 4, 1887.

od survive. But only two years after the Pickens County Courthouse was completed, Bruce and Morgan virtually duplicated this building at Camilla with their 1890 Mitchell County Courthouse. Except for a few minor details, the two buildings appear to have been identical. Such similarity supplies ample authority to attribute the 1888 Pickens County Courthouse at Jasper to Bruce and Morgan.

Indeed, Bruce's touch is unmistakable. The building bears a marked similarity to the architect's very first courthouse design, the 1871 Loudon County Courthouse, which still stands in Loudon, Tennessee. In addition, Bruce's plan here at Jasper is similar to his earlier Second Empire courthouses at Sparta, Monroe and Gainesville. Gone are the lavish Parisian details, and in their place we find brick corbeling decorating the cornice, flat unadorned exterior walls and a simple pediment with an uncomplicated fanlight. Bruce's 1890 Mitchell Count Courthouse had a central clock tower with a multifaceted dome similar to the architect's tower designs at Sparta and Gainesville. Old photographs reveal a substantial, flat-roofed pedestal at the crown of the old Pickens County Courthouse,

and it is probably safe to assume that this building once had a similar tower, although no early photographs survive to confirm such speculation.

Architecturally the Spartan lines of Alexander Bruce's 1888 Pickens County Courthouse may not have fully reflected the euphoria of New South passion expressed by many Georgia court buildings of the era. Nonetheless, it replaced the county's first courthouse, which was less than thirty years old when it was destroyed. In the conservative mountain air of Pickens County, Bruce's building must have appeared a wildly expressive and fanciful monument to a new age of industry and rail.

Plate 18.4: The depot at Jasper, built in 1905.

When the L&N acquired the Atlanta, Knoxville and Northern Railroad in 1902, the purchase included the old rails of the Marietta and North Georgia Railway, which had become part of the Atlanta, Knoxville and Northern in 1895. Almost immediately the L&N began to replace the old depots up and down the line. One of the first of the L&N's new generation of depots was this fine station at Jasper. Ironically, just as this building was completed, the L&N opened its "New Line" to Knoxville from Cartersville up through Chatsworth. The serpentine rails of "The Old Line" from Marietta through Canton, Jasper, Ellijay and Blue Ridge were no longer the L&N's main artery to Knoxville.

This depot looks back down a railroad with a checkered history. In the post-war era, the driving force behind the old Marietta and North Georgia Railway was General William Phillips of Marietta. Phillips was a well-known and powerful figure in Georgia, and he undoubtedly played a substantial role in the acquisition of the state's endorsement of the road's bonds and in the acquisition of convict labor from the state.

The line's use of convict labor is well documented. In 1875, all convict leases to the Marietta and North Georgia Railway were revoked after the line had attempted to divide work gangs, farm out convict laborers as agricultural workers and march fifty convicts 130 miles south to plantations on the Flint River in Taylor County.[8] The reason for the division of

Plate 18.4: The 1905 L&N depot at Jasper looks back down a railroad with a checkered history. (Photo: Wilber W. Caldwell.)

[8] Judson Clements Ward, Jr., *Georgia Under the Bourbon Democrats* (Chapel Hill: University of North Carolina Press, 1947) 385.

[9] Mike McKinney in Dale Dyer Jones, *Facts of Fannin, The History of Fannin County* (Dallas GA: Curtis Media, 1989) 41.

[10] Ward, Jr., *Georgia Under the Bourbon Democrats* (Chapel Hill, 1947), 384-88.

this labor force is not known, but accounts in Fannin County contend that in the early years of the line's construction, funds were so scarce that there was not always food for the convict workers. Thus, foremen were forced to hire them out for work in copper mines at Ducktown, Tennessee.[9] In 1875, short-term leases were being blamed for the many abuses within the convict lease system in Georgia including extremely high escape and death rates among the convicts. Reform of the system was attempted in 1876. Curiously, the new Act also provided that the state furnish, free of charge, 250 convicts for work on the Marietta and North Georgia Railway for a period of three years. This portion of the Act was declared unconstitutional by the Georgia Supreme Court in 1883, but the line continued to work convicts until 1884.[10]

The use of convict labor to build so many of Georgia's postbellum railroads recalls a dark chapter in the state's railroad history. Although convicts were not widely used for railroad construction after 1890, the state of Georgia would continue to lease convict laborers to private contractors until the system was finally abolished in 1908, three years after this depot was constructed at Jasper.

GILMER COUNTY: ELLIJAY

Plate 18.5: The depot at Ellijay, built in 1912.

Among the last of the old Marietta and Northern Georgia depots to be replaced along the "Old Line" from Atlanta to Knoxville, was the depot at Ellijay. In 1912, ten years after the L &N acquired the rickety line, sister depots rose at Ellijay and Woodstock. Typical of the L&N's rather traditional depot style, this building was erected just in time to hear the final gasp of New South passion aroused by the railroad in Gilmer County.

In 1884, the arrival of the Marietta and North Georgia Railway at Ellijay had marked the end of a long period of waiting. As early as 1876, convicts had graded 30 miles of roadbed in Gilmer County,[11] but it would be eight more years before the railroad would reach Ellijay. There followed a brief boom, and the town's population reached 437 in 1890. But fol-

Plate 18.5: The L&N's 1912 depot at Ellijay was erected just in time to hear the final gasp of dwindling New South passion aroused by the railroad in Gilmer County. (Photo: Wilber W. Caldwell.)

lowing this initial surge, growth was slow. Twenty-two years later, as this depot rose, Ellijay counted only about 600 residents with another 200 or 300 in the adjoining village of East Ellijay, which had sprung up beside the railroad.

Plate 18.6: The Hyatt Hotel, built in 1898. Converted for use as the Gilmer County Courthouse in 1934.

Created in 1832, Gilmer County was one of ten counties carved from Cherokee County, which had been created from the vast lands of the "Cherokee Nation." A log courthouse was erected at Ellijay in 1833. Although the building had dirt floors in the rooms adjoining courtroom, it served the remote mountain county for over twenty years. In 1837, Adiel Sherwood described Ellijay as a village of twenty dwellings and three stores, and according to George White's *Statistics of the State of Georgia* the town had a population of only about 300 in 1849. In 1854, a brick courthouse replaced the old log structure. With its great parapets terminating the roofline, it was similar to the 1860 White County Courthouse at Cleveland. Times were hard in Gilmer County in the decades surrounding the Civil War and this is made clear by the fact that the county was unable to pay for its new courthouse. The builder finally resorted to legal action in 1877. Twenty-three years after the 1854 Gilmer County Courthouse was completed, the

Plate 18.6: The Gilmer County Courthouse was fashioned from the old Hyatt Hotel in 1934. (Photo: Wilber W. Caldwell.)

Plate 18.7: Between Blue Ridge and Murphy, North Carolina, this old depot at Mineral Bluff is all that is left of the original nineteenth century depots built by the Marietta and North Georgia Railway. (Photo: Wilber W. Caldwell.)

builder won his judgment and was eventually paid his fee along with considerable accrued interest.[12]

The old 1854 brick vernacular court building would serve the county for eighty years only to be replaced by a converted hotel. This building stands in bold contrast to the grand new courthouses that rose at Jasper and Blue Ridge after the arrival of the Marietta and North Georgia Railway. Jasper reacted quickly to the promise of her new railroad and to hope for the crossing rails of the Augusta and Chattanooga. Blue Ridge was born of the railroad, quickly became a junction town and captured the county seat away from bypassed Morganton only a few years after her birth. But with little hope for crossing rails, no great natural resources except her timber, and only the subsistence agriculture of an impoverished mountain county, Gilmer was not tempted to believe in the New South myth. After a movement for a new courthouse fizzled in 1901, the town would make do with her old 1854 brick court building for another thirty-four years. Then in the heart of the depression, unable to afford a new building, she would again have to "make do," this time with the old hotel. It is interesting to note that in remodeling the old building for use as a courthouse, the wooden porches of the Hyatt Hotel were removed and the obligatory columns of Neoclassical Revival were applied. The columns of the Old South were still very much in vogue well into the hardships of the twentieth century.

FANNIN COUNTY: BLUE RIDGE

Plate 18.7: The depot at Mineral Bluff, built c. 1890.

This charming brick depot at Mineral Bluff, between Blue Ridge and Murphy, North Carolina, is all that is left of the original nineteenth century depots built by the Marietta and North Georgia Railway. After acquiring the line in 1902, the L&N replaced most of the early depots with new buildings like those we find today in Woodstock, Jasper, Tate, Ellijay, and Blue Ridge. The survival of this little depot is dramatic testimony to the secondary status of the branch from Blue Ridge to Murphy. Originally intended as the main line to Knoxville, plans for the route beyond

Murphy were scrapped in the late 1880s after the builders of the Knoxville and Southern Railroad (a Tennessee corporation controlled by the Marietta and North Georgia) found that the right-of-way west of Murphy had already been secured by a forerunner of the North Carolina and Western Railroad.[13]

With this dead-end at Murphy, a new route to Knoxville had to be found. Capitalizing on earlier plans to build from the East Tennessee, Virginia and Georgia Railroad's mainline south of Knoxville to the copper mines at Copperhill, Tennessee, the Knoxville Southern embarked upon one of the wildest journeys in American railroad engineering history. North of Copperhill, the mountain terrain presented engineers with a series of challenges. The most formidable of these was the descent into the Hiawassee River valley, a feat that was first accomplished by a series of switch-backs that severely limited train length. This limitation proved economically unworkable, and in 1891, only a year after the first train ran from Blue Ridge to Knoxville, the Marietta and North Georgia declared bankruptcy. Reorganized in 1895 as the Atlanta, Knoxville and Northern Railroad, the new company replaced the switchbacks with the ingenious "Hiawassee Loop" in 1898. Descending by circling Bald Mountain, the road crossed over itself and circled the mountain again in order to reach the river valley. All of this was accomplished only a few years before the L&N acquired the line, and began construction of the "New Line" to perfect its link between Cincinnati and Atlanta. This connection would render the Georgia portion of the "Old Line" through Blue Ridge all but obsolete.

Plate 18.8: The Fannin County Courthouse at Morganton, built in 1855.

This unusual courthouse with its great flaring square columns and crude clerestory was constructed around 1855 at Morganton, the original county seat of Fannin County. Cut from Gilmer and Union Counties in 1854, Fannin County remained a remote wilderness until 1886 when the Marietta and North Georgia Railway arrived at the place that was soon to be called Blue Ridge. Laid out in 1887 at an elevation above 1700 feet, Blue Ridge boasted the highest depot

Plate 18.8: The 1855 Fannin County Courthouse at the old county seat at Morganton.

in Georgia. As lots were sold in the new town, the line pressed northward, arriving at Murphy, North Carolina, in 1888. By 1890, with their junction just north of Blue Ridge, rails to both Murphy and Knoxville were operational, and the new town counted 264 residents.

Plate 18.9: The Fannin County Courthouse at Blue Ridge, built in 1901. Burned 1936. James W. Golucke, architect.

As the first buildings rose at Blue Ridge, there was agitation to relocate the county seat. As early as 1887, *The Ellijay Courier* called Blue Ridge "The Coming City of the Skies" and speculated: "In the case the courthouse is ever removed to any point on the Marietta and North Georgia Railway, Blue Ridge will be the most suitable location, and the founders of the town could not have appropriated a more desirable spot than the plot of ground they so generously offer, which...affords ample room for all of the public buildings of the county."[14]

By the mid-1890s, a considerable battle raged over the site of the Fannin County seat. In September

---

[11] George Gordon Ward, Jr., *The Annals of Upper Georgia* (1965; reprint, Nashville: Parthenon Press, 1974) 354.

[12] Ward, Jr., *The Annals of Upper Georgia*, 449.

[13] R. E. Barkley, *The Railroad Comes to Ducktown* (Knoxville GA: n.p., 1973) 128-29.

[14] *The Ellijay Courier*, September 30, 1887.

Plate 18.9: Until it burned in 1936 James Golucke's 1901 Fannin County Courthouse stood to remind Blue Ridge of its brief flirtation with the capricious New South. (Photo: Courtesy of Ted Brooke.)

of 1895, seeking to secure Morgantown's position as the center of county government, county leaders accepted plans for a new courthouse at Morganton by Atlanta architect, Andrew J. Bryan.[15] This building was never built, for shortly thereafter, Blue Ridge won her bid for the county seat. In 1900, with her population swollen to an incredible 1148, James Wingfield Golucke's wildly ornate Fannin County Courthouse began to rise in Blue Ridge. It was in many ways a copy of Golucke's 1900 Clayton County Courthouse at Jonesboro, which had been completed shortly after the Fannin County Courthouse at Blue Ridge was begun. The flowery ornament of the 1901 Fannin County Courthouse is perhaps the best mirror we have to reflect the wild aspirations that swirled about

Plate 18.10: The 1887 Murray County Courthouse at Spring Place was one of the last brick vernacular courthouses to be built in Georgia. (Photo: Courtesy of the Georgia Dept. of Archives & History.)

the streets of Blue Ridge at the turn of the century. Golucke's fundamentally Romanesque form was decorated with classical exuberance. At the heart of the decoration is a bold polychrome achieved through the use of light colored rusticated stone quoining, keystones and window splays.

Sadly, Blue Ridge's boom was short-lived, and the flamboyant decoration of James Golucke's 1901 Fannin County Courthouse would quickly come to represent yet another irony. With the 1905 completion of the L&N's "New Line" to Knoxville from Cartersville via Chatsworth, Georgia, and Etowah, Tennessee, Blue Ridge's population had dipped below 400 by 1910. It had been a wild ride on a rickety mountain railroad. James Golucke's courthouse stood to remind the village of its brief flirtation with the capricious New South until it burned in 1936.

MURRAY COUNTY: CHATSWORTH

Plate 18.10: The Murray County Courthouse at Spring Place, built in 1887. Demolished in the 1980s.

Murray County was the largest and the least populous of the ten counties cut from the vast expanses of Cherokee County in 1832. The original boundaries of Cherokee County included all of Walker, Whitfield, Gordon, Dade, Catoosa, Murray, and Fannin and parts of Bartow and Gilmer Counties. The first court was held in the old 1805 Moravian Mission at Spring Place near the plantation of James Vann, a trader and farmer who had settled in the "Cherokee Nation" before 1800. By 1839, agitation for a proper courthouse began, and a brick building "like the one at Cassville" was completed at Spring Place sometime around 1843.[16] The simple structure served the county until it burned in 1884. In 1887, it was replaced by this three-story court building, one of the last brick vernacular courthouses to be erected in Georgia. Except for the high mansard roof enclosing the upper story, this building, with its bracketed eaves and bold brick pilasters, resembles the 1874 Bartow County Courthouse at Cartersville.

Despite the fact that the county's first railroad scheme, the Murray County Mining and Railroad

Company, had failed to get beyond the planning stages back in the 1875, by 1887, when this courthouse was completed, the atmosphere in Spring Place was charged with railroad speculation. At that time, it appeared that the Augusta and Chattanooga Railroad would build through the village, and in 1888 *The North Georgia Citizen* was advocating a locally financed railroad from Dalton to Spring Place.[17] Neither of these roads were built, and Spring Place remained a village of only about 200 residents. But by the turn of the century, the town was again afire with railroad-fueled aspirations as the Dalton and Alaculsey Railroad began grading from Dalton via Spring Place to Murphy, North Carolina. In 1902, as grading neared completion, the usual speculations appeared. A letter from a north Georgia resident survives to attest to the spirit instilled by the prospect of rails in Murray County: "It has been said that Spring Place was finished, but it is booming now with a first class school, livery stable, telephone, big flour mill, cotton gin, railroad, and lots of things we never dreamed of…"[18] This may not sound like the stuff of modern industrial dreams, but, more often than not in these rural places, the promises of the New South appeared disarmingly modest. Indeed, they were often more a testament to the poverty of the region than to the limitation of the myth. In truth, the prospect of schools and stables and gins constituted high hopes for many Georgians in 1900. But in Spring Place, as elsewhere, these promises proved hollow, and hopes were dashed as the Dalton and Alaculsey Railroad failed before any track was laid.

Plate 18.11: The Murray County Courthouse, built in 1916. Alexander Blair, architect.

Although Alexander Blair's 1916 Murray County Courthouse rose at Chatsworth well after the end of the period of our interest, this building and the circumstances surrounding its construction deserve inclusion here for several reasons. First, this was the seventh and last Georgia courthouse designed by Macon architect, Alexander Blair III, the son of Macon's pre-eminent architect of the 1880s, Alexander Blair II (see Appendix C). Second, the creation of the city of Chatsworth is one of the last in a

Plate 18.11: Alexander Blair's fine 1916 Murray County Courthouse at Chatsworth is perhaps the last of a long line of Georgia courthouses that reflect the stubborn pride and blind hope, which accompanied so many innocent aspirations for progress. (Photo: Wilber W. Caldwell.)

long saga of railroad-created county towns in Georgia. The story of Chatsworth's battle to wrestle the county seat away from Spring Place is reminiscent of similar battles that had been fought all across the state in the preceding decades. Last, unlike so many of the court buildings erected in Georgia after 1910, Alexander Blair's Murray County Courthouse at Chatsworth is an architectural reflection of the exuberance, aspirations and hope that typified the late nineteenth century and the first decade of the twentieth century when the myth of the New South shone like a beacon. Like so many earlier court buildings, it symbolized a hope born of a railroad that promised a path up and out of the poverty that shackled the region.

The "Old Line" of the L&N, had been built from Marietta via Blue Ridge to Knoxville by the Marietta and North Railroad between the mid-1870s and 1890. Later called the Atlanta, Knoxville and Northern, the line was a characterized by sharp turns and steep grades. As the new century began, the L&N planned a main trunk railroad from Atlanta to Cincinnati. It was a modern version of the dreams of

---

[15] *The Manufacturer's Record*, September 13, 1895.

[16] Murray County Historical Society, *Murray County Heritage* (Roswell GA: Murray County Historical Society, 1987) 56.

[17] The North Georgia Citizen, September 20, 1888, in *Murray County Historical Society*, Murray County Heritage, 98-99.

Georgia's earliest railroads. In the late 1830s, the merchants of Athens, Augusta and Charleston had hungrily eyed railroad schemes emanating from Cincinnati. In 1905, work began on the L&N's latter day reincarnation of this old dream, and the "New Line" was graded up from Junta just north of Cartersville on the Western and Atlantic Railroad, to Etowah, Tennessee. The completion of this modern railroad with its sweeping curves and gentle grades rendered the precarious "Old Line" a nearly forgotten "local" railroad, and created great excitement in the long valley west of the Cohutta Mountains.

The story of the birth of Chatsworth is apocryphal in the context of the railroad's power to create towns. Here the Chatsworth Land Company had not only secured property along the "New Line" and laid out town lots, but had even gone so far as to erect a brick yard and three lumber companies to furnish materials for the town that speculators knew would rise. In an equally foresighted and bold move, an entire block was left open and designated "Reserved for Courthouse Square."[19] Among the first buildings to rise at Chatsworth was the L&N's fine frame depot. It still stands today in stunning restoration only two blocks off the square. Founded in 1906, Chatsworth's population had reached 314 by 1910, while Spring Place languished only three miles away, her population only 194 and falling as residents moved to the new town beside the railroad.

The battle for the county seat began in 1912. It would take four years to resolve the question. Finally in 1913, Chatsworth won the day, but a new battle then flared up over the erection and financing of a new courthouse. An injunction was sought to delay the collection of taxes to pay for a new building at Chatsworth, and along the way the county commissioners were briefly jailed for contempt of court. Emotions ran high in Murray County. Here is a very late artifact pointing to the divided mind of rural Georgia, the conflict between Old South and New, between town and county, between tradition and progress.

The forces of tradition had, as always, fought well. Alexander Blair's fine 1916 Murray County Courthouse is perhaps the last in a long line of Georgia courthouses to reflect the stubborn pride and blind hope which accompanied so many innocent aspirations for progress. The great octagonal dome is unique in Georgia, and the grand portico with its high balustrade looks out across an enormous square to the peaks of the high Cohutta Mountains. Indeed, it is the site, as much as the design that makes this a compelling public building.

SOME LAST THOUGHTS ON THE MARIETTA AND NORTH GEORGIA RAILWAY

The story of the Marietta and North Georgia Railway typifies the history of so many of Georgia's railroads of the postbellum period. Born of purely local passions and built to further the economic interests of Cobb, Cherokee, Pickens, Gilmer and Fannin Counties, the narrow gauge mountain railroad struggled to secure funding, struggled to lay track and then struggled to survive. With the early aid of state endorsed bonds, the line was financed primarily by local subscriptions from the counties it served. Grading began in the mid-1870s and was accomplished largely using convict labor leased from the state. Progress was excruciatingly slow. Rails finally reached Blue Ridge in 1886 and did not arrive in Murphy, North Carolina until 1888. In the meantime, early operations were sluggish, and as finances deteriorated, Northern capitalists acquired control of the company, planning an extension to Knoxville, Tennessee.

With the widening of the rails to standard gauge in 1889 and the completion of a rickety connection between Blue Ridge and Knoxville in 1890, the line began to take on a more regional character, as the first direct link between Atlanta and Knoxville. But the Marietta and North Georgia was not built as a main trunk railroad. Grades were steep, curves were severe and despite her strategic connection, the line fell on hard times and failed in the economic turbulence that preceded the Panic of 1893. Reorganized out of bankruptcy in 1895 as the Atlanta, Knoxville and Northern Railroad, the new company was acquired by the Louisville and Nashville Railroad in 1902. Thus, the

Marietta and North Georgia had run the familiar gauntlet, from local servant to exploitive corporate giant.

Along the way the road had inspired its fair share of New South passion and grand aspirations in the otherwise conservative mountain country of north Georgia. This spirit was reflected at Jasper with the completion of Bruce and Morgan's 1888 Pickens County Courthouse, and in Blue Ridge, a town created by the railroad, where James Golucke's Fannin County Courthouse rose in 1901. In Canton, spirits also ran high, but Cherokee County had completed a new courthouse on the very eve of the railroad's arrival. Only tiny Ellijay failed to catch the fever. There a new courthouse movement sputtered in 1901, and the town utilized the 1854 courthouse until 1934.

The last page in the story of the Marietta and North Georgia Railway is equally typical. It illustrates the capricious nature of the myth of the New South and its railroad purveyors. In 1905, the L&N built the "New Line" from Atlanta to Knoxville, and the "Old Line" through Canton, Jasper, Ellijay and Blue Ridge once again became a local affair. The boomtown of Blue Ridge, whose population had reached almost 1200 in 1900, was reduced to a village of fewer than 400 by 1910. Across the mountains to the west, along the L&N's "New Line," the village of Chatsworth appeared in Murray County, to steal the county seat away from the venerable Spring Place and employ Macon's Alexander Blair III to design the last of Georgia's great fantasy courthouses in 1916.

•

[18] Martha Durham to Mrs. Richard Bramblett, January 18, 1902, in Murray County Historica Society, *Murray County Heritage*, 100.

[19] Murray County Historical Society, *Murray County Heritage*, 411

The Atlanta and Florida Railroad

Fulton County: Atlanta (see chapters 4, 11, 26 & 32) • Fayette County: Fayetteville
Pike County: Zebulon • Crawford County: Knoxville • Peach County: Fort Valley (see chapter 6)
Some Last Thoughts on the Atlanta and Florida Railroad

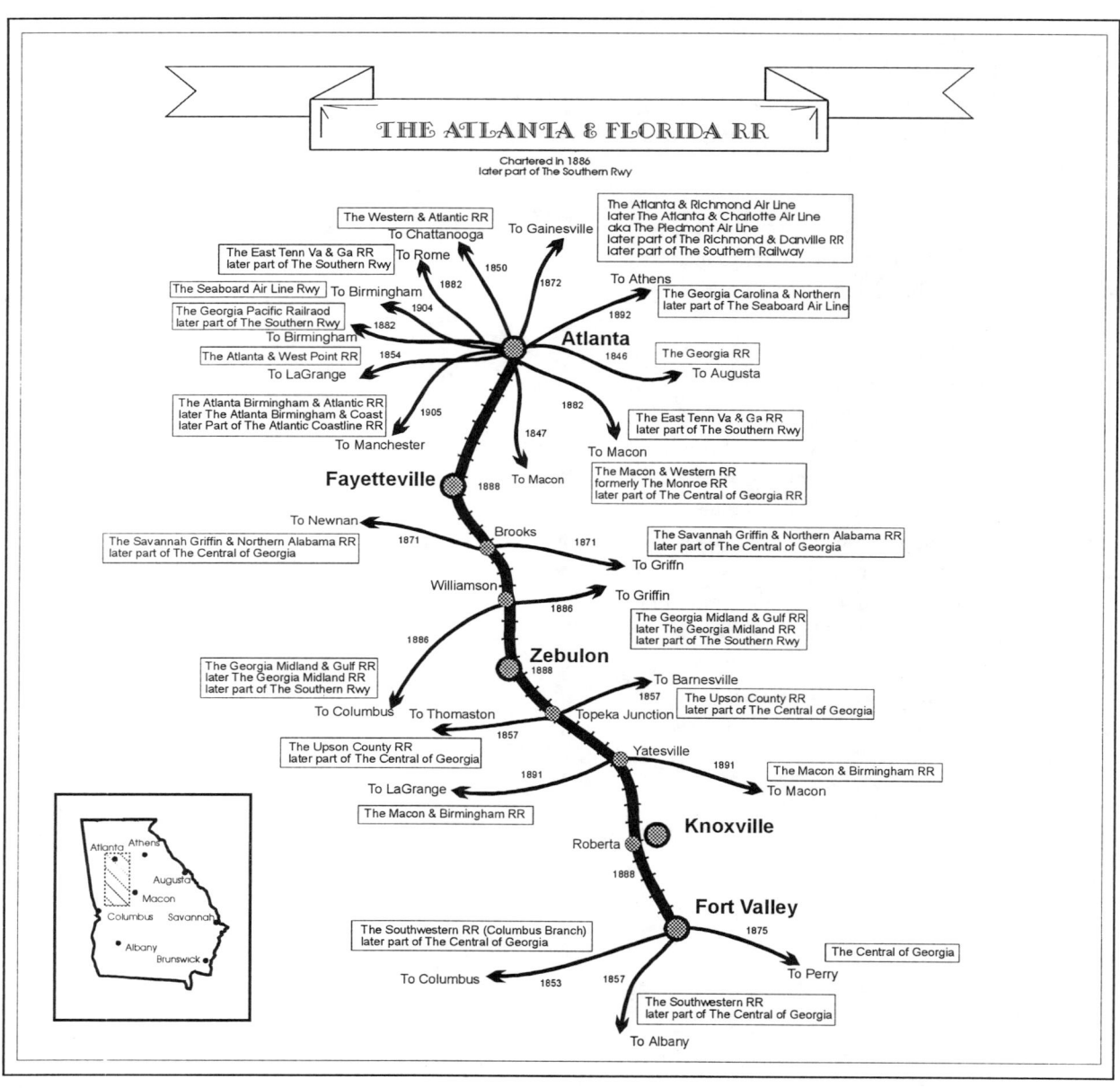

19 | The Atlanta and Florida Railroad

FAYETTE COUNTY: FAYETTEVILLE

Plate 19.1: The Fayette County Courthouse, built 1825-1831. Remodeled in 1888. Bruce and Morgan, remodeling architects. Burned 1982. Rebuilt in 1983.

Fayette County was one of the five original counties forged from the enormous tract of land between the Ocmulgee and Flint Rivers that made up the Creek Indian Cession of 1821. The construction of a brick courthouse of this size as early as 1825 was a convincing testament to the rapid growth of the county after the initial land lottery of 1821. The complete written instructions that constitute the plan for this building survive, and the document offers insight into the design process of vernacular public buildings of the era. Dimensions and structural matters are included in detail, and materials are prescribed including "smooth well-burnt brick," and a roof of "good heart pine shingles." But architectural details are sketchy. The color scheme, arched entrances and cupola are specified, but the builder was left with considerable latitude concerning the look of the structure.[1]

The building we find on the square at Fayetteville today bears little resemblance to the original Fayette County Courthouse. In 1888, a major remodeling added considerable detail to the old structure, most notably the tower, modillions beneath the eaves, dormers and elaborate Queen Anne chimneys. A 1965 remodeling transformed the original two-story structure into a three-story affair, and to complete the disguise, the building burned in 1982. In a laudable effort, it was rebuilt on its old foundations in the center of Fayetteville's ample square in 1983.

---

[1] Fayette County Historical Society, *The History of Fayette County, 1821-1971* (Fayetteville GA: Fayette County Historical Society, 1971) 17.

That Fayette County kept her original court building after the arrival of the Atlanta and Florida Railroad in 1888 is testament to the region's frugal agrarian soul. Nonetheless, considerable New South zeal was ignited by the arrival of steel rails. Atlanta architects, Bruce and Morgan's extensive 1888 remodeling of the old building spoke for the new spirit of progress that burned in Fayetteville as the town finally achieved this long awaited rail connection.

The Atlanta and Florida Railroad was chartered in 1886 as the Atlanta and Hawkinsville Railroad. By 1888, rails were complete from Atlanta through Fayetteville to a connection with the Southwestern Railroad at Fort Valley. The atmosphere in Fayetteville became highly charged as soon as plans for the line were announced. In 1886, *The Fayetteville Chronicle* observed that the town had been "awakened to the fact that she is behind the times," declared that "public spirit predominates," and predicted that Fayetteville

Plate 19.1: The building we find on the square at Fayetteville today bears little resemblance to the original 1825 Fayette County Courthouse. (Photo: Wilber W. Caldwell.)

would soon, "lead the race." The Chronicle continued its euphoric harangue, stating that the $15,000 the town had subscribed in the new railroad's stock was "a good and safe investment," and that, "No event in the history of the county is of greater importance to the entire county than this railroad project." [2] In this context, Bruce and Morgan's grand tower with its convex roof and broad cornice must have seemed a fitting symbol for what appeared to be Fayetteville's emergence into the pure light of New South prosperity. Sadly, little of that illumination came Fayetteville's way. Four years after Fayette County's grand new courthouse tower rose on the square, the contractor on the job was still unpaid, and in 1892 he had to sue the county in order to gain satisfaction.[3]

Plate 19.2: The depot at Fayetteville, built in 1902.

All along the line, the mythical progress that everyone thought would arrive on the rails of the Atlanta and Florida Railroad was slow to materialize. The Atlanta and Florida had struggled from its beginning. The line was never extended beyond Fort Valley to Hawkinsville, much less to Florida as the ambitious name implied, and only a year after the rails were laid, the new road's stock was declared "without value."[4] Four years after its completion to Fort Valley, the company declared bankruptcy. When the silver rails arrived at Fayetteville, the village counted about 350 residents, and the town's first depot was little more than a shed. By the turn of the century, twelve years after the arrival of the railroad, Fayetteville remained unchanged, its population still only 430. Citizens had been partitioning the Southern Railway, which had acquired the failed Atlanta and Florida in 1894, to build a new depot when the old building burned in 1900.[5] A replacement depot was completed early in 1901, and the structure was declared "the pride of the town." Less than a year after its completion, the Southern's new depot burned and was replaced by this simple combined passenger and freight station, which still stands in Fayetteville today.[6]

Fayetteville's odyssey is typical of many Southern towns seduced by the tempting myth of the New South. So impressed were town leaders with the few brick buildings that rose, and so convinced were they that progress was at hand, that most turned a blind eye to the county's continued poverty. Such was the power of the myth of the New South, and it is little wonder that such a potent mythology would often be manipulated by powerful interest groups that opposed change. Paul Gaston writes. "Time and again, attempts to expose the poverty and want of the region have been frustrated by appeals to the myth, a fact all the more remarkable because of the continuing failure of the Southern economy."[7]

No mills appeared in Fayetteville, and the town continued to struggle to garner even a fraction of area agricultural trade. By 1938, the rails of the old Atlanta and Florida were being pulled up for scrap. In that year there was still only one paved road running into Fayetteville.[8]

PIKE COUNTY: ZEBULON

Plate 19.3: The Pike County Courthouse, built in 1844. Demolished in 1895.

By the 1840s, many rural Southern builders were beginning to ascertain at least some of the logic that underlay the Greek orders. This fine courthouse at Zebulon exemplifies a growing sophistication that was no doubt accelerated by the widespread popularity of builder's guides. Books like Asher Benjamin's *The American Builder's Companion* (1827) and *The Practical House Carpenter* (1830) and Milard Lefever's *The Beauties of Modern Architecture* (1837) contained details of classical orders for a new generation of American builders. In contrast to the more vernacular "carpenter Greek" courthouses of the 1820s and 1830s, like the one at nearby Newnan (1829), the elegant stucco-covered brick 1844 Pike County Courthouse at Zebulon, with its massive Doric columns and board entablature, begins to capture the true essence of classical proportion despite vernacular departures.

In the decades before the Civil War, as the vernacular expressions of the Greek Revival in Georgia sought to voice an elusive architectural ideal, the symbols attached to the style were evolving to articulate a perverse regional socio-economic ideal. Driven largely by the rhetoric of John C. Calhoun in South Carolina,

Plate **19.2:** In 1902, less than a year after its completion, the Southern Railway's new depot at Fayetteville burned and was replaced by this simple combined passenger and freight station (Photo: Wilber W. Caldwell.)

Plate **19.3:** The 1844 Pike County Courthouse at Zebulon evidenced a growing sophistication among local builders in rural Georgia.

the Greek democracy in the American South came to stand not only for democracy and justice as it did in the rest of the country, but also for an idealized myth-

[2] *The Fayetteville Chronicle*, November 5, 1886.

[3] Janice Hardy, *Preservation of Georgia's Courthouses Through Historic Documentation and Photography* (Milledgeville GA: Georgia College, 1980).

[4] *The Pike County Journal*, February 26, 1883.

[5] *The Fayetteville News*, August 10, 1900.

[6] *The Fayetteville News*, February 14, 1902.

[7] Paul M. Gaston, *The New South Creed, A Study in Southern Mythmaking* (1970; reprint, Baton Rouge LA: Louisiana State University, 1970) 222.

[8] Fayette County Sesquicentennial Committee, *The Fayette County Sesquicentennial Program* (Fayetteville GA: Fayette County Sesquicentennial Committee, 1971).

Plate 19.4: The depot at Zebulon, built in 1888. (Photo: Wilber W. Caldwell.)

ical society, which prospered on the backs of slaves.[9] Such distortions lead to the wild enthusiasm for the style in the South both before and after the war, and to a premature waning of the popularity of the Greek Revival in the North.[10]

Only two years after the Creek Indians ceded the vast tract between the Ocmulgee and the Flint Rivers to the state of Georgia in 1821, Pike County was cut from Monroe County. The new county established its first county seat at Riley's Crossroads, a place later called Newnan (not to be confused with Newnan in Coweta County). A log courthouse was erected there, but in 1824, when Upson County was created from Pike, the site at Newnan was abandoned in favor of a more central location. A new county town was laid

out in 1825 and called Zebulon. A two-story frame courthouse was erected, and it stood until this building rose in 1844. By then, the original county town of Newnan was only a memory.

In antebellum times, Zebulon prospered on the success of her cotton growers and on the strength of a robust wagon trade. Local histories contend that L. L. Griffin's 1840s scheme for an early railroad or plank road from Griffin to West Point was discouraged by powerful teamster's interests in Zebulon.[11] In truth, General Griffin had many more pressing problems than local opposition in Zebulon, and his east-west road was never to be. Meanwhile, along the rails of L. L. Griffin's Monroe Railroad from Macon to Atlanta, the city of Griffin prospered, her population exceeding 2000 in 1849 according to White's *Statistics of the State of Georgia*. Likewise, the town of Barnesville sprang up in the Southern portion of Pike County, and prospered on wagon trade between the railroad and the city of Columbus. With the completion of the Atlanta and West Point Railroad in 1853 and the spur of the Upson County Railroad from Barnesville to Thomaston in 1857, Zebulon's thriving wagon trade was eclipsed, and the town settled back into obscurity. In 1860, Adiel Sherwood would write in his updated *Gazetteer of the State of Georgia*, "Since the railroad brings everything to Griffin and Barnesville, Zebulon out of the way is rather in decline." When the Atlanta and Florida Railroad arrived in Zebulon in 1888, the town counted only about 300 residents.

Plate 19.4: The depot at Zebulon, built in 1888.[12]

By the 1880s, Zebulon's attitude toward the railroads was much changed. The town had actively sought a rail connection when the Georgia Midland and Gulf was built from Griffin to Columbus in 1885, but hopes were dashed as the line was surveyed on the high ground west of Zebulon through Concord and Molena. When word of the Atlanta and Hawkinsville Railroad reached Zebulon in 1886, spirits soared on the news, and as this fine depot rose, agitation for a new courthouse simultaneously surfaced.

[9] Vernon L. Parrington, *Main Currents in American Thought, The Romantic Revolution in America*, 3 vols. (New York: Harcourt, Brace, and World, Inc., 1927) 2: xii.

[10] James Marston Fitch, *American Building and the Historical Forces that Shaped It* (1947; rev. ed, Boston: Houghton Mufflin Company, 1966) 88: and Robert J. Brink, ed., *Courthouses of the Commonwealth* (Amhurst MA: University of Massachusetts Press, 1984) 99.

[11] Lizzie R. Mitchell, *History of Pike County, 1822-1932* (1932; reprint, Spartanburg GA: Reprint Company, 1980) 34.

[12] *The Knoxville Journal*, April 13, 1888.

[13] *The Pike County Journal*, March 18, 1890.

[14] *The Pike County Journal*, October 23, 1891.

[15] *The Pike County Journal*, April 22, 1892.

[16] *The Pike County Journal*, February 26, 1889.

[17] *The Pike County Journal*, March 23, 1894.

Plate 19.5: The Pike County Courthouse, built in 1895. James W. Golucke, architect.

In 1890, county leader, J. H. Mitchell, wrote to *The Pike County Journal:* "The rapid development of the county in population, wealth and material prosperity entitles it to a better courthouse. We are now 12th or 14th in the state in this regard."[13] Just exactly where Mr. Mitchell got his statistics is not known, but as we have seen, reality rarely stood in the way of the soaring New South convictions delivered by a new railroad. Although Pike's agricultural production ranked seventeenth among Georgia's 127 counties, according to the 1890 census, the county stood 41st in population, and 33rd in capital invested in manufacturing. Nonetheless, as elsewhere in rural Georgia, believing made it so. By 1891, the grand jury declared the old Pike County Courthouse unsafe, and *The Journal* predictably added that a new courthouse was not a matter of "pride, but of general necessity."[14] By 1892, the grand jury reported to the citizens of Pike County that the old courthouse was not only "unsafe," but was now "unsuited" and "insufficient," and that to "defer action" in the matter of a new courthouse would be "the acme of folly." [15]

Pike County's new courthouse movement, which bloomed in the teeth of the depression following the Panic of 1893, offers compelling evidence of the blind faith the early railroads instilled in the residents of the towns they served. In Zebulon, momentum gathered for a new courthouse while the railroad, that had inspired the movement in the first place, slowly collapsed. In 1889, only a year after its completion, the stock of the Atlanta and Florida Railroad was deemed "without value" by *The Pike County Journal.* [16] By 1891, the line was in deep financial trouble, and the company declared bankruptcy in 1894. All of this seemed to escape county leaders in Zebulon, who in March of 1894, viewed the plans for Atlanta architects Bruce and Morgan's newly completed courthouse at Talbotton as well as a locally drawn design while paying only lip service to the far reaching financial woes that surrounded the tiny village and her failing railroad. Even though its planners were, "...aware of the great depression that exists in all branches of industry and trade," the new courthouse was to go forward.[17]

Nonetheless, it may have been in a spirit of frugality that moved county leaders in Zebulon to select a design by Atlanta's newest architect, James Wingfield Golucke, over the work of preeminent Southern architectural firm of Bruce and Morgan. Golucke, who in 1890 was listed in an Atlanta City Directory as an employee of the Woodward Lumber Company, became an "architect" in the 1891 edition. We know little of his early commissions. Golucke's almost identical Johnson County Courthouse at Wrightsville and the Emanuel County Courthouse at Swainsboro rose in the same year as his design at Zebulon, and these three court buildings mark the beginning of a remarkable career. Golucke would go on to design twenty-six courthouses in Georgia (see Appendix C) and 4 in Alabama.

The building we see today on the square in Zebulon has lost much of its original charm. Gone is Golucke's grand classical tower. Gone also is the colorfully painted pressed tin decoration which once adorned broad entablatures with decorative scrolling motifs. The original building with its central tower was a picture of classical symmetry. The ingenious square plan combined four equal cubic modules to

Plate 19.5: The 1895 Pike County Courthouse as it looks today. In Zebulon, momentum gathered for a new courthouse, while the railroad, that had inspired the movement in the first place, slowly collapsed. (Photo: Wilber W. Caldwell.)

create the four mirror-image elevations, each composed of two identical bays flanking a recessed entrance. As was usual in almost all of Golucke's court buildings, the second floor contains great arched windows that press down on the segmentally arched fenestration of the story below. This original form was much altered over the years as a series of natural disasters transformed the once stunning building into the simple structure we see today.

Plate 19.6: The Pike County Courthouse built in 1895. James W. Golucke, architect. Tower added in 1898. Bruce and Morgan, remodeling architects.

In 1898, only three years after its completion, lightening struck James Golucke's Pike County Courthouse, damaging the grand tower which, with its delicate lantern, originally rose from the exact center of the structure. An inspection of the damage revealed that the structural members were inadequate to support the tower's weight. Atlanta architects, Bruce and Morgan, whose designs had been considered by the county leaders back in 1894, were called

Plate 19.6: In Zebulon in 1898, Alexander Bruce's fine tower crowned James Golucke's simple classicism with the Parisian elegance of and earlier age.

in to fashion a replacement clock tower. The new tower was a stunning mix, recalling both early Second Empire Style designs of the 1880s and the popular Romanesque Revival Style, which had earned Bruce such acclaim in the early 1890s. We find this kind of ornamental classicism in much of Bruce's late work. The clean lines of Golucke's design at Zebulon called for a classical approach, and Bruce responded with the Parisian elegance of an earlier era. Although the new tower moved the building a long distance from Golucke's original intent, the result was strangely compatible and unquestionably monumental.

Over the years, a number of James Wingfield Golucke's court buildings have evidenced structural design flaws. The original towers of both the Union County Courthouse of 1899 and the Baker County Courthouse of 1907 are gone, and the tower of the 1900 Schley County Courthouse at Ellaville developed a disturbing lean. The citizens of Wrightsville found similar structural deficiencies in the 1895 Johnson County Courthouse, the nearly identical twin of Golucke's Pike County Courthouse. Golucke's tower at Wrightsville was removed in 1938 owing to its unstable condition. The original towers, both at Wrightsville and at Zebulon, were supported by two enormous wooden beams that spanned an incredible 74 feet. Hip trusses were added (probably by the builder in an effort to compensate for Golucke's folly), but these carry only a small percentage of the weight. Undoubtedly it was this structural shortcoming that compelled Bruce and Morgan to relocate the 1888 tower to the south elevation of Golucke's building at Zebulon.

It is little wonder that James Golucke's engineering know-how was lacking, for as far as we know, the architect had no formal training. Nonetheless, his artistic skills were well honed, and in fairness, many shaky buildings rose in the era before sound engineering principles were codified. Even the buildings of the well-respected firm of Bruce and Morgan were not always a match for the forces of nature. Only two years after its completion, the tower blew off Alexander Bruce's 1883 Walton County Courthouse at Monroe.[18]

The last, and surely the most devastating event, in the history of James Golucke's Pike County Courthouse occurred in 1949, when a tornado struck the building, completely destroying the upper portion of Alexander Bruce's fine tower. By this time, Pike County's population had dwindled to less than half its 1900 level, and the remodeling of the old building was a sadly half-hearted affair. Thus, the building we see today at Zebulon is a dim reflection of the art of Georgia's two most prolific courthouse architects, James Wingfield Golucke and Alexander Campbell Bruce.

CRAWFORD COUNTY: KNOXVILLE

Plate 19.7: The Crawford County Courthouse, built in 1831-1832.

As the rails of the Atlanta and Florida Railroad approached Knoxville, Georgia, waves of New South aspiration washed over the village. *The Knoxville Journal* was quick to admit that the village of 200, which lay beside this simple antebellum courthouse had "never been a place of much note," and that area farmers were slaves to the cotton king, practicing a primitive agriculture, growing "their bread and meat, and selling cotton and cotton only." Indeed this was a poor area. The entire county produced only about 10,000 bales in 1890, and hauled their harvest all the way to Macon in wagons.[19] As a point of comparison, in that same year, 23,000 bales were produced in neighboring Monroe County. But despite the depressed state of affairs in Crawford County, *The Journal* continued on according to the myth, declaring that the arrival of the railroad would change all of this overnight, creating "opportunities as are rarely known," and "building up an immense trade...not surpassed anywhere." In addition to the speculation surrounding the arrival of the Atlanta and Florida Railroad, spirits were further bolstered by news that "The Macon and Opelika Railroad" (as the Macon and Birmingham was often called in its early organizational days) would also pass through Knoxville, creating "an important railroad Junction" there.[20] As the rails of the Atlanta and Florida were completed through Fayette and Pike Counties, accounts of

Plate 19.7: The 1832 Crawford County Courthouse at Knoxville. In 1888, Knoxville's simple vision of railroad imported progress was a far cry from the complex industrial dreams of the full-blown myth of the New South, and it was certainly not powerful or ambitious enough to beget a new courthouse. (Photo: Wilber W. Caldwell.)

"booms" in both Fayetteville and Zebulon were reported by *The Journal*.[21]

But as track-laying crews neared Knoxville, it became clear that the rails would bypass Knoxville. Missing the courthouse by about a mile, the new road placed its 89-mile post at a place first dubbed New Knoxville and later called Roberta for the daughter of the farmer who donated the right of way. Today in Crawford County, the usual myth of the bypassed town is alive. Many residents are convinced that the railroad bypassed Knoxville owning to local opposition to the modern intrusion of the railroad. While such myths may have contained some small grain of truth in the antebellum period, by 1888 it is highly unlikely that even the most unsophisticated locals would have viewed the railroad as anything other than a windfall. *The Knoxville Journal* bears this out, reporting solidarity in March of 1888: "We have no soreheads or croakers, but every citizen of the place wants to see Knoxville improve as a business location, and all believe that it will. We want men of enterprise to come here, and will give them a royal wel-

[18]   *The Banner-Messenger* (Buchanan GA), March 7, 1890.

[19]   *The Knoxville Journal*, January 27, 1888.

[20]   *The Knoxville Journal*, January 27, 1888.

[21]   *The Knoxville Journal*, January 27, 1888, and March 30, 1888.

come."[22] Nonetheless, the Atlanta and Florida Railroad bypassed the county seat, probably more by reason of friendly geography at Roberta than unfriendly citizens in Knoxville. Few would foresee the implications of this near miss. At first, a mile away seemed close enough, and in a whirl of wild New South rhetoric, *The Journal* predicted that Knoxville would soon be a city of 3000 inhabitants.[23] But in 1888, a miss was indeed as good as mile, and Knoxville was doomed to obscurity.

Cut from the enormous Houston County in 1822, Crawford County had laid out its county seat at Knoxville and incorporated the town in 1825. The county's original courthouse burned in 1830, and was replaced by this sturdy building, which remains one of only fifteen antebellum court buildings still standing in Georgia today (see Appendix A). Only six are still in use as courthouses. Although the Crawford County Courthouse has seen many remodelings, and despite the fact that the original brick exterior walls have been stuccoed over, it retains its original exterior lines, free from the encumbrances and prostitutions of later renovations and additions. An imposing second story beneath a broad wooden cornice and ample eaves are divided into small bays by rudimentary brick pilasters whose only ornament derives from simple brick caps. All of this presses down on an unadorned lower story, which has the appearance of a half basement.

Less than twenty years after this building was constructed, the reliable George White in his 1849 *Statistics of the State of Georgia* described Knoxville as a village containing a courthouse, a jail, 4 stores, two churches and about 250 residents. Almost forty years

later, on the eve of the railroad's arrival in Crawford County, Knoxville had not changed much.

In July of 1888, just as the rails arrived, we find ads in *The Knoxville Journal* for property in "The New Railroad Town One Mile from Knoxville."[24] Here was boomtown speculation in a town that had yet to be named. In 1890, we first encounter the name Roberta, and by February of 1892, the official county newspaper, *The Crawford County Herald* was suddenly being published in Roberta, not in Knoxville. In the meantime, desperate concern arose over the route of the Macon and Birmingham, and speculators worried that, "Crawford County will be doomed to do forever without a market town, compelled to scatter its trade to the four winds, unless the road shall pass near the center of the county."[25] This would prove prophetic. As the Macon and Birmingham laid track in Monroe County well to the north of Knoxville, progress at Roberta was slow. Surprisingly, Knoxville briefly experienced a modest boom, fueled in part by rumors of a branch of the Atlanta and Florida from Knoxville to Macon.[26] Friction surfaced over cotton trading, and the seemingly inevitable squabble over the courthouse began. In 1899, *The Crawford County Correspondent* published the following: "Already it had been talked by some of our largest tax payers to move the courthouse and the jail to Roberta, as Roberta is near the center of the county and is the most suitable place for it from every standpoint.... Roberta is willing to buy the (courthouse) lot and give it to the county."[27] But Roberta was not strong enough to accomplish such a coup. By 1910, Knoxville had more than doubled in sized, boasting over 500 residents, and Roberta was a village of only 227. Although spirits had briefly soared with the arrival of the Atlanta and Florida, Knoxville's expectations had, in truth, been quite modest. She wanted a cotton market of her own. This simple vision was a far cry from the complex industrial dreams of the full-blown myth of the New South, and it was certainly not a vision powerful or ambitious enough to beget a new courthouse. Although Atlanta's S. M. Inman & Company employed buyers in Knoxville in 1889,[28] there was never to be cotton market of any significance in Crawford County. As the new century progressed,

[22] *The Knoxville Journal*, March 30, 1888.

[23] *The Knoxville Journal*, March 30, 1888.

[24] *The Knoxville Journal*, December 7, 1888.

[25] *The Knoxville Journal*, June 29, 1889.

[26] *The Knoxville Journal*, February 8, 1889.

[27] *The Crawford County Correspondent*, July 28, 1899.

[28] *The Knoxville Journal*, September 7, 1889.

[29] *The Pike County Journal*, May 28, 1889.

[30] *Waycross Evening Herald*, January 4, 1890.

[31] *The Knoxville Journal*, February 8, 1889

Roberta grew, while only a mile away Knoxville withered. Today the rails of the old Atlanta and Florida are gone, and what little prosperity they brought to Crawford County is evidenced by a cluster of brick buildings beside the old roadbed at Roberta. Only a mile away, this courthouse is about all that remains of Knoxville.

SOME LAST THOUGHTS ON THE ATLANTA AND FLORIDA RAILROAD

In 1888, when the Atlanta and Florida Railroad was completed from Atlanta, via Fayetteville, Zebulon and Roberta, to Fort Valley, there was speculation all up and down the newly laid rails concerning extension of the fledgling railroad. There were reports of continuing the line to Hawkinsville as originally planned. Another extensive scheme involved the Cordele, Waynesville and South Brunswick Railroad, which was chartered in 1888. A survey was reportedly completed to Cordele[29] and later to Waycross.'[30] Further conjecture circulated regarding a Florida destination as far away as Tampa. In 1889, spirits in Knoxville soared on the rumor of a branch line of the Atlanta and Florida from Knoxville to Macon.[31]

Despite such lofty plans and the considerable agricultural bounty of Pike and Fayette Counties, the Atlanta and Florida was financially weak from the beginning. Like many of the railroads of the last part of the century, this line was redundant, and thus superfluous. The road paralleled a portion of the Georgia Midland and Gulf from Griffin to Columbus and both the Macon and Western, and the East Tennessee, Virginia and Georgia from Atlanta to Macon. The value of a line from Atlanta to Florida would later prove enormous, but in 1888, the value of a line from Atlanta to Fort Valley was highly questionable. The Atlanta and Florida Railroad Company passed into the hands of a receiver as soon as the financial troubles of the early 1890s began. After Americus's renowned railroad builder, Samuel Hawkins, failed in his attempt to acquire the line, the great grasping hydra of J. P. Morgan's Southern Railway acquired the company out of bankruptcy in 1894. But even as a branch of the mighty Southern

Railway, this was never much of a railroad. One indication of the line's impotence was its failure to create boomtowns where it crossed other railroads. Though villages sprung up at Brooks (crossing with the Central's Savannah and Western Division), Williamson (crossing with the Georgia Midland) Topeka Junction (crossing with the old Upson County Railroad from Barnesville to Thomaston) and at Yatesville (crossing with the Macon and Birmingham), none of these places were destined to become much more than whistle stops.

Thus, as James Golucke's fine courthouse rose at Zebulon and as Fayette County remodeled her old court building and erected Alexander Bruce's stunning 1888 clock tower, the railroad that inspired such grand monuments was already falling apart. And thus, the story of the courthouse and the depot in Pike and Fayette Counties is all the more compelling. As we have seen, once geminated, the seeds of the myth of the New South would grow even in the most infertile of soils. Only in the sandy fields of Crawford County west of Macon where tiny Knoxville and her new rival Roberta toiled to establish a cotton market, would the myth prove impotent. Meanwhile not far away the seeds of the same powerful myth had been sown east of Macon, and a new crop of courthouses was blooming there.

•

The Macon and Northern Railroad

Bibb County: Macon (see chapters 3 & 8) • Jones County: Gray • Jasper County: Monticello
Morgan County: Madison (see chapter 1) • Oconee County: Watkinsville • Clarke County: Athens
(See chapter 13) • Some Last Thoughts on the Macon and Northern Railroad

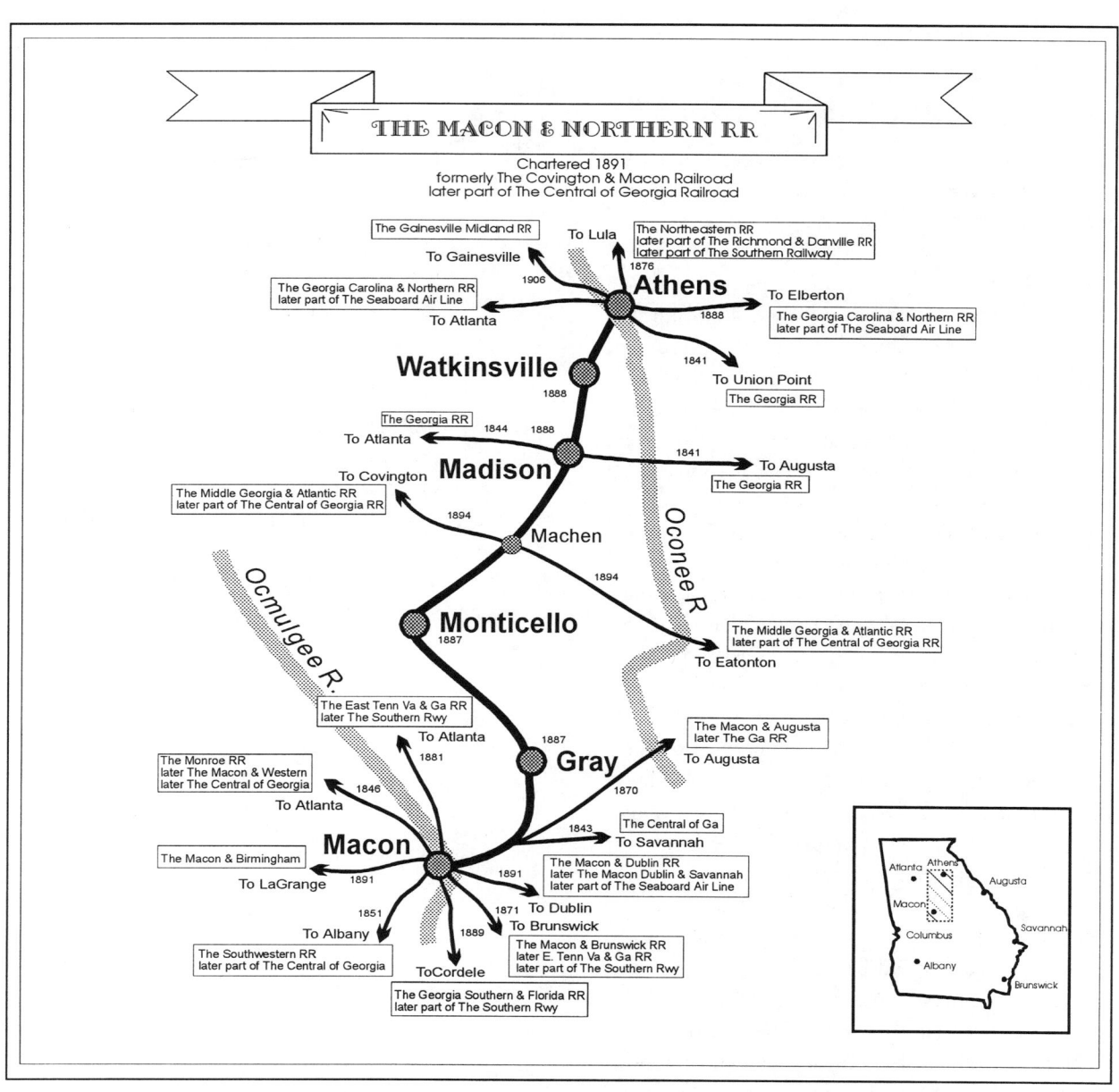

20 | The Macon and Northern Railroad

Plate 20.1: The Jones County Courthouse, built in 1905-1906. James W. Golucke, architect.

In 1905, the construction of this courthouse at Gray marked the end of a fierce battle. The venerable village of Clinton, the county's original county town, had been assaulted by the upstart village of Gray, which had sprung up beside the newly laid rails of the Covington and Macon Railroad. The story of Gray's successful campaign to capture the county seat of Jones County clearly reveals the character of the opposing forces that divided the mind of the American South throughout the closing decades of the nineteenth century and well into the twentieth. With the railroad as their champion, the forces of the mythical New South, led by a rising merchant elite clashed head-on with the entrenched armies of an equally mythical Old South, positioned behind barricades of intransigence and nostalgia.

In 1886, the year before the railroad arrived at the place that was soon to be called Gray, the old Jones County Courthouse stood on the square in Clinton, the county's largest town. According to Sholes's *Gazetteer of Georgia,* published in that same year, Clinton was a village of about 200 residents. Built in 1818, the old brick vernacular courthouse had replaced the county's first permanent court building, which had been erected in 1808 only a year after Jones County was cut from Baldwin. Clinton's history consisted of a brief period of growth, followed by a long, slow decline. By 1840, the moment of her fullness had passed. At its peak, Clinton boasted a number of "small manufacturing plants" including a tannery, several gins and mills as well as two taverns, two hotels and a notable academy, the Clinton Female Seminary, which like most everything else in Clinton eventually located to Macon.[1] Eclipsed by Macon's railroad driven success in the late 1840s, by 1860 Clinton had settled back into obscurity only to be brutalized by Sherman in 1864. The extent of the damage is unclear. One report declared that one third of the town was "in ashes."[2] Whatever the damage, the old courthouse was left untouched and as Reconstruction began, old Clinton, now a little more worse for wear, continued her slow decline.

In 1886, two Confederate Veterans, E. C. Machen and James H. Blount, set in motion a series of events that would spell the end for Old Clinton. E. C. Machen, then living in New York, came to Macon and organized the Covington and Macon Railroad. In the original charter, Machen's railroad was to be part of a line planned to connect Knoxville, Tennesssee, and the Florida coast. In a notable personal effort, he completed rails from Macon via Gray to Monticello in 1887. Bypassing Covington, Machen pressed the line northward through Madison, arriving at Athens in January of 1889. Largely through a plucky individual effort, he managed to finance, promote and construct his railroad despite limited financial resources. Along the way, Machen overcame skepticism and survived

Plate 20.1: James Golucke's 1905 Jones County Courthouse is a remarkable reminder of an obscure architect's unique ability to fashion comfortable, rural, public buildings from the monumental and often imposing vocabulary of the popular Richardsonian Romanesque Style. (Photo: Wilber W. Caldwell.)

bankruptcy. Meanwhile, Jones County resident, Macon lawyer and United States Congressman, James Blount, one of the largest land owners in Georgia,[3] laid out a new town along Machen's rails only three miles from Clinton. First called Blountston, the tiny village became known as Gray's Station and later simply Gray. Despite her efforts to secure a depot, Clinton had failed to attract Machen's railroad.

Almost ten years after the first train steamed into Gray, Clinton counted 350 residents according to Sholes's 1896 *Gazetteer of Georgia,* and Gray had a population of only 20. By that time, E. C. Machen had long since left his struggling enterprise, and the Covington and Macon Railroad had undergone several reorganizations, changed its name to the Macon and Northern and become part of the Central of Georgia. Meanwhile, James Blount had retired from public life after his bizarre involvement in the United States' acquisition of Hawaii.

All the while, Clinton's venerable courthouse was slowly deteriorating. In 1900, as the inevitable cries went out for a new courthouse, the expected agitation commenced for removal of the county seat from Clinton to Gray, despite the fact that, in that year, Gray could claim only 70 residents[4] and Clinton was still a village of 324. Supporters of Gray contended that Clinton was "slowly dying," while Gray boasted "the hopes of a railroad town."[5]

In Gray, the forces of the New South rallied behind their powerful myth, declaring that a courthouse beside the railroad at Gray would act as the "nucleus of a thriving manufacturing town," create a "market for county truck farmers" and produce "a high school of which the county would be proud."[6] Here were the three fundamental pillars of New South mythology: manufacturing diversified agriculture and education. Three miles away, Clinton's forces huddled behind barricades composed of more emotional material. According to *The Jones County News,* Clinton's Old South defenders insisted that "the ancient associations which hover around Clinton, should entitle her to a clam of the people."[7] Thus in 1900, Gray wrapped herself in blind hope, while Clinton wrapped herself in blind tradition. It was the classic Southern confrontation, and it was a battle that Clinton would win. In 1900, even though Clinton's eminent decline had been obvious, tiny Gray's progress was not dynamic enough to convince a county of farmers that the New South myth was real.

Following this initial defeat, progressive forces in Gray were strong enough to prevent the construction of new courthouse at Clinton, and in 1905 the railroad town tried again. By this time, the trappings of New South prosperity must have been everywhere to be seen in Gray. *The News* declared that "in the past two years more buildings have been built a Gray that have been built in Clinton in the past fifty years."[8] Meanwhile, Clinton had been reportedly reduced to a community of "court officials, lawyers, and physicians…who would get away if they could."[9] Through it all, the railroad had been firmly in Gray's corner. In 1900, the Central of Georgia, which had acquired the Macon and Northern in 1894, had offered to haul all courthouse materials to Gray for half rate should the courthouse be constructed there. In 1905, the line offered to build a new depot at Gray should the town prevail in the election for removal. Leaders in Gray formed the Jones County Land Development Company and offered to donate the courthouse lot in Gray to the county. The vote in 1905 was 1289 for removal of the courthouse to Gray and 51 against the removal.

It is interesting and perhaps telling that Gray's victory was so decisive only five years after her initial defeat. Although we have no specific population figures for the year 1905, it is unlikely that Gray was more than half the size of Clinton in that year. Nonetheless, attitudes were changing. After the uncertainties of the 1890s, the years between 1900 and 1905 saw things get steadily better for most farmers in Georgia. Cotton prices were rising, banks were appearing even in remote places, the new class of merchants and professionals was amassing political power and the railroads were completing their web of connectivity. In Gray, as elsewhere in the Deep South, the architecture of progress was suddenly manifest in rows of new brick commercial buildings. Men who had been skeptical of the New South's promises in 1900, were not so sure in 1905. While many still doubted, most were not willing to risk missing any opportunity

that might arise. In Jones County, everyone agreed that, even if the New South were real, it would never take shape in Clinton. So it happened that tiny town of Gray won the day.

It appears that county leaders had selected Atlanta architect James W. Golucke's plan before Gray won the county seat. This was Golucke's finest Romanesque revival courthouse design, and he must have recognized it as such, for he sold the plan with minor variations five times in Georgia. In 1905, as this building rose in Gray, three similar Golucke-designed buildings already graced the squares at McDonough, Blairsville and Ellaville. The last of these quintuplet courthouses rose in Baker County at Newton, Georgia, in 1907.

All of these buildings were so similar, that it is easier to discuss their differences than their similarities. Variations centered around the use of granite banding and voussoirs at McDonough and Blairsville, a bold detail that effected a distinct polychromy and placed these buildings much more in the mold of the Richardsonian Romanesque Style. At Gray, as at Ellaville and at Newton, a brick sting course replaced the more monumental stone details, and voussoirs were also suggested in brick relief. The results, although less imposing, still communicated power and grace. Additional variations are found in the towers. Golucke's designs at McDonough and at Ellaville carried towers capped with the ubiquitous Romanesque triple arch. These are quoined with column-like piers with flared capitals. Here in Gray, as in Newton and at

[1] Carolyn White Williams, *History of Jones County, Georgia* (Macon GA: JW Burke, 1957) 25.

[2] Macon Daily Telegraph and Confederate, November 26th, 1864 in Williams, *History of Jones County, Georgia*, 133.

[3] Allan David Candler and Clement A. Evans, eds., *The National Cyclopedia of American Biography*, 63 vols. (Atlanta: State Historical Association, 1893-1984) 13: 372.

[4] Candler and Evans, eds., *The National Cyclopedia of American Biography*, 2: 150.

[5] *The Jones County News*, March 29, 1900.

[6] *The Jones County News*, February 22, 1900.

[7] *The Jones County News*, February 22, 1900.

[8] *The Jones County News*, May 25, 1905.

[9] *The Jones County News*, June 6, 1905.

Blairsville, the tower's central feature is a single large arch supported by bold piers echoing the main entrance. The signature of all of these buildings is a satisfying symmetry which emphasizes verticality and is composed of a high tower flanked by two vertical pedimented bays, each adorned with elongated triple arches pressing down on a lower story of more massive arched openings. The corner bays are quoined with turret-like decorations and Golucke's favored pressed metal ornament is the Classical scrolling motif that appears above the entrance and on the cornice of the high tower.

All five of Golucke's quintuplet courthouses still stand today. They are remarkable reminders of an obscure architect's unique ability to fashion comfortable, rural public buildings from the monumental vocabulary of Henry Hobson Richardson. Sadly the towers have not survived at Blairsville and at Newton.

Plate 20.2: The Jones County Courthouse, built in 1818. Demolished in 1919.

Clinton was once one of the most revered towns in central Georgia. Today, little remains. The old 1818 courthouse at Clinton is gone, pulled down in 1919 after it was damaged by high winds. Despite the abiding brand of hope inspired by the Macon and Northern Railroad, at Gray, dreams of New South prosperity were not to come true there either. Like Clinton, Gray remained in Macon's shadow. In the

end, the great mills, which so many thought were sure to rise beside the Macon and Northern, amounted to nothing more than a handful of mythical dreams.

JASPER COUNTY: MONTICELLO

Plate 20.3: The Jasper County Courthouse built in 1839. Demolished 1909.

Before the arrival of E. C. Machen's Covington and Macon Railroad in 1887, hopes in Monticello had been alternately lifted and dashed by a long series of failed railroad schemes that began back in the 1850s with the ill-fated Monticello and Griffin Railroad (see Table 20.1). With such a dubious railroad history, this comfortable trading town in the heart of Georgia's rich cotton growing central Piedmont grew skeptical of railroad promises. Thus, the usual New South euphoria that was so often imported by postbellum rails was slow to arrive in Monticello. With a population of about 500 in 1887, Monticello had not changed a great deal from the village George White documented in his 1849 *Statistics of the State of Georgia*. White described a modest town surrounding this simple three-story brick courthouse, which had been erected in 1839 to replace the county's original log court building built in 1811, only three years after Jasper County (originally called Randolph County) had been created from Baldwin. A series of notable fires had swept through the town in the dark days of the 1870s,

Plate 20.2: The 1818 Jones County Courthouse at Clinton. Today little remains of old Clinton. (Photo: Courtesy of the Georgia Department of Archives and History.)

Plate 20.3: The 1839 Jasper County Courthouse stood on the Square at Monticello for over 80 years. (Photo: Courtesy of the Georgia Dept. of Archives and History.)

and by 1887 a few brick stores had appeared on the square. But although Monticello had doubled in size by the turn of the century, this growth was not accompanied by the soaring New South spirit usually found beside postbellum rails. A locally funded attempt to organize a cotton mill at Monticello fizzled in 1899.

Plate 20.4: The depot at Monticello, built in 1901. Demolished 1996.

After the turn of the century, a new wave of hope began to bolster expectations in many county towns in the cotton growing South. As this depot rose, Monticello appeared to slowly shed her conservative ways. The Southern Bobbin Company was chartered in 1899, and with it, electric power arrived in 1901, followed by a new water works five years later. By 1905, flush times appeared to be at last abroad in cotton's kingdom. There was talk of 15-cent cotton, and some of the county's efforts toward agricultural diversity that had arrived with the railroad were beginning to pay off. By 1900, Jasper County reported 10,000 acres of peach orchards.[10] By 1906, in the spirit of optimism, *The Monticello News* was beginning to insert pithy slogans, like "Watch Monticello Grow" between articles detailing plans for new brick buildings. All of this had the ring of boosterism, the verbose language of the myth of the New South. As plans were unveiled for the Middle Georgia Interurban Railroad, an electric commuter line from Griffin to Monticello, a new line from Griffin to Social Circle was also contemplated. The lure of crossing rails at last sparked agitation for a new courthouse in Monticello.

Plate 20.5: The Jasper County Courthouse, built in 1907. T. F. Lockwood, architect.

After the Grand Jury of 1906 recommended a new courthouse, the Lockwood Brothers of Columbus were selected to design a symbol to flaunt both Monticello's past and her desire for progress. Four years earlier, the firm had designed the 1903 Dougherty County Courthouse at Albany, and their

[10] Jasper County Historical Foundation, Inc., *History of Jasper County, Georgia* (Roswell GA: WH Wolfe, 1976) 98.

Table 20.1
MONTICELLO RAILROADS CHARTERED BUT NEVER BUILT
The Monticello & Griffin RR, 1852
The Eatonton & Monticello RR, 1854
The Macon, Monticello & Atlanta RR, 1872
The Monticello, Eudora & Social Circle RR. 1885
The Monticello & Eatonton RR, 1886
The Middle Georgia Interurban RR, c. 1906
Griffin to Social Circle via Monticello, c.1907

Plate 20. 4: As this depot rose at Monticello in 1901, the town appeared to shed some of its conservative ways. (Photo: Wilber W. Caldwell.)

Plate 20.5: The Lockwood Brothers of Columbus designed the 1907 Jasper County Courthouse in the mold of their 1903 court building at Albany. (Photo: Wilber W. Caldwell.)

design here at Monticello mirrors this earlier building. Lockwood's courthouse at Albany had been one of the first of the new wave of neoclassical court buildings to be erected in Georgia. Despite its modernity, it paled in comparison to the stunning neoclassical public buildings of James Golucke and Frank Milburn. The Lockwood Brothers' reputation was centered in the talent of New Jersey born and New York trained architect, Frank Lockwood, who in 1895, had moved from Columbus to Montgomery, Alabama, to open an office there, leaving the Columbus office in the charge of brother, Thomas Firth Lockwood.

The Lockwood Brothers' 1903 court building at Albany featured a fine portico attached to a rather clumsy rectangular mass beneath an awkwardly proportioned domed lantern. Here in Monticello in 1907, we find a derivative but inferior work. Albany's great Ionic hexastyle portico is here reduced to four widely spaced columns, and the detail of the brick work in the lower story is simplified to mimic banded rustication instead of the more elegant patterns that once emanated from the gauged arches of the ground floor at Albany. Both buildings featured light gray brick, which when new, must have sparkled with classical brilliance, but with age, had developed the unlovely soiled hue of Georgia red clay.

All of this notwithstanding, the Lockwood Brothers' creation in Monticello was an accurate reflection of the true state of affairs. In 1907, like so many Southern towns, the place was trapped between a newfound lust for progress, and a deep-seeded fascination with the past. Romantic images of the Old South clashed with visions of an industrial New South as two seemingly contradictory myths rose up to taunt the citizens of Jasper County. This courthouse straddled both myths. The modern Neoclassical Style was part of an "American Renaissance" in the North where it reflected American financial and industrial might. At the same time, Lockwood's great portico with is classical columns recalled the enduring myth of the Lost Cause, which by 1907 had grow into a cult of sweeping dimensions. It is a strange quirk of history that just as the promises of the myth of the New South seemed to be becoming real in places like Monticello, the myth of the Old South shone the brightest. The

period between 1900 and 1910 saw the apex of the cult of the Lost Cause. Thus, just as a modern economic recovery beckoned, the archaic notions that had plagued the South since the time of Jefferson loomed larger than ever. That the image of a New South, rising from the ashes of the Old could simultaneously exist along side such archaic romanticism, is an enigma. Like most complex human emotions, its true essence is revealed only in symbols like the columns of T. F. Lockwood's 1907 Jasper County Courthouse.

OCONEE COUNTY: WATKINSVILLE

Plate 20.6: The Oconee County Courthouse, built in 1888. Burned 1938. William W. Thomas, architect.

Originally the county seat of Clarke County, Watkinsville erected her first courthouse in 1806 only five years after the county had been cut from Jackson County. The simple frame building was replaced by a substantial brick courthouse in 1829. The builder of that 40' x 50' two-story brick vernacular structure was James Carlton, who had just completed the 1828 Taliaferro County Courthouse at Crawfordville.

The contrast between Athens and Watkinsville became pronounced well before the Civil War. In 1849, when George White published his *Statistics of the State of Georgia,* Watkinsville was described as a village of about 240 residents, while Athens was a city of over 3000. Watkinsville lost the county seat to Athens in 1871. But as Athens grew, farmers in rural areas wanted no part of the booming railroad city's modern ways. Dissatisfaction was so strong in the southern portion of the county around the comfortable old county seat of Watkinsville, that a new county, Oconee, was created in 1875. The old 1829 courthouse once again presided over local governmental affairs. In 1888, when William Thomas's Oconee County Courthouse replaced the county's 1829 brick court building at Watkinsville, which had burned in 1887, its Spartan form reaffirmed the region's stubborn independence.

William W. Thomas was born in Athens in 1849 just as George White completed his statewide survey and only eight years after the Georgia Railroad built its branch from Union Point to Athens. Two years after his death in 1904, the last of the city's five rail lines, the Gainesville Midland, would arrive. In the short life of William Thomas, we find the two major elements of this book: architecture and the railroads. In 1872, as a young civil engineer, he surveyed the route of the Northeastern Railroad, a milepost in Athens's Faustian and often frustrated railroading bargains.

Although William W. Thomas's career would be that of a prominent Athens business man (president of the Southern Mutual Insurance Company, Trustee of the University of Georgia and Director of the Georgia Railroad), his love and talent for architecture are apparent in the impressive array of stylish buildings that he designed in the years between 1879 and 1896. His work in Athens displays a remarkable familiarity with a number of popular styles of the day. It includes the unique octagonal plan for 1882 Seney-Stovall Chapel; several fine Queen Anne homes, like the 1890 William P. Walsh home and the 1895 J. H. Flemming House; the stunning Richardsonian Romanesque design of the 1891 White Hall Mansion (attributed) and his own home, the remarkable 1896 Thomas-Carithers House, which was the first Beaux-Arts Style building in Athens. W. W. Thomas was the last of the old school of Southern architects. Something of a Renaissance man(an engineer, not a schooled architect(he was a man who, despite his obvious architectural skills, practiced the art more as a pastime than a vocation.

Just as the life of William Thomas would find connection with the depots in Athens, it would find connection with the courthouse in two rural hamlets. Among Thomas's architectural accomplishments are the 1879 Jackson County Courthouse at Jefferson and the 1888 Oconee County Courthouse at Watkinsville. Unlike most of Georgia's rural court buildings of the era, neither of these structures were products of local railroad inspired New South ravings.

The Covington and Macon Railroad arrived in Watkinsville in the very same year that William Thomas's 1888 Oconee County Courthouse was built, and although the town had every right to indulge in the usual wild aspirations for railroad-borne

Plate 20.6: William Thomas's 1888 Oconee County Courthouse at Watkinsville was a building of sober practicality reflecting little of the New South's shinning promises. (Photo: Courtesy of Ted Brooke.)

New South prosperity, we find little record of such euphoria. As Thomas's sturdy building rose, Populism was gaining strength in Oconee County. Accordingly, Thomas's courthouse is a rather stern affair, lacking the exuberant styling of contemporary court buildings erected in surrounding counties like Oglethorpe (1887) and Walton (1883) where the New South myth was popular. Here was a structure of sober practicality. Built on the usual Greek Cross plan, the building's flat unadorned brick walls recalled earlier vernacular court buildings of the antebellum period, despite its picturesque pedimented central bay and Romanesque arched entrance. As we have seen, in places where Populism flourished, few were seduced by the myth of a bountiful New South, and even fewer saw the railroad as anything other than a ruthless exploiter of poor farmers. Oconee County was such a place, and she would build no fantasy courthouse.

William Thomas's austere symbol for Oconee County's agrarian individualism burned in 1938 and was replaced by the present Oconee County Courthouse at Watkinsville.

Plate 20.7: The depot at Farmington.

The old Macon and Northern tracks from Madison to Athens have been abandoned. The old depot at Watkinsville is today nowhere to be found, but its sister still stands in Oconee County seven miles south of Watkinsville in the village of Farmington, which was once a town of over 500 residents.[11] This

Plate 20.7: The old depot at Watkinsville is gone, but its sister still stands in the nearby village of Farmington. (Photo: Wilber W. Caldwell)

depot and a few brick stores are all that remain of Farmington to remind us of the stubborn farmers along the line of the Macon and Northern who spat in the face of the New South with its Yankee industrialism as they resolutely turned the fields white with cotton each Fall.

SOME LAST THOUGHTS ON THE MACON AND NORTHERN RAILROAD

The travails of E. C. Machen and his Covington and Macon Railroad illustrate the fragile and tentative nature of Georgia's new crop of "home grown" railroads that had germinated in the decade after Reconstruction. Local investors hungry for connection encountered a new breed of railroad promoters hungry for the mythical economic potential of the New South. Thus, an odd assortment of ne'er-do-well railroad companies were born in the 1880s only to find themselves unequal to the financial nightmares of the early 1890s. Machen's road was typical. Born of a grand plan to connect the Florida coast and Knoxville, Tennessee, the line had struggled almost from the onset, and before it reached Monticello in 1887, reorganization and refinancing had dictated a new route.

[11] Margaret F. Sommer, *The History of Oconee County* (Dallas GA: Curtis Media, 1983) 54.

[12] *The Jones County Headlight*, July 14, 1888. Machen was a railroad man through and through, after his struggles with the Covington and Macon and the Middle Georgia and Atlantic, he was instrumental in the progress of the Brunswick and Birmingham Railroad in south Georgia after the turn of the century

Bypassing Covington in 1889, the line was completed via Madison to Athens despite financial difficulties. By 1891, the Covington and Macon was again in trouble, and a tedious series of mergers, failures and acquisitions found the road renamed the Macon and Northern in 1891 and in the hands of the Central of Georgia by 1894. Meanwhile, Machen remained undaunted. Determined that Covington held some key to success, he began to promote the Middle Georgia and Atlantic Railroad, which in 1894 completed track from Eatonton to Covington crossing the rails of the Macon and Northern at the village appropriately named Machen.

Although the record of courthouse building is not so compelling along the rails of the Macon and Northern as elsewhere in this era, the line was not without its impact in this regard. It would take the newly created village of Gray in Jones County almost twenty years to wrestle the county seat away from venerable old Clinton. Along the way, the power of rail to create New South fervor even in the smallest hamlet was clearly illustrated by the fact that in 1900 Gray, with a population of only 70, made a credible assault on the courthouse. The tiny village attempted the charge with the railroad as her only ally, and only five years later in 1905, Gray won the prize. James W. Golucke's remarkable Jones County Courthouse rose the next year. Clinton never recovered.

Farther up the rails Monticello and Madison were both slow to swallow the tempting bait of New South promise delivered by the Macon and Northern. But after the turn of the century, both would eventually feel the pull of the myth, and both would construct courthouses which reflected duel symbols. The year 1907 saw the completion of T. F. Lockwood's Jasper County Courthouse at Monticello and James W. Golucke's Morgan County Courthouse at Madison. Here were two grand neoclassical monuments to symbolize both the growing myth of the Old South and the irresistible myth of the New.

Only tiny Watkinsville would remain untempted by the New South's Yankee-inspired bargain. William Thomas's simple 1888 Oconee County Courthouse did not celebrate the arrival of the railroad or the dreams of the New South. It was simply a replacement for the 1829 court building that had burned in 1887. The winds of change that blew in Watkinsville were not promising breezes of New South bounty, but radical gales of Populist upheaval.

Through all of this, in Jones and Jasper Counties, E. C. Machen was regarded as something of a hero. Here was a Southerner, a Confederate veteran in Yankee clothing. In 1888, this rebel-turned-financier had, according to the Jones County Headlight, almost single-handedly carried his railroad "through from beginning to end," and was "being loaded down with compliments on every side."[12] Surely here was a shinning product of the New South. But like almost all of the New South's gleaming wares, E. C. Machen's Covington and Macon Railroad was to find it difficult to fulfill the wild expectations that so many promises and promotions had fabricated

As the Covington and Macon struggled to reach Athens, back in Macon three new lines were chartered, and that city's already formidable railroad might was coming into full bloom. As the Covington and Macon became the Macon and Northern, the Macon Construction Company received charters for the Georgia Southern and Florida, the Macon and Birmingham and the Macon and Atlantic Railroads. By 1891, nine railroads radiated outward from Macon.

Plate 20.8: Athens. (Photo: Wilber W. Caldwell.)

The Georgia Southern and Florida Railroad

Bibb County: Macon (see chapters 3 & 8) • Dooly County: Vienna • Crisp County: Cordele
(see chapter 23) • Turner County: Ashburn • Tift County: Tifton (see chapter 10)
Cook County: Adel Lowndes County: Valdosta (See chapter 7)
Some Last Thoughts on the Georgia Southern and Florida Railroad

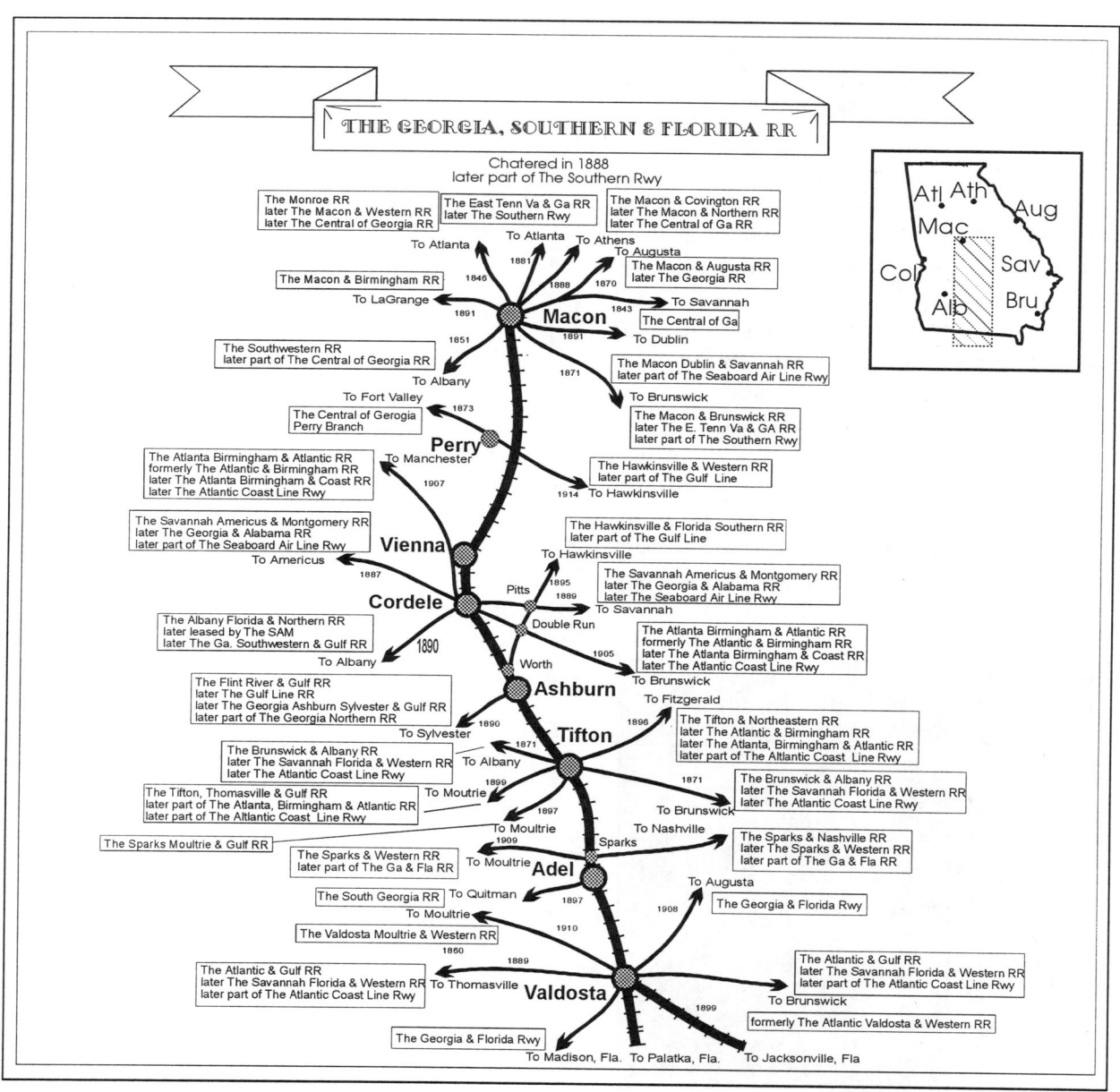

21 | The Georgia Southern and Florida Railroad

DOOLY COUNTY: VIENNA

Plate 21.1: The Dooly County Courthouse, built in 1890. William Parkins, architect.

In Vienna, agitation for a new courthouse commenced just as the rails of the Georgia Southern and Florida Railroad arrived in 1888. Almost straight away county leaders commissioned the noted Atlanta Architect, William Parkins to design a symbol for Dooly County's newfound railroad-inspired aspirations.

After his brief partnership with Alexander Bruce and a subsequent association with New York architect, Lorenzo Wheeler, and New South promoter, Hannibal Kimball, William Parkins resumed architectural practice on his own. Between 1888 and 1892, he designed four of Georgia's most picturesque court buildings: the 1888 Gordon County Courthouse at Calhoun, the 1892 Polk County Courthouse at Cedartown, the 1892 Terrell County Courthouse at Dawson and his exceptional Dooly County Courthouse at Vienna also completed in 1892. It is no coincidence that such fanciful public architecture was created by Parkins immediately following his association with Wheeler and Kimball. Surely William Parkins had been influenced by the charisma of Hannibal Kimball and his compelling New South propaganda. There were few men in Georgia who had been able to resist Kimball's seductive intensity and conviction. Just as surely, Parkins had been deeply influenced by the wild eclectic fantasies of architect, Lorenzo Wheeler, who had come south to join Kimball in 1884 as the designer of Atlanta's fabulous Kimball House II. After his collaboration with Wheeler on the 1886 Randolph County Courthouse at Cuthbert and the 1887 Oglethorpe County Courthouse at Lexington, Parkins created his most overtly fanciful courthouse designs. Here was a modern flamboyant voice for the unfettered aspirations of four Georgia villages seduced by the mythical railroad-borne promises of New South.

The 1960 remodeling of the old 1890 Dooly County Courthouse presents attractive and functional modifications to the old building, and thus it is a long distance from a pure restoration. The glassed-in enclosure of the second story porch

Plate 21.1: William Parkins's 1890 Dooly County Courthouse was a fantastic symbol for Vienna's fantastic vision. (Photo Wilber W. Caldwell.)

now appears massive where originally an airy open-arched balcony overlooked Vienna's public square. In addition, the great conical dome of the high tower was not replaced, leaving a rather incomplete, unbalanced stub in place of what was once the building's most fanciful element. Happily the impossibly slender tourelle still decorates the low tower with its Romanesque arcaded arched corbeling. Despite its modern facelift, the picture beside the square at Vienna today is still evocative of the era when everyone thought that the rails of the Georgia Southern and Florida Railroad were about to lift the tiny village up and out of the sea of poverty that surrounded it and cast the place headlong into the abundance of the industrial age. Such a fantastic vision, required a fantastic symbol, and William Parkins, perhaps more than any other regional architect of the period, was adroit at delivering Romantic fantasies for a people who were desperately clinging to the crumbling remnants of the Romantic age.

Indeed, the picturesque as an expression of an artistic ideal was closely tied to Romanticism. Certainly this connection, along with its reliance on powerful historical associations, accounted for the popularity of picturesque architecture in the Deep South. There were forty-nine picturesque court buildings erected in Georgia between 1880 and 1907 (see Appendix C). The dominance of the Picturesque in the Romantic Age has been described as the "triumph of picture over geometry…the conquest of poetry over mathematics." This suggested of course, "the victory of imagination over reason."[1] Certainly nothing could have been more apt for rural Georgia in the era when the railroads were spreading the wildly imaginative hopes of a largely mythical New South.

In 1824, only three years after the creation of Dooly County, the town of Vienna, originally called Berrien, was laid out. By 1833, the village had a population of 33,[2] but no courthouse was constructed. In 1836, the county seat was moved to the larger village of Drayton on the banks of the Flint River at the western boundary of the sprawling new county. A small courthouse was erected there, but this arrangement did not last long. Probably owing to pressure for a more central location, the seat of county government was returned to Berrien in 1839. At this time, there was a movement to change the name of the place to Centerville, but in 1841, residents settled on the name Vienna. A log courthouse was constructed at about this time. This building burned in 1847 destroying all of the county's records, and in 1848 a 40' x 50' two-story frame courthouse, probably similar to those at nearby Tazwell, Preston and Cusseta was erected on Vienna's ample square. In his 1849 *Statistics of the State of Georgia,* George White could only say that Dooly County roads were good, but "the situation (in Vienna)…renders unhealthy." He estimated the town's population to be about 100.

With the 1888 arrival of the Georgia Southern and Florida Railroad, Vienna began to stir. The town's population exceeded 500 in 1890, and by the end of the decade, Vienna boasted a few sawmills. In 1897, the Dooly Southern Railroad had been constructed from nearby Richwood to Penia, a distance of nine miles. But for all of her New South dreams, Vienna never became more than a local market town in the service of King Cotton. In 1902, the county produced over 26,000 bales.[3] Only a year or so later, the Dooly Southern was abandoned.

By the early years of the new century, when the Atlantic and Birmingham Railroad, the predecessor of the Atlanta, Birmingham and Atlantic, built its depot at Vienna, the village had become a town of over 1000. By 1910, her population had reached 1500. But as elsewhere, agriculture, and specifically the growing of cotton, remained the county's economic mainstay. By 1904, as investors in Vienna petitioned the state legislature for a charter for the Georgia Eastern Railroad Company to run the 82 miles from Eastman via Vienna to Americus, two depots and thirty-eight brick buildings stood at Vienna.[4] A few new towns had appeared beside the new rails in Dooly County, but this brief and shallow boom was only a faint and disappointing shadow of those vibrant promises of New South industrial bounty that had inspired the wild flight of fancy that was the Dooly County Courthouse. Vienna received little of the New South's mythical bounty, and the Georgia Eastern Railroad was never built.

TURNER COUNTY: ASHBURN

Plate 21.2: The Turner County Courthouse, built in 1907-1908. Alexander Blair III and Peter E. Dennis, architects.

With his design for the 1907 Turner County Courthouse, Macon architect, Alexander Blair III completed the architectural songs he had begun to voice in his first court building, the 1902 Decatur County Courthouse at Bainbridge. Like most of the region's trained architects in the years surrounding the turn of the century, Blair was struggling to find architectural forms to stand for both the South's obsession with its past and the region's growing perception that modern economic prosperity was just around the corner. Four of Alexander Blair's eight courthouses in Georgia (see Appendix C) reflected more traditional neoclassical styling. But here in Ashburn, as in Bainbridge, Blair relied on vaguely neo-colonial imagery of a loosely Georgian composition to supply an appropriately historical air. As a part of a sweeping national architectural return to order, Georgian forms were in vogue in 1907. Working in Ashburn in concert with Macon architect Peter Dennis, Blair moved a step beyond his creation at Bainbridge, and draped his Turner County Courthouse in even more flamboy-

ant classical grab. The paired columns of the two grand porticos reflect the popular American Beaux-Arts Style, and the bold rusticated quoining accomplishes an up-to-date and strikingly polychromatic effect in yellow brick. Additional Renaissance details, like the splayed window headers and the pedimented entrances, successfully marry Georgian

Plate 21.2: In Ashburn, as in Bainbridge, Alexander Blair relied on vaguely neocolonial imagery of a loosely Georgian composition to supply an appropriately historical air. (Photo: Wilber W. Caldwell.)

[1] J. M. Crook, *The Dilemma of Style* (London: Murray, 1987) 40.

[2] Fort Early Chapter of the Daughters of the American Revolution, *The History of Crisp County* (Cordele GA: Fort Early Chapter of the Daughters of the American Revolution, 1916) 24.

[3] From Greater Vienna, a promotional leaflet published by promoters of the city of Vienna, c.1904.

[4] From Greater Vienna, a promotional leaflet published by promoters of the city of Vienna, c.1904.

elements to modern Parisian details. Here is a stunning symbol for Ashburn's seemingly meteoric rise from an empty place in the piney woods in 1888 to the county seat of the newly created Turner County in 1905.

Ashburn was not alone in her boom. In 1905, South Georgia was alive with a short-lived progress, which at the time, appeared to reflect the blossoming prosperity of the New South. In 1904, the state legislature finally lifted the ban on the creation of new counties, which, since 1877, had fixed the number of counties in Georgia at 137. Originally promoted as Henderson County, Turner County was the first of eight new Georgia counties created in 1905.[5] Of the new counties created since 1904, four lie in a neat line beside the Georgia Southern and Florida Railroad. In 1905, Crisp, Turner and Tift Counties would appear along these rails, followed by Cook County in 1918. What had once been a sparsely populated region of pine forests, subsistence farming and herding was transformed into millions of board feet of lumber and rivers of turpentine. By 1910, Ashburn, which had hardly been a place at all in 1890, was a village of over 2000 residents, and her story is a tale of several vast personal empires of timber.

Just as H. H. Tift began his lumber-driven miracle at Tifton and on the eve of the completion of the Georgia Southern and Florida Railroad, William Warren Ashburn, a budding lumber baron in Eastman, and J. S. Betts purchased a large tract surrounding present day Ashburn and christened the new town of "Marion." Betts erected a sawmill, and when the town was chartered in 1891 the name was changed to Ashburn. Despite this honor, W. W. Ashburn continued to reside in Moultrie, where he owned even more extensive timber interests. In 1896, J. S. Shingler, another self-styled lumber and turpentine baron from Dodge County, bought Ashburn's interest in the timberlands in what was soon to be Turner County and continued to develop and exploit the substantial timber and naval stores resources of the area.

The Georgia Southern and Florida Railroad had been completed in 1888. Shortly thereafter, a depot was established to serve the sawmills at Ashburn. In 1894, the Hawkinsville and Florida Southern Railroad

was completed to a junction with the Georgia Southern and Florida at the town of Worth just to the north of Ashburn, and beginning in 1904, J. S. Betts was instrumental in the creation of the northern end of the Flint River and Gulf Railroad from Ashburn southwestward through Sylvester. W. W. Ashburn died in 1906. In that same year, just as the Flint River and Gulf Railroad was completed from Ashburn to Sylvester, the first grand jury in the newly created Turner County recommend that a courthouse be erected in a location "convenient to the depot,"[6] which by that time serviced 10 passenger trains a day.[7]

Despite her promising start and her unshakable New South faith, hard times lay ahead for Turner County. When the great pine forests were gone, and the saw mills had all moved away, cotton was planted in the empty expanses once shaded by stately pines. The first crops blossomed just in time for the boll weevil. As late as 1926, Turner County contained the only unpaved section of Georgia's US Highway 41. Today the pleasant town of Ashburn recalls the memory of William Warren Ashburn, but along the roadbed of the old Flint River and Gulf, the village of Shingler has all but disappeared. Ironically, on the same old roadbed, the town of Betts, named for the man who created those rails, and thus the town, is today nowhere to be found. Likewise at Worth, which once stood at the junction of the Hawkinsville and Florida Southern and the Georgia Southern and Florida no trace of a town remains.

The Georgia Southern and Florida was acquired by the Southern Railway in 1903. The Hawkinsville and Florida Southern, which later became the Gulf Line, was abandoned from Worth to Hawkinsville in 1921. The Flint River and Gulf was acquired by the ill-fated Hawkinsville and Florida Southern, but was revived in 1922 as the Georgia, Ashburn, Sylvester and Camilla Railroad. This became part of the Georgia Northern Railroad in 1972 and was abandoned in 1982. Such is the sad testament to the railroads that built Turner County and inspired her stunning courthouse. Today not a single depot remains beside any of her arrow-straight rights-of-way. Like the great stands of virgin pine and the abundant rivers of turpentine, these simple wooden buildings are today barely even memories.

Cook County: Adel

In 1906, the year after Crisp, Turner and Tift Counties were created beside the Georgia Southern and Florida Railroad, a new county movement surfaced farther to the south along the same rails in Berrien County at the town of Adel. Although Cook County was not created until 1919, and a courthouse was not erected at Adel until 1939, the railroad's role in the creation of the new county is undeniable, and Adel's story is instructive. Sadly, the sprawling old wooden depot at Adel has been demolished, and today no depots stand in Cook County to remind us that the railroads once brought life to this sparsely populated section of the piney woods.

In 1888, when the Georgia Southern and Florida Railroad passed by the village formerly called Puddleville, it missed the town by about a quarter of a mile. Quick to seize the opportunity, local landowners made the usual bargain with the railroad. In return for the depot site, free right-of-way and one-half of the new business and residential lots, they contracted with the Macon Construction Company, the owner, promoter and builder of the Georgia Southern and Florida Railroad, to survey and lay out a new town of Adel beside the newly laid rails.[8]

Adel's growth was notable. In 1897, the South Georgia Railroad was built to Quitman from the village of Heartpine south of Adel on the Georgia Southern and Florida. The northern terminus of this line was later moved to Adel. Lumber interests built tram roads into the piney woods from the village of Sparks, just two miles north of Adel. Two of these became common carriers. The Sparks and Nashville and the Sparks and Western Railroads later became part of the Georgia and Florida Railroad's branch from Nashville to Moultrie. Adel, a village of about 500 in 1890, became a town of almost 2000 by 1910.

The driving force behind the new county movement in Adel was local merchant, landowner and timberman Homer L. Parrish. A local account of Cook County's struggle to be born recalls that in 1906 at the first meeting to discuss the possibility of a new county, the usual litany of arguments had been recited: increased population around Adel, distance to the county seat at Nashville, and so on. After plans were laid to legally petition the state legislature with a well rounded proposal, H. H. Tift who had been instrumental in the creation of Tift County the year before, is reported to have offered his sage advise. After hearing the long list of justifications for a new county, without rising from his seat Tift, had reportedly said, "I tell you men, just get your bill drawn, put fifteen thousand dollars in your pocket, go to Atlanta when the legislature meets, buy your county, and come home."[9] After twelve years of formal solicitation presenting all of the data they could muster, the story goes that in 1918, delegates in support of the creation of Cook County finally took Henry Tift's advice and "forgot about showing of evidence and dire need for its creation…," and took, "a sizable sum of money…to Atlanta…."[10] Thus, Cook County was born, and it is perhaps fair to infer that many of Georgia's counties born in the New County Movement of the early part of this century were created with similar "political contributions."

Some Last Thoughts on the Georgia Southern and Florida Railroad

The Georgia Southern and Florida Railroad was the only successful child of the Macon Construction Company. In 1888, this bold group of Macon investors undertook to build three railroads radiating outward from Macon. To connect Macon with Savannah, the company planned the Macon and

[5] The others were Stephens, Toombs, Tift, Crisp, Jeff Davis, Grady and Jenkins.

[6] John Ben Pate, *The History of Turner County* (Spartanburg GA: Reprint Company, 1979) 97.

[7] Turner County Diamond Jubilee, Inc., *The Turner County Diamond Jubilee* (Ashburn GA: n.p., 1955).

[8] June Jackson Parrish, *The History of Cook County, Georgia and Its Municipalities* (Adel GA: n.p., 1967) 56.

[9] Parrish, *The History of Cook County, Georgia and Its Municipalities*, 8.

Atlantic. This ill-fated endeavor accomplished considerable grading but constructed only 12 miles of track near Brewton, a village 50 miles east of Macon. Working westward form Macon the company also built the Macon and Birmingham, which reached LaGrange in 1890. Here construction was halted owing to increasing financial difficulties. Only a year after its arrival in LaGrange, this line was in bankruptcy. After a series of reorganizations and failures the Macon and Birmingham Railroad was abandoned in 1923. Only the Georgia Southern and Florida proved profitable for the Macon Construction Company. Reaching Valdosta in 1888, this line, known as "The Suwanee River Route," stretched southward from

Plate 21: Ashburn. (Photo: Wilber W. Caldwell.)

[10] Parrish, *The History of Cook County, Georgia and Its Municipalities*, 9.

[11] Parrish, *The History of Cook County, Georgia and Its Municipalities*, 56.

[12] Parrish, *The History of Cook County, Georgia and Its Municipalities*, 98

Macon. By 1890, tracks had been completed over the entire 230 miles to a terminus at Palatka, Florida. Despite the success of the Georgia Florida and Southern, the line failed in 1895, pulled down by national depression and a monumental debt stemming from efforts to sustain the struggling Macon and Brunswick Railroad. The line was immediately acquired by J. P. Morgan's ravenous Southern Railway, which soon acquired the Atlantic, Valdosta and Western, connecting to Jacksonville, Florida, at Valdosta. After substantial improvements in the early years of the twentieth century, the road would become the Southern's main line to Florida, replacing the old Macon and Brunswick through Jesup.

Like most locally funded railroads of the era, the Georgia Southern and Florida and its parent, the Macon Construction Company, contemplated more than just a railroad. By the mid 1880s, the railroads' power to create towns and inflate land prices was abundantly clear. Accordingly, most railroading ventures operated in close harmony with "development" companies that sought to take full advantage of real estate speculation and land booms so often created by new railroads even before rails were laid. This was especially true in the case of railroads that probed deep into theretofore isolated and inaccessible areas. It was customary for these land development companies to not only secure depot sites and rights-of-way in established towns along the proposed routes, but also to acquire raw land for future development and sale. In addition to their demands for stock subscriptions from towns along the way, in many cases, railroad companies demanded large tracts of land at little or no cost. In the case of the Georgia Southern and Florida, we find that the original survey for the road charted a route through Quitman. But when citizens there refused free right-of-way and free land for development, the line was built through Valdosta where the depot site, right-of-way and substantial lands were ceded to the railroad.[11] In Adel, where a new town was created about a quarter mile from old Puddleville, railroad surveyors laid out the town in exchange for one-half of the business and residential lots in the new village Adel.[12] Although Cordele, the quintessential boom town, had already been fully exploited by the

Savannah, Americus and Montgomery Railroad and its allied Americus Land Development Company, the Georgia, Southern and Florida was given half interest in 200 acres there on the assumption that the crossing rails would further inflate the value of the Savannah, Americus and Montgomery's already substantial holdings.

In the decades following the completion of the Georgia Southern and Florida, new counties sprouted like so many seedlings along the arrow-straight rails, and courthouses blossomed like Spring flowers. At Vienna, William Parkins's 1890 Dooly County Courthouse appeared only two years after the rails arrived, and Frank Milburn's grand Lowndes County Courthouse rose at Valdosta in 1903.

By 1910, miracles of growth had followed the railroad's arrival, as the junction town of Cordele mushroomed from an empty place in the woods in 1888 to a city of almost 6000 by 1910. The once crude sawmills at Tifton stood among almost 3000 residents at the junction of three mainline railroads in that same year, and Valdosta, where five railroads crossed, was a city of over 7500. In 1905, three of the first eight counties of the New County Movement appeared along the line of the Georgia Southern and Florida as Crisp, Turner and Tift Counties were created. Cordele and Ashburn immediately set to work to erect grand classical courthouses. Although Cook County would not emerge, until 1919, there can be little doubt that its creation was a late harvest of the seeds of New South aspiration and hope planted thirty years before as the Georgia Southern and Florida laid out the new town of Adel a few hundred yards from the old village once called Puddleville.

The Georgia Southern and Florida offers a compelling example of the early power of Georgia's railroads to disseminate New South mythology into some of the wildest and most remote country in the state. But as the twentieth century wore on and the great stands of virgin pine were depleted, these rails began to relate a very different story. They told of the capricious reality of the new age, and the unreliable nature of its myths. While the New South seemed real at places like Cordele, Tifton and Valdosta where many rails crossed, it brought only shallow booms followed by more poverty and want to Vienna, Ashburn and Adel. While the new "business elite" in these towns clung to their faith in the promise of a new economic age, for the timbermen, farmers and herders along the rails, talk of the New South had developed a uniquely hollow ring by 1920.

•

The Macon, Dublin and Savannah Railroad

Bibb County: Macon (see chapters 3 & 8) • Twiggs County: Jeffersonville • Laurens County: Dublin
Treutlen County: Soperton • Some Last Thoughts on The Macon, Dublin and Savannah Railroad

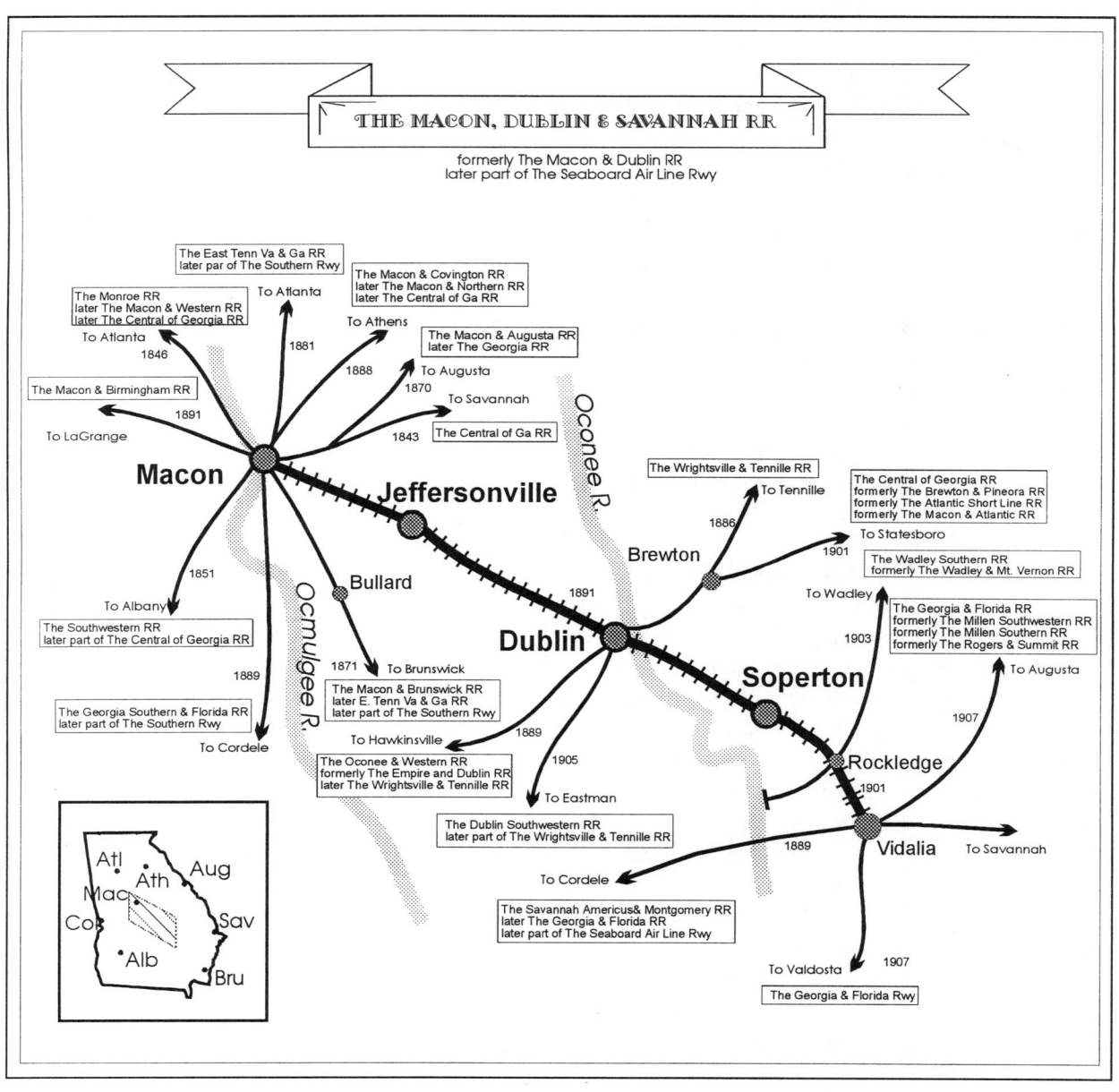

22 | The Macon, Dublin and Savannah Railroad

Plate 22.1: The Twiggs County Courthouse, built c.1810, Burned 1901.

In 1809, when Twiggs County was created from Wilkinson, a courthouse was already under construction at the new and yet unnamed county town of Wilkinson County, which had been laid out about 5 miles from present-day Jeffersonville. Since the new county seat of Wilkinson County lay in the center of the newly created Twiggs County, work on that building was halted, and Wilkinson relocated her county town at Irwinton. Not far from the abandoned site, the citizens of Twiggs built their own county town and called it Marion. This fine two-story frame courthouse rose sometime around 1810. Like Clinton in Jones County, the little village knew an early rush of success in the 1820s and 1830s only to be overshadowed by the extraordinary progress of the state-created trading center at nearby Macon. Macon's location on the Ocmulgee and the arrival of the Central of Georgia Railroad at Macon in 1842 sealed Marion's fate. The village of Marion was in full decline by 1850, when the citizens of Twiggs County voted to move the county seat to Jeffersonville (originally called Raines Store) only 6 miles away.

The history of old Marion is today shrouded in myth. As is usual in places by-passed by the railroads, the traditional myth in Twiggs County is that the Central was originally surveyed through Marion, but that the town opposed change of any sort, and there arose such opposition to the railroad that the Central was obliged to change its route. Like all of these tales, the story centers on a charming and self-effacing image of simpler times. According to the official history of Twiggs County: "Many citizens feared the advent of the horseless carriage, believed it to be a curse on their welfare, and stated publicly and emphatically that they wanted no part of any untried gadget running loose in their midst."[1]

---

[1] J. Lanette O'Neal Faulk and Betty Walker Jones, eds, *History of Twiggs County, Georgia* (Jeffersonville GA: Major General John Twiggs Chapter, American Daughters of the American Revolution, 1960) 51.

Plate 22.1: In 1868, the old Twiggs County Courthouse at Marion was dismantled, moved to Jeffersonville and reassembled.

To be sure, there were some in Marion who harbored such opinions. But as we have seen, the Central had little interest in any of the towns along its route, and the choice of the northern route through Burke, Jefferson and Washington Counties was based on hard economics and modern engineering. It is highly unlikely that local opposition had much influence on the decisions of this powerful company, which had behind it the power of law and considerable public support.

Other myths regarding Marion center on that odd and often contradictory mix of the legends of the Old South and the American frontier. We are told that that the town enjoyed a "gay society," while elsewhere it seems that social activity centered around drinking, gambling and "street brawls."[2] According to George White, the town once had a branch of the Bank of Darien, but by 1849, when White listed Marion in his 1849 *Statistics of the State of Georgia,* he described a village of about sixty residents, containing only a courthouse, a jail and two stores.

The reasons for the relocation of the Twiggs County seat from Marion to Jeffersonville remains something of a mystery. In 1849, the old town of Raines Store became officially known as Jeffersonville, and White tells us only that the town had a population of about 100 and was "considered healthy." Certainly, Marion was on the decline in 1850 and Jeffersonville was growing, but White supplies a clue when he describes Jeffersonville as "healthy." Marion was built at the very edge of a swamp, and it may have

been this poor site that prompted the move to Jeffersonville. Controversy would rage for almost twenty years, and although it was first decided to move the courthouse in 1850, the actual removal was not accomplished until 1868, when the old frame building, along with the jail, a hotel and several other buildings, were dismantled and reconstructed in Jeffersonville. This rang the death knell for Marion, which completely disappeared shortly thereafter. Today no trace of the village remains.

Plate 22.2: The depot at Jeffersonville.

In the same year that the Twiggs County Courthouse was moved to Jeffersonville, the Macon and Brunswick Railroad began service between Macon and Hawkinsville. One of the first of the Reconstruction railroads backed by the state's guarantee of its bonded debt, the Macon and Brunswick skirted the western boundary of Twiggs County. The fact that Jeffersonville was 6 miles closer to the depot at Bullard may well have been a factor in the decision to finally move the county seat. Whatever the case, while Marion disappeared and was forgotten, Jeffersonville, 12 miles from the railroad, simply stagnated. Five years later in 1873, the Central surveyed a line from its main line at Griswold to Jeffersonville, but nothing came of this plan. Jeffersonville continued to languish,[3] and in 1886, according to Sholes's *Gazetteer of Georgia,* Jeffersonville's population was still below 250. At about this time, the Macon and Dublin Railroad was born. Chartered in 1885, the Macon and Dublin was the brain-child of its first president, Twiggs County planter, Dudley Hughes, and his associate John M. Stubbs of Dublin. Financed entirely from local stock subscriptions and without bonded debt,[4] the Macon to Dublin struggled in its early years. Convict labor was initially employed,[5] but after only 14 miles were graded, work was stopped as a grander scheme surfaced. In 1886, the Savannah, Dublin and Western Short Line Company was chartered to link Macon and Savannah via Dublin. This plan included a branch from Dublin via Hawkinsville to Americus. All of this came to nothing, and in 1890 work resumed on the original Macon to Dublin line, now reorganized as the Macon, Dublin and Savannah

Railroad. The fifty-mile long railroad was completed to Dublin in 1891, and in 1901 it was extended to Vidalia where it linked to Savannah via the Seaboard Air Line Railway.

Plate 22.3: The Twiggs County Courthouse, built in 1902-1903. James W. Golucke, architect.

By 1901, when plans surfaced to extend the Macon, Dublin and Savannah to Vidalia, Jeffersonville's population had doubled in only five years. In that same year, the wooden relic of the 1810 Twiggs County Courthouse burned to the ground. With such a sudden and pressing need for a new courthouse, it is difficult to attribute the construction of Atlanta architect, James W. Golucke's 1903 Twiggs County Courthouse to New South zeal fired by the prospect of a rail link from Jeffersonville to Savannah. Nonetheless, aspirations were aloft in Jeffersonville in 1901. In May of that year, *The Twiggs Herald* contemplated the extension of the line:

> If the Macon and Dublin is to be extended to Savannah, our town has a growing chance if our businessmen are public spirited enough to organize an enterprise that will attract moneyed men. It is necessary to the welfare of our town that we have a bank and a cotton market; a cotton mill will be a splendid money making investment, and we would be glad to see a move in this direction.[6]

Here is a clear reflection of railroad-inspired dreams of commerce and an excellent example of the odd mixture of business and benevolent civic-mindedness that had characterized the early cotton mill movement in Georgia. "Build the mill to save the town" often seemed to be a more compelling motivation than dreams of profit.

As usual, out in the red hills of Twiggs County, the myth of the New South had not captured the imagination of the county's farmers the way it had seduced the merchants in town. It took three elections to get two-thirds of the county's 710 qualified voters to cast ballots in favor of courthouse bonds, and in

Plate 22.2: When the Seaboard Air Line acquired the old Macon, Dublin and Savannah Railroad, Jeffersonville found itself on the main line from Macon to Savannah. (Photo: Wilber W. Caldwell.)

Plate 22.3: James Golucke's 1903 Twiggs County Courthouse at Jeffersonville replaced the county's old frame court building which burned in 1901. (Photo: Wilber W. Caldwell.)

[2] Faulk and Jones, *History of Twiggs County, Georgia*, 50.

[3] Virgil Powers, *Annual Reports to the President of the Central Railroad and Banking Company* 3/37 (Savannah GA: 1873) 35-36.

[4] Faulk and Jones, eds, *History of Twiggs County, Georgia* (Jeffersonville, 1960) 159-60

[5] *The Wrightsville Recorder*, December 20, 1884.

[6] *The Twiggs Herald*, May 3, 1901.

1902 bonds to fund a courthouse and jail were finally issued.

James Golucke's Twiggs County Courthouse was dedicated in April of 1903. It was built on the same plan as three other Golucke designed court buildings in Georgia: the 1900 Clayton County Courthouse at Jonesboro, the 1901 Madison County Courthouse at Danielsville and the 1901 Fannin County Courthouse at Blue Ridge. All of these buildings display subtle differences in fenestration and decoration, but with their front corner pavilions capped with pyramidal roofs, octagonal rear corner pavilions and slender central towers, their similarities are striking. Of these four sister courthouses, this building at Jeffersonville is by far the most Spartan owing largely to smaller, simpler fenestration and to the absence of bold quoining, keystones and splayed headers.

No cotton mill appeared in Jeffersonville, and despite her location on the railroad, the place never became much of a cotton market. In 1903, as James Golucke's new courthouse rose, the town did acquire a bank, but the place remained a simple county town with twelve stores, three lawyers, three doctors, two livery stables, two repair shops, two gins and two hotels.[7] In short, the New South passed Jeffersonville by. Between 1900 and 1901, Jeffersonville added only about 180 new residents. Meanwhile, only 30 miles down the rails of the Macon, Dublin and Savannah, at the crossing of the old Wrightsville and Tennille Railroad, Dublin had grown from a village of 800 in 1890 to a city of almost 6000 by 1910.

LAURENS COUNTY: DUBLIN

Plate 22.4: The Laurens County Courthouse, built in 1895. Demolished in 1962. Bruce and Morgan, architects.[8]

In 1891, when the Macon, Dublin and Savannah Railroad made its junction with the Wrightsville and Tennille at Dublin, the event marked the beginning of a period of growth in that city that was every bit as impressive as the phenomena at Waycross, Tifton and Cordele. On the surface, Dublin suddenly appeared to be a model of New South prosperity and growth. The

Queen Anne details of Bruce and Morgan's 1895 Laurens County Court surely reflected the high hopes and grand aspirations that soared on the banks of the Oconee River, where Dublin had become a railroad junction town.

If we scrape away the glitter of the myth, and inquire into the reason for the success at Dublin, we find at the heart of the boom, not the modern songs of industrial development nor the diversified agriculture that New South spokesmen so ardently promoted, but the same old monotonous Southern melody of cotton. Late arriving railroads had opened the piney woods in Laurens County to the exploitation of the area's timber resources, and once the mighty pine forests were gone, it was abundantly clear that, if only enough fertilizer could be applied, the sandy soil here was better for the raising of cotton than many of the washed out farms of the old cotton belt.

Again it was the railroads that supplied the needed ingredient. As tons of guano were spread across Laurens County, her fields turned white with the capricious prosperity of cotton while Dublin became a formidable cotton market. In 1879, Sholes's *Gazetteer of Georgia* placed Dublin's population at 490, and the next year, Laurens produced about 7000 bales of cotton on 20,000 acres. By 1910, the county harvested an incredible 42,000 bales cultivated on over 100,000 acres. In that year, Dublin's population was almost 6000, and the town counted over 100 retail stores and eight enormous wholesalers. In 1900, over 1000 mules were traded at Dublin.[9] A cotton mill, which like so many others across the state claimed to be "the largest in the South," opened in 1902, and by 1905, the place boasted 22 passenger trains a day. In 1913, in an act worthy of the most ostentatious braggadocio, a seven-story building was erected in Dublin.

But what appeared to be a paragon of New South progress was built on the flimsy foundations of cotton. In 1918, Laurens County harvested over 55,000 bales of cotton. Three years later, the boll weevil appeared, and the county produced only 11,000 bales. It was a disaster, and it marked the beginning of a period of deep decline for middle Georgia.

Like all of Bruce and Morgan's late nineteenth century court buildings, the 1895 Laurens County

Courthouse follows a highly picturesque agenda. classically inspired Queen Anne decoration allowed Alexander Bruce to create a modern look, while clinging to what was by 1895 the fading star of the Romanesque Revival in America. Distinctly Queen Anne elements are evident in Bruce and Morgan's court buildings at Talbotton, Buchanan and Dallas, all built in 1892, and in their 1894 Bulloch County Courthouse at Statesboro. Bruce's last two courthouses, the 1896 Monroe County Courthouse at Forsyth and the 1898 Butts County Courthouse at Jackson, carried classical ornamentation beyond the Queen Anne. They gave voice to an eclectic style that acknowledged the new American classicism, which was sweeping the American North, without giving in to it by discarding Alexander Bruce's deeply etched Romantic sensitivities. Here in Dublin, elaborate terra cotta and complex multi-paned windows, decorate Bruce's fittingly up-to-date symbol for the blossoming city's modern aspirations. In an ironic way, the building is a fitting symbol for the illusive New South as well. Its modern Queen Anne trappings are charming but transparent attempts to disguise a singularly retardate core.

In 1807, when Laurens County was cut from Wilkinson, the region was a vast empty wilderness of pine. The first county seat was established at Sumpterville, and a makeshift temporary courthouse was erected. In 1811, eight years before the first steamboat appeared on the Oconee River, the seat of government of the new county was moved to Dublin on the banks of that stream, and a more permanent public building was completed sometime before 1828. In 1849, a two-story frame courthouse rose at Dublin, and in that same year, George White described the place in his *Statistics of the State of Georgia* as having about 180 inhabitants and "a good courthouse, several stores and 65 houses." A little over a year before, the Central Railroad and Banking Company had completed its surveys from Savannah to Macon, and Dublin lay on the southern route. Here again we find

Plate 22.4: Bruce and Morgan's 1895 Laurens County Courthouse was a fitting symbol for Dublin and the New South: distinctly modern Queen Anne trappings disguised a singularly retardate core. (Photo: Courtesy of Georgia Department of Archives and History.)

the usual myth surrounding local opposition to early railroads. According to The Official History of Laurens County, "...fearing that the railroad might be an invasion of private rights and would give unpleasant publicity, citizens refused a right of way."[10] It is unlikely that such opposition had much effect on the Central's decision to build its looping northern route, which avoided the swamps west of Savannah and the lonely stretches of pine barrens and instead traversed the rich fields of Georgia's Cotton Belt.

Bypassed by the Central in 1840, Dublin would rely on the Oconee River as her primary transportation link for the next fifty years. In the early days, pole boats and cotton boxes filled the unreliable channel, and although steamboats remained active well into the twentieth century, the Oconee was filled with snags and often too low to support traffic for as much as six months out of the year. By the time the Wrightsville and Tennille Railroad arrived in Dublin in 1886, atti-

[7] *The Twiggs Herald*, July 26, 1901.

[8] The Minutes of the Ordinary's Court of Laurens County for the year 1895 record a payment to Bruce and Morgan for courthouse design on page 371.

[9] Don and Mildred Lamb, *A Profile of Dublin and Laurens County* (Macon GA: Williams and Canady, 1995) 19.

[10] Bertha Sheppard Hart, *The Official History of Laurens County* (Athens GA: John Lauren Chapter, Daughters of the American Revolution, 1987) 49.

tudes toward the railroad were much changed. An iron bridge was erected to span the Oconee in 1891. In that same year, the Macon, Dublin and Savannah joined the Wrightsville and Tennille at Dublin, and the town began to blossom. Two more railroads would make their junction at Dublin (see Table 22.1). By the first decade of the new century, two fine passenger depots stood in Dublin, one served the Macon, Dublin and Savannah, the other the Wrightsville and Tennille. Like Alexander Bruce's elegant Queen Anne courthouse, both are gone today.

TREUTLEN COUNTY: SOPERTON

Georgia's New County Movement began in 1904 when the state legislature lifted the 27 year-old constitutional ban on the creation of new counties in the state. Almost immediately twenty-one prospective new counties sought recognition, and eight new counties were created in 1905. Between 1906 and 1924, sixteen more new Georgia counties would be created.

There can be little doubt that the railroads lay at the heart of all of this. In the years since the Constitution of 1877 had fixed the number of counties in Georgia at 137, the railroads had changed the map of the state. By 1905, towns, which had not existed at all in 1877, had mushroomed into prosperous trading centers, and in many cases these newcomers sought to steal away the courthouses from traditional regional market towns. With the constitutional amendment of 1904, Georgia's brash new railroad boom towns suddenly ceased their efforts to capture county seats away from older towns and began to redraw the map of Georgia with successful efforts to

create new counties. Most of the new counties appeared in the Pine Barrens. By 1905, the enormous expanses of the Wiregrass were no longer empty forests, and the huge counties of south Georgia began to be partitioned around the boom towns created by the very rails that had hauled off the region's timber and hauled in the new settlers to people new towns.

Soperton is a late example of such a place. Before 1901, when the Macon, Dublin and Savannah Railroad extended its rails from Dublin to Vidalia, Soperton was nothing but piney woods and farm land, and present-day Trentlen County was originally part of Montgomery, Emanuel and Tattnall Counties. In 1905, part of this area had been included in the failed attempt to create James County with the booming village of Adrian as the county seat. When Adrian, at the junction of the Wadley Southern and the Central of Georgia, failed in her bid for new county status, Soperton was only three years old. But the growth of this new village beside the Macon, Dublin and Savannah was so great that, before the end of the decade, talk began to center around a new county with Soperton as the county seat.

Indeed, early accounts of Soperton's growth are startling. The first mention of the town comes in June of 1902, when *The Montgomery (County) Monitor* reported that "30 or 40 lots had been sold," at Soperton, where there was one general store and "several families."[11] Only four months later *The Monitor* informed readers that Soperton was "on a boom" with five stores and "several dwellings going up."[12] Less than a year later, we find an account of "fourteen stores packed with new goods." This article featured a description of the place as a "live town with every house new and a new stock of goods in every store." Included in this was the prediction that "Soperton will expand until it takes in Mount Vernon and all of the towns on this side of the (Oconee) River."[13] The Bank of Soperton opened for business only a year after the town was laid out, and by 1910 Soperton counted almost 500 residents. In 1915, and early attempt to create Treutlen County failed to pass the state legislature. Three years later, the Durden Lumber Company employed over 200 at Soperton, and the area was leading the state in the harvesting of

---

Table 22.1

RAILROADS AT DUBLIN

1886-The Wrightsville and Tennille Raiload. Tennille via Dublin to Hawkinsville and Eastman.

1891-The Macon, Dublin and Savannah Railroad. Macon via Dublin to Vidalia. (later part of the Seaboard Air Line.)

1889-The Empire and Dublin Railroad. Dublin to Hawkinsville. (later the Oconee and Western, later part of the Wrightsville and Tennille.)

1904-The Dublin and Southwestern Railroad. Dublin to Eastman. (later part of the Wrightsville and Tennille.)

second-generation stands of slash pine. The new county became a reality in 1918.

Architect, J. J. Baldwin's, Treutlen County Courthouse was completed in 1920. Its traditional lines are typical of the new era of courthouse building in Georgia after 1910. Such designs are not a part of this study.

SOME LAST THOUGHTS ON THE MACON, DUBLIN AND SAVANNAH RAILROAD

In the late 1880s five new railroads began construction in Macon. In addition to the Georgia Southern and Florida; the Macon and Birmingham and the ill-fated Macon and Atlantic, E. C. Machen's Covington and Macon built northward toward Athens, and a locally conceived and financed line, the Macon and Dublin, began grading eastward toward Dublin. After considerable delays precipitated by more ambitious schemes including a branch to Americus, the Macon and Dublin was reorganized as the Macon, Dublin and Savannah and completed to Dublin in 1891. With its completion, ten railroads radiated from Macon.

In 1901, the Macon, Dublin and Savannah extended its rails to Vidalia where it joined the Seaboard Air Line, which had acquired the old Savannah, Americus, and Montogomery Railroad line in that same year. Villages along the right-of-way suddenly found themselves on the main line between Macon and Savannah. In Jeffersonville, a dusty village of only a few hundred residents, hopes soared as the town's population had doubled between 1895 and 1900. But the town lay in Macon's shadow, and without crossing rails, Jeffersonville was destined to remain an obscure place. The county's old frame courthouse burned in 1901, and not surprisingly James Golucke's Romanesque Revival replacement is among that architect's most uninspiring creations. By that time, only 30 miles to the east beside the Oconee River at Dublin, where the rails of the Macon, Dublin and Savannah crossed the Wrightsville and Tennille, a period of extraordinary growth was well underway. A town of 800 in 1890, Dublin's population would exceed 5700 by 1910. Here an early wave of New South frenzy begot Alexander Bruce's elegant 1895 Laurens County Courthouse, an exuberant Queen Anne expression of hope and high spirits.

At Soperton, a village laid out in 1902, we find a late example of the railroad's enduring power to create towns and inspire courthouses. Before Soperton was twenty years old, it was the county seat of a new county called Treutlen, and a courthouse rose there in 1920.

The Macon, Dublin and Savannah Railroad is typical of the evolution of Georgia's railroads in the late nineteenth and early twentieth century. The story of the 1880s is the story of New South passion and of local railroad building in Georgia. The story of the 1890s is the story of acquisition and consolidation by Northern railroad conglomerates. The ensuing story is a tale of exploitation and disappointment as, one by one, the promises of the New South were found to be hollow. They were balanced on the flimsy foundations of cotton and propped up by the disappearing buttresses of once vast forests of pine.

•

[11] *The Montgomery Monitor*, June 19, 1902.

[12] *The Montgomery Monitor*, October 6, 1902.

[13] *The Montgomery Monitor*, March 26, 1903

The Savannah, Americus and Montgomery Railroad

Stewart County: Lumpkin • Webster County: Preston • Sumter County: Americus (see chapter 6)
Crisp County: Cordele • Wilcox County: Abbeville • Telfair County: McRae (see chapter 9)
Wheeler County: Alamo • Montgomery County: Mount Vernon • Toombs County: Lyons

THE SAVANNAH AND WESTERN RAILROAD
Evans County: Claxton • Bryan County: Pembroke • Chatham County: Savannah (see chapter 2)
Some Last Thoughts on the Savannah, Americus & Montgomery Railroad

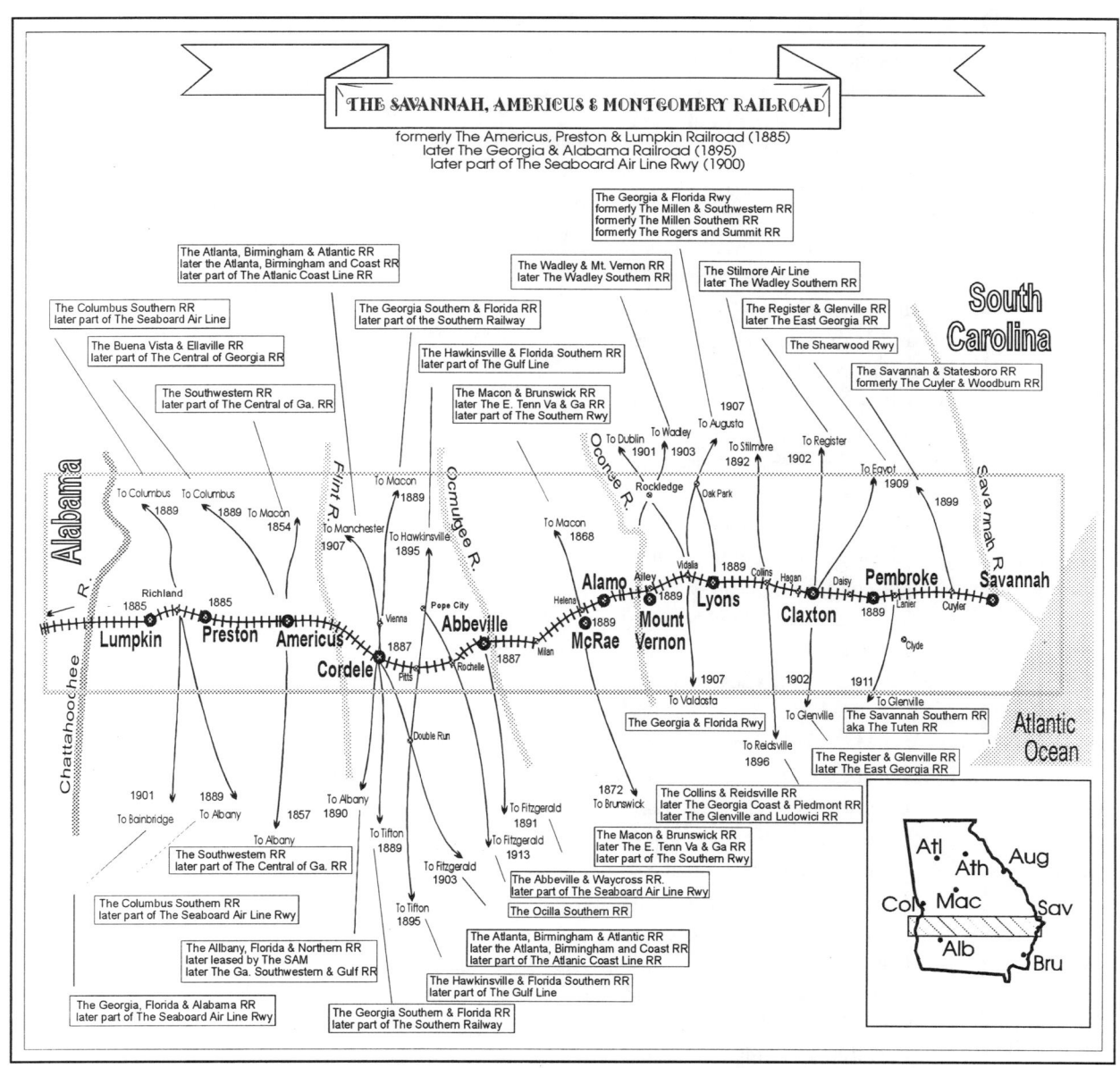

23 | The Savannah, Americus and Montgomery Railroad

STEWART COUNTY: LUMPKIN

Plate 23.1: The Stewart County Courthouse, built in 1895. Andrew J. Bryan, architect. Burned 1922. Rebuilt 1923, T. F. Lockwood, architect.

In 1895, when Atlanta architect, Andrew Bryan, drew the plans for the Stewart County Courthouse at Lumpkin, few in Georgia understood the far-reaching implications of his design. Here was the first court building in Georgia to express the "new classicism" that was to sweep the nation into the new century. Two years before, the flamboyant arcades of Chicago's 1893 Columbian Exposition had awed visitors with its "Florentine" finery and begun the so-called American Renaissance. Ironically, this gushing display of classical ornament had been strongly opposed by Lumpkin's native son, the prominent Chicago architect, John Wellborn Root. As one of America's leading architects and the consulting architect for the design of the buildings at the Chicago fair, Root had sought to embellish the great exposition with elaborately picturesque buildings of "variety and color."[1] But in 1890, while the fair was in its planning stages, Root died in an untimely death. His romantic ideas for the architecture at the grand exposition, along with those of Louis Sullivan, were quickly swept aside by the proponents of the new classicism led by Eastern architects like Charles McKim and Richard Morris Hunt. As the Chicago Fair opened, great spasms of Beaux-Arts classicism spewed forth in an orgy of Baroque excess, and the picturesque in America was quickly engulfed.

John Wellborn Root had traveled a long way from the rural Stewart County of his youth. Likewise, in 1893, the architecture of the proposed "White City" at Chicago was a great distance from the simple country courthouse at Lumpkin,

---

[1] Donald Hofmann, *The Architecture of John Wellborn Root* (Baltimore: John Hopkins University Press, 1975) 232.

Georgia. Despite her ancient ties to classical forms, the American South would be slow to embrace the new styles unveiled at Chicago. Chief architect Bradford Gilbert's buildings at the 1895 Cotton States Exposition in Atlanta confirm the region's intransigence. Although the buildings in Atlanta's Piedmont Park manifested a return to symmetry, their thrust was still decidedly picturesque. With their romantic gray and green color scheme and their rustic shingle and stone textures, Gilbert's highly influential designs at Atlanta would further retard the progress of the new classicism in the region.

Nonetheless, classical seeds were on the wind, and men like Andrew Bryan understood how seductive these classical images would be for the American South. He also knew that such a seduction could never be accomplished by flashy displays of Beaux-Arts ornament alone. Like James Golucke and Frank Milburn after him, Bryan began the process of neoclassical revival in Georgia with a bit of an "end run." He eschewed fashionable Parisian forms and returned to the vocabulary of Georgian England so familiar to the South. His 1895 Stewart County Courthouse at Lumpkin paved the way for the classical revival in Georgia. Although the first properly neoclassical court building in the state rose in Columbus in 1896, it would be almost a decade before classical forms were firmly entrenched in Georgia. By then, the South

Plate 23.1: Atlanta architect, Andrew J. Bryan's, 1895 Stewart County Courthouse was the first court building in Georgia to express the "new classicism" that swept the nation into the new century. (Photo: Wilber W. Caldwell.)

would have manipulated the symbols attached to the new style to suit her own peculiar needs. Meanwhile, here in Lumpkin, the Federal Style details of Andrew J. Bryan's Stewart County Courthouse, which was originally crowned with a stunning Neocolonial lantern, appeared to be more a voice from the past than from the future. Perhaps nothing could have been more appropriate.

Originally the county seat of Randolph County, Lumpkin had been laid out in February of 1830 as the partition of the enormous Lee County began. The town had become the Stewart County seat when that county was created from Randolph in December of the same year. The town's early progress was exceptional. A log courthouse was erected at Lumpkin in 1831 and was replaced by a sturdy frame court building in 1837. In that same year, Adiel Sherwood described the town as having 36 dwellings. As the lure of its new cotton growing lands filled Stewart County with eager farmers, Lumpkin continued to grow. In his 1849 *Statistics of the State of Georgia,* George White catalogued Lumpkin's successes, listing three hotels, twelve stores, ten lawyers and a population numbering between 800 and 1000. White adds, "considerable business is done in this place." But Lumpkin's early growth was not to continue. A long period of stagnancy followed the end of the war. The simple wooden courthouse and the flimsy wooden buildings that had ringed the square before the Civil War would stand well into the 1890s. In 1885, Stewart County produced only 15,000 bales of cotton, a figure that barely surpassed her antebellum output. Sholes's *Gazetteer of Georgia* for 1879, 1886 and 1896 all list Lumpkin's population at about 1000.

Lumpkin's period of dormancy had not been without episodes of railroad speculation. The first of Lumpkin's failed railroad encounters, occurred way back in 1847 when the original survey of the Southwestern Railroad proposed a line through Stewart County. A local legend contends that a powerful Stewart County landowner, not wanting to grant right of way to the Southwestern, had avoided negotiations by continually "going fishing," and thus forced the railroad to build along the eastern route through Sumter County.[2] This makes colorful reading, but as we have seen, the Southwestern's decision to build along an eastern route through Sumter County was the result of substantial stock subscriptions in Americus, and the promise of a connection with the locally funded Georgia and Florida Railroad then planned from Albany to Americus.

After the Civil War, Lumpkin eyed its share of Reconstruction railroad building schemes, but none had appeared promising enough to spark the New South spirit that briefly lifted so many Georgia communities of the era. Perhaps the most notable of these was Hannibal Kimball's ill-fated Bainbridge, Cuthbert and Columbus Railroad. This flimsy scheme failed in 1872. In 1884, the town's hopes were again stirred as *The Lumpkin Independent* informed readers that the Kimball's bankrupted railroad, renamed the Chattanooga, Columbus and Florida Railroad, was "at work re-grading the old line near Cuthbert," and that the road would undoubtedly "go by or near Lumpkin."[3] In that same year, there was speculation that the Central of Georgia was planning to build a line from Smithville just north of Albany to Columbus through either Lumpkin or Preston. Rumors of a line to Eufaula, Alabama were equally enticing.[4]

As the grand plans of both the Central and the Chattanooga, Columbus and Florida dissolved into thin air, Samuel Hawkins and a group of ambitious investors in Americus pressed ahead with their plans to break the monopolistic grip of the Central of Georgia by laying rails from Eufaula via Americus to either Hawkinsville or Eastman. The line initially had the backing of the East Tennessee, Virginia and Georgia Railroad, which had acquired the failed Macon and Brunswick in 1882. Apparently the East Tennessee, Virginia and Georgia's interest in the project waned, but Hawkins persevered. Abbreviating his grand plan, he led efforts to build the Americus Preston and Lumpkin Railroad, a narrow gauge line spanning the 45 miles from Americus via Lumpkin to the Chattahoochee River. Hawkins assured investors that the river "cannot be pooled against us." As "God's highway," Hawkins concluded, a river "could not be used to oppress."[5] With this, he set about to raise the capital for his line.

Despite the fact that torrential rains had spoiled Lumpkin's grand barbecue of "50 carcasses" organized in June of 1884 to promote Colonel Hawkins's tiny railroad,[6] Stewart County demonstrated her zeal for the new line by subscribing almost $30,000 of the road's $85,000 cost. By December, *The Independent* reported that over 300 hands were at work in Stewart County grading the Americus, Preston and Lumpkin Railroad,[7] and in an apt metaphor for the railroad's perceived healing economic power, the paper's editor declared: "The railroad will be a great throbbing pulse through which must flow the warm life blood of social and financial prosperity."[8]

As the railroad reached Preston in 1885, Lumpkin was "anxiously looking eastward," and there were many "evidences of energy and enterprise." Citizens awaited the rails whose arrival would surely "mark a period of peace, plenty and prosperity."[9] The mood was expectant as the first train steamed into Lumpkin in February of 1886. Amid a rush of high expectations and billowing steam everyone assumed that Lumpkin was about to "speedily grow to the magnitude of a commercial city."[10]

Sadly, the initial effect of the Americus Preston and Lumpkin Railroad on Lumpkin's struggling economy bore little resemblance to her visions of New South wealth. The road's first depot was an old fertilizer warehouse, and the shabby wooden buildings that still ringed the 1837 frame Stewart County Courthouse looked nothing like the grand New South monuments of brick that everyone thought would rise. Expectations were quickly tempered by reality,

---

[2] Helen Eliza Terrill, *The History of Stewart County, Georgia* (Columbus GA: Columbus Office Supply, 1958) 331.

[3] *The Lumpkin Independent*, December 6, 1884.

[4] Terrill, *The History of Stewart County, Georgia*, 371; and the *Lumpkin Independent*, September 5, 1885.

[5] J. E. D. Shipp, "Samuel Hugh Hawkins", in William J. Northen, ed., *Men of Mark in Georgia*, 6 vols. (Atlanta: A.B. Caldwell, 1906-12) 2:407.

[6] *The Lumpkin Independent*, June 28, 1884.

[7] *The Lumpkin Independent*, December 6, 1884.

[8] *The Lumpkin Independent*, July 26, 1884.

[9] *The Lumpkin Independent*, September 12, 1885.

[10] *The Lumpkin Independent*, March 3, 1886.

and throughout the late 1880s, successive grand juries found the old wooden courthouse totally acceptable.

But Samuel Hawkins was far from finished. By the end of the decade, the Americus, Preston and Lumpkin had become the nucleus of the mighty Savannah, Americus and Montgomery Railroad, affectionately known as the SAM. By 1891 the entire line was converted to standard gauge and the rails stretched all the way from Montgomery, Alabama, to Lyons, Georgia, where its trains ran into Savannah on the newly completed rails of the Savannah and Western. The effect in Lumpkin was electric. Brick buildings began to materialize, and the Bank of Sumter County rose in 1891. By 1893, two grand juries had recommended a new courthouse, and in May of 1895 *The Independent* issued a scathing indictment of the old court building: "…there is not a county in this or any other state in this Republic of 70 million inhabitants, that is commensurate in population and wealth with Stewart County, so poorly provided with public buildings."[11] By the first of June, courthouse designs had been submitted by "half a dozen" architects, and a plan by Atlanta's Andrew Bryan had been selected.[12]

Ironically, the very expansion that so lifted spirits in Lumpkin proved fatal for the Savannah, Americus and Montgomery. Extending the road westward to Montgomery had proved far more expensive than Samuel Hawkins and his engineers had originally calculated. The national depression of the early nineties coupled with the failure of the Central and the Savannah and Western's sudden refusal to allow the SAM use of its tracks into Savannah, put an abrupt end to Colonel Hawkins's dreams.

Despite the failure of the SAM and the national depression that surrounded its collapse, the seeds of New South spirit were now firmly rooted in Lumpkin, and seemingly nothing could shake the town's faith in a future harvest of prosperity. The naïveté of those seduced by New South mythology is clearly illustrated here. In April of 1893, *The Independent* declared: "If capitalists make a visit to our town and see a great many new buildings going up, they will be at once captivated by the enterprise of the place and want to invest some of their money here."[13] Here again was

the rotten core of the New South myth: a continuing tendency to confuse the superficial trappings of a hollow and short-lived commercial boom with the foundations of lasting industrial progress.

In another irony, the few manifestations of the new age that did make their way into Stewart County would not find their center in Lumpkin, but in tiny Richland on the county's eastern border, where in 1889 the rails of the Columbus Southern Railroad crossed the SAM. By 1901, the Georgia, Florida and Alabama had extended its rails northward from Cuthbert toward Columbus, and three railroads met at Richland.

Plate 23.2: The Seaboard Air Line Depot at Richland, built in 1913.

The construction of this fine brick depot in 1913 may have marked the exact moment of Richland's fullness. The tiny village of only about 100 had seen the arrival of the SAM in 1885. In 1889, she had watched as that railroad's real estate investment arm, the Americus Investment Company, erected the massive Richland Hotel at the very crossing of the rails of the SAM and the Columbus Southern. Richland suddenly found herself at the junction of southwestern Georgia's main rail arteries: Savannah to Montgomery and Columbus to Albany. Here we find a manifestation of the fabled power of the railroad to create both boom and bust. In 1913, when this depot appeared across the street from the Richland Hotel, Richland had swept past Lumpkin as the area's leading trading center. In that year, she boasted 3 hotels, 2 banks, 25 stores, a fertilizer factory, a cottonseed oil factory and over 1500 residents. By that time, both the SAM and the Columbus Southern had long since failed. Both lines were acquired by the Georgia and Alabama Railroad, which in 1901 became the core of the soon-to-be-mighty Seaboard Air Line. The Seaboard later acquired the Georgia, Florida and Alabama as well, and suddenly Richland lay at the center of that great railroad's operations in western Georgia.

In 1922, Andrew Bryan's Stewart County Courthouse at Lumpkin burned, and Richland made a futile bid to wrestle the county seat away from hapless Lumpkin. It was to be the one prize that the bold upstart would not garner. Lumpkin retained the county seat and a sadly inferior reconstruction of Bryan's 1895 Stewart County Courthouse, designed by Columbus architect T. F. Lockwood, rose in 1923.

Today in Richland, at the junction of these all but forgotten rusty rails, the Seaboard's old depot stands empty. Across the street looms the eerie abandoned hulk of the old Richland Hotel. These buildings recall a time when the mythical New South seemed very real in Stewart County. Today, the evidence of this fleeting prosperity is cloaked by the ravages of a long and relentless period of decline. Here beside these rusting rails lies the real architecture of the New South: the architecture of hope, transformed by years of neglect into the architecture of broken dreams.

WEBSTER COUNTY: PRESTON

Plate 23.3: The Webster County Courthouse, built in 1915. T. F. Lockwood, architect.

T. F. Lockwood's rather Spartan courthouse at Preston was built after the end of the period of our interest, but it's humble predecessor speaks clearly of that day in 1885 when the rails of Samuel Hawkins's Americus Preston and Lumpkin Railroad arrived in Webster County. Originally chartered in 1853 as Kinchafoonee County, the county's was re-named Webster in 1856. In that same year, its county town, a place first known as Lannahassee and later called McIntosh was re-named Preston, and a two-story frame courthouse was erected. Similar to the nearby frame courthouses at Cusseta in nearby Chattahoochee County and at Tazwell in Marion County, this simple wooden court building stood on Preston's square for almost sixty years. Here was convincing testament to the fact that Webster County residents received little in return for the $15,000 that they subscribed toward the construction of Colonel Hawkins's railroad. The usual myths of impending New South progress were not delivered in this tiny village by the Americus, Preston and Lumpkin Railroad in 1885. Her continued use of the old frame court building further suggests that the zeal for progress failed to later rise in Preston as it had in Lumpkin after the lowly narrow gauge Americus, Preston and

Plate 23.2: Today in Richland, beside the old SAM's all but forgotten rusty rails, the Seaboard's 1913 depot stands empty. Across the street looms the eerie abandoned hulk of the old Richland Hotel. (Photo: Wilber W. Caldwell.)

Plate 23.3: Built well after the end of the period of our interest, T. F. Lockwood's 1915 Webster County Courthouse reflects little of the hope that characterized so many Georgia court buildings of the earlier era. (Photo: Wilber W. Caldwell.)

[11] *The Lumpkin Independent*, May 11, 1895.

[12] *The Lumpkin Independent*, June 1, 1895.

[13] *The Lumpkin Independent*, April 29, 1893.

Lumpkin became the mighty Savannah, Americus and Montgomery Railroad.

Statistical evidence bares out this humble building's story. According to A. C. Sholes's *Gazetteer of Georgia,* Preston had a population of 135 in 1879. Although the arrival of the Americus, Preston, and Lumpkin sparked some local cotton and lumber trade, and the village counted 350 residents in 1886, Preston's population was back down to around 200 by 1896. A county history recounts that around the turn of the century Preston contained two saw mills, two gins and a turpentine still. [14] This was surely not the sturdy foundation upon which to build New South dreams.

The reasons for Preston's stagnancy are clear. Eclipsed by the stunning growth of the nearby rail junctions at Richland and Americus, Preston was destined to watch the New South's pageant of dreams from the wings. With no prospect for a rail junction, tiny Preston lay in the midst of a poor agricultural area, and was peopled by a sturdy breed of individualists. Not surprisingly, many in Webster County welcomed Populism with open arms. As in other counties where Populists were strong, these sturdy farmers would shun the railroad's shinny promises of a new industrial age.

When Webster County finally erected a new courthouse in 1915, it was only because the old 1856 frame building burned. The devastating courthouse fire broke out in the midst of an investigation concerning missing county funds, and many locals remembered that the scent of kerosene "filled the air."[15]

Architecturally, the 1915 Webster County Courthouse reflects little of the hope that characterizes so many Georgia court buildings of the earlier era. It fails to approach any of Columbus architect T. F. Lockwood's earlier designs in Georgia. If it reflects anything at all, it is the practical and frugal nature of the farmers of Webster County and an admiration for Andrew J. Bryan's 1895 Stewart County Counthouse at Lumpkin. A simple classical portico and a few splayed window headers comprise this building's only decoration. These appear to be pale attempts to copy Bryan's Georgian details at nearby Lumpkin.

The tiny wooden depot that once stood beside the rails that passed only 3/4 of a mile from this courthouse has been moved to a nearby farm. The much altered and dilapidated building is today used as a storage shed, a sad and ironic testament to Samuel Hawkins's mighty Savannah, Americus and Montgomery Railroad and its forerunner the Americus Preston and Lumpkin.

CRISP COUNTY: CORDELE

Plate 23.4: Union Depot at Cordele, built c.1901, demolished 1954.

Of the many grand monuments to New South aspirations that blossomed at Cordele, there was perhaps no better symbol for the city's extraordinary growth than this fine depot built by the Seaboard Air Line and the Southern Railway in 1901.[16] The building stood at the intersection of the rails of the old Savannah, Americus and Montgomery and those of the Georgia Southern and Florida Railroads, which crossed here in 1888.

Cordele was the creation of the Americus Investment Company, the holding company that built the SAM and aggressively exploited the commercial potential of the many towns the new road created as it expanded across Georgia. In 1886, less than a year after completing his Americus, Preston and Lumpkin Railroad from Americus to Lumpkin, Samuel Hawkins obtained an amendment to the road's charter allowing him to extend the line eastward from Americus to the Ocmulgee River at Abbeville. At that time, one of the directors of Colonel Hawkins's railroad was Sumter County native, Henry Clay Bagley, who, along with Hawkins, had been a partner in the People's Bank of Americus, which Hawkins had founded back in 1883. In 1887, the twenty-seven year old Bagley was made president of the Americus Investment Company. Here was a man of penetrating vision despite his youth. He quickly grasped the opportunities presented by the collision course of the SAM as it pressed eastward from Americus and the Georgia Southern and Florida as it laid its rails southward from Macon. In 1887, it was clear that the two roads would cross somewhere, and H. C. Bagley intended to dictate the location of this crossing and to reap the financial rewards.

By no coincidence, Henry Bagley was the owner of 1200 acres then in Dooly County. In a story which, according to Georgia chronicler, Lucian Lamar Knight, "read like a modernized fable of Aesop," he sold this land to the Americus Investment Company with the knowledge that the SAM would run through the center of the property. He then divided the tract into town lots and gave half interest in 200 acres of his future "city" to the Macon Construction Company, which controlled the Georgia Southern and Florida Railroad. In exchange he received that company's promise to build its line through the place he had recently named Cordele, to honor Samuel Hawkins's wife and daughter, both named Cordelia.[17] By early 1888, Cordele was a village of 300 people, "a few wooden shacks°and numerous pine trees."[18] By 1890, the town had its third railroad, Nelson Tift's Albany, Florida and Northern. This line immediately fell on hard times and was leased to the SAM, giving Samuel Hawkins a vital link to Albany. By 1893, Cordele was a city of almost 1500. Ironically, just as Cordele began to surge towards real commercial power, the SAM and the Georgia Southern and Florida collapsed.

The story of the rise and fall of the Savannah, Americus and Montgomery Railroad and of Samuel Hawkins and Henry Bagley is surely one of the most compelling and romantic episodes of the era. Accounts of the fall of Hawkins's empire are all the more gripping when viewed against the backdrop of the commercial success at Cordele. As early as 1893, Colonel Hawkins's railroading exploits were being recognized for their dramatic appeal. As the SAM crumbled, *The Vienna Progress* observed:

> The history of 'the Sam'…reads more like a romance…. By the building of the road Col. Hawkins became, from an ordinary bank president, the Great Railroad king of Southwest Georgia. He virtually dictated the great business interests of this section, and those who opposed him or his plans or did not "bow the knee" were made to feel his displeasure.[19]

Plate 23.4: The 1901 Union Depot at Cordele stood at the intersection of the rails of the old Savannah, Americus and Montgomery and those of the Georgia Southern and Florida Railroads, which crossed here in 1888.

Interestingly, this account, published as the SAM collapsed, provides us with a view of Hawkins that flies in the face of his popular legend. Accounts in Vienna, a town spurned by the SAM in favor of the future city of Cordele, paint a picture of Hawkins as a grasping power broker. This portrait befits the Northern stereotype of a denizen of the Gilded Age and is a long distance from the familiar popular image of Colonel Hawkins as the self-sacrificing, civic spirited, Southern entrepreneur who fought to overcome the grasping exploitation of the mighty Central of Georgia Railroad. The Vienna account characterizes Samuel Hawkins as "ambitious," informs us that he "borrowed left and right" and implies that his "SAM city council" gutted the Bank of Americus and bankrupted the city. Further, Hawkins's extension of his railroad to Montgomery is described as stubborn and in imprudent opposition the advise of his friends and advisors.[20] What is more, William Williford in his *Americus Through the Years*, informs us that there had been "hints of irregularities" in the operations of

[14] Webster Women's Club, *History of Webster County* (Roswell GA: Webster Women's Club, 1980) 49.

[15] Webster Women's Club, *History of Webster County*, 51.

[16] *The Abbeville Chronicle*, August 22, 1901.

[17] Lucian Lamar Knight, *Georgia's Landmarks, Memorials and Legends,* 2 vols. (Atlanta: Lucian Lamar Knight, 1913) 1: 499-500.

[18] An undated newspaper clipping from The Cordele Daily News, c.1905, reproduced in Crisp County Anniversary Album, 1905 - 1955 (Cordele: 1955).

[19] *The Vienna Progress*, February 14, 1893.

[20] *The Vienna Progress*, February 14, 1893.

the Americus Investment Company. And according to Williford, in December of 1892, Henry Clay Bagley suddenly resigned, sold his home in Americus and moved to Atlanta where he later made a notable success in the insurance business.[21]

All of this calls into question the usual glowing rhetoric of Hawkins's biographers. In his sketch of Colonel Hawkins in *Men of Mark in Georgia* J. E. D. Shipp, an early civic leader in Cordele, describes Hawkins as "unselfishly devoted to some great patriotic measure" and a man who made "the sacrifice of self for the love of his fellow man."[22] Sadly, we will never know Samuel Hawkins's motives, but his sacrifice is well documented. His personal efforts to save the SAM, resulted in the loss a great personal fortune. Reportedly, he lost over a million dollars of his own money in efforts to save the railroad.[23]

Samuel Hawkins died in 1905, just as Cordele became the county seat of the newly created Crisp County. The collapse of the SAM may have ruined Hawkins, but it had little long-term effect on Cordele's growth. By the time Crisp County was born, the old SAM had become the main artery of the mighty Seaboard Air Line, and the Georgia Southern and Florida had become part of J. P. Morgan's sprawling Southern Railway. The Albany, Florida and Northern was back on its feet as the Georgia Southwestern and Gulf, and the new and powerful

Atlanta, Birmingham and Atlantic Railroad crossed all of these older roads at Cordele. Henry Clay Bagley's vision was being called the "The Magic City," "South Georgia's Rising Star," "The Gate City to Southern Georgia" and "The Birmingham of the Pines." Suddenly, Americus had a new rival. As that old city of 7500 paid its final respects to Samuel Hawkins, Cordele boasted over 6500 residents, 128 retails stores, four hotels, a large foundry, two newspapers, electric lights, paved sidewalks, a steam laundry and this depot, which stood at the junction of three of the most powerful railroads in Georgia.

Plate 23.5: The Crisp County Courthouse, built in 1907. Demolished 1950. T. F. Lockwood, architect.

The New County Movement of 1905 brings the power of Cordele's railroads into focus. Four of the eight new counties created in that year lay either on the Georgia Southern and Florida or on the old line of the SAM.[24] The citizens of Cordele petitioned the state legislature with compelling arguments for the creation of Crisp County, and although the old rationales concerning the distance to be traveled by rural residents to the county seat were included, they were far down the list. Cordele's most convincing arguments were built on hard statistics: Cordele was the largest city in Georgia that was not a county seat. It had four railways, ten warehouses and 128 retails stores. The proposed Crisp County would contain more wealth and population than any other proposed new county, and the new county would contain more railroad mileage than 123 of Georgia's 137 counties. Opposition in Dooly was vigorous, but futile. It centered not on any compelling logic, but rather on disputing Cordele's statistics. Orators before the state legislature called Cordele's claim to $37 million in business receipts a "Great Fish Story," and placed the true total at under $1 million.[25]

One of Cordele's arguments for her new county was the fact that she already had a building suitable for use as a courthouse. While this may have been true, as soon as the new county of Crisp was created, the citizens of Cordele, fueled by new zeal and unfettered aspirations, set about to build a monument to their railroad driven success. The choice of T. F. Lockwood

Plate 23.5: Despite architect T. F. Lockwood's rather lack-luster neoclassical efforts at Albany and later at Monticello, his design for the 1907 Crisp County Courthouse at Cordele answered to a higher muse. Photo: Courtesy of the Georgia Dept. of Archives and History. (Photo: Courtesy of the Georgia Dept. of Archives and History.)

is not surprising. With his brother, the New York trained architect, Frank Lockwood, T. F. Lockwood began his practice in Columbus in the late 1890s. In 1895, Frank moved to Montgomery, Alabama, and most of his best work is in that state. Nonetheless, the Lockwood Brother's 1903 Dougherty County Courthouse at Albany was one of the state's first court buildings built in the style of the emerging American Neoclassical Revival and in 1905 Cordele must have looked to the great success that was blossoming at Albany for more than architectural models. Despite its importance in the early American Neoclassical Revival in Georgia, Lockwood's courthouse at Albany was inferior to many of the early neoclassical court building that began to cover the state in the early years of the new century. Notable superior examples stood just down the rails from Cordele. At Abbeville Frank Milburn's exceptional Wilcox County Courthouse rose in 1903, and at Valdosta that same architect created his fine Lowndes County Courthouse in 1905. It is not surprising that the brash upstart, Cordele, would grasp at the most modern of symbols to speak for her meteoric success. Indeed, the streets of Cordele were lined with Beaux-Arts finery by 1910. Notable examples are James Golucke's Carnegie Library and T. F. Lockwood's grand Cordele Masonic Lodge both completed in 1907.

Despite Lockwood's rather lack-luster neoclassical efforts at Albany and later at Monticello, here in Cordele his design answered to a higher muse. Perhaps it was the opulent $80,000 budget that allowed Lockwood to soar. Whatever the case, the addition of the attic story allowed the grand Ionic porticos to reflect a lofty and graceful verticality absent at Albany, and the addition of the half basement afforded the opportunity to set the great columns atop monumental stairs. Perhaps these were lessons gleaned from Frank Milburn's skillful examples at nearby Abbeville and Valdosta. Whatever the source, they represent an advancement in Lockwood's classical education, and his 1907 Crisp County house was a fitting monument for both Cordele's already substantial successes and for her even more ambitious aspirations.

Here, as in Valdosta, Tifton, Albany and Waycross, the New South was spreading a few crumbs

of prosperity in the piney woods. In 1905, the region was quickly being stripped of its last stands of virgin timber and the resulting empty expanses were just as quickly being covered with cotton. Few could call this kind of progress mythical, but neither would any come to call it permanent.

The story of Cordele's decline is a story that unfolded after the period of our interest. Today, the city is lined with the crumbling architecture of its initial boom. Still, despite demolitions and decay, including the destruction of T. F. Lockwood's Crisp County Courthouse and Cordele's old Union Depot in the early 1950s, the city today contains some remarkable treasures of turn of the century architecture. Like Richland, but on a much grander scale, we find in Cordele the architecture of the New South. Here are the flamboyant structures of the pride and hope of a simple rural people who were briefly propelled to the very edge of the new age, only to be unceremoniously cast back into the old.

WILCOX COUNTY: ABBEVILLE

Plate 23.6: The Wilcox County Courthouse, built in 1903. Frank P. Milburn, architect.

Along with the early neoclassical designs of James Golucke, Frank Pierce Milburn's grand Wilcox County Courthouse at Abbeville led the way to a new era of courthouse design in Georgia and opened the door for the American Neoclassical Revival. In the North, in the years following Chicago's 1893 Columbian Exposition, the new classicism had come to symbolize the nation's emerging financial and industrial progress. Thus, it is not surprising that the style was slow to take root in the impoverished soil of the America South. In Georgia, late nineteenth century efforts like Andrew Bryan's rather neocolonial 1895

[21] William Bailey Williford, *Americus Through the Years*, revised ed. (Atlanta: Cherokee Press, 1975) 215-17.

[22] J. E. D. Shipp, "Samuel Hugh Hawkins" in Northen, ed., *Men of Mark in Georgia*, 3: 401.

[23] Williford, *Americus Through the Years*, 217.

[24] Tift, Turner and Crisp Counties were located on the Georgia Southern and Florida, and Toombs County was located on the old SAM.

[25] *The Vienna Progress*, July 18, 1905.

Stewart County Courthouse at Lumpkin and the more purely neoclassical lines of his 1896 Muscogee County Courthouse at Columbus had failed to inspire the great waves of classical excess that were engulfing the North. Only after the success of carefully nostalgic designs by Milburn and Golucke in the first years of the new century, were Georgians moved to embrace the new architecture of the so-called "American Renaissance."

Of all the early neoclassical court buildings in the state, Milburn's Wilcox County Courthouse is certainly one of the finest. Frank Milburn understood the historical allure of both Jeffersonian Classicism and the Greek Revival in the American South. More than

Plate 23.6: Frank Pierce Milburn's 1903 Wilcox County Courthouse at Abbeville led the way to a new era of courthouse design in Georgia. (Photo: Wilber W. Caldwell.)

any of his contemporaries in Georgia, he was thoroughly versed in the vocabulary of the Italian Renaissance and thus comfortable with the baroque ornament of the new Beaux-Arts classicism. It was Milburn's marriage of modern Beaux-Arts elements to familiar, Old South architectural forms that supplied the region with acceptable symbols for both the past and the future. Here, draped in all the finery of the emerging industrial age, we find the grand temple-like portico attached to a rectangular mass, the same classical form that had remained so dear to the nostalgic, agrarian Southern heart. Here, in one enigmatic and inherently contradictory symbol, is the architecture of the New South, an architecture that embraced the new in order to recall and preserve the old.

Frank Pierce Milburn was born in Louisville, Kentucky in 1868. The son of an architect and builder, Milburn worked first in West Virginia, later in Kentucky and then in Charlotte, North Carolina. He finally settled in Columbia, South Carolina, where he became one of the most prolific Southern architects of the era. Between 1895 and his death in 1926, he designed over 250 major structures in the South including 4 courthouses in Georgia, at least 6 in North Carolina and 2 in South Carolina, as well as court buildings in Kentucky, Florida, Oklahoma and elsewhere. He worked on three state capitol buildings and would later become the chief architect for the Southern Railway, designing depots at Durham and Salisbury, North Carolina; Charleston, Columbia, Spartanburg, and Greenville, South Carolina, and Augusta and Savannah, Georgia, to name but a few.[26]

Exactly how county leaders in Abbeville, Georgia, came to commission Frank Milburn in 1903 is not known. Although the town had experienced considerable growth after the arrival of the Savannah, Americus and Montgomery Railroad in 1887, Abbeville's boom was pale when compared to the miracles the SAM would perform at Richland, Cordele, and Vidalia. Although the town was built on the banks on the Ocmulgee River, her early history lay in the shadow of Hawkinsville, and Abbeville's significance as a river port was negligible before the arrival of the SAM.

In 1857, the year after Wilcox County was created from Pulaski and Irwin Counties, a log courthouse was built at Abbeville. In the 1860 edition of Adiel Sherwood's *Gazetteer of Georgia,* the village was described as "a new and small place." Almost twenty years later, Sholes's 1879 *Gazetteer of Georgia* lists Abbeville as a town of only 50 residents with a small store and a sawmill. In that year, the old courthouse burned and a two-story frame building replaced it. As the simple wooden structure rose, Wilcox County was still a sparsely populated region not much changed from its frontier beginnings and inhabited by highly individualistic stockmen, subsistence farmers and the new breed of rough and ready independent timbermen. By 1886, Abbeville counted 150 inhabitants, but it was not until after the arrival of the railroad that the town began to earn her reputation as a river port. In an 1886 revision to the charter of the Savannah, Americus and Montgomery Railroad, the company obtained the state's permission to operate steamboats on the Ocmulgee, and soon the SAM had built a sizable wharf at Abbeville and had constructed three steamboats there.[27] In the years that followed, five steamboats operated on the Ocmulgee between Abbeville and the ports of Brunswick and Savannah, and the steamer, J. C. Stewart, made the trip from Abbeville to Hawkinsville and back three times a week.[28] In 1890, Abbeville boasted 657 residents. By 1900, her population exceeded 1100. By this time, the town had begun to sip the intoxicating wine of the New South myth.

As was usually the case, a great portion of these heady spirits arrived by rail. Only two years after the arrival of the SAM, the Abbeville and Tifton Railroad was chartered, but these plans came to nothing. At the same time speculation surrounding an Abbeville to Waycross connection further lifted expectations, and in 1891, this line was built to Fitzgerald making Abbeville a junction town. This perceived triumph was followed by speculation surrounding a railroad from Abbeville to Eastman.[29]

By 1901, *The Abbeville Chronicle* was filled with the rose-colored boosterism that so often accompanied the drunken swagger of those who had drunk too deeply of the New South's potent and blinding elixir.

According to *The Chronicle,* Abbeville was ripe for industrial development, for the town was "endowed by nature with peculiar and special facilities for the establishment of such enterprises." A list of these "facilities" included a navigable river, ample railroad facilities and "inestimable and inexhaustible timber resources."[30]

In a more sober moment earlier in that same year, *The Chronicle* had informed readers that: "The ravages of the lumbermen and turpentine men have left but a vestige of the magnificent pines that abounded just a few years ago. To such extent has the devastation gone, that saw mills and turpentine farms are being abandoned on every hand."[31] In 1900, a movement to build a cotton mill at Abbeville fizzled, and in the next year *The Chronicle* published a list of the town's commercial and "industrial" enterprises, which included a saw mill, a large shingle mill, one gin, one bank, 4 hotels and 30 mercantile houses.[32] There was growth here, but it was hardly the stuff of industrial success.

Nonetheless, as was usually the case, a few sips of the sweet wine of the myth of the New South had been enough to spark agitation for a new courthouse at Abbeville. In 1897, the Wilcox County Commissioners selected a plan by Atlanta architect, Andrew J. Bryan.[33] But while Abbeville planned her trendy new wardrobe of progress, the SAM had created another success beside her rails in Wilcox County.

[26] John E. Wells and Robert E. Dalton, South Carolina Architects, 1885-1935, A Biographical Dictionary (Richmond: The New South Architectural Press, 1992) 122-7; and Lawrence Wodehouse, "Frank Pierce Milburn (1868-1926), A Major Southern Architect " in The North Carolina Historical Review 50/2 (Chapel Hill: 1973) 289-303.

[27] Mary Lou McDonald and Samuel Jordon Lawson III, *The Passing of the Pines, A History of Wilcox County, Georgia* (Roswell GA: W.H. Wolfe, 1984) 5; and Williford, *Americus Through the Years,* 186.

[28] Mary Lou McDonald and Samuel Jordon Lawson III, *The Passing of the Pines, A History of Wilcox County, Georgia,* 5.

[29] *The Abbeville Chronicle,* February 17, 1898.

[30] *The Abbeville Chronicle,* February 24, 1898.

[31] *The Abbeville Chronicle,* January 27, 1898.

[32] *The Abbeville Chronicle,* 1901, quoted in Mary Lou McDonald and Samuel Jordon Lawson III, *The Passing of the Pines, A History of Wilcox County, Georgia,* 36.

[33] Mary Lou McDonald and Samuel Jordon Lawson III, *The Passing of the Pines, A History of Wilcox County, Georgia* (Roswell, 1984) 24.

Plate 23.7: This substantial brick depot at Rochelle is a fitting reminder of the power of early railroads to create places of importance almost overnight. (Photo: Wilber W. Caldwell.)

Plate 23.7: The depot at Rochelle.

The old depot at Abbeville is gone, but this fine brick depot at Rochelle stands on the spot where, in 1913, the new rails of the Ocilla Southern Railroad crossed the old SAM. This building and the village of Rochelle are fitting reminders of the power of railroads to create places of importance almost overnight. In 1887, as grading on the SAM began in Wilcox County, the town of Rochelle was laid out along the right-of-way near the exact center of the county. Ten years later the place boasted a population of almost 800. Beginning in 1897, the upstart town, which had been first called "Center," waged a formidable campaign to wrestle the county seat away from Abbeville on the county's eastern boarder.

Between 1897 and 1902, political war raged in Wilcox County. Several elections were held, and each was contested on the grounds of certain "irregularities." Appeals before the Secretary of State, the state legislature and the various courts followed. In 1897, Rochelle filed suit demanding that the county cease plans for the construction of Andrew Bryan's new courthouse at Abbeville. Then, in a much-contested countywide election held in November of 1898, Rochelle won the county seat away from Abbeville. But Abbeville was not about to surrender without a fight.[34] After an election in 1900, ballot boxes were stolen from the courthouse at Abbeville.[35] As emotions flared, increasingly angry rhetoric and threats of

violence marked the contest. Along the way, *The Rochelle New Era* published a letter suggesting that the matter be settled with shotguns.[36] Finally, the Oconee Circuit court rendered judgment in favor of Abbeville, and the town retained architect Frank Milburn and rushed to build a new courthouse in order to cement her hold on the prize.

But the war was far from over. The grand jury was split of the question of a new court building at Abbeville, and their presentments of April 1903 contained conflicting majority and a minority report concerning new construction. More injunctions followed, and more threats. Despite the grand jury's split decision, the county commissioners pressed forward with plans to hire a contractor. In April of 1903, *The Fitzgerald Enterprise* reported that Wilcox County Commissioner T. M. Parson's "found an ugly coffin at his door decorated with a skull and cross bones warning that if he signed the contract, he would be dead before the ink of his signature dried."[37] In May, *The Chronicle* finally reported that the matter was settled, "Winchesters and pistols notwithstanding,"[38] and the old frame courthouse was moved from Abbeville's square. It would later serve the town simultaneously as both a warehouse and an Opera house.[39]

So it was that the 1903 Wilcox County Courthouse began as a building to celebrate Abbeville's New South commercial aspirations and ended up as a culmination of a desperate battle to retain the town's status as county seat in the face of a tenacious onslaught from neighboring Rochelle. *The Fitzgerald Enterprise* clearly grasped Abbeville's evolving motivation. Writing in 1903, the editor noted that the construction of the building "would settle the courthouse question for a long time to come."[40] And so it did.

To the extent that Frank Milburn's courthouse at Abbeville stood for that town's New South aspirations, the building symbolizes the usual irony. As the new century unfolded, Abbeville's hopes were dashed as her railroads failed. Like the SAM, the old branch from Abbeville to Fitzgerald was acquired first by the Georgia and Alabama Railroad and then by the Seaboard Air Line in 1900. Efforts to extend the line northward came to nothing. In 1907, hope was still alive as the Abbeville and Northwestern Railroad was chartered to cross the Hawkinsville and Florida Southern at Pineview and make a junction with the Georgia Southern and Florida at Unadilla. Although no rails were ever laid, these plans briefly sparked renewed hopes for "an international trading center" at Abbeville based on the fact that the town still offered steamboat connections to Brunswick.[41] But in 1907, commercial traffic on the Ocmulgee was beginning to disappear, and Abbeville, with a population of about 1200, was about to enter a period of decline. By 1930, the town counted only 1000 residents, and by 1950, the year before the last passenger train stopped at Abbeville, this number was down to 890. The branch from Abbeville to Fitzgerald was abandoned in 1970, and today the monumental grandeur of Frank Milburn's courthouse at Abbeville is magnified by the rural nature of its immediate surroundings.

In the end, Milburn's courthouse at Abbeville turned out to be not so much a building of hope, as a building of desperation. The irony here lies in the fact that a building of such grace and grandeur could rise as the culmination of an episode of such violence and anger. The violent side of the American South is a well-worn theme. It is most often-recalled in connection with accounts of vigilante justice, lynching and racially motivated atrocities. But here we find that this pension for violence, which seemed to be the birthright of so many Southerners, extended well beyond racial issues. W. J. Cash notes, that the roots of this behavior lay in "the tendency for violence that had grown up in the Southern backwoods as it naturally grows up on all frontiers."[42] As we have seen, in 1903, Wilcox County was still not very far from the frontier.

WHEELER COUNTY: ALAMO

Plate 23.8: The Wheeler County Courthouse, built in 1913. Burned 1916. Rebuilt 1917. Ed C. Hosford architect.

By 1910, town building in rural Georgia had reached its high water mark in most counties. Although the myth of the New South still had an allure for a few, most were beginning to recognize the

modern age for what it really was: a cold, competitive, exploitive tyrant heedless to the needs of the small farmer, determined to concentrate its industry in cities and obsessed with the excesses of big business, big government and unfettered urbanization. The Myth of the New South was dying, and the age of grand courthouse building in Georgia was coming to and end. Along with Alexander Blair's 1916 Murray County Courthouse at Chatsworth, Ed Hosford's Wheeler County Courthouse was one of the last designs to reflect the aspirations of the earlier period.

Ed Hosford's 1913 Wheeler County Courthouse at Alamo was his last courthouse design in Georgia. Although it is similar in silhouette to his 1908 Harris County Courthouse at Hamilton, the flamboyance of a grand tower was omitted. Likewise, Hosford's design here at Alamo is a far cry from the buoyant

Plate 23.8: Ed C. Hosford's 1913 Wheeler County Courthouse was one of the last designs in Georgia to reflect the aspirations of the earlier period. (Photo: Wilber W. Caldwell.)

[34] *The Abbeville Chronicle,* November 10, 1898.

[35] *The Abbeville Chronicle,* August 9, 1900.

[36] *The Abbeville Chronicle,* August 13, 1903.

[37] *The Fitzgerald Enterprise* in *The Abbeville Chronicle,* April 16, 1903.

[38] *The Abbeville Chronicle,* May 7, 1903.

[39] *The Abbeville Chronicle,* June 4, 1903.

[40] *The Fitzgerald Enterprise* quoted in *The Abbeville Chronicle,* February 26, 1903.

[41] *Abbeville Chronicle,* January 31, 1907 in Mary Lou McDonald and Samuel Jordon Lawson III, *The Passing of the Pines, A History of Wilcox County, Georgia,* 33.

[42] W. J. Cash, *The Mind of the South* (1941; reprint, New York: Vintage Books, 1991) 43.

Renaissance classicism of his 1906 Dodge County Courthouse at Eastman. This building is transitional. Although enormous columns with expressive Corinthian capitals reflect a measure of optimism and flare, its simple unadorned lines lack the kind of expressive exuberance displayed by most of the state's early neoclassical court buildings erected in the first decade of the new century. Here we find the beginning of a new civic architecture characterized by restraint and, in some cases, even by resignation.

The end of the great stands of virgin pine came late to Wheeler County. By 1900, lumber companies were deserting the empty expanses of neighboring Dodge, Telfair and Wilcox Counties. But in 1912, when Wheeler County was created from Montgomery, Alamo was still on a modest boom and her saw mills were still busy ravenously devouring her natural wealth. The village had been created in 1889 after the arrival of the Savannah, Americus and Montgomery Railroad. By 1900, Alamo had a population of 183.[43] By 1910, this number had only reached 249. In 1905, despite her diminutive size, the village led a campaign to create a new county called Stephens. This effort was one of thirteen failed new county campaigns in the state in 1905, and only eight new counties were created in that year. The name Stephens was allotted to the new county in the northeast of the state with Toccoa as her county seat, but residents in Alamo were not deterred. By 1911,

despite her lack of a significant urban center, the region was again lobbying to split off from Montgomery County first as Hoke Smith County, and then as Kent County, after local politician William Kent.[44] The fact that William Kent was subsequently disbarred from the practice of law in Georgia and later jailed for malpractice is perhaps indicative of the shabby ethics which governed many of the state's local political struggles in the early part of the century.[45]

MONTGOMERY COUNTY: MOUNT VERNON

Plate 23.9: The depot at Ailey, built in 1904. [46]

Erected by the Savannah, Americus and Montgomery Railroad in 1890,[47] the ancestor of this unassuming little depot was the center of enormous controversy when the railroad first arrived in Montgomery County. The SAM and her affiliate, the Americus Investment Company, had a history of bypassing existing towns in areas where the development of new ones seemed feasible. The road's logical path through Vienna had been ignored in favor of the southern route that created the extraordinary boomtown Cordele. Likewise the line had by-passed McRae, crossing the old Macon and Brunswick about mile away at the place railroad executives would call Helena after the wife of Henry Bagley, the president of the Americus Investment Company. When a similar tactic was planned a mile or so from Mount Vernon, residents where irate. *The Montgomery Monitor* reported the news with bitter accusations: "As is often the case, the new railroad will not have stations in existing towns, but close enough by to sap their foundations and suck them dry."[48] According to *The Monitor,* the SAM's survey was deliberately designed to ruin Mount Vernon,[49] and by August of 1890, the town had sued the SAM, charging that instead of honoring her bargain to build a depot at Mount Vernon, the company had built its station 2 1/2 miles away and simply called it "Mount Vernon."[50] In April of 1891, the citizens of tiny Peterson, only 2 miles from Mount Vernon, donated a depot site. A depot was erected there and called Ailey after the town's old post

Plate 23.9: The ancestor of this unassuming little depot at Ailey was the center of enormous controversy when the railroad first arrived in Montgomery County. (Photo: Wilber W. Caldwell.)

office. It was just another disappointment in a long line of disappointments for Mount Vernon.

Beginning with the Central of Georgia's original "southern survey" that had been abandoned back in the late 1830s, Mount Vernon had seen a parade of failed railroad schemes. As the SAM approached, Mount Vernon was courting an extension of the Macon, Dublin and Savannah Railroad. At the same time, the town sought to attract the Central's plan for a Savannah to Columbus line. Neither of these railroads would be built, but in 1903 the Wadley and Mount Vernon Railroad, a late 1890s lumber road chartered as a common carrier, did eventually extend its old line all the way to the Oconee River only a few miles north of Mount Vernon.[51] Still, in 1888, the outlook in Mount Vernon was bleak. *The Monitor* mourned: "We have had so many propositions for railroads through our county...all to be abandoned before work had been commenced, that we have come to regard these proceedings with little confidence."[52] The maladjusted child of unfulfilled expectations is cynicism, and as Mount Vernon encounter one disappointment after another, she grew glib on the subject of railroads. In 1888, *The Monitor* sarcastically warned: "if something isn't done, the Central is going to build the Savannah and Columbus right through our county."[53] As the Central's plans dissolved, *The Monitor* responded: "...hopes for our railroad are dead....if we can't have a railroad, can't we at least have a telephone?"[54] Just a year before, *The Monitor* had speculated that "if Mount Vernon is in the wrong place, it isn't so large that it can't be moved."[55]

Indeed, Mount Vernon had always been a small place. In his *Statistics of the State of Georgia,* George White described Mount Vernon in 1849 as a healthy place with a courthouse and one store. Various Sholes's *Gazetteers of Georgia* reflect a static population of about 150 between 1879 and 1886. In 1878, 5 stores, 2 hotels and only 24 dwellings surrounded Mount Vernon's old frame courthouse.[56] Before the arrival of the SAM, the town had relied on the capricious waters of the Oconee River and on the Macon and Brunswick Railroad, which passed through neighboring Telfair County 17 miles to the west. At this time,

Mount Vernon was the center of the county's substantial wool trade, an early economic mainstay of many Wiregrass counties. The village also boasted a small cotton market. So critical was the early link to the Macon and Brunswick, that Montgomery County actually paid to maintain bridges and roads in Telfair County between Mount Vernon and the railroad.[57] But this tenuous connection brought only a trickle of the modern waters of growth.

The very first Montgomery County Courthouse was lost to Emanuel County when that county was created from Montgomery in 1812. The next year a small court building was erected at Mount Vernon. This structure was replaced by a larger frame building in 1857. Forty years later, the town's hopes rode on the approaching rails of the SAM, and predictably agitation began for a new courthouse. An 1889 letter to *The Montgomery Monitor* described the old courthouse as "one of the worst in the state."[58] Despite the fact

[43] Allen D. Candler and Clement H. Evans, *The National Cyclopedia of American Biography,* 63 vols. (Atlanta: State Historical Association, 1906) 33.

[44] *The Montgomery Monitor,* July 7, 1911.

[45] *The Montgomery Monitor,* October 14, 1915.

[46] *The Montgomery Monitor,* January 28, 1904 in Robert Scott Davis, History of Montgomery County, Georgia, to 1918 (Roswell GA: WH Wolfe, 1992) 389.

[47] *The Montgomery Monitor,* August 29, 1891 in *Davis, History of Montgomery County, Georgia, to 1918,* 371.

[48] *The Montgomery Monitor,* February 6, 1890 in *Davis, History of Montgomery County, Georgia, to 1918,* 369.

[49] *The Montgomery Monitor,* April 3, 1890, in *Davis, History of Montgomery County, Georgia, to 1918,* 370.

[50] *The Montgomery Monitor,* August 28, 1890, in *Davis, History of Montgomery County, Georgia, to 1918,* 371.

[51] Les R. Winn, *Ghost Trains and Depots in Georgia* (Chamblee GA: Big Shanty Press, 1995) 325.

[52] *The Montgomery Monitor,* April 4, 1888 in *Davis, History of Montgomery County, Georgia, to 1918,* 367.

[53] *The Montgomery Monitor,* April 18, 1888 in *Davis, History of Montgomery County, Georgia, to 1918,* 367.

[54] *The Montgomery Monitor,* January 24, 1889 in *Davis, History of Montgomery County, Georgia, to 1918,* 368.

[55] *The Montgomery Monitor,* April 13, 1887, in *Davis, History of Montgomery County, Georgia, to 1918,* 365.

[56] Mark V. Wetherington, *The New South Comes to Wiregrass Georgia* (Knoxville: University of Tennessee Press, 1994) 226.

[57] Wetherington, *The New South Comes to Wiregrass Georgia,* 226.

that the railroad missed the county seat by over a mile, by 1890 Mount Vernon had grown into a town of over 700 residents. By 1893, serious plans for a new building were being considered.[59]

Plate 23.10: The Montgomery County Courthouse, built in 1907. Alexander Blair III, architect.

There can be little doubt that in 1893 the agitation for a new courthouse in Montgomery County was a direct result of the brief boom precipitated by the arrival of the Savannah, Americus and Montgomery Railroad. But as the new courthouse movement fizzled, the SAM was creating formidable competition for the venerable town. Nearby, new railroad towns bloomed.

By 1905, Mount Vernon was under siege. The passage of statewide legislation to allow new counties in Georgia had opened the floodgates of ambition, and three new counties were proposed to be cut from

Plate 23.10: Mount Vernon erected Alexander Blair's 1907 Montgomery County Courthouse in order to defend herself against the new dogs of commercial and industrial ambition that nipped at her flanks from every side. (Photo: Wilber W. Caldwell.)

[58] *The Montgomery Monitor,* November 21, 1889, in *Davis, History of Montgomery County, Georgia, to 1918,* 369.

[59] *The Montgomery Monitor,* March 23, 1893, in *Davis, History of Montgomery County, Georgia, to 1918,* 376.

[60] *The Montgomery Monitor,* August 31 1905, in *Davis, History of Montgomery County, Georgia, to 1918,* 391.

[61] *The Montgomery Monitor,* June 8, 1905 in *Davis, History of Montgomery County, Georgia, to 1918,* 390.

Montgomery. To the west, residents campaigned for the creation of Stephens County with tiny Alamo as her county town. To the north, the new village of Adrian, at the junction of the old Wadley and Mount Vernon Railroad and the Central of Georgia's Dublin to Savannah route led the battle to create James County. And to the east, powerful forces in the new railroad town of Lyons proposed the creation of Toombs County. The growing city of Vidalia hung in the balance between old Montgomery County and the emerging upstart Toombs. Mount Vernon was in a quandary. If Vidalia were included in the proposed new county, enormous tax revenues would be lost. If Vidalia stayed in Montgomery County, many feared that she would attempt to capture the county seat away from Mount Vernon. Even tiny Ailey made a brief bid for the county seat.[60]

Thus, in the midst of the siege, Montgomery County retained Macon architect Alexander Blair III to build a new courthouse in order to secure Mount Vernon's position as the county town. By the time Blair's Montgomery County Courthouse was completed, James and Stephens Counties had failed in their bids for new county status, and only Toombs County, which claimed both Lyons and Vidalia, had succeeded in breaking away. By 1910, Mount Vernon's population had again stagnated at around 600, and the battle continued to rage. In 1912, Wheeler County was created from Montgomery with Alamo as the county town, and in 1918, Treutlen County was chartered with Soperton as her administrative center. A shadow of its former self, Montgomery County had become one of the smallest counties in the state.

By July of 1905, a new era of courthouse design had begun in Georgia, and examples of the new style were popping up all across the state. Frank Milburn's stunning 1903 Wilcox County Courthouse stood beside the Ocmulgee at Abbeville, W. F. Denny's elegant 1904 Jefferson County Courthouse occupied the site of the old State Capitol Building at Louisville. Before selecting a design by Macon's Alexander Blair III, the Montgomery County Commissioners reviewed plans by Atlanta architect, James W. Golucke, who had just completed his remarkable Coweta County Courthouse at Newnan. Blair's plan was selected largely on the strength of the architect's recent design for the Miller County Courthouse at Colquitt, [61] and the Montgomery County Courthouse would emerge as a slightly larger sister of that earlier building. A similar design with only few alterations would later rise in a third iteration at Cairo. Of Blair's three similar neoclassical court buildings built between 1905 and 1908, only this one at Mount Vernon survives.

Here was an early glimpse of the architecture of the new era. Although it still recalled earlier Southern classical models, the 1907 Montgomery County Courthouse also flaunts the modern Renaissance-inspired details of Beaux-Arts Classicism. For example, the entablature above the bold portico displays the familiar triglyph in the Greek mode, but gone is the temple-like pediment and in its place we find a decorative Beaux-Arts parapet. Renaissance details characterize the fenestration. Splayed headers cap window openings below, while elaborate cornices are supported by scrolling brackets above. Large corner pavilions with emphatic rusticated yellow brick quoining and low pyramidal roofs flank the central portico beneath a massive octagonal dome topped with a simple Greek lantern. To be sure, the grand columns must have evoked memories of the architecture of the Old South, but a flashy New South exuberance had crept into the traditional blend.

It is difficult to deny that Mount Vernon's 1907 Montgomery County Courthouse was a product of the railroads. But here, the impact of the SAM was nothing like the wild frenzies of New South expectations at Richland, Americus and Cordele. This courthouse rose not in celebration of, but in opposition to, such visions of progress. In a microcosm of Southern logic, Mount Vernon erected the modern walls of Alexander Blair's courthouse in order to defend herself against the new dogs of commercial and industrial ambition that nipped at her flanks from every side. Like the South itself, Mount Vernon would don the clothing of Yankee success in order to secure her ancient prerogatives. Blair's building secured the county seat for the traditional village of Mount Vernon, defending it against the onslaught of a cash register mentality spawned by the railroads in newly

created railroad towns like Lyons, Alamo, Vidalia and Soperton.

TOOMBS COUNTY: LYONS

Plate 23.11: Union Depot at Vidalia, built c. 1910.

This extraordinary depot tells a tale of two cities, Vidalia and Lyons. It is the familiar story of the railroad's capricious power. One small village became a boomtown while another languished beside the same rails. Like so many of the towns along the Savannah, Americus and Montgomery Railroad, Lyons and Vidalia were the creations of Henry Clay Bagley's Americus Investment Company, which sought to exploit the real estate boom created by the construction of that railroad. Building eastward from Cordele in the late 1880s, the SAM created a string of towns across Wilcox, Dodge, Telfair, and Montgomery Counties. Substantial new villages appeared beside the line's new depots at Seville, Pitts, Rochelle, Rhine, Milan, Helena, Alamo, Vidalia and Lyons. The depot at Lyons would be the SAM's last in Georgia, for this was as far east as Colonel Hawkins's railroad would go. Here the line met the rails of the Central of Georgia's Savannah and Western Railroad, and by reciprocal agreement, the SAM's trains rode the Central's rails into Savannah. When the Central failed in 1892, and trackage rights from Lyons to Savannah were rescinded, it spelled the beginning if the end for the SAM.

After a modest initial boom, Vidalia and Lyons were both slow to develop. Before the turn of the century, population was thin in these remote reaches of

Plate 23.11: This extraordinary depot at Vidalia tells a tale of two cities.

Plate 23.12: With the completion the 1906 Toombs County Courthouse at Lyons, we find one of the first local attempts to portray the kind of governmental monumentality that had been so carefully avoided by courthouse designers in the American South.(Photo: Courtesy of Ted Brooke.)

the piney woods, and initially the railroad did little more than expose the region's vast forests to the exploitation of independent timbermen and turpentiners. In 1900, Vidalia counted only 503 citizens and Lyons only 534. But with the arrival of the Millen Southwestern Railroad around 1898 and the extension of the Macon, Dublin and Savannah from Dublin in 1901, Vidalia became an important railroad junction and began a remarkable railroad-inspired boom. Chartered in 1901, the Citizens Bank of Vidalia became the first bank on the new line between Cordele and Savannah. Before the end of the first decade of the new century, the mighty Seaboard Air Line controlled all of the track between Savannah and Montgomery as well as the old Macon, Dublin and Savannah from Vidalia to Macon. By this time, the old Millen Southwestern had become part of the Georgia and Florida Railroad whose main line had been built through Vidalia, stretching all the way from Augusta to Madison, Florida. By 1910, Vidalia counted almost 1800 residents, and by 1920, it was a city of almost 3000.

Meanwhile, Lyons had achieved only modest growth counting fewer than 1000 residents in 1910. Unlike Vidalia, with her web of mighty railroads, only one tiny spur joined the Seaboard's rails at Lyons. Chartered in 1904, the Garbutt and Donovan Short

Line Railway managed to span the 14 miles from Lyons to Oak Park and a junction with the Georgia and Florida Railroad before it was abandoned in 1911. Despite the limited progress in Lyons, this shaky railroad added fuel to New South fires already burning there. In 1905, political forces in Lyons spurred the creation of Toombs County from Montgomery, Emanuel and Tattnall. Behind the newly created voice of *The Lyons Progress*, a local paper created "for no other purpose than to create a new county,"[62] leaders in Lyons not only succeeded in creating a new county but cleverly corralled the booming Vidalia into the bargain.

When the new county movement began in Lyons, Vidalia had been focusing its attention on wrestling the county seat of Montgomery County away from hapless Mount Vernon. Vidalia's leaders reasoned that if the Toombs County movement in Lyons failed and the Stephens County movement in Alamo succeeded Mount Vernon would end up on the western edge of a newly partitioned Montgomery County, and the much larger and more progressive Vidalia would suddenly find herself in the center.[63] Thus, confusion reigned as the citizens of Vidalia initially opposed the creation of Toombs County. Only after it became clear that the forces supporting the creation of Stephens County were weak, did Vidalia join the Toombs County movement. By then, leaders in Lyons were firmly in charge of the new county's fate, and the smaller and more centrally located Lyons became the county seat.

Plate 23.12: The Toombs County Courthouse, built in 1906. James Wingfield Golucke, architect (attributed). Burned 1917. Rebuilt 1919. Alexander Blair III, architect. Demolished 1964.

Bolstered by their success, Toombs County organizers were quick to erect a courthouse at Lyons. The building not only secured the town's lock on the county seat in the face of nearby Vidalia's unprecedented growth, but also served to celebrate the new county's creation and soaring aspirations. The new courthouse at Lyons embodied a form that was deeply etched in the Southern psyche. In the nation's infancy, Southern architects like Thomas Jefferson and Robert Mills had fashioned public buildings featuring light second-story porticos supported by massive masonry arcades. Here in Lyons, similar historical elements were designed to appeal to conservative Southern sensibilities while, at a second level, the ongoing thrust of the new American classicism was allowed to shine through. Here again was an architecture for the New South. Both modern and traditional at the same time, it balanced duel symbols. Here was an architecture to soothe both sides of the divided and tortured mind of the South.

Antebellum models for an airy pedimented portico supported by a massive arcade are many. The form traces its roots to the Italian Renaissance, and early American classicists had been quick to employ this simple but monumental design. Both Charles Bullfinch's 1795 Massachusetts State House and Thomas Jefferson's 1817 Pavilion VII at the University of Virginia feature this arrangement. In the 1820s, Robert Mills often employed a similar approach when he covered South Carolina with stunning courthouses in the Greek mode. A decade later, the most popular and influential of the American builder's guides of the 1830s, Asher Benjamin's *The American Builder's Companion*, featured a "Design for a Courthouse" featuring three massive arches supporting a portico of six Ionic columns. Eighty years after Benjamin's design, the architect of the Toombs County Courthouse would arrange the outside columns in pairs to close the composition just as Benjamin had demonstrated in 1837.

But by the end of the first decade of the new century, the county courthouse in Georgia was loosing some of its appeal as a symbol for individualism. Comfortable symbols for local aspirations and individual hope were disappearing. In their place rose awe-inspiring symbols for the pomp and power of emerging governmental might, imposing glimpses of the modern age. In Lyons, we find one of the first local attempts to portray the kind of governmental monumentality that had been so carefully avoided by courthouse designers of the earlier period in the American South.

Although the 1906 Toombs County Courthouse burned in 1917 taking with it all record of its design-

er, we can make a good case for James Golucke as the architect. In 1906, the only other postbellum court building in Georgia to employ a similar portico was James Golucke's courthouse at nearby Reidsville. Although Golucke's courthouse at Reidsville is today much altered from its original form and the original roof and high clock are gone, photographs of the old building reveal certain details which are quite similar to the 1906 Toombs County Courthouse. Both buildings feature arcades decorated with a bold banded polychromy of alternating brick and stone supporting airy porticos, and both display fashionable splayed window headers. Splayed window lentils like those at Lyons were a favorite ornament of James W. Golucke, and identical details appear in his courthouse designs at Newnan, Sylvester, Madison and Eatonton. In the post war period, no other courthouse architect in Georgia created designs of this nature, but as early as 1900, James Golucke had designed two courthouses in Alabama, at Anniston and LaFayette, featuring similar porticos and similar splayed window headers. These designs may have been attempts to copy Frank Milburn's stunning 1896 neoclassical Courthouse at Charlotte, North Carolina. The tiny lantern atop the dome is also telltale. Although most domes of the period featured a crowning lantern, Golucke employed a unique style with this detail. Supported by unusually thin columnettes, many of his lanterns, like the one here at Lyons, appear disproportionately open and light. Notable examples are found at Newnan, Sylvester, and LaFayette, Alabama. To further the case for Golucke, we know that he was soliciting commissions in the area in this period, for *The Montgomery Monitor* informs us that he submitted plans for nearby Mount Vernon's new courthouse in 1905.[64] To be sure, this evidence in support of James Golucke as the architect of the 1906 Toombs County Courthouse is far from conclusive. But in addition to these facts detailing similarities between this building and Golucke's known work, we are left with the fact that

[62] Amos Milton Teasley, *The History of Toombs County,* Masters Thesis (Athens: The University of Georgia, 1940) 3.

[63] *The Montgomery Monitor,* June 8, 1905.

[64] *The Montgomery Monitor,* June 8, 1905.

none of the other architects who designed courthouses in Georgia in the first decade of the new century created anything even remotely resembling the form of this remarkable courthouse at Lyons.

The 1907 Toombs County Courthouse burned in 1917 and was replaced in 1919 by a design by Macon's Alexander Blair III. It appears that the loss was not complete, for the corner pavilions and much of the fenestration of Blair's replacement are identical to the original design, but gone were the grand clock tower, the grand arcade and the elevated portico. In their place was a massive portico of the so-called "Giant Order" supporting a bold entablature similar to Blair's entrances at Mount Vernon and Cairo.

Alexander Blair's Toombs County Courthouse was demolished in 1964 to make way for a modern replacement. The destruction of the original court building and Alexander Blair's replacement were followed by aggressive attempts by the larger and more prosperous Vidalia to steal the Toombs Court seat away from Lyons. But Lyons clung tenaciously to the prize.

EVANS COUNTY: CLAXTON

Plate 23.13: The depot at Daisy.

A surprising number of these old wooden depots are still standing along the rails of the old Savannah and Western Railroad between Savannah and the line's junction with the old SAM at Lyons. In addition to this romantic old hulk at Daisy in Evans County, early wooden depots can still be found beside the rails at Manassas, and Bellville. Moved from their original locations but still standing, the old depots that once stood at Pembroke and Collins are today privately owned. These buildings vibrantly illustrate one of the central ironies of this book, that such an unassuming architecture could serve such a powerful master. These simple structures stand to remind us of the might of the Savannah and Western Railroad. Chartered in 1885 and built by the Central of Georgia between 1888 and 1890, the line briefly served as the perfecting link in Samuel Hawkins's grand scheme to connect Savannah via Americus to Montgomery, Alabama, and to break the Central of Georgia's strangle-hold on the west Georgia Cotton Belt.

In east Georgia, the history of the Savannah and Western is the story of an area that was once one of the most deserted parts of piney woods. In 1845, the enormous Tattnall County, which at that time included all of Evans County and most of Toombs, had a population of only 1302, and her county seat, Reidsville, counted less than 50 residents. When the Savannah and Western cut through the county in 1889, bypassing Reidsville by only 7 miles, the village probably contained about 150 residents. By 1897, the Collins and Reidsville Railroad had connected Reidsville with the Savannah and Western, but in 1900 Reidsville's population was still only around 250.

As the Savannah and Western placed its depots in the empty expanses of old Tattnall County, villages emerged. Notable among these were Claxton and Hagan. Laid out by railroad engineers less than two miles apart, the twin hamlets vied for influence and power. In 1898, the powerful Perkins Lumber Company began operating a large mill at Hagan, but Claxton would win the day after that company chartered the Register and Glenville Railroad in 1902. This line was an expansion of an older logging railroad built by the Perkins Lumber Company, and it ran from Register on the Central via Claxton to Glenville where it later made a junction with the Glenville and Southern, a predecessor of the Georgia Coast and Piedmont. To seal Claxton's victory, a second rail crossing was accomplished there in 1909 as the Shearwood Railway was chartered to build from Claxton to Clyo in Effingham County. Progress on this shaky line was slow, and after ten years the road had only managed to reach Egypt on the Central's main line between Savannah and Macon. The Shearwood Railway was abandoned in 1935.

Thus by 1910, with three railroads and a population of over 1000, Claxton had grown to the very doorstep of nearby Hagan, which counted 784 residents. Meanwhile Reidsville's population remained under 500. Local political power was shifting. As the New County Movement gained strength in Georgia, it is not surprising that efforts to cut a new county from

Tattnall began in 1912 with the publication of *The Claxton Enterprise*. By 1914, Evans County was a reality, and Claxton was her county seat. But J. J. Baldwin's Evans County Courthouse would not rise until 1923. Another of that architect's restrained public monuments, the building is not included in this study.

BRYAN COUNTY: PEMBROKE

Plate 23.14: The Bryan County Courthouse at Clyde, built in 1901. Demolished c.1940.

When the Savannah and Western Railroad built through Bryan County in 1889, it established depots and thus towns at Ellabell, Lanier, Pembroke and Groveland. Far to the south of this line lay the tiny village of Clyde, the Bryan County seat. The history of Clyde is shrouded in mystery. Today nothing remains, and the site is inaccessible, lying within the vast confines of Fort Stewart, which swallowed up the town and enormous portions of Bryan, Liberty, Tattnall and Long Counties in 1940.

Bryan County was created in 1793 from Liberty and Effingham. The first county seat was established at Hardwick, but there is no record of a courthouse there. There is evidence that the county seat was moved to a place called Crossroads in 1797, but the record is a bit unclear. Likewise the exact date and circumstance of the removal of the county seat to Clyde are the subjects of considerable conjecture. A number of places are mentioned as subsequent locations of the county seat including "Bryan Courthouse" and a village called Eden, but it seems likely that these are simply earlier names for Clyde. It appears that a courthouse was erected there, perhaps as early as 1814. County records contain an 1316 deed to the courthouse lot, and it is possible that the building was already complete when the land was deeded to the county. In 1901, this large frame courthouse was erected at Clyde and served the county until the county seat was moved to Pembroke in 1937.

By all accounts, Clyde was never much of a place, a courthouse, a jail, a store and a few dwellings. But then Bryan County was not much of a place when it came to towns. Even after the arrival of the railroad,

Plate 23.13: Ironically, simple structures like this little depot at Daisy in Evans County often stood for the nearly boundless power of the railroad. (Photo: Wilber W. Caldwell.)

Plate 23.14: The 1901 Bryan County Courthouse at Clyde was the last frame court building erected in Georgia.

Pembroke, the most successful of the new breed of railroad towns in the county, remained small. The Cuyler and Woodburn Railroad had skirted the northern edge of Bryan County in the late 1890s. By 1899, this line reached all the way to Statesboro as the Savannah and Statesboro Railroad. But even as late as 1910, Pembroke's population was still below 500. In 1911, a short line railroad called the Savannah Southern (a.k.a. the Tuten Railroad) was completed from Lanier to Glenville, but Lanier realized little growth, and the line was abandoned in 1923. Bryan county history records "discussions" of moving the county seat to the railroad town Ellabell in 1901.[65] Little came of the movement, but it was probably this threat of removal that spurred the construction of a

new courthouse at Clyde in that same year. This was the last frame courthouse built in Georgia.

If Pembroke was small, then Clyde was minuscule. No reliable figures are available to document the town's population, but in 1936, when county voters finally approved the removal of the county seat to Pembroke, *The Pembroke Journal* reported that Clyde had long been the "smallest county seat in the state" and that "for many years there was only one resident at Clyde, excepting the sheriff and the jailer."[66] Many older county residents discount this story, claiming that Clyde was a town of about 20 or 30 inhabitants. Even in the 1930s, Clyde had its supporters, for we find that when the present courthouse at Pembroke rose in 1938, its was constructed from plans drawn years earlier for a new courthouse at Clyde.[67]

Whatever its size, the lesson of Clyde and this old courthouse is clear. It reminds us that there were many places in the piney woods, which remained untouched by the railroads, places where the myth of the New South had simply failed to arrive.

SOME LAST THOUGHTS ON THE SAVANNAH, AMERICUS AND MONTGOMERY RAILROAD.

After acquiring the Southwestern Railroad in 1869, the Central of Georgia had held the rich cotton growing areas of southwestern Georgia in a monopolistic strangle hold. With the construction of the SAM, Samuel Hawkins sought to break the Central's tyrant grip. Hawkins also struggled to preserve the power of the city of Americus, which in 1886 was about to be bypassed by the Central's new branch from Andersonville to Columbus, an extension of the old Buena Vista and Ellaville Railroad. To add to the perceived nobility of Hawkins's enterprise, the Savannah, Americus and Montgomery was one of the first postbellum railroads in Georgia to be financed wholly by local subscription. But perhaps the greatest appeal of the SAM was its meteoric but remarkably brief success. With the completion of the line to Montgomery, the signing of the short-lived reciprocal arrangement with the Savannah and Western for the

Plate 23.15: Cordele.Photo: (Wilber W. Caldwell.)

use of the trackage from Lyons to Savannah and the lease of the old Albany, Florida and Northern from Cordele to Albany, the SAM briefly supplied the Central with all of the competition she could handle. In response, the Central's subsidiary, the Savannah and Western, rescinded the SAM's trackage rights into Savannah. As the financial panic of the early 1890s began, the SAM's days were numbered. Thus, like the legends of the Old South, the legend of the SAM would end in defeat. Poetically, just as the Savannah, Americus and Montgomery Railroad was entering its finest hour, the great Central of Georgia crumbled as the result a complex fraud that burdened the company with enormous debt and left the vast road unable to met its obligations.

The reasons for the failure of the SAM are many. Surely the unpredictably high cost of completing the line to Montgomery and loss of trackage rights from Lyons to Savannah were key factors, as was an 1892 state law limiting new stock subscriptions for existing railroads in Georgia. But in the final analysis, it was the national economic crisis of contracting credit, the resulting Panic of 1893 and the ensuing national depression that brought the SAM down. Like most Georgia railroads built between the end of the war and 1890, the SAM fell before the consolidating forces of Northern financial might. The story of another Southern Camelot had reached its inevitable conclusion, and her Arthur, Colonel Samuel Hawkins, had come tumbling down with her.

The character of Samuel Hugh Hawkins is something of an enigma. Legend presents us with a Southern gentleman, who, having heroically survived the war, adapted to the times by attempting to lift his native South out of economic darkness and into the pure light of the new industrial age. In legend, Hawkins's motives are pure: to break the exploitive grip of the Central of Georgia, to save the city of Americus, and to lift the region to new economic heights. But the record of history is a bit less kind. Hawkins's original plan for his railroad involved the financial support of the Northern owned exploitive railroad juggernaut, the East Tennessee, Virginia and Georgia Railroad. It was only after this conglomerate

giant withdrew its support that Hawkins set out on his own. His initial scheme belies the image of Hawkins as a visionary. The original plan relied heavily on river transportation, first on the Chattahoochee west of Lumpkin, and later on the Ocmulgee at Abbeville where the SAM would operate steamboats of her own. Hawkins's perception of these rivers as "God's highway" which "could not be used to oppress"[68] was romantic enough to be the stuff of legend, but these were hardly the utterings of a visionary. Indeed, it appears that Hawkins's dream of a railroad from Savannah to Montgomery did not begin as a unified vision, but unfolded little by little, building confidence with its own evolving success and perhaps with Samuel Hawkins's evolving personal ambitions. Contemporary accounts suggest that Hawkins had a substantial ego and became stubbornly and perhaps imprudently committed to the expansion of his empire. While critics stop short of accusing Hawkins of avarice, much of this suggests that he was nothing more than a shrewd and calculating citizen of the Gilded Age in America, a period populated with men of unbridled greed and questionable ethics. The real Samuel Hawkins probably fell somewhere in the middle. He surely sought to behave according to the perceived code of the Old South while at the same time he struggled to achieve success in an arena governed by a more modern grasping ethic. Like most Southerners of the era, Samuel Hawkins found himself trapped between opposing myths, and thus he struggled to reason with a divided mind.

The record of courthouse building along the line of the Savannah, Americus and Montgomery Railroad is a document filled with the power of the railroad to inspire grand architecture. Here is a blueprint for

[65] The Bryan Historical Society, *The History of Bryan County* (1985), 6.

[66] *The Pembroke Journal*, July 10, 1936.

[67] *The Pembroke Journal*, February 19, 1937.

[68] J. E. D. Shipp, "Samuel Hugh Hawkins" in William J. Northen, ed., *Men of Mark in Georgia*, 2: 407

buildings whose duel symbolism echoed the dilemma that confronted Samuel Hawkins. Fittingly the first, and perhaps the best, of these structures rose at Americus in 1887. Only a year after the Americus, Preston and Lumpkin Railroad reached Lumpkin, a building committee in Americus headed by Samuel Hawkins himself, commissioned Atlanta architects, Bruce and Morgan, to erect a monument to the city's soaring railroad-inspired dreams. The resulting 1887 Sumter County Courthouse at Americus was the firm's first in a series of triumphant Romanesque revival court buildings. Bruce's romantic towers would soon come to stand for dreams of New South progress in county towns from Rome to Dublin.

All of the other architectural voices which were to sing along the line of the of the Savannah, Americus and Montgomery Railroad were neoclassical. Beginning with a rather Neocolonial song, Andrew Bryan's 1895 Stewart County Courthouse at Lumpkin sounded Georgia's first note of the new classicism which was soon to engulf the South. The mighty Seaboard Air Line acquired the old SAM in 1900, and between 1903 and 1907 classical court buildings rose at Abbeville, McRae, Lyons, Mount Vernon and Cordele.

The power of the SAM's rails to create new courthouses lingered long after the end of the period of our interest as new counties popped up along the line. The Ed Hosford's 1914 Wheeler County Courthouse was among the last neoclassical designs in the state to reflect the exuberance of the earlier period, while J. J. Baldwin's 1923 Evans County Courthouse at Claxton communicated the more reserved reality of the modern age. Likewise in counties where the myth of the New South had failed to arrive and the power of crossing rails was not felt, T. F. Lockwood's 1915 Webster County Courthouse at Preston and the 1938 Bryan County Courthouse at Pembroke mirror classical forms but with little flare.

Interestingly, with the exception of the old depots at Richland and at Rochelle, all of the grand brick depots built by the Seaboard Air Line along the line of the old SAM are gone. Like Alexander Bruce's stunning Sumter County Courthouse, no trace remains of the fine late-century brick depots at Americus,

Cordele, and Vidalia. Ironically, a number of the old wooden depots still stand along these rails in small towns like Plains, Milan, Daisy, Manassas and Bellville.

•

24 | The Buena Vista and Ellaville Railroad

MARION COUNTY: BUENA VISTA

Plate 24.1: The Marion County Courthouse at Tazwell, built in 1848.

Six miles northeast of the present-day county seat of Marion County at Buena Vista lies the tiny hamlet of Tazwell. Here we find one of only five frame court buildings still standing Georgia (see Table II of the Introduction). Typical of scores of these simple structures that stood on courthouse squares all across the state, this building sings songs of a sturdy, rural population who remained philosophically close to frontier. It is telling to note that buildings just like this were being erected in South Georgia right up to the turn of the century.[1]

Created from Lee and Muscogee Counties in 1827, Marion County was part of the partition of the enormous tract between the Chattahoochee and the Flint Rivers that was ceded to the state by the Creek Indians in 1825. The county's first courthouse, a simple log structure, rose about 7 miles from Tazwell at the village of Horrey shortly after the creation of the new county. In 1838, the county seat moved to Tazwell, and a second court building was erected there. That building burned in 1845, and this sturdy heart pine courthouse was begun the following year. Completed in 1848, the building hosted only one court session, before the voters of Marion County elected to move the county seat to the village of Pea Ridge, which they renamed Buena Vista to commemorate the recent American victory in the Mexican American War. By this time, Marion County had a population of over 10,000 and was teeming with new arrivals eager to share in the bounty of the new cotton growing lands in the western part of the state. In 1849, the reliable traveler, George White described Buena Vista in his *Statistics of the State of Georgia* as a village of 200 residents with six stores, seven lawyers and two large

---

[1] The last frame courthouse in Georgia was erected in Bryan County at Clyde in 1901.

The Buena Vista and Ellaville Railroad

Marion County: Buena Vista • Schley County: Ellaville • Chattahoochee County: Cusseta
Some Last Thoughts on the Buena Vista and Ellaville Railroad

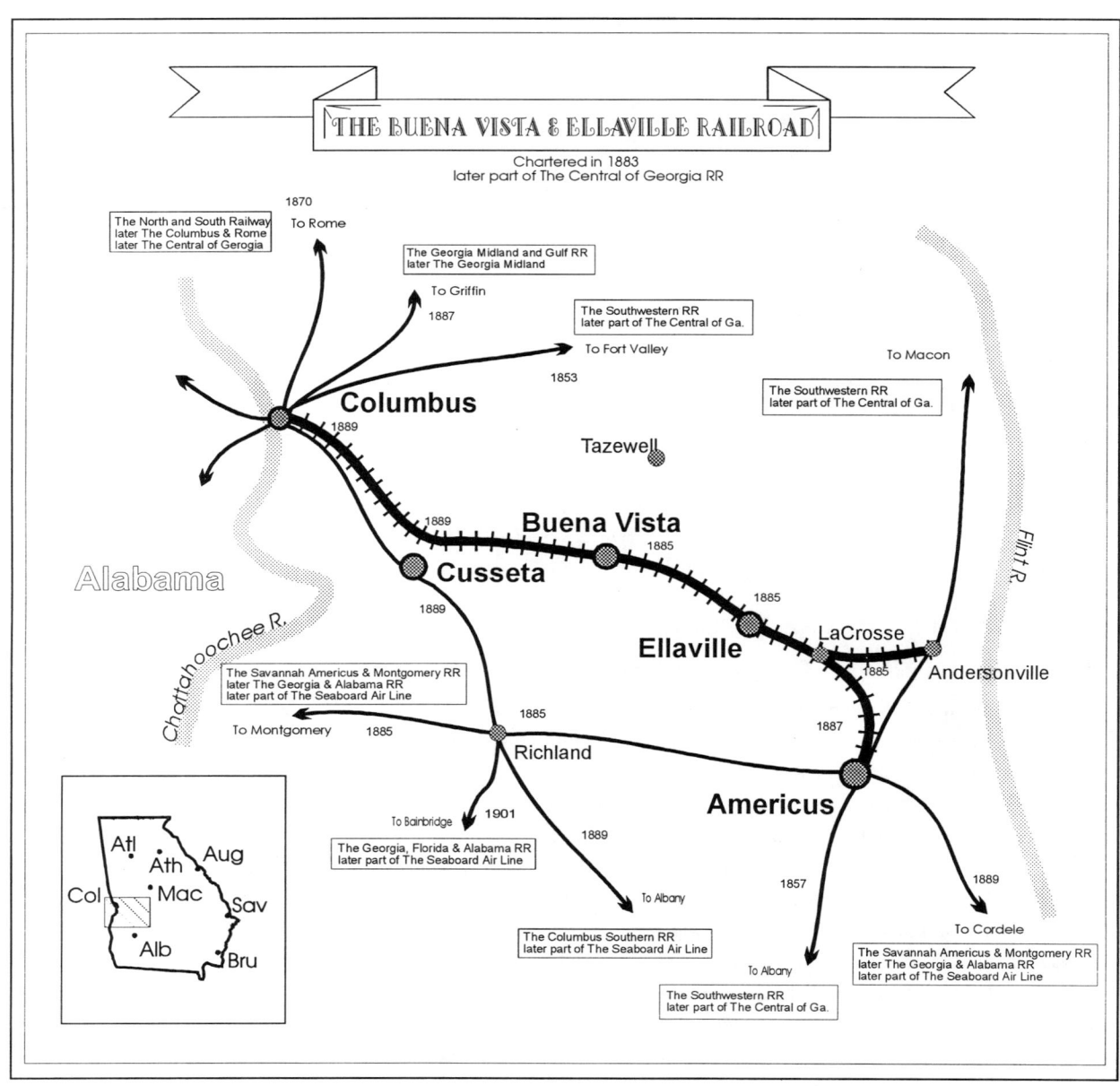

taverns. Of Tazwell, White could only say, "since the removal of the county buildings, the place has declined." Today Tazwell is little more than a crossroads.

Plate 24.2: The Marion County Courthouse, built 1849-1850. Remodeled in 1928.

In 1849, when the brick for this fine courthouse was fired at the new brickyard at Buena Vista, it was clear that the aspiring citizens of Marion County meant to place themselves in the company of their more prosperous neighbors. In that year, brick courthouses stood on the courthouse squares in nearby Muscogee, Talbot, Crawford, and Sumter Counties. Completed in 1850, the Marion County Courthouse at Buena Vista is a massive structure.

Almost thirty years later, in 1880, the Buena Vista Railroad was chartered in an effort to connect Buena Vista with Columbus, Oglethorpe or Americus. At that time, Buena Vista was a town of about 500 residents. By 1883, extensive talks with both Columbus and Americus had yielded little. At one time, Americus had promised to subscribe $25,000 toward the road's construction, but the deal disintegrated as the dispute over control of the line ended in an impasse.[2] Leaders in Buena Vista finally realized that, if they wanted a railroad, they would have to build it themselves, and the Buena Vista and Ellaville Railroad was chartered in 1883. By 1885, with substantial help from the Central of Georgia Railroad, which supplied the track and the rolling stock, a line was complete from Buena Vista, via Ellaville, to a junction with the Central's Southwestern Railroad at Andersonville.[3]

Just as the first train arrived in Buena Vista, Samuel Hawkins's Americus Preston and Lumpkin Railroad began to lay track from Americus toward the Chattahoochee River in Stewart County. Within the space of a few years Hawkins's short line would emerge as the Savannah, Americus and Montgomery Railroad. In 1887, as Hawkins began to lay track east of Americus toward Savannah, the Central ended its threat to bypass Americus by constructing a branch line from LaCrosse on the Buena Vista and Ellaville to Americus. Hawkins had won a great victory. In 1889,

Plate 24.1: Typical of scores of simple frame structures that stood on courthouse squares all across the state, the 1848 Marion County Courthouse at Tazwell sings songs of a sturdy, rural population who remained philosophically close to frontier. (Photo: Wilber W. Caldwell.)

the Central purchased the Buena Vista and Ellaville outright and extended its rails to Columbus. The original portion of the line from LaCrosse to Andersonville fell into disuse and was abandoned, probably sometime right after the turn of the century.

Plate 24.2: The original vernacular form of the 1850 Marion County Courthouse at Buena Vista is today partly masked by a 1928 remodeling that included the addition of a classical portico. (Photo: Wilber W. Caldwell.)

[2]   Nettie Powell, *History of Marion County, Georgia* (Columbus GA: Historical Publishing Company, 1931) 87.

[3]   Powell, *History of Marion County, Georgia*, 87-88.

Thus, by 1890, Buena Vista was connected to both Americus and Columbus. A few brick buildings appeared on the square, but, as cotton prices sank and the depression of the early nineties deepened, there was little in Marion County to arouse zeal for a new economic era and many struggling farmers took up the banner of Populism. In the election of 1894, Marion County along with her neighbor Taylor County became the only two Populist strongholds south of Macon. The power of the New South myth was weak here, for as Populists, these farmers opposed any government that danced to the tune of American big business. Perhaps the most despised of all American business interests were the railroads, which Georgia's Populists sought to nationalize. It was an odd mixture of grassroots republicanism and selective socialism. While nearby county towns like Columbus, Talbotton, Oglethorpe and Lumpkin erected fantasy courthouses to celebrate their aspirations for a place in a New South of economic promise, Marion and Taylor Counties clung to their antebellum court buildings.

In Populism, many farmers found a political voice in the ongoing dialogue between mercantile New South ambition and agrarian Old South conservatism, between town and country, between the emerging business elite and the traditional yeoman farmer-individualist. In speeches like the one delivered in 1893 at Dranesville, only 8 miles from Buena Vista, Thomas Watson characterized Populism as a the champion of Jeffersonian ideals and a renewal of the classic struggle to check the unfettered Hamiltonian forces that controlled the money supply. Whatever it was, Populism stood firmly in the path of the juggernaut of American big business, and its was soon brushed aside just another battle the South would loose against the seemingly inexorable forces of Northern economic might.

With such a conservative mind set and little or no prospect for crossing rails, progress in Buena Vista was slow. Although tons of railroad-imported guano boosted cotton production in Marion County, in 1887, as the first train steamed into town, *The Marion Sentinel* described Buena Vista as having only 900 residents, thirteen stores, and one hotel.[4] By 1900, the town had not grown much, counting 1016 inhabitants. Countywide population remained near its 1850 level of about 10,000. Although Buena Vista had added electric lights, a new water works and a new brick depot (completed in 1904), by 1910, the village contained only 1161 residents. By 1920, Marion County's population was down to 7600, and ten years later it was below 7000. Little New South hope had arrived on the rails of the Buena Vista and Ellaville Railroad, and little had been warranted. As cotton's kingdom crumbled, Marion County languished. In 1928, an extensive remodeling masked the vernacular form of the old 1850 court building, which included the addition of a classical portico. The old courthouse still serves the county today, one of fifteen antebellum court buildings still standing in Georgia today (see Appendix A).

SCHLEY COUNTY: ELLAVILLE

Plate 24.3: The Schley County Courthouse, built in 1899. James W. Golucke, architect.

Although the People's Party did not carry Schley County in 1894 as they had neighboring Marion and Taylor Counties, Georgia's Populists enjoyed notable support here. Central to this cause was the agrarian's deep mistrust of industrialization. Especially suspect were the railroads with their exploitive rate policies. As the depression of the early 1890s deepened, many farmers united in political rebellion against what they perceived to be the grasping juggernaut of American big business, which dominated government and controlled farm prices through manipulations of the money supply. Ten years after the first train arrived in Ellaville, any New South zeal that may have arrived in Schley County on the Buena Vista and Ellaville Railroad was all but forgotten. By 1894, Populists armies of hapless tenants and sharecroppers were renouncing the New South's Faustian bargain with Northern industrial interests. Ellaville remained a village of only about 350 residents, and although the arrival of the railroad had established the place as a minor cotton market, the appeal of the New South myth and the power of the region's new business elite were never strong here.

The area around Ellaville was originally called Pond Town, and in 1854, when Schley County was created from Marion and Sumter Counties, the new county seat of Ellaville was laid out only about a half a mile from old Pond Town. A brick courthouse was erected on the square sometime around 1858. In 1884, the first train on the Buena Vista and Ellaville Railroad arrived to shorten the 12-mile journey from Ellaville to the Southwestern Railroad's depot at Andersonville to the impossibly brief span of only one hour. But the tiny railroad was not an immediate success, and it was not until the Central of Georgia acquired the line and extended it all the way from Americus to Columbus that there existed any possibility for the prosperity of the new age to flow along these rails. By this time, the farmers of Schley County were entangled in a predicament of tenancy poverty that typified the age. Populism was on the rise, and the brick walls of the old courthouse at Ellaville were crumbling.

With the approach of the new century, economic depression abated and the Populist cause began to fade, but the old 1858 Schley County Courthouse continued to deteriorate. By 1898, the grand jury declared the old building to be in "dangerous condition," and before another year had passed they recommended a new one. But Schley County was a conservative place, and county leaders viewed the new age and a new courthouse with the same skepticism. If the old building could be repaired, then they were not about to replace it. In May of 1899, a contractor from Americus was hired to inspect the old building, and although his report stopped short of saying that the old building was unsafe, he characterized the structure as "yielding continually," constructed of inferior materials and of questionable structural integrity.[5] In short, the old building was strong enough to support the roof, but there was no guarantee that the rickety thing would not blow down in the first strong gust. This was enough to turn the tide of conservatism. Within a year, Schley County had demolished the old court building, selected a design by Atlanta architect, James Golucke, issued bonds to fund construction, erected a new building and celebrated their work with

Plate 24.3: James Golucke's 1899 Schley County Courthouse at Ellaville evokes little of Henry Hobson Richardson's grand visions for evolving modern American architectural forms, but from Richardson's rustic Romanesque vocabulary, Golucke created comfortable buildings which, although modern, also sang ancient and strangely agrarian songs. (Photo: Wilber W. Caldwell.)

a grand outdoor banquet consumed at a table which measured over 250 feet in length.[6]

Only two years before the new courthouse began to rise in Ellaville, James Wingfield Golucke had designed his first Richardsonian Romanesque court building, the 1897 Henry County Courthouse at McDonough. Despite Golucke's lack of formal architectural training, the design at McDonough would confirm the ex-cabinetmaker as a major force in Georgia's quest for suitable public architectural symbols. Golucke's plan for the Henry County Courthouse became the template for four more

[4]   The Marion Sentinel in Nettie Powell, *The History of Marion County, Georgia*, 90.

[5]   *The Schley County News*, May 25, 1899.

[6]   *The Schley County News*, October 19, 1899.

Romanesque court buildings in the state. The second of these rose at Blairsville in Union County in 1899 where Golucke perfected his model, altering the fenestration to effect a more Richardsonian impression while retaining the polychromy accomplished through the use of granite voussoirs and banding. Sadly the highly Richardsonian granite trim is omitted in the last three of these quintuple sisters, the 1899 Schley County Courthouse at Ellaville, the 1905 Jones County Courthouse at Gray and the 1907 Baker County Courthouse at Newton. Today the ravages of time have taken their toll. Still, except for variations in the tower design, these three buildings were once virtually identical.

Here again, Golucke's engineering skills are called into question. Sadly, few of his towers have stood the test of time. Golucke's grand towers at Wrightsville, Zebulon and Blairsville are gone. On the banks of the Flint at Newton, where Golucke died, a grotesque replacement tower violates the building's original Romantic charm. Here in Ellaville, serious structural problems appeared as the tower developed a pronounced lean. The structure was stabilized in 1992.

Despite their lack of structural integrity, Golucke's towers endowed his buildings with much of their Romantic imagery. Romanesque spires evoked a sense of monumentality despite these buildings' otherwise diminutive proportions. James Golucke had struck a balance. He had tamed the Richardsonian beast, wrestling Richardson's awe-inspiring forms down from their lofty heights and into the dusty soil of rural Georgia. Surely, Golucke sensed little of Richardson's grand visions for evolving modern American architectural forms. But from the master's rustic Romanesque vocabulary, Golucke created comfortable buildings, which although modern, also sang the ancient and strangely agrarian songs of an era when Europe lay in cultural ruin, helplessly fixed in the grasp of futile economic masters. Here is a fitting metaphor for rural Georgia in the decades that followed defeat.

CHATTAHOOCHEE COUNTY: CUSSETA

The Chattahoochee County Courthouse built in 1854. Formerly at Cusseta, moved to Westville for restoration in 1975. (See Plate 3 in the Introduction.)

The last gavel fell in a wooden courthouse in Georgia at Cusseta in 1975. Across the state, over a hundred-frame court buildings had been erected. The last appeared in Bryan County at Clyde in 1901. In that year, twenty-three vernacular frame courthouses, very much like this one, were still in use in Georgia. Today only five remain standing (see Table II of the Introduction). Such buildings speak volumes about the seemingly countless county towns where the myth of the New South had been slow to arrive. They reveal places where a cycle of poverty refuted the hopeful sermons so zealously preached by New South spokesmen who predicted a new era of prosperity along an ever widening web of rail. In this context, this fine restoration is a historical gem. Built of heart pine and erected by slaves immediately after Chattahoochee County was created from Muscogee and Marion Counties in 1854, the old courthouse from Cusseta narrates a compelling tale of a New South that never arrived.

Although there was a depot called "Cusseta" on the Central's 1889 Columbus extension of the Buena Vista and Ellaville Railroad, the line missed the town by some distance. About the same time that the Central bypassed Cusseta, the Columbus Southern was built from Columbus to Albany, and although that line did pass through the county seat, Chattahoochee County would experience little of the passion aroused by the New South's gleaming promises. Located in hilly terrain, Cusseta was wedged between the industrial miracle at Columbus and the railroad boom at Richland. In the shadow of such success, the village found it difficult to garner any of the progress of the new age. Therefore, as the Central's first train steamed by in May of 1889 followed by the first train on the Columbus Southern in October of that same year, Cusseta counted only 241 residents. By 1910, she could count only 341.

---

[7] Powell, *History of Marion County, Georgia*, 87-88.

[8] Powell, *History of Marion County, Georgia*, 88.

SOME LAST THOUGHTS ON THE BUENA VISTA AND ELLAVILLE RAILROAD

By the early 1890s, the Central Railroad and Banking Company controlled some 2700 miles of track in Georgia, South Carolina and Alabama. Almost from her beginning, the company had exhibited an expansionist's appetite, as she provided the financial impetus for the construction of the Southwestern Railroad in the late 1840s. In the turbulent times that followed the war, the Central adopted an even more opportunistic policy characterized by the acquisition of established lines, which were foundering on the nightmarish shoals of the post-war economy. As the 1870s ended, the Central's tactics again subtly changed, and the company was quick to come to the aid of under funded local railroad companies struggling to lay new track.

Such was the case with the Buena Vista and Ellaville Railroad. Although the grading of this line had been accomplished with local capital, the Central supplied the rails and the rolling stock for the new road.[7] It is questionable whether the Buena Vista and Ellaville could have been completed without the Central's support. Not surprisingly, this assistance came with a substantial price. The new railroad struggled from the beginning, and in 1886, the Central bought the Buena Vista and Ellaville for 30 cents on the dollar,[8] extending its rails to Columbus. This was part of the Central Railroad and Banking Company's larger scheme to connect Savannah with Birmingham via Columbus. It is certainly no coincidence that, in that same year, the SAM joined rails with the Central's subsidiary, the Savannah and Western at Lyons. Thus, with trackage rights granted by the SAM from Lyons to Americus and the acquisition of the Buena Vista and Ellaville from Americus to Columbus, the Central briefly enjoyed a direct route from Savannah to Columbus.

However, the rails through Buena Vista and Ellaville were not to remain a main trunk railroad for long. In 1891, the Savannah and Western canceled the reciprocal trackage agreements with the SAM. This spelled the beginning of the end for the SAM, which would eventually become a key link in the Seaboard

Air Line. In the wake of all of this, along the rails of the old Buena Vista and Ellaville Railroad, traffic was once again mostly local. Cotton flowed out of Marion and Schley Counties, but little of the myth of a modern New South flowed in. A few brick buildings rose at Buena Vista and at Ellaville, but these towns experienced only modest growth between 1890 and 1910.

The record of courthouse building in Schley, Marion and Chattahoochee Counties confirms this scenario. Only James Golucke's 1900 Schley County Courthouse at Ellaville rose to sing the songs of progress. Although out of fashion in the rest of the nation, at the turn of the century the Romanesque Revival still appeared modern in the American South, where new ideas continued to be viewed with skepticism, and where a notable stylistic lag had characterized the region's architecture since before the Civil War. Although Golucke's courthouse at Ellaville wore the clothing of the new age, it was in fact, little more than a manifestation of the county's pressing need for a new court building, which had surfaced in 1899 when the crumbling walls of the old 1858 Schley County Courthouse were condemned. Down the rails at Buena Vista, the old 1856 Marion County Courthouse was standing solid as a rock as the new century arrived, just as it stands today. In tiny Cusseta in Chattahoochee County, where the rails of the Central's Columbus extension had missed the village altogether in 1889, the 1854 frame courthouse would serve until 1975.

•

The Wrightsville and Tennille Railroad
The Augusta, Gibson and Sandersville Railroad

Richmond County: Augusta (see chapter 1) • Glascock County: Gibson • Washington County: Sandersville
Johnson County: Wrightsville • Laurens County: Dublin (see chapter 22)
Some Last Thoughts on the Wrightsville and Tennille and the Augusta Gibson and Sandersville Railroads

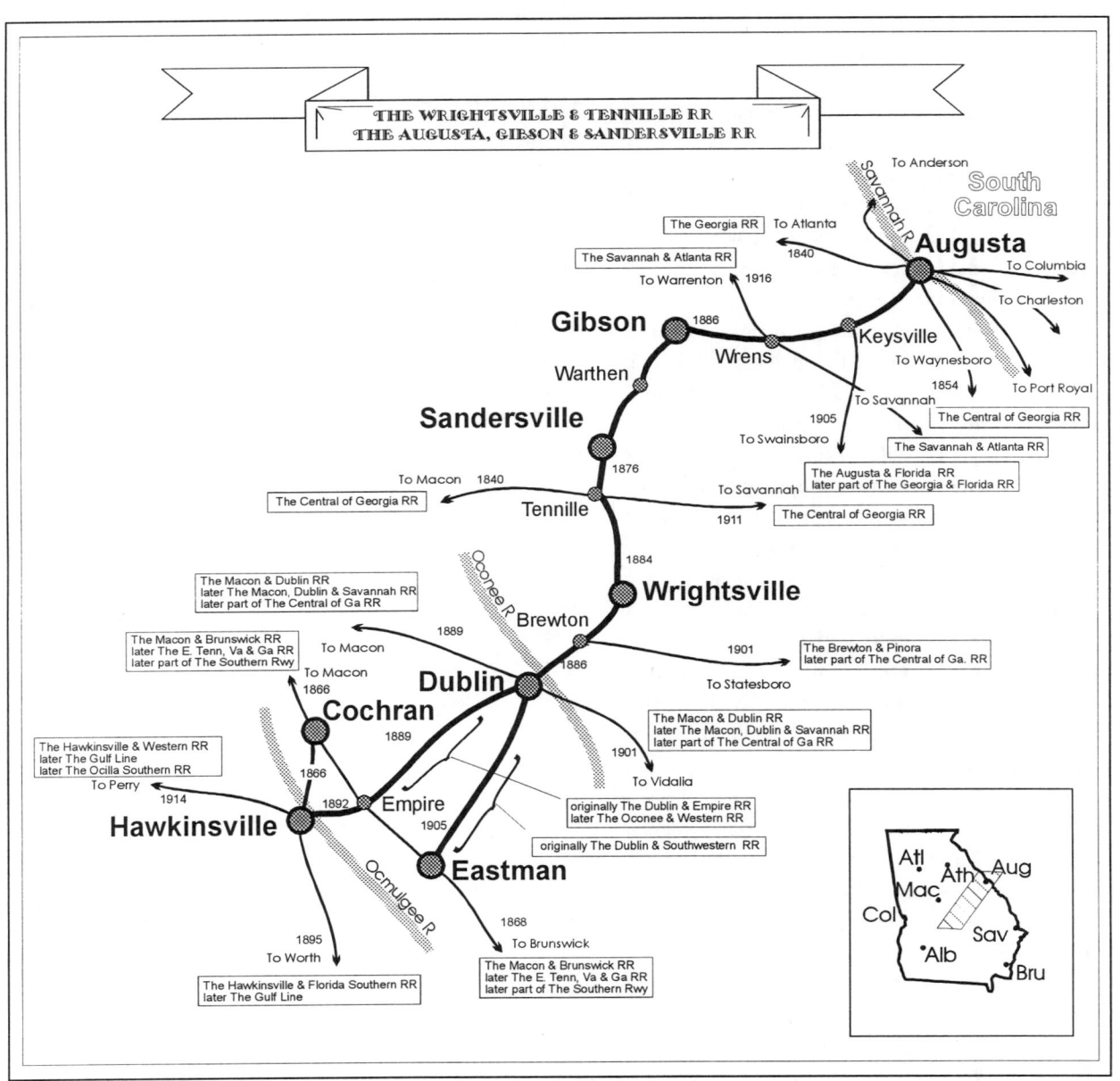

25 | The Wrightsville and Tennille Railroad
The Augusta, Gibson and Sandersville Railroad

WASHINGTON COUNTY: SANDERSVILLE

Plate 25.1: The Washington County Courthouse, built in 1855-1856. Burned in 1864. Architect, unknown.

In 1836, when a simple brick vernacular courthouse rose to replace Washington County's original 1812 frame courthouse, Sandersville was a village of fewer than 100 residents,[1] and no one could have guessed that this tiny county town was to become the home to one of Georgia's most important architectural symbols. In 1855, the 1836 Washington County Courthouse burned to the ground in a fire that destroyed most of Sandersville, a town, which by then, according to George White's earlier account, counted about 400 residents. This extraordinary courthouse rose in that same year to celebrate cotton and the wealth that had blossomed in Georgia's Eastern Cotton Belt in the middle of the nineteenth century.

Here is a building of unique refinement. By the 1850s, many brick courthouses had risen in the Piedmont, and some, like those at Macon and Columbus, were quite large. But few approached the sophisticated styling found here at Sandersville. In Georgia in 1855, only the 1833 Greek revival courthouse at Savannah and the 1821 Federal Style courthouse at Augusta rivaled the Washington County Courthouse. There was undoubtedly an architect involved here, but sadly, his identity has been lost in history.

From an early date, the national architecture of the new and idealistic nation was firmly set in the mold of classical revival. Jefferson, himself, had labored to set the tone and to fix the symbolism. In concept, the new American architecture

---

[1] Mary Alice Jordan, *From Cotton to Kaolin, A History of Washington County, Georgia* (Sandersville GA: Washington County Historical Society, 1989) 15.

Plate 25.1: The 1855 Washington County Courthouse at Sandersville constituted one of the most important architectural symbols of its day in Georgia. (Photo: Courtesy of the Georgia Department of Archives and History.)

embodied simplified forms, loosely fashioned after Greek and Roman models. These buildings stood for sweeping ideals: Democracy, Wisdom, Justice, and the like. Despite a symbolism rooted in classical imagery, the new American classicism wandered freely from ancient to neoclassical forms. The Georgian and the so-called Palladian styles that had characterized the Colonial Period were still very much alive after the Revolution in the work of Charles Bulfinch, Asher Benjamin, and other European trained early American architects. At the same time, a new architectural sub-style was emerging. In America and elsewhere, what Henry Russell Hitchcock calls Romantic Classicism in his definitive study of nineteenth century architecture is sometimes termed the "Revolutionary Democratic" style.[2] Characterized buy an almost abstract use of classical geometric shapes and a stark monochrome, this most modern of classically inspired styles carried with it the most powerful and idealistic of the democratic symbols born of the Enlightenment. American practitioners include Jefferson himself and Benjamin Henry Latrobe. The simple, elegant lines of the Regency Style work of William Jay in Savannah might also be included in this category. Despite such revolutionary forms, the most powerful and pervasive voice in America's classical love affair was to be the Greek revival. But here in Sandersville, we find neither of

these classical models, but rather the vestigial neoclassical side of American Classicism. Here we find a glowing reflection of the Italian Renaissance.

General Sherman burned this extraordinary courthouse in 1864. It was one of only ten courthouses destroyed by Federal forces in Georgia. In this case, orders to torch the building were issued in response to Confederate resistance to Sherman's advance into Sandersville, which although described as light in most reports, did include rebel snipers firing from the courthouse. In retaliation, Sherman declared that only the courthouse and the jail would be burned, and straight away, the Yankees left Sandersville to burn the Central of Georgia's depot at Tennille 3 miles to the South.

Plate 25.2: The depot at Tennille, built in 1869.

In 1840, in a headlong rush from Savannah to Macon, the main trunk of the Central Railroad bypassed Sandersville. Struggling to outlast the economic depression that lingered in the wake of the Panic of 1837, the road established its Station Number 13 at the village first known as Franklinville, also referred to as "Sandersville Station" and later called Tennille. Today, the usual myth of the bypassed town is still alive in Sandersville. This story holds that the railroad was not wanted in the county town, and thus had to be routed through Tennille. While there may be some truth in this, the Central had paid little attention to any of the towns along its route. It is unlikely that tiny Sandersville, a village of less than 100 residents in 1840, could have tempted the road to alter its straight course along the low ridge that led from the crossing of Williamson Swamp Creek at Davisboro to the crossing of the Oconee River near Oconee.

This fine depot, completed in 1869, was one of many built by the Central in the late 1860s and early 1870s to replace those destroyed by Sherman on his March to the Sea. Once adorned with the scrolling brackets of what many have termed the American Railroad Style, the building is similar to warehouses still standing today at Millen, Bartow, Toomsboro and Milledgeville on the Central, and at Fort Valley and Montezuma on the Central's subsidiary, the

Plate 25.2: The imposing depot at Tennille, completed in 1869, was one of many built by the Central in the late 1860s and early 1870s to replace those destroyed by Sherman on his March to the Sea. (Photo: Wilber W. Caldwell.)

Southwestern Railroad. The American Railroad Style was an offspring of the Italianate Style, which blossomed in the 1850s. Depots of this type often incorporated elaborate towers, classical fenestration, and scrolling brackets supporting the eaves. In Georgia, the depots built by the Central in the heart of the Reconstruction period gained entry into this class solely through their use of delicate curved brackets.

The 1870s began with considerable railroad speculation in Sandersville as plans were laid for the Sandersville Branch Railroad in 1872 and later for the Goodrich Railroad from Sandersville to Davisboro on the Central in 1873. Neither of these lines got beyond the planning stages. But in 1876, business leaders in Sandersville completed the Sandersville and Tennille Branch Railroad. At this time, Tennille was still little more than a dusty hamlet of fewer than 90 residents[3] and Sandersville boasted a population above 1000. As the two towns were connected by rail, cotton's tyranny of increased production and dwindling returns gripped Washington County. When this depot was completed in 1869, cotton production in Washington County was already approaching its prewar level. The county produced over 11,000 bales in 1870. By 1880, this figure had more than doubled.

Meanwhile, vast stands of timber were being exploited to the south. In 1884, with the considerable

help of the Central, the Wrightsville and Tennille Railroad was constructed by the Perkins Lumber Company, which operated a sizable mill south of Tennille at Harrison. Originally organized in 1883 as the Wrightsville and Sun Hill Railroad, the line was not an immediate success. The Central, which had supplied the rails and rolling stock for the fledgling road,[4] purchased a large block of the new road's nearly worthless stock before the end of 1884,[5] and acquired the Wrightsville and Dublin Railroad in 1886, thus extending the line all the way to Dublin. As a pawn of the Central, the Wrightsville and Tennille would later acquire branches to Hawkinsville and to Eastman.

Despite the new railroad's ongoing financial problems, Tennille prospered. No longer a dusty depot town serving the 3-mile branch line to Sandersville, crossing rails made the village a full-fledged junction town. With the construction of the Wrightsville and

[2] Alan Gowans, *Styles and Types of American Architecture, Social Function and Cultural Expression* (1992; reprint, New York: Icon Editions, 1993) 103-110.

[3] Jordan, *From Cotton to Kaolin, A History of Washington County, Georgia*, 42.

[4] Jordan, *From Cotton to Kaolin, A History of Washington County, Georgia*, 50.

[5] Les R. Winn, *Ghost Trains and Depots in Georgia* (Chamblee GA: Big Shanty Press, 1995) 137.

Tennille's shops and yards, her population soared. By 1890, Tennille counted almost 1000 residents, and by 1910 her population exceeded 1600. In 1903, as Augusta architect Charles E. Choate's stunning Wrightsville and Tennille Office building rose only a stone's throw from this old depot, Tennille had a new passenger depot (demolished in 1969), electric lights, a new water works, twenty-four retail stores, six manufacturing concerns including a cotton mill and twenty passenger trains a day.[6] Meanwhile, 3 miles to the north in Sandersville, another Augusta architect had been at work.

Plate 25.3: The Washington County Courthouse, built in 1868-1869. Expanded and remodeled 1899. Lewis F. Goodrich, remodeling architect.

By 1869, despite the economic hardships of Reconstruction, Washington County had managed to replace the rather spectacular ruins of the old 1856 courthouse which, like the charred columns of the 1852 Cobb County Courthouse at Marietta, had become locally known as "Sherman's Sentinels." The 1869 Washington County Courthouse was a simple two-story brick affair and, in the hard times of the late 1860s, the builder had used bricks salvaged from the ruins.

Plate 25.3: The Queen Anne elegance of Augusta architect Lewis Goodrich's 1899 remodeling of the Washington County Courthouse celebrated Sandersville's late nineteenth century boom. (Photo: Wilber W. Caldwell.)

With the construction of the short but vital link of the Sandersville and Tennille Railroad in 1876, Sandersville finally avoided the fate of the bypassed town. As the first depot for the Sandersville and Tennille Railroad rose at Sandersville in 1876, a modest building boom blossomed. According to Sholes's *Gazetteer of Georgia*, Sandersville had a population of about 1000 in 1879. This number had doubled by 1886, when the Augusta, Gibson and Sandersville Railroad arrived in Sandersville from Augusta. After fire destroyed a sizable portion of the town in 1888, new brick buildings began to sprout around the square.

Things seemed to be looking up for Sandersville, but the Augusta, Gibson and Sandersville Railroad was a narrow gauge road, and the connection with the standard gauge rails of the Sandersville and Tennille created something of a bottleneck. The Augusta, Gibson and Sandersville failed in 1891, and was reorganized in 1893 as the Augusta Southern. Two years later, the tracks were widened to standard gauge, and finally, spirits in Sandersville again soared.

Meanwhile, out in the countryside of Washington County, the 1890s had not kindled the kind of hope that had smoldered in Sandersville. Populism was strong here. Farmers and Aliencemen had little faith in railroads with their easy promise of a new era of prosperity. So skeptical were some Washington Countians, that a second rail line, the Sandersville Railroad was constructed in 1894 to redundantly span the 3 miles from Sandersville to Tennille. The new line was built to compete with the Augusta Southern, which had acquired the Sandersville and Tennille Railroad in that same year. Although the atmosphere in Sandersville was ripe for courthouse building, the mood of the county's rural population was guarded, and when the rickety portico of the 1868 courthouse was removed in 1896, the grand jury began to call for a remodeling of the old building rather than a total replacement.[7] However, what a remodeling it was to be.

So extensive were the additions and alterations, that the old courthouse was effectively encased in the new structure. The result was a remodeling in name only. Here is a voice of hope rising to scribe the high-water mark of Sandersville's late nineteenth century boom. Building upon the success of his newly completed 1897 Screven County Courthouse at Sylvania, Augusta architect, Lewis F. Goodrich, employed a distinctly Queen Anne approach here in Sandersville. The fluted chimneys, the picturesque tower with its classical trim, and the high pedimented dormers are characteristic of Queen Anne ornament. However, like Lewis Goodrich's later 1904 Taliaferro County Courthouse at Crawfordville, the 1899 Washington County Courthouse at Sandersville stops short of the full exuberance inherent in the Queen Anne Style. Nowhere to be found are the highly picturesque bell-like roofs and the lacy entrance porticos with their delicate groupings of tiny columns that decorated Goodrich's courthouse at Sylvania. At Sandersville, we find large expanses of flat brick wall space, the simple elegance of a formal tower and the sober rustication of brick banding in the lower story. All of this reflects a restrained approach.

In America, the Queen Anne was the last, and perhaps the most elaborate of the picturesque styles. Endowed with a highly eclectic license, it combined picturesque forms with classically inspired detail. This complex Swan Song of Queen Anne finery brought the picturesque movement full circle. In its lust for electric freedom, in the end, it finally embraced the classicism it had once sought to replace.

Here in Washington County, where the promises of the New South were still subject to the scrutiny of a highly skeptical agrarian rural population, it is indeed fitting that, at the turn of the century, a generous helping of vernacular restraint crept into the architecture of the county's most poignant and enduring symbol. After a series of failures and reorganizations, the Southern Railway acquired the Augusta Southern in 1901. By 1905, two brand new depots had replaced the railroad's original "old cow barns" in Sandersville,[8] but the hope for New South progress that had arrived by rail in the previous decades was disappearing. The entire line of the original Augusta, Gibson and Sandersville Railroad was abandoned in 1934, and Sandersville once again found herself at the end of an remote spur.

JOHNSON COUNTY: WRIGHTSVILLE

When the first depot was erected at Wrightsville around 1884, the simple building breathed life into to the tiny village. Johnson County had been created from Washington, Emanuel and Laurens Counties in 1858. The following year, Wrightsville had been laid out, and a two-story frame courthouse was erected. Twenty years later, according to Sholes's *Gazetteer of Georgia*, the population was less than 100 residents, but railroad dreams were on the wind. In 1876, neighboring Sandersville had been connected to the main line of the Central at Tennille. As early as 1880 *The Wrightsville Recorder* was heralding plans by both the Sandersville and Tennille Railroad and the Central of Georgia to construct a new line southward from Tennille, via Wrightsville, to Dublin.[9] Three years later, the Wrightsville and Tennille Railroad was chartered, and in 1884, as the rails neared Wrightsville, the Wrightsville and Dublin Railroad was born. New South zeal filled the streets of Wrightsville, and *The Recorder* waxed optimistic: "Steam is the great civilizer, and the completion of this road will mark a new era in the advancement of our county."[10]

By 1886, the Central of Georgia Railroad controlled the rails from Tennille to Dublin. In that year, according to Sholes, Wrightsville's population had surged to over 600, and *The Recorder* measured the town's success in terms that everyone could understand. "Ten yeas ago not ten bales of cotton were brought here," the editor declared, and he went on to boast that, since the arrival of the railroad, the town handled "an average of over 2000 bales per year." The 1885 article further predicted that this number would soon reach 5000 bales, and *The Recorder* concluded, "Now that the railroad has arrived, Wrightsville will no longer black the boots of other towns."[11] So it

[6] Jordan, *From Cotton to Kaolin, A History of Washington County, Georgia*, 42.

[7] *Middle Georgia Progress*, September 13, 1898.

[8] Jordan, *From Cotton to Kaolin, A History of Washington County, Georgia*, 43.

[9] *The Wrightsville Recorder*, September 25, 1880.

[10] *The Wrightsville Recorder*, November 29, 1884.

[11] *The Wrightsville Recorder*, July 11, 1885.

Plate 25.4: The 1895 Johnson County Courthouse at Wrightsville was the first of James W. Golucke's 26 court buildings in Georgia. (Photo: Wilber W. Caldwell.)

Plate 25.5: Golucke's original clock tower. (Photo: Courtesy of Ted Brooke.)

[12] Allen D. Candler and Clement A. Evans, *The Cyclopedia of Georgia* 3 vols. (Atlanta: State Historical Association, 1906) 644.

[13] Barton C. Shaw, *The Wool Hat Boys* (Baton Rouge: Louisiana State University Press, 1984) 2.

[14] *The Glascock Banner*, February 7, 1895.

was to be. By 1900, Wrightsville's population was above 1000, and according to the 1906 *Cyclopedia of Georgia,* in addition to hosting a booming lumber and naval stores trade, the town shipped 5000 bales of cotton on the Wrightsville and Tennille Railroad.[12]

Plate 25.4: The Johnson County Courthouse, built in 1895. Golucke & Stewart, architects.

Wrightsville's sudden surge was propelled by a chain of railroad related events beginning with the Wrightsville and Tennille's connection to Dublin in 1886. This was followed by the completion of the Augusta, Gibson and the Sandersville Railroad in that same year. By 1891, when the Macon and Dublin entered Dublin, Wrightsville found herself with convenient rail connections to Savannah, Macon and Augusta. By this time, the seemingly obligatory movement for a new courthouse was under way.

In 1895 and 1896, Johnson County erected the first of Atlanta architect James Wingfield Golucke's 26 courthouses in Georgia. Like its nearly identical twin, which was begun only months later at Zebulon in Pike County, the 1895 Johnson County Courthouse employed a unique classical plan composed of four equal cubical pedimented modules whose entablatures were wrapped in a colorful wreath of painted pressed metal. All of this supported an enormous central classical clock tower crowned with a delicate Greek lantern. Golucke's original towers, both here and at Zebulon, were later replaced owing to inadequate structural support. But in Wrightsville, the original tower stood until 1938 when its was removed and the present neocolonial tower was constructed. Golucke's models for these monumental towers are not known, but the year before this courthouse was begun, R. H. Hunt completed his stunning Elbert County Courthouse at Elberton, which was capped with a very similar tower. Whatever its source and despite its rickety structural design, the original tower supplied an awe-inspiring crown to this prolific architect's first courthouse.

In 1995, the Johnson County Courthouse underwent an extensive restoration returning the exterior of the building to its original brick color and beautifully refurbishing all of the original window sashes and frames. Extensive interior work included restoration of plaster walls and extensive work in the courtroom including the restoration of the balcony. Despite this fine makeover, the 1938 neocolonial replacement tower is a mere shadow of the elegance of the building's original tower, and the simplified entrances are artistically no match for Golucke's curious entrance arches supported by groups of tiny columnettes. Despite the fact that the re-creation of such refinements were beyond Johnson County's present means, this is still a restoration to be applauded. Today this building is a credit to county leaders and to the memory of the enigmatic James Wingfield Golucke.

GLASCOCK COUNTY: GIBSON

Plate 25.6: The Depot at Mitchell.

Today the old depot at Gibson is gone, but its nearly identical sister still stands in Glascock County in the tiny hamlet of Mitchell, 7 miles east of Gibson. Here is a fitting symbol for a railroad that knew nothing but hard times. In 1884, the Augusta, Gibson and Sandersville Railroad Company was chartered to build a narrow gauge railroad south from Augusta to connect with the Sandersville and Tennille Railroad in Washington County. The line was completed in 1886, immediately experienced financial difficulties and failed in the economic nightmare of the early 1890s. In 1893, the Augusta Southern Railroad Company was chartered to acquire the failed line. This company operated the ne'er-do-well road until in 1897 when it leased the line to the South Carolina and Georgia Railroad, which became part of the Southern Railway in 1899. In 1917, the line was sold to the Georgia and Florida Railroad. The entire line through Glascock and Washington Counties was abandoned in 1934. Clearly this was not the glorious industrial triumph that New South promoters had so freely vouched safe. All through the five decades of the Augusta Southern's futile struggle, the tiny village of Gibson waited skeptically beside a depot very similar to this one.

Here we find the enigmatic roots of Populism. In the heart of Georgia's "terrible Tenth" Congressional District, Glascock County offers compelling insight into the strange phenomenon that was the People's

Plate 25.6: This depot at Mitchell is a fitting symbol for the struggle of the Augusta Southern Railroad. (Photo: Wilber W. Caldwell.)

Party in Georgia. Why Populism found fertile soil in some counties and was rejected in others is a challenging question. On the surface it would seem that opposition to the perceived manipulation of the nation's farmers by an economy, "rigged" to favor the rich, would have aroused strong Populist support in most rural areas of the state in the mid 1890s. But this was not the case. Some scholars suggest that Populism most often emerged in backwoods districts away from the railroads, while others suggest that it was reaction to the railroad's exploitive freight rates that supplied the key. In this connection, some seek a connection between Populist strength and fruit growing in a region. Others contend that the third party movement most often flourished in areas where there were many new settlers and few blacks.[13]

None of these scenarios seem to fit the mold of Glascock county, where in 1894, a Populist newspaper in Gibson began to publish some of the most extreme Populist rhetoric in the nation. In 1895, just as the Augusta Southern was widened to standard gauge, *The Glascock Banner* warned readers, "the greed of Capitalists, if permitted to continue, must result in absolute servitude."[14] Such categorical notions suggest deep roots. In his fine study, *The Wool Hat Boys*, Barton C. Shaw suggests that the foundation for Populist successes in the "terrible Tenth" was laid well before the war by antebellum Whigs, when "the northern Cotton Belt was tutoring its citizens in political nonconformity."[15] Thus, according to Shaw, as the difficulties of the 1890s unfolded: "(the terrible Tenth already possessed a strong anti-Bourbon tradition. Indeed, the spirit of Robert Toombs was still abroad in the Region."[16]

Whatever its roots, Populism was strong in Glascock County, and in 1895, The Banner boasted that Populist candidates in the county had encountered "no opposition." In the same issue the editor offered his readers a scathing condemnation of bonded public debt, declaring, "Agents of the Rothchilds are busy attending to the business of their masters.[17]" This was not the stuff that that built new courthouses.

Plate 25.7: The 1858 Glascock County Courthouse at Gibson is one of only five remaining frame court buildings in Georgia. (Photo: Wilber W. Caldwell.)

Plate 25.7: The Glascock County Courthouse, built in 1858.

Once scores of court buildings like this one stood on courthouse squares all across the state. Today only five remain (see Table II of the Introduction). These sturdy hipped roof structures were generally of a vernacular sort, but many incorporated simple classical details, like the elegant pilasters, which framed what was once the main entrance of the old courthouse here in Gibson. Despite the economic potential that beckoned with the arrival of the Augusta, Gibson and Sandersville Railroad in 1886, the citizens of Glascock County would place little faith in promises imported by steel rails. Immobile within their reactionary economic and political mind-sets, these farmers harbored intransigent attitudes. Such philosophies were typical of a large but often politically impotent force that inhabited the rural South well into this century. Here in Glascock County, these deep-seeded convictions gained political momentum in the 1890s. They came bubbling to the surface in the form of Populism and its radical and often contradictory political organization known as the Peoples Party. Although its surge was brief, the third party movement in Georgia revealed widely held popular attitudes and emotions regarding economic progress that could not have been more at odds with the grasping philosophies of New South spokesmen and the rising business elite. Few new courthouses rose where Populism flourished. According to Sholes's *Gazetteer of Georgia,* Gibson was a hamlet of only 100 residents in 1879. By 1890, the place had six stores, but only 197 residents, and in 1910 Gibson counted only 367 inhabitants. The county's original courthouse would serve until 1918, and in that year, this frame building was moved from it original site. In converting the old building to a private home, a large portico was added and the main entrance was covered over.

[15] Shaw, *The Wool Hat Boys,* 3.

[16] Shaw, *The Wool Hat Boys,* 42.

[17] *The Glascock Banner,* January 3, 1895.

SOME LAST THOUGHTS ON THE WRIGHTSVILLE AND TENNILLE AND THE AUGUSTA, GIBSON AND SANDERSVILLE RAILROADS

In 1840, when the Central Railroad and Banking Company erected the first tiny depot at Station #13 in Washington County, few could have foreseen that the tiny village that sprang up beside the rails would later become the bustling railroad junction town of Tennille. In the decades that followed Appomattox, the Central's rails from Savannah to Macon became the spine of a web of connectivity. Short lines, spurs and ne'er-do-well local branch lines snaked their way from various bypassed towns to join the main trunk of this pioneer antebellum railroad. Among the first to seek such a connection was Sandersville, which in 1876 issued $10,000 in city bonds to build the 3-mile spur of the Sandersville and Tennille Railroad. Through the efforts of the Perkins family, which operated a large lumber mill at Harrison south of Tennille, and with the considerable aid of the Central, the Wrightsville and Tennille Railroad was completed from Tennille to Wrightsville in 1884 and extended southward to Dublin in 1886. Meanwhile, another railroad was snaking its way southward from Augusta. The narrow gauge rails of the Augusta Gibson and Sandersville Railroad completed the link all the way from Augusta to Dublin when they arrived in Sandersville in 1886.

At the center of all of this was the village of Tennille, which briefly appeared destined to become the dominant junction city of the region. But after 1891, when the Macon, Dublin and Savannah Railroad was completed from Macon to Dublin, it became clear that Dublin was to be the railroad's city of destiny, and Alexander Bruce's stunning Laurens County Courthouse rose in 1895 to celebrate Dublin's success. With a new connection to Savannah via Vidalia and subsequent new lines to Hawkinsville and to Eastman, Dublin secured her role. To the north, Wrightsville, Tennille, Sandersville and Gibson could only look on in envy.

North of Dublin, other obstacles impeded the construction of architectural symbols of hope. In the early 1890s, New South zeal was weakened in Glascock and Washington Counties by strong Populist sentiments. Leading Glascock's fight against the exploitation of American big business, the village of Gibson would keep her 1858 frame courthouse well in to the twentieth century. Farther south along the bankrupt rails of the Augusta Gibson and Sandersville Railroad, Sandersville also kept her old vernacular courthouse, but by 1899, the spirit of progress was strong enough to warrant extensive remodeling and addition. In Wrightsville where political patterns were more typical of the Wiregrass than the old Cotton Belt, Populist skepticism was not so strong, and here we find the classic courthouse depot scenario. With the connection to Dublin in 1886, the town began a period of enthusiastic growth the center piece of which was James Golucke's 1895 Johnson County Courthouse with its once monumental clock tower.

Plate 25.8: Tennille: The Wrightsville and Tennille Office Building, built in 1903. Charles E. Choate, architect. (Photo: Wilber W. Caldwell.)

The Georgia, Carolina and Northern Railroad

Gwinnett County: Lawrenceville • Barrow County: Winder (see chapter 16) • Clarke County: Athens (see chapter 13) Madison County: Danielsville • Elbert County: Elberton (see chapter 14)
Fulton County: Atlanta (also see chapters 4, 11 & 32)
Some Last Thoughts on the Georgia, Carolina and Northern Railroad

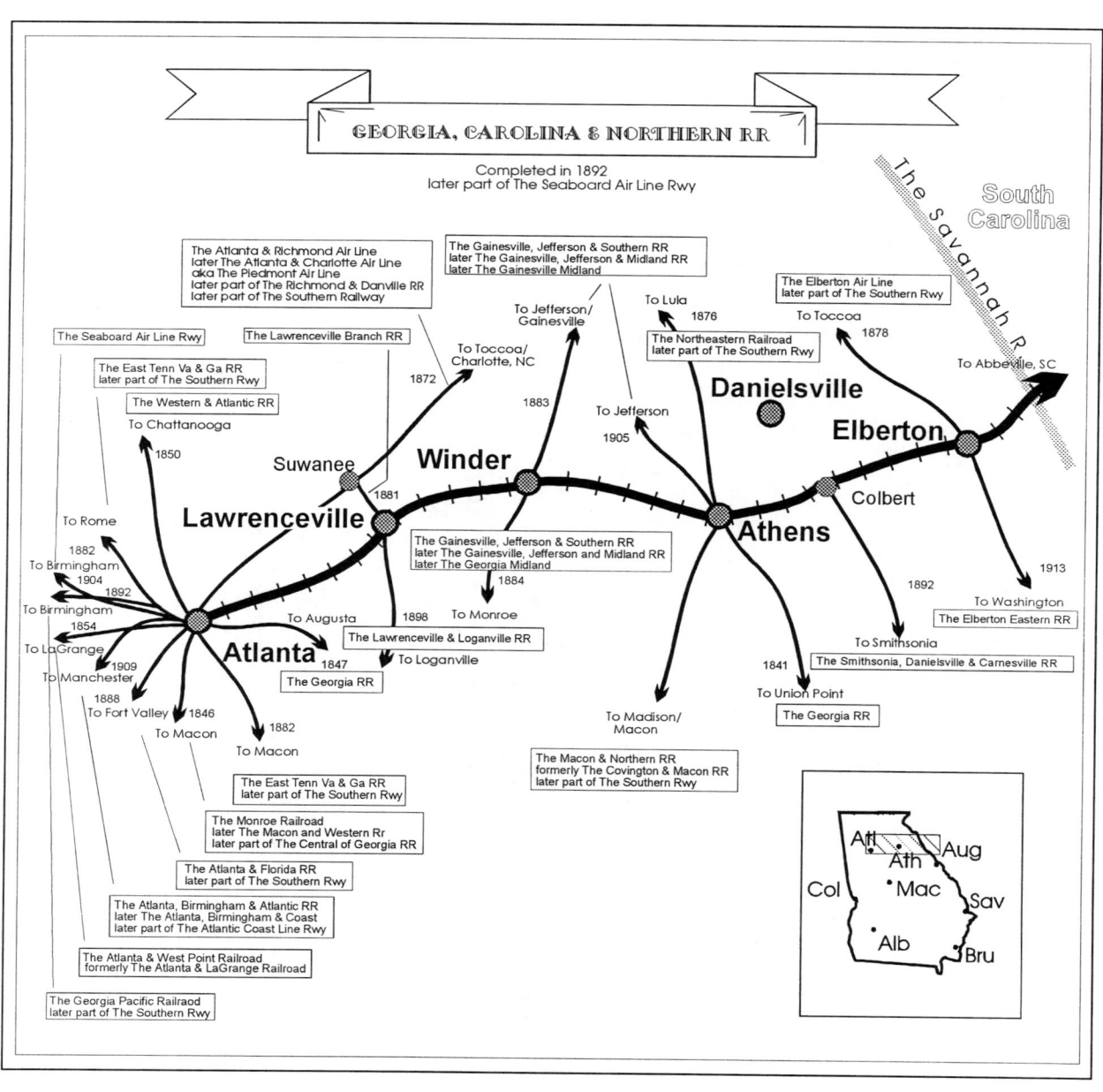

26 | Georgia, Carolina and Northern Railroad

Plate 26.1: The Gwinnett County Courthouse at Lawrenceville, built in 1884-1885, E. G. Lind, architect.

In 1885, just as the first court was called to order in Atlanta architect E. G. Lind's sparkling new Gwinnett County Courthouse, the Seaboard Air Line, though its pawn the Georgia, Carolina and Northern, began construction of its main line through the Carolinas toward Atlanta. It would be seven years before this mighty rail artery reached Lawrenceville to make its junction with the tiny Lawrenceville Branch Railroad whose narrow gauge rails had spanned the 10 miles from Lawrenceville to Suwanee in 1881. At Suwanee, the Lawrenceville Branch intersected the Atlanta and Charlotte Air Line, which later became the very heart of J. P. Morgan's powerful Southern Railway. Only three years after the town celebrated the completion of its tiny spur, *The Weekly Gwinnett Herald* "rejoiced to see fruits so abundant," declared that the miniature spur had "added new life and enterprise to a dying town," and discussed bids for the construction of a new courthouse.[1]

Gwinnett County had been created in 1818 from lands ceded to the state by Cherokee Indians and from parts of Jackson County. After two temporary log court buildings briefly served the new county in two temporary locations, the permanent county site was established at Lawrenceville, and a brick courthouse was erected there in 1824. Five years later, Adiel Sherwood described Lawrenceville in his *Gazetteer of Georgia* as a village of forty dwellings, ten stores, and three churches. By 1849, when George White published his *Statistics of the State of Georgia,* Lawrenceville had changed little; her population remained at about 400. Although one of Georgia's 33 antebellum cotton mills was erected at Lawrenceville in

---

[1] *Weekly Gwinnett Herald*, March 25, 1884.

Plate 26.1: Edmund Lind's 1884 Gwinnett County Courthouse at Lawrenceville was an early example of picturesque eclecticism in Georgia. (Photo: Courtesy of the Georgia Department of Archives and History.)

the 1850s, Federal forces burned the factory in 1864, and when the old courthouse burned in 1871, Lawrenceville still counted only about 400 residents. We know little of the courthouse that was erected in 1874, except that before the steel rails arrived in Lawrenceville, the grand jury found the building in good condition[2] and after the arrival of the first train, it was described as "inadequate" and "nearly useless."[3]

With the completion of the Lawrenceville Branch Railroad in 1881, an unrealistic helping of New South zeal steamed into Lawrenceville. As the rails neared, expectations ran high, and *The Herald* declared that the railroad was as welcome as "the approach of Blucher at Waterloo."[4] On the eve of the tiny spur's completion, the editor predicted that the arrival of the first train would: "...mark a new epoch in its (Lawrenceville's) history and will build up rapidly a fine business for our citizens....Already the old town is being awakened to new life and the next year will make wonderful changes."[5]

However, in the early 1880s, as the county's second railroad, the Gainesville, Jefferson and Southern, built across northern Gwinnett, and as hopes were stirred by prospects for a line from Covington to Lawrenceville,[6] expectations gave way to fantasies. *The Herald* declared that, with the arrival of the railroads, the county's "haunts of ignorance and vice" were being transformed into "school houses and

churches" and that the once "dark corners" of the county were suddenly "competing with more favored places for the palm of intelligence, morality and progress."[7] With such railroad induced illusions abroad in the streets of Lawrenceville, euphoric public symbols seemed bound to rise. In August of 1883, *The Herald* reported that "a strong current of public opinion is getting up in this county for a new courthouse,"[8] and in September of that year, the grand jury recommended a new court building.[9] In January of 1884, Atlanta architect, E. G. Lind presented his plans for a new Gwinnett County Courthouse to the county commissioners.[10]

Edmund George Lind was born in London in 1829. He studied architecture at the Government School of Design and apprenticed in London from 1849 to 1855, when he sailed to Baltimore to work in the offices of the noted church architect, N. G. Starkeweather. In 1857, he was elected a charter member of the American Institute of Architects. After the Civil War, Lind began his own practice and is best known for his designs for the Peabody Institute in Baltimore, the Arlington Hotel in Washington, D. C., and for numerous Italian Villa Style private mansions in Maryland, Virginia and North Carolina. During the Grant administration, he worked as assistant to the government's noted Supervising Architect, Alfred B. Mullet. Lind moved to Atlanta around 1881 and practiced in Georgia for over ten years before returning to Baltimore in 1892.

Few of Edmund Lind's designs still stand in Georgia today, but this building at Lawrenceville and Atlanta's Central Presbyterian Church remain to celebrate the work of one of the first architects to practice in Atlanta after the Civil War. In 1879, according to Thomas Henry Morgan's recollections published in The Atlanta Historical Bulletin, there were only three architectural firms in Atlanta, Parkins and Bruce, Fay and Bruyn and the office of Gustav Leo. Edmund Lind and G. L. Norrman both arrived around 1881.[11] This group was typical of the era in that Lind and Norrman were both foreign born and trained. The first architectural school in the United States was not established until 1869. Thus, the first crop of American architects to practice after the Civil

War were a mix of European trained professionals and a rather uneven group of American born journeymen who had learned their profession indirectly as civil engineers or in the nation's informal system of apprenticeship and a rather laisse-faire school of "hard knocks."

Edmund Lind's creation at Lawrenceville is an early example of picturesque eclecticism in Georgia. Fundamentally an echo of the older Romantic music of the Italian Villa Style, the building features an elegant broken based pediment above the entrance and graceful scrolling modillions supporting the eaves. Lind's original tower was a massive, squat affair of a vaguely Norman design crowned with a picturesque round lantern with a conical cap. The result was fanciful and imposing, but like the American South itself in 1885, this building seems to look both forward and back at the same time. Despite its modern romantic lantern and up-to-date arched entrance, in the final analysis, Edmund G. Lind's 1885 Gwinnett County Courthouse was as much a voice from the past, as a reflection of the future.

Plate 26.2: The Gwinnett County Courthouse at Lawrenceville, built in 1884, E. G. Lind, architect. Tower remodeled in 1908.

Despite her shiny new railroad and her sparkling new courthouse, Lawrenceville saw little progress in the 1880s. According to Sholes's 1879 *Gazetteer of Georgia*, as the decade began, the town had a population of 480. Ten years later Lawrenceville could count only 566 residents. But with the arrival of the main line of the Georgia, Carolina and Northern Railroad in 1892, the pace in Gwinnett began to quicken. By 1900, Lawrenceville's population had reached 853, the Lawrenceville and Loganville Railroad had been completed, and a cotton mill was under construction. As the end of the first decade of the new century approached, Lawrenceville was a city of almost 1500. Although E. G. Lind's 1885 Gwinnett County Courthouse still nobly reflected the county's newly charged aspirations, the roof leaked perennially and the absence of a clock tower placed the old building sadly behind the times in the eyes of Gwinnett's rising

new class of professionals and business elite in Lawrenceville.

Beginning in 1880s, the clock tower had become a standard feature of Georgia court buildings, and by 1910, in all but the poorest of counties, courthouse clocks were pounding out the hours from picturesque squares all across in the state. Accordingly, in 1908, E.

Plate 26.2: With the 1908 addition of a neoclassical clock tower, the architecture of the Gwinnett County Courthouse appeared to look both forward and back at the same time. (Photo: Wilber W. Caldwell.)

[2] *Weekly Gwinnett Herald*, March 17, 1880.

[3] *Weekly Gwinnett Herald*, September 19, 1883.

[4] *Weekly Gwinnett Herald*, March 30, 1881.

[5] *Weekly Gwinnett Herald*, February 2, 1881.

[6] *Weekly Gwinnett Herald*, January 15, 188 .

[7] *Weekly Gwinnett Herald*, March 25, 1884.

[8] *Weekly Gwinnett Herald*, August 29, 1883.

[9] *Weekly Gwinnett Herald*, September 19, 1883.

[10] *Weekly Gwinnett Herald*, January 29, 1884

[11] Thomas Henry Morgan, "The Georgia Chapter of The American Institute of Architects," *The Atlanta Historical Bulletin* 7/28 (September 1943): 140-41.

G. Lind's romantic lantern at Lawrenceville was removed and the crown of his rather medieval low tower blossomed into an elaborate neoclassical affair that recalled earlier Second Empire towers as much as it did the new American neoclassicism. In fact, Lawrenceville's tower, which was designed by "Mr. McKinney,"[12] presumably a local builder, bore a strong resemblance to several of Alexander Bruce's earlier clock towers, most notably the crown atop Bruce's replacement tower that was added to the 1894 Pike County Courthouse at Zebulon in 1898. Despite what might have been an unpleasant collision of mismatched styles, the ornate neoclassical decoration of the new tower and the earlier Italian elements of the old court building both looked to the Italian Renaissance for their inspiration, and the resulting blend is remarkably pleasing. Once again, the architecture of the New South had managed to look both forward and back at the same time.

The elegant tower at Lawrenceville had set a high-water mark for the town. As the new century worn on, new troubles surfaced in rural Georgia. The Lawrenceville Branch Railroad was abandoned in 1920. Four years later, there was still only one paved road in all of Gwinnett County. Hard times wore on and on, and over twenty years later, in 1943, the county could count only three paved highways and the courthouse roof still leaked. As the New South proved mythical, the grand courthouses that had reflected the grand hopes of an earlier era were cloaked in irony as they decayed. Here in Lawrenceville, the County's stunning 1992 restoration and adaptive reuse of E. G. Lind's 1885 Gwinnett County Courthouse is a fitting tribute to the dreams of a little remembered era, dreams that had required almost 100 years to come true.

MADISON COUNTY: DANIELSVILLE

Plate 26.3: The Madison County Courthouse at Danielsville, built in 1901. James W. Golucke, architect.

Ten miles north of Athens, tiny Danielsville is the quintessential bypassed town. Here we find the compelling drama of hope and disappointment created by

a seemingly endless stream of unfulfilled railroad promises, dubious freight imported on an illusory river of railroads that never arrived. In 1841, the Georgia Railroad was completed to Athens. Eight years later, George White's reliable *Statistics of the State of Georgia* described Danielsville as a hamlet of only thirty-five residents. The county seat of Madison County, Danielsville had seen the erection of a log courthouse just after the county was created in 1812. In 1834 a frame court building replaced this building. By 1880, Madison County was bound by railroads. To the east, the Northeastern Railroad was creating a notable commercial success at Harmony Grove (later called Commerce), and to the west, the Elberton Air Line was sparking similar prosperity at Royston. When the Georgia, Carolina and Northern Railroad completed track along the county's eastern boarder in 1891, Danielsville, a village of about 150 residents, found itself boxed by rails on three sides but touched by none.

Throughout the 1880s, the village had been enticed by numerous railroad-building schemes, including several plans for a line from Athens via Danielsville to Carnesville. The original plan for the Georgia Midland and Gulf had been for a line through Athens and Danielsville all the way to Hartwell, and the vision of north Georgia's perennial railroad dream, the Augusta and Chattanooga Railroad, had once included a depot at Danielsville. In 1890, when the Georgia, Carolina and Northern Railroad was building southward from Carolina, three different surveys were completed for that road's route into Athens. One of these ran through Danielsville.[13] At about the same time, James Smith, a wealthy farmer in Oglethorpe County, was planning his Smithsonia, Danielsville and Carnesville Railroad, and in 1891, eager investors in Madison County subscribed $15,000 to bring Col. Smith's line to Danielsville.[14] The next year, a section of this line was built from Smithsonia to Colbert, on the Georgia, Carolina and Northern, five miles east of Danielsville. Despite this broad spectrum of railroad promises, Danielsville remained unconnected.

In 1900, notwithstanding past disappointments, Madison County made plans for a new courthouse. In

September of 1900, the grand jury found the old 1834 frame building "too small" and in November of that same year, Atlanta architect, James W. Golucke was hired to design a new court building. As Golucke's new courthouse rose, *The Danielsville Monitor* was mute on the subject of impending New South progress and prosperity, and the editor printed little of the usual public spirit that so often accompanied the promise of rail and the construction of new court buildings. It is little wonder that such spirit was absent, for as the new century began, Danielsville still had no railroad, and her population was down to only 104.

Despite *The Monitor's* lack of euphoric rhetoric, there is ample evidence that the town's railroad dreams were very much alive in 1900. Visions of the Augusta and Chattanooga Railroad were far from dead, and one faction was urging a route through Danielsville to Gainesville.[15] But Danielsville's firmest hope lay with the Smithsonia, Danielsville and Carnesville. In 1896, the extension of this line to Danielsville seemed so certain that Sholes's *Gazetteer of Georgia* actually listed Danielsville as a stop on the line. Surely, hope sprang eternal in Danielsville as James Golucke's 1901 Madison County Courthouse rose on the square, for in 1902 the citizens of the tiny village again supported James Smith's line from Colbert, this time subscribing $10,000 toward its extension.[16]

James Golucke's Madison County Courthouse at Danielsville was one of four similar Romanesque designs created by the Atlanta architect in the years surrounding the turn of the century. The first of these rose at Jonesboro in Clayton County in 1898 and the last was completed in 1903 at Jeffersonville in Twiggs County. In 1901, as Danielsville celebrated her new courthouse, a similar court building was erected at Blue Ridge in Fannin County. All of these buildings display considerable variation in their ornamentation. Nonetheless, they are part of a highly symmetrical common vision, a slender central Romanesque tower flanked by rather squat pyramidal roofed corner pavilions in front and octagonal corner pavilions in the rear. This arrangement certainly owes a debt to H. H. Richardson's celebrated 1888 Allegheny County Courthouse at Pittsburgh. The form appeared in

Plate 26.3: The 1901 Madison County Courthouse at Danielsville was one of four similar Romanesque designs created by James Golucke in the years surrounding the turn of the century. (Photo: Wilber W. Caldwell.)

Georgia in 1896 with the completion of the stunning Elbert County Courthouse at Elberton designed by the noted Chattanooga architect and Elbert County native son, Reuben H. Hunt. Golucke first employed the central tower with flanking pavilions in his 1895 Emanuel County Courthouse at Swainsboro. It is highly likely that Golucke's design was inspired by Hunt's earlier court building at Elberton. Likewise, the proximity of Hunt's monumental work in neighboring Elbert County must have influenced the Madison County Commissioners in their selection of Golucke's apparently derivative design. After all, in 1901, the mighty Seaboard Air Line had just absorbed the old Georgia, Carolina and Northern, and most Danielsville residents suddenly found Elberton only a brief train ride away on the rails that everyone was sure would soon arrive in Danielsville.

[12] Jaeger/Pyburn, Inc. "Historic Research" in Preservation. Restoration and Adaptive Reuse, Historic Gwinnett County Courthouse, Lawrenceville, Georgia, an unpublished document in the Gwinnett County Historical Society in Lawrenceville.

[13] Paul Tabor, *The History of Madison County, Georgia* (Danielsville GA: n.p., 1974) 87.

[14] E. Merton Coulter, James Monroe Smith, *Georgia Planter, Before and After Death* (Athens GA: University of Georgia Press, 1961) 60.

[15] *The Danielsville Monitor*, September 29, 1899.

[16] Tabor, "The History of Madison County, Georgia," 87.

However, the mythical rails did not arrive. A petition for a new charter for the Smithsonia, Danielsville and Carnesville Railroad was drafted in 1903. Seven Danielsville businessmen were listed among the petitioners.[17] *The Cyclopedia of Georgia,* published in 1906, informed readers that "a railroad to connect with the Seaboard was in contemplation" at Danielsville,[18] and in 1907, there was talk of a line through Danielsville from Anderson, South Carolina, to Athens. In 1910, the Augusta, Lincolnton and Northern Railroad was chartered and surveyed through Danielsville.[19] All of these schemes came to nothing, and as the decade wore on, the irony of James Golucke's grand courthouse was made all the more poignant by the diminutive size of the town which lay beside it.

FULTON COUNTY: ATLANTA, PART 3

By the end of the Reconstruction period, Atlanta had captured the state capitol from Milledgeville and cemented her position as the transportation hub of the South. In 1892, when the Georgia, Carolina and Northern Railroad arrived, the city was traversed by eleven meandering rail lines radiating out from the old Union Depot like the spokes of a great rickety wheel. With the completion of her pawn, the Georgia, Carolina and Northern, the Seaboard Air Line Railway gained entrance into Atlanta. Initially the company was denied track rights into the center of the city, and passengers had to transfer near Inman Park to a street railway for the short ride downtown. This situation was soon rectified when the Seaboard built a rather circuitous link, skirting north of the city to join the Western and Atlantic's tracks near today's Inman Yard.

The so-called Gilded Age had blessed Atlanta like no other place in the South. Just as the crude Second Empire styling of Max Corput's 1871 Union Depot II and the more pleasing French and Italian lines of Parkins and Bruce's 1883 Fulton County Courthouse had announced the beginning of the period, the Renaissance pomp of Edbrooke and Burnham's Georgia State Capitol Building and the careful symmetry of Bradford Gilbert's buildings at the 1895 Cotton States Exposition heralded the end of the era.

Plate 26.4: The Georgia State Capitol Building, begun in 1884, completed in 1889. Edbrooke and Burnham, architects.

To no one's surprise, Hannibal Kimball's Atlanta Opera House, which had been scandalously acquired by the state for use as a capitol building in 1869, proved less than satisfactory. In the early 1880s, Milledgeville began the last of her efforts to recapture the state capitol, and state leaders rushed to build a new capitol building to cement Atlanta's hold on the prize. The Georgia Capitol Commission began its search for a design under the supervision of its architectural advisor, George Post, one of New York's most prominent architects. Ten designs were submitted, including one by the eminent public designer, E. E. Meyers, who had just been awarded the commission for the Texas State Capitol Building at Austin. Surprisingly Meyer's design was rejected in favor of the "simpler and more elegant detail" of Chicago architects, Willoughby J. Edbrooke and Franklin P. Burnham, whose credentials included grand classical courthouses all across the Midwest beginning in the 1870s.[20]

In 1884, Columbus Hughes's 1854 Federal style combination Fulton County Courthouse and Atlanta City Hall Building was demolished. On this commodious site, where Union troops had camped only twenty years before, Georgia's new State Capitol Building began to rise. Like most of the classically inspired state capitol buildings of the era, Georgia's owes a sizable debt to the United States Capitol Building in Washington, whose wings and great dome were completed in 1865. Notable examples of this trend are E. E. Meyers' Texas (1882-1888) and Colorado (1886-1906) State Capitol Buildings. The well-known architectural historian, Henry Russell Hitchcock, terms Meyer's designs "parodies" of the United States Capitol. To be sure, Georgia's new capitol building was also such a parody. In fact, Hitchcock is harsh indeed in his assessment of Edbrooke and Burnham's design, charging that the building has a "naked look" and stands "stiff, uncertain and seemingly incomplete behind a hesitatingly academic facade."[21] There may be some truth in this assessment, but in the American South of 1889, this building was nothing less than a triumph.

As successful as Edbrooke and Burnham's new state capitol building was, it was little copied in Georgia. In the mind of most Georgians, such architecture was acceptable when it represented the power of the Federal government or even the bureaucracy of the state. However, before 1910, when it came to local public architecture in the South, less pretentious approaches were generally preferred. The symbolism embodied in the Southern county courthouse was a great deal more complex and infinitely more personal than any celebration of mere governmental might. In fact, the whole idea of governmental might was largely repugnant in the Southern mind. This was especially true for those who lived out in the country. And most did.

Thus, while a grand Renaissance Revival monument rose at Atlanta, all across Georgia, local public architecture continued to reflect picturesque motifs. And when the new classicism finally crept southward after the turn of the century, the classical buildings that rose were generally simpler—more in the mold of the Greek Revival of the Old South than reflections of the rococo Beaux Arts classicism of Northern industrial and financial might.

Plate 26.5: The Agricultural Building at the 1895 Cotton State Exposition at Atlanta. Bradford Gilbert, architect.

Only six years after the completion of Edbrooke and Burnham's Renaissance extravagance at Atlanta and only two years after the wild classical success of the architecture of the 1893 Colombian Exposition at Chicago, the buildings of Atlanta's 1895 Cotton States Exposition rose to reaffirm the South's unswerving attachment to picturesque architectural forms. The promoters of this grand exposition sought to lift the South out of the decades of hard times that had followed defeat, to establish Atlanta as the center of a new Southern brand of prosperity and to propel the city out of the financial doldrums that had followed the Panic of 1893. Taking their cue from the success

Plate 26.4: Although many critics have characterized Edbrooke and Burnham's Georgia State Capitol Building as a poor "parody" of the US Capitol, in 1889 the building was a triumph in the American South. (Photo: Wilber W. Caldwell.)

Plate 26.5: Unlike the formal classical raiments that adorned Chicago's 1893 "White City," the principal buildings at Atlanta's 1895 Cotton States Exposition were cloaked in picturesque garments. (Photo: Courtesy of the Georgia Department of Archives and History.)

[17] E. Merton Coulter, James Monroe Smith, *Georgia Planter, Before and After Death* (Athens GA: University of Georgia Press, 1961) 60-61.

[18] Allen D. Candler and Clement A. Evans, eds., *The Cyclopedia of Georgia* (Atlanta: State Historical Association, 1906) 564.

[19] Tabor, *The History of Madison County, Georgia*, 87.

[20] Henry Russell Hitchcock and William Seale, *Temples of Democracy, State Capitols of the U. S. A.* (New York: Harcourt, Bruce, Jovanovich, 1976) 196.

of Chicago's so-called "White City," promoters in Atlanta planned a uniform architectural agenda presented in a landscape setting. But unlike the flamboyant classical raiments that adorned Chicago's "City Beautiful" the principal buildings at Atlanta were cloaked in soft, rather rustic garments.

Thus, the architecture of the Cotton States Exposition is a great deal more noteworthy for what it was not than for what it was—it was not the "neoclassical Florentine"[22] extravagance of the 1893 Columbian Exposition. It was simple, symmetrical, sparsely decorated and powerfully in the mold of the Romanesque.

Like the buildings in Chicago, the Atlanta structures were temporary, but instead of the flowering plaster and staff columns of Richard Morris Hunt and Charles McKim, Atlanta flaunted the gray-shingled and green-roofed discipline of Bradford Gilbert, with its simple Richardsonian arches, bold tourelles and straight-forward massing. Gilbert, a New Yorker, won the competition against the best Atlanta architects including Bruce and Morgan. He was known primarily for his work for the railroads, having designed the celebrated and monumentally Richardsonian 1892 Illinois Central Station at Chicago,[23] redesigned the Old Grand Central Station in New York (although with less than popular results) and fashioned numerous depots on the New York, Lake Erie and Western Railroad.[24] Gilbert designed four of the five main buildings in Atlanta's Piedmont Park, and his direct approach made its point with shapes and lines, not with ornament.[25] This, combined with the subdued colors and the rustic stone masonry, produced a result that was not only different from Chicago's "White City," but was perhaps as far from that opulent neoclassicism as possible. It was another compelling example of the slow Southern reaction to Northern architectural trends.

Gilbert's understated designs were no accident. Georgia and the South had much to sell to the world in 1895. The promoters of the Cotton States Exposition were proponents of the New South: new Southern industry, new Southern agriculture, new Southern race relations, and most of all new Southern dreams as receptacles for old Northern capital. With such visions for sale, these men were little distracted by realities. Nonetheless, they had their practical side. In the selling of the New South to Northerners, they shunned any reference to the tarnished columns of the Old South. Accordingly, carefully ordered elements of the currently popular Shingle Style organized along simple Romanesque lines proved contemporary and impressive, yet still appropriately humble. Of the designs in Piedmont Park, only W. T. Downing's Fine Arts Building, Elsie Mercur's Women's Building, and Gilbert's Electricity Building recalled the architecture of the Chicago Fair.

Despite such fundamental differences, the architecture of the 1893 Columbian Exposition and the 1895 Cotton States Exposition did share a common element. All of these buildings were studies in symmetry. Taken in the context of the nearly pervasive picturesque aesthetic that had dominated American architecture for almost a quarter of a century, this was quite a departure. The very concept the picturesque is rooted in asymmetry. So most of the buildings of the Romanesque and Gothic Revivals had relied on asymmetrical silhouettes to achieve artistic effects contrived to recall "pictures" of the European countryside. To all of this Richardson had added a bold and singularly American character, but much of his work was still firmly rooted in the picturesque. Subsequent eclecticism had taken asymmetry almost to the limit: especially notable in this regard are the Queen Anne Style, the Shingle Style, the Eastlake Style and the other derivative domestic styles of the era. Suddenly, just before the turn of the century, the architecture of these two expositions confronted both North and South with a return to order in alternately neoclassical and Romanesque clothing.

[21] Hitchcock and Seale, Temples of Democracy, *State Capitols of the U. S. A.*, 196.

[22] John Allwood, *The Great Exhibition* (London: Studio Vista, 1977) 84. According to Mr. Allwood this is the term used by the promoters of the 1893 Columbian Exposition to describe the architecture of the Fair.

[23] Carrol L. V. Meeks, *The Railroad Station* (New Haven, 1959), 107-8.

[24] Henry F. Withey and Elsie Rathburn Withey, *Biographical Dictionary of American Architects* (Los Angeles: New Age Publishing, 1970) 233.

[25] Franklin M. Garrett, *Atlanta and Environs, A Chronicle of Its People and Events* 3 vols. (New York: Lewis Publishing Company, 1954) 321-22

SOME LAST THOUGHTS ON THE GEORGIA, CAROLINA AND NORTHERN RAILROAD

As the Georgia, Carolina and Northern Railroad bridged the Savannah River in 1890, expectations soared all along the proposed route. At Elberton, where the line crossed the old Elberton Air Line, county leaders commissioned the noted Chattanooga architect and Elbert County native son, Reuben H. Hunt, to design a symbol for Elberton's grand aspirations. Hunt's stunning Elbert County Courthouse rose in 1892. At Athens, where Leon Henri Charbonnier's 1876 Clarke County Courthouse had celebrated the construction of the Northeastern Railroad fifteen years earlier, the Georgia, Carolina and Northern's depot would be the blossoming city's fourth. Farther to the west, the new rails crossed the Gainesville, Jefferson and Southern Railroad at the old village of Jug Tavern, and the city of Winder emerged to later demand its own county and its own courthouse. Finally, as the Georgia Carolina and Northern approached Atlanta, it crossed the spur of the Lawrenceville Branch Railroad, which had inspired Atlanta architect E. G. Lind's exuberantly picturesque 1884 Gwinnett County Courthouse at Lawrenceville.

Only tiny Danielsville was bypassed. Although one of the original surveys for the Georgia, Carolina and Northern had proposed a line right through this tiny village, in the end, this apparent good fortune proved just another frustration in a long list of railroad disappointments for hapless Danielsville. Nonetheless, hope sprang eternal in Madison County, and just after the turn of the century, as the extension of the Smithsonia, Danielsville and Carnesville Railroad appeared eminent, the county erected the stern Romanesque walls of James Golucke's 1901 Madison County Courthouse at Danielsville.

Chartered to connect the Seaboard Air Line's growing web of rail in North and South Carolina with the great rail terminus at Atlanta, the Georgia, Carolina and Northern Railroad was begun in 1885. With its completion in 1892, the line became the first of the Seaboard's three main arteries in Georgia. Before the end of the century, the Seaboard merged with two other Georgia railroads, both completed in the early 1890s: the Georgia and Alabama Railroad, the successor of the old Savannah, Americus and Montgomery Railroad, crossed the middle of the state to connect Savannah with Montgomery, Alabama; and the Florida Central and Peninsular Railroad skirted the coast and stretched all the way from Columbia, South Carolina, to Tampa, Florida.

•

The Southeastern Georgia Tidewater

THE FLORIDA CENTRAL AND PENINSULAR RAILROAD
Chatham County: Savannah (see chapter 2) • Camden County: Woodbine

THE JESUP SHORT LINE ATLANTIC COAST LINE RAILWAY
Wayne County: Jesup (see chapter 7) • Charlton County: Folkston

THE GEORGIA COAST AND PIEDMONT RAILROAD
Tattnall County: Reidsville (see chapter 28) • Long County: Ludowici (see chapter 7)
McIntosh County: Darien Glynn County: Brunswick (see chapter 9)

SOME LAST THOUGHTS ON THE SOUTHEASTERN GEORGIA TIDEWATER

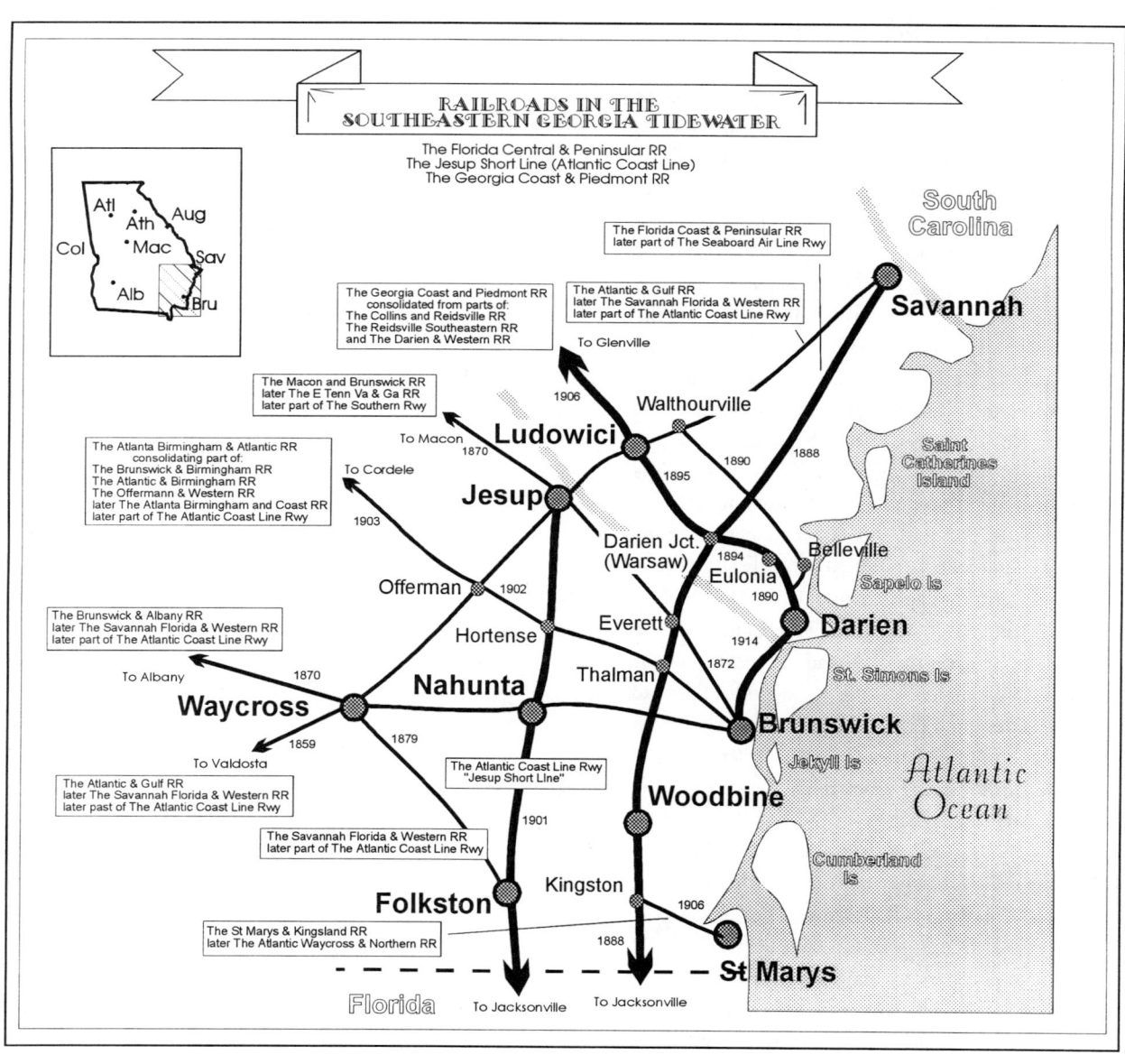

RAILROADS IN THE
SOUTHEASTERN GEORGIA TIDEWATER
The Florida Central & Peninsular RR
The Jesup Short Line (Atlantic Coast Line)
The Georgia Coast & Piedmont RR

27 | The Southeastern Georgia Tidewater

CAMDEN COUNTY: WOODBINE

Plate 27.1: The Camden County Courthouse at St. Marys, built in 1872. Burned c. 1965.

The courthouses of Camden County constitute an eloquent record of the struggle between those who favored a central governmental location in the county's sparsely populated interior and those who preferred a county seat convenient to the coast. One of the state's original eight counties, Camden was created in Georgia's Constitution of 1777. In 1788, the first county seat was established at St. Patricks, later called St. Marys. A crude courthouse was erected there at an early date, but the record is sketchy, and we have only one description of a courthouse at St. Marys before 1872. This account recalls a two-story frame building with a "covered piazza" all the way around.[1] In 1800, a new centrally located county town was laid out at Jeffersonton on the banks of the Satilla River, and a court building rose there in 1802. This 25 by 35-foot, two-story frame building served the county until 1870, when the county seat was re-established on the coast. This simple Carpenter Greek court building was erected at St. Marys in 1872. Today, no trace remains of Jeffersonton, but before the arrival of the railroads, Jeffersonton and St. Marys were the only real towns in Camden County.[2]

The early history of this region is a story of timber and water transportation. Saw mills were humming in the area as early as 1766, and a steam-powered saw mill was operating at Burnt Fort Lake around 1830.[3] By the time this simple courthouse rose at St. Marys in 1872, scores of small mills dotted the county, and the decades that followed the Civil War witnessed the exploitation by large Northern timber interests, including those of the lumber baron, William E. Dodge.

---

[1] J. S. Silva's recollections of early St. Marys, reprinted as "Paper No. 9," in *The Southeastern Georgian,* August 27, 1953.

[2] James T. Vocelle, *History of Camden County, Georgia* (Jacksonville FL: Kennedy Brown-Hall Co., 1914) 133.

[3] Marguerite Reddick, *Camden's Challenge, A History of Camden County, Georgia* (St. Marys GA: Camden Historical Commission, 1976) 73-74.

From the beginning of railroading in America, timber and rail went hand in hand. The tale is told that in 1835 the US Army Corps of Engineers planned a wood-railed, mule-powered railroad from Charleston, through Camden County, to Gainesville, Florida.[4] Just how much of this line was graded or built is not known. We do know that Camden was the scene of considerable railroad scheming beginning with the charter of the St. Marys and Columbus Railroad in 1836. The St. Marys Railroad was chartered in 1856, and the St. Marys and Western in 1870. Both sought a connection to the Atlantic and Gulf, near Waycross. Likewise, the Jacksonville, St. Marys, and Jesup Railroad was chartered in 1901.[5] All of these schemes came to nothing. In 1882, the Georgia and Florida Railroad Company began a line from Jesup via St. Marys to Florida. By 1887, considerable

Plate 27.1: The old 1872 Camden County Courthouse at St. Marys was used as a school after the county seat was moved to Woodbine in 1923. (Photo: Courtesy of the Georgia Department of Archives and History.)

[4] Reddick, *Camden's Challenge, A History of Camden County, Georgia*, 92.

[5] *The Jesup Sentinel*, April 5, 1901.

[6] *The Southeastern Georgian*, February 2, 1908.

[7] Lucian Lamar Knight, *Georgia's Memorials, Landmarks and Legends*, 2 vols. (Atlanta: 1916) 1: 351.

grading had been completed and two bridges constructed, but the company stopped work after it was purchased by Henry Plant who feared completion for his Savannah, Florida and Western.

When the railroad finally came to Camden County, the immediate effect was not so dramatic as elsewhere in Georgia. Nonetheless, in the 1890s, a string of towns appeared beside the shining new rails of the Florida Central and Peninsular Railroad. With extensive connections in Florida, this line was built in 1893 from Savannah, through coastal Georgia. From its connection with the Richmond and Danville in South Carolina, the Florida Central and Peninsular represented the perfecting link between Washington, D.C., and Tampa, Florida. In Camden County, villages sprouted around the new depots at Kingsland, Woodbine, White Oak, Tarboro, and Waverly. Today, only the simple frame depot at Kingsland remains to recount the railroad's story.

Despite the powerful new railroad, water travel was still a key to Camden's economy. In the early 1890s, the Suwanee Canal was completed from the sawmills on the edge of the great Okefenokee Swamp to Bull's Head Bluff on the Satilla River. In 1907, seven years after the Florida Central and Peninsular became part of the mighty Seaboard Air Line, the steam ship C. H. Evans still made three trips a week up the Satilla. Most travelers arrived in St. Marys by boat even after the town was connected to the Seaboard Air Line by the St. Marys and Kingsland Railroad in 1906. The St. Marys and Kingsland became the Atlantic, Waycross and Northern in 1911 after grand plans were revealed for an extension of the tiny line all the way to Unadilla south of Macon. Like most of Camden County's early railroad schemes this, too, came to nothing.

Ironically, when St. Marys finally achieved her rail link, pressure was already mounting to move the county seat back to the center of the county. In 1910, the new railroad village of Woodbine had a population of only 155, while St. Marys boasted almost 700 residents. However, the interior railroad town was growing, and with the myth of the New South exposed for the half lie that it was, the tiny spur from Kingsland had not created the usual aspirations for a modern age in old St. Marys. By all appearances, St. Marys looked on her railroad not as a source of economic rebirth but as a defense against those who sought a new location for the courthouse. In 1908, with the new rail connection complete, *The Southeastern Georgian* made this position clear. St. Marys, the editor declared, would "rebound to the credit of the entire" county, and he jumped from this conclusion directly to a recommendation for the construction of a "modern courthouse and jail" at St. Marys.[6] This was not to be, and a 1916 description of St. Marys leaves little doubt about the town's sleepy persona: "There is no mad and feverish rush after mammon—no seething vortex of trade—no Babble of commerce...."[7]

As the new century wore on and the battle lines were drawn in Camden County, the weapons of war in the fight for the county seat slowly changed from railroads to roads. Following the completion of a toll bridge across the Satilla in 1917, Woodbine redoubled its efforts, capturing the county seat in 1923. Four years later, US Highway 17 was built through the new county town, and the next year the strangely Gothic tabby walls of the present Camden County Courthouse rose at Woodbine. The motorcar was making its mark, and the era of the courthouse and the depot was over.

CHARLTON COUNTY: FOLKSTON

Plate 27.2: The depot at Folkston, built in 1914.[8]

Charlton County was created in 1854, from the vast almost empty expanses of Camden County between the Tidewater and the great swamp. With a population of less than 1750 at the time of its creation, Charlton was one of Georgia's largest and least populous counties. A two-story wooden courthouse was erected at the old trading village known as Traders Hill. This building burned in 1877 and was replaced by a simple frame court building. Four years later, the village of Folkston appeared beside the shining new rails of Henry Plant's ambitious new branch railroad from Waycross to Florida. From its very inception, Folkston seem destined to become Charlton's county

Plate 27. 2: The depot at Folkston. Just after the turn of the century the creation of a railroad junction supplied the thrust to propel Folkston to prominence. (Photo: Wilber W. Caldwell.)

seat, just as the venerable old village of Traders Hill seem destined to become a ghost town.

As usual, it was the creation of a railroad junction that acted as the catalyst to propel Folkston to prominence. In 1901, the Atlantic Coast Line Railroad had acquired Henry Plant's old Savannah, Florida and Western, and the new company began the construction of a 55-mile branch line from Jesup to Folkston. A short cut from Savannah to Jacksonville, the line came to be called "The Jesup Short Line." By 1902, as this important link joined the old Waycross to Jacksonville branch at Folkston, the village had captured the county seat away from Traders Hill, and begun construction of the town's first brick building, T. J. Darling's 1902 Charlton County Courthouse. This simple frame depot rose twelve years later.

Plate 27.3: The Charlton County Courthouse at Folkston, built in 1902. Burned 1928. T. J. Darling, architect / builder.

T. J. Darling, a prominent Waycross builder, may have been an accomplished contractor, but he was certainly not an accomplish architect. Darling's first courthouse at Waycross, the 1891 Ware County Courthouse had surely represented a notable departure from the building's original design by noted Atlanta architect, G. L. Norrman. The bastardized result was a rather crude, picturesque structure known as "The Castle." Here in Folkston, we find Darling's own design, an architectural calamity, typical of many builder designed structures of the era. Darling's work reflects a deadly combination: restricted budget and the desire to voice virtually all the popular styles of the day in one building. The resulting confusion of unadorned brick was an unfortunate combination of both Romanesque and classical elements. Despite this jumble of modern architectural vocabularies, the completed building appeared vernacular. Here is the old hipped-roofed cube of the antebellum vernacular court building disguised by Romanesque corner pavilions, a Richardsonian entrance, and an ungainly pair of columns.

Nonetheless, T. J. Darling's 1902 Charlton County Courthouse spoke with the voice of progress. Here, despite their grotesque application, modern architectural elements expressed hope with the same optimism that had been inspired by so many railroads all across Georgia. Folkston was a village of about 170 residents when this courthouse rose. By 1910, the town had doubled its size, and Charlton County boasted over 4000 residents, almost twice the population recorded when Henry Plant's Savannah, Florida and Western arrived in 1881. To be sure, the Wiregrass region on the edge of the great swamp was still a wild and impoverished place at the turn of the century. However, the songs of the courthouse and the depot were heard just as clearly way out in the piney woods as they were on the airy verandahs of the Piedmont.

Plate 27.3: Despite its crude jumble of architectural vocabularies, T. J. Darling's 1902 Charlton County Courthouse spoke with the voice of progress.

McINTOSH COUNTY: DARIEN

In the decades that followed defeat, an expanding web of rail imported hope to scores of otherwise despondent country villages all across Georgia, and elaborate court buildings rose in response to railroad-inspired dreams. In Darien however, we find a compelling exception to prove the rule of the connection between courthouse and depot.

In the late 1830s, the construction of Georgia's very first railroads had marked the beginning of a period of decline for the bustling little seaport at the mount of the Altamaha River in McIntosh County. In the first decades of the nineteenth century, Darien had thrived on cargoes of rice, indigo and sugar and from the bounty of cotton and timber flowing down the Oconee and the Ocmulgee Rivers from the interior of the state. In 1817, Darien was the site of one of the first steam powered saw mills in the United States. Standing as an impressive testament to the port's economic importance was the Bank of Darien, established in 1818. With branches at Savannah, Augusta, Milledgeville, Dahlonega, and Auraria, this institution was among the first to bring financial sophistication to an independent plantation economy, pressing its influence to the very edges of the frontier. However, in the late 1830s, the construction of the Central Railroad from Savannah to Macon put and end to Darien's prominence as a cotton market, and as the new rails were laid, the Bank of Darien failed in the depression following the Panic of 1837.

By 1849, when the insightful traveler, George White, wrote of Darien in his *Statistics of the State of Georgia,* he described a village of about 600 residents containing a courthouse, a jail, one hotel and twelve stores. White's comments cut to the quick of the situation: "...formerly a place of much business...construction of the Central Railroad has taken much of the produce which used to come to Darien." But just as White gleaned the cause of Darien's decline, he also foresaw the town's coming salvation: "Situated on a river which furnishes inexhaustible supplies of the best pine lumber in the world, and accessible to ships of heavy burthen, nothing is wanted but perseverance to insure prosperity to the town. Immense quantities of timber and turpentine are now brought to Darien."

White's insights are penetrating, and the great timber boom of the last third of the nineteenth century is today legendary in Darien. The port lay at the end of a romanticized journey for countless timber raftsmen, who each year floated down the Ohoopee, the Oconee and the Ocmulgee to jam the channel at Darien with the bounty of Georgia's virgin pine forests. During the 1880s and 1890s Darien received as many as eighty-five great log rafts a day, each containing as many as 100,000 board feet of lumber.[9] In 1868, the mills at Darien had produced 20 million board feet of finished lumber for export. By 1874, this figure was above 100 million.[10] Across the marshes on Saint Simons Island, the enormous mills of William E. Dodge were producing similar quantities. In 1879, Sholes's *Gazetteer of Georgia* listed Darien's population at 2000, and called the city "one of the principle timber markets in the world."

White's prediction had proved correct, save one detail: Georgia's great pine forests were not "inexhaustible." After the turn of the century, the timber boom at Darien disappeared just as quickly as it had appeared. By 1900, most of eastern Georgia's virgin pine was gone. The big gang saws were growing silent, and Georgia's forests were filled with smaller portable sawmills and tram railroads. Timber rafting on the Altamaha was disappearing, and an ever-increasing network of railroads was replacing river rafting as the primary transportation modem in the lumber industry. Darien was again in decline. The end came quickly. The high point of Darien's timber export was the year 1900, when 112 million board feet cleared the port. In that year, 101 vessels had loaded cargo at Darien for foreign ports. Two years later, only 59 million board feet cleared the port on a mere thirty-one vessels. It was clearly a disaster. Timber recorded at the public boom in Darien dropped from 51 million board feet in 1900 to 6 million board feet in 1905.[11] The great forests were disappearing, timber buyers and portable mills moved up-stream and were beginning to ship by rail to better harbors at Brunswick and Savannah, and timber prices were falling fast as the Panic of 1907 set in.

In the midst of all of this, Darien built a railroad of her own. However, it was too little, too late. In 1885, a group of investors in Darien procured a charter for the Darien Short Line Railroad, which planned a rail link from Darien to Belleview on the Sapelo River. The initial plan was for a rail connection to offset the diminishing importance of river transportation and to exploit the natural deep-water harbor potential of Sapelo Sound. Progress was excruciatingly slow. By 1890, a Liberty County short line railroad had completed track to Belleview from Walthoursville on the Savannah, Florida and Western, but the Darien Short Line failed before it reached Belleview to capitalize on this windfall.

In 1894, the struggling road was reorganized as the Darien and Western Railroad. By this time, the Florida Central and Peninsular was completed from Savannah, southward through McIntosh County into Florida. With the completion of this powerful road, the newly re-organized Darien and Western changed its focus, seeking a connection with this newly completed main trunk line. By the end of 1894, the Darien and Western had built 21 miles of track from Crescent on the Darien-Belleview line to Darien Junction (later Warsaw) on the Florida Central and Peninsular. The next year, the last few miles of track were completed into Darien, and a depot was erected on Columbus Square. The Crescent to Darien Junction branch was extended 10 miles westward to the tiny village of Middleton, but this section of the road saw little use and was quickly abandoned. Despite the usual wave of railroad-imported euphoria in Darien, the tiny new railroad was powerless against the forces that propelled Darien's decline. The new rails could not replace Georgia's dwindling stands of virgin pine. Competition from nearby Brunswick was growing, and Darien's location on her mighty river was being rendered meaningless by so many railroads.

---

[8] *The Southeastern Georgian,* June 17, 1954.

[9] Buddy Sullivan, *Early Days on the Georgia Tidewater, The Story of McIntosh County and Sapelo* (Darien GA: Mcintosh County Board of Commissioners, 1990) 456.

[10] Sullivan, *Early Days on the Georgia Tidewater, The Story of McIntosh County and Sapelo,* 348.

[11] Sullivan, *Early Days on the Georgia Tidewater, The Story of McIntosh County and Sapelo,* 539.

As the new century unfolded, Brunswick grew, and the last of the state's great main trunk railroads began to build into the interior. By 1906, it appeared to many that the construction of the Atlanta, Birmingham and Atlantic Railroad would thrust Brunswick toward increased commercial success. At about the same time, a group of investors purchased the Darien and Western and two nearby short line railroads, the Reidsville and Southeastern Railroad and the Collins and Reidsville Railroad, with the idea of connecting Brunswick to Collins on the Seaboard Air Line in Tattnall County. The new line was chartered in 1906 as the Georgia Coast and Piedmont Railroad. By 1914, the line had built a sturdy steel bridge at Darien, bridged the mighty Altamaha River and completed track from Darien into Brunswick in order to perfect her connection with the Atlanta Birmingham and Atlantic. Here was a final blow to fell the already wounded port of Darien. The railroad, which she had begun in order to compensate for the diminishing importance of river transportation, had, in the end, been employed to boost harbor traffic at nearby Brunswick. Darien was demoted to just another stop along the way.

However, the Georgia Coast and Piedmont was destined to boost neither Brunswick nor Darien. The

Plate 27.4: This unusual stone courthouse at Darien was begun in 1874 and complete around 1876.

[12] The Darien Gazette, May 25, 1874.

line served some of the poorest areas in the state, and in 1916, as the last of the virgin timber was stripped from Tattnall and Liberty Counties; the tiny railroad plummeted into receivership. Abandoning the line from Ludowici to Brunswick, a reorganized company, known as the Collins and Ludowici Railroad, met a similar financial demise in 1921. A second reorganization abandoned all of the line except the profitable 20 miles from Glenville to Collins, and the Glenville and Collins Railroad managed to operate until 1941. Thus in 1919, only twenty-four years after the first train arrived in Darien, the old depot there saw the last train pass into history. The depot at Darien burned in 1976.

Plate 27.4: The McIntosh County Courthouse, built in 1874-1876. Architect unknown

Although the usual helping of high hopes had arrived in Darien on the Darien and Western Railroad, these aspirations were not sufficient to beget a new courthouse in McIntosh County. The county's first courthouse had been erected at the first county seat of Sapelo Bridge (later called Eulonia) shortly after the county was created from Liberty County in 1793. The seat of local government was moved to Darien in 1818, and it appears that a courthouse was erected shortly thereafter. Sadly, no description of this building comes down to us. The first mention of a courthouse at Darien comes in 1863, when Federal raiders destroyed the courthouse and most of the county's records. A replacement court building rose immediately following the war, but this structure burned in 1873. This unusual two-story courthouse was begun in 1874 and completed sometime around 1876. This building was partially destroyed by fire in 1931, but its distinctive low pediment remains at the core of the present McIntosh County Courthouse.

Strangely, Darien, a village desperately in need of a railroad to save her failing harbor, had failed to build a monument to hope after the first train arrived. This may seem an odd exception to the pattern of the courthouse and the depot, but the myth of the New South was undoubtedly weak here, for the village had seen many notable economic difficulties. In addition, only three years after the rails of the Darien and Western arrived in Darien, the town experienced one of the worst disasters in a history filled with disasters. In 1898, a powerful hurricane swept across the South Georgia coast. This sturdy courthouse at Darien withstood the wind and water, but the rest of the town was reduced to ruin.

All of this notwithstanding, there is a more fundamental reason for Darien's lack of faith in her new railroad. This was a maritime town. From the beginning, all her successes and failures had centered on the river and the sea. Accordingly, there were undoubtedly many in Darien in 1895, who viewed the railroad with extreme skepticism. In fact, from the very beginning railroad schemes had met with something less than unanimous support in Darien. In 1874, *The Darien Gazette* had published letters speculating "a rale rode [sic]" would only "ad [sic] another convenience for cut throts [sic] and theves (sic)," and asking "haven't we a great river full of boats?"[12] In this climate, little zeal for a new courthouse was forthcoming.

SOME LAST THOUGHTS ON THE SOUTHEASTERN GEORGIA TIDEWATER

In Camden, Charlton, Glynn, and McIntosh Counties, the vast stretches of piney woods that lay just inland from the coast, constituted one of the most sparsely populated and economically stunted regions in Georgia. Here, even in the railroad-building boom of the last decades of the nineteenth century, the crossing rails did not create boomtowns and excitement like so many of its upcountry counterparts. Built in 1893, the section of the line from Savannah to Jacksonville, Florida crossed the old Macon and Brunswick at the village of Everett and the old Brunswick and Albany near Bladden, both in Glynn County. Neither of these towns rose to prominence. Likewise, as the new century dawned and the myth of the New South waned, crossing rails on the Florida Central and Peninsular created by the Georgia Coast and Piedmont at Darien Junction (later called Warsaw) and by the Atlanta, Birmingham and Atlantic at Thalman begot little growth. Most of these places would be difficult to find today, were it not for the rail junctions that remain.

Nonetheless, in 1901, the construction of "The Jesup Short Line" spawned as notable success at Folkston as that town captured the Charlton County seat and built a sturdy brick courthouse. By 1910, Folkston's population had doubled. In neighboring Camden County similar stirrings occurred after the completion of the Florida Coast and Peninsular in 1894. However, the venerable port of St. Marys was by far the county's largest and most powerful town, and it would take almost thirty years before the new breed of railroad towns grew strong enough to capture the county seat. It was not until 1923 that Woodbine became the Camden County seat, and a new courthouse did not rise there until 1928. In McIntosh County, the Darien and Western Railroad, which was completed to Darien in 1895, proved impotent to save the port from the inevitable decline that followed the demise of the state's once abundant stands of virgin pine. No new courthouse rose to celebrate Darien's waning prospects, and even the 1914 extension of the Georgia Coast and Piedmont from Darien to Brunswick failed to inspire much in the way of New South zeal.

Perhaps Southeastern Georgia's best illustration of the power of new rails to inspire fantasy court buildings occurred in Brunswick in 1907 when New York architect Charles Gifford's Glynn County Courthouse rose to celebrate the completion of the last of the great main trunk railroads built in Georgia. Most in Brunswick viewed the Atlanta, Birmingham and Atlantic as the key to that city's maritime future. In the minds of many, this rail link to the steel mills at Birmingham was Brunswick's ticket to a grand banquet of New South bounty. Sadly, this was not to be, for by 1900 Georgia's railroads were no longer just channeling freight to the coast, but competing head on with coastwise maritime traffic. A competition that would spell disaster for both Brunswick and Savannah and render the hopeful symbolism of Gifford's grand courthouse at Brunswick all the more ironic.

•

Short Lines in Eastern Georgia

Bulloch County: Statesboro • Candler County: Metter • Tattnall County: Reidsville
Emanuel County: Swainsboro • Jefferson County: Louisville
Some Last Thoughts on Short Lines in Eastern Georgia

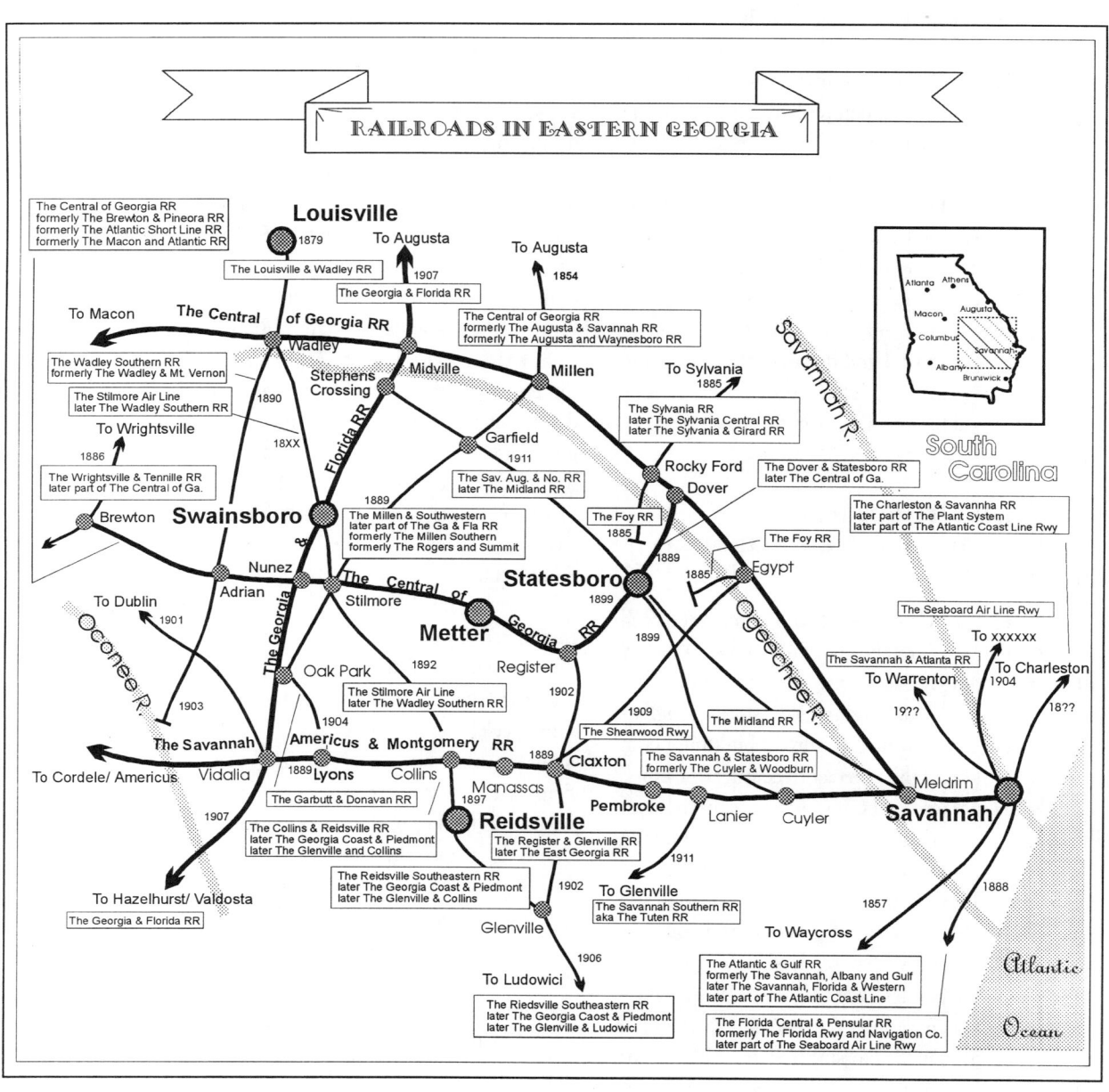

RAILROADS IN EASTERN GEORGIA

The Central of Georgia RR
formerly The Brewton & Pineora RR
formerly The Atlantic Short Line RR
formerly The Macon and Atlantic RR

Louisville   1879

To Augusta

To Augusta

The Louisville & Wadley RR

1907

The Georgia & Florida RR   1854

To Macon   The Central of Georgia RR

The Central of Georgia RR
formerly The Augusta & Savannah RR
formerly The Augusta and Waynesboro RR

Wadley

The Wadley Southern RR
formerly The Wadley & Mt. Vernon

Stephens Crossing   Midville   Millen   To Sylvania   1885

The Stilmore Air Line
later The Wadley Southern RR   1890

The Sylvania RR
later The Sylvania Central RR
later The Sylvania & Girard RR

To Wrightsville   18XX   Garfield   1911   Rocky Ford   Dover

The Dover & Statesboro RR
later The Central of Ga.

1886   The Sav. Aug. & No. RR
later The Midland RR

The Wrightsville & Tennille RR
later part of The Central of Ga.   1889   The Foy RR   1885

The Charleston & Savannha RR
later part of The Plant System
later part of The Atlantic Coast Line Rwy

Brewton   Swainsboro

The Millen & Southwestern
later part of The Ga & Fla RR
formerly The Millen Southern
formerly The Rogers and Summit   1889   The Foy RR

Nunez   Statesboro   1885   Egypt

Adrian   The Central of   Stilmore   1899   The Seaboard Air Line Rwy

To Dublin   1901   Metter   1899   To xxxxxx

The Savannah & Atlanta RR   To Charleston
1904

Oak Park   1892   Register   To Warrenton   19??   18??

The Stilmore Air Line
later The Wadley Southern RR   1902

1903   1909   The Shearwood Rwy   The Midland RR

The Savannah   1904   Americus & Montgomery RR   1889   Claxton

The Savannah & Statesboro RR
formerly The Cuyler & Woodburn

To Cordele/ Americus   Vidalia   1889 Lyons   Collins   Manassas   Pembroke   Lanier   Cuyler   Meldrim   Savannah

The Garbutt & Donavan RR   1897

1907   The Collins & Reidsville RR
later The Georgia Coast & Piedmont
later The Glenville and Collins   Reidsville   The Register & Glenville RR
later The East Georgia RR   1911

The Reidsville Southeastern RR
later The Georgia Coast & Piedmont
later The Glenville & Collins   1902   To Glenville   1888

To Hazelhurst/ Valdosta   The Savannah Southern RR
aka The Tuten RR   1857

The Georgia & Florida RR   Glenville   To Waycross

1906   The Atlantic & Gulf RR
formerly The Savannah, Albany and Gulf
later The Savannah, Florida & Western
later part of The Atlantic Coast Line

To Ludowici

The Riedsville Southeastern RR
later The Georgia Caost & Piedmont
later The Glenville & Ludowici   The Florida Central & Pensular RR
formerly The Florida Rwy and Navigation Co.
later part of The Seaboard Air Line Rwy

Savannah R.

South Carolina

Oconee R.   The Georgia &   Florida RR   Ogeechee R.

Atlanta   Athens
Macon   Augusta
Columbus   Savannah
Albany   Brunswick

Atlantic

Ocean

28 | Short Lines in Eastern Georgia

BULLOCH COUNTY: STATESBORO

Visions of a New South were delivered to Statesboro as the first train steamed into town on the rails of the Dover and Statesboro Railroad in 1889. By 1894, Alexander Bruce's grand Bulloch County Courthouse had risen on the square, and by the middle of the first decade of the new century, the citizens of Statesboro were envisioning a great railroad center in the piney woods of Bulloch County. However, the foundations upon which Statesboro built her dreams of a railroad empire were shaky.

The first rails in Bulloch County were laid by timbermen and terpentiners seeking access to the county's vast forests of virgin pine. Spidery fingers of steel rail snaked their way toward tiny Statesboro as the town grew from a hamlet of twenty-five inhabitants in 1880[1] to a town of 425 by 1890. In 1885, lumber baron, E. E. Foy built two rail lines from the Central of Georgia's main line, southward into Bulloch, one from Rocky Ford and one from Egypt. Neither reached Statesboro. Farther south around 1890, the local lumberman and turpentine king, J. N. Woods built a spur beginning in Bulloch County at Woodburn and extending to Cuyler on the old Savannah, Americus and Montgomery Railroad. Just to the west, the Perkins Lumber Company built from Register to Glenville crossing the old S. A. M. at Claxton around the turn of the century. All of these lines contemplated extensions to Statesboro, but only the Cuyler and Woodburn would make the jump. Reorganized as the Savannah and Statesboro Railroad, the line reached Statesboro in 1899. Just as the Savannah and Statesboro's first train steamed in to Statesboro, an extension of the Brewton and Pineora Railroad was completed. The Central acquired this line, along with the Dover and Statesboro Railroad, in 1901, making Statesboro a stop on a circuitous through-line from Dublin to Savannah.

---

[1] Leodel Coleman, ed., *Statesboro, A Century of Progress, 1866-1966* (Statesboro GA: The Bulloch Herald, 1969) 6. Sholes's 1879 *Gazetteer of Georgia* places Statesboro's population at 22.

By the turn of the century, Statesboro was a town of 1200 residents most of whom must have been thoroughly blinded by the light of New South myth shining from this handful of ne'er-do-well lumber roads and from the Central's serpentine route through Statesboro to Savannah. Despite such dubious beginnings, Statesboro began to see herself as the center of a vast rail network. In the decades that followed the turn of the century, a wild and unrealistic series of rail-

RAILROAD SPECULATION AT STATESBORO AFTER 1900

Table 28.1

The Atlanta and Savannah Air Line, Savannah via Statesboro to Atlanta, 1902.

The Statesboro and Northern, Statesboro to Wrightsville, 1904.

The Swainsboro and Statesboro, Statesboro to Wrightsville, 1904.

The Savannah, Statesboro and Northern, Savannah to Athens, 1904.

The Savannah, Statesboro and Western, Savannah to Atlanta, 1906.

The Georgia and Florida Railroad, branch via Statesboro from Summit to Savannah, 1907.

The Savannah, Augusta and Northern, Savannah via Statesboro to Chattanooga, 1907.[2]

road schemes rained down in Bulloch County, each begetting a new wave of euphoria in an ongoing flood of expectations (See Table 28.1). At the end of all of this, only one railroad laid any track. In 1907, the Savannah, Augusta and Northern began construction of a 26 mile stretch from Statesboro to a junction with the Georgia and Florida Railroad, reaching the place soon to be called Stephens Crossing near Midville in 1911.

Despite the fact that all of her lofty railroad dreams turned out to be little more than dust in the wind, the sheer energy created by such wild aspirations begot considerable progress in Statesboro. By 1910, the town boasted 2500 citizens. Here, as in so many Georgia towns tempted by the gleaming wares of the New South myth, believing made it so. Bolstered by her shining new symbols of New South progress, the growing town reveled in a new water works in 1901, a new ice plant in 1902, and the mir-

acle of electric lights in 1904. The 1907 acquisition of one of the state's regional agricultural colleges would eventually prove the city's crowning glory. Of course, in 1907, all of this revolved around the South's perennially fickle nemesis, cotton. By the middle of the first decade of the new century, Statesboro had become the world's largest Sea Island cotton market, trading one-eighth of the world's supply of that long-fibered staple.[3] However, as the first buildings of Statesboro's new college rose, hard times lay ahead in cotton's teetering kingdom.

As her cotton market bloomed and railroad speculations swirled, Statesboro was blind to the sea of rural poverty that lay all around it. As the vast forests of pine began to disappear, cotton's ruthless grip tightened, and the railroads that had promised so much, began to disappear. The Midland Railroad, which had acquired the old Savannah, Augusta and Northern in 1915, abandoned her rails from Statesboro to Savannah in 1923, and the Savannah and Statesboro was pulled up only ten years later. Finally, the portion of the Central of Georgia from Brewton to Metter was abandoned in 1938, leaving Statesboro once again an out-of-the-way stop on an insignificant spur, just as Sea Island cotton was becoming a rarity in Georgia.

As the new century unfolded, Bulloch County was loosing more than her railroads. In 1904, the state legislature repealed the law limiting the number of counties in Georgia, and citizens at Millen and at Dover began lobbying for a new county to be cut from Bulloch's northern flank. Millen won the day in 1905 with the creation of Jenkins County. By 1908, the town of Metter to the east of Statesboro began to campaign for a new county constructed from western Bulloch. By the second decade of the new century, the new county madness was at its peak, and petitions for new county seats were filed from Metter, Pulaski, Stillmore, Brooklet, and Claxton. In 1914, Bulloch shrank again as Metter and Claxton prevailed, establishing the new Georgia counties of Candler and Evans. Less than a decade later, the impossible dream of a great rail center at Statesboro would be long forgotten.

Plate 28.1: The Bulloch County Courthouse at Statesboro, built in 1894. Bruce and Morgan architects.

In 1889, the completion of the tiny spur from Statesboro to Dover on the Central of Georgia's main line sparked almost immediate agitation for a new courthouse. By the spring of 1894, the grand jury had recommended a new courthouse, and county officials had completed an inspection of new court buildings at Vienna, Oglethorpe, and "several other county seat towns."[4] There can be little doubt that one of these "other towns" was Talbotton, where Atlanta architect Alexander Bruce's fine 1892 Talbot County Courthouse had just been completed. In a matter of only a few weeks after this inspection tour, an invitation to contractors was published in *The Statesboro Star,* and Bruce and Morgan's 1894 Bulloch County Courthouse began to rise on the square at Statesboro. The building was an almost exact copy of the firm's 1892 court building at Talbotton. Bulloch's new courthouse was complete before the end of 1894, and citizens marveled at "its dimensions and magnificence."[5]

For those who could remember the Statesboro of only a few years before, the new building must have appeared impossibly lavish. In 1904, *The Statesboro News* published a letter that recalled the Statesboro of 1890 as a town of "three or four old dilapidated wooden stores and an old frame courthouse."[6] The frame court building of this recollection was erected shortly after the end of the Civil War to replace the crude country courthouse at Statesboro that had been burned by Federal forces in 1864.

There are no detailed records regarding Bulloch's early court buildings. By one account, the county's first courthouse was a log structure, built on the square at Statesboro before 1806.[7] Another recalls a frame court building built in 1800 and a later antebellum brick courthouse.[8] It is not known which building was burned by Sherman's troops, but whatever the Yankees burned, it must have been a rude affair, for only three families resided in Statesboro in 1864. Certainly, Alexander Bruce's elaborate Queen Anne monument of 1894 appeared even grander

when viewed in contrast to these crude early structures.

In 1894, the forward-looking architectural symbol for modernity in the South was the American Queen Anne Style. In the closing years of the nineteenth century, New World adaptations of Norman Shaw's English Queen Anne Style were tailor-made for the American South. The region was hesitant to embrace the exuberant classical excesses that were

Plate 28.1: Alexander Bruce's 1894 Bulloch County Courthouse was an almost exact replica of the Atlanta architect's 1892 Talbot County Courthouse at Talbotton.

---

[2] Coleman, ed., *Statesboro, A Century of Progress, 1866-1966*, 81-85.

[3] Coleman, ed., *Statesboro, A Century of Progress, 1866-1966*, 10.

[4] Coleman, ed., *Statesboro, A Century of Progress, 1866-1966*, 92.

[5] *The Bulloch Times*, November 8, 1894, in Coleman, ed., Statesboro, *A Century of Progress, 1866-1966*, 92.

[6] *The Statesboro News*, September 27, 1904, quoted in Hulda K. Kelly, ed., *I See By the Paper, Bulloch County Georgia. 1899-1946* (Statesboro GA: Bulloch County Historical Society, 1984) 46.

[7] Coleman, ed., *Statesboro, A Century of Progress, 1866-1966*, 91.

[8] Eugenia Wasden Payne, *Historic Survey of 159 County Courthouses in the State of Georgia for the National Society of Colonial Dames of America Colonial Dames* (Macon GA: n.p., 1976).

sweeping the nation after the success of the buildings of the 1893 Columbian Exposition at Chicago. Nonetheless, Southerners sought modern symbols in their quest for the riches of the mythical New South. At the same time, they fought any idiom that might ignore cherished references to the past. The Queen Anne in its "free classical" phase supplied the perfect answer to this uniquely Southern dilemma. The style embodied perhaps the ultimate eclectic license: the freedom to cover picturesque buildings with all manner of classical decoration. Like the Southern mind, the American Queen Anne Style was a confusion of inherent contradictions. It adorned picturesque forms with the ornament of the very classicism, which the picturesque had originally sought to replace. In similar fashion, Southerners sought New South progress in order to gain the power to preserve the cherished institutions of the Old South.

Between 1887 and 1898, Bruce and Morgan designed thirteen Romanesque courthouses in Georgia. Six of these incorporate predominately Queen Anne detail (see Appendix C). This building

Plate 28.2: After its 1914 remodeling, the Bulloch County Courthouse at Statesboro presented two distinct architectural voices for the town's railroad inspired aspirations. (Photo: Wilber W. Caldwell.)

and its almost identical sister at Talbotton are arguably Bruce's best Queen Anne court buildings. Like all of the Atlanta architect's Queen Anne courthouses, the building projected a rather fundamental Romanesque form with hints of Richardsonian influence. Overlaid is an array of classically inspired decoration. Most notable are the broken based pediments that crown the large tower and the distinctive classical pediments in the side elevations above the courtroom windows. The bell shaped low tower roof is typically Queen Anne, as is the extensive use of terra cotta decoration.

Plate 28.2: The Bulloch County Courthouse at Statesboro, built in 1894. Bruce and Morgan architects. Remodeled in 1914. Ed C. Hosford, remodeling architect.

Clear testament to Statesboro's growth was heard in 1914, when only twenty years after its completion, Bruce and Morgan's new courthouse proved too small for the blossoming needs of Bulloch. Architect, Ed C. Hosford of Eastman, was commissioned to enlarge the building. Great classical porticos obscured the original Romanesque entrance arches. The fine Queen Anne lower tower with its distinctive bell-like dome was covered in a blocky attempt to achieve symmetry by matching the lower section of the main tower and altogether featureless corner pavilions were added. It was an obvious and clumsy attempt not only to enlarge the structure, but also to bring it up-to-date by draping it in the finery of American Beaux-Arts Classicism. The result is unfortunate. No longer the Queen Anne gem of Alexander Bruce's vision, or an appealing statement of the new American classicism, the enlarged Bulloch County Courthouse had become an architectural jumble. A coat of white paint has further obscured the original picturesque polychromy, masking the contrasting textures of brick, terra cotta, and stone. Today the building retains distinction and power solely through the enduring vehicle of Bruce's grand tower, which was thankfully untouched by Hosford's well-meaning but nonetheless brutal bastardization.

Shining through all of this architectural butchery is the clear voice of history. In 1914, the new classicism was the well-established bearer of the torch of

American progress. Even in the back eddies of the Deep South, the picturesque had run its course, and the Queen Anne Style suddenly appeared old and out-of-date. Places like Statesboro were still desperately trying to grasp the ring of a fading New South myth, but the new century brought new symbols for the same old dilemmas. It can be no coincidence that the lavish columns of American classicism were attached to the Bulloch County Courthouse only a year before the charter of the Midland Railroad, Statesboro's third and final attempt at a viable rail connection to Savannah.

Here in Statesboro, in one building, we find two distinct architectural voices for the town's railroad-imported aspirations. First Alexander Bruce's stunning Queen Anne courthouse of 1894, which celebrated the progress sparked by 1889 the Dover and Statesboro Railroad, and later E. C. Hosford's exuberant, if not graceful, 1914 neoclassical remodeling of this building on the eve of the Midland Railroad's new line from Statesboro to Savannah.

CANDLER COUNTY: METTER

Plate 28.3: The depot at Metter, built in 1902.

In the late 1880s, the Macon Construction Company began work on three new railroads emanating from Macon. The Georgia Southern and Florida pressed southward through Cordele and Valdosta into Florida in 1889. The Macon and Birmingham struggled westward, finally reaching LaGrange in 1890, and the least successful of these, the Macon and Atlantic Railroad, sought a direct easterly route from Macon to Savannah. This enterprise managed to build only 8 miles of track eastward from Brewton, Georgia, just north of Dublin, before it failed in 1892. Reorganized as the Atlantic Short Line Railway, the new company extended the line another 16 miles before it was sold in foreclosure to the newly chartered Brewton and Pineora Railroad in 1898. By 1901, when the Central acquired the Brewton and Pineora, the line was completed all the way from Brewton to Statesboro. At this point, the Central abandoned her plans for a new, direct connection into Savannah, opt-

Plate 28.3: This sturdy depot, built by the Central of Georgia in 1902, rose at Metter only four years after the town was laid out. (Photo: Wilber W. Caldwell.)

ing for a circuitous route with the purchase of the Dover and Statesboro Railroad.

Along the line of the old Brewton and Pineora, three towns surged to brief prominence in the early years of the new century. Where these rails crossed the old Wadley and Mount Vernon Railroad, the village of Adrian sprang to life in the 1890s. At about the same time, 25 miles to the east at the junction of the Central, the Stillmore Air Line and the old Millen and Southwestern Railroad, the notable railroad boom-town of Stillmore surged to prominence. Lastly, on the boundary between Emanuel and Bulloch County, the village of Metter was laid out in 1898. All of these places would make a bid to become the county seat of new counties. Adrian proposed the creation James County in 1905, and Stillmore unsuccessfully lobbied for the creation of Stonewall County in 1913. Only Metter would succeed.

As early as 1904, *The Bulloch Times* would observe, "hustling Metter, a town that is growing, wants to become a county seat."[9] Metter's first serious new county campaign was mounted in 1908 when county leaders proposed the creation of first "Georgia County" and later "Dixie County." By this time, the new village by the rails of the Central of Georgia had a population of almost 400. Subsequent efforts to create a new county around the success at Metter followed in 1912 and 1913. In 1914, Metter finally won the day, and Candler County was finally created from portions of Emanuel, Bulloch and Tattnall in 1914. J. J. Baldwin's Candler County Courthouse rose in 1921, and by 1930, Metter counted 1424 residents. However, like Adrian and Stillmore, this fragile rose of progress, which had blossomed in east Georgia's sandy soil proved just another fading flower in cotton's neglected garden. All three towns experienced a meteoric rise followed by lofty expectations, and a swift decline. And all tumbled back into the chasm of hard times that was underlined by the abandonment of the Central's tracks from Brewton to Metter in 1938.

Tattnall County: Reidsville

Plate 28.4: The depot at Manassas.

This tiny depot at Manassas is about all that remains today to remind us of the early railroads in Tattnall County.[10] In 1888, on its way to a connection with the Savannah, Americus and Montgomery Railroad at Lyons, The Central's Savannah and Western Railroad was the first to pierce the wild expanses of this remote area of the piney woods. Along these rails, a host of tiny depots like this one sprang up. On the same line, 5 miles to the west, a depot was erected at Collins. There in 1897, the Collins and Reidsville Railroad forged a southward spur to connect the Tattnall County seat at Reidsville to the Central's main line. Not four years after the first train arrived at Reidsville, one of Georgia's most flamboyant neoclassical court buildings began to rise beside the town's new depot.

Tattnall County was created in 1801 from the vast expanses of Montgomery County. At the time of its creation, there were no towns in the new county, and the first county seat was established at Drake's Ferry. In 1807, the seat of local government was moved to a place called Ohoopee Mills, and a 16' x 20' log courthouse was erected there. In 1830, the centrally located town of Reidsville was laid out, and a crude temporary courthouse was built. Finally, in 1837, a substantial frame court building was completed. Early accounts describe a two-story structure with a portico supported by fluted columns in the Greek mode.[11] Sadly, no photographs of this building survive. In 1849, George White found only about fifty residents at Reidsville. According to a questionable local legend, the village was so small in 1860 that elements of Sherman's advancing army passed through Reidsville without recognizing it for a town. By 1900, three years after the first train steamed in from Collins, Reidsville counted 257 inhabitants. By 1906, the rails stretched southward to Ludowici as the Reidsville and Southeastern Railroad, and in that same year, the Georgia Coast and Piedmont Railroad, which would extend all the way to Brunswick by 1914, acquired the entire line. However, hard times followed. The line from Brunswick to Ludowici was abandoned in 1919, and the link from Ludowici to Glenville was scrapped two years later. The Glenville and Collins Railroad operated the remaining rails from Collins through Reidsville to Glenville until 1941 when the entire line was abandoned.

Plate 28.5: The Tattnall County Courthouse at Reidsville, built in 1902. James W. Golucke, architect.

All of this was a long distance from the abiding prosperity of the New South myth. Nevertheless in 1897, when the rails of the Collins and Reidsville Railroad reached Reidsville, the usual euphoric overreaction occurred. Less than four years later, the county began the construction of a grand courthouse unlike anything in Georgia. Sadly, newspaper accounts from this era are not to be found, and there are few local records to detail the mood in Reidsville around the turn of the century. Nonetheless, photographs of James Golucke's grandiose architectural expression of New South zeal speak eloquently for what could only have been soaring aspirations in the tiny village.

Just as the new century began, Golucke experimented with the new classicism in Alabama in Chambers and Calhoun Counties. His flamboyant courthouse at Reidsville represented one of the first attempts in rural Georgia to mimic the Baroque frippery of American Beaux-Arts classicism. This often-excessive new style had swept the nation after Chicago's 1893 Columbian Exposition. The buildings at Chicago quickly galvanized new, classically inspired architectural trends and created the utopian notions surrounding the American "City Beautiful Movement." The American Northeast sought wide boulevards and gleaming white temples to hide the growing squalor of her slums and tenements, and Northern industrialists hungered for opulent symbols to reflect their newfound material progress. All the while, the American South remained in large part a rural place. She counted few tenements and enjoyed no such progress. Thus, the region was slow in her acceptance of this flowery architecture of "American Renaissance." As we have seen, in the American South, the new classicism was first manifested in nostalgic neocolonial forms. For most Southerners, this careful classicism tended to recall the uncomplicated agrarian reveries of the antebellum era rather than Baroque orgies of American, turn-of-the-century, industrial success. Here in Reidsville, we find a notable exception.

Despite the Renaissance arcades and French finery of James Golucke's 1902 Tattnall County Courthouse at Reidsville, there were retardate forces at work here. To be sure, modern Beaux-Arts elements abound in the rusticated columns, limestone

Plate 28.4: This tiny depot at Manassas is about all that remains today to remind us of the early railroads in Tattnall County. (Photo: Wilber W. Caldwell.)

Plate 28.5: James Golucke's 1902 Tattnall County Courthouse at Reidsville represented one of the first attempts in rural Georgia to mimic the Baroque frippery of American Beaux Arts classicism. (Photo: Courtesy of the Georgia Dept. of Archives and History.)

[9] *The Bulloch Times*, April 30, 1904.

[10] The depot at Collins has been moved to a private farm in Tattnall County. The depots at Reidsville and Glenville are no longer standing.

[11] John P. Rabun Jr., "A History of Tattnall County" (master's thesis, Mercer University, 1954). Research paper submitted at Mercer University, a copy of which can be found in the Tattnall County Library at Reidsville.

balustrades and in the elaborate scrolling decorations that adorned the cornice. But with its great mansard roof and multifoliate dormers, the building also suggested the much older French Neoclassicism of the Second Empire Style. In this sense, Golucke's courthouse at Reidsville is yet another example of that seemingly ubiquitous stylistic lag which had characterized Southern architecture for decades.

Plate 28.6: The Tattnall County Courthouse, built in 1902. James W. Golucke, architect. Remodeled 1961.

In the early 1960s, a brutal renovation of the 1902 Tattnall County Courthouse left this extraordinary building permanently maimed. The old building had fallen pray to years of neglect, and by 1961, citing the "deplorable condition" of the structure; several grand juries had recommended the renovation of Golucke's Beaux Arts oddity.[12] In a countywide election, county leaders proposed a $200,000 bond issue to fund a "new roof" and a 5000 square foot addition. In support of the bond issue, *The Tattnall Journal* made no mention of the demolition of the tower or the removal of the great mansard roof.[13] In February of 1961, Tattnall County voters soundly rejected the proposed bond issue, and in April of that year, the matter was back before the grand jury that

Plate 28.6: Today, what remains of James Golucke's Parisian symbol for Reidsville's turn-of-the-century aspirations stands as a deformed reminder of the many stunning court buildings that were demolished in the 1950s, 1960s and 1970s. (Photo: Wilber W. Caldwell.)

approved $80,000 for the building's "preservation."[14] There was still no mention of the demolition of the tower. In July of 1961, *The Tattnall Journal* announced that the clock tower along with the dormers and chimneys would be removed and the courtroom ceiling would be lowered. According to *The Journal* these modifications were aimed at changing the building's architectural style from "French to Georgian." This rationale would be laughable had it not been fabricated to defend such tragic mutilations. There was no further mention of the project, and *The Journal* did not even report the demolition of the grand tower, which must have been quite an event. Today it is difficult to find anyone in Reidsville who is not sickened by the loss of this treasure, but in 1961, the great tower came tumbling down apparently without public comment.

Today, James Golucke's Parisian symbol for Reidsville's turn-of-the-century aspirations stands as a deformed reminder of the many stunning court buildings that were demolished in the 1950s, 1960s and 1970s. As a casualty of one of many misguided mid-century campaigns to remodel Georgia's historic public architecture, the denuded building today recalls the shocking price of these atrocities (see Appendix D).

EMANUEL COUNTY: SWAINSBORO

Plate 28.7: The Emanuel County Courthouse, built in 1895.[15] Burned 1919. James Wingfield Golucke, architect.

Emanuel County was created in 1812 from parts of Bulloch and Tattnall Counties. The first log courthouse was erected at Swainsboro in 1814. When George White passed through that village in 1849, he found only "two or three families" living there. According to White's *Statistics of the State of Georgia*, the town consisted of little more than a courthouse, a jail, and a small cluster of dwellings. The courthouse that White found at Swainsboro in 1849 was Emanuel County's third. The two-story frame structure had been erected in 1840 to replace the 1822 log courthouse that had burned earlier that year. The simple frame court building would serve for over 50 years. It was removed from the square in 1895 and used as a private residence until its demolition in the 1960s. Decades after White's visit, not much had changed in Swainsboro. In 1880, the village was still quite small, counting only 186 residents.[16] However, when the first locomotive steamed into Swainsboro around 1895, things began to change, and the Romanesque extravagance of James Golucke's Emanuel County Courthouse rose to meet the first train.

Trains had long been on the minds of county leaders in Emanuel. Even in the staggering economic aftermath of war, the residents of tiny Swainsboro were seduced by the promise of rail. In June of 1867, *The Sandersville Central Georgian* reported a plan for a railroad from Swainsboro to some point on the Central's antebellum main line just to the north in Burke County. Proponents of the new road cited the "untold wealth" of Emanuel's "lofty pines" and "undeveloped" area agriculture.[17] By August, the spur from "No. 9" (Millen) to Swainsboro was being promoted as a main trunk line via Swainsboro and Dublin to Fort Valley, where it would connect with the Central's branches to Columbus and southwestern Georgia.[18] But in the late 1860s as cotton prices fell, support for this ambitious plan faded. It would be another twenty-five years before the steam whistle would pierce the silence of the vast pine forests around Swainsboro.

Throughout the 1870s and 1880s, tiny tram railroads snaked their way southward from the Central's main trunk into the pine forests of Emanuel County. Many of these rickety lines were simple "gravity" railroads without steam power. The Central's well-known president, William Wadley, who owned considerable timber interests in the area, constructed one of the first of these logging roads. By 1870, local speculation centered on plans for the extension of the line from Wadley's mill, located about three miles south of Millen, to Swainsboro. For twenty years, nothing came of this scheme, but finally in 1889, the Rogers and Summit Railroad was chartered and built from Rogers, near Millen on the Central, to the village of Summit (later called Twin City) to the east of Swainsboro. In 1897, this line was reorganized as the Millen and Southwestern Railroad, and in 1906, it was extended southward to Normantown where it

would soon become part of the new Georgia and Florida Railroad on its way from Augusta, via Vidalia and Valdosta, to Madison, Florida.

As the 1890s began, another logging line appeared in Emanuel County. Timber baron and future railroad promoter, George Brinson, built the first leg of his Stillmore Air Line from Collins to the newly created village of Stillmore in 1889. By 1895, Brinson's line was laying track toward Swainsboro, and by 1901 his "Air Line" would connect to the Central at Wadley where it would later become part of the

Plate 28.7: In 1895, the Stillmore Air Line was extended northward to Swainsboro, and James Golucke's Emanuel County Courthouse rose to meet the first train. (Photo: Courtesy of Ted Brooke.)

[12] *Tattnall Journal*, April 21, 1960.

[13] *Tattnall Journal*, November 24, 1960, and January 12, 1961.

[14] *Tattnall Journal*, April 20 1961.

[15] *The Manufacturer's Record*, May 3, 1895.

[16] James E. Dorsey, ed., *Footprints on the Hoopee, A History of Emanuel County, 1812-1906* (Spartanburg GA: Reprint Company, 1978) 156.

[17] *The Central Georgian*, June 12, 1867 in W. C. Rogers, ed., Emanuel Memories (Swainsboro GA: Swainsboro Forest Blade Publishing Company, 1976) 45.

[18] *The Central Georgian*, August 14, 1867 in Rogers, ed., Emanuel Memories, 46.

Wadley Southern Railroad. By this time, the rails of the Midville, Swainsboro, and Red Bluff had also reached Swainsboro, and the now booming town of almost 900 had its second railroad.

In 1895, as George Brinson's steel rails snaked their way up from Stillmore toward Swainsboro, James Golucke's Emanuel County Courthouse began to rise on the square. In that same year, Golucke-designed courthouses were also under construction at Wrightsville and at Zebulon. These were the Atlanta architect's first court buildings. The classical styling of the twin court buildings at Wrightsville and Zebulon offers a striking contrast to Golucke's Romanesque design here at Swainsboro. Although all three buildings display symmetry reflecting the emerging architectural "return to order" which would soon vanquish the Picturesque, Golucke's design at Swainsboro was one of the first courthouses in Georgia to employ Romanesque vocabulary to achieve symmetry. Undoubtedly inspired by H. H. Richardson's masterpiece, the 1888 Allegheny County Courthouse at Pittsburgh, the front elevation of Golucke's Emanuel County Courthouse was a miniature of this American master's popular form. It featured a slender central tower flanked by bold corner pavilions with steep roofs. However, here Golucke departed from Richardson's plan. Discarding the careful and poignant use of the massive Romanesque detail for which Richardson had become famous, Golucke

opted for an assortment of classical ornament including scrolling motifs of pressed metal banding on the cornice. Pressed metal like this would later become this architect's signature. It adorned many of Golucke early courthouses including those at Wrightsville, Zebulon, and McDonough. Additional classical elements are found in the rounded pediments of the dormers on the corner pavilions and in the flowery relief of the capitols atop the slender pilasters that quoin the tower. Much of this, along with the bell shaped roof of the central tower, reflects Queen Anne influence, but the overall effect here was decidedly Romanesque. This early court building became Golucke's model for future Romanesque designs like those at McDonough, Blairsville, Ellaville, Gray, and Newton. All of these buildings display the same fundamental massing, but tall pedimented bays replaced corner pavilions, and Golucke's early classical ornamentation gave way to more fundamentally Richardsonian motifs.

Plate 28.8: The Stillmore Air Line Depot at Stillmore built c.1890.

Farther to the south, along the line of the Stillmore Air Line, the village of Stillmore had been little more than a rickety sawmill when the line was chartered in 1889. Suddenly it became a boomtown. By 1900, three railroads crossed at Stillmore (see Table 28.2). Local lore contends that Stillmore's population reached 2100 before 1910. However, the United State Census for that year records only 645 residents, while Swainsboro counted over 1300. Although exact figures will never be known, Stillmore may have actually been larger than Swainsboro at some point near the end of the first decade of the twentieth century. Boom towns, like Stillmore were filled with transient populations, and with her notorious barrooms, sprawling hotels, busy railroad shops and twelve passenger trains a day, Stillmore was undoubtedly more active in 1910 than sleepy Swainsboro.[19]

Railroads were fickle lovers. As the vast pine forests of Emanuel County were converted into oceans of stumps, the boll weevil wrought his insidious devastation. By 1920, the rails at Stillmore no longer hummed with the music of progress. The Wadley

Plate 28.8: The Stillmore Air Line's depot at Stillmore.

Southern abandoned its line through Stillmore in 1929. The Georgia and Florida scrapped her rails through the town in that same year, and nine years later in 1938, when the Central abandoned her track from Brewton to Metter, the last rails in Stillmore were pulled up for scrap. Although the remains of this elegant little depot can still be found in Stillmore, a drive through the village today does little to reveal the source of the wild aspirations that must have swirled around this tiny building in 1910.

JEFFERSON COUNTY: LOUISVILLE

Plate 28.9: The Central of Georgia Depot at Bartow, built in 1869.

Bypassing the old state capitol of Louisville, the Central of Georgia Railroad built Station #11 in southern Jefferson County in 1839. The original name of the place was Spier's Turnout, an appellation that attests to its railroad origins. However, the arrival of the railroad did not result in instant growth. Twenty years later in 1859, Spiers Turnout contained only two dwellings.[20] During the war, the place was called Bartow in honor of Francis S. Bartow, a Confederate leader killed in the First Battle of Manassas. As for Sherman's destructive passage in 1864, Jefferson County histories only say that he "came and tore up the railroad." After the war, the depot at Bartow was one of the first to be rebuilt by the Central. This sturdy warehouse stands today to attest to Jefferson County's importance in the oppressive economics of cotton in the postbellum era. Although the initial period of growth in Bartow began around 1880, the row of brick stores that stand empty today can reasonably be dated around 1900, for in December of 1899 a large portion of the then mostly wooden town burned to the ground.[21]

At about that time, 12 miles to the north, the venerable village of Louisville was beginning to stir from her long numbing sleep. Four years after the disastrous fire at Bartow, Louisville erected a grand monument to emerging New South aspirations on the site of Georgia's old capitol building. The old capitol building at Louisville was the first government building erected by the State of Georgia. After the revolution,

RAILROADS AT STILLMORE IN 1900	Table 28.2
The Millen Southwestern, later part of the Georgia and Florida Railroad.	
The Brewton and Pineora, later part of the Central of Georgia.	
The Stillmore Air Line, later part of the Wadley Southern.	

the state conducted its business in rented buildings first at Savannah and later at Augusta. By 1796, the General Assembly had legislated the new capitol city of Louisville into existence and built the simple government building in the center of the newly laid out town. Jefferson County was created in that same year. Although the first capitol building would stand on the square at Louisville for over fifty years, we know little of its nature except that its was a 50' x 50' two-story brick structure with three rooms on each floor.[22] Following the decision to move the state capitol to Milledgeville in 1804, the old building served as an arsenal until 1812, the Jefferson County Courthouse from 1813 to 1816, and later as a Masonic lodge. In

Plate 28.9: A testament to the bounty of cotton in Jefferson County, the Central of Georgia's 1869 depot at Bartow was among the first to be rebuilt after Sherman's fiery march. (Photo: Wilber W. Caldwell.)

[19] Rogers, ed., *Emanuel Memories*, 127-31.

[20] Z. V. Thomas, *History of Jefferson County* (1927; reprint, Macon GA: Reprint Company, 1927) 81.

[21] *The True Citizen*, December 16, 1899.

[22] Mills Lane, ed., *The Rambler in Georgia* (Savannah 1973) in Joan Niles Sears, *The First Hundred Years of Town Planning in Georgia* (Atlanta: Cherokee Press, 1979) 167.

1816, Jefferson County erected its first court building, a simple frame structure that served until 1824 when the old state house was again employed as the county courthouse. In 1847, Georgia's first capitol building was demolished to make way for the 1848 Jefferson County Courthouse, a two-story brick vernacular court building built in part from material salvaged from the old state house.

Louisville's hold on the state capitol had seemed shaky from the very beginning. Although the town briefly flourished as a tobacco market, its swampy site immediately proved unhealthy, and its location at the head of navigation on the Ogeechee River offered limited commercial possibilities. Efforts to clear the Ogeechee began as early as 1796 and continued well into the nineteenth century but nothing came of the efforts. Perhaps the most crippling blow to Louisville's hold on the state capitol was struck almost before the town was laid out. By the closing years of the eighteenth century, the discovery of the cotton gin had created enormous demand for the cotton growing lands to the west, and by 1800, Louisville was far to the east of Georgia's growing population center.

Louisville declined substantially after the removal of the capitol to Milledgeville. Efforts to clear the Ocmulgee continued as cotton replaced tobacco in the town's economy. In 1829, Adiel Sherwood's *Gazetteer of Georgia* reported that $10,000 had been subscribed to clear the channel, and that boats containing 200 to 300 bags of cotton had descended to Savannah. The Ogeechee remained a capricious shallow tangle, and after the Central of Georgia passed her by in 1839, Louisville continued to struggle. An 1806 source described the town as having ten dry goods stores and 100 dwellings.[23] In his 1849 *Statistics of the State of Georgia*, George White reported that the town had "deteriorated," into a village containing only a courthouse, a jail, one academy, one tavern, five stores and a population of about 100.

After the war, Louisville experienced a sizable boom. In 1872, the Louisville and Wadley Railroad was chartered from Louisville to connect with the Central of Georgia at Wadley. It took eight years to complete the 10-mile spur. By 1879, Louisville counted almost 800 residents according to Sholes's *Gazetteer*

of Georgia. However, despite the emergence of a considerable cotton trade, the town again stagnated after her initial boom. In the early 1890s, Jefferson County became a formidable stronghold for Georgia's People's Party, and, as usual, the New South myth was slow to bloom in Populism's agrarian garden. By 1900, Louisville's population was barely above 1000.

Nonetheless, as the new century dawned, Louisville began to stir. Aspiring to end her isolation at the end of the tiny spur, Louisville entertained railroad promoters in surprising numbers. In this highly charged atmosphere, a movement for a new courthouse quickly materialized. In 1901, George Brinson spoke in Louisville to announce the extension of his Stillmore Air Line to Wadley. The new stretch of track meant that Brinson's line suddenly connected Collins on the Seaboard Air Line with Wadley on the Central of Georgia. Some of the speculation in Louisville centered on further extension of this line to "allow an outlet both north and south."[24] A year later, *The Louisville News and Farmer* reported that railroad schemes pointed outward from Louisville to "all points of the compass."[25] One of the most promising of these was the Wrens and Louisville Railroad, which sought to connect Louisville to the village Wrens on the Augusta Southern Railroad in northern Jefferson County. For a brief moment, this line appeared to represent Louisville's long awaited link to "Augusta and to the world in general."[26] At the center of this speculation was Louisville's own William Phillips, a local jurist, farmer, banker, and self-style railroad promoter. In 1902, *The News and Farmer* summed up the intoxicating myth of railroad promise, predicting that the new line would "lead to wealth, happiness and convenience," and christening William Phillips the town's "Moses."[27]

Plate 28.10: The Jefferson County Courthouse at Louisville, built in 1904. Willis Denny, architect.

In this fertile hothouse of railroad expectations, plans for a new courthouse quickly blossomed. Beginning in November of 1902, successive grand juries found the old 1848 court building first "in bad condition," and later "unsafe and dangerous."[28] By June of the following year, the voters of Jefferson

County had approved bonds to fund a new building by the incredible majority of 456 for and 20 against.[29]

In 1903, the choice of Atlanta architect and Jefferson County native, Willis Denny was probably a foregone conclusion. Although Denny was only thirty years old when he drew the plans of the Jefferson County Courthouse, his work in Atlanta was fast earning him a place among that city's best architectural talent. One of a rising new generation of home-trained American architects, Denny had studied at Cornell University and apprenticed in the office of Atlanta's preeminent architectural firm, Bruce and Morgan. Denny opened his own office in 1897, and by 1903, he had already designed several stunning churches in Atlanta along with a number of hotels, including the elaborate Majestic Hotel and his masterpiece, the A. G. Rhodes House, one of Atlanta's architectural treasures.

In Louisville, Denny created one of a growing number of courthouses in Georgia to wear the clothing of the blossoming "American Renaissance." As we have seen, the South was slow to accept the new classicism owing to its associations with the vast urban centers in the North and its national association with American industrial and financial might. However, by 1904, thirteen classical courthouses stood on Georgia squares (see Appendix A), and a new and uniquely Southern symbolism was emerging to drape these grand structures simultaneously in the mythology of both the Old and the New South. Although Willis Denny was careful to follow the lead of James Golucke and Frank Milburn, adorning a fundamental rectangular mass with the familiar paristyle portico of the earlier age, he was quick to add skillful hints of the rising tide of Beaux-Arts classicism in America. Windows framed by grand Renaissance pediments and delicate classical pilasters, bold cartouches and graceful roundels decorate multifaceted elevations that project the three dimensional plasticity of modern Parisian forms. Like Frank Milburn, Willis Denny was obviously comfortable with both the vocabulary and the symbolism of the new American classicism. Sadly, only a year after the cornerstone of his grand Jefferson

Plate **28.10**: Built on the site of Georgia's old capitol building, Willis Denny's 1904 Jefferson County Courthouse rose amid a flurry of railroad speculation in Louisville. (Photo: Wilber W. Caldwell.)

County Courthouse was laid, Denny died suddenly at the age of 31.

The cornerstone for Willis Denny's grand courthouse at Louisville was laid in March of 1904. As if to prove the connection between the courthouse and the depot, the keynote speaker for the occasion was none other than Louisville's "Moses," railroad promoter, William Phillips. Phillips delivered a rousing speech that hammered home the New South notion that the construction of the new courthouse was an indication that the citizens of Louisville were "not satisfied with the achievements of the past," and that a new kind of Progress had "taken hold" in the old capitol. It must have appeared that way in 1904, but the events of the following decades would prove otherwise. William Phillip's Louisville and Wrens Railroad was never built.

[23] Yulssus Lynn Holmes, *Those Glorious Days, A History of Louisville as Georgia's Capitol, 1796-1807* (Macon GA: Mercer University Press, 1996) 52.

[24] *The News and Farmer*, June 22, 1901.

[25] *The News and Farmer*, June 19, 1902.

[26] *The News and Farmer*, June 19, 1902.

[27] *The News and Farmer*, June 19, 1902.

[28] *The News and Farmer*, November 20, 1902 and May 21, 1903.

[29] *The News and Farmer*, June 18, 1903.

SOME LAST THOUGHTS ON SHORT LINES IN EASTERN GEORGIA

In his 1913 *History of Transportation in the Eastern Cotton Belt to 1860,* Ulrich B. Phillips sums up the saga of Georgia's antebellum railroads:

> The transportation problem was crossing the barrier (the vast empty expanses of the Pine Barrens) and connecting the coast with the cotton growing areas. The obvious method in the railway era was to build a single trunk line from each seaport across the barriers, and then lay out a system of radiating lines in the cotton belt which would gather freight and serve as feeders to the main stems."[30]

The Central of Georgia, which began in the late 1830s at Savannah, is a perfect example. In antebellum times, the Central ignored the vast timber lands of the Pine Barrens and bypassed most of the county towns of the old eastern cotton belt in a head long rush to Macon. From there the "feeders" sprouted out into the rich cotton growing regions of Southwestern Georgia and the western Piedmont.

Initially, the only antebellum branch lines to the Central between Savannah and Macon were to Augusta and to Milledgeville and Eatonton. But between the late 1870s and 1915 a vast network of railroad "feeder" lines to the Central and to the old Savannah, Americus and Montgomery Railroad materialized in the Pine Barrens and the eastern cotton belt. For the most part, this later spidery web of steel was not built to serve "King Cotton." It knelt before a new king, "King Timber." Nevertheless, in the end, the new king would prove every bit as disappointing as the old.

The story of the courthouse and the depot in eastern Georgia along the old Central of Georgia Railroad and the old Savannah, Americus and Montgomery Railroad is the story of a complex tangle of track originally built to serve scores of hungry lumber mills. Along the way, these lines connected theretofore-bypassed towns and nurtured, in these out-of-the-way places, late blossoms of the myth of the New South.

The usual bumper crop of grand courthouses followed the flower of New South promise. In Bulloch County, in 1894, not five years after the arrival of the first train on the Dover and Statesboro Railroad, Bruce and Morgan's Queen Anne gem rose on the square in Statesboro. Likewise in Tattnall County, James Golucke's stunning Beaux-Arts creation was under construction less than five years after the Collins and Reidsville Railroad reached Reidsville. In Swainsboro, Golucke's 1895 Emanuel County courthouse was rising just as the rails of George Brinson's Stillmore Air Line were extended to that county town. Three years later in 1898, as the Brewton and Pineora Railroad built eastward toward Statesboro, the village of Metter was laid out. Within a decade, a movement for the creation of new county was underway in Metter, and Candler County was created in 1914. Inspired by lofty speculation surrounding ill-fated plans to extend the Louisville and Wadley Railroad to Wrens, and thus connect to Augusta, Willis Denny's exquisite Jefferson County Courthouse rose in 1904.

Just after the turn of the century, the piney woods came alive along the new rails. Prosperous towns sprouted at places like Adrian, Stillmore, Garfield, Twin City, Register, and Portal. All had their brief day in the sun. But as the great forests were cleared and the boll weevil made his way up from Mexico, the shinny rails of eastern Georgia's ambitious new short line railroads began to rust.

•

---

[30] U. B. Phillips, *History of Transportation in the Eastern Cotton Belt to 1860* (1908; reprint, New York: McMillan, 1913) 4

29 | The Georgia, Florida and Alabama Railroad

MILLER COUNTY: COLQUITT

Plate 29.1: The Miller County Courthouse, built in 1906. Burned in 1974. Alexander Blair III, architect.

In 1856, as new settlers continued to flow into the rich cotton growing lands of southwest Georgia, Miller County was created from Early and Baker Counties, and the village of Colquitt was laid out as the new county's seat of government. A wooden courthouse was erected sometime before 1860. This first court building burned in 1872, and was replaced by a second frame building in 1873. By this time, the Central of Georgia had completed her "Blakely Extension" from Albany as far west as Arlington, 18 miles north of Colquitt, and a considerable boom began there despite the national financial crisis of 1873 and the economic nightmare that attended Reconstruction. By 1879, Sholes's *Gazetteer of Georgia* described Arlington as a town of 400 residents. Meanwhile, tiny Colquitt languished, tantalized by a series of grand railroad schemes that began in 1869 with the charter of the ill-fated Bainbridge, Cuthbert and Columbus Railroad. Amid accusations of irregularities regarding the issuing of state endorsed bonds and despite the efforts of Hannibal Kimball, Georgia's most notorious railroad promoter of the day, the line failed in 1872 after grading only 35 miles of roadbed and laying no track at all. Arlington continued to flourish and the Central completed the "Blakely Extension" all the way to Blakely in 1881. Colquitt remained unconnected, mired in railroad speculation, first centering on the 1880 charter of the Chattanooga, Columbus and Southern and ten years later on the hopes for the Bainbridge, Columbus and Western. But the rails failed to materialize.

Finally, in 1895, the Georgia Pine Railroad managed to complete a section track northward from Bainbridge through Colquitt to Arlington. This created a wave of optimism in Colquitt, and in that same year the old wooden 1873 courthouse was remodeled to include a Greek style portico supported by columns.[1] By 1901, the directors of the Georgia Pine Railroad were dreaming larger dreams. The line had become the Georgia, Florida and Alabama Railroad and was extend-

[1] The Colquitt Garden Club, *The History of Miller County, 1856-1980* (Colquitt GA: The Colquitt Garden Club, 1980) 104.

The Georgia, Florida & Alabama Railroad

Stewart County: Richland (see chapter 23) • Randolph County: Cuthbert (see chapter 6)
Calhoun County: Morgan • Miller County: Colquitt • Baker County: Newton
Decatur County: Bainbridge (see chapter 12)
Some Last Thoughts on the Georgia, Florida & Alabama Railroad

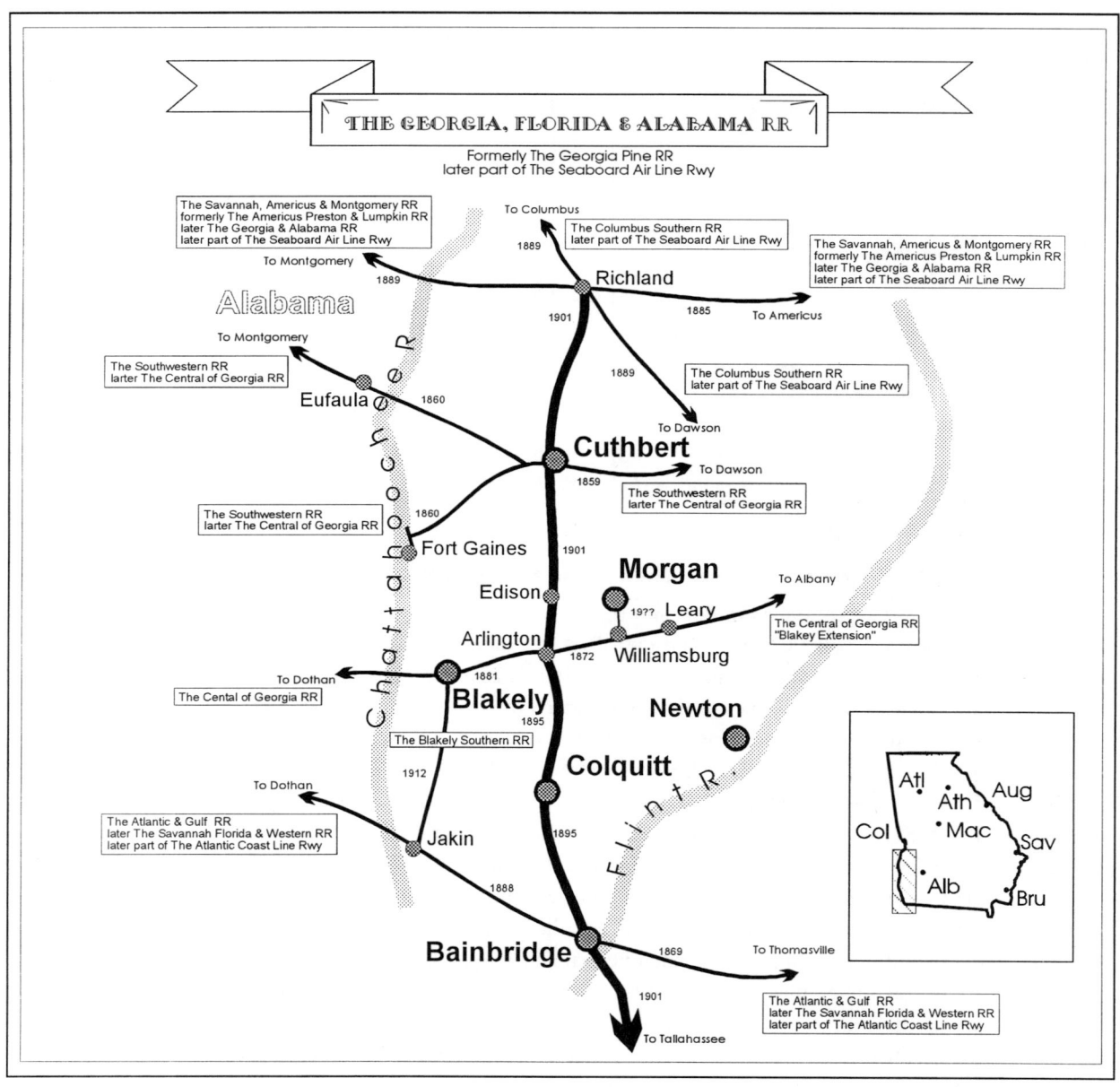

Plate 29.1: The 1904 Miller County Courthouse. By 1904 neoclassical court buildings were beginning to sprout all across Georgia. (Photo: Courtesy of Ted Brooke.)

ed from Arlington all the way to Richland where it joined the old Savannah, Americus and Montgomery and the Columbus Southern Railroads, thus completing the long-awaited connection to Columbus. By this time, powerful timber and turpentine interests were busy in Miller County, and Colquitt counted her population above 300. It would be convenient to conclude that all of this railroad-born success sparked agitation for a new courthouse in Miller County. This may indeed have been the case, but in October of 1904, the old Miller County Courthouse burned to the ground.

The Deep South had been slow to accept the flowery neoclassicism born of the architectural successes of the 1893 Columbian Exposition at Chicago, but by 1904, neoclassical court buildings were beginning to sprout all across Georgia. Not far from Colquitt in nearby Blakely, Morgan and Dillon's grand Early County Courthouse was beginning to rise, and at the other end of the "Blakely Extension" at Albany, T. F. Lockwood's Dougherty County Courthouse was nearing completion. The selection of Macon architect, Alexander Blair III, speaks to tiny Colquitt's determination to mimic the success at nearby Bainbridge. There in 1902 Blair had designed his Decatur County Courthouse not far from the shiny new rails of the Georgia, Florida and Alabama Railroad.

The 1906 Miller County Courthouse was the second of Alexander Blair's eight courthouse designs in Georgia. It was the first of three courthouses that the architect would design in popular classical form first seen in James Golucke's 1900 DeKalb County Courthouse at Decatur and later so articulately voiced in Frank Milburn's 1903 Wilcox County Courthouse at Abbeville. With its simple rectangular silhouette, massive domed clock tower, and grand tetrastyle portico, Blair's 1906 Miller County Courthouse at Colquitt was another in a growing number of neoclassical court buildings that were proving so popular in the first decade of the new century. This would be the model for Blair's later court buildings at Mount Vernon (1907) and at Cairo (1908). Here was another ambitious symbol for the South's precarious dilemma. It was a duel symbol, that mimicked the modern forms of neoclassical Revival, Beaux-Arts classicism and the "City Beautiful" movement so popular in the North, while at the same time it recalled the shady verandahs of "old times not forgotten" in the rural South. Only in the American South could such complex and confused symbols be attached to such simple architecture. Only the deeply troubled Southern mind could perceive without contradiction an architecture that satisfied both her aspirations for American industrial and financial success and her equally compelling yearnings for an agrarian past draped in the brooding bittersweet nostalgia of the Lost Cause. Here, in tiny Colquitt was a symbol for both the seductive myth of the Old South and the illusive myth of the New South.

CALHOUN COUNTY: MORGAN

Plate 29.2: The Union Depot at Arlington, built in 1898.[2]

This fine depot is a convincing testament to the notable turn-of-the-century economic success at Arlington. In 1898, when this building rose at the junction of the Central's "Blakely Extension" and the newly completed Georgia Pine Railroad, Arlington had blossomed into a substantial commercial center

---

[2] *The Manufacturer's Record*, December 2, 1898.

boasting over 700 residents. By 1910, the town would nearly double in size. Meanwhile, 12 miles to the northeast, bypassed by the railroads, the county town of Morgan languished, and her population was below 250. As if to underline the contrast between sleepy Morgan and bustling Arlington, hopes for a branch of the Georgia Pine Railroad from Arlington via Morgan to Dawson were dashed just as the construction of this depot began.[3]

Arlington's boom had begun back in 1873. In that year, passing along the southern border of Calhoun County, the Central of Georgia had completed her "Blakely Extension" from Albany as far west as the village of Lick Skillet, later renamed Arlington. In the economic depression that followed the Panic of 1873, it would be eight years before the line was complete to Blakely. Despite the hard times, Arlington prospered in the mid-1870s as the railhead for a rich agricultural area. By 1879, the town counted about 400 residents according to Sholes's 1870 *Gazetteer of Georgia.* Laid out by railroad surveyors, the original town plan had two depot lots: one for the Central, and one for the notorious Hannibal Kimball and his ill fated Bainbridge, Cuthbert and Columbus Railroad. Kimball's line had been graded through Arlington around 1872, but no track was ever laid. Amid scandalous allegations of fraud, the road failed in the ensuing economic collapse of 1873. Despite continuing agitation, the vision of a north-south railroad did not begin to materialize until 1895 when Savannah entrepreneur, J. D. Williams, constructed his Georgia Pine Railroad from Bainbridge to Arlington. In addition, it was not until 1901, that Kimball's dream became a reality. In that year, the Georgia, Florida and

Alabama Railroad completed the line all the way from Tallahassee to Richland where it made connections to Columbus. It is interesting to note that in 1905, Hannibal Kimball, often written off as a scoundrel, was held in high esteem in Calhoun County and is described by a local editor as a visionary "who saw the future back in 1870."[4]

Through it all, the county town of Morgan would remain without a rail connection. The grand fantasy court building would not rise in Calhoun County to celebrate the myth of the New South, because no railroad had been constructed to import grand visions to Morgan. As the county town languished, the railroad towns of Arlington, Edison, and Leary fought for the removal of the courthouse.

The first and perhaps the fiercest of these battles occurred in 1892, when the original Calhoun County Courthouse burned. The building had been erected in 1854 when Calhoun County was created from Early County. In 1892, Arlington offered to build a new court building at no cost to taxpayers, if the county seat were moved to Arlington. *The Calhoun Courier* published an article supporting these efforts. Here was the pure essence of the New South dogma that lay at the heart of the complex relationship between the courthouse and the depot. According to *The Courier,* capital flowed to "enterprise," and "capitalists can see the enterprise of the people in the public buildings."[5] The editor went on to speculate that with the new courthouse beside her crossing railroads, Arlington would soon be a city of 5000 residents. Despite Arlington's two railroads and her euphoric but singularly unrealistic rhetoric, Morgan won the day based on tradition and her central location. A frame court building was completed on the square at Morgan in 1893. The designer of this building was Calhoun County resident, W. H. Parkins, who bore the same name but no relation to the notable Atlanta architect, William Parkins.

The railroad's promise would continue to drive Arlington in her quest for power. In 1905, leaders in Arlington proposed the creation Griggs County with Arlington as the county seat. This movement failed to garner support in the State Legislature, but in 1929, when the Calhoun County Courthouse at Morgan

Plate 29.2: The depot at Arlington. (Photo: Wilber W. Caldwell.)

again burned to the ground, both Arlington and neighboring Edison once more fought for removal of the courthouse. However, Morgan again retained the prize, having by this time constructed a spur from Morgan to the Central at Williamsburg. Local tradition has it that the present Calhoun County Courthouse at Morgan faces east, with its back to Edison and Arlington in order to snub these two aggressive railroad-inspired pretenders.

BAKER COUNTY: NEWTON

Plate 29.3: The Baker County Courthouse, built in 1906-1907. James W. Golucke, architect.

Ever since Nelson Tift established his trading post on the Flint River at Albany in 1836, Newton, the county town of Baker County, has languished in Albany's shadow. Baker County was cut from Early County in 1825, and shortly thereafter, the first crude wooden courthouse was erected at Byron, not far from present day Albany. The county seat was soon moved to Newton which was laid out on Flint River well to the south of Tift's future enterprise, and the county's second courthouse rose at Newton around 1832. Five years later, the building witnessed the passage of Tift's first steamboat, the Mary Emeline, on its way from Apalachicola to Albany.

All Newton could do was watch as Albany passed her by, and by 1849, in his *Statistics of the State of Georgia,* the reliable George White informs us that Albany had a population of about 800, while the county seat at Newton counted only 30 residents. In 1853, the creation of Dougherty County with Albany as the county town doomed Newton to an obscure fate. Her 1832 frame courthouse burned in 1873, only to be replaced by a similar two-story wooden building.

As we have seen, it was not the river that ultimately drove Albany's success, it was the railroad. As the early voyages of the Mary Emeline proved, steamboating on the Flint was a perilous and uncertain enterprise. Despite considerable effort to dredge, blast, and clear a channel, the Flint remained a capricious highway. In 1873, just as Newton's second new courthouse rose, the United States Corps of Engineers

made of survey of the Flint. Their report describes Newton as "small village" with "a courthouse, a jail, a few stores and a population of about 150." The report goes on to describe the Flint below Newton as far south as Bainbridge as containing, "many serious and almost impossible obstructions."[6] A plan for clearing the Flint was adopted by the Corps in 1874, but the undertaking was still not complete in 1910. Defying all efforts to dredge a navigable channel, the river remained "narrow" with "many shoals."[7] In the

Plate 29.3: When the 1906 Baker County Courthouse rose at Newton, the Romanesque Revival was long dead in most of America, but the rural South clung to symbols of the past with a tenacity unmatched elsewhere in the country. (Photo: Wilber W. Caldwell.)

[3] *The Morgan Monitor*, in the Calhoun County Historical Society, *Against Oblivion, A History of Calhoun County Georgia* (Alpharetta GA: W. H. Wolfe, 1994) 102.

[4] *The Edison News*, 1905, in The Calhoun County Historical Society, *Against Oblivion, A History of Calhoun County Georgia*, 73-74.

[5] *The Calhoun Courier*, May 13 and May 20, 1898.

[6] US Corps of Engineers Report on a Survey of the Flint River, in Baker County Historical Society, *The History of Baker County, Georgia* (Roswell GA: The Baker County Historical Society,1991) 35.

[7] Baker County Historical Society, *The History of Baker County, Georgia*, 35.

meantime, seven railroads had met at Albany, and her population exceeded 8000.

In 1900, tiny Newton remained completely bypassed, counted just over 300 residents and harbored little hope for a railroad of her own. The great east-west lines ran through Albany to the north and Bainbridge to the south, while north-south railroads skirted Baker County passing through Camilla to the east and Colquitt to the west. Nevertheless, at one point, a connecting scheme did emerge. In 1906, amid the various plans for a railroad from Albany via Cairo to Quincy, Florida, speculation for the construction of the Albany, Camilla and Newton railroad swept through Baker County.[8] In the end, this grand railroading scheme came to nothing, and we have little documentation of the effects of such speculation in Newton. Baker County did not have its own newspaper until 1912, and no Albany papers from 1906 survive today. Nonetheless, we know that the county's first bank, the Bank of Baker County, was established in that same year, and it cannot be a coincidence that the last of Georgia's Romanesque Revival courthouses rose on the square in Newton in 1906 amid talk of a railroad in Baker County.

By 1906, the Romanesque Revival was long dead in most of America, but as we have seen, the rural American South clung to symbols of the past with a tenacity unmatched elsewhere in the country. James W. Golucke's 1906 Baker County Courthouse was a near copy of his 1905 Jones County Courthouse at Gray. Except for the design of the original tower and a few details in the banding and fenestration, this building also matches Golucke's court buildings at McDonough (1897), Blairsville (1899), and Ellaville (1900).

Sadly, like many of Golucke's court buildings, the original tower did not stand the test of time. In 1925, the Flint River flooded Newton. When the river

returned to its banks, the high water mark was 6 feet up the side of this courthouse. The footings beneath the tower were seriously weakened. Shortly thereafter, the original tower was demolished, and the grotesque replacement we see today was erected in its place. In the Flint River flood of 1994, the high water mark was nearly 17 feet up the walls of the old courthouse, and the old building was abandoned leaving Newton a near ghost town. Today the building has been restored and designated a historical landmark.

In a quirk of history, just as the Romanesque Revival breathed a dying breath in Georgia, James Wingfield Golucke, the architect of so many of its most enduring monuments, died in the obscure village of Newton. In 1907, as Golucke's courthouse neared completion, the architect was arrested and placed in the Baker County jail for alleged misappropriation of county funds in connection with the construction of the Baker County Courthouse. The frail Golucke was crushed by these accusations and deeply shamed by his incarceration. On October 7, 1907, he unsuccessfully attempted suicide, and on October 26, 1907, he died at the age of 50 while still in prison. A contemporary Baker County history suggests that Golucke may have been wrongfully accused by local culprits, who were attempting to cover their own crimes.[9]

In 1907, the premature death of James Golucke marked the end of an era for public architecture in Georgia. Alexander Bruce, arguably the master of the picturesque in Georgia, had retired in 1904. Although the popularity of the picturesque had lingered in the American South, the Romantic architectural epic came to an abrupt end in Georgia with the erection of the Baker County Courthouse and the sudden death of its creator. Perhaps it was a fitting end. The picturesque had come to a sudden end in the North fifteen years earlier, and its great guiding genius, Henry Hobson Richardson, had met an equally sudden death in 1886.

Surely, James Golucke was no Richardson. Nonetheless, the comparison is interesting. In the growing urban centers of the North and Midwest, Richardson and his followers sought to create a distinctly American architectural style to boldly flaunt

[8] R. H. Wind, *Grady, 1904-1953* (Cairo GA: Messenger Publishing Co., 1983) 8-9.

[9] Baker County Historical Society, *The History of Baker County, Georgia*, 29.

[10] The last wooden courthouse to be built in Georgia rose at Clyde in Bryan County in 1901.

the emerging nation's industrial and financial success. Meanwhile, way out in the dusty fields of rural Georgia, James Golucke sought to tame the massive Richardsonian beast. He designed soft, simple, pastoral Romantic forms that stood for a less ambitious form of progress and simultaneously recalled an ancient age. Toward the end of his career, H. H. Richardson had begun to create a uniquely modern idiom that few would immediately comprehend. Golucke on the other hand, showed no such originality. He was one of the first architects in the Deep South to embrace the new classicism, and with the same zeal he had lavished on the picturesque, he fashioned duel symbols to soothe the troubled and divided mind of the South.

SOME LAST THOUGHTS ON THE GEORGIA, FLORIDA AND ALABAMA RAILROAD

Plans for what was to become the Georgia, Florida and Alabama Railroad go all the way back to 1869 and the charter of the ill-fated Bainbridge, Cuthbert and Columbus Railroad. In 1872, this early scheme for a north-south line through southwestern Georgia disintegrated into a cloud of allegations involving the illegal endorsement of state guaranteed bonds and the questionable financial dealings of the notorious railroad promoter, Hannibal I. Kimball. All through the 1880s and early 1890s, plans for the line's revival continued to tantalize residents in Cuthbert, Colquitt, and Bainbridge. At last, in 1895, the Georgia Pine Railroad was completed from Bainbridge to join the Central's "Blakely Extension" at Arlington. In Arlington, a notable boom followed, but the full flowering of Kimball's lingering railroad vision did not blossom until 1901, when the line, which by then was called the Georgia, Florida and Alabama Railroad, completed track from Tallahassee all the way to Richland where it made a connection to Columbus. Shortly after its completion, the Georgia, Florida and Alabama became part of the Seaboard Air Line Railway.

As we have noted, in the mid 1880s, the renewal of grading on the old Bainbridge, Cuthbert and

Columbus sparked such hope at Cuthbert that Kimball Wheeler and Parkins's extraordinary 1886 Randolph County Courthouse rose to celebrate the prospect of crossing rails. Likewise, the completion of the entire line from Columbus via Bainbridge to Tallahassee supplied Bainbridge with crossing rails in 1901, and Alexander Blair's stunning Decatur County Courthouse rose in 1902. By 1906, the new rails had even delivered some of the passion for a new age to tiny Colquitt where Macon's Alexander Blair was also commissioned to design a new court building after the old Miller County Courthouse burned in 1904. In the meantime, the success of the Georgia, Florida and Alabama Railroad had spawned considerable booms at Arlington and Richland.

Despite these grand monuments at Bainbridge, Cuthbert and Colquitt, the story of the courthouses and the depots along the rails of the old Georgia, Florida and Alabama is perhaps best told from the tiny bypassed town of Morgan where the residents successfully fended off continued efforts to capture the Calhoun County seat following railroad-inspired booms at Arlington, Edison and Leary, and where one of the last vernacular wooden county houses to be erected in Georgia rose in 1893.[10] Meanwhile, just to the east, on the banks of the Flint River, tiny Newton, the county seat of Baker County, remained bypassed by rail. Newton finally built a new court building, possibly inspired by hopes for the Albany, Camilla and Newton Railroad, which had been chartered in 1906. But no steel rails arrived at Newton, and fittingly, James Golucke's Baker County Courthouse, which rose at Newton in 1907, was the last Romanesque Revival court building erected in the state.

•

The Mountains of North Central Georgia

Dawson County: Dawsonville • White County: Cleveland • Lumpkin County: Dahlonega
Towns County: Hiawassee • Forsyth County: Cumming • Union County: Blairsville
Some Last Thoughts on the North Georgia Mountains

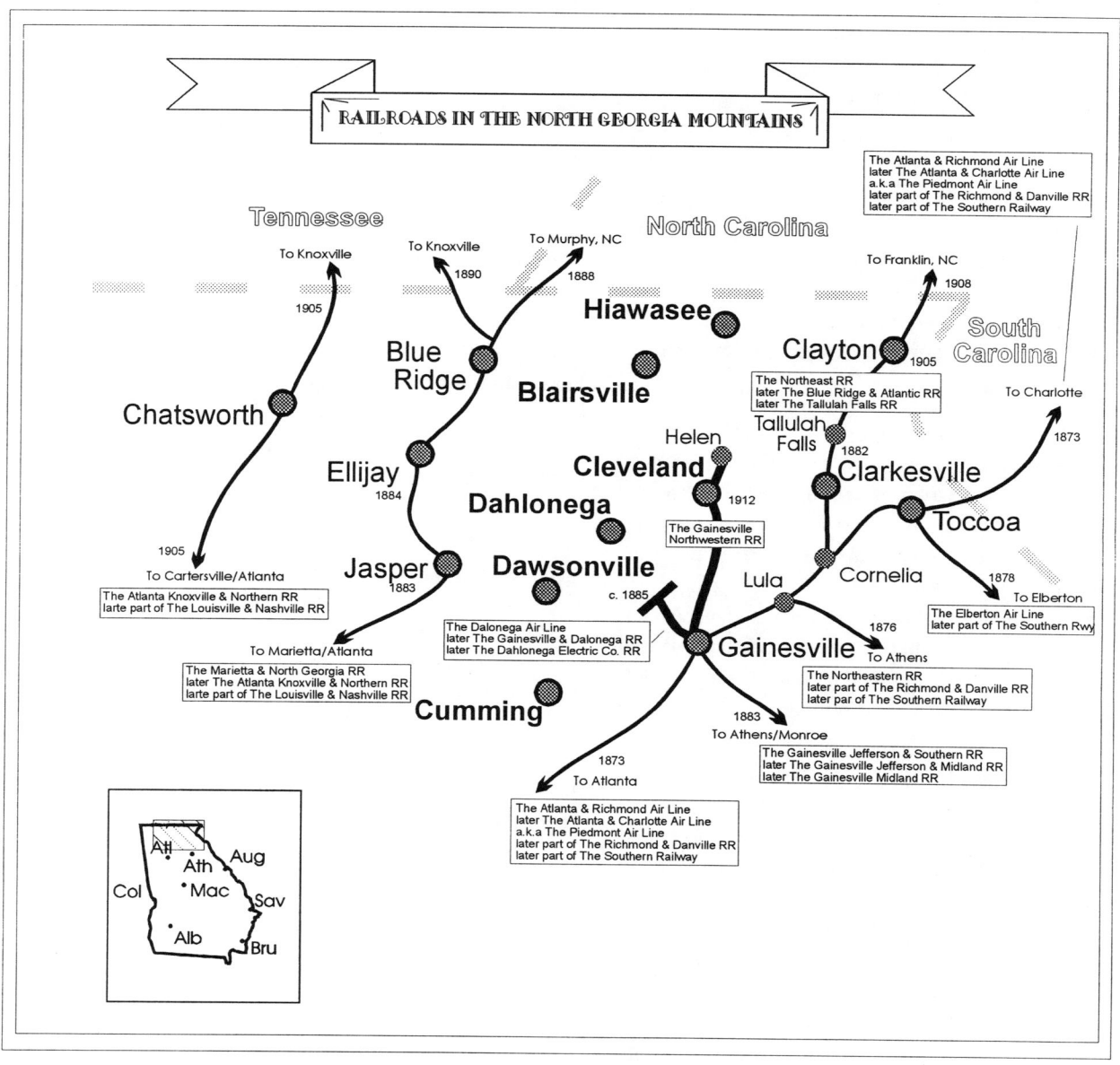

RAILROADS IN THE NORTH GEORGIA MOUNTAINS

Tennessee

North Carolina

To Knoxville

To Knoxville
1890

To Murphy, NC
1888

The Atlanta & Richmond Air Line
later The Atlanta & Charlotte Air Line
a.k.a The Piedmont Air Line
later part of The Richmond & Danville RR
later part of The Southern Railway

To Franklin, NC
1908

1905

Hiawasee

Clayton
1905

South Carolina

Blue Ridge

Blairsville

Tallulah Falls

To Charlotte

Chatsworth

Helen

Clarkesville
1882

1873

Ellijay
1884

Cleveland

The Northeast RR
later The Blue Ridge & Atlantic RR
later The Tallulah Falls RR

Dahlonega

Toccoa

1905

Jasper
1883

Dawsonville
c. 1885

1912

The Gainesville
Northwestern RR

Lula

Cornelia

1878

To Cartersville/Atlanta

To Elberton

The Atlanta Knoxville & Northern RR
larte part of The Louisville & Nashville RR

The Elberton Air Line
later part of The Southern Rwy

The Dalonega Air Line
later The Gainesville & Dalonega RR
later The Dahlonega Electric Co. RR

1876

To Marietta/Atlanta

Gainesville

To Athens

The Marietta & North Georgia RR
later The Atlanta Knoxville & Northern RR
larte part of The Louisville & Nashville RR

The Northeastern RR
later part of The Richmond & Danville RR
later par of The Southern Railway

Cumming

1883

To Athens/Monroe

The Gainesville Jefferson & Southern RR
later The Gainesville Jefferson & Midland RR
later The Gainesville Midland RR

1873

To Atlanta

The Atlanta & Richmond Air Line
later The Atlanta & Charlotte Air Line
a.k.a The Piedmont Air Line
later part of The Richmond & Danville RR
later part of The Southern Railway

Aug
Ath
Col
Mac
Sav
Alb
Bru

30 | The Mountains of North Central Georgia

DAWSON COUNTY: DAWSONVILLE

Plate 30.1: The Dawson County Courthouse, built in 1857-1860.

Of the seven brick antebellum court buildings still standing in Georgia (see Table I in the Introduction), the 1860 Dawson County Courthouse at Dawsonville may best represent the simple vernacular architectural style that once covered the state's courthouse squares with sturdy uncomplicated two-story brick buildings. Here is that unadorned and fundamentally Georgian form that had remained unchanged since the first American courthouses rose in the seventeenth century.

It is no coincidence that so many of the remaining examples of this once pervasive building form are in the mountain counties of north central Georgia. Here, frozen in time, in one of its most fiercely defended bastions, the uncomplicated practical architecture of the American frontier still broadcasts its uncomplicated symbols. This a building to remind us of a nearly forgotten American ideal, and the uncompromising individualism, which on the American frontier, was virtually unencumbered by governmental intervention. Here the rule of law was exercised only to preserve those freedoms necessary to maintain such individualism. Accordingly, architecture like this remained untainted by the complex myths and symbols that would soon separate the nation. Elsewhere, Georgia's courthouses would begin to reflect monumental struggles: industrialism vs. agrarianism, governmental might vs. local and individual prerogatives, Realism vs. Romanticism. However, up in the mountains, these simple buildings would continue to serve while the rest of the state embraced the complex architecture of a dubious progress. On the edge of the high mountains, the Dawson County Courthouse stood firm, while the legions of industrialism rode through the gardens of the American heartland, and transformed a rural nation of farmers into an urban nation of workers and clerks.

Plate 30.1: It is no coincidence that many of the remaining examples of this once pervasive vernacular building form are in the mountain counties of north central Georgia where the railroads failed to penetrate. (Photo: Wilber W. Caldwell.)

Such intransigence was not without a numbing price. When Dawson County was created in 1857 from parts of Pickens, Gilmer, Lumpkin, and Forsyth, the population of the entire county was under 1000 persons. Although population would grow in the late nineteenth century, reaching almost 6000 in 1880, farming in these hills was difficult, and the region remained among the poorest in the state. Although a railroad was surveyed from Gainesville to Dahlonega through the northern section of Dawson County, the project eventually fizzled. In 1900, Dawsonville counted only about 200 residents. By 1910, this number was down to 179, as mountain families began to stream down out of the hills in search of jobs in the cotton mills that were readily available in the Piedmont. Dawson County had a population of about 5500 in 1900. By 1930, this was down to 3500. The rails had never arrived to deliver New South promises, and the old courthouse at Dawsonville spoke only of the disappearing frontier. Ironically, as the new century unfolded, enough of the mythology of prosperity and progress had crept up into these hills to lure almost half of the county's population down to the sprawling mill villages. The cramped conformity of the villages must have offered a stark contrast to the free-spirited frontier individualism so eloquently voiced by the 1860 Dawson County Courthouse and by the wilderness that once surrounded it.

WHITE COUNTY: CLEVELAND

Plate 30.2: The White County Courthouse, built in 1860.

White County's story is similar to that of Dawson County. Created form Habersham County in 1857, White County also completed a brick court building in 1860. This sturdy structure is one of only seven standing examples of that simple brick vernacular courthouse form that covered Georgia's squares in the antebellum period (see Table 1 in the Introduction). The county seat at Mount Yonah, later called Cleveland, was surveyed in 1858, and this courthouse was begun in that same year. According to the county records, the original plan for the building called for columns, probably in the Greek mode, but these were omitted in the revised plan of 1859. The completed building, with its wood shingle roof and brick flooring on the ground floor, originally had an external stairway leading to the second floor courtroom.[1] Great brick walls, 16 inches thick at the base, rise to high parapets on the north and south elevations to terminate the roof.

Here gold mining continued on a limited scale well into the twentieth century, but White County remained remote and sparsely populated throughout the nineteenth century. Sholes's *Gazetteer of Georgia* reports that the population of Cleveland was only about 200 persons in 1879. In 1901, as the great textile mills began to rise at Gainesville, the population began to trickle down out of the hills to the sprawling mill villages that were beginning to cover the Piedmont. In 1910, no railroad had arrived in White County to import dreams of New South prosperity, and those few families that remained continued on in the simple time-honored ways of the north Georgia mountains.

It was not until after the period of our interest that the railroad finally came to White County. Nonetheless, the events that followed the construction of the Gainesville and Northwestern Railroad in 1912 were reminiscent of the earlier period. The Gainesville and Northwestern was built to serve the enormous Byrd-Mathews Lumber Company, which had acquired extensive timber interests around Helen and Robertstown on the edge of the high mountains in northern White County. By the early 1920s, the usual array of tiny tramlines had snaked their way into the hills to haul out a rich harvest of timber, and a spur line was built from Clermont in northern Hall County to the pyrite mines in Lumpkin County. However, by the early 1930s, the vast stands of timber were gone, the great mills at Helen and Robertstown were closed, and the Gainesville and Northwestern Railroad had been abandoned for scrap. Here is a late chapter in that all-too-familiar story that had already been played out all across the South in the decades surrounding the turn of the century. It had been just another episode in an on-going tale of exploitation and abandonment, and it left behind little of the illusive prosperity of the mythical New South for the residents of White County to enjoy.

LUMPKIN COUNTY: DAHLONEGA

The Lumpkin County Courthouse at Dahlonega, built in 1836. (See Plate 2 in the Introduction)

In 1828, the discovery of gold in the wild mountain country of north Georgia added urgency to an already ugly dispute between the Cherokee Indians and the state of Georgia. Despite the fact that the State had no legal claim to the vast tract then known as "The Cherokee Nation," settlers began to pour into the region in search of El Dorado. A period of land grabbing ensued, and despite the fact that Federal authorities strongly opposed the settlement of Cherokee land, the state of Georgia proceeded to annex all of north Georgia. Long before a treaty

was signed in 1835 and the Cherokee were packed away to Oklahoma in 1838, the state legislature had created the enormous Cherokee County, held a Land Lottery to distribute its lands, chartered the Western and Atlantic Railroad to run through the middle of the area, and divided the vast tract into ten new counties. One of these was Lumpkin County.

Plate 30.2: According to county records, the original plan for the White County Courthouse called for columns, probably in the Greek mode, but these were omitted in the revised plan of 1859. (Photo: Wilber W. Caldwell.)

In Lumpkin County, the extraordinarily rapid growth of towns like Auraria and Dahlonega attests to the intensity of Georgia's "gold rush." In the summer of 1832, two cabins were built at the future site of the city of Auraria in Lumpkin County. By November of that year, the village had a population of 500 according to Lumpkin County historian Andrew Cain.[2] *Nile's Register*, published in Baltimore in May of 1833, offers a description of this boom town less than a year after its founding, listing over 100 dwellings, eighteen or twenty stores, twelve or fifteens lawyers, and a population of around

---

[1] Grant Keene, "White County Courthouse," *North Georgia Journal of History* 1/1 (Fall 1984).

[2] Andrew W. Cain, *History of Lumpkin County for the first One Hundred Years, 1832-1932* (Atlanta: Stein Printing Company, 1932) 42.

[3] *Nile's Register*, May 4, 1833 in Cain, *History of Lumpkin County for the first One Hundred Years, 1832-1932*, 43.

1000.[3] The more centrally located village of Dahlonega was settled at about the same time. Following an early dispute over the legality of the title to property in and around Auraria, Dahlonega became the county seat and a temporary log courthouse was built there in 1832. By 1836, when this fine brick court building was completed, Dahlonega's fate as the principle city of the area was firmly rooted. In 1835, the United States Mint established one of its three new branch mints at Dahlonega (the others were at Charlotte and New Orleans). By 1849, George White describes Dahlonega as a town of about 1000 residents, but gives no details regarding Aururia. The old mint building was to remain for many years the largest building in north Georgia. It continued to operate until the outbreak of war in 1861, and ten years later, the building was sold to North Georgia Agricultural College. It burned in 1879 and was replaced by Parkins and Bruce's stunning design, the first and perhaps the finest picturesque building in north Georgia. The elegant structure stands today as one of the state's best examples of Alexander Bruce's early work.

Just as the walls of Parkins and Bruce's new college building began to rise, Dahlonega began to stir with aspirations created by the charter of the Dahlonega Air Line. By this time, Lumpkin County residents were no strangers to railroad speculation. The Gainesville and Dahlonega Railroad had been chartered back in 1866, but after much agitation, the line failed to progress. The Dahlonega Air Line may have been a revival of that earlier scheme. Whatever the case, local papers of the era continued to refer to the "Gainesville and Dahlonega" railroad. Several surveys were completed, and the depot site at Dahlonega was selected. There followed considerable controversy over the route of the new line. At one point, it appears that a branch to Auraria was planned, and later the main line seems to have been bound for Auraria with a branch to Dahlonega.[4] Portions of this railroad were graded, and it appears that 15 miles of track was laid from Gainesville to a point near the Chestatee River. This was abandoned in 1893 when the company was sold.[5] In the meantime, the 1889 charter of the Marietta and Dahlonega Railroad had stirred hope. Sadly, this line, too, came to nothing. Even as late as 1903 brief hopes for the old Gainesville and Dahlonega scheme were rekindled by an ill-fated plan put forward by the Gainesville and Dahlonega Electric Railroad Company.[6]

Through it all, Dahlonega remained unconnected, and the old courthouse would serve Lumpkin County until 1965 when it was refurbished for use as a museum. Meanwhile, population figures in Dahlonega offer striking testament to the exodus that was occurring all across north Georgia in the first decades of the new century. In 1900, revived interest in gold mining by large commercial mining firms put Dahlonega's population at 1255 residents. By 1910, this number was down to 829.

TOWNS COUNTY: HIAWASSEE

Plate 30.3: The Towns County Courthouse, built in 1899. Demolished in 1963.

Towns County was cut from Union County in 1856, and the county seat was laid out at a place then called Watson's Crossroads and later renamed Hiawassee. A "temporary" log courthouse was erected in 1857. A more substantial wooden court building probably replaced the first structure, but the record here is unclear. Whatever the case, by the end of the nineteenth century, the old courthouse was declared unsafe, and the grand jury recommended a brick structure. In 1899, this rather Spartan brick building rose at Hiawassee. Although in May of 1899 *Bricklayer and Mason* informed its readers that

---

[4] Olin Jackson and Michael A. Miller, "Early Railroads in Lumpkin and Dawson Counties," *A North Georgia Journal of History 1* (1989): 48-52.

[5] Hugh M. Comer, "Railroad Abandonments in Georgia" (masters thesis, Macon, 1985) 89.

[6] *The Atlanta Constitution*, October 15, 1903.

Towns County leaders had selected a design by Atlanta architects, Golucke and Stewart, this building is unlike any of James Golucke's grand creations of that period. It is more likely that Golucke and Stewart simply submitted plans for a new courthouse at Hiawassee, and that their design was not used.

There is little in this simple vernacular building to suggest the work of a professional architect. Conversely, there is much to suggest the design of an unsophisticated local builder. The basic form of the building recalls scores of earlier vernacular court buildings characterized by the ubiquitous rectangular brick two-story box with its familiar hipped roof. The exterior walls carry no decoration save the bold pilasters that divide each elevation into vertical bays. The building's only ornament is found in the paired brackets that support the eaves. This detail was typical of vernacular court buildings erected in Georgia in the 1850s and had not been seen in the state since the 1870s. On the brink of the modern era, it seems highly unlikely that any professional architect would have created a design so unmistakably out of date.

According to Sholes's *Gazetteer of Georgia*, Hiawassee was a village of about 300 residents in 1896. Isolated deep in the high mountains of north Georgia it is doubtful that much of the optimism attached to the myth of the New South had made its way up through the high passes to Towns County. Appropriately, this courthouse reflected no high hopes and little exuberance. It is noteworthy, however, that less than ten years before this courthouse was begun, the North Carolina and Western Railroad had been completed through Hayesville, North Carolina, only 15 miles to the north of Hiawassee, on its way to Murphy, North Carolina. All of this notwithstanding, it was a treacherous 15 miles to Hayesville in 1899, and Hiawassee would remain in a state of virtual isolation for decades to come.

Plate 30.3: In 1899, this rather Spartan brick building rose at Hiawassee after the old wooden Towns County courthouse was declared unsafe. (Photo: Courtesy of Ted Brooke.)

The 1899, Towns County Courthouse was the last brick vernacular court building to be erected in Georgia. It was demolished in 1963.

FORSYTH COUNTY: CUMMING

Plate 30.4: The Forsyth County Courthouse built in 1905. Burned in 1973. James W. Golucke, architect.

Plate 30.4: Despite the original Romanesque design, by the time the 1905 Forsyth County Courthouse rose at Cumming a generous helping of classical ornament had crept in. (Photo: Courtesy of Ted Brooke.)

For the most part, the railroads had failed to penetrate the mountain country of north central Georgia. Although six mountain counties would remain unconnected by rail, two of these erected stylish new court buildings just after the turn of the century. Union County began construction of a grand new courthouse in 1900, and Forsyth County followed in 1905. Both erected Romanesque designs by Atlanta architect, James W. Golucke.

When Forsyth County was created from Cherokee County in 1832, a log courthouse was erected at Cumming. In 1839, a frame building replaced the original structure. It was removed from the square in 1854 to make way for a brick court building patterned after the 1836 Lumpkin County Courthouse at Dahlonega. By 1900, Cumming was a comfortable village of about 250 residents. Notwithstanding the pervasive poverty that prolonged the region's frontier individualism and nurtured a deep-rooted conservatism, and despite the absence of a rail connection, in December of 1904 county leaders in Forsyth accepted Golucke's design for a Romanesque courthouse at Cumming.

By the turn of the century, the Romanesque Revival had died a sudden death in the American North, but the style lingered in the Deep South. Here an impoverished rural population had been slow to embrace the flamboyant ornamental excesses of the new American classicism. Elsewhere, the lavish Beaux-Arts finery of the so-called "American Renaissance" flaunted the young nation's grasping ambitions for financial and industrial progress. Not only did this kind of symbolism have little relevance in the hills of north Georgia, such concepts were repugnant to many. Thus, it is not surprising that county leaders in Union and Forsyth Counties took a backward glance in fashioning their own personal architectural symbols for the future. As we have seen, a nostalgic focus dominated at least one side of the Southern mind, and Romantic notions lingered here well into the twentieth century, despite the growing national trend toward critical realism. In this regard, Golucke's Romanesque designs were ideal. They not only offered a look back at the picturesque era in American architecture, they harkened all the way back to the architecture of an agrarian and feudal Europe in a much-romanticized age of chivalry.

James Golucke's 1905 Forsyth County Courthouse at Cumming was originally planned to mirror the architect's earlier Richardsonian Romanesque work in Henry (1897) and Union (1900) Counties. In November of 1904, *The Forsyth County North Georgian* published Golucke's rending of the proposed building that appears identical to these earlier designs.[7] However, by the time the corner stone was laid in June of 1905, the plan had been considerably altered. Some of these alterations came as county officials sought to rein in the budget for the new building. It appears Golucke seized this opportunity to add "modern" touches to his creation and a generous helping of classical ornament crept in. The basic design reflected Golucke's preferred Romanesque massing; a slender central tower flanked by corner pavilions with low pyramidal roofs. But overlaid classical decoration abounded. Arched hoodmolds appeared above the second story windows. The clock tower was completely transformed into a neoclassical affair reminiscent of Golucke's 1902 Tattnall County Courthouse at Reidsville and the traditional lantern was crowned with a low, distinctly Beaux-Arts dome.

The result fell short of Golucke's stunning neoclassical court buildings that were rising at Newnan and Eatonton. At the same time, it failed to evoke the simple power that flowed from the architect's more purely Romanesque designs that were going up at Blairsville and Gray. Here was a last gasp of the free eclecticism of the earlier age, an attempt to cloak a massive ancient form in flowery ornament. Golucke's Forsyth County Courthouse at Cumming attempted to pay tribute to both old and new styles. Sadly, it failed to dignify either. Nonetheless, it was a grand symbol for the citizens of Cumming, and a notable structure for its day, for it rose in an atmosphere untainted by the far-fetched railroad-imported visions of prosperity that inspired so many court buildings of the era.

Forsyth County's choice of James Golucke in late 1904 is illustrative of the prolific power and popularity of this architect at the height of his productivity. In his brief career, James Golucke designed twenty-six courthouses in Georgia (see Appendix C). Until it burned in 1973, James Golucke's 1905 Forsyth County Courthouse at Cumming stood as one of the few exceptions to prove the rule that insists that, in the years surrounding the turn of the century, grand courthouses were inspired by the railroad-imported hope. It is interesting to note that two of these rare exceptions were in the mountains, where the modern hopes carried by the railroads never arrived and the frontier spirit of the early nineteenth century remained robust despite the modern notions that were infecting the rest of the state.

UNION COUNTY: BLAIRSVILLE

Plate 30.5: The Union County Courthouse built in 1900. James W. Golucke, architect.

High up in the north Georgia mountains at the tiny village of Blairsville, a brick vernacular courthouse replaced Union County's original log court building in 1859. Patterned after the White County Courthouse at Cleveland that was under construction in that same year, the sturdy brick building burned to the ground in 1899. Out of its ashes, James Wingfield Golucke's stunning Union County Courthouse rose in 1900.

In 1900, Blairsville was a village of only 141 residents, and Union County was effectively sealed off from the emerging modern world by the highest mountains in Georgia. The nearest railroad was the North Carolina and Western, which ran through Culberson, North Carolina, 15 difficult miles to the north. This was not a

Plate 30.5: As this 1950s photograph clearly reveals, the tower of James Golucke's 1900 Union County Courthouse at Blairsville developed a disturbing lean. (Photo: Courtesy of Ted Brooke.)

place for dreams of industrial revolution or for the budding mythology of New South prosperity. Yet inexplicably, Golucke's flamboyant symbol for progress rose here in 1900.

We know little of the details surrounding the construction of this building, but it is clear that the project was far from unilaterally popular in Union County. Local historians recount an emotional political battle involving a movement to relocate the county seat to a place then known as Bunker Hill. This was followed by a fierce battle over the site of the new building in Blairsville, a lawsuit that sought an injunction to halt construction and the refusal of Union County voters to approve a bond issue to fund the new building. Despite such opposition, county leaders pressed ahead with construction, funding the building by direct tax, which reportedly sorely burdened many of the taxpayers of Union County. [8]

Although none of this is the stuff of the New South myth, James Golucke's 1900 Union County Courthouse is not without its lofty symbolism. By 1900, the Romanesque Revival was

[7] *The North Georgian*, November 30, 1904.

[8] C. R. Collin and Jan H. Devereaux, *Sketches of Union County* (Blairsville GA: Union County Historical Society, 1974) 22.

long dead in the North. However, in the Deep South, it continued to carry its duel symbols well into the new century. Here was both the modern force of the monumental Romanesque buildings in the American North and a uniquely Southern look backwards not only to the earlier American era, but also to Europe and her medieval age of Chivalry and Romance so soothing to the festering Southern psyche.

Testifying to the style's lingering polarity, Golucke designed five Romanesque courthouses in Georgia from almost identical plans. The first of these was his stunning 1897 Henry County Courthouse at McDonough. This success was followed by the court buildings in Schley County at Ellaville and by this building at Blairsville, both completed in 1900. Two subsequent courthouses rose using the same general plan: the 1905 Jones County Courthouse at Gray and the 1907 Baker County Courthouse at Newton. Except for details in the towers, trim and fenestration, these buildings are identical. Interestingly, only this building at Blairsville and its predecessor at McDonough, were detailed with the bold granite banding and heavy stone voussoirs so typical of the work of the American master, Henry Hobson Richardson, whose influence here can not be overstated. The other three of Golucke's Richardsonian court buildings were erected using brick trim and thus lack the dramatic contrast and the ancient aura created at McDonough and here at Blairsville.

As this 1950s photograph clearly reveals, Golucke's engineering of the supports for the tower was suspect here at Blairsville. As we have seen, many of the architect's towers have not stood the test of time. The central towers have been condemned and removed from Golucke's twin courthouses at Zebulon and at Wrightsville, and from his 1907 courthouse at Newton. Like its sister at Ellaville, Golucke's tower here at Blairsville developed a disturbing lean. It was condemned and removed in 1959, and the entire building was declared unsafe in 1971. Happily,

the Union County Courthouse is presently undergoing extensive renovation.

SOME LAST THOUGHTS ON THE MOUNTAINS OF NORTH CENTRAL GEORGIA

By the early 1880s, the mills at Augusta and Columbus were producing a great deal more than coarse cotton cloth. A comprehensive New South mythology was being spun, and the new dogma was tailor-made to soothe the South's festering wounds. It promised the prosperity of the industrial age, while at the same time it sought to wrap itself in the romantic mythology of the Lost Cause and the cherished social fabric of the past. The prospect of a New South inspired visions of battlements of modern industry and diversified agriculture rising to protect archaic institutions. Just as the mills at Augusta and Columbus inspired faith in the possibility of a New South, the railroads emanating from Atlanta and Macon supplied the messengers for the new creed. Wherever the shining new rails went, they delivered gleaming new promises. All across Georgia, the old antebellum vernacular courthouses were coming down to make way for symbols of the promises of the New South.

It is not surprising then, that the few places in Georgia where we still find brick vernacular court buildings are places that were either untouched by rail or places that mounted strong Populist opposition to the railroads. The best example of this is in the mountains of north central Georgia. Here six counties remained untouched by rail before 1910. At Dawsonville, Cleveland and Dahlonega we find three of the best standing examples of antebellum brick vernacular court buildings in the state. All three buildings would serve well into the twentieth century, while at Hiawassee, the last of the brick vernacular courthouses to be built in Georgia rose in 1899.

In the high mountains, the last bastions of frontier individualism were seldom breached by the myths of either the Old or New South. Here before the war there had been few slaves and little cotton, and here after the war the railroads had failed to deliver the promises of the new era. Ironically, around the turn of the century, when the myths of the new order finally began to find their way up into the hills, late Romanesque Revival court buildings were erected at Cumming and at Blairsville. By this time, the Romanesque Revival was long dead in the American North, and these architectural anachronisms rose in the midst of a great exodus down out of the mountains to the sprawling mill villages that were beginning to cover the Piedmont.

•

The Georgia and Florida Railway

Richmond County: Augusta (see chapter 1) • Emanuel County: Swainsboro (see chapter 27)
Jeff Davis County: Hazlehurst (see chapter 9) • Coffee County: Douglas (see chapter 32)
Berrien County: Nashville • Irwin County: Ocilla • Lowndes County: Valdosta (see chapter 7)
Some Last Thoughts on the Georgia and Florida Railway

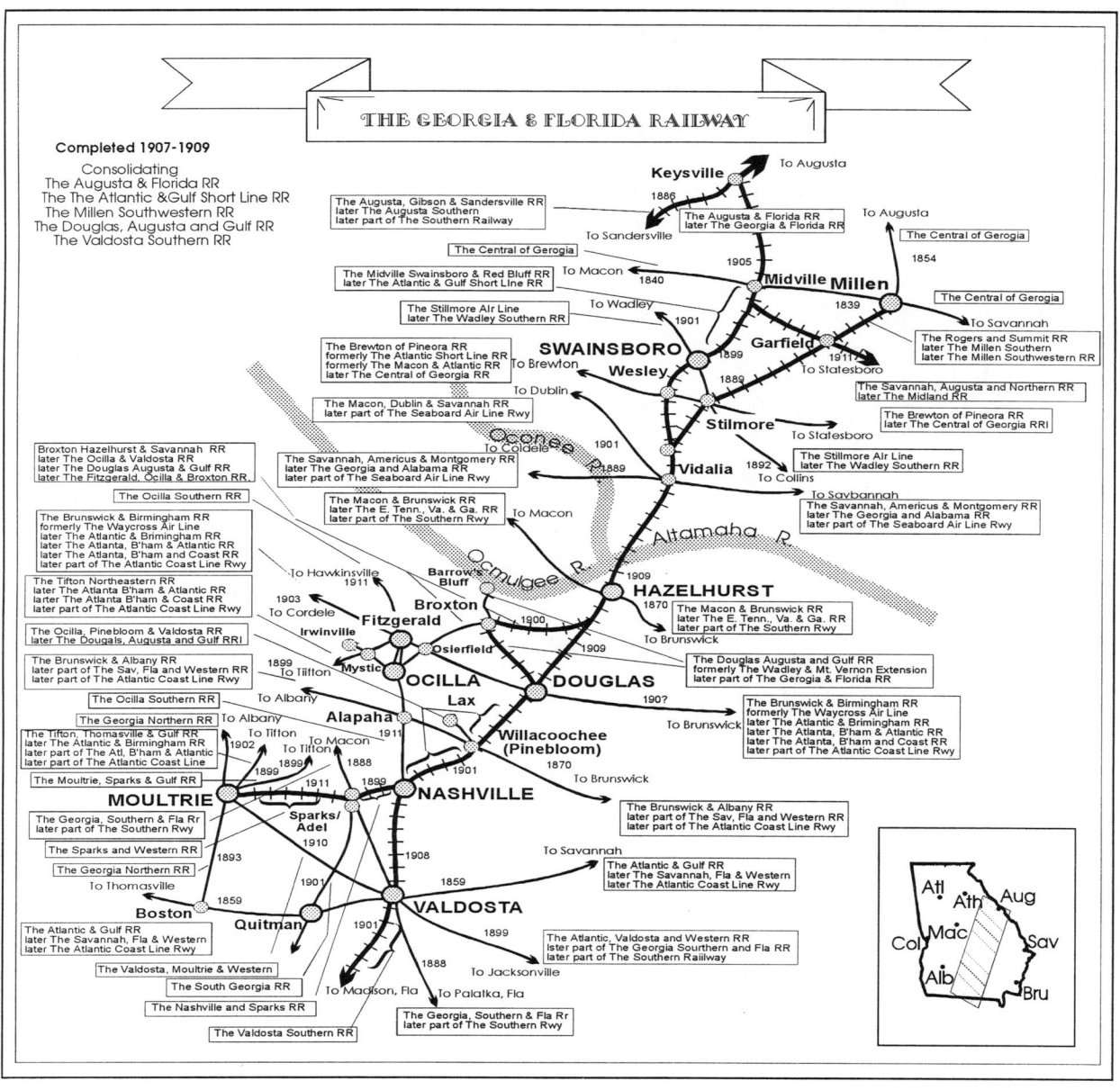

31 | The Georgia and Florida Railway

BERRIEN COUNTY: NASHVILLE

Plate 31.1: The Berrien County Courthouse, built in 1898. Walter Chamberlain, architect.

Berrien County's first courthouse was begun in 1856, the same year the county was created from Irwin, Coffee and Lowndes Counties. In 1898, the old two-story frame building was moved to the corner of the square, and plans for a new brick courthouse were presented to the Berrien County Commissioners. *The Tifton Gazette* described, "a handsome and tasty building, in the latest style of the builder's art."[1] This local perception of what constituted "the latest style" clearly reveals just how far the rural South stood from the American architectural mainstream at the turn of the century.

In 1898, this courthouse, designed by Walter Chamberlain of Knoxville, Tennessee, not only recalls the Romanesque Revival, which had died a rather sudden death in the North five years earlier, but also reflects vernacular masonry decorations typical of the many simple builder-designed brick commercial buildings. Such buildings were beginning to line the streets of so many South Georgia railroad boomtowns around 1900. Walter Chamberlain's six court buildings in Georgia (see Appendix C) include two other Romanesque designs. One of these, the 1894 Macon County Courthouse at Oglethorpe, is virtually identical to this courthouse at Nashville. Chamberlain used this design in other courthouses as well, notably in his 1897 Crenshaw County Courthouse at Luverne, Alabama, and his 1899 Gibson County Courthouse at Trenton, Tennessee.

Despite the dated architectural vocabulary, the building was not totally without modern tone. A trendy national return to architectural symmetry is clear here, and the details of the unusual tower hint at the Neoclassical Revival, which, at the turn of the century, was taking the American North by storm. Notwithstanding these crude attempts at trendy details, this

---

[1] *The Tifton Gazette*, March 25, 1898.

Plate 31.1: The 1898 Berrien County Courthouse at Nashville was considered up-to-date in the South in 1900, and it further documents the on-going stylistic architectural lag that had characterized Southern building since before the Civil War. (Photo: Wilber W. Caldwell)

building documents the on-going stylistic architectural lag that had characterized Southern building from before the Civil War.

Despite its retardate design, the 1898 Berrien County Courthouse stood for powerful illusions of progress in the piney woods. As the nineteenth century ended in south central Georgia, "King Timber" was in full swing. By 1898, the enormous expanses of Berrien County were being covered with a tangle of logging tram roads. There can be little doubt that this courthouse was built on the foundations of economic zeal created by these railroads. In October of 1899, *The Tifton Gazette* reported that six new lines had been chartered in Berrien, and that if all were built, nine railroads would traverse the county. Of course, all these lines were not built, but one of these, the Nashville and Sparks Railroad, arrived in Nashville just as the last bricks of Nashville's new court building were put into place. The 13 rickety miles of the Nashville and Sparks represented the end of Nashville's long quest to obtain a rail connection to the Georgia Southern and Florida Railroad's main line.

While Nashville struggled to build this spur, neighboring towns in Berrien County were teeming with the power of timber and rail. Tifton had grown from a dusty sawmill in 1872 to a city of 1300 by

1900. As the new courthouse rose at Nashville, Tifton erected a grand Union Depot to serve her five railroads. Farther South, the combined twin towns of Adel and Sparks, which had been laid out beside the Georgia Southern and Florida Railroad in 1888, boasted crossing rails and over 1400 residents by the turn of the century. Even the remote village of Milltown, which would later be called Lakeland, would boast 1200 residents by 1910. All the while, tiny Nashville languished, her population below 300 as the new century dawned. By 1910, Tifton and Adel were towns of about 2000 residents, and in that year, *The Nashville Herald* reported that there were ten banks in Berrien County, two each at Nashville, Sparks, Adel, and Milltown and one each at Alapaha and Lenox.[2]

The great railroad and timber boom in south central Georgia around Berrien and Irwin Counties would later result in the creation of six new counties.[3] In the years after 1905, courthouses would be built at Tifton, Ashburn and Fitzgerald, and by the 1920s, new courthouses would rise at Pearson, Adel and Lakeland. With all of this progress on the wind, it is perhaps fitting that here in Nashville, the old 1898 Berrien County Courthouse still stands, to echo a late gasp of the Romanesque Revival in America. When this building was new, it must have appeared that the New South myth was coming true in Berrien County. But as the new century unfolded, "King Timber" was dying, and his successor; "King Cotton" would soon prove a ruthless monarch.

Plate 31.2: The depot at Alapaha.

The fine detail of this simple depot at Alapaha on the old Brunswick and Albany Railroad is all that remains today in Berrien to remind us of the web of rail that once covered the county. In 1907, John Skeleton Williams, whose brilliance had been behind the success of the Seaboard Air Line in 1901, had purchased four short line railroads between Augusta and Madison, Florida. The next year, he began to build short links of new track to connect these acquisitions (see Table 31.1). The result was the Georgia and Florida Railway.

One of Williams's four acquisitions was the Douglas, Augusta and Gulf, which had been chartered to consolidate lines between Hazlehurst and Valdosta. From its very beginnings, this line had had been the tool of the Georgia and Florida Railway. In the middle of the first decade of the new century, the Douglas, Augusta and Gulf acquired the Ocilla, Pinebloom and Valdosta, the Ocilla, Broxton and Hazlehurst, and the Ocilla and Valdosta Railroads. In 1907, the Georgia and Florida Railway purchased the Douglas, Augusta and Gulf, and by 1910, 28 miles of new track had been laid between Nashville and Valdosta thus completing Williams's dream of a line all the way from Augusta to Madison, Florida. Meanwhile, the Georgia and Florida had had leased the Nashville and Sparks Railroad in 1906. Williams later acquired the Sparks and Western Railroad and completed a branch from Nashville to Moultrie in 1911.

But as the great huffing locomotives of the Georgia and Florida Railway steamed into Moultrie, William's dreams were beginning to unravel. By 1913, the Georgia and Florida was in the hands of receiver. Despite his clever manipulation of so many failing lumber roads in the era when the last of Georgia's great pine forests were disappearing, the fact remained that John Skelton William's new railroad served some of the most sparsely populated areas in the state. Although it brought new life and a late glimmer of the New South myth to places like Nashville, the Georgia and Florida Railway was doomed to failure almost before it began.

Walter Chamberlain's Berrien County Courthouse had been completed just as the first train arrived in Nashville on the Nashville and Sparks Railroad. It would preside over a brief period of economic vigor punctuated by the arrival of the Georgia and Florida and the Ocilla Southern Railroads. But the perceived progress symbolized by Chamberlain's grand new courthouse proved largely mythical. By the early 1920s, the Ocilla Southern was failing fast, and the doomed company abandoned its track from Nashville to Fitzgerald in 1924. Throughout the new century, the Georgia and Florida remained a ne'er-do-well railroad struggling from bankruptcy to bankruptcy. Just as John Skelton Williams's ragtag rail-

Plate 31.2: The fine detail of this simple depot at Alapaha on the old Brunswick and Albany Railroad is all that remains in Berrien to remind us of the web of rail that once covered the county. (Photo: Wilber W. Caldwell.)

PARTS OF THE GEORGIA AND FLORIDA RAILWAY	Table 31.1

Trackage leased from the Augusta Southern from Augusta to Keysville.

Purchase of the Augusta and Florida Railroad, 1907, Keysville to Midville

Purchase of the Atlantic & Gulf Short Line Railroad, 1907, (formerly the Midville, Swainsboro and Red Bluff Railroad), Midville to Swainsboro.

Georgia and Florida Railway new track c.1908, Swainsboro to Millen Jct.

Purchase of the Millen Southwestern Railroad, 1907, Millen Jct. to Vidalia.

Georgia and Florida Railway new track c.1908, Vidalia to Hazlehurst.

Purchase of the Douglas, Augusta and Gulf Railroad, 1907 including part of the Ocilla and Valdosta Railroad, Broxton to Hazlehurst (formerly the Broxton, Hazlehurst and Savannah Railroad), and the Ocilla, Pinebloom and Valdosta Railroad, Nashville to near Douglas

Georgia and Florida Railway new track c.1908, Nashville to Valdosta.

Purchase of the Valdosta Southern Railroad, 1907, Valdosta to Madison, Florida.

[2] *The Nashville Herald*, October 14, 1910.

[3] In 1905, Tift and Turner Counties were created, followed by Ben Hill (1906), Atkinson (1917), Cook (1919), and Lanier (1920).

road had been put together piece-meal, it would be dismantled in a like manner. The last train on the Nashville and Sparks Railroad ran in 1967 and by 1983 almost all of the old Georgia and Florida Railway between Hazlehurst and Nashville had been pulled up for scrap.

IRWIN COUNTY: OCILLA

Plate 31.3: The Irwin County Courthouse at Ocilla, built in 1909. H. L. Lewman, architect.

In the early 1830s, the famous Coffee Road was built from the south bank of the "Big Bend" of the Ocmulgee River across the empty expanses of the Wiregrass to Lowndes County. Over seventy years later, this ancient trail would mark much of the route of John Skelton William's Georgia and Florida Railway. The Coffee Road passed through the heart that section of the piney woods known as Irwin County. Surveyed in 1818 on lands ceded to the State of Georgia by the Creek Indians, the county first held court in private homes near the Ocmulgee River on her northern boundary. It was not until 1830 that the village of Irwinville was laid out and a crude wooden courthouse of "rough hewn timber" was erected.[4] This building was replaced by a larger wooden building in 1854. In 1883, a large frame courthouse rose at Irwinville. All the while, the great expanses of Irwin

Plate 31.3: Fresh from her victory over Irwinville, Ocilla surged forward on dreams of New South prosperity symbolized by H. L. Lewman's 1909 Irwin County Courthouse. (Photo: Wilber W. Caldwell.)

County were dwindling. Eventually Irwin would contribute lands for the creation of all or part of twenty-one new counties.

As late as 1897, the old county seat of Irwinville, contained little more than a courthouse, a hotel, a few stores and a handful of dwellings.[5] In that year, the upstart boomtown of Fitzgerald mustered her first attempt to capture the Irwin County seat away from the hapless village of Irwinville. A remarkable success story laid out in 1895 as a "colony" for Union Soldiers, Fitzgerald had blossomed almost overnight into a city of several thousand in the northern part of old Irwin County. Although in many ways Fitzgerald represented a tangible manifestation of the New South myth, in the eyes of many native Georgians, this elaborate "Yankee" development appeared tainted by the stain of "Carpetbaggers." Not surprisingly and despite several attempts, the so-called "Magic City" failed to steal the courthouse away from tiny Irwinville. Meanwhile, just to the south of Fitzgerald, the town of Ocilla, which had consisted of little more than a turpentine still, a saw mill and a store in 1895, was also on a boom as the new century dawned. Ocilla's population reached 800 in 1900, and by 1910, the village was a city of over 2000.

The first train had steamed into Ocilla in 1897. Two years earlier, the railroad visionary, John Skelton Williams, had acquired the old Savannah, Americus and Montgomery Railroad and reorganized the failed line as the Georgia and Alabama Railroad. At about the same time, Williams purchased a branch line from Abbeville to Lulaville known as the Abbeville and Waycross Railroad, and in 1896-1897, he extended this spur via Fitzgerald to Ocilla. These were among the first in a series of acquisitions that were to produce Williams's mighty Seaboard Air Line Railway

By 1907, when John Skelton Williams began to assemble the pieces of his Georgia and Florida Railway (see Table 31.1), the map of south-central Georgia below the "Big Bend" in the Ocmulgee River had been radically altered. Not only had a web of rail traced its way across the face of the land, creating boom towns at Tifton, Fitzgerald, Ashburn, Douglas and Ocilla, but in 1905 and 1906 three new counties had been carved from Irwin's once vast expanses. After the loss of vast tracts to the upstarts, Turner, Tift and Ben Hill Counties, the once central county town of Irwinville suddenly found itself located on the Irwin's western edge. The time was ripe for Ocilla to make her bid for the county seat. The battle raged throughout out the year 1907, each side claiming election irregularities and fraud. In the end, Ocilla won the day when the Supreme Court of Georgia finally decided in her favor.[6]

Fresh from her victory over Irwinville, Ocilla surged forward on New South dreams of impending prosperity. Meanwhile, great railroad consolidations were creating the Georgia and Florida Railway and the Atlanta, Birmingham and Atlantic Railroad, but neither line would pass through Ocilla. Nonetheless, the growing town was not without a tangle of track to import wild visions of a bright economic future. The Seaboard Air Line connected Ocilla with the main line of the Atlanta, Birmingham and Atlantic at Fitzgerald, and the Fitzgerald, Ocilla and Broxton connected to the ABA's Tifton / Thomasville branch at Mystic. As plans for a new courthouse were drawn, the first rumblings were heard concerning the construction of the Ocilla Southern Railroad, which would soon connect Ocilla with Nashville to the South and with Hawkinsville and Perry to the North.[7] In an orgy of urban zeal, there was even talk of a street railway from Ocilla to Fitzgerald.[8] Only a few months before the contract for the construction of H. L. Lewman's grand Irwin County Courthouse was let, a proposal was on the table for the creation of the Ocilla Cotton Mill.[9] Amid such clamor, there can be little doubt that in 1909, the myth of the New South had won many converts in the streets of Ocilla.

As usual, the arrival of the New South myth demanded a grand architectural symbol. In 1909, the county commissioners of Irwin County did not have to look far to find a model. Just a year before, the Falls City Construction Company of Louisville, Kentucky had completed H. L. Lewman's Appling County Courthouse at Baxley, a building which was to become the toast of the Wiregrass. As we have seen, this court building was much copied in Georgia in the closing years of the first decade of the new century. County leaders at Toccoa in the newly created Stephens

County and at Summerville in Chattooga County had selected plans similar to Lewman's Appling County Courthouse. In May of 1909, the Irwin County Commissioners expressed their admiration for Lewman's building at Baxley; by early July plans had been drawn and approved and in July, Fall City Construction had been awarded the contract to build a building similar to Lewman's courthouse in Appling County. [10]

Irwin County records name Falls City Construction as the architect of the 1909 courthouse at Ocilla. There is no specific mention of H. L. Lewman, but along with his two brothers, Lewman was a principle of that company, and he is specifically credited with the 1907 design for the courthouse at Baxley. Thus, is almost certain that he prepared the plans for the Falls City Construction Company here at Ocilla. To be sure, the two buildings were derived from the same basic plan, and accordingly, it is easier to recount their differences that it is their similarities. The most notable difference is that Lewman's courthouse at Baxley was constructed entirely of limestone, while at Ocilla his plan called for brownish "No. 1 Washington hydraulic pressed brick," with limestone trim.[11] At Ocilla, Lewman's courthouse stands on a spacious square, while his building at Baxley rests on a corner lot. Thus all four entrances at Ocilla are framed by classical porticos vaguely reflecting the Composite Order. At Baxley only the front entrance flaunts such columns. Another notable difference is the presence of the half basement at Ocilla. This device, although constructed of drab concrete, lifts the building and allows it to project a more monumental silhouette than Lewman's court building at Baxley. There are also

[4] James B. Clements, *The History of Irwin County* (Atlanta: Foote and Davies, 1930) 435.

[5] An 1896 address by Dr. Jay Shrader, "The New Caanan, Fitzgerald and the Old Soldiers' Colony" (Fitzgerald: n.p., 1971) 52.

[6] *The Ocilla Star*, January 31, 1908.

[7] *The Ocilla Star*, March 21, 1909.

[8] *The Ocilla Star*, February 5, 1909.

[9] *The Ocilla Star*, January 29, 1909

[10] *The Ocilla Star*, May 21, June 11 and July 9, 1909.

[11] *The Ocilla Star*, June 6, 1909.

minor differences of ornament like the fenestration in cupola. But generally these buildings are sisters, and their message is the same: a modern lust for the New South prosperity promised by the railroads and a simultaneous and seemingly contradictory desire to return to the Romantic gentility of a similarly mythical and equally unreachable past.

SOME LAST THOUGHTS OF THE GEORGIA AND FLORIDA RAILWAY

The Georgia and Florida Railway was the brainchild of John Skelton Williams, who had masterminded the enormously successful railroad acquisitions and consolidations of the Seaboard Air Line in 1901. Forced out as president of the Seaboard in 1903, Williams began work on a second grand railroad consolidation.

In one sense, the time was right for such a venture. The central part of the state was a tangle of short lines and logging roads, all constructed around the turn of the century to exploit the state's vast stands of virgin timber crop. By 1906, when Williams began to create the Georgia and Florida Railway, the great forests were quickly disappearing, and miles of rail languished, rusting amid the sea of stumps that had once been Georgia's deep piney woods. Between 1906 and 1910, Williams fashioned his new line from Augusta all the way to Madison, Florida. Buying up four struggling railroads, two of which were already consolidations in their own right, Williams completed his line by linking these unconnected pieces.

Table 31.2	BRANCH LINES OF THE GEORGIA & FLORIDA RAILWAY

The Augusta Southern Railroad RR, acquired in 1917, abandoned 1934.

The Millen Southwestern Railroad, acquired in 1906, abandoned in 1929.

The Nashville and Sparks Railroad and the Sparks and Western Railroad acquired in 1911, abandoned in 1967.

Various branches of the Douglas, Augusta and Gulf Railroad including lines to Broxton and Barrows Bluff, acquired in 1906, abandoned piece-meal beginning around 1920.

The Statesboro and Northern, acquired in 1924, abandoned in 1950.

Miraculously, he was able to do this by building new links totaling only about 80 miles of track (see Table 31.1).

Unfortunately, the situation, which made the purchase of Williams's string of short line railroads financially feasible in the first place was also contributed to the Georgia and Florida's lack of success. The sad fact was that the rails Williams had purchased meandered through some of the wildest county in Georgia. Although the Georgia and Florida Railway spawned countless new towns, and added vigor to the economies of Swainsboro, Vidalia, Hazlehurst, Douglas, and even tiny Nashville, these were hardly urban population centers in 1910, and by 1913 the Georgia and Florida was in the hands of a receiver. The ne'er-do-well company would limp along through most of the twentieth century. In a long series of reorganizations and the acquisitions, the company acquired and later abandoned numerous branches (see Table 31.2). The failing line was finally absorbed by the Southern Railway in 1983, and large portions of the main line were scrapped.

Despite the fact that from it's very beginning the Georgia and Florida Railway had teetered on unsure financial footings, the record of courthouse building along its main line offers strong evidence that, even as late as the first decade of the new century, ne'er-do-well railroads could still deliver generous helpings of New South mythology to the county towns along their rights-of-way. Most notable in this regard are Andrew J Bryan's 1900 Coffee County Courthouse, which rose only four years after the steel rails reached Douglas in 1896 and Walter Chamberlain's 1898 Berrien County Courthouse, which was completed just as the first train arrived in Nashville on the Nashville and Sparks Railroad. Likewise, Ocilla boomed after the 1897 arrival of the Georgia and Alabama Railroad's (later the Seaboard Air Line Railway) spur from Abbeville via Fitzgerald. Ten years later Ocilla would wage a battle to capture the Irwin County seat from tiny Irwinville, and H. L. Lewman's Irwin County Courthouse rose at Ocilla in 1909.

By 1906, when John Skelton Williams began the acquisitions and consolidations that would become the Georgia and Florida Railway, two new counties had already been created along the route of his new main trunk. Toombs County had emerged, sweeping up the booming town of Vidalia on its coattails, and farther south, Jeff Davis County voiced its aspirations with the erection of Walter Chamberlain's 1906 courthouse at Hazlehurst. Finally, there can be little doubt that the Georgia and Florida Railroad's acquisition of its branch from Nashville to Moultrie in 1911 added considerable fuel to the fires of the new county movement that burned at Sparks and Adel and that resulted in the creation of Cook County in 1919.

•

The Atlanta, Birmingham and Atlantic Railroad

Glynn County: Brunswick (see chapter 9) • Bacon County: Alma
Coffee County: Douglas • Ben Hill County: Fitzgerald • Colquitt County: Moultrie
Crisp County: Cordele (see chapter 23) • Dooly County: Vienna (see chapter 21)
Macon County: Oglethorpe (see chapter 6) • Talbot County: Talbotton
Troup County: LaGrange (see chapter 4)

ATLANTA BRANCH

Fulton County: Atlanta (Part 4, also see chapters 4, 11 & 26)
Some Last Thoughts on the Atlanta, Birmingham and Atlantic Railroad.

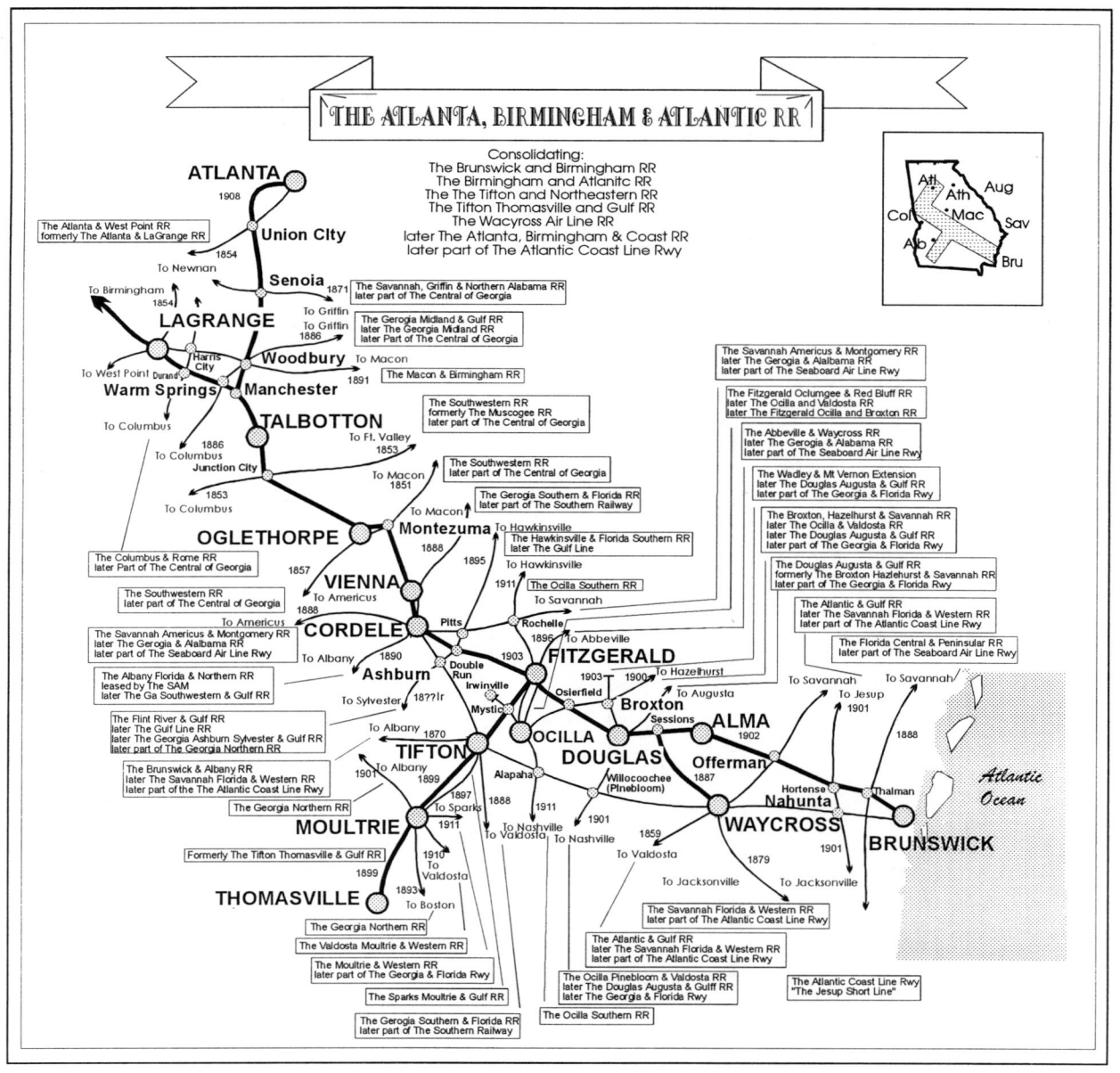

32 | The Atlanta Birmingham & Atlantic RR

BACON COUNTY: ALMA

The most important of the great rail systems built in Georgia after the turn of the century was the Atlanta, Birmingham and Atlantic. Like the Georgia and Florida, it had its beginnings in a tangle of older logging tram roads and short lines.

In 1902, two of these ne'er-do-well railroads met in what is today Bacon County. In that year, the Offerman and Western upgraded the old logging road of the Southern Pine Lumber Company through the village soon to be called Alma. Just to the west, it joined the Waycross Air Line at the tiny hamlet of Sessions. By 1903, the rails of the Offerman and Western had become part of the Brunswick and Birmingham Railroad and connected all the way eastward to Brunswick. Meanwhile, the Waycross Air Line had become part of the Atlantic and Birmingham Railroad and stretched westward all the way through Fitzgerald and Cordele to Montezuma. In that same year, the Atlantic and Birmingham purchased the Brunswick and Birmingham, and in 1906, the entire line was acquired by the Atlanta, Birmingham and Atlantic.

Meanwhile, in the wild and nearly empty pine forests that were to become Bacon County, a notable enterprise was underway only 6 miles east of the junction at Sessions along the rails of the old Offerman and Western. Here at Alma, we find late testimony of the power of railroads to create towns and to ultimately build courthouses. In 1898, Alma was nothing more than a large turpentine still. The first real settlers at the tiny post office called Lola came on the Offerman and Western. Within a few years, the crude shacks and huts of the turpentiners were evolving into a town. Alma was incorporated in 1904. Typical of so many late blossoms in the railroads' fertile garden, real growth in Alma came with the efforts of land speculators. In 1907, the Alma Land Improvement Company surveyed and graded streets; planted 1600 shade trees, built an $8000 brick school, and began selling town lots. By 1910, Alma had a population of almost 500.

As further testament to the power of the once mighty Atlanta, Birmingham and Atlantic Railroad, Alma successfully lobbied for the creation of a new county in 1914. Originally promoted as Haldeman County, and ultimately called Bacon, the new county was cut from parts of Appling, Ware, and Pierce. After a brief battle with nearby Nichols over the county seat, court was convened at Alma on the upper floor of a commercial building. J. J. Baldwin's Bacon County Courthouse was built in 1920, and is not part of this study.

COFFEE COUNTY: DOUGLAS

Plate 32.1: The Coffee County Courthouse built in 1889. Burned in 1898.

Coffee County was created from Appling, Telfair and Irwin Counties in 1854. In that year, lumber for the county's first courthouse was milled at one of the early saw mills along the Ocmulgee River and floated down river to Barrow's Bluff on the county's northern border. From there, it was hauled the last 20 miles to Douglas by ox cart.[1] The building served until 1889 when this two-story, frame courthouse replaced it. Typical of scores of vernacular frame court buildings that covered Georgia's squares in the early period, this one presided over a vast wilderness of pine that contained no real towns and little population. In 1860, the United States Census reported that all of Coffee County contained fewer than 3000 residents. For the next forty years, Douglas remained a singularly remote hamlet, little more than a few dusty dwellings and a store beside the simple frame courthouse. Regarding Douglas, Sholes's 1879 *Gazetteer of Georgia* could only report that "repeated efforts have failed to secure infor-

Plate 32.1: In 1889, when this frame courthouse rose at Douglas, it presided over a vast wilderness of pine that contained no real towns.

mation on this place." The 1886 edition reported that the town only had a population of 50.

By the beginning of the 1890s, the fingers of tiny logging railroads were snaking their way into the forests of Coffee County, and things began to stir in Douglas. In 1896, town leaders accomplished a rail connection to the old Brunswick and Albany Railroad at Axson by extending a rickety logging line. Although this line, known briefly as the Douglas and McDonald Railroad, was not a state chartered commercial carrier, the first train carried a load of brick for Douglas's first brick building. In addition, in 1898, when the old frame courthouse burned, bricks for a new court building arrived by rail. Around the turn of the century, Douglas enthusiastically supported the Wadley and Mount Vernon Extension, which completed track from Douglas through Broxton to the "Great Bend" of the Ocmulgee at Barrow's Bluff in 1903. This line, which was originally planned to cross the river and connect to the Wadley and Mount Vernon Railroad, was acquired by the Douglas, Augusta and Gulf Railroad in 1905. It became a branch of the Georgia and Florida Railway in 1906.

By the time the Wadley and Mount Vernon Extension reached the Ocmulgee River in 1903, the Atlantic and Birmingham Railroad had glued together the pieces of the old Waycross Air Line and the Brunswick and Birmingham Railroad to fashion a main trunk railroad from Brunswick, through Douglas, Fitzgerald and Cordele all the way to Montezuma. By the end of the decade, when the Georgia and Florida Railway completed her main line from Augusta through Douglas to Madison, Florida, the Atlanta, Birmingham and Atlantic Railroad had gobbled up the Atlantic and Birmingham and completed her grand scheme to connect Birmingham with Brunswick.

Thus, the last two great main trunk railroads to be built in Georgia crossed at Douglas, and as the new century dawned, the town was booming. Population rose from around 600 in 1900 to over 3500 in 1910. Long before the Georgia and Florida Railway completed extensive shops at Douglas, *The Douglas Weekly Breeze* was spewing forth the usual excitement of the era. As early as 1904, the editor related that, Douglas had twenty-five brick stores, two banks and "one of the most systematic and artistically designed courthouse in the state."[2]

Plate 32.2: The Coffee County Courthouse at Douglas, built in 1900. Burned in 1939. Andrew J. Bryan, architect.

When the old Coffee County Courthouse burned in 1898, citizens in Douglas were suddenly confronted with not only a pressing need for a new court building but also with a desire to create a grand symbol to voice their new-found railroad imported aspirations. The design that Andrew J. Bryan presented may have appeared new to Coffee County leaders in 1899, but it was virtually the same drawing that the Atlanta architect had presented to business leaders in Toccoa two years earlier when that town made its unsuccessful bid for the Habersham County seat.[3]

The elevation presented at Toccoa is that of the late French Renaissance, sometimes called the Francois I Style and often referred to as the Chateauesque Style in America. Round towers with conical caps and ornate high dormers epitomize this style. Before Bryan presented his plan in Coffee County, he altered his design pushing it subtly back in time toward Romanesque imagery. Gone was the Francois I "basket handle" arch in the high tower that was originally proposed for Toccoa. In its place was the familiar triple arch, typical of Romanesque designs of the era. These adjustments accomplished only the first in a series of Romanesque alterations to Bryan's original Toccoa design. By the time the building was completed in 1900, the bold lintels of the French Renaissance had been replaced with sashed windows, and the heavy window headers on the second story had become the graceful round-arched openings of the Romanesque Revival.

We might assume from all of this that the fundamental mass and masculinity of H. H. Richardson's Romanesque designs were more attractive to rural Southerners in 1900 than the frilly pomp of the French Renaissance. This was true, but we must also keep in mind that in creating the style that we have come to call the Richardsonian Romanesque, Richardson himself often overlaid his massive

medieval forms with French Renaissance motifs. Especially notable in this regard is Richardson's favored use of ornate French Renaissance peaked gables. His pension for heavy masonry window lintels and mulls is also typical of the French Renaissance.

Whatever the stylistic description of Andrew J. Bryan's 1900 Coffee County Courthouse at Douglas, it supplied local business leaders with the symbol they required to announce their great expectations. For a brief moment, it appeared that these lofty dreams would materialize. However, by the time, the rails of the Georgia and Florida Railway crossed the Atlanta, Birmingham and Atlantic at Douglas, Georgia's great pine forests were gone. The sea of cotton, which sprouted in their place, would run dry by 1920. For

Plate 32.2: Andrew J. Bryan's 1900 Coffee County Courthouse supplied business leaders in Douglas with just the symbol they required to announce their great expectations. (Photo: Courtesy of Ted Brooke.)

[1] Warren P. Ward, *Ward's History of Coffee County* (Atlanta: Foote and Davies, 1930) 297.

[2] *Douglas Weekly Breeze*, October 1, 1904.

[3] *The Southern Record* (Toccoa GA), August 16, 1897, and *The Douglas Weekly Breeze*, October 1, 1904.

Douglas, like so many Southern towns that had sailed on the waters of New South promise, the middle of the twentieth century would prove a disappointing destination. Andrew Bryan's Coffee County Courthouse burned in 1939.

BEN HILL COUNTY: FITZGERALD

One of the most compelling examples of the distortions generated by the New South myth is found in the stories that detail the creation of the city of Fitzgerald. Accounts of Fitzgerald's beginning as a planned "colony" for Union Civil War veterans have reached legendary proportions. The story is centered in real events, but the historical facts of the episode are clouded by exaggerations and far fetched fabrications, products of the blatant boosterism and distorted self-promotion that surrounded so many New South enterprises.

Fitzgerald's story, which has largely grown out of original promotional material, begins with what promoters hailed as "the most stupendous colonization scheme even conceived in America."[4] The scheme was the brainchild of Indiana newspaper editor, Philander H. Fitzgerald, who, in 1895, began promoting his American Tribune Soldiers Colony. Accounts of the boom at Fitzgerald boarder on the exaggerated. According to one account, only a year after the site was selected, Fitzgerald contained "one bank, three newspapers, two railroads, twenty-five

mills and industrial establishments, over two hundred fifty business houses of various kinds…and a population of seven thousand or more."[5] Another account related that the town's population went from 100 to 4000 in the space of only sixty days.[6] Yet, another claims that 20 to 300 new settlers arrived daily.[7] An 1896 promotion urged capitalists to "plant your money here" and predicted that the new city would contain 15,000 residents by January of 1897 and 40,000 to 60,000 within a year.[8] Northern veterans were joined by locals, and the myth of Fitzgerald as a the epitome of New South progress was further enhanced by the image of the place as a model for reconciliation and good will between North and South.

In the muddle of such optimism, it is difficult to assess the true state of affairs in Fitzgerald in 1896. To be sure, there was a large response to Philander Fitzgerald's glowing promotions. In that year, the Midwest had been devastated by drought, and settlers flocked to the new "colony." However, it appears that P. H. Fitzgerald had promoted his "New Canaan" before he purchased the land. As settlers began to arrive, his deal to purchase a site in Montgomery County had fallen through, and Fitzgerald was scrambling to acquire the tract in Irwin County near the tiny village of Swan. When the settlers arrived at Swan, they found nothing but a few wooden buildings and a rickety saw mill. Within a few months a sprawling slum, known as "Shacktown," appeared, and the Northern press was decrying the horrid conditions of the place. Nonetheless, the streets of the city that was to become Fitzgerald were laid out in 1895, and a permanent town began to rise. The exact size of the initial boom will never be known, but there can be little doubt that it was not nearly so large as promoters claimed. In addition, many of the early settlers must have simply left after one look at "Shacktown." In a much-needed benchmark to reality, the 1900 United States Census places Fitzgerald's population at 1817.

By 1901, Philander Fitzgerald was beset by myriad lawsuits, and his American Tribune Soldiers' Colony Company was in the hands of a receiver. In that year, Fitzgerald left Georgia, attempting a similar real estate promotion in Texas. But he was besieged with similar legal problems there. Finally, he attempt-

[4] An 1896 address by Dr. Jay Shrader in *The Savannah Morning News* in 1896 and reprinted in *The New Canaan, Fitzgerald and The Old Soldier Colony* (Fitzgerald GA: n.p., 1971) 3.

[5] An 1896 address by Dr. Jay Shrader in *The Savannah Morning News* in 1896 and reprinted in *The New Canaan, Fitzgerald and The Old Soldier Colony*.

[6] Russell M. Chalker, "Fitzgerald, Place of Reconciliation," *The Georgia Historical Quarterly* 55/3 (1971): 402.

[7] Patricia Holt Yarborough, "A Historical Perspective of the Founding of Fitzgerald, Georgia" (master's thesis, Milledgeville, 1986) 10.

[8] An 1896 address by Dr. Jay Shrader in *The Savannah Morning News* in 1896 and reprinted in *The New Canaan, Fitzgerald and The Old Soldier Colony*, 10-11.

[9] Yarborough, *A Historical Perspective of the Founding of Fitzgerald, Georgia*, 53.

[10] *The Fitzgerald Enterprise*, December 12, 1908.

ed to establish a second "colony" in Georgia, but by then he was entangled in countless suits and indictments and his credibility was low.[9]

Plate 32.3: The Atlanta, Birmingham and Atlantic Depot at Fitzgerald, built 1907-1910.

Philander Fitzgerald was finally convicted of mail fraud in 1907. In that same year, the Atlanta, Birmingham and Atlantic Railroad began what was to become arguably the finest depot on its line at Fitzgerald. A vague imitation of the Spanish Mission Style depots so popular with the Atlantic Coast Line Railroad, the A. B. A.'s great depot at Fitzgerald offers convincing testimony to the town's considerable progress. Despite the exaggerations surrounding her beginnings and the questionable dealings of her founder, by 1907, Fitzgerald, with over 6000 residents, had eclipsed Tifton as the principal rail center in south-central Georgia, was as large as Cordele and nearly as large as Valdosta.

At the heart of Fitzgerald's real boom had been the arrival of the Atlantic and Birmingham Railroad in 1902. This line had consolidated the rails of the old Brunswick and Birmingham Railroad and those of the Waycross Air Line to form the foundation of a modern scheme that sought to link the port at Brunswick with the steel mills at Birmingham. By 1903, the Birmingham and Atlantic had pieced together its line from Brunswick through Fitzgerald and Cordele, all the way to Montezuma. In the last half of the first decade of the new century, this line was acquired by the last of the great main trunk railroads to be built in Georgia, the Atlanta, Birmingham and Atlantic, which completed rails to Birmingham and a branch to Atlanta. Expectations for this powerful new line pumped more life into Fitzgerald, which lay at the junction of the new road's main line and its branch to Thomasville. By 1911, five railroads met at Fitzgerald (see Table 32.1). By this time, the town had a cotton mill, four banks, one of the largest hotels in the state, a five-story office building, twenty-two blocks of brick paving, and the sprawling shops of the A. B. A.

Plate 32.3: In 1907 The Atlanta, Birmingham and Atlantic Railroad began what was arguably its finest depot at Fitzgerald. (Photo: Wilber W. Caldwell.)

Plate 32.4: The Ben Hill County Courthouse, built in 1909. Henry H. Huggins, architect.

In 1907, as the plans for Fitzgerald's fine depot were drawn, Ben Hill County was created from Irwin and Wilcox with Fitzgerald as the county seat. By 1908, bonds had been approved, and county leaders had selected a courthouse plan by Virginia architect, H. H. Huggins.

We know little of the selection process, except that fourteen architects presented plans in Fitzgerald in December of 1908 and that Huggins's plan was selected from this group by the county commissioners.[10] This was to be Huggins's only courthouse in

---

RAILROADS AT FITZGERALD 1911

Table 32.2

1896 The Abbeville & Waycross RR (later the Georgia & Alabama RR, later part of the Seaboard Air Line Railway), Abbeville to Ocilla

1899 The Tifton & Northeastern (later part of the Atlantic and Birmingham RR, later part of the Atlanta, Birmingham & Atlantic RR), Fitzgerald to Thomasville.

1902 The Fitzgerald, Ocmulgee & Red Bluff RR (later the Ocilla and Valdosta RR, later the Fitzgerald, Ocilla & Broxton RR), Fitzgerald to Ocilla.

1903 The Atlantic and Birmingham RR (later the Atlanta, Birmingham and Atlantic RR, later the Atlanta, Birmingham and Coast RR, later part of the Atlantic Coast Line Railway), Brunswick to Birmingham.

1911 The Ocilla Southern RR, Nashville to Perry.

Plate 32.4: The 1909 Ben Hill County Courthouse at Fitzgerald is Virginia architect H. H. Huggins's only courthouse in Georgia. (Photo: Wilber W. Caldwell.)

Georgia, and it bears resemblance to his Roanoke County Courthouse in Roanoke, Virginia, which rose at about the same time.

Henry Hartwell Huggins was a man of his times. With very little architectural training to support a great deal of ambition, audacity, and swagger, he fashioned a successful architectural practice in Roanoke, Virginia, beginning in the 1890s. His brash and boastful promotional style, along with Roanoke's considerable boom, had propelled Huggins's career forward into the new century. Roanoke, like Fitzgerald was known as "The Magic City," and riding the wave of new building there, Huggins boasted in his advertising that he had designed more Roanoke housing "than any other twelve architects, and I can prove it."[11] It appears that this boastful approach won the day in Fitzgerald.

Also wining the day in Fitzgerald was Huggins's personal version of the architectural style that was by

then coming to be called "Southern Colonial." The Georgian or "Colonial" Revival, which had been underway in the North for decades, had gained strength by the turn of the century. This classical revival was freely interpreted in the American South to satisfy Southerners' peculiar desires for both "monumentality and neighborliness."[12] Inherent in most Southern solutions were columns. For Southerners, "the fact that columns were rarely if ever found on true Colonial homes mattered little. Anything that smacked of antiquity was termed 'Colonial.'"[13] Here was the same freewheeling neoclassical solution, that had appeared in Georgia in the public buildings of James Golucke, T. F. Lockwood and Frank Milburn. Huggins added his own personal twist, resting the grand portico on top of the cornice of the main mass of the composition, and thus creating a kind of extended dormer terminating in the great pediment with its frilly plaster decoration in the tympanum.

In an interesting footnote to Fitzgerald's architectural history, Henry H. Huggins died in Richmond, Virginia, under mysterious circumstances in 1912, only three years after the completion of this courthouse. According to *The Richmond Times-Dispatch*, the architect had been leading a double life, with a wife and child in Roanoke and another wife in Richmond.[14] If the exaggerations surrounding the creation of the city of Fitzgerald and the lives of Philander Fitzgerald and Henry Huggins are any barometer, the New South was indeed a mythical place, built on the flimsy foundations of unrealized dreams and populated by brash promoters with feet of clay.

COLQUITT COUNTY: MOULTRIE

Plate 32.5: The Colquitt County Courthouse, built in 1902-1903. Andrew J. Bryan, architect.

Andrew J. Bryan's stunning 1903 Colquitt County Courthouse at Moultrie stands on the town's spacious square as a monument to the exploitation of one of the last great stands of virgin pine in Georgia. In 1886, when W. W. Ashburn arrived in South Georgia to purchase vast tracts of untouched woodlands northeast of Moultrie, the town was a dusty hamlet of about fifty residents. Ashburn was fresh from a notable success in the timber business in Dodge County, and he quickly began a rich harvest in and around Colquitt County. Charles Pidcock also arrived in Colquitt County the late 1880s, and with the support of his farther, James Nelson Pidcock, a New Jersey railroad promoter and builder, he began logging operations south of Moultrie in Thomas and Brooks Counties.

Lumbermen Ashburn and Pidcock, along with Colquitt County's pioneer timber baron, J. B. Norman, would all play roles in the creation of Moultrie's railroads. In February of 1893, the Pidcock family piloted the first train into Moultrie. The line was called the Georgia Northern Railroad and it was an extension of a lumber tram road from Pidcock to Hollis. Begun without a charter from the state, the road first operated on the charter of the Boston and Albany Railroad, which had failed in 1892 before laying any track. In 1893, the line was completed to Moultrie. By 1902, the southern terminus had been moved to Boston, on the old Atlantic and Gulf Railroad, and the line stretched northward all the way to the Atlantic Coast Line Railway's branch at Darrow just south of Albany. By 1905, the Georgia Northern had bridged the Flint River and controlled its own rails into Albany.

Meanwhile J. B. Norman, who controlled vast timber interests east of Moultrie, chartered his Sparks, Moultrie and Gulf Railroad in 1897. At about the same time, H. H. Tift and W. W. Ashburn began promoting the Tifton, Thomasville and Gulf Railroad, which was completed via Moultrie all the way from Thomasville to Tifton in 1899. By 1903, when this fine courthouse rose at Moultrie, the ambitious new Atlantic and Birmingham Railroad, the forerunner of the Atlanta, Birmingham and Atlantic, purchased Tift's Tifton, Thomasville and Gulf as well as his Tifton Northeastern Railroad. The new line then controlled a branch from Fitzgerald through Tifton all the way to Thomasville. With its three railroads, Moultrie was an important stop along the way, and the town was booming.

Plate 32.5: By the 1920s, Moultrie would find that the promising gleam of the steel rails that inspired Andrew J. Bryan's stunning 1903 Colquitt County Courthouse were nothing more than a fleeting glimpse of that largely mythical notion called the New South. (Photo: Wilber W. Caldwell.)

Colquitt County had been created from Thomas County in 1856, and the town of Moultrie was established beside the tiny Post Office, which had originally been called Ocklockney. Little is known about the first Colquitt County Courthouse except that it was quite modest. One account describes a one-story log structure built in 1859.[15] This simple building burned in 1888, and a two-story frame courthouse was erected in that year. With the arrival of the Georgia Northern Railroad in 1893, things began to stir in Moultrie. In 1895, a promotional piece declared, "Three years ago Moultrie had a population of 50 inhabitants, now she is a thriving little town of 1200 busy, stirring souls."[16] Various accounts place Moultrie's 1893 population between 50 and 300. County records relate that there were no brick buildings in Moultrie in 1895, but by 1901, brick buildings lined the square,

[11] A 1909 Roanoke City Directory quoted in Charles E. Bromwell, Calder Loth, William M. S. Rasmussen and Richard Guy Wilson, *The Making of Virginia Architects* (Richmond: Virginia Museum of Fine Arts, 1992) 334.

[12] Bromwell, Loth, Rasmussen and Wilson, *The Making of Virginia Architects*, 334.

[13] Bromwell, Loth, Rasmussen and Wilson, *The Making of Virginia Architects*, 334.

[14] *Times-Dispatch* (Richmond VA), December 9, 1912 in Bromwell, Loth, Rasmussen and Wilson, *The Making of Virginia Architects*, 334.

[15] *The Moultrie Observer*, July 11, 1975.

[16] W. A. Covington, *The History of Colquitt County* (Atlanta: Foote and Davies, 1980) 160.

the town had three railroads, three banks, a cotton mill, and a population exceeding 2200. When the new century dawned the vast stands of pine were disappearing from Colquitt County. But the railroads were still hauling carloads of New South promises into Moultrie and the time was ripe for a new courthouse.

In 1901, when Andrew J. Bryan presented the plan for his stunning Colquitt County Courthouse to county leaders in Moultrie, James W. Golucke's 1900 DeKalb County Courthouse at Decatur was the toast of Georgia. Golucke's courthouse at Decatur was the third in the state to reflect the up-to-date styling of the Neoclassical Revival that had swept the American North after the success of the "Florentine Renaissance" buildings of the 1893 Columbia Exposition at Chicago. Oddly, Andrew Bryan himself had designed the first two neoclassical court buildings in Georgia. The first was the 1895 Stewart County Courthouse at Lumpkin. This was followed by Bryan's 1896 Muscogee County Courthouse at Columbus.

Bryan's 1895 courthouse at Lumpkin mirrored older Georgian motifs, while his strictly neoclassical creation at Columbus with its trendy Beaux-Arts ornament copied lavish Northern models, which symbolized the nation's lusty materialism. At the turn of the century, such symbolism was not completely welcome in the American South. Thus, despite the fact that Andrew Bryan had pioneered the introduction of the new classicism into the Deep South, it would be Golucke's courthouse at Decatur, completed in 1900 that became the model for a new kind of public building in Georgia. In DeKalb County, James Golucke successfully captured the Southern imagination with his marriage of the flowery new American neoclassicism to the simple classical forms associated with the architecture of the Old South. Golucke understood that the South's quest for modern progress was impossibly encumbered by the brooding burden of her past. At Decatur, he fashioned a perfect duel symbol for the Southern dilemma, a building that represented the region's modern material aspirations and, at the same time, nostalgically recalled a romantic image of an age long past but not forgotten. By 1903, six new court buildings based on Golucke's Decatur plan rose in Georgia (see Appendix A).

One of these was Andrew J. Bryan's Colquitt County Courthouse. Like Golucke, Bryan began with the dome of a central clock tower, squared it, and attached grand porticos to each of the four sides. Thus, all four sides of Moultrie's large square were afforded equal entrances, and each reflected Old South imagery in a grand classical portico centered on a rectangular mass.[17] Following Golucke's lead, Andrew Bryan then decorated his creation in the ornament of the day, flowery capitals, scrolling brackets supporting ornate stone window headers, two high balustrades, and an octagonal clock tower with broken based pediments supported by paired columnettes to frame the four faces of an enormous clock.

Despite such modern imagery, Andrew J. Bryan was still drawn to the picturesque. Multi-paned windows and an eight-sided flared roof with a pointed lantern adorn the great tower. These elements represent a retreat to the architectural styles of the earlier Romantic era, and suggest that Bryan's building is transitional. The subsequent removal of the original balustrades and the addition of modillions supporting the broad eaves add to the picturesque affect. These elements, along with the simplification of the fenestration after a 1959 remodeling that turned the two-story building into a three-story affair, draw attention to the ornate tower. Simplification such as this presses the entire building farther back in time and away from the strict order of the new American classicism of the turn of the century.

Moultrie's population exceeded 3000 in 1910, but by then the great pine forests were gone. The end of Colquitt County's vast stands of pine brought hard times for the tiny railroads that had carried the harvest away. In 1910, the next to the last of Moultrie's railroads, the Valdosta, Moultrie and Western, was completed from Valdosta to Moultrie. By 1921, the entire line had been abandoned. As the new century progressed, the tangle of rails that had once served the great mills and turpentine stills of H. H. Tift, W. W. Ashburn, J. B. Norman and the Pidcock family began to rust. As early as 1903, Henry Tift sold his Tifton, Thomasville and Gulf Railroad to the Atlantic and Birmingham Railroad, the forerunner of the emerging giant, the Atlanta, Birmingham and Atlanta Railroad.

This was the beginning of a period of consolidation in which ne'er-do-well lumber roads were gobbled up by larger companies seeking branches to support main line railroads. In 1911, the Georgia and Florida Railway completed a branch to Moultrie with the purchase of the Nashville and Sparks Railroad and the Sparks and Western.

Meanwhile, as cotton began to cover the barren expanses left by the timber barons, the Pidcock family carefully expanded their tiny Georgia Northern railroad, acquiring J. L. Hand's Flint River and Gulf in 1910, and 42 miles of the old Hawkinsville and Florida Southern Railroad from Ashburn to Camilla in 1922. However, in the end, cotton would prove every bit as fickle as timber. In the 1920s and 1930s, like most of the rural South, Moultrie would find that the promising gleam of the steel rails that had inspired her stunning new courthouse, had been nothing more than a fleeting glimpse of that largely mythical notion called the New South.

TALBOT COUNTY: TALBOTTON

In 1853, when the Southwestern Railroad completed the link begun by the Muscogee Railroad from Columbus to Fort Valley, Talbot County was flush with the prosperity of cotton. In 1850, the county's plantations had produced over 15,000 bales of the white fiber. The new railroad that passed through the town of Geneva, only 7 miles south of the county seat at Talbotton, added yet more fuel to the economic fires that burned in this corner of Cotton's Kingdom. According to George White's Statistics of the State of Georgia, Talbotton's population had reached almost 1500 in 1849, and the town contained a "large and well arranged" brick courthouse, a jail, two churches, two academies and seven or eight stores.

Talbot County had been cut from Muscogee County in 1827. The courthouse that George White described had been erected in 1831. It was the county's first permanent court building. The two-story brick vernacular structure was built by the Birch brothers who had been involved in the additions to the Georgia state capital building at Milledgeville in the late 1820s and who erected similar excellent early

brick court buildings at Watkinsville (1829) and at Greenville (1832). By the time the Southwestern Railroad arrived in Talbot County, Talbotton already boasted a host of fine examples of wooden architecture from the plantation era. Many still stand today. Especially notable in this regard are the Zion Episcopal Church (1848), an excellent early example of the American Gothic Style, and an array of Greek Revival residences.

In 1838, only ten years after Talbotton was laid out, and just as Georgia's earliest railroads were getting underway, progressive leaders in the new county town chartered the Talbotton Railroad. This early plan called for a line from Macon via Talbotton to Columbus, but in the depressed financial atmosphere of the late 1830s, organizers were unable to garner enough support to fund the scheme, and no track was laid. It would be more than forty years before steel rails arrived in Talbotton. The Talbotton Branch Railroad was chartered in the railroad building frenzy of the early 1870s. However, like most cotton growing regions, so hard hit was Talbot County in the aftermath of war, that it would take nine years to build the 7 miles of track from Talbotton to a junction with the Southwestern at Bostwick, (later called Pascal, later Junction City). The Talbotton Branch Railroad was finally completed in 1881, but by the time the first train came into town, Talbotton had begun to decline, with her population down to around 750 according to Sholes's 1879 *Gazetteer of Georgia*. Surely, the new railroad brought with it some glimmer of hope, but in 1881, hard times lay ahead for Talbotton, and the hour of her fullness was past.

Plate 32.6: The Talbot County Courthouse, built in 1892. Bruce and Morgan, architects.

Entrenched in the myths of the past, Talbotton was slow to acquire the trappings of the new age. Nonetheless, the Talbotton Branch Railroad imported a small helping of the New South myth. The 1890s saw a small resurgence at the end of this lonely spur.

---

[17] Golucke's 1900 DeKalb County Courthouse originally had four porticoed entrances. Two of these disappeared with the later addition of wings.

Plate 32.6: Although impressive and monumental to a degree, Bruce and Morgan's 1892 Talbot County Courthouse at Talbotton emanates a distinctly rural charm. (Photo: Wilber W. Caldwell.)

As Talbotton's population neared 1000, the Peoples Bank of Talbotton was chartered and the simple brick commercial architecture that had begun to surround so many Georgia squares around the turn of the century began to appear.[18] Meanwhile, on February 12, 1892, the old Talbot County Courthouse burned to the ground. The subsequent commission of Atlanta

architects, Bruce and Morgan, supplies further evidence that at least some New South passion had trickled into Talbotton.

When the old courthouse at Talbotton burned, Bruce and Morgan were busy covering Georgia's squares with Romanesque court buildings. Between 1892 and 1895, the firm designed thirteen Romanesque Revival courthouses in Georgia, many with elaborate Queen Anne details. Seven of these still stand today. (see Appendix C). This building at Talbotton, begun in 1892, and its virtual twin in Statesboro (1895) are among the finest of these.

Whether we call this building Romanesque Revival or Queen Anne is something of a mute point. In America, the Queen Anne Style, inspired by the great English architect Norman Shaw, had quickly evolved into a rather confused mix of English Renaissance, Tudor, and Elizabethan elements often lavishly overlaid with classical decoration. In addition, Richardsonian elements were also common. As Alan Gowans so aptly puts it, American Queen Anne buildings "sometimes seemed to look back to the Italianate, and sometimes sideways to Richardsonian Romanesque."[19] Here in Talbotton we find an appealing model. The high tower with its steep pyramidal roof, the great arched entrance with its wide brick voussoirs and the triple arched window grouping above is purely Richardsonian. Nevertheless, Queen Anne elements abound in the bell shaped roof of the low tower, the lacy central pediment with its fan-shaped window and lacy cornice, and the many decorative panels displaying both repetitive terra-cotta motifs and scrolling floral designs.

Although impressive and monumental to a degree, this building, like much of Bruce and Morgan's work in Georgia, embodies a distinctly rural charm. Here is the reason for these prolific architects' success in the South. They were able to fashion from the contemporary vocabulary of the day a comfortable, even pastoral, architecture that satisfied that odd mixture of contradictions that made up the Southern psyche of the late nineteenth century. It was a public architecture tailor-made for a people of divided mind. A people who sought at the same time the prosperity of the modern age and the archaic traditions of a

[18] The last of the old wooden business houses on the square in Talbotton was demolished in 1901. William Davidson, *A Rockaway in Talbot, Travels in an Old Georgia County,* 4 vols. (West Point GA: W. H. Davidson, 1983) 8.

[19] Alan Cowans, *Styles and Types of North American Architecture, Social Function and Cultural Expression* (1992; reprint, New York: Icon Editions, 1993) 199.

[20] James Michael Russell, *Atlanta, 1847-1890, City Building in the Old South and the New* (Baton Rouge: Louisiana State University Press, 1988) 117.

bygone era; a people who desired monumentality in a public building but abhorred any hint of the symbolism of governmental power; a people who wanted to appear up-to-date, but at the same time, labored to preserve a distinctly rural and agrarian society and who immersed themselves in a deeply nostalgic mythology of the most shamelessly Romantic sort. The Romanesque Revival was the perfect vehicle for such dual symbolism. At its heart, it was the rural architecture of a feudal era, but with the addition of a little Queen Anne trim, buildings could sing distinctly modern songs in a comfortable homespun way. Although some of the vocabulary here is that of Richardson, and to a lesser degree of Norman Shaw, the convoluted symbolism that the South evolved for these idioms could not have been farther from these masters' original intents.

ATLANTA: FULTON COUNTY PART 4

Plate 32.7: Atlanta's Terminal Station built 1903-1905. Demolished 1971. P. Thornton Marye, architect.

In 1871, Atlanta's second Union Depot, Max Corput's crude architectural vision of Second Empire styling, rose to serve Atlanta's four railroads. At that time, the city's population numbered around 20,000. When Parkins and Bruce's more gracefully appointed Second Empire Fulton County Courthouse was completed in 1883, eight railroads met at Atlanta (see Table 32.2). Population had nearly doubled its 1870 count,[20] and Corput's ungainly depot was quickly becoming out moded. By the early 1890s, Atlanta's population was nearing 65,000, and two more railroads had reached the city to crowd passengers into the old depot. In the decade following the turn of the century, the population exploded again. By this time, three more railroads had joined the fray at the old Union Depot. The Seaboard Air Line completed a line from Atlanta to Birmingham in 1904, and at about the same time, the L&N acquired trackage rights into Atlanta. Finally, in 1908, the Atlanta, Birmingham and Atlantic completed its branch from Manchester to Atlanta. It was the thirteenth railroad for a city of almost 150,000 residents.

RAILROAD LINES AT ATLANTA 1908
The Georgia Railroad
From Augusta 1847
The Atlanta and West Point Railroad
To West Point 1854
The Central of Georgia Railroad
From Macon 1847 (formerly the Macon and Western)
The Southern Railway
To Charlotte 1872 (formerly Atlanta and Richmond Air Line)
To Macon 1882 (formerly E. Tenn. Va. & Ga. RR)
To Birmingham 1882 (formerly Georgia Pacific RR)
To Rome 1882 (formerly E. Tenn. Va. & Ga. RR)
To Fort Valley 1888 (formerly Atlanta and Florida RR)
The Louisville and Nashville Railroad
To Knoxville 1891(formerly Marietta and North Georgia RR)
The Western and Atlantic Railroad
To Chattanooga 1850 (leased to the N, C & L RR)
The Seaboard Air Line
To Richmond 1892 (formerly Georgia, Carolina and Northern RR)
To Birmingham 1904
The Atlanta, Birmingham and Atlantic Railroad
To Manchester 1908

Table 32.2

Plate 32.7: Construction of Atlanta's Terminal Station was begun in 1903 under the direction of the Atlanta Terminal Company, an organization financed and controlled largely by the Southern Railway. (Photo: Courtesy of the Atlanta History Center.)

As early as 1890, pressure was mounting to replace Corput's 1871 Union Depot. In 1891, the famous financier, Jay Gould, visited Atlanta "in connection with the selection of a site for a new depot."[21] Searching for a new site was one of the many late century schemes aimed at the construction of a new depot. However, all attempts came to nothing. The most the city and its railroads were able to muster was a remodeling of the old building in 1901.[22] In that year, struck by the inadequacy of the remodeling scheme, Atlanta's newspapers began to aggressively agitate for a new passenger station. At the center of the campaign was an all-out assault on Union Depot. *The Atlanta Journal* referred to the old building as "the alleged depot," termed passengers "suffers," and described a virtual Bedlam overflowing with "seething masses of disgusted humanity."[23]

Construction of Atlanta's Terminal Station began in 1903 under the direction of the Atlanta Terminal Company, an organization financed and controlled largely by the Southern Railway. Architect, Philip Thornton Marye, received the commission in 1903 and moved to Atlanta from his native Virginia in 1904. In a career that lasted until 1935, Marye designed numerous public buildings. Notable among these were grand passenger depots for Mobile and Birmingham, Alabama, and fine courthouses for Wake County, North Carolina, and Greenville County, South Carolina. Undoubtedly his crowning achievement was Atlanta's Shrine Mosque (Fox Theater Building) completed in 1929.

In 1904, Marye's selection of the Spanish Renaissance style for Atlanta's Terminal Station is not hard to reckon. Only three years before, both Savannah and Augusta had completed grand Spanish Renaissance style passenger depots designed by the Southern Railway's chief architect, Frank Milburn. Indeed, by 1904, the style had become a favorite with the Southern Railway. Like so many of the Neoclassical Revival styles that were sweeping the country around the turn of the century, the popularity of the Spanish Renaissance Revival in America owed a great deal to the buildings of the 1893 Colombian Exposition at Chicago. Although many promoters termed the predominant architectural style of the great fair "Florentine Renaissance," in truth, the buildings of Chicago's so-called "White City" incorporated a complex blend of Academic traditions. This architecture was more accurately characterized in the 1893 *History of the World's Fair* where it was described as "the style of the Romans as adapted for modern uses by the Italian, French and Spanish Renaissance."[24] As Marye's grand depot rose at Atlanta, similar and even more flamboyant Renaissance-inspired public buildings were the toast of the 1904 Louisiana Purchase Exposition at Saint Louis.

But unlike the Rococo buildings of the Saint Louis World's Fair and unlike Frank Milburn's utilitarian Spanish Renaissance brick depots at Augusta and Savannah, Marye pioneered the use of a new material with his Terminal Station at Atlanta. The building was one of the first reinforced concrete structures in the South. As we have seen, in the decade following the turn of the century, the use of cast concrete block was becoming commonplace, but poured reinforced concrete was something all together new. At this time, the new material was also used to fashion great viaducts to connect the new depot to the center of town, passing over the tangle of track that had snarled the city's traffic since its very beginnings. However, reinforced concrete was a technology that would not be fully perfected for decades to come, and although the new viaducts did much to ease Atlanta's traffic problems, Marye's great Terminal Station was something of a dark old pile. Nonetheless, when it opened to serve the Southern and the Atlanta and

[21] Franklin Garrett, *Atlanta and Environs, A Chronicle of Its People and Events*, 3 vols. (New York: Lewis Publishing Company, 1954) 4: 204.

[22] Garrett, *Atlanta and Environs, A Chronicle of Its People and Events*, 408.

[22] Garrett, *Atlanta and Environs, A Chronicle of Its People and Events*, 408.

[23] The Atlanta Journal, October 25, 1901 in Garrett, *Atlanta and Environs, A Chronicle of Its People and Events*, 406.

[24] Henry B. Fuller, *History of the World's Fair* (Chicago: 1893) 85, 101, quoted in Carroll L. V. Meeks, *The Railroad Station* (New Haven: Yale University Press, 1978) 126-27.

[25] *The Atlanta Journal*, May 14, 1905. The original train shed was enclosed. It was replaced by an open "butterfly" style shed in 1925.

[26] *The Manufacturer's Record*, July 23, 1897.

[27] *The Manufacturer's Record*, June 10, 1898.

West Point and the Central of Georgia Railroads, in May 1905, it was heralded as the "gateway to the South," with "one of the largest train sheds in the country."[25] Meanwhile the L & N, the Western and Atlantic, the Seaboard Airline and the Georgia Railroad all continued to use the old Union Depot until it was demolished in 1930.

Plate 32.8: The Fulton County Courthouse, begun in 1907, completed in 1914. Morgan and Dillon, architects.

It is perhaps no coincidence that in 1907, just as the Atlanta, Birmingham and Atlantic Railroad began construction of its connection to Atlanta, Fulton County began construction of a new courthouse. Parkins and Bruce's fine 1883 picturesque court building had served the county well both as a seat of government and a symbol for Atlanta's late nineteenth-century railroad-inspired aspirations. However, even as early as 1897 there had been agitation for a new courthouse at Atlanta. In that year, Atlanta architects, J. H. Dinnwiddle and W. T. Downing had proposed plans for a new Futon County Courthouse.[26] Although it was decided to remodel and expand the old structure with the addition of a $100,000 annex,[27] it was already clear to many that the old building was inadequate for a city that was soon to count 150,000 inhabitants. Likewise, the symbols of the old Second Empire Style were sadly out of date among the grand new tall building that were rising in the capitol city.

Indeed, from its very beginnings, Atlanta had been something apart from the rest of Georgia. Thus, it is not surprising that, as the twentieth century blossomed, the city chose to set aside the warm, nostalgic, architectural symbols embodied in the picturesque public buildings of the ninetieth century. Nor would she embrace the exuberant new turn-of-the-century American classicism. Rather Atlanta chose the cold academic lines of a modern institutional classicism that was to cover the nation in the coming decades.

Begun in 1907, Morgan and Dillon's great courthouse at Atlanta was seven years under construction. Here was a looming monolithic symbol for a place where the promises of the New South were in many

ways being realized along with an attendant American cash register morality. This is not the architecture of the people but rather the architecture of bureaucratic power wielded by an increasingly distant government. Along the way in 1911, Parkins and Bruce's proud 1883 Fulton County Courthouse was demolished.[28]

SOME LAST THOUGHTS ON THE ATLANTA, BIRMINGHAM AND ATLANTIC RAILROAD

Although blurred by disappointment, railroad-imported, New South promises were still inspiring courthouse building in many places at the end of the first decade of the new century. There is perhaps no better illustration of this lingering phenomena that the court buildings that rose along the last of the

Plate 32.8: Begun in 1907, Morgan and Dillon's great courthouse at Atlanta was seven years under construction. (Photo: Wilber W. Caldwell)

great main line railroads to be built in Georgia, the Atlanta, Birmingham and Atlantic.

The Atlanta Birmingham and Atlantic (later called the Atlanta Birmingham and Coast and even later part of the mighty Atlantic Coast Line Railway) emerged as the product of a grand scheme to connect the iron and steel mills at Birmingham with the port of Brunswick, Georgia. Like so many railroads of the era, it began with a patchwork consolidation of obscure public carriers and a tangle of makeshift logging lines.

It all began in 1902, when the Offerman and Western upgraded the old logging road of the Southern Pine Lumber Company from Offerman westward through present-day Bacon County where the line joined the Waycross Air Line at the tiny ham-

Plate 32.9: Fitzgerald (Photo: Wilber W. Caldwell)

let of Sessions. By 1903, the rails of the Offerman and Western had become part of the Brunswick and Birmingham Railroad and connected all the way eastward to Brunswick. At the about same time, the Waycross Air Line became part of the Atlantic and Birmingham Railroad and stretched track northwestward all the way from Waycross, through Sessions, and then eastward to Fitzgerald, Cordele and Montezuma. In that same year, the Atlantic and Birmingham acquired H. H. Tift's Tifton, Thomasville and Gulf Railroad along with his Tifton and Northern Railroad, thus adding a branch line from Fitzgerald all the way to Thomasville. Before the year was out, the Atlantic and Birmingham purchased the Brunswick and Birmingham, and three years later in 1906, the entire line was acquired by the Atlanta, Birmingham and Atlantic. New track was laid across western Georgia. The ABA acquired the old Talbotton Branch Railroad from Junction City to Talbotton and at the emerging boomtown of Manchester, where the new road established extensive shops and yards; a branch line was begun to Atlanta arriving in 1908. In the meantime, the line completed track westward through LaGrange. After the acquisition of several smaller lines in Alabama, the first train ran from Brunswick to Birmingham in 1908. The last leg of that first run was on track owned by the L&N, but the ABA completed its own main line to Birmingham in 1910.

Nevertheless, Brunswick was a harbor of limited potential, and powerful northern financial interests methodically sought to stifle Birmingham's steel industry. Therefore, as the new century wore on, the Atlanta, Birmingham and Atlantic Railroad constantly flirted with bankruptcy. It underwent several reorganizations, first as the Atlanta, Birmingham and Atlantic Railway in 1909, later as the Atlantic Coast Line's pawn, the Atlanta, Birmingham and Coast, in 1926 and finally as part of the giant Atlantic Coast Line Railway, which acquired complete interest in the line in 1946.[29]

Despite the fact that the ABA failed to live up to the financial expectations of its organizers, it nonetheless sparked irrational hopes and wild aspirations in towns across the face of Georgia. As always, these vibrant dreams were the stuff that new courthouses were made of. At the places where the Atlanta, Birmingham and Atlantic crossed other main line railroads some of Georgia's finest public buildings rose. Notable in this regard is Andrew Bryan's 1900 Coffee County Courthouse completed only two years after the first rails arrived in Douglas. That town's railroad-inspired aspirations would briefly soar as the new century unfolded and two of Georgia's newest mainline railroads (the Georgia and Florida and the Atlanta, Birmingham and Atlantic) crossed in the shadow of Bryan's new Coffee County Courthouse. Likewise in 1902, Moultrie, along the line of the ABA's Thomasville branch, commissioned Andrew Bryan to design a public symbol for her own railroad-inspired dreams. In that year, speculation centered on the recent arrival of several new rail lines. Among these was H. H. Tift's Tifton Thomasville and Gulf Railroad, which had been completed in 1899. The ABA's forerunner, the Atlantic and Birmingham Railroad acquired this line just as Bryan's new Colquitt County Courthouse began to rise in Moultrie.

However, it was not only in the old, established county towns of South Georgia that the ABA spread its beguiling messages of hope and progress. The new line and its branches bolstered the power of the emerging new rail hubs at Tifton, Cordele, and Fitzgerald. In 1905 as the new county movement began, three new Georgia county seats were created along the ABA's shinny new rails. Tifton became in county town of Tift County in 1905, and in that same year, Cordele was named a new county town. T. F. Lockwood's grand Crisp County Courthouse was completed at Cordele in 1907. In 1906, Fitzgerald mustered the power and support to create a new county, and H. H. Huggins' Ben Hill County Courthouse was completed in 1909.

All along the right of way of the Atlanta, Birmingham and Atlantic, new towns sprang up in the wilderness. The village of Alma grew strong enough to

demand a new county of her own and in 1914, Bacon County was created. J. J. Baldwin's Bacon County Courthouse was completed in 1920. Although this building suggests little in the way of flamboyant exuberance or flare, it is nonetheless a compelling a late illustration of the railroads' power to create hope and erect courthouses even in the most remote corners of the piney woods.

•

[28] Garrett, *Atlanta and Environs, A Chronicle of Its People and Events*, 577.

[29] Les R. Winn, *Ghost Trains and Depots of Georgia* (Chamblee GA: Big Shanty Press, 1995) 312

The Atlanta and Savannah Railroad

Chatham County, Savannah (see chapter 2)—Effingham County, Springfield—Screven County,
Sylvania —Warren County, Warrenton (See chapter 8) • Effingham County, Springfield
Some Last Thoughts on the Atlanta and Savannah Railroad

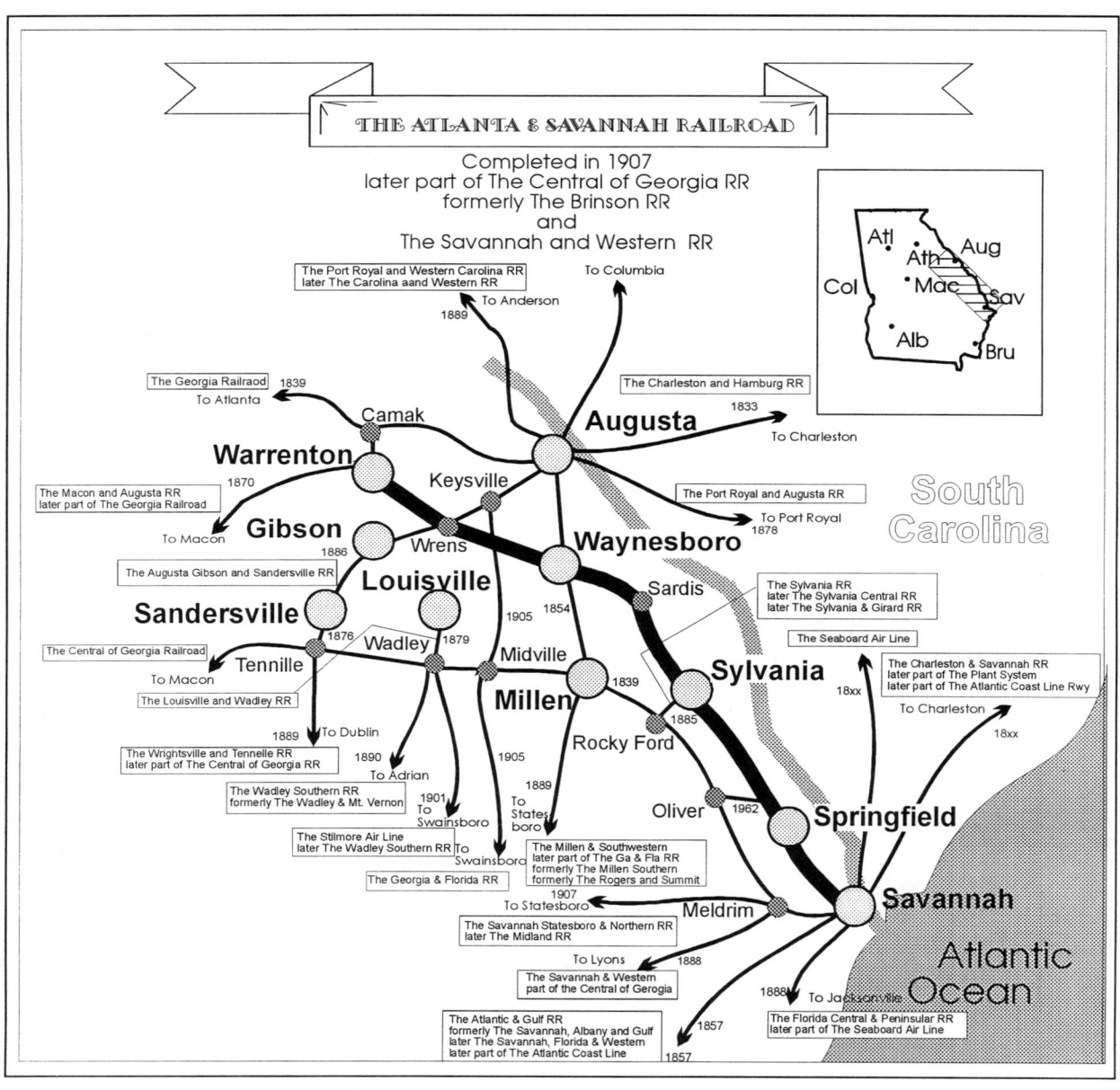

33 | The Atlanta and Savannah Railroad

Plate 33.1: The Effingham County Courthouse at Springfield, built in 1909. Hyman C. Whitcover, architect.

Built at the close of the first decade of the twentieth century, Savannah architect Hyman C. Whitcover's Effingham County Courthouse offers convincing testament to the lingering myth of the New South. It also demonstrates that fact that, even as late as 1909, new rails still had the power to create the kind of railroad-inspired civic and economic euphoria that had been so common in rural Georgia at the end of the previous century.

One of Georgia's original counties, Effingham, is situated in the low coastal plane between the Ogeechee and Savannah Rivers. Like so many Pine Barrens counties, Effingham never enjoyed the prosperity that her old Cotton Belt neighbors to the north and west knew. Throughout the nineteenth century, times remained tough in these dense piney woods and populations remained relatively small. The construction of the Central of Georgia Railroad along the county's western border in 1839 began the slow exploitation of area timber resources, but according to the great traveler, George White, in 1849 Effingham county counted only 3457 inhabitants. Even as late as 1880, the US Census listed Effingham's population at a mere 5979. Countywide population was down to 5599 ten years later.

In revolutionary times, the county seat was established at Tuckseeking. It was later moved to Elberton. Both of these villages disappeared long ago. The seat of county government was then placed at Ebenezer and still later established at the village of Effingham before finally moving to Springfield, which was incorporated in 1833.[1] Before the construction of a frame courthouse at Springfield, we know little of court buildings in any of these places, but in the early period, court was probably held in private homes. George White informs us that a frame courthouse stood on the square in Springfield in 1849, but in a rare unflattering remark he describes the village as a "place of little note." White was undoubtedly right, for a review of various Sholes's *Gazeteers of Georgia* reveals little growth in Springfield as the century wore on. Sholes relates

---

[1] *The Atlanta Constitution*, November 10, 1958.

Plate 33.1: The story of Hyman C. Whitcover's 1909 Effingham County Courthouse clearly demonstrates the lingering power of new rails to create the kind of railroad-inspired civic and economic euphoria that had been so common in rural Georgia at the end of the previous century. (Photo: Wilber W. Caldwell.)

that the town contained about forty citizens in 1879, about 100 in 1887 and less than 200 in 1896. A 1901 photograph of a portion of the old wooden court building depicts a crude, two-story, Carpenter Greek design. Although the simple building stood on Springfield's square for more than half a century, it witnessed little change. Meanwhile, just to the west, the town of Guyton had sprung up on the Central's mainline. By 1900, Guyton boasted an astonishing 2379 residents according to the US Census. Like so many county towns adjacent to the Central's early line from Savannah to Macon, Springfield was bypassed by the railroad, and progress was focused in the newly created depot towns on the county's western border. However, in the end of the first decade of the new century, all of this was on the verge of change.

The promise for change came with the inspirational George Mills Brinson, who in 1906 chartered a railroad to run from Savannah westward to Springfield and beyond. Brinson was a railroad promoter and tim-

ber baron of considerable note. He had been key in promoting the Wadley Southern Railroad and later of the Brewton and Pineora Railroad (see chapter 28). Along the way he had acquired tens of thousands of acres of timber land and had played a notable hand in founding the town of Stillmore and in the extraordinary boom that occurred there in the decades surrounding the turn of the century.[2] So when the first train steamed into Springfield in August of 1907, expectations were high. By early 1909, Brinson's railroad was complete from Savannah all the way to Sylvania in Screven County, and plans were underway to build on to Waynesboro and a connection with the Central's Augusta line. To celebrate all of this, Effingham built a new courthouse.

There can be little doubt that Hyman Whitcover's grand neoclassical palace of justice owes a debt to the designs of Thomas Jefferson as well as to the flamboyant American Neoclassical Revival that had swept the country a decade or more earlier. It is equally clear that the building symbolized the progress that everyone knew the shiny new rails would bring to Springfield. According to *The Springfield Herald* of February 19, 1909, the new courthouse was "the harbinger of a new day," "the herald of a new civilization," and the "pacesetter for a forward march."[3] *The Herald* also sang the usual New South songs of progress, crooning about "fifty new buildings in Springfield since the railroad arrived—many of brick,"[4] and applauding entrepreneur Brinson as "far-sighted" and "broad minded."[5] Just three weeks before the cornerstone was laid for Whitcover's grand symbol for progress, *The Herald* published an article entitled "Hurrah for Springfield" in which the editor painted a glowing picture of a town that was suddenly "climbing to the top of the latter."[6]

However, as usual, real progress was a long distance away. Although George Brinson's railroad would continue its westward expansion over the next decade, its history would remain checkered, and financial difficulties lay ahead for the celebrated entrepreneur. Reorganized first as the Brinson Railway Company and later as the Savannah and Western Railroad, the line was completed as the Atlanta and Savannah Railroad all the way through Warrenton to Camak on

[2] Dixon Hollingsworth, ed. *The History of Screven County, Georgia* (Dallas TX: Curtis Media, 1989) 69.

[3] *Springfield Herald*, February 19, 1909.

[4] *Springfield Herald*, February 05, 1909.

[5] *Springfield Herald*, January 29, 1909.

[6] *Springfield Herald*, January 29, 1909.

[7] Angela Lee-Ford, *Screven and Jenkins Counties* (Charleston: Arcadia, 1999) 16.

the Georgia Railroad in 1918. Three years later, the Atlanta and Savannah declared bankruptcy. By this time, most dreams of New South resurgence in Springfield were long forgotten. The Central of Georgia acquired the entire line in 1951 and portions of the route have since been abandoned.

SCREVEN COUNTY: SYLVANIA

Screven was cut from Effingham and Burke Counties in 1793. In the early years, court was held in a private home, and it was not until 1797 that county leaders designated the first county site at Jacksonborough and built a small courthouse there. This was probably a log structure, but the only description of this early building that is recorded simply states that it was "small and rustic." In 1832, a more substantial frame and brick courthouse replaced the county's original court building.[7] In 1847, for reasons that are shrouded in myth and conjecture, and after considerable controversy, the county seat was moved to the new town of Sylvania. The old 1832 courthouse at Jacksonborough was demolished, and salvaged materials were used in the construction of a new courthouse at Sylvania, only 5 miles away. After the removal of the courthouse, Jacksonborough quickly disappeared. In 1849, the reliable traveler, George White, reported that Sylvania consisted of "a courthouse, a jail, 1 tavern, 2 stores, 1 church and 1 school." White went on to say that "4 or 5 families" resided there and that the town was "considered healthy." As for Jacksonborough in 1849, White reports an already "deserted village." Although some accounts maintain that Sherman burned the courthouse at Sylvania on his March to the Sea, there is no documented support for this theory, and it appears that the old 1847 two-story frame court building stood on Sylvania's square for fifty years.

Meanwhile, beginning in the late 1830s, the Central of Georgia constructed its line from Savannah to Macon, establishing a string of stops along the eastern bank of the Ogeechee River, which formed Screven's western boundary. Towns sprang up at Oliver, Halcyondale, Dover, Rocky Ford, Scarborough and Millen.

Plate 33.2: The Screven County Courthouse at Sylvania, built in 1897. Lewis F. Goodrich, architect.

These new towns along the Central flourished while Sylvania languished. Notable among the upstarts was Rocky Ford, which by the 1880s had become the center of considerable industry revolving around E. E. Foy's timber enterprises. These included several tram railroads, a bridge across the Ogeechee River and a lumber mill employing over 100 people in 1887. In 1884, businessmen from Rocky Ford, Sylvania and Savannah banded together to charter the Sylvania Railroad, a 15 mile spur line from the Central's depot at Rocky Ford to Sylvania. It did not take long for the little railroad to get into financial trouble, and by 1903 the line had been renamed the Sylvania Central Railroad and had been gobbled up by the Central of Georgia, which had underwritten its debts back in 1886. By this time, Rocky Ford boasted expanded timber enterprises, a new hotel, an enor-

Plate **33.2:** The towering Queen Anne design of the 1897 Screven County Courthouse must have been quite popular, for Goodrich employed the very same plan twice more after the turn of the century.

mous brickyard, and even a town band, while Sylvania, at the end of her near-do-well spur, counted only about 500 residents. [8]

To add to Sylvania's woes, a large portion of the town, including the old courthouse, burned to the ground in 1897. In the wake of this fire, new brick buildings rose. By far the most impressive of these was Augusta architect Lewis Goodrich's 1897 Screven County Courthouse. The towering Queen Anne structure must have been quite popular, for Goodrich employed the very same design twice more after the turn of the century, once in South Carolina and once in Taliaferro County where an identical courthouse rose at Crawfordville in 1903.

Probably influenced by earlier Queen Anne designs by Atlanta architects, Bruce and Morgan, in Talbotton (1892), Buchanan (1892), Statesboro (1894) and Dublin (1895), Goodrich employed similar Queen Anne detail in Sylvania. The picturesque asymmetrical massing of the two corner towers with their bell domes, as well as the ornate chimneys and dormers that break the silhouette of the roof line and the sashed windows with grids of tiny panes above are all characteristic of the Queen Anne Style. Like Bruce and Morgan, Goodrich undoubtedly employed Queen Anne ornament in order to achieve a more modern effect, dressing an older, fundamentally Romanesque form in up-to-date finery. But despite all of this decoration, the 1897 Screven County Courthouses broadcast a rather Spartan visage when compared to older brick Queen Anne buildings in the North, where picturesque styles had fallen from favor in the wake of the American Neoclassical Revival, which had gained momentum after the success of the buildings at the 1893 Colombian Exposition in Chicago.

Nine years after the construction of Lewis Goodrich's 1897 Screven County Courthouse, George Brinson chartered his Brinson Railway. By 1909, this line had acquired some of E. E. Foy's old tramlines, which had been incorporated as the Savannah Valley Railroad. The enterprising Brinson tied this web together to create a connection from Savannah through Springfield and Sylvania all the way to Millhaven. By 1913, the line had reached

Waynesboro, and by 1913, it stretched all the way to St. Claire. Brinson's railroad fell on hard times in 1915, and by 1917, it had been purchased by the newly created Savannah and Atlanta Railroad, which had just completed track from St. Claire to a connection with the Georgia Railroad at Camak.

The new track from St. Claire to Camak inspired hope in Sylvania, while out in the piney woods the great virgin stands were disappearing and the boomtowns along the Central's main line were drying up. Today Halcyondale, Dover, Rocky Ford, and Scarborough are hard to find, and Sylvania remains the only town of significance in Screven County. Sadly, Lewis Goodrich's 1897 Screven County Court House was demolished in 1965.

SOME LAST THOUGHTS ON THE ATLANTA AND SAVANNAH RAILROAD

The construction of the Atlanta and Savannah Railroad supplies us with a late example of the power of rail to bolster economic expectations and to inspire fantasy courthouses even in the most out-of-the-way places. Here is proof that as late as the end of the first decade of the new century, the myth of a railroad-driven New South was still alive in remote corners of Georgia's piney woods.

Originally begun as the Brinson Railroad, the Atlanta and Savannah was in many ways typical of rail lines of the earlier period. It began as the dream of timber man and railroad entrepreneur, George Brinson, who managed to consolidate and connect several old timber company tram railroads in Effingham and Screven Counties. By 1909 Brinson's new line stretched all the way from Savannah to Sylvania in Screven County, passing through the previously by-passed county town of Springfield in Effingham county, where spirits soared and a grand new courthouse rose in that same year. Hope was fired in Sylvania as well. Where for decades progress had failed to ride on her tiny spur line. Doubtless the arrival of mainline rails would have inspired a court building in Sylvania had the town not just built a new one to replace Screven's old wooden courthouse that had burned in Sylvania's disastrous fire in 1897.

However, as elsewhere in the piney woods, the promises of the New South proved hollow. The great virgin pine forests of Effingham and Screven Counties slowly disappeared. By the beginning on the second decade of the new century, the Brinson Railroad had undergone several reorganizations and even though it was eventually completed all the way to Camak and a connection with the Georgia Railroad, the line never flourished. In 1921 the Atlanta and Savannah Railroad declared bankruptcy and later became part of the Central of Georgia, which used a short section of her of track out from Savannah as a new main line before tying back into the Central's original main line at Oliver. This effectively diverted traffic away from Springfield and Sylvania, and the portion of the old Atlanta and Savannah Railroad west of Sylvania was pulled up from scrap in 1962.

•

[8] Lee-Ford, *Screven and Jenkins Counties*, 75.

Appendix A: Georgia Courthouses: A Chronological Listing

Standing Court Buildings (1998) Are Listed In Bold Type

Built	County	City	Style	Material	Architect	Demo
1760c	Chatham	Savannah	Vernacular	brick	N/A	1831
1786	Greene	Greensboro	Vernacular	log	N/A	1787
1788	Greene	Greensboro	Vernacular	log	N/A	1805
1788c	Camden	St Marys	Vernacular	frame	N/A	
1789	Burke	Waynesboro	Vernacular	frame	N/A	1825
1791	Elbert	Elberton	Vernacular	unknown	N/A	
1793	Franklin	Carnesville	Vernacular	log	N/A	
1793	Oglethorpe	Pilomoth	Vernacular	log	N/A	
1793c	Hancock	Sparta	Vernacular	frame	N/A	1806
1794c	McInstosh	Sapelo bridge	Vernacular	log	N/A	
1797	Warren	Warrenton	Vernacular	frame	N/A	1853
1797c	Screven	Jacksonboro	Vernacular	log?	N/A	1832
1798	Liberty	Riceboro	Vernacular	log	N/A	
1800	Lincoln	Lincolnton	Vernacular	unknown	N/A	1874
1801	Richmond	Augusta	Vernacular	brick	N/A	
1802	Camden	Jeffersonton	Vernacular	frame	N/A	
1806	Clarke	Watkinsville	Vernacular	frame	N/A	1829
1806	Franklin	Carnesville	Vernacular	frame	N/A	1826
1806	Jackson	Jefferson	Vernacular	log	N/A	
1806c	Bulloch	Statesboro	Vernacular	log	N/A	
1806c	Hancock	Sparta	Vernacular	brick	N/A	1882
1807	Greene	Greensboro	Vernacular	brick	N/A	1849
1807	Morgan	Madison	Vernacular	brick	N/A	1844
1807c	Tattnall	Ohoopee mills	Vernacular	log	N/A	
1808	Elbert	Elberton	Vernacular	frame	N/A	
1808	Jones	Clinton	Vernacular	frame	N/A	1818
1808c	Laurens	Summerville	Vernacular	frame	N/A	
1808c	Wilkinson	Irwinton	Vernacular	frame	N/A	1828
1810	Pulaski	Hartford	Vernacular	frame	N/A	1857
1810	Twiggs	Marion	Vernacular	frame	N/A	
1811	Jasper	Monticello	Vernacular	log	N/A	1839
1811c	Laurens	Dublin	Vernacular	frame	N/A	
1812	Telfair	Jacksonville	Vernacular	log	N/A	186?
1812	Washington	Sandersville	Vernacular	frame	N/A	1836
1813	Madison	Danielsville	Vernacular	log	N/A	1834
1813	Montgomery	Mt. Vernon	Vernacular	frame	N/A	1857c
1814	Baldwin	Milledgeville	unknown	brick	N/A	1838
1814	Emanuel	Swainsboro	Vernacular	log	N/A	

Built	County	City	Style	Material	Architect	Demo
1814c	Bryan	Clyde	Vernacular	frame	N/A	1901
1816	Elbert	Elberton	Vernacular	frame	N/A	
1816	Jefferson	Louisville	Vernacular	frame	N/A	
1817	Jackson	Jefferson	Vernacular	brick	N/A	
1817	Wilkes	Washington	Federal	brick	Ball, Fredrick	1902
1818	Hall	Gainesville	Vernacular	log	N/A	
1818	Jones	Clinton	Vernacular	brick	N/A	1920c
1818c	Gwinnett	Unknown	Vernacular	log	N/A	
1818c	McInstosh	Darien	Vernacular	frame	N/A	1863
1819	Oglethorpe	Lexington	Vernacular	brick	N/A	1887
1820c	Gwinnett	Unknown	Vernacular	log	N/A	
1820c	Hall	Gainesville	Vernacular	frame	N/A	
1821	Habersham	Clarkesville	Vernacular	frame	N/A	1980?
1821	Richmond	Augusta	Federal	brick	Middleton, James	1959
1821	Walton	Monroe	Vernacular	log	N/A	1823
1822	Emanuel	Swainsboro	Vernacular	log	N/A	1840
1822	Newton	Covington	Vernacular	log	N/A	1824c
1823	Fayette	Fayetteville	Vernacular	frame	N/A	
1823	Pike	Old Newnan	Vernacular	log	N/A	
1823	Walton	Monroe	Vernacular	brick	N/A	1841
1823?	Bibb	Macon	Vernacular	frame	N/A	1828
1824	Dekalb	Decatur	Vernacular	log	N/A	1829
1824	Gwinnett	Lawrenceville	Vernacular	brick	N/A	1871
1824	Henry	McDonough	Vernacular	frame	N/A	1824
1824	Houston	Perry	Vernacular	frame	N/A	1855
1824	Monroe	Forsyth	Vernacular	log	N/A	1825
1824	Newton	Covington	Vernacular	brick	N/A	1856
1824	Rabun	Clayton	Vernacular	log	N/A	1838
1825	Butts	Jackson	Vernacular	log	N/A	1828
1825	Early	Blakely	Vernacular	log	N/A	1836
1825	**Fayette**	**Fayetteville**	**Vernacular**	**brick**	**N/A**	**standing**
1825	Monroe	Forsyth	Vernacular	brick	N/A	1896
1825?	Burke	Waynesboro	Vernacular	brick	N/A	1856
1825c	Baker	Byron	Vernacular	frame	N/A	
1825c	Ware	Waresboro	Vernacular	log	N/A	
1826	Dade	Trenton	Vernacular	brick	N/A	
1826	Decatur	Bainbridge	Vernacular	frame	N/A	1831
1826	Franklin	Carnesville	Vernacular	brick	N/A	1906
1826	Pike	Zebulon	Vernacular	frame	N/A	1844
1827	Butts	Jackson	Vernacular	brick	N/A	1828
1827	Thomas	Thomasville	Vernacular	log	N/A	1846
1827c	Bulloch	Statesboro	Vernacular	frame	N/A	1864
1828	Appling	Holmesville	Vernacular	log	N/A	

Built	County	City	Style	Material	Architect	Demo
1828	Butts	Jackson	Vernacular	brick	N/A	1864
1828	Campbell	Campbellton	Vernacular	brick	N/A	1912
1828	Lowndes	Franklinville	Vernacular	log	N/A	
1828	Marion	Horry	Vernacular	log	N/A	
1828	Taliaferro	Crawfordville	Vernacular	brick	N/A	1902c
1828	Upson	Thomaston	Vernacular	brick	N/A	1852
1828c	Muscogee	Columbus	Vernacular	frame	N/A	1838
1828c	Wilkinson	Irwinton	Vernacular	frame	N/A	1854
1829	Campbell	Campbellton	Vernacular	frame	N/A	1835
1829	Clarke	Watkinsville	Vernacular	brick	N/A	1887
1829	Coweta	Newnan	Vernacular	brick	N/A	1904
1829	Dekalb	Decatur	Vernacular	brick	N/A	1842
1829	Glynn	Brunswick	Vernacular	unknown	N/A	
1829	Harris	Hamilton	Vernacular	log	N/A	1831
1829	Oconee	Watkinsville	Vernacular	brick	N/A	1887
183?	Chatooga	Summerville	Vernacular	log	N/A	1841?
1830	Bibb	Macon	Greek Revival	brick	Alexander, Elam	1872
1830	Carroll	Carrollton	Vernacular	log	N/A	1837
1830	Irwin	Irwinville	Vernacular	unknown	N/A	
1830	Troup	Lagrange	Vernacular	brick	N/A	1904
1830c	Tattnall	Reidsville	Vernacular	log	N/A	
1830c	Wayne	Waynesville	Vernacular	log	N/A	
1831	Harris	Hamilton	Vernacular	brick	N/A	1907
1831	Henry	McDonough	Vernacular	brick	N/A	1896
1831	Stewart	Lumpkin	Vernacular	log	N/A	1837
1831	Talbot	Talbotton	Vernacular	brick	N/A	1892
1831–1832	**Crawford**	**Knoxville**	**Vernacular**	**brick**	**N/A**	**in use**
1831c	Heard	Franklin	Vernacular	brick	N/A	1894
1832	Forsyth	Cummings	Vernacular	log	N/A	
1832	Habersham	Clarkesville	Vernacular	brick	N/A	1898
1832	Hall	Gainesville	Vernacular	brick	N/A	1852
1832	Meriwether	Greenville	Vernacular	brick	N/A	1901
1832	Putnam	Eatonton	Vernacular	brick	N/A	1904
1832	Screven	Jacksonboro	Vernacular	frame	N/A	1847
1832c	Baker	Newton	Vernacular	frame	N/A	1873
1833	Chatham	Savannah	Greek Revival	brick	Warren, Russell	1898
1833	Floyd	Livingston	Vernacular	log	N/A	1835
1833	Gilmer	Ellijay	Vernacular	log	N/A	1854
1833	Lumpkin	Dahlonega	Vernacular	log	N/A	
1834	Cobb	Marietta	Vernacular	log	N/A	1838
1834	Lowndes	Loudenville	Vernacular	log	N/A	
1834	Madison	Danielsville	Vernacular	frame	N/A	1900
1834	Murray	Spring place	Vernacular	brick	N/A	

Built	County	City	Style	Material	Architect	Demo
1834	Sumter	Americus	Vernacular	frame	N/A	1850c
1835	Floyd	Rome	Vernacular	brick	N/A	1892?
1836	Bartow	Cassville	Vernacular	brick	N/A	1864
1836	Dooly	Drayton	Vernacular	log	N/A	
1836	Early	Blakely	Vernacular	frame	N/A	1857
1836	**Lumpkin**	**Dahlonega**	**Vernacular**	**brick**	**N/A**	**standing**
1836	Paulding	Van wert	Vernacular	frame	N/A	
1836	Washington	Sandersville	Neoclassical	brick	unknown	1855
1837	Carroll	Carrollton	Vernacular	frame	N/A	1860?
1837	Lee	Starkville	Vernacular	frame	N/A	1858
1837	Liberty	Hinesville	Vernacular	frame	N/A	1925
1837	Randolph	Cuthbert	Vernacular	frame	N/A	1840
1837	Stewart	Lumpkin	Vernacular	brick	N/A	1895
1837	Tattnall	Reidsville	Vernacular	frame	N/A	
1838	**Cobb**	**Marietta**	**Vernacular**	**frame**	**N/A**	
1838	Decatur	Bainbridge	Vernacular	brick	N/A	1855
1838	Macon	Lanier	Vernacular	frame	N/A	1972c
1838	Muscogee	Columbus	Vernacular	brick	N/A	1896
1838	Rabun	Clayton	Vernacular	log	N/A	1878
1838	Walker	Lafayette	Vernacular	brick	N/A	1882
1839	Forsyth	Cummings	Vernacular	frame	N/A	1854
1839	Jasper	Monticello	Vernacular	brick	N/A	1909
1839	Marion	Tazwell	Vernacular	frame	N/A	1845
1840	Cherokee	Canton	Vernacular	brick	N/A	1864
1840	Emanuel	Swainsboro	Vernacular	frame	N/A	1960s
1840	Randolph	Cuthbert	Vernacular	brick	N/A	1885
1840c	Effingham	Springfield	Vernacular	frame	N/A	1909
1841	Chatooga	Summerville	Vernacular	brick	N/A	1909
1841	Dooly	Berrien(vienna)	Vernacular	log	N/A	1847
1841	Walton	Monroe	Vernacular	brick	N/A	1882
1842?	Dade	Trenton	Vernacular	frame	N/A	1853
1843c	Murray	Spring place	Vernacular	brick	N/A	1884
1844	Morgan	Madison	Vernacular	brick	N/A	1917
1844	Pike	Zebulon	Greek Revival	unknown	unknown	1895
1845	Lowndes	Troopville	Vernacular	frame	N/A	1858
1845c	Ware	Waycross	Vernacular	frame	N/A	
1846	Thomas	Thomasville	Vernacular	brick	N/A	1858
1847	Baldwin	Milledgeville	Vernacular	brick	N/A	1861
1847	Dekalb	Decatur	Vernacular	brick	N/A	1900
1847	Dooly	Vienna	Vernacular	frame	N/A	1892
1847	Screven	Sylvania	Vernacular	frame	N/A	1897
1847	Sumter	Americus	Vernacular	brick	N/A	1887
1848	Jefferson	Louisville	Vernacular	brick	N/A	1904

Built	County	City	Style	Material	Architect	Demo
1848	Marion	Tazwell	Vernacular	frame	N/A	standing
1848–1849	Greene	Greensboro	Greek Revival	brick	Demarest, David	in use
1849	Laurens	Dublin	Vernacular	frame	N/A	1895
1849–1856	Marion	Buena vista	Vernacular	brick	N/A	in use
1851	Gordon	Calhoun	Vernacular	brick	N/A	1888
1852	Clinch	Magnolia	Vernacular	frame	N/A	1856
1852	Hall	Gainesville	Vernacular	brick	N/A	1882
1852	Paulding	Dallas	Vernacular	brick	N/A	1924
1852	Polk	Cedartown	Vernacular	brick	N/A	1964
1852	Upson	Thomaston	Vernacular	brick	N/A	1908
1852c	Whitfield	Dalton	Vernacular	brick	N/A	1891
1853	Cobb	Marietta	Greek Revival	brick	Hunt, William	1864
1853	Pickens	Jasper	Vernacular	brick	N/A	
1853	Warren	Warrenton	Vernacular	brick	N/A	1908
1853c	Elbert	Elberton	Vernacular	brick	N/A	1893
1854	Calhoun	Morgan	Vernacular	frame	N/A	1892
1854	Chattahoochee	Cusseta	Vernacular	frame	N/A	standing
1854	Clay	Fort Gaines	Vernacular	frame	N/A	in use
1854	Coffee	Douglas	Vernacular	frame	N/A	
1854	Dade	Trenton	Vernacular	brick	N/A	1926
1854	Fannin	Morganton	Vernacular	brick	N/A	
1854	Forsyth	Cummings	Vernacular	brick	N/A	1905
1854	Gilmer	Ellijay	Vernacular	brick	N/A	1934
1854	Hart	Hartwell	Vernacular	frame	N/A	
1854	Irwin	Irwinville	Vernacular	frame	N/A	
1854	Lee	Starkville	Vernacular	frame	N/A	1858
1854	Lee	Webster	Vernacular	frame	N/A	
1854	Macon	Oglethorpe	Vernacular	frame	N/A	1857
1854	Taylor	Butler	Vernacular	brick	N/A	1935
1854	Wilkinson	Irwinton	Vernacular	frame	N/A	1864
1854	Worth	Isabella	Vernacular	frame	N/A	1879
1855	Decatur	Bainbridge	Vernacular	brick	N/A	1902
1855	Dougherty	Albany	Vernacular	brick	N/A	1903
1855	Houston	Perry	Vernacular	brick	N/A	1948
1856	Berrien	Nashville	Vernacular	brick	N/A	1928c
1856	Catoosa	Ringgold	Vernacular	brick	N/A	1939
1856	Charlton	Trader's Hill	Vernacular	log	N/A	1877
1856	Clinch	Magnolia	Vernacular	frame	N/A	1867
1856	Columbia	Appling	Vernacular	brick	N/A	in use
1856	Hart	Hartwell	Vernacular	brick	N/A	1900
1856	Newton	Covington	Vernacular	brick	N/A	1884
1856	Terrell	Dawson	Vernacular	frame	N/A	
1856	Union	Blairsville	Vernacular	log	N/A	

Built	County	City	Style	Material	Architect	Demo
1856	Webster	Preston	Vernacular	frame	N/A	1915
1857	**Burke**	**Waynesboro**	**Vernacular**	**brick**	**N/A**	**in use**
1857	Carroll	Carrollton	Vernacular	brick	N/A	1892
1857	Early	Blakely	Vernacular	brick	N/A	1904
1857	Fulton	Atlanta	Federal	brick	Hughes, C.	1883
1857	Haralson	Buchanan	Vernacular	brick	N/A	1891
1857	**Macon**	**Oglethorpe**	**Vernacular**	**brick**	**N/A**	**standing**
1857	Milton	Alpharetta	Vernacular	brick	N/A	1955
1857	Montgomery	Mt. Vernon	Vernacular	frame	N/A	1907
1857	Towns	Hiawassee	Vernacular	log	N/A	
1858	**Dawson**	**Dawsonville**	**Vernacular**	**brick**	**N/A**	**standing**
1858	**Glascock**	**Gibson**	**Vernacular**	**frame**	**N/A**	**standing**
1858	Mitchell	Camilla	Vernacular	frame	N/A	1869
1858	Schley	Ellaville	Vernacular	brick	N/A	1900
1858	**Thomas**	**Thomasville**	**Vernacular**	**brick**	**Wind, John**	**in use**
1858	Washington	Sandersville	Neoclassical	brick	Wetter, A. P.	1864
1858	Wilcox	Abbeville	Vernacular	log	N/A	1879
1858c	Pierce	Blackshear	Vernacular	log	N/A	1859c
1859	Colquitt	Moultrie	Vernacular	log	N/A	1881
1859	Johnson	Wrightsville	Vernacular	frame	N/A	1894
1859	Lowndes	Valdosta	Vernacular	frame	N/A	1869
1859	Quitman	Georgetown	Vernacular	frame	N/A	1939
1859	**Spalding**	**Griffin**	**Italianate**	**brick**	**Hughes, C.**	**standing**
1859	Union	Blairsville	Vernacular	brick	N/A	1899
1859–1864	Brooks	Quitman	Federal	brick	Wind, John	in use
1859c	Pierce	Blackshear	Vernacular	frame	N/A	1875
1860	Miller	Colquitt	Vernacular	frame	N/A	1872
1860	Telfair	Jacksonville	Vernacular	frame	N/A	
1860	**White**	**Cleveland**	**Vernacular**	**brick**	**N/A**	**standing**
1860–1865	**Banks**	**Homer**	**Vernacular**	**brick**	**N/A**	**standing**
1861	Clayton	Jonesboro	Vernacular	brick	Vanloan, Abe	1864
1861	Lee	Starkville	Vernacular	brick	N/A	
1865c	McInstosh	Darien	Vernacular	frame	N/A	1873
1867	Clinch	Homerville	Vernacular	frame	N/A	
1867	Polk	Cedartown	Vernacular	brick	N/A	1888c
1868–1869	**Washington**	**Sandersville**	**Vernacular**	**brick**	**N/A**	**in use**
1868c	Bulloch	Statesboro	Vernacular	frame	N/A	
1869	**Clayton**	**Jonesboro**	**Vernacular**	**brick**	**Fay & Corput**	**standing**
1869	Mitchell	Camilla	Vernacular	frame	N/A	1890
1870	Butts	Jackson	Vernacular	brick	N/A	1897
1870	Wilkinson	Irwinton	Vernacular	brick	N/A	1924
1870c	Towns	Hiawassee	Vernacular	frame	N/A	1899
1870c	Ware	Waycross	Vernacular	frame	N/A	1872

Built	County	City	Style	Material	Architect	Demo
1871	**Campbell**	**Fairburn**	**Greek Revival**	brick	**unknown**	standing
1871	Lowndes	Valdosta	Vernacular	frame	N/A	
1871–1873	**Clay**	**Fort Gaines**	**Vernacular**	brick	**N/A**	in use
1872	Camden	St. Mary's	Vernacular	frame	N/A	1965
1872	Lee	Leesburg	Vernacular	frame	N/A	1873
1872	**McDuffie**	**Thomson**	**Vernacular**	brick	**N/A**	in use
1872	Rockdale	Conyers	Vernacular	brick	N/A	1939
1872	Telfair	McRae	Vernacular	frame	N/A	1888
1872c	Ware	Waycross	Vernacular	frame	N/A	
1873	Baker	Newton	Vernacular	brick	N/A	1906
1873	**Bartow**	**Cartersville**	**Italianate**	brick	**unknown**	standing
1873	Bibb	Macon	2nd Empire	brick	Randall, G. P.	1924
1873	Cobb	Marietta	Greek Revival	brick	Hunt, William	1969
1873	Miller	Colquitt	Vernacular	frame	N/A	1904
1873	Wayne	Jesup	Vernacular	frame	N/A	1903
1874	Appling	Baxley	Vernacular	frame	N/A	1876
1874	Cherokee	Canton	Vernacular?	brick	N/A	1926
1874	Dodge	Eastman	Vernacular	frame	N/A	1907
1874	Gwinnett	Lawrenceville	Vernacular	brick	N/A	1884
1874	Lincoln	Lincolnton	Vernacular	brick	N/A	1916
1874	**McInstosh**	**Darien**	**Vernacular**	brick	**N/A**	in use
1874	**Pulaski**	**Hawkinsville**	**Vernacular**	brick	**Bryan, A. J.**	in use
1874c	Douglas	Douglasville	Vernacular	frame	N/A	
1875	Lowndes	Valdosta	Vernacular	brick	N/A	
1875	**Pierce**	**Blackshear**	**Vernacular**	frame	**N/A**	standing
1876	Appling	Baxley	Vernacular	frame	N/A	1886
1876	Clarke	Athens	2nd Empire	brick	Charbonnier, H.	1951
1876	Douglas	Douglasville	Vernacular	brick	N/A	1884
1877	Charlton	Trader's Hill	Vernacular	frame	N/A	
1878	Rabun	Clayton	Vernacular	frame	N/A	1908
1879	**Jackson**	**Jefferson**	**Italianate**	brick	**Thomas, W.W.**	in use
1880	Lee	Leesburg	Vernacular	brick	N/A	1921
1880	Wilcox	Abbeville	Vernacular	frame	N/A	
1880	Worht	Isabella	Vernacular	frame	N/A	1893
1881	Colquitt	Moultrie	Vernacular	frame	N/A	1903?
1881–1883	**Hancock**	**Sparta**	**2nd Empire**	brick	**Parkins & Bruce**	in use
1883	Fulton	Atlanta	2nd Empire	brick	Parkins & Bruce	1911
1883	Irwin	Irwinville	Vernacular	frame	N/A	
1883	Walker	Lafayette	Vernacular	brick	Patton, J. B. ?	1922
1883–1884	**Walton**	**Monroe**	**2nd Empire**	brick	**Bruce and Morgan**	in use
1884	Glynn	Brunswick	Vernacular	frame	N/A	
1884	**Newton**	**Covington**	**2nd Empire**	brick	**Bruce and Morgan**	in use
1884–1885	**Gwinnett**	**Lawerenceville**	**Romanesque**	brick	**Lind , E. G.**	standing

Built	County	City	Style	Material	Architect	Demo
1885	Hall	Gainesville	2nd Empire	brick	Bruce & Morgan	1936
1886	Appling	Baxley	Vernacular	brick	N/A	1907
1886	**Randolph**	**Cuthbert**	**Romanesque**	**brick**	**Kimball/Wheeler/Parkins**	**in use**
1887	**Baldwin**	**Milledgeville**	**Vernacular**	**brick**	**Dennis, P. E.**	**in use**
1887	Murray	Spring Place	Vernacular	brick	N/A	1990
1887	**Oglethorpe**	**Lexington**	**Romanesque**	**brick**	**Kimball/Wheeler/Parkins**	**in use**
1887	Sumter	Americus	Romanesque	brick	Bruce&Morgan	1959
1888	Gordon	Calhoun	Romanesque	brick	Parkins, William	1961
1888	Oconee	Watkinsville	Romanesque	brick	Thomas, W. W.	1939
1888	Pickens	Jasper	Romanesque	brick	Bruce & Morgan	1947
1888	Telfair	McRae	Vernacular	brick	N/A	1906
1889	**Chatham**	**Savannah**	**Romanesque**	**brick**	**Preston, William G.**	**standing**
1889	Coffee	Douglas	Vernacular	frame	N\A	1900
1890	**Dooly**	**Vienna**	**Romanesque**	**brick**	**Parkins, William**	**in use**
1890	Mitchell	Camilla	Vernacular	brick	Bruce & Morgan	1937
1890	Polk	Cedartown	Romanesque	brick	Parkins, William	1951
1891–1892	**Haralson**	**Buchanan**	**Romanesque**	**brick**	**Bruce & Morgan**	**standing**
1892	**Paulding**	**Dallas**	**Romanesque**	**brick**	**Bruce & Morgan**	**in use**
1892	**Talbot**	**Talbotton**	**Romanesque**	**brick**	**Bruce & Morgan**	**in use**
1892	**Terrell**	**Dawson**	**Romanesque**	**brick**	**Parkins, William**	**in use**
1892	Ware	Waycross	Romanesque	brick	Norman, G. L.	1977
1892	Whitfield	Dalton	Romanesque	brick	Chamberlain, W.	1961
1893	Calhoun	Morgan	Vernacular	frame	N/A	1929
1893	Carroll	Carrollton	Romanesque	brick	Bruce & Morgan	1927?
1893	**Floyd**	**Rome**	**Romanesque**	**brick**	**Bruce & Morgan**	**standing**
1893	Worth	Isabella	Vernacular	frame	N/A	1894
1893–1894	**Elbert**	**Elberton**	**Romanesque**	**brick**	**Hunt & Lamar**	**in use**
1894	**Bulloch**	**Statesboro**	**Romanesque**	**brick**	**Bruce & Morgan**	**in use**
1894	Heard	Franklin	Romanesque	brick	Bruce & Morgan	1964
1894	**Macon**	**Oglethorpe**	**Romanesque**	**brick**	**Chamberlain, W.**	**in use**
1894	Worth	Isabella	Vernacular	brick	unknown	1960c
1895	Emanuel	Swainsboro	Romanesque	brick	Golucke, J. W.	1919
1895	**Johnson**	**Wrightsville**	**Noeclassical**	**brick**	**Golucke &Stewart**	**in use**
1895	Laurens	Dublin	Romanesque	brick	Bruce & Morgan	1962
1895	**Pike**	**Zebulon**	**Neoclassical**	**brick**	**Golucke & Stewart**	**in use**
1895	**Stewart**	**Lumpkin**	**Neoclassical**	**brick**	**Bryan, A. J.**	**in use**
1896	**Clinch**	**Homerville**	**Vernacular**	**brick**	**unknown**	**in use**
1896	Douglas	Douglasville	Romanesque	brick	Bryan, A. J.	1956
1896	**Monroe**	**Forsyth**	**Romanesque**	**brick**	**Bruce & Morgan**	**in use**
1896	Muscogee	[missing info]	Neoclassical	brick	Bryan, A. J.	1969
1897	**Henry**	**McDonough**	**Romanesque**	**brick**	**Golucke & Stewart**	**in use**
1897	Screven	Sylvania	Romanesque	brick	Goodrich, L. F.	1965
1898	**Berrien**	**Nashville**	**Romanesque**	**brick**	**Chamberlain, W.**	**in use**

Built	County	City	Style	Material	Architect	Demo
1898	Butts	Jackson	Romanesque	brick	Bruce & Morgan	in use
1898	Clayton	Jonesboro	Romanesque	brick	Golucke, J. W.	in use
1898	Gilmer	Ellijay	Neoclassical	brick	unknown	in use
1898	Habersham	Clarkesville	Romanesque	brick	Golucke, J. W.	1965
1898	Washington	Sandersville	Romanesque	brick	Goodrich, L. F.*	in use
1898–1900	Dekalb	Decatur	Neoclassical	stone	Golucke, J. W.	standing
1899	Cobb	Marietta	Romanesque	brick	Golucke, J. W.	1969
1899	Echols	Statenville	Vernacular	frame	unknown	19??
1899	Towns	Hiawassee	Vernacular	brick	unknown	1963
1899	Union	Blairsville	Romanesque	brick	Golucke, J. W.	standing
1899	Washington	Sandersville	Romanesque	brick	Goodrich, L. F.*	in use
1900	Coffee	Douglas	Romanesque	brick	Bryan, A. J.	1939
1900	Schley	Ellaville	Romanesque	brick	Golucke & Stewart	in use
1901	Bryan	Clyde	Vernacular	frame	unknown	1940c
1901	Charlton	Folkston	Romanesque	brick	Darling T. J.	1928
1901	Fannin	Blue ridge	Vernacular	brick	Golucke, J. W.	1936
1901	Hart	Hartwell	Neoclassical	brick	Golucke, J. W.	1967
1901	Madison	Danielsville	Romanesque	brick	Golucke, J. W.	in use
1902	Decatur	Bainbridge	Neoclassical	brick	Blair, Alexander	in use
1902	Taliaferro	Crawfordsville	Romanesque	brick	Goodrich, L. F.	in use
1902	Tattnall	Riedsville	Neoclassical	brick	Golucke, J. W.	in use
1902–1903	Bartow	Cartersville	Neoclassical	brick	Golucke, J. W.	in use
1902–1903	Colquitt	Moultrie	Neoclassical	brick	Bryan, A. J.	in use
1902–1903	Meriwether	Greenville	Neoclassical	brick	Golucke, J. W.	in use
1902–1903	Pierce	Blackshear	Neoclassical	brick	Golucke, J. W.	in use
1902–1903	Twiggs	Jeffersonville	Romanesque	brick	Golucke, J. W.	in use
1903	Dougherty	Albany	Neoclassical	brick	Lockwood T. F.	1966
1903	Wayne	Jesup	Romanesque	brick	unknown	in use
1903	Wilkes	Washington	Romanesque	brick	Milburn, Frank	in use
1903–1904	Wilcox	Abbeville	Neoclassical	brick	Milburn, Frank	in use
1904	Jefferson	Louisville	Neoclassical	brick	Denny, W. F	in use
1904	Troup	Lagrange	Neoclassical	brick	Bryan, A. J.	1936
1904–1905	Coweta	Newnan	Neoclassical	brick	Golucke, J. W.	in use
1904–1905	Early	Blakely	Neoclassical	brick	Morgan & Dillion	in use
1904–1905	Lowndes	Valdosta	Neoclassical	brick	Milburn, Frank	in use
1905	Forsyth	Cummings	Romanesque	brick	Golucke, J. W.	1973
1905	Morgan	Madison	Neoclassical	brick	Golucke, J. W.	in use
1905	Putnam	Eatonton	Neoclassical	brick	Golucke, J. W.	in use
1905–1906	Jones	Gray	Romanesque	brick	Golucke, J. W.	in use
1905–1906	Worth	Sylvester	Neoclassical	brick	Golucke, J. W.	in use
1906	Franklin	Carnesville	Neoclassical	concret	Chamberlain, W.	in use
1906	Miller	Colquitt	Neoclassical	brick	Blair, Alexander	1974
1906	Telfair	McRae	Neoclassical	brick	Blair, Alexander	1934

Built	County	City	Style	Material	Architect	Demo
1906	Toombs	Lyons	Neoclassical	brick	Golucke, J. W.(Attr)	1917
1906–1907	Baker	Newton	Romanesque	brick	Golucke, J. W.	standing
1906–1907	Jeff Davis	Hazlehurst	Romanesque	concret	Chamberlain, W.	in use
1907	Glynn	Brunswick	Neoclassical	brick	Gifford & Betts	in use
1907	Montgomery	Mt. Vernon	Neoclassical	brick	Blair, Alexander	in use
1907	Turner	Ashburn	Neoclassical	brick	Blair, Alexander	in use
1907–1908	Appling	Baxley	Neoclassical	stone	Lewman, H. L.	in use
1907–1908	Dodge	Eastman	Neoclassical	brick	Hosford, E. C.	in use
1907–1908	Stephens	Toccoa	Neoclassical	brick	Lewman, H. L.	in use
1908	Crisp	Cordele	Neoclassical	brick	Lockwood, T. F.	1950
1908	Harris	Hamilton	Neoclassical	brick	Hosford, E. C.	in use
1908	Jasper	Monticello	Neoclassical	brick	Lockwood, Bros	in use
1908	Rabun	Clayton	Vernacular	concrte	Lewman, H. L.	1960
1908	Upson	Thomaston	Neoclassical	brick	Milburn, Frank	in use
1908–1909	Grady	Cairo	Neoclassical	brick	Blair, Alexander	1980?
1909	Ben Hill	Fitzgerald	Neoclassical	brick	Huggins, H. H.	in use
1909	Chatooga	Summerville	Neoclassical	brick	Bryan & Co.	in use
1909	Effingham	Springfield	Neoclassical	brick	Whitcover, W. H.	in use
1909–1910	Warren	Warrenton	Neoclassical	brick	Chamberlain, W.	in use
1910	Irwin	Ocilla	Neoclassical	brick	unknown	in use
1910	Jenkins	Millen	Neoclassical	brick	Goodrich, L. F.	in use

Appendix B: Georgia Courthouses: Alphabetically by County

Built	County	City	Style	Material	Architect	Demo
1828	Appling	Holmesville	Vernacular	log	N/A	
1874	Appling	Baxley	Vernacular	frame	N/A	1876
1876	Appling	Baxley	Vernacular	frame	N/A	1886
1886	Appling	Baxley	Vernacular	brick	N/A	1907
1907–1908	**Appling**	**Baxley**	**Neoclassical**	**stone**	**Lewman, H. L.**	**in use**
1847	Baldwin	Milledgeville	Vernacular	brick	N/A	1861
1825c	Baker	Byron	Vernacular	frame	N/A	
1832c	Baker	Newton	Vernacular	frame	N/A	1873
1873	Baker	Newton	Vernacular	brick	N/A	1906
1906–1907	**Baker**	**Newton**	**Romanesque**	**brick**	**Golucke, J. W.**	**standing**
1814	Baldwin	Milledgeville	unknown	brick	N/A	1838
1887	Baldwin	Milledgeville	Vernacular	brick	Dennis, P. E.	in use
1860–1865	**Banks**	**Homer**	**Vernacular**	**brick**	**N/A**	**standing**
1836	Bartow	Cassville	Vernacular	brick	N/A	1864
1873	**Bartow**	**Cartersville**	**Italianate**	**brick**	**unknown**	**standing**
1902–1903	**Bartow**	**Cartersville**	**Neoclassical**	**brick**	**Golucke, J. W.**	**in use**
1909	**Ben Hill**	**Fitzgerald**	**Neoclassical**	**brick**	**Huggins, H. H.**	**in use**
1856	Berrien	Nashville	Vernacular	brick	N/A	1928c
1898	**Berrien**	**Nashville**	**Romanesque**	**brick**	**Chamberlain, W.**	**in use**
1823?	Bibb	Macon	Vernacular	frame	N/A	1828
1830	Bibb	Macon	Greek Revival	brick	Alexander, Elam	1872
1873	Bibb	Macon	2nd Empire	brick	Randall, G. P.	1924
1859–1864	**Brooks**	**Quitman**	**Federal**	**brick**	**Wind, John**	**in use**
1814c	Bryan	Clyde	Vernacular	frame	N/A	1901
1901	Bryan	Clyde	Vernacular	frame	unknown	1940c
1806c	Bulloch	Statesboro	Vernacular	log	N/A	
1827c	Bulloch	Statesboro	Vernacular	frame	N/A	1864
1868c	Bulloch	Statesboro	Vernacular	frame	N/A	
1894	**Bulloch**	**Statesboro**	**Romanesque**	**brick**	**Bruce & Morgan**	**in use**
1789	Burke	Waynesboro	Vernacular	frame	N/A	1825
1825?	Burke	Waynesboro	Vernacular	brick	N/A	1856
1857	**Burke**	**Waynesboro**	**Vernacular**	**brick**	**N/A**	**in use**
1825	Butts	Jackson	Vernacular	log	N/A	1828
1827	Butts	Jackson	Vernacular	brick	N/A	1828
1828	Butts	Jackson	Vernacular	brick	N/A	1864
1870	Butts	Jackson	Vernacular	brick	N/A	1897
1898	**Butts**	**Jackson**	**Romanesque**	**brick**	**Bruce & Morgan**	**in use**
1854	Calhoun	Morgan	Vernacular	frame	N/A	1892
1893	Calhoun	Morgan	Vernacular	frame	N/A	1929
1788c	Camden	St. Marys	Vernacular	frame	N/A	

Built	County	City	Style	Material	Architect	Demo
1802	Camden	Jeffersonton	Vernacular	frame	N/A	
1872	Camden	St Mary's	Vernacular	frame	N/A	1965
1828	Campbell	Campbellton	Vernacular	brick	N/A	1912
1829	Campbell	Campbellton	Vernacular	frame	N/A	1835
1871	**Campbell**	**Fairburn**	**Greek Revival**	**brick**	**unknown**	**standing**
1830	Carroll	Carrollton	Vernacular	log	N/A	1837
1837	Carroll	Carrollton	Vernacular	frame	N/A	1860?
1857	Carroll	Carrollton	Vernacular	brick	N/A	1892
1893	Carroll	Carrollton	Romanesque	brick	Bruce & Morgan	1927?
1856	Catoosa	Ringgold	Vernacular	brick	N/A	1939
1856	Charlton	Trader's Hill	Vernacular	log	N/A	1877
1877	Charlton	Trader's Hill	Vernacular	frame	N/A	
1901	Charlton	Folkston	Romanesque	brick	Darling, T. J.	1928
1760c	Chatham	Savannah	Vernacular	brick	N/A	1831
1833	Chatham	Savannah	Grk_revival	brick	Warren, Russell	1898
1889	**Chatham**	**Savannah**	**Romanesque**	**brick**	**Preston, William G.**	**standing**
183?	Chatooga	Summerville	Vernacular	log	N/A	1841?
1841	Chatooga	Summerville	Vernacular	brick	N/A	1909
1909	Chatooga	Summerville	Neoclassical	brick	Bryan & Co.	in use
1854	**Chattahoochee**	**Cusseta**	**Vernacular**	**frame**	**N/A**	**standing**
1840	Cherokee	Canton	Vernacular	brick	N/A	1864
1874	Cherokee	Canton	Vernacular?	brick	N/A	1926
1806	Clarke	Watkinsville	Vernacular	frame	N/A	1829
1829	Clarke	Watkinsville	Vernacular	brick	N/A	1887
1876	Clarke	Athens	2nd empire	brick	Charbonnier, H.	1951
1854	**Clay**	**Fort Gaines**	**Vernacular**	**frame**	**N/A**	**in use**
1871–1873	**Clay**	**Fort Gaines**	**Vernacular**	**brick**	**N/A**	**in use**
1861	Clayton	Jonesboro	Vernacular	brick	Vanloan, ABE	1864
1869	**Clayton**	**Jonesboro**	**Vernacular**	**brick**	**Fay & Corput**	**standing**
1898	**Clayton**	**Jonesboro**	**Romanesque**	**brick**	**Golucke, J. W.**	**in use**
1852	Clinch	Magnolia	Vernacular	frame	N/A	1856
1856	Clinch	Magnolia	Vernacular	frame	N/A	1867
1867	Clinch	Homerville	Vernacular	frame	N/A	
1896	**Clinch**	**Homerville**	**Vernacular**	**brick**	**unknown**	**in use**
1834	Cobb	Marietta	Vernacular	log	N/A	1838
1838	Cobb	Marietta	Vernacular	frame	N/A	
1853	Cobb	Marietta	Greek Revival	brick	Hunt, William	1864
1873	Cobb	Marietta	Greek Revival	brick	Hunt, William	1969
1899	Cobb	Marietta	Romanesque	brick	Golucke, J. W.	1969
1854	Coffee	Douglas	Vernacular	frame	N/A	
1889	Coffee	Douglas	Vernacular	frame	N\A	1900
1900	Coffee	Douglas	Romanesque	brick	Bryan, A. J.	1939
1859	Colquitt	Moultrie	Vernacular	log	N/A	1881

Built	County	City	Style	Material	Architect	Demo
1881	Colquitt	Moultrie	Vernacular	frame	N/A	1903?
1902–1903	**Colquitt**	**Moultrie**	**Neoclassical**	**brick**	**Bryan, A. J.**	in use
1856	**Columbia**	**Appling**	**Vernacular**	**brick**	**N/A**	in use
1829	Coweta	Newnan	Vernacular	brick	N/A	1904
1904–1905	**Coweta**	**Newnan**	**Neoclassical**	**brick**	**Golucke, J. W.**	in use
1831–1832	**Crawford**	**Knoxville**	**Vernacular**	**brick**	**N/A**	in use
1908	Crisp	Cordele	Neoclassical	brick	Lockwood, T. F.	1950
1826	Dade	Trenton	Vernacular	brick	N/A	
1842?	Dade	Trenton	Vernacular	frame	N/A	1853
1854	Dade	Trenton	Vernacular	brick	N/A	1926
1858	**Dawson**	**Dawsonville**	**Vernacular**	**brick**	**N/A**	standing
1826	Decatur	Bainbridge	Vernacular	frame	N/A	1831
1838	Decatur	Bainbridge	Vernacular	brick	N/A	1855
1855	Decatur	Bainbridge	Vernacular	brick	N/A	1902
1902	**Decatur**	**Bainbridge**	**Neoclassical**	**brick**	**Blair, Alexander**	in use
1824	Dekalb	Decatur	Vernacular	log	N/A	1829
1829	Dekalb	Decatur	Vernacular	brick	N/A	1842
1847	Dekalb	Decatur	Vernacular	brick	N/A	1900
1898–1900	**Dekalb**	**Decatur**	**Neoclassical**	**stone**	**Golucke, J. W.**	standing
1874	Dodge	Eastman	Vernacular	frame	N/A	1907
1907–1908	**Dodge**	**Eastman**	**Neoclassical**	**brick**	**Hosford, E. C.**	in use
1836	Dooly	Drayton	Vernacular	log	N/A	
1841	Dooly	Berrien (Vienna)	Vernacular	log	N/A	1847
1847	Dooly	Vienna	Vernacular	frame	N/A	1892
1890	**Dooly**	**Vienna**	**Romanesque**	**brick**	**Parkins, William**	in use
1855	Dougherty	Albany	Vernacular	brick	N/A	1903
1903	Dougherty	Albany	Neoclassical	brick	Lockwood, T. F.	1966
1874c	Douglas	Douglasville	Vernacular	frame	N/A	
1876	Douglas	Douglasville	Vernacular	brick	N/A	1884
1896	Douglas	Douglasville	Romanesque	brick	Bryan, A. J.	1956
1825	Early	Blakely	Vernacular	log	N/A	1836
1836	Early	Blakely	Vernacular	frame	N/A	1857
1857	Early	Blakely	Vernacular	brick	N/A	1904
1904–1905	**Early**	**Blakely**	**Neoclassical**	**brick**	**Morgan & Dillion**	in use
1899	Echols	Statenville	Vernacular	frame	unknown	19??
1840c	Effingham	Springfield	Vernacular	frame	N/A	1909
1909	**Effingham**	**Springfield**	**Neoclassical**	**brick**	**Whitcover, W. H.**	in use
1791	Elbert	Elberton	Vernacular	unknown	N/A	
1808	Elbert	Elberton	Vernacular	frame	N/A	
1816	Elbert	Elberton	Vernacular	frame	N/A	
1853c	Elbert	Elberton	Vernacular	brick	N/A	1893
1893–1894	**Elbert**	**Elberton**	**Romanesque**	**brick**	**Hunt & Lamar**	in use
1814	Emanuel	Swainsboro	Vernacular	log	N/A	

Built	County	City	Style	Material	Architect	Demo
1822	Emanuel	Swainsboro	Vernacular	log	N/A	1840
1840	Emanuel	Swainsboro	Vernacular	frame	N/A	1960s
1895	Emanuel	Swainsboro	Romanesque	brick	Golucke, J. W.	1919
1854	Fannin	Morganton	Vernacular	brick	N/A	
1901	Fannin	Blue ridge	Vernacular	brick	Golucke, J. W.	1936
1825	**Fayette**	**Fayetteville**	**Vernacular**	**brick**	**N/A**	**standing**
1823	Fayette	Fayetteville	Vernacular	frame	N/A	
1833	Floyd	Livingston	Vernacular	log	N/A	1835
1835	Floyd	Rome	Vernacular	brick	N/A	1892?
1893	**Floyd**	**Rome**	**Romanesque**	**brick**	**Bruce & Morgan**	**standing**
1832	Forsyth	Cummings	Vernacular	log	N/A	
1839	Forsyth	Cummings	Vernacular	frame	N/A	1854
1854	Forsyth	Cummings	Vernacular	brick	N/A	1905
1905	Forsyth	Cummings	Romanesque	brick	Golucke, J. W.	1973
1793	Franklin	Carnesville	Vernacular	log	N/A	
1806	Franklin	Carnesville	Vernacular	frame	N/A	1826
1826	Franklin	Carnesville	Vernacular	brick	N/A	1906
1906	**Franklin**	**Carnesville**	**Neoclassical**	**concret**	**Chamberlain, W.**	**in use**
1857	Fulton	Atlanta	Federal	brick	Hughes, C.	1883
1883	Fulton	Atlanta	2nd Empire	brick	Parkins & Bruce	1911
1833	Gilmer	Ellijay	Vernacular	log	N/A	1854
1854	Gilmer	Ellijay	Vernacular	brick	N/A	1934
1898	**Gilmer**	**Ellijay**	**Neoclassical**	**brick**	**unknown**	**in use**
1858	**Glascock**	**Gibson**	**Vernacular**	**frame**	**N/A**	**standing**
1829	Glynn	Brunswick	Vernacular	unknown	N/A	
1884	Glynn	Brunswick	Vernacular	frame	N/A	
1907	**Glynn**	**Brunswick**	**Neoclassical**	**brick**	**Gifford & Betts**	**in use**
1851	Gordon	Calhoun	Vernacular	brick	N/A	1888
1888	Gordon	Calhoun	Romanesque	brick	Parkins, William	1961
1908–1909	Grady	Cairo	Neoclassical	brick	Blair, Alexander	1980?
1786	Greene	Greensboro	Vernacular	log	N/A	1787
1788	Greene	Greensboro	Vernacular	log	N/A	1805
1807	Greene	Greensboro	Vernacular	brick	N/A	1849
1848–1849	**Greene**	**Greensboro**	**Greek Revival**	**brick**	**Demarest, David**	**in use**
1818c	Gwinnett	Unknown	Vernacular	log	N/A	
1820c	Gwinnett	Unknown	Vernacular	log	N/A	
1824	Gwinnett	Lawrenceville	Vernacular	brick	N/A	1871
1874	Gwinnett	Lawrenceville	Vernacular	brick	N/A	1884
1884–1885	**Gwinnett**	**Lawerenceville**	**Romanesque**	**brick**	**Lind, E. G.**	**standing**
1821	Habersham	Clarkesville	Vernacular	frame	N/A	1980?
1832	Habersham	Clarkesville	Vernacular	brick	N/A	1898
1898	Habersham	Clarkesville	Romanesque	brick	Golucke, J. W.	1965
1818	Hall	Gainesville	Vernacular	log	N/A	

Built	County	City	Style	Material	Architect	Demo
1820c	Hall	Gainesville	Vernacular	frame	N/A	
1832	Hall	Gainesville	Vernacular	brick	N/A	1852
1852	Hall	Gainesville	Vernacular	brick	N/A	1882
1885	Hall	Gainesville	2nd Empire	brick	Bruce & Morgan	1936
1793c	Hancock	Sparta	Vernacular	frame	N/A	1806
1806c	Hancock	Sparta	Vernacular	brick	N/A	1882
1881–1883	**Hancock**	**Sparta**	**2nd Empire**	**brick**	**Parkins & Bruce**	**in use**
1857	Haralson	Buchanan	Vernacular	brick	N/A	1891
1891–1892	**Haralson**	**Buchanan**	**Romanesque**	**brick**	**Bruce & Morgan**	**standing**
1829	Harris	Hamilton	Vernacular	log	N/A	1831
1831	Harris	Hamilton	Vernacular	brick	N/A	1907
1908	**Harris**	**Hamilton**	**Neoclassical**	**brick**	**Hosford, E. C.**	**in use**
1854	Hart	Hartwell	Vernacular	frame	N/A	
1856	Hart	Hartwell	Vernacular	brick	N/A	1900
1901	Hart	Hartwell	Neoclassical	brick	Golucke, J. W.	1967
1831c	Heard	Franklin	Vernacular	brick	N/A	1894
1894	Heard	Franklin	Romanesque	brick	Bruce & Morgan	1964
1824	Henry	McDonough	Vernacular	frame	N/A	1824
1831	Henry	McDonough	Vernacular	brick	N/A	1896
1897	**Henry**	**McDonough**	**Romanesque**	**brick**	**Golucke & Stewart**	**in use**
1824	Houston	Perry	Vernacular	frame	N/A	1855
1855	Houston	Perry	Vernacular	brick	N/A	1948
1830	Irwin	Irwinville	Vernacular	unknown	N/A	
1854	Irwin	Irwinville	Vernacular	frame	N/A	
1883	Irwin	Irwinville	Vernacular	frame	N/A	
1910	**Irwin**	**Ocilla**	**Neoclassical**	**brick**	**unknown**	**in use**
1806	Jackson	Jefferson	Vernacular	log	N/A	
1817	Jackson	Jefferson	Vernacular	brick	N/A	
1879	**Jackson**	**Jefferson**	**Italianate**	**brick**	**Thomas, W W.**	**in use**
1811	Jasper	Monticello	Vernacular	log	N/A	1839
1839	Jasper	Monticello	Vernacular	brick	N/A	1909
1908	**Jasper**	**Monticello**	**Neoclassical**	**brick**	**Lockwood, Bros**	**in use**
1906–1907	**Jeff Davis**	**Hazlehurst**	**Romanesque**	**concret**	**Chamberlain, W.**	**in use**
1816	Jefferson	Louisville	Vernacular	frame	N/A	
1848	Jefferson	Louisville	Vernacular	brick	N/A	1904
1904	**Jefferson**	**Louisville**	**Neoclassical**	**brick**	**Denny, W. F.**	**in use**
1910	**Jenkins**	**Millen**	**Neoclassical**	**brick**	**Goodrich, L. F.**	**in use**
1859	Johnson	Wrightsville	Vernacular	frame	N/A	1894
1895	**Johnson**	**Wrightsville**	**Noeclassical**	**brick**	**Golucke &Stewart**	**in use**
1808	Jones	Clinton	Vernacular	frame	N/A	1818
1818	Jones	Clinton	Vernacular	brick	N/A	1920c
1905–1906	**Jones**	**Gray**	**Romanesque**	**brick**	**Golucke, J. W.**	**in use**
1808c	Laurens	Summerville	Vernacular	frame	N/A	

Built	County	City	Style	Material	Architect	Demo
1811c	Laurens	Dublin	Vernacular	frame	N/A	
1849	Laurens	Dublin	Vernacular	frame	N/A	1895
1895	Laurens	Dublin	Romanesque	brick	Bruce & Morgan	1962
1837	Lee	Starkville	Vernacular	frame	N/A	1858
1854	Lee	Starkville	Vernacular	frame	N/A	1858
1854	Lee	Webster	Vernacular	frame	N/A	
1861	Lee	Starkville	Vernacular	brick	N/A	
1872	Lee	Leesburg	Vernacular	frame	N/A	1873
1880	Lee	Leesburg	Vernacular	brick	N/A	1921
1798	Liberty	Riceboro	Vernacular	log	N/A	
1837	Liberty	Hinesville	Vernacular	frame	N/A	1925
1800	Lincoln	Lincolnton	Vernacular	unknown	N/A	1874
1874	Lincoln	Lincolnton	Vernacular	brick	N/A	1916
1828	Lowndes	Franklinville	Vernacular	log	N/A	
1834	Lowndes	Loudenville	Vernacular	log	N/A	
1845	Lowndes	Troopville	Vernacular	frame	N/A	1858
1859	Lowndes	Valdosta	Vernacular	frame	N/A	1869
1871	Lowndes	Valdosta	Vernacular	frame	N/A	
1875	Lowndes	Valdosta	Vernacular	brick	N/A	
1904–1905	**Lowndes**	**Valdosta**	**Neoclassical**	**brick**	**Milburn, Frank**	**in use**
1833	Lumpkin	Dahlonega	Vernacular	log	N/A	
1836	**Lumpkin**	**Dahlonega**	**Vernacular**	**brick**	**N/A**	**standing**
1838	Macon	Lanier	Vernacular	frame	N/A	1972c
1854	Macon	Oglethorpe	Vernacular	frame	N/A	1857
1857	**Macon**	**Oglethorpe**	**Vernacular**	**brick**	**N/A**	**standing**
1894	**Macon**	**Oglethorpe**	**Romanesque**	**brick**	**Chamberlain, W.**	**in use**
1813	Madison	Danielsville	Vernacular	log	N/A	1834
1834	Madison	Danielsville	Vernacular	frame	N/A	1900
1901	**Madison**	**Danielsville**	**Romanesque**	**brick**	**Golucke, J. W.**	**in use**
1828	Marion	Horry	Vernacular	log	N/A	
1839	Marion	Tazwell	Vernacular	frame	N/A	1845
1848	**Marion**	**Tazwell**	**Vernacular**	**frame**	**N/A**	**standing**
1849–1856	**Marion**	**Buena vista**	**Vernacular**	**brick**	**N/A**	**in use**
1872	**McDuffie**	**Thomson**	**Vernacular**	**brick**	**N/A**	**in use**
1794c	McInstosh	Sapelo Bridge	Vernacular	log	N/A	
1818c	McInstosh	Darien	Vernacular	frame	N/A	1863
1865c	McInstosh	Darien	Vernacular	frame	N/A	1873
1874	**McInstosh**	**Darien**	**Vernacular**	**brick**	**N/A**	**in use**
1902–1903	**Meriwether**	**Greenville**	**Neoclassical**	**brick**	**Golucke, J. W.**	**in use**
1832	Meriwether	Greenville	Vernacular	brick	N/A	1901
1860	Miller	Colquitt	Vernacular	frame	N/A	1872
1873	Miller	Colquitt	Vernacular	frame	N/A	1904
1906	Miller	Colquitt	Neoclassical	brick	Blair, Alexander	1974

Built	County	City	Style	Material	Architect	Demo
1857	Milton	Alpharetta	Vernacular	brick	N/A	1955
1858	Mitchell	Camilla	Vernacular	frame	N/A	1869
1869	Mitchell	Camilla	Vernacular	frame	N/A	1890
1890	Mitchell	Camilla	Vernacular	brick	Bruce & Morgan	1937
1824	Monroe	Forsyth	Vernacular	log	N/A	1825
1825	Monroe	Forsyth	Vernacular	brick	N/A	1896
1896	**Monroe**	**Forsyth**	**Romanesque**	**brick**	**Bruce & Morgan**	**in use**
1907	**Montgomery**	**Mt. Vernon**	**Neoclassical**	**brick**	**Blair, Alexander**	**in use**
1813	Montgomery	Mt. Vernon	Vernacular	frame	N/A	1857c
1857	Montgomery	Mt. Vernon	Vernacular	frame	N/A	1907
1807	Morgan	Madison	Vernacular	brick	N/A	1844
1844	Morgan	Madison	Vernacular	brick	N/A	1917
1905	**Morgan**	**Madison**	**Neoclassical**	**brick**	**Golucke, J. W.**	**in use**
1834	Murray	Spring place	Vernacular	brick	N/A	
1843c	Murray	Spring place	Vernacular	brick	N/A	1884
1887	Murray	Spring place	Vernacular	brick	N/A	1990
1828c	Muscogee	Columbus	Vernacular	frame	N/A	1838
1838	Muscogee	Columbus	Vernacular	brick	N/A	1896
1896	Muscogee	1896	Neoclassical	brick	Bryan, A. J.	1969
1822	Newton	Covington	Vernacular	log	N/A	1824c
1824	Newton	Covington	Vernacular	brick	N/A	1856
1856	Newton	Covington	Vernacular	brick	N/A	1884
1884	**Newton**	**Covington**	**2nd Empire**	**brick**	**Bruce & Morgan**	**in use**
1829	Oconee	Watkinsville	Vernacular	brick	N/A	1887
1888	Oconee	Watkinsville	Romanesque	brick	Thomas, W. W.	1939
1793	Oglethorpe	Pilomoth	Vernacular	log	N/A	
1819	Oglethorpe	Lexington	Vernacular	brick	N/A	1887
1887	**Oglethorpe**	**Lexington**	**Romanesque**	**brick**	**Kimball/Wheeler/Parkins**	**in use**
1836	Paulding	Van Wert	Vernacular	frame	N/A	
1852	Paulding	Dallas	Vernacular	brick	N/A	1924
1892	**Paulding**	**Dallas**	**Romanesque**	**brick**	**Bruce & Morgan**	**in use**
1888	Pickens	Jasper	Romanesque	brick	Bruce & Morgan	1947
1853	Pickens	Jasper	Vernacular	brick	N/A	
1858c	Pierce	Blackshear	Vernacular	log	N/A	1859c
1859c	Pierce	Blackshear	Vernacular	frame	N/A	1875
1875	**Pierce**	**Blackshear**	**Vernacular**	**frame**	**N/A**	**standing**
1902–1903	**Pierce**	**Blackshear**	**Neoclassical**	**brick**	**Golucke, J. W.**	**in use**
1823	Pike	Old newnan	Vernacular	log	N/A	
1826	Pike	Zebulon	Vernacular	frame	N/A	1844
1844	Pike	Zebulon	Greek Revival	unknown	unknown	1895
1895	**Pike**	**Zebulon**	**Neoclassical**	**brick**	**Golucke & Stewart**	**in use**
1852	Polk	Cedartown	Vernacular	brick	N/A	1964
1867	Polk	Cedartown	Vernacular	brick	N/A	1888c

Built	County	City	Style	Material	Architect	Demo
1890	Polk	Cedartown	Romanesque	brick	Parkins, William	1951
1810	Pulaski	Hartford	Vernacular	frame	N/A	1857
1874	**Pulaski**	**Hawkinsville**	**Vernacular**	**brick**	**Bryan, A. J.**	**in use**
1832	Putnam	Eatonton	Vernacular	brick	N/A	1904
1905	**Putnam**	**Eatonton**	**Neoclassical**	**brick**	**Golucke, J. W.**	**in use**
1859	Quitman	Georgetown	Vernacular	frame	N/A	1939
1824	Rabun	Clayton	Vernacular	log	N/A	1838
1838	Rabun	Clayton	Vernacular	log	N/A	1878
1878	Rabun	Clayton	Vernacular	frame	N/A	1908
1908	Rabun	Clayton	Vernacular	concrte	Lewman, H. L.	1960
1837	Randolph	Cuthbert	Vernacular	frame	N/A	1840
1840	Randolph	Cuthbert	Vernacular	brick	N/A	1885
1886	**Randolph**	**Cuthbert**	**Romanesque**	**brick**	**Kimball/Wheeler/Parkins**	**in use**
1801	Richmond	Augusta	Vernacular	brick	N/A	
1821	Richmond	Augusta	Federal	brick	Middleton, James	1959
1872	Rockdale	Conyers	Vernacular	brick	N/A	1939
1858	Schley	Ellaville	Vernacular	brick	N/A	1900
1900	**Schley**	**Ellaville**	**Romanesque**	**brick**	**Golucke & Stewart**	**in use**
1797c	Screven	Jacksonboro	Vernacular	log?	N/A	1832
1832	Screven	Jacksonboro	Vernacular	frame	N/A	1847
1847	Screven	Sylvania	Vernacular	frame	N/A	1897
1897	Screven	Sylvania	Romanesque	brick	Goodrich, L. F.	1965
1859	**Spalding**	**Griffin**	**Italianate**	**brick**	**Hughes, C.**	**standing**
1907–1908	**Stephens**	**Toccoa**	**Neoclassical**	**brick**	**Lewman, H. L.**	**in use**
1831	Stewart	Lumpkin	Vernacular	log	N/A	1837
1837	Stewart	Lumpkin	Vernacular	brick	N/A	1895
1895	**Stewart**	**Lumpkin**	**Neoclassical**	**brick**	**Bryan, A. J.**	**in use**
1834	Sumter	Americus	Vernacular	frame	N/A	1850c
1847	Sumter	Americus	Vernacular	brick	N/A	1887
1887	Sumter	Americus	Romanesque	brick	Bruce&Morgan	1959
1831	Talbot	Talbotton	Vernacular	brick	N/A	1892
1892	**Talbot**	**Talbotton**	**Romanesque**	**brick**	**Bruce & Morgan**	**in use**
1828	Taliaferro	Crawfordville	Vernacular	brick	N/A	1902c
1902	**Taliaferro**	**Crawfordsville**	**Romanesque**	**brick**	**Goodrich, L. F.**	**in use**
1807c	Tattnall	Ohoopee mills	Vernacular	log	N/A	
1830c	Tattnall	Reidsville	Vernacular	log	N/A	
1837	Tattnall	Reidsville	Vernacular	frame	N/A	
1902	**Tattnall**	**Riedsville**	**Neoclassical**	**brick**	**Golucke, J. W.**	**in use**
1854	Taylor	Butler	Vernacular	brick	N/A	1935
1812	Telfair	Jacksonville	Vernacular	log	N/A	186?
1860	Telfair	Jacksonville	Vernacular	frame	N/A	
1872	Telfair	McRae	Vernacular	frame	N/A	1888
1888	Telfair	McRae	Vernacular	brick	N/A	1906

Built	County	City	Style	Material	Architect	Demo
1906	Telfair	McRae	Neoclassical	brick	Blair,Alexander	1934
1856	Terrell	Dawson	Vernacular	frame	N/A	
1892	**Terrell**	**Dawson**	**Romanesque**	**brick**	**Parkins, William**	in use
1827	Thomas	Thomasville	Vernacular	log	N/A	1846
1846	Thomas	Thomasville	Vernacular	brick	N/A	1858
1858	**Thomas**	**Thomasville**	**Vernacular**	**brick**	**Wind, John**	in use
1906	Toombs	Lyons	Neoclassical	brick	Golucke, J. W.(Attr)	1917
1857	Towns	Hiawassee	Vernacular	log	N/A	
1870c	Towns	Hiawassee	Vernacular	frame	N/A	1899
1899	Towns	Hiawassee	Vernacular	brick	unknown	1963
1830	Troup	Lagrange	Vernacular	brick	N/A	1904
1904	Troup	Lagrange	Neoclassical	brick	Bryan, A. J.	1936
1907	**Turner**	**Ashburn**	**Neoclassical**	**brick**	**Blair, Alexander**	in use
1810	Twiggs	Marion	Vernacular	frame	N/A	
1902–1903	**Twiggs**	**Jeffersonville**	**Romanesque**	**brick**	**Golucke, J. W.**	in use
1856	Union	Blairsville	Vernacular	log	N/A	
1859	Union	Blairsville	Vernacular	brick	N/A	1899
1899	**Union**	**Blairsville**	**Romanesque**	**brick**	**Golucke, J. W.**	standing
1828	Upson	Thomaston	Vernacular	brick	N/A	1852
1852	Upson	Thomaston	Vernacular	brick	N/A	1908
1908	**Upson**	**Thomaston**	**Neoclassical**	**brick**	**Milburn, Frank**	in use
1838	Walker	Lafayette	Vernacular	brick	N/A	1882
1883	Walker	Lafayette	Vernacular	brick	Patton, J. B.?	1922
1821	Walton	Monroe	Vernacular	log	N/A	1823
1823	Walton	Monroe	Vernacular	brick	N/A	1841
1841	Walton	Monroe	Vernacular	brick	N/A	1882
1883–1884	**Walton**	**Monroe**	**2nd Empire**	**brick**	**Bruce & Morgan**	in use
1825c	Ware	Waresboro	Vernacular	log	N/A	
1845c	Ware	Waycross	Vernacular	frame	N/A	
1870c	Ware	Waycross	Vernacular	frame	N/A	1872
1872c	Ware	Waycross	Vernacular	frame	N/A	
1892	Ware	Waycross	Romanesque	brick	Norman, G. L.	1977
1797	Warren	Warrenton	Vernacular	frame	N/A	1853
1853	Warren	Warrenton	Vernacular	brick	N/A	1908
1909–1910	**Warren**	**Warrenton**	**Neoclassical**	**brick**	**Chamberlain, W.**	in use
1812	Washington	Sandersville	Vernacular	frame	N/A	1836
1836	Washington	Sandersville	Neoclassical	brick	unknown	1855
1858	Washington	Sandersville	Neoclassical	brick	Wetter, A. P.	1864
1868–1869	**Washington**	**Sandersville**	**Vernacular**	**brick**	**N/A**	in use
1898	**Washington**	**Sandersville**	**Romanesque**	**brick**	**Goodrich, L. F. ***	in use
1899	**Washington**	**Sandersville**	**Romanesque**	**brick**	**Goodrich, L. F.***	in use
1830c	Wayne	Waynesville	Vernacular	log	N/A	

Built	County	City	Style	Material	Architect	Demo
1873	Wayne	Jesup	Vernacular	frame	N/A	1903
1903	**Wayne**	**Jesup**	**Romanesque**	**brick**	**unknown**	**in use**
1856	Webster	Preston	Vernacular	frame	N/A	1915
1860	**White**	**Cleveland**	**Vernacular**	**brick**	**N/A**	**standing**
1852c	Whitfield	Dalton	Vernacular	brick	N/A	1891
1892	Whitfield	Dalton	Romanesque	brick	Chamberlain, W.	1961
1858	Wilcox	Abbeville	Vernacular	log	N/A	1879
1880	Wilcox	Abbeville	Vernacular	frame	N/A	
1903–1904	**Wilcox**	**Abbeville**	**Neoclassical**	**brick**	**Milburn, Frank**	**in use**
1817	Wilkes	Washington	Federal	brick	Ball, Fredrick	1902
1903	**Wilkes**	**Washington**	**Romanesque**	**brick**	**Milburn, Frank**	**in use**
1808c	Wilkinson	Irwinton	Vernacular	frame	N/A	1828
1828c	Wilkinson	Irwinton	Vernacular	frame	N/A	1854
1854	Wilkinson	Irwinton	Vernacular	frame	N/A	1864
1870	Wilkinson	Irwinton	Vernacular	brick	N/A	1924
1854	Worth	Isabella	Vernacular	frame	N/A	1879
1880	Worth	Isabella	Vernacular	frame	N/A	1893
1893	Worth	Isabella	Vernacular	frame	N/A	1894
1894	Worth	Isabella	Vernacular	brick	unknown	1960c
1905–1906	**Worth**	**Sylvester**	**Neoclassical**	**brick**	**Golucke, J. W.**	**in use**

Appendix C: Georgia Courthouses 1870–1910, Listed by Architect

ALEXANDER BLAIR III, 18XX–1931 (MACON)

	Built	County	City	Style	Material	Demo
1	1902	**Decatur**	**Bainbridge**	**Neoclassical**	**brick**	**in use**
2	1906	Miller	Colquitt	Neoclassical	brick	1974
3	1906	Telfair	Mcrea	Neoclassical	brick	1934
4	1907	**Montgomery**	**Mt. Vernon**	**Neoclassical**	**brick**	**in use**
5	1907	**Turner***	**Ashburn**	**Neoclassical**	**brick**	**in use**
6	1908	Grady	Cairo	Neoclassical	brick	1980?
7	1916	**Murray**	**Chatsworth**	**Neoclassical**	**brick**	**in use**
8	1917	Toombs	Lyons	Neoclassical	brick	1964

* With P. E. Dennis

Other public buildings of note designed by Alexander Blair III include the Macon City Auditorium (1920), the remodeling of the Monroe Railroad Building to become Macon City Hall and numerous schools all across Georgia including Mount de Sales Academy, Lanier High School and the Georgia Academy for the Blind all in Macon.

ALEXANDER BRUCE, 1835–1927 & **THOMAS HENRY MORGAN**, 1857–1940
PARKINS AND BRUCE 1879 (Atlanta)
BRUCE & MORGAN 1883 (Atlanta)
MORGAN AND DILLION 1904 (Atlanta)

	Built	County	City	Style	Material	Demo
1	1882	Hancock*	Sparta	2nd Empire	brick	in use
2	1883	Fulton*	Atlanta	2nd Empire	brick	1911
3	1883	Walton	Monroe	2nd Empire	brick	in use
4	1884	Newton	Covington	2nd Empire	brick	in use
5	1885	Hall	Gainesville	2nd Empire	brick	1936
6	1887	Sumter	Americus	Romanesque	brick	1959
7	1888	Pickens	Jasper	Romanesque	brick	1947
8	1890	Mitchell	Camilla	Romanesque	brick	1937
9	1892	Haralson	Buchanan	Romanesque	brick	standing
10	1892	Talbot	Talbotton	Romanesque	brick	in use
11	1892	Paulding	Dallas	Romanesque	brick	in use
12	1893	Floyd	Rome	Romanesque	brick	standing
13	1893	Carroll	Carrollton	Romanesque	brick	1927?
14	1894	Heard	Franklin	Romanesque	brick	1964
15	1894	Bulloch	Statesboro	Romanesque	brick	in use
16	1895	Laurens	Dublin	Romanesque	brick	1962
17	1896	Monroe	Forsyth	Romanesque	brick	in use
18	1898	Butts	Jackson	Romanesque	brick	in use
19	1906	Early**	Blakely	Neoclassical	brick	in use

*Bruce with William Parkins
**Morgan and Dillion

Before moving to Atlanta in 1879, Alexander Bruce practiced in Knoxville, Tennessee, designing Tennessee courthouses for Loudon (1871), McMinn (1875), Smith (1879), Hamblen (1874), and Hamilton (1875) Counties, as well as other public buildings including Rome's Cherokee Lodge, Nevin Opera House, and the Second Empire buildings at Shorter College. After establishing their practice in Atlanta, Bruce and Morgan were responsible for a remarkable number of college buildings across the South, including Tilman Hall at Clemson University (1893), Pell Hall at Converse College in Spartanburg, South Carolina (1892), additions to Macon's Weslyan Female College, Atkinson Hall at Georgia Normal and Industrial College in Milledgeville, Samford and Harris Halls at Auburn University, and the administration buildings at both Agnus Scott College and the Georgia Institute of Technology (1888) in Atlanta. Depots in Georgia designed by Bruce and Morgan include the Central of Georgia Office Building and train Shed at Columbus (1882), the Macon and Western Depot at Forsyth (1999) and Union Depots at Americus (1900) and at Columbus (1901). Other public and commercial buildings of note designed by Bruce and Morgan include Concordia Hall, the Grant Prudential Building, the Law Building of M. C. Kiser, All Saints Episcopal Church (1904–1906), North Avenue Presbyterian Church (1901), the Empire Building (1901) and the Century Building (1901), all in Atlanta.

ANDREW J. BRYAN, active 1894–1913, (Atlanta, New Orleans, Louisville)

	Built	County	City	Style	Material	Demo
1	1874	Pulaski	Hawkinsville	Vernacular	brick	in use
2	1895	Stewart	Lumpkin	Neoclassical	brick	in use
3	1896	Muscogee	1896 [HEH?]	Neoclassical	brick	1969
4	1896	Douglas	Douglasville	Romanesque	brick	1956
5	1898	Habersham	Clarkesville	Romanesque	brick	1965
6	1900	Coffee	Douglas	Romanesque	brick	1939
7	1903	Colquitt	Moultrie	Neoclassical	brick	in use
8	1904	Troup	Lagrange	Colonial	brick	1936

In addition to these eight courthouses in Georgia, Andrew J. Bryan designed court buildings all across the South including those at Opelika (1998), Alabama; Booneville, Brookhaven, Forest, Indianola, Louisville, and Macon, Mississippi; Franklinton, New Rhodes, and St. Francaisville, Louisiana, and Moncks Corner and Dillon, South Carolina.

WALTER CHAMBERLAIN Active c.1890–c.1911.
W. CHAMBERLAIN & COMPANY (Knoxville)
FALLS CITY CONSTRUCTION COMPANY (Knoxville)

	Built	County	City	Style	Material	Demo
1	1892	Whitfield	Dalton	Romanesque	brick	1961
2	1894	Macon	Oglethorpe	Romanesque	brick	in use
3	1898	Berrien	Nashville	Romanesque	brick	in use
4	1905	Jeff Davis	Hazlehurst	Romanesque	concrete	in use
5	1906	Franklin	Carnesville	Neoclassical	concrete	in use
6	1909	Warren	Warrenton	Neoclassical	brick	in use

In addition to these six courthouses in Georgia, Walter Chamberlain designed court buildings all across the South including those in Talapoosa (1901), St. Claire (1902), and Dallas (1902) Counties in Alabama; Rhea (1891), Morgan (1904), and Gibson (1901) Counties in Tennessee, and Deaf Smith (1910) and San Saba (1911) Counties in Texas.

JAMES WINGFIELD GOLUCKE, 1857–1907
GOLUCKE & STEWART, 1891 (ATLANTA)
J. W. GOLUCKE & COMPANY, 1900 (Atlanta, Anniston & Jacksonville)

	Built	County	City	Style	Material	Demo
1	1895	Pike	Zebulon	Neoclassical	brick	in use
2	1895	Johnson	Wrightsville	Neoclassical	brick	in use
3	1895	Emanuel	Statesboro	Romanesque	brick	1919
4	1897	Henry	McDonough	Romanesque	brick	in use
5	1898	Habersham	Clarkesville	Romanesque	brick	in use
6	1898	Clayton	Jonesboro	Romanesque	brick	in use
7	1899	Cobb	Marietta	Romanesque	brick	1969
8	1899	Union	Blairsville	Romanesque	brick	standing
9	1900	Dekalb	Decatur	Romanesque	stone	standing
10	1900	Schley	Ellaville	Romanesque	brick	in use
11	1901	Fannin	Blue Ridge	Vernacular	brick	1936
12	1901	Hart	Hartwell	Neoclassical	brick	1967
13	1901	Madison	Danielsville	Romanesque	brick	in use
14	1902	Tattnall	Reidsville	Neoclassical	brick	in use
15	1903	Meriwether	Greenville	Neoclassical	brick	in use
16	1903	Twiggs	Jeffersonville	Romanesque	brick	in use
17	1906	Worth	Sylvester	Neoclassical	brick	in use
18	1903	Pierce	Blackshear	Neoclassical	brick	in use
19	1903	Bartow	Cartersville	Neoclassical	brick	in use
20	1903	Ware*	Jesup	Romanesque	brick	in use
21	1904	Coweta	Newnan	Neoclassical	brick	in use
22	1905	Morgan	Madison	Neoclassical	brick	in use
23	1905	Jones	Gray	Romanesque	brick	in use
24	1905	Forsyth	Cumming	Romanesque	brick	1973
25	1905	Putnam	Eatonton	Neoclassical	brick	in use
26	1906	Toombs*	Lyons	Neoclassical	brick	1917
27	1907	Baker	Newton	Romanesque	brick	standing

* attributed

In addition to these twenty-seven courthouses in Georgia, James Golucke designed four court buildings in Alabama, specifically those of Chambers (1899), Calhoun (1900), Lauderdale (1901), and Macon (1905) Counties. Other Georgia public and commercial buildings designed by James Golucke include the Rockdale County Jail at Conyers (1897), a fine hotel in Washington (1898), the Macon County Jail in Oglethorpe (1899), the Twiggs County Jail at Jeffersonville (1902), the Cordele Carnaige Library (1903), the Covington City Hall, the First Baptist Church at Cartersville, the Pickens County Jail at Jasper, Terrell Hall at Georgia College in Milledgeville, the Whitfield County Jail at Dalton, the Locust Grove Institute, and the Twin Buildings at Central State Hospital in Milledgeville.

LEWIS F. GOODRICH, c.1848–1917 (Augusta)

	Built	County	City	Style	Demo
1	1898*	Burke	Waynesboro	Vernacular	in use
2	1899	Washington	Sandersville	Romanesque	in use
3	1897	Screven	Sylvania	Romanesque	1965
4	1902	Taliaferro	Crawfordsvillel	Romanesque	in use
5	1910	Jenkins	Millen	Neoclassical	in use

*remodeling

In addition to these five courthouses in Georgia, Lewis Goodrich's other designs include the Athens City Hall Building and the Aiken Institute and Opera House in Aiken SC.

ED C. HOSFORD (Atlanta, Eastman)

	Built	County	City	Style	Material	Demo
1	1907	Dodge	Eastman	Neoclassical	Brick	in use
2	1908	Harris	Hamilton	Neoclassical	Brick	in use
3	1914	Wheeler	Alamo	Neoclassical	Brick	1916
4	1917	Wheeler	Alamo	Neoclassical	Brick	in use

In addition to these four courthouses in Georgia, Ed Hosford designed a number of court buildings in Florida including those in New LaFayette (1908), Jefferson (1909), Henry (1926), and Glade (1926) Counties. He also designed courthouses for Glascock (1909), and Mason (1909) Counties in Texas.

H. L. LEWMAN, (Louisville KY)
FALLS CITY CONSTRUCTION COMPANY

	Built	County	City	Style	Material	Demo
1	1907	Stephens	Toccoa	Neoclassical	brick	in use
2	1907	Appling	Baxley	Neoclassical	log	in use
3	1908	Rabun	Clayton	Vernacular	[missing info]	1960

LOCKWOOD BROTHERS
THOMAS FRITH LOCKWOOD (Columbus)
FRANK LOCKWOOD, 1865–1936 (Columbus, Montgomery)

	Built	County	City	Style	Material	Demo
1	1903	Dougherty	Albany	Neoclassical	brick	1966
2	1908	Jasper	Monticello	Neoclassical	brick	in use
3	1908	Crisp	Cordele	Neoclassical	brick	1950
4	1915	Webster	Preston	Neoclassical	brick	in use
5	1935	Calhoun	Morgan	Neoclassical	brick	in use

Frank Lockwood, the brother of T. F. Lockwood, was well known for his remodeling of the Alabama State Capitol building (1906–1910) and for court buildings in Baldwin (1901), Conecuh, Escambia (1902), Russell (remodeling, 1908), and Calhoun Counties in Alabama and in Washington County, Florida. Practicing in Columbus, often with his better-known brother in Montgomery, Alabama, T. F. Lockwood lent his name to the designs of these five Georgia courthouses, as well as numerous other public and commercial buildings including the Investment Building in Columbus and the Cordele Masonic Lodge (1907).

FRANK MILBURN, 1868–1926 (Charlotte, Columbia, Washington, DC)
MILBURN & HESTER (Columbia SC)

	Built	County	City	Style	Material	Demo
1	1903	Wilcox	Abbeville	Neoclassical	brick	in use
2	1903	Wilkes	Washington	Romanesque	brick	in use
3	1905	Lowdens	Valdosta	Neoclassical	brick	in use
4	1908	Upson	Thomaston	Neoclassical	brick	in use

Frank Milburn was arguably the most prolific Southern architect of the era. During his long career, he worked on three state capitol buildings and designed over 250 public and commercial buildings all across the South in virtually all of the popular styles of the day. In addition to these four courthouses in Georgia, a partial listing of Milburn-designed court buildings includes those in Clay (1889), Magoffin (1892), and Bourbon (1905) Counties in Kentucky; Forsyth (1893), Mecklenburg (1896), Buncombe, and Wayne (1913) Counties in North Carolina; Anderson (1897), Newberry (1907), and Greenville (1900) Counties in South Carolina; Grayson (1908) and Buchanan (1906) Counties in Virginia; Putnam (1900), Ming (n.d.), and McDowell (1894) Counties in West Virginia and in Columbia (1905) County, Florida. As the chief architect for the Southern Railway, Milburn designed numerous depots for that line and associated railroad companies including major depots at Augusta (1901) and Savannah (1901), Georgia; Blackville (1899), Columbia (1902), Summerville (1900), Sumter (1901), Spartanburg (1904), Greenville (1904), Charleston (1905), and Union (1905), South Carolina; and in Durham (1904), Asheville, Charlotte, and Salisbury (1908), North Carolina. [1]

[1] Lawrence Wodehouse contends that Milburn designed twenty-six courthouses and nineteen railroad depots, but he fails to include a list. Lawrence Wodehouse, "Frank Pierce Milburn (1868–1926), A Major Southern Architect," *The North Carolina Historical Review* 50/3 (1973): 289-303.

WILLIAM PARKINS, 1836–1894 (Atlanta)
PARKINS & ALLEN (1871)
PARKINS & BRUCE (1879)
KIMBALL, WHEELER AND PARKINS (1885)
WHEELER AND PARKINS (1886)
WHEELER AND PARKINS (1888)

	Built	County	City	Style	Material	Demo
1	1882	Hancock	Sparta	2nd Empire	brick	in use
2	1883	Fulton	Atlanta	2nd Empire	brick	1911
3	1886	Randolph	Cuthbert	Romanesque	brick	in use
4	1887	Oglethorpe	Lexington	Romanesque	brick	in use
5	1888	Gordon	Calhoun	Romanesque	brick	1961
6	1890	Polk	Cedartown	Romanesque	brick	1951
7	1892	Dooly	Vienna	Romanesque	brick	in use
8	1892	Terrell	Dawson	Romanesque	brick	in use

W. W. THOMAS, 1849–1904 (Athens)

	Built	County	City	Style	Material	Demo
1	1879	Jackson	Jefferson	Italianate	brick	in use
2	1888	Oconee	Watkinson	Romanesque	brick	1939

OTHERS

Built	Architect	County	City	Style	Material	Demo
1885	Lind, E. G.	Gwinnett	Lawerenceville	Romanesque	brick	standing
1887	Dennis, P. E.	Baldwin	Milledgeville	Vernacular	brick	in use
1892	Norman, G. L.	Ware	Waycross	Romanesque	brick	1977
1894	Hunt & Lamar	Elbert	Elberton	Romanesque	brick	in use
1904	Denny, W. F	Jefferson	Louisville	Neoclassical	brick	in use
1907	Huggins, H. H.	Ben hill	Fitzgerald	Neoclassical	brick	in use
1907	Gifford & Betts	Glynn	Brunswick	Neoclassical	brick	standing
1907	Dennis, P. E. *	Turner*	Ashburn	Neoclassical	brick	in use

* with Alexander Blair III

Selected Historical Bibliography

PRIMARY

Books

Atlanta City Directory. 15 vols. Richmond: R. L. Polk, 1891-1892, 1896-1899, 1902-1910.

Bennett, Mark, ed. *History of the Louisiana Purchase Exposition*. 1904. Reprint, New York, The New York *Times*, 1976.

Biographical Souvenir of the State of Georgia. Chicago: F. A. Battey Company, 1899.

Candler, Allen David and Clement A. Evans, eds. 3 vols. *The Cyclopedia of Georgia*. Atlanta: State Historical Association, 1906.

Georgia Historical and Industrial. Atlanta: Georgia Department of Agriculture, 1901

Greater Vienna. Vienna GA: n.p., 1902.

Houston, James. *The Port of Brunswick, Georgia, The Safest, Most Capacious and Best Situated Harbor on the Southeastern Atlantic Coast*. Brunswick GA: The Office of the Mayor of the City of Brunswick, 1869.

Industrial Georgia: Cotton Manufacturers. Atlanta: The Georgia Power Company, 1923.

Industries of Savannah. Savannah GA: JM Elstner, 1886.

Irvine, William S. *Brunswick and Glynn County, Georgia*. Brunswick GA: Brunswick Board of Trade, 1902.

Janes, Thomas P. *The Handbook of Georgia*. New York: Russell Brothers, 1876.

Prospectus of the City of Tallapoosa, Haralson County, Georgia. Boston: The Georgia-Alabama Investment and Development Company, 1891.

Poor, Henry V. *Poor's Manual of Railroads in the United States*. New York: HV& HW Poor, 1868-1894.

Report of the Presidents, Chief Engineers and Superintendents of the Central Railroad and Banking Company of Georgia. 6 vols. Savannah GA: JM Cooper & Co., 1854-1895.

Reports to the Presidents, Chief Engineers and Superintendents of the Southwestern Railroad Company. Macon GA: The JW Burke & Company, 1869.

Semiannual Reports of the Railroad Commission of the State of Georgia. Atlanta: Constitution Publishing Company, 1886-1910.

Sherwood, Adiel. *A Gazetteer of Georgia. Containing Particular Descriptions of the State, Its Resources, Counties, Towns, Villages and Weather etc.* Philadelphia: JW Martin and WK Boden, 1829.

———. *A Gazetteer of Georgia. Containing Particular Descriptions of the State, Its Resources, Counties, Towns, Villages and Weather etc.* Washington: P Force, 1839.

———. *A Gazetteer of Georgia. Containing Particular Descriptions of the State, Its Resources, Counties, Towns, Villages and Weather etc.* Macon GA: S Boykin, 1860.

Sholes's Directory of the City of Macon. Macon GA: A. E. Sholes, 1878.

Sholes's Georgia State Gazetteer and Business Directory. 3 vols. Atlanta: AE Sholes and Company, 1879, 1886, 1896.

Singleton, D. T. *Putnam County, Georgia and Its Resources*. Atlanta: Methodist Book & Publishing Co., 1895.

Thomas, Henry W., ed. *Digest of the Railroad Laws of Georgia*. Atlanta: Franklin Printing and Publishing Co., 1895.

Truman, Benjamin C. *History of the World's Fair, Being a Complete and Authentic Description of the Columbian Exposition From Its Inception*. 1893. Reprint, New York: The New York Times, 1976.

White, George. *Statistics of the State of Georgia*. Savannah GA: W Thorne Williams, 1849.

———. *Historical Collections of Georgia, Containing the Most Interesting Facts, Traditions, Biographical Sketches, Anecdotes etc.* New York: Pudney and Russell, 1854.

Young and Company's Business and Professional Directory of Georgia. Atlanta: Young and Company, 1904.

Newspapers

The Abbeville *Chronicle*. The University of Georgia.

The Advocate Democrat (Crawfordville GA). The University of Georgia.

The Albany *Daily Herald*. The University of Georgia.

The Albany *Herald*. The University of Georgia.

Albany *Patriot*. The University of Georgia.

Americus *Times-Reporter*. The University of Georgia.
Atlanta *Constitution*. The University of Georgia.
Atlanta *Evening News*. The University of Georgia.
The Atlanta *Journal*. The University of Georgia.
The Augusta *Constitutionalist*. The University of Georgia.
Augusta *Chronicle*. The University of Georgia.
The Bainbridge *Search Light*. The University of Georgia.
The Baxley *News-Banner*. The University of Georgia.
The Blackshear *Times*. The University of Georgia.
Brunswick *Advertiser and Appeal*. The University of Georgia.
The Bulloch *Times*. The University of Georgia.
The Cairo *Messenger*. The University of Georgia.
The Calhoun (County) *Courier*. The University of Georgia.
Calhoun *Times*. The University of Georgia.
Campbell *News* (Fairburn GA). The University of Georgia.
The Camilla *Enterprise*. The University of Georgia.
Carnesville *Advance*. The University of Georgia.
The Carroll County *Times*. (Carrollton GA). The University of Georgia.
The Cherokee *Advance*. The University of Georgia.
The Cherokee *Georgian* (Canton GA). The University of Georgia.
The Chronicle (Washington GA). The University of Georgia.
The Columbus *Inquirer*. The University of Georgia.
The (Conyers, Georgia) *Solid South*, University of Georgia.
The Cordele *Dispatch*. The University of Georgia.
The Crawford County *Correspondent* (Roberta GA). The University of Georgia.
Daily Citizen and News (Dalton GA). The University of Georgia.
The Dalton *Argus*. The University of Georgia.
The Darien *Gazette*. The University of Georgia.
The Danielsville *Monitor*. The University of Georgia.
The Dawson *News*. The University of Georgia.
The Decatur *New Era*. The University of Georgia.
The Douglas *Weekly Breeze*. The University of Georgia.
Early County *News*. The University of Georgia.
The Eatonton *Messenger*. The University of Georgia.
The Edison *News*. The University of Georgia.
The Ellijay *Courier*. The University of Georgia.
The Enterprise (Thomasville GA). The University of Georgia.
The Enterprise and Appeal (Cuthbert GA). The University of Georgia.
The Fayetteville *Chronicle*. The University of Georgia.
The Fayetteville *News*. August The University of Georgia.
The Fitzgerald *Enterprise*. The University of Georgia.
The Forest News (Jefferson GA). The University of Georgia.
The (Forsyth County) *North Georgian*. The University of Georgia.
The Fort Valley *Enterprise*. The University of Georgia.
The Franklin County *Register*. The University of Georgia.
The Free Press (Carrollton GA). The University of Georgia.
The (Gainesville) *Eagle*. The University of Georgia.
The Glascock *Banner*. The University of Georgia.
The Gwinnett *Herald*. The University of Georgia.
The Hamilton *Journal*. The University of Georgia.
The Haralson *Banner-Messenger*. The University of Georgia.
The Harris County *Banner-Messenger*. The University of Georgia.
The Hartwell *Sun*. The University of Georgia.
The Hawkinsville *Dispatch and News*. The University of Georgia.
The Hawkinsville *News*. The University of Georgia.
The Henry County *Weekly*. The University of Georgia.

The Herald (Dallas GA). The University of Georgia.

The Houston *Home Journal*. The University of Georgia.

The Ishmaelite. The University of Georgia.

The Jackson *Argus*. The University of Georgia.

The Jackson *Herald* (Jefferson GA). The University of Georgia.

The Jackson *News*. The University of Georgia.

The Jasper County *News*. The University of Georgia.

Jeff Davis *Ledger*. The University of Georgia.

The Jesup *Sentinel*. The University of Georgia.

The Jones County *Herald*. The University of Georgia.

The Jones County *Headlight*. The University of Georgia.

The Jones County *News*. The University of Georgia.

The (Kingsland) *Southeastern Georgian*. The University of Georgia.

The Knoxville *Journal*. The University of Georgia.

The Lawrenceville *News Herald*. The University of Georgia.

The Lee County *Journal*. The University of Georgia.

The Louisville *News and Farmer*. The University of Georgia.

The Lumpkin *Independent*. The University of Georgia.

The Macon *Evening News*. The University of Georgia.

The Macon *Telegraph and Confederate*. The University of Georgia.

The Macon Telegraph. The University of Georgia.

The (Macon) *Georgia Journal and Messenger*.

The Manufacturers Record. The University of Georgia.

The Marietta *Journal*. The University of Georgia.

The Marion (County) *Sentinel*. The University of Georgia.

The McDuffie *Progress*. The University of Georgia.

The Meriwether *Vindicator* (Greenville GA). The University of Georgia.

The Middle Georgia Argus (Jackson GA). The University of Georgia.

The Monroe *Advertiser*. The University of Georgia.

The Monticello *News*. The University of Georgia.

The Montgomery *Monitor*. The University of Georgia.

The Morgan *Monitor*. The University of Georgia.

The Moultrie *Observer*. The University of Georgia.

The Nashville *Herald*. The University of Georgia.

National Headlight (Flovilla GA). The University of Georgia.

The News and Banner (Franklin GA). The University of Georgia.

The News and Courant (Cartersville GA). The University of Georgia.

The North Georgia Citizen (Dalton GA). The University of Georgia.

The Ocilla *Star*. The University of Georgia.

The Paulding *New Era*. The University of Georgia.

The Pike County *Journal*. The University of Georgia.

The Richland *Banner*. The University of Georgia.

Rome *Tri-weekly Courier*. The University of Georgia.

The Sandersville *Central Georgian*. The University of Georgia.

The (Sandersville) *Middle Georgia Press*. The University of Georgia.

The Sandersville *True Citizen*. The University of Georgia.

The Savannah *Morning News*. The University of Georgia.

The Schley *County News*. The University of Georgia.

The Southern Banner. The University of Georgia.

The Southern Recorder (Milledgeville GA). The University of Georgia.

The Sparta *Times and Planter*. The University of Georgia.

The Star (Elberton GA). The University of Georgia.

The Statesboro *News*. The University of Georgia.

The Summerville *News*. The University of Georgia.

The Tattnall *Journal*. The University of Georgia.

The Telfair *Enterprise*. The University of Georgia.

The Thomasville *Times.* The University of Georgia.

The Tifton *Gazette.* The University of Georgia.

The Times *Journal* (Eastman GA). The University of Georgia.

Tri-County *Advertiser* (Clarksville GA). The University of Georgia.

The Turner County *Banner.* The University of Georgia.

The Twiggs *Herald.* The University of Georgia.

The Valdosta *Times.* The University of Georgia.

The Vienna *Progress.* The University of Georgia.

The Vienna *News.* The University of Georgia.

Walker County *Messenger* (Lafayette GA). The University of Georgia.

The Walton (County) *News.* The University of Georgia.

The Warrenton *Clipper.* The University of Georgia.

The Waycross *Evening Herald.* The University of Georgia.

The Washington *Gazette.* The University of Georgia.

The Waycross *Herald.* The University of Georgia.

The Weekly *Star* (Douglasville GA). The University of Georgia.

The Weekly Sumter *Republican.* The University of Georgia.

The Wheeler County *Eagle.* The University of Georgia.

The Winder *News.* The University of Georgia.

Worth County *Local.* The University of Georgia.

The Wrightsville *Recorder.* The University of Georgia.

SECONDARY

United States History
Books

Carlton, David L. *Mill and Town in South Carolina, 1880-1920.* Baton Rouge LA: Louisiana State University Press.

Coleman, Kenneth and Charles Stephen, eds. 2 vols. *Dictionary of Georgia Biography.* Athens GA: University of Georgia Press, 1983.

Gibson, John W. *Those 163 Days, A Southern Account of Sherman's March from Atlanta to Raleigh.* New York: Coward-McCann 1961.

Howard, Major General O. O. in US War Department *The War of the Rebellion, Official Records of Union and Confederate Armies,* series 1, vol. 39, Part 3, Orders, 532.

Lowitt, Richard. *Merchant Prince of the Nineteenth Century,* William E. Dodge. New York: Columbia University Press, 1954.

Morrison, Samuel. *The Oxford History of the American People.* New York: Oxford University Press, 1965.

Parrington, Vernon L. *Main Currents in American Thought.* 3 vols. "The Romantic Revolution in America, 1800-1860." New York: Harcourt, Brace & World, Inc., 1927.

———. *Main Currents in American Thought.* 3 vols. "The Beginnings of Critical Realism in America, 1860-1920." New York: Harcourt, Brace & World, Inc., 1930.

Schlereth, Thomas J. *Victorian America. Transformations in Everyday Life.* 1991. Reprint, New York: Harpers Perennial, 1992.

Wells, Louis Ray. *The Industrial History of the United States.* New York: McMillan, 1923.

Railroad History
Books

Barkley, R. E. "The Railroad Comes to Ducktown." Knoxville: n.p., 1973.

Carver, Kaye and Myra Queen. *Memories of a Mountain Short Line, The Story of the Tallulah Falls Railroad.* Rabun Gap GA: Foxfire Press, 1976.

Cumming, Mary Gardner Smith. *The Georgia Railroad and Banking Company, 1833-1945, An Historic Narrative.* Augusta GA: Walton Printing Company, 1945.

Dozier, Howard Douglas. *A History of the Atlantic Coast Line Railroad.* New York: AM Kelly, 1971.

Ferguson, Maxwell. *State Regulation of Railroads in the South.* New York: Columbia University Press, 1916.

Jackson, Olin and Michael A. Miller. "Early Railroads in Lumpkin and Dawson Counties." Vol. 1, *A North Georgia Journal of History,* eds. Olin Jackson and Michael A. Miller. Woodstock GA: Legacy Communications, 1989.

Klein, Maury D. *History of the Louisville and Nashville Railroad.* New York: MacMillan, 1972.

Kyper, Frank. "Retracing the Route of the Tallulah Falls Railroad." Vol. 3, *A Journal of North Georgia History,* ed. Olin Jackson. Woodstock GA: Legacy Communications, 1995.

Moreland, Nancy. "North Georgia's Old L&N Depots." Vol. 3, *A North Georgia Journal of History,* ed. Olin Jackson. Woodstock GA: Legacy Communications, 1995.

Pidcock, Frank R. Jr. *Rails, Quails and Ashburn Hill.* Moultrie GA: Frank R. Pidcock, 1988.

Phillips, Ulrich B. *History of Transportation in the Eastern Cotton Belt to 1860.* 1908. Reprint, New York: McMillan, 1913.

Schivelbush, Wolfgang. *The Railway Journey, The Industrialization of Space and Time in the 19th Century.* 1941. Reprint, Leamington Spa, Hamburg and New York: Berg Publishers, Ltd., 1986.

Smith, John W. *Building a Railroad, 1832-1952, The Seaboard Air Line, Its Beginnings and Its Contributions.* New York: Newcomen Society in North America, 1952.

Stover, John F. *The Railroads of the South, 1865-1900, A Study in Finance and Control.* Chapel Hill:University of North Carolina Press, 1955.

Smyth, George Hutchinson. *The Life of Henry Bradley Plant.* New York and London: G. P. Putnam & Sons, 1989..

Summers, Mark W. *Railroads, Reconstruction and the Gospel of Prosperity.* Princeton NJ: Princeton University Press, 1984.

Wadley, William. *In Report of the Superintendent of The Western and Atlantic Railroad to his Excellency* Howell Cobb. Atlanta: Cherokee Publishing Company, 1852.

Ward, James A. *Railroads and the Character of America, 1820-1887.* Knoxville: University of Tennessee Press, 1986.

Winn, Les R. *Ghost Trains and Depots of Georgia.* Chamblee GA: Big Shanty Press, 1995.

Articles

Chalker, Fussell. "Irish Catholics in the Building of the Ocmulgee and Flint Railroad." *The Georgia Historical Quarterly* 54/4 (1970): 507-15.

Goff, John H. "The Steamboat Period in Georgia." *The Georgia Historical Quarterly* 12/3 (1928): 236-54.

Mc Guire, Peter S. "Athens and the Railroads, The Georgia and the Northeastern Railroads." *The Georgia Historical Quarterly* 18/1 (1934): 1-26.

———. "Athens and the Railroads, The Northeastern Extension, the Macon and Northern and the Georgia, Carolina and Northern Railroads." *The Georgia Historical Quarterly* 18/2 (1934): 118-44.

———. "The Railroads of Georgia, 1860-1880." *The Georgia Historical Quarterly* 16/3 (1932): 179-213.

Stover, John F. "The Ruined Railroads of the Confederacy." *The Georgia Historical Quarterly* 42/4 (1958): 376-88.

Theses, Dissertations and Unpublished Manuscripts

Comer, Hugh. "Railroad Abandonments in Georgia." Macon GA: 1985.

Dixon, Max Jefferson. "Georgia Railroad Growth and Consolidation 1860-1917." Thesis, Emory University, 1949.

———. "The Central of Georgia, 1833-1892, An Abstract."Atlanta: Peabody Teachers College, 1953.

The Georgia Historical Society's Collections of the Central of Georgia Railway. "Geographical Location Finding Aid." Atlanta: The Georgia Department of Archives and History, n.d.

Southern History
Books

Ayers, Edward L. *Promise of the New South, Life After Reconstruction.* Oxford and New York: Oxford University Press, 1992.

———. *Southern Crossing, A History of the American South, 1877-1906.* Oxford and New York: Oxford University Press, 1995.

Cash, W. J. *The Mind of the South.* 1941. Reprint, New York: Vintage Books, 1991.

Carlton, David L. *Mill and Town in South Carolina, 1880-1920.* Baton Rouge LA: Louisiana State University Press, 1982.

Coulter, Ellis Merton. *The South During Reconstruction, 1865-1877.* 1947. Reprint, Baton Rouge: University of Louisiana Press, 1947.

Galensen, A. C. *Migration of Cotton Textile Industry from New England to the South, 1880-1930.* New York: Garland, 1985.

Gaston, Paul M. *The New South Creed, A Study in Southern Mythmaking.* 1970. Reprint, Baton Rouge: Louisiana State University Press, 1976.

Gibson, John M. *Those 163 Days, A Southern Account of Sherman's March from Atlanta to Raleigh.* New York: Coward-McCann, 1961.

Grester, Patrick and Nichols Cords, eds. *Myth and Southern History,* 2nd ed. 2 vols. Urbana and Chicago: University of Illinois Press, 1989.

Mitchell, Broadus. *The Rise of Cotton Mills in the South.* Baltimore: Johns Hopkins University Press, 1921.

Oates, Mary J. *The Role of the Cotton Textile Industry in the Economic Development of the American South.* New York: Arno Press, 1975.

Page, Walter Hines. *The Rebuilding of the Old Commonwealth.* New York: Doubleday, Page and Company, 1905.

Tindall, George Brown. *Emergence of the New South.* Baton Rouge: Louisiana State University Press, 1967.

Wheeler, Richard. *Sherman's March.* New York: Crowell, 1978.

Woodward, C. Vann. *Origins of the New South, 1877-1913.* 1951. Reprint, Baton Rouge: Louisiana State University Press, 1993.

————. *The Burden of Southern History.* 1960. Reprint, Baton Rouge and London: Louisiana State University Press, 1993.

Wright, Gavin. *Old South - New South, Revolution in the Southern Economy Since the Civil War.* 1986. Reprint, Baton Rouge: Louisiana State University Press, 1996.

Georgia History
Books

Bartley, Numan V. *The Creation of Modern Georgia.* 1983. Reprint, Athens and London: University of Georgia Press, 1990.

Chapman, William. *The Madison Historic Preservation Manual.* Madison: n.p., 1990.

Coleman, Kenneth and Charles Stephen Gurr. *Dictionary of Georgia Biography.* 2 vols. Athens: University of Georgia Press, 1983.

————. *History of Georgia.* Athens: University of Georgia Press, 1977.

Conway, Alan. *The Reconstruction of Georgia.* Minneapolis: University of Minnesota Press, 1966.

Coulter, E. Merton. *Georgia: A Short History.* Chapel Hill: University of North Carolina Press, 1960.

————. James Monroe Smith, *Georgia Planter, Before and After Death.* Athens GA: University of Georgia Press, 1961.

Georgia Humanities Council. *The New Georgia Guide.* Athens and London: The University of Georgia Press, 1996.

Hodler, Thomas W. and Howard A. Schretter. *The Atlas of Georgia.* Athens GA: Institute of Community and Area Development, 1986.

Knight, Lucian Lamar. *A Standard History of Georgia and Georgians.* 6 vols. New York and Chicago: Lewis Publishing Company, 1917.

————. *Georgia's Landmarks, Memorials and Legends.* 2 vols. Atlanta: Lucian Lamar Knight, 1914.

Meuller, Edward A. *Perilous Journey, A History of Steamboating on the Chattahoochee, Apalachicola and Flint Rivers, 1828-1928.* Eufaula GA: Historic Chattahoochee Commission, 1990.

Northen, William J., ed. *Men of Mark in Georgia.* 6 vols. Atlanta: A. B. Caldwell, 1906-1912.

Range, Willard. *A Century of Georgia Agriculture.* 1954. Reprint, Athens: University of Georgia Press, 1969.

Regan, Alice E. *H. I. Kimball, Entrepreneur.* Atlanta: Cherokee Publishing Company, 1983.

Sears, Joan Niles. *The First Years of Town Planning in Georgia.* Atlanta: Cherokee Press, 1979.

Shaw, Barton, C. *The Wool Hat Boys, Georgia's Populist Party.* Baton Rouge and London: Louisiana State University Press, 1984.

Ward, Judson Clements, Jr. *Georgia Under the Bourbon Democrats, 1872-1890.* Chapel Hill: University of North Carolina Press, 1947.

Articles

Goff, John H. "Georgia in the Steamboat Period." *The Georgia Historical Quarterly* 12/3 (1928): 236-54.

Griffin, Richard W. "The Origins of Industrial Revolution in Georgia, Cotton Textiles, 1810-1865." *The Georgia Historical Quarterly* 42/4 (1958): 355-75.

Johnson, J. G. "Notes on Manufacturing." *The Georgia Historical Quarterly* 16/3 (1932): 214-31.

Shryock, Richard H. "The Early Industrial Revolution on the Empire State." *The Georgia Historical Quarterly* 11/2 (1927): 109-28.

Local History
Books

Against Oblivion, *A History of Calhoun County Georgia*. Alpharetta: WH Wolfe, 1994.

Anderson, Mary Ann. *A Town at the Crossroads, Celebrating the 125th Anniversary of the Founding of Hazlehurst, Georgia*. Hazlehurst GA: 1995.

As Sweet as Its Namesake, The Story of Vidalia. Vidalia GA: Vidalia Centennial Inc., 1990.

Aycock, Roger D. *All Roads Lead to Rome*. Rome GA: The Rome Heritage Foundation, 1981.

Bagley, Garland C. *History of Forsyth County*. Easley SC: Southern Historical Press, 1985.

Baker, Paul R. *Richard Morris Hunt*. Cambridge MA: MIT Press, 1980.

Baker, Taylor Bonnie. *History of Alma and Bacon County, Georgia*. Alma GA: Historical Society of Alma and Gerster, Patrick and Nicholas Cords, eds. *Myth and Southern History*. 2 vols. Urbana and Chicago: University of Illinois Press, 1989. Bacon County, 1984.

Baker, John William. *History of Hart County*. Atlanta: Foote and Davies, 1933.

Baker, Robert S. *Chattooga County, A Story of a County and Its People*. Roswell GA: WH Wolfe Associates, 1988.

Baldwin, Nell H. and Albert M. Hillhouse. *An Intelligent Student's Guide to Burke County, Georgia, History*. Waynesboro GA: Nell H. Baldwin and Albert M. Hillhouse, 1956.

Bankston, Emmie Carnes. *History of Roberta and Crawford County, Georgia*. Macon GA: 1976.

Barfield, Louise Calhoun. *History of Harris County Georgia*. Columbus GA: 1961.

Barksdale, Margaret G., E. L. Cowan and Francais A. King, eds. *A History of Rockdale County*. Conyers GA: THP, 1978.

Barron, Ruth T. *Footprints in Appling County*. Baxley GA: The Appling County Board of Commissioners, 1981.

Battey, George M. *History of Rome and Floyd County*. Atlanta: Webb, 1922.

Beeson, Leola. *History Stories of Milledgeville and Baldwin County*. Milledgeville GA: Omni Press, 1943.

Bennett, Kenneth A. *Chronicle of Clinch County*. Waycross GA: Brantley Printing Company, 1991.

Bonner, James C. *A Short History of Heard County*. Milledgeville GA: Georgia College, 1967.

————. *Georgia's Last Frontier, The Development of Carroll County*. Athens GA: University of Georgia Press, 1971.

————. *Milledgeville, Georgia's Antebellum Capital*. Athens GA: University of Georgia Press, 1978.

Boone, Dean. *History of Pierce County, Georgia*. Blackshear GA: Broome Printing, 1973.

Brannen, Dorothy. *Life in Old Bulloch, The Story of a Wiregrass County in Georgia*. Gainesville GA: Magnolia Press, 1987.

Brunton, Yvonne Miller. *Grady County, Georgia, Some of Its History, Folk Architecture and Families*. Jackson MS: Quality Printers, 1979.

Butler, John C. *Historical Record of Macon and Central Georgia*. Macon GA: National Association of the Colonial Dames of America, 1858.

Cain, Andrew W. *History of Lumpkin County for the first One Hundred Years, 1832-1932*. Atlanta: Stein Printing Company, 1932.

Cashin, Edward. *The Story of Augusta*. Augusta GA: Richmond County Board of Education, 1980.

Cate, Margaret Davis. *Our Todays and Yesterdays, A Study of Brunswick and the Coastal Islands*. Brunswick GA: Glover Brothers, 1930.

Charlton County, Georgia, *Historical Notes*. Jesup GA: Charlton County Historical Commission, 1972.

Church, Mary L. *The Hills of Habersham*. Clarkesville GA: n.p., 1962.

Clarke, Caroline McKinney. *The Story of Decatur*. Decatur GA: Caroline McKinney Clarke, 1973.

Clements, James B. *The History of Irwin County*. Atlanta: Foote and Davies, 1930.

Cliver, Carolyn, Francais Davis and Tom Liner, eds. "Clarkesville, Early Days." Vol. 1, *The Journal of North Georgia History*, eds., Olin Jackson and Michael A Miller. Woodstock GA: Legacy Communications, 1977-1984.

Cobb, Private Joe. *Carroll County and Her People.* Carrollton GA: Private Joe Cobb, 1906.Cobb, W. P. *History of Dodge County, Georgia, 1832-1992.* Atlanta: Foote and Davies, 1992.

Coleman, Leodel, ed. *Statesboro, A Century of Progress, 1866-1966.* Statesboro GA: The Bulloch *Herald,* 1969.

Collections of the DeKalb County Historical Society. 2 vols. Decatur GA: DeKalb County Historical Society, 1980.

Collections of the Early County Historical Society. 2 vols. Blakely GA: The Early County Historical Society, 1971.

Collin, C. R. and Jan H. Devereaux. *Sketches of Union County.* Blairsville GA: Union County Historical Society, 1974.

Commons, W. C. and Clara Stovall. *History of McDuffie County, Georgia.* Tignall GA: Boyd Publishing, 1988.

Cook, Anna Maria Green. *History of Baldwin County, Georgia.* Anderson SC: Keys Hearns, 1925.

Cook, Jimmy, Mrs., Mrs. Sidney Johnson and Mrs. Ralph Jackson. *History of Johnson County.* Wrightsville GA: 1968.

Cooper, Walter G., *The Official History of Fulton County.* 1934. Reprint, Spartanburg: Reprint Company, 1978.

Corley, Florence F. *Augusta, Georgia: A Confederate City.* Columbia: University of South Carolina Press, 1960.

Covington, W. A. *The History of Colquitt County.* Atlanta: Foote and Davies, 1937.

Cox, Jack F. *History of Sumter County, Georgia.* Roswell GA: WH Wolfe, 1978.

Cunyus, Lucy Josephine. *The History of Bartow County, Formerly Cass.* Cartersville GA: Tribune Publishing, 1933.

Davidson, Victor. *History of Wilkinson County.* Macon GA: JW Burke, 1930.

Davidson, William H. A *Rockaway in Talbot, Travels in an Old Georgia County,* 4 vols. West Point GA: WH Davidson, 1983.

————. *Brooks of Honey and Butter, Plantations and People of Meriwether County, Georgia.* Alexander City AL: Outlook Publishing Company, 1971.

Davis, Fannie Mae. *Douglas County, Georgia, From Indian Trails to Interstate 20.* Roswell GA: WH Wolfe, 1987.

Davis, Robert S and James E. Dorsey. *Lincoln County Genealogy and History.* Swainsboro GA: Magnolia Press, 1987.

Davis, Robert Scott. *History of Montgomery County, Georgia, to 1918.* Roswell GA: WH Wolfe, 1992.

————. *Pickens Past, A Photographic History of Pickens County, Georgia.* Roswell GA: WH Wolfe, 1995.

Dawson County Heritage. Dawsonville GA: Dawson County Historical and Genealogical Society, 1997.

Decatur County Past and Present, 1823-1991. Roswell GA: The Decatur County Historical Society, 1991.

Dorsey, James E., ed. *Emanuel County, Georgia, A Collection of Newspaper Sources.* Swainsboro GA: Emanuel Historic Preservation Society, 1982.

————. *Footprints on the Hoopee, A History of Emanuel County, 1812-1906.* Spartanburg SC: Reprint Company, 1978.

————. *History of Hall County, Georgia.* Gainesville GA: Magnolia Press, 1991.

————. *Jefferson County, Georgia, 1871-1900, A Collection of Newspaper Sources.* Swainsboro GA: Emanuel County Junior College Library, 1979.

Dowell, Spright. *The History of Mercer University.* Macon GA: Mercer University Press, 1958.

Du Bose, Louise Jones. *A History of Columbus, Georgia, 1828-1928.* Columbus GA: The Historical Publishing Company, 1929.

Eller, Lynda S. *Heard County Georgia, A History of Its People.* Huguley AL: Genealogical Records Roving Press, 1980.

Elrod, Frary. *Historical Notes on Jackson County, Georgia.* Jefferson GA: n.p., 1967.

Evans, Virginia Fraiser, ed. *Liberty County Georgia, A Pictorial History.* Statesville NC: Liberty County Library Board of Commissioners 1979.

Faulk, J. Lanette O'Neal and Betty Walker Jones, eds. *History of Twiggs County, Georgia.* Jeffersonville GA: Major General John Twiggs Chapter, American Daughters of the American Revolution, 1960.

Flanigan, James C. *History of Gwinnett County, 1818-1943.* 2 vols. 1943. Reprint, Lawrenceville GA: Gwinnett Historical Society, 1959.

Foster, W. A., Jr. *Paulding County, Its People and Places.* Roswell GA: WH Wolfe, 1983.

Fowler, Ryland D. *Macon County Life.* Montezuma GA: Macon County Historical Society, 1983.

Garrett, Franklin M. *Atlanta and Environs; A Chronicle of Its People and Events.* 3 vols. New York: Lewis Publishing Company, 1954.

Garrison, Webb B. *The Legacy of Atlanta.* Atlanta: Peachtree Publishing, 1987.

Gibson, Mary Jones and Lily Elizabeth Reynolds. *The Coweta Chronicles for one Hundred Years, with an Account of the Indians from whom the Land was Acquired and Some Historical Papers Relating to its Acquisition.* Atlanta:

Stein Printing Company, 1928.Ginn, Leonora, ed. *Barnesville Days to Remember, 1826-1976.* Barnesville GA: Barnesville Lamar County Historical Society, 1976.

Glancing Backward, Albany, Georgia, 1836-1976. Albany GA: Dougherty County Public School System, Sesquicentennial Committee, 1986.

Glimpses of Cherokee County. Canton: Cherokee County Historical Society, 1988.

Goolsby, Ira, Florence Moye and Cornelia Mattox. *Randolph County, A Compilation of Facts, Recollections and Family Sketches.* Cuthbert GA: Randolph County Historical Society, 1977.

Grice, Warren, ed. *History of Houston County, Georgia.* Perry GA: 1934.

Griffin, Ben. *At Home in Carrollton, A History Illustrated.* Roswell GA: WH Wolfe, 1995.

Groover, Robert Long. *Sweet Land of Liberty, A History of Liberty County.* Roswell GA: WH Wolfe, 1987.

Grubbs, Lillie Martha. *History of Worth County, Georgia, for its First Eighty Years.* Macon GA: JW Burke Company, 1934.

Gurr, Stephen. *The Windsor of Victorian Americus.* Americus GA: n.p., 1973.

Haralson County History Book. Dallas TX: The Haralson County Historical Society, 1983.

Harris, Mrs. Wallace Leigh, ed. *History of Pulaski and Bleckley Counties.* Macon GA: Daughters of the American Revolution, Georgia State Society, Hawkinsville Chapter, 1957.

Hardee, Charles Seaton Henry. *Reminiscences and Recollections of Old Savannah.* Savannah GA: n.p., 1928.

Harden, William. *History of Savannah and South Georgia.* Atlanta: Cherokee Publishing Company, 1969.

Hardman, Thomas Colquitt. *History of Harmony Grove - Commerce, Jackson County, Georgia.* Athens GA: n.p., 1949.

Hart, Bertha Sheppard. *The Official History of Laurens County.* Athens GA: John Lauren Chapter, Daughters of the American Revolution, 1987.

Hays, Louise Frederick. *History of Macon County, Georgia. 1933.* Reprint, Spartanburg SC: Reprint Company, Atlanta: 1979.

Hickey, Louise McHenry. *Rambles Through Morgan County.* Monroe GA: Walton Press, 1989.

Hickson, Bobbe S. *A Land So Dedicated, A History of Houston County.* Perry GA: Houston County Library Board, 1976.

Hillhouse, Albert M. *The History of Burke County, Georgia, 1777-1950.* Swainsboro GA: Magnolia Press, 1985.

Hinton, E. H. *A Historical Sketch of the Solution of Trade and Transportation at Macon, Georgia, Together with a Synopsis of the Rate Adjustment from the East.* Macon GA: n.p., 1912.

Historical Background of Dougherty County, 1836 - 1941. 1941. Reprint, Atlanta: Cherokee Publishing Company, 1981.

History and Remembrances of Dougherty County. 1924. Reprint, Spartanburg SC: Reprint Company, 1978.

History of Athens and Clarke County. Athens GA: H. J. Rowe, 1922.

History of Baker County, Georgia. Roswell GA: Baker County Historical Society, 1991.

History of Bryan County. Pembroke GA: The Bryan Historical Society, 1985.

History of Candler County, Georgia. Metter GA: Candler County Historical Society, 1994.

History of Coweta County, Georgia. Roswell GA: Newnan and Coweta County Historical Society, 1988.

History of Crisp County. Cordele GA: The Fort Early Chapter of the Daughters of the American Revolution, 1916.

History of Fayette County, 1821-1971. Fayetteville GA: Fayette County Historical Society, 1971.

History of Franklin County, Georgia. Roswell GA: WH Wolfe, 1986.

History of Heard County, Georgia. Dallas TX: The Heard County Historical Society, 1991.

History of Jasper County, Georgia. Roswell GA: WH Wolfe, 1984.

History of Lee County, Georgia. Leesburg: Lee County Historical Society, 1983.

History of Miller County, 1856-1980. Colquitt GA: The Colquitt Garden Club, 1980.

History of Newton County, Georgia. Covington GA: The Newton County Historical Society, 1988.

History of Peach County, Georgia. Fort Valley GA: Governor Treutlen Chapter of the Daughters of the American Revolution, 1973.

History of Schley County, Georgia. Roswell GA: WH Wolfe, 1982.

History of Telfair County, Georgia. Dallas TX: Curtis Media, 1987.

History of Webster County. Roswell GA: Webster Women's Club, 1980.

History of White County, Georgia, 1857-1980. Cleveland GA: White County Book Committee, 1981.

Hodges, Lucile. *A History of Our Locale, Mainly Evans County, Georgia.* Macon GA: Southern Press, 1965.

Hollingsworth, Dixon, ed. *The History of Screven County, Georgia.* Dallas TX: Curtis Media, 1989.

Holmes, Yulssus Lynn. *Those Glorious Days, A History of Louisville as Georgia's Capital, 1796-1807*. Macon GA: Mercer University Press, 1996.

Hull, Augustus Longstreet. *Annals of Athens, Georgia, 1801-1901*. Athens GA: The Athens Banner, 1906.

Hurst, Robert L. *This Magic Wilderness, Historical Features of the Wiregrass*. Waycross GA: Brantley Printing, 1982.

Huxford, Folks. *History of Clinch County, Georgia*. Macon GA: JW Burke, 1916.

———. *History of Brooks County, Georgia 1858-1948*. 1948. Reprint, Spartanburg SC: Reprint Company, 1948.

Hynds, Earnest C. *Antebellum Athens and Clarke County, Georgia*. Athens GA: University of Georgia Press, 1974.

Ingram, Culpepper Fred. *Beadland to Barrow, History of Barrow County, Georgia, from the Earliest Days to the Present*. Atlanta: Cherokee Publishing Company, 1978.

Jones, Charles C. and Salem Dutcher. *The Memorial History of Augusta*. Syracuse GA: D. Mason, 1890.

Jones, Frank F. *History of Decatur County, Georgia*. 1971. Reprint, Spartanburg: Reprint Company, 1980.

Jones, Dale Dyer, ed. *Facets of Fannin, The History of Fannin County*. Dallas GA: Curtis Media, 1989.

Jones, Mary G. and Lily Richards. *Coweta Chronicles*. Atlanta: Stein Printing, 1928.

Jordan, Margaret Coleman. *Wayne Miscellany*. Jordan: n.p., 1976.

Jordan, Mary Alice. *From Cotton to Kaolin, A History of Washington County, Georgia*. Sandersville GA: Washington County Historical Society, 1989.

Jordan, Robert H. *There was a Land, A Story of Talbot County, Georgia and Its People*. Columbus GA: Columbus Office Supply Co., 1971.

Kaufhold, Shirley and Tony Bryant, eds. *The Hart of Georgia, A History of Hart County, Georgia*. Alpharetta GA: WH Wolfe, 1992.

Kelly, Hulda K. ed. *I See By the Paper, Bulloch County Georgia, 1899-1946*. Statesboro GA: Bulloch County Historical Society, 1984.

King, P. C. *Fort Gaines and Environs*. Alburn AL: Warren Enterprises, 1976.

Kriby, Bill. *Dynamic Gwinnett, Legacy, Life and Vision*. Atlanta: Longstreet Press, 1993.

Kirkland, Mary, ed. *Cornerstone of Georgia, Seminole County, 1920-1991*. Roswell GA: Seminole County Historical Society, 1991.

Kyle, F. Clason. *Images, A Pictorial History of Columbus, Georgia*. Norfolk GA: Donning Company, 1986.

Lamb, Don and Mildred Lamb. *Profile of Dublin and Laurens County*. Macon GA: Williams and Canady, 1995.

Lambdin, Augusta, ed. *The History of Lamar County*. Barnesville GA: The Barnesville News Gazette, 1932.

Lane, Mills, *Savannah Revisited, A Pictorial History*. Rev. ed. Savannah: Beehive Press, 1969.

———. *Savannah Revisited, A Pictorial History*. Rev. ed. Savannah GA: Beehive Press, 1977.

Lupold, John S. *Columbus, Georgia, 1828-1978*. Columbus GA: Columbus Sesquicentennial, Inc., 1978.

Lunceford, Alvin Mell. *Taliaferro County Records and Notes*. Spartanburg SC: Reprint Company, 1988.

Mahan, Joseph B. Jr., *The History of Old Cassville, 1833-1866*. 1950. Reprint, Cartersville: n.p.,1994.

Majors, Glenda and Forest Cluch. *Treasures of Troup County*. LaGrange GA: Troup County Historical Society, 1993.

Mann, Floris Perkins. *History of Telfair County from 1812 to 1949*. 1949. Reprint, Spartanburg: Reprint Company, 1978.

Marlin, Lloyd G. *The History of Cherokee County*. Atlanta: Walter W. Brown Publishing Co., 1932.

Martin, Bobby M., ed. *Wayne County, Georgia, Its History and Its People*. Dallas GA: Curtis Media, 1990.

McCash, William Barton and June Hall McCash. *The Jekyll Island Club, Southern Haven for America's Millionaires*. Athens and London: University of Georgia Press, 1989.

MacCommons, William C. and Clara Stoval, *The History of McDuffie County, Georgia*. Tignall GA: Boyd Publishing, 1988.

Maddox, Joseph T. *Wilkinson County Historical Collections*. Irwinton GA: n.p., 1978.

McDaniel, Susie Blaylock. *Official History of Catoosa County, Georgia, 1853-1953*. Ringgold GA: n.p., 1953.

McDonald, Mary Lou and Samuel Jordon Lawson III. *The Passing of the Pines, A History of Wilcox County, Georgia*. Roswell GA: WH Wolfe, 1984.

McIntosh, John Hawes. *Official History of Elbert County, 1796-1936*. 1936. Reprint, Atlanta: Cherokee Publishing Co., 1968.

McGuffey, Charles D., ed. *The Standard History of Chattanooga, Tennessee*. Knoxville TN: Crew and Dorey, 1911.

McMichael, Lois, ed. *History of Butts County, Georgia, 1825-1976.* Atlanta: Cherokee Publishing Company, 1978.

McQuinn, Alex S. *History of Charlton County. 1932.* Reprint, Spartanburg SC: Reprint Company, 1988.

McRae, Sybil, ed. *A Pictorial History of Hall County, Georgia.* Gainesville GA: The Hall County Library Committee, 1985.

Melton, Ella C. and Augusta Griggs Raines. *History of Terrell County, Georgia.* Roswell GA: WH Wolfe, 1980.

———. *History of Washington County, Georgia.* Atlanta: Boyd Printing, 1924.

Melton, Quimby, Jr. *History of Griffin, 1840-1900.* Griffin GA: Quimbly Melton, Jr., 1959.

Mitchell, Lizzie R. *History of Pike County, 1822-1932.* 1932. Reprint, Spartanburg SC: Reprint Company, 1980.

Monroe County, Georgia, A History. Forsyth GA: Monroe County Historical Society, 1979.

Moore, Joseph Henry Hightower. *A History of Clayton County, 1821-1983.* College Park GA: Ancestors Unlimited, Genealogical Society of Clayton County, Georgia, 1983.

Murray County Heritage, Roswell GA: The Murray County Historical Society, 1987.

Newnan, Lois Owen. *Haralson County, Georgia.* Roswell GA: WH Wolfe, 1994.

Nottingham, Carolyn Walker and Evelyn Hannah. *The Early History of Upson County, Georgia.* Thomaston GA: Georgia Genealogical Reprints, 1930.

O'Kelly, T. D. and A. J. Guinn, eds. *Historical Souvenir of Conyers.* Conyers GA: n.p., n.d.

Official History of Whitfield County. Dalton GA: Whitfield County History Commission, 1936.

Parrish, June Jackson. *The History of Cook County, Georgia and Its Municipalities.* Adel GA: n.p., 1967.

Pate, John Ben. *The History of Turner County.* Spartanburg SC: Reprint Company, 1979.

Payne, Lois. *Historical Sketches of Oglethorpe.* Butter GA: Benns, 1979.

Perryman, Clinton J. *History of Lincoln County, 1933.* Reprint, Tignall GA: Boyd Publishing Company, 1985.

Pinkston, Regina P. *Historical Account of Meriwether County, Georgia, 1827-1974.* Greenville GA: Gresham Printing Company, 1974.

Pitts, Lucie. *History of Gordon County.* Calhoun: Press of The Calhoun *Times,* 1933.

Powell, Nattie. *History of Marion County, Georgia.* Columbus GA: Historical Publishing Company, 1931.

Powell, Nora and Watts Powell, eds., *Historical and Genealogical Collections of Dooly County, Georgia.* 3 vols. Vienna GA: Nora Powell and Watts Powell, 1973.

Rainer, Vessie Thrasher. *Henry County, Georgia, The Mother of Counties.* McDonough, GA: Boyd Publishing Company, 1971.

Raines, Augustus Griggs. *History of Terrell County, Georgia.* Roswell GA: WH Wolfe, 1980.

Rapier, A. F. *Tenants of the Almighty.* New York: MacMillan, 1943.

Reddick, Marguerite. *Camden's Challenge, A History of Camden County, Georgia.* St. Marys GA: Camden Historical Commission, 1976.

Register of Deaths in Savannah, Georgia. 6 vols. September 1818-1832. Savannah GA: The Georgia Historical Society, 1989.

Reynolds, Lily Elizabeth. *Coweta Chronicles for One Hundred Years with an account of the Indians from whom the Land was Acquired and Some Historical Papers Relating to its Acquisition.* Atlanta: Stein Printing Company, 1928.

Rice, Thaddeus B. *The History of Greene County, Georgia.* Macon GA: JW Burke Company, 1961.

Ritchie, Andrew Jackson. J. *Sketches of Rabun Count History, 1819-1948.* Atlanta: Foote and Davies, 1948.

Rome and Floyd County, An Illustrated History, 1834-1984. Rome GA: Sesquicentennial Committee of the City of Rome, 1985.

Roberts, Lucien. *A History of Paulding County.* Dallas GA: Lucien Roberts, 1933.

Rogers, Norma Kate. *History of Chattahoochee County, Georgia.* Easley SC: Southern Historical Press, 1976.

Russell, James Michael. *Atlanta, 1847-1890, City Building in the Old South and the New.* Bator Rouge and London: Louisiana State University of Press, 1988.

Sams, Anita. *Wayfarers in Walton.* Monroe GA: General Charitable Foundation of Monroe, 1967.

Sargent, Gordon D. "The Legacy of Charles Adamson," *The Journal of North Georgia History* 3, ed., Olin Jackson. Woodstock GA: Legacy Communications 1995, 337-39.

Sartain, James Alfred. *History of Walker County, Georgia.* Dalton GA: Showalter, 1932.

Saurez, Annette McDonald. *A Source Book History of Cuthbert and Randolph County.* Atlanta: Cherokee Publishing Company, 1982.

Schmier, Louis E. *Valdosta and Lowndes County, A Ray in the Sunbelt.* Northridge CA: Windsor Publications, 1988.

Scott, Thomas Allan. "Cobb County Georgia, 1880-1900, A Socioeconomic Study of an Upper Piedmont County.": n.p., 1978.

Shadburn, D. L. *A Pioneer History of Forsyth County, Georgia.* Roswell GA: WH Wolfe, 1981.

Shelton, Jane Twitty. *Pines and Pioneers, A History of Lowndes County, 1826-1900.* Atlanta: Cherokee Publishing, 1976.

Shivers, Forrest. *The Land Between, A History of Hancock County, Georgia to 1940.* 1940. Reprint, Spartanburg SC: Reprint Company, 1990.

Smith, Clifford L. *History of Troup County.* Atlanta: Foote and Davies, 1933.

Smith, F. C. *The History of Oglethorpe County.* Washington GA: Wilkes Publishing Company, 1970.

Sommer, Margret F., ed. *The History of Oconee County.* Dallas GA: Curtis Media, 1993.

Spence, Margaret and Anna M. Flemming. *History of Mitchell County, Georgia, 1857-1976.* Camilla GA: Camilla Rotary Club, 1976.

Stancil, W. Dorsey. *Vanishing Gwinnett, A Pictorial History of Bygone Days.* Lawrenceville GA: Gwinnett County Historical Society, 1984.

Strain, Jane M., ed., *History of the Town of Hogansville, 1870 - 1970.* Hogansville GA: n.p., 1970.

Straham, Charles Martin. *Clarke County and the City of Athens.* Athens GA: C. P. Byrd, 1993.

Story of Washington-Wilkes. Athens GA: The Writer's Program of the Works Projects Administration, 1941.

Sullivan, Buddy. *Early Days on the Georgia Tidewater, The Story of McIntosh County and Sapelo. Being a Narrative Account, with Particular Attention to the County's Waterway and Maritime Heritage; Plantation Culture and Uses of the Land in the 19th Century; and a Detailed Analysis of the History of Sapelo Island.* 1990. Reprint, Darien GA: Mcintosh County Board of Commissioners, 1990.

Tabor, Paul. "The History of Madison County, Georgia." Danielsville GA: n.p., 1974.

Tate, Luke E. *History of Pickens County.* Spartanburg SC: Reprint Company, 1978.

Temple, Sarah Blackwell Gober. *The First Hundred Years.* Atlanta: Walter W. Brown, 1935.

Terrill, Helen Eliza. *The History of Stewart County, Georgia,* Columbus GA: Columbus Office Supply, 1958.

Thomas, F. T. *A Portrait of Historic Athens.* Athens: University of Georgia Press, n.d.

Thomas, Z. V. *History of Jefferson County.* 1927. Reprint, Spartanburg SC: Reprint Company, 1978.

Thompson, K. *Touching Home, A Collection of History and Folklore from the Copper Basin and Fannin County Area.* Blue Ridge GA: n.p., 1976.

Trogdon, Kathryn C., ed. *The History of Stephens County, 1715-1972,* Toccoa GA: Toccoa Women's Club, 1973.

Vocelle, James T. *History of Camden County, Georgia.* Jacksonville FL: Kennedy Brown-Hall Co., 1914.

Walker, Anne Kendrick. *Backtracking in Barbour County, A Narrative of the Last Alabama Frontier.* Richmond GA: Dietz Press, 1941.

Walker County Heritage. Dallas GA: Walker County History Committee, 1984.

Walker, Laura Singleton. *History of Ware County.* Macon GA: JW Burke, 1934.

Ward, George Gordon, Jr. *The Annals of Upper Georgia.* 1965. Reprint, Nashville: Parthenon Press, 1974.

Ward, Warren P. Ward's *History of Coffee County.* Atlanta: Foote and Davies, 1930.

Wetherington, Mark V. *The New South Comes to Wiregrass Georgia, 1860-1910.* Knoxville: University of Tennessee Press, 1994.

Wilburn, R. Allen. *Haralson Heritage.* Columbus GA: n.p., 1995.

Wilhoit, Virginia Hill. *History of Warren County Georgia. 1793-1974.* Washington GA: Wilkes Publishing Company, 1976.

William, O. B. *Americus Through the Years.* 1960. Revised Edition, Atlanta: Cherokee Publishing, 1975.

Williams, Carolyn White. *History of Jones County.* Macon GA: JW Burke, 1957.

Williams, Ida Belle. *History of Tift County.* Macon GA: JW Burke, 1948.

Williams, Marie Haley. *Lavonia, Gem of the Piedmont.* Lavonia GA: Library Committee, Lavonia Carnegie Library, 1977.

Wind, R. H. *Grady, 1904-1953.* Cairo GA: n.p., 1983.

Wise, Lena Smith. *The Story of Oglethorpe County.* Lexington GA: Historic Oglethorpe County, 1980.

Young, Ida, Julius Gholson and Clara Nell Hargrove. *The History of Macon, Georgia.* Macon GA: Lyon, Marshall and Brooks, 1950.

Articles

Chalker, Russell M. "Fitzgerald, Place of Reconciliation." *The Georgia Historical Quarterly* 55/3 (1971): 397-405.

DeVine, Jerry, W. "Town Development in Wiregrass, Georgia." *The Journal of Southwest Georgia History* 1 (1983): 1-37.

Mallard, Daisy and Virginia Culpepper, "Americus." *The Georgia Review* 4/1 (1950): 115-24.

O'Donovan, Susan E., ed. "The Journal of Nelson Tift, Part I." *The Journal of Southwest Georgia History* 3 (1985): 64-100.

————. "The Journal of Nelson Tift, Part II." *The Journal of Southwest Georgia History* 4 (1986): 89-121.

Phillips, Ulrich B. "Historical Notes of Milledgeville, Georgia." *Gulf States Historical Magazine* (1903): 1-11.

Theses, Dissertations and Unpublished Manuscripts.

Cook, John Homer. "History of Chattooga County." Thesis, Mercer University, 1931.

Henderson, Charles K. 'Polk County Persons and Things." Cedartown GA: Polk County Library, Cedartown GA, 1937.

Hinton, E. H. "A Historical Sketch of the Solution of Trade and Transportation at Macon, Georgia, Together with a Synopsis of the Rate Adjustment from the East." Macon GA: n.p., 1912.

Rabun, John P. Jr. "A History of Tattnall County." [Ph.D.?] dissertation, Mercer University, 1954.

Teasley, Amos Milton. "The History of Toombs County." Thesis, The University of Georgia, 1940.

Yarborough, Patricia Holt. "A Historical Perspective of the Founding of Fitzgerald, Georgia." Milledgeville GA: Georgia College, 1985.

Selected Architectural Bibliography

PRIMARY

Books

Arnold, C. D. *Official Views: Cotton States and International Exhibition, Atlanta, 1895.* St. Louis: C. B. Woodward Printing, 1895.

Ascher, Benjamin. *The American Builder's Companion, or A System of Architecture Particularly adapted to the present style of Building.* 6th Edition. 1827. Reprint, New York: Dover Publications, 1969.

————. *The Practical House Carpenter, Being a Complete Development of the Grecian Orders of Architecture, Each Example Being Fashioned According to the Style and Practice of the Present Day.* 1830. Reprint, New York: Da Capo Press, 1972.

Bricknell's Village Builder and Supplement. 1876. Reprint, Watkins Glen NY: Athenaeum, 1976.

Bruce and Morgan, *Architects and Superintendents.* Atlanta: Bruce and Morgan, 1883.

Cooper, Walter G. *The Cotton States International Exposition.* Atlanta: The Illustrator Company 1896.

Downing Andrew Jackson. *The Architecture of County Houses, Including Designs of Cottages, Farm Houses and Villas with Remarks on Interiors, Furniture and the Latest Modes of Warming and Ventilation.* New York: D. Appleton and Company, 1850.

Lefevre, Millard, *The Modern Builder's Guide.* 1833. Reprint, New York: Dover Publications, 1969.

————. *The Beauties of Modern Architecture.* New York and London: D. Appleton, 1855.

Official Catalogue of the Cotton States Exposition and International Exposition. Atlanta: Claflin and Mellinchamp, 1895.

Schuyler, Montgomery. *American Architecture and Other Writings by Montgomery Schuyler.* 2 vols. Edited by W. H. Jordy and Ralph Coe. Cambridge: Belknap Press of Harvard University Press, 1961.

Sloan, Samuel. *The Modern Architect.* 2 vols. 1851. Reprint, Sloan's Victorian Buildings. New York: Dover Publications, 1890.

Van Brunt, Henry. *Architecture and Society: Selected Essays of Henry Van Brunt* edited by William A. Coles. Cambridge: Belknap Press of Harvard University, 1969.

Vaux, Calvert. *Villas and Cottages, A Series of Designs Prepared for Execution in the United States.* 1859. Reprint, New York: Dover Publications, 1970.

Journals

The American Architect and Builder. The Georgia Institute of Technology.
The Architectural Record. The Georgia Institute of Technology.
The Manufactures Record, Georgia State University.

SECONDARY

General
Books

Ackerman, James S. *Palladio.* New York: Penguin Books, 1966.

Allwood, John. *The Great Exhibitions.* London: Studio Vista, 1977.

Banham, Reyner. *A Concrete Atlantis, U. S. Industrial Building and European Modern Architecture, 1900-1923.* Cambridge MA: MIT Press, 1986.

Brink, Robert J., ed. *Courthouses of the Commonwealth.* Amherst: University of Massaschusetts Press, 1984.

Carley, Rachel. *The Visual Dictionary of American Architecture.* New York: Henry Holt, 1994.

Colquhoun, Alan. "The Beaux Arts Plan" in *The Beaux Arts* ed. Robin Middleton, 80-83. London: Architecture Design, 1978.

Condit, Carl W. *The Chicago School of Architecture: A History of Commercial and Public Building in the Chicago Area, 1875-1925.* Chicago and London: The University of Chicago Press, 1964.

Crook, J. Mordaunt. *The Dilemma of Style, Architectural Ideas from the Picturesque to the Post Modern.* London: Murray, 1987.

Curl, James Stevens. *Victorian Architecture.* New Abbot and London: David and Charles, 1990.

Floyd, Margaret Henderson. *Architecture After Richardson, Regionalism and Modernism - Longfellow, Alden and Harlow in Boston and Pittsburgh.* Chicago and London: University of Chicago Press, 1994.

Fitch, James Marston. *American Building and the Environmental Forces that Shaped It.* 1947. Revised Edition, Boston: Houghton Mufflin Company, 1972.

———. *American Building and the Historical Forces that Shaped It.* 1947. Revised Edition, Boston: Houghton Mufflin Company, 1966.

Gowans, Alan. *Styles and Types of North American Architecture: Social Function and Cultural Expression.* 1992. Reprint, New York: Icon Editions, 1993.

Hamlin, Talbot. *Greek Revival in America, Being an Account of Important American Architecture and American Life prior to the War Between the States.* 1944. Reprint, New York: Dover Publications, 1964.

Hitchcock, Henry Russell. *The Architecture of H. H. Richardson and His Times.* New York: Museum of Modern Art, 1936.

———. *Architecture: Nineteenth and Twentieth Century.* 1958. Reprint, New Haven and London: Yale University Press, 1977.

———. "French Influence on 19th Century Architecture in the USA." *In The Beaux Arts* ed. Robin Middleton, 80-83. London: Architectural Design, 1978.

——— and William Seale. *Temples of Democracy, State Capitols of The U. S.* A. New York: Harcourt, Bruce, Jovanovich, 1976.

Hofmann, Donald. *The Architecture of John Wellborn Root.* Edited by William Jordy et al. Baltimore MD: Johns Hopkins University Press, 1975.

Mumford, Lewis. *The Brown Decades: A Study of the Arts in America, 1865-1895.* 1931. Reprint, New York: Dover Publications, 1971.

O'Goman, James F. *H. H. Richardson, Architectural Forms for American Society.* Chicago: University of Chicago Press, 1987.

Ochsner, Karl. *H. H. Richardson, Complete Architectural Works.* Cambridge MA: MIT Press, 1982.

Pare, Richard, ed. *Courthouse, A Photographic Document.* New York: Horizon Press, 1978.

Roth, Leland. *McKim, Mead and White, Architects.* New York: Harper & Row, 1983.

Rydell, Robert W. *All the World's Fair, Visions of Empire at American International Expositions, 1876- 1916.* Chicago: University of Chicago Press, 1984.

Scully, Vincent J. Jr. *The Shingle Style and The Stick Style: Architectural Theory and Design from Downing to the Origins of Wright.* 1955. Revised Edition, New Haven and London: Yale University Press, 1971.

————. *American Architecture and Urbanism.* 1969. Revised Edition, New York: Henry Hold and Company, 1988.

Smith, G. E. Kidder. *The Architecture of the United States.* 3 vols. Garden City NY: Anchor Books, 1981.

Stern, Robert A. M., *Gergroy Gilmartin and Hohn Massengale.* New York 1900: Metropolitan Architecture and Urbanism 1890-1915. 1983. Reprint, New York: Rizzoli International Publications, 1992.

Van Zanten, David. "Le Systeme Des Beaux Arts," *The Beaux Arts* ed. Robin Middleton.

Vogt, A. M. *The Universe History of Art and Architecture: The Nineteenth Century.* 1973. English Translation, New York: Universe Books, 1989.

Wadell, Gene and Rhodri W. Liscomb. *Robert Mills' Courthouses and Jails.* Easley SC: 1981.

Whiffen, Marcus. *American Architecture Since 1780: A Guide to Styles.* 1969. Reprint, Cambridge MA and London: MIT Press, 1981.

Whittkower, Rudolf. *Architectural Principles in the Age of Humanism.* New York: WW Norton and Company, 1962.

Withey, Henry F. and Elsie Rathburn Withey, eds. *Biographical Dictionary of American Architects.* Los Angeles: New Age Publishing, 1956.

Articles

Curran, Kathleen. "The German Rundbogenstil and Reflections of the American Round-Arched Style." *The Journal of the Society of Architectural Historians* 47/4 (1988): 351-73.

Woods, Mary. "The First American Architectural Journals: The Profession's Voice." *The Journal of the Society of Architectural Historians* 48/2 (1989): 117-38.

Railroad Architecture
Books

Binney, Marcus and David Pearce. *Railway Architecture.* 1979. Reprint, New York: Van Norstrand Reidhold Company, 1980.

Cavalier, Julian. *Classic American Railroad Stations.* San Diago: A. S. Barnes, 1980.

Grant, H. Roger and Charles W. Bohi, *The Country Railroad Station in America.* Boulder: Pruett Publishing Company, 1978.

Meeks, L. V. Carroll. *The Railroad Station.* New Haven: Yale University Press, 1956.

Richards, Jeffery and John M. MacKenzie. *The Railway Station, A Social History.* Oxford and New York: Oxford University Press, 1986.

Regional and Local Architecture
Books

Andrews, Wayne. *Pride of the South: A Social History of Southern Architecture.* New York: Athenaeum, 1979.

Bromwell, Charles R., Calder Loth and William M. S. Rasmussen. *The Making of Virginia Architecture.* Richmond VA: Virginia Museum of Fine Arts, 1992.

Chapman, William *The Madison Historic Preservation Manual.* Madison: n.p., 1990.

Crane, Sophia and Paul Crane. *Tennessee Taproots.* Old Hickory TN: Earle-Shields, 1976.

Guide to the Architecture of Atlanta. Atlanta: The American Institute of Architects, North Georgia Chapter, 1975.

Hardy, Janice A. *Georgia County Courthouses.* Atlanta: Georgia Trust for Historic Preservation, 1979.

Historic Preservation in Columbus Georgia. Columbus GA: Columbus Area Bicentennial Committee, 1976.

Historic Savannah, A Survey of Significant Buildings in the Historic and Victorian Districts of Savannah. Savannah GA: Savannah Historical Foundation, 1968.

Jordan, Robert and Gregg Puster. *Courthouses in Georgia, 1825-1983.* Norcross GA: The Harrison Company, 1984.

Kelsey, Mavis. *The Courthouses of Texas.* College Station: Texas A & M University Press. 1993.

Lane, Mills. *Architecture of the Old South: Georgia.* Savannah GA: Beehive Press, 1985.

————. *Architecture of the Old South: South Carolina.* Savannah GA: Beehive Press, 1984.

————. *Savannah Revisited, A Pictorial History.* Athens GA: University of Georgia Press, 1969.

————. *Savannah Revisited, A Pictorial History.* Rev. ed. Savannah GA: BeeHive Press.

Lindlay, John. *The Georgia Catalogue, Historical American Building Survey.* Athens GA: University of Georgia Press, 1982.

Lyon, Elizabeth Anne Mack. *Atlanta Architecture, The Victorian Heritage.* Atlanta: Atlanta Historical Society, 1976.

Marshall, Charlotte. *Historic Houses of Athens.* Athens GA: Athens Historical Society, 1987.

Mitchell, William, Jr. *Landmarks, The Architecture of Thomasville and Thomas County, Georgia.* Thomasville GA: Thomasville Landmarks, 1980.

Mitchell, William Robert. *Classic Savannah.* Savannah GA: Golden Coast Publishing, 1987.

Morgan, Thomas Henry. "Architects in Atlanta and Suburbs." In *History of Fulton County* by Walter G. Cooper, 437-45. 1934. Reprint, Spartanburg SC: Reprint Company, 1978.

Peet, George and Gabrielle Keller. *Courthouses and the Commonwealth.* Amhurst MA: University of Massachusetts Press, 1984.

Sieg, Chan. *The Squares of Savannah.* Norfolk GA: Donning, 1984.

Spector, Tom. *The Guide to the Architecture of Georgia.* Columbia SC: University of South Carolina Press, 1993.

Wells, John E. and Robert E. Dalton. *South Carolina Architects, 1885-1935, A Biographical Dictionary.* Richmond: The New South Architectural Press, 1992.

Williford, William B. *The Glory of Covington.* Atlanta: Cherokee Publishing Company, 1973.

Wilson, Adelaide. *Historic and Picturesque Savannah.* Boston MA: n.p., 1899.

Wilson, Charles R. and William Ferris, eds. *Encyclopedia of Southern Culture.* Chapel Hill: University of North Carolina Press, 1989.

Articles

Keene, Grant "White County Court House." *Journal of North Georgia History Journal.* 1/2 (1984): 5-8.

King, Spencer Bidwell. "Atlanta's Early Builders." *Atlanta Historical Bulletin* 15/4 (1970): 88-96.

————. "*Rebel Lawyer: The Letters of Lt. Theodorick W. Montfort, 1861-1862.*" The Georgia Historical Quarterly 68/3 (June 1964): 319.

Morgan, Thomas Henry. "The Georgia Chapter of the American Institute of Architects." *The Georgia Historical Quarterly* 7/28 (1943): 89-167.

————. "Reminiscences of the Architecture and Architects of Atlanta." *The Atlanta Historical Bulletin* 2/10 (1937): 5-14.

Rumore, Samuel A. "Building Alabama's Courthouses." *The Alabama Lawyer.* 1990-1998.

Wodehouse, Lawrence. "Frank Pierce Milburn, A Major Southern Architect." *The North Carolina Historical Review* 50/3 (1973): 280-303.

Theses, Dissertations and Unpublished Manuscripts

Edge, Carolyne. "Early Architecture of Athens, Georgia." Thesis, The University of Georgia, 1986.

Hardy, Janice. "Preservation of Georgia Courthouses Through Historic Documentation and Photography." Milledgeville GA: Georgia College, c.1980.

———— and Anne Harmon. "Thematic National Register Nomination of Georgia Courthouses." Atlanta: 1979.

Lyon, Elizabeth Mack. "Business Buildings in Atlanta, A Study in Urban Growth and Form." Dissertation, Emory University, 1971.

Payne, Eugenia Wasden. "Historical Survey of 159 County Court Houses in the State of Georgia for the National Society of Colonial Dames of America." Macon GA: Washington Library, Macon GA, 1976.

Index

Notes regarding the Index.

All references to specific courthouses are listed by county name under "courthouses." These references do not appear elsewhere in the index under county names or county town names.

All references to specific depots are listed by town name under "depots" and under specific town names elsewhere in the index.

All references to specific railroad companies are listed alphabetically under "railroads." These references do not appear elsewhere in the index.

Atlanta and Charlotte Air Line, The: (also see The Atlanta and Richmond Air Line and
the Richmond and Danville Railroad) 49, 126, 277-92, 317, 321, 324, 326, 334, 350,
356, 359, 475.

Atlanta and Florida Railroad, The: 74, 96, 105, 107, 109, 163, 211, 248, 397-405,
543.

Atlanta and Hawkinsville Railroad, The: 163, 248, 398, 400.

Atlanta and LaGrange Railroad, The: 134, 159.

Atlanta and Richmond Air Line, The: (also see The Atlanta and Charlotte Air Line and
the Richmond and Danville Railroad) 49, 276, 277-92, 311, 316-7, 319, 323, 332.

Atlanta and Savannah Air Line, The: 494.

Atlanta and Savannah Railroad, The: 63, 74, 241, 549-53.

Atlanta and West Point Railroad, The (also see The Atlanta and LaGrange Railroad):
39, 43, 101, 142-59, 192, 301, 366, 369, 400, 543, 545.

Atlanta Americus and Florida Railroad, The: 169, 173, 226.

Atlanta Atlantic and Great Western Railway, The: 238.

Atlanta Birmingham and Atlantic Railroad, The: 14, 164, 208, 212, 227, 258-9, 263-5,
268-9, 271, 364, 367, 369, 419, 440, 490-1, 529, 533-47.

Atlanta Birmingham and Coast Railroad, The (also see The Atlanta Birmingham and
Atlantic Railroad,): 537, 545.

Atlanta Knoxville and Northern Railroad, The: 119, 124, 386, 388, 391, 394.

Atlantic and Birmingham Railroad, The: 206, 227, 263, 270, 364-5, 418, 533-4, 537,
539-40, 546.

Atlantic and Gulf Railroad, The: 63, 177-8, 199-229, 260, 275, 293-5. 300-1, 311,
350, 486.

Atlantic and Gulf Short Line Railroad, The: 527, 539.

Atlantic and Mississippi Railroad, The: 113, 315.

Atlantic Coast Line Railway, The: 63, 66, 199-229, 266-76, 293-9, 302-3, 305, 311,
369, 487, 533-47, 539, 533-47.

Atlantic Fort Valley and Memphis Railroad, The: 248.

Atlantic Short Line Railway, The: 497.

Atlantic Valdosta and Western Railroad, The: 214-6, 218, 422.

Atlantic Waycross and Northern Railroad, The: 486.

Augusta and Chattanooga Railroad, The: 56-8, 126, 131, 285, 387, 390, 393, 478-9.

Augusta and Eatonton Railroad, The: 84.

Augusta and Eatonton Turnpike and Railroad Company, The: 24, 83.

Augusta and Florida Railroad, The: 74, 256, 527.

Augusta and Hartwell Railway, The: 332.

Augusta and Hawkinsville Railroad, The: 248, 398.

Augusta and Knoxville Railroad, The: 332.

Augusta and Savannah Railroad, The: 74.

Augusta and Summerville Railroad Company, The: 26.

Augusta and West Florida Railroad, The: 226.

Augusta and Waynesboro Railroad, The: 69, 74.

Augusta Gibson and Sandersville Railroad, The: 26, 89, 465-73.

Augusta Southern Railroad, The: 26, 256, 468, 471, 504, 527, 530.

Augusta Douglas and Gulf Railroad, The

Augusta Lincolnton and Northern Railroad, The: 480.

Augusta Tallahassee and Gulf Railroad, The: 226.

Augusta Thomasville and Gulf Railroad, The: 226.

Bainbridge and Northeastern Railroad, The: 297.

Bainbridge Columbus and Western Railroad, The: 507.

Bainbridge Cuthbert and Columbus Railroad, The: 184-7, 297, 311, 435, 507, 510, 512.

Bainbridge Cuthbert and Western Railroad, The: 297.

Bainbridge Northern Railroad, The: 297.

Barnesville and Thomaston Railroad, The: 99.

Birmingham Columbus and St. Andrews Railroad, The: 305.

Blakely Extension, The: 304-7, 507, 509-10, 513.

Blakely Southern Railroad, The: 305, 307.

Blue Mountain Line, The: 134.

Blue Ridge and Atlantic Railroad, The: 316, 319, 323.

Blue Ridge Railroad, The: 316, 321-3.

Bostick Railroad, The: 38.

Boston and Albany Railroad, The: 177, 539.

Bowdon Railroad, The: 372.

Brewton and Pineora Railroad, The: 493, 497, 503, 506, 550.

Brinson Railroad, The: 63, 89, 241, 357, 549-53.

Broxton, Hazlehurst and Savannah Railroad, The: 256.

Brunswick and Albany Railroad, The: 177-9, 184, 209-11. 229, 260-1, 265, 266-76,
301, 311, 350, 491, 526, 534.

Brunswick and Atlanta Railroad, The: 261.

Brunswick and Augusta Railroad, The: 261.

Brunswick and Birmingham Railroad, The: 206, 270, 367, 533-4, 537, 546.

Brunswick and Chattahoochee Railroad, The: 216.

Brunswick and Flint River Railroad, The: 261.

Brunswick and Florida Railroad, The: 178, 211, 216, 260, 267-8, 301.

Brunswick and Great Northern Railroad, The: 261.

Brunswick and St. Simon's Railway, The: 261.

Brunswick St. Mary's and Florida Railroad, The: 261.

Brunswick Athens and Northwestern Railroad, The: 261, 316.

Brunswick, LaGrange and Northwestern Railroad, The: 151.

Buck Line Railroad, The: 49, 282, 292.

Buena Vista and Ellaville Railroad, The: 170, 454, 457-463.

Buena Vista Railroad, The: 459.

Camilla and Cuthbert Railroad, The, 185, 302.

Carrabelle and Thomasville Railroad, The: 226.

Carrabelle, Tallahassee and Georgia Railroad, The: 226.

Carrollton, Marietta and Western Railroad, The: 119.

Cartersville and Gainesville Air Line, The: 124, 285.

Cartersville and Van Wert Railroad, The: 124, 184, 311, 376.

Cartersville, Gainesville and Augusta Railroad, The: 124, 285.

Cartersville, Gainesville and Port Royal Railroad, The: 124, 285.

Cartersville, Gainesville, Augusta and Charleston Railroad, The

Central of Georgia Railroad, The (also see The Central Railroad and Banking Company
of Georgia): 11-3, 26 39, 60, 61-89, 91-110, 111, 113, 115, 128, 134, 139-40, 148,
150, 157-9, 161-97, 228-9, 236-8, 242-3, 249, 263, 297, 301, 304-5, 311, 350, 361,
362-382, 405, 407-415, 425-6, 430, 435, 447, 449, 452, 454-5, 457-463, 465-73, 488,
493-5, 497-8, 501, 503-4, 506-7, 509-11, 513, 543, 545, 549-53.

The Central Railroad and Banking Company of Georgia, The (also see the Central of

Thomaston and Barnesville Railroad, The (also see the Barnesville and Thomaston
Railroad and the Thomaston Branch Railroad): 99, 107-108.
Thomaston (Branch) Railroad, The: 99, 107-108.
Thomasville and Augusta Railroad, The: 226.
Thomasville and Cordele Railroad, The: 226.
Thomasville and Gulf Railroad, The: 296.
Thomasville and Northern Railroad, The: 226.
Thomasville and Ty Ty Railroac, The: 226.
Thomasville Branch of the Atlanta and Florida Railroad, The: 226.
Thomasville Branch of the Georgia Southern and Florida Railroad, The: 226.
Thomasville Railroad, The: 226.
Thomasville, Florida and Western Railroad, The: 226.
Thomasville, Tallahassee and Gulf Railroad, The: 226.
Tifton and Northeastern Railroad, The: 270, 537, 539, 546.
Tifton, Thomasville and Gulf Railroad, The: 227, 270, 539, 540, 546-7.
Tuten Railroad The: 454.
Union Pacific of Georgia, The: 267, 269, 274.
Union Pacific Railroad, The: 274.
Upson County Railroad, The (also see the Thomaston and Barnesville Railroad): 107,
400, 405.
Valdosta Southern Railroad, The: 256.
Valdosta, Moultrie and Western Railroad, The: 216, 540.
Vicksburg and Brunswick Railroad, The: 187-8.
Waco and Bowdon Railroad, The: 372.
Wadley and Mount Vernon Railroad, The: 89, 447-8, 497, 503, 534.
Wadley Southern Railroad, The: 430, 502-3, 550.
Wainhurst Railroad, The: 300
Walton Railroad, The: 286, 358-9, 361.
Washington and Elberton, Railroad: 55.
Washington and Lincolnton Railroad, The: 58-9.
Washington Railroad and Banking Company, The: 54.
Waycross Air Line, The: 212, 533-4, 537, 546.
Waycross and Florida Railroad, The: 210.
Waycross Short Line Railroad, The: 210-1, 213.
Waycross, Baxley and Vidalia Railroad, The: 258.
Waycross, Chattanooga and Jacksonville Railroad, The: 251.

Western and Atlantic Railroad, The: 11-2, 32, 39, 43, 48, 50, 52, 59, 88, 92, 100, 109, 111-41, 157, 184, 190, 192, 229, 241, 279, 284, 301, 311, 315-6, 350, 394, 517,
543, 545.
Will's Valley Railroad, The: 309.
Wrens and Louisville Railroad, The: 504.
Wrightsville and Dublin Railroad, The: 467, 469.
Wrightsville and Sun Hill Railroad, The: 467.
Wrightsville and Tennille Railroad, The: 249, 428-30, 431, 465-73.
Raines Store GA: 425.
Randall, Gourdon P.: 77, 81, 235, 265, 281, 310, 360, 385.
Randolph County GA: 173, 183-7, 188, 434.
Randolph County GA (see Jasper County GA): 410.
Ransom, Earnest L.: 257.
Raymond GA: 158, 364-5.
Register GA: 506.
Reidsville GA: 200-1, 452, 498-500, 506.
Renaissance Revival Style: 53, 98, 180, 182, 193, 207, 221, 225, 257, 264, 318, 328,
367, 387, 449, 481, 505.
Rhine GA: 173, 449.
rice production in Georgia: 199-200.
Riceboro GA: 201.
Richardson, Henry Hobson: 8-9, 18, 45, 53, 64, 97-8, 106, 117, 120, 127, 137-8, 147,
156, 171-2, 193, 325, 329, 341, 347, 351, 356, 371, 377, 410, 462, 479, 482, 502, 512,
522, 535, 543.
Richardsonian Romanesque Style: 8-9, 53, 57, 63-4, 106, 108, 117, 120, 127, 137-8,
156, 171-2, 195, 263, 321, 329, 341, 343, 347, 351-2, 377, 413, 461-2, 482, 488, 502,
512-3, 520, 522, 535, 542.
Symbolism: 8-9, 156, 347, 351, 462, 512-3.
Richland GA: 169, 187, 253, 436-7, 438, 441-2, 449, 456, 462, 509-10, 513.
Richmond Academy
Richmond County GA: 23-7.
Richmond VA: 280, 286, 292.
Richwood GA: 418.
Ringgold GA: 12, 131-3.
Rising Fawn GA: 309, 376.
River Junction FL: 210.
Roberta GA: 403-5.
Robertstown GA: 517.
Rockdale County GA: 45-7, 282.
Rockmart GA: 376.
Rocky Ford GA: 68, 493, 551-2.
Rochelle GA: 173, 253, 444-5, 449, 456.
Romanticism in the South: 17-8, 418.

Romantic Classicism: 17, 147, 466.
Romanesque Revival Style: 6-9, 15, 45, 53, 57, 64, 70, 75, 97-8, 101, 106, 122, 127,
131, 137-8, 154-5, 165, 171-2, 182-3, 206, 212, 242, 257, 289, 299, 305-6, 320-1, 325,
341, 343, 347, 351, 371-2, 376, 381-2, 392, 402, 409, 417, 429, 462, 479, 481, 488,
502, 512, 520-3, 525-6, 535, 542-3, 552.
Symbolism: 7-8, 462-3, 520, 522, 543.
Rome GA: 57, 118, 121, 130, 133-9, 141, 148, 155, 158, 276, 333, 340, 351, 361,
363-82, 385.
Root, John Wellborn: 9, 18, 138, 172, 193, 433.
Rosier GA: 74.
Roswell GA: 49, 282, 292.
Roswell Junction GA: 43.
Royston GA: 478.
Rumph, Samuel: 162-163.
Rundbogenstil: 53, 321.
Ruskin, John: 76-7.

S
Saint Claire GA: 552.
Saint Mary's GA: 204, 485-7, 491.
Saint Pancras Station: 16, 278.
Saint Patricks GA: 485.
Saint Simon's Island GA: 250, 260-1.
Salt Springs GA: 343, 374.
San Bernard GA: 272.
Sandersville GA: 66, 89, 243, 465-9, 473.
Sapelo River: 200, 489.
Sardis GA: 74.
Satilla River: 25-6, 268, 485-7, 549.
Savannah GA: 11-2, 15, 24, 26, 57, 59-60, 61-7, 70, 76-7, 79, 88, 91, 95-6, 109,
112-3, 115, 140-1, 162, 165, 169, 188, 192, 194, 216, 222, 227-8, 243, 259-60, 280,
290, 297, 300, 316, 345, 357, 370, 427, 429, 431, 436, 442-3, 450, 452, 455, 463, 470,
473, 483, 486, 491, 493-4, 496-7, 506, 544, 550.
Savannah Cotton Exchange Building: 64.
Savannah River: 59, 63, 73, 75, 93, 325, 332, 483.
Sawdust GA: 27.
Scarboro GA: 68, 551-2.
Schley County GA: 460-2.
Schuyler, Montgomery
Schwab, Augustus: 12, 67, 345.
Scott, George Gilbert: 16, 76.
Screven County GA: 68.
Screven, GA: 204, 551-2.
Screven, James: 204.
Scully, Vincent: 147.
Sea Island cotton 199, 209, 494.